KU-778-424

4000372?

ADMINISTRATIVE LAW IN IRELAND

SECOND EDITION

by

DAVID GWYNN MORGAN, LL.M. (LOND.),
of the Middle Temple, Barrister,
Dean and Associate Professor of Law, University College, Cork

and

GERARD HOGAN, B.C.L., LL.M. (N.U.I.),
LL.M. (PENN.), M.A.,
of King's Inns, Barrister,
Lecturer in Law, Trinity College, Dublin

LONDON
SWEET & MAXWELL
1991

Published in 1991 by
Sweet & Maxwell Limited of
South Quay Plaza, 183 Marsh Wall,
London, E14 9FT
Computerset by
Promenade Graphics Ltd., Cheltenham
Printed by
Butler and Tanner of Frome, Somerset

A catalogue record for this book is available from the British Library

ISBN 0 421 42550 4

All rights reserved.
No part of this publication may be reproduced
or transmitted, in any form or by any means, electronic,
mechanical, photocopying, recording or otherwise,
or stored in any retrieval system of any nature,
without the written permission of the copyright
holder and the publisher, application for which
shall be made to the publisher.

©
Sweet & Maxwell Limited
1991

To Deirdre, Declan, Gwendolen, Daniel and Gareth
(D.G.M.)

To my parents and Karen
(G.H.)

PREFACE

It is impossible to doubt the large and growing need for Administrative Law in this jurisdiction. The prevalence of Leviathan in all our lives can be demonstrated, for instance, by the large sums of money of which he disposes. Moreover, State authority in its multi-various forms looms especially large in any small country like Ireland, which traditionally has lacked any significant private institutions (like, say, an equivalent of the City of London) which would act as a counter-weight. Yet pulling in the opposite direction is a strong national preference for the individualistic rights such as private property, political freedom and privacy: a preference which is conveniently implemented via a written Constitution containing an entrenched Bill of Rights, administered by an activist judiciary.

In spite of this rich raw material, lawyers have been slow (for reasons examined briefly in Chapter 1) to admit Administrative Law to the charmed circle of blocs of law which are officially regarded as discrete legal subjects. Even in Britain, the sounds of self-congratulation celebrating the coming of age of Administrative Law have only recently died down. In this jurisdiction, although the last 20 years have witnessed many important developments, the law in this area remains rather immature. While the majority of recent developments certainly represent an improvement on what went before (*e.g.* the removal of State immunity in *Byrne* v. *Ireland* [1972] I.R. 241) some of their implications have not always been fully worked out.

Moreover, there is one unfortunate trend which was noted in the preface to the first edition of the work in 1986 which has persisted and, indeed, has become very pronounced during the intervening period. This is the general lack of respect for precedent. It is not simply fastidiousness or a sense of legal tidiness which prompts us to express concern, since respect for precedent is the vital vehicle to ensure certainty and consistency and lack of judicial subjectivity, which are the essential features of any legal system. It is, of course, one thing to say, as did Lord Diplock in *R.* v. *Inland Revenue Commissioners, ex p. National Association of Self-Employed Ltd.* [1982] A.C. 617, that judicial pronouncements on matters of public law delivered before 1950 should now be viewed with caution, but it is quite another to disregard recent decisions of relevance. To speak of a breakdown in the system of precedent is an assertion which requires justification, but, unfortunately, the evidence is writ large all over the recent law reports.

Consider the following eight examples (which are elaborated in the text, at the points indicated) of areas in which relevant precedents have apparently been disregarded, and where, as a result, the law is in doubt: the circumstances in which an error of law is jurisdictional rather than being concerned only with the merits (pages 342–354); whether the *delegatus non potest delegare* principle applies stringently to the acts of civil servants within a Department of State (pages 404–405); whether a refusal of constitutional justice is justifiable on the grounds either that the applicant had no case on the merits or that constitutional justice was available on appeal (pages 454–457 and 497–501); whether the exhaustion of alternative remedies is essential before judicial review of an administrative action will lie (pages 605–609); the scope of the courts' discretion to refuse to quash an administrative decision (pages 605–609 and 609–611); whether there remain any circumstances in which the Attorney-General's authority to launch judicial review proceedings by way of a relator action can ever be exclusive (pages 626–632) and the extent to which administrative bodies retain a quasi-immunity in tort actions (compare, for example, *Pine Valley Developments Ltd.* v. *Minister for Environment* [1987] I.R. 23 on the one hand with *Ryan* v. *Ireland* [1989] I.R. 177 and *Bakth* v. *Medical Council* [1990] 1 I.R.515 on the other). On many points, therefore, there are two lines of authority. The unfortunate legal adviser is thus unable to give definite advice to his client because he is uncertain which line will find favour with the court. A less significant consequence is that this book is longer than it would otherwise have been since we have thought it necessary, where there are two divergent lines of authority, to include both of them.

There have also been some major doctrinal developments—such as, for example, the doctrine of legitimate expectations; the duty to give reasons and State liability. In regard to the latter, divergent attitudes have been expressed as to the inter-relationship between the emerging torts of misfeasance of public office and liability for the negligent exercise of a discretionary power on the one hand and the action for damages for breach of constitutional rights on the other. These developments, however, have emerged very much as result of a tendency of *de leges ferenda* on the part of the judiciary, rather than as a result of the natural, incremental development supported by reliance on precedent. It would appear that, following a period of rapid reform, a period of reflection and consolidation is now needed.

Not all of the developments charted here have come through the judiciary. The position of the Ombudsman was filled in 1984 and several interesting reports have been published. Indeed, to judge by the case-load of the office and the central position which it has quickly assumed in the polity, its establishment was a much needed reform. The new provisions of Order 84 of the Rules of the Superior Courts 1986 introduced the essence of the judicial review procedure recommended by the Law Reform Commission in their 8th Working Paper in 1979. The present Coalition Government has also promised widespread reform of the system of local government and at the time of writing, the various committees of experts have just reported: *Local Government Reorganisation and Reform* (1991, Pl. 7918). Unfortunately, the Local Government Act 1991 (which implements certain of the recommendations of the Report such as the relaxation of the *ultra vires* rule and changes in regard to section 4 motions in planning matters) came too late for inclusion in the text: the principal changes are therefore summarised in an appendix. There has also been a partial, but long overdue, overhaul of the fleet of state-sponsored bodies: the privatisation of Irish Life is imminent as is the demise of Foir Teoranta and the Irish Land Commission. On the debit side, the zeal for public service reform has quietened and little has been done to implement the proposals contained in the 1985 White Paper on reform of the public service.

Traditionally among lawyers, in the common law world, the lion's share of whatever attention was given to Administrative Law was lavished upon the segment known as "judicial review of administrative action". More recently a reaction against this tendency has developed, in part on account of the artificial, technical nature of judicial review. In Britain, its relevance has been questioned on the ground that compared to the vast number of administrative decisions taken each day, very few give rise to applications for judicial review. However, such figures as are available seem to show that there is vastly more litigation *per capita* here than in Britain. The growing importance of Administrative Law is evidenced by the fact that in recent years, more than 50 per cent. of the written judgments emanating from the Supreme Court are concerned with public law issues. Indeed, according to evidence given by the senior legal assistant at the Attorney-General's Office to the Dáil Committee on Public Accounts, there has been a 53 per cent increase in the number of judicial review applications between 1986 and 1989: see *The Irish Times*, May 4, 1990.

At a more political level, it has also been suggested that over emphasis upon the constraints on administration militated against good administration and pushed the balance between the needs of the community and individual rights too far in favour of the individual. This debate has been characterised as a controversy between "red-" and "green-light" theorists (see Davis, "English Administrative Law—An American View" [1962] *Public Law* 139 and Harlow and Rawlings, *Law and Administration* (1984)). Here the imbalance between the present, individualistic temper of the Irish judiciary (*"fiat justitia, ruat coelum"*) and, on the other side, the rather conservative public service may be in danger of creating a lop-sidedness at some points in our system of Administrative Law. Indeed, we may be approaching the situation where—in contrast to the traditional privileges enjoyed by the State in litigation—the State and public authorities may actually be at a disadvantage. This is certainly true of the modern standing rules, but there are also other areas (such as, perhaps, the extension of control of discretionary powers, and some of the developments in the area of constitutional justice and State liability) where the law may possibly have tilted too much against the State.

It would, however, be an affectation to claim that the second edition of this work is dedicated to either the thesis or antithesis identified in the previous paragraph. Rather it attempts to steer a middle course, dealing first with certain of the instruments of government, namely, Ministers, Departments and the civil service; state-sponsored bodies and local government. Bearing in mind the exigencies of the economics of legal publishing in a small jurisdiction we have dealt very briefly with local government (and, in particular, with planning law) because the needs of the reader in these areas have been met elsewhere. For the same reason, we have kept our account of the constitutional law background to a minimum. After the instruments of government, we described the instruments of control, namely tribunals and inquiries, the Ombudsman, (Chapters 6 and 7) judicial review (in Chapters 8–11) and the modifications in ordinary litigation when public authorities are involved (in Chapters 12–14).

The emphasis is very much on the law and practice of the Republic, although we have endeavoured to cite the relevant Northern Irish authorities where appropriate. We have attempted to cover developments up to the end of the Hilary law term 1991 (including the Supreme Court's decision in *O'Keefe* v. *An Bord Pleanála*), whilst, in some instances, referring to later material. As regards the readership: we have tried to cater both for the needs of practitioners and students by providing a detailed analysis of recent developments and fairly comprehensive footnote references for the former, while at the same time taking care to outline fundamental principles and to describe certain concepts whose artificiality requires some explanation.

It is a pleasure to record our thanks to the many people who have given so freely of their time and wisdom to add to, or improve, the contents of this book: Mr. Brendan Dineen; Ms. Marcella Doyle; Mr. Seamus Given; Mr. Dermot Gleeson S.C.; Mr. Eamonn Hall; Mr. Patrick McGovern; Mr. Michael Murphy; Mr. Maurice O'Connell; Ms. Valerie O'Connell; Mr. Declan Quigley; Her Excellency, President Mary Robinson; Dr. Yvonne Scannell; Mr. Morgan Sheedy and Mr. Gerry Whyte. Part of the chapter on the Ombudsman is taken from an article by one of the authors which appeared in the 17th volume of the Irish Jurist in 1982 and we are grateful to Professor W. N. Osborough for allowing us to reproduce this material. Part of the material from Chapters 13 and 14 was taken from the Irish submission to the United Kingdom National Committee of Comparative Law Colloquium on Governmental Liability, Compensation and the Law of Civil Wrongs which was held in Birmingham in September 1985. The Irish submission was prepared jointly by Mr. A. Kerr and one of the authors. The authors are grateful to Mr. Kerr and Professor A. W. Bradley for permission to use this material. We must record our gratitude to our indexer, Ms. Julitta Clancy, whose compilation of the table of cases and statutes and the index is in itself a tribute to her skill and professionalism. We also thank our publishers for their sterling work, especially on the copy-editing of a difficult manuscript. Finally, we must pay a special tribute and thanks to our respective wives, Karen Quirk and Deirdre Morgan, for their constant encouragement and forbearance.

Gerard Hogan
David Gwynn Morgan
May 1991

TABLE OF CONTENTS

Table of Contents

TABLE OF CASES

Table of Cases

Table of Cases

Table of Cases

Table of Cases

Table of Cases

Table of Cases

Table of Cases

Table of Cases

Table of Cases

TABLE OF STATUTES

1. Acts of the Parliament of Great Britain, Ireland and the United Kingdom (pre-1922 Acts and post-1922 United Kingdom and Northern Ireland Acts)

2. Acts of the Irish Free State and Ireland (post-1922 Acts)

Table of Statutes

Table of Statutes

3. Other jurisdictions

TABLE OF STATUTORY INSTRUMENTS

lvii

TABLE OF RULES OF THE SUPERIOR COURTS

TABLE OF CONSTITUTIONAL PROVISIONS

TABLE OF EUROPEAN COMMUNITIES LEGISLATION

R.T.C. LIBRARY
LETTERKENNY

PART I

INTRODUCTION

CHAPTER 1

INTRODUCTION

1. Flavour of Administrative Law

Administrative law is conventionally defined as the law regulating the organisation, composition, functions and procedures of public authorities[1]; their impact on the citizen; and the restraints to which they are subject. By public authorities, we mean (to list the examples principally covered in this book): the Government in the sense, which is the one employed in Article 28 of the Constitution, of the 15 Ministers who are the central directorate of the executive; a Minister in his Department[2] state-sponsored bodies[3] like CIE or RTE and local authorities.[4] There are other public bodies, such as the Universities; the Gardai Siochána; and the Defence Forces, which there is no space to cover specifically here, apart from noticing that the general ideas and rules of administrative law apply to them. It ought also to be noted that there are certain private bodies which discharge public (or "quasi-public") functions, for example, the trade unions or professional associations, like the Incorporated Law Society or the Medical Council. Such bodies have been characterised as "domestic governments" and it has accordingly seemed appropriate to the courts and legislature, to extend to them certain of the characteristic principles of administrative law, for example, the rules of constitutional justice.

Administrative law is clearly a public law subject, that is to say, that its focus is relations between the individual and the state, in contrast with private law (for example, the law of contract or tort), which regulates relations—mainly between private individuals. Classification of administrative law as public law raises the difficult question of the boundary and, be it said, the substantial overlap, with constitutional law. One point of distinction stems from the fact that administrative law focuses on the executive and the other two major organs (legislature and judicature) are important only so far as they impact on the executive—by contrast, constitutional law covers all three organs equally. The second point of distinction is that, generally speaking, matters of principle are fixed by constitutional law; whereas administrative law looks more to questions of detail and to matters of function more than structure. Thirdly, constitutional law includes as a major component the law of fundamental rights—those legal rights which are regarded as so essential to decent, digni-

---

[1] Of course large public companies may be as much in need of control by the law as public authorities. Companies are, in fact, controlled by company law and labour law and an interesting book remains to be written comparing these controls with those imposed by administrative law. For the present, see Chap. 8 on "The Reach of Public Law."
[2] See pp. 57–62.
[3] See Chap. 4.
[4] See Chap. 5.

R.T.C. LIBRARY, LETTERKENNY

fied life as a human being that they are established by the Constitution and judicial exegesis and prevail over all other types of law. Yet it must be admitted that it is very often in cases involving the administrative actions of the executive that the fundamental rights have to be invoked. Thus there is a substantial, if adventitious, connection between administrative and constitutional law and at various points[5] we shall notice the fundamental rights as part of the controls upon administrative actions.

In the mid-nineteenth century, following the Industrial Revolution, and with the rise of political democracy, there was a vast increase in the activity of the executive and its intervention in the affairs of the citizen. This has taken various forms, including the regulation of land use and commercial trans-actions; the provision of social welfare benefits and free or subsidised health and education services; and the management of the economy by such measures as the control of prices and incomes, tax actions, subsidies, etc.[6] Since administrative law is the law regulating the administration of the executive arm of government one might have expected such trends to be reflected in the development of administrative law as a coherent subject.

Yet the reality is that in the common law world, administrative law has only recently come to be acknowledged and studied as a unified discipline.[7] There are at least three reasons for this, the first of which is historical and is common to Ireland and Britain. The Parliamentary victory in the British Civil War in the seventeenth century led to the eradication of the central executive machinery built around the Privy Council. The organs which evolved to fill these gaps did so in a cramped, ad hoc way. It is to this historical factor that is owed such features of our system of administrative law as the absence of the specialised administrative courts which exist on the Continent; the distorting fiction that public law is simply a special case of private law; the crab-like growth of our system of judicial review, proceeding from the baseline of the *ultra vires* doctrine[8]; the formal significance of the legislature in the control of governmental administration[9]; and the late development of professionalism in the public service. At the local level too, the institutions of government were not tailormade for their tasks. Before the nineteenth century, the principal institution was the amphibious justices of the peace, who also acted as local courts of law. When, as a result of the Civil War, the justices were released

---

[5] See pp. 374–375, 412–415 and 538–541.
[6] See Holdsworth, *History of English Law*, Vol. xiv, pp. 90–204.
[7] The first lectures on Administrative Law in Irish Universities were given as indicated: T.C.D. (1946, F. C. King); U.C.D. (early 1950s, P. McGilligan); U.C.G. (1975, J. M. G. Sweeney); U.C.C. (1978, D. Gwynn Morgan); Q.U.B. (1953). For recent works on Irish Administrative Law (or aspects thereof), see—Stout, *Administrative Law in Ireland* (Dublin, 1985); Casey, "Ireland" (written in English) in *Gesichte der Verwaltungsrecht wissenschaft in Europa* (ed. Hegen) (Frankfurt am Main, 1982); Koekkoek, "Ierland" (written in Dutch) in *Het bestuursrecht van de landen der Europese Gemeenschappen* (ed. Prakke and Kortmann) (Kluwer, 1986); Collins and O'Reilly, *Civil Proceedings and the State in Ireland* (Dublin, 1989).
[8] See pp. 328–335.
[9] See pp. 53–57.

from the control of the Privy Council, they could only be called to account by the Court of King's Bench. It seemed natural simply to apply to the justices in their administrative role the same remedies as those which controlled them in their judicial duties. By another apparently natural development, the courts extended these remedies and, with them, the substantive law for the control of the justices' administrative action to cover all the other public authorities as these grew up.

The second factor was the enormous, ideological influence of the turn-of-the-century scholar, Dicey. His principal tenet was that Ministers and other state organs ought to be subject to the same law, administered by the same courts, as a private individual and that this ideal was achieved in the British system of law. Contrasted with this was the French institution of the *droit administratif* in which specialised tribunals applied law to the acts of the executive and, it was implied, gave the executive an easy ride. From such an outlook, it was a short step to the conclusion that a system of administrative law, which acknowledged the unique position of the state and systematically granted it special powers and subjected it to special controls, was anathema. It followed that to embark on a study of such elements of administrative law as there happened to be in British law was to court disaster.

The third reason why administrative law has been so slow to develop as a coherent, unified whole is that the territory which it covers is so voluminous and diverse. The subject really consists of general principles, with the substantive details being contained in such subjects as: planning law; housing and public health law; social welfare law; licensing law; and economic law. Throughout this work, we shall be examining material which could be relocated in one or other of these categories. This is a feature which distinguishes administrative law from discrete subject-blocs, like tort or criminal law, where a single book can cover more or less the whole area and where the overlap with neighbouring subjects is less significant. The result of this feature is that the most fruitful approach in explaining administrative law is to describe the leading principles and to observe their operation in certain specimen areas.

Administrative law may be regarded as made up of two components: the instruments of government and the instruments of control. The instruments of government—Ministers and Departments, state-sponsored bodies, local authorities, etc.—are, or should be, designed to enable administrators, working under the control, direct or indirect, of elected politicians, to take decisions and provide services which are in the best interests of the community. But the powers of these agencies are delineated by the law—albeit a law which allows them a great deal of latitude. The law is administered by the instruments of control: the tribunals[10]; the Ombudsman[11]; and, most important of all, the courts, enforcing a bloc of law known as judicial review.

---

[10] See Chap. 6.
[11] See Chap. 7.

2. Two Distinctions

The major difficulty inherent in administrative law is the sheer diversity of the decisions, powers, functions, etc. (these words mean more or less the same) which it comprehends. Here are some examples of typical governmental decisions; the expulsion of an undesirable alien; a local authority's decision to build a concert hall or theatre under the Local Government Act 1960; the making of a statutory instrument regulating the procedure of An Bord Pleanála; the making of a development plan by a local planning authority; a decision whether to grant planning permission in respect of a particular building; assessment of capital gains following the sale of a piece of land; award of a social welfare benefit; allocation of a corporation house. In ordering these disparate functions and in understanding the controls which administrative law imposes on them, we shall be assisted by two sets of distinctions: first, policy and administration; and secondly, legislative and individual decisions.

Policy-administration

Put briefly, administration[12] assumes that there is already in existence a principle and that all the administrator has to do is to establish the facts and circumstances and then to apply the principle. It is of the essence of good administration that the principle must be fairly clear and precise so that, in any given situation, the result should be the same, whether it is administrator A or administrator B who has taken the decision. For, in its purest form, administration requires only a knowledge of the pre-existing principle and an appreciation of the facts to which it is being applied: it is an intellectual process involving little discretion. By contrast, policy-making is largely discretionary: the policy-maker must decide, as between two alternatives, the one which he considers best in the interest of the community. He must take into account all the relevant factors and which factors are relevant is, to a considerable extent, left to him. In doing this, the policy-maker will have to draw on his own values and, in the light of this, it is no coincidence that the words policy and politics come from the same Greek root (*polis*, meaning city). For each word relates to choice in the affairs of the community and it is natural, in a democracy, that major policy questions should be taken by politicians (often on the advice of senior public servants), whether Ministers or, at local government level, elected councillors. As Mèndes-France observed: "To govern is to choose." According to the democratic ideal, one elected politician is chosen in preference to another politician just because it is his policy which finds favour with the electorate.

Applying the policy-administration dichotomy to the list of governmental functions given earlier, we can say that matters such as the expulsion of an

---

[12] Administration is one of these awkward words which takes its meaning from the word to which it is opposed—*i.e.* in this Part, to "policy." Unfortunately for clarity, it can also be used in other senses as when it is opposed to legislation or when an administrative decision is contrasted with a quasi-judicial decision (on which, see pp. 485–486).

alien; building of a concert hall; making of procedural regulations; making of a development plan—are policy matters, whereas the grant of planning permission; assessment of capital gains; award of a welfare benefit; and allocation of a corporation house are acts of administration. Indeed, the planning functions afford particularly neat illustrations in that the development plan is the pre-existing standard on which the administrator bases his decision whether to grant permission for a specific development. The first is policy; the second is administration. It must of course be admitted that such classifications over-estimates the neatness of reality; policy and administration really represent the opposite poles of a scale and most decisions fall at some intermediate point on the scale. It would, for instance, be plainly wrong to suppose that a manager or planning officer deciding whether to grant planning permission for a small bungalow in an area zoned as "primarily agricultural" would not have to use some of his own discretion.

Clearly the question of whether a decision is one of policy or of administration will depend in part on the wording of the statute or other instrument creating the decision. For instance, section 5(1) of the Aliens Act 1935 provides that the Minister for Justice may "if and whenever he thinks proper" expel an alien.[13] Plainly, this is a policy decision. However, the legislature might have provided that the alien could only be expelled on (say) "health grounds" or in the case of "criminal activity." Such a test would be closer to the administrative end of the scale, but would still leave considerable discretion to the Minister. The decision could have been rendered entirely administrative by providing that an alien could only be expelled if (say) he were suffering from one of a list of specified diseases or if he had been convicted of any indictable offence.

Legislative—individual decisions

The second major distinction in the field of governmental decision-making lies between legislative and individual decisions. A legislative decision affects a potentially unlimited category of persons or situations which share the specified common characteristics; whereas an individual decision is directed to, and affects only, some particular individual(s). It will be seen immediately than an Act of the Oireachtas is an example of a legislative decision. This is true but the Act is not the only example for the meaning of "legislation" invoked here is wider than the artificially-restricted meaning which has been imposed upon "law-making" in the context of Article 15.2.1[14] which provides that only the Oireachtas may "make laws for the State." The definition used here is intended to comprehend any rule: for instance, a statutory instrument or by-law.

Before a legislative decision has any effect in a particular instance, an individual decision[15] is necessary, to apply the rule to the particular situation to

[13] For control of a discretionary (policy) decision, see Chap. 10.
[14] See further, pp. 12–16.
[15] As used here, "individual decision" comprehends both an "administration of justice" Art. 34.1.

which it is relevant. One way in which this may be done is by the application of a law by a court. But it often happens that law, especially public law, is applied not by a court but by an administrative agency and, of the list of examples given earlier, the grant of planning permission (local planning authority: county or city manager); the assessment of capital gains (the Revenue Commissioners); and the award of a social welfare benefit (deciding officer in the Department of Social Welfare) are all instances of individual decisions taken by the administrative agency indicated in brackets.

We can summarise the relationship between the two sets of distinctions by saying that a legislative decision is inevitably a policy decision. On the other hand, an individual decision will usually be nearer the administrative end of the spectrum in that it is the product of the application of some (more or less) precise standard—and three examples of this were listed previously. However, in some cases, an individual decision will be the direct result of the decision maker's discretion and such individual policy decisions include, for example, the expulsion of an alien or the building of a concert hall.

Application of the two classifications

The significance of these two types of classification lies in the part they have played in influencing the design of the organs and procedures of government administration and of the controls which are exercised over this administration. Much of the remainder of the book consists of illustrations of this observation. Thus, here we can only advert to a few examples of it and direct the reader to the place where they are amplified. For example, consider the design of governmental structures at the local government level: broadly speaking, the reserved functions, which are the preserve of the elected councillors, deal with policy matters; whereas the executive functions, which are vested in the top official, the county or city manager, consist of administrative acts.[16] For historical reasons, the picture is not so clear when one examines the central government, Ministers and Departments though here, too, there is an approximate observation of the distinction.[17]

Where there are pre-existing rules, the control exercised over the decision will be necessarily stricter. In the first place, the legislature is more likely to have established a tribunal to take the decision[18] and/or to have created an appeal to a court in respect of the decision. Secondly, even where this has not been done, a court may intervene on the ground of error of law.[19] Policy decisions may, it is true, be reviewed by a court—but it is only in a very clear case that they will be struck down and at an earlier stage in the development of administrative law, courts have been heard to say that they must leave policy questions to be dealt with through the agency of ministerial responsibility to the legislature.[20] These results flow from the idea that elected persons

[16] See pp. 165–171.
[17] See pp. 57–62 but see also, pp. 400–405.
[18] See pp. 225–226 and 231–232.
[19] See pp. 354–358.
[20] See p. 56.

or bodies take policy decisions, whilst courts customarily take decisions on the basis of pre-existing principles.

Reinforcing the trend noted in the previous paragraph is the fact that administrative decisions are always individual decisions. It is because individual decisions have a direct effect on individual rights that they are more stringently controlled than legislative decisions: for example certain types of decision must be taken by a Minister personally rather than through his civil servants.[21] Again, where the significant procedural safeguard of constitutional justice is concerned, we find that these rules are less likely to apply to policy than to administrative decisions and usually do not apply to legislation.[22] The law of remedies also formerly observed the two distinctions we have described.[23] Finally, the Ombudsman's jurisdiction is confined to "action[s] taken in the performance of administrative functions"[24] thereby excluding legislative, though not other types of policy, decision.

[21] See pp. 400–405.
[22] See pp. 485–488.
[23] See p. 583.
[24] Ombudsman Act 1980, s.4(2). See further, pp. 285–286.

CHAPTER 2

FUNDAMENTAL PRINCIPLES AND SOURCES OF
ADMINISTRATIVE LAW

1. Fundamental Constitutional Principles: Rule of Law

The twin concepts of the rule of law[1] and the separation of powers[2] are the most fundamental principles of Irish administrative law. Both the structure of our system of government and the basis of judicial review of administrative action are founded on these principles. While a thorough analysis of these constitutional doctrines more properly belongs to a textbook on constitutional law, some of the major aspects of these principles may be sketched here.

At the heart of the rule of law there are four interrelated notions.[3] The first is the principle of legality. Every executive or administrative act which affects legal rights, interests or legitimate expectations must have legal justification. Where no such authority exists, the aggrieved party may have recourse to the courts where this decision will be invalidated. This is no more than an application of the principle of *ultra vires*. And it is not enough for the administrative authority concerned to show that it possessed ostensible legal authority, for the courts will review the exercise of discretionary power according to settled principles of reasonableness, proper motives and compliance with natural justice.[4] The second principle is that everyone, including the Government and its servants, is subject to the law. This principle received graphic affirmation in cases such as *Macauley* v. *Minister for Posts and Telegraphs*,[5] (where a statutory provision requiring the prior permission, or *fiat*, of the Attorney-General before an action could be taken against a Minister of State was found to be unconstitutional) and *Byrne* v. *Ireland*[6] (holding that the former Crown immunity from suit had not survived the enactment of the Constitution). The third meaning of the rule of law is that the legality of executive or administrative acts is to be determined by judges who are independent of the Government. The principle of judicial independence is enshrined in Article 34.1 of the Constitution,[7] and the courts have always jealously safeguarded their powers to review administrative action. Thus, legislative attempts to

---

[1] Gwynn Morgan, *Constitutional Law of Ireland* (Dublin, 1985), pp. 42–45; Wade, *Administrative Law* (Oxford, 1988), pp. 23–32.
[2] Gwynn Morgan, *op. cit.* pp. 36–41; Kelly, *The Irish Constitution* (Dublin, 1984), pp. 28–32.
[3] There are other aspects of the rule of law which pertain to the administration of criminal justice, and thus are not our present concern. For example, the prohibition of retroactive penal legislation contained in Art. 15.5 of the Constitution may be said to a feature of the rule of law.
[4] See Chaps. 9 and 10.
[5] [1966] I.R. 345.
[6] [1972] I.R. 241. See pp. 701–705.
[7] Kelly, *op. cit.* pp. 232–255. See generally, *Buckley* v. *Att.-Gen.* [1950] I.R. 67; *Re Haughey* [1971] I.R. 217 and *The State (McEldowney)* v. *Kelleher* [1983] I.R. 289.

curb—or even altogether to prevent—review of administrative action have been viewed with disfavour by the judiciary.[8]

The final aspect of the rule of law is that the law must be public and precise: the law should be ascertainable and its operation predictable. This principle underlies a number of important rules of statutory construction such as the presumption against retrospectivity[9] and the principle that taxing statutes must be strictly construed.[10] This allows the citizen to arrange his behaviour to conform with the law.

2. Fundamental Constitutional Principles: Separation of Powers

Article 6 assumes that the powers of government are of three types: legislative, executive and judicial. Article 6 does not in terms prescribe a separation of powers, but the effect of other constitutional provisions—most notably, Articles 15, 28 and 34—is to "entrench the different arms of government in varying degrees and prescribe their sovereignty in their own areas, without, however, hermetically insulating the different powers from one another in all respects."[11] The constitutional distribution of powers, is, however, an imperfect one, and this is recognised by the very terms of the Constitution itself. The central exception, indeed, constitutes the main feature of our governmental system, namely, the fused legislature-executive and such is the strength of the party whip system, that the Oireachtas is almost completely under the control of the Government of the day. It is only the judiciary who enjoy a secure position *vis-à-vis* the other branches of government.[12]

Four aspects of the separation of powers are of particular importance for administrative law. These arise in the contexts of executive privilege; ouster and preclusive clauses; Article 15.2.1 (which vests the Oireachtas with sole and exclusive legislative power) and Articles 34.1 and 37 (which collectively forbid the Oireachtas to confer judicial functions on bodies other than courts, save only where the functions are of a limited kind).

As executive privilege, ouster clauses and Articles 34 and 37 are examined

---

[8] In *The State (Pine Valley Developments Ltd.)* v. *Dublin C.C.* [1984] I.R. 407, 426 Henchy J. commented that the courts "should be reluctant to surrender their inherent right to enter on a question of the validity of what are prima facie justiciable matters," and see further, pp. 374–378 on the issue of ouster and preclusive clauses. See also the comments of O'Higgins C.J. in *Condon* v. *Minister for Labour* [1981] I.R. 62, 69: "A strong, healthy and concerned public opinion may, in the words of Edmund Burke, 'snuff the approach of tyranny in every tainted breeze,' but effective resistance to unwarranted encroachment on constitutional guarantees and rights, depends, in the ultimate analysis on the courts. If access to the courts is denied or prevented or obstructed, then such encroachment, being unchallenged, may become habitual, and, therefore, unacceptable."

[9] *Hamilton* v. *Hamilton* [1982] I.R. 466; *Doyle* v. *An Taoiseach* [1986] I.L.R.M. 693.

[10] For a general exposition of this principle, see, *e.g. Inspector of Taxes* v. *Kiernan* [1981] I.R. 117 and *McGrath* v. *McDermott* [1988] I.R. 258. See also, *Att.-Gen.* v. *Wilts United Dairies Ltd.* (1921) 39 T.L.R. 781 (administrative body had no power to levy charges for public purposes, save where this is expressly authorised by statute).

[11] Kelly, *op. cit.* p. 29.

[12] Kelly, *op. cit.* pp. 232–255.

elsewhere,[13] it remains to consider here the provisions of Article 15.2.1. While Article 15.2.1. vests the Oireachtas with exclusive power of legislation, it is nevertheless permissible for the Oireachtas to delegate power to make regulations which will give effect to the principles and policies contained in the parent Act. The question therefore is whether the parent Act has actually sanctioned the delegation of a power which goes beyond the mere giving effect to its principles and policies. In the first case of its kind, *Pigs Marketing Board* v. *Donnelly*[14] Hanna J. rejected the argument that the price-fixing powers given to the defendant board by the Pigs and Bacon Acts 1935–1937 amounted to an unconstitutional delegation of legislative power. The board in exercising these powers was not making new law, but was merely giving effect to the statutory provisions as to how they should determine that price.

In the past decade, the number of significant cases in this area has shown an increase with two leading modern cases: *City View Press Ltd.* v. *An Comhairle Oiliúna*[15] and *Cooke* v. *Walsh.*[16] In the former case the provisions of the Industrial Training Act 1967 had been challenged as granting an unconstitutional delegation of legislative power. The defendants were empowered to fix the amount of a levy to be collected from industrial enterprises which was then used to train apprentices in that industry. O'Higgins C.J. observed that in this instance the Oireachtas had reserved unto itself the right to annul regulations made under the Act, and that this power of annulment was a common feature of many items of legislation. While this was a safeguard, the ultimate responsibility of ensuring that there had not been an unconstitutional delegation of power rested with the courts. The relevant test was whether the impugned legislation was more than:

> "[A] mere giving effect to principles and policies contained in the statute itself. If it be, then it is not authorised, for such would constitute a purported exercise of legislative power by an authority which is not entitled to do so under the Constitution. On the other hand, if it be within the permitted limits—if the law is laid down in the statute and details only filled in or completed by the designated Minister or subordinate body—there is no unauthorised delegation of legislative power."[17]

Judged by these standards there had not been any unconstitutional delegation of legislative power, as the court found (rather surprisingly in view of the actual provisions of the 1967 Act) that it contained clear statements of policies and objectives, and the only task left to the defendants was to calculate the size of the levy for any particular industry by reference to these principles.

In *Cooke* v. *Walsh* the validity of certain ministerial regulations purpor-

---

[13] At pp. 729–735 (executive privilege); at pp. 374–378 (ouster clauses) and pp. 236–239 (Art. 37).
[14] [1939] I.R. 413. See also, *National Union of Railwaymen* v. *Sullivan* [1947] I.R. 77; *de Burca* v. *Att.-Gen.* [1976] I.R. 38; *The State (Devine)* v. *Larkin* [1977] I.R. 24; *The State (Gilliland)* v. *Governor of Mountjoy Prison* [1987] I.R. 201 and Kelly, *op. cit.* pp. 74–79.
[15] [1980] I.R. 381.
[16] [1984] I.L.R.M. 208. See also, *The State (Gallagher, Shatter and Co.)* v. *de Valera* [1986] I.L.R.M. 3.
[17] [1980] I.R. 381, 399.

tedly made pursuant to the Health Act 1970 was at issue. This Act conferred full eligibility to receive free health services on certain classes of individuals (of which the infant plaintiff was one). But another section of the Act, section 72, enabled the Minister for Health to make regulations providing for any service "being made available only to a particular class of the person" who had eligibility for that service. Ministerial regulations made pursuant to this latter provision purported to exclude persons otherwise entitled under the Act to free medical services from such entitlements where their injuries were sustained as a result of a road accident and where they were entitled to receive compensation in respect of their injuries. Read at its full width, section 72 would probably have permitted the Minister to alter the eligibility provisions contained in the Act itself. But such a construction would render section 72 invalid having regard to Article 15.2, as the Minister would have been authorised to change or alter the Act by executive decree. Accordingly, section 72 was given a more limited construction in the light of the presumption of constitutionality. While the validity of section 72 was thus saved, it rendered the impugned regulations *ultra vires*, because the section, as interpreted (which, in reality, had been radically re-interpreted) did not permit the Minister to alter the eligibility requirements when making regulations thereunder.[18]

Very similar reasoning was applied by the Supreme Court in *Harvey* v. *Minister for Social Welfare*,[19] where the validity of section 75 of the Social Welfare Act 1952 was challenged. This section allows the Minister to adjust the payments made to a person who is in receipt of more than one benefit, pension or allowance. Regulations had been made in 1979 pursuant to section 75 whereby persons potentially entitled to several such payments were confined to obtaining only one payment. However, section 7 of the Social Welfare Act 1979 provides that a widow's pension shall be payable until she remarries and the applicant argued that inasmuch as section 75 allowed the Minister to make regulations which overrode other statutory provisions, it amounted to an unconstitutional delegation of legislative power. The Court rejected that submission, but did so only on the basis that the 1979 Regulations were *ultra vires* inasmuch as they had purported to vary or alter the terms of section 7 of the 1979 Act. The Court thus paralleled the reasoning in *Cooke* v. *Walsh*. As far as the legislative power point was concerned, Finlay C.J.[20] put it thus:

"The Court is satisfied that the terms of section 75 of the Act of 1952 do not make it necessary or inevitable that a Minister . . . making regulations pursuant to the power therein created must invade the function of the Oireachtas in a manner which would constitute a breach of the provisions of Article

---

[18] O'Higgins C.J. thought that s.72 might enable the Minister to regulate the provision of certain services provided by the Health Boards. See now Health (Amendment) Act 1986, which reverses the decision of the Supreme Court as far as hospital charges are concerned.
[19] [1990] I.L.R.M. 185.
[20] *Ibid*. 188.

15.2. The wide scope and unfettered discretion contained in the section can only be exercised by a Minister making regulations so as to ensure that what is done is truly regulatory or administrative only and does not constitute the making, repealing or amending of law in a manner which would be invalid having regard to the provisions of the Constitution."

One important statute has already proved vulnerable to challenge in line with these developments. Section 1 of the Imposition of Duties Act 1957[21] gives the Government power by order to impose, vary or terminate any excise, customs or stamp duty. The only check on this raising of taxation by executive decree is contained in section 2(1) of the Act: any such order will expire at the end of the year following that in which it is made unless confirmed by the Act of the Oireachtas.[22] Such is the comprehensiveness of the statutory language that it is almost impossible to contend that orders made thereunder are *ultra vires*.[23] It is difficult therefore to see how section 1 could withstand challenge in view of the test articulated in *City View Press*. The Government has been given power to amend earlier legislation and to raise taxes by executive decree, thus going far beyond the mere giving effect to "principles and policies" contained in the legislation which has been amended. It is true that such orders had to be confirmed by legislation by the end of the following year,[24] but even where the order lapses for want of statutory confirmation, this was without prejudice to all acts done under cover of the order. In any event, given the clear infringement of Article 15.2, it would seem that this feature of the Act could save it from constitutional challenge. This was the view of Blayney J. in *McDaid* v. *Sheehy*[25] where he held that section 1 of the 1957 Act was unconstitutional.

Blayney J. observed that the 1957 Act did not contain any principles or policies and that the powers thereby conferred on the Government were powers to legislate:

"It is left to the Government to determine what imported goods are to have a customs or excise duty imposed on them and to determine the amount of such a duty . . . It is far from the case of the Government simply filling in the details. The fundamental question in regard to the imposition of customs or excise duties on imported goods is, firstly, on what goods should a duty be imposed and, secondly, what should be the amount of the duty. The decision on both these matters is left to the Government. In my view, it

---

[21] As amended by s.22 of the Finance Act 1962. See generally, Hogan, "Note on the Imposition of Duties Act 1957" (1985) 7 D.U.L.J.(N.S.) 134.
[22] In *Doyle* v. *An Taoiseach* [1986] I.L.R.M. 693 Barrington J. suggested that the confirmation procedure provided for by s.2(1) of the Act might not apply to orders which were void *ab initio*.
[23] But the Act does not give the power to the Government to create new duties; it simply allows the Government to vary or amend *existing* duties: see Barrington J. in *Doyle's* case. Such an order may also be void for unreasonableness: *Doyle* v. *An Taoiseach* [1986] I.L.R.M. 693.
[24] Imposition of Duties Act 1957, s.2(1).
[25] [1989] I.L.R.M. 342. Blayney J.'s decision was, however, reversed by the Supreme Court on the technical ground that it was not, on the facts, necessary for him to have addressed the constitutional issue: Supreme Court, December 5, 1990.

was a proper subject for legislation and could not be delegated by the Oireachtas."[26]

This quartet of cases—*City View Press, Cooke* v. *Walsh, Harvey* and *McDaid*—severely limits and marks off the boundaries of delegated legislation and it is probable that the full significance of these cases has only been partially realised. There have been several recent statutory provisions which purport to enable the relevant Minister to make regulations within a specified time period (usually three years) amending the parent Act.[27] A good recent example of this statutory formula is provided by section 5 of the Trustee Savings Bank Act 1989 which provides that:

"If, in any respect, any difficulty arises in bringing any provision of this Act into operation or in relation to the operation of such provision, the Minister for Finance may by regulations do anything which appears to him to be necessary or expedient for removing that difficulty, for bringing that provision into operation or for securing and facilitating its operation, and such regulations may modify any provision of this Act so far as may be necessary or expedient for carrying such provision into effect for the purposes as aforesaid but no regulations shall be made under this section in relation to any provisions of this Act after the expiration of three years commencing on the day when the relevant provision of this Act came into operation."

While the utility and convenience of this provision was defended by the Minister for Finance[28] during the Second Stage of the Dáil debate, it is not surprising that other deputies questioned the constitutionality of such a provision.[29] In view of the recent authorities, it is difficult to see how the Oireachtas can validly delegate the power to amend a statute by statutory instrument on a Minister, even if that power contains certain safeguards.

European Communities Act 1972: the implementation of directives

Similar difficulties exist in the case of the European Communities Act 1972 and the European Communities (Amendment) Act 1973. The 1972 Act provides, *inter alia*, that future acts adopted by the institutions of the Communi-

---

[26] *Ibid.* 346.
[27] Other recent examples of this statutory formula (which are generally headed "Regulations to remove difficulties") include s.25 of the Farm Tax Act 1985; s.13 of the Canals Act 1986, s.10 of the Valuation Act 1988 and s.4 of the Building Societies Act 1989. S.6 of the Trustee Savings Bank Act 1989 is an even more remarkable provision in that it enables the Minister to make regulations amending the Act "for the purpose of assimilating the law relating to Trustee Savings Banks to the modifications of the law relating to companies, banks or building societies."
[28] The Minister said (*Dáil Debates*, Vol. 392, col. 1273):
"[This Act] is the first 'root and branch' reform of [Trustee Savings Bank Act 1863] in the history of this State. There is a strong possibility of unforeseen technical difficulties arising in giving effect to the provisions of the present Bill to enable the Minister to deal with them. . . . There is no possibility of the provision being used to subvert the intention of the legislation and there are precedents for it."
[29] See the comments of Deputies Noonan and Taylor at *Dáil Debates*, Vol. 393, cols. 424–428.

ties shall be binding on the state and "shall be part of the domestic law thereof under the conditions laid down in those treaties." In the case of directives issued by Community institutions, Article 189(3) of the EEC Treaty provides that: "A directive shall be binding, as to the result but shall leave to the national authorities the choice of the form and methods."

In nearly all cases implementing measures will be necessary on the part of the Member State in order to give the directive full force and effect.[30] One of the principle methods of implementing directives in this jurisdiction is contained in section 3 of the European Communities Act 1972, which enables a Minister of State to implement such directives by statutory order. Section 3(2) states:

> "Regulations made under this section may contain such incidental, supplementary and consequential provisions as appear to the Minister . . . to be necessary for the purposes of the regulations (including provisions repealing, amending or applying, with or without modification, other law, exclusive of this Act)."[31]

Section 4 of the 1972 Act had originally provided that such ministerial regulations required legislative confirmation, but it was later felt that this method was too cumbersome.[32] Section 4 was amended by section 1 of the European Communities (Amendment) Act 1973, and it now provides that ministerial regulations made under the Act shall have statutory effect.[33]

This method of implementing directives would appear to be in conflict with Article 15.2, as section 4 permits a Minister of State to make regulations which in some cases do more than give effect to the principles and policies contained in the 1972 Act. A regulation of this nature could effect a far-reaching change in the existing law. It is true that Article 29.4.3 gives constitutional cover to "measures adopted by the State necessitated by the obligations of membership of the Communities" and that the State is obliged by Article 189 of the Treaty to implement such directives. But as we have seen, Article 189 deliberately leaves the *method of implementation* of directives to the Member States, and does not require or prescribe that these directives be implemented by ministerial order. Article 29.4.3 cannot therefore be called in aid to justify

---

[30] Community directives, unlike Community regulations, are not usually directly applicable, *i.e.* they do not immediately become part of the domestic law of each Member State. However, the European Court has made it clear that the implementation of EC directives may in certain cases be superfluous, but in such cases Member States must ensure that their nationals are aware of their rights under such a directive: *Commission* v. *Germany* (Case 29/84) [1985] E.C.R. 166.

[31] However, such regulations may not create an indictable offence: s.3(4).

[32] In fact one such confirming measure was enacted: see European Communities (Confirmation of Regulations) Act 1973.

[33] The amended s.4 provides for an elaborate system of parliamentary scrutiny by the Joint Committee on the Secondary Legislation of the European Communities (now vested in the Joint Oireachtas Committee on Legislation) and also includes procedures whereby regulations made under the Act may be annulled by either House of the Oireachtas. For an account of the work of the Joint Committee, see Robinson, "Irish Parliamentary Scrutiny of European Community Legislation" (1979) 16 C.M.L.R. 9.

what would otherwise be a breach of Article 15.2.[34] Of course, no such difficulties arise where the directive is implemented by an Act of the Oireachtas.

Another interesting example is afforded by the European Communities
(Environmental Impact Assessment) Regulations 1989,[35] whereby the Environmental Impact Assessment directive was implemented by a statutory
instrument following an abortive attempt to do so through the use of an
administrative circular.[36] The implementing instrument is entirely legislative
in character, in that it purports to effect no less than six separate (and extensive) amendments to the Local Government (Planning and Development)
Acts 1963–1983 and amends 11 other diverse items of legislation, ranging
from the Public Health (Ireland) Act 1878 through to the Urban Renewal Act
1986.

Since these views were put first forward in the 1986 edition, a different view
has been advanced. Curtin,[37] for example, has argued that the discretion conferred by Article 189(3) is not unlimited:

> "It must be read in conjunction with Article 5 of the EEC Treaty which
> obligates Member States to take all appropriate measures to give effect to
> Community law, an obligation clearly 'necessitated' by membership of the
> Community. It follows that Member States must recognise the conse-
> quences, in their internal legal order, of their adherence to the Community
> and, if necessary, adapt their procedures in such a way that they do not
> form an obstacle to the implementation, within the prescribed time limits,
> of their obligations within the framework of the Treaty.
>
> The duty to give full effect to Community law means first and foremost
> that the legislature of a given Member State must ensure that the obli-
> gations of membership are implemented in time. In Ireland, where an aver-
> age of 36 Acts manage to become law every year and where well over 500
> statutory instruments have been adopted on the basis of the European

---

[34] However, the Joint Committee on Secondary Legislation of the European Communities
appear to have taken a contrary view on this question. In their Twenty-Second Report (Prl. 5141)
(1975), the Committee commenting (pp. 17–18) on European Communities (Road Traffic)
(Compulsory Insurance) Regulations 1975 (S.I. 1975 No. 178) which amended the Road Traffic
Act 1961, observe as follows:
"The Joint Committee accepts that Ministerial Regulations made under section 3 of the European Communities Act 1972 may lawfully amend Acts of the Oireachtas or other statutes in
force if such is required by the Community secondary legislation which the Regulations are to
implement. However, the fact that the power exists ought not, in the Joint Committee's
opinion, to mean that it is appropriate to use it in every case. Regard should be had to the relative importance of the statute to be amended and to the range of its application to determine
whether the amendment should be effected by a statutory instrument or amending statute. In
the case of a statute such as the Road Traffic Act 1961 which is of such importance in the everyday life of citizens the Joint Committee considers that any proposals for its amendment should
be initiated by a Bill introduced in the Dáil or Seanad. It recommends that when opportunity
offers Regulation S.I. No. 178 of 1975 should be repealed and its terms incorporated in an
amending statute."
[35] S.I. 1989 No. 349.
[36] *Browne* v. *An Bord Pleanála* [1989] I.L.R.M. 865. See pp. 44–45.
[37] Curtin, "Some Reflections on European Community Law in Ireland" (1989) 11 D.U.L.J.
(N.S.) 207, 211–212.

Communities Act 1972 alone, it does not require any great mathematical ability to calculate that, at the pace the Oireachtas currently operates, it would not be an appropriate form and method of ensuring the timely entry into force to provide that in each and every case for their approval by Parliament."

The essential premise of this passage is that there is no alternative to this statutory mechanism, since without it, Ireland would fall behind in its Community obligation to give effect to such directives in national law.

This assumption would not seem to be correct. First, it is not, of course, in every case that the use of the 1973 Act would involve a breach of the constitutional requirements. There are numerous examples of EC directives (such as, for example, labelling requirements) which do not involve the amendment of earlier legislation and which are purely administrative or regulatory in nature. Secondly, to cater for change of a more radical type, there is no constitutional objection to a procedure by which effect is given to such directives via an omnibus statute. Finally, if changes to the present method of implementing directives via the 1973 Act required the Oireachtas to take a more active legislative role, that would be no bad thing. "Lack of parliamentary time" is an argument often advanced in this context, but this is an excuse which is increasingly difficult to accept given that the Dáil sits only about 87 days in the average year.[38]

"Henry VIII clauses"

One other feature of Article 15.2.1 which may be mentioned here is that this sub-Article in conjunction with other constitutional principles[39] prevents the statutory exclusion of judicial review of delegated legislation. In *Institute of Patent Agents* v. *Lockwood*[40] the House of Lords held that rules which "were to have the same effect as if they were contained in [the parent statute]" ("Henry VIII clauses") could not be examined by the courts. The Irish courts—even prior to independence—have never been willing to assent to this proposition, and *Lockwood* has been distinguished—rather unconvincingly— in a series of subsequent Irish cases.[41] However *Lockwood* is now simply of historical interest only as this decision and the principle which it embodies cannot have survived the enactment of the Constitution. Any statutory provision which purported to confer such an immunity on delegated legislation

---

[38] Casey, "Constitutional Law in Ireland" (London, 1987), p. 123.

[39] Art. 34.3.1 (High Court's original jurisdiction) and Art. 40.3 (guarantee of fair procedures). See *Tormey* v. *Att.-Gen.* [1985] I.R. 283 and Pye, "The s.104 Certificate of Registration—The Impenetrable Shield No More?" (1985) 3 I.L.T.(N.S.) 213 and Hogan, "Reflections on Tormey v. Attorney-General" (1986) 8 D.U.L.J.(N.S.) 31. The entire subject of the exclusion of judicial review is examined at pp. 374–378.

[40] [1894] A.C. 347.

[41] *R. (Conyngham)* v. *Pharmaceutical Society of Ireland* [1894] 2 I.R. 132; *Commissioners of Public Works* v. *Monaghan* [1909] 2 I.R. 718; *Mackey* v. *Monks* [1916] 2 I.R. 200 (reversed on other grounds by the House of Lords): [1918] A.C. 59 and *Waterford Corporation* v. *Murphy* [1920] 2 I.R. 165. See Donaldson, *Some Comparative Aspects of Irish Law* (Duke, 1957), pp. 200–203.

4000033327

342.06

T.C. LIBRARY, LETTERKENNY

would be the equivalent of a delegation of legislative power, and this would be contrary to Article 15.2.1 for the reasons given in *City View Press*.

3. Sources of Administrative Law

Introduction

The sources of administrative law are various and heterogeneous, but five principal sources can be identified: the Constitution, common law, primary legislation, delegated legislation and administrative circulars. Many administrative law cases raise issues drawn from more than one of these diverse sources. A good modern example is provided by *O'Flynn* v. *Mid-Western Health Board*,[42] which neatly illustrates the interaction of some of these sources.

Section 72(1) of the Health Act 1970 allows the Minister for Health to prescribe regulations concerning the administration of schemes administered by Health Boards. The Minister duly made a statutory instrument under this section: Health Services Regulations 1972.[43] These regulations establish the entire administrative structure on which is erected the medical card system (by which patients with "full" or "partial eligibility" within the meaning of the 1970 Act are entitled to free or partially free medical care). The making of arrangements between medical practitioners and the Health Boards and the establishment of a complaints committee are required by the Regulations. However, the detailed practical arrangements and the obligations of medical practitioners taking part in the scheme are set out in a ministerial circular of 1972. Furthermore, it is a requirement of participation in the scheme that practitioners should enter into a contract[44] which incorporates the Regulations and the administrative schemes prescribed by the circular with their local Health Boards. In the *O'Flynn* case itself, the applicant doctors were charged with various alleged improprieties and requested further information from the Chief Executive Officer of the respondent board. This information was not forthcoming, but the official nonetheless requested the Minister, pursuant to Article 8(1) of the 1972 Regulations, to convene a committee to investigate these complaints. Barr J. quashed the order establishing such a committee, as he held that the official had not complied with an important precondition prior to invoking this Article 8(1) procedure:

---

[42] [1989] I.R. 429.

[43] S.I. 1972 No. 88.

[44] Thus, in *The State (Boyle)* v. *General Medical Services (Payment) Board* [1981] I.L.R.M. 14 the applicant sought to challenge Art. 8(1) of the 1972 Regulations (which allows for an investigating committee to be established) as *ultra vires* the 1972 Act. Keane J. would not permit such a challenge, since he pointed out (at 15) that:

> "Even if it were held to be *ultra vires*, this would not avail the [applicant], since as a matter of contract, irrespective of any question of statute, he has bound himself to accept the jurisdiction of the appeal committee appointed by the Minister under the terms of this Article."

See also, *Grehan* v. *North Eastern Health Board* [1989] I.R. 422, where Costello J. granted the plaintiff doctor a declaration that the respondents were not unilaterally entitled to alter the terms of her contract by issuing a new circular purporting to alter the contractual terms of doctors participating in the scheme.

"This is a patently important step which has potentially far-reaching consequences for the doctor in question. Article 24 clearly envisages that it ought not to be taken until the doctor has had an opportunity to consider the complaint and to respond to it within a specified time limit. He cannot make a meaningful response if he is not as fully informed as the complaint alleged."[45]

We see here common law and constitutional principles being brought to bear on the proper construction of the Article in question. Since the doctors were not fully informed of the case they had to meet (a conclusion drawn variously from common law and constitutional principles as applied to statutory interpretation), Barr J. went on to hold that the convening of the committee was invalid for want of compliance with these formal requirements.

The law of judicial review is, of course, very largely a creation of the common law in the form of rules of statutory interpretation for there is no Irish equivalent of the United States Administrative Procedure Act 1946. Accordingly, key principles—such as the scope of error of law[46] and the doctrine of reasonableness[47] have been formulated entirely by the judiciary. The development of these principles has, in turn, been buttressed and extended by the Constitution.[48] In addition, doctrines of sovereign immunity[49] and executive privilege[50] have been declared to be unconstitutional and constitutional principles have been introduced to support other far-reaching judicial developments. Primary legislation has been of lesser importance as far as the field of judicial review is concerned, as there are few statutory provisions containing principles of general application in this sphere and, indeed, the task of the administrative lawyer when confronted with primary legislation is quite often confined to engaging in a textual exegesis of the statutory language to ascertain whether administrative decisions taken pursuant to such legislation are truly *intra vires*. However, primary legislation has been the main source of what might be termed organic administrative law, *i.e.* the law relating to the structure and functions of the law relating to Government administration— Ministers and Departments, local authorities, state-sponsored bodies, etc. Moreover, apart from judicial review, the other institution of controls of administrative action—such as the Ombudsman[51] and tribunals—are also the product of statute.

Accordingly, most of the other chapters in this book are taken up with a study of statute law in the field of Government, together with the specialised common law rules of statutory interpretation. Since the principal sources such as the Constitution, statute law and the general common law principles of

---

[45] [1989] I.R. 429, 438.
[46] See pp. 341–354.
[47] See Chap. 10.
[48] See pp. 534–541.
[49] *Byrne* v. *Ireland* [1972] I.R. 241.
[50] *Murphy* v. *Dublin Corporation* [1972] I.R. 215.
[51] See Chap. 7.

judicial review are considered generally throughout this book, and are, in any case, not peculiar to administrative law, the remainder of this chapter is, accordingly, devoted to a consideration of the two remaining principal sources of administrative law: delegated legislation and the use of circulars and non-statutory administrative schemes.

4. Delegated Legislation

Delegated legislation is legislation which has been made by some person or body other than the Oireachtas and to whom the Oireachtas had delegated its legislative functions for strictly limited purposes. While delegated legislation is now an established feature of our law, it could scarcely be otherwise given the growth of the modern state. There are several practical reasons which justify the existence of delegated legislation. Parliamentary time is scarce and the Oireachtas could not reasonably be expected to legislate for every administrative detail. It is, therefore, content to state the general principles in legislation and to allow the details to be regulated by ministerial order. There is also a need for flexibility and the law must be capable of rapid adjustment to meet changing circumstances.[52] In some cases regulations giving effect to the principles enshrined in the parent Act are drawn by a specialist body possessing particular expertise.[53]

Statutory Instruments Act 1947

The Statutory Instruments Act 1947 is designed to ensure the publication of all items of delegated legislation, thus rendering academic any doubts as to whether the Rules Publication Act 1893 applied to Ireland.[54] The term "statutory instrument" is defined by section 1(1) as meaning every "order, regulation, rule, scheme or by-law" made in the exercise of a statutory power. However, the Act then goes on to make the quite unnecessary distinction between statutory instruments to which the Act primarily applies, and other statutory instruments to which the Act's provisions may apply. In fact, the phrase "primarily applies" is something of a misnomer, for the Act does not apply in a secondary sense to other delegated legislation. In other words, if the Act does not primarily apply to certain instruments, then they fall outside the scope of the Act. The matter is further complicated by the fact that the Attorney-General is given power to exempt from the provisions of the Act a particular instrument of a type or class on the grounds that it is only of local or

---

[52] *Craies on Statute Law* (7th ed., Edgar), pp. 290–292.
[53] *e.g.* orders made by the Joint Labour Committee under the Industrial Relations Act 1946 fixing minimum wages for certain industries.
[54] In *The State (Quinlan)* v. *Kavanagh* [1935] I.R. 249, Kennedy C.J. had assumed that the Rules Publications Act 1893 applied to Ireland, but in *Re McGrath and Harte* [1941] I.R. 68, Sullivan C.J. pointed out that this Act had not been adapted for application in this jurisdiction. In fact, the 1893 Act was repealed by s.7 of the 1947 Act.

personal or temporary application or for "any other reason."[55] The Act "primarily applies"[56] to statutory instruments made after January 1, 1948 by either the President; Government; Minister; Minister of State; an authority having for the time being power to make rules of court; or: "[A]ny person or body, whether corporate or unincorporate, exercising throughout the State any functions of government or discharging throughout the State any public duties in relation to public administration."[57] This last category would include, for example, state-sponsored bodies and the Commissioners of Public Works.

Section 1 of the Statutory Instruments (Amendment) Act 1955 requires that a copy of each statutory instrument be sent to 10 listed libraries within 10 days of its being made and that each instrument must also be published by the Stationery Office. Section 3(2) of the 1947 Act provides that in civil cases the validity or effect or coming into operation of any statutory instrument shall not be affected by non-compliance with these publication requirements. As far as criminal cases are concerned, section 3(3) provides that where a person has been charged with the offence of contravening a provision in a statutory instrument to which the Act applies, the prosecution must prove that notice of the making of the order had been published at the date of the alleged offence unless the prosecutor can satisfy the court that reasonable steps have been taken to bring the purport of the statutory instrument to the attention of the public.[58]

In the case of statutory instruments, the common law remains to govern the requirements as to publication to which the Act does not primarily apply. In *The People* v. *Kennedy*[59] the Court of Criminal Appeal held that orders made under the Emergency Powers Act 1939 were not in the same position as a stat-

---

[55] s.2(3)(4). Notice of exemption must be published in *Iris Oifigiúil*. The compatibility of this exemption procedure with the equality guarantee contained in Art. 40.1 of the Constitution seems doubtful. For a more extensive discussion of the 1947 Act, see Jackson, "Delegated Legislation in Ireland" [1962] *Public Law* 417. It is understood that Bord Telecom Éireann sought an exemption under the 1947 Act from the Attorney-General in respect of statutory instruments under the Postal and Telecommunications Services Act 1983 which authorised price increases, but this was refused, presumably on the basis that such orders ought to be published.

[56] The certificate of the Attorney-General to the effect that in his opinion a particular instrument is one to which the Act primarily applies is conclusive: s.2(2). S.4(1) of the Documentary Evidence Act 1925 provides that prima facie evidence of the making of any delegated legislation by the Government, a Minister, or any statutory body, corporate or unincorporate exercising any function of government or discharging throughout the State "any public duties in relation to public administration," may be given by production of a copy of *Iris Oifigiúil* purporting to contain such regulations or the production of a copy of the instrument or regulation purporting to be published under the "superintendence or authority" of the Stationery Office.

[57] The instrument must also be one which is required by statute to be laid before both or either Houses of the Oireachtas or is of such a character as affects the public generally or any particular class or classes of the public (s.2(2)) and must not be a statutory instrument which is required by statute to be published in *Iris Oifigiúil* (s.2(1)).

[58] s.3(3) thus preserves the common law principles recognised in cases such as *Lim Chin Aik* v. *R.* [1963] A.C. 160.

[59] [1946] I.R. 517. See also, *People* v. *Griffin* [1974] I.R. 416.

ute (*i.e.* not in the public domain), and therefore, upon a prosecution for a contravention of the order, must be proved in evidence. This decision was later distinguished in *The State (Taylor)* v. *Wicklow Circuit Judge*,[60] where it was sought to quash a conviction under the provisions of the Road Traffic Act 1933 on the grounds that the existence of a ministerial order bringing into force the relevant portions of the Act had not been formally proved in evidence. Davitt J. observed that the relevant order in *Kennedy's* case was:

> "Substantive legislation made by exercise of delegated authority; that it was continuous in its effect and that from day to day it affected personal rights and liabilities; whereas the order in question here was but momentary in its operation, bringing into force a piece of legislation enacted by the Oireachtas."[61]

By contrast Davitt J. held in *Taylor's* case that the Circuit Court judge who had been administering the Road Traffic Act 1933 for many years was entitled to take judicial notice of the ministerial order without the need for formal proof of its making. Another restriction on the general principle was laid down in *D.P.P.* v. *Collins*.[62] It concerned the need to prove in evidence the existence of regulations implementing the Road Traffic Act 1978. Henchy J. conceded that while formal proof of the legislative provisions may be necessary where the precise ingredients of the offence are uncertain, it was otherwise where (as here):

> "[A] course of judicial conduct is so inveterate and unquestioned and of such a nature that it necessarily postulates the existence and validity of a statutory instrument. In such circumstances the court is entitled to take judicial notice of the statutory instrument.[63]

Given that in *Collins* the regulations were ones to which the 1947 Act primarily applied,[64] the court could have arrived at the same result by reference to section 3(3) of that Act. The necessity for the prosecution to prove that the order had been published could have been thereby dispensed with, as it seems clear that "reasonable steps" had been taken for the purpose of bringing the regulations to the attention of the public.

Section 11 of the Interpretation Act 1937 permits a Minister to make regulations and orders in advance of the Act coming into force, where this is necessary to enable the Act to have "full force and effect on the coming into force of the Act." It was on this basis that in *The State (McColgan)* v. *Clifford*[65] the Supreme Court upheld the validity of advance regulations made by

[60] [1951] I.R. 311.
[61] [1951] I.R. 319.
[62] [1981] I.L.R.M. 447. See Stevenson (1983) 19 Ir.Jur.(N.S.) 95.
[63] [1981] I.L.R.M. 450.
[64] *I.e.* regulations made by a Minister of State after January 1, 1948, which were not of a purely "local or personal" application.
[65] [1980] I.L.R.M. 75.

the Minister for the Environment prior to the coming into force of the Road Traffic Act 1978. Henchy J. declared that the court could take judicial notice of the fact that the earlier legislation had broken down, and that fresh legislation was imperative. Given these circumstances, advance regulations were necessary in order to give the Act "full force and effect" once it became operational.

While there is some English authority for the proposition that delegated legislation does not come into force until it is published,[66] this point is dealt with by section 9(2) of the Interpretation Act 1937 which provides:

"Every instrument made wholly or partly under an Act of the Oireachtas shall, unless the contrary intention is expressed in such instrument, be deemed to be in operation as from the end of the day before the day on which such instrument is made."

However, the idea that delegated legislation should have the force of law in advance of its publication would seem to be inimical to constitutional values such as fair procedures.

In most cases the parent statute will require that the statutory instrument be "laid" before the Houses of the Oireachtas within a specified period— generally, 21 sitting days.[67] Such authority as there is suggests that failure to comply with this "laying" requirement does not invalidate the statutory instrument.[68]

Judicial control

In the first place, as mentioned above, the delegation of power must not be in breach of Article 15.2.1. In addition the courts must examine the validity of any delegated legislation according to the standard criteria of *vires* or reasonableness. As executive or administrative bodies do not possess an inherent legislative power, the validity of delegated legislation falls to be tested against the background of what is authorised by the parent statute either expressly or by necessary implication and in just the same way as any administrative action effecting only an individual change. The question of whether a statutory instrument is *ultra vires* the parent statute is essentially one of statutory interpretation. In determining the issue of *vires*, there are a number of standard presumptions which are employed by the courts. Thus, the Oireachtas is pre-

---

[66] *Johnson* v. *Sargant* [1918] 1 K.B. 101. See Lanham, "Delegated Legislation and Publication" (1974) 37 M.L.R. 510.
[67] The "laying procedure" is regulated by statute: see Houses of the Oireachtas (Laying of Documents) Act 1966.
[68] *Premier Meat Packers Ltd.* v. *Minister for Agriculture*, High Court, July 28, 1971. See also, *R.* v. *Sheer Metalcraft Ltd.* [1951] 1 Q.B. 586. But given that the object of the 1966 Act is to enable the Houses of the Oireachtas to examine a statutory instrument with a view to its possible annulment, it could be argued that the "laying requirement" is mandatory, and not merely directory. However, the Attorney-General's office has advised that failure to lay does not render a statutory instrument invalid: Report of Senate Select Committee on Statutory Instruments (T.162) (Pr. 4685), p. 15. On mandatory/directory requirements, see pp. 361–371.

sumed not to have delegated the power to raise taxes[69]; or to oust the jurisdiction of the courts[70]; or to encroach upon the liberty of the citizen[71]; or to give retrospective effect to delegated legislation[72] or to infringe any provisions of the Constitution.[73] Subject to these presumptions, the task of the courts is to ascertain the true intent of the enabling Act, and, as Butler J. said in *Minister for Industry & Commerce* v. *Hales*:

> "Considerations of constitutionality apart, the judicial control of subordinate legislation operates only through the doctrine of *ultra vires* and the function of the courts can only be fulfilled by enquiry as to whether the statutory rule or order falls within the scope of the enactment from which it purports to derive its authority. This is the check placed upon arbitrary government by the executive. In a consideration of any given power, the court must not only interpret the terms in which the statutory power is expressed to see that it is not given any wider power than is necessary, but must also see that the power does not exceed or interfere with or negative the provisions and intention of the enactment as a whole."[74]

There are a number of modern illustrations of this principle in cases where statutory instruments have been declared to be *ultra vires*. In *Minister for Industry & Commerce* v. *Hales*[75] the question at issue was whether insurance agents employed under a contract of service were "workers" for the purposes

---

[69] *Att.-Gen.* v. *Wilts United Dairies Ltd.* (1921) 39 T.L.R. 781. For a discussion of whether the Oireachtas may validly delegate the power to raise taxes in view of the provisions of Arts. 17 and 22 of the Constitution, see Hogan, "A Note on the Imposition of Duties Act 1957" (1985) 7 D.U.L.J.(N.S.) 134.

[70] *Newcastle Breweries Ltd.* v. *The King* [1920] 1 K.B. 854; *Commissioners of Customs and Excise* v. *Cure and Deeley Ltd.* [1962] 1 Q.B. 340 and see generally, *Tormey* v. *Att.-Gen.* [1985] I.R. 289.

[71] *The State (O'Flaherty)* v. *O'Floinn* [1954] I.R. 295; *Murphy* v. *P.M.P.A. Insurance Co. Ltd.*, [1978] I.L.R.M. 25 (presumption against interference with right to privacy); *The State (Lynch)* v. *Ballagh* [1986] I.R. 203.

[72] This is a general presumption of statutory interpretation: *Hamilton* v. *Hamilton* [1982] I.R. 466; *Doyle* v. *An Taoiseach*. But *cf. Re McGrath and Harte* [1941] I.R. 68 and *Minister for Agriculture* v. *O'Connell* [1942] I.R. 600. The Joint Oireachtas Committee on the Secondary Legislation of the European Communities has drawn attention to the fact that the European Communities Act 1972 does not authorise the making of delegated legislation with retrospective effect: see p. 38.

[73] There is a presumption that statutory powers (including power to make delegated legislation) granted by an Act of the Oireachtas do not authorise the donee of such powers to infringe the Constitution: *East Donegal Co-operatives Ltd.* v. *Att.-Gen.* [1970] I.R. 317. An extradition treaty which was promulgated by means of statutory instrument pursuant to s.8 of the Extradition Act 1965 was declared unconstitutional as it created a charge on public funds without the approval of Dáil Éireann contrary to Art. 29.5.2: *The State (Gilliland)* v. *Governor of Mountjoy Prison*, [1986] I.L.R.M. 381. Statutory instruments which effected unconstitutional religious discrimination contrary to Art. 44.2.3 were declared invalid in *Quinn's Supermarket Ltd.* v. *Att.-Gen.* [1972] I.R. 1 and *Mulloy* v. *Minister for Education* [1975] I.R. 88. It appears that delegated legislation can qualify as an "enactment" for the purposes of Art. 40.1, thus bringing the "proviso" to that sub-Article into play: *Dillane* v. *Ireland* [1980] I.L.R.M. 167. But *cf.* the views of Walsh J. in *East Donegal Co-operatives Ltd.* v. *Att.-Gen.* [1970] I.R. 317. See generally, Kelly, *op. cit.* pp. 447–449.

[74] [1967] I.R. 50, 83.

[75] [1967] I.R. 50.

of the Holidays (Employees) Act 1961. Although the Act was expressly confined in its general application to employees and apprentices, the Minister
was empowered by section 3(3) to extend its application in respect of holiday
pay to any "class or description of . . . persons" who could be deemed to be
workers for the purposes of the Act. The Minister had purported by statutory
instrument made under section 3(3) to so extend the Act to insurance agents,
but this order was held to be *ultra vires* the parent Act by a Divisional High
Court. As Henchy J. remarked:

> "It is not conceivable that the legislature, having indicated that the scope
> of the Act was to be limited to persons employed under a contract of ser-
> vice or a contract of apprenticeship, should by the use of general words
> in section 3(3) of the Act have given the Minister power to broaden the
> scope of the Act to such an extent that he could, by the making of regu-
> lations, import into work-contracts made with independent contractors a
> series of statutory terms as to holiday allowances, the breach of which
> would result in criminal liability. I cannot believe that the power to effect
> such radical and far-reaching changes in the law of contract was
> intended, or should be deemed to have been so intended, by a loosely
> drafted sub-section in an Act that has declared its purpose and scope to
> be otherwise."[76]

Other cases are more straightforward and so, for example, in *The State
(Carney)* v. *Governor of Portlaoise Prison*,[77] rule 38(2) of the Rules for the
Government of Prisons 1947 was held by the Supreme Court to be *ultra
vires*. This sub-rule allowed for the remission of one-fourth of a sentence of
penal servitude for good conduct, yet the Penal Servitude Acts 1854–1863
made no provision for such a rule. Another example in a similar context is
furnished by the decision of McWilliam J. in *Incorporated Law Society of
Ireland* v. *Minister for Justice*.[78] Here rule 2 of the Government of Prisons
Rules 1976 purported to allow the Minister, where he considered this necessary in the interests of the "security of the State," to restrict access of particular legal advisers to a given prison. McWilliam J. pointed out that the
General Prisons (Ireland) Act 1877 did not enable the Minister to make rules
in the interests of the security of the State and held that the Rules were
accordingly *ultra vires*.

But by far the greatest number of challenges have been to the *vires* of Rules
of Court. The various Rules Committees for the District Court, Circuit Court

---

[76] *Ibid.* 76–77.
[77] [1957] I.R. 25.
[78] [1978] I.L.R.M. 112. Other examples include *The State (McLoughlin)* v. *Eastern Health Board*
[1986] I.R. 416 (where ministerial regulations restricting the statutory right of claimants to certain
fuel allowances were held to be *ultra vires*) and *American International Tobacco Co.* v. *Att.-Gen.*
[1990] 1 I.R. 394 (where Hamilton P. held that s.65 of the Health Act 1947 confined the Minister
to declaring certain medical preparations to be "restricted articles" and that the Minister could
not avail of this section to restrict the sale of non-medical articles such as tobacco sachets).

and the Superior Courts have been given statutory jurisdiction to make rules concerning the "practice and procedure" of their respective courts and several cases turn on the question of whether a particular rule is properly a matter of practice and procedure.[79] In *Woolf* v. *Ó Gríobhta*,[80] Davitt P. held that rule 85 of the District Court Rules 1948 was *ultra vires*. This rule had purported to confer the right, upon payment of the precribed fee, to obtain copies of depositions taken in a criminal trial upon "any person who satisfies the Clerk that he has a bona fide interest in the matter." These words were, said Davitt P., of "very wide application" and not at all confined to parties to the proceedings before the District Court. By purporting to confer such rights on persons who might be "in no way concerned with the exercise by the District Court of its jurisdiction," the Rules went beyond matters of practice and procedure and were *ultra vires*. A similar approach is evident in the judgment of the Supreme Court in *The State (Lynch)* v. *Ballagh*,[81] where the validity of the District Court (Criminal Procedure Act 1967) Rules 1985 was at issue. These Rules allowed a member of the Gardaí to decide to release a suspect on station bail and direct his appearance at a sitting of the District Court within 30 days. A majority of the Supreme Court held these Rules to be *ultra vires* in that they regulated the procedure to be adopted by a member of an Garda Síochána and were not concerned with the practice and procedure before the District Court.

Other cases have concerned attempted alterations—as opposed to mere necessary adaptions or modifications—of statutory requirements by the Rules Committees. In *The State (O'Flaherty)* v. *Ó Floinn*[82] the Supreme Court held that rule 55(4) of the District Court Rules (which had purported to enlarge the period by which a District Justice could remand a suspect in custody to 15 days) was *ultra vires* the provisions of section 21 of the Indictable Offences (Ireland) Act 1849. O'Dalaigh J. described the proposed change as "radical" and as something "more than the mere modification" of the 1849 Act. In *Thompson* v. *Curry*,[83] the provisions of Order 62, rule 5 of the Rules of the Superior Courts 1962 which attempted to reverse a statutory sequence prescribed by section 2 of the Summary Jurisdiction Act 1857 were found to be *ultra vires* by the Supreme Court. Walsh J. described this as an attempt to amend a condition precedent to jurisdiction and, hence, beyond the powers

---

[79] The power of the Superior Court Rules Committee to make Rules of Court governing "pleading, practice and procedure generally" is contained in s.36 of the Courts of Justice Act 1924, as applied by ss.14(2) and 48 of the Courts (Supplemental Provisions) Act 1961. It is interesting to note that s.36(ix) of the 1924 Act purports to confer the Committee with power to secure the "adaptation or modification of any statute that may be requisite for any of the purposes of this Act." However, this power to modify or adapt an Act is one that cannot validly be delegated to the Rules Committee by virtue of Art. 15.2.1 in view of the reasoning of the Supreme Court in cases such as *City View Press Ltd.* v. *AnCO* [1980] I.R. 381.

[80] [1953] I.R. 267.

[81] [1986] I.R. 203.

[82] [1954] I.R. 295.

[83] [1970] I.R. 61.

of the Superior Court Rules Committee. Finally, in *Rainey* v. *Delap*[84] the Supreme Court held rules 29 and 30 of the District Court Rules 1948 to be *ultra vires*. Section 10(1) of the Petty Sessions (Ireland) Act 1851 confers power on a District Justice to hear and determine a complaint and to issue a summons accordingly. Rules 29 and 30 purported to confer this power on a District Court clerk, but this was held by Finlay C.J. to go beyond the mere modification of an earlier statutory provision and was thus *ultra vires*.

The validity of Order 31, rule 29 of the Rules of the Superior Courts 1986 (which provides for the making of an order for discovery against a person who is not a party to the proceedings) has been challenged in several cases, but has been upheld on each such occasion on the ground that it does not involve any substantive change in the law. Barron J. described the change in *Holloway* v. *Belenos Publications Ltd.*[85] as a new rule "regulating the exercise of the inherent jurisdiction of the court,"[86] a view echoed by Costello J. in *Fitzpatrick* v. *Independent Newspapers plc*,[87] who said of the rule that it was "procedural," adding that the "Rules Committee is clearly empowered to enable the courts to make such orders."[88]

As stated already, the courts exercise control over delegated legislation in the same manner as other administrative actions and thus delegated legislation may be condemned as invalid on the ground that it is unreasonable[89] or has been made in bad faith or (possibly) in breach of natural justice.[90] However, because of the legislative character of statutory instruments or other delegated legislation, it seems likely that the rules of constitutional justice will apply—if at all—only in an attenuated form.[91]

Procedure

One practical problem relates to the methods by which a statutory instrument may be challenged. Invalidity can certainly be raised by way of defence[92] in either civil or criminal proceedings or, indeed, by way of plenary proceedings. The majority of challenges, however, arise in judicial review

[84] [1988] I.R. 470. Compare this reasoning with the unduly permissive approach of cases such as *Att.-Gen.* v. *Bruen and Kelly* [1935] I.R. 615, where it was held that the relevant District Court Rule permitting a summons to be signed by a District Court clerk was *intra vires*, despite the express provisions of s.36 of the Illicit Distillation (Ireland) Act 1831 and s.11 of the Petty Sessions (Ireland) Act 1851 which required the summons to be signed by a Justice of the Peace and now a District Justice.
[85] [1988] I.R. 494.
[86] *Ibid.* 498.
[87] [1988] I.R. 132.
[88] *Ibid.* 135.
[89] See, *e.g. Cassidy* v. *Minister for Industry & Commerce* [1978] I.R. 297; *Doyle* v. *An Taoiseach* [1986] I.L.R.M. 693.
[90] *Burke* v. *Minister for Labour* [1979] I.R. 354; *The State (Lynch)* v. *Cooney* [1982] I.R. 337.
[91] *Bates* v. *Lord Hailsham* [1972] 1 W.L.R. 1373; *Cassidy* v. *Minister for Industry & Commerce* [1978] I.R. 297. See Casey, "Ministerial Orders and Review for Reasonableness" [1978] *Public Law* 130.
[92] As happened in *Listowel U.D.C.* v. *McDonagh* [1968] I.R. 312. But while the District and Circuit Courts may rule on the validity of a statutory instrument (excepting, of course, cases where a post-1937 instrument is alleged to be inconsistent with the Constitution), regard must be had to the jurisdictional limits imposed by s.25 of the Courts (Supplemental Provisions) Act 1961.

proceedings. It is also well established that the invalidity of a statutory instrument can be challenged by way of case stated.[93] Where it is alleged that the statutory instrument is invalid on constitutional grounds a complication arises. Article 34.3.2 provides that the constitutionality of any post-1937 law can only be determined by the High Court and this has been held to mean that such issues cannot even be raised by way of case stated in the District or Circuit Courts.[94] As a result of the Supreme Court's decision in *The State (Gilliland)* v. *Governor of Mountjoy Prison*,[95] it would appear that a statutory instrument made pursuant to a post-1937 statute is also a "law" for the purposes of Article 34.3.2. In the *Gilliland* case, the statutory instrument had been made pursuant to the Extradition Act 1965. Accordingly, in the extradition proceedings before the District Court it might have been open to the requested person to allege that the order in question was *ultra vires* the parent Act. These issues (provided that they did not raise constitutional questions) might also have been the subject of a case stated. However, if it had been alleged that the order were *ultra vires* the Constitution, this could only have been done by way of proceedings (such as judicial review) which were actually commenced in the High Court.

Parent statutes and confirmation orders

One significant practical point which arises concerns the continuing validity of delegated legislation made under a parent statute when that parent statute has itself been repealed. Despite the general statutory saving clause contained in section 21(1) of the Interpretation Act 1937, it would seem that, in the event of a repeal, as might be expected, the delegated legislation will also lapse: the branch falls with the tree, unless some statute expressly provides to the contrary.[96]

Moreover, inconveniently enough, this would seem to remain true even though that parent statute is repealed and replaced by another similar statute or even by a consolidation Act. There is no general doctrine of "implicit survivorship." The exception, already alluded to, is where the delegated legislation is thrown a statutory life-line. A typical example is section 312(2) of the Social Welfare (Consolidation) Act 1981 which provides:

"All instruments and documents made or issued under the replaced enactments and in force immediately before the commencement of this Act (other than the provisions of any instruments which are incorporated in this Act) shall continue in force as if made or issued under this Act."[97]

---

[93] As happened in *Minister for Industry & Commerce* v. *Hales* [1967] I.R. 50.
[94] *Foyle Fisheries Commission* v. *Gallen* (1960) Ir.Jur.Rep. 35; *Minister for Labour* v. *Costello* [1988] I.R. 235.
[95] [1987] I.R. 201.
[96] *Watson* v. *Winch* [1916] 1 K.B. 688.
[97] This provision was considered in *The State (Kenny)* v. *Minister for Social Welfare* [1986] I.R. 693, 695 where Egan J. considered it "strange" that a statutory instrument made in 1973 should now be examined as to its *vires* in relation to the Social Welfare (Consolidation) Act 1981. However, he pointed out that the Order had been carried over by s.312(2) of the 1981 Act. Another example of this statutory technique is provided by the Restrictive Practices Act 1972, s.26(2) of which carries over statutory instruments previously made pursuant to s.9 of the (now repealed) Restrictive Trade Practices Act 1953.

This obviously sensible device raises a novel constitutional point. As we have seen, the effect of Article 15.2.1 of the Constitution is that delegated legislation can do no more than fill in the details of principles which have been laid down by some Act of the Oireachtas. This, presumably, must mean laid down by parent legislation which is in force, but the issue is whether this has also to be the original parent legislation. It would seem, however, that this is not constitutionally required. The object of the constitutional provision is to ensure that there is no new principle of policy enunciated in delegated legislation which has not been authorised by some existing Act of the Oireachtas. There is no reason why this Act has to be the same as that which initially authorised the delegated legislation.

A further practical question has been raised by a number of recent cases. If a statutory instrument is found to be *ultra vires*, can this order be subsequently confirmed with prospective effect by a later Act of the Oireachtas? The principle behind the doctrine of *ultra vires* in this context is that an order is invalid if it exceeds the scope of the statutory powers vested in the maker of the legislation *by the Oireachtas*. Accordingly, it would not seem inconsistent with this principle if the Oireachtas was subsequently to confirm and validate the order in question. This is illustrated by two cases concerning orders made under the Imposition of Duties Act 1957. In the first of these cases, *Doyle* v. *An Taoiseach*,[98] Barrington J. held that an order made under this Act was void for unreasonableness. Section 79 of the Finance Act 1980 had purported to confirm this order (as is required under the machinery of the 1957 Act), but at the time of confirmation the Oireachtas had not realised that the order was actually invalid. Barrington J. doubted whether such a void order could be thus confirmed, but in the Supreme Court, Henchy J. appeared to suggest that an invalid order could be confirmed in this way, at least where the confirming legislation did not operate retrospectively. The restriction would seem to be correct given that the usual problems associated with retrospective legislation could arise if the Oireachtas were to purport to validate an *ultra vires* statutory instrument by a later Act.

This matter also arose in *McDaid* v. *Sheehy*[99] which concerned the validity of the Imposition of Duties (No. 221) (Excise Duties) Order 1975 which had been subsequently confirmed by section 46 of the Finance Act 1976. Blayney J. held that as the enabling provision (section 1) of the Imposition of Duties Act 1957 was unconstitutional, it followed that the 1975 Order was invalid. But could section 46 of the 1976 Act have the effect of supplying the validity which the 1975 Order had previously lacked? Blayney J. thought it could:

"The confirmation of the Order was a clear expression of [the] intention [of the Oireachtas]. At that time it was believed that the order was valid but that confirmation was necessary so that it would continue to have statutory

---

[98] [1986] I.L.R.M. 693. The Supreme Court held that the confirming legislation could not operate retrospectively, since this would have had the effect of creating retroactive criminal sanctions, contrary to Art. 15.5 of the Constitution.
[99] [1989] I.L.R.M. 342.

31

force after the end of 1976 . . . So the intention in confirming was to give it the status of a permanent statutory provision deriving its validity as from the end of 1976 from section 46 and it seems to me to be perfectly reasonable to interpret section 46 as giving effect to that intention.

The alternative is to say that section 46 had no effect whatever—that because such orders mentioned in the section were invalid they could not be confirmed. But such an interpretation would not . . . be reasonable. Firstly, it is at variance with the clear intention of the Oireachtas that the orders mentioned in the section should have the force of law, and, secondly, it proceeds on the assumption, which has not been supported by any authority, that an invalid order cannot be confirmed. There is no doubt that an invalid order can be rendered valid by being made the subject of a statutory provision . . . "[1]

Blayney J.'s reasoning would appear to be a straightforward application of the principle of *ut res magis valeat quam pereat*. In this case, section 46 of the 1976 Act had simply provided that:

"The orders mentioned in the table to this section are hereby confirmed."

and this formula can hardly be considered to be objectionable.

Categories of delegated legislation

Orders. We have already seen that section 1(1) of the Statutory Instruments Act 1947 defines a statutory instrument as meaning "an order, regulation, rule, scheme or by-law" made in the exercise of a statutory power. An order may be contrasted with regulations and rules in that it refers (or, at any rate, ought to refer) to the single exercise of an administrative power in relation to a particular person or situation[2] and random examples include commencement orders bringing statutes into force, judicial appointments and compulsory purchase orders. However, the nomenclature employed in the case of delegated legislation is not consistent and there are many examples of delegated legislation which are referred to as "orders" when, strictly speaking, they should be designated as "regulations."[3]

Regulations and Rules. Regulations, like by-laws, have a definite legislative character. Rules have the same character as regulations, save that this term is usually reserved for orders describing and regulating the procedure of courts,[4] tribunals or other statutory bodies.

Schemes. Schemes, like orders, tend to be administrative in character, but this nomenclature is often employed where the instrument involves figures or gradations, or where it prescribes the details of fees or charges. A good

---

[1] *Ibid.* 348. Blayney J. added ([1989] I.L.R.M. 347–348) that it was unreasonable to construe s.46 of the 1976 Act "as having no effect."
[2] See Report of the Senate Select Committee on Statutory Instruments (T. 162) (Pr. 4685), p. 15.
[3] For example, statutory instruments made under the Restrictive Practices Acts 1972–1987 are designated as orders, even though such orders are essentially legislative in character.
[4] S.I. 1986 No. 78.

example is provided by section 90(2) of the Postal and Telecommunications Services Act 1983 which allows Bord Telecom to make a scheme detailing charges for its telecommunications services and the terms and conditions applicable to such charges. Thus, for example, the Telephone (Amendment) Scheme 1986 prescribes rules in respect of telephone charges and itemises such matters as differing costs depending on the length of the phone-call, distance between caller and receiver and so forth.

By-laws. By-laws are another category of delegated legislation. As their title implies, these rules have a legislative character, but differ from regulations in that they are restricted in their ambit or field of application. By-laws are typically made by local authorities in respect of their own functional area, but other examples include by-laws made by railway companies or airport authorities. One element of what constitutes a by-law was explained by Lord Russell in *Kruse* v. *Johnson*:

> "An ordinance affecting the public, or some portion of the public, imposed by some authority clothed with statutory powers ordering something to be done or not to be done, and accompanied by some sanction or penalty for its non-compliance."[5]

This definition was recently approved by Walsh J. in *The State (Harrington)* v. *Wallace*.[6] Here the question was whether certain sheep-dipping regulations made by Cork County Council could properly be regarded as by-laws. Walsh J. agreed that not every administrative regulation made by a local authority could be regarded as a by-law and where the regulation did not itself contain a sanction it could not be regarded as a by-law. Here the regulations did contain a criminal sanction for non-observance and this fact, coupled with the local character of the regulations, was enough to make them by-laws.

Section 4(1) of the Documentary Evidence Act 1925 provides that prima facie evidence of any by-law may be given by the production of a copy of *Iris Oifigiúil* purporting to contain such a by-law. However, this subsection does *not* apply to by-laws made by local authorities, as individual local authorities cannot be said "to be exercising throughout the State any functions of government or discharging throughout the State any public duties in relation to public administration" within the meaning of section 4(2)(*d*) of the 1925 Act. For the same reason, local authorities fall outside the scope of the Statutory Instruments Act 1947.

Sections 125–127 of the Municipal Corporations (Ireland) Act 1840 enable certain local authorities to make by-laws "for the good rule and government of the borough." County councils were given similar powers by section 16 of the Local Government (Ireland) Act 1898. Other legislation vests local authorities with power to make by-laws in relation to specific subjects, especially in relation to environmental and public health matters.[7]

---

[5] [1898] 2 Q.B. 91, 96.
[6] [1988] I.R. 290.
[7] See, *e.g.* Public Health (Ire.) Act 1878.

In addition to the specific controls contained in the particular statutory provisions the courts may, as with other forms of delegated legislation, invalidate by-laws on the grounds of lack of *vires*, unreasonableness, etc.[8]

Parliamentary control

Many hundreds of statutory instruments are promulgated each year, some of them of a very far-reaching nature. In an attempt to deal with this difficulty the Oireachtas often seeks to retain some measure of parliamentary control. The parent statute typically provides that every regulation made pursuant to that Act must be laid before each House of the Oireachtas. Either House may then pass a resolution within 21 sitting days annulling any such regulation but without prejudice to anything previously done thereunder.[9] While this procedure is of some value in permitting the discussion of a contentious statutory instrument, it ignores the reality of a Government majority in both Houses of the Oireachtas, so that this method of control remains largely theoretical. One might also mention that while this annulment procedure has been described by O'Higgins C.J. as a "valuable safeguard," it cannot authorise that which is not otherwise sanctioned by Article 15.2.[10]

Occasionally a statute may require that confirming legislation be passed within a particular stated period[11]; or that the draft instrument will not come into force unless confirmed by Act of the Oireachtas[12] or resolution of each House[13]; or provide for an appeal by any person aggrieved against the making of the instrument to the High Court.[14]

Save in the case of statutory instruments made under the European Communities Act 1972, there is currently (1991) no parliamentary scrutiny of delegated legislation. This is in contrast with the position which obtained between 1948 and 1983 when this function was discharged by a Senate Select Com-

---

[8] See, *e.g. Kruse* v. *Johnson* [1898] 2 Q.B. 91 (by-law prohibiting singing within 50 yards of a dwelling-house not void for unreasonableness); *Dublin Corporation* v. *Irish Church Missions* [1901] 1 I.R. 387; *Enniscorthy U.D.C.* v. *Field* [1904] 2 I.R. 518; *Dun Laoghaire Corporation* v. *Brock* (1952) Ir.Jur.Rep. 37; *Limerick Corporation* v. *Sheridan* (1956) 90 I.L.T.R. 56; *Listowel U.D.C.* v. *McDonagh* [1968] I.R. 312 and see generally, pp. 514–515.

[9] On this "laying" procedure, see p. 25. Note that in *Immigration and Naturalisation Service* v. *Chada*, 462 U.S. 919 (1983) a majority of the U.S. Supreme Court held that the "legislative veto" was unconstitutional. This decision was the outcome of a formal, logical application of the separation of powers: if the veto were to be classified as an executive or judicial function it would not be for Congress, alternatively, if it were a legislative function it should have been decided by both Houses and signed by the President rather than through the resolution of one House acting alone. If *Chada* were applied in this jurisdiction it would probably render unconstitutional the power to annul statutory instruments given to both individual Houses of the Oireachtas. It is unlikely that *Chada* would be followed in this jurisdiction if only because in Ireland the legislature is not just a law-making organ since, in addition, the Government is responsible to the Dáil. However, this result could also be avoided if the Houses of the Oireachtas were to be characterised as being merely designated bodies to whom an administrative power (*viz.* the power of annulment) has been given.

[10] *City View Press Ltd.* v. *AnCO* [1980] I.R. 380.

[11] *e.g.* Imposition of Duties Act 1957, s.2; Provisional Collection of Taxes Act 1927, s.3.

[12] Restrictive Practices Act 1972, s.8(3).

[13] *e.g.* Electoral Act 1963, s.6(3); Health Act 1970, s.4(5).

[14] *e.g.* Fisheries (Consolidation) Act 1959, s.8 (appeal to High Court). See *Moloney* v. *Minister for Fisheries*, High Court, February 28, 1979; *Dunne* v. *Minister for Fisheries* [1984] I.R. 230 and *Courtney* v. *Minister for Fisheries* [1989] I.L.R.M. 605.

mittee on Statutory Instruments. This function then devolved on the Joint Oireachtas Committee on Legislation between 1983 and 1987, but neither Committee was re-established in the wake of either the 1987 or 1989 General Elections. This is a pity, since that Committee performed quite valuable work in highlighting deficiencies in statutory instruments promulgated otherwise than in accordance with the European Communities Act 1972. Since it is possible that such a Committee may be established at some time in the future, and given that the past publications of both the Senate Committee and the Joint Oireachtas Committee are largely inaccessible to the legal community, it is proposed here to give a short account of the work of these Committees.

Senate Select Committee on Statutory Instruments/Joint Oireachtas Committee on Legislation

Because the Joint Oireachtas Committee which sat between 1983 and 1987 did not have any set criteria against which to judge statutory instruments, it is instructive to refer to the terms of reference of the former Senate Committee. This Committee was required to report to the Houses of the Oireachtas the existence of a statutory instrument on the following grounds:

"(i) that it imposes a charge on the public revenues or contains provisions requiring payments to be made to the Exchequer or any Government Department or to any local or public authority in consideration of any licence or consent, or of any services to be rendered or prescribes the amount of any such charge or payments;

(ii) that it appears to make some unusual or unexpected use of the powers conferred by the statute under which it was made;

(iii) that it purports to have retrospective effect where the parent statute confers no express authority so to provide;

(iv) that there appears to have been unjustifiable delay either in the laying of it before either House of the Oireachtas or in its publication;

(v) that for any special reason its form or purport calls for elucidation;

(vi) that its drafting appears to be defective; or
on any other ground which does not impinge on its merits or on the policy behind it; . . . "[15]

The high constitutional significance of the first and third heads requires no underlining. In fact, the former Senate Committee seldom had to invoke these grounds. The second ground covers a noticeably diverse collection of blemishes. For example, one instrument raised by several million pounds the maximum borrowings of a certain body which could be guaranteed by the Minister for Finance.[16] In another case, a statutory instrument which attempted to control the sale of commercial cream was cast so widely that it

---

[15] Second Report of the Select Committee on Statutory Rules, Orders and Regulations (1949) (T. 122), p. vii. The instrument in question was the Emergency Powers (No. 157) Order 1942 (Seventh Amendment) Order 1948 (S.I. 1948 No. 357).
[16] First Report of the Select Committee on Statutory Rules, Orders and Regulations (1949) (T. 121), pp. xii–xviii.

even caught a householder skimming cream off a bottle of milk with a tea-spoon.[17]

The remaining heads may be illustrated by reference to the last Report (1978–1981) of the former Senate Committee[18] which considered 333 instruments. The attention of the Senate was drawn to 36 of them. Twenty-one instruments were reported on the grounds of "unjustifiable delay" under head (iv). The criterion set by previous select committees was that a delay of more than seven days was "unjustifiable" and the delays in respect of which the Committee complained averaged 18 days and ranged from nine days to three months. The significance of these delays lies in the fact that, as the Committee observed, a member of either the Dáil or the Senate may put down a motion for annulment only after the instrument has been laid, yet the instrument comes into force at the date it is made and the annulment is not retrospective.

In the Senate Committee's last report, 14 statutory instruments succumbed under the miscellaneous head (v) (" . . . for any special reason its form or purport calls for elucidation"). The two most significant defects were: first, the lack of a brief explanatory memorandum describing the general purport of the instrument, in spite of a Department of Finance instruction to all Departments that this should be provided, and, secondly, the absence of a precise citation of the parent sections of the legislation under which the instrument had been made. The point underlying this defect is the need for persons affected by the instrument to be able to check whether the instrument is *ultra vires* the enabling power contained in the parent legislation. In earlier reports, the Committee had complained that the titles of certain instruments had failed to identify the subject-matter. The Committee also condemned the practice of expressing regulations as amendments to existing regulations so that their effect could only be discovered by reference to the other regulations. Each of these defects is of importance in the context of the rule of law and is an issue on which the Committee has had to return to the attack on more than one occasion.[19]

An example of head (vi) (" . . . drafting appears to be defective . . . ") is to be found in the 1978–1981 Report of the former Senate Committee. This concerned an order made under section 31 of the Broadcasting Authority Act 1960 which purported to ban interviews with a spokesman "for any other or more of the following organisations. . . . " The Committee took the view that the words which it had underlined rendered the instrument meaningless. The Department of Posts and Telegraphs had replied that in the original instrument the underlined phrase read "any one or more." The Committee reported to the Senate that the Department had failed in its duty to supply an accurate copy of the instrument to the House.

The inclusion of the final, unnumbered residual head ("any other

---

[17] First Report of the Select Committee on Statutory Instruments (1978, Prl. 9747).
[18] Report of the Select Committee on Statutory Instruments (1981).
[19] Second Report of the Select Committee on Statutory Instruments (1954, Pr. 3864), p. 17.

ground . . . ") meant that the former Senate Committee's jurisdiction was very wide and went beyond the grounds of review exercisable by a court. On the other hand, the Joint Committee's only sanction was to report an instrument to the Houses and the Senate Select Committee's annual reports were seldom debated. Nevertheless, the Senate Committee received consistent co-operation from Departments of State and other instrument-making bodies and difficulties were often resolved in a satisfactory manner by an exchange of correspondence.

Joint Committee on the Secondary Legislation of the European Communities

At present, therefore, the parliamentary scrutiny is confined to the work of the Joint Committee on the Secondary Legislation of the European Communities, which, by virtue of section 4 of the European Communities (Amendment) Act 1973 performs the statutory function of reviewing statutory instruments made pursuant to the European Communities Act 1972.[20] The Committee's brief is to examine such instruments as it "may select and to report thereon to both Houses of the Oireachtas."[21]

The Committee has drawn attention to a variety of blemishes and, in particular, has increasingly questioned the use of the 1972 Act in cases where it feels that primary legislation would have been more appropriate. Thus, for example, when considering the European Communities (Life Assurance Accounts, Statements and Valuations) Regulations 1986[22] the Committee observed that:

"The main provisions regulating insurance companies are contained in regulations made under the European Communities Act, 1972 and so have never been considered by the Houses of the Oireachtas. In the Committee's view, this is unsatisfactory and it considers that there is a clear need for a consolidation statute in this area."[23]

The Committee had previously expressed itself in similar language with regard to the European Communities (Removal of Restrictions on Immature Spirits) Regulations 1985[24] (which had repealed two earlier Acts of the Oireachtas) where it said that:

"It is undesirable that amendments of Acts of the Oireachtas should remain indefinitely embodied in subordinate legislation. Opportunity should be taken to include such amendments in primary legislation when it presents itself."[25]

---

[20] See Robinson, "Irish Parliamentary Scrutiny of European Community Legislation" (1979) 16 C.M.L.Rev. 9.
[21] See the Committee's latest terms of reference and appointment: *Dáil Debates*, Vol. 333, cols. 2063–2065 (November 29, 1989).
[22] S.I. 1986 No. 436.
[23] Report of the Fifth Joint Committee on the Secondary Legislation of the European Communities, Report No. 8 (December 14, 1988), p. 10.
[24] S.I. 1985 No. 368. See also, p. 18.
[25] Report of the Fifth Joint Committee on the Secondary Legislation of the European Communities, Report No. 2 (January 20, 1988), pp. 4–5.

To judge by some of the published responses to the Committee's queries about this point, it does not appear that as yet the various Government Departments share these concerns. Thus, for example, the Department of Finance responded to a query from the Committee about the Immature Spirits Regulations 1985 by saying that regulations made under the 1972 Act have "statutory effect" and that therefore "it is not necessary to incorporate in primary legislation the amendments and repeals included in the Regulations", which rather misses the point.[26]

The retrospective operation of regulations made under the 1972 Act has also been the subject of the Committee's attention. One such example is the European Communities (Exemption from Value-Added Tax on the Permanent Importation of Certain Goods) Regulations 1985[27] which was made with retrospective effect from July 1, 1984. The Committee considered that this practice was objectionable, bearing in mind that there was ample time for the Minister for Finance to make regulations before the period for which they were required to come into operation.

> "The present Joint Committee considers it objectionable that Ministers should make regulations under the 1972 Act with retrospective effect when there is no specific authority to do so. In the Joint Committee's view, the Houses of the Oireachtas should have the opportunity of considering in every case whether they are prepared to delegate power to legislate retrospectively. If it considered that such a power is essential in order to fulfil Community obligations, an amendment of the 1972 Act should be proposed in order that the Houses should have the opportunity of fully considering the matter."[28]

One might add in this context that, in the absence of express statutory authority, any attempt to give a statutory instrument retrospective effect is almost certainly *ultra vires* the 1972 Act.

In other cases, a Minister has attempted to reserve a power of exemption from the application of the particular statutory instrument in question. One such example is provided by Article 4 of the European Communities (Life Assurance, Accounts, Statements and Valuations) Regulations 1986 which allows the Minister for Industry and Commerce to provide that these Regulations shall not apply to a specified undertaking. The Joint Committee could not accept that such a power was properly contemplated by the 1972 Act:

> "A power conferred on a Minister by statute to make a statutory instrument ought not, in the Joint Committee's view, to be regarded as enabling the Minister to assume a power therein to grant administratively a dispensation from an obligation to comply with it."[29]

---

[26] Text of a letter dated February 3, 1987, from the Department of Finance to the Committee reproduced in the Second Report of the Fifth Joint Committee, p. 2.
[27] S.I. 1985 No. 183.
[28] Second Report of the Fifth Committee, p. 2.
[29] Eighth Report of the Fifth Committee, p. 8.

Once again it would seem that these powers of exemption are, in fact, *ultra vires* the 1972 Act.

It is clear that the Committee's deliberations are most interesting and their comments are invariably well-taken. Whether such observations, which have received scant publicity, carry much weight with the Government Departments in question is a matter of conjecture, but the evidence to date shows that many of the criticisms have not been followed by the Departments in question. Certainly, the threat of annulment of a statutory instrument is one which carries little weight in practice.

Another consideration is that statutory instruments of far-reaching importance are regularly promulgated without any reference to the Oireachtas, so that—as the Joint Committee has recognised—many areas of the law are regulated by delegated legislation made under the 1972 Act which in turn has either substantially amended or repealed primary legislation passed by the Oireachtas. If the Joint Committee was designed to be the bulwark against the erosion of parliamentary sovereignty, then—despite the excellence of its reports—it has clearly failed in its task. If the present practice of widespread reliance upon statutory instruments is to be retained, then perhaps there is room for the strengthening of the Committee's powers. Thus, for instance, it might be provided that instruments promulgated under the 1972 Act should have legal effect unless the Joint Committee recommended by a certain date that they be confirmed by primary legislation enacted within a further date.

5. Administrative Rules and Circulars

Introduction

One of the most remarkable features of the many diverse Government schemes and licensing arrangements currently in existence is the extent to which they are derived from administrative (*i.e.* non-statutory) rules and circulars.[30] Why this should be is largely a matter for conjecture. The civil service may find it convenient and may also be concerned that a statutory structure might prove to be inflexible. Parliamentary time is scarce and there may be difficulties in securing the assistance of a parliamentary draftsman to prepare the appropriate legislation or statutory instrument. Thus, one study on the method of implementing Community legislation in the various Member States found that Irish officials did not like to have to implement directives by means of primary legislation:

"The process of drafting a primary piece of legislation is time consuming because it requires extensive consultation with interested organisations,

---

[30] Somewhat surprisingly, there is not a huge amount in the literature on this topic, but see Ganz, *Quasi-Legislation: Recent Developments in Secondary Legislation* (London, 1987); Wade, *Administrative Law* (6th ed.), pp. 858–862; Baldwin & Houghton, "Circular Arguments: the Status and Legitimacy of Administrative Rules" [1986] *Public Law* 231; Hogan, "The Legal Status of Administrative Rules and Circulars" (1987) 22 Ir.Jur.(N.S.) 194 and Hadfield, "The Doctrine of Legitimate Expectations" (1988) 39 N.I.L.Q. 103.

adequate attention from the Parliamentary Draftsman, discussion in Cabinet and parliamentary time."[31]

Although the use of delegated legislation was found to be less time-consuming than an Act of the Oireachtas, this nevertheless brought its own difficulties:

"The drafting of statutory instruments is not a simple procedure. A proposed legal instrument makes its way slowly from the sponsoring department, to the Attorney-General's office, and finally to the Parliamentary Draftsman. This process is repeated until all interests are satisfied with the statutory instrument. Delays are generated not only by policy conflict, but also because of bureaucratic blockages in the system."[32]

Moreover, there is some evidence that some Government Departments prefer to issue—almost as a matter of policy—administrative rules and circulars rather than opt for legislation.[33] The main culprits in this regard appear to be the Departments of Agriculture, Education and the Environment. It is quite remarkable, for example, that there is virtually no legislation regulating primary education or many various schemes administered by the Department

---

[31] Laffan, Manning, Kelly, "Ireland" in *Making European Policies Work: The Implementation of Community Legislation in the Member States* (Siedentopf & Ziller) (European Institute of Public Administration, 1986), p. 383.
[32] Laffan, Manning, Kelly, *loc. cit.* p. 392.
[33] This reluctance on the part of the Government and the civil service to use primary legislation unless this is strictly necessary is by no means confined to Community matters. A good example of this is provided by the Government's decision to oppose the establishment by legislation of the National Curriculum Council. The Council has advisory functions in relation to the school curriculum. The Minister for Education (Mrs. O'Rourke) gave the following reasons for refusing to place the Council on a statutory framework (*Dáil Debates*, Vol. 374, cols. 2186–2187) (November 3, 1987):
> "There is no need to enshrine advisory functions in legislation. These functions will not be enhanced in any way by putting them into a statute. An Act of the Oireachtas will not confer any greater powers for advising upon the curriculum Council. Neither will the Council's powers to advise the Minister be reduced in any way by failing to confer them by statute. Once terms of reference for a body such as a Curriculum Council are laid down in an Act of the Oireachtas, they become quite inflexible. They cannot be adjusted in any way except by [an Act] of the Oireachtas. The Curriculum Council which I intend to establish on a non-statutory basis will have more flexible terms of reference."

This statement tends to explain the Department of Education's preference for regulation utilising of non-statutory rules rather than the use of primary legislation. This informal attitude has been increasingly questioned, as witnessed by the remarks of Costello J. in *O'Callaghan* v. *Meath V.E.C.*, High Court, November 20, 1990, where he said (at p. 1 of his judgment):
> "It is a remarkable feature of the Irish system of education that its administration by the Department of Education is largely uncontrolled by statute or statutory instruments and that many hundreds, perhaps thousands, of rules and regulations, memoranda, circulars and decisions are issued and made by the Department and the Minister (dealing sometimes with the most important aspects of education policy) not under any statutory power but merely as administrative measures. These measures are not, of course, illegal. But they have no statutory force and the sanction which ensures compliance with them is not a legal one, but the undeclared understanding that the Department will withhold financial assistance in the event of non-compliance."

However, see now the announcement by the Minister for Education (Mrs. Mary O'Rourke T.D.) to the effect that the administrative schemes and circulars governing the educational sector would shortly be put on a statutory footing: *The Irish Times*, November 27, 1990.

of Agriculture. One consequence of this non-statutory framework is that it is not necessary for the relevant Minister to secure parliamentary approval. One graphic illustration of this occurred in 1987 when the Minister for Education decided to reduce the pupil/teacher ratio in primary schools. This was done by means of a circular and the matter only came before the Oireachtas because the issue was raised by the opposition parties.[34] A defeat for the Government on this issue would not necessarily have resulted in the withdrawal of the circular, since the circular—unlike an ordinary Bill—does not require a majority in each House of the Oireachtas and—unlike a statutory instrument—is not subject to annulment by either House of the Oireachtas.[35]

It will be seen, therefore, that circulars and administrative rules are an increasingly common form of quasi-legislation. This feature may be heightened by comparison with Article 15.2.1. The essential point is that circulars are not law because they do not derive from a law-making source. This, in fact, is a more fundamental flaw than that created by Article 15.2.1 which, as interpreted in the case law described above, states only that law which introduces a new principle must be made by the Oireachtas, whilst for less ambitious law, different sources may serve. In contrast, circulars are not the progeny of any recognised law-making process.

The difficulty of analysing the status and effect of circulars is compounded by the fact that there are circulars of many different types. A significant point of distinction is whether or not a circular has been expressly authorised by a statute. For example, the Rules for National Schools[36] or the scheme governing the Criminal Injuries Compensation Tribunal[37] have no obvious statutory provenance, yet both have been judicially interpreted and construed. On the other hand, section 56 of the Insurance Act 1989 allows the Minister for Industry and Commerce to make an order "prescribing codes of conduct" to be observed by insurance agents or insurance brokers. Assuming such an order were made, could such codes as were made thereunder be regarded as having the force of law? The problem here lies in the fact that the major conceptual topic of the legal status of circulars and other administrative statements is, as yet, imperfectly explored. However, the following principles can be suggested.

First, circulars and the rest of their family are not law. As a consequence, the public authority which issued such a circular may not rely on that circular

---

[34] This was the celebrated Circular 20/87 issued by the Department of Education which sought by circular to effect a reduction in the pupil/teacher ratio in primary schools. There was a series of rather inconclusive votes in the Dáil, which resulted in a defeat for the Government on one of these votes, but in the event, the Government narrowly won on the major vote on this issue: see *Dáil Debates*, Vol. 375, cols. 1645–1657 (November 24, 1987).

[35] See pp. 34–35, *infra*.

[36] The cases where the Rules for the National Schools have been construed include: *Newell* v. *Starkie* [1917] 2 I.R. 73; *Leyden* v. *Attorney-General* [1926] I.R. 334; *Maunsell* v. *Minister for Education* [1940] I.R. 213; *McEneaney* v. *Minister for Education* [1941] I.R. 430; *Cotter* v. *Aherne* [1976–1977] I.L.R.M. 248; and *Crowley* v. *Ireland* [1980] I.R. 102.

[37] The cases where the Criminal Injuries Compensation Rules have been considered include *The State (Hayes)* v. *Criminal Injuries Compensation Tribunal* [1982] I.L.R.M. 210 and *The State (Creedon)* v. *Criminal Injuries Compensation Tribunal* [1988] I.R. 51.

as against the private citizen in order to affect or prejudice his strict legal rights nor may such a circular be relied on by one citizen against another. Secondly, this proposition begs the question of whether a citizen may invoke a circular as against the public authority. The answer is that, although as stated, a circular may not, as a matter of strict law, alter the law, it may, and often has been, the basis of a legitimate expectation. There is nothing unique to circulars in this, as a legitimate expectation can be created in a variety of ways, ranging from an official letter to an express oral representation. The decided cases tend to show, however, that circulars appear to be the most common source of legitimate expectations. This rapidly developing area is now covered separately in Chapter 13.[38]

Finally, although circulars do not in themselves have a legal status, they tend to have enormous impact as many will assume that they have an official legal standing. Accordingly, that is why the courts will, exceptionally, entertain proceedings challenging the *vires* of a circular. In strict law, such a circular is of no more potency than (say) an opinion of counsel which a public authority had reason to disseminate to the public at large. However, for the sorts of reasons just mentioned, such a circular has immense practical weight and the courts properly assume the jurisdiction to declare that any statement of law contained therein is erroneous in law. It remains to elaborate on these propositions.

Can administrative circulars alter existing procedural or substantive law?

Principle and authority seem to argue against the suggestion that procedural or substantive law could be changed by administrative circular. The abolition of corporal punishment by circular provides a particularly good example of an attempt to change substantive law through administrative rules. This was purportedly done in 1982 by a circular emanating from the Department of Education,[39] but it is difficult to see how such a circular could have been legally effective for this purpose. There is a further point: at common law, it was permissible for a teacher and those *in loco parentis* (such as a teacher) to administer reasonable corporal punishment to a child. It seems clear that this common law right[40] can only be altered by an Act of the Oir-

---

[38] See Chap. 13.

[39] Rule 130 of the Rules for National Schools, 1965 (which provided for corporal punishment in certain circumstances) was amended by Circulars 9/82 and 7/88. The change in practice was announced in the Dáil by the Minister for Education (Professor O'Donoghue) in March 1982: see *Dáil Debates*, Vol. 333, cols. 1430–1431. It may be, however, that teachers could lawfully be bound as a matter of contract to observe the terms of this circular and, furthermore, pupils might possibly be in a position to assert that this circular (directed as it was to the public at large) created a legitimate expectation that they should not be subjected to corporal punishment.

[40] It is difficult to find judicial authority for this proposition, but this fact was conceded by the British Government in *Campbell & Cosans* v. *United Kingdom* (1983) 4 E.H.R.R. 293, 297. This concession would appear to be undoubtedly correct. *Cf. Carberry* v. *Yates* (1935) 69 I.L.T.R. 86, 88 where Devitt J. held, in effect, that a ministerial circular prescribing the teaching of Irish as a compulsory requirement of the primary curriculum was unlawful, describing it as a ministerial "ukase for which there is not any statutory authority." Subsequent attempts to reverse this decision through legislation failed: see Osborough, "Education in the Irish law and Constitution" (1978) 13 Ir.Jur. (N.S.) 145, 176–180.

eachtas and not by circular. The topic of corporal punishment in schools is one which has proved controversial in the past and is a subject on which there are many different views. How can it be correct, therefore, as a matter of either constitutional or political propriety, for such a decision to be taken in private by a Government department without the matter receiving the approval of the Oireachtas via legislation?

A second example is afforded by *Colman (J.J.) Ltd.* v. *Commissioners of Customs and Excise*[41] in which the English Court of Appeal held that notices issued by the defendants could not be conclusive as to the level of import duty payable on a consignment of goods. Under the Import Duties Act 1958, goods transhipped to the United Kingdom from a Commonwealth country were entitled to preferential treatment for import duty purposes. In this case, mustard seed was shipped from Canada via Rotterdam to the United Kingdom. At the time of the consignment, the plaintiffs did not realise that the defendants had issued new guidelines which indicated that the goods transhipped via third countries would not qualify for preferential treatment. The Court of Appeal held that the plaintiffs qualified for preferential treatment under the 1958 Act because the goods had never been in free circulation so that although the plaintiffs had not complied with the terms of the notices issued by the defendants, this could not disqualify them from a preferential treatment to which they were entitled:

> "[A]lthough the new notice was not satisfied, I think that the parcels qualify for Commonwealth preference. The Customs authorities cannot, by these notices, make the law or alter it."[42]

Several recent High Court decisions also tend to support this view. In *Donohue* v. *Dillon*,[43] Lynch J. said of a Practice Direction that as it did not have statutory force, it could not be used as an aid to the construction of the Rules of the Superior Courts 1986. In effect, Lynch J. appeared to say—as did Lord Denning in the *Colman* case—that these administrative notices "cannot change the law or alter it."

A similar approach is evident in the judgment of Lardner J. in *Devitt* v. *Minister for Education*.[44] In this case the applicant had been appointed by the County Dublin Vocational Education Committee as a temporary whole-time teacher rather than as a permanent whole-time teacher. Under section 23 of the Vocational Education Act 1930, an application for a full-time position was to be made in the first instance to the Vocational Education Committee. Any

---

[41] [1968] 1 W.L.R. 1286.

[42] [1968] 1 W.L.R. 1291. Note that in *Crowley* v. *Ireland* [1980] I.R. 112 Kenny J. said that the use by the Minister of unqualified teachers in an industrial dispute would be a breach of the Rules for National Schools and hence an unlawful use of public funds. But this would appear to attach to the Rules a form of legal status which is not warranted.

[43] [1988] I.L.R.M. 654. Yet another example is provided by *Grehan* v. *North Eastern Health Board* [1989] I.R. 422, where Costello J. held that the terms of the plaintiff's contract with the defendants could not be unilaterally altered by circular. Had such changes been effected by either primary or delegated legislation, then of course, this would have superseded the terms of the contract between the parties.

[44] [1989] I.L.R.M. 639.

appointment to that position by the Committee was in turn subject to the Minister's approval. A ministerial circular entitled Memorandum V7, issued in 1967 appeared to indicate that the Minister would abide by the Committee's decision, provided the person in question was duly qualified and there was satisfactory evidence of age, health and character. In this case, the Minister—in an apparent effort to reduce the number of permanent teaching posts created by local Vocational Education Committees—invoked her powers under section 23(2) of the 1930 Act and refused to give her consent to the appointment. It was said on behalf of the applicant that the Minister was confined to the matters (qualifications, age and health of applicant) referred to in the ministerial circular and could not invoke other matters in seeking to justify the exercise of her discretion. Lardner J. could not accept this submission:

> "No doubt in relation to the exercise of this statutory discretion the Minister may adopt general rules or procedures to guide herself or to notify other concerned persons as to the manner in which she will exercise her discretion provided that they are relevant to the exercise of her powers and are reasonable. But she is not in my view entitled by such rules or procedure to limit the scope of the discretion entrusted to her or disable herself from the full exercise of it. Nor in my judgment may such a practice be relied upon by the applicant as estopping the Minister from the full exercise of the discretion vested in her by the Act."[45]

Lardner J.'s comments necessarily imply that a circular cannot qualify or modify the terms of an Act of the Oireachtas. But the most graphic confirmation to date of this principle comes with the decision of Barron J. in *Browne* v. *An Bord Pleanála*.[46] This case concerned the manner in which the EC Environmental Impact Assessment Directive had been purportedly implemented by administrative circular. Barron J. referred to several decisions of the European Court of Justice which had found such methods of implementing a directive to be unlawful. Thus, in *Commission* v. *Belgium*,[47] the European Court held that:

> "Mere administrative practices which, by their nature, can be changed as

---

[45] *Ibid.* 649. Lardner J. relied on the comments of Henchy J. in *Re Greendale Properties Ltd.* [1977] I.R. 256, 264 as authority for the proposition that a public body cannot be estopped from performing a statutory duty. But *cf.* the comments of McWilliam J. in *Phelan* v. *Laois Vocational Education Committee*, High Court, February 28, 1977, where he acknowledged that even though a circular might not bind the Minister, it might be evidence "of improper exercise of his powers if he were to ignore his own requirements without good reason." It should be noted that the very same ministerial circular prescribed an Irish qualification for all applicant teachers employed by vocational education authorities and that the legality of this qualification was challenged in judicial review proceedings before Blayney J. in the High Court. This requirement was subsequently upheld by the European Court of Justice in *Groener* v. *Minister for Education* [1990] I.L.R.M. 335. Note also that in *O'Callaghan* v. *Meath V.E.C.*, High Court, November 20, 1990, Costello J. held that these Ministerial Circulars "were quite clearly not made under . . . statutory power. They are merely administrative measures with no statutory force."
[46] [1989] I.L.R.M. 865.
[47] (Case 102/79) [1980] E.C.R. 1473.

the authorities please and which are not published widely enough cannot be regarded [as proper means of implementing a directive.]"[48]

Barron J. thus concluded that the directive had not been validly implemented by circular, since this "did not have the force of law and for this reason cannot have incorporated any of the provisions of the Directive into our domestic law."[49]

A supporting policy reason why circulars should not be regarded as law is that they are not formally published and accessible. The limited circulation of such circulars and their general inaccessibility may mean that the reliance on such circulars could be contrary to the guarantee of fair procedures, since it might well be thought that "any rule which is applied on the basis of an internal memorandum which is not available to the public may lack the characteristic of true law and could possibly be challenged on that ground."[50] These principles would certainly seem to have considerable relevance as far as the operation of the Tuberculosis and Brucellosis Schemes are concerned, as in *McKerring* v. *Minister for Agriculture*[51] O'Hanlon J. found it remarkable that the only guidance to be found regarding the grant scheme was to be found in the conditions on the back of the cattle movement permit and any changes in these conditions "were notified to the farming community by way of newspaper advertisement."[52] The issue of fair procedures arising from the restricted publication of this circular had not, however, been argued before him.

Judicial review of administrative circulars

It now seems clear that administrative circulars may be subject to judicial review. Given the ubiquitous nature of circulars it would be ill-advised to attempt an exhaustive classification of the circumstances in which judicial review may lie. The purpose of the present section is merely to present cases in which the issue of judicial review of circulars has been (more or less addressed) by the courts. However, the following three situations exist and have yielded a fair amount of case law. The first concerns circulars of a particular and not unusual type, namely, those which do not purport to change the law but merely to state the law.[53] It not infrequently happens that Government Departments will issue a circular by way of guidance for the benefit of local authorities. It would be unrealistic to pretend that such circu-

---

[48] *Ibid.* 1486.
[49] [1990] I.L.R.M. 364.
[50] Byrne (1987) 22 Ir.Jur. 326–327. See also, the comments of Scott L.J. in *Blackpool Corporation* v. *Locker* [1948] 1 K.B. 349, 361:
 "The very justification for the basic maxim [that ignorance of the law is no excuse] is that the whole of our law, written or unwritten, is accessible to the public—in the sense, of course, that, at any rate, its legal advisers have access to it, at any moment, as of right."
[51] [1989] I.L.R.M. 82.
[52] *Ibid.* 83–84.
[53] See, *e.g. McNamee* v. *Buncrana U.D.C.* [1983] I.R. 213, where the Supreme Court made reference to a circular issued by the Department of the Environment which (incorrectly, as it happened) sought to explain the duties of housing authorities in the wake of the earlier decision of the Supreme Court in *McDonald* v. *Feeley*, July 23, 1980.

lars have only the same status and influence *de facto* as counsel's opinion or a legal textbook in the same area of law and, it seems, that even this type of circular is amenable to judicial review in a suitable case. The second type of circular is where the authority purports either to change the law or, alternatively, to create some form of administrative scheme which affects individual rights or liabilities.[54] Finally, the more common type of circular is one which in effect may be categorised as a series of administrative decisions. Since such a circular does not change the law, it is subject to the same disciplines—*vires*, reasonableness, etc., as an ordinary administrative action. If the circular satisfies these tests, well and good. If not, then again it is in the same position as an individual administrative action and will be struck down.

Prior to the decision of Murphy J. in *Greene* v. *Minister for Agriculture*[55] the question of the courts' jurisdiction to review the legality of such administrative schemes had never received elaborate judicial consideration in this jurisdiction. Murphy J. did not appear to question his entitlement to subject such a scheme to judicial review on ordinary grounds of *vires*, reasonableness, etc. The plaintiffs in *Greene* succeeded in their claim that the manner in which the means test was imposed in a ministerial circular dealing with headage payments to farmers as a form of grant-aid discriminated against married couples and was contrary to Article 41. Murphy J. said that Article 15.4.1[56] had no relevance to the present case, as this ministerial scheme was not a "law" within the meaning of that subsection, but he could nonetheless intervene to declare the offending portion of the scheme to be unconstitutional:

> "[Article 15.4.1] would have no application and would provide no direct assistance in determining the extent to which the schemes would be invalidated or the date from which they would cease to have operative effect. The Ministerial schemes are defective and must be condemned because they fail to respect and vindicate express constitutional rights."[57]

While *Greene* is a clear authority to the effect that administrative circulars of this kind are subject to judicial review, the theoretical basis for this assertion of judicial power was more fully explored by the House of Lords in *Gillick* v. *West Norfolk and Wisbech Health Authority*.[58]

In this case, the plaintiff challenged the legality of a departmental "memor-

---

[54] A good example is the establishment by administrative scheme of the Milk Quota Appeals Tribunal which is designed to deal with hardship cases arising from the operation of the milk super-levy system. This tribunal does not, of course, have any statutory backing and, in this respect, may be compared to the operation of the Criminal Injuries Compensation Tribunal. The Milk Quota Appeal Tribunal's full terms of reference and rules of procedure do not appear ever to have been formally published, but an outline of its terms of reference was published in the advertisements in the national newspapers on May 30, 1990.

[55] [1990] I.L.R.M. 364.

[56] Art. 15.4.1 provides that:
"The Oireachtas shall not enact any law which is any respect repugnant to this Constitution or to any provisions thereof."
See generally, Kelly, *op. cit.* pp. 83–84 and 1987 Supplement, pp. 18–19.

[57] [1990] I.L.R.M. 364, 373–374.

[58] [1986] A.C. 112.

andum of guidance" issued to local health authorities giving advice in relation to the provision of contraception for children under 16. A majority of the House concluded that the provision of such advice was not unlawful. While Lords Fraser and Scarman were willing to hold that any such error would be *ultra vires*, Lords Bridge and Templeman concluded that it could have no legal effect, yet was subject to judicial review. Lord Bridge put the matter thus:

> "The issue by a department of government with administrative responsibility in a particular field of non-statutory guidance to subordinate authorities operating in the same field is a familiar feature of modern administration. The innumerable circulars issued over the years by successive departments spring to mind as presenting a familiar example. The question whether the advice tendered in non-statutory guidance is good or bad, reasonable or unreasonable, cannot, as a general rule, be subject to any form of judicial review."[59]

Lord Bridge then went on to refer to *Royal College of Nursing* v. *Department of Health and Social Security*.[60] In these proceedings the legality of a memorandum issued by the defendants concerning certain procedures to be followed under the Abortion Act 1967 was challenged by the plaintiffs. In the event, the defendants' contentions were upheld and Lord Bridge added that, as against this background, it would have been surprising "if the courts had declined jurisdiction."[61] He continued by saying:

> "But I think it must be recognised that the [*Royal College of Nursing*] decision (whether or not it was so intended) does effect a significant extension of the court's power of judicial review. We must now say that if a government department, in a field of administration in which it exercises responsibility, promulgates in a public document, albeit non-statutory in form, advice which is erroneous in law, then the court . . . has jurisdiction to correct the error of law by an appropriate declaration. Such an extended jurisdiction is no doubt a salutary and indeed a necessary one in certain cir-

[59] [1986] A.C. 912–913. *Cf.* the comments of Finlay P. in *The State (Kershaw)* v. *Minister for Social Welfare* [1985] I.L.R.M. 235 where he said (at 239) that in so far as a ministerial circular provided guidance concerning the operation of the fuel scheme operated under the terms of the Social Welfare (Consolidation) Act 1981, it was "clearly a proper and valid administrative act." In the present case, however, social welfare appeals officers relied on the circular in the holding that the applicant was not entitled to certain social welfare benefits. Finlay P. held that this was unlawful, as the terms of such a circular could not deprive either a deciding or appeals officer from exercising their statutory powers under the 1981 Act to decide whether the applicant was entitled to the benefits claimed. For other cases where the courts took on the task of reviewing administrative decisions by reference to criteria prescribed by a circular, see *The State (Melbarien Enterprises Ltd.)* v. *Revenue Commissioners* [1985] I.R. 706 (Commissioners took into account irrelevant consideration not permitted by non-statutory administrative scheme) and *Reidy* v. *Minister for Agriculture and Food*, High Court, June 9, 1989 (where the Department purported, pursuant to the terms of a ministerial circular, to impose a disciplinary penalty which was not authorised by the Civil Service Regulation Acts 1956–1958).
[60] [1981] A.C. 800.
[61] [1986] A.C. 122. This language is very reminiscent of the language used by Gavan Duffy J. almost 50 years previously in *Maunsell* v. *Minister for Education*: see p. 48.

cumstances, as the *Royal College of Nursing* case itself well illustrates. But the occasions of a departmental non-statutory publication raising, as in that case, a clearly defined issue of law, unclouded by political, social or moral overtones, will be rare."[62]

This is perhaps the best exposition to date of the true legal status of this type of administrative circular. While it cannot be equated with either primary or secondary legislation, such a circular can be subjected to judicial review. This reasoning was taken a step further in *R.* v. *Secretary of State for the Environment, ex p. Greenwich L.B.C.*,[63] where judicial review was sought of a Government leaflet purporting to explain a new local government tax ("community charge"). While the application was dismissed on the merits, Woolf L.J. held that the courts could intervene if the publication in question "was manifestly inaccurate or misleading." Applying this principle in an Irish context, it might mean that, in an appropriately exceptional case, judicial review could lie in respect of an explanatory memorandum to a Bill or, even, to officially sponsored Government leaflets or advertisements such as are now common in the run-up to polling day in a referendum.[64]

The other categories of circulars have also been subjected to judicial review by the courts. Certainly the courts have been prepared to construe the non-statutory Rules for National Schools and, in appropriate cases, to grant relief in respect of breaches of these Rules. In *Maunsell* v. *Minister for Education*[65] Gavan Duffy J. held that the defendants had misconstrued Rule 82 of the 1932 Rules for the National Schools in the course of taking an administrative decision against the plaintiff teacher and rejected the argument that he had no jurisdiction to do so because of the non-statutory nature of the Rules in question:

> "[O]ur law would be deplorably inadequate if the High Court were in the humiliating position of being compelled to refuse all relief to a citizen whose rights are denied as a direct result of a serious misconstruction by a Department of State of an important regulation vitally affecting him."[66]

Moreover, in another case involving a challenge to an administrative decision

---

[62] [1986] A.C. 122.

[63] *The Times*, May 17, 1989.

[64] In *The Irish Times*, June 16, 1990, the Revenue Commissioners were reported as having said that they would continue to apply the "forty-eight hour rule" on travellers' allowances for dutiable goods, despite a ruling by the European Court of Justice in *E.C. Commission* v. *Ireland, The Times*, June 14, 1990 that this rule was contrary to Community law. This is, perhaps, an example of the type of case where the the courts might intervene to declare invalid a statement of this kind.

[65] [1940] I.R. 213.

[66] *Ibid*. 235–236. Gavan Duffy J. did, however, regard such an error as an "error in the exercise of a statutory duty." This is obviously fallacious, since the Rules for the National Schools are not "law" in the sense of imposing statutory duties on the persons or bodies to whom they are addressed. However, Barron J. has held that issues of construction arising from these Rules have a sufficient public law dimension to permit a challenge to the validity of a suspension from primary school to be taken by way of judicial review: *Murtagh* v. *Board of Management of St. Emer's National School*, High Court, November 27, 1989.

taken on foot of a circular, *Mulloy* v. *Minister for Education*,[67] the Supreme Court held that a departmental circular which discriminated against priests and members of religious orders was a discrimination on the grounds of religious belief or status, contrary to Article 44.2.4. No question was raised in this case as to the court's jurisdiction to make such a pronouncement in view of the non-statutory (and presumably non-binding) nature of such a departmental circular. And the courts have also entertained challenges to decisions of the Criminal Injuries Compensation Tribunal, despite the fact that the tribunal has no statutory basis and thus, here again, we find examples of administrative decisions taken on foot of a circular.

Conclusion

We have seen, therefore, that despite the fact that administrative circulars may create legal rights and obligations and are subject to judicial review, their legal status defies exact classification. In a seminal article published in 1944[68] Sir Robert Megarry described such legislation as a form of "quasi-legislation" and this seems as good as description as any of the effect in practice of such circulars. But no legal system can be content with a situation whereby public authorities and Government Departments habitually resort to circulars in an attempt to regulate legal rights.[69] Such a practice was roundly condemned by Streatfield J. in a notable passage:

> "Whereas ordinary legislation, by passing through both Houses of Parliament or, at least, lying on the table of both Houses, is thus twice blessed, this type of so-called legislation is at least four times cursed. First, it has seen neither House of Parliament; secondly, it is unpublished and is inaccessible even to those whose valuable rights or property may be affected; thirdly, it is a jumble of provisions, legislative, administrative, or directive in character, and sometimes difficult to disentangle one from the other; and, fourthly, it is expressed not in the precise language of an Act of Parliament or an Order in Council but in the more colloquial language of correspondence, which is not always susceptible of the ordinary canons of construction."[70]

Streatfield J.'s comments are pertinent in this jurisdiction, since, as we have seen, the very inaccessibility of such circulars might well be regarded as a breach of constitutional justice. Given that the Statutory Instruments Act 1947 takes great pains to ensure that statutory instruments are published, why should a Government Department be permitted through the use of circulars

---

[67] [1975] I.R. 88.

[68] "Quasi-Legislation" (1944) 60 L.Q.R. 125.

[69] Sir Robert Megarry's comments (*loc. cit.* p. 127) apply *a fortiori* to our modern legal system:
"A system under which the practitioner may have to search Hansard, the Stationery Office list of official publications and the weekly law papers to find out how far up-to-date text-books and the statute book itself can be relied upon as stating the effective law will commend itself to few."
And as Ganz, *op. cit.* sardonically observed (p. 2), the practitioner "would have to look a great deal further afield today."

[70] *Patchett* v. *Leathem* (1949) 65 T.L.R. 69, 70.

R.T.C. LIBRARY
LETTERKENNY

to by-pass these requirements? And, as far as the constitutional dimension is concerned, while Scott L.J.'s comment in *Blackpool Corporation* v. *Locker*[71] that such circulars were examples "of the very worst kind of bureaucracy" may be going too far, it would be difficult to argue against the proposition that the systematic use of such circulars by Government Departments so as in effect to create a quasi-legislative code, and hence withdraw the matter from the purview of the Oireachtas, is contrary to the spirit, if not quite the letter, of Article 15.2.1.

---

[71] [1948] 1 K.B. 349.

Part II

INSTITUTIONS OF GOVERNMENT

CHAPTER 3

DÁIL, MINISTERS, DEPARTMENTS AND CIVIL SERVANTS

The object of this chapter is to sketch the constitutional and legal framework within which the administration of central government proceeds, dealing, in Part 1, with the part played by the Dáil; in Part 2, with the legal persona of a Minister; and in the remaining Parts with the civil service. However, no attempt is made to deal with the process of law-making.

1. Formal Control by the Dáil

Following the British model[1] the members of the Government (Cabinet) are formally responsible to the Dáil, though not the Senate,[2] in two ways.

(a) **Collective Government responsibility.** The principal form of responsibility is collective. The Constitution makes the Government collectively responsible to the Dáil. This means that, after an election, the Dáil elects a Government and also that it can remove and, without reference to the people, replace it with a new Government. However, its power to elect a replacement Government is restricted by the provision that even a Taoiseach who has been defeated in the Dáil may advise a dissolution followed by a general election and, thus far, no President has seen fit to reject such advice.[3] Moreover, all the Dáil's powers over the Government are conditioned by the basic fact of political life which is that a Government can almost always command the support of a majority of deputies, because deputies are elected principally on the basis of the party which they have pledged themselves to support in the Dáil. Such is the strength of the whip-system that the legislature cannot be regarded as speaking with a voice independent of the executive

---

[1] Though at the inception of the State, some efforts were made to modify this model: on this and on the entire subject, see Gwynn Morgan, *Constitutional Law of Ireland* (Dublin, 1990), pp. 54–87.

[2] The Government is not formally responsible to the Senate in the way that it is to the Dáil. Informally, the Senate's position in regard to publicising and criticising the Government's activities and policy decisions is similar to, though less important than, that of the Dáil. For instance, the select committees constituted to review a specific area of government activity (*e.g.* the Joint Committee on Commercial State Sponsored Bodies) are invariably joint committees, but with a minority of members from the Senate. Accordingly in the limited space available the role of the Senate has not been examined.

[3] See generally, Arts. 13.1; 13.2; 28.4.1; and 28.10. Notice, however, this observation of a former Secretary of the Department of Finance and former Governor of the Central Bank: "It is doubtful if the normal life of a government of four years or so is now adequate for the preparation and implementation of national plans. . . . This 'efficiency argument' points to the advisability of providing, by statute, that parliament should have a fixed, rather than a maximum, life of five years. This would not necessarily mean that governments would have a correspondingly fixed life of five years, but it could be a significant step in that direction": Murray, "Irish Government Further Observed" (1983) 31 *Administration* 284, 287.

and, so, it is realistic to characterise the central element in the Irish governmental system as a fused executive-legislature.

The epithet "collective" means, first, that the Government, as a collective authority, speaks with one voice and, secondly, that if the Taoiseach resigns from office (or is removed), the other members of the Government also leave office.[4] In other words, the Government stands, or falls, as a single, united entity.

(b) Individual ministerial responsibility. A governmental decision is seldom so grave that an error in relation to it would warrant the bringing down of a Government. Thus, although from the broad constitutional perspective, collective responsibility is the more important element, it is the individual ministerial doctrine which could potentially be of greater significance in checking undesirable governmental action. According to the individual ministerial doctrine, if a Minister commits certain types of error then there is an obligation on him, and on him alone, to resign. In appropriate circumstances, so the theory runs, a Minister is supposed to resign of his own accord; but if he fails to do this, he must certainly resign if a vote of no confidence in him is passed by the Dáil. The type of error which attracts this duty may be: a personal act of dishonour or indiscretion; a failure of policy; or an act of maladministration, within his Department—the latter of which is, *par excellence*, the focus of administrative law.

As is well known, the individual ministerial doctrine has received mainly lip-service and there have been very few resignations for breach of the doctrine since 1922.[5] The principal reason for the failure of the doctrine is the lack of a non-partisan agency to determine conclusively when a Minister should resign and then, if necessary, to enforce this sanction: as with the collective responsibility doctrine, the Dáil is prevented from playing this part because of the strict party system. There are other reasons for the failure: the single sanction of resignation affords no gradation of sanctions to deal with the varied offences of widely varying culpability which may arise; again, resignation would not even be available as a sanction where the responsible Minister had left office before the error came to light. Moreover, a particular difficulty arises in relation to a type of error which is common in the area of administrative law, namely, abuse of power or an act of maladministration,

---

[4] Arts. 28.4.2; 28.11.1.

[4a] There is no reference to this doctrine in the Constitution. However it has been accepted that the rule exists as a convention derived from the relationship of Ministers to the Dáil: see, *e.g.* *Dáil Debates*, Vol. 187, cols. 19–59, March 7, 1961 (second stage of the Mental Treatment (Detention in Approved Institutions) Bill 1961), *Dáil Debates*, Vol. 256, cols. 1473–1501, (November 9, 1970), cols. 1732–1766, (November 10, 1970) (motion of no confidence in Minister for Agriculture, consequent on the Arms Trial).

[5] One definite example involved the resignation of a Parliamentary Secretary in 1946 because of allegations of a conflict of interest between his official duties and a firm in which he had an interest: see *Report of the Tribunal appointed by the Taoiseach on November 7, 1947* (P.No. 8576). It is often difficult, and seldom profitable, to determine whether a resignation is an act of individual responsibility or an act of collective responsibility stemming from the fact that the Minister resigning disagrees with the rest of the Government.

occurring during the course of routine administration. For in any Department of State, there will be hundreds or thousands of civil servants serving under a Minister and such an error may be wholly the fault of a civil servant.[6] Where the Minister is not personally involved in the error, is it not dogmatic to expect his head to roll?[7] This situation was illustrated in 1961 in the context of the involuntary detention of mental patients. According to the relevant statute, the Minister for Health's permission had to be renewed after every six-month period of detention. The junior civil servant whose task it was to pass on the applications for the Minister's permission fell ill and failed to perform this task, with the result that almost 300 patients were illegally detained. Yet the Minister convincingly brushed aside calls for his resignation as unrealistic.[8]

Before going further, it ought to be mentioned, for the sake of completeness, that, apart from theoretically controlling the Government and making laws, the Dáil has a third function, namely, acting as the "Grand Inquest of the Nation."[9] What this rather grandiloquent phrase means is that the House investigates, appraises, publicises and even dramatises the Government's decisions and highlights the alternatives. It provides a continuous critical commentary on the Government's performance and, thereby, it is hoped, helps to educate the individual members of the public in casting their vote at the subsequent election. This is a peculiarly elusive function with the result that the Dáil's performance is difficult to assess, especially as the effect of the "Grand Inquest" is more likely to be preventative, rather than curative, *i.e.* to discourage a Government from doing something which will not bear the light of day. However, it is reasonable to suppose that in this role, the Dáil has some effect in forestalling the worst excesses.

Consequences of individual ministerial doctrine

Although the ministerial responsibility doctrine is such a broken-backed rule, it bears mentioning because its existence (real or supposed) has had a formative influence upon the machinery for the performance and control of Ministers and Departments in the following ways.

(1) It remains the formal position that a Minister is responsible to the Dáil for all activities going on within his Department. In part, as a result of this, the Dáil attempts to cover too wide an area and has insufficient time and attention for what should be its principal concern, namely major matters of policy. Thus, for instance, one element of ministerial responsibility to the Dáil is the Minister's duty to answer questions on behalf of his Department. A large proportion of these questions relate to the personal minutiae of con-

---

[6] See *Dáil Debates*, Vol. 187, cols. 19–59 (March 7, 1961).
[7] Murray, "A Working and Changeable Instrument" (1982) 30 *Administration* 43, 52. See also, Wheare, *Maladministration and its Remedies* (London, 1973), Chap. 3; and Murray, "Irish Government Further Observed" (1983) 31 *Administration* 284, 288–298.
[8] See *Dáil Debates*, Vol. 187, cols. 19–59 (March 7, 1961).
[9] On which see Gwynn Morgan, *op. cit.* pp. 144–151.

stituents[10] and the discussion of these issues tends to crowd out the examination of policy issues. Again, the Dáil's supposed power and duty to police all of a Department's activities may impede the development of other, more effective means of controlling routine actions, for instance, along the lines proposed in the note on Administrative Law and Procedure appended to the Devlin Report.[11]

(2) Another effect of the doctrine is to "politicise" every decision taken in a Department by converting every decision—however minor, technical or inherently non-controversial—into a potential bone of contention in a parliamentary dog-fight, which may affect the credit of the entire Government. One consequence of this is that the caution of an already-cautious civil service is increased in order to obey the supreme obligation of "protecting the Minister." Thus, for instance, files are pushed up from one level of the civil service hierarchy to another so that issues have to be resolved at a higher level than would otherwise be considered necessary. Another result is " 'the representations' system [which] helps to perpetuate the misconception that everything can be 'fixed.' "[12]

(3) The personification of the entire activity of the Department in its Minister (politically, by the ministerial responsibility doctrine and, legally, through the Ministers and Secretaries Act 1924) leaves no formal position for anyone else, even senior management. The effect of this arrangement is to militate against personal responsibility and initiative on the part of civil servants. One symbol of this is the practice, now fallen into disuse, of civil servants commencing routine letters with the formula, "I am directed by the Minister to. . . ."

(4) In the past, courts have offered it as a reason (or pretext) to justify a refusal to review some administration actions that "this is a matter for which the Minister is responsible to Parliament." This traditional and unrealistic view—which relies upon a model of Parliament which existed, only for a brief period in mid-nineteenth century Britain, before the growth of the party system and "big government"—is not part of the thinking of the contemporary Irish judiciary. Nevertheless, it was an influence in shaping the doctrine of judicial review, which exists in Ireland today.[13]

(5) To set against these disadvantages, it should be said that the ministerial responsibility principle underpins the so-called *Carltona* doctrine[14] by which

---

[10] One-half of all questions to the Minister for the Environment concern individual constituents' problems. This figure is exceeded in the case of the questions for the Minister for Social Welfare: see *The Irish Times*, January 20, 1984.

[11] Prl. 792, App. 1.

[12] *Ibid*. 448.

[13] See, *e.g. Liversidge* v. *Anderson* [1942] A.C. 206 (a case involving individual liberty). See also, the comments of Shaw L.J. in *Raymond* v. *Att.-Gen.* [1982] Q.B. 839, 847 on political responsibility for decisions of the D.P.P.: "The safeguard against an unnecessary or gratuitous exercise of this power [to enter a *nolle prosequi*] is that . . . the Director's duties are exercised under the superintendence of the Attorney-General. That officer of the Crown is, in his turn, answerable to Parliament, if it should appear that his or the Director's powers have . . . in any case been abused." See also, Gearty, "Administrative law in the 1980s" (1987) 9 D.U.L.J.(N.S.) 21, 39–42.

[14] See further, pp. 400–405.

duties and powers vested in a Minister may be performed or exercised by officials in his Department. As it was put in *Carltona* v. *Commissioners of Works*[15]:

"Constitutionally the decision of such an official is, of course, the decision of the minister. The minister is responsible. It is he who must answer before Parliament for anything that his officials have done under his authority. . . . The whole system of departmental organisation and administration is based on the view that ministers, being responsible to Parliament, will see that important duties are committed to experienced officials. If they do not do that, Parliament is the place where complaint must be made against them."

We shall return to some of these features in Part 3, which deals with the reform of the civil service.

2. Legal Structure of the Ministers and Departments

Before independence, the separate executive which was the great anomaly of the Act of Union which fused the British and Irish Parliaments, consisted of about 50 units described variously as "departments," "boards" or "offices." Ireland, it was said, had "as many boards as would make her coffin". The administrative units, some of which were merely the Irish branches of a mainland Department, enjoyed a variety of relationships with the Lord Lieutenant (the formal head of the executive) and the Chief Secretary (a sort of Minister for Irish Affairs who represented the Irish administration in the House of Commons).[16]

The objective of the post-independence Government was to sweep away this *disjecta membra* and to replace it with a uniform system in which the central executive power of the State flowed directly through the members of the Government, so that the Dáil could exercise control over the entire administration (for in those heady days, it was hoped that the Dáil would wield substantial influence over governments). A complementary change was made on the legal plane by the Ministers and Secretaries Act 1924 (a code contemplated at Article 28.12 of the Constitution) which is the chief organic law determining the framework of the executive arm of government.[17]

The 1924 Act established the (say) Minister for Justice as a statutorily-created corporation sole,[18] distinct from the temporary incumbent of the office. Linked with this development was the practice of vesting almost all

---

[15] [1943] 2 All E.R. 560, 563. The final, rather dated, sentence in this passage is an example of the point made in para. 4.
[16] McDowell, *The Irish Administration* (London, 1964); McColgan, "Partition and the Irish Administration 1920–1922" (1980) 28 *Administration* 147.
[17] Minister and Secretaries Act 1924, s.9.
[18] 1924 Act, s.2(1). On the Minister as corporation sole, see further, pp. 709–713.

central government functions[19] in a particular Minister.[20] The 1924 Act provides that "each . . . Department . . . and the powers, duties and functions thereof shall be assigned to and administered by the Minister"[21] but that whenever any power is vested by statute in a Minister, the administration entailed in the exercise of that power is deemed to be allocated to the Department of that Minister.[22] The result of these provisions is that the Minister is not only head of the Department; he also personifies the Department and, as corporation sole, bears responsibility in law for its every action. At the same time, most, at least, of these actions may be performed by departmental civil servants, rather than the Minister himself.

The Ministers and Secretaries Act 1924 "establishe[s] . . . the several (eleven in the original 1924 Act) Departments of State amongst which the administration and business of the public services in [the State] shall be distributed."[23] The Act also gives a generalised description of the duties of the Departments which it establishes, of which the following may be taken as representative:

> "The Department of Justice shall comprise the administration and business generally of public services in connection with law, justice, public order and police, and all powers, duties and functions connected with the same except such powers . . . as are by law reserved to the Executive Council [now Government] and such powers . . . as are by the Constitution or by law excepted from the authority of the Executive Council or of an Executive Minister and shall include in particular the business, powers, duties and functions of the branches and officers of the public service specified in the Second Part of the Schedule to this Act [which includes the Courts, the Public Record Office and the Registry of Deeds] and of which Department the head shall be, and shall be styled, an t-Aire Dlí agus Cirt or (in English) the Minister for Justice."

---

[19] There are a few functions which, in order to mark their importance or to add lustre, are vested in the President or the Government. In addition, a very few functions are vested in designated civil servants. The principal example is the deciding officer/appeals officer in the Department of Social Welfare: see pp. 241–248. Plainly, too, the generalisation in the text does not refer to the functions vested in a state-sponsored body.

[20] Though this is subject to the overriding imperative contained in Art. 28.4 of the Constitution that "The Government . . . shall be collectively responsible for the Departments of State administered by the members of the Government." See also Ministers and Secretaries Act 1924, s.5: "Nothing in this Act contained shall derogate from the collective responsibility of the [Government] as provided by the Constitution notwithstanding that members of the [Government] may be appointed individually to be Ministers, heads of particular Departments of State." It is thus open to the Government to direct a Minister as to how a decision should be taken, although the decision has been statutorily vested in a Minister.

[21] 1924 Act, s.1.

[22] Ministers and Secretaries (Amendment) Act 1939, s.6(3). See also, Art. 28.12 of the Constitution and Kiely, "Ministers and Departments" (1986) 7 *Seirbhís Phoiblí* 7. But for *delegatus non potest delegare*, see pp. 396–400.

[23] As of 1991, the full list of Departments of State is as follows: the Taoiseach; Energy; Foreign Affairs; Industry and Commerce; Environment; Defence; the Marine; Tourism and Transport; Communications; Finance; Health; Social Welfare; Agriculture and Food; Justice; Labour; Education; and the Gaeltacht.

Nevertheless, it is to be noted that almost all governmental functions are created by a specific statute. Such a statute would prevail against the job-description given in the 1924 Act, (of which that of the Minister for Justice has just been quoted as an example) even if it involved vesting a function in what would seem, according to that Act, to be an inappropriate Department. What then is the legal (as opposed to informative) purpose of a statutory job-description? In the first place, a Minister is a corporation sole and, as such, he has the capacity to contract, but only for the purpose of his authorised function or purposes incidental thereto. The description in the 1924 Act[24] would be significant in divining what these purposes were and, thus, in determining whether a particular contract were *ultra vires* the Minister's power. In addition the description might be helpful in fixing the scope of a civil servant's employment in the context, for instance, of a tort action against the State.[25] It might also be invoked by the Controller and Auditor General, if he were deciding whether some item fell outside an imprecisely worded vote. And in the context of the Dáil, the statutory description is an indication of the matters for which a Minister is responsible.

Where a new Department, with its ministerial head, is established, then a statute (called a Ministers and Secretaries (Amendment) Act) usually has to be passed. A statute is necessary because the creation (or dissolution) of a corporation sole requires an Act of the Oireachtas. Thus the Ministers for (for example) Supplies,[26] Health,[27] Social Welfare,[28] the Gaeltacht,[29] Labour[30] and the Public Service,[31] were not created by the Ministers and Secretaries Act 1924 and so each had to be created by its own amending statute. A statute was also passed when the office of Minister for Supplies was dissolved.[32] However, as we shall see when we come to the demise of the Minister for the Public Service and the constitution of the Minister for Tourism and Transport (covered below under the heading "Recent Changes"), a new statute is not always necessary because of the device of "the shell of the corporation sole." Under the Ministers and Secretaries (Amendment) Act 1939, the Government has extensive powers, exercisable by order, to alter the name of any Department or the title of any Minister; to transfer powers between Ministers and the administration of a public service between Departments; or to allocate to a Department the administration of a public service not expressly allocated to a Department. The Government is even empowered to

---

[24] 1924 Act, s.1. For the supersession of the title Ministry by Department in 1924, see Fanning, *The Irish Department of Finance, 1922–1958* (Dublin, 1978), p. 39.
[25] See pp. 710 and 713.
[26] Ministers and Secretaries (Amendment) Act 1939.
[27] Ministers and Secretaries (Amendment) Act 1946.
[28] *Ibid.*
[29] Ministers and Secretaries (Amendment) Act 1956. For the distinction between industrial and non-industrial civil servants, see p. 68, n. 74.
[30] Ministers and Secretaries (Amendment) Act 1959.
[31] Ministers and Secretaries (Amendment) Act 1973.
[32] Minister for Supplies (Transfer of Functions) Act No. 21 of 1945, s.3.

make "such adaptations of enactments as shall appear to the Government to be consequential on anything done under [these powers]."[33]

The 1922 Constitution allowed for a maximum of 12 Ministers[34] (although in the Irish Free State only nine, 10 or 11 were actually appointed) whilst the 1924 Act constituted 11 Departments. By today, there are 17 Departments,[35] whilst a maximum number of Ministers is fixed at 15 by Article 28.1. However, no difficulty arises from this apparent mis-match, because the Taoiseach, who determines which members of the Government are to be assigned as Ministers to which Department, is free to assign more than one Department to the same member of the Government[36] (for example, the Departments of Health and Social Welfare are often assigned to the same Minister, though this has not been the case from 1986 to date). The Taoiseach may also appoint a member of the Government who does not have responsibility for a Department, that is a Minister without portfolio.[37]

Ministers of State.

The Ministers and Secretaries Act 1924 provided for the appointment by the Executive Council of a maximum of seven "parliamentary secretaries" to act as junior Ministers.[38] In 1977, this provision was repealed and replaced by a measure allowing for the appointment of "Ministers of State" from among members of either House to a maximum of initially 10 and, since 1980, 15.[39] The increase in the number of junior Ministers was explained in the Dáil on the grounds of the greater volume of government business by comparison with that in 1924. The increase also had the effect of enlarging the "pay roll" vote.[40]

In spite of this change of name, the function of these junior Ministers remains the same, that is, to assist the Minister at the head of the Department to which they are assigned by their appointment. A Government order[41] may be made on the request of a Minister, delegating to his Minister of State all the Minister's powers and duties under a particular Act or, more narrowly, any particular statutory power or duty.

Since the functions of a Minister of State are largely the same as those formerly performed by a parliamentary secretary, the change is merely a matter

[33] Act No. 36 of 1939, s.6(1). The words quoted in the text constitute a rare example of a "Henry VIII clause," on which see pp. 13–16 and 19–20.
[34] Art. 55.
[35] See p. 58, n. 23.
[36] Ministers and Secretaries (Amendment) Act 1946, s.4, replacing Ministers and Secretaries Act 1924, s.3 which had significantly limited wording.
[37] Ministers and Secretaries (Amendment) Act 1939, s.4. The device of a Minister without portfolio has only been availed of twice: once during 1939–1945 when a Minister for the Co-ordination of Defensive Measures was appointed; and, secondly, for a few months in 1977, during a period when a Minister for Economic Planning and Development was appointed before the office had been constituted by the Ministers and Secretaries (Amendment) Act 1977.
[38] Ministers and Secretaries Act 1924, s.7.
[39] Ministers and Secretaries (Amendment) (No. 2) Act 1977, s.1; Ministers and Secretaries (Amendment) (No. 2) Act 1980, s.2.
[40] *Dáil Debates*, Vol. 301, cols. 59–62, November 2, 1977 (Mr. Colley).
[41] For example, Public Service (Delegation of Ministerial Functions) Order (S.I. 1978 No. 117).

of "image," the need for which has been explained on the grounds that the title "parliamentary secretary" gave people, both at home and internationally, the impression that a very junior Minister was involved. Accordingly, the new title was decreed for the position of junior Minister. Probably because of its use in Britain, the title "Minister of State" was invoked. However, the same style was already in use for "members of the Government having charge of a Department of State,"[42] that is, Government Ministers. This change therefore required a new name for Government Ministers and this is now (in respect of statutes passed after 1977), provided by the title "Minister of the Government."[43]

Recent changes

It may be useful to trace the most recent developments in the organisation of the structure of government business. First, on the reorganisation of the Coalition Government (1982–1987) in February 1986[44] the tourism functions of the Minister for Industry, Trade, Commerce and Tourism were transferred to the Minister for Fisheries and Forestry, who thus became the Minister for Tourism, Fisheries and Forestry, leaving the original Minister retitled simply the Minister for Industry and Commerce.

Then, when the Fianna Fáil Government was formed in 1987, further extensive changes to the structure of government were made in order, it was said, to reinforce the portfolios with the greatest potential for wealth and employment creation.[45] The first two of these changes involved the creation of new Ministers and Departments. The Minister for Tourism, Fisheries and Forestry was rechristened the Minister for the Marine,[46] retaining the marine functions of the original Minister, receiving a transfer of transport functions from the Minister for Communications[47] but losing its tourism functions. The second new Minister, the Minister for Tourism and Transport (the derivation of whose corporation sole is explained below), received transfers of the remaining transport functions from the Minister for Communications,[48] and of tourism functions from the Minister for the Marine.[49] This combination was based on the idea that the transport system should be regarded as an aspect of tourism policy. To complete this series of changes, responsibility for certain forestry and wildlife functions was transferred to the Minister for Energy from the for-

---

[42] Interpretation Act No. 38 of 1937, Schedule, item 18; Civil Service Regulation Act 1956, s.2(1)(*d*).
[43] Ministers and Secretaries (Amendment) (No. 2) Act 1977, s.4; *Dáil Debates*, Vol. 301, cols. 62–63.
[44] *Dáil Debates*, Vol. 363, col. 2774.
[45] *Dáil Debates*, Vol. 371, cols. 52–59.
[46] Tourism, Fisheries and Forestry (Alteration of Name of Department and Title of Minister) Order (S.I. 1987 No. 82).
[47] Communications (Transfer of Departmental Administration and Ministerial Functions) Order (S.I. 1987 No. 91). See also, Arramara Teoranta (Transfer of Departmental Administration and Ministerial Functions) Order (S.I. 1987 No. 93).
[48] Communications (Transfer of Departmental Administration and Ministerial Functions) (No. 2) Order (S.I. 1987 No. 92).
[49] Tourism (Transfer of Departmental Administration and Ministerial Functions) Order (S.I. 1987 No. 95).

mer Minister for Tourism.[50] Following the loss of transport, the Minister for Communications was reduced to a rump of functions, consisting mainly of the supervision of broadcasting, An Post and Bord Telecom Éireann. While the Minister remains as a separate corporation sole the incumbent has always held Communications in tandem with another portfolio.

The third change was that all the functions of the Minister for the Public Service were transferred to the Minister for Finance.[51]

The statutory shell—the corporation sole—thus vacated by the Minister for the Public Service was used to constitute the Minister for Tourism and Transport[52] so that there was no need for a Ministers and Secretaries (Amendment) Act to create a new corporation sole.

Fourthly the Minister for Agriculture was renamed the Minister for Agriculture and Food.[53]

Finally, according to the Taoiseach, Mr. Haughey[54]:

"In order to give greater thrust to certain development areas, I intend to create Offices attached to a number of Departments. Each of these Offices will be under the direct control of a Minister of State. A headline for this kind of Office already exists, in the Office of Public Works and the Office of the Revenue Commissioners, which are attached to the Department of Finance, but which exercise separately their own distinct functions and responsibilities."

However, the only legislation found necessary to implement this change was the delegation, under the Ministers and Secretaries Code of, for example, certain functions of the Minister for Agriculture and Food to each of the Ministers of State in that Department.[55] In particular, no mention was made of the neglected provision which empowers the Government, by order "to prescribe the organisation of any Department of State and for that purpose to create units of administration within such Department of State."[56]

The changes made in 1987 were substantially retained following the 1989 Election.

[50] Forestry and Wildlife (Transfer of Departmental Administration and Ministerial Functions) Order (S.I. 1987 No. 96).
[51] Public Service (Transfer of Departmental Administration and Ministerial Functions) Order (S.I. 1987 No. 81).
[52] Public Service (Alteration of Name of Department and Title of Minister) Order (S.I. 1987 No. 83). A similar stratagem was employed in early 1980, when the Minister for Economic Planning was abolished and the Minister for Energy was constituted. See S.I. 1980 Nos. 1, 8–12.
[53] Agriculture (Alteration of Name of Department and Title of Minister) Order (S.I. 1987 No. 97).
[54] *Dáil Debates*, Vol. 371, cols. 56–57. The Offices are: the Office of Science and Technology and the Office of Trade and Marketing (each attached to the Department of Industry and Commerce); the Office of Food Industry and the Office of Horticulture (each attached to the Department of Agriculture); the Office of Forestry (attached to the Department of Energy).
[55] Agriculture and Food (Delegation of Ministerial Functions) Orders (S.I. 1987 Nos. 163 and 164). The impression that some change had taken place was probably caused by the popular practice of adopting titles derived from their assigned functions, such as "Minister of State for Horticulture" whereas the correct legal form would be "Minister of State at the Department of Arigiculture and Food."
[56] Ministers and Secretaries (Amendment) Act 1939, s.6(1)(*e*).

3. Reform in the Civil Service:[57]

1981–1987

Save for the 1973–1987 period, the personnel and organisation functions for the entire civil service has always been vested in the Minister for Finance. Because the civil service pay and pensions bill accounts for a large and increasing share of public expenditure, this function had been regarded since the foundation of the State as an intrinsic element in the control of Government expenditure. However, with the economic programming of the late 1950s, the civil service was required to play a new and more dynamic part in the economic life of the country. To assist it to adapt to this change, the Minister for Finance constituted the Public Services Organisation Review Group ("the Devlin Report"), which reported in 1969.[58] One of its major proposals was implemented fairly quickly. This was the creation of a Minister for the Public Service, with a separate Department of State, freed of the shadows cast by preoccupation with the functions of the Department of Finance and the transfer to the new Minister of powers over the civil service.[59] The object of this change, effected by the Ministers and Secretaries (Amendment) Act 1973,[60] was to promote a more positive attitude towards matters of organisation and personnel, as contrasted with the exclusive emphasis on cost-consciousness natural to the Department of Finance. In particular, it was hoped that the new Department would possess sufficient authority and enthusiasm to push through the other reforms proposed by the Devlin Report. In fact, for wider political reasons, very little happened until the mid 1980s.

The Governments of 1981–1982 and 1982–1987 were elected on a programme which included public service reform, symbolised by the fact that, between 1982 and 1986, for the first time ever, the incumbent of the office of Minister for the Public Service did not hold a second portfolio. The result was a number of specific reforms, including: the articulation of major expenditure programmes in each Department so as to pin-point the link between costs and performance; the appointment, with effect from early 1984, of an Ombudsman to hold the office which had remained vacant since it was constituted in 1980; the establishment, in 1984, of the Top Level Appointments Committee to make

[57] R. Boyle and L. Joyce, *Making Change Work* (I.P.A.; 1988); R. Boyle, *Managing Public Sector Performance* (I.P.A.; 1989) C. Murray, *Civil Service Observed* (I.P.A., 1990); J. Dunne, "Politics of Institutional Reform" (1989) 4 *Irish Political Studies* 1.
[58] Prl. 792. For comment, see J. J. Lee, *Ireland 1912–1985* (Cambridge University Press, 1989), pp. 547–554; S. Calleary, "Devlin—ten years on" (1979) 27 *Administration* 4, 395; N. Whelan, "Public service adaptation—its nature and requirements" (1979) 27 *Administration* 1, 96; C. Ó Nualláin, "Public service reform" (1978) 26 *Administration* 3, 301–302; R. Chapman, "The Irish public service: change or reform?" (1975) 23 *Administration* 2, 138 and Seán Dooney, "1969–1979: a decade of development?" (1980) 1 *Seirbhís Phoiblí* 2, 29, 32.
[59] Public Service (Transfer of Departmental Administration and Ministerial Functions) Order (S.I. 1973 No. 294).
[60] 1973 Act, s.2. It was provided by the 1973 Act, that the Minister for the Public Service should always be the same person as the Minister for Finance. This provision was revoked by the Ministers and Secretaries Act 1980, s.7. Ss.4 and 5 of the 1973 Act also established the Public Service Advisory Council on which see n. 68 below.

recommendations for filling posts at Assistant Secretary level or above, apply-ing the criterion of merit rather than seniority[61]; the opening up of a number of principal and assistant principal posts[62] to selection along similar lines; and the appointment of Secretaries for a maximum period of seven years. (By 1991, the term of office of the first of the Secretaries appointed on this basis was drawing to a close and it was unclear whether the limitation would be observed.) In addition: a wider and more attractive presentation of infor-mation was established, civil servants dealing with the public were required to give their names and a special unit of the Department of the Public Service (which has now been lodged in the Government Supplies Agency) undertook responsibility to "dejargonise" (*sic*) all Government or departmental forms. The Review Body on Higher Remeration in the Public Sector[63] recom-mended that increments for Assistant Secretaries should not be virtually auto-matic (as formerly) but should be performance-related. This change was effected from 1989. If it proves successful, it will presumably spread, in time, to other grades.

Finally, *Serving the Country Better: A White Paper on the Public Service* was published in 1985.[64] The major constitutional-legal change proposed by the White Paper was a modification of the ministerial responsibility doctrine. This change followed from an analysis of a defect in the governmental system which has been explained by Dr. Barrington as follows:

> "The basic system established to ensure the democratic accountability of government rested on the idea that the job of a Minister in charge of a Government Department is very like that of a manager of a small business. He should take all the decisions and have his finger in every pie. [But] government is not small business, but very big business indeed."[65]

Although the White Paper was still born, the idea on which it was based (which was along the same lines as the Devlin Report's old concept of the *Aireacht*) remains of interest. Accordingly it is worth quoting a passage from the White Paper which envisaged a remedy for the ill, identified by Dr. Barrington:

> "Where departments have a sufficiently large volume of purely executive work, Ministers will be enabled by legislation to transfer such work to sep-arate offices to be known as executive offices which will have full responsi-bility for discharging it effectively. The transfer will be effected by order made by the Minister with the consent of the Ministers for Finance and the Public Service and subject to affirmative resolution of each House of the Oireachtas. The purpose of establishing executive offices is twofold: to free

[61] See further, pp. 76–77.
[62] A similar scheme had been in existence for Higher Executive Officers since 1973.
[63] Pl. 5244, paras 7.22–35.
[64] Pl. 3262. The sub-title was a misnomer since the White Paper dealt almost exclusively with the civil service. Most of these reforms are summarised in *Serving the Country Better: A White Paper on the Public Service* (1985, Pl. 3262) ("The White Paper"). For comment, see "A special issue on the White Paper." (1985) 6 *Seirbhís Phoiblí* 4. The full implications of some of the changes suggested here will be appreciated when the rest of this chapter has been read.
[65] *The Irish Administrative System* (Dublin, 1980), p. 32.

Ministers of involvement in time-consuming day-to-day administration and to enable the officials responsible for the delivery of services to concentrate on good management. This approach will be followed in departments where there is sufficient volume of executive work to make it feasible to set up separate organisations for its performance.

Examples of possible areas where executive offices might be set up are the payment of social insurance benefits and social assistance by the Department of Social Welfare; Central Statistics Office; school building work in the Department of Education; and the Air Navigation Services Office and the Meteorological Service, which at present operate in many respects as executive offices of the Department of Communications on a non-statutory basis.

The work transferred will no longer be regarded as part of the business of the department for which the Minister is responsible and, accordingly, the Minister will not be answerable to the Dáil for the day-to-day operations of the office. (He will, of course, remain responsible for the policy under which it operates). The following arrangements will generally apply:

Ministers will have power to appoint and, if necessary, replace the chief executives of such offices, subject to normal procedures. The chief executive and other staff will be civil servants who will be graded in accordance with their responsibilities.

Each executive office will have a separate vote for which the chief executive will be the Accounting Officer, *i.e.* the official statutorily accountable to the Dáil.

The statutory orders setting up the individual executive offices will spell out in more detail the relationship between the offices and their departments and Ministers.

To improve management, the chief executives of the executive offices will be given greater managerial autonomy than is normally possible within the civil service context, including authority in relation to appointment, discipline and dismissal of staff."[66]

1987–1991

The major preoccupation of the Governments in power since 1987 has been retrenchment in public expenditure so as to reduce the public debt to a more manageable level. Against this background, the view has been taken that public service reform might involve additional expenditure and, in any case, was something which could wait. Thus the Minister for—and Department

---

[66] (Pl. 3262), pp. 27–28. The legislation to implement the new régime was considered but never published. The equivalent British development is the transfer of certain types of executive work to "agencies" run by chief executives who are responsible for delivering specified services within policy and resources agreed with the appropriate Minister and with the assistance of staff who are subject to a more flexible pay and conditions régime. By mid-1989, eight of these agencies (*e.g.* Vehicle Inspectorate, Companies House, HMSO, Civil Service College) had been set up. See Flynn, Grey and Jenkins, "Taking the Next Steps: the Changing Management of Government" (1990) *Parliamentary Affairs* 159.

of—the Public Service were abolished as an independent entity and the functions and personnel of the former Minister were restored to the Minister for Finance, as in the pre-1973 era.[67] The Public Service Advisory Council was laid to rest alongside its former sponsoring Department.[68] Again, while the detailed reforms made during the period 1981–1987 (listed above) were retained, the comprehensive initiative towards Devlinisation proclaimed in *Serving the Country Better* has been terminated.[69]

The two major post-1987 reforms are Administrative Budgets and the Efficiency Audit Group.[70] As the name indicates, Administrative Budgets are concerned with such administrative costs as: salaries, consultancy services and travelling and office expenses. One feature of the new scheme is that a commitment of funds is made on a three-yearly basis so that planning and organisation is located within a wider frame of reference and administrator are freed from obedience to the annual cycle (which as Aneurin Bevan pointed out, is more appropriate to a pastoral society dependent on the ebb and flow of the seasons than a modern polity). However Dáil approval and review will continue to be based on the present annual system[70a] and no device has been established to overcome this disjointure.

The most important feature of the Administrative Budgets is that by introducing the new scheme, the Minister for Finance made an unprecedented delegation of his power to consent to expenditure. This power was delegated to the Secretary of each Department (who, is of course, the accounting office for each Department vote). Thus there has been a delegation of authority: to

[67] At the time of the transfer, there was talk of retaining some status for public service reform by rechristening the Minister for Finance as the Minister for Finance and the Public Service. But this came to nothing.

The Department of Finance is now divided into five divisions: Finance; Public Expenditure; Budget and Planning; Personnel and Remuneration; and Organisation, Management and Training. The last two divisions are under the control of a Secretary, who was formerly at the head of the Department of Public Service.

[68] The Council's final annual report (No. 13, Pl. 5197) is for the period ended November 1986 but was obviously (see p. 7) prepared after the demise of the Department of the Public Service. At pp. 8–9 the Report states:

"We have discussed the relevance of the Council among ourselves during the past three years. We have come to the conclusion that it has made no impact. It is our view that it has not a useful role at the present time. It doesn't have an audience. Only on one occasion did the Oireachtas debate a Report and that was in the Senate. . . . The sponsoring Department, the DPS, has been absorbed by the Department of Finance and it would seem appropriate that consideration should now be given to resting the Public Service Advisory Council, pending a new approach to the reorganisation of the Public Service."

The legality of this rest may be questioned in view of the widespread use of the word "shall", in the Ministers and Secretaries (Amendment) Act 1973 and its Schedule, in regard to the PSAC, *e.g.* s.4(1) states: " . . . there shall . . . be established a Public Service Advisory Council. . . . "

[69] Though note that: the Social Welfare Services Office (within the Department of Social Welfare) which deals with the mechanism for actually paying social welfare benefits; the Air Navigation Services Office (within the Department of Tourism and Transport); and the Government Supplies Agency (within the Office of Public Works which is itself semi-independent of the Department of Finance) have been organised outside the normal hierarchy of the Department and with an independent link to the Minister. There are a few other examples of such embryonic Devlinisation.

[70] See, generally, *Dáil Debates*, Vol 386, col. 235–236; January 25, 1989; Vol 395, col. 197, January 31, 1990; Vol 403, col. 1801–1804, December 11, 1990.

[70a] For details of financial procedure, see Gwynn Morgan, *Constitutional Law of Ireland*, Chap 8.

expend money to a higher maxima than before; to vire (transfer) money between sub-heads of a vote; to create posts up to and including the level of Higher Executive Officer; and to purchase computer equipment up to a value of £100,000. Concurrently with this change, there will be a substantial delegation of authority to line managers in each particular Department. These changes came into effect, for the first time, in respect of all Departments of State, for the trienium, 1991–1993 (following an experiment in the Department of Social Welfare in 1989).

The intended effect of the changes will be to increase the authority and, therefore, responsibility of Secretaries and line managers and, inevitably other civil servants too. This amounts to, *inter alia*, a long overdue recognition of the decay of the individual ministerial doctrine, considered in Part I of this chapter. It should also remove some of the Department of Finance's minute powers of control and bring the administration of a Department of State closer to that of a large private organisation.

The establishment of the Efficiency Audit Group, like the introduction of Administrative Budgets, was accomplished by administrative memorandum, no legislative instrument being considered necessary. The changes are alike too in that they have not attracted the degree of even specialised interest, which their potential importance might be thought to warrant. The essence of the Audit is a periodic, critical, pragmatic examination of the working of each Department. The examination is intended to be more radical and far-reaching than that carried out by say the Operations and Management Unit of the Department of Finance. It will embrace not only the particular Department but also its relationship with associated branches of administration, whatever form these take. For example, the first investigation (which commenced in 1988 and was still not complete by early 1991) was into the Department of Defence including its links with the Defence Forces. The examination is carried out by a committee, comprising representatives from the Departments of Finance (two members) and the Department of the Taoiseach as well as the Department under investigation together with three private sector managers, and chaired by a Professor of Economics. It is serviced by a secretary who is a civil servant in the Department of the Taoiseach. The Audit, which is modelled on a similar scrutiny of the British Departments, is known to enjoy the support of the present Taoiseach, Mr. Haughey, and so it is likely that any recommendations which the Group makes will be adopted and that the legislative, financial or administrative changes necessary for their implementation will be made.

4. Civil Service: Definitions and Context

The widest term used in this area (though not generally in the context of legislation) is the "public sector," a category which embraces not merely civil servants but all those who are employed, directly or indirectly, by some public body. This comprises in all about 270,000 people, compared with a gross figure for national employment (excluding the self-employed) of 900,000.

A slightly narrower term than the public sector[71] is the public service[72]—those employees whose salary and pension bill (approx. £3 billion) is paid for, directly or indirectly, out of public funds—a term which is obviously very significant in economic and financial contexts. Broadly speaking, the public service comprises the public sector less employees of commercial state-sponsored bodies. At the centre of the public service lies the civil service manning, *inter alia*, the Departments of State. The number of civil servants increased from 28,000 in 1960 to 70,000 in 1983 just before the establishment of *An Post* and *Bord Telecom Éireann*.[73] In 1986, there were 35,000 civil servants and by 1990 (as a result of the restriction on recruitment and the early retirement scheme) the figure had fallen to 27,000.[74] The numbers and remuneration of the civil servants in each Department, formerly shown in the Book of Estimates, have appeared since 1966 in a separate publication, the *Directory of State Services*.

Civil servant

It is necessary to define the terms "civil servant" and "civil service" more precisely: for these terms are used in various statutes which provide no definition for the terms and, when it comes to applying the terms, there are some marginal public posts whose constituent statute does not make it clear whether or not they are civil servants.[75] Most important, the term "civil servant" is used to indicate the scope of both the Civil Service Commissioners Act 1956 which regulates the selection of civil servants and the Civil Service

---

[71] Those employed in the public sector are those made up roughly as follows: civil servants (27,000); employees of the health boards (57,000); the state-sponsored bodies (84,000); the local authorities and county committees of agriculture (27,000); security forces (25,000); and educational sector (52,000).

In a study comparing Ireland with Sweden, Britain, Italy and U.S., Dr. Murray concludes that the Irish public employment of labour ratio is somewhat below average and that its rate of increase in recent years was also below average and has indeed been reversed in recent years: Murray, "Public Employment Observed" (1989) 10 *Seirbhís Phoiblí* 32.

[72] For a rare statutory example of the use of "public service," see Ministers and Secretaries (Amendment) Act 1973, ss.1, 3 and 5 (setting up the Minister for the Public Service and the Public Service Advisory Council). See further, Chap. 4, p. 104, n. 4.

[73] For a point arising out of the transfer of staff to these new bodies, see *Flynn* v. *An Post* [1987] I.R. 68, 75, 80–81.

[74] This figure includes 5,000 industrial civil servants, most of whom are craftsmen or general workers employed in the Department of Fisheries and Forestry or the Office of Public Works. The rules regarding the employment of these civil servants differ to a considerable extent from those affecting the non-industrial civil service, for instance, industrial civil servants are usually in "scheduled" positions (see p. 79, para. 1) and thus not recruited by the Civil Service Commissioners. The closest we can come to a definition of an industrial civil servant is to say that they are those grades which have been designated as "workers" by the Minister for the Public Service for the purposes of the Industrial Relations Act 1946, Pt. VI (which gives the Labour Court power to investigate trade disputes). See also Industrial Relations Act 1969, s.17(1) and Public Service (Transfer of Departmental Administration and Ministerial Functions) Order (S.I. 1973 No. 294). The remaining Parts of the chapter will deal principally with non-industrial civil servants.

[75] Though modern statutes frequently state explicitly that the posts they create are to be civil servants, *e.g.* Law Reform Commission Act, s.10(6)(*b*); Ombudsman Act, s.10(2); Staff of the Houses of the Oireachtas Act 1959, s.3; Presidential Establishment Act 1938, s.6. The Ministers and Secretaries Act 1924, s.2(2) does not do this but it is clear that the positions which it contemplates meet the tests for a civil servant given in the text.

Regulation Act 1956 (which deals with the terms and conditions of civil servants). A useful historical sketch of the terms was given by Kingsmill Moore J. in *McLoughlin* v. *Minister for Social Welfare* (the facts of which will be given below)[76]:

"The words 'civil service' and 'civil servant' though in frequent use on the lips of politicans and members of the general public, are not terms of legal art. The British Royal Commission on the Civil Service which reported in 1931 stated that 'there is nowhere any authoritative or exhaustive definition of the civil service.' The phrase seems to have been first used to describe the non-combatant service of the East India Company, and was well established in English political language by the middle of the nineteenth century.

Though it may be difficult to frame an exact definition, it does not seem in any way impossible to reach an approximation to the meaning of the words sufficient to meet the requirements of the present case. In Britain civil servants were servants of the Crown, that is to say, servants of the King in his politic capacity, but not all servants of the Crown were civil servants. Those who used the strong arm—military, naval and police forces—were excluded from the conception, for the service was civil, not combatant; and so also, by tradition, were judges and holders of political offices. Civil servants were paid out of monies voted by parliament and if permanent, had the benefit of the Superannuation Acts. In theory, as servants of the King, they held their positions at pleasure but in practice they were treated as holding during good behaviour. . . .

The bulk of British civil servants working in Ireland, were taken into the service of Saorstat Éireann and the phrase, with the ideas attached to it, was assimilated into Irish political life. Soon it made its appearance in the Irish statute book, and after the passing of our present Constitution, in statutes of the Republic. Borderline cases have been dealt with by special legislation. Persons have been deemed to be civil servants for one purpose and deemed not to be civil servants for another. But, if we substitute 'State' for 'King' the summary which I have already given corresponds to the present conception of civil servants in Ireland.

I have no doubt that Mr. McLoughlin is a civil servant. He is a state servant engaged in administering one of the most important of State functions, that of justice: he is paid out of monies voted by the Oireachtas: the situation which he holds was dealt with by a scheduling order under section 10 of the Civil Service Regulation Act, 1924, and such an order could only be properly applicable to a post in the civil service—for its effect is to exclude a situation in the civil service from the operation of the Act."

Partly in the light of this evolution, we can suggest the following guidelines in defining a civil servant. First, civil servants are paid out of moneys provided annually, through the Appropriation Act, by the Oireachtas.[77] Secondly, they serve the various organs of State created by the Constitution, including the

[76] [1958] I.R. 1, 14–15.
[77] Civil Service Regulation Act 1956, s.18.

President, the Dáil and Senate, the Attorney-General, the Comptroller and
Auditor General, the Taoiseach and the other Ministers who are in charge of
Departments of State. To this list must be added other offices, like the Ombudsman, which, although established by Act of Parliament,[78] rather than by the
Constitution, are plainly constitutional in nature. As might be expected from the
term "servant," the actual incumbents of these offices themselves—for instance,
the Ministers or the Comptroller and Auditor General or the Ombudsman are
not created civil servants and other political appointees are also excluded from
the category of "civil servants." So, too, are those who help to exercise the
military, police or judicial function. Although it involves an element of circular-
ity, it should be noted that civil servants are public officials who are subject to the
régime (described in subsequent Parts) which is created by the two 1956 Acts.
Finally, the Civil Service Regulations Act 1956, section 20 provides that "for the
purposes of this Act," the question of whether a person is a civil servant "shall be
decided by the Minister [for Finance], whose decision shall be final."

Kingsmill Moore J.'s analysis of the concept of a "civil servant" in
McLoughlin was quoted with approval in *Murphy* v. *Minister for Social Welfare*.[79] Here the applicant had been appointed under the Industrial Relations
Act 1946, as an ordinary member of the Labour Court. The main issue before
the court was the question of whether the applicant was insurable under the
Social Welfare (Consolidation) Act 1981. This, in turn depended on whether
the applicant was "employ[ed] in the civil service of the Government or the
civil service of the State" (in the language of the First Schedule to the Act). In
elucidating this difficult problem, Blayney J. first quoted the passage from
McLoughlin which is reproduced above and then went on to address the question which was before him, as follows:

"In the light of this very useful exposition of the meaning to be attached to
the expressions 'civil service' and 'civil servant,' the correct test to be
applied in determining whether the applicant was a civil servant would
appear to be whether he was a servant of the State in its politic capacity,
and in my opinion he was. He was a state servant exercising an important
function in the area of industrial relations; he was paid out of monies voted
by the Oireachtas for the Department of Labour, and he was under the
control of the Minister for Labour who could remove him from office for
stated reasons: see section 10 of the Industrial Relations Act 1946. The
preamble to the same Act stated that it was an 'Act to make further and
better provision for promoting harmonious relations between workers and
their employers and for this purpose to establish machinery for regulating
rates of remuneration and conditions of employment and for the prevention and settlement of trade disputes, and to provide for certain other
matters connected with the matters aforesaid.' The Labour Court was one
of the instruments created to achieve the aims outlined in the preamble and
to implement the terms of the Act. It was created to fulfil an important

[78] Ombudsman Act 1980, s.2.
[79] [1987] I.R. 295. See also, *Power* v. *Minister for Social Welfare* [1987] I.R. 307.

function in the area of industrial relations. As a member of that court, the applicant was executing the policy of the State and so was engaged in the service of the State."[80]

Yet the problem is surely more difficult than might appear from this passage. It is certainly true that the applicant was paid out of a Departmental Estimate. The second half of the passage seems to hint that industrial relations is a characteristic governmental function. But then the dirigiste state has taken to itself such a diverse collection of functions that this factor does not take the argument very far. More difficulty stems from the statement, in the final sentence, that since "the applicant was executing the policy of the State [he] was engaged in the service of the State." (Is State used here as a loose synonym for "Minister" or "Government"?) In any case, this assertion brings us up against the major difficulty. This difficulty can be raised by way of a statement from Kerr and Whyte's *Irish Trade Union Law* (which was written before *Murphy* was decided):

> "The members are paid out of public funds but they are not civil servants nor do they act under instruction from the Minister. In fact, when the Minister for Labour performed the official opening ceremony of the Court's new headquarters in 1984, he expressly rejected doubts about the Court's independence and stressed that the Government in which he participated was committed to maintaining the Court's unbiased role. At the same ceremony the then Chairman of the Court stressed his determination that the Court would remain a wholly independent forum for the settlement of disputes, which would not act as an arm of government economic policy."[81]

In addition to this significant point about independence, one ought to note that while an ordinary member of the Labour Court is appointed by the Minister for Labour, before doing so, admittedly only as a matter of practice, the Minister consults trade unions. Even more significant is the fact that the Minister must appoint a person who has been nominated, not by the Civil Service Commissioners, but by a "trade union of workers [or employers]." Next, the member's term of office is fixed by the Minister but may not exceed five years. These are not normal features of a civil servant's employment. Finally, it is incomplete to state (as the passage quoted from *Murphy* does) that he may be removed by the Minister since as a matter of law, the consent of the organisation which nominated the member is also necessary. This is a far cry from the traditional notion of the will and pleasure of the Government.[82]

---

[80] *Ibid.* 305. Blayney J. buttressed his conclusion by a distinct argument which is not of such general interest, namely that s.10(6) of the Industrial Relations Act 1946 provides that the Civil Service Regulation Acts 1924 and 1926 shall not apply to members of the Labour Court. "Since these Acts applied to civil servants only, if the ordinary members of the Labour Court were not civil servants, the exclusion would not have been necessary." (p. 305) This surely is not a very strong argument: for the provisions in the 1946 Act may have been inserted *ex abundante cautela*.
[81] Professional Books 1985, p. 339 (footnotes omitted).
[82] For the statutory references, see Industrial Relations Act 1946, s.10(8).

71

On what has been said so far, it might seem that the decision, in *Murphy*, is at best a marginal one, influenced by a desire to make the applicant eligible for social welfare entitlements. However, there is another point which, it is respectfully suggested, puts it beyond doubt that the applicant was not a civil servant. This argument depends on the fact that, as was stated in the passage quoted from *McLoughlin*, judges and the holders of political office are excluded from the category of civil servants.[83] Now the Labour Court is not, of course, a court of law; nor are its members judges. Rather its basic functions are the provision of conciliation and mediation services. However, it is suggested that the factors adduced in the paragraph quoted from Messrs. Kerr and Whyte's book mean that, so far as distance from the civil service is concerned, Labour Court members may, by analogy, be regarded as on a par with such personages as judges, politicians or the Ombudsman.

To generalise the issue: there are a number of what may be regarded as satellites of Departments which for policy reasons have always been regarded as needing some independence from the Minister. Among them are: the Revenue Commissioners; the Land Registry; the Civil Service Commission; the Local Appointments Commission.[84] These entities are usually staffed by civil servants (a matter to which we shall return in the context of the distinction between civil servants of the Government and of the State). In some cases, the heads of these entities, like the members of the Labour Court, enjoy some distinctive element in their statutory position which reflects the convention upholding their independence. If *Murphy* is to be followed faithfully, the heads of these bodies must also be classified as civil servants. It is suggested that because of the need for independence, this is an undesirable result and, in a broad sense, unconstitutional. This view certainly derives some support from the underlying tenor of the major judgments in the Supreme Court in *McLoughlin* though, as we shall see, the precise issue in that case was different from that in *Murphy*.

A further point which emerges from this discussion is that it is possible to be in the service of the State, yet not in the *civil* service of the State. This is clear from the passage quoted from Kingsmill Moore J.'s judgment in *McLoughlin*, in particular from the following:

" . . . not all servants of the Crown were civil servants. Those who used the strong arm—military, naval and police forces—were excluded from the conception, for the service was civil, not combatant; and so also, by tradition, were judges and holders of political office."[85]

It has also been suggested, in the previous paragraphs, that members of the Labour Court might be added to this intermediate category. More difficult is

---

[83] The argument examined here was not considered in *Murphy* where Blayney J. said, in a different context, that Kingsmill Moore J. had stated in *McLoughlin* that "any service of the State which is not 'combatant' is entitled to be described as 'civil' " [1987] I.R. 305. As can be seen from the quotation in the text, this overlooks Kingsmill Moore J.'s reference to judges and politicians.

[84] See pp. 77–78 (Civil Service Commissioners) and pp. 105–106 (Revenue Commissioners).

[85] [1958] I.R. 14–15. See also, *Murphy* v. *Minister for Social Welfare* [1987] I.R. 305.

the question of what meaning can be given to this category of non-civil-servant State servants. The most that can be said is that, negatively, they are not subject to the 1956 Acts and on the positive side, the State is vicariously liable for their torts.[86]

Finally, one should note that the action *per quod servitium amisit* cannot be taken by the State in respect of its "servants" (regardless of whether they are civil servants or not). This was established in *Attorney-General* v. *Ryan's Car Hire Ltd.*[87] on the ground that "service [to the State] is different in kind from that required or existing in the ordinary master and servant relationship."[88]

Civil servant of the Government or the State?

The distinction between a civil servant of the State and a civil servant of the Government was not at issue in *Murphy*, since the statutory category which was at the heart of that case embraced both types of civil servant. By contrast, this distinction was the central issue, indeed was drawn for the first time, in *McLoughlin*. The plaintiff was a temporary assistant solicitor in the Chief State Solicitor's office, which is one of the services assigned to the Attorney-General by the Ninth Part of the Schedule to the Ministers and Secretaries Act 1924. He argued that he was not to be regarded as being employed in the "civil service of the Government" and hence was not an "employed contributor" for the purposes of the Social Welfare Act 1952. The majority of the Supreme Court ignored the powerful literal argument which swayed the dissenting judge,[89] founding itself instead on the following high constitutional principle: a civil servant is a servant of the State and the State has many organs, including not only the Government, but also the President, the Oireachtas, the Comptroller and Auditor General and the Attorney-General. It is necessary for the proper functioning of each organ that it should be free and independent of any other organ of the State. Specifically, it is vital for the Attorney-General to be independent of the Government. It follows that the Attorney's staff should not be subject to the instructions of the Government or any of its Ministers and, thus, that they should be classified as civil servants of the State and not of the Government. Following this line of reasoning, the term "civil servant of the State" is now applied, by statute, to the staff of other major organs of State including the President, the Oireachtas and the Ombudsman.[90] Not only the Attorney-General, but also the other organs of State listed earlier, need to be independent of the Government and its Ministers and so it seems that their staff too must be classed as being in the civil

[86] See pp. 710–713.
[87] [1965] I.R. 642. This case reversed a stream of contrary authority: *Attorney-General* v. *Dublin United Tramways Co.* [1939] I.R. 590; *Minister for Finance* v. *O'Brien* [1949] I.R. 91; *Attorney-General* v. *Coras Iompair Éireann* 90 I.L.T.R. 139.
[88] [1965] I.R. 664.
[89] The dissenting judge, Maguire C.J., relied on a narrower argument, which is peculiar to the Attorney-General (and does not extend to the President, etc.), namely, that by the 1924 Act, s.1 the administration of any public services which are not located in any of the other Departments of State is vested in the Department of the Taoiseach: see [1958] I.R. 11–12, 19–20, 23–24.
[90] See p. 68, n. 75.

service of the State. The term "civil servant of the State" has been applied, by some statutes, not only to those who serve bodies established by the Constitution, but also to the servants of certain bodies constituted by statute—such as the Ombudsman—whose functions require them to be independent.[91] The logic of the derivation of the two terms is such that the term "civil service of the State" ought to include both the "civil service of the Government" and the staff working for the Attorney-General, etc.[92] In fact, common usage is to treat the two terms as if they were mutually exclusive.

The basis of the decision in *McLoughlin* was that since, in respect of some of his functions, the Attorney-General needed to be independent so, too, did his staff. If this be true of the Attorney, how much more so is it true of the judiciary? For the Attorney might himself be regarded as at least a semi-detached politician in that as one of his functions (by today his only substantial function) he is the Government's legal adviser. In addition, he leaves office with the Government. By contrast, the independence of the judiciary is a major premise of the Constitution and, indeed, is stated expressly in Article 34.5.1 of the Constitution. In the light of this, it is striking that court staff are regarded as civil servants of the Government, indeed, operate as a unit of the Department of Justice. The possibility for a conflict of interest appears obvious. It seems clear then, following the reasoning in *McLoughlin*, that court staff ought to enjoy the status of civil servants of the State. For this change to have substance, rather than just being a colourable device (which would not, it is submitted, satisfy the Constitution), certain statutory amendments removing any say in the appointment and dismissal of court staff from the Government would have to be made. An analogous, though less powerful, argument could be made for saying that the staff of such independent and semi-independent bodies as the Labour Court and the Revenue Commissioners ought also to enjoy the status of civil servants of the State.

The need, referred to in the last paragraph to mark the significance of the distinction between a civil servant of the Government and the State by some real differences in regard to the appointment and removal of the two categories of civil servant has not been taken into account in the legislation. For in face of the fundamental principle enunciated by the Supreme Court in *McLoughlin* at a time just before the Civil Service Commissioners Act 1956 and the Civil Service Regulation Act 1956 were enacted, each of these Acts applies a common régime to the civil service of the State and of the Government. The distinction between these two categories has thus been collapsed in that each statute is made to apply to the "civil service" which is defined in the interpretation sections to include both the civil service of the State and of the Government.[93] But this draftsman's legerdemain cannot dissolve a difference of substance which stems from the special position of independence which (in most cases) the Constitution requires the organs of State to possess. Thus the

---

[91] See, *e.g.* Civil Service Commissioners Act 1956, s.2; Civil Service Regulation Act 1956, s.2.
[92] *Cf. Byrne* v. *Ireland* [1972] I.R. 241, 286.
[93] The Acts define the terms very slightly differently: see Civil Service Commissioners Act, s.3(1) and Civil Service Regulation Act, s.2(1).

present law which does not take account of the need for independence from the Government—for example, the rule that it is the Government which dismisses established civil servants who are servants of the State (but not of the Government)—is probably unconstitutional.

5. Appointment and Selection

The framework of rules governing the appointment, selection, dismissal and conditions of employment of civil servants is largely statutory. However, by way of warning, in connection with the description which follows, it must be emphasised that there are also extra-statutory rules, often contained in circulars, which in practice often make a greater impact than the statute.

In the first place, it must be noted that decisions regarding the creation of new posts in the civil service, including their numbers and the grade at which they are located, are, by statute, taken by the Minister for Finance.[94] However, as mentioned in Part 3, since Administrative Budgets were established in 1991, there has been a substantial delegation of this function.

The senior civil servant in a Department, the Secretary, is appointed by the Government on the recommendation of the Minister responsible for the Department involved.[95] Otherwise, all the civil servants in a Department are formally appointed by the Minister of that Department, though subject to the power of veto of the Minister for Finance[96] (which has been waived in the case of higher executive officers and posts at lower levels).[97] But it must be noted that, as explained below, the authority of each Minister will be overridden in the many cases in which the candidate is actually selected either by the Civil Service Commissioners or by the Top Level Appointments Committee.

Although promotions are, technically, appointments, an important initial question is whether or not the post is to be "promotional" in the sense that competition for it is to be confined to existing civil servants, either in the Department in which it arises or throughout the entire civil service. This ques- with the Minister for Finance, following negotiations with the civil service

---

[94] Civil Service Regulation Act 1956, s.17(1)(*b*); Ministers and Secretaries Act 1924, s.2(2).
[95] Ministers and Secretaries Act, 1924, s.2(2). Note that most personnel functions in respect of individual civil servants of the State are vested in a Minister. The reason is, perhaps, a desire to retain responsibility and answerability to the Dáil for these functions. In any case, the way in which this result has been achieved is to create the position of "appropriate authority" in whom the 1956 Acts vest the powers, for instance, to discipline or to seek an exclusion order in respect of a civil servant. However, the appropriate authority may delegate his powers (*e.g.* to the Attorney-General in respect of the Attorney-General's staff) and such a delegation has usually been made: see Ministers and Secretaries Act 1924, s.2(2); Civil Service Commissioners Act tion is settled by the Minister for the Department involved, in consultation 1956, s.3; Civil Service Regulation Act 1956, s.2; Ombudsman Act 1980, s.10(3).
[96] Ministers and Secretaries Act 1924, s.2(2).
[97] The White Paper (*Serving the Country Better*: Pl. 3262) proposed (at para. 7.12) that the law should be changed so that Secretaries and other designated officials will have power to appoint staff up to levels prescribed by the Minister in charge of the Department, but, in any case, not above Higher Executive Officer level. However, the White Paper envisaged that staff would continue to be selected through normal procedures.

unions. Where the post is not promotional, it will usually be because the post is at a basic recruitment grade: competition for it will necessarily be open to all and selection will usually be by the Civil Service Commissioners: see below. As mentioned already, when this is so, appointment becomes merely a formal function.[98]

Promotional posts

For higher posts, the competition will usually be promotional, *i.e.* confined either to the particular Department or at least to the civil service. In this case, the *modus operandi* for selection is not fixed by statute, but is determined by the Minister in whose Department the vacancy exists,[99] in consultation with his senior officials. There is an exception to this in the case of senior appointments which fall within the jurisdiction of the Top Level Appointments Committee, described in the following paragraph. However, where the exception does not apply and the *modus operandi* is determined by the Minister, he may hold a formal competition of the interview-board type, possibly operated by the Civil Service Commissioners on an agency basis; or he may observe the "seniority rule."[1] Where, unusually, the outcome of the selection process is a promotion which is not "in the customary course of promotion or transfer," as that course had been decided by the Commissioners, for instance from Engineer to Assistant Principal (crossing class barriers) the Civil Service Commissioners must be involved because the appointment is subject to the Commissioners certifying (by a process commonly known as "recertification") that the person selected is qualified as regards knowledge, ability and health for the post.[2]

Promotion via the Top Level Appointments Committee[3]

The jurisdiction of this Committee extends to posts at Assistant Secretary level or above (including non-general service grades) in all Departments, apart from Foreign Affairs and the Revenue Commissioners. Its main purpose was to get away from the tendency, which existed before the Committee was established in January 1984, for a post to go to a senior, if not the most senior, contender from within the same Department. While the new system does accommodate the possibility of open competition its main element is automatic, inter-departmental competition for the posts to which it applies. The Committee is also supposed, where this is possible, to make its decision irrespective of a

---

[98] Civil Servants of the State are usually appointed by a Minister: see, *e.g.* Civil Service Regulation Act 1956, s.19; Ombudsman Act 1980, s.10(1)(*b*). But *cf.* Staff of the Houses of the Oireachtas Act 1959, s.8.

[99] Ministers and Secretaries Act 1924, s.2(2); Civil Service Commissioners Act 1956, ss.13(2), 14(2). Sometimes, even in these circumstances, the Minister for the Public Service may prefer to ask the Commissioners to hold a competition under the Civil Service Commissioners Act 1956, s.29(1)(*b*). Such competitions are often held on a service-wide basis for promotion from Executive Officer to Higher Executive Officer.

[1] For an account of a dispute arising from the Minister for the Public Service's decision to appoint a candidate who was fifteenth in order of seniority, see *The Irish Press*, November 10, 1983.

[2] Civil Service Commissioners Act 1956, ss.18–24.

[3] This section draws heavily on C. H. Murray, "The Top Level Appointments Committee" (1988) 9 *Seirbhís Phoiblí* 1, 10.

candidate's background, in other words to overlook the dual structure of professional and general service streams.

The Committee consists of: the Secretary to the Government; the Secretary (Public Service Management and Development) Department of Finance; two Secretaries of Departments chosen by the Taoiseach after consultation with the Minister for Finance; and, in the case of the appointment of a Secretary, the outgoing incumbent. The new system is not established by statute and so it is still subject to the statutory provisions, already mentioned, by which it is the Government which appoints the Secretary of a Department and the responsible Minister who appoints to the other posts. Accordingly as a matter of law (leaving aside the possibility of the new doctrine of legitimate expectations), all that the committee may do is to make recommendations. No information has been published as to whether the Committee's recommendations have been accepted in all cases. However, it seems likely that with one exception,[4] this has been the case. Other more serious restrictions have been built into the process. Thus, the Secretary of the Department in which the vacancy exists may nominate two applicants who appear before the committee without having to be interviewed by the Civil Service Commissioners, which is a part of the process for the other candidates. Secondly, in the case of a post of Secretary, since 1987 the Committee has been required to recommend three candidates, without ranking them so that the Government may choose among them.

As regards the success of the Committee in achieving its objectives, Dr. Murray (Secretary in the Department of Finance, 1969–1976) concludes "[t]he Committee has achieved some success in promoting inter-departmental mobility at senior level, but the record is hardly outstanding, except perhaps at Secretary level."[5]

Basic recruitment posts: selection by Civil Service Commissioners

As already stated, appointment to most basic recruitment posts is a formality since the selection for most of these posts must be made by the inde-

---

[4] Murray, *loc. cit.* 12 refers to a rumour that one recommendation involving an Assistant Secretary post was not accepted.

[5] *Ibid.* 15. This conclusion is drawn from the figures for the Committee's work during the period January 1984 to mid-1987. The chart given below updates the figures in Dr. Murray's article by adding in the details of later appointments by the TLAC (the figures were published in (1988) 9 *Seirbhís Phoiblí* 9, 20 and (1989) 10, 51) so bringing the figures up to the end of 1989. However the later figures appear to lead to the same conclusion as the earlier ones.

	Filled Outside Dept.	Filled Inside Dept.	Total
Secretaries and Equivalent	5	8	13
Deputy and Assistant Secretaries	13	55	68
Professional Technical Posts	3	18	21

pendent Civil Service Commissioners,[6] first set up in 1923,[7] but presently constituted under the Civil Service Commissioners Act 1956. The object of this system is to prevent jobbery and nepotism. Although the Act purports to state that the Commissioners are dismissible at "the will and pleasure of the Government,"[8] their independence has been consistently respected since the foundation of the State. They have carried their independence to the lengths of (for example) giving the Department involved the name of only the candidate placed first in the competition for a particular post and refusing to disclose whether any other candidates were regarded as qualified for the post. According to the Act, the Commissioners are appointed by the Government, but the convention is for the Ceann Comhairle to be *ex officio* Chairman of the Commissioners and the other two members to be the Secretary to the Government and an official from the Department of Finance (usually the Director of Recruitment in the Department (an Assistant Secretary)). Their staff, who are appointed by the Minister for Finance[9] service both the Civil Service Commissioners and the Local Appointments Commission.

Subject to the exceptions to be outlined below, all civil servants must be selected by the Commissioners, and the person whom they recommend is invariably appointed.[10] Indeed, in practice the names of persons selected for appointment to the basic general service grades are not even submitted to the Minister concerned.

In filling an established or an unestablished post, the Commissioners must hold a competition.[11] The competition is governed by regulations made by the Commissioners (subject to the consent of the Minister for Finance), dealing with such matters as, for example, the qualifications of candidates (*e.g.* Irish citizens only, or certain specified academic qualifications).[12] The Com-

[6] Civil Service Commissioners Act 1956, ss.13(1), 14(1).
[7] Civil Service Regulation Act 1923; Civil Service Regulation Act 1924. See also Fanning, *The Irish Department of Finance 1922–1958* (Dublin, 1978), pp. 63–72. Lee, *Ireland 1912–1985*, p. 107 comments: "Perhaps the major achievement of the early years, and it remains one of the most remarkable achievements in the history of the state, was the creation of a Civil Service Commission, consisting of the Ceann Comhairle (Speaker), and two civil servants, to preside over the public appointments process. The new government was naturally deluged with importunities for jobs. The scope for casualness in the appointments process was considerable. The Civil Service Commission did the state great service in setting ethical standards. Given the scope for corruption permitted by the feeble sense of public morality, the imposition of a high degree of integrity in appointments to the central administration verged on the miraculous. The same considerations did not apply to promotion within the civil service, where the criterion of seniority soon took precedence over that of merit even among men themselves originally appointed on grounds of merit. Nevertheless, this was at the time a relatively venial transgression of the code of strict personal integrity which would be rightly regarded as one of the glories of the civil service."
[8] Civil Service Commissioners Act 1956, s.10(1).
[9] *Ibid.* ss.13(1), 14(1).
[10] The language of the statute makes this point even clearer in the case of the Local Appointments Commission: see Local Authorities (Officers and Servants) Act 1926, s.6(4) and *The State (Minister for Local Government)* v. *Sligo Corporation* (1935) 69 I.L.T.R. 72. See also, *Local Appointments 1926–1972* (Anniversary Booklet), p. 11.
[11] Civil Service Commissioners Act 1956, s.13(1), 14(1).
[12] *Ibid.* ss.15, 16 and 30. For an example, see *The State (Cussen)* v. *Brennan* [1981] I.R. 181, 305.

missioners must make their selection in accordance with the order of merit, as determined under the regulations, but only from amongst candidates whom they regard as qualified for appointment.[13]

Appointments in which Commissioners not involved

There are various exceptional initial appointments in which the Commissioners are not involved. In addition to the appointment of Secretaries of Departments and promotions, already described, these exceptions include the following posts.

(1) Certain posts are listed in the Schedule to the Civil Service Commissioners Act, for instance, porters, messengers and cleaners.[14] The method of recruitment to such posts is left to the individual Departments.

(2) The Commissioners may, on the request of "the appropriate authority" (almost always the Minister for the Department involved) and with the consent of the Minister for Finance, (assuming that he is not the appropriate authority) declare that posts of a specified grade are an "excluded position." In this case too, recruitment is done by the individual Department and is often a patronage appointment. "Excluded position" orders (which are usually only for a limited period) must be publicised by a notice in *Iris Oifigiuil* and can only be made in respect of unestablished positions.[15] The Commissioners will only give their permission if the appropriate authority can make a good case (*e.g.* need for speed in obtaining staff or need to recruit local staff).

(3) An individual may be appointed to a particular post (either established or unestablished), without the intervention of the Commissioners, if the appropriate authority with the consent of the Minister for Finance recommends the appointment and the Government decides that it would be "in the public interest."[16] Publicity must be given to such unusual appointments in the form of a notice in *Iris Oifigiuil*.[17] This exemption has been used, for instance, in the appointment of persons formerly employed by public bodies which have become defunct, such as the Hospitals Commission. Personal political advisers to a Minister are usually appointed to an unestablished, temporary post for the life of the Government, by an excluding order (described in the previous paragraph). However, in 1979 there were protests when the Government used the public interest exemption to appoint their political advisers as established civil servants.

(4) Women in the civil service, who under the pre-1973 rules had been

---

[13] Civil Service Commissioners Act 1956, s.17.

[14] *Ibid.* ss.4.6(2)(*b*) and First Sched.

[15] *Ibid.* ss.5, 6(2)(*c*). Cf. *The State (Minister for Local Government)* v. *Ennis U.D.C.* [1939] I.R. 258.

[16] Civil Service Commissioners Act 1956, ss.13(3), 14(3). See *Aughey* v. *Ireland* [1986] I.L.R.M. 206 for discontent with possible abuses of the analogous "exceptional" system of promotion in the Garda Síochána (authorised by Garda Síochána (Promotion) Regulations 1960 (S.I. 1960 No. 203), Art. 5(2): "Promotion of Guards who have shown special zeal and ability in the performance of their duties notwithstanding that they may not have passed class 3 promotion examinations or the Irish proficiency test").

[17] Civil Service Commissioners Act 1956, s.27(1).

forced to retire on marriage,[18] may, if their husbands die, be readmitted to their old Departments or offices by the appropriate authority without undergoing the usual selection process; but subject to the consent of the Minister for Finance and subject to the Commissioners certifying that an applicant is qualified as regards knowledge, ability and health.[19]

6. Dismissal and Discipline

Dismissal

For certain purposes, the régime for the employment of civil servants distinguishes between established and unestablished positions, according to whether the position is one in respect of which a pension may be granted under the Superannuation Act 1834.[20] One context in which this distinction is important is dismissal. Under the Civil Service Regulation Act 1956, section 5, every established civil servant (a category which now catches the bulk of civil servants) "shall hold office at the will and pleasure of the Government." On its own, this would mean that established civil servants could be dismissed for any or no reason and that the procedure followed would be immaterial. The inspiration behind this remarkable provision is the legally insecure position of the British Crown servant.[21] This owes its origin to the exigencies of British history—frequently in the military and/or colonial context—which were thought to require the power of immediate dismissal of a Crown servant unhampered by any fear of legal consequences[22]; and also to the authoritarian culture which underlay the Royal Prerogative.

The power to dismiss at pleasure, bestowed by a literal reading of section 5, is probably unconstitutional on two counts.[23] First, it violates the civil servant's right to constitutional justice. Secondly, unless the provision were reinterpreted very drastically in the light of the presumption of constitutionality, it would allow dismissal on unreasonable or unconstitutional grounds, for instance, a dismissal which was motivated by religious discrimination.

---

[18] Civil Service Regulation Act 1956, s.10. See now Civil Service (Employment of Married Women) Act 1973.

[19] Civil Service Commissioners Act 1956, s.2.

[20] Note that as regards pension rights, the Superannuation Acts of 1936, 1942, 1946, 1947 and 1954 have merely incorporated 19th-century British legislation (see Superannuation Act 1834, s.30; Superannuation Act 1859). By virtue of s.2 of the 1859 Act the decision of the Minister for Finance as to any claim for a pension "shall be final." See further Emden, *The Civil Servant in the Law and the Constitution* (London, 1923), pp. 25–31 and App. I. There is now also a non-statutory pension scheme for unestablished civil servants.

[21] For a summary of the legal position of the Crown servants in Britain and the Commonwealth, see Marshall, "The Legal relationship between the State and its Servants in the Commonwealth" (1966) 15 I.C.L.Q. 150 and Fredman and Morris, "Civil Servants: A Contract of Employment?" [1988] P.L. 58. See also, *B.B.C.* v. *Johns* [1965] Ch. 32 and *Council of Civil Service Unions* v. *Minister for the Public Service* [1985] A.C. 385. For the wider rule that the executive cannot fetter its discretionary powers, see pp. 672–674.

[22] *Cf. Garvey* v. *Ireland* [1981] I.R. 75, 95–97.

[23] See Casey, "Natural and Constitutional Justice: The Policeman's Lot Improved" (1979–1980) 2 D.U.L.J.(N.S.) 95, 99–100. An unestablished civil servant may be removed by the appropriate authority: Civil Service Regulation Act 1956, s.6.

In fact, the practice is such that those dismissals as do occur are almost certainly within the Constitution. For dismissals only occur on plainly justifiable grounds, often where a crime of dishonesty has either been proved before a court or, at least, is strongly suspected. And as regards procedure, the practice is to inform the civil servant why his dismissal is being contemplated and to allow him an opportunity to put his side of the case to the entire Government in written form.

The legislation controlling dismissal was given a particularly stringent interpretation in *Whelan* v. *Minister for Justice*[24] a case stemming from the dismissal of a probationer civil servant (a prison officer). The salient point in the case was that the applicant had not been dismissed until a few weeks after the termination of his two-year probationary period. However, by the governing legislation in the case of probationers (section 7 of the 1956 Act, as amended by section 3 of the Civil Service Regulation (Amendment) Act 1958) it is "during the civil servant's probationary period" that the appropriate authority—in this case, the Minister for Justice—is required to be "satisfied that [a probationer] has failed to fulfil the conditions of probation attaching to his probationary position."[25] The only evidence before the High Court was a minute issued by the Prisons' Personnel Section of the Department of Justice, stating that the Minister for Justice had determined that the applicant had failed to fulfil the conditions of his probation in that his sick absence record was unsatisfactory (a point which was not contested). The significant finding of fact was that this communication was dated *after* the termination of the probationary period. And, according to Blayney J: "there is no evidence that prior to that date the respondent was satisfied that the applicant had failed to fulfil the conditions of his probation."[26] If this case teaches any general lesson, it is that many judges will construe the law very strictly against the Minister or the State.

The applicant also had an alternative argument, namely that the actual decision terminating the probationer's services must have been taken and communicated to the probationer, before his period of probation expired. In regard to this argument, Blayney J. stated:

"It seems to me that there are two separate parts to section 7. The first is that the appropriate authority must be satisfied during the period of probation that the probationer has not fulfilled the conditions of his probation; the second is that the appropriate authority, on being so satisfied, shall terminate the services of the civil servant. But there is no requirement that the termination shall occur prior to the expiration of the period of probation. It

---

[24] High Court, June 29, 1990.

[25] *Ibid.* pp. 6, 7 of the judgment.

[26] *Ibid.* p. 5. Did this mean that, as a matter of fact, the applicant's sick record became unsatisfactory only after the end of the probationary period? Such a thing appears inherently unlikely and there is nothing in the judgment to show that it was (or was not) so. If we assume that the sick record was bad during the probationary period, then it seems that the judge was focusing, rather literally, on the point in time at which the Minister actually became satisfied that the applicant had failed to fulfil the probation conditions, as opposed to the time when the failure occurred.

seems to me, accordingly, that the section envisages that the appropriate authority, having been satisfied during the period of probation that the particular civil servant had failed to fulfil the conditions of his probation, would then have a reasonable time after the period had expired in which to terminate his services."[27]

In any case, as a matter of fact, the percentage of established civil servants who have had to be dismissed has always been unnaturally low, by comparison either with employees in the private sector or even with unestablished civil servants. In part, this is a consequence of the cumbersome procedure which requires every dismissal to go before the Government.[28]

At present, non-industrial civil servants and established civil servants are excluded from the protection of the Unfair Dismissals Act 1977[29] and the Minimum Notice and Terms of Employment Act 1973,[30] respectively. Moreover, no period of notice is stipulated in a civil servant's terms and conditions of service; in practice, however an *ex gratia* period of two or three weeks is usually allowed. Most civil servants are excluded from the scope of the Redundancy Payments Act 1967.[31] However, all categories of civil servant come within the Anti-Discrimination (Pay) Act 1974, the Employment Equality Act 1977 and the Maternity Protection of Employees Act 1981.

Discipline

The granting of the annual salary increase is usually automatic but a civil servant's conditions of employment provide that it may be withheld if the Minister of the particular Department considers it appropriate. In addition, the Civil Service Regulation Act 1956 creates a number of other disciplinary powers. The "suspending authority"—almost always the Minister for the Department in which the civil servant works—may suspend a civil servant if, for example, "it appears to the suspending authority that the civil servant has been guilty of grave misconduct."[32] The suspension is without pay though in certain circumstances it may be reimbursed.[33] This power is invariably dele-

---

[27] *Ibid.* p. 7. However, the judge went on to consider an argument grounded on one of the conditions of probation, fixed by the Minister for Justice. This provided: "Should the officer's services be unsatisfactory [as regards health, conduct and efficiency generally], the appointment may be terminated at any time *during the period.*" (Author's italics). Without deciding the matter finally, Blayney J. suggested that this provision had qualified section 7 of the 1956 Act and might be "open to the construction that if the Applicant's services were unsatisfactory it was only during his probationary period that his appointment could be terminated." (at p. 7).

[28] *Serving the Country Better*, para. 7.12 proposed, as part of its policy of giving Secretaries greater legal responsibility for the management of their Departments, that subject to an appropriate right of appeal, they should be empowered to dismiss staff up to clerical level.

[29] 1977 Act, s.2(1)(*h*).

[30] 1973 Act, s.3(1)(*c*). *Serving the Country Better* proposed (at para. 7.2) that the law be changed to give civil servants the benefit of the Minimum Notice and Terms of Employment Act 1973 and the Unfair Dismissals Act 1977.

[31] 1967 Act, s.4(1).

[32] Civil Service Regulation Act 1956, ss.3(1), 13.

[33] *Ibid.* s.14.

gated to Higher Executive Officers.[34] The appropriate authority—usually the responsible Minister—is also authorised to make reductions in the pay or grading of civil servants.[35] Finally, a civil servant will not be paid his remuneration for any period of unauthorised absence.[36]

It has been assumed, justifiably we think, that the general principles of administrative (or public) law apply in the field of the employment—including the dismissal and discipline—of civil servants. Three illustrations of this general precept may be offered. In the first place, each of the disciplinary powers is now conditioned by procedural rules.[37] If there are no specific procedural rules, then the general precepts of constitutional justice are usually[38] available to control the exercise of a disciplinary power. A case in point is *Ahern* v. *Minister for Industry and Commerce*.[39] Here the relationship between the applicant and his colleagues and superiors, in the Patents Office within the Department of Industry and Commerce, had been strained for some years. The latest episode consisted of the disclosure by the applicant of a document which he had been specifically instructed to keep confidential. At first, disciplinary proceedings against him were initiated. However, these were aborted and the matter was referred to the Chief Medical Officer in the Department. He advised that the opinion of a psychiatrist was needed and that if the applicant refused to attend the psychiatrist, it would be necessary to place him on compulsory sick leave until he was certified as fit to resume his duties. It appears that the High Court accepted the respondents' contention that authority for such suspension could be derived from Public Circular 25/78 which states that " . . . no officer who appears to require medical attention should be allowed to remain on duty." The applicant did refuse to consult a psychiatrist and, as a result, he was placed on "compulsory sick leave" until he had submitted a certificate signed by a psychiatrist, a period which, in the event, lasted for almost three months. The instruction to the applicant was in the form of a "minute" signed by the Personnel Officer, but prefaced by the conventional formula "I am directed by the Minister for Industry and Commerce. . . . " It was accepted, as Blayney J. stated, that the net question was whether the court should: "quash . . . the decision of the Personnel Officer . . . , taken at the direction of the Minister . . . to place the applicant on compulsory sick leave."[40]

---

[34] *Ibid*. s.3(2). Although where there has been a loss of money, the decision is vested in the first place in the Minister for Finance but is usually delegated to the responsible Minister. *Serving the Country Better* proposes (at para. 7.12) that Secretaries and other nominating officers should be empowered, subject to appropriate appeals procedures, to take disciplinary measures. For a case involving delegation, see *Flynn* v. *An Post* [1987] I.R. 68, 75, 80, 81, below at pp. 466–467. Another aspect covered in *Flynn* was the period for which the delegation was permitted.

[35] *Ibid*. s.15.

[36] *Ibid*. s.15(5).

[37] See Department of the Public Service Circular 9/84, which governs procedures for dealing with grievance, disciplinary and promotion eligibility problems.

[38] There is a possibility that constitutional justice does not apply where, because of the seriousness of the situation, immediate removal from duty is necessary.

[39] High Court, July 6, 1990. See also, *The Revenue Commissioners* v. *O'Callaghan* High Court, January 11, 1991.

[40] *Ibid*. p. 9 of the judgment.

The respondents' first line of defence was to submit that this question was not justiciable. This was rejected by the judge, "on balance." He held that the decision was justiciable on the basis that although the applicant had been on full pay whilst he was on leave, nevertheless his right to work was affected in that he was barred from carrying out his normal work. In addition, the decision carried with it the innuendo that the applicant was unfit for work by reason of some psychotic disease.

The main argument, however, concerned the *audi alteram partem* limb of constitutional justice. Upholding the applicant's submission on this point, Blayney J. stated:

"Reports were . . . obtained from [the applicant's superiors and colleagues] and sent to [the Chief Medical Officer]. The applicant did not see any of these reports and was unaware of their existence. The first time he had an opportunity of reading them was when he obtained discovery in the course of these proceedings. The reports were not confined to the [disclosure of the confidential document by the applicant] but dealt with the entire of the applicant's career since entering the Patents Office in 1971. The applicant had no opportunity of refuting any of the matters contained in the reports."[41]

(From a general perspective, wider than the civil service, it is noteworthy that, in *Ahern*, constitutional justice was held to apply to a holding in a novel area, namely a person's health.)

However, notwithstanding his finding on this point Blayney J. decided that for three reasons he would exercise his discretion not to grant the applicant an order quashing the decision to put him on compulsory sick leave. The first reason was that he was, in a significant sense, the author of his own downfall, in that he had, for some time, unreasonably refused to attend a psychiatrist. Secondly, the judge was influenced by the fact that it was only out of consideration for the applicant, and in spite of the applicant's intransigence, that the Personnel Officer had referred the matter to the Chief Medical Officer rather than continuing with the disciplinary proceedings which had, at an early stage of the episode, been initiated and then aborted. Finally, Blayney J. took the view that the order would not advantage the applicant in any way in that the

---

[41] *Ibid*. p. 12. The judge went on to adopt a distinct, though supporting, argument. He stated (at pp. 12–13):

"Apart from this, Dr. Finucane [the Chief Medical Officer] had no medical report before him when advising that the applicant should be put on compulsory sick leave. He had not examined the Applicant himself, nor had he obtained the opinion of a psychiatrist since the applicant had refused to see one. In these circumstances, I consider that Dr. Finucane had no evidence to support his opinion that the applicant ought to be put on sick leave and that Mr. Bennett [the Personnel Officer] accordingly had no good ground for giving his direction.

In his first advice to Mr. Bennett, Dr. Finucane stated that the opinion of a psychiatrist was needed and that, if the applicant did not attend one, a direction to do so on pain of suspension might be necessary. It is unfortunate that Finucane then altered his advice to placing the applicant on compulsory sick leave if he was not prepared to see Dr. Ryan. A direction to suspend the applicant for refusing to comply with what in the circumstances was a not unreasonable direction and one which would have been easier to stand over."

presence of the decision as regards compulsory sick leave on his file would not prejudice him as regards his promotion prospects or in any other way.

A second general doctrine which has been observed in the field of dismissal and discipline is the *ultra vires* principle which received a straightforward, though strict, application in the case of *Reidy* v. *Minister for Agriculture*[42] which arose out of the punishment of a civil servant in the Department of Agriculture. In judicial review proceedings, he took a number of points, two of which are relevant here. The first concerned the withholding of his annual salary increment. The procedure governing this sanction was set out in Department of Finance Circular 9/87. However, by an oversight on the part of one of the personnel officers, the procedure set out in an earlier circular— which had been superseded by the new circular—was followed. The practical difference between the two circulars was between a decision to defer payment for a specified period, subject to review at the end of that period (as was the correct course required by the new circular) and a simple decision not to pay the increment due (as had actually occurred). Because of this difference, O'Hanlon J. held that the decision not to pay the increment was invalid.

The other sanction which had been applied against the applicant in *Reidy* was that he would not be allowed to compete for any promotion competitions. This was held invalid, again because there was no authority for it. O'Hanlon J. stated:

" . . . The issue of promotion is dealt with in Circular No. 12/49 which stipulates (*inter alia*) that before promotion is made to any post of a type referred to in the Circular (which would appear to incorporate any categories of promotion which might be open to the applicant) the Head of the Department was required to certify, '(b) that the officer is fully qualified for the higher post and that he is the best qualified of the officers in the Department eligible for the post.' In the event of any dereliction of duty occurring on the part of an officer it is to be expected that the record of his service will contain particulars of any such matters which might count against him when the possibility of his promotion to a higher post is under consideration, but it appears to me that the decision taken in relation to the applicant—if upheld—would have the effect of blocking all hope of promotion for him for a fixed period of two years in a manner which seems to be incompatible with the general discretion to promote subject only to compliance with the conditions outlined in Circular No. 12/49. This penalty is one of such significance that it cannot be regarded as one capable of being imposed independently of the disciplinary powers conferred expressly by the Acts, and the further conditions of service dealt with by circulars emanating from the Department of Finance."[43]

[42] High Court, June 9, 1989.
[43] *Ibid.* pp. 6–7. In regard to the final sentence of this passage, it may be observed that it is unfortunate that nothing further was said to elucidate what penalties, if any, were sufficiently insignificant to be imposed independently of the sources listed by the judge or what alternative sources are acceptable—possibly, agreements worked out between the Departments and the unions representing civil servants.

A third general principle is the precept that a power granted for one purpose cannot be used for a different purpose. More specifically in the present context, it was implicit in *Reidy* that the power of transferring a civil servant may not be used to effect what is intended as a punishment. In that case, O'Hanlon J. appraised a direction that the applicant had been moved from Kilmeedy to the District Livestock Office in Limerick (a distance of about 30 miles), as follows:

> "I am satisfied that the decision to move the applicant from his previous place of employment to a new headquarters, (which involved the applicant in some additional travel each week), was based on the *bona fide* belief arising as a result of the matters of complaint against the applicant which had been investigated, that there was a danger that the applicant was tending to relax the strict requirements of the Beef Premium Scheme when dealing with farmers close to home with whom he would be acquainted personally, and that it would be preferable to locate him in new headquarters somewhat removed from his home area. I am satisfied that this was a decision made in good faith for administrative reasons and should not be regarded as a punishment or penalty imposed on the applicant, although referred to as 'disciplinary action' in the letter of the 27th July, 1988, addressed to the applicant."[44]

Accordingly, the applicant's submission on this issue failed on the facts. However, the point was well made that the power of transfer could not be used as a punishment.

There is a further reason why the characterisation of the power of transfer as a punishment (or not) could be significant. This is in the context of the rules of constitutional justice. As mentioned already, these rules of course apply to a punishment. But it is a more open question whether they would apply to an exclusively administrative arrangement for the well-being of the Department. On the one hand, it could be said that the effect upon the individual involved—which could be significant—is the same in terms of upheaval on himself and his family, irrespective of whether a punishment was intended or not. On the other hand, the application of the rules of constitutional justice in the case of punishment is long established and dependent in part upon the damage to reputation which it carries with it. This is not true of a transfer arising out of administrative rearrangements which may, moreover, depend upon wider changes of policy or public demand. These changes, in contrast to disciplinary offences, are not well fitted to be examined by a procedure governed by the rules of constitutional justice.

[44] High Court, June 9, 1989 at p. 8 of the judgment. Compare this aspect of O'Hanlon J.'s judgment with *Merricks* v. *Nott-Bower* [1964] 1 All E.R. 717 (where the English Court of Appeal held that the plaintiff policemen were entitled to challenge the validity of a transfer order on the ground that its real purpose was to impose disciplinary punishment) and *Re Murray's Application* [1987] 12 N.I.J.B. 1. In the latter case, Higgins J. quashed a similar transfer order on the ground that the evidence disclosed that the Chief Constable "must have been materially influenced" by the desire to impose a form of disciplinary punishment on the policemen.

7. Terms and Conditions of Employment

The basic legal provision in this field is section 17 of the Civil Service Regulation Act 1956,[45] which provides as follows:

"(1) The Minister shall be responsible for the following matters—
 (*a*) the regulation and control of the Civil Service,
 (*b*) the classification, re-classification, numbers and remuneration of civil servants,
 (*c*) the fixing of—
  (i) the terms and conditions of service of civil servants, and
  (ii) the conditions governing the promotion of civil servants.
 (2) The Minister may, for the purpose of subsection (1) of this section, make such arrangements as he thinks fit and may cancel or vary those arrangements."

It is under this provision that the Minister for Finance: fixes a civil servant's conditions of employment including such matters as pay-scale, hours of work and holidays; issues personnel circulars altering these conditions; creates new posts; divides civil servants into classes and grades[46]; agreed the Conciliation and Arbitration Scheme; imposed the 1987 embargo on the refilling of vacancies in the civil service and announced its replacement, in 1986, by a more discriminating embargo which depended on the Minister of Finance's determination of the staffing needs of each Department. In 1990, a further relaxation associated with Administrative Budgets was made: see Part 3.

It seems likely, because of their importance, that the section 17 powers must be exercised by the Minister himself. However, a distinct and more difficult question arises: after the section 17 power has been exercised to establish some general precept, who exactly must apply the precept in an individual case? This was one of the broad questions raised by *Reidy* v. *Minister for Agriculture*, though on its actual facts, the outcome turned on the particular wording of the appropriate conditions of service. As mentioned earlier, the facts were that the applicant had been transferred. This change was effected under his conditions of service, which provided as follows: "An officer's headquarters will be such as may be designated from time to time by the Head of the Department." There was no reason for O'Hanlon J. not to apply this provision literally and he did so, finding for the applicant on the following basis:

"The decision, however, was taken by the Personnel Officer in the Department, who, at the time was a Principal Officer, and does not appear to have been ratified by the Head of the Department, as envisaged by the Conditions of Service, nor has it been shown to my satisfaction that the power to make this decision was lawfully delegated to the officer who made it."[47]

Three points of elaboration may be ventured on this brief passage. First, it

---

[45] This section replaced the Ministers and Secretaries Act 1924, s.2(3).
[46] *Inspector of Taxes* v. *Minister for the Public Service* [1986] I.L.R.M. 296, 300.
[47] *Reidy* v. *Minister for Agriculture* High Court, June 9, 1989 at p. 8

appears implicitly to reject the *Carltona* doctrine,[48] by which anything done by a civil servant is *ipso facto* regarded as having been done by the Minister. Secondly, on the other hand, it only appears to require "ratification" by the Minister. This is rather vague but it sounds as if not very much actual involvement of the Minister is required to satisfy it. Finally, the passage appears to contemplate that the power could have been "lawfully delegated"[49] by the Minister provided that this had been done by a sufficiently explicit (and possibly specific?) act.

Sources of law regulating employment

A difficult question which has not yet been thoroughly or comprehensively examined by the courts is the issue of what are the sources of law governing a civil servant's conditions of employment. A convenient point of departure is the following passage from *Reidy* (the facts of which have already been given):

> "In addition, matters such as entitlement to payment of increments, the rules governing promotion within the Civil Service, and the determination of the officer's place of work from time to time, were regulated in part by the conditions of service accepted by the officer on taking up his appointment, and in part by Departmental Circulars issued from time to time, incorporating decisions made pursuant to section 17 of the Civil Service Regulation Act, 1956."[50]

It emerges from this passage that there are two main sources of law (in addition, it goes without saying, to the 1956 Act itself) governing a civil servant's employment: first, an officer's "terms and conditions of employment," to use the normal terminology employed in the civil service, (the question of whether these conditions amount to a contract is discussed below); and, secondly, circulars incorporating decisions made under the 1956 Act.

This suggests the difficult question: what is the legal status of such circulars? It is suggested that the admittedly ambiguous phrase, used in the passage, "circulars . . . incorporating decisions made pursuant to . . . the Civil Service Regulation Act, 1956" should not be taken so far as to mean that such a circular is a statutory instrument. The persuasive, though not conclusive, reason for this suggestion is that it seems that such circulars are not intended by their maker to be statutory instruments. Such a classification would fly in the face of the customary assumption within the Government bureaucracy. For in the first place, there is no reference in such circulars to the parent legislation. Secondly, they are not couched in the precise legal language characteristic of a statutory instrument. Finally, a circular made in virtue of section 17 is not promulgated as a statutory instrument as would be required, in the case of a statutory instrument by the Statutory Instruments Act 1947.[51]

---

[48] On which see pp. 56–57.
[49] For the *delegatus* doctrine, see pp. 396–400.
[50] *Reidy* v. *Minister for Agriculture* at p. 3. See also, p. 6.
[51] See further, pp. 22–25.

It is suggested rather, that a circular made under section 17 should be regarded simply as a rule of practice made in the exercise of a statutory discretion. As such, it would be as binding as any other administrative action authorised by statute[52] but is not a statutory instrument.

There remains the other possibility, which for reasons to be explained, is rejected by the authors, namely that a circular should be regarded as being an implied term in the contract between the civil servant and the State (assuming that there is a contract, a point to which we return below). Some indirect support for this view can be obtained from a statement made in *McMahon* v. *Minister for Finance*.[53] In *McMahon*, the subject was the legal status of the Civil Service Conciliation and Arbitration Scheme. However, the approach taken by Kenny J. in that case appears to have been wide enough to embrace anything done under section 17 and thus to be relevant here. Kenny J. stated[54]:

"Throughout the case the plaintiffs' counsel have referred to it as a 'statutory scheme' with the implication that it has been confirmed by statute or that it has in some undefined way the force of statute. Section 17 of the Civil Service Regulations Act 1956, seems to me to be intended to give the Minister for the Public Service power to make schemes or contracts for the regulation of civil service pay: it is a section which enables the Minister to make schemes or contracts (I think that this is what 'arrangement' means) but it does not follow that an arrangement made by the Minister is 'a statutory scheme' or 'a statutory arrangement.' The scheme is a contract and nothing more."

The reasoning in this passage is rather bold. The second sentence in the passage overlooks the fact that, as a result of the Ministers and Secretaries Code, the Minister is a corporation sole and, hence, already has nearly the same capacity to make a contract as a natural person. Section 17 must, therefore, have been intended to give him additional capacity to make schemes, etc., which thus derive their authority from the statute and not from contract. Moreover, the Conciliation and Arbitration Scheme appears to be just the type of *sui generis* artefact which it was sought to capture by the use of what is (for statutory language) the uncharacteristically vague term "arrangement" in section 17(2). Admittedly this last argument would not apply if it is sought to invoke *McMahon* as indirect authority for saying (in respect of the point which was at issue in *Reidy*) that a circular is to be regarded as binding by virtue of being an implied term in a contract. But the main point made earlier is still relevant,

---

[52] In contrast with certain other types of circular: see, *e.g. O'Callaghan* v. *Department of Education*, Supreme Court, November 21, 1955, in which it was held that a circular issued by the Department of Education and not made under statute could not be invoked so as to override the terms of a contract between a teacher and the Department of Education, nor so as to prejudice the teacher's rights under that contract.

[53] High Court, May 13, 1963. For further details, see pp. 98–99.

[54] *Ibid.* p. 50 of the judgment.

namely that the Minister's authority to make such a circular is grounded on statute and there is no need to invoke the artificial device of an implied term to make it binding.

Now it is true that a civil servant's terms and conditions sometimes state expressly that the civil servant's conditions may be altered by any circulars which may be made from time to time. However, this begs the central question which is whether the circular is binding even without such mention. Such statements may have been included in the civil servant's conditions, simply as a result of a prudent civil service lawyer wishing to provide his employer with both belt and braces.

The more important issue, in any case, is the issue on which *Reidy* and *McMahon* appear to agree,[55] namely that civil service conditions of employ-

---

[55] A query to which no very satisfactory answer can as yet be given is as to the circumstance in which the difference between *Reidy* and *McMahon* might be of significance. One context concerns the major doctrinal principle that both the procedure by way of an application for judicial review and the substantive principles of administrative law only apply where an issue of "public law" is involved and the mere fact that the employer is a public authority does not *per se* inject the necessary public law element. In regard to the problem of characterisation which this demarcation line creates, there is some English authority for saying that the presence of a contract militates against the existence of the necessary public law element (*R.* v. *East Berkshire Area Health Authority* [1985] Q.B. 152). However, in Ireland, this doctrinal point has not even been raised in *Reidy* or any of the other civil service cases, which have taken the form of judicial review applications, without any protest being raised by the respondents. (See Hogan, "Public Remedies and Judicial Review in the Context of Employment Law" (1984) 4 J.I.S.L.L. 19; *R.* v. *Home Secretary, ex p. Benwell* [1985] Q.B. 554; Fredman and Morris, "Civil Servants: A Contract of Employment" (1988) 58, 71–76.

There is another reason why it might be significant whether, as *Reidy* suggests, the conditions of employment of a civil servant are determined not only by his contract but also by the 1956 Act and circulars made thereunder. This may be demonstrated by reference to *Glover* v. *BLN Ltd.* [1973] I.R. 388, where it was stated (at 414) "[An office-holder] may have a contract under which he may be entitled to retain [the office] for a fixed period. . . . But the holder of an office does not hold it under a contract: he holds it under the terms of the instrument which created it." This ruling was followed in *Murphy* v. *Minister for Social Welfare* [1987] I.R. 303 where one of the points at issue (in determining whether the applicant was in "insurable employment" for the purposes of the Social Welfare (Consolidation) Act 1981 was whether the applicant was "employ[ed] . . . under any contract of service." In holding that the applicant was not employed under a contract, Blayney J. stated in *Murphy* (at 303):

"The only effect of Glover's contract was to give him the right to retain his office for a given period. It did not in any way alter the nature of his office. So, in the present case, even if the applicant could establish some contract with the Minister, that would not in any way alter the fact that the origin of his employment was his appointment to a statutory office and not his entering into any contract of service. In the circumstances it is not necessary to go into the question of whether the applicant had any contract with the Minister. Even if he had, it would not have affected the basis of the applicant's employment which was his being appointed to any office. It could not have altered that situation into one in which the applicant held under a contract of service."

To go back to civil servants: it appears likely that a civil servant is an office-holder just because of the fact that his employment is authorised by statute (" . . . each Minister may appoint . . . other officers and servants to serve in the Department of which he is the head . . . ." Ministers and Secretaries Act 1924, s.2(2)). Given this statutory underpinning it could hardly be said that a civil servant holds his employment *under* a contract. This categorisation will not, however, be significant in regard to the question at issue in *Murphy*, namely whether a civil servant is in "insurable employment" for the purposes of the Social Welfare (Consolidation) Act 1981 because it is an alternative ground for falling within this category that a person should be employed in the civil service.

ment are governed by at least some type of law which binds both the Minister/ State and the individual civil servant and not by something less than law, such as the device of legitimate expectations.

Contract of Employment

In Britain,[56] and elsewhere, there has been much debate as to whether a contract of employment exists between a civil servant and the State.[57] This speculation has been prompted, at least partly, by the fact that a civil servant may be dismissed at will. But as the Privy Council has observed "a power to determine a contract at will is not inconsistent with the existence of a contract until it is so determined."[58] In Ireland—though in *Reidy*, O'Hanlon J. did not need to decide the matter and did not do so (referring only to "conditions of service")—there is some, admittedly, not conclusive, authority favouring the existence of a contract. First, in *McMahon*[59] (which is criticised above), Kenny J., without hesitation, characterised the Conciliation and Arbitration Scheme as a contract, and the terms of employment of an individual civil servant look even more like a typical contract than does the Scheme itself. Again, as noted already in the fairly similar situation of the Defence Forces, the Supreme Court has described the relationship between the State and a member of the Defence Forces as a "statutory contract."[60] This question was also at issue in *Inspector of Taxes Association* v. *Minister for the Public Service*,[61] a case which arose out of the defendant's refusal to recognise the plaintiff's association for the purposes of the Civil Service Conciliation and Arbitration Scheme. The aspect of the case which is relevant here is that the plaintiffs were confronted with the difficulty that, even assuming that the Scheme was a contract, the plaintiffs were not parties to it, and, consequently, were incapable of asserting any rights which arose under it. However, Murphy J. was prepared to adopt a roundabout way to find in favour of the plaintiffs.

"In my view the only basis on which the plaintiffs could rely upon the [Conciliation and Arbitration] scheme and the contract which constitutes it is on the basis that the members of the plaintiff association are officers or

---

[56] Logan, "A Civil Servant and his Pay" (1945) 61 L.Q.R. 240. Fredman and Morris, *op. cit.* and the authorities referred to at n. 1 thereof. In the U.K., the Civil Service Pay and Conditions Code, para. 14 states that civil servants do not have a contract of employment enforceable in the courts. This was drawn upon in the most recent case on the subject, *R.* v. *Civil Service Appeal Board, ex p. Bruce* [1988] 3 All E.R. 686, to hold that the Crown did not have the requisite intention to be bound and, thus, there could be no contract.

[57] Thus the White Paper proclaimed (at p. 63) that civil servants up to and including Clerical Officers will be given "contracts of employment" but it seems that all this meant was that the conditions on which they could be dismissed were to be amended, by statute, so that these civil servants would be no longer dismissible at pleasure.

[58] *Reilly* v. *R.* [1934] A.C. 176, 179–180.

[59] High Court, May 3, 1963.

[60] *The State (Gleeson)* v. *Minister for Defence* [1976] I.R. 280, 296. Exactly the same phrase is used in *Egan* v. *Ireland*, High Court, October 24, 1988, p. 10 of the judgment. At p. 11 of *Egan*, Barr J. stated: "a regular officer on being commissioned for an indefinite period contracts to remain in the permanent defence force until he reaches the retirement age. . . . "

[61] High Court, March 24, 1983. See also, the interlocutory decision, High Court, November 30, 1981.

employees of the State whose terms of employment include by implication a provision that each of them shall have the benefit of the contract and scheme in accordance with its terms and provisions. Whilst the facts which would support such an inference were not canvassed in great detail, I would be satisfied to accept for the purposes of this judgment that the plaintiffs, as representing employees of the State, are entitled in contract to have the terms of the scheme implemented by the Minister. . . . It seems to me the high-water mark of *the contractual rights of the plaintiff association derived from its members* is to have an application made by a staff association fairly considered by the Minister and that being done this bona fide decision to grant or withhold recognition is conclusive."[62] (Authors' italics)

This admittedly rather novel analysis depends on the assumption that there is a contract between a civil servant and the State which creates legally enforceable rights. (On appeal to the Supreme Court,[63] this preliminary point as to the plaintiff's authority to bring the case appears not to have been taken. However, the court rejected the plaintiff's case on the ground that the Minister's decision regarding regrading had been properly taken.)

As well as these persuasive rather than compelling judicial authorities, the Constitution, with its preference for individual rights, militates in favour of a civil servant enjoying some sort of legal right in respect of his employment.

However, the standard civil service conditions of employment explicitly (and, perhaps, unnecessarily) preserve the power, bestowed on the Minister by the 1956 Act, section 17(2) namely to "cancel or vary [the terms and conditions of service]." Thus, the terms could be altered unilaterally by the Minister (though presumably, not retrospectively, because of the Constitution's protection of property rights) without violating a civil servant's contract of employment. In view of this and (where it still applies) of the power to dismiss at will, a civil servant's contract, if there be one, would seem to be an unusual one, from which not all the normal legal consequences flow.

What, in any case, is the practical significance of whether such an unusual contract exists or not? In the first place, it may be relevant in regard to remedies. Thus, if, for instance, the State were refusing to pay a civil servant's salary, it seems that he could claim for damages for breach of contract rather than just suing on a *quantum meruit* (which might mean a different amount of damages). Secondly, as recent British case law shows, this question can be of significance in a number of unexpected, adventitious ways.[64] One context in which it can arise in industrial relations is the tort of inducing a breach of contract. (However, it should also be noted that a significant difference between British and Irish law is that Irish civil servants who go on strike would commit

---

[62] High Court, March 24, 1983.
[63] *Inspector of Taxes Association* v. *Minister for Public Service* [1986] I.L.R.M. 296. See further, pp. 549–550.
[64] Fredman and Morris, *loc. cit.*

a criminal offence, although it might be considered impolitic to prosecute).[65] Again, one or the other party, but probably the Minister/State, may wish to claim that there is a contract in order to invoke some implied term, for instance, a duty of confidentiality.

Structure of the civil service: classes and grades[66]

There are three broad (non-statutory) divisions among civil servants: the general service; the departmental; and the professional and technical classes. The general service officers perform the general duties of their department from routine clerical operations to the higher advisory or managerial work. They are subdivided into—in ascending order in the pyramid—sub-clerical, clerical, executive and administrative classes.[67] The other two broad divisions are specialists. The members of the departmental classes are recruited with a general educational qualification, but are assigned to work peculiar to a Department in which they specialise, *e.g.* the Taxes Classes in the Office of the Revenue Commissioners or the Social Welfare Inspectorate in the Department of Social Welfare. In contrast, the members of the professional and technical classes specialise in work which is performed outside, as well as within, government service, for example engineers or electricians.

Within these broad groupings, there are divisions into grades. The significance of this administrative classification is that positions in the same grade share the same type of qualification, work and conditions, including a common pay scale; progress from one point on the scale to the next is usually automatic. Thus, grading affects not only pay and the other conditions of work, but also career prospects. Throughout the civil service there are about 700 different grades[68]: proliferation is assisted by the fact that equivalent grades in different departments usually bear different titles. The relationship between grades and classes is as follows. In the original conception, as it operated in the Irish Free State and earlier, a class meant a grouping of grades engaged on a particular type of work within which an officer would expect to make his civil service career, entering at the bottom and working up towards the top. But his final grade was normally dependent on the grade at which he entered and thus on his educational qualifications at that time. However, for the past 30 years or so, this strict concept of class has been modified so that promotion between classes is fairly common.

---

[65] Offences Against the State Act 1939, s.9(2). The Report of the Commission of Inquiry on Industrial Relations (Pl. 114), paras. 787–789 recommended the amendment of this provision "to remove any doubt that it might apply to legitimate trade union activities in the public service."
[66] Devlin Report, paras. 7.3.1–7.8.5. Dooney, *The Irish Civil Service* (Dublin, 1976), Chap. 3 and pp. 147–152.
[67] The grades within the administrative classes are as follows: Secretary, Deputy Secretary, Assistant Secretary; Principal; Assistant Principal; Administrative Officer (A.O.); Higher Executive Officer (H.E.O.). A.O. and H.E.O. are equivalent grades; the difference is that A.O.s enter straight from university; whereas the H.E.O. is a promotional post.
[68] " . . . Fewer than 200 grades account for two-thirds of staff. At the higher levels, there are many single person grades with identical or similar pay scales. This pattern will be progressively simplified but it is recognised that this will take some time.": *Serving the Country Better*, para. 4.10.

R.T.C. LIBRARY LETTERKENNY

The question of grading was at the centre of *Inspector of Taxes Association* v. *Minister for the Public Service*[69] which took the form of a claim by the plaintiff association that the Minister's refusal to recognise it for the purposes of the Concilition and Arbitration Scheme, on the sole ground that the Inspectors of Taxes (Technical) were not a separate grade, was invalid. To appreciate this claim, it is necessary to recall that in 1960, the PAYE system of income tax collection, which had formerly been confined to the public sector, was extended to cover all employees. One consequence of this was the creation of a new post of Inspector of Taxes, holders of which were recruited from persons in the tax clerical grades; they possessed no technical qualifications; were not granted a commission by the Minister; and were designated "Clerical Inspector" as distinct from the traditional Inspector of Taxes (which then became known as "Technical Inspector"). The occasion for the case, in 1983, was that proposals were being prepared which would fundamentally alter the entire career structure open to Inspectors of Taxes. Accordingly, the plaintiff association, which had been formed in 1980 to represent only Technical Inspectors, wrote to the Minister for the Public Service requesting recognition for the purposes of the Conciliation and Arbitration scheme. The Minister rejected the plaintiff's application for recognition because it was established administrative policy (the propriety of which was not challenged) to confine recognition to only one association in respect of each grade and the constitution of the plaintiff association was confined to Technical Inspectors and excluded Clerical Inspectors from its membership.

Thus the case came down to the issue of whether the Technical Inspectors and the Clerical Inspectors constituted separate grades, even though the Minister had taken a decision not to create separate grades. According to Finlay C.J.:

"It would be quite inconsistent with the responsibilities thus placed by [the Civil Service Regulation Act 1956, s.17] on the Minister, if his overall power to run and regulate the civil service within the terms of that section were subject to concepts of grading arising from a legal definition of what constituted a grade capable of being imposed upon him by the decision of a Court. In so far, therefore, as the plaintiff's claim in this case consisted of an assertion that a grading of Inspector of Taxes (Technical) had spontaneously occurred as a result of the development of the work of the Revenue Commissioners between 1960 and 1980 and without a decision made by the Minister under section 17, I would affirm the dismissal of that portion of the claim."[70]

[69] [1986] I.L.R.M. 296 (S.C.); High Court, March 24, 1983.
[70] [1986] I.L.R.M. 300. The analogous authority to the *Inspector of Taxes Association* in respect of the Garda Síochána is the case of *Aughey* v. *Ireland* [1986] I.L.R.M. 206; [1989] I.L.R.M. 87. The basis of this case was that the plaintiffs—who were detective officers and detective garda—believed that the existing Garda representative associations were not representing adequately their special interests as detective members of the force. However, permission to form a new association to exclusively represent detectives had been refused by the Commissioner of the Gardái on the ground that to do so would contravene s.1 of the Garda Síochána Act 1977. This provision authorises the establishment of "an association or associations for all or any one or more of

However it is significant that the Chief Justice went on to hold that the Minister's decision whether to create a new grade was, like any other administrative action, subject to judicial review. But, on the facts of the case, he found against the plaintiff:

> "It could not be said that the differences established between the workload, responsibility, qualifications and training of Inspectors of Taxes (Technical) and Inspectors of Taxes (Non-Technical) were such that having regard to other considerations it was not open to the Minister to decide to leave both of these categories of Inspectors of Taxes in the same grade."[71]

Conciliation and Arbitration Schemes

It is a cardinal point that notwithstanding the wide discretionary powers conferred upon the Minister for Finance by the 1956 Act, section 17, these powers are not usually exercised in regard to conditions of service, including pay. In the first place, any increases made under the Public Service Pay Agreement (or, formerly, the National Wage Agreement) are granted automatically. Secondly, in the case of the higher civil servants—the 150 or so Secretaries, Deputy Secretaries and Assistant Secretaries and their equivalent in the professional classes—the Minister has always accepted the recommendations of the "Review Body on Higher Remuneration in the Public Sector." This body was established in 1972, at first under the chairmanship of Mr. Liam St. John Devlin and now of Mr. Dermot Gleeson S.C., as a standing body to advise the Government on the level of pay for civil servants and local authority officers outside the scope of Conciliation and Arbitration Schemes as well as the chief executives of state-sponsored bodies and the judiciary.

In the case of the great majority of the civil service, pay increases are deter-

---

the ranks of the Garda Síochána below the rank of sergeant." It was held in the High Court, and appears to have been accepted in the Supreme Court (although the point does not seem to be beyond controversy) that the provision authorises the establishment of only one association for any particular rank. Given the existence at the time of the decision of representative associations, for all members of all ranks, the issue in the part of the case with which we are concerned came down to the question of whether the rank of Detective Officer or Detective Garda were separate ranks from their equivalents in the uniformed branch.

In the High Court the situation in the case of the civil service (which was examined in the *Inspector of Taxes Association* case) was distinguished on the basis that the question of what was a separate grade was a matter for an administrative decision by the (then) Minister for the Public Service whereas with the Garda the division into ranks was fixed by statutory instrument. Yet this overlooks the fact that a statutory instrument, just as much as an administrative action, may be *ultra vires* for unreasonableness.

However, in the Supreme Court, Walsh J. addressed the issue squarely in the following passage (at 90):

> "It is clear from an examination of the structure of the Garda Síochána as a police force that a detective officer below the rank of Sergeant enjoys the same rank as any other member of the Garda Síochána below the rank of Sergeant. The difference in duties or operational methods does not affect the matter. There is no recognised rank of 'Detective Officer' although the expression is commonly used to distinguish them from their uniformed colleagues. The same applies to those members of the detective branch or section who have the rank of Sergeant or Inspector. The Court is of opinion that the claim that a Detective Officer or a Detective Garda is an officer of a separate rank in the Garda Síochána is not established."

[71] [1986] I.L.R.M. 303.

95

mined by negotiation within the framework of the Conciliation and Arbitration Schemes. Up until 1983, Principals and Assistant Principals were included among the so-called "Devlin Grades" but now they have their own Conciliation and Arbitration Scheme which is modelled on the older-established scheme which serves all non-industrial civil servants at the level of Higher Executive Officer or below.[72] This Scheme[73] comprises two parallel and similar systems. The first and most important involves a General Council which deals with problems which are not peculiar to any one Department (often claims from grades which are common to more than one Department). The other system consists of Departmental Councils which deal with matters which are relevant only to a particular Department, for example, claims by Departmental classes like the building inspectors in the Department of the Environment. The official representatives on either type of council consist of no more than six (on the General Council) or four (on a Departmental Council) members nominated by the Minister for Finance (one of whom is nominated as chairman), almost always from among his officers. On the other side are an equal number of staff representatives, drawn from the various staff associations/unions—some 50 or so—which have been recognised by the Minister. It is not within the competence of either type of council to make binding agreements but only to make agreed recommendations or, at the request of either side, to record disagreement.

The Scheme lists the subjects which are appropriate for discussion by the General Council, among them not only pay, allowances and hours of work but also: principles governing recruitment, discipline and promotion; suggestions by the staff for promoting efficiency in the civil service; and questions of doubt as to subjects appropriate for discussion at Departmental Council. According to one summary of the Scheme[74]:

"It is open to either side to put forward items for inclusion in the agenda. In practice, of course, the vast majority of the items are put forward by the staff side. Whether items so put forward come within the province of the council is a matter for the chairman to decide. However, before any item is excluded, the scheme provides that the council must be given a chance of expressing its views whether it should be included or excluded."

The Civil Service Conciliation and Arbitration Scheme is only the earliest of a number of such schemes, each modelled on the same pattern and covering a particular area of public sector employment, including the Gardaí, teachers, local authority, and health board officials. The role of the chairman of the

[72] The first Scheme was established in 1950. The present Scheme established in 1955 and revised in 1976 is an appendix to Department of the Public Service Circular 6/76; for a summary of it see Dooney, *op. cit.* App. 7. See also, McGinley, "Pay Negotiation in the Public Service" (1976) 24 *Administration* 76, 80–84; Massey, "A New Approach to Public Service Pay" (1986) 34 *Administration* 455; Keating, "Civil Service Negotiation Machinery—C and A or Labour Court" (1988) 9 *Seirbhís Phoiblí* 28.
[73] The Scheme excludes individual cases which are dealt with according to procedures laid down in Department of Public Services Circular 9, 1984 ("Procedures for dealing with grievance, disciplinary and promotion eligibility problems.")
[74] Dooney, *op. cit.* App. 7.

Conciliation Council in the Garda Conciliation and Arbitration Scheme—the equivalent of the General Council in the Civil Service Scheme—came up for examination before the High Court in *Garda Representative Association* v. *Ireland*.[75] The net issue was the chairman's refusal to place on the agenda for discussion by the Council, a proposal by the Commissioner to abolish overtime payments in respect of parading time and rostering for special duties. The detailed arguments for and against inclusion need not detain us, since Murphy J. held that under the terms of the Scheme, as with the Civil Service Scheme, it was for the chairman to decide. In a passage which is of relevance also to the Civil Service Scheme, Murphy J. stated:

> "It is not disputed that a subordinate tribunal may be compelled to exercise its authority. In the present case, however, the right and duty of the conciliation council to discuss any matter (or at any rate to discuss any matter at the behest of the staff side) was conditional upon the matter in question being 'appropriate for discussion by the council.' As the chairman of the council has clearly purported to exercise the jurisdiction undoubtedly vested in him to rule on the appropriateness of any given matter which the staff side seek to list for discussion, and has in the purported exercise of that jurisdiction rejected the application of the staff side to place on the agenda the relevant decisions of the Commissioner, the council does not have jurisdiction to discuss these decisions. Such jurisdiction would not exist unless the decision made by the chairman . . . is set aside and a decision favourable to the staff side substituted therefor. Accordingly, it is necessary for the plaintiffs to satisfy the court that this decision was invalid."[76]

The applicant trade union offered three grounds on which the decision should be set aside, all to no avail. Two of these—unreasonableness and legitimate expectations—are considered elsewhere.[77] The third was examined and rejected in the following passage:

> "In the present case counsel for the plaintiffs have adverted to the fact that the chairman of the council is a permanent civil servant and was appointed to his office as chairman by the Minister for Justice. On the other hand there was nothing sinister or improper in that appointment. The bargain between the parties expressly provided for such an appointment to be made by the Minister. In relation to the procedure adopted I do not see how the conduct of Mr. Crowley could be challenged in any respect. He heard both parties. He considered their submissions and not only did he give his decision but he gave his reasons therefor. Insofar as judicial review concerns the manner in which a decision is made rather than the substance of the decision, it seems to me that Mr. Crowley's conduct was impeccable."[78]

---

[75] [1989] I.R. 193.
[76] [1989] I.R. 202–203.
[77] See Chap. 10.2 and p. 682 respectively.
[78] [1989] I.R. 202.

To return to our account of the Civil Service Scheme: in practice, if the official side agrees with the staff side, it does so because the terms of the agreement are acceptable to the Minister. Thus, it will invariably happen that if there is an agreed recommendation to the Minister for Finance it will be accepted though in the case of a pay increase, it is often introduced "in phases." Alternatively, where the two sides disagree, the Minister's response to the report will not be favourable to the staff side. In this case, the second stage comes into play and the staff representatives have the right to refer the matter to arbitration provided that it is an "arbitrable claim." This phrase covers a narrower category than the subjects which may be discussed at a Council. It includes for instance issues such as pay and allowances which, it is assumed, can be resolved by reference to comparable terms outside the service, but excludes matters of policy such as regrading or productivity claims.

The Arbitration Board is a standing body with a chairman (usually a lawyer) chosen by the Minister for Finance. In addition, each side chooses two members.[79] In addition, there may be one workers' member and one employers' member of the Labour Court, nominated by the Chairman of the Court, when requested for a particular claim. The Board's report, which does not have to be unanimous, is sent to the Minister.

At the third and final stage, if the Government wishes to reject or modify a recommendation from the Board, then it may only do so by securing the passage of a Dáil motion to this effect.[80]

Legal status of the Scheme

The legal status of the Scheme was examined in *McMahon* v. *Minister for Finance*,[81] a case brought by a dissident member of the staff side. The significant part of Kenny J.'s judgment is his finding that the Scheme was legally binding (albeit as a contract rather than "a statutory scheme."[82]) After making this fundamental finding, the judge went on to hold that there were three irregularities in connection with a General Council meeting and thus a declaration was granted that the meeting was invalid.[83] As a consequence,

---

[79] Recognition will not be accorded to any association which is affiliated to any political organisation unless the affiliation subsisted prior to 1949. (This restriction is a device to include the Post Office Workers' Union. It was introduced at a time when William Norton, formerly Secretary General of the P.O.W.U., was a member of the Government).

[80] Such a motion has only been passed once, in 1953. However, a motion to this effect was passed, in 1986, under a similar Conciliation and Arbitration Scheme for teachers: see *Dáil Debates*, Vol. 363, cols. 1839–2005 (February 6, 1986). The teachers claimed that the passing of such a motion was unfair, although there is no doubt that it is part of the Scheme.

[81] High Court, May 13, 1963.

[82] This nuance was explored at pp. 89–91.

[83] The Scheme had been violated in that (1) the chairman of the staff panel had been regarded as *ex officio* "principal staff representative" (that is, the leader of the staff representatives) on the General Council; (2) one of the staff representatives who was absent from the Council meeting had been represented by a substitute, (3) one person had been wrongfully barred from standing for election as a staff representative.

there could be no valid report from the meeting and, since a report is an essential preliminary to arbitration, the arbitration could not proceed.

However, in addition to this case, we must bear in mind that the 1956 Act, section 17(2) (which was quoted in full *supra*) explicitly authorises the Minister to "cancel or vary those arrangements" which may be taken to mean, *inter alia*, that the Minister may abrogate the Scheme unilaterally. Furthermore, Article 2 of the Scheme itself states (possibly *ex abundante cautela*):

"The existence of this scheme does not imply that the Government have surrendered or can surrender their liberty of action in the exercise of their constitutional authority and the discharge of their responsibilities in the public interest."

Bearing all this in mind, the following propositions may be tentatively suggested:

(1) The Minister is free to revoke the Scheme.
(2) He is also free not to use it, though in fact, for political reasons, most "conciliable" matters are negotiated through the Scheme.
(3) However, once a matter has been entrusted to the machinery created by the Scheme, it must be pursued to its conclusion, following the procedure laid down in the Scheme (a point illustrated by both the *Garda Representative Association* and the *McMahon* case) and including, if necessary, a Dáil vote.

Politics

Finally, two aspects of a civil servant's terms of employment which have wider constitutional implications may be mentioned.[84] Essentially, there is a complete embargo on political activity. There are two sets of restrictions. In the first place, in general, no civil servant, whether temporary or permanent, may be elected or sit as a member of the Dáil or Senate.[85] There is a possibility that this restriction violates the constitutional right to stand for election,

---

[84] Note also, the Prevention of Corruption Acts 1889–1916, as adapted by Adaption Order No. 37 of 1928 which deals with corruption among civil servants and Department of Finance Circulars 50/1929 and 16/1936 on outside employment and conflict of interest. Section 34 of the Offences Against the State Act 1939) has been held unconstitutional in *Cox* v. *Ireland* High Court, October 2, 1990. This provision stated that whenever a person who is convicted by a Special Criminal Court of a scheduled offence for the purpose of Pt. V of the 1939 Act, holds a post in the public sector, then he shall forfeit that employment. This decision was based on a number of grounds. Barr J.'s key finding was that the disabilities imposed on the plaintiff by the section were not matters related to his employment but were in the nature of a punishment which was (unreasonably) confined to those working in the public sector. The section was erratic in other ways too, for example it did not apply to all serious crimes and it only applied where the prosecution occurred in the Special Criminal Court. On these grounds, there was discrimination contrary to Art. 40.1 and a violation of the plaintiff's right to earn his livelihood under Art. 40.3.1.
[85] Electoral Act 1923, s.51; Constitution, Art. 18.2.

bestowed by Article 16.1.1. While this right is not absolute, it can, like other constitutional rights, only be qualified where this can be justified as being, objectively, in the public interest.[86] This test is manifestly satisfied in the case of higher civil servants who are required to give impartial and independent advice to the Government and individual Ministers. However, there is a possibility that it would be unconstitutional as regards its application to lower civil servants (say telephonists or messengers) whose work is not really part of the political process.

The other restriction is contained in Department of Finance Circular 21/32 which is still in force:

"The Minister is aware that it is the view of the Civil Service itself that the action of an official who identifies himself actively or publicly with political matters is indefensible, and that such conduct is detrimental to the interests of the Service as a whole. The nature and conditions of a Civil Servant's employment should, of themselves, suggest to him that he must maintain a reserve in political matters, and not put himself forward on one side or another and, further, that he should be careful to do nothing that would give colour to any suggestion that his official actions are in any way influenced or capable of being influenced, by party motives. That is the attitude which the Minister, while not wishing in any way to interfere with or influence political views privately held, expects Civil Servants at all times to observe. Should any departures from official impartiality occur it will be followed by disciplinary action. If the Head of Department (after such consultation as he may think fit with his Minister) takes the view that the official has overstepped the bounds of propriety, he should send for him, point out to him the gravity of his fault, and obtain from him an undertaking that there will be no recurrence of similar impropriety in the future. If more severe action is called for, its severity will be related to the time and place, the standing of the official concerned, and the degree of publicity, but the Minister will look to Heads of Departments to ensure that, where punishment is deserved, it will follow.

While the Minister appreciates that it would not be feasible to anticipate every occasion of the kind in question that might arise for consideration, he desires to lay down specific directions on the following points, namely,

(1) An official shall not be a member of an Association or serve on a Committee having for its object the promotion of the interests of a political party or the promotion or prevention of the return of a particular candidate to the Dáil.

(2) An official shall not support or oppose any particular candidate or party either by public statement or writing.

(3) An official shall not make any verbal statements in public (or which are liable to be published), and shall not contribute to newspapers or other

---

[86] *King* v. *Attorney-General* [1981] I.R. 233.

publications any letters or articles, conveying information, comment or criticism on any matter of current political interest, or which concerns the political action or position of the Government or of any member or group of members of the Oireachtas."

Again it might be queried whether (assuming for the sake of argument that this circular is binding either as a term of the condition of service or as an "arrangement" under section 17 of the 1956 Act) in its application to the lower grades in the civil service, this circular violates the Constitution, Article 40.3.1 of which protects the right to communicate and Article 40.6 of which protects freedom of expression and the right to hold political opinions. In any case, it should be noted that since 1974, this ban has been modified, but only in its application to industrial civil servants and (subject to a proviso that officers engaged in a particular category of work may be excluded from this freedom) clerical workers.[87] Civil servants in these groups may engage in political activity, including standing for election to local authorities, but may not stand as candidates for either House of the Oireachtas.

There are, however, more insidious ways in which the impartiality of the civil service may be eroded and, in 1982, various practices gave rise to protests from, *inter alia*, the Association of Higher Civil Servants.[88] First, there had been an increase in the size of "private offices," *i.e.* offices within a Department, which may be staffed by as many as 20 civil servants under a Higher Executive Officer and which assist the Minister in dealing with a range of constituency and party political activities, including obtaining a health card for a constituent, sending circulars to all of a Minister's constituents; or helping to organise the Minister's local party branch. Sometimes this involves civil servants in working in the constituencies of members of the Government. This development carries obvious dangers that the civil servants involved will be, or will be regarded as being, politicised. Connected with this is the older problem of the extent to which civil servants should prepare material for ministerial speeches to party meetings. The conventional rule is that when civil servants are asked to provide such material, they should ensure that it is balanced and objective. One compromise would be for this range of functions to be performed by a restricted number of temporary civil servants, appointed on a contract basis, for the life of the Government. This approach, which may be the lesser of two evils, has, however, also been criticised by the Association of Higher Civil Servants, on the grounds that it may injure civil service structures and morale.

---

[87] Department of the Public Service Circular No. 22 of 1974: see statement made by the Minister for the Public Service on March 6, 1974 (reproduced by Dooney, *op. cit.* App. 8). See also, Department of Finance Circulars Nos. 23/1925 and 20/1934.
[88] See Association of Higher Civil Servants, *Discussion Paper on Civil Servants and Politics* (April 1983). For a broader discussion, see P. Honohan, "The Role of the Adviser and the Evolution of the Public Service" in Hederman (ed.) *Essays in Honour of Patrick Lynch* (Gill and Macmillan, 1988).

Confidentiality

It has been suggested that ministerial confidentiality is one of the causes of our secretive system of government.[89] In any event, for whatever reason of constitutional system or inherited political culture, it is clear from paragraph 3 of the Circular quoted above that civil servants are barred from publishing material on public affairs or appearing on radio or television, without permission "and in practice have found it quite hard to get this permission even for innocuous material."[90] This state of affairs may be inevitable but one consequence of it is to further reduce the sluggish flow of expert information available to the general public and to keep the level of public debate low.

On the plane of criminal law, the most stringent provision is section 4(1) of the Official Secrets Act 1963, which forbids any person to communicate:

"[A]ny official information to any other person unless he is duly authorised to do so or does so in the course of and in accordance with his duties as the holder of a public office or when it is his duty in the interests of the State to communicate it."[91]

The remarkably wide sweep of this provision arises from the definition of "official information" as, *inter alia*, "any . . . information which is secret or confidential or is expressed to be either. . . . " In the light of the reasoning used in *Maher* v. *Attorney-General*,[92] it is probable that the extension of the definition to catch information which is "expressed to be either . . . " is unconstitutional. The phrase "duly authorised" in section 4(1) is amplified in a later subsection, which provides that a person may be authorised to disclose information by a Minister or State authority. It is also an offence to obtain official information where a person is aware or has reasonable grounds to believe that the communication of the information to him would contravene section 4(1).[93] Each of these offences normally carries a maximum penalty of six months' imprisonment and/or a £100 fine, on summary conviction.[94]

---

[89] P. Cook, "Why we need open government in Ireland" (1984) 5 *Seirbhís Phoiblí* 23, 25. "[A] small nation with a written constitution and a neutral standing in international affairs has virtually the same draconic powers of Government secrecy as [Britain] a front-line NATO state with no written constitution." There is no equivalent of the U.S. Civil Service Reform Act 1978 which protects civil servants who leak information which they believe reveals: mismanagement; a gross waste of funds; an abuse of authority or a substantial and specific danger to public health or safety: see Murphy, "A changing civil service" (1986) 34 *Administration* 345, 350. See also, Ryan "Let the People Know" (1986) 7 *Seirbhís Phoiblí* 20. This article describes the Freedom of Information Bill 1985 which Senator Ryan introduced, unsuccessfully, into the Senate on September 25, 1985.
[90] Chubb, *The Government and Politics of Ireland* (Stanford, 1982), p. 326.
[91] There has only been one prosecution for breach of the 1963 Act but that prosecution (which was brought against *The Irish Independent* in 1984, for publishing an identikit picture of a suspect, which had been sent to every Garda station in the country) concerned Pt. III, which creates the more serious type of offence involving the safety of the State. The only case involving the precursor Official Secrets Act 1911–1920 was brought in 1933 and resulted in an acquittal.
[92] *Maher* v. *Att.-Gen.*, [1973] I.R. 140.
[93] 1963 Act, s.4(3).
[94] *Ibid.* s.13.

CHAPTER 4

STATE-SPONSORED BODIES[1]

1. Introduction

The principal objective of the Ministers and Secretaries Act 1924 was, as has been seen, to provide that all the central, executive power of the state should flow through Ministers responsible to the Dáil. However, by 1927, the first four state-sponsored bodies had been established. The functions of these four give some idea of the work of the state-sponsored sector: the Electricity Supply Board was set up to provide public financing of a huge investment project which, it was believed, could not be privately financed; the Agricultural Credit Corporation was constituted to make loans to farmers and to promote the co-operative movement; the Dairy Disposal Co. Ltd. was set up to acquire, and thus prevent a foreign take-over of, Newmarket Creameries; the purpose of the Medical Registration Council—whose functions were passed on to the newly-constituted Medical Council in 1978—was to regulate the practice of medicine in the state.

By 1991, on the Department of Finance's count[2] there were about 70 state-sponsored bodies. The total number employed in the entire sector was approximately 84,000 (or 7 per cent. of the total work-force, or 9 per cent. of the total number of employees). The sector accounted for 10 per cent. of gross national product and consumed one-half of the state's annual investment programme. The lion's share of all these figures is taken up by the 30 or

---

[1] See Chubb, *The Government and Politics of Ireland* (London, 1982), Chap. 14; Chubb, *A Source Book of Irish Government* (Dublin, 1981), Chap. 10; Fitzgerald, *State-Sponsored Bodies* (Dublin, 1963); *Industrial Policy* (Dublin: The Stationery Office, 1984); N.E.S.C., *Enterprise in the Public Sector* (Dublin: The Stationery Office); Covery and McDowell, *Privatisation: Issues of Principle and Implementation in Ireland* (Dublin, 1990); Zimmerman, "Irish State-Sponsored Bodies: The Fractionalization of Authority and Responsibility" (1986) 7 *Seirbhís Phoiblí*, 2, 27; D. A. O'Callaghan, "Controlling the State-Sponsored Bodies" (1983) 31 *Administration* 346; B. Walsh, "Commercial State-Sponsored Bodies" *The Irish Banking Review*, Summer 1987, 27; P. Massey, "Privatisation: Time for a Closer Look" (1987) 8 *Seirbhís Phoiblí* 2, 2; N. McMahon "The Role of the State Organisation" (1987) 8 *Seirbhís Phoiblí* 2, 60; P. Sweeney, "Public Enterprise in Ireland: A Statistical Description and Analysis": a paper given to the Statistical and Social Enquiry Society of Ireland on February 15, 1990.
[2] For the list of 1961 state-sponsored bodies, see *Dáil Debates*, Vol. 311, cols. 868–886 (February 8, 1979). Notice, however, that the parliamentary question, to which this list (together with informative comments) was the answer defined "state-sponsored body" in fairly expansive terms. By contrast, the Public Expenditure Division of the Department of Finance, which operates a general overview of the entire state-sponsored body sector, requires that to qualify as a state-sponsored body: all or almost all members of the board should be appointed by a Minister; (in the case of a non-commercial body) the bulk of the funds should emanate from the Government; and the auditor should be the Comptroller and Auditor General as opposed to a private auditor. Also the Department's definition excludes advisory agencies. See also, n. 4 below.

so commercial state-sponsored bodies.[3] Because of their diverse tasks, state bodies vary considerably in terms of capital, staffing, etc., ranging from a dozen staff (at the Law Reform Commission) to 14,500 employees (at Bord Telecom).

By way of introduction, it ought to be stressed that our concern is with the structure of state bodies and their relationship with the Government, rather than their performance, which is a matter of economics and public adminis-tration. However, to exclude entirely reference to these subjects would be rather like portraying *Hamlet* as a play about a Second Grave-Digger.

Meaning of "state-sponsored body"

There is no general statutory definition of a state-sponsored body[4] for the reason that the term is seldom used in statute law, which almost always directs itself to a specific body as opposed to the entire sector. Yet although there is a variation from one body to another, (so that propositions in this field are inevitably generalisations) the term is useful for descriptive purposes because these bodies do raise common problems of accountability, patronage, staff-ing, control, organisation and legal status. Broadly speaking, the term "state-sponsored body" denotes an authority which discharges specialised, central functions usually of a governmental nature, yet which is set at a distance from the Government and Ministers. This last point is the central feature in the concept of the state-sponsored body. For, on the one hand, these agencies exercising public functions are owned by the State and rely, in the case of non-commercial bodies, substantially on State finance; and are controlled by boards whose members are selected by the Government or a Minister. But, on the other hand, they are subject to a lesser degree of control, by the responsible Minister and the Dáil, than would apply to the activities of a Department of State. As was said by the Minister when piloting the Bill to constitute the ESB through the Dáil:

" . . . [T]here are going to be no Parliamentary questions with regard to this Board. There are going to be no complaints from a Deputy that his

---

[3] We return at pp. 116–118 to the differences between the commercial and non-commercial state bodies and to a list of commercial state bodies.

[4] But see Ministers and Secretaries (Amendment) Act 1973, s.1 (which in defining the catchment area of the former P.S.A.C. refers to "the public service" which means "the Civil Service of the Government and the Civil Service of the State" and (in what may be regarded as a definition of a state body) "such bodies established by or under statute and financed wholly or partly by means of grants or loans made by a Minister of State or the issue of shares taken up by a Minister of State as may stand designated for the time being by regulations made by the Minister [for the Public Service]." No such regulations has been made. See also Ryan, "The Role of the State-Sponsored Body in the new Public Service" (1973) 21 *Administration* 387, 397. A further example is provided by the National Development Corporation Act 1986, s.10(1)(*a*) which uses the term "state-sponsored commercial enterprise" in the context of entities with which the NDC may establish joint enterprises. The term is defined by reference to a list in the Second Sched. to the Act, which enumerates all the bodies usually regarded as commercial state bodies. In s.10(1)(*b*) of the same Act, the term "state-sponsored body" is employed to catch the entities (certain of the non-commercial state bodies, which are listed in the First Sched. to the Act) which the Corpor-ation must consult, where appropriate, before making an investment. See also, n. 2 above.

area is not served at such a rate as some other Deputy . . . this Board is not going to be regarded as a machine for wiping off all political obligations of this, that and the other Deputy."[5]

In addition, a state-sponsored body is usually constituted by its own distinctive statute, a point developed in Part 3. The staff of state bodies are usually not civil servants.[6] Finally as stated already, a state-sponsored body administers a central, specialised, governmental function. Thus, local or regional bodies—such as health boards or harbour boards—are usually excluded. Again the epithet "governmental"—deliberately a rather vague term—alludes to the fact that it is conventional to exclude quasi-judicial bodies, *e.g.* An Bord Pleanála, or the Adoption Board. Also excluded are the three traditional specialist services of education,[7] police and defence are not regarded as being part of the state-sponsored body sector and those entities, like the Mines and Quarries Advisory Council or the Public Service Advisory Council, which are exclusively concerned with giving advice to a Minister. However bodies, like the Combat Poverty Agency or the National Social Service Board, which have a wider competence as regards promotion and publication are treated as non-commercial state bodies.

Commissions

There are, however, other functions in regard to which it is desirable that a steady policy, which is not blown by the political wind, should be followed. However, such functions are not always housed in a state-sponsored body. This is the explanation for the existence of the Revenue Commissioners (1923); Civil Service Commission (1924)[8] and the Local Appointments Commission (1926).[9] These bodies are not state bodies: because their staff are civil servants of the Government; because they are not constituted as independent legal entities (whether as corporations sole or companies); and because, historically, apart from the Local Appointments Commission, they were set up before the earliest state-sponsored bodies. However, what is more important is that they do enjoy the same kind of arm's length relationship with the responsible Minister. This has been achieved by vesting their functions in statutory commissioners who are free of interference in day-to-day matters,

---

[5] *Dáil Debates*, Vol. 18, col. 1919 (March 15, 1927).
[6] Another troublesome term, examined at pp. 68–73.
[7] In the case of the Universities, see also the Ministers and Secretaries Act 1924, s.9(4).
[8] "The fact that the Civil Service Commissioners hold office at the pleasure of the Executive Council would appear . . . unsatisfactory in view of the statutory intention that they should exercise a more or less judicial independence in certain matters . . . [we] hope that the steady development of a sound practice over a considerable number of years will eventually prove a better safeguard than might be afforded by some other system of a more logical character" (*Commission of Inquiry into the Civil Service 1932–35*, Vol. 1, p. 82).
[9] The Irish Land Commission, established in 1881, is being dissolved by the Irish Land Commission (Dissolution) Bill 1989 and its powers and duties are being transferred to the Minister for Agriculture and Food. The reason is that the former Commission's task of transferring land from landowners to tenant farmers has been effectively complete for some decades.

largely as a result of convention. Such commissioners usually have their own separate estimate. Since these bodies have so much in common with state-sponsored bodies it may be instructive to examine here the structure of one of them briefly.

The Revenue Commissioners were constituted in 1923 to take over the functions of tax assessment and collection formerly exercised by the British Commissioners of Inland Revenue and the British Commissioners of Customs and Excise. The three Revenue Commissioners are appointed for an indefinite term, at the pleasure of the Taoiseach, from among the existing officials of the Commissioners.[10] Finance Acts traditionally embody a provision to the effect that all taxes or duties imposed or continued by the Act "are hereby placed under the care and management of the Revenue Commissioners." It is true that the Revenue Commissioners Order of 1923 requires the Commissioners to obey any instructions which may be issued to them by the Minister for Finance. However, this provision has been substantially glossed by a convention which has frequently been enunciated by Ministers in reply to deputies' questions in the Dáil. One of its earliest formulations (in 1923) is contained in a letter sent, on the Minister's behalf, to the Commissioners' first chairman. The following is an extract from this letter:

" . . . [W]hile the Revenue Commissioners will be responsible directly to the Minister for Finance for the administration of the Revenue Services, the Commissioners will act independently of Ministerial control in exercising the statutory powers vested in them in regard to the liability to tax of the individual taxpayer."[11]

Plainly, a well-understood convention to this effect is helpful to Ministers and deputies in warding off importuning taxpayers. Indeed it may be that, in general—and certainly in the case of the Revenue Commissioners—the *de facto* independence of government of a commission is often greater than that of a state-sponsored body.

Inevitably, some taxpayers will be dissatisfied with the decisions of the Commissioners' staff and these disputes may be resolved by appeal to the tribunal known as the Appeal Commissioners appointed by the Minister for Finance, from among the senior staff of the Revenue Commissioners in the case of one Commissioner and the other from the Bar. Their jurisdiction covers income taxes but not Customs and Excise.[12]

---

[10] Revenue Commissioners Order of 1923 made under Adaptation of Enactments Act 1922, s.7. Read literally the Ministers and Secretaries Act 1924, s.1(ii) (" . . . The Department of Finance which shall comprise . . . the collection . . . of the revenues of [the State] . . . ") and Schedule, First Part could be taken to mean that the Department of Finance had swallowed the Revenue Commissioners, but this result was not intended: see *Re Irish Insurance Association Ltd.* [1955] I.R. 176, 182–183 and Sean Reamon, *History of the Revenue Commissioners* (Dublin, 1981), Chap. 5.
[11] The letter is quoted in Reamon, *op. cit.* pp. 56–61 where other evidence for the convention is given.
[12] Income Tax Act 1967, s.156(1); Finance (Miscellaneous Provisions) Act 1968, s.1(1).

Introduction

A note on legal status

State-sponsored bodies are generally subject to the ordinary law, for example, as to torts or tax, save where they enjoy some specific statutory exemption. Yet there are a number of contexts in which they might enjoy some special position. In determining whether they do, it is necessary to consider the legal status of the body. More precisely, its degree of independence of the central executive organ, is significant.[13] The first context stems from the international law precept, followed by most national courts, that "foreign states" are exempt from their jurisdiction. Thus, in *Gibbons* v. *Udarás na Gaeltachta*,[14] the question arose before the New York courts in the course of an action for breach of contract and fraudulent misrepresentation allegedly arising from a joint venture agreement partially concluded in New York, as to whether Udara, a state body, which acts as a promotional agency for the Gaeltacht, fell within the ambit of this immunity.[15] The courts rejected the agency's claim for sovereign immunity, emphasising its view of the Udarás operation as being "no different . . . from the promotional activities engaged in by a private public relations firm."

Secondly, a number of diverse statutes employ some such term as "public authority" or "public body," usually without offering any assistance by way of definition of the critical term. The question could arise as to whether some particular state body is within the term. In fact, the only form in which this problem has presented itself in recent Irish law concerned the General Medical (Payments) Board (which might be classified not as a state body but as a tribunal which also discharges some routine, executive functions). In any case, the net question in *The General Medical Services (Payments) Board* v. *Minister for Social Welfare*[16] was whether an employee of the plaintiff board was insurable for the Social Welfare Act 1952 at the ordinary rate of contribution or at the special rate applicable to employment by a "public authority" pursuant to Article 5(1)(c) of the Social Welfare (Modification of Insurance) Regulations 1956. In short, the question for the High Court was whether the plaintiff board was a public authority. Hamilton J. commenced by observing that:

" . . . it is surprising that there does not exist any general definition of what is or what is not a public authority either in statute or in court decisions."[17]

---

[13] Note that "State authority" is defined, for the purpose of the Postal and Telecommunications Services Act 1983, s.1(10(1)) to include only Ministers of the Government, Commissioners of Public Works and the Irish Land Commission, and, for the purpose of the Statute of Limitations 1957, s.2(1), in the same way but with the addition of two other entities, the Revenue Commissioners and the Attorney-General.

[14] 549 F.Supp. 1094 (S.D.N.Y. 1982). An identical conclusion as to the agency's immunity was reached in *Gibson* v. *The Republic of Ireland* 682 F. 2d. 1022 (D.C. Cir. 1982).

[15] As established by s.1605 of the U.S. Foreign Sovereign Immunities Act.

[16] [1976–1977] I.L.R.M. 210.

[17] *Ibid.* 211. Many of the authorities opened to the judge by counsel were concerned with the interpretation of s.1 of the Public Authorities Protection Act 1893 (which is no longer law here or in England) on which see p. 640. Notice that, by the Transport Act 1950, s.10, CIE was made exempt from the 1893 Act.

107

Later, the judge, adopted the following definition taken from *Halsbury's Laws of England*[18]:

"A public authority is a body, not necessarily a county council, municipal corporation or other local authority, which has public or statutory duties to perform and which performs these duties and carries out its transactions for the benefit of the public and not for private profit."

The judge also summarised the function and status of the plaintiff board as follows[19]:

"It is a board established by a ministerial order made in pursuance of the powers given to the Minister for Health by s.11(2) of the Health Act 1970, which Act was enacted by the legislature, *inter alia*, to provide for the establishment of bodies for the administration of the health services; it is one of the bodies established for the administration of the health services; its function is admittedly a limited one namely:

(a) The calculation of payments to be made for the services provided by the health boards under s.58 and s.59(1) of the Health Act 1970.

(b) The verification of the accuracy and reasonableness of claims in relation to such services.

(c) The compilation of statistics and other information in relation to such services and the communications of such information to persons concerned with the operation of such services.

It cannot make a profit and its members do not receive any remuneration."

The judge's conclusion that the plaintiff was, indeed, a public authority, then flowed naturally from the definition quoted earlier.

Another example of a statute employing the phrase "public body" is the Prevention of Corruption Act 1906—which is still law in Ireland, By this Act, it is an offence for an employee of a "public body" to corruptly accept a gift as an inducement to show favour to persons doing business with the body. In *R. v. Manners*,[20] the House of Lords held that the North Thames Gas Board came within the definition of a "public body" for the purposes of the 1906 Act. A similar question could arise in an Irish court in a case in which the employee of a state-sponsored body was being prosecuted for the same offence.

---

[18] *Ibid.* 217. The quotation is from *Halsbury* (3rd ed.), Vol. 30, p. 682. This passage does not really address the difficulties with the concept of a public body.

[19] [1976-1977] I.L.R.M. 215. Two subsidiary points, in the case, may be worthy of note. The first of these appears to be directed to rebutting what is anyway a rather unconvincing argument, namely that the board was set up by ministerial order rather than directly by statute. This argument was rejected on the basis that this distinction does not cause any difference in the "fundamental nature [of the functions of the board]" (p. 217). Secondly, the functions of the plaintiff board are of "an internal administrative nature" (p. 217) in that it does not involve the making available of a general medical service to the public. However, in response to this, the court held that the plaintiff's functions could not be considered in isolation from the duties of the health boards, which they service and which plainly are "public."

[20] [1978] A.C. 43.

Thirdly, it may just be arguable that a state-sponsored body would be regarded as part of the State for the purposes of any former prerogative right (such as the presumption that the State is not bound by statute)[21] which may persist in independent Ireland. This argument appears unlikely to succeed however, given the historical development of the prerogative, coupled with the tenor of the reasoning in *Re Irish Employers' Mutual Insurance Association Ltd.*[22] and also the Irish courts' dislike of special privileges.

Such questions, each of which may require a slightly different categorisation, have generated a certain amount of case law, in Britain and elsewhere in the common law world[23] but not in Ireland. However, the principle is not in doubt. As was said by Kingsmill Moore J. in regard to an analogous issue (involving, be it noted, the Commissioners of Public Works, who are less autonomous than a state-sponsored body):

"The degree of direction and control which is exercised by the executive over the conduct of the work may afford an indication as to whether the Commissioners in executing the work are acting as servants of the State."[24]

European Community Law[25]

The novel concepts of European Community law have introduced a further need to categorise public authorities (embracing, *inter alia*, state-sponsored bodies) in order to resolve a number of different issues, three of which will be mentioned here.[26] These questions are complicated by the fact that, in the interests of maintaining uniformity from Member State to Member State, they should be regarded as mixed questions of Community and national law.

The first of these questions arises from the fact that Article 48 of the EC Treaty which establishes the right to free movement of workers permits a derogation in the case of "the public service". The Court of Justice has stressed the need for a restrictive interpretation of the exemption from such a

---

[21] See pp. 725–729.
[22] [1955] I.R. 176. For the facts in this case, see n. 24.
[23] Foulkes, *Administrative Law* (London, 1982), pp. 12–17; Hogg, *Liability of the Crown* (Toronto, 1989), Chap. 8.
[24] *Re Irish Employers' Mutual Insurance Association Ltd.* [1955] I.R. 176. The facts of the case were that the Commissioners of Public Works had taken out insurance with a company which subsequently went into liquidation. The Commissioners claimed that the moneys due to them from the company should, as a matter of prerogative right, be paid in priority to the debts due to other creditors. For present purposes, the relevant question was whether assuming that this prerogative existed, the Commissioners would be characterised as sufficiently part of the State to be able to invoke it. It was held that, in general, the Commissioners were to be regarded as servants of the State. However, where the Commissioners were performing work on behalf of local authorities, then they were not acting as servants of the State. See also, *Re Maloney* [1926] I.R. 202, 206; *Irish Land Commission* v. *Ruane* [1938] I.R. 148, 152–157, 161 (Irish Land Commission characterised as a servant of the State).
[25] On this subject, see an excellent monograph by Deirdre Curtin, "The Province of Government: Delimiting the Direct Effect of Directives in the Common Law Context."(1990) 15 E.L. Rev. 195.
[26] The authorities are listed in Curtin, *loc. cit.*

fundamental principle. Thus in several rulings, the Court has confined this exemption to posts involved in activities which are peculiar to public service, such as the armed forces, the judiciary, the diplomatic corps and local authorities, as contradistinguished from activities such as health-care or education, which may also be performed by the private sector.[27] What this means, in the context of state-sponsored bodies, is that commercial bodies are excluded from the exemption in that they involve industrial or commercial enterprises, whereas several of the non-commercial bodies are within the exemption because they entail distinctively public functions, such as economic regulation.

Another context in which a similar question arises is the free movement of goods. An example occurred in *R* v. *The Royal Pharmaceutical Society of Great Britain et al.*[28] Here the Court of Justice, notwithstanding that the respondent professional body could not be regarded as an organ of state so far as operational control was concerned, held that the measures which it had adopted to regulate the pharmaceutical profession could be equated with those of the state on the basis of their purpose and of the type of powers with which the respondent had been endowed.

The remaining point of classification required by European Community law arises when an EC Directive has either not been implemented by a Member State after the requisite time allowed for implementation has passed or has been inaccurately translated into its national law. It has now been established that, while such Directives do not operate against a private individual or company, they do, provided that they are unconditional and sufficiently precise, have direct effect against the State concerned, on the basis that the State is estopped from benefiting from the consequence of its own default.[29] This ruling immediately raises the question of the extent of "the State" and, in particular in the present context, whether it would embrace a state-sponsored body. The leading authority is *Foster* v. *British Gas plc.*[30] where the substantive issue here, involved Directive 76/207, the Equal Treatment Directive. The relevant issue for present purposes was whether the defendant which was, at the relevant time, a nationalised industry (as the British call their commercial state bodies) should be classified as an organ of the State. The English Court of Appeal concluded that it should not so be classified, saying that the defendant was not subject to the day-to-day control of a Minister and that its powers were original rather than delegated by a Minister or other state

---

[27] Other examples include the question of whether a state body is a "public body or undertaking" for the purposes of public works contracts (or which, see pp. 114–116) or for Art. 90(1) of the EC Treaty, which deals with monopoly power (on which, see pp. 155–157).

[28] Joined Cases 266 and 267/87 [1990] 1 Q.B. 534.

[29] *Marshall* v. *Southampton and South-West Hampshire Area Health Authority (Teaching)* case 152/84 [1987] E.C.R. 723.

[30] [1988] I.C.R. 584. (Court of Appeal); [1990] 2 C.M.L.R. 833 (E.C. Court of Justice) Notice also, *Turpie* v. *University of Glasgow* (Decision of the Industrial Tribunal (Scotland) of September 26, 1986, holding that a university is not to be regarded as part of the State for the instant purpose).

organ.[31] In addition, the Court relied on the fact that the defendant could not be regarded as performing any of the classic duties of the State.[32]

The plaintiff appealed to the House of Lords, which referred the case to the European Court of Justice and this court sounded a very different note from that heard in the Court of Appeal. The kernel of the Court of Justice's judgment is the following passage[33]:

" . . . the Court has held in a series of cases that unconditional and sufficiently precise provisions of a directive could be relied on against organisations or bodies which were subject to the authority or control of the State or had special powers beyond those which result from the normal rules applicable to relations between individuals.

[19] The Court has accordingly held that provisions of a directive could be relied on against tax authorities (Case 8/81, *Becker*, and 22 February 1990 in Case C-221/88, *Fratelli Costanzo* v. *Comune Di Milano*), constitutionally independent authorities responsible for the maintentance of public order and safety (Case 222/84, *Johnston* v. *Chief Constable of the Royal Ulster Constabulary*), and public authorities providing public health services (Case 152/84, *Marshall*).

[20] It follows from the foregoing that a body, whatever its legal form, which has been made responsible, pursuant to a measure adopted by the State, for providing a public service under the control of the State and has for that purpose special powers beyond those which result from the normal rules applicable in relations between individuals is included in any event among the bodies against which the provisions of a directive capable of having direct effect may be relied upon."

Unfortunately the last paragraph of this passage is a little inexact. In the first place, does the reference to "the control of the State" mean legal control or real, effective control and, secondly, how close must the control be? It is relevant here that the Advocate General's opinion, in this case, is much longer and better reasoned and can be used to amplify the court's judgment. The Advocate General is explicit that, generally, the "concept of a public body must be understood very broadly."[34] In particular, it extends[35]:

" . . . so far as 'the State' has given itself powers which place it in a position to decisively influence the conduct of persons—whatever their nature, public or private, or their sphere of activity—with regard to the subject-matter of the directive which has not been correctly implemented. It is

---

[31] This was a point of distinction from *Marshall* in which part of the reason for the plaintiff's success was that the defendant area health authority could be regarded as acting as an agent for a Minister.

[32] Success in regard to this factor was the basis of the plaintiff's victory in *Johnston* v. *Chief Constable of the Royal Ulster Constabulary* case 222/84 [1986] E.C.R. 1651.

[33] [1990] 2 C.M.L.R. 833, 856–857. Footnotes omitted. An example of "special powers" in the Irish context would be Bord Telecom's and An Post's monopolies, which are examined at pp. 120–121.

[34] *Ibid.* 850.

[35] *Ibid.* 851.

immaterial in that regard in what manner 'the State' can influence the conduct of those persons: de jure or de factor, for example because the organ of authority has a general or specific power (or is simply able as a matter of fact) to give that person binding directions, whether or not by the exercise of rights as a shareholder, to approve its decisions in advance or suspend or annul them after the fact, to appoint or dismiss (the majority of) its directors, or to interrupt its funding wholly or in part so as to threaten its continued existence, with, however, the proviso [that] the possibility exercising influence must stem from something other than a general legislative power . . .."

In addition, the passage quoted from the court's judgment left it doubtful whether the requirements it mentioned—"a public service under the control of the State" and "[possessing] special powers beyond those which result from the normal rules . . ."—must both be satisfied. The Advocate General, however, is definite, that to bring a body within the broad category of the State, it suffices if *any* of the requirements is met. Moreover, the Advocate General mentions another ground of qualification which has no counterpart in the court's judgment, namely: "bodies which pursuant to the constitutional structure of a Member-State can exercise any authority over individuals . . . "[36]

It appears likely, from the test enunciated by the Court of Justice in *Foster*, especially when read in the light of the Advocate General's opinion, that an Irish state-sponsored body (even a commercial body) would come within the category of a public body for the purpose of being bound by an EC Directive. As it happens, there is, as yet, only one domestic Irish case which is even remotely in point and this authority involved not a state body but a tribunal. Moreover the reasoning in the case is so divergent from that in *Foster* as to be now of doubtful authority.

The case in question is *Browne* v. *An Bord Pleanála*[37] in which the nett question was whether a grant of planning permission was invalid because the application did not comply with the provisions of Directive 85/337 in that it omitted certain requisite information from the environmental impact study. Addressing the point rather briefly, Barron J. stated[38]:

> "the respondent has [no] wider powers than those of an Appellate Tribunal. In my view, the respondent can in no way be held responsible for the failure of the state to implement the directive, if failed they have."

In the light of *Foster*, this approach appears to be founded too squarely upon the notion that for an entity to be regarded as a public body, it should, in some sense, share reponsibility for the failure in the relevant Member-State

[36] *Ibid.* 850–851.
[37] [1989] I.L.R.M. 865. Note that, in *Murphy* v. *An Bord Telecom* [1989] I.L.R.M. 53 one of the preliminary questions referred to the Court of Justice by the High Court involved the status of Bord Telecom for the present purpose. However, since the discrimination in question fell within Art. 119 of the EC Treaty, it was not necessary to determine the applicability of the Equal Pay Directive (75/117).
[38] [1989] I.L.R.M. 865, 873–874.

to implement the directive in national law. This approach has been rejected by the European Court, as is clear from the facts of the cases listed in paragraph [19] of the passage for *Foster* quoted earlier.

Other forms of state involvement in the economy

State-sponsored agencies are comparatively straightforward in that they are bodies which, subject to some exceptions, are under the exclusive and visible control and ownership of the State. If we range even further away from the traditional arrangement of public functions being discharged by a Department of State with a Minister at the head, we encounter manifold and subtle (even subterranean) forms of state involvement in the economy. It would be beyond our brief to do more than allude to the novel questions of control, responsibility, consistency and adequate public debate raised by arrangements like these. However, the following examples may be mentioned briefly. The first concerns the State's capacity to make contracts, a phenomenon which was sketched briefly by the then Minister for Finance in the following passage:

"Where in the past a civil service of limited size carried out the administrative functions of the state, today the range of instruments required by government for the achievement of its objectives goes well beyond the traditional concept of the organs of the State. At its extreme, this tendency has gone farthest in the United States where the phenomenon is common of the large private sector corporation almost entirely dependent on public contracts and producing almost exclusively for government. The development of bodies of this type side by side with the more familiar agencies of government has led to questioning in some countries of the traditional institutional arrangements of the performance of the executive functions of government. It has produced the concept of the 'contract state' where executive functions are performed by a range of bodies included in the broad category of 'quasi autonomous non-governmental institutions' with an emphasis on the contractual rather than the structural relationships between government and these bodies.

It would be interesting to analyse the instruments through which the purposes of government are achieved in this country and to ascertain the extent, if any, to which there has been a move towards performance by contract rather than by traditional agencies. . . . I don't think there has been any large scale move in this direction, but I think that the idea of a contractual relationship between government and its traditional agencies is emerging behind some of the thinking here in recent years. What is valuable about this thinking is that it concentrates attention on the problem of what government can and should do directly and what it can and should have undertaken for it by other means."[39]

Other examples of the State spreading its tentacles through the economy by

[39] Ryan, "The Role of the State Sponsored Body in the New Public Service" (1973) 21 *Administration* 387–388.

means other than complete ownership include: wage-control through the (extra-statutory) annual National Wage Agreements[40]; statutory control over prices for various goods and services under the Prices Acts 1958–1972[41]; informal attempts by the Minister for the Environment to influence building society interest rates and by the Minister for Justice to encourage the Incorporated Law Society to expand the intake to its solicitors training course[42]; a complex of industrial grants and subsidies to set beside the system of taxes[43]; joint ventures between state bodies and other (often foreign) business organisations; and state shareholding in private companies, either directly through the Minister for Finance or by way of a state-sponsored body, like the Industrial Development Association.[44]

Procedure for Government contracts

Formerly the procedure for Government contracts (which are almost all made in the name of a Minister) was dealt with by the issue of circulars from the Minister of Finance, some of which go back to the 1920s. Presumably these circulars derived their authority from the Minister for Finance's statutory powers in regard to "the supervision and control of all purchases made for or on behalf of, and all supplies of commodities and goods held by any Department of State and the disposal thereof . . .."[45] This provision is confined to "Departments of State." For the Minister for Finance's authority over the other entities, one has to go to the fact that (presumably) the contracts into which they are entering will be funded by Exchequer money. The Minister's authorisation is necessary before such funds are spent[46] so that, by implication, he also has authority to fix conditions. Where the contract is not funded by the Exchequer as in the case of contracts entered into by commercial state sponsored bodies, the question of the Minister's authority is more problematic.

By the 1980s there was a clear need for co-ordinating and updating these procedures in the light of changed conditions, and for making them available in a convenient format. The changes which have occurred include the fact that in recent years there has been a considerable increase in the value of purchasing by public bodies, accompanied by an increased level of delegation to Government Departments of their own purchasing requirements. Previously, purchases were handled centrally by such specialised bodies as the Office of Public Works or the Stationery Office which are satellites of the Minister for

---

[40] For a case arising from statutory wage control, see *Burke* v. *Minister for Labour* [1979] I.R. 354.

[41] See, *e.g. Cassidy* v. *Minister for Industry* [1978] I.R. 197.

[42] *Dáil Debates*, Vol. 399, col. 2311–2312 (June 13, 1990).

[43] See McMahon, *Economic Law in Ireland* (Brussels, 1977), Chap. 3 and generally.

[44] Notice also that in 1925 the Abbey Theatre became the first state-subsidised theatre in the English-speaking world: Drabble, *The Oxford Companion to English Literature* (Oxford, 1984), p. 1.

[45] Ministers and Secretaries Act 1924, s.1(ii).

[46] Ministers and Secretaries Act 1924, s.2(4); Exchequer and Audit Department Act 1921. For the detailed position, see Gwynn Morgan, *Constitutional Law of Ireland*, pp.126–127.

Finance. In addition, there are a number of EC Directives relating to public contracts.

The response to these needs was the establishment of a Working Group comprising the representatives of the Ministers for Finance, the Environment, Education, Labour, Industry Trade Commerce and Tourism and the Minister of State at the Department of Finance. This group produced the document, "An Outline of Government Contracts Procedures."[47]

The *Outline* deals with works, supply and service contracts and contracts for the disposal of public property. It applies to contracts, one of the parties to which is a Department of State or office or a local or regional authority. These rules in the *Outline* are subject to modification and qualification by the Department of Finance and in most cases only apply where the contract is worth more than £10,000. The major policy underlying the procedures and the conditions fixed by the *Outline* is to encourage fair and open competition among businesses which trade with public authorities. Thus, save in exceptional cases, the public authority should try to obtain "five but not less than three tenders."[48] Invitations must state that the public authority will not be bound to accept the lowest or, indeed, any tender. The adoption of "restricted" tendering procedures (*i.e.* invitation of tenders is confined to firms on an official list) is permissible so long as the public authority concerned is satisfied that the list is reasonably comprehensive. At the same time, there should be a conscious policy to encourage recently-established firms, as for instance by awarding smaller contracts to them at first. Other more detailed aspects are that there should be a preference for fixed contracts and, secondly (in the case of building works contracts) a preference against nominated sub-contractors since such nomination tends to blur responsibility. In addition, a contractor must be able to produce a certificate from the Revenue Commissioners establishing that he is up to date in paying his taxes. In the case of the acquisition of goods or services, public authorities are admonished that purchase contracts will generally be better value for money in the long run than leasing contracts.[49]

The *Outline* also notes that there are a number of international obligations, in this field. Thus there are European Community Directives dealing with the award of public works contracts above a value of 1 million ECU and supply

---

[47] Pl. 4120—Department of Finance, 1986.
[48] *Ibid.* 22.
[49] One difficult question which arises in regard to the Outline is its precise legal status. Its Preface states that: "under no circumstances should this document be regarded as being legally binding on public contracting authorities." The question arises whether this would be taken at its face value in face of a claim by (say) a business which had failed to secure a contract with a public authority, following a procedure which did not comply with the rules in the Outline? Of course, this query raises the subject of legitimate expectations, on which see Chap. 13. More generally, the law relating to the legal status of such informal instruments as the *Outline* is examined at pp. 39–47. See also, *The State (Melbarien Enterprises Ltd.)* v. *Revenue Commissioners* [1985] I.R. 706 (tax clearance certificate refused because a company with connections with the applicant company owed arrears of tax) is discussed.

contracts above a threshold of 200,000 European Units of Account.[50] In addition, there is a *GATT* (General Agreement on Tariffs and Trade) *Agreement on Government Procurement*[51] which applies to supply contracts above a minimum of 150,000 Special Drawing Rights.

2. Functional Classification

Commercial and non-commercial state-sponsored bodies

Commercial state-sponsored bodies, known in other countries as "public enterprises," are under some kind of notional duty (though one which is only occasionally mentioned in legislation) to make sufficient profit to cover capital expenditure and, in practice, they do receive at least a substantial portion of their revenue from the sale of their products or services. By contrast, non-commercial bodies are agencies for the disbursement of state funds, which are given to them as grants-in-aid which appear as sub-heads of their parent Department's estimates. These funds may only be released with the permission of the Minister for Finance and the responsible Minister. Stemming from this difference, the Government has a much closer control, in some cases statutory,[52] over the salaries and numbers of persons employed in the case of a non-commercial agency. For example, non-commercial state-sponsored bodies must make quarterly returns to the parent Department supplying this information. In addition, they were subject to the one-in-three embargo on the filling of vacancies within the public service, which existed in the early and mid-1980s.

With commercial state-sponsored bodies, control is slightly less tight. There is no direct control over numbers of staff. However, as part of the policy that there should be a co-ordinated approach to pay in the entire public sector, all state-sponsored bodies are subject to central control over wages, including National Wage Agreements. There is, however, no legal basis for this particular control save in some of the statutes enacted or articles of association, drafted since the late sixties.[53]

---

[50] See European Community, Directives 71/304/EEC; 71/305/EEC and 77/62, which are referred to in the *Outline*, pp. 17 and 28; see further, Collins and O'Reilly, *Civil Proceedings and the State in Ireland: a practitioner's guide (The Round Hall Press, 1990)*, p. 192.

[51] This is implemented by European Community Directive 80/767.

[52] *e.g.* Combat Poverty Agency Act 1986, s.13, Urban Renewal Act 1986, s.20.

[53] *Serving the Country Better* (1985, Pl. 3262), para. 8.14 proposed to extend this statutory control to all commercial bodies. For an example of one modern statute effecting this change, see the Turf Development Act 1990, s.10 and for an example of Articles of Association, see Art. 70 of Bord Telecom Éireann which provides:" "In determining the remuneration or allowances for expenses to be paid to any of its officers or servants or the terms or conditions subject to which any such officer or servant holds or is to hold his employment, the Directors shall have regard either to Government or nationally agreed guidelines which are for the time being extant, or to Government policy concerning remuneration and conditions of employment which is so extant, of which the Minister may notify the Company from time to time with the consent of the Minister for the Public Service." Though note that even without legal control, in 1978 the Minister for Finance instructed a state-sponsored company to cut the salary of its chief executive by 25 per cent. and this instruction was obeyed.

The Government's involvement in the narrower question of the chief executives' salaries has attracted a good deal of attention (not least among chief executives). It is worthy of note because it is symptomatic of the general tension arising from the amphibious position of state bodies. On the one hand, Feargal Quinn, who was Chairman of An Post 1984–1989, has remarked that Government restrictions on executive salaries limit the ability of commercial state bodies to recruit the best managers.[54] On the other hand, the large state bodies have an important trend-setting effect, particularly in the area of pay and conditions of employment, and it is reasonable therefore that central Government should retain overall control.

The legal position here is more clear-cut than in regard to the issue of the payment of other members of staff (though it is worthy of note that any decision in regard to the salary of the top person in any organisation is bound to have trickle-down effect at lower levels). The Gleeson Report on Higher Remuneration in the Public Sector deals with the question of the salaries of chief executives as follows:

"Characteristically the constitution of a state-sponsored body (whether statutory or contained in Memorandum and Articles of Association) provides that the remuneration of the chief executive shall be determined by the board with the consent of the relevant Minister. In other words the board fixes remuneration and the Minister grants or refuses consent to the board's decision. As prevailing statutory or contractual provisions clearly give the primary role in pay determination to the boards of state-sponsored bodies, it appears to us that the function of the Review Body is to furnish advice to the relevant Ministers so as to facilitate the giving or refusing of properly informed consent to proposals by boards.[55]"

The report then went on to make recommendations as to pay for chief executives, which were accepted by the Government (or, strictly speaking, by the respective Ministers). It can be expected that the Review Body will also be involved in advising on the pay of chief executives in the future.

---

[54] "State Companies and Commercial Freedom" *Management*, March, 1981.
[55] (1987, Pl. 5244), para 4.9. For examples of the statutes referred to in the quotation, see: Air Companies (Amendment) Act 1976, s.6; Agricultural Credit Act 1978, s.19; Transport (Miscellaneous Provisions) Act 1979, s.7; Electricity (Supply) (Amendment) Act 1988, s.7. Notice that these are all amending statutes, altering the original position, which was that no ministerial consent was required. The expression used in the statutory provision is usually "the Chief Officer, however styled." For an example drawn from Articles of Association, take Art. 69 of Bord Telecom, which provides as follows:

" . . . officers and servants of the Company shall be paid by the Company such remuneration and allowances for expenses and shall hold office on such terms and conditions as the Directors think fit subject to in the case of its chief officer (whether that officer is described as the chief officer or otherwise), the approval of the Minister given with the consent of the Minister for the Public Service."

Commercial state-sponsored bodies

Although there are only 30 or so[56] commercial bodies (just over 40 per cent. of the total), they employ approximately 74,000 people (as against nearly 10,000 in the non-commercial sector). The sector has some of the largest employers in the country, accounting (in 1987) for the first four of the largest employers (Bord Telecom, CIE, ESB and An Post) and for seven (with the addition, to the bodies already mentioned, of Aer Lingus, Bórd na Móna and RTE) of the 17 companies which employed more than 2,000 staff. In 1987, the aggregate capital stock was £5½ billion and the contribution to g.n.p. was £2 billion or 10 per cent. of total g.n.p. (a third of this contributed by the recently established state bodies, Bord Telecom and An Post). However by the standards of other developed States, on the criterion of fraction of g.n.p. contributed by state bodies, Ireland is in the middle range (*cf.* France: 17 per cent. in 1983; Ireland: 10 per cent. in 1987; United Kingdom: 11 per cent. in 1978–1981; Germany: 1 per cent. in 1979).[57]

The birth-rate of commercial state bodies has fluctuated, being particularly high at times of economic change. Thus most of them were established during one of the following three periods; the drive for self-sufficiency in 1932–1939; the post-Second World War recovery period; or the years of economic expansion immediately after 1958. Professor Bristow has given the following historical sketch of the growth of this sector:

"The 1930s saw the nearest thing Ireland has experienced to the use of public enterprise in pursuit of an ideology—that is, economic self-sufficiency (which was an ideology rather than merely a development strategy in that it was the reflection of a political philosophy). The Irish Sugar Company was set up in 1933 and the decade saw the beginnings of governmental involvement in peat production (which led to the eventual establishment of Bord na Mona in 1946) and in air transport with the foundation of Aer Rianta in

[56] The classifications are not rigorous, and each category has fuzzy edges. Some bodies which the Department of Finance deems commercial for some purposes are nonetheless excluded from the annual published assessment of the performance of the commercial state-sector (Table 6 of the Public Capital Programme) on the ground that they do not derive the entirety of the revenue from trading. There are other slight anomalies. The Department of Finance regards the following as being commercial state bodies:

Agricultural Credit Corporation plc, Aer Lingus plc/Aerlinte Éireann plc, Aer Rianta, Arramara Teo., Blood Transfusion Service Board, Bord Gáis Éireann, Bord na Móna, Bord Telecom Éireann, British & Irish Steam Packet Company Ltd, Coillte Teo., Coras Iompair Éireann, Custom House Docks Development Authority, Electricity Supply Board, Housing Finance Agency Ltd, Industrial Credit Corporation plc, Irish National Petroleum Corporation Ltd, Irish National Stud Ltd, Irish Steel Ltd, National Building Agency Ltd, National Concert Hall Company, An Post National Lottery Company, Nitrigin Éireann Teo., An Post, Racing Board, Radio Telefis Éireann, Royal Hospital Kilmainham Company, Voluntary Health Insurance Board,

Note: Irish Life Assurance plc and Siuicre Éireann Teo are in the process of being privatised; such surprising inclusions as the Blood Transfusion Service Board or the National Concert Hall Co. qualify because their income does almost cover their outgoings.

[57] Information based on Sweeney, "Public Enterprise in Ireland: A Statistical Description and Analysis", 3–6.

1937. Import substitution continued to be important in the 1940s with the nationalisation of Irish Steel in 1947 and even after self-sufficiency had ceased to occupy a central position in development policy (Nitrigin Éireann and the British and Irish Steam Packet Company were set up as late as 1961 and 1965 respectively). A variant of it—security of supply of imports in times of international trouble—is still alive today. Not only did this idea provide the rationale for the foundation of Irish Shipping in 1941 but, in 1979, it was the stated justification for the establishment of the Irish National Petroleum Corporation (INPC) and the taking over by that company of the Whitegate refinery in 1982. . . .

The Industrial Credit Company [now Corporation] was created in 1933 to remedy a lack of underwriting facilities and to provide a channel of industrial finance. Ceimici Teoranta was established in 1938 to use surplus potatoes to produce industrial alcohol (no such surplus ever materialised and this operation has always had to rely on imported molasses), and Coras Iompair Éireann was set up in its present form in 1950 because the market mechanism was in danger of eliminating the railways."[58]

The most natural question to ask is why a particular commercial enterprise is not in the private sector rather than why it is not vested in some Minister for execution by the civil service. Often, the reason why the work is not done by private enterprise is that it is not profitable. Why then does the State undertake the burden? There are a number of reasons. In the first place, the activity may form part of the infrastructure for the entire economy, frequently in sectors in which, irrespective of profit, the amount of capital required was, at the time it was set up—though possibly this is no longer the case—too great for the Irish private sector.[59] Secondly, the objective may be to develop natural resources.[60] Thirdly, the state-sponsored body may originate as a rescue operation designed to maintain employment after the demise of some private company.[61] The postal and telecommunication services were, until 1983, vested in the Department of Posts and Telegraphs. They were transferred to state-sponsored bodies in the anticipation that this change would promote a more flexible response to the challenges of the technological and commercial world.[62] The broadcasting service was also vested in the Department of Posts

---

[58] Bristow, "State-Sponsored Bodies" (1982) 30 *Administration* 165, 166.
[59] *e.g.* ESB; Aer Lingus; British and Irish Steam Packet Co. Ltd.; Irish Shipping Ltd. (now defunct); An Post; Bord Telecom Éireann.
[60] *e.g.* Bord na Móna; C.S.E.T.; National Stud Co. Ltd.; Coillte Teo (set up by the Forestry Act 1988).
[61] *e.g.* Irish Life Assurance Co. Ltd.; Irish Steel Holdings Ltd.; Coras Iompair Éireann.
[62] See *Report of the Posts and Telegraph Review Group* 1978–1979 (Prl. 7883) ("the Dargan Report"), which concluded, at p. 2, that "the restrictions, practices, and precedents within which [the Department of Posts and Telegraphs] functions make it an unsuitable structure for management of a business such as telecommunications"; see also *Reorganisation of Postal and Telecommunication Services* (Prl. 8809), Chaps. II and III. A point of interest is that when An Bord Post and An Bord Telecom were constituted it was the objective of the Postal and Telecommunications Services Act 1983 to transfer all liabilities, arising out of postal and telephone services and extant on vesting day, to the new boards. However, the relevant provisions—ss.56 and 57 of the 1983 Act—refer only to proceedings and claims brought by and against "the Minister [for Posts

and Telegraphs until the establishment of Radio Éireann (which became Radio Telefis Éireann in 1966) by the Broadcasting Authority Act 1960. In this case, the major reason for the change was the need to give some measure of independence of the government of the day to such a politically-significant organ of communication. More recently the National Treasury Management Agency (covered at note 77 below) is being established to enable salaries to be offered to its staff which are comparable with those paid in the private sector.

Thus, as a conclusion, it may be suggested that commercial state bodies have been set up as ad hoc responses to various needs and not as a device to supplant private enterprise for ideological reasons. Indeed the Directive Principles of state policy contained in Article 45.3.1 of the Constitution enjoin the state "[to] favour and, where necessary, supplement private initiative in industry and commerce."

The importance of being state-sponsored[62a]

A number of state-sponsored bodies have been granted monopolies by their constituent statute. The objective is to enable them to provide a comprehensive range of service, even in rural areas where this is not profitable, free of the danger that some private business will "cream off" the profitable areas. The constitutionality of one such monopoly was upheld in *Attorney-General and Minister for Posts and Telegraphs* v. *Paperlink Ltd.*[63] The defendants, who operated a substantial courier service, were breaching a monopoly, granted to the Department of Posts, by the precursor of section 63 of the Postal and Telecommunications Services Act 1983.[64] They defended themselves, unsuccessfully, against the plaintiffs' claim for an injunction to restrain them, by attacking the monopoly. Their major argument was that the monopoly vio-

---

and Telegraphs]" leaving out of account the possibility that, as a matter of law, the appropriate person might be the State or the Minister for Finance (on which see pp. 709–713). This defect is rectified, with retrospective effect, by the Postal and Telecommunications Services (Amendment) Act 1984, ss.2–4.

[62a] For the Government's direct financial assistance to the state-sponsored sector, see pp. 129–131.

[63] [1984] I.L.R.M. 373. See also, *Nova Media Services Ltd.* v. *Minister for Posts and Telegraphs* [1984] I.L.R.M. 161, 167; *Ulster Transport Authority* v. *Brown* [1953] N.I. 70; McCormack, "Monopoly Power in the High Court" (1984) 6 D.U.L.J. (N.S.) 152. For the suggestion that RTE's former *de facto* monopoly broadcasting power was unconstitutional on the ground of infringement of the constitutional right to free speech, see Kelly, "The Constitutional Position of R.T.E." (1967) 15 *Administration* 205; Kelly (1978) *Irish Broadcasting Review* 5; McRedmond (1978) *Irish Broadcasting Review* 62. For more recent developments in connection with monopolies, see pp. 154–157.

[64] It is noteworthy that, most unusually for a legal provision, s.63(2) of the 1983 Act includes a policy justification for itself. It reads as follows: "The said privilege is granted to the company—

   (*a*) in view of its primary purpose of providing a national postal service and of the general duty imposed on it by *section 13*, and
   (*b*) in recognition of the fact that a privilege of this kind is appropriate having regard to the area and population of the State and the present state of development of postal technology, and
   (*c*) because a viable national postal system involves subsidisation of some loss-making services by profit-making services."

(See, to similar effect, for Bord Telecom, s.87 of the 1983 Act).

lated their right to earn a livelihood and carry on a business which is one of the unspecified rights bestowed by Article 40.3.1. Costello J. accepted this argument in principle but went on to hold that the monopoly could be justified as enhancing "the common good." He also accepted that he could utilise Article 45.3.1 for the purpose of determining what limitations were legitimate and in the interests of the common good. The judge, however, rejected the defendants' interpretation of this provision. It admittedly demonstrated a preference for private enterprise, albeit with an explicit recognition of the state's role *faute de mieux*; yet it did not follow from this very general guideline that there was an onus of proof upon the state to justify the existence of a state monopoly in legal proceedings. The defendants' second argument was that the postal monopoly did not promote "the common good," first because it was being operated inefficiently and, secondly—a related point—because it would be possible to gain the advantages claimed for the monopoly by a system which was less restrictive of the defendants' rights. To support these claims, the defendants wished to call economists and accountants to give evidence that, for instance, the Department was paying wages which were above the market rate; that the accounting system was a bad one; and that "overnight" money was not properly invested. Costello J. refused to hear such evidence because he held that to determine the legal arguments founded on it—in other words to determine whether a particular postal service serves the common good—was the prerogative of the legislature rather than a court. This attitude, rather surprisingly, harks back to an earlier era of constitutional jurisprudence.[65] Nevertheless, considering the multifarious controversial issues which such a quest would present for decision, it is understandable that the judge chose not to embark on such a quest.

A second type of accusation which surfaces periodically is that the Government is abusing its powers in order to give a state-sponsored body some unjustified immunity[66] or some unfair advantage over trade competitors as, for instance, when £13 million of taxes owed by Ostann Éireann in respect of Great Southern Hotels was waived by the Revenue Commissioners; or when the Government promoted the Air Transport Bill 1986, which, as originally drafted, would have inflicted penalties on four operators cutting their prices below Aer Lingus rates.[67]

Cross-subsidisation is a feature which may be an advantage or a disadvantage to a state body. For example, the ESB has been instructed to purchase natural gas from Bord Gáis Éireann below, and later above, the oil-related price and to purchase peat from Bord na Móna, though it might be possible

---

[65] Principally in the interpretation of Arts. 40.3.2 and 43, on which see Kelly, *The Irish Constitution* (Dublin, 1984), pp. 644–661.
[66] Such actions could possibly be contrary to Art. 92 of the Treaty of Rome as an unauthorised state aid.
[67] The offending provision was removed, following Dáil protests: see *Dáil Debates*, Vol. 352, cols. 853–910 (June 27, 1984). See also, Lemass, "The Role of the State-Sponsored Body in the Economy" (1958) 6 *Administration* 277, 278.

for it to purchase cheaper raw material abroad. And NET receives gas from BGE on favourable terms.[68] It has also been said that:

"discriminatory pricing may have reduced the surpluses of profitable State companies in order to reduce the published losses of other public enterprises. Indeed, such transfer pricing appears to be a rather common practice in the State company sector."[69]

In 1989 the Minister for Communications discouraged the sale, by a subsidiary of RTE, of Cablelink to a United States company (a potential competitor of Bord Telecom). Cablelink was sold, the following year to Bord Telecom, the Minister for Industry and Commerce having given his consent following a reference to the Fair Trade Commission under the Mergers, Take-overs and Monopolies (Control) Acts 1978 and 1987.

Situations which certainly represent a loss to a state body are those in which it is obliged to take some action on social, rather than economic, grounds. One example of this concerns the fact that the ESB has been instructed to charge urban and rural consumers at the same rates and thus to cause one group of electricity users to subsidise another group and, also, to distort the ESB's income. The protest of state-sponsored bodies at this type of behaviour by Ministers has taken the form of suggesting that, in the interests of presenting a fair picture of the agency's performance, allowance should be made in its accounts—or even a grant paid—to allow for the value of the social benefits.[70] At present, CIE's railway company and its urban transport subsidiary receive the only subsidy for social obligations.

Non-commercial state-sponsored bodies

Non-commercial bodies are even more difficult to schematise. On one classification, they can be grouped into four types. First, there are those promotional bodies which operate as a stimulus and back-up to private enterprise.[71] Secondly, there are research and promotional bodies.[72] Thirdly, there are bodies which regulate a particular profession or business, dealing with education and entry, maintaining proper standards and sanctions for breach of these standards. These bodies are at the fringe furthest away from the civil

[68] Compare comment of the Joint Committee on Commercial State-Sponsored Bodies *Report on Irish Shipping* (1985, Pl. 3091) on the fact that ESB had awarded only a half of the contract to carry coal from U.S. to Moneypoint to Irish Shipping, with the other half going to a Japanese company. The Joint Committee said that "appropriate Government guidelines should be developed which, on the one hand, would not impinge on the competitiveness of open market quotations but, on the other hand, would provide for due consideration of the Exchequer's involvement in both bodies."

[69] Massey, "Privatisation: Time for a Closer Look," (1987) 8 *Seirbhís Phoiblí*, 2. 2.

[70] NESC Report; Bristow *op. cit.* p. 180. See also, Postal and Telecommunications Services Act 1983, s.51 ("Loss-making services provided by direction of the Minister") and s.75 ("Recoupment of the postage, elections, referenda and messages to certain organs of state"). For history of these sections see Byrnes, "Profitability *vis-à-vis* the Public Interest" (1984) 31 *Administration* 372.

[71] *e.g.* Industrial Development Authority; Irish Export Board (Coras Trachtala); Bord Failte Éireann.

[72] *e.g.* Irish Science and Technology Agency, *Teagasc* (on which see p. 146, n. 58).

service and closest to the private sector (indeed, on some classifications are not regarded as state bodies at all) in that some of their funds are provided by the profession itself; and a minority of their controlling boards are usually appointed by the Minister, whilst the majority are elected by members of the profession. For instance, one member of the Dental Board is nominated by the Government and three by the Medical Council, whilst the remaining five are elected by dentists. This characteristic is present, though in a weaker form, outside the professions. Thus, the members of Bord na gCon, which regulates the greyhound racing industry, are all appointed by the Minister for Agriculture, but three out of the seven members must be members of the Standing Committee of the Irish Coursing Club.[73] A different type of shared control is represented by the Foyle Fisheries Commission where control is divided between the Governments of the Republic and the United Kingdom.[74] Fourthly, there is a large group, which provide miscellaneous services frequently in the health field.[75]

Because the non-commercial state body group spans such a diverse range, it follows that the reasons why the functions they perform have not been vested in Departments of State are various. In the case of the promotional bodies, the same sort of reasons apply as in the case of the commercial state bodies, namely that their duties require "exceptional initiative and innovation,"[76] qualities which are not always to be found in the civil service. Again, the civil service culture may be regarded as an inappropriate milieu for research. In regard to the third category (bodies regulating the professions etc.) it is plain too that, given the attitude of uncritical trust adopted by successive Governments towards the professions, their domestic arrangements will always be placed at arm's length from the Government. In addition, the state body form is useful in that it can accommodate the election or selection of some members of a state body's controlling agency by persons other than the Minister.

However, many of the non-commercial state bodies—including several in the miscellaneous category—are discharging functions which could equally well have been assigned to executive branches of Departments of State. Why, for instance, should the National Authority for Occupational Safety and Health, established under the Safety, Health, and Welfare at Work Act 1989 to enforce the relevant statutory provisions be a separate state body with independent powers, when the Air Navigation Services Office is part of the Department of Tourism and Transport and is staffed by civil servants? In an area where ad hocery abounds and fashions change, this type of anomaly is

---

[73] See Greyhound Industry Act 1958, s.9.

[74] See Foyle Fisheries Act 1952 and Foyle Fisheries (Northern Ireland) Act 1952.

[75] *e.g.* Medical Bureau of Road Safety, and the Agency for Personal Service Overseas. Following EEC entry, agricultural marketing bodies concerned with the disposal of agricultural products surplus to commercial requirements, which were formerly state-sponsored bodies, were converted into co-operatives; see, *e.g.* An Bord Bainne Co-operative Ltd. This point is authoritatively explained at *Kerry Co-Op Creameries* v. *An Bord Bainne* [1990] I.L.R.M. 664, 671.

[76] Lemass, "The Organisation behind the Economic Programme" (1961) 9 *Administration* 3, 4–6.

common. It led the Devlin Report to propose that while the commercial state bodies should be allowed to operate with the maximum permissible freedom, the activities of non-commercial bodies and executive branches of departments dealing with similar subject-matter should be pooled and reallocated to a common executive unit which would be subject to the control of a central Aireacht.[77]

3. Legal Form

A state-sponsored body must have a legal existence, which is independent not only of the Government but also of its members and staff. The reason for this is the need for it to be a continuing entity, endowed with the legal capacity to: own property, make contracts, employ servants, sue and be sued, etc. This distinct legal existence may be achieved in either of two ways. First, a state-sponsored body may be constituted as a statutory corporation (or board) by its own separate statute[78] which typically provides that:

> "(1) As soon as may be after the passing of this Act a board to be styled and known as [*e.g.*] the Electricity Supply Board . . . shall be established in accordance with this Act to fulfil the functions assigned to it by this Act.
> (2) The Board shall be a body corporate having perpetual succession and may sue and be sued under its said style and name."[79]

Alternatively, it may be a statutory company, *i.e.* an ordinary company (usually registered under the Companies Act 1963), in which almost all the shares are held by a Minister. (The exceptions are often confined to the shares, which, as a matter of general company law, are required to be held by one other person). In this case, the corporate nature of the body arises from the companies legislation and not from its own tailor-made statute, which

[77] Gaffney, "The Central Administration" (1982) 30 *Administration* 115, 122.
   Though note, as an example of the flexibility of the state-sponsored body form, the National Treasury Management Agency (constituted by the National Treasury Management Agency Act 1990) whose principal duty is to manage the borrowing of moneys for the Exchequer. It was accepted that the main reason for the Agency was that staff skilled and knowledgeable in the area of finance were not attracted by civil service salaries. Three of the Agency's features bear emphasis. First of all, the Government was empowered to delegate, by order, to the Agency "the functions of the Minister specified in the First Schedule and any other functions of the Minister in relation to the management of the national debt or the borrowing of moneys for the Exchequer that the Minister considers appropriate and are specified in the order" (s.5(1)). However the Agency's functions are to be performed "subject to the control and general superintendence of the Minister" (s.4(3)). Moreover whilst in every other state body, the actual legal persona is a board or authority with flesh and blood incumbents, in the case of the Agency, there is no such central directorate, merely a body corporate supervised by the Minister and served by the chief executive and his staff. In short, as one might expect, given its function, the Agency enjoys next to no autonomy from the Minister.
[78] Or statutory instrument: see Blood Transfusion Service Board (Establishment) Order (S.I. 1965 No. 78) made under Health (Corporate Bodies) Act 1961, s.3. A second parent statute authorising the establishment of state bodies by statutory instrument is the Local Government (Corporate Body) Staff Act 1971 which may be used to set up bodies which service all the local authorities in the State.
[79] Electricity Supply Act 1927, s.2.

only provides typically that "the Minister shall take steps to procure that a limited company conforming to the conditions laid down in the schedule to the Act shall be registered under the Companies Act."[80] Indeed as a matter of law, a special statute is unnecessary since, provided that any necessary expenditure is authorised by the Appropriation Act, a Minister, as a corporation sole, under the Ministers and Secretaries Act, is free, like any natural person, to set up a company either by drawing up a memorandum and articles of association or by taking over all the shares in an existing company. This occurred, for instance, in 1946 when the State purchased the Irish Steel Holdings Ltd., which was in the hands of the receiver. The reason why it is usual for the creation of a state-sponsored body, even as a company, to be preceded by an enabling statute is a political one, namely to afford the Oireachtas some opportunity to discuss its objectives and structure and the sources of its investment capital. Consonant with this, the enabling statute usually contains a broad description of the functions, duties and powers of the state body in addition to the more detailed statement which is contained in the articles of association.[81] These are necessarily stated broadly (*inter alia*, so as not to be enforceable in a court). For example:

"The principal objects of [An Post] shall be stated in its memorandum of association to be—
(*a*) to provide a national postal service within the State and between the State and places outside the State,
(*b*) to meet the industrial, commercial, social and household needs of the State for comprehensive and efficient postal services and, so far as the company considers reasonably practicable, to satisfy all reasonable demands for such services throughout the State,
(*c*) to provide services by which money may be remitted (whether by means of money orders, postal orders or otherwise) as the company thinks fit,
(*d*) to provide counter services for the company's own and Government business and, provided that they are compatible with those services and with the other principal objects set out in this subsection, for others as the company thinks fit, and
(*e*) to provide such consultancy, advisory, training and contract services inside and outside the State as the company thinks fit."[82]

The consequence of the *ultra vires* doctrine is that state bodies may only exercise their powers, for example, to contract, in order to achieve certain types of object.[83] The objects are those specified (in the case of statutory corporations) in their constituent statute or (in the case of statutory companies)

---

[80] Sugar Manufacturing Act 1933, s.4 constituting Suicre Éireann c.p.t.
[81] Deputy Cooney suggested that the Articles of Association should be laid before the Oireachtas: see, *Dáil Debates*, Vol. 256, col. 2215 (November 17, 1971).
[82] Postal and Telecommunications Services Act 1983, s.12(1). In some cases the lack of enforceability in a court is express, *e.g.* 1983 Act, ss.13(2), 15(2); Transport Act 1958, s.7(3).
[83] For some examples of the extension of these powers, see pp. 147–148.

in the memorandum of association, or objects reasonably incidental thereto. Contracts to achieve purposes outside these objects would be void.

The obvious question which arises is: on what criterion is it determined whether a state-sponsored body should be poured into the vessel of a statutory corporation rather than a statutory company? Here, as elsewhere in this area, there is no firm rule. As has been said of the variety of organisational forms for public bodies in Britain: "Like the flowers in spring, they have grown as variously and as profusely and with as little regard for conventional patterns."[84] So far as there is any guide, it is that more than two-thirds of commercial bodies are statutory companies, whereas non-commercial bodies are almost all cast as boards (or even "councils"). One significant reason for this is that it is easier to change the memorandum and articles of a company than it is to pass the necessary legislation to alter a board and such flexibility may be important to a commercial body. It was, for instance, decided to cast An Post and Bord Telecom Éireann as registered companies. The reasons given by the Post and Telegraphs Review Group Report was that a company may be altered more easily and can take quicker decisions.[85] Secondly, the division of a company's assets would have been facilitated by the existence of shares and, in the first decade of the state-sponsored sector's existence, the public was usually invited—though without success—to subscribe for shares in the companies (hence the original name—"semi-state bodies"). In line with this trend, Comhlucht Siuicre Éireann (which is now Siuicre Éireann c.p.t.) was set up in 1933 in the form of a (public) company because it was expected that it would be sold off sooner or later,[86] whereas bodies like ESB or Bord na Móna were never expected to go into private hands and so were created as statutory boards. Again, if a private company becomes the subject of a Government take-over then it will naturally remain as a company.

In principle, in the case of statutory companies, general company law applies, though it may not be well adapted to the artificial circumstances involved.[87] The position of a state-sponsored body which wears the guise of a statutory corporation is even more cloudy. It has been suggested:

" . . . that the general common law of corporations will govern [statutory corporations] except in so far as this is expressly or impliedly modified and that many of the judge-made principles of company law will be equally applicable to this more recent growth. But in applying common law principles recognition must be given to the consequences flowing from their dual role as commercial enterprises and public authorities. . . . [In

[84] Street, "Quasi-Governmental Bodies since 1918." *British Government since 1918* (ed., Campion) (London, 1948).

[85] *Report of (Dargan) Posts and Telegraphs Review Group 1978–79* (Prl. 7883), p. 63. (The earlier stages of the Bill were promoted by a Fianna Fail Government, the later stages by a Coalition Government). See *Dáil Debates*, Vol. 343, col. 1526 (June 15, 1983).

[86] Indeed some shares in it—though only amounting to a single figure percentage—are in private hands and, like the Industrial Credit Corporation, it has a stock exchange quotation though there has been no dealing for some time.

[87] Golding, "The Juristic Basis of the Irish State Enterprise" (1978) 13 Ir.Jur. (N.S.) 302, 310–312.

addition] the absence of shares and shareholders automatically renders large and important branches of company law totally inapplicable. . . . "[88]

This guideline means, *inter alia*, that the *ultra vires* principle, in its pristine common law form,[89] would apply to statutory corporations.

4. Control by the Minister[90]

In most cases, the Minister who controls and is ultimately responsible for a state-sponsored body is the Minister whose departmental duties fall closest to the work of the body.[91] Thus, for example, the Agricultural Credit Corporation is responsible to the Minister for Finance; Irish Steel Holdings Ltd. (Industry and Commerce); ESB (Energy); Aer Lingus Teo (Communications); National Rehabilitation Board Ltd. (Health).

Vested in the responsible Minister (or, very occasionally, in the Government) are six statutory powers which may be used to control a state-sponsored body. After these legal powers have been described, the factors which determine the use which the Minister actually makes of his formal ascendancy will be examined.

Appointment of board members/directors

In the case of statutory corporations, members of the board are usually selected by the responsible Minister but either with the consent of or, after consulting, the Minister for Finance. The chairman is chosen usually by the responsible Minister but occasionally by the board, subject to the Minister's approval. The term of office is typically three to five years, after which a director may be reappointed (or disappointed) for an unlimited number of further terms. The terms and conditions of employment are usually fixed by the responsible Minister with the consent of the Minister for Finance. There will usually be four to nine directors. However, in bodies to which the Worker Participation (State Enterprises) Acts 1977 and 1988[92] apply, the size of the board has been increased to accommodate the workers' directors. Large boards are also a feature of those non-commercial bodies which include the

---

[88] Gower, *Modern Company Law* (London, 1979), pp. 287–288.

[89] *I.e.* unaffected by Companies Act 1963, s.8; and European Communities (Companies) Regulations 1973 (S.I. 1973 No. 163).

[90] For a study of independence-control in relation to the Central Bank of Ireland (a somewhat untypical state body) in a comparative setting, by its former Governor, see Murray, "The Independence of Central Banks: An Irish Perspective" (1982) 30 *Administration* 33.

[91] Note, however, that the Minister for Finance was responsible for Siuicre Éireann c.p.t. before responsibility was transferred to the Minister for Agriculture and Food by the Sugar Manufacture (Transfer of Departmental Administration and Ministerial Functions) Order (S.I. 1980 No. 55); and also had some limited statutory functions (*e.g.* appointment of directors, approval of borrowing) in relation to the now defunct Ceimici Teo and Irish Shipping.

[92] On worker participation, see further, pp. 134–136.

(usually elected) representatives of different interests, *e.g.* the Nursing Board or the Medical Council (29 and 25-member boards, respectively).

The position is similar for statutory companies save that their boards are usually smaller and that, in accordance with general company law, board members retire by rotation, two at each Annual General Meeting.

It often happens that a Minister will appoint one or two of his departmental civil servants as board members, a practice which has been justified as aiding smooth communication and attacked as subverting the independence of state-sponsored bodies by in effect imposing a Trojan horse upon the state body. Apart from five years in the 1950s, the Secretary of the Department of Finance has always been a "service director" of the Central Bank of Ireland.

Dismissal

With a statutory company, the responsible Minister possesses the power of dismissal of directors, *qua* shareholder. In the case of a statutory corporation the constituent statute vests the power of dismissal of board members in the responsible Minister, in some cases subject to the consent of the Minister for Finance. Occasionally, the power is vested in the Government. However, dismissal is an extreme step and, whatever the statutory provision may say, this is a decision which would only be taken following anxious deliberation by the entire Government.[93] Frequently, the power of removal is conditioned on such grounds as ill-health, stated misbehaviour or failure to perform duties effectively.[94] Where a state-sponsored body is a company, removal is usually not dealt with in the body's own statute, but in the articles of association which list specific grounds on which the shareholder, *i.e.* the Minister, may dismiss a director.

A *cause célébre* in this field occurred in 1972 and involved the members of the RTE Authority (for whom the appointing and dismissing agency is now, and was then, the Government). The episode arose out of the Minister for Posts and Telegraph's use of his power under the Broadcasting Authority Act 1960, section 31 to issue an order which forbade RTE from broadcasting any matter calculated to promote the aims of "any organisation which engages in, promotes, encourages or advocates the attaining of any political objectives by violent means." The Authority protested against the vagueness of this wording and a month after the order had been made RTE broadcast an interview[95] with the IRA Chief of Staff. The Government gave the Authority the option of dismissing the interviewer or of all members of the Authority being removed from office and the Authority took the second option. The sequel came in the Broadcasting Authority (Amendment) Act 1976 which, first, narrowed the

[93] But for the resignation of Dr. Joseph Brennan from the Central Bank in 1953, see Murray, *op. cit.* 41–42; see also Lemass, "The Role of the State-Sponsored Body in the Economy" (1958) 6 *Administration* 277, 289.
[94] *e.g.* Gas Act 1976, Sched. 1, Art. 4(7); Transport Act 1950, s.7.
[95] This interview also led to *Re Kevin O'Kelly* (1974) 108 I.L.T.R. 97.

scope of section 31[96] and, secondly, provided some additional protection for the members of the Authority. Thenceforth, a member could only be removed "by the Government from office, for stated reasons if, and only if, resolutions are passed by both Houses of the Oireachtas calling for his removal."[97]

A second instance occurred, in 1983, when the Minister for the Gaeltacht dismissed three members of Udarás na Gaeltachta.[98]

Dissolution

It is uncertain whether, absent legislation, a Minister has the authority to dissolve a state-sponsored body. The constituent statute typically states, in the case of a statutory corporation, "the Electricity Supply Board . . . shall be established" or, in the case of a statutory company, "the Minister shall take steps to procure that a limited company . . . shall be registered . . . ."[99] These provisions might suggest that having set up the state body, the Minister could not then turn round and dissolve it. However, as against this, section 9(1)(a) the Ministers and Secretaries Act 1924, states that: "[i]t shall be lawful for the [Government] . . . to dissolve any . . . statutory body" which category is defined widely enough to embrace a state-sponsored body.[1]

In any case, the common practice is that when state bodies are dissolved (as part of a reorganisation, for none has so far been dissolved as a matter of discipline or because of a policy disagreement), the change is effected by Act of the Oireachtas. The main reason for this is to afford the Houses of the Oireachtas an opportunity of debating the change.

Finance[2]

The control of finance affords the Government a range of convenient levers over most spheres of activity. In the first place, in the case of non-commercial bodies, funds are delivered in the form of grants-in-aid which can only be released with the permission of the responsible Minister and the Minister for Finance.

With commercial bodies, the position is more complicated. Investment capital may be raised by borrowing (either from the Exchequer or private sources) or, in the case of companies, by the issue of shares to a Minister, almost always to the Minister for Finance. Among the key provisions in the

---

[96] On which, see pp. 535–539.
[97] Broadcasting Authority (Amendment) Act 1976, s.2.
[98] In 1987, the ESB were disputing (before the Circuit Court) their liability to pay rates. The (Fianna Fail) Government publicly threatened to remove the board unless (as happened) the rates were paid. The obligation to pay rates is now made clear by the Electricity (Supply) (Amendment) Act 1988, ss.8–10. See also, Postal and Telecommunications Services Act 1983, s.54.
[99] For the references, see pp. 124–125, nts. 79 and 80.
[1] See Central Bank Act 1942, s.5(b) excluding the Bank from the sweep of s.9 of the 1924 Act.
[2] For the law on central Government finance, see generally, Gwynn Morgan, *op.cit.* pp. 112–132.

constituent statute of a state-sponsored body are those which fix the maximum amounts which it is empowered to raise, by borrowing or issuing shares. These limits take the form of legislation and thus their alteration provides an opportunity for the Oireachtas to review the policy and performance of the body involved. It is customary to fix the limits at such a level that if the organisation is expanding fairly rapidly, amending legislation is necessary every four to six years. As well as the Oireachtas' authorisation, the consents of the responsible Ministers and the Minister for Finance are necessary where shares are issued or money is borrowed from the Exchequer.

Where loss on current expenditure is involved or pre-existing debts have to be written off, constituent statutes or amendments may provide for the making of a subsidy by the Minister for Finance.

Where funds are borrowed from a private source, (in some cases, by issuing stock) the Minister for Finance, after consultation with the responsible Minister, may guarantee repayment and such a guarantee constitutes a charge on the central fund. Until 1984,[3] these guarantees were given very readily. However, the Minister for Finance has now announced that such guarantees will only be given for good cause and that the State will not undertake responsibility for loans which are not guaranteed. The fact that this announcement was made contemporaneously with the Government's unprecedented decision to allow Irish Shipping to go into liquidation drove home the message that it was a significant element in the Government's change to a more businesslike policy in relation to the commercial state-sponsored sector. Its significance is clear from the fact that in 1987, continuing Government guarantees totalled £2.7 billion (against a total capital base for the entire sector of £5.5 billion) and covered almost all long-term and some short-term loans, from banks and other private creditors. These guarantees mean that it is the taxpayer rather than the creditor who bears the risk of the debt not being repaid and, accordingly, the interest rate is lower than would otherwise be the case.[4]

The expectation, which is sometimes expressed in the parent statute,[5] is that taking account of the need to make an adequate return on capital, a commercial body should at least break even, taking one year with another. In fact, in recent years, only two of the bodies (Irish Life and the Industrial Credit Corporation) have regularly paid any dividend. However, in the past two or three years other statutory companies, including Aer Lingus and Bord Telecom have begun to pay dividends. In addition, for most years since natu-

---

[3] The occasion for the change of policy (announced by the Minister for Finance in a speech made to the Institute of Bankers on November 16, 1984) was the Irish Shipping liquidation. Irish Shipping Ltd. had liabilities estimated at £114 million of which only some were state guaranteed and the (substantial) remainder went unpaid: see *Business and Finance*, November 22 and 29, 1984. See, further, *Dáil Debates*, Vol. 353, cols. 2077–2158, December 3, 1984.
[4] Joint Oireachtas Committee on State-Sponsored Bodies: *Second Report: Irish Shipping Ltd.* (1985, Pl. 3091), para. 35.
[5] *e.g.* Electricity (Supply) Act 1927, s.21(2); Gas Act 1976, s.10; *cf.* Transport Act 1958, s.7(2).

ral gas came on stream in 1981, Bord Gais has remitted profits to the Exchequer.

Information

All state bodies are under duties—stated, variously, in the parent statute or articles of association—to give their Minister important information as to, for instance, profit and loss account, capital account, revenue account, etc. Frequently, the Minister has power to settle the form of annual reports and accounts and also to be given whatever specific information he requests. There is often a statutory obligation, failing which there is a practice, that the annual report and accounts should then be laid before each House of the Oireachtas. In fact, it often happened in the past that these annual reports and accounts were not published until two or more years after the year to which they relate. However, in 1986 the Government established a rule of practice (which has been followed) that, save in the case of an authorised derogation, reports should be published within six months of the year to which they relate.

Shareholding

In the case of state bodies which take the legal form of companies, there is, theoretically, a further source of authority. This arises from the fact that the Minister effectively owns all the shares. Accordingly, he has the same powers to pass whatever resolution, special resolution or extraordinary resolution he wishes. Obviously, a full-blooded use of this power would subvert the whole *raison d'être* of a state body and, by a convention described in the next section, it has never been used.

5. Balance of Authority between Minister and State-Sponsored Body

Whilst many of these powers are seldom used, their very existence shapes the relationship between the state body and the responsible Minister. This naturally means that a state body is often acutely sensitive to the wishes of the responsible Minister, even on a point in regard to which the Minister has no specific legal authority, a phenomenon which has been felicitously described in the United States as "raised-eyebrow regulation." Take, as an Irish example, the intervention by the Minister for Industry and Commerce in the CIE bus strike in 1963. The Minister had written a letter encouraging CIE to reach a settlement and the letter used the phrases "strongly request" and "direct" pretty well interchangeably. Questioned in the Dáil on the source of his power to intervene, the Minister said:

> "I have no statutory power to issue directions to CIE in relation to trade disputes between the company and its employees. In view of the functions assigned to me under the Ministers and Secretaries Act, I do not need to have special powers to enable me to make a strong request to the company. . . . When I issued a request to the company in the first place, the

company knew well that I was making an attempt to solve the strike and they agreed to accept my direction in the matter."[6]

It often suits a Minister to intervene without appearing to do so, as in another CIE labour dispute, at a time when Todd Andrews was the (full-time) chairman of CIE. Mr. Andrews wrote in his autobiography:

"Finally the Taoiseach, Sean Lemass, decided that the lock-out should be lifted and the bus services restored. Jack Lynch phoned me to say that 'the boss' (*i.e.* Lemass) wanted me to take the men back. I told him I would refuse to do so unless I got a directive either from the Taoiseach or from himself as Minister for Industry and Commerce to end the lock-out and that the terms of the directive be published. . . .

Later [Mr. Lynch] phoned to say that he had read over the directive to 'the Boss' who agreed with the wording but did not think it was necessary to publish it. I replied that unless it was published the lock-out would not be lifted by me. He phoned me back again in due course to say that publication had been arranged."[7]

The division of jurisdiction is usually taken to be that, in principle, "day-to-day" decisions are for the state body itself; whereas strategic and policy issues have to be resolved, if possible, by agreement between the board and the Minister, but with the Minister having the last word. Thus, for instance, whilst capital investment by ESB would involve the Minister for Energy, decisions as to staff allocation or electricity load management would not.[8]

It is a striking feature of the constituent statutes of state-sponsored bodies that, with a few exceptions, they do not deal directly with the overall relationship between the Minister and the body and, at least up to the 1970s, the responsible Minister was granted no formal power to give directions of any kind. However, the practice has now changed to the extent of granting such power explicitly. Typical of recent statutes is the Postal and Telecommunications Services Act 1983. According to section 110(1) of the 1983 Act:

"The Minister [for Communications] may issue directions in writing to either company [*sc.* An Post or Bord Telecom Éireann] requiring the company:

(*a*) to comply with policy decisions of a general kind made by the Government concerning the development of the postal or telecommunications services . . .

(*b*) to do (or refrain from doing) anything which he may specify from time to time as necessary in the national interest. . . .

(*c*) to perform such work or provide such work or provide or maintain

---

[6] *Dáil Debates*, Vol. 202, col. 34 (April 23, 1963). The Minister's reference to the Ministers and Secretaries Act might be a reference to his general job description powers under the Ministers and Secretaries Act 1924, s.1(vii) on which see pp. 58–59.

[7] Andrews, *Man of No Property* (Cork, 1982), p. 257. Note also the episode in which the Minister for Agriculture "instructed" RTE not to carry a report of a National Farmers Association's criticism of him, see: *Dáil Debates*, Vol. 227, cols. 1661–1664 (April 13, 1967).

[8] See *Dáil Debates*, Vol. 311, col. 868 (February 8, 1979).

such services for a state authority as may be specified in the direction. . . ."[9]

This statutory division of responsibilities of course, accords with the conventional division explained in the previous paragraph. The Minister threatened to issue a direction, under the provision just quoted, in 1991, as part of his campaign to pressurise An Post into modifying its plan to close 500 sub-post offices.[10]

Four glosses

To obtain some idea of how the Minister/state-sponsored body relationship operates in practice, one needs to add at least four glosses or exceptions to the policy/operational demarcation just outlined.

(1) Government's power of control is much greater over a non-commercial, than a commercial, body. The reasons are, first, that the commercial bodies are already subject to the discipline of the market-place (of which there is no equivalent for the non-commercial bodies which are usually little more than executive agencies) and, secondly, that the Government control over the provision of grants is even more significant where this is a state-sponsored body's only source of funds. As has been said earlier, a non-commercial body often amount to little more than an agency of the responsible department.

(2) A Minister must ensure—said Sean Lemass—that a state-sponsored body is "kept in line . . . with the overall development plans of the Government."[11] This means that the Government will often use its convenient hold over a large sector of industry and commerce to impose its line on economic, social or other issues. In several cases, Ministers have intervened to require a decision to be taken in order to maintain employment, even though this is not in line with commercial considerations. Take, for instance, the following Dáil question:

[9] As variations on the theme, consider: the Housing Finance Agency Act 1981, s.6 ("The Minister [for the Environment] may . . . with the consent of the Minister for Finance, give such general directions as to policy . . . " Such directions must be laid before each House and published in *Iris Oifigiuil*); Dublin Transport Authority Act 1986, s.12 ("The Minister may with the consent of any other Minister involved give to the Authority such general directions in writing concerning the traffic management objectives of the Authority or its administration as he considers appropriate." The 1986 Act has now been repealed.); National Lottery Act 1986, s.29 ("Whenever the Minister [for Finance] considers it necessary to do so in the public interest, he may give a direction in writing . . . relating to the National Lottery"). See also, Gas Act 1976, s.11; Central Bank Act 1971, s.43 and the *Programme for Economic and Social Progress* (1990, Pl. 7829), para. 89.1.
[10] See *Irish Times* February 21, 1991.
[11] Lemass, "The Role of the State-Sponsored Body in the Economy" (1958) 6 *Administration* 278, 288. Note the episode in which the Taoiseach informed the chairman of RTE that in the opinion of the Government "the best interests of the nation would not be served by sending an RTE team to Vietnam": *Dáil Debates*, Vol. 227, cols. 1661–1664 (April 13, 1967) and also the remark of Mr. Pat Dineen, Chief Executive of BGE that "BGE, purely from a business point of view, was most reluctant to take over the company [Dublin Gas]. We took it over because the Government wanted us to." (*Business and Finance*, 1987); and the report that Aer Lingus had successfully resisted Government pressure to sell certain of its hotels: *The Irish Times*, July 10, 1982, p. 1.

"Mr. Hegarty asked the Minister for Tourism and Transport [who was then responsible for British and Irish Steampacket Co. Ltd.] in view of the likelihood of redundancies at Verolme Cork Dockyard, will he consider giving the green light to have the new B. and I. roll-on roll-off car ferry built at the yard immediately."[12]

There is no concession in this question—nor was there in the answer—to the notion that B. & I. is a separate entity from what was then the Department of Tourism and Transport, responsible for taking its own decisions along commercial lines and it is normal political practice that there should have been no such concession.

However, by the mid-1980s, the Government was grappling desperately with an economic crisis, a major element in which was massive expenditure—both on capital investment and the financing of a current deficit—by state-sponsored bodies. With the total reaction of the Government to this crisis, we shall deal later.[13] For the moment, it is only necessary to notice how faithfully the change in Government was reflected in employment by the state bodies: during the period 1980–1987, 15 of the major commercial state companies shed an average of 18 per cent. of their workforce, which thus fell from 7.2 per cent. to 6.3 per cent. of the total number of those employed in Ireland.

Another substantial example of the Government using its convenient hold over the state-sponsored sector to impose a particular (social) policy concerns worker participation, which is established by the Worker Participation (State Enterprises) Acts 1977 and 1988. The 1977 Act provided for the election[14] of worker-director board members in the case of the seven largest commercial enterprises: Electricity Supply Board; Coras Iompair Éireann, Siuicre Éireann c.p.t. (now on the point of privatisation); Nitrigin Éireann Teo; Aer Lingus; British and Irish Steam Packet Co. Ltd.; and Bord na Móna. Bord Telecom Éireann and An Post were added to the ranks by the Postal and Telecommunications Act 1983. However, the relevant provisions of the 1983 Act were repealed and replaced by the 1988 Act which thus brought these two state bodies within the same legislative scheme as the original seven. The 1988 Act also bestowed worker directors/members upon a further two state bodies: Aer Rianta and the National Rehabilitation Board. The advent of worker-directors/members means that the total numbers may have to be increased. Accordingly, in order to accommodate the extra numbers, the Minister for Labour is empowered, after consultation with the Minister for Finance and the Minister responsible for the particular body, to make an order prescribing the number of directors or board members on the state bodies to which

---

[12] *Dáil Debates*, Vol. 307, cols. 2429–2430 (June 29, 1978).

[13] See pp. 144–151.

[14] Worker Participation (State Enterprises) (General Regulations) (S.I. 1988 No. 170) specify the general rules for elections under the 1977 and 1988 Acts. See also, The Worker Participation (State Enterprises) (Postal Voting) Regulations (S.I. 1988 No. 171) and the Worker Participation (State Enterprises) (Preliminary Poll) Regulations (S.I. 1988 No. 172).

worker-directors/members may be appointed.[15] Save in one case,[16] the worker directors/members must amount to a third of the entire number.[17] The Minister for Labour's powers have been utilised[18] to provide that, with three exceptions, each of the state bodies listed earlier has 12 directors/members of whom four represent the work force. The exceptions are An Post (15 members with five representing the employees); National Rehabilitation Board (15: three) and Aer Rianta. It is also significant that the Minister for Labour, again following consultation with the Minister for Finance and the responsible Minister, may by order add fresh bodies to, or remove bodies from, the scope of the Workers' Participation Acts[19] (though this has not, so far, been done). Each of the orders mentioned in this paragraph is subject to the affirmative resolution of each House.[20] The 1988 Act also introduced for the first time, in Irish law, the concept of worker-participation by way of sub-board arrangements. These arrangements are required to cater for[21]:

"(*a*) the exchange of views and clear and reliable information on a regular basis between the specified body and such persons as the agreement may provide concerning such affairs of the specified body as may be provided in the agreement;

(*b*) the giving by the specified body of relevant information in good time to such persons as the agreement may provide concerning such decisions of the specified body as may be so provided and which are liable to have a significant effect on the interests of employees of the specified body; and

(*c*) the dissemination of the information and views referred to in *paragraphs (a)* and *(b)* of this subsection to the employees of the specified body, except in the circumstances, if any, provided for in the agreement,

and the arrangements shall contain such other provisions as may be agreed by the parties thereto."

This innovation applies potentially to all of the 39 state bodies listed in the schedule to the 1988 Act. This schedule includes all the commercial enterprises and the larger of the other state bodies. However, these arrangements do not apply automatically but will only apply if they are invoked. This may be done in either of two ways: first, by application from either a trade union (or trade unions) representing a majority of employees, secondly, provided that at least 15 per cent. of the employees request it, by the holding of a poll

---

[15] 1977 Act, s.23(1).
[16] The exception is the National Rehabilitation Board for which the legislation specifies a maximum of one third of all board members and a minimum of two members.
[17] 1977 Act, s.23 as amended by 1988 Act, s.24 and the Second schedule to the 1977 Act. (which is inserted by 1988 Act, s.24(1)).
[18] Worker Participation (State Enterprises) Orders (S.I. 1978 No. 186; S.I. 1980 No. 100; S.I. 1988 No. 149; S.I. 1988 No. 337).
[19] 1977 Act, s.4(4).
[20] 1988 Act, s.24(2)(*a*), (*b*).
[21] *Ibid.* s.6(2).

R.T.C. LIBRARY
LETTERKENNY

of the entire work force on the establishment of the arrangements for participation.

What is of particular significance here is the fact that it is only the state section of commercial enterprise which has been caught by any form of a development which, for numerous good and bad reasons, management and shareholders have generally viewed without exaggerated enthusiasm. Some statements have been made about extending this change to the private sector[22]; but legislation to implement it has never, so far, appeared to be a practical possibility.

(3) Closely related to the impact which a state body can make on the Government's general policies is the question of party-political advantage. This is the very factor which the state-sponsored body form of organisation was designed to exclude. But, in a highly-politicised environment, this is a counsel of perfection and, as Sean Lemass remarked in 1958,[23] the main danger with state bodies is that politicians might endanger the system by interfering too much in their activities. The average voter may know little about the constitutional position of a state body but he knows that it is in "the public domain" and accordingly (he may think) under the Government's control. To a considerable extent, the state-sponsored sector's deeds, whether good or bad, will tend to rub off on the Government and so here is another motive for intervention, in some cases even in day-to-day activities. Thus, state bodies have sometimes delayed impending price rises where these rises would have coincided with a general election. To take a further example, given by Dr. Sweeney[24]:

"In the 1988 Budget, the Minister of Finance, Mr. McSharry, persuaded the ESB to repay £31.4m debt outstanding instead of a planned £2m in interest and capital, and he also imposed a 5% VAT charge on electricity, stating that there 'will be no increase in consumer prices' (1988 Budget Statement). In the 1990 Budget, the Minister for Finance, Mr. Reynolds,

---

[22] See the commentary on the 1988 Act in the Irish Current Law Statutes Annotated (Tony Kerr) in which it is noted that the then (Labour Party) Minister for Labour insisted that the 1977 Act was the beginning of a trend which would eventually engulf the private sector. Again, when the *Advisory Committee on Worker Participation* (1986, Prl. 4339) was eventually appointed, its members were unanimous that:
> "increased employee participation was desirable but were not unanimous as to how impetus could be given to the development of participation in the private sector. The majority, including the Chairman, recommended the introduction of enabling legislation in the private sector for all organisations employing more than one hundred people (see paras. 172–188). Those members representing the Federated Union of Employers preferred a purely voluntary approach."

Kerr, *op. cit.* In fact, nothing has yet come of the Committee's recommendation. It may be mentioned that, at the relevant time, the first four of the five largest employers in the country were state bodies and that of the enterprises employing over 2,000 employees, eight were state bodies and the remaining 10 were private companies.

[23] Lemass, *op. cit.* 291. In "The Organisation behind the Economic Programme" (p. 7) Mr. Lemass also predicted that whenever a SSB becomes controversial, the parent Minister will exercise closer control over the body as criticisms of it reflect upon the Minister.

[24] *Public Enterprise in Ireland*: paper given to Statistical and Social Enquiry Society of Ireland on February 15, 1990, p. 30.

136

increased the rate of VAT to 10% saying that 'I am arranging that the additional costs be absorbed by the ESB.' (They will be £18m in a full year). He also imposed 10% VAT on Telecom Éireann services stating that 'I am confident that this can be implemented without increased cost to Telecom users' (Cost of £11m in a full year) (Budget Speech 1990). He was supported by the Minister for Energy, Mr. Molloy, on the issue of the ESB increase, who, when questioned on whether the board would obey the 'suggestion' said 'the Government has made its intentions clear. The ESB is a semi-state organisation and the new policy has been defined' (*Irish Times*, 1990)."

(4) It emerges, from what has been said so far, that there is a potential source of conflict of interests between the Government's role *qua* owner of a state body and its roles *qua* Government or *qua* political partisan. There is a further possible source of conflict where the state body is not a monopoly[25] and a Minister has a function as a licensing authority, so that he may be required to choose between the state body and its competitors.

Two recent episodes involving RTE illustrate rather surprisingly the potential for a conflict of interest arising from the four capacities (just identified) in which the Government may relate to a state body. The background to each was the removal, by the Radio and Television Act 1988[26] of RTE's effective monopoly.

It was relevant in regard to the first episode that section 16(1) of the 1988 Act provides that: "the Minister may at the request of the Commission and after consultation with RTE" require the latter to provide facilities needed in connection with the independent sound broadcasting services. And the independent contractor must make such payments to RTE "as the Minister, after consultation with RTE and the Commission, directs." In 1989, there was an absence of agreement between one of the independent contractors and RTE as to the amount, the Minister having fixed a figure which RTE regarded as unfairly low.[27] In the end, a rather higher figure was agreed upon, but not before RTE had threatened the Minister with an application for judicial review proceedings, the first such threat ever to have been issued, at any rate in public.

The occasion for the second episode[28] was that even after the admission of competition, almost all of the proceeds of the television licence fee (apart from the cost of collection) continued to go to RTE. This represented, according to the 1989 figures, about £44m out of RTE's total income of about £110m. This subvention meant, said the Government, that RTE's competitors were at a substantial disadvantage. Thus it was necessary, to adopt the metaphor used by the proponents of change, to level the playing field. RTE's response was that the extra finance was necessary because of the high cost of

[25] On monopolies, see further, pp. 154–157.
[26] See pp. 248–251.
[27] See *The Irish Times,* March 20–30, 1989.
[28] See *The Irish Times,* June 29, 1990; *Dáil Debates,* Vol. 400, col. 1215–1219 (June 28, 1990).

public service broadcasting. The motivation imputed to the Government by the Opposition was that, in its news and current affairs programmes, RTE had examined the Government's performance in a thorough and impartial fashion.

As first announced, the Government proposed a package of three measures to improve the position of the independent broadcasters. The first of these was the Minister for Communication's proposal that Radio 2 FM, which was then a pop station, should become more of a cultural service. The striking point, about this proposal, for present purposes is that there was never any suggestion that it should be implemented by way of legislation: it was to stand or fall on its inherent merits and the Minister's power of persuasion. The second suggestion did appear in the Broadcasting Bill 1990, as originally drafted, though it was dropped at Second Stage: it was that up to 25 per cent. (*i.e.* £11m at 1989 figures) of the T.V. licence fee revenue should be withheld from RTE and apportioned among the commercial broadcasters in amounts to be determined by the Independent Radio and Television Commission. The first two proposals were dropped apparently because of their unpopularity with the public. The third measure, however, became law. Thitherto, the position had been that the total time for broadcasting advertisements and the maximum period to be given to advertisements in any hour were fixed by the RTE Authority subject to the approval of the Minister.[29] The effect of the change was that first, the total daily broadcasting time was not to exceed 7.5 per cent. of total daily transmission time and the maximum hourly time was not to exceed five minutes (as compared with 10 per cent. and six months per hour, respectively, before the 1990 Act). Secondly, the Authority was required not to make any more money in receipts from advertising, sponsorship or other forms of commercial promotion than its receipts from broadcasting licence fees (on pain of a corresponding reduction in its income from licence fees).[30] In contrast, in 1989, its income from licensing fees was £45 million and, from advertising, £55 million, with a further £10 million from miscellaneous sources, such as publications.

Special statutory controls over RTE

Broadly speaking, state-sponsored bodies are subject to the same law as other persons. In some cases there are modifications and of these, RTE affords the most striking examples. The best known of these controls is the Broadcasting Authority Act 1960, section 31 (as amended).[31] There is another analogous but broader provision which prohibits the authority from broadcasting "anything which may reasonably be regarded as being likely to promote, or incite to, crime or as tending to undermine the authority of the

---

[29] Broadcasting Authority Act 1960, s.20(3) as inserted by the Broadcasting Authority (Amendment) Act 1976, s.14.
[30] Broadcasting Authority Act, 1990, s.3.
[31] For this provision, see pp. 535–539.

State."[32] On a broader front, the Authority is under a duty to broadcast news and current affairs "in an objective and impartial manner" without giving its own views (save on broadcasting policy) and to ensure that its programmes do not "unreasonably encroach on the privacy of an individual."[33] The Authority is under positive, though necessarily imprecise, duties: to uphold "rightful liberty of expression"; to pay regard to the values and traditions of foreign states, particularly EEC Member States; and

> "to be responsive to the interests and concerns of the whole community, be mindful of the need for understanding and peace within the whole island of Ireland, ensure that the programmes reflect the varied elements which make up the culture of the people of the whole island of Ireland, and have special regard for the elements which distinguish that culture and in particular for the Irish language."[34]

The length of advertising permitted has already been explained. Advertisements on certain subjects—those directed towards any religious or political end or related to any industrial dispute—must not be accepted.[35] Finally, it should be noted that the Minister retains the power of fixing the amount of the broadcasting licence fee, RTE's major source of income.[36]

There is a Broadcasting Complaints Commission to consider complaints against RTE, such as that any of the obligations outlined in the previous paragraph have been broken, that the Authority's advertising code has been violated or that "an assertion was made in a broadcast of inaccurate facts or information in relation to an individual which constituted an attack on the dignity, honour or reputation of that individual."[37] To assist the Commission, the Authority must record and retain for at least 180 days a copy of every broadcast. The Commission has no power to award damages or enforce any other sanction save that it may require the Authority to publish its decision on a complaint.[38] (This is done through the *RTE Guide*). Furthermore, if the Commission's findings favour the complainant, then, unless the Commission considers it inappropriate, RTE must broadcast the findings at a time and in a manner corresponding to those of the offending broadcast.[39]

In addition the RTE Authority may, with the consent of the Minister for Communications, appoint advisory committees.[40] This power has been exer-

---

[32] Broadcasting Authority (Amendment) Act 1976, s.3. The relationship of this provision with s.3 (as amended) has not been judicially explored. In 1984, when a Noraid spokesman was banned from the airwaves by the Minister for Communications because Noraid was not on the list of proscribed organisations authorised by s.31, the Minister relied upon his power under s.3 of the 1976 Act.

[33] 1976 Act, s.3. The duty of impartiality does not affect the Authority's right to transmit "political party broadcasts" (a phrase which is not defined): 1960 Act, s.18(2).

[34] 1976 Act, s.13.

[35] 1960 Act, s.20. See generally, Hall and McGovern, "Regulation of the Media: Irish and European Community Dimensions" (1986) 8 D.U.L.J. 1 (N.S.).

[36] 1976 Act, ss.1, 8; 1960 Act, ss.1(b), 22; Wireless Telegraphy Act 1926, s.5.

[37] 1976 Act, s.4 Broadcasting Act 1990, s.8.

[38] 1976 Act, s.4. See also Hall and McGovern, *loc. cit.*

[39] 1990 Act, s.8.

[40] 1976 Act, s.5.

cised to appoint the Radio 2 Advisory Committee, which has now lapsed and the Council for Radio na Gaeltachta, which exerts a significant influence upon Radio na Gaeltachta.

6. Control by the Oireachtas

One of the points which emerges from a survey of the Government's controls over a state body is that the occasions on which the most effective controls are exercisable are usually points at which the Oireachtas is not involved. The Oireachtas is, of course, involved in the legislation designing a state body and any amending legislation which may be necessary, for instance to authorise an increase in share capital. But this operates spasmodically and not necessarily at the times of greatest significance not, for instance: when a new board is being appointed; when a decision whether to withdraw or to go into a certain area of activity is taken; or when a guarantee is given by the Minister for Finance to a private lender. By contrast, in respect of administration going on within a Department of State is concerned, these lacunae do not exist because the Government is responsible, to the Dáil, for all administrative acts even if these do not require a change of law. This means that such activity may be debated and Ministers may be questioned in the Dáil about them. In contrast, where any question is raised as to the activity of a state-sponsored body, it is likely to be met by the imprecise rule which excludes responsibility for day-to-day matters. And where a state body is operating in the commercial world there is obviously an additional reason for confidentiality.

Nevertheless, the performance of state-sponsored bodies is sometimes discussed in the Oireachtas. Where money is given (whether in exchange for shares or simply as a grant) or lent to commercial state bodies, this is usually done on the authority of the constituent Act or an amendment thereof, rather than during the Estimates or by way of an Appropriation Act. However, in spite of this, during the Estimates debate, deputies are permitted to discuss the performance of a state-sponsored body which comes under the wing of the Department whose vote is under examination and a Minister does sometimes take the opportunity to give an account of the past record and prospects of a state body which comes within his jurisdiction. However, the reality is, first, that many estimates go undebated for lack of time and, secondly, even where there is a debate, discussion ranges over the entire field of a Department's activities. Thus it is inappropriate as a vehicle for the kind of detailed, technical debate necessary to a state-sponsored body because such a debate would have had to be at a broad level. Again, although annual reports from each body have to be laid before each House, they have seldom, if ever, been made the occasion for a "take note" debate. The conclusion must be that debate in the Oireachtas is spasmodic and often superficial.

Joint Oireachtas committee

It is true that it was precisely to achieve substantial exclusion of the Oireachtas that the state body form was invented. Nevertheless it came to be felt, especially in the light of the recent huge expenditure of public funds by the state body sector and of greater control over this sector, by the Government, that this process had gone too far. To meet such criticisms the Joint Oireachtas Committee on State-Sponsored Bodies was established. It was anticipated, correctly, that the technique of a small select committee would create the kind of non-partisan, technical milieu which is appropriate for discussion of this area. Following suggestions down the years that such a committee be established, it was eventually constituted in 1976.[41] Its jurisdiction is confined to all the commercial bodies, including Udaras na Gaeltachta but excluding the National Lottery Co. and the Housing Finance Agency Ltd. The reasons given[42] for the exclusion of the non-commercial bodies were, first, that with virtually all the commercial bodies, profit and loss provides an objective yardstick for evaluating their success—which is lacking in the case of the non-commercial sector; and secondly, that the performance of non-commercial bodies could not be examined in isolation from the policy, including allocation of resources, of their parent department. It is unfortunate that the Committee's reports[43] have been of variable quality.

Comptroller and Auditor General

The question of whether the Comptroller and Auditor General should audit state-sponsored bodies is as old as state bodies themselves. When the ESB was being set up in 1926 the appointment of auditors from the private sector rather than the CAG caused divisions in Dáil Éireann. In the early 1960s a policy decision was taken that, in the case of well-established commercial state bodies, the Ministers concerned would not oppose any request from them to engage private sector auditors. Four bodies took the oppor-

---

[41] See *Dáil Debates*, Vol. 293, col. 1403 (November 10, 1976). It has been reconstituted in subsequent Houses (apart from the 1981–1982 Houses). For the present (1990) Committee, see Dáil Debates, Vol. 394, col. 2069–2071 (December 5, 1989).

The Joint Committee on Public Expenditure whose remit included both the Departments of State and the non-commercial state-sponsored bodies associated with each of them was not reconstituted after 1987.

[42] *Dáil Debates*, Vol. 319, cols. 169–199, (March 19, 1980) (unsuccessful motion to extend the Committee's bailiwick to the non-commercial sector).

[43] The Committee on State-Sponsored Bodies has issued reports on the following bodies: National Stud (1979, Prl. 7869); B. & I. (1979, Prl. 8063); Min Fheir (1979, Prl. 8242); CIE/OIE (1979, Prl. 8438); Ceimici Teo (1979, Prl. 8475); Aer Rianta (1979, Prl. 8582); Arramara Teo. (1980, Prl. 8686); Bord na Móna (1980, Prl. 8808); VHI (1980, Prl. 8899); ACC (1980, Prl. 8944); ICC (1980, Prl. 9261); NBA (1980, Prl. 9480); CSET (1980, Prl. 9555); Aer Lingus/Aer Linte (1980, Prl. 9584); Irish Shipping Ltd. (1981, Prl. 9663); NET (1981, Prl. 9752); Foir Teo (1981, Prl. 9944); RTE (1981, Prl. 9945); Ostann Iompair Éireann (1984, Pl. 2); Irish Shipping Ltd. (1985, Pl. 3091); Bord Gáis Éireann (1985, Pl. 3638); Udarás na Gaeltachta (1986, Pl. 3747). Analysis of Financial Position of Commercial State-Sponsored Bodies (1986, Pl. 4487); Electricity Supply Board (1987, Pl. 4487); Bord Telecom Éireann (1987, Pl. 4718); Irish Life Assurance plc. (1988, Pl 5451); An Post (1988, Pl. 5731); B & I Line (1988, Pl. 5779); Irish Steel Limited (1988, Pl. 5924); Aer Lingus plc and Aer Linte Éireann plc (1989, Pl. 6554); Report on certain allegations levelled at the former Chairman of the Committee (1989, Pl. 6607); Irish National Stud Company Limited (1990, Pl. 7135); Irish National Petroleum Corporation Limited (1990, Pl. 7381); An Post – An Post National Lottery Company (1990, Pl.7382).

tunity to move to private sector auditors—Irish Life, the Air Companies (Aer Lingus and Aer Linte), Irish Shipping and Ceimici Teo. and subsequently Irish Steel and NET also changed auditors. Although there appears to be no coherent policy on this question, a general pattern with some exceptions has emerged over the years—the allocation of the audit of non-commercial bodies to the CAG and that of the commercial bodies to private sector auditors.[44]

The Committee of Public Accounts *Special Report on the Future Role of the Comptroller and Auditor General and the Committee of Public Accounts* devotes a section to the question of whether the CAG should audit the state bodies. Extracts from this section, with its recurrent theme of the accountability of state bodies, are given in an Appendix to this chapter.

6. Board and Chief Executive

In theory, the rights, duties and identity of a state-sponsored body are concentrated in the board. The board is the body corporate, the legal personality of the body: everyone else is merely a creature, whether an officer or servant, of the board. In practice, the position is radically different. In practice, the Devlin Report offered the following list of the usual duties discharged by a board:

"(a) Implement government policy; (b) Appoint top management; (c) exercise financial control; (d) stimulate development; (e) maintain liaison with the minister; (f) supervise personnel policy; (g) measure management performance."[45]

Dr. Barrington is less expansive: according to him, the principal task of the board is to integrate two major influences, first, the overall policy of the responsible Minister; secondly, the stream of advice from management based on operational experience. Both these contributions are "discussed and weighed by board members of broad general experience from many walks of life. The development of policy, therefore, is a broadly participatory affair in which the board plays a central role."[46]

However even these accounts would appear to exaggerate the usual influence of the board. The central facts are that there are no statutory quali-

---

[44] The information in this para. comes from the Committee of Public Accounts *Special Report on the future role of the CAG and the PAC* (1988, Pl. 5645), para. 35. The exceptions to the general pattern described in the text were that the constituent statutes required RTE's (Broadcasting Authority Act 1960, s.25) and ESB's (Electricity (Supply) Act 1927, s.7) accounts to be audited by an Auditor appointed by the responsible Minister (in practice, the CAG). In the case of RTE, this requirement was removed by the Broadcasting Act 1990, s.7. This provision, however, also states that, whoever does act as auditor must submit to the Minister for Communications a certified statement as to the total revenue derived by the RTE Authority from advertising and sponsorship.

[45] Devlin Report, para. 5.2.21.

[46] Barrington, *The Irish Administrative System* (Dublin, 1980), p. 59. See also Kenny, "Boards of Directors in Ireland" (1978) 26 *Administration* 107.

fications for membership (other than not being a deputy or senator) and members are often chosen as a reward for their political loyalties. The duties of membership are usually allowed to take up only a few hours at once-monthly meetings. The remeration for an ordinary member remains £800 with chairmen usually being paid in the range £1,000–1,200 and civil servant members not being paid.[47] By contrast, a state-sponsored body's senior officials will be full-time experts who are in frequent, informal contact with the civil servants in the responsible Department. The board's effective authority is, thus (in an analagous way to that of local councillors) curtailed from above by the Minister and Department as seen in Part 4 but also from below, by the officials. In reality, the average board member's contribution is likely to be small and may amount merely to confirming proposals brought before it by the management. This poses a classic danger, namely that there may be a divorce between responsibility and effective power. Something of the sort materialised in the events leading up to the liquidation of Irish Shipping in 1984. One significant factor in the company's losses arose from imprudent long-term chartering agreements entered into by the company. Another source of loss was the formation (with a private shipping line) of a joint pool of shipping known as Celtic Bulk Carriers. In each case the board was not properly informed and, thus, was not properly in control.[48]

In an area where anomalies are almost the norm, it would be surprising if there were no exceptions to this general pattern. And, sure enough, we find, for instance, that in the case of the ESB (the earliest of the commercial state bodies) section 2(6) of the Electricity (Supply) Act 1927 originally stated that the chairman of the Board was to be full time. However this provision was revoked by section 6 of the Electricity (Supply) (Amendment) Act 1988, as a result of which the terms and conditions of the chairman of the ESB as with other chairmen, are left to the responsible Minister acting with the consent of the Minister of Finance and, at present, the chairman remains full time.[49] Again, certain Ministers, or possibly Ministers making appointments in regard to certain particularly significant state bodies (*e.g.* the Central Bank), will recognise that too much is at stake for the appointments to be made of anyone other than diligent, well-qualified persons. And in other cases, individual appointees who do not, at first sight appear appropriate, turn in, for whatever reasons of patriotism or pride, first rate performances. Again certain boards have a collective reputation for vigour and intelligence. However, the system as it is usually operated, is not likely to produce such results and the old gibe—that appointments are the Irish equivalent of the Honours system—remains substantially true. The natural outcome is that the effective decision-making is done by the chief executive and his senior management and/or the Minister and his civil servants. This state of affairs, is of course, not very different from that which often prevails in the private sector.

[47] For the prerequisites, see *Magill*, September 1980.
[48] Pl. 3091, paras. 17, 23.
[49] In addition, in the 1980s, the chairman of CIE's terms and conditions provided that he was retained for four days per week.

Oddly enough, the constituent statutes scarcely ever mention the chief executive (save in the context of his salary, a point discussed in Part 2) and never provide a description of his functions. Nevertheless—and regardless of whether the chief executive has or has not been made a member of the board, as is increasingly coming to be the case—there is no doubt of his position as effectively the "managing director."[50]

As a matter of law, it follows from the board's general power in appointing staff that (with a very few exceptions[51]) it is the board which selects and appoints, the chief executive. It is, indeed, their principal function. As a matter of practice, too, the decision is usually left to the board.

7. Contemporary Government Policy towards the State-Sponsored Sector

Until the public-debt crisis of the mid-1980s little attention, official or scholarly, had been devoted to these agencies. Plainly, they were constitutional novelties; yet the implications which their peculiar status (neither Government nor private enterprise nor good red herring) had, both for the performance which could be expected from them and for the state policy to be adopted towards them, had been neglected. However by the mid-1980s, the air was heavy with the sound of lame ducks coming home to roost. The economic performance of the state-sponsored sector in the 1980s can be illustrated by the following facts. First, the 15 major, non-financial commercial bodies made an aggregate net loss (after depreciation and the payment of interest) during the period 1980–1983. Secondly, even during the post-1983 period, the interest payments to the Exchequer as a percentage of the total government investment (by way of equity, government loans and capital grants) was very low by comparison with commercial standards. The figures for net assets and the net profits/net assets ratio for some recent years are as follows: 1980: £1.5 bn, − 5.4 per cent.; 1983: £2.5 bn, − 1.5 per cent.; 1984: £3.8 bn, + 0.8 per cent.; 1987: £4.4 bn, + 0.7 per cent.[52]

[50] The title used is usually "chief executive," save that certain state bodies (*e.g.* ICC and Siuicre Éireann c.p.t.) have a "managing director."
[51] Though in the case of RTE, the Minister for Communication's consent is necessary for an appointment to the position of Director General. (Broadcasting Authority Act 1960, s.13(4)) an arrangement which caused tension, over an appointment, in 1985. For similar provisions, see Turf Development Act 1946, s.8(3); Combat Poverty Agency Act 1986, s.12.
[52] See P. Sweeney, "Public Enterprise in Ireland" 13 and 14. The figures for 1984 and 1987 include Bord Telecom and An Post in addition to the original 15 state bodies. The figures include the current grant to CIE but exclude ESB's amortisation charge. The 15 state bodies referred to in the text are as follows: Aer Lingus; Aer Rianta; Arramara; Bord Gas Éireann; Bord na Móna; B & T; Ceimici Teo (in liquidation, 1984); CIE, Irish Sugar; ESB; INPC; Irish Shipping (in Liquidation, 1984); Irish Steel; NET; RTE. The financial, commercial state bodies are not included because of difficulties in the definition of profits: Agricultural Credit Corporation; Foir Teo; Industrial Credit Corporation; Irish Life; Voluntary Health Insurance Co. Coillte Teo which is concerned with the corporatisation of the forestry service was not established until 1989.

One of the causes underlying these significant improvements was "a new emphasis on financial performance, judged by the criterion of profit, with social objectives, particularly employment, being relegated."[53] In addition, as might have been expected, a certain amount of new thinking in relation to the state-sponsored sector was done in the late 1980s and continues. In the first place, a number of independent scholarly or semi-official studies of the question were published, by economists and public administrators,[54] and were broadly critical of the intellectual neglect which had gone before. Next, the incoming Fianna Fail Government of 1987–1989 (continued, as a Coalition with the Progressive Democrats, 1989–date) responded with the publication of the *Programme for National Recovery* which made a point of stating that:

> "The state-sponsored bodies will be actively encouraged and facilitated to develop and diversify their economic employment-creating activities. Where new legislation is required to achieve this, it will be brought forward."[55]

In the present short survey of the contemporary debate on the role of state sponsored bodies, matters under consideration may be listed under the following heads.

(i) Rationalisation

Since 1987 as a response to the need for economy in the public sector—there has been fairly extensive rationalisation for example, Bord Na gCapall and Foir Teo have been terminated by the Board Na gCapall (Dissolution) Act 1991 and the Foir Teo (Dissolution) Act, 1990 and their functions transferred to the Minister for Agriculture and food and the Industrial Credit Corporation, respectively.[56] There has also been extensive reorganisation to rationalise the ad hocery of the years. Originally, for instance, state activity in encouraging unemployment was divided among three agencies: An Co (the Industrial Training Authority) a board constructed to deal with the training and employment of adults; the Youth Employment Agency, a company constituted to do similar work for young persons; and the National Manpower Service, a unit of the Department of Labour which dealt with placement and occupational guidance. The Labour Services Act 1987 dissolves An Co and wound up the YEA and the NMS and then created FAS,[57] to take over their functions. However the administration

---

[53] Sweeney, *op. cit.* 33.
[54] See recent monographs listed at n. 1.
[55] Pl. 5213, p. 17. See, to similar effect, *Programme for Economic and Social Progress* (Pl. 7829, 1990), para. 83–93.
[56] See also the Exported Live Stock (Insurance) Act 1984 (dissolving the Exported Live Stock (Insurance) Board); and the Wool Marketing Act 1984 (dissolving An Chomairle).
[57] FAS is an acronym for Foras Aiseanna Saothaoir (Institute for Labour Facilities). However the word, *Fas*, also means growth.

of unemployment benefits still remains vested in the Department of Social Welfare.[58]

However where there is specific reason to do so, the Government has been prepared to promote legislation constituting new state bodies. Thus, for example, to give greater thrust to two areas of anticipated economic growth— forestry and horticulture—Coillte Teoranta (Forestry Act 1988) and An Bord Glas (Bord Glas Act 1990) were created. Again it was thought appropriate, presumably to distance the enterprise from the Government of the day, to establish the National Lottery Co. (by the National Lottery Act, 1986) to run the Lottery, though note that the allocation of proceeds from the Lottery is left to the Government.

In addition, structural re-organisation has been provided by the Transport (Reorganisation of Coras Iompair Éireann) Act, 1986 by which CIE was required to form three companies—Iarnród Éireann (Irish Rail), Bus Éireann (Irish Buses); and Bus Atha Cliath (Dublin Buses)—as units by which the different segments of the enterprise, formerly run by CIE directly, are to be run.

(ii) Greater discrimination and flexibility

According to the National Economic and Social Council,[59] some of the problems of the state bodies stemmed from the fact that the Government and responsible Departments had tended to treat them too much as a homogeneous group, notwithstanding the fact that they were set up to serve diverse purposes and to operate in different milieux.

Since 1987, the Government has shown itself to be more sophisticated and discriminating in appraising the potential of state bodies and more innovative in the courses which it has allowed them to pursue. Thus, it has been more prepared to give the economically stronger bodies their head.

Consider, for example, the legislation presaged in the *Programme for National Recovery*. The first items in what may be a longer legislation programme are the Electricity Supply (Amendment) Act 1988 and the Turf Development Act 1990, which effect a number of changes. To take the 1990 Act first: when Bord na Móna was first set up in 1946, its functions were restricted essentially to the extraction, production, marketing and sale of turf and turf products and all ancillary requirements necessary for this purpose.

---

[58] Similarly as a result of the Agricultural (Research, Training and Advice) Act, 1988, ACOT, AFT and BNCOT were wound up and their functions united in Teagasc—the Agricultural and Development Authority. In addition, by the Science and Technology Act 1987, Eolas (the National Board for Science and Technology) and the Institute for Industrial Research and Standards were replaced by the Irish Science and Technology Agency. Again in 1987, most of the functions of An Foras Forbartha Teo (National Institute for Physical Planning) which was a town planning ministerial advisory body, were subsumed within the Department of the Environment.

The National Development Corporation Act 1986 established the National Development Corporation as a venture capital agency to take equity stakes in industry. However by 1990 when the IDA was expected to dispose of about £190 million (compared with £7 million in the case of Nadcorp) and to do so increasingly by way of taking equity stakes, there were rumours about the winding-up of Nadcorp and its amalgamation with the IDA. See *The Irish Times* editorial of June 26, 1990.

[59] NESC, *Enterprise in the Public Sector* (Dublin, Stationery Office, no date), p. 16.

The 1990 Act extends the Board's powers into other areas in which it has, or is likely to acquire, expertise. Specifically, it is empowered to "execute engineering and building works of any kind whatsoever and research of any kind whatsoever which the Board in its discretion considers desirable."[60] Furthermore, the Board is for the first time given power to use cutaway bog for any activity unrelated to peat production for which there may be a commercial opportunity, such as tourism. However, the exercise of this power is subject to the Board giving the right of first refusal, for a 12-month period, to Coillte Teoranta (the Forestry Company).[61]

The *Programme* also states that it envisages, within the subsequent five years, a threefold expansion of turnover in overseas consultancies by "State Agencies"[62] and accordingly the Act gives Bord na Móna power to "provide . . . consultancy services and advisory services . . . and the training of persons."[63]

In the case of the ESB, the Electricity (Supply) Act 1927 confined its activities fairly narrowly to the generation, production and supply of electricity. Accordingly when it began to diversify it was considered advisable to provide, in the Electricity (Supply) (Amendment) Act 1982 that "the Board may engage in aquaculture, that is to say the culture of any species of fish . . . ," thereby empowering the ESB to set up Salmara, a commercial fish-farming subsidiary. In the 1988 Act, powers are given to the ESB to distribute and sell coal or any other substance or produce specified by the Minister for Energy by regulations; to manufacture and sell coal-based products, and to distribute and sell any by-product of the generation of electricity.[64]

To facilitate and enhance their activities, each board is empowered to promote, form or take part in or acquire companies.[65] As another aspect of increased flexibility, the *Programme* envisages state agencies entering joint ventures, and power to do this is granted to each state body.[66]

The Acts also increase the boards' range by making it clear that most of the board's functions may be performed abroad as well as within Ireland.[67] However, the requirement of ministerial consent in regard to the exercise of many functions, for example the formation of companies[68] or the commercial development of cutaway bogs,[69] is retained.

---

[60] s.7 of the 1990 Act creating an amended s.20(1)(*k*) in the Turf Development Act 1946.
[61] s.7(*j*): as of 1988, the acreage depleted of peat was 3,770 hectares of which, however, 2,824 hectares had been transferred to the Forestry Service: *Dáil Debates*, Vol. 384, col. 2477, debate on Turf Development Bill 1988 (1 hectare = 2.4 acres.)
[62] Pl. 5213, p. 25.
[63] s.7(*k*).
[64] 1988 Act, ss.3–5.
[65] 1988 Act, s.2; 1989 Act, s.2.
[66] 1990 Act, s.8(a) creating an amended s.20(1)(*h*) of the 1988 Act, s.2. Power is also given to Bord na Móna by s.3, to form sub-boards and to delegate some of its functions to them.
[67] 1988 Act, ss.3–5, 1990 Act, s.4.
[68] 1988 Act, s.2(b); 1990 Act, s.2.
[69] 1990 Act, s.8(b).

Three tentative comments may be made on these two measures. In the first place, it is questionable in regard to certain of the changes whether, legally speaking, legislation was required. For example, given that all state bodies are corporate bodies, it seems clear that, as a consequence, they would have had anyway the capacity to form companies. The question of joint ventures is perhaps less clear. It may be thought that the *delegatus non potest delegare* doctrine[70] would prevent the performance of a board's statutory functions by a distinct entity. It seems, however, unlikely that this rather archaic doctrine would be extended into the commercial sphere. There may have perhaps been an element of *ex abundante cautela* on the part of the Government's legal adviser.

Secondly, consider the changes effected in the boards' substantive functions, for example Bord na Móna's enhanced capacity in engineering and building. Additional legal authority would certainly appear necessary for such functions in that they are not incidental to the functions bestowed by the 1946 Act.

Finally, it is surprising, given that the Government has set out in the *Programme* various general policies, for example as to joint ventures and consultancies—in regard to all "State Agencies"—that the legislation is still grounded on a piecemeal basis. (The precedent offered by the Health (Corporate Bodies) Act 1961 and Local Authority (Corporate Bodies) Act 1971 has not been followed in this area.)[71] Would it not make more sense if the desired powers were given generally to state bodies, whose identity would be determined by ministerial order? Legally speaking, it certainly would. The reason, presumably, why this obvious course has not been adopted is that the Government is being true to the convention by which the Houses of the Oireachtas are afforded an opportunity to discuss the progress and needs of each state body, separately.

(iii) Control

The problem of control is, of course, peculiarly difficult in regard to state-sponsored bodies. Where there is too much control, initiative and flexibility are low and the function may as well have been vested in a Department of State in the first place. Indeed the result may be actually worse because the state body may feel itself so inhibited as not to react to commercial opportunities or difficulties, whilst the Department of State may lack the knowledge and resources to do what is not really its job.[72] It is of interest that in

---

[70] On which, see pp. 396–400.

[71] See p. 124, n. 78.

[72] However, the Joint Oireachtas Committee on State-sponsored Bodies concluded that in spite of its extensive powers of surveillance, the Department of Communications was not sufficiently aware of the crisis into which Irish Shipping was sailing during the period 1979–1984: see Second Report: Irish Shipping Ltd. (1985, Pl. 3091), paras. 1, 23 and 24. It has been suggested (see Sweeney, *op. cit.* p. 31) that the collapse could have been prevented had the monitoring been adequate.

1979, Padraic O'Halpin, a former chief executive of a state body interviewed 20 chief executives and reported that "several found the absence of a definite policy on joint ventures with either foreign or home enterprises a barrier to potential development."[72a] The opposite extreme is that there is too little control by the responsible Minister. This is particulary undesirable where one is dealing with a commercial state body, enjoying a partial or complete monopoly. In this case, by definition there is no market-place to discipline the body and, if management is slack, it may start to free-wheel at the cost of the tax-payer and/or its customers. Considering the state body's position *vis-à-vis* its customers, it has to be said that the arrangements for state bodies include little in the way of consumer protection. It is a remarkable fact that only two state bodies—An Post and Bord Telecom—have ever been subject to surveillance by a user's council[73] and that even these provisions were dropped when these bodies were brought within the Ombudsman's remit.

A few bodies, it is true, are subject to such a control as the following[74]:

> "It shall be the general duty of the telecommunications company to conduct the company's affairs so as to ensure that:
> (a) charges for services are kept at the minimum rates consistent with meeting approved financial targets, and
> (b) revenues of the company are not less than sufficient to:
>> (i) meet all charges properly chargeable to revenue account (including depreciation of assets and property allocation to general reserve) taking one year with another,
>> (ii) generate a reasonable proportion of capital needs, and
>> (iii) remunerate capital and repay borrowings.
> (2) Nothing in this section shall be construed as imposing on the company, either directly or indirectly, any form of duty or liability enforceable by proceedings before any court to which it would not otherwise be subject."

But this is a rather negative control: there are no signs that it has had the desired consequence.

It has been suggested that a number of proxies for market forces should be used. Among the possibilities are[75]:

> "i. *Borrowing limits.* The total amount that a company can borrow during a year should be agreed in consultation with the relevant government department. This would replace the present practice of giving approval to borrowing as the need arises.

[72a] "The Chief Executive in State Enterprise" (Dublin: Irish Productivity Centre), p. 4 quoted in Zimmerman (1987) 8 *Seirbhís Phoiblí* 2, 2, 31.
[73] RTE has a Broadcasting Complaints Commission (see p. 139) but this has a different function in that its role is much wider than simply protecting the interests of the consumer, *e.g.* it must ensure impartial presentation of the material broadcast television programmes rather than protecting the viewer against, for instance, too much football on the screen.
[74] 1983 Act, s.14. See also, 1983 Act, s.13 (An Post); Electricity Supply Act 1976, s.21(2).
[75] B. Walsh, "Commercial State-Sponsored Bodies" *The Irish Banking Review* 27, 3 Summer 1987.

    ii. *Investment criteria.* Proposed investments by CSSBs should be eva-
luated using a standard project appraisal methodology. Only projects
that can meet the target rate of return equal to the cost of the funds to
the Exchequer plus five per cent should be approved.

    iii. *Pricing policy.* The goal should be to bring the prices of the goods and
services provided by CSSBs into line with the prices prevailing in other
countries, especially in the EEC."

(iv) Co-ordination

A related problem concerns the need to ensure good communication and a
concerted approach as between the Government and commercial state-
sponsored bodies and also as between different bodies. As part of a survey
based on interviews with 38 chairmen, chief executives and officials of state
bodies, civil servants and informed observers, Professor Zimmerman
writes[76]:

> "A parallel exists between the development of public organizations in the
> Irish Republic and in individual American states in the latter part of the
> 19th century and the early part of the 20th century. With growing urbaniza-
> tion and industrialization, a popular demand arose in the United States for
> state governments to assume responsibility for new functions. In respond-
> ing to the demand, the state legislature created a new agency to administer
> each new function. The unplanned proliferation of agencies created in time
> serious organizational problems: lack of co-ordination, overlapping of
> responsibility, and rivalry among agencies were common and wasted public
> resources."

Professor Zimmerman then goes on to appraise a number of suggested
devices for improving co-ordination: information consultation and information exchange; interagency committees and agreements; a consultative
body; the National Development Corporation; the Department of the Taoiseach and "the partnership approach."

In fact, apart from individual, informal contacts, the only arrangements
which presently exist are: the Consultative Group of Chief Executives of
State Organisations, composed of chief executives of mainly commercial
bodies, which is an informal group serving as a forum for the discussion of
common problems; a similar grouping in the form of the Irish section of
Centre European de l'Entreprise Publique; and, by far the most important, the
Department of Finance. For within the Public Expenditure Division (one of
the three divisions into which the Department of Finance is divided) there are
a number of Principals/Assistant Principals, each being responsible both for a
particular departmental vote and for the state-sponsored bodies which are

---

[76] "Irish State-Sponsored Bodies: The Fractionalization of Authority and Responsibility," (1986)
7 *Seirbhís Phoiblí*, 2, 27, 32.

associated with that Department. Thus there exists, in Finance, a fair concentration of expertise about the state-sponsored sector, more especially so since many of the contacts between a body and the Government involve finance and since the Minister for Finance's consent (as well as that of the responsible Minister) is often required for the activities of a body. The Department of Finance then is the *de facto* central office for the state-sponsored sector. The Department also shapes overall Government policy and certain specific policies in this area.

(v) Privatisation

Privatisation holds a high place on the agenda of public debate not least because it is part of the Zeitgeist against state involvement which is running so strongly in North America and Western and Eastern Europe. A part of the motivation is that, as it was put by an Irish economist in 1987[77]:

"Technology, capital markets, the supply of entrepreneurship and attitudes towards state activity have changed dramatically since most CSSBs were established in Ireland. In the 1930s it was plausible to argue that, if the state had not undertaken radio broadcasting or sugar production or the provision of industrial credit, worthwhile employment and profit opportunities would have been missed."

The writer goes on to note that, in the Irish context, the most compelling argument in favour of privatisation is that the proceeds would mean a substantial reduction in public indebtedness.[78] This line of argument is reinforced where one is considering a state body which is likely to require heavy capital investment (*e.g.* Aer Lingus—a new fleet).

The present Irish Government's approach to privatisation has been cautious because of its unpopularity with the public sector trade unions. It is worth noting that when An Post and Bord Telecom were created, at a time when privatisation was in the air wafting across the Irish Sea, care was taken, because of union pressure, to include in the parent statute a provision to the effect that only the then Minister for Posts and Telegraphs could own shares.[79]

As of late 1990, the main legislative[80] initiatives were the Insurance Act 1990 and the Sugar Act 1991 and the following account is based on these two measures.

True to the idea that the ex-state bodies will be treated in law simply as ordinary large companies, they will be governed largely by company law. It bears noting that this is, itself, an idea which, in view of the particular nature and public perception, of some state bodies and the dominant market which

---

[77] Walsh, *op. cit.* 34.
[78] A guestimate of the proceeds of sale of the entire enterprise (in late 1990) is as follows: ESB—£500m; Irish Life—£400m; Telecom Éireann—£800m; Bord Gais—£300m; Aer Lingus—£100m.
[79] Postal and Telecommunications Act 1983, s.21. See also, *Dáil Debates*: Vol. 337, cols. 1573–1577, July 7, 1982; *Senate Debates*, Vol. 101, cols. 498 and 560 (July 5, 1983).
[80] Notice also the merger of NET's operating company with a Northern Ireland Irish Fertiliser subsidiary of ICI and the sale of the Joint Hospital Services Board and of Irish Ferries.

they often enjoy, contains a number of policy assumptions.[81] It does, however, reflect the Anglo-Irish Law's fundamental antipathy towards the establishment of specialist legal régimes to reflect varied social and/or economic circumstances; indeed, as noted earlier, the law governing the present state bodies, which are cast in the form of companies, is largely private law. Accordingly the role of public law in regard to privatisation is limited.

The changes in relation to both the Irish Life Assurance plc and Siuicre Éireann, c.p.t. employ the normal company law technique of establishing a holding company to own, respectively, a new restructured Insurance company and the existing Sugar Company. The responsible Minister is then empowered to exchange his shares in the existing company for shares in the (new) holding company and also to acquire further shares in the holding company. (These are powers, for which, strictly speaking, legislation is probably unnecessary since each Minister is anyway a corporation sole.[82]) There will also, of course, be features which are peculiar to each individual state body, which is being privatised and of these Irish Life affords a good example. This state body was in fact a particularly appropriate candidate for privatisation because, as a result of its origin in a rescue operation of existing privately owned companies and its profitability, it had long been permitted an unusually high degree of autonomy.[83] In addition to the State's natural desire to capitalise on its assets, the need for a major change in the Company was put on two grounds. The first of these was that certain foreign States, for example about half of the states in the United States would not permit companies owned by foreign Governments to take over native companies and this was impeding the Company's development. The other factor did not necessarily require privatisation. It was the fact that at an earlier stage in the history of the evolution of life assurance business, the Company has been virtually mutualised by virtue of the inclusion of a provision in the Company's Articles of Association that with-profits policy-holders were to have a right to 98 per cent. of the total profits. This naturally represented a substantial disincentive to any private share-holding in the Company (even though, latterly, the Company's business had evolved away from with-profits policies and towards unit-linked policies). The Articles of Association of the successor company to Irish Life allow for a more realistic dividend to be paid to share holders and thus the Company will be able to expand. However, in order to safeguard the vested rights of the with-profits policy holders, the approval of the courts in Ireland and United Kingdom was necessary and has been granted, for the transfer of business from Irish Life to the new company.

From the perspective of public law, the major issue in regard to privatisation remains basically the same as for state bodies, namely should the State

---

[81] See, generally, C. Graham and T. Prosser, "Privatising Nationalised Industries: Constitutional Issues and Legal Techniques," (1987) *Modern Law Review* 16–51; C. Graham and T. Prosser, *Golden Shares: Industrial Policy by Stealth?* (1988) *Public Law* 413.

[82] See pp. 57–60.

[83] On the rationales for the privatisation of Irish Life see *Dáil Debates*, Vol. 401, cols. 10–71; 238–255; 287–359; July 4–5, 1990; Joint Oireachtas Committee Report (1988, Pl. 5451).

exercise any control over the former state bodies and, if so, according to what criteria and through what technique? In the first place, in regard to the Insurance Company, the Minister for Finance intends to retain 34 per cent. of the shares, which is sufficient to veto any special resolution and also, under the Stock Exchange Rules, to attract certain rights in the event of a predatory take-over. In the case of the Sugar Company, the figure for shares retained is 45 per cent. The reasons for this comparatively high figure are, first, stock-exchange liquidity (availability of sufficient funds on the market) and, secondly, industrial relations grounds (to reassure unions and other interested parties that the State will be retaining a substantial shareholding in the company and therefore a strong influence on its operations for some time to come). In addition, the Minister's influence will be enhanced by the fact that in each case, the responsible Minister intends to make provision, in the Memoranda and Articles of Association,[84] for a so-called "Golden Share." Such a share has been explained, in the British context, as follows[85]:

> "The basis, in general, for a golden share scheme is that the share capital of the company will contain one special rights redeemable preference share of £1 held by the government or their nominee. Certain matters are then specified as being deemed to be a variation of the rights of the Special Share and therefore can only be effective with the consent in writing of the Special Shareholder . . . The most common of these matters are: any amendments to the article relating to the Special Share, the article defining the restrictions on shareholding and the definitions of various terms. Also usually included are a prohibition on a voluntary winding up and on the creation of new shares, other than ordinary equity shares."

The Minister for Finance has indicated that in the case of the Insurance Company, the golden share will be so drafted that during the five year period following the flotation of the company the Minister will be able to prevent individuals or groups gaining more than a 15 per cent. holding. Such special arrangements are not of themselves contrary to the anti-discrimination provision (Article 7) and the pro-competition provisions (Articles 85–94) of the Treaty of Rome. However, the Minister went further and promised to use his powers to preserve the "Irish ethos" and "local base" of Irish Life by vetoing hostile (and foreign) take-over bids.[86] Now the anti-discrimination and pro-competition provisions, just mentioned, are very general in scope. Moreover Article 90(1) of the Rome Treaty (which is quoted in full, below) states explicitly that they do apply to "public undertakings and undertakings to which Member States grant special or exclusive rights." And it has been held that this formula covers undertakings "for whose actions the State must take special responsibility by reason of the influence which they may exert over

---

[84] The possibility is also mentioned in s.2(2) of the Sugar Act 1991, though not the Insurance Act 1990.
[85] C. Graham and T. Prosser (1988) *Public Law* 413, 414.
[86] *Dáil Debates*, Vol. 401, col. 15, July 4, 1990. On the Treaty of Rome, see further pp. 155–157.

such actions."[87] Thus, it would seem that Article 90 will apply to the Minister for Finance's golden share and that if the Minister's powers are used to veto bids because he does not want to see the company fall into foreign hands, this would be a clear breach of Article 7, which prevents discrimination on the grounds of nationality.

A related issue concerns whether the State should attempt to exercise some degree of positive control over the ownership of the former state body to favour some group such as employees or customers of the company; the "small investor"; institutional investor, etc.[88] The usual instrument for achieving this includes the way the shares are first marketed. In addition however section 2 of the Sugar Act 1991 even goes beyond this to attempt to influence subsequent transactions:

"(7) The Minister [for Finance], following consultation with the Minister for Agriculture and Food, may sell or dispose of shares held by him in the Holding Company on prescribed terms and conditions to such specified persons as he may prescribe.

(8) The Minister may prescribe different terms and conditions for classes of specified persons and may prescribe conditions as to consideration including conditions concerning sale or disposal for no consideration or for consideration less that the market value of the said shares at the time of their sale or disposal.

. . ..

(10) In this section—
'prescribed' means prescribed by regulations under this section and 'prescribe' shall be construed in like manner;
'specified persons' means employees or former employees of the Company and beet growers."

(vi) Monopolies

At this point, it ought to be emphasised that some discussions of privatisation issues confuse privatisation—that is the transfer into private ownership of an enterprise originally owned by the State—with the fact that such enterprises often enjoy a "legal monopoly," as distinct from a "natural" monopoly (which arises from economic and social realities, such as the nature and cost of the enterprise and the size of the market). About a natural monopoly little can be done, so that the following remarks are directed to legal monopolies. The coincidence between state ownership and a legal monopoly is not inevitable. One theoretical alternative would be a monopoly which is in private hands, though there are obvious dangers in such a situation. Another more likely possibility would be that whilst the state body is retained, its legal monopoly is broken so that the state body is open to the competition of pri-

---

[87] (Cases 188–190/80) *France* v. *Commission* [1982] E.C.R. 2454.
[88] In France where there is a lack of large institutional shareholders, the State has been afraid of the possibility of "raiders" if all the shares were divided among a large number of small holdings. Accordingly the responsible Minister is empowered to place a substantial number of shares with "hard cores" of investors from outside the financial markets. He exercises this power after receiving the opinion of the "Privatisation Commission."

vate enterprise. This has happened recently, in the field of broadcasting, inter-city buses and international air transport.

A further example is section 111 of the Postal and Telecommunications Services Act 1983, by which a licensing system was created for the supply of equipment for connection to the telecommunications network. This means that Bord Telecom may have competition in areas in which it has hitherto had a monopoly (for example, the supply of equipment—receivers, etc.—for connection to the telecommunications network). In this case the licensing authority is the Minister for Communications. However, in the case of licenses to run buses, it is anticipated that, as with broadcasting, new legislation will create licensing authority distinct from the responsible Minister.

Most state bodies are usually exempted from the Restrictive Practices Act 1972 and the Mergers, Take-overs and Monopolies (Control) Act 1978.[89] However state bodies are broadly subject to the Treaty of Rome. The joint effect of Articles 37 and 90[90] of the Treaty is to permit Member States to maintain public undertakings with special or exclusive rights while at the same time ensuring that any such special regime does not effect unfair discrimination against persons or goods on the grounds of nationality[91] or otherwise effect a breach of the competition rules.

Article 37(1) is concerned with State monopolies enjoying exclusive rights in the procurement and distribution of goods and provides that:

"Member States shall progressively adjust any State monopolies of a commercial character so as to ensure that when the transitional period has ended no discrimination regarding the conditions under which goods are procured and marketed exists between nationals of Member States.

The provisions of this Article shall apply to any body through which a Member State, in law or in fact, either directly or indirectly supervises, determines or appreciably influences imports or exports between Member States. These provisions shall likewise apply to monopolies delegated by the State to others."

To fall within the ambit of Article 37, it is necessary that the monopoly body, first, has, as its object, trade in commercial goods capable of being the subject-matter of competition and trade between Member States and, secondly, plays an effective part in such trade.[92] There have been no Irish cases involving Article 37, but since the German and French alcohol[93] mon-

---

[89] Though in the case of Bord Telecom Éireann and An Post, this dispensation was removed by s.3 and the Second Sched. of the Restricture Practices (Amendment) Act 1987.
[90] See generally in relation to Arts. 37 and 90, Wyatt and Dashwood, *The Substantive Law of the EEC* (London, 1986), Chaps. 7 and 19; Bellamy and Child, *Common Market Law of Competition* (London, 1987), Chap. 13; McMahon and Murphy, *European Community Law in Ireland* (Dublin, 1989), Chap. 21.
[91] Art. 90(1) forbids discrimination contrary to Art. 7, which in turn prohibits discrimination based on nationality.
[92] (Case 6/64) *Costa* v. *ENEL* [1964] E.C.R. 585; (Case 91/78) *Hansen* v. *Hauptzollamt Flensburg* [1979] E.C.R. 935.
[93] See *Fifteenth Report on Competition Policy* (1986), para. 262.

opolies and the French potash fertilizer monopoly[94] have all been held to be within the scope of Article 37, it would seem that commercial state bodies such as Bord na Móna, Bord Gáis Éireann and Nitrigin Éireann Teo. would all come within its scope. Likewise, if the Deutsche Bundespost[95] can be held to come within the scope of Article 37 insofar as its monopoly in cordless telephones is concerned, the same might well be true of the special rights conferred on Bord Telecom Éireann by section 87(1) of the Postal and Telecommunications Services Act 1983.

Article 37(1) does not require the entire abolition of State commercial monopolies, but rather that they should be adjusted in such a way as to ensure that no discrimination regarding the conditions under which goods are procured and marketed exists between nationals of Member States.[96] As a result, a national monopoly may not enjoy exclusive importation rights and exporters from other Member States must retain the right to sell their product directly in the Member State.[97] In addition, the rules regulating the state monopoly may not have a discriminatory effect in practice on imported products.[98]

Article 90 is a complementary provision designed to ensure that public undertakings may not engage in discriminatory conduct or otherwise infringe the competition rules. Article 90(1) provides:

> "In the case of public undertakings and undertakings to which Member States grant special or exclusive rights, Member States shall neither enact nor maintain in force any measure contrary to the rules contained in this Treaty, in particular to those rules provided for in Article 7 and Articles 85 to 94."

Article 90(1) appears to have been inserted *ex abundante cautela* to provide that the State may give a state-sponsored body exclusive privileges in relation to, say, broadcasting, but could not go further and allow that body to discriminate in favour of Irish goods. It may be questioned whether this provision was really necessary, since the position would be the same for a private entity, for the reason that the very existence of a monopoly or dominant position is not in itself a breach of Article 86 (or the other competition rules), as Article 86 only prohibits an *abuse* of a dominant or monopoly position. Article 90(1) therefore only confirms the applicability of the non-discrimination and competition rules to state-sponsored bodies.

Italy v. *Saachi*[99] is the leading case on Article 90(1). Here the Court of Justice upheld the compatibility with the Treaty of Rome of the broadcasting monopoly given to RAI (the Italian equivalent of RTE). However, the Court

---

[94] See *Fourteenth Report on Competition Policy* (1985), para. 288.
[95] See the approach taken by the EC Commission in their decision, *Re Cordless Telephones in Germany* [1985] 2 C.M.L.R. 397.
[96] (Case 59/75) *Pubblico Ministero* v. *Manghera* [1976] E.C.R. 91; (Case 91/78) *Hansen* v. *Hauptzollamt Flensburg* [1979] E.C.R. 935.
[97] (Case 78/82) *Commission* v. *Italy* [1983] E.C.R. 1955.
[98] (Case 90/82) *Commission* v. *France* [1983] E.C.R. 2011.
[99] (Case 155/73) [1974] E.C.R. 409.

indicated that had RAI discriminated in favour of Italian products in, for example, its advertising rates, this would have been a breach of Article 90(1).

Article 90(2) makes some concession to the special position of state bodies. It provides that:—

"Undertakings entrusted with the operation of services of general economic interest or having the character of a revenue-producing monopoly shall be subject to the rules contained in this Treaty, in particular to the rules on competition, in so far as the application of such rules does not obstruct the performance, in law or in fact, of the particular tasks assigned to them. The development of trade must not be affected to such an extent as would be contrary to the interests of the Community."

While this provision gives commercial state bodies some room for manoeuvre, the onus is on the body in question to show that the application of the competition rules would obstruct the performance of their duties. There appears to be no case to date in which Article 90(2) has been successfully invoked. Thus, in *Nungesser K.G.* v. *Commission*,[1] the Court of Justice held that a French agricultural research body could not invoke Article 90(2) to justify export bans (which prima facie infringe Article 85(1)) contained in contracts for the marketing of maize seeds.

---

[1] [1982] E.C.R. 2015.

APPENDIX TO CHAPTER 4

EXTRACTS FROM THE COMMITTEE OF PUBLIC ACCOUNTS SPECIAL REPORT ON THE FUTURE ROLE OF THE COMPTROLLER AND AUDITOR GENERAL AND THE COMMITTEE OF PUBLIC ACCOUNTS (Pl 5645, 1988)

Commercial State-sponsored Bodies

3.7 In the case of the commercial SSBs it is appropriate that they should have sufficient flexibility of action to operate profitably in their respective sectors though special considerations apply in the case of those SSBs which are in a monopoly situation. Regardless of their form commercial SSBs owe their existence to the State and were set up with finance provided by Dáil Éireann. From time to time they have received Exchequer funds as equity capital, loans, grants and subsidies. In some instances guarantees have been given by the State on foot of loans raised by these bodies. In times of difficulty the SSBs usually turn to Parliament for assistance. In short, in all cases there is an express or implicit dependence on the State. The Group feels that this dependence should be reflected in their accountability arrangements.

3.8 Concern has long been expressed at the lack of accountability of commercial SSBs. As far back as 1950 a motion was introduced and debated in the Seanad to provide that a Joint Committee should be set up to review the operations of State companies. Throughout the late 1960s and the early 1970s the matter was a recurrent theme in Oireachtas debates and committee meetings. This concern ultimately led to the establishment of the Joint Committee on Commercial State-sponsored Bodies in 1978 with a brief to examine the Reports and Accounts and overall operational results of SSBs engaged in trading or commercial activities. Successive Joint Committees have contributed to an improvement in the public accountability process for these bodies although the cyclical nature of the reviews can result in many years passing before a body comes under scrutiny. Furthermore, no structured process was ever developed for responding to the recommendations or criticisms of the Joint Committee in the same way as the Department of Finance responds to those of the PAC.

3.9 In this situation there should be some compensating procedure to fill the accountability void. The Group believes that the PAC has an important role to play in this context. In view of the primacy which the Constitution confers on Dáil Éireann in financial matters, it is the only parliamentary committee which is concerned with the audit aspects of public expenditure. The PAC, working through the C. & A.G., should therefore supplement the periodic performance reviews of the Joint Committee. The C. & A.G. should be relieved of responsibility for direct audit of the commercial SSBs which he now audits, but he should have access inspection rights in relation to all commercial SSBs and his reports thereon should be subject to PAC examination

158

and report. It is in the public interest that the C. & A.G. should be an informed, independent contributor to the accountability process for these bodies. The exercise of such rights should obviously involve consultation, as appropriate, with the private sector auditors of the bodies. The proposed arrangement would appear to achieve the balance between the necessary operational freedom for the bodies on the one hand and the need to protect the State's overall interests on the other. The protection of these interests would include such matters as:

— verifying that Ministerial directives are not being circumvented;
— identifying instances of wasteful competition between SSBs and areas of overlap;
— examining the activities of subsidiaries;
— identifying the use of tax avoidance schemes.

Non-commercial State-sponsored Bodies

3.10   The position with regard to the non-commercial SSBs is completely differ- **3.10**
ent. At the time of the establishment of the Joint Committee the Minister for Finance intimated that accountability for the non-commercial SSBs hinged on the fact that they were generally funded from voted moneys which were open to annual parliamentary debate and to the scrutiny of the C. & A.G. It was not until 1983 that a mechanism for partial accountability of these bodies was devised with the establishment of the Committee on Public Expenditure (PEC). The orders of reference for that Committee included reviewing the justification for and the effectiveness of ongoing expenditure of the non-commercial SSBs. The PEC has not been reconstituted by the new Dáil so we have returned to the pre-1983 position.

3.11   In examining the question of accountability of the non-commercial SSBs **3.11**
the viability criteria applying to commercial SSBs do not arise. The Group considered whether audit should be viewed as an intrinsic part of the parliamentary accountability process in the case of non-commercial SSBs. We are referring here to financial audit as distinct from Value-for-Money (VFM) audit which will be dealt with in the next chapter. It can be argued that financial audit is a fairly straightforward legal requirement and that it is immaterial who undertakes the audit once access inspection rights are granted to the C. & A.G. There is justification for that view. However the Group feels that this does not recognise the C. & A.G.'s primary responsibility for audit of moneys which are, after all, voted moneys at one remove and as such, should be subject to the rigours of public audit and accountability. We feel that the appointment of the C. & A.G. as auditor of these bodies does tend to add a degree of assurance in the public's mind that the management of State moneys is being thoroughly scrutinised. On a more practical level the allocation of these audits to the C. & A.G. overcomes the possibility of duplication in any exercise of an inspection function.

3.12   While the Group proposes that the audit of non-commercial SSBs should **3.12**

continue to be carried out by the C. & A.G., we recommend that the C. & A.G. should examine the feasibility of using private sector auditors working under his direction to undertake the detailed audit work where it is more economical and practical to do so.

Audit Report—State-sponsored Bodies

3.13   The Group wishes to draw attention to the situation in relation to the audit **3.13** reports of SSBs generally. At present the formal audit opinion is the only report made available to Parliament by way of tabling the accounts in the House. In no sense is there a report to Dáil Éireann. Because of the very nature of their establishment and funding, SSBs cannot be regarded in the same light as private sector firms in so far as reporting responsibilities are concerned. The Irish public is the ultimate owner of SSBs and therefore there must be a reporting requirement to their representatives, *i.e.* Dáil Éireann. The Group feels that there should be an audit report on all SSBs to Dáil Éireann, over and above the audit "opinion" or "certificate," which would give detailed comments on the results of the audit perhaps along the lines of the content of the management letter. This would enhance SSBs' public accountability and such a report should serve as a basis for PAC examination and report.

CHAPTER 5

ASPECTS OF LOCAL GOVERNMENT LAW

1. Historical Introduction and Modern Developments

Pre–1922 Developments

It has been stated that the "basic structure of [Irish] local government has remained that enacted by the British parliament in 1898."[1] In that year the Local Government (Ireland) Act 1898 was passed, and this legislation effected a major reorganisation of the system of local government which had operated prior to that date. Until 1898 the functions of local government had been discharged by a range of diverse and often single-function bodies, of which only the most important can be mentioned. First, the construction, repair and maintenance of roads and bridges lay in the hands of the grand jury, who also had a supervisory function in relation to other public works.[2] The grand jury was appointed by the assize judge, who was required to approve the grand jury's "presentments," *i.e.* expenditure proposals. The grand jury raised revenue by means of taxes on local landowners, and these taxes were known as the "grand jury cess." The corrupt[3] and undemocratic nature of this system led to the reform, which was to come when the grand juries were relieved of their local government functions by the Local Government (Ireland) Act 1898.

Secondly, the poor law and sanitary services were administered, in most parts of the country, by boards of guardians. In Ireland, the poor law union was an area 10 miles in radius around each of the 130 market towns,[4] and the guardians were elected by the poor-law ratepayers. Local ratepayers also sat, *ex officio*, on the board of guardians. Because the guardians—unlike the grand juries—were permanent bodies holding regular meetings, their functions were extended by legislation throughout the nineteenth century.[5] By 1840 there were also 68 borough corporations to certain of which some or all of the powers of grand juries had been transferred. Ten of these (Dublin,

---

[1] Alexander, "Local Government in Ireland" (1979) 27 *Administration* 3, 7. What follows is necessarily a brief and very selective account of the principal features of local government law. Readers who desire a fuller treatment of this complicated subject are referred to Keane, *The Law of Local Government in the Republic of Ireland* (Dublin, 1982); Street, *The Law of Local Government* (Dublin, 1955) and Roche, *Local Government in Ireland* (Dublin, 1982).

[2] The grand jury system, which had originated in the Grand Jury Act 1634 had been reorganised by the Grand Jury (Ireland) Act 1836.

[3] See generally, Roche, *op. cit.* pp. 29–43.

[4] See Alexander, *loc. cit.* 6. The numbers were increased to 163 after the Famine.

[5] See, *e.g.* Births and Deaths Registration Act 1863 which required the compilation of mortality statistics by local authorities.

Cork, Belfast, Limerick, Waterford, Londonderry, Sligo, Kilkenny and Clonmel) were retained as municipal boroughs by section 12 of the Municipal Corporations (Ireland) Act 1840. Borough status was later granted to Wexford (by petition, 1845); Dún Laoghaire (by petition, 1930) and Galway (by private Act of the Oireachtas, 1937). Further reform came with the passage of the Local Government Act 1871, which gave a centralised body—the Local Government Board—control over the activities of local boards. By the end of the nineteenth century the local guardians enjoyed wide powers and "not only relieved destitution and furnished public and personal health services, but, from 1893, provided rural housing as well."[6] Side by side with the boards of guardians system, town commissioners were elected in the towns which had adopted the Towns Improvement (Ireland) Act 1854 or which had been appointed under the Lighting of Towns (Ireland) Act 1828 or other local Acts.[7] The town commissioners had functions in relation to lighting, draining, paving, water supplies, land acquisition, railways, and in some cases, policing.

Major reform of this system was not to come until the Local Government (Ireland) Act 1898. This Act set up a two-tier system of local government, organised along county lines.[8] Each county was to have a county council, apart from Tipperary which is divided into North and South Riding.[9] In addition, Galway was established as a county borough by section 5 of the Local Government (Re-organisation) Act 1985.[10] The same Act also provided for the dissolution of the existing Dublin County Council and Dún Laoghaire Corporation and their replacement by three new county councils: the electoral counties of Dublin-Fingal; Dublin-Belgard and Dún Laoghaire-Rathdown. However, no commencement order has been made in respect of this later change and none is expected for the foreseeable future.[11] Returning to the 1898 Act, Dublin, Cork, Belfast, Waterford, Londonderry and Sligo were made county boroughs in which the Corporations were to have the functions of a county council, together with those functions which as borough councils they had previously enjoyed. Each county was divided into local districts, with an urban or rural district council. In rural areas, the public health functions of the boards of guardians were transferred to the rural district councils. The power to levy the poor law rates was assigned to the county councils, but the boards of guardians were still responsible for the administration of the poor law system, including the provision of medical relief. Finally, and perhaps most importantly, the franchise was extended to all adult male

---

[6] Chubb, *The Government and Politics of Ireland* (Stanford, 1982), p. 292.
[7] Some towns had elected representatives by virtue of local Acts: see Vanston's *Law of Municipal Towns*, pp. 6 and 358.
[8] See generally, Roche, *op. cit.* pp. 32–36.
[9] For the reasons as to why Tipperary was divided into North and South Ridings, see App. IX to Roche, *op. cit.*
[10] For commentary, see Hogan (1985) I.C.L.S.A. 7–01.
[11] Staff and trade union difficulties are apparently impeding the making of such a commencement order.

ratepayers.[12] This extension of the franchise not only ensured that local government was to be more representative in nature, but also created a form of local politics in Ireland which, in the following 20 years or so, was to be the backbone of the nationalist struggle for Irish independence.

Post-1922 developments

The first major piece of local government legislation following the establishment of the Irish Free State in 1922 was the Local Government (Temporary Provisions) Act 1923. This was enacted at a time when the country was split between pro- and anti-Treaty factions. Against this background, it seemed natural to the Government of the day to promote a policy of taking greater control over local authorities. For example, the Minister for Local Government's power to "dissolve and transfer functions to any body or persons or person he shall think fit" which had hitherto applied only to boards of guardians was extended to all local authorities.[13] And, indeed, this power was to be frequently availed of in the next few years.[14] Secondly:

> "Sinn Féin policy on local government, from which much of the reform thinking of this time derives, was aimed at clearing away most, if not all, of the undergrowth of small local bodies at sub-county level."[15]

Accordingly, boards of guardians (outside Dublin) were abolished by the 1923 Act, replacing them with boards of health, which were statutory committees of county councils.[16] Health and sanitary functions were discharged by the boards of health which were abolished in 1940 when these functions became the direct responsibility of the county councils.[17] Eventually, by the Health Act 1970, the health functions (but not the sanitary functions) were transferred to eight regional health boards. In the same vein of thinning out the undergrowth of small bodies, the Local Government Act 1925 abolished rural district councils and their functions were assigned to the appropriate county council.[18]

The Local Government (Officers and Employees) Acts 1926–1983 provide that the appointment of most major local authority officers cannot be filled

---

[12] The franchise was extended to women aged 30 years and upwards by the Representation of the People Act 1918. This 30-year limit was removed by the Local Government (Extension of Franchise) Act 1935, which also granted the vote to all Irish citizens aged 21 years and upwards who were not subject to legal incapacity. The citizenship requirement was deleted by the Local Elections Act 1972, and the franchise was granted to all persons aged 18 years and upwards resident in the locality who have duly complied with the registration requirements: see Electoral (Amendment) Act 1973, s.2. The Local Government (Ireland) Act 1918 had previously introduced proportional representation for local elections.

[13] 1923 Act, s.12. Similar provisions are now contained in the Local Government Acts 1941–46, save that under this later legislation the Minister for the Environment is not entitled to direct the removal of the elected representatives but only to dissolve the Council.

[14] In 1923 five authorities were dissolved. The corresponding figures for 1924 and 1925 were 13 and five respectively.

[15] Roche, *op. cit.* p. 52.

[16] 1923 Act, ss.3–7 and Local Government Act 1923, ss.9 and 10.

[17] County Management Act 1940, s.36.

[18] Local Government Act 1925, s.3.

save on the recommendation of the Local Appointments Commissioners.[19] This process of selection by an independent body was a desirable reform, and guards against the political and other forms of patronage which are an all-too-common feature of Irish life. Another major step in the same direction was the introduction of the management system by the County Management Act 1940.[20] This constitutes the most far-reaching change in the local government system since the passing of the Local Government (Ireland) Act 1898, and is described below.

The Health Act 1970 represented the next major change in the local government system. This legislation established eight regional health boards composed of representatives of local authorities, the medical and other professions and ministerial nominees. The Act removed the administration of the health services from the local authorities, a stark reminder of the stringent control of local authorities by centralised government. 1971 saw the publication of a White Paper[21] on local government reorganisation and this was the first comprehensive review of local government since 1922. The White Paper proposed the abolition of the *ultra vires* rule; new legislation on the modernisation of the constitution, membership and procedure of local authorities; new accounting and auditing procedures; and the concentration of central government controls on "key points" only, while at the same time allowing local authorities "the greatest possible discretion in the exercise of their powers." These proposals remain unimplemented, but meanwhile the trend of centralisation continued with the Local Government (Financial Provisions) Act 1978 which effectively abolished domestic rates. The difficulties faced by local authorities were rendered even more acute by the Supreme Court's decision in *Brennan* v. *Attorney-General*[22]—which held that the method of collecting rates on agricultural land was unconstitutional—and made urgent reform of the local government system imperative.[23] The critical financial position of local authorities was alleviated to an extent by the passage of the Local Government (Financial Provisions) (No. 2) Act 1983[24] which substantially extended the power of the local authority to charge for certain essential services (*e.g.* water supply and refuse collection) but this was recognised as a stop-gap measure and one which was not intended to be a substitute for a

---

[19] There are some exceptions to this general rule including the posts of part-time professional staff, nurses, midwives and technical posts.

[20] The management system had earlier been imposed by a series of separate Acts on Cork, Dublin, Limerick and Waterford county boroughs. See Roche, *op. cit.* pp. 100–104.

[21] *Local Government Reorganisation: Proposals for the reorganisation of the existing structure of local government and for modifications and improvements in the operation of the system* (Dublin, 1971).

[22] [1984] I.L.R.M. 355.

[23] The Supreme Court observed that an anomalous, or even unjust method of valuing property was not of itself unconstitutional. However, once the anomalous method of valuing agricultural land contained in the Valuation (Ireland) Act 1852 was used as the basis for assessing rates, then the method of collecting such rates (s.11 of the Local Government Act 1946) infringed the plaintiff's property rights as guaranteed by Art. 40.3, and was unconstitutional.

[24] See O'Hagan, McBride, Sanfey, "Local Government Finance: The Irish Experience" [1985] B.T.R. 235.

radical overhaul of the entire local government system. The present Government has announced yet a further review of local government structures and financing. The local elections originally scheduled for 1990 have been deferred for one year pending the outcome of this review.[25]

2. The Management System

The essence of the management system is that certain functions (known as "reserved functions") may be exercised by the elected members, while all other functions ("executive functions") are discharged by a salaried officer, known as "the City Manager" or "the County Manager," as the case may be. However, the elected members are entitled to give the Manager binding directions as to the manner in which certain executive functions shall be discharged.[26] Draft estimates of expenditure must be prepared by either the Estimates Committee of the council or, if, as is far more usual, there is no such committee, by the Manager unless, as is most unusual, there is an Estimates Committee.[27] In either case, the estimates must then be adopted at a full meeting of the council at which "the Manager shall be present."[28] The Manager's status *vis-à-vis* the local authority is further enhanced by the provisions regarding his appointment and renewal. Selection is by the Local Appointments Commissioners,[29] who, as a matter of law, may recommend either one or two persons for the post. However, by an inveterate practice, the Commissioners recommend only one person who is then automatically appointed by the particular local authority. In addition, a Manager can only be removed from office with the sanction of the Minister for the Environment[30] and following the passage of a resolution, of which at least seven days' notice has been given, by a two-thirds' majority of the councillors. No Manager has as yet been removed. However, a few have been suspended, a process which requires a resolution of the same type as for a removal, but no ministerial consent.[31] Given the need for consistency between a county council and any lower authority within its area, it is most important that a County Manager is *ex officio* made Manager for every elective body within the county.

---

[25] *The Irish Times*, March 21, 1990. The Review Group reported in March 1991: *Local Government Reorganisation and Reform* (Pl. 7918)
[26] City and County Management (Amendment) Act 1955, s.4. See pp. 171–175.
[27] 1955 Act, s.7.
[28] *Ibid.* s.10(1).
[29] Local Authorities (Officers and Employees) Act 1926, s.6; City and County Management (Amendment) Act 1955, s.6.
[30] County Management Act 1940, s.6. S.13(5) permits the City Manager to delegate his executive powers to an Assistant Manager: *Cassels* v. *Dublin Corporation* [1963] I.R. 193. S.17(9)(a) of the City and County Management (Amendment) Act 1955 allows the Manager to revoke that delegation, in which case, he resumes the power to discharge the statutory function in question: *Dublin Corporation* v. *McDonnell* High Court, July 3, 1968.
[31] County Management Act 1940, s.7.

Reserved executive functions

The reserved functions of local authorities are set out in the Second Schedule to the County Management Act 1940.[32] Section 16(3) of that Act provides that the Minister for the Environment may by order direct that certain functions or powers should also be reserved functions in addition to those scheduled to the 1940 Act. The number of reserved functions has thus been increased by both ministerial orders and subsequent legislation.[33] Section 17 of the 1940 Act states that every power, function or duty of a local authority or elected body which is not declared to be a reserved function shall be an "executive function" of such council or body and exercisable by the Manager. An executive function must be performed by the Manager by way of a signed order in writing.[34] A register must be kept of all such orders made by him for inspection by the elected representatives at a council meeting. However, it is of practical importance that the Manager has extensive powers of delegation to an assistant County Manager, or to a County Manager or to a county secretary, town clerk or other "approved officer".[35] Within this category come specified senior administrative officers, of the equivalent in local government to the grade principal in central government. A curious and amusing example of the legal relationship between the Manager and the elected members is provided by *Waterford Corporation* v. *O'Toole*.[36] The defendant was interested in the life and works of the composer William Vincent Wallace[37] and he sought to erect two stone plaques commemorating the composer on his own hotel premises. The plaques had come into the possession of the Corporation and the City Manager agreed to the defendant's proposal that he should take possession of the plaques for this purpose. This decision was subject to ratification by the council, but Mr. O'Toole was given to understand that this would be a mere formality. In fact, the City Council refused to give their consent to this arrangement and the Corporation sub-

---

[32] A full list of the reserved functions is to be found in Keane, *op. cit.* pp. 20–30.

[33] See, *e.g.* County Management (Reserved Functions) Order 1985 (S.I. 1985 No. 341) (making of domestic service charges under ss.2 and 8 of the Local Government (Financial Provisions) (No. 2) Act 1983 to be a reserved function) Air Pollution Act 1987, ss.39, 46 (making of special control areas and air quality management plans) and Housing Act 1988, s.11(6) (making of scheme of priority for letting of houses to be a reserved function). S.13 of the 1988 Act also empowers a housing authority to provide halting sites for travellers, but since "this not expressed to be a reserved function . . . the Manger can exercise the statutory powers thus conferred," *per* Costello J. in *Wilkinson* v. *Dublin County Council*, High Court, September 7, 1990, at p. 10 of the judgment. A similar view was taken by Finlay C.J. in *Ferris* v. *Dublin County Council*, Supreme Court, November 7, 1990.

[34] 1940 Act, s.19. Moreover, the courts will not go behind a Manager's signed order "to supply any want or deficiency in it by evidence of the process of discussion or agreement between officers of the authority which led to the making of the order": *Athlone U.D.C.* v. *Gavin* [1985] I.R. 434, 443, *per* Finlay C.J.

[35] *Ibid.* s.13.

[36] High Court, November 9, 1973.

[37] William Vincent Wallace was born in Waterford in 1812 and died in France in 1865 after an eventful and colourful career. No less a figure than Wagner was compared favourably with Wallace by many local enthusiasts, but, alas, *Die Walküre* has proved more durable than *Maritana* and, in terms of international reputation, the Waterford Light Opera Festival cannot as yet compete with Bayreuth.

sequently sought the return of the plaques which, by this time, had been embedded in concrete. The question arose as to whether the City Manager had power to make these arrangements with the defendant. Finlay J. held that such ratification was not required:

> "[A]s a matter of law, the disposal or, more properly, the erection and display of these plaques on any particular premises was not a reserved function . . . and that it was within the power of the City Manager to have made any arrangement he liked with Mr. O'Toole in regard to the plaques without obtaining the ratification or approval of the City Council."

However, Finlay J. further found, on the facts, that as Mr. O'Toole was aware that the City Manager had not intended to transfer the plaques without such consent and, in the absence of such consent, a condition of Mr. O'-Toole's bailment failed, with the result that he committed a detinue of the goods.[38]

Section 17 of the 1940 Act appears to have received judicial consideration in only one other case: *The State (Harrington)* v. *Wallace*.[39] The Second Schedule to the 1940 Act provides, *inter alia*, that the "making, amending or revoking of a bye-law" shall be a reserved function. Cork County Council promulgated certain sheep-dipping regulations and the question arose as to whether these regulations were a by-law within the meaning of the 1940 Act. Walsh J. accepted that if they were not, then they would be invalid in that the making of such regulations would not have been a reserved function within the meaning of the Act and that such powers could only have been exercised by the County Manager. However, Walsh J. decided, without much discussion, that, on their true construction, the regulations were, in fact, by-laws.[40] This case illustrates what, in any event, are unexceptionable propositions, namely, that it is unlawful for the City or County Manager to exercise reserved functions and, conversely, that subject to one important statutory exception presently to be considered, the elected representatives may not usurp the executive functions of the Manager.

Moreover, it is quite clear that the elected members may not delegate their reserved powers to the Manager. This point is illustrated by *Grange Developments Ltd.* v. *Dublin County Council (No. 2)*,[41] where the terms of the Dublin City development plan (the making of which is a reserved function) purported to invest the City Manager with a power to grant undertakings to

---

[38] The Corporation were awarded £1 nominal damages for detinue and Finlay J. refused on discretionary grounds to order the return of the plaques, since the cost and likely damage of removing the plaques from the concrete structure in which they were now embedded would be out of all proportion to their intrinisic value.
[39] [1988] I.R. 290.
[40] Walsh J. thought (*ibid.* 294) that it "would be hard to improve on" the definition of a by-law given by *Kruse* v. *Johnson* [1898] 2 Q.B. 91, 96:

> "An ordinance affecting the public, or some portion of the public, imposed by some authority clothed with statutory powers ordering something to be done or not to be done, and accompanied by some sanction or penalty for its non-observance."

[41] [1989] I.R. 296.

grant planning permissions where this was considered by him to be expedient so as to avoid a claim for compensation under the Local Government (Planning and Development) Act 1963. Both Murphy J. and the Supreme Court considered that the effect of this clause was to attempt to give the Manager power to rewrite the terms of the development plan as and when it seemed convenient to do so and that this represented an illegal delegation of powers. As Murphy J. said:

> "As the making of a development plan and any variation of such plan is a reserved function by virtue of s.19(7) of the 1963 Act, it seems to me that the wide-ranging powers conferred on the executive authority by . . . the 1983 development plan is an illegal and invalid intrusion on that power."[42]

It should be noted that the exercise of a reserved function by the elected members does not involve any special procedures and a simple majority of members at a quorate meeting will suffice. As Finlay C.J. said in *P. & F. Sharpe Ltd.* v. *Dublin City & County Manager*[43]:

> "A reserved function can be carried out by a local authority by any lawful method of procedure which is contained in the rules of its proceedings and does not require any specific majority or number of persons voting in favour of it. [It may also] be carried out without the necessity for any specific notice of its intention to do so to be given to the county manager or to anyone else."[44]

There is no comprehensive method of characterising reserved as distinct from executive functions; nevertheless, it is generally true to say that the latter are of an administrative nature. Reserved functions tend to deal with political and policy-making matters, or involve quasi-legislative or financial powers. Section 13 of the Local Government (Financial Provisions) Act 1978 provides a good example of this distinction. The section provides that "the making of a rate" (*i.e.* the individual assessment of a multitude of rateable properties) shall not be a reserved function, but section 13(2) stipulates that this shall not be taken to affect the local authorities' power to strike a rate in the pound.[45] Accordingly, the power of the elected local representatives to levy finance is not affected,[46] but the execution of that policy decision—essentially an administrative function—is assigned to the Manager. Naturally, too, dignified and representational functions, such as making someone a freeman,

---

[42] *Ibid.* 312.
[43] [1989] I.L.R.M. 565.
[44] *Ibid.* 577.
[45] This power is contained in s.10(4) of the City and County Management (Amendment) Act 1955. S.4 of the 1955 Act requires that the notice of the resolution must specify a day not later than seven days after the receipt of the notice by the Manager for the holding of the meeting at which the resolution is to be considered. This is to be contrasted with the ordinary procedures to be followed in the case of reserved functions: *P. and F. Sharpe Ltd.* v. *Dublin City and County Manager* [1989] I.L.R.M. 565, 577, *per* Finlay C.J.
[46] However, from a practical point of view, the abolition of domestic rates has diminished the power of the elected representatives. The local authorities are now increasingly dependent on central government as a source of revenue.

electing a member of the council to represent it on a harbour authority or nominating a Presidential candidate are also reserved functions.

In many cases, the relevant provisions will expressly state that the power in question is to be a reserved function. Section 19(7) of the Local Government (Planning and Development) Act 1963 provides, for example, that:

"The making of a development plan or any variations thereof shall be a reserved function."

In some cases, however, this is not expressly stated and an example is provided by section 13(1) of the Gaming and Lotteries Act 1956:

"A local authority may by resolution adopt this Part in respect of the whole or a specified part of its administrative area and by resolution rescind such resolution."

In the absence of an express statement to the contrary, it might be thought, on the one hand, that the effect of section 17(1) of the County Management Act 1940 was that this function was to be an executive function. This sub-section provides that:

"Every power, function or duty of the council . . . or of an elective body which is not a reserved function shall . . . be an executive function."

Support for this view is also provided by section 19(1) of the 1940 Act:

"Every act or thing done or decision taken by a county manager for the council . . . or an elective body which, if done or taken by such council or elective body would be required by law (other than this Act) to be done or taken by resolution of such council or elective body, shall be done or taken by such county manager by an order in writing signed by him. . . . "

This would seem to suggest that, where subsequent legislation merely refers to powers to be exercised by the local authority and omits to define such a power as a reserved function, then the power is properly regarded as an executive function and exercisable by the Manager. On the other hand, the very wording of section 13 of the 1956 Act (which refers to a "resolution") and the policy nature of the decision in question would all seem to imply that the function should be regarded as being a reserved function. Moreover, the powers of local authorities under section 13 of the 1956 Act have to date been regarded as reserved functions exercisable by the elected members and this does not appear to have attracted any judicial comment.[47]

An executive function must be performed by the Manager by way of a

---

[47] See, *e.g. The State (Divito)* v. *Arklow U.D.C.* [1986] I.L.R.M. 123; *Re Camillo's Application* [1988] I.R. 104. Note that Keane, *op. cit.* p. 27 characterises this function as being a reserved function. On the other hand, in *Ferris* v. *Dublin County Council*, Supreme Court, November 7, 1990, Finlay C.J. rejected the argument that the reserved nature of a local authority function might arise by implication. He said (at p. 4 of the judgment):

"The existence of a reserved function within the code of local authority law with which I am concerned, must be expressly provided and cannot be implied in the manner in which it was submitted in this case."

signed order in writing.[48] Although there does not appear to be any authority directly in point, first principles would seem to require that the Manager must identify the legal source of his powers on the face of the order, at least where the order is such as to affect individual rights or liberties. Should the Manager fail to identify the correct legal basis of his powers in the order, then the order will fall as *ultra vires*. This happened in *Lyons* v. *Kilkenny Corporation*,[49] where the services charged imposed by the County Manager incorrectly referred to the Casual Trading Act 1980, instead of the Local Government (Financial Provisions) (No. 2) Act 1983. In this respect, it may also be significant that in *Dublin Corporation* v. *Ashley*[50] the Supreme Court was prepared to condemn as invalid a managerial order that was "uncertain and ambiguous" and which failed clearly "to comply with the limits of the statutory power of Dublin Corporation as a sanitary authority."[51] These observations of Finlay C.J. might be taken to suggest that a managerial order must show jurisdiction on its face.

As a matter of practicability, an inflexible operation of the separation of powers between the elected members and the Manager would plainly be unworkable. Although under this demarcation of functions the Manager is theoretically consigned to a purely administrative role, in practice, the council will rely on the Manager's expertise for advice and guidance, and the Manager's "contribution to the development of local policy is considerable."[52] On the one hand, a Manager has the right to attend council meetings and the duty to advise the council, generally and particularly, in regard to the exercise of their functions.[53] In the other direction, the City and County Management Act 1955 was passed after a series of Departmental circulars designed to enhance the status of the councillors *vis-à-vis* the Manager had been ignored by many Managers. This Act clearly strengthened the position of the councillors.

In the first place, the councillors' right to information has been improved. In relation to either any, or every, performance of a specified executive function (other than staffing), the councillors may by resolution direct that before the Manager exercises that function, he must inform them of the manner in which he proposes to perform that function.[54] Again, even without a resolution, the Manager shall inform the councillors before any works are under-

---

[48] County Management Act 1940, s.19(1). Thus, in *Relihan* v. *Kerry County Council* Supreme Court, May 14, 1970, Ó Dálaigh C.J. held that as local authority appointment were placed (by s.16 of the 1940 Act) in the hands of the County Manager, he can only act by order under s.19(1). In the absence, therefore, of a signed order under s.19(1), the plaintiff could not have been appointed as the holder of a permanent office with the authority.

[49] High Court, February 14, 1987.

[50] [1986] I.R. 781.

[51] *Ibid.* 787.

[52] *Report of the Public Services Organisation Review Group* ("the Devlin Report") (1969, Prl. 792), para. 25.2.12.

[53] 1940 Act, ss.30 and 31.

[54] 1955 Act, s.2.

taken or expenditure for work is committed.[55] Furthermore, the elected representatives may direct that the works be not proceeded with.[56]

Section 4

Most important of all, section 4 of the City and County Management (Amendment) Act 1955 enables the elected members to give the Manager directions as to how certain of his executive functions shall be performed. Section 4(1) of the 1955 Act provides:

"[A] local authority may by resolution require any particular act, matter or thing specifically mentioned in the resolution and which the local authority or the Manager can lawfully do or effect to be done or effected in performance of the executive functions of the local authority."

The power of the local authority to pass such a resolution is, however, subject to a number of important qualifications. Special notice must be given[57] and not only must there be a majority of members in favour of the resolution, but that majority must exceed at least one-third of the total number of the members of the local authority. A resolution of this nature can only require the performance of an executive function in a lawful manner, and it seems clear that a resolution which required the Manager to act in an unreasonable or arbitrary manner, or in a manner contrary to the requirements of constitutional justice, would be *ultra vires*.[58] Furthermore, section 4(9)(*a*) states that a resolution may not "apply or extend" to:

"[T]he performance of any function or duty of a local authority generally [or] to every case or occasion of the performance of any such function or to a number or class of such cases or occasions so extended as to be substantially or in effect every case or occasion on which any such function is performed in that area. . . . "

The purpose of this subsection is to ensure that the Manager is not stripped of an entire executive function by means of a general resolution. So, for example, while a section 4 resolution may validly direct that a particular planning permission should be granted, it may *not* require that all applications of that type should be acceded to.[59] In addition, it would seem that this procedure cannot be used to compel the Manager not to do any particular act, matter or thing, *i.e.* it can only be used to direct the Manager to take some positive step.[60]

---

[55] *Ibid.* s.2(7).
[56] *Ibid.* s.3.
[57] s.4 of the 1955 Act requires that notice of the resolution must specify a day not later than seven days after the receipt of the notice by the Manager for the holding of the meeting at which the resolution is to be considered.
[58] *McDonald* v. *Feeley*, Supreme Court, July 23, 1980; *P. and F. Sharpe Ltd.* v. *Dublin Corporation* [1989] I.L.R.M. 565.
[59] However, such resolutions do not extend to the exercise or performance of the Manager's executive functions in relation to the control, remuneration, etc., of the council's officers or servants.
[60] See Keane, *op. cit.* pp. 35–36.

This very question might have—but ultimately did not—arise in the aftermath of the long-running *Grange Developments* case. On March 14, 1989, Murphy J. granted leave to the developers to enforce an arbitrator's award for £1.9 million under the Arbitration Act 1954 and, following a decision by the Supreme Court not to put a stay on the payment of the award, Dublin County Council were faced with the prospect of an immediate payment of this sum.[61] Following a special meeting of the County Council, it was suggested that the councillors were about to order the Manager not to pay over the sum of money, but this was later denied.[62] Although this matter does not appear to have been finally judicially decided, it is arguable that a section 4 motion could not have been used for this negative purpose. Section 4 expressly refers to any "act, matter or thing" which the local authority or Manager "can lawfully do" but, significantly, omits any reference to a negative act or deed. And, as section 4 represents an exception to the separation of powers between the Manager and the elected members, it is to be expected that—like all statutory exceptions—it will be strictly construed. On the other hand, in *P. J. Sharpe Ltd.* v. *Dublin City Manager*, Finlay C.J. said in passing that s.4 applied to the whole range of "executive functions, namely, those associated with the granting or refusing of planning permissions."[63]

There is a further reason why the councillors could not have lawfully instructed the Manager not to pay the arbitrator's award in the *Grange Developments* case. Section 4 refers to any act which the local authority or the Manager can "lawfully do." Thus, the mechanism of a section 4 motion cannot be used to achieve an unlawful object and the Manager may decline to obey a section 4 resolution where it is clear that the resolution would require the performance of an illegal act.[64] In addition, section 16 provides that if the proposed resolution would involve an illegal payment, or would likely result in a deficiency or loss of the authority's funds, then the names of the persons voting for such a proposal must be recorded, and those voting in favour of the resolution are liable to be surcharged. Of course, as O'Hanlon J. pointed out in *P. & F. Sharpe Ltd.* v. *Dublin Corporation*,[65] the mere fact that a local authority receives certain legal advice does not decide the issue "beyond yea or nay." A local authority may elect to ignore the advice tendered, but they clearly do so at their own risk:

> "They may be vindicated by a later decision of the courts confirming the validity of what was done, or they may face a finding that their action was unlawful and have to pay the penalty for such unlawfulness."[66]

[61] *The Irish Times*, March 22, 1989.
[62] The County Manager handed over the sums in question to the receiver appointed by the High Court, *The Irish Times*, March 23, 1989.
[63] [1989] I.R. 701, 714.
[64] Where the case involves an "obvious and patent illegality, the Manager would be not only entitled, but in duty bound, to refuse to comply with the directions given to him by the Council": *P. and F. Sharpe Ltd.* v. *Dublin City Manager* [1989] I.L.R.M. 565, 571, *per* O'Hanlon J.
[65] [1989] I.L.R.M. 565.
[66] *Ibid.* 571.

Section 4 in the planning context

Most section 4 resolutions arise in the context of the granting of planning permission and section 26(3)(c) of the Local Government (Planning and Development) Act 1963 prescribes a special procedure where the City Manager is of opinion that the granting of such permission pursuant to a section 4 resolution would materially contravene the provisions of either the development plan or a special amenity order. In such a case the Manager must ensure that the provisions of section 26(3)(a) of the 1963 Act are complied with, which include, *inter alia*, the publication of a newspaper notice indicating the intention of the authority to grant the permission,[67] the invitation of submissions from members of the public within 21 days of the publication of such newspaper notice and, finally, the passage of a resolution by the local authority.

The general scope of the powers conferred by section 4 was considered by the Supreme Court in the important case of *P. & F. Sharpe Ltd.* v. *Dublin City and County Manager.*[68] In this case the applicants had obtained planning permission to erect a large housing development in the vicinity of a dual carriage-way. The applicants then sought permission for access to the dual carriage-way from the housing estate. Despite the fact that there were several reports before the City Council strongly recommending against acceding to this request for road safety reasons, a section 4 motion requiring the City Manager to grant the permission in the terms sought was carried. The City Manager, however, refused to comply with the resolution on the ground that he considered that it was *ultra vires* and mandamus proceedings were then commenced by the applicants.

Finlay C.J. first rejected the respondents' contention that the scope of section 4 did not extend to planning matters by reason of the express provision made for a number of reserved functions by the terms of the Local Government (Planning and Development) Act 1963. Such a contention would have blurred the distinction between the two types of functions and such a construction of the relevant statutory provisions would have been unacceptable having regard to the unambiguous terms of section 17 of the 1940 Act. He then went on to consider how the principles of fair procedures and the reasonable exercise of a quasi-judicial function could be applied in the case of a section 4 resolution of this nature. It was clear that the granting of planning permission involved the exercise of quasi-judicial powers and that a planning authority was required to act reasonably and exclude all irrelevant considerations. In the context of a section 4 resolution this did not mean that the Manager was required to exercise a discretion independently of the members, but rather that:

"[T]he obligation to act in a judicial [sc. quasi-judicial] manner is by virtue

---

[67] For a case raising evidential issues concerning proof of whether the appropriate newspaper notices were circulated in the context of a resolution rescinding the application of Pt. III of the Gaming and Lotteries Act 1956, see *Re Murphy's Application* [1987] I.R. 667.
[68] [1989] I.L.R.M. 578–579.

of the service of notice of intention to propose a resolution under section 4 of the 1955 Act transferred from the County Manager to the elected members. They must act in a judicial manner . . . before reaching any conclusion on the resolution. If, however, having done so they resolve to give a direction to the County Manager, I have no doubt but that the proper construction of section 4 is that he carries that out as part of his statutory duty as a mere executive duty and is not entitled, provided the resolution is valid and lawful, to exercise any separate or independent discretion as to whether or not he will obey it. If, of course, the elected members do not resolve to operate section 4 of the 1955 Act, the County Manager's duty to act in a judicial manner in considering the application for permission revives."[69]

Here the uncontradicted evidence pointed to the fact that the access road would have involved a material contravention of the development plan. At a minimum—and in line with the special statutory procedures envisaged by section 26(3)(c) of the Local Government (Planning and Development) Act 1963—fair procedures and the general requirement that the elected members discharge their functions in planning matters in a quasi-judicial manner meant that "specific public notice of their intention to consider this resolution" should have been given by the elected representatives. Accordingly, the section 4 resolution was a nullity in law. It followed that if the elected members still wished to put down such a resolution in relation to the access road, they would be required to serve a fresh notice on the Manager. The Manager would then be required to implement the special statutory procedure under section 26(3) of the 1963 Act and, once that was done, it would be open to the elected members "to consider this application anew, having served the appropriate notices and having heard and considered all matters concerning it."[70]

This principle regarding reasonableness was applied by Blayney J. in *Flanagan* v. *Galway County Council*,[71] where the elected representatives had directed the County Manager by way of section 4 resolution to grant the applicant the planning permission sought by him. The evidence showed that the Council had been heavily influenced by the personal circumstances of the applicant and it had been stated on the applicant's behalf by the proposer of the motion that he would otherwise be obliged to emigrate. Blayney J., however, decided that the elected members were confined to a consideration of the proper planning and development of their own functional area and that matters such as the personal circumstances were irrelevant. Accordingly, the section 4 resolution was invalid because such irrelevant considerations had been taken into account by the elected members and mandamus would not

---

[69] *Ibid.* 581.
[70] *Ibid.*
[71] High Court, May 25, 1989. See also, *Griffin* v. *Galway City and County Manager*, High Court, October 31, 1990, a case with similar facts, where Blayney J. held that a s.4 motion was invalid as it failed to have regard to the fact that the proposed grant of planning permission would breach the development plan and the councillors proposing the motion failed to disregard irrelevant considerations.

therefore issue to compel the County Manager to implement it. The practical effect of *P. & F. Sharpe* and *Flanagan* will almost certainly be to curb the excessive use of section 4 motions in planning matters.

3. The Doctrine of Ultra Vires

Corporations could be created at common law by virtue of the royal pre- rogative, but even prior to 1922 the tendency was very much to favour the cre- ation of corporations by statute. Nowadays, the number of corporations in existence which have been created otherwise than by statute is insignificant, but the theoretical difference as to the true scope of their respective powers still remains:

> "A corporation [incorporated by royal charter] stands on a different foot- ing from a statutory corporation, the difference being that the latter species of corporation can only do such acts as are authorised directly or indirectly by the statute creating it; whereas the former can, speaking generally, do anything that an ordinary individual can do."[72]

Borough corporations were originally created by royal charter but their status as statutory corporations was recognised and confirmed by section 12 of the Municipal Corporations (Ireland) Act 1840. County councils and urban district councils were designated as statutory corporations by Article 13(1) of the Local Government (Application of Enactments) Order 1898 and section 65 of the Local Government Act 1955 is to the same effect as far as Town Commissioners are concerned. Accordingly, the doctrine of *ultra vires* applies quite rigidly in the case of all local authorities, since they all have the status of statutory corporations. This has meant that enabling legislation tends to be very specific. Thus, section 56 of the Local Government Act 1941 invests local authorities with the power to decorate their functional area "on the occasion of public rejoicing" and section 113 of the Housing Act 1966 permits a hous- ing authority to award prizes to householders for the tidy maintenance of houses and gardens. The *ultra vires* rule assumes particular importance in the area of compulsory acquisition and the principal statutory provision—section 10 of the Local Government (No. 2) Act 1960—is comprehensive in its scope.[73] But even here there are restrictions. Thus, section 10 of the Public Libraries (Ireland) Act 1855 specifically prohibits the use of compulsory powers of acquisition to acquire land on which to build a library.

The consequence of the *ultra vires* rule and this approach to drafting is that a local authority might find itself without power to do something which one might reasonably expect it to be able to do. This difficulty might arise not because there was any reason why it should not have such a power but simply because this had not previously been anticipated. This restriction tends to induce a sense of caution on the part of local authority officialdom who may

---

[72] *Att.-Gen.* v. *Leeds Corporation* [1929] 2 Ch. 291, 295, *per* Luxmoore J.
[73] This section could "hardly be more comprehensive in its terms": *Leinster Importing Co. Ltd.* v. *Dublin County Council* [1984] I.L.R.M. 605, 607, *per* McWilliam J.

think in the absence of express statutory authorisation that discretion was the better part of valour and prefer not to take the risk. There are several consequences attendant on the doing of an *ultra vires* act. First, there is the risk of surcharge if the act requires the expenditure of money.[74] Secondly, if it involved the making of a contract, then the authority might be debarred from suing a creditor on that contract or *vice-versa*. Thirdly, there is a likelihood that if a local authority commits a tort in the course of an *ultra vires* activity, it would be held that the local authority was not vicariously liable for the tort. Finally, an *ultra vires* act will be invalidated by the courts. For all these reasons it has been suggested that the *ultra vires* rule might at least be modified to enable authorities to have a general power to act bona fide in the interests of the residents within their functional area.[75]

However, it should be noted that *express* statutory authorisation is not necessary, for it will be enough if the powers in question may be necessarily inferred from the terms of the enabling statute:

> "Whatever may be fairly regarded as incidental to, or consequential upon, those things which the legislature has authorised, ought not (unless expressly prohibited) to be held by judicial construction to be *ultra vires*. . . ."[76]

Many of the reported cases turn on the question of whether the actions of the local authority may be said to be reasonably incidental to the powers expressly conferred, and a number of miscellaneous examples will now be given. For instance, in *Hendron* v. *Dublin Corporation*[77] it was held that the Housing (Miscellaneous Provisions) Act 1931, the law which then governed compulsory acquisition for housing purposes, simply conferred on the local authority the right to acquire land compulsorily where such land was required immediately for housing purposes; no such power of compulsory acquisition existed where the land was to be used for future housing purposes, or where (as in the instant case) the authority had yet to reach a final decision on the matter. Many other "incidental powers" cases have arisen in the context of planning law, as conditions may be imposed by the planning authority where they are necessary "for the proper planning and development" of the area.

In *Dublin Corporation* v. *Raso*[78] the defendant had obtained planning per-

---

[74] See pp. 178–181.
[75] The Devlin Report recommended in 1969 (para. 25.3.8) that local authorities should have a general competence to act for the good of the community, a view which is endorsed at para. 14.2.1 of the 1971 White Paper. *Cf.* the English Local Government Act 1972, s.137 which empowers a local authority to incur expenditure of a two-penny rate if in their opinion it is in the interests of their area or its inhabitants.
[76] *Att.-Gen.* v. *Great Eastern Ry. Co.* (1880) 5 App.Cas. 473, 478, *per* Lord Selborne L.C. *Cf.* the comments of the Devlin Report at para. 25.3.8: "The current application of the doctrine of *ultra vires*, together with the specific terms in which local government statutes tend to be drawn, encourage rigid control over local authority activities by the Department and deter local authority initiative. In a number of other countries, local authorities operate successfully within a general competence to act for the good of the community. Similar powers could be extended to local authorities, subject to such specific limitations as were considered necessary."
[77] [1943] I.R. 566.
[78] [1976–1977] I.L.R.M. 139.

mission for use of premises as a "fish and chips" shop on condition that the premises were not used for this purpose between the hours of 11 p.m. and 8 a.m. Finlay P. held that this condition was *intra vires* as it was up to the planning authority to impose conditions of this kind with a view to:

"[C]utting down nuisance, noise and the frequenting or gathering of people which would disturb the residential aspect of a neighbourhood. Such an object and condition is clearly within the planning code."

This conclusion seems questionable, given that the Planning Acts are not generally designed to deal with questions such as noise control and nuisance. Indeed, the decision in *Raso* may be compared with other decisions where a less generous attitude to what may be said to be "reasonably incidental" to the powers of planning authorities has been taken. In *Frank Dunne Ltd.* v. *Dublin County Council*[79] Pringle J. held that a planning condition which sought to impose noise control was *ultra vires* in that it had "no relation to the planning and development" of the area.[80] A stricter attitude is taken in cases where property rights might be affected. Thus, in *The State (F.P.H. Properties S.A.)* v. *An Bord Pleanála*[81] the Supreme Court held that certain conditions requiring the restoration of Furry Park House, a house of considerable architectural significance (which was owned by the applicant) were invalid. The applicants had sought and obtained planning permission for the building of luxury apartments in the grounds of Furry Park House on condition that the house (which was not within the scope of the application) was so restored, but McCarthy J. could not accept that such conditions regulated the "development or use" of the lands in respect of which planning permission was sought, namely, the grounds of Furry Park House.

Another good example is provided by *Re Cook's Application*[82] which concerned the legality of certain actions taken by the Unionist majority of Belfast City Council in opposition to the Anglo-Irish Agreement of 1985. The applicants—who were Alliance Party councillors—challenged the *vires* of resolutions which had been passed by the Council delegating its functions to the Town Clerk and affixing a banner—bearing the legend "Belfast says No"—to the City Hall. These resolutions had been passed as part of the Council's campaign against the Anglo-Irish Agreement, but this campaign, it was submitted, did not constitute a local government function and, consequently, that these functions were *ultra vires*. Both Hutton J. and the Northern Irish Court of Appeal held, in the first instance, that the *ultra vires* doctrine applies, not only to the exercise of powers and the expenditure of monies by a council, but also to a council resolution.[83] However, it was held these acts

---

[79] [1974] I.R. 566. See also, *Killiney & Ballybrack Residents Assoc. Ltd.* v. *Minister for Local Government (No. 2)* [1978] I.L.R.M. 78.
[80] But such a condition is now expressly authorised by the Local Government (Planning and Development) Act 1963, s.26(2)(bb), as inserted by s.39(c) of the Local Government (Planning and Development) Act 1976.
[81] [1987] I.R. 698.
[82] [1986] 11 N.I.J.B. 43.
[83] A view adopted by Blayney J. in *Ahern* v. *Kerry County Council.*

were *intra vires* the Council because the workings of the Agreement could affect functions—such as transport, parks and recreation—which are either the functions of, or are incidental to, the functions of Belfast City Council.[84] Likewise, in *Hazell* v. *Hammersmith and Fulham Council*[85] the English Court of Appeal held that interest risk management was reasonably incidental to a local authority's duty to manage borrowings and investments. (However, where, as in this case, there had been no attempt by the authority's financial officers to match the Council's debts and investments, the authority had by, entering into sophisticated transactions on the spot and capital markets, simply engaged in speculative trading and this was held to violate a rather different aspect of *ultra vires*.)

An even stricter attitude is taken towards the question of *ultra vires* where the authority's action involves the imposition of financial charges. If a local authority is vested with a discretionary power, it may not lawfully impose a charge as a condition of exercising that power unless this is clearly authorised by statute.[86] While the Local Government (Financial Provisions) (No. 2) Act 1983 does introduce such charges, there have been quite a number of decided cases in which such service charges have been found to be *ultra vires* as a result of such strict construction.[87]

Even though the local authority may have the legal capacity to do certain acts, its decision may well be flawed by some procedural irregularity or abuse of discretionary power. These general principles of administrative law which apply to all public bodies are explained elsewhere. Thus, a local authority may not abdicate, surrender or contract out of its statutory powers and it must exercise its discretionary powers in good faith[88] and in a reasonable manner.[89]

4. The Audit System

A local authority owes a fiduciary duty to its ratepayers,[90] and it seems that a ratepayer may take appropriate action to restrain proposed expenditure which is *ultra vires* the local authority.[91] But the audit system which operates *ex post facto* to expose financial irregularities and surcharges those responsible[92] is an even more effective means of ensuring that local authority

---

[84] Nevertheless, these actions were held to be *ultra vires* on the grounds of unreasonableness: the delegation of local authority functions to the Town Clerk amounted to an abdication of statutory responsibilities, see pp. 520–521.

[85] [1990] 2 W.L.R. 17.

[86] *City Brick and Terra Cotta Ltd.* v. *Belfast Corporation* [1958] N.I. 44; *Commissioners of Customs and Excise* v. *Cure and Deeley Ltd.* [1962] 1 Q.B. 340 and *The State (Finglas Industrial Estates Ltd.)* v. *Dublin County Council*, Supreme Court, February 17, 1983.

[87] See pp. 193–196.

[88] *The State (O'Mahony)* v. *Cork Board of Health* [1941] Ir.Jur.Rep. 79; *Limerick Corporation* v. *Sheridan* (1956) 90 I.L.T.R. 59 and *The State (Divito)* v. *Arklow U.D.C.* [1986] I.L.R.M. 123.

[89] *Limerick Corporation* v. *Sheridan* (1956) 90 I.L.T.R. 59; *P. and F. Sharpe Ltd.* v. *Dublin County Council* [1989] I.L.R.M. 565.

[90] *Prescott* v. *Birmingham Corporation* [1955] Ch. 210; *Bromley L.B.C.* v. *Greater London Council* [1983] 1 A.C. 789.

[91] *R. (Bridgeman)* v. *Drury* [1894] 2 I.R. 489; *Arsenal F.C.* v. *Ende* [1977] A.C. 1. But see *Weir* v. *Fermanagh County Council* [1913] 1 I.R. 193.

[92] County Management Act 1940, s.10.

finances are strictly controlled.[93] An auditor, known as the local government auditor (usually a fee-earning accountant retained for a few weeks in the financial year), is appointed each year by the Minister for the Environment[94] and the Minister may also decide to hold an extraordinary audit.[95]

By virtue of section 12 of the Local Government (Ireland) Act 1871 a person aggrieved by an auditor's decision has two distinct remedies. First, he may apply to the High Court for an order of certiorari. The High Court's jurisdiction to hear a certiorari application under section 12 of the 1871 Act is plenary in nature, and is not confined to issues of law, but can also deal wth issues of fact.[96]

If the person aggrieved adopts this first alternative and the surcharge is confirmed by the High Court, then he may apply to the Minister by way of administrative appeal, who is empowered to remit the surcharge "if [he] is of opinion that the circumstances of the case make it fair and equitable that this should be done." The second alternative is that the person aggrieved may apply directly to the Minister to inquire into and to decide upon the lawfulness of the reasons stated by the auditor.[97]

Originally, the councillors were the persons who in law authorised expenditure. And it is the person who authorises an illegal payment who may be surcharged and consequently, formerly, it was the councillors who were surcharged. However, as a result of the establishment of the management system, it is the Manager who authorises the payment and he would have been surcharged had there been no adjustment of the law. Because of the nature of reserved functions, their exercise does not generally lead to expenditure, or, at any rate, the expenditure of significant sums. However, it is possible for the elected representatives to take over an executive function via a section 4 motion.[98] Accordingly, section 16 of the City and County Management (Amendment) Act 1955 provides that councillors who vote in favour of a section 4 resolution involving the making of an illegal payment are liable to be surcharged instead of the Manager.[99]

Although in some respects a local government auditor may be compared to a company auditor, his functions are altogether more onerous. Although not

[93] But see the comments of the Devlin Report (at para. 25.3.10): "The practice of surcharge should be abolished. Surcharges are rarely upheld on appeal and adequate alternative sanctions exist with which to discipline inefficient local authority officers." On the other hand, however seldom used, the existence of the surcharge power is long-established and well known among councillors and officials and will sometimes be a factor of some weight in their calculations.
[94] Local Government Act 1941, s.68.
[95] Local Government (Ireland) Act 1902, s.21. For an instance of where an extraordinary audit was held to be warranted, see *Asher* v. *Environment Secretary* [1974] Ch. 208.
[96] *R. (King-Kerr)* v. *Newell* [1903] 2 I.R. 335; *R. (Ferguson)* v. *Moore O'Ferrall* [1903] 2 I.R. 141; *Walsh* v. *Minister for Local Government* [1929] I.R. 377 (Murnaghan J. (*dubitante*)); *The State (Raftis)* v. *Leonard* [1960] I.R. 381. An appeal also lies (by virtue of s.12) to the Minister for the Environment against the making of a surcharge.
[97] Local Government Act 1946, s.68(8).
[98] Local Government (Ireland) Act 1871, s.12.
[99] The City Manager is obliged to inform the members that if they vote in favour of such a resolution that they will be surcharged; and the names of those voting in favour of the resolution are recorded in the minutes.

bound by any rules of procedure, he must act in an independent manner[1] and he is obliged to give all interested parties a fair hearing, and to give them an opportunity to show why they should not be surcharged.[2] The auditor is entitled to take evidence on oath, and he can also compel the attendance of any person at an extraordinary audit and issue the equivalent of a *subpoena duces tecum* to that person.[3] Nevertheless, the auditor cannot be compelled to turn the audit into a judicial inquiry. In *The State (Deane and Walsh)* v. *Moran*[4] the applicants objected to the auditor's allowance of certain expenditure on what were claimed to be private roads. They contended that the only way in which the matter could have been satisfactorily resolved was if a sworn inquiry had been conducted, with legal representation and an opportunity to cross-examine witnesses. Davitt P. rejected this suggestion. He agreed that the auditor was obliged to act fairly and to give the parties concerned a fair opportunity of making their case, but he stressed that an audit:

> "[W]as primarily and essentially an examination of accounts which was usually conducted by a person whose qualifications were those of an auditor and accountant and not those of a judge. . . . A close examination of the enactments . . . left the impression that it was never intended that such an audit could be turned into something essentially different such as a sworn inquiry or a judicial trial at the mere wish of some interested person, no matter how well intentioned."[5]

Power to charge

Section 12 of the 1871 Act entitles the auditor to raise a surcharge in respect of payments which are "contrary to law, or which he deems unfounded." The phrase "contrary to law" clearly deals with *ultra vires* payments,[6] but the phrase "one which he deems unfounded" has given rise to some difficulty. Is the phrase "unfounded" simply a synonym for *ultra vires*, or does it extend to expenditure on the part of the local authority which in the circumstances is "unnecessary and extravagant?" The weight of authority now supports the latter construction, and indeed, the matter can now be regarded as settled. However, some doubts had been created by the observations of Palles C.B. in *R. (Duckett)* v. *Calvert*[7] to the effect that while the auditor might surcharge councillors for a breach of trust, this must be established in substantive proceedings. In other words, it was only where a court had ruled that the pay-

---

[1] *R. (Local Government Board)* v. *McLoughlin* [1917] 2 I.R. 174; *The State (Deane & Walsh)* v. *Moran* (1954) 88 I.L.T.R. 37.
[2] *The State (Dowling)* v. *Leonard* [1960] I.R. 421; *R. (Butler)* v. *Browne* [1909] 2 I.R. 333; *R. (Kennedy)* v. *Browne* [1907] 2 I.R. 505.
[3] Local Government Act 1941, s.86.
[4] (1954) 88 I.L.T.R. 37.
[5] (1954) 88 I.L.T.R. 43.
[6] *R. (Bridgeman)* v. *Drury* [1894] 2 I.R. 489; *R. (Ferguson)* v. *Moore O'Ferrall* [1903] 2 I.R. 141.
[7] [1898] 2 I.R. 511. Palles C.B. adhered to this view in *R. (King-Kerr)* v. *Newell* [1903] 2 I.R. 355. A Divisional Court had earlier reached the contrary conclusion in *R. (Inglis)* v. *Drury* [1898] 2 I.R. 528; and this was affirmed in *R. (Kennedy)* v. *Browne* [1907] 2 I.R. 505. See also, *Hazell* v. *Hammersmith and Fulham D.C.* [1990] 2 W.L.R. 17, 46–48, *per* Woolf L.J.

ments were unnecessary and extravagant that the auditor could surcharge on the grounds that such expenditure had been "unfounded." The other pre-independence authorities disputed this view, and it was stated that the auditor was entitled to surcharge not only in the case of *ultra vires* expenditure, but also where the authority had entered into contracts which imposed an unnecessary burden on the ratepayers.

Not surprisingly, given the unsatisfactory nature of these authorities, Davitt P. in *The State (Raftis)* v. *Leonard*[8] felt he was justified in taking a fresh approach to the interpretation of the section. In his view the purpose of the section was to prevent the ratepayer "from being burdened with expenses for which there was no proper justification." Accordingly, the auditor was entitled to surcharge, not only in respect of *ultra vires* payments, but also payments which are *intra vires*, and which are, in the opinion of the auditor, unfounded, and the judge instanced a payment under an enforceable contract which was wholly unnecessary as an example of expenditure of the latter variety. He conceded that the court might be bound to follow *Calvert* as an authority for the proposition that the payment of a judgment debt cannot be deemed by the auditor to be unfounded,[9] but he did not think that the principle of that case should be further extended.

Section 20 of the Local Government (Ireland) Act 1902 also enables the auditor to impose a charge on any member or officer of a local authority in respect of "any deficiency or loss incurred by his negligence or misconduct." Although the matter is not entirely free from doubt, it would seem that the negligence referred to in the section is the ordinary standard of negligence applied in civil cases.[10]

5. The Rating System

Up to quite recently the rating system was the principal source of revenue for local authority expenditure. With the passage of the Local Government (Financial Provisions) Act 1978 rates on domestic dwellings were relieved and local authorities came to rely heavily on grants in aid from the Exchequer for financial support. The technique by which this was achieved was that the authority was required "to make an allowance to the [ratepayer] . . . and, accordingly, the rate so made shall be abated."[11] In this way, domestic rates were kept in being, in some conceptual sense, although no domestic rates

---

[8] [1960] I.R. 381.
[9] In *Calvert*, a Divisional Court quashed a surcharge which had been imposed in respect of a street lighting contract. Judgment had been entered against the Council, and although the Court's reasoning was not unanimous, all were agreed that payment of a sum due on a judgment could not be regarded as unnecessary or unfounded.
[10] See Keane, *op. cit.* pp. 313–314. But *cf.* the comments of Lord O'Brien C.J. in *R. (Kennedy)* v. *Browne* [1907] 2 I.R. 505. However, the Supreme Court has confirmed that there is no intermediate standard of proof in civil cases—the test in all cases is that of the balance of probabilities: *Banco Ambrosiano* v. *Ansbacher and Co.* [1987] I.L.R.M. 669.
[11] Local Government (Financial Provisions) Act 1978, s.3.

R.T.C. LIBRARY, LETTERKENNY

were actually paid. The reason for this indirect approach was, presumably, because of the use of rateable valuations (such as a leaseholder buying out his freehold under Part II of the Landlord and Tenant (Ground Rents) (No. 2) Act 1978) or the status of a ratepayer (*e.g. locus standi*)[12] in other areas of the law. However, the Minister for the Environment was obliged to compensate each local authority, at first, by making "a grant equal to the aggregate of the allowances made by the authority." This would have necessarily imposed some pressure on the Central Exchequer because, in general, it is the councillors who fixed the rate in the pound and, hence, it might seem, the amount which the Minister would have to pay. This in turn would have tended to encourage local authorities to spend freely since they were in large measure absolved (with the exception of business rates which are fixed at the same rate as domestic rates) from the obligation to answer to their local electorates for large rate bills. To meet this possible danger, section 10 of the Local Government (Financial Provisions) Act 1978 empowered the Minister, with the consent of the Minister for Finance, to issue directions to rating authorities and fixing limits upon their expenditure estimates and/or the rate in the pound. During the 1978–1983 period the Minister fixed the rate in the pound via the mechanism of circulars which specified the maximum permissible percentage increase (at a percentage invariably less than the rate of inflation). Then, by section 9 of the Local Government (Financial Provisions) (No. 2) Act 1983, the Minister's obligation to compensate local authorities for the rates forgone was substantially modified: the compensation no longer *equals* the amounts notionally refunded; rather, it must "not exceed" that figure. Naturally, in view of this change, since 1983 it has not been necessary for the Minister to use the other controls.

A second severe—and, perhaps, fatal—blow to the viability of the present rating system came with the decision of the Supreme Court in *Brennan* v. *Attorney-General*[13] where it held that the system of collecting rates on agricultural land was unconstitutional. The Court observed that the method of collecting rates contained in section 11 of the Local Government Act 1941 was based on the anomalous Griffiths poor law valuation of agricultural land in 1852, and the use of such an outdated system combined with the absence of any effective review mechanism constituted, in the circumstances, an unjust attack on the plaintiff's property rights.[14] However, the anomalies do not exist to the same extent in the case of non-agricultural land, not least now because of the possibility of an appeal to the new Valuation Tribunal, established by the Valuation Act 1988. The net result is that the only type of rates remaining are those on business premises.

As far as urban houses and buildings are concerned, the valuation was orig-

---

[12] See pp. 611–626.

[13] [1984] I.L.R.M. 355.

[14] O'Higgins C.J. was of the opinion that a valuation system—even one which was anomalous or unjust—was in and of itself neutral as far as constitutional rights were concerned. It was only when the valuation system was used as the basis of assessing rates that the method of collecting these rates could be attacked as unconstitutional.

inally based upon "an estimate of the net annual value thereof."[15] These valuations are also based on the Griffiths valuation survey, and they bear scant relation to present letting values. Unlike the position which formerly existed in relation to agricultural land, the valuations can be revised in various ways. First, there is the possibility of a general revision.[16] Secondly, each clerk of a local authority may send to the Commissioner of Valuation a list of specific items of property for revision.[17] But by far the most important method of revision or creating new valuations is that provided for by section 3 of the Valuation Act 1988.[18] Section 3(1) states that:

> "An owner or any occupier of property, the rating authority or an officer of the Commissioner of Valuation may apply at any time for a revision of the valuation of any property entered in the Valuation Lists or for the inclusion of any property not so entered."

It would, perhaps, have been preferable had the 1988 Act abolished the other methods of obtaining a valuation revision. For example, section 3(1) would seem to have overtaken the second method just referred to (sending by local authority clerk a list of specific items of property for revision) but section 4 of the Valuation (Ireland) Amendment Act 1854 which provided for this procedure has not been formally repealed. It is true that section 3(7) appears to contemplate some form of implied repeal of older statutory procedures in that it declares that this section shall have effect "notwithstanding" anything to the contrary in the Valuation Acts," but this formula seems awkward and much less desirable than that of express repeal.

Section 3(2) of the 1988 Act contemplates that such applications shall be made in the first instance to the rating authority who, in turn, will forward them on a monthly basis to the Commissioner of Valuation. The Commissioner is then obliged to determine the application within six months after receiving the application or "as soon as may be thereafter." The owner and occupier of the property may then appeal on an informal basis (known as a "first appeal") against the decision of the Commisioner under sections 19, 20 and 31 of the Valuation (Ireland) Act 1852. The Commissioner then directs that a valuer who has not previously been employed in making the original valuation to inspect the hereditament and investigate the complaint and report to him. This method of appeal has been described in the following terms:

---

[15] But *cf.* the comments contained in the White Paper, *Local Finance and Taxation* (1972, Prl. 2745), para. 51.2: "The defects in the system have given rise to inequities which have become more pronounced with the passage of time and have been aggravated by the constant and substantial increases in rate poundages." See de Buitléir, *Problems of Irish Local Finance* (Dublin, 1974), pp. 9–16.
[16] Valuation (Ireland) Act 1852, s.11.
[17] Under s.34 of the Valuation (Ireland) Act 1852 a County Council may apply to the Minister for the Environment for a general revision of lands in the county, but no such valuation has ever been carried out. By virtue of s.65 of the Local Government (Ireland) Act 1898 the Corporations of the cities of Dublin, Cork, Limerick and Waterford may apply for a general revision of 14 years. Dublin City was revalued in 1908–1915 and Waterford in 1924–1926. See de Buitléir, *op. cit.* pp. 11–12.
[18] See Ó Caoimh (1988) I.C.L.S.A. 2–01.

"The 'first appeal' is normally informal and usually involves a fresh survey of the property in question by a valuer, normally referred to as the 'appeal valuer,' who reports on his findings to the Commissioner of Valuation."[19]

The rating authority is obliged by s.4(b) of the 1988 Act to inform the owner or occupier of the outcome of the "first appeal." There is a further possibility of appeal in that the owner/occupier may appeal within a further 28 days to the Valuation Tribunal and the notice of appeal must contain particulars of the valuation and a "statement of the specific grounds of appeal." Section 3(5)(c) provides that the Tribunal shall then:

"[T]ransmit a copy of every notice received by it to the Commissioner of Valuation (who shall be respondent in and entitled to be heard and adduce evidence at the hearing of, the appeal concerned), to the rating authority or authorities concerned and to any other person appearing to the Tribunal to be directly affected by the determination and any such person shall be entitled to be heard and to adduce evidence at the hearing of the appeal."

A further appeal lies by section 5 on a point of law by way of case stated[20] to the High Court which has extensive powers "to reverse, affirm or amend the determination in respect of which the case has been stated." The High Court has also power to "remit the matter to the Tribunal with the opinion of the Court thereon, or make such other order in relation to the matter as the Court thinks fit." However, a party wishing to appeal by way of case stated is required by section 5(1) "immediately after the determination of an appeal by the Tribunal" to "declare his dissatisfaction to the Tribunal."

Section 5 is modelled on sections 22 and 23 of the 1852 Act (which allowed an appeal from the Commissioner to the Circuit Court) and section 10 and 11 of the Valuation (Ireland) Act 1860 (which permitted a further appeal by way of case stated to the High Court). These provisions of the 1852 and 1860 Acts could—and should—have been repealed without any loss by the Valuation Act 1988, but these old statutory procedures remain and may still be used as an alternative to the new appeal procedures under section 5 of the 1988 Act. Nevertheless, the old procedures provide a guide as to how the High Court's powers under section 5 will be interpreted. Thus, in *Pfizer Chemical Corporation* v. *Commissioner of Valuation*[21] Costello J. said, of the power to reverse, confirm or amend conferred on the High Court by section 11 of the 1860 Act, that it "could not have been wider" and that it clearly extended to the power "to amend an error in the valuation lists." This reasoning will presumably apply, *mutatis mutandis*, to appeals under section 5 of the 1988 Act.

[19] Ó Caoimh, *loc. cit.* 2–05.
[20] Dissatisfaction with the termination of the appeal must be expressed "immediately after the determination" of any appeal by the Tribunal: s.5(1). This provision appears to be modelled on s.428(1) of the Income Tax Act 1967. In *The State (Multi-Print Labels Ltd.)* v. *Neylon* [1984] I.L.R.M. 545 Finlay P. held that the similar provisions of s.428(1) of the 1967 Act were not mandatory and, moreover, should not be given "the extraordinarily strict meaning which would involve an expression of dissatisfaction at the conclusion of the actual hearing."
[21] High Court, May 9, 1989.

It is also esential that, as far as section 5 appeals are concerned, that the case stated should set out the facts as found by the Valuation Tribunal. This point was made by Blayney J. in *Mitchelstown Co-operative Agricultural Society Ltd.* v. *Commissioner of Valuation*[22] which was the first appeal under the 1988 Act. Here the Tribunal had simply annexed the entire transcript of the evidence to the case stated, but there was no "clear statement of the facts" as found by the Tribunal. Blayney J. ruled that this was not an acceptable form of case stated:

> "There must be a finding of fact based on . . . evidence. There is no finding in the case. Furthermore, it is the case that the facts must be found and stated. This Court should not be required to go outside the case stated to some other document in order to discover them."[23]

Apart from the appellate procedures provided for by the 1988 Act and the older statutory appeal mechanisms, an appeal also lies against the "making of the rate" (*i.e.*, the fixing of the actual amount to be paid by the occupier of a hereditament which is simply the product of the rateable value and the rate in the pound)[24] and thus it is open to the Commissioner of Valuation to hold that any persons have been wrongly included or excluded from the rate, or that the rate itself is illegal. A rate may also be quashed on certiorari,[25] but a ratepayer who fails to avail of the statutory procedures to correct the determination of the Commissioner, will be later estopped from doing so. A local authority is empowered to amend the rates "so as to make them conform with the enactments relating thereto."[26]

Method of valuation

The principal method of valuing units of property (upon which the assessment of rates is then based) is now contained in the Valuation Acts 1852–1988, but—in a manner characteristic of the needless intricacies[27] of the rating code—this cannot be fully understood without reference to the provisions of section 64 of the Poor Relief (Ireland) Act 1838. This section provided for a uniform method of valuation of rateable hereditaments (known as the "hypothetical rent" basis) and stated that every rate shall be:

> "[A] poundage rate made upon the estimate of the net annual value of the

---

[22] [1989] I.R. 210.

[23] *Ibid.* 212.

[24] Poor Relief (Ireland) Act 1838, ss.106–112, as amended by Valuation (Ireland) Act 1852, s.28 and ss.22, 23, 29 and 30 of the Poor Relief (Ireland) Act 1849.

[25] *R. (McEvoy)* v. *Dublin Corporation* (1878) 2 L.R.Ir. 371.

[26] *Whaley* v. *Great Northern Ry. Co.* [1913] 2 I.R. 142; *Stevenson* v. *Orr* [1916] 2 I.R. 619. But this estoppel does not apply to entries which are *ultra vires*: *Dublin Corporation* v. *Dublin Cemeteries Committee*, Supreme Court, November 12, 1975.

[27] Thus, Costello J. could comment in *Pfizer Chemical Corporation* v. *Commissioner of Valuation*, High Court, May 9, 1989 (at p. 19 of the judgment):

> "The rating and valuation code is a confusing mosaic of partly repealed and imperfectly drafted Victorian statutes encrusted with a century and a half's judicial decisions. It should long ago have been repealed and modernised."

several hereditaments rated thereunto; that is to say, of the rent at which one year with another the same might in their actual state be reasonably expected to let from year to year, the probable average cost of the repairs, insurance and other expenses, if any, necessary to maintain the hereditaments in their actual state, and all rates, taxes and public charges, if any . . . being paid by the tenant."

Section 11 of the Valuation (Ireland) Act 1852 effected a change in the method of assessing the rates for certain types of rateable hereditaments. Henceforth land was to be valued having regard to the "net annual value thereof" with reference to the average price of certain types of agricultural produce. The reference to "land" in section 11 of the 1852 Act was held by the Supreme Court in *Roadstone Ltd.* v. *Commissioner of Valuation*[28] to refer only to land that had preserved its original pastoral or agricultural nature. Land used for business, commercial or manufacturing purposes was not valued on the agricultural price basis of section 11 of the 1852 Act, but was instead valued by reference to the hypothetical rent basis of section 64 of the 1838 Act. "Houses and buildings" were to be valued on the same "hypothetical rent" basis as heretofore, save that now section 11 required that every tenement or rateable hereditament must be separately valued. This has been held to mean that:

"[T]he characteristic of a tenement to be separately valued, is a tenement, all of which is under the occupation of the same occupier, under the same immediate lessor, under one contract of tenancy."[29]

Thus, in *Coal Distributors Ltd.* v. *Commissioner of Valuation*[30] Blayney J. held that the Commissioner was wrong in not separately valuing two separate lots of property held under different titles by the same occupier.

How is the hypothetical rent to be arrived at? A good recent example of where this issue was considered is provided by the judgment of Barron J. in *Rosses Point Hotel Co. Ltd.* v. *Commissioner of Valuation*.[31] Here the plaintiff company ran a hotel which was initially successful, but then encountered financial problems due to the then unfavourable economic and financial climate. The Circuit Court held that these factors could not be relied upon in order to reduce the valuation of the hotel property where the intrinsic value of the hotel property remained the same, but Barron J. held that this ruling was incorrect in law:

"Profit earning ability is the basic element in determining the net annual value. It is based not on actual profits but on what the prospective tenant would anticipate would be his profits. Again, it is not the termination or curtailment or curtailment of the business or an identifiable part of the business which will justify a reduction in the valuation. It is the effect which

[28] [1961] I.R. 239.
[29] *Switzer & Co.* v. *Commissioner of Valuation* [1902] 2 I.R. 275, 281, *per* Palles C.B.
[30] [1989] I.R. 472.
[31] [1987] I.L.R.M. 512.

such cesser or curtailment will have on the prospective tenant which is material."[32]

Because of the difficulties which obtained prior to the passage of the Valuation Act 1988 of ensuring that the majority of valuations were up to date, a practice had evolved from about 1947 of fixing the valuation at about one-third of the net rental value and of giving revised valuations broadly in line with the general run of figures for similar properties in the areas involved. This practice had no statutory foundation and was held to be illegal, on at least two occasions,[33] by the High Court. In response, section 5(1) of the Valuation Act 1986 now provides that the amount of a valuation may be reduced by such amount as is necessary to ensure, in so far as it is reasonably practicable, that:

"[T]he amount of the valuation bears the same relationship to the valuations of other tenements and rateable hereditaments as the net annual value of the tenement bears to the net annual values of the other tenements or rateable hereditaments."

By way of a further exception to section 11 of the 1852 Act, a special régime for the valuation of "public utility undertakings" (including those belonging to the Electricity Supply Board, Bord Telecom Éireann, Bord Gáis Éireann and piped television networks) on a global basis was established by section 4 of the Valuation Act 1988. Section 4 allows the Minister for the Environment to order that certain types of public utility undertakings shall henceforth be valued on a global valuation basis. The net annual value of such property is deemed to be 5 per cent. of the effective capital value of the undertaking, although this is expressed to be subject to section 5 of the 1988 Act which enables the valuations to be decreased having regard to comparisons with other relevant properties in the area. Such valuations are to be revised on a five-yearly basis and there is a right of appeal to the Valuation Tribunal. Section 7(4) envisages an apportionment procedure whereby the global valuations shall be apportioned between the rating authorities.

Rateable hereditaments

Section 24 of the 1838 Act provides that rates are to be levied on the "occupier" of "rateable hereditaments."[34] The word "occupier" has, however, been given a special extended meaning by virtue of sections 14 and 23 of the Local Government Act 1946 and the term now includes the owner of the building where it is unoccupied.[35] These sections also provide for rebates where the building is unoccupied because of the execution of repairs, alter-

---

[32] *Ibid.* 515–516.
[33] *Scholfield* v. *Commissioner of Valuation*, High Court, July 24, 1972; *Munster & Leinster Bank Ltd.* v. *Commissioner of Valuation* [1979] I.L.R.M. 246.
[34] Poor Relief (Ireland) Act 1838, s.24.
[35] The test as regards occupancy is the *de facto* position, and, accordingly, mere licensees or even trespassers may be liable for rates if they have the unrestricted use and enjoyment of the hereditament: see *Carroll* v. *Mayo County Council* [1967] I.R. 364.

ations or additions[36] or where the owner is bona fide unable to find a tenant at a reasonable rent. The occupation of the hereditament must be permanent and not merely transitory in nature.[37]

Section 63 of the 1838 Act set out a list of hereditaments which were to be rateable for the purposes of the Act:

> "[A]ll lands, buildings, and opened mines; all commons and rights of commons to be had, received or taken out of any land; all rights of fishery; all canals, navigations and rights of navigation; and rights of way and other rights or easements over land and the tolls levied in respect of such rights and easements, and all other tolls. . . . "

An important rating exemption was, however, provided by section 7 of the Annual Revision of Rateable Property (Ireland) Act 1860 which provides that in making the valuation of any "manufactory" or building erected or used for such purpose, the Commissioner shall not take into account the value of any "machinery" therein, save only such as shall have been erected and used for the purpose of motive power. This exemption has received generous judicial interpretation in a series of cases in the last two decades and this judicial trend is, perhaps, best exemplified by the judgment of the Supreme Court in *Beamish and Crawford Ltd.* v. *Commissioner of Valuation.*[38] Here the question was whether certain fermentation and conditioning tanks used by the appellants in the brewing process constituted "machinery" within the meaning of section 7 of the 1860 Act and, hence, exempt from rating liability. O'Higgins C.J. answered in the affirmative, saying that the word "machine" within the meaning of section 7:

> "[C]onnotes apparatus by means of which force is applied, modified or used by mechanical means for a specific purpose, whether such apparatus is moving or fixed, and that in determining whether the apparatus so qualifies as a machine or machinery the components should not be regarded separately or piecemeal but as integral parts of the process in which they are used."[39]

This reasoning was followed in a series of cases and had the effect of greatly extending the scope of section 7 beyond that which had previously been thought to be the case. Thus, in *Pfizer Chemical Corporation* v. *Commissioner of Valuation*[40] Costello J. held that "thickener tanks" (which were part of the manufacturing process by which dolomite rock was converted into magnesium) were "machinery" and a similar view was taken by Hamilton P. in *Siúicre Éireann Cpt* v. *Commissioner of Valuation*[41] where he held that heavy fuel tanks used for the process of manufacture in the plant were

---

[36] The term includes the demolition of the premises: see *Carlisle Trust Ltd.* v. *Commissioner of Valuation* [1965] I.R. 456.
[37] Keane, *op. cit.* pp. 185–186.
[38] [1980] I.L.R.M. 149.
[39] *Ibid.* 151.
[40] High Court, July 31, 1984.
[41] High Court, October 5, 1988.

"machinery." Perhaps most strikingly of all, Barrington J. held in *Mitchel-stown Co-operative Agricultural Society Ltd.* v. *Commissioner of Valuation*[42] that a grain bin used for the conversion of barley into malting barley was "machinery" and was not a "building" for the purposes of the Valuation Acts.

The general thrust of the Valuation Act 1986 was to restore the status quo *ante* prior to this series of decisions. Sections 2 and 3 of the 1986 Act create categories of fixed property which shall be deemed to be rateable hereditaments. Moreover, the new section 7 of the 1860 Act (as inserted by section 7(1) of the 1986 Act) now provides as follows:

"(a) In making the valuation of any mill or manufactory or any building used or erected for any such purpose, the Commissioner of Valuation shall in each case value the water or other motive power thereof, but shall not take into account the value of any machinery therein, save only such as shall be erected and used for production of motive power.
 (b) For the purposes of this subsection, machinery erected and used for the production of motive power includes electrical power connections."

The effect of these statutory changes is to permit the Commissioner of Valuation to continue to value most kinds of industrial plant as if it were not "machinery" for the purposes of section 7 of the 1860 Act, recent judicial decisions to the contrary notwithstanding.

The 1986 Act also took the opportunity to include certain categories of fixed property within the scope of the valuation code. Section 7(2) refers to certain items of fixed property (such as car-parks, furnaces, ovens and reservoirs) so as to ensure that they are to be valued and are rateable.

Exemptions for charitable or public purposes

Hereditaments, which would otherwise be rateable, are exempt if they are used for charitable or public purposes. However, the subject of rating exemption "is one of considerable difficulty and obscurity, even by the standards of our law of local government"[43] and much of the difficulty has been caused by the diverging views as to what is the appropriate statutory basis for the exemption. Apart from certain specific statutory exceptions, the principal statutory basis[44] is contained in the proviso to the Poor Law (Ireland) Act 1838 which exempts buildings used "exclusively for religious worship, or for the education of the poor, cemeteries, burial grounds and hospitals or other

[42] High Court, July 27, 1989.
[43] Keane, *op. cit.* p. 289.
[44] Certain relief is provided in the case of secondary schools and community halls by s.2 of the Local Government (Financial Provisions) Act 1978. There are a number of local and private Acts which provide either full or partial relief for certain notable important buildings, *e.g.* Local Government (Dublin) Act 1930 (which gives exemptions in respect of, *inter alia*, the King's Inns, Corn Exchange and the College of Surgeons). The exemption for Trinity College, Dublin only applies to buildings occupied as of the date of the passage of the 1930 Act: *Dublin Corporation* v. *Trinity College, Dublin* [1985] I.L.R.M. 283.

buildings used exclusively for charitable or public purposes". It might have been supposed that this proviso would have been overtaken by section 2 of the Valuation (Ireland) Act 1854 which required the Commissioner of Valuation to distinguish for valuation purposes:

> "[A]ll hereditaments and tenements, or portions of same, of a public nature, or used for charitable purposes, or for the purposes of science, literature and the fine arts."

However, in *Londonderry Union* v. *Londonderry Bridge Commissioners*[45] the Court of Exchequer Chamber held that the 1854 Act was not designed "to create new, or abolish old, rating obligations" but only "to provide a machinery for valuing standards according to the standards provided by the existing legislation."[46] Accordingly, the court held that the words of section 2 of the 1854 Act must be read subject to the words of the proviso to section 63 of the 1838 Act. This rather strained construction was confirmed by the Irish Court of Appeal in *O'Neill* v. *Commissioner of Valuation*[47] and the matter was put beyond all doubt by the Supreme Court decision in *McGahan & Ryan* v. *Commissioner of Valuation*[48] where Murnaghan J. said of the *Londonderry Union* case that:

> "[I]t involves that the exemption from the poor rate is to be ascertained, not from the language of [section 2 of the 1854 Act], but from the rating provisions of the Poor Relief (Ireland) Act 1838, section 63 with its proviso. We do not think that the decision can now be departed from. It explains how section 63 has been considered as the guiding section governing rateability and has never been treated as repealed. In subsequent legislation the basis of the poor rate has been adopted widely for rating purposes outside the scope of the original Poor Relief Act 1838 and it would, in our opinion, bring about results not intended by the Legislature, if the exemption were now to be sought, not in the proviso to section 63 of the Poor Relief Act 1838, but in the Valuation Act 1854."[49]

This view was, however, rejected by the House of Lords in *Governors of Campbell College, Belfast* v. *Commissioner of Valuation for Northern Ireland*[50] who took the view that the statutory basis for the exemption was to be found in section 2 of the 1854 Act. Lord Radcliffe described the *Londonderry Bridge* and *O'Neill* cases as "unsatisfactory" and as involving "an incoherent rule of construction," saying that there was no justification for limiting the ambit of the exemption conferred by the words "of a public nature, or used for charitable purposes" in section 2 of the 1854 Act as being coterminous with the exemptions set out in the proviso to section 63 of the 1838 Act. Yet in its latest pronouncement on this issue, *Governors of Wesley College* v.

---

[45] [1868] I.R. 2 C.L. 577.
[46] *Ibid.* 586, *per* O'Hagan J.
[47] [1914] 2 I.R. 447.
[48] [1934] I.R. 736.
[49] *Ibid.* 752.
[50] [1964] N.I. 107.

Commissioner of Valuation,[51] the Supreme Court reaffirmed that the statutory basis for the exemption is the proviso to section 63 of the 1838 Act. In view of the fact that counsel for Wesley College had initially suggested that the decision of the House of Lords in the *Campbell College* case should be followed,[52] it is surprising that the Supreme Court did not reply to the criticisms of the *Londonderry Bridge* and *O'Neill* cases which had been voiced in the *Campbell College* case. Of course, even if the reasoning in the *Campbell College* is to be preferred—and there is much to be said for this particular point of view—it may be that the earlier Irish decisions have become so embedded in the fabric of our law that they can only be reversed by legislation.[53] We must now consider the main heads of exemption under section 63 of the 1838 Act.

"Charitable purposes"

It has been held that the term "charitable" in the proviso to section 63 does not include any charitable purpose which is not mentioned therein.[54] Accordingly, it was thought up to quite recently that buildings used for educational purposes must be confined to the education of the poor.[55] But in its most recent pronouncement on this vexed question, *Governors of Wesley College v. Commissioner for Valuation*,[56] the Supreme Court has struck a slightly different note. In that case an exemption had been claimed on behalf of a private fee-paying school which was geared towards making a profit. It was this fact, rather than that the education provided was not exclusively for the benefit of the poor, which meant that the plaintiffs could not obtain the benefit of the exemption. The *Wesley College* decision may well extend the grounds for exemption, for the test now appears to be whether the buildings are used exclusively for charitable or public purposes (*i.e.* in the sense of no private gain), and a building is not precluded from being considered charitable simply because is benefits are not confined to the poor.

The decision in *Wesley College* may well have other implications in this area, for in *Maynooth College v. Commissioners for Valuation*,[57] it was held that a Catholic seminary was a rateable hereditament. The building was not "exclusively dedicated to religious worship" (to use the language of the pro-

---

[51] [1984] I.L.R.M. 117.
[52] Henchy J. adverted to this at 119.
[53] Thus, Murnaghan J. remarked in *Kerry County Council* v. *Commissioner of Valuation* [1934] I.R. 527, 538:

> "I am of opinion that it is futile at this lapse of time to seek to interpret the [*Londonderry Bridge* case] in a sense different to that in which it has so long been understood in this country, and that if any change in the law is to be made it should be sought from the Legislature."

Likewise, Keane, *op. cit.* p. 293 considers that, given that these decisions are of such long standing, the Supreme Court, even if "unhappy" about this line of authority, might "apply the maxim *communis error facit jus.*"

[54] *Barrington's Hospital* v. *Commissioner of Valuation* [1957] I.R. 299.
[55] *O'Neill* v. *Commissioner of Valuation* [1914] 2 I.R. 447; *McGahan and Ryan* v. *Commissioner of Valuation* [1934] I.R. 736.
[56] [1984] I.L.R.M. 117. Neither *O'Neill* nor *McGahan and Ryan* are referred to in Henchy J.'s judgment for the Supreme Court.
[57] [1958] I.R. 189.

viso to section 63 of the 1838 Act), and as the word "charitable" excluded any charitable purpose expressly mentioned earlier in the proviso, the seminary could not be said to be used for charitable purposes merely because it was for the advancement of religion.[58] In the light of the *Wesley College* decision, it may be that an institution of this nature could now claim to be charitable *if it were non-profit*-making in nature, and which would otherwise be regarded as charitable for tax purposes.[59]

Infirmaries, hospitals . . . or other buildings used exclusively for charitable purposes

The same difficulties do not arise in the case of the final ground of exemption in favour of "infirmaries, hospitals . . . or other buildings used exclusively for charitable purposes" because such charitable purposes have not already been expressly mentioned in the proviso. Thus, in *Barrington's Hospital* v. *Commissioner for Valuation*,[60] a public voluntary hospital was held to be charitable in its purpose, despite the fact that some of its patients were fee-paying, as these fees were not used for private profit. It may well be argued that in the *Wesley College* decision the Supreme Court effectively applied this test to *all* charitable or public institutions, despite the fact that in the case of educational and religious institutions the scope for exemption would appear to have been severely limited by the terms of the proviso.

"Public purposes"

This head of exemption has also been considered in a series of decisions commencing with *Londonderry Union* v. *Londonderry Bridge Commissioners*,[61] where the issue was whether the tolls received by the defendants from the operation of a bridge were exempt from rating. The Court of Exchequer Chamber held that as the basis of exemption from rating was to be found in the proviso to section 63 of the 1838 Act, this question turned on the meaning of "public purposes" in the 1838 Act. The bridge in question was open for use by all members of the public subject to payment of a toll and, hence, it was held that the tolls themselves were exempt from rating on the public purposes ground. This decision was narrowly distinguished in *Mayor of Limerick* v. *Commissioner of Valuation*[62] (where it was held that a gas works operated by Limerick Corporation was carried on for the benefit of a limited class of ratepayers in a defined locality and, hence, was not exempt), but otherwise

---

[58] Even though the building would be regarded as charitable for ordinary tax purposes under the test laid down by the House of Lords in *Income Tax Special Purposes Commissioners* v. *Pemsel* [1891] A.C. 531. See also *Brendan* v. *Commissioner of Valuation* [1969] I.R. 202.
[59] Though note that in *St. Macartan's Diocesan Trust* v. *Commissioner of Valuation* [1990] 1 I.R. 508, it was conceded before Gannon J. (at p. 512) that "the question of charitable purpose [did] not arise . . . because the use of the hereditaments, although being for [non-profit making] education, [was] not for the education of the poor."
[60] [1957] I.R. 299. See also, *Dublin Corporation* v. *Dublin Cemeteries Committee*, Supreme Court, November 12, 1975.
[61] (1868) I.R. 2 C.L. 577.
[62] (1872) I.R. 6 C.L. 420.

retained its authority. Indeed, by an application of this principle, Belfast[63] and Sligo[64] harbours, technical schools[65] and the constituent colleges of the National University of Ireland[66] all succeeded in securing rating exemption. The rationale of the *Mayor of Limerick* decision was confirmed by the Supreme Court in *Kerry County Council* v. *Commissioner of Valuation*,[67] where it was held that premises occupied by Kerry County Council did not qualify for an exemption. Murnaghan J. agreed that this was a case where a "limited and defined class of the public has an interest" in the property in question (in this case, the ratepayers of Kerry), but, on the authority of the *Londonderry Bridge* case, this did not suffice to enable an exemption to be claimed.

This question was recently examined by Gannon J. in *St. Macartan's Diocesan Trust* v. *Commissioner of Valuation*.[68] In this case an agricultural college was established in the 1940s and organised along denominational lines. Some time later the college began to receive considerable financial support from the State and it became non-denominational in character. It was also non-profit-making, although students were required to pay relatively sizeable fees. Gannon J. concluded, although not without some regret, that the college could not be regarded as being used for "public purposes" within the meaning of the 1838 Act:

> "The educational establishment comprised of these hereditaments was originally founded for the benefit of a limited section of the public. It was later adapted and adopted by the State for wider public service. That educational establishment has never been taken over by the State, although it has been staffed and maintained with the aid of money provided by the State . . . Nevertheless, the vicarious State involvement in the use by the occupiers of the hereditament could not . . . reasonably qualify them as 'dedicated to or used for public purposes' as these words of the proviso of section 63 of the 1838 Act have been interpreted. . . . "[69]

Interestingly enough, it was conceded that, since the educational establishment was not dedicated exclusively for the use of the poor, it could not avail itself of the charitable exemption. As we have seen, given that the college was operated on a non-profit-making basis, this concession would seem questionable in view of the reasoning of Henchy J. in the *Wesley College* case.

Service charges

By 1983 the financial state of so many local authorities had become so parlous following the effective abolition of rates on domestic dwellings and agricultural land that it was considered desirable that they should have the power

---

[63] *Belfast Harbour Commissioners* v. *Commissioner of Valuation* [1897] 2 I.R. 516.
[64] *Sligo Harbour Commissioners* v. *Commissioner of Valuation* [1899] 2 I.R. 214.
[65] *Pembroke U.D.C.* v. *Commissioner of Valuation* [1904] 2 I.R. 429.
[66] *Governing Body of University College, Cork* v. *Commissioner of Valuation* [1912] 2 I.R. 328.
[67] [1934] I.R. 734.
[68] [1990] 1 I.R. 508.
[69] *Ibid.* 513.

to impose charges in respect of a diverse number of services provided by them. The Local Government (Financial Provisions) (No. 2) Act 1983 was designed to this end and by extending the power of local authorities to impose such charges, it was intended to restore some measure of fiscal autonomy to local government. However, the charges have proved to be controversial, and this legislation cannot be regarded as an adequate substitute for some proper form of local taxation. The question of service charges was a major issue at the 1985 local elections but, nevertheless charges have been retained by all authorities apart from Dublin Corporation.[70] Originally, the making of service charges was an executive function for the Manager, but since the County Management (Reserved Functions) Order 1985,[71] the making of domestic service charges was made a matter for the elected representatives.

Section 2 is the key section of the 1983 Act:

(1) Subject to section 4 of this Act, any existing enactment which requires or enables a local authority to provide a service but which, apart from this subsection, does not empower the authority to charge for the provision of the service shall be deemed so to provide.

(2) Subsection 1 . . . shall have effect as regards an enactment notwithstanding the inclusion in the enactment of a provision which either precludes a local authority from charging for the provision of a service or requires that a service be provided by such authority free of charge.

(3) Subject to section 4 of this Act, notwithstanding any provision in any existing enactment whereby there is specified—

(a) the amount of the charge which may be made by a local authority in respect of a service which the authority is required or enabled to provide, or

(b) an amount which a charge described in paragraph (a) of this subsection is not to exceed,

the local authority may make a charge which exceeds the amount so specified and any charge made by virtue of this subsection shall for all purposes be deemed to have been duly made under this enactment.

Section 3 provides that the amount of such charges shall be such that as "the authority considers appropriate" and further states that the charge shall:

"be payable and recoverable from the person for whom the charge is provided, or, where the service is provided in respect of premises—

(a) in case the premises are not owned by a local authority and comprise more than one dwelling, the owner of the premises, and

(b) in any other case, the occupier of the premises,

and different such charges may be made by an authority in respect of persons, premises or services of different classes or descriptions."

---

[70] For amounts due to local authorities in services charges and the total amounts collected up to September 30, 1985, see the replies given by the Minister for the Environment (Mr. Liam Kavanagh T.D.) to parliamentary questions, *Dáil Debates*, Vol. 363, cols. 2418–2422 (February 12, 1986).

[71] S.I. 1985 No. 341.

Ministerial control is provided for under section 4. The Minister for the Environment is empowered to exclude certain classes of services from the scope of section 2 charges, but no such order appears to have been made to date. Section 5 empowers a local authority via the Manager (since this is an executive function) to waive "all or portion of a charge" if it is satisfied that "it is appropriate to do so on the ground of personal hardship, a power which has been extensively used to exempt, for example, the old and the unemployed."

The validity of the imposition of service charges has been challenged in a series of cases, all of which illustrate the principle that as the 1983 Act is, in effect, a taxing statute, it must be strictly construed. *Athlone U.D.C.* v. *Gavin*[72] concerned the validity of a charge of £60 levied on every domestic dwelling for water, refuse and sewage services for a particular year. Finlay C.J. held that the charge was invalid in that section 2(1) of the 1983 Act conferred a power to make a charge for a single service and could not, said Finlay C.J., be construed "as enabling a local authority to fix a single charge for a number of services."[73]

Finally, section 8 amends the provisions of section 65A of the Public Health (Ireland) Act 1878 and allows for the imposition of water charges which are made payable on an instalment basis and the strict construction approach was continued in *Dublin Corporation* v. *Ashley*.[74] Here the local authority had sought to impose water charges payable on demand and not on instalment, as contemplated by section 65A of the Public Health (Ireland) Act 1878, as amended by section 8 of the 1983 Act. Finlay C.J. said that the word "instalment" when applied to payment meant "part of the payment and could not be construed as the entire of it." Accordingly, the County Manager had acted *ultra vires* in seeking to provide for the fixing of a charge "payable in one single amount."

The word "service" is given a broad definition by section 1 as meaning:

> "any service, facility, licence, permit, certificate, approval or thing which a local authority may render, supply, grant or issue or otherwise provide in the performance or exercise of any of its functions, powers or duties to any person or in respect of any premises and includes the processing of an application for such a licence, permit, certificate or approval."

However, even this definition has been narrowly construed. In *Ballybay Meat Exports Ltd.* v. *Monaghan County Council*[75] the applicants had attempted to connect their drains with the respondent's sewers, but the respondents claimed to be entitled to impose service charges in respect of this connection. Gannon J. held that an owner or occupier of premises enjoyed a right to cause

---

[72] [1985] I.R. 434.
[73] *Ibid.* 442. See also, *O'Donnell* v. *Dún Laoghoire Corporation (No. 1)* High Court, July 17, 1990 (where orders which failed to specify the dates on which instalment payments were to be made were held to be invalid).
[74] [1986] I.R. 781.
[75] [1990] I.L.R.M. 864.

R.T.C. LIBRARY
LETTERKENNY

his drains to empty into a sewer without charge was a public right conferred by section 23 of the Public Health (Ireland) Act 1878. Accordingly, this right was not "merely an individual service provided by the sanitary authority to such owner or occupier" and the charges were to that extent *ultra vires*. This decision might have far-reaching consequences for local authorities in that it means that their power to impose service charges is not as broad as had been imagined.

Moreover, a local authority may not seek to collect service charges where the service has not been availed of. This emerges from another judgment of Gannon J. on this issue, *Louth County Council* v. *Matthews*,[76] where the defendant had refused to pay service charges for refuse collection when he had not availed of the collection service. Gannon J. said that he could not accept the submission that:

> "[T]he word "service" . . . when used in sections 2 and 3 should be interpreted as being provided for a person without regard to whether or not it was provided to that person. The wording of section 3 which empowers the plaintiff to prescribe appropriate different charges for different classes of persons, when coupled with section 5 in relation to giving relief in cases of hardship seems to me more consistent with creating a contractual relationship."[77]

In consequence, since the defendant had not actually used the service, he should not be charged for it.

Finally, it should be noted that where a local authority has already imposed a charge in virtue of another statutory enactment, it may not proceed to impose a further charge under the terms of the 1983 Act. This occurred in *Lyons* v. *Kilkenny Corporation*[78] where the holders of casual trading permits under the Casual Trading Act 1980 had previously paid a charge in respect of the granting of such a permit. The Corporation then sought to levy an additional sum from them by way of a service charge under the 1983 Act, but Barron J. ruled that this was *ultra vires*. The permit holders were entitled to park their vehicles at designated areas for trading purposes and "have, in effect, paid for the right to do so, but are now being compelled to pay a further sum."[79]

6. Conduct of Meetings

As a matter of general principle and subject to certain express and implied legal restraints, local authorities are free to conduct their business in whatever manner they see fit. By section 61(1) of the Local Government Act 1955, the Minister for the Environment is empowered to make regulations governing the summoning and holding of meetings and the procedures to be followed at

[76] High Court, April 14, 1989.
[77] *Ibid.* p. 14.
[78] High Court, February 14, 1987.
[79] *Ibid.* p. 5.

such meetings, but to date, no such regulations have been made. However, section 62(1) of the 1955 Act permits local authorities to adopt their own standing orders:

> "A local authority may make standing orders for the regulation of their procedures, other than proceedings, the regulation of which is provided for by, or under statute (including this Act), and may amend or revoke such standing orders."

Most local authorities have adopted standing orders which are occasionally revised from time to time.

Accordingly, the special procedures provided for by statutory provisions such as section 4 of the City and County Management (Amendment) Act 1955 cannot be defeated by the operation of a local authority's standing orders.

Section 41 of the Local Government Act 1941 specifies the method by which votes at such meeting may be decided:

> "Notwithstanding anything in any enactment in force immediately before the commencement of this section or commencing at the same time as this section:
>
> (a) any act done which, by virtue of such enactment may be done at a duly constituted meeting of a local authority by a majority of the members present at such meeting, may be done by a majority of those members present at such meeting, may be decided by a majority of those members present at such meeting, may be decided by a majority of those members who vote at such meeting for and against the doing of such act, and
>
> (b) any question which, by virtue of any such enactment may be decided at a duly constituted meeting of a local authority by a majority of those members who vote at such meeting on the decision of such question."

It should be noted that this section does not apply to subsequent enactments prescribing special voting procedures, section 4 of the 1955 Act (which requires, *inter alia*, that the number of members of the local authority voting in favour of the resolution must exceed one-third of the total members of the authority) being a notable case in point. The matter of an equality of votes is dealt with by sections 62 and 63 of the Local Government Act 1946. Save where the chairman is not a member of the local authority, the chairman has "a second or casting vote" in the case of a tied vote.

The procedure to be followed at meetings to consider the estimates of annual expenditure and the striking of a rate is regulated by section 10(1) of the City and County Management (Amendment) Act 1955:

> "An estimate of expenses shall be considered by the local authority at a meeting . . . of the local authority at which the manager shall be present and which shall be held during the prescribed period and of which not less than seven days' notice shall have been given to every person who is a member of the local authority when such notice is given."

In *Ahern* v. *Kerry County Council*[80] Blayney J. was required to consider whether the procedures adopted at an estimates meeting complied with the terms of this section. At the estimates meeting it had been initially decided that the councillors should consider a particular group of estimates first. The chairman originally confined the speakers to this group of estimates. However, after this group had been considered, it was then decided that all the other estimates should immediately be put to the vote together, without further discussion and the rate thereby struck.

Blayney J. held that the procedures adopted were not in compliance with section 10, since all that had been done was that only some of the expenses had been considered:

"Obviously, it may not be asked that every single page of the estimates should be considered but, nonetheless, it seems to me that it would at least be necessary that each programme group should come up for consideration. It may that on each consideration there would be very little discussion on them, but at least once every programme had been brought up for the Council's consideration then it would be possible to say that each programme group was considered. In this case, where each programme group was not considered, it cannot be said that the estimate of expenses was considered."[81]

The judge was not impressed by the argument that, since the councillors had a copy of the book of estimates a week before the meeting (as required by section 10(2)(b)), each councillor had individually considered the estimates and that this was sufficient compliance with the statutory requirements:

"It is not a question of each councillor considering the estimates separately, on his own. It has to be done at a meeting of the local authority and, of course, there is a very great difference between considering something on one's own and considering it at a meeting where there would be available to each member the views of the other members and, obviously, there is always a possibility that a person may come to a very different view and obtain greater insight into a particular matter when he is assisted by the views of others. I think it is clear that this is what the sub-section requires."[82]

Nor did it matter that the majority had simply adopted what seemed to them to be the most convenient way of dealing with the matter:

"The sub-section clearly imposes a duty on the local authority and the majority is clearly under an obligation to comply with that particular duty. Accordingly, I do not think that one can say that there has been a compliance with the section simply because the majority took a different view.

---

[80] [1988] I.L.R.M. 392.
[81] *Ibid.* 397.
[82] *Ibid.* 398.

There would, in my mind, have to be an objective compliance and I do not see, on the facts, that there was such a compliance."[83]

Blayney J. accordingly quashed the decision to adopt the estimates and to strike the rate. This decision illustrates once more the scrupulousness with which the courts will scrutinise decisions of public bodies, even deliberative public bodies.

The power to suspend and exclude councillors from meetings

The *Ahern* case also touches on something which has been considered at length in a series of Northern Irish cases, namely, the extent to which the majority can adopt a procedure at a meeting which would either defeat the performance of local authority functions and obligations or otherwise unfairly prejudice those councillors forming a minority at a particular meeting. These cases have all arisen either in the context of protests at the presence of Sinn Féin councillors or in the wake of the Anglo-Irish Agreement and they raise many interesting and hitherto relatively unexplored questions touching on the conduct of local authority business.

The standing orders adopted by almost all local authorities contain powers to suspend and exclude councillors from meetings following disorderly conduct. At common law, however, the only powers of suspension given to authorities are those which are necessary to the existence of such a body.[84] Such powers have been described as "protective and self-defensive powers only, and not punitive."[85] Accordingly, it seems that local authorities may not exercise this power to suspend or exclude in a manner which goes beyond the common law power and thus cannot be used to ensure the indefinite exclusion of a member.

This emerges from the judgment of Hutton J. in *Re McAnulty's Application*.[86] A nationalist councillor had referred in offensive terms to the Union Jack at a meeting of Belfast City Council and it was resolved that he should be suspended and excluded from meetings until he apologised. Hutton J. held that the standing orders which provided for exclusion pending an apology were *ultra vires* and that the suspension was invalid. As Hutton J. pointed out, the effect of standing orders was that a member might be excluded indefinitely; yet such a power was not reasonably necessary for "the protection and self-defence" of the Council:

"[T]he power given by the Standing Order to suspend indefinitely until the submission of an apology in every case of obstructive or offensive conduct is too wide and is therefore invalid. The reason why I consider that the power in every instance to continue the suspension after the particular sitting is not reasonably necessary, is because the period between the end of

---

[83] *Ibid.*
[84] *Barton* v. *Taylor* (1886) 11 App.Cas. 197; *Re McAnulty's Application* [1985] N.I. 37; *Re Curran and McCann's Application* [1985] N.I. 261.
[85] *Barton* v. *Taylor* (1886) 11 App.Cas. 197, 203, *per* Lord Selborne.
[86] [1985] N.I. 37.

the sitting and the commencement of the next sitting will give time for tempers to cool."[87]

The judge did observe, however, that the power to suspend pending an apology in the case of wilful and persistent obstruction of business might be justified as being necessary for the protection of the Council, but the standing orders were not drafted in such terms. It also seems that the common law protective and self-defensive power of local authorities does not extend outside the "sphere of control of its proceedings" for in *Re French's Application*[88] Carswell J. held that a local authority did not have authority to require that members must subscribe to a declaration that they would not support violence, even where the ostensible reason for this requirement was that it was in the interests of safety of councillors. In addition, Carswell J. strongly suggested that local authorities did not have the power to expel or exclude members on security grounds.

This judicial trend was continued in *Re Curran and McCann's Application*[89] where Hutton J. held that the effective exclusion of two Sinn Féin councillors and the purported delegation of council business to a special committee (from which the applicants were also excluded) following a majority vote of Craigavon Borough Council was unlawful. Hutton J. held that the protective and defensive powers of a local authority council did not embrace the exclusion of the applicants, despite their membership of a party which supported and espoused terrorist violence:

> "Because I am of opinion that the question whether or not Sinn Féin councillors should be excluded from a council is a matter to be decided by the government and Parliament, I consider that the power of a council to exclude members of Sinn Féin is not a power which should be implied by the common law. Therefore I would hold that a council does not have the power in law to exclude Sinn Féin councillors on the ground that they are members of a party which, outside the council chamber, proclaims its support for terrorist violence."[90]

The power to delegate local authority functions

It is also clear that the courts will not permit a local authority to abandon or sub-delegate its statutory functions. We have already seen that it is unlawful for the elected representatives to delegate their reserved powers to the Manager. This point has also been made in a series of remarkable decisions of the Northern Irish courts.

In *Re Curran and McCann's Application*[91] Hutton J. held that it was not permissible for the Council to hive off the vast majority of its business to a special committee to the exclusion of the applicant councillors. This question

[87] *Ibid.* 42.
[88] [1985] N.I. 310.
[89] [1985] N.I. 261.
[90] *Ibid.* 277.
[91] [1985] N.I. 310.

was further explored by the Northern Irish Court of Appeal in *Re Cook's Application*[92] where Belfast City Council had resolved not to hold meetings in protest against the signing of the Anglo-Irish Agreement. The Council decided to delegate its functions to the town clerk and two councillors challenged the validity of these resolutions. The Northern Irish Court of Appeal agreed that a resolution expressing opposition to the Agreement would have been *intra vires* the Council, since the workings of the Agreement could affect the "functions carried out by the Council or in respect of which the Council has an interest to it by statute." However, Lord Lowry L.C.J. continued:

> "What . . . the Council is not entitled to do is to refuse or deliberately neglect to discharge its statutory obligations as the elected local authority for the Belfast District and thereby to deprive the ratepayers and citizens of Belfast of the Council's services."[93]

Lord Lowry went on to emphasise that such a decision on the part of the Council was, in the local government context, unreasonable in law:

> "The Council's decision was from the local government standpoint, and we emphasise these words (*the local government standpoint*) the negation of all the principles according to which local government is carried on through discussion and debate among elected representatives, culminating in decisions on a wide variety of important matters. To say this is not to call in question the ability of the Town Clerk; but to leave all these matters to a paid official, no matter how competent is simply not the way to carry on local government. It is, in fact, completely unreasonable in [law] and (we emphasise these words again) *in the local government context.*"[94]

7. Specimen Functions

Over the centuries, local authorities gathered accretions of diverse statutory functions and powers of varying importance. This may be illustrated by listing the programme groups in which they are categorised by the Public Bodies (Amendment) Order 1975 for estimates of expenditure purposes and giving the amounts allocated to each programme in the local authority estimates for 1987: housing and building (£436m); road transportation and safety (£361m); water supply and sewerage (£222m); environmental protection (£149m); recreation and amenity (£104m); miscellaneous services (£82m); agriculture, education, services, health and welfare (£70m); and development incentives and controls (£28m).

A question of some complexity is the demarcation line in respect of responsibility for each function as between any lower tier authority (non-county borough; urban district council or town commissioners) and the county council. This is a difficult matter depending as it does on transfers from grand

---

[92] [1986] 1 N.I. J.B. 43.
[93] *Ibid.* 92.
[94] *Ibid.* 92–93.

juries and an intricate analysis of "the tortuous labyrinth of an unexplored administrative code."[95] However, as a generalisation, it may be said that, leaving aside town commissioners, each type of authority bears responsibility in law for each type of function within its own functional area. Where the more important functions are concerned, the major exception to this is that the maintenance and construction of all county and main roads shall be the responsibility of the county councils, even if the roads run through an urban district council. But besides this exception, there are a number of cases, where because of the inadequate size and resouces of the lower-tier authority the formal position created by the legislation would be thoroughly impracticable. To circumvent this difficulty, the Local Government Act 1955 provides that the power of one authority may be exercised on its behalf by another authority.[96] This device has been frequently used to enable a county council to exercise many of the functions of the lower-tier authorities, for instance, urban roads and aspects of water supply.

Local authorities have been vested with a variety of important functions and statutory powers. Thus, local authorities have responsibility for such matters as the maintenance and improvement of roads[97]; the protection of the environment[98]; fire services[99]; vocational education[1] the licensing of gaming and amusement halls; street trading[2] the maintenance of a register of all multi-storey buildings in its functional area[3] the compilation of electoral registers[4] and miscellaneous functions relating to the administration of justice, such as the appointment of coroners and the provision of courthouses.[5] We can now examine briefly three separate specimen functions—planning control; housing and certain functions under the Gaming and Lotteries Act 1956.

Planning control[6]

Although the potential for planning control has been in existence in Ireland since 1934,[7] it was not until the coming into force of the Local Government (Planning and Development) Act 1963 that a comprehensive scheme of planning control was established. Local authorities were designated by this Act as

---

[95] *Devanney* v. *Dublin Board of Assistance* (1949) 83 I.L.T.R. 113, *per* Gavan Duffy J.

[96] s.59.

[97] See generally, Roche, *op. cit.* pp. 244–256.

[98] Scannell, *The Law and Practice relating to Pollution Control in Ireland* (London, 1982).

[99] Fire Services Act 1981.

[1] Roche, *op. cit.* pp. 273–275.

[2] Local authorities are designated as licensing authorities under the Casual Trading Act 1980.

[3] Local Government (Multi-Storey Buildings) Act 1988, s.2(1).

[4] Electoral Act 1963, ss.6 and 7.

[5] Courthouses (Provisions and Maintenance) Act 1935, s.3.

[6] See generally, Walsh, *Planning and Development Law*, (2nd ed.); O'Sullivan and Sheppard, *A Sourcebook on Planning Law in Ireland* (Abingdon, 1984 and 1987 Supplement); Scannell, *Planning Control: Twenty Years On* (1982) 4 D.U.L.J.(N.S.) 41 (Part 1); (1983) 5 D.U.L.J.(N.S.) 225 (Part 2).

[7] Town and Regional Planning Act 1934; Town and Regional Planning Act (Amendment) Act 1939. For an account of this legislation (which was repealed in its entirety in 1963) see Miley and King, *Town and Regional Planning in Ireland* (Dublin, 1951).

planning authorities for their functional area,[8] and were now obliged to produce, and regularly to update, a development plan. Furthermore, enforcement powers and the power to restrain unauthorised developments were greatly increased.

But even this legislation proved to be defective in a number of important respects. An appeal lay to the Minister for Local Government, who in practice was susceptible to local political pressures[9] and who often granted permissions which materially contravened the development plan.[10] Moreover, the enforcement powers while frequently utilised, proved cumbersome in dealing with the growing problem of unauthorised developments. The Local Government (Planning and Development) Act 1976 sought to deal with these problems. It transferred the Minister's appellate functions to an independent body, known as An Bord Pleanála. In addition, the enforcement controls were strengthened, and the Act envisaged a greater role for third-party objectors. Further detailed changes were made both to the planning process and to An Bord Pleanála by legislation enacted in 1982 and 1983[11] respectively.

While undoubtedly the most important function of a planning authority—the granting or refusing a planning permission—is an executive function, and vested in the City or County Manager, nevertheless the elected representatives do have an important say in the planning process. It is the task of the local councillors to make a development plan,[12] and they may also revoke or modify a planning permission.[13] In addition, the councillors may declare any particular area to be one of special amenity.[14]

A development plan drawn up by a local authority must identify certain objectives.[15] A local authority is required to keep a draft of the development

---

[8] Local Government (Planning and Development) Act 1963 ("the 1963 Act") s.2(2). An exception arises in the case of town commissioners, who, although they are local authorities, are not designated as planning authorities. These functions are discharged in the case of a town with commissioners by the county council of the county in which the town is situated.

[9] *Cf.* the comments of Henchy J. in *The State (Pine Valley Develoments Ltd.)* v. *Dublin County Council* [1984] I.R. 417, 425 and see pp. 374–378.

[10] This was held to be *ultra vires* by the Supreme Court in *The State (Pine Valley Developments Ltd.)* v. *Dublin County Council* [1984] I.R. 417. This decision was reversed by the Local Government (Planning and Development) Act 1982, s.6. An Bord Pleanála is expressly vested with a jurisdiction to depart from the terms of the development plan: Local Government (Planning and Development) Act 1976, s.14(8).

[11] The Local Government (Planning and Development) Act 1983 sets out the procedure governing the appointment of the chairman and members of An Bord Pleanála. This Act represents yet another legislative attempt to augment the impartiality of the Board and to reduce political interference with its operations. For a fuller account of this legislation, see Walsh, *op. cit.* pp. 79–83; Stevenson, "Planning Appeals in the Republic of Ireland" (1985) 7 *Urban Law and Policy* 170, and see p. 240.

[12] s.19(7) of the 1963 Act.

[13] s.30 of the 1963 Act.

[14] s.42 of the 1963 Act, as amended by s.40 of the 1976 Act.

[15] s.19(2)(a) of the 1963 Act. In the case of urban areas, a local authority is required to have regard to the following objectives: (a) indicating the zoning of particular areas for particular purposes; (b) improving road safety by the provision of parking places or road improvements; (c) the development and renewal of obsolete areas; (d) the preservation, improvement and extension of amenities. In rural areas, the objectives include (c) and (d), but also the improvement and extension of water and sewage supplies.

plan on public display for at least three months, and to take into consideration any objections or representations made with regard to the draft plan. The authority is entitled to make non-material alterations to the draft plan without going through the statutory notification and exhibition procedure again.

Subject to one important qualification, the planning authority is bound by the terms of the development plan and is not entitled to grant a permission which materially contravenes the terms of the development plan. This is a matter which was considered by O'Hanlon J. in *O'Leary* v. *Dublin County Council*[16] where the issue was whether the respondents were entitled to provide a halting site for members of the travelling community in an area of high amenity which had been designated as such in the relevant development plan. O'Hanlon J. accepted that this proposal constituted a material contravention of the development plan, observing that the "praiseworthy motives of the County Council" were not sufficient to absolve them from compliance with the planning law. He added that:

"I think that the requirements of the planning law have to be applied with the same stringency against the local authority, in this case, as would be the case if the proposal came from a private developer."[17]

A similar approach is manifest in the judgments of the Supreme Court in both *Grange Developments Ltd.* v. *Dublin County Council*[18] and *P. & F. Sharpe Ltd.* v. *Dublin County Council.*[19] In the *Grange Developments* case, an undertaking to grant planning permission in respect of an unspecified number of industrial buildings and hotels was purportedly given by the planning authority pursuant to section 57 of the Local Government (Planning and Development) Act 1963. This undertaking was apparently granted in an effort to avoid a large compensation claim by the developer, who had been refused planning permission to develop some 500 residential houses. The Supreme Court held that the undertaking was invalid on the ground that, *inter alia*, it involved the planning authority violating the terms of its own develop-

---

[16] [1988] I.R. 150. See also, *Wilkinson* v. *Dublin County Council*, High Court, September 7, 1990, where Costello J., following the principles of *O'Leary*, held that the provision of a halting site catering for at least 400 members of the travelling community by the local authority for an indefinite period was a material contravention of the development. Costello J. reached this conclusion (at p. 9 of his judgment) because:

"No reasonable planning authority could regard this development as being consistent with the proper planning and development of the area. For this reason, the Manager's order was ultra vires and should be quashed. This does not mean that the site cannot be developed as a halting site; it means that it cannot be developed as a halting site on the scale now proposed."

However, in *Ferris* v. *Dublin County Council*, the Supreme Court, November 7, 1990 upheld the creation of a temporary halting site, set on seven acres, catering for 30 families for a period of not more than five years. Finlay C.J. drew attention to the need for urgency and, emphasising the temporary nature of the site, said that the Manager's decision could not be regarded as unreasonable within the meaning of the principle enunciated by Henchy J. in *The State (Keegan)* v. *Stardust Compensation Tribunal* [1986] I.R. 642, 658.

[17] *Ibid.* 154.

[18] [1986] I.R. 246.

[19] [1989] I.L.R.M. 565.

ment plan. The lands in question were zoned for agricultural use and, as Finlay C.J. observed, "the erection of industrial buildings or structures for recreational purposes would have been inconsistent with that zoning."[20] In *P. & F. Sharpe*, the Supreme Court held that the planning authority would have acted *ultra vires* were it to grant a particular planning permission in respect of a road access to a dual carriage-way. The evidence showed that such permission would have involved "a significant and very important road hazard." Yet road safety was a major feature of the planning authority's development plan and, hence, the granting of such permission would have involved a material contravention of its own development plan.[21]

However, the elected members are entitled to grant such a permission following a passing of a special resolution to that effect.[22] The Manager can also be required to grant planning permission if directed by a valid resolution under section 4 of the City and County Management (Amendment) Act 1955, where the proposed development would not materially contravene the development plan.

The planning authority is entitled by virtue of section 26(1) of the 1963 Act to attach conditions to a grant of permission, but all such conditions imposed must be in furtherance of the proper planning and development. Section 26(2) states that, without prejudice to the generality of section 26(1), the conditions attached may include "any and all" of a list of specified conditions.[23] The planning authority is required to give reasons in respect of each condition imposed.[24] The discretionary power to attach conditions is, of course, governed by ordinary principles of administrative law. The conditions imposed must fairly and reasonably relate to the proposed development, and the reasons given in support of the condition must be capable of justifying the imposition of the condition.[25] Not only that, but the courts will quash the decision to attach conditions—even where the conditions are valid on their face—where it has been shown that the decision has been actuated by improper motives, or that the planning authority has rejected legitimate considerations, or has introduced irrelevant considerations, or has otherwise manifested unreasonableness in arriving at its decision.[26]

[20] [1986] I.R. 246, 255.
[21] 1976 Act, s.37.
[22] Generally speaking only An Bord Pleanála is entitled to grant a permission which materially contravenes the terms of the development plan. S.39(g) of the 1976 Act also permits the planning authority to contravene materially the development plan in certain circumstances once the elaborate procedure specified in the subsection has been followed.
[23] Among the conditions specifically authorised are included conditions requiring the carrying out of works (including the provision of car parks) which the authority consider are required for the purposes of the development authorised by the permission, conditions abating noise or vibration levels and conditions requiring contributions in respect of local authority expenditure.
[24] Local Government (Planning and Development) Act 1963, s.26(8), as inserted by Local Government (Planning and Development) Act 1976, s.39(9).
[25] *Killiney and Ballybrack Residents Assoc. Ltd.* v. *Minister for Local Government (No. 2)* [1978] I.L.R.M. 78.
[26] *The State (Fitzgerald)* v. *An Bord Pleanála* [1985] I.L.R.M. 117; *P. and F. Sharpe Ltd.* v. *Dublin County Council* [1989] I.L.R.M. 565; *Flanagan* v. *Galway County Council*, High Court, May 25, 1989.

An applicant may also obtain planning permission in default, for section 26(4) of the 1963 Act provides that where an application has been made to a planning authority in accordance with the regulations for the time being in force[27]; then if notice of the decision has not been given to the applicant within the appropriate period (which is generally two months),[28] a decision by the planning authority to grant permission shall be regarded as having been granted on the last day of the period. It is of some practical significance that if the planning authority acting bona fide requires the developer to provide further information, time starts to run again from the date when the information was provided. The purpose of these default provisions is to compel the planning authority to direct its mind to the planning application and to adjudicate upon such application within the appropriate period.

It is now clear that even a decision which, is *ultra vires* (and thus liable to be set aside as a nullity), is still a "decision" for the purposes of section 26(4), and thus the applicant cannot claim that "no decision" has been given in such a case and that he is consequently entitled to permission in default.[29]

An Bord Pleanála

Any person may appeal[30] against the decision of the planning authority to An Bord Pleanála. An Bord Pleanála is required to act judicially and there have been several cases where decisions have been quashed either because the Board breached the rules of constitutional justice, or because it was held to have abused its power, topics which are considered elsewhere,[31] where it acted on irrelevant considerations. The procedures governing planning appeals are contained in section 18(1) of the Local Government (Planning and Development) Act 1983:

"Where the Board is of opinion that any document, particulars or other information is necessary for the purpose of enabling it to determine an appeal . . . , the Board may serve on any person who is a party to the

[27] The following are the principal regulations currently in force: Local Government (Planning and Development) Regulations 1977 (S.I. 1977 No. 65); Local Government (Planning and Development) Regulations 1982 (S.I. 1982 No. 342); Local Government (Planning and Development) (Exempted Development and Amendment) Regulations 1984 (S.I. 1984 No. 348); Local Government (Planning and Development) (Exempted Development) Regulations 1985 (S.I. 1985 No. 130); European Communities (Environmental Impact Assessment) Regulations 1989 (S.I. 1989 No. 349) and Local Government (Planning and Development) Regulations 1990 (S.I. 1990 No. 89). For a recent example of a case where the applicant was held to have failed to comply with these regulations, (and was, thus, disentitled to default permission) see *Crodaun Homes Ltd.* v. *Kildare C.C.* [1983] I.L.R.M. 1. But see *Mulloy and Walsh* v. *Dublin C.C.* [1990] I.L.R.M. 633 (where Blayney J. held that the non-compliance with the Regulations could be ignored as *de minimis* so that the plaintiffs were held to be entitled to a default permission).
[28] Although the time period is extended where the local authority makes a bona fide request for further information: see s.26(4)(*b*) of the 1963 Act or if the applicant consents or if the Environmental Impact Assessment Regulations are involved.
[29] *The State (Abenglen Properties Ltd.)* v. *Dublin Corporation* [1984] I.R. 381: *Creedon* v. *Dublin Corporation* [1984] I.R. 428 (reaching similar conclusions in respect of the analogous default provisions contained in s.10 of the (now lapsed) Housing Act 1969).
[30] One may also simply appeal against a condition imposed by a planning authority: see Local Government (Planning and Development) Act 1983, s.19.
[31] See Chaps. 9 and 10.

appeal, or on any other person who has made submission or observations to the Board as regards the appeal, a notice under this section

(a) requiring that person . . . to submit to the Board such document, particulars or other information . . . and,

(b) stating that, in default of compliance with the requirements of the notice, the Board will . . . and without further notice to the person, pursuant to this section dismiss or otherwise determine the appeal.''

In contrast, however, the Local Government (Planning and Development) Regulations 1977, Article 38 requires the Board to give a copy of the appeal "to each other party to the appeal" and Article 35 defines "a party to the appeal" as including the appellant, the relevant planning authority, the applicant for a planning permission and the recipient of any warning notice. A curious result of this definition is that a successful third-party objector is not necessarily entitled—or, indeed, perhaps, at all—to a hearing on appeal before An Bord Pleanála. This emerged from the judgment of Murphy J. in *The State (Haverty)* v. *An Bord Pleanála*.[32] Here the applicant had successfully objected to the decision to planning permission before the planning authority, but this decision was reversed on appeal by An Bord Pleanála. As the applicant was not a "party to the appeal," she was not automatically supplied with a copy of the appeal. However, a planning consultant retained by the applicant duly applied to the Board for a copy of the grounds of appeal and thus obtained a copy. The applicant then made detailed comments in respect of the appeal but the appellants were given a further opportunity to provide further written replies in response to these submissions. The applicant was unaware of this further written reply until after the determination of the appeal and she claimed that the procedures adopted by the Board breached the rules of constitutional justice.

Murphy J. first drew attention to the lacuna in the 1977 Regulations inasmuch as they did not appear to recognise the rights of persons who had originally made submissions before the planning authority. However, it was clear from the terms of section 18 of the 1983 Act that such persons had rights to a fair hearing. Nevertheless, Murphy J. found no breach of constitutional justice in that he thought that fair procedures in this case merely ensured that a successful objector would have the right to make "informal objections," but no more than this. The judge stressed the need for finality and that some party "must have the last word." The reality was that the applicant had put forward a detailed professional argument before An Bord Pleanála and while Murphy J. accepted that the applicant was concerned that she might have:

"[W]ished to expand upon her argument or to raise counter-arguments to those made in reply by the developers but I have no doubt that the real substance of her case was before An Bord Pleanála and duly considered by it."[33]

[32] [1987] I.R. 485.
[33] *Ibid.* 493.

As a general rule, a party aggrieved by a planning decision should first exhaust his appellate remedies by appealing to An Bord Pleanála. However, where the applicant wishes to impugn the *vires* of a planning decision, it may be that he may now apply directly to the High Court for judicial review of that decision at least in certain circumstances.[34]

The Board is alone entitled to determine whether development has taken place, and, if so, whether it is exempted development[35] for the purpose of the planning code. The Board is also entitled to refer any point of law to the High Court for determination.[36]

Enforcement

The planning code may be enforced by way of criminal sanctions, enforcement or warning notices or by the granting of injunctive relief. By virtue of section 24 of the 1963 Act a person who carries out any development in respect of which permission is required without or in contravention of such permission is guilty of an offence. The prosecution may proceed summarily or by way of an indictment.[37] On the other hand, the planning authority may choose to take the less drastic step of issuing an enforcement notice or a warning notice, if of the opinion that a development is being carried out in an unauthorised manner, or contrary to the requirements of conditions attached to the permission. The enforcement notice[38] must specify the nature of the unauthorised development, or the development constituting non-compliance with a condition, and require the developer to take such steps as are necessary to restore the land to its original condition. Alternatively, a warning notice may be issued by a planning authority where it appears that the land is being, or is likely to be, developed in an unauthorised manner,[39] or where unauthorised *use* is being made of the land, or where any structural or natural feature of the land, the preservation of which is required by a condition subject to which a permission for the development of any land was granted, may be removed or damaged.

The planning injunction is undoubtedly the most effective method of ensuring compliance with the planning code. Section 27(1) of the 1963 Act authorises the High Court to restrain unauthorised development or use of land. The High Court is empowered by section 27(2) to require any specified person to do or not to do or to cease to do anything which the court considers necessary to ensure that the development is carried out in conformity with the planning

---

[34] *P. and F. Sharpe Ltd.* v. *Dublin County Council* [1989] I.L.R.M. 565, but *cf.* the decision of the Supreme Court in *The State (Abenglen Properties Ltd.)* v. *Dublin Corporation* [1984] I.R. 381.

[35] s.14(2) of the 1976 Act.

[36] s.42 of the 1976 Act.

[37] s.24 of the 1963 Act, as amended by s.8 of the Local Government (Planning and Development) Act 1982.

[38] The differing types of enforcement notices which may be issued are discussed by Walsh, *op. cit.* pp. 145–154. Failure to comply with an enforcement notice is an offence: Local Government (Planning and Development) Act 1963, s.37(7).

[39] s.26 of the 1976 Act. This matter is discussed by Walsh, *op. cit.* pp. 154–155.

permission.[40] Section 27 expressly provides that an applicant need not satisfy ordinary *locus standi* requirements:

> "We are all, as users and enjoyers of the environment in which we live, given a standing to go to the Court and to seek an order compelling those who have been given a development permission to carry out the development in accordance with the terms of that permission. And the Court is given a discretion sufficiently wide to make whatever order is necessary to achieve that objective."[41]

The effectiveness of the section 27 remedy has been strengthened by a series of decisions which make it plain that it would require exceptional circumstances for the court to refrain from exercising its powers under this section in the case of unauthorised development or use of land.[42]

The planning authority is also entitled in certain limited situations to revoke or modify a permission granted.[43] This is a reserved function, and is exercisable only by the elected representatives. The power to modify or revoke such a permission may itself only be used where (if the permission relates to the carrying out of works) such works have not been commenced or (if the permission relates to a change of use of land) at any time prior to a change of use. A person affected by a revocation notice may appeal to An Bord Pleanála. This power of revocation was granted to planning authorities to deal with the problem of unimplemented permissions. Passage of time, or changes in the development plan may make it desirable that a particular permission should not be implemented. Accordingly, the revocation power must be exercised with these objectives in mind, and it would not seem that this power may be validly exercised for no better reason than that a particular permission has been granted on appeal,[44] or because the applicant has succeeded in obtaining permission in default.

Housing

Numerous pieces of legislation dating from the mid-nineteenth century have sought to deal with the problem of poor and overcrowded housing, and to provide suitable accommodation for persons of modest means. The principal legislation on this topic is now contained in the Housing Act 1966, although this reforming and consolidating Act has been amended on a number of occasions, most notably by the Housing (Miscellaneous Provisions) Act 1979, and the Housing Act 1988.[45]

Local authorities are vested with the powers of a housing authority for their

---

[40] However, the Court will not make a mandatory order in s.27(2) proceedings: see *Dublin C.C. v. Kirby* [1985] I.L.R.M. 325.

[41] *Morris* v. *Garvey* [1983] I.R. 319, 323, *per* Henchy J.

[42] *Morris* v. *Garvey* [1983] I.R. 319; *Stafford and Bates* v. *Roadstone Ltd.* [1980] I.L.R.M. 1 and see generally, Scannell, "Planning Control—Twenty Years On II" (1983) 5 D.U.L.J.(N.S.) 225, 241–247.

[43] s.30 of the 1963 Act. See Walsh, *op. cit.* pp. 99–102.

[44] *The State (Cogley)* v. *Dublin Corporation* [1970] I.R. 244.

[45] See Keane, *op. cit.* pp. 128–147: Roche, *op. cit.* pp. 220–243.

functional area. Section 8 of the Housing Act 1988[46] now requires housing authorities to prepare an estimate of existing and prospective housing requirements at any time that appears to them expedient or as they may be directed to do so by the Minister for the Environment. In making such assessment, the housing authority are required to have regard, *inter alia*, to information:

> "[I]n relation to the housing conditions in the area, including the number of houses which are in any respect unfit or unsuitable for human habitation, are over-crowded,[47] are shared involuntarily or are expected (through obsolescence, demolition or conversion to other uses) to be lost to the supply of housing over the period to which the estimate relates."

Section 9 requires a housing authority to make an assessment, on at least a three-yearly basis, of the need for provision by the authority:

> "[O]f adequate and suitable housing accommodation for persons—
> (a) whom the authority have reason to believe, or are likely to require, accommodation from the authority, and
> (b) who, in the opinion of the authority, are in need of such accommodation and are unable to provide from their own resources."

Section 9(2) provides that, without prejudice to the generality of section 9(1), a housing authority is enjoined to have regard, *inter alia*, to the housing needs of the homeless; travellers; persons living in sub-standard or overcrowded accommodation; young persons leaving institutional care or without family accommodation; persons in need of accommodation for medical or compassionate reasons; the elderly or those who are disabled or handicapped. Section 11 (which replaces the previous section 60 of the Housing Act 1966) requires the housing authority to draw up a scheme of priorities for the letting of dwellings to persons in need of accommodation and who have insufficient means to provide for their own accommodation. Section 11(2)(a) permits the authority to reserve a particular number or proportion of dwellings for "persons of such category or categories" as it may determine.

The purpose and effect of section 60 of the Housing Act 1966 (which corresponded to the present section 11 of the 1988 Act) was examined by the Supreme Court in *McDonald* v. *Feeley*.[48] In this case, itinerants residing within the County Council's functional area had trespassed on lands belonging to the Council. The Council members resolved, pursuant to section 4 of the City and County Management (Amendment) Act 1955 that the County Manager should take action to evict the itinerants. Initially, no alternative

---

[46] See Maher (1988) I.C.L.S.A. 28/01–28/33.

[47] By virtue of s.63 of the Housing Act 1966, a house is deemed to be overcrowded when the number of persons ordinarily sleeping in the house and the number of rooms therein either: (1) are such that any two of those persons, being persons of 10 years of age or more of opposite sexes and not being persons living together as man and wife must sleep in the same room, or (2) are such that the free air space in any room used as a sleeping apartment for any person is less than 400 cubic feet.

[48] Supreme Court, July 23, 1980.

accommodation had been offered to the itinerants. The Supreme Court noted
that a County Manager could only be required to perform a lawful act by lawful means, and hinted that action of this nature would not have been lawful
had not alternative accommodation been offered at the eleventh hour by the
County Council. Such action might not have been lawful because the housing
authority would have acted without having regard to the housing needs of
persons resident within their functional area.

As far as the specific housing needs of the travelling community are concerned, section 13 of the Housing Act 1988 now provides that:

> "A housing authority may provide, improve, manage and control sites for
> caravans used by [members of the travelling community] and may carry out
> any works incidental to such provision, improvement, management or con-
> trol, including the provision of such services for such sites."

This provision is permissive only and would not seem to give rise to any
enforceable statutory duty.[49]

In some respects, the Housing Act 1988 represents a dilution of the obligations formerly imposed by the Housing Act 1966. For example, section 55
of the 1966 Act obliged the local authority to draw up a building programme,
but this section is now expressly repealed by section 30 of the 1988 Act. This
repeal was justified[50] on the basis that as the cost of local authority building
programmes were increasingly met by central government funds, the importance of the building programme had accordingly diminished to the point of
redundancy. On the other hand, some statutory obligations contained in the
1966 Act have been strengthened and added to by the latest legislation.
Section 56(1) provides that a housing authority:

> "may erect, acquire, purchase, convert or reconstruct, lease or otherwise
> provide dwellings (including houses, flats, maisonettes and hostels) and
> such dwellings may be temporary or permanent."

Section 13(2) of the 1988 Act now extends these powers of housing authorities
to include the management and control sites for caravans used by members of
the travelling community.

Lettings made by a housing authority under the provisions of the Housing
Acts are subject to an implied warranty that the premises are fit for human
habitation. This was decided by the Supreme Court in *Siney* v. *Dublin Corporation*,[51] where two months after the plaintiffs moved into a flat provided
by the defendants under the Housing Act 1966 water appeared under the

---

[49] In *University of Limerick* v. *Ryan*, High Court, February 21, 1991, Barron J. agreed that s.13
was permissive, but said that the authority's discretion was one "which must in appropriate circumstances be exercised". He added that, by virtue of s.13, "a housing authority cannot meet its
statutory obligations by offering only a conventional dwelling to travellers".
[50] See the comments of the Minister for the Environment (Mr. Padraic Flynn T.D.) at *Seanad
Debates*, Vol. 120, col. 2171.
[51] [1980] I.R. 400. For an excellent account of this case, see Kerr and Clarke, "Council Housing,
Implied terms and Negligence—A Critique of *Siney* v. *Dublin Corporation*" (1980) 15
Ir.Jur.(N.S.) 32. See also, *Coleman* v. *Dundalk U.D.C.*, Supreme Court, July 17, 1985.

floor covering of the bedroom of the flat and a fungus spread over the walls. Eventually the plaintiff and his family were compelled to leave the flat and they were housed elsewhere by the Corporation. O'Higgins C.J. held that the plaintiff was entitled to damages for breach of an implied warranty contained in the lease:

> "[T]his was a letting made by the defendant corporation of a dwelling provided under its building programme and let by it in accordance with its scheme of priority for, *inter alia*, the ending of overcrowding and the elimination of houses unfit in any respect for human habitation. . . . It seems to me that not to imply such a condition or warranty would be to assume that the defendant corporation was entitled to disregard, and was disregarding, the responsibilities cast upon it by the very Act which authorised the building and letting of the accommodation in question."[52]

This entire question was further explored by Blayney J. in *Burke* v. *Dublin Corporation*,[53] where the defendants had installed a defective heating system (which apparently had caused asthma and other bronchial conditions) into a number of houses let by them under the Housing Act 1966. The defendants argued that the house was not unfit for human habitation within the meaning of section 66(2) of the Housing Act 1966:

> "The housing authority in considering whether a house is unfit for human habitation shall have regard to the extent (if any) to which the house is deficient as respects each of the matters set out in the Second Schedule to the Act."

The matters expressly referred to in the Second Schedule did not include heating systems, but Blayney J. could not accept that the standards in the Second Schedule by reference to which the fitness for human habitation was to be determined were exclusive. In his view, the houses were not fit for human habitation at the time of the letting by reason of the defects in the heating system:

> "Suppose at the time of the letting it was known that there was a risk that the use of the heating [system] might cause one of the tenants to develop asthma, would the house have been let to the [plaintiff]? I have no doubt but that it would not. The defendants would have taken the view that it was unfit for letting in the condition in which it was, and would have substiuted some other form of heating [system]. And this would have rendered the house unfit for human habitation."[54]

Blayney J. then proceeded to consider the claim of another plaintiff who had actually purchased the dwelling that had been originally let to her under the Housing Act 1966 by the authority, but whose case was otherwise on all

---

[52] *Ibid*. 410.
[53] [1990] 1 I.R. 18.
[54] *Ibid*. 27. The reasoning of Blayney J. was expressly approved by the Supreme Court: *Burke* v. *Dublin Corporation*, Supreme Court, July 16, 1990.

fours with that of the other plaintiffs. The judge referred to section 90(1) of the 1966 Act under which the sale was effected:

" . . . [A] housing authority may, if they think fit, sell or lease any dwelling to which this section applies, in case the dwelling is occupied by a tenant, to the tenant, or, in case the dwelling is not so occupied, to any other person."

Blayney J. then went on to say that the reasoning of O'Higgins C.J. in *Siney* would appear to apply, *mutatis mutandis*, to this type of case:

"If a warranty is not to be implied, that would amount to say that the housing authority was entitled to disregard the responsibilities cast upon it by the Act which authorised the building and selling of the house . . . [A] dwelling newly built by a housing authority might be immediately leased or sold rather than let on a weekly tenancy. If a housing authority were to do this, it seems to me that it would be wholly illogical that they could escape the duty of ensuring that the dwelling was reasonably fit for human habitation, although they would have had such a duty if they were letting the dwelling on a weekly tenancy."[55]

Damages were accordingly awarded to the tenant-purchaser for breach of the implied warranty. This might be thought to be a far-reaching extension of the duties of a housing authority under the Housing Act 1966, but, of course, the *Burke* decision does not mean that the authority will have a potential liability in perpetuity, as it were, to tenant-purchasers and their successors in title. The essential element of this part of Blayney J.'s judgment is that a local authority is responsible for any breach of implied warranties at the time of the sale of the premises to a tenant-purchaser, but not for any defects that subsequently arise.

As far as private accommodation is concerned, a local authority is entitled to send the equivalent of what in the planning process are called warning notices where it is satisfied that a particular house is overcrowded or is unfit for human habitation. Section 65 of the 1966 Act entitles the authority to serve a notice on the owner of the premises requiring him to desist from causing or permitting the overcrowding. Failure to comply with such a notice is an offence.[56] In the case of unfit houses, the authority may serve a notice on the owner of such premises requiring him within 28 days to carry out specified works. If the house is unfit for human habitation, but is not capable of being rendered habitable at a reasonable expense, then the owner must be afforded the opportunity of carrying out such specified works, or using the house in a particular manner. If this is not possible, the authority may make a closing order (which prohibits the use of the house or any part thereof for any purpose specified by the housing authority) or a demolition order. A person

---

[55] *Ibid.* 29.
[56] s.65(4) of the 1966 Act. The maximum penalty which may be imposed is £100 and one month's imprisonment.

aggrieved by a closing order or a demolition order may generally appeal to the Circuit Court.[57]

Now that the Housing Act 1969[58] has been repealed by the Housing Act 1988, the demolition of habitable houses is dealt with by the Local Government (Planning and Development) (Exempted Development and Amendment) Regulations 1984.[59] These regulations have amended the classes of development which are exempted from the requirement of obtaining planning permission contained in the Third Schedule to the Local Government (Planning and Development) Regulations 1977.[60] The demolition of a habitable house is no longer regarded as an exempted development and consequently planning permission is required.

Functions under the Gaming and Lotteries Act 1956

Part III of the Gaming and Lotteries Act 1956 confers important functions on local authorities in that such authorities can by resolution determine whether they wish to permit the operation of gaming at amusement halls and funfairs within their functional area. Unless the local authority has resolved that the provisions of Part III shall be so applied within their functional area, the operation of gaming at amusement halls or funfairs is unlawful.

Once such a resolution is in force, then the District Court has jurisdiction to grant a certificate authorising the issue of a gaming licence, to which conditions may be attached. The District Court is required to have regard to various statutory criteria, including the character of the applicant or the persons exercising control and management; the number of gaming licences already in the vicinity; the suitability of the premises and the class of persons likely to have resort to it.[61] The Revenue Commissioners are then obliged to grant a gaming licence on payment of the appropriate excise duty.[62] However, a certificate of this kind has been held to be an annual certificate of limited duration and it is not in the nature of a permanent property right which attaches to the premises. This was decided by Johnson J. in *Dublin Corporation* v. *O'Hanrahan*,[63] where he held that a certificate granted by the District Court must be renewed annually and that a "certificate can be refused in respect of a premises which was previously certified."[64]

The vast majority of local authorities did exercise their powers under Part III of the Acts, but increased social concern as to the perceived evils associated with such gaming halls led to many local authorities exercising their

---

[57] ss.72 and 73 of the 1966 Act.
[58] The Act required permission from a housing authority for the demolition of a habitable house, or the use "otherwise than for human habitation" of any habitable house. The Act lapsed on December 31, 1984.
[59] S.I. 1984 No. 348.
[60] S.I. 1977 No. 65.
[61] s.17.
[62] s.19.
[63] [1988] I.R. 121.
[64] *Ibid.* 124.

powers under section 13 to rescind such resolutions, at least in part.[65] This in turn has given rise to litigation, but the courts have displayed a marked disinclination to interfere with the exercise of such discretion by local authorities.

A good example is supplied by *The State (Divito)* v. *Arklow U.D.C.*[66] Here the local authority, anticipating an application by the applicant to the District Court for a gaming licence, rescinded an earlier resolution which had applied Part III of the 1956 Act to the entirety of their functional area. The authority then readopted Part III for part of their functional area, but excluded a stretch of the street where the applicant's premises were situated. This resolution was assailed on a number of grounds and among them was the argument that the local authority was motivated by bias. Henchy J. said:

> "I have no doubt that in the eyes of the applicant, the council's resolutions appear as a personalised obstruction of his efforts to convert his premises into a licensed amusement hall. However, looking at the situation objectively, I cannot hold that he has shown that the council were actuated, wholly or primarily by personal considerations . . . [T]here is ample evidence to lend support to the council's claim that, in removing the application of Part III of the Act from a stretch of Upper Main St. which contains the applicant's premises, they were motivated by considerations such as the undesirability of having an amusement arcade in the vicinity of five schools, the adequacy for the town of Arklow of the four existing amusement arcades, and the declared wishes of the local community."[67]

Accordingly, therefore, a resolution to rescind or vary the extent of a previous resolution under Part III of the 1956 Act will be upheld where it is based on objective considerations. Once such a resolution has been passed, then it is clear that the District Court has no further jurisdiction to grant certificates under the terms of Part III of the 1956 Act and that any gaming on premises within the area specified by the rescinding resolution becomes unlawful.[68]

8. Central Government Controls

The powers of the elected representatives have not only been eroded from below by the management system, but also reduced from above by the ascendency of the Minister for the Environment. For local authorities are subject to extensive and diverse controls exercised by the Minister for the Environment, of which there is one at almost every aspect of a local authority's structure and functions. The most significant single control probably flows from the replacement of almost all forms of income from rates with rate support grants, a matter covered in Part 5. But there are a myriad of other forms of control. Local authorities, for instance, enjoy a general power to borrow

[65] For the background to the recission of the Part III resolution by Dublin Corporation, see *Re Murphy's Application* [1987] I.R. 667.
[66] [1986] I.L.R.M. 123.
[67] *Ibid.* 126.
[68] *Re Camillo's Application* [1988] I.R. 104.

money, but subject to the control of the Minister.[69] In practice, most local authorities borrow from either the Local Loan Fund[70] (which is under the control of the Minister for Finance) or (for short term loans) from the banks. Dealing with the former, more important source, Roche states:

"In applying for sanction, the local authority submits details of the proposed work. The Minister has professional and technical staff who examine the proposals. If there is no technical objection and the Minister is satisfied that the project is one for which borrowing should be permitted, that the authority has power to borrow for this purpose and the ability to repay, sanction is given. By this the Minister does not assume any responsibility for the plans or schemes put forward. If the loan is sought from the Local Loans Fund, the Minister will recommend the issue from the Fund."[71]

In more specific matters, the Minister for the Environment enjoys a power of consent or veto, for example, with regard to the making of by-laws.[72] Some statutes even give the Minister power to make regulations for local authorities, as, for example, in planning matters.[73] Even when this is not the formal legal position, substantially the same result is achieved (in terms of uniformity throughout the country and Ministerial ascendancy) by the Department of the Environment issuing circulars containing model by-laws or other regulations which most local authorities are pleased to adopt. In certain cases (such as dispute as to whether a local authority dwelling which is being sold to a former tenant has been put into "good structural condition,")[74] an individual may appeal to the Minister against a decision of the local authority. In other cases, the Minister's power of command is given specific statutory foundation. For example, section 15 of the Public Health (Ireland) Act 1896 provides:

"Where complaint is made to the [Minister for the Environment] that a sanitary authority has made default in providing their district with sufficient sewers . . . .[the Minister], if satisfied, after due inquiry that the authority has been guilty of the alleged default shall make an order limiting a time for the performance of their duty in the matter of such complaint. If such duty is not performed by the time limited in the order, such order may be

[69] Local Government (No. 2) Act 1960, s.4.
[70] Constituted by the Local Loan Funds Acts 1935–1987. The maximum aggregate amount which can be advanced by the Fund is increased every few years. By the Local Loan Funds (Amendment) Act 1986, it was fixed at £4.5 billion. Note that by s.1 of the Local Loans Fund (Amendment) Act 1987, the Minister is empowered to waive the whole or part of any local loan "if it seems to him desirable so to do."
[71] Roche, *op. cit.* p. 182. However, the effect of the 1987 Act is that all major local authority capital projects are now funded by way of capital grants, thereby eliminating the circular transfers of the local loans fund.
[72] Local Government (Ireland) Act 1898, s.16; Municipal Corporations (Ireland) Act 1840, s.125 (by-law must be fixed to outer door of town hall for 40 days after council resolution, during which period Minister may veto it). Again, s.26(1) of the Local Government Act 1941 provides that the consent of the Minister for Environment is necessary before an officer of any local authority may lawfully be removed from his post: see *O'Mahony* v. *Arklow U.D.C.* [1965] I.R. 710.
[73] Local Government (Planning and Development) Act 1963, s.10; Local Government (Water Pollution) Act 1977, ss.26, 27 and 30.
[74] Housing Act 1966, s.106(1).

enforced by mandamus or [the Minister] may appoint some person to perform such duty . . . .''

A modern example is to be found in sections 11 and 12 of the Local
Government (Roads and Motorways) Act 1974. These sections provide that a
road authority must comply with any direction in relation to a "national road
or motorway"[75] which is given by the Minister. If the authority fails to do so,
the Minister may make an order requiring the authority to comply; foiling
obedience to this, the Minister may make an order investing himself with such
of the functions of the road authority as he considers necessary.

The Minister is even entitled to make two steps which penetrate to the very
heart of local democracy. First, he may remove the elected members on any
number of specific grounds:

(i) where he is satisfied following a local inquiry that the authority is not
effectively performing its duties;
(ii) where the local authority refuses to obey any court order,
(iii) where the authority refuses to permit its accounts to be duly audited;
(iv) where the number of members is not sufficient to permit a quorum to
be formed for meetings[76];
(v) where the authority refuses to strike an adequate rate,[77]
(vi) where the authority refuses or wilfully neglects to comply with an
express requirement which is imposed upon them by any enactment or
order.[78]

It should be noted that ground (vi) would authorise the Minister to dismiss
the elected members if, for example, they refused to comply with his directive
that the rate struck in the pound should not exceed a specific amount. These
powers were employed in 1969 to dismiss the members of Dublin Corporation
where the Council had deliberately struck a rate less than the full amount
required to meet the demand for health services.[79] Where the elected members are dismissed, the Minister may appoint one or more persons to act as
commissioners for the local authority.[80] The commissioner discharges the
reserved functions of the elected members in the interim period pending the
next elections.[81]

Secondly, by section 2 of the Local Elections Act 1972, the Minister has the
power to order that local elections be postponed, although this order is made
subject to confirmation by Dáil and Senate resolutions. Indeed, this power

---

[75] As defined in s.1 of the 1974 Act (in effect, a road becomes a "national road" or "motorway"
when it is delcared to be such by the Minister). For a further example of a power to give directions, see Local Government (Financial Provisions) Act 1978, s.15.
[76] Grounds (i)–(iv) are contained in the Local Government Act 1941, s.44.
[77] Local Government Act 1946, s.30(4).
[78] Local Government Act 1941, s.44 as inserted by s.64 of the Local Government Act 1946.
[79] Roche, *op. cit.* p. 123. The members of Naas U.D.C. were dismissed in similar circumstances
in 1985; see *The Irish Times*, August 3, 1985.
[80] Local Government Act 1941, s.48.
[81] s.49 of the 1941 Act. Local authorities now come within the Ombudsman's remit: see Ombudsman Act 1980 (Second Schedule) (Amendment) Order 1985 (S.I. 1985 No. 69).

has been exercised surprisingly often.[82] In May 1973, the then Minister for Environment (or Local Government, as it was then known) stated that his order postponing the local elections from 1973 to 1974 was the fifteenth such postponment since 1919 and the fourth such postponment in the preceding eight years.[83] Since 1974, the elections have been postponed in 1984 and 1990.[84]

Naturally, the very existence of these powers presupposes that they will be exercised on an informed basis. Accordingly, the Minister may require a local authority:

"to make to him any return or report or furnish him with any information in relation to their functions which he may consider necessary or desirable . . . ."[85]

Moreover, the Minister may even cause a local inquiry to be held for the purpose or any of his powers or duties.[86]

In reality, of course, even without particular legal warrant, a Minister or Departmental civil servant's suggestion will carry enormous weight becaue of the relationship of ascendancy and subservience within which it is made. It would be difficult to gainsay the observation of one commentator to the effect that "local authorities are little more than executive agencies,"[87] nor, indeed, the more figurative comments of Dr. Barrington:

"Local government is like any other historical ruin: something that we are perhaps reluctant to see removed wholly, but which we are prepared to see moulder away."[88]

---

[82] Local Elections Act 1973, s.2(4).
[83] *Dáil Debates*, Vol. 265, col. 1050 (May 15, 1973).
[84] The present Coalition Government have announced a postponement in March 1990 to allow for fundamental reform of local government in advance of the next local elections scheduled in June 1990. The Advisory Expert Committee has now reported: *Local Government Reorganisation* (Pl. 7918) (March, 1991).
[85] Local Government Act 1941, s.84.
[86] *Ibid.* s.83.
[87] Walker, *Local Government Finance in Ireland* (E.R.S.I., 1962), p. 4.
[88] Barrington, *The Irish Administrative System* (Dublin, 1988), p. 40.

PART III

INSTITUTIONS OF CONTROL

CHAPTER 6

TRIBUNALS, INQUIRIES AND LICENSING[1]

1. Introduction

One may begin an explanation of the nature of tribunals by listing a few examples (most of which are considered *infra*). In the fields of taxation and compulsory acquisition, there are: Appeal Commissioners[2]; the Valuation Tribunal[3]; Employment Appeals Tribunal[4]; the Mining Board[5]; and arbitrators appointed by the Land Values Reference Committee under various statutes to fix compensation for land compulsorily acquired.[6] Tribunals which resolve disputes arising from the running of the welfare state include the appeals officers in the Department of Social Welfare,[7] and the General Medical Services Payments Board.[8] In related fields there are the Criminal Injuries Compensation Tribunal[9] and the Legal Aid Board.[10] Several tribunals have been set up to operate the various types of control and regulation in the public interest, often by way of a licensing system. These include the Censorship of Films Board[11]; the Censorship of Publications Board[12]; An Bord Pleanála[13]; the Registrar of Friendly Societies[14] and the Independent Radio and Tele-

---

[1] See generally, Stout, *Administrative Law in Ireland* (1985, I.P.A.), Chaps. 7–9 and App. 1; Grogan, *Administrative Tribunals* in F. G. King (ed.) *Public Administration in Ireland* III (Dublin, 1954), p. 32; Donaldson, *Some Comparative Aspects of Irish Law* (Duke, 1957), pp. 192–198 and Grogan, *Administrative Tribunals in the Public Service* (Dublin, 1961).
[2] Income Tax Act 1967, Pt. XXVI.
[3] Valuation Act 1988.
[4] Redundancy Payments Act 1967, s.39, as amended by s.1 of the Unfair Dismissals Act 1977. The Employment Appeals Tribunal has replaced the former Redundancy Payments Tribunals which had been established under the 1967 Act. For an account of the work of this tribunal, see Redmond, *Dismissal Law in the Republic of Ireland* (Dublin, 1982), pp. 120–128.
[5] Minerals Development Act 1940, s.33.
[6] Acquisition of Land (Assessment of Compensation) Act 1919, as amended by Acquisition of Land (Reference Committee) Act 1925. Notice that following the change of government in 1987, it was announced that the farm tax was no longer to be collected. Accordingly, although the Farm Tax Act 1985 has not been repealed, the Farm Tax Tribunal which it constituted is no longer *de facto* extant: see further, *Duggan* v. *An Taoiseach* [1989] I.L.R.M. 712.
[7] See further, Pt. 4, pp. 241–248.
[8] See pp. 241–248.
[9] *Scheme of Compensation for Personal Injuries Criminally Inflicted* (1974) (Prl. 3658). See Osborough, "The Work of the Criminal Injuries Compensation Tribunal" (1978) 13 Ir.Jur.(N.S.) 320.
[10] *Scheme of Legal Aid and Advice* (1979, Prl. 8534), pp. 7–11. See Whyte, "And Justice for Some" (1984) 6 D.U.L.J.(N.S.) 88.
[11] Censorship of Films Act 1923, s.1. See also, Video Recordings Act 1989, s.10.
[12] Censorship of Publications Act 1946, s.2. Nowadays, the Censorship Board is rarely used.
[13] Local Government (Planning and Development) Act 1976, ss.3–13 and Schedule to the Act. See Stevenson, "Planning Appeals in the Republic of Ireland" (1985) 7 *Urban Law and Policy* 170.
[14] For an account of the miscellaneous work of the Registrar, see Kerr and Whyte, *Irish Trade Union Law* (Professional Books, 1985), pp. 41–48.

vision Commission.[15] A number of tribunals exist to discipline members within the public service, for instance in the police and defence forces and in the prison service.[16]

As can be seen, the majority of the tribunals operate in the field of public law, assisting in the dirigiste and welfare aspects of the State's responsibilities. However, when creating a statutory innovation in the private law area, the Oireachtas sometimes chooses to vest responsibility for implementing the scheme in a tribunal, rather than a court. Examples include An Bord Uchtála[17]; the Labour Court[18]; the Employment Appeals Tribunal[19]; the Rent Tribunal[20]; the Pensions Tribunal[21] and the Controller of Patents, Designs and Trade Marks.[22]

A further anomaly is that, while most tribunals have been established by statute, in some cases—for instance, the Criminal Injuries Compensation Tribunal, Legal Aid Board, Motor Insurance Bureau and the Stardust Compensation Scheme—they are established merely by administrative scheme. The extra-statutory character of these tribunals does not, however, preclude judicial review of their decisions. This question was raised in *R.* v. *Criminal Injuries Compensation Board, ex p. Lain*,[23] where, following the English case of *The State (Hayes)* v. *Criminal Injuries Compensation Tribunal*,[24] Finlay P. said that the High Court would review a decision of the tribunal in appropriate cases, such as where the principles of constitutional justice had been violated, or where the scheme of compensation had been misinterpreted.

We ought to mention here a sub-group which are sometimes called (in a further example of the vague terminology endemic in this field) "domestic tribunals." Any profession, trade union, organisation or even club may have rules for dealing, itself, with the discipline of its own members. Quite often, in the interest of fairness, a domestic tribunal will be set up to apply these disciplinary rules so as to determine whether the member is guilty of some transgression and, if so, what his punishment should be. In some cases the rules will be statutory in origin. Examples are those relating to the legal, medical and dental[25] professions. In other cases, notably trade unions[26] but

---

[15] Radio and Television Act 1988.
[16] See, *e.g.* the disciplinary mechanism established by the Garda Síochána (Discipline) Regulations 1971 (S.I. 1971 No. 316) and the Garda Síochána (Complaints) Act 1986; for the latter see pp. 230–231.
[17] Adoption Act 1952, s.8.
[18] Industrial Relations Act 1946, Pt. II. See Mortished, "The Industrial Relations Act 1946" in King (ed.) *Public Administration in Ireland* II (Dublin, 1949).
[19] See n. 4, *supra*.
[20] Housing (Private Rented Dwellings) (Amendment) Act 1983, ss.2–4. For an account of the procedure before the Rent Tribunal, see de Blacam, *The Control of Private Rented Dwellings* (Dublin, 1984), pp. 55–62.
[21] Pensions Act 1990, Pt. II.
[22] Patents Act 1964, ss.77 and 78.
[23] [1967] 2 Q.B. 864.
[24] [1982] I.L.R.M. 210.
[25] See, respectively, Solicitors (Amendment) Act 1960, Pt. II; Medical Practitioners Act 1978, Pt. V; Dentists Act 1985, Pt. II.
[26] See Kerr and Whyte, *Irish Trade Union Law* (Professional Books 1985), pp. 100–102.

also sports associations, like the G.A.A., they will derive their authority ultimately from the agreement of their members. In both cases, but especially
where the tribunal is constituted by statute, it will probably be subject to
judicial control and at least some of the principles of substantive public law
will apply.[27] The rationale for this intervention is doubtless that while these
bodies may not be formally or completely "public" in nature, they make such
a crucial impact on their members and on the rest of the community that their
affairs warrant the attention of the court. In *Abbott* v. *Sullivan*[28] Denning L.J.
said of trade union committees:

> "These bodies, which exercise a monopoly in an important sphere of
> human activity, with the power of depriving a man of his livelihood, must
> act in accordance with the elementary rules of justice. They must not con-
> demn a man without giving him an opportunity to be heard in his own
> defence: and any agreement or practice to the contrary would be invalid."[29]

Although Denning L.J. was in dissent, it is these views which represent the
modern law.[30] However, notwithstanding this principle, in practice, a court
will sometimes resile from interfering in certain cases with the internal affairs
of a tribunal whose authority derives from contract. Thus, in *McGrath and
O'Ruairc* v. *Trustees of Maynooth College*[31] Henchy J. observed that a civil
court was not the ideal forum in which to decide what was a "grave delin-
quency against clerical obligations" within the meaning of the college's own
internal statutes. The court could only reject the conclusion of a domestic tribunal when it was one "that could not reasonably have been come to in the
circumstances," or where the decisions had been arrived at in breach of natural justice or other internal procedure prerequisites.

   As with Cleopatra, so with tribunals: "Age cannot wither them nor custom
stale their infinite variety." This lack of uniformity extends even to the
nomenclature. Not only do the names of tribunals differ—board, commission,
tribunal, officer, registrar, controller, referee, umpire—but different authorities use different titles for the entire species. Thus one finds tribunals described as: administrative tribunals; special tribunals; statutory tribunals, or,
even, quasi-judicial tribunals. Modern usage, adopted here, prefers—simply—
"tribunals."

   Before going further, we ought to offer a summary of the commonly-
accepted meaning of the term "tribunal." It is a body, independent of the
Government or any other entity but at the same time not a court, which takes

---

[27] See, *e.g. O'Donoghue* v. *Veterinary Council* [1975] I.R. 398 and *Re M., a Doctor* [1984] I.R.
479 (review of statutory tribunals) and *McGrath and O'Ruairc* v. *Trustees of Maynooth College*
[1979] I.L.R.M. 166 and *Connolly* v. *McConnell* [1983] I.R. 172 (domestic tribunals). See
further, pp. 321–328.
[28] [1952] 1 K.B. 189.
[29] *Ibid.* 198.
[30] See, *e.g. Edwards* v. *SOGAT* [1971] Ch. 354; *Enderby Town F.C.* v. *Football Association*
[1971] Ch. 591; *N.E.E.T.U.* v. *McConnell* (1983) 2 J.I.S.L.L. 97 and *Connolly* v. *McConnell*
[1983] I.R. 172.
[31] [1979] I.L.R.M. 166.

decisions affecting individual rights, according to some fairly precise (and usually legal) guidelines and by following a regular and fairly formal procedure.[32] This is an explanation on whose elements we shall enlarge in Part 3.

Such a definition leads straightaway to the question: why does it matter whether or not a body is classified as a tribunal? It should be made clear, first of all, that the term tribunal (just like "state-sponsored body") is not a statutory category from membership of which certain definite legal consequences flow. Rather it is a term popularised by academic lawyers as an organising principle for books, lectures, etc. and as a basis for comparisons. Secondly, and more importantly, a court exercising the power of judicial review over a public body may be more likely to insist on rigorous standards of constitutional justice, reasonableness, etc., if it takes the view that the body before it possesses the attributes of a tribunal. However, this is merely a question of degree, for given that a certain type of decision is involved, a court will apply stringent standards whatever the nature of the body before it.

It ought to be stated, parenthetically, that naturally in a large number of judicial review cases, the body whose decision is under review is indeed a tribunal. However, in general, such cases will be considered together with similar cases involving other bodies, in the appropriate chapter on judicial review, and not here.

2. Why a Tribunal?

Not only is uniformity lacking from tribunal to tribunal, there is also a lack of consistency as to whether a tribunal should be created at all. If one leaves aside local authorities, semi-state bodies and other specialist institutions, it may be said that an individual decision may be vested in any one of three

---

[32] The Data Protection Commissioner, established by the Data Protection Act 1988, s.9 and Second Sched., and examined in R. Clarke, *Data Protection Law in Ireland* (Round Hall Press, 1988) Chap. 8, is a borderline candidate for the designation "tribunal." In regard to this point of classification, first, it is not significant that he has functions (in regard, for example, to promoting codes of practice (s.13); or prosecuting for offences under the Act (s.30))—in addition to those in respect of which he might be thought to be acting as a tribunal. (See pp. 228). This consideration is more than outweighed by the fact that by his constitution, and indeed by express declaration, he is made "independent in the performance of his functions." The most important of the functions in the performance of which he might be thought to act as a tribunal is the issuing of an enforcement notice (s.10). This is issued where the Commissioner is of the opinion that a data controller (one who controls the contents of personal data) is contravening a provision of the Act, which is not itself designated as directly attracting criminal liability. An example would be an individual's right of access to data about himself or his right of rectification or erasure (ss.4–6). If the data controller fails to comply with an enforcement notice, he commits a criminal offence. Thus the Commissioner does make a substantial impact on individual rights. However this impact is at once removed from the Commissioner since a criminal prosecution is necessary before a data controller suffers any sanction. Moreover, on turning to examine procedure, it seems even less likely that the Commissioner can be regarded as a tribunal. For the salient and connected facts are that, first, there is a full right of appeal to the Circuit Court against the issue of an enforcement notice and, secondly, the Second Schedule to the Act contains none of the procedural formalities which are normally laid down for a tribunal (although the Commissioner does in fact permit informal representations to be made). Accordingly the Commissioner must be regarded as probably falling just outside that nebulous category, the "tribunal."

different types of body: a Minister and his Department; a court, or a tribunal. Let us now review these options.

Tribunal or Minister?

It would certainly make for consistency if the following demarcation line for functions between a Minister and a tribunal were consistently observed by the Oireachtas: matters should be allocated to a tribunal where they require a decision to be taken independently of the executive by the determination of facts according to a fairly formalised procedure, and the application to the facts of a fairly precise set of rules. In short, a tribunal would take all quasi-judicial decisions. This would leave to the Minister and his Department decisions containing a high policy content, which are not susceptible to regulation by a code of law.[33]

In fact, this division of functions as between a tribunal and a Minister fails as an adequate description of reality at two points. First, by no means all of the decisions of a type suitable for resolution by a tribunal are actually vested in a tribunal. Dealing with the question of allocation of functions in Britain, the Council of Tribunals remarked frankly:

"[T]he choice is influenced by the interplay of various factors—the nature of decision, accidents of history, departmental preferences and political considerations—rather than by the application of a set of coherent principles."[34]

This is at least as true in Ireland as it is in Britain. Occasionally, functions which one would expect to be located in a tribunal are, for historical or other reasons, vested in a court, or, more often, in a Minister. The lack of correlation between a particular type of decision and a particular forum can be illustrated by the fact that in regard to three important functions, a decision is taken in the first instance by a body which is part of the executive arm of government; thence an appeal may be taken to a tribunal, with a further right of appeal from the tribunal (in the first two of the examples to be given, on a point of law only) to the High Court. One can see this pattern in the areas of planning, social welfare and tax law. Moreover, the transfer of planning appeals from the Minister for Local Government to An Bord Pleanála in 1977 does not appear to have radically altered the decisions emerging from the planning appeals process.[35]

As compared with a Minister, tribunals possess various advantages. The first of these was adverted to by Henchy J. in *The State (Pine Valley Developments Ltd.) v. Dublin C.C.*[36] Speaking in the context of an "aberrant" and

---

[33] This allocation of functions would be in line with the proposals contained in the Devlin Report: see Prl. 792, App. 1.
[34] *The Functions of the Council on Tribunals* (1980) (Cmd. 7805), para. 1.7.
[35] But for the advantages of An Bord Pleanála over the Minister for Local Government, see Stevenson, "Planning Appeals in the Republic of Ireland" (1985) 7 *Journal of Urban Law and Policy* 170.
[36] [1984] I.R. 407.

ultra vires grant of outline planning permission by the Minister for Local Government, Henchy J. said that the Minister had:

> "[I]gnored the rights of the respondent planning authority and of those who were entitled to get notices and to be heard before such a material contravention could take place. It is no wonder that Parliament, in its wisdom, by the [Local Government (Planning and Development) Act 1976] transferred to an independent appeal board the appellate power which had been vested by the [Local Government (Planning and Development) Act 1963] in an individual who might be influenced in his decisions by political pressures or other extraneous or unworthy considerations."[37]

Secondly, a tribunal is less affected by changes of government than a Minister and Department would be and thus there may be some gain in consistency, a quality very desirable in an area in which the policy-content is usually low. Finally, the amorphous quality of a Department of State with its various activities and interests may mean that an individual would be more confident that his arguments had been fully taken into account by a tribunal. In short, tribunals are regarded as more likely to be fair and to provide greater safeguards for the individual than would be the case with a Minister. It follows that a tribunal is more often created where the area of government administration involved requires interference with valuable private property rights.

There is a qualification to the principle that decisions for which guidelines are provided are vested in tribunals. This is pin-pointed in the subtle difference which has been drawn between "court-substitute tribunals" which conform more or less to this criterion, and "policy-orientated tribunals," which do not.[38] For the purpose of a policy-orientated tribunal is a slightly different one, namely to allow policy, in a narrow field, to be worked out case by case by a specialist body, free of day-to-day interference by party politics and party politicians. One example of a tribunal of this type is administered by An Bord Pleanála.[39] The Labour Court, which is vested, *inter alia*, with the function of making "recommendation[s] setting forth its opinion on the merits of the [trade] dispute and the terms on which it should be settled"[40] provides another example of a "policy-orientated tribunal" at work.

Tribunal or court?

The other general perspective from which to survey tribunals is by a comparison with the courts. Since most Irish tribunals are of the court-substitute type, could their functions not simply have been vested in a court of the

[37] *Ibid.* 425.
[38] Farmer, *Tribunals and Government* (London, 1984), Chap. 8.
[39] Note that s.7 of the Local Government (Planning and Development) Act 1976 allows the Minister for the Environment to issue general policy directives to local authorities. This power was exercised once in 1982: see Local Government (Planning and Development) General Policy Directive 1982 (S.I. 1982 No. 264).
[40] Industrial Relations Act 1946, s.68(1), as inserted by s.19 of the Industrial Relations Act 1969. See Von Prondzynski and McCarthy, *Employment Law* (London, 1988): "This new criterion [*sc.* of the 1969 Act] was intended to reflect a belief, current in the [Labour] Court itself, that it should approach its task in a wholly pragmatic and flexible way."

appropriate level?[41] The short answer is that the growth of tribunals is largely due to the failure of the legal system to respond in a flexible manner to new challenges. Indeed, the creation of one of the first modern tribunals—the court of referees system, established under the National Insurance Act 1911 to hear national insurance claims—occurred because of the dissatisfaction with the handling of workmen's compensation cases by the County Court.[42]

It is usually agreed that, by comparison with courts, tribunals carry certain practical advantages. In the first place, the procedure before a tribunal is simpler and more flexible than that of a court. Although a tribunal may not adopt procedures which are unfair or which imperil a just result, it is nonetheless master of its own procedures, and enjoys a considerable discretion as to whether to depart from the strict rules of evidence or permit legal representation or cross-examination of witnesses.[43] These features, together with the frequent absence of an adversarial framework,[44] the fact that the proceedings are often held in private,[45] and the less formal atmosphere of a tribunal combine to make an appearance before a tribunal a less daunting experience than the "day in court." Often, especially to people from a humbler background, the very image of a court—with its criminal connotations—is unwelcome. For example, the Housing (Private Rented Dwellings) Act 1982—which provides for a new system of rent assessment following the invalidation of the former Rent Restrictions Act 1960[46]—originally vested this jurisdiction in the District Court. This jurisdiction was subsequently transferred to a Rent Tribunal by the Housing (Private Rented Dwellings) (Amendment) Act 1983 because of the concern aroused among the tenants by the prospect of the courtroom.[47]

A further example of a tribunal being substituted for a court occurred recently in the field of rating valuation. Until the Valuation Act 1988, an appeal lay from a determination of the Commissioner of Valuation to the Circuit Court. As a result of the Act, an appeal now lies to the Valuation Tribunal, which it establishes. From the tribunal there is an appeal on a point of law (just as, before, there was an appeal from the Circuit Court) to the High Court and thence to the Supreme Court.[48]

Secondly, many tribunals possess a particular expertise. This would be true, for example, in the case of bodies such as An Bord Pleanála, the Appeal

---

[41] Indeed, because tribunals are so similar to courts, the question has arisen in Britain as to whether they are to be treated as courts for particular purposes such as contempt of court (*Att.-Gen.* v. *British Broadcasting Corporation* [1981] A.C. 303) and immunity from defamation proceedings for witnesses (*Trapp* v. *Mackie* [1979] 1 W.L.R. 377). See further, p. 234.
[42] Abel Smith and Stevens, *Lawyers and the Courts* (London, 1967), pp. 111–118.
[43] See the comments of *Report of the Public Services Organisation Review Group* ("the Devlin Report") (1969, Prl. 792), App. I, pp. 448–449, on this aspect of tribunals.
[44] For tribunal procedure, see pp. 233–235.
[45] Contrast Art. 34.1 which requires that the administration of justice by courts shall be in public, save in "such limited and special cases as may be prescribed by law."
[46] *Blake* v. *Att.-Gen.* [1982] I.R. 117. For an account of this decision, and the flurry of legislative activity which followed in its wake, see McCormack, "Blake-Madigan and its Aftermath" (1983) 5 D.U.L.J.(N.s.) 205.
[47] See generally, *Dáil Debates*, Vol. 344, cols. 2514–2544 (July 7, 1983).
[48] See generally, Valuation Act 1988, ss.2 and 5 and First Sched. See further, pp. 183–185.

Commissioners for Income Tax and the Employment Appeals Tribunal. The courts take cognisance of this fact, for they are sometimes reluctant to interfere with the workings of specialist tribunals.

Thirdly, tribunals are quicker and cheaper for all the parties concerned. Their simpler procedure means that it is usually unnecessary for a lawyer to appear.[49]

Fourthly, tribunals can be incorporated within a variety of institutional frameworks, and it will often be appropriate for the legislature to constitute an agency which is not only a tribunal but also possesses a number of other regulatory, promotional, advisory functions along the lines of a United States "administrative agency." Such tribunals are often vested with diverse non-judicial functions. A leading example is the Labour Court, which combines general arbitration functions in the field of industrial relations with quasi-judicial (or, indeed, possibly judicial) functions under the Redundancy Payments Act 1967, and the Anti-Discrimination (Pay) Act 1974. A second example is the Pensions Board constituted by Part II of the Pensions Act 1990. The Board is not only a tribunal; it also bears the functions of: devising guidelines on the duties of the trustees of pensions schemes; encouraging the provision of training schemes for them; advising the Minister for Social Welfare; and monitoring the operation of the Act and pensions developments generally.[50] Concomitant with its responsibilities, the Board is also an example of a "balanced" or representative tribunal[51] in that 10 of its 12 ordinary members must be nominated by bodies representing variously: employees, employers, occupational pension schemes, accountants, lawyers or actuaries.[52] However, notwithstanding its many other functions just listed in regard to certain types of decision, the Board is required to act as a tribunal. For the technique employed in the Act is that certain fairly detailed standards are fixed, either by the Act or regulations made under it, in regard to such matters as the preservation of benefits; adequate funding; the disclosure of information to interested parties; and equal treatment of men and women.[53] The Act then provides that where there is any conflict between any of these standards and the rules of a pension scheme, it is the statutory standards which prevail. The duty of administering these standards to determine whether there is any conflict is vested in the Board.

Where a court is involved in such a combination of roles it has been successfully argued, elsewhere in the common law world, that the arrangement con-

---

[49] *Cf.* Employment Appeals Tribunal Sixteenth Annual Report (1983, Pl. 2733): "While the procedures of the Tribunal were intended to be informal, speedy and inexpensive, the increasing involvement by the legal profession, particularly in claims under the Unfair Dismissals Act 1977, has tended to make the hearings more formal, prolonged and costly, with an over-emphasis on legal procedures and technicalities" (p. 4). According to the 1983 Report, 19.7 per cent. of employees and 23.9 per cent. of employers opted for legal representation in all claims coming before the Tribunal.
[50] Pensions Act 1990, s.10.
[51] For this phrase, see p. 240.
[52] 1990 Act, First Sched., para. 8.
[53] See especially, ss.26, 38, 53, 58 and 75 of the Act.

travened the equivalent of Article 34.1,[54] and it would certainly be regarded as undesirable and unconventional.

Finally, tribunals tend to take a less rigid attitude to questions of statutory interpretation and to precedent. Indeed, it is possible that a tribunal which adhered rigidly to a doctrine of precedent, as far as its *own* decisions are concerned, would run foul of the rule against inflexible policies.[55] However, in the very interests of consistency, tribunals do follow precedent to some extent. In particular where points of law are concerned, tribunals must apply the law, employing the standard principles of statutory interpretation and following the decisions of the High Court and Supreme Court. This point was made emphatically by McCarthy J. in *McGrath* v. *McDermott*,[56] where the Supreme Court was considering a decision of the Appeal Commissioners. This decision had purported to adopt the doctrine of "fiscal nullity" (a British principle by which financial transactions, which had no purpose other than the avoidance of tax and which did not involve a real loss, should be disregarded). The Commissioners had either ignored or been unaware of the relevant decisions of the Supreme Court. The Commissioners' decision was reversed on appeal to the High Court—whose reversal was upheld in the Supreme Court—on the ground that the doctrine of "fiscal nullity" had not been accepted by the Irish courts.

As against these advantages, the wisdom of allocating certain judicial functions to tribunals rather than courts has been questioned, by Walsh J. Writing in the context of the work of An Bord Uchtála the judge opined, extracurially, that:

> "[C]ertain aspects of family law are of such fundamental importance, such as those cases which can alter the legal status of a person, that they should be decided in the High Court. . . . This prompts one to question the wisdom or desirability of permitting the legal adoptions to take effect without judicial intervention or confirmation. . . . [The powers of the An Bord Uchtála] are limited. It cannot decide questions concerning the validity of the marriage of couples who seek to adopt. Yet if adoption is approved for a couple whose marriage is not a valid subsisting marriage in the eyes of the law of the State the resulting invalidity of the adoption may not be discovered until it is too late to avoid . . . the inevitable legal consequences."[57]

Webster J. made similar observations about the functions of prison disciplin-

---

[54] Legislation which vested a court with non-judicial arbitral functions in the area of industrial relations was held to be contrary to s.71 of the Commonwealth Constitution in *Att.-Gen. of Australia* v. *R. and the Boilermakers' Society of Australia* [1957] A.C. 288. Keane J. appeared to endorse this view in *The People* v. *Neilan*, High Court, April 25, 1990.

[55] *Merchandise Transport Ltd.* v. *British Transport Commission* [1962] 2 Q.B. 173, 197; *R.* v. *Greater Birmingham Appeal Tribunal, ex p. Simper* [1974] Q.B. 543 (tribunal cannot consider itself bound by its own "rules of thumb"). For this rule, see pp. 545–548.

[56] *McGrath* v. *McDermott* [1988] I.R. 258, 278.

[57] In foreword to Binchy, *A Casebook on Irish Family Law* (Abingdon, 1984), p. vii.

ary tribunals in *R*. v. *Home Secretary, ex p. Tarrant*[58] when listing a number of considerations which the prison authorities should take into account before deciding whether to permit the prisoner to be legally represented. These factors included: the seriousness and gravity of the charge; whether any points of law are likely to arise; the capacity of a particular prisoner to present his own case; the need for reasonable speed in making the adjudication and the need for fairness as between prisoners, and as between prisoners and prison officers. If the result of this decision was that serious disciplinary offences were more frequently referred to the criminal courts, then Webster J. did not regard such a result "as a matter of regret,"[59] and it seems fair to infer that he considered that prison tribunals were inherently unsuited to the task of adjudication in cases involving serious disciplinary charges.

No tribunal goes further in the direction of the court-model than do the tribunals constituted under the Garda Síochána (Complaints) Act 1986. This Act provides for a scheme of independent investigation and adjudication in regard to complaints made about Gardaí by members of the public.[60] The complaints must relate to a breach of discipline—principally conduct specified in the Fourth Schedule to the Act, which includes: abuse of authority; corrupt or improper practice; and misuse of property or money belonging to a member of the public. However it would be most unusual for proceedings under the Act to go ahead where a criminal prosecution is to be instituted in respect of the same conduct.[61] On receipt by the Commissioner of the Garda Síochána of a complaint, he must first consider whether the complaint is suitable for informal resolution.[62] (Any statement made by the Gardaí involved, for the purpose of informal resolution, will not be admissible in any informal proceedings[63]). If there is no informal resolution, then the Commissioner must appoint a member of the Gardaí to investigate the complaint.[64]

The investigating officer's report is referred to the Garda Síochána Complaints Board (at least three of whose nine members must be barristers or solicitors), which bears responsibility for administering the Act. After considering this report, the Board must, in certain circumstances, refer the matter to a tribunal constituted under the Second Schedule to the Act.[65] Two of the members of the tribunal must be Board members and at least one of these must be a barrister of solicitor and the third member of the tribunal must be a Garda nominated by the Commissioner.[66] Although it sits in private, the tribunal's procedure is close to that of court, with the chief executive

---

[58] [1985] Q.B. 251.
[59] *Ibid.* p. 287.
[60] Garda Síochána (Complaints) Act 1986, s.5. Apart from the requirement of reference by a member of the public, the demarcation line between the disciplinary scheme established by the Act and that which was instituted by the Garda Síochána (Discipline Regulations) 1971 (S.I. 1971 No. 316) remains unclear.
[61] Though this is not absolutely forbidden by the Act: see ss.6(6), 7(1)(8).
[62] 1986 Act, s.5.
[63] *Ibid.* s.5(6).
[64] *Ibid.* s.6.
[65] *Ibid.* s.7.
[66] *Ibid.* Second Sched., para. 1.

presenting the case against the Garda and the Garda either presenting his own case or being represented by another Garda.[67] The Second Schedule also provides for: the tribunal having the power to subpoena witnesses and administer oaths; a witness's privileges being the same as a witness before court; and the giving of false evidence being an offence. Any person who does anything else in relation to the proceedings, which if done *vis-à-vis* a court would amount to contempt of court, is also an offence. A sufficient record of the proceedings must be kept.

Where a breach of discipline is either admitted or found to exist by the tribunal, it is for the tribunal to decide whether disciplinary action should be taken and if so, which of the specified forms of disciplinary action—dismissal, compulsory retirement, reduction in rank or pay, reprimand or caution—should be adopted.[68]

Appeal from the tribunal, against either a finding that the Gardái was in breach of discipline and/or the punishment, lies to the Garda Síochána Complaints Appeal Board, constituted by the Third Schedule to the Act. The chairman of the Board must be a Circuit Court judge and one of the two ordinary members must be a barrister or solicitor. The appeal must be grounded on the record of the tribunal proceedings together with: such other evidence "as the Appeal Board thinks fit"; and "any observations of the tribunal which relate to any matter arising on the record aforesaid and which the Appeal Board requests the tribunal to furnish."[69]

3. Common Features

We must now elaborate on the remarks, made in Part I, about the types of feature which distinguish a tribunal.

Rule bound

As far as one can generalise about tribunals it can be said that they take decisions in regard to which the range of options is sufficiently narrow and predictable for it to be crystallised in the form of a reasonably precise set of rules or at least a specific catalogue of factors. This is in contrast with the wide discretionary power which, for instance, permits a Minister to exercise a particular power if he deems it "necessary in the public interest."[70] To take some examples: first, An Bord Uchtála must not make an adoption order unless it is satisfied "that the applicant is of good moral character, has sufficient means to support the child, and is a suitable person to have parental rights and duties in respect of the child."[71] Again, the Rent Tribunal is required to fix the rent in respect of formerly rent-controlled tenancies by having regard to the:

"[N]ature, character and location of the dwelling, the other terms of the

[67] *Ibid.* para. 5.
[68] 1986 Act, s.9.
[69] *Ibid.* Third Sched., para. 3.
[70] For controls of discretionary powers, see Chap. 10.
[71] Adoption Act 1952, s.13(1).

tenancy; the means of the landlord and the tenant; the date of purchase of the dwelling by the landlord and the amount paid by him therefor; the length of the tenant's occupancy of the dwelling and the number and ages of the tenant's family residing in the dwelling."[72]

Law administered by a tribunal is more likely than law administered by a court to include a range of factors which tends to create a discretion and, secondly, to be expressed in terms of standards as opposed to rules.[73] In contrast to rules, standards—such as "good moral character"—call for the exercise of some discretion. It is, however, a discretion which must be exercised reasonably, objectively and judicially. This means that even where the wording of the statutory test administered by the tribunal is vague, the effect of the open, formal procedure, together with an accumulation of informal precedents, will have the effect of restricting its discretion. This is especially so when the tribunal maintains a public register of its decisions, as does the Employment Appeal Tribunal. However, it must be said that often a tribunal does not publish its decision, much less its reasons. For example, the reports submitted by the planning inspector—who chairs an oral inquiry—to An Bord Pleanála are not published at all. This effectively means that no system of precedent is established whereby the members of the public can assess the likelihood of a successful appeal.[74]

Appeals

Since decisions taken by tribunals are, first, bound by fairly precise rules and, secondly, involve questions of individual rights, it might be predicted on the basis of earlier discussion[75] that a statutory appeal would be created from a tribunal to a court. In fact, provision is generally made for an appeal to the High Court but this is usually confined to points of law.[76] In some cases an appeal will lie to a specialised appellate tribunal. For instance, a party aggrieved by a prohibition order made by the Censorship of Publications Board—nowadays, happily, a comparatively rare event—may appeal *de novo*

---

[72] Housing (Private Rented Dwellings) Act 1982, s.13(2). However, these criteria are not in the nature of an "automatic check list, they are only to be considered when they are relevant": *Quirke* v. *Folio Homes Ltd.* [1989] I.L.R.M. 496, 499, *per* McCarthy J.
[73] But this is not always the case: see, *e.g.* Succession Act 1965, s.117 (which allows the court to make provision for the child out of a deceased parent's estate where it is of opinion "that the testator has failed to make proper provision for the child in accordance with its means").
[74] Clark, "Social Welfare Insurance Appeals" (1978) 13 Ir.Jur.(N.S.) 265, 282 makes the same point about the non-publication of decisions of social welfare appeals officers' decisions: "If decisions are at present poorly recorded, this will hinder even the most primitive and informal system of *stare decisis*. Appeals officers may then run the risk of operating within an appeals system in which uniformity of decision making is singularly absent."
[75] See p. 8.
[76] See, *e.g.* Adoption Act 1952, s.30(1); Local Government (Planning and Development) Act 1976, s.42(*a*); Social Welfare (Consolidation) Act 1981, s.299; Housing (Private Rented Dwellings) (Amendment) Act 1983, ss.12 and 13; Farm Tax Act 1985, s.8(4); Valuation Act 1988, s.5. In the case of the Appeals Commissioners for Income Tax, the tax-payer may appeal *de novo* to the Circuit Court. Either party may ask for a case stated on a point of law from the decisions of the Appeal Commissioners or the Circuit Court: Income Tax Act 1967, ss.428–431. For the difficult distinction between law and fact, see *Rahill* v. *Brady* [1971] I.R. 69.

to the Censorship of Publications Appeal Board.[77] A further example is provided by the Seanad Electoral (Panel Members) Act 1947, whereby an appeal
lies to a Judicial Referee from a decision of the returning officer on the eligibility of a candidate for a particular electoral panel.[78] In other cases, an appeal
will lie to a Minister.[79] However, occasionally the decision of the tribunal will
be declared to be final, and no appeal will lie.[80]

The High Court retains an inherent right of review of decisions of tribunals,
irrespective of any appeal mechanism.[81] However, there is a view that the
applicant must, in general, exhaust all other rights of appeal before he can
seek judicial review of a tribunal's decision.[82]

Procedure

Procedure is laid down, in the first instance, by the constituent statute, and
is generally supplemented by procedural regulations made pursuant to statutory instrument or contained in the Schedule to the constituent statute[83] or
both. These provisions typically deal with matters such as the following: how
many members constitute a quorum and a majority; the circumstances in
which an oral hearing is required; whether the tribunal has the power to subpoena witnesses and to administer oaths; whether the witness commits an
offence if he gives false evidence and whether the witness enjoys the same
privileges as a witness before a court. The provisions may also specify:
whether certain types of hearings are to be in public or in private; whether the
tribunal may sit in divisions; and whether it may delegate its powers to a
smaller group of members. These issues aside, the tribunal is generally authorised to regulate its own procedure.[84]

In the case of a few modern tribunals, the constituent statute states that
"[a] witness . . . before a tribunal shall be entitled to the same privileges and

[77] Censorship of Publications Act 1946, ss.2 and 3.
[78] ss.36–38 of the 1947 Act. In *Ormonde and Dolan* v. *MacGabhann*, High Court, July 9, 1969,
Pringle J. held that the plaintiffs were entitled to by-pass this judicial referee procedure in order
to seek a declaration from the High Court that they had the proper and appropriate qualifications
for nomination on the Labour Panel.
[79] See, *e.g.* Local Government (Water Pollution) Act 1977, s.8 (appeal to Minister for the
Environment against local authority decision to refuse, or to attach conditions to, grant of trade
and/or sewage effluent licence).
[80] Social Welfare (Consolidation) Act 1981, s.299. But *cf. Kingham* v. *Minister for Social Welfare*, High Court, November 25, 1985 at pp. 246–247.
[81] *Tormey* v. *Att.-Gen.* [1985] I.R. 289 .
[82] *The State (Abenglen Properties Ltd.)* v. *Dublin Corporation* [1984] I.R. 381; *Creedon* v. *Dublin
Corporation* [1984] I.R. 427. The alternative views are canvassed at pp. 605–609.
[83] For modern examples, see Farm Tax Act 1985, Schedule; Valuation Act 1988, Schedule.
Notice an unusual feature of the Valuation Tribunal, namely that, by para. 3 of the Schedule, the
tribunal is required to issue a written judgment.
[84] See, *e.g.* Adoption Act 1952, First Sched.; Social Welfare (Insurance Appeals) Regulations
1952 (S.I. 1952 No. 376), Art. 54–11 (appeals officers); Local Government (Planning and Development) Regulations 1977 (S.I. 1977 No. 65), Art. 45 (An Bord Pleanála). In *The State (Casey)*
v. *Labour Court* (1984) 3 J.I.S.L.L. 135, 138, O'Hanlon J. observed that the Labour Court was
given a discretion by s.21 of the Industrial Relations Act 1946 to regulate its own procedures in
relation to the taking of evidence on oath. Accordingly, neither the parties nor the High Court
could dictate to the Labour Court the manner in which it conducts its own procedures "once it
exercises its powers in accordance with the statute from which it derives its authority to act."

immunities as a witness before a court."[85] This, be it noted, is a rather restricted protection in that it only covers actions against witnesses in respect of evidence given by them. However, even in the case of statements not within this limited protection or, alternatively, where the tribunal enjoys no statutory protection whatsoever, it is clear that proceedings before a tribunal attract qualified privilege on the ground that the performance of a public duty is involved.[86] The more difficult question is whether common law absolute privilege would apply, in the same way as if the tribunal were a court. As yet, there appears to be no Irish authority on this point (though given the national predeliction for defamation proceedings, this seems unlikely to last). In the most recent English authority, *Trapp* v. *Mackie*,[87] the House of Lords held that, provided that the body in question was one "recognised by law," there was no single element which would be conclusive to show that—adopting the conventionally-accepted test[88]—it had attributes sufficiently similar to those of a court to create absolute privilege. Lord Diplock then went on to list certain characteristics of the body in question—which was inquiring into the dismissal of a teacher—which cumulatively were more than enough to justify the granting of absolute privilege.[89]

But irrespective of what the constituent statute may say or what administrative practice may develop, a tribunal is always subject to constitutional justice in its more stringent form and, so, it is the courts which have the last word on such questions as whether an oral hearing should have been held.[90] The impact of constitutional justice is demonstrated by a British parallel: out of the three examples cited by Professor Wade[91] of amendments to draft procedural regulations secured by the British Council on Tribunals, all of these changes (disclosure to both sides of information given to the tribunal; a right to representation and the duty imposed on persons discharging quasi-judicial

---

[85] Valuation Act 1988, First Sched., para. 6; Garda Síochána (Complaints) Act 1986, Second Sched., para. 6.

[86] *Royal Aquarium Society* v. *Parkinson* [1892] 1 Q.B. 431, 443, 454.

[87] [1979] 1 W.L.R. 377.

[88] *Royal Aquarium Society* v. *Parkinson* [1892] 1 Q.B. 443, 448, 452.

[89] With particular reference to the Labour Court, Kerr and Whyte, *Irish Trade Union Law* (Professional Books, 1985), p. 356 state:

> "The Labour Court is recognised by law. The Court is empowered to summon witnesses before it, to examine witnesses on oath and require any such witnesses to produce documents. The investigation can be held in public and witnesses can be cross-examined. The relative informality of procedure does not outweigh those factors, and the authors would submit that the general principle expressed by Lopes L.J. [in *Royal Aquarium Society*] should be extended to [give absolute privilege to] Labour Court investigations but not to conciliation proceedings with an Industrial Relations Officer."

[90] "Tribunals exercising quasi-judicial functions are frequently allowed to act informally—to receive unsworn evidence, to act on hearsay, to depart from the rules of evidence, to ignore courtroom procedures and the like—but they may not act in such a way as to imperil a fair hearing or a fair result," *per* Henchy J. in *Kiely* v. *Minister for Social Welfare* [1977] I.R. 267, 281. See generally at pp. 446–452.

[91] *Administrative Law* (1988), pp. 924, 934.

functions to give reasons for their decisions) have been effected in Ireland through the courts.[92]

Accusatorial v. inquisitorial style

There are two other factors which it might be expected would draw many tribunals towards the inquisitorial model. First, as regards subject-matter, the accusatorial model is appropriate in ordinary civil proceedings where the court is usually deciding a *lis inter partes* involving two identifiable private parties, each with diametrically opposing interests. By contrast there is often only one individual interest at a hearing before a tribunal, as, *e.g.* in an application for a grant or a licence.

There is, secondly, a practical factor militating in favour of the inquisitorial system, namely, that the accusatorial system works best when the two adversaries are equally experienced and informed. This requirement will often not be met in the case of tribunals where the private individuals involved are often not legally represented.

However, there are two other factors which pull in favour of the accusatorial system. First, the rules of constitutional justice—which are imposed by judges with the court system, no doubt, in mind, as a role model—apply to hearings before tribunals. Secondly, in certain tribunals it has been thought necessary to establish a *legitimus contradictor* and this tends to give a hearing an adversarial flavour. Thus, the responsible Inspector of Taxes appears in front of the Appeal Commissioners to argue in support of his earlier decision.

Independence

Tribunals exercising public law powers are required to strike an even balance between the individual on the one hand and the administrative authorities who represent the public interest on the other: they should be guided only by the law and their own non-partisan discretion. At times, queries have been raised—either in regard to tribunals as a whole or in regard to specified tribunals—as to whether they measure up to these standards. In the first place, tribunals lack the tradition, status and institutional arrangements necessary to promote independence which the courts have long enjoyed. Moreover, the fact that all the cases before a particular tribunal often involve the same administrative agency may breed a certain cosiness.

Particular doubt has arisen about the independence of the deciding officer/appeals officer system for determining social welfare claims because it is manned by serving civil servants operating within a Department of State. Deciding officers are selected by the Minister for Social Welfare at executive or staff officer level and they hold this position at the pleasure of the Minister.

---

[92] *Geraghty v. Minister for Local Government* [1976] I.R. 153; *Nolan v. Irish Land Commission* [1981] I.R. 23; *The State (Williams) v. Army Pensions Board* [1983] I.R. 308; (disclosure of information); *McGrath & O'Ruairc v. Trustees of Maynooth College* [1979] I.L.R.M. 166; *Flanagan v. University College, Dublin* [1988] I.R. 724 (legal representation); *The State (Creedon) v. Criminal Injuries Compensation Board* [1988] I.R. 51 and *International Fishing Ltd. v. Minister for Marine* [1989] I.R. 149 (duty to give reasons). For further detail on these points, see pp. 446–448, 449–452 and 457–465, respectively.

Deciding officers appear to regard themselves as subject to departmental directions and policy considerations, although it seems likely that it was the intention of the Oireachtas to give the deciding officer a similar status to that of the appeals officer. After some years as a deciding officer a civil servant will generally return to service within the Department. Later he may be appointed, usually at assistant principal grade, as an appeals officer by the Minister and again holds his position at pleasure.[93]

Suspicion of the appeals officer's independence—and, by implication, that of the deciding officer—had been fuelled by decisions such as *McLoughlin* v. *Minister for Social Welfare*.[94] In this case the question arose as to whether the plaintiff was employed "in the civil service of the Government" for social insurance purposes. The appeals officer considered that he was bound to adhere to the terms of a minute from the Minister for Finance which, in effect, directed the officer to find that the plaintiff was so employed. This decision was reversed by the Supreme Court, with O'Daly J. stating that the appeals officer had abdicated his duty to act in an impartial and independent fashion:

> "The Appeals Officer said that he was bound to adhere to a direction, pur- porting to have been given to him by the Minister for Finance, an obser- vation which disclosed not a concern for the niceties of the probative value, but the belief that a public servant in his position had no option but to act on the direction of a Minister of State. Such a belief on his part was an abdi- cation by him from his duty as an Appeals Officer. That duty is laid upon him by the Oireachtas and he is required to perform it as between the par- ties that appear before him freely and fairly as becomes anyone who is called upon to decide on matters of right or obligation."[95]

Further recognition of the anomalous position of the social welfare appeals system is provided by the fact that decisions of both the deciding officer and the appeals officer come within the scope of the Ombudsman's jurisdiction.[96]

Constitution: Articles 34.1 and 37

Doubts about the independence of the tribunals were probably part of the inspiration for the constitutional rule, Article 34.1, which provides that (sub- ject to certain exceptions) "justice shall be administered in courts established by law by judges . . . " and not by tribunals. Article 37 provides the exception to the pure milk of the separation of powers principle in that it permits the Oireachtas to vest "limited functions and powers of a judicial nature in matters other than criminal matters" in a body which is not a court. The wording of Article 34.1 and Article 37 is unsatisfactory in that it does not appear to provide any clear criteria which would enable the courts to deter- mine (1) the distinction between judicial and non-judicial powers; (2) what is

[93] See generally Clark, "Social Welfare Insurance Appeals" (1978) 13 Ir.Jur.(N.S.) 165.
[94] [1958] I.R. 1. See further, on this case, pp. 405–406.
[95] *Ibid.* 27.
[96] Ombudsman Act 1980, s.5(1)(*a*)(iii).

a "limited" judicial function; and (3) what is a "criminal matter". These are matters of constitutional definition which are discussed in constitutional law books.[97] It is not intended to attempt to cover the same ground here but merely to describe a few of the cases in order to alert the reader to the constitutional time-bomb which may be ticking away under any tribunal of which it can be said that it is administering justice without coming within the exceptional category. At the same time, it must be emphasised that there are several tribunals which are plainly out of danger because they do not administer justice. An example is An Bord Pleanála: it has been held[98] that this tribunal is not administering justice when it grants (or withholds) planning permission because such a large measure of policy discretion is involved; and, secondly, in respect of another of the Board's powers, that although the function of determining what is "development" or "exempted development" constitutes an administration of justice, it falls within the Article 37 exception.

A case which falls on the other side of the line is *Re Solicitors' Act 1954*,[99] in which the power of the Disciplinary Committee of the Incorporated Law Society to strike off solicitors who had been found guilty of serious disciplinary offences was held to be an administration of justice. Moreover the Supreme Court also held that even if there were a full appeal, by way of rehearing from the Disciplinary Committee's decision to the High Court, this appeal would not restore constitutionality to the Committee's decision.

In order to avoid the difficulties disclosed by the *Re Solicitors Act 1954* decision, certain crucial features were included when the medical disciplinary system was restructured in the Medical Practitioners Act 1978. First, the Medical Council does not have the power to strike off a doctor, although it does have the significant power and duty of making an elaborate inquiry as a result of which it may decide that the doctor should be struck off. If it does so decide, then the doctor has the right to apply within 21 days to the High Court, which may either cancel or confirm the decision. Finally, the Council bears the onus of proving before the court, in the usual way, any contested facts.

The disciplinary system constituted by the 1978 Act was upheld, in *Re M*.[1] by Finlay P. (as he then was) in the High Court. The *Solicitors' Act* decision was distinguished in *Re M*. on the basis that one criterion for an "administration of justice" is that it must be "final and conclusive," as opposed to recommendatory. Since the Medical Council's decision was not blessed with the quality of conclusiveness it was held that the Council was not "administering justice." In a related case, *M. v. Medical Council*,[2] it was accepted that, in the situation in which the professional body makes the necessary recommen-

[97] See Kelly, *The Irish Constitution* (Dublin, 1990), pp. 363–368; Kelly, Hogan and Whyte, Supplement to *The Irish Constitution* (1987), pp. 51–65; Casey, *Constitutional Law in Ireland* (London, 1987), pp. 200–212; Forde, *Constitutional Law of Ireland* (Cork, 1987), pp. 152–160. Gwynn Morgan, *Constitutional Law of Ireland* (Dublin, 1990), pp. 36–40.
[98] *Central Dublin Development Association* v. *Attorney-General* 109 (1975) I.L.T.R. 69, 93–96.
[99] [1960] I.R. 239. See also, the extraordinary *Canada* v. *E.A.T.* High Court, March 14, 1991.
[1] [1984] I.R. 479.
[2] [1984] I.R. 485.

dation and the practitioner does not object, the legislation meant that the court must accept the professional body's decision unless it sees good reason to do otherwise. This was found to be constitutional.

These authorities appear to represent an advance in the development of the law as enunciated in the *Solicitors Act* decision. It is now possible, if the correct formula be used—that is, "confirmation" by the High Court rather than appeal—to allow some involvement by the relevant professional body. It may be commented that it does seem desirable, as a matter of policy, that the relevant factual points and professional standards should be allowed to be settled—as they are in most cases in the United States (another jurisdiction in which the Constitution imposes a strong form of the separation of powers)—by experienced members of the profession who are appointed or elected to represent the entire profession. For there seems little danger in Ireland, where the independence of the professions is a fundamental tenet, that a disciplinary tribunal would be less independent of the executive branch than are the courts.

Designed according to the same specification and to meet the same Constitutional imperative—satisfying Article 34.1 of the Constitution—as the medical disciplinary system is the nurses' disciplinary system constituted by the Nurses Act 1985. This system came up for constitutional scrutiny before the Supreme Court in *Kerrigan* v. *An Bord Altranais*.[3] Following the statutory procedure, allegations against the plaintiff had been heard by the Fitness to Practice Committee of the Board in an oral inquiry which lasted for 12 sittings. The Committee's report, finding that the plaintiff was guilty of professional misconduct, was submitted to the Board which gave the plaintiff and her legal representatives an opportunity to be heard and then decided that her name should be erased from the Register of Nurses. Nevertheless the Supreme Court held that before the High Court could confirm this decision, the High Court must hold a full oral hearing (at any rate where, as in the instant case, there were disputed questions of fact). According to Finlay C.J.: "The necessity for that procedure arises from the constitutional frailty that would attach to the delegation of any such power to a body which was not a court established under the Constitution, having regard to the decision of the former Supreme Court in *Re Solicitors' Act*."[4]

In a number of cases, however, the courts have been prepared to uphold the constitutionality of a tribunal on the basis that it fell within Article 37.1 (quoted above) in that the function being exercised was "limited." This argument was, however, tried, unsuccessfully, in *Re Solicitors Act 1954*, where the appellants had actually been struck off the roll of solicitors. Finding that the powers thus exercised were not limited, Kingsmill Moore J. observed:

> "It is the 'powers and functions' which must be 'limited,' not the ambit of
> their exercise. Nor is the test of limitation to be sought in the number of

---

[3] Supreme Court, March 21, 1990. A similar system is followed in the Dentists Act 1985, ss.39–42.
[4] *Ibid.* p. 8 of the judgment.

powers and functions which are exercised. The Constitution does not say 'powers and functions limited in number'. . . . A tribunal having few powers and functions but those of far-reaching effect and importance could not properly be regarded as exercising 'limited' powers and functions. . . .
The test as to whether a power is or is not 'limited' in the opinion of the Court, lies in the effect of the assigned power when exercised. If the exercise of the assigned powers and functions is calculated ordinarily to affect in the most profound and far-reaching way the lives, liberties, fortunes and reputations of those against whom they are exercised, they cannot properly be described as 'limited.' "[5]

However, a slightly more flexible approach may be discerned in the judgment of McMahon J. in *Madden* v. *Ireland*.[6] At issue in this case was the power of the Land Commission's lay commissioners and appeal tribunal to fix the price of land in cases of compulsory acquisition. McMahon J. first accepted that this was not merely the exercise of an administrative function, but involved the administration of justice, as there was no room "for policy concepts, and what is being decided is solely a question of legal right." But the judge went on to hold that this was a power of a limited nature and he adverted to the role which Article 37 had obviously been intended to play:

"Experience has shown that modern government cannot be carried on without many regulatory bodies and those bodies cannot function effectively under a rigid separation of powers. Article 37 had no counterpart in the Constitution of Saorstat Éireann and in my view introduction of it to the Constitution is to be attributed to a realisation of the needs of modern Government. The ascertainment of the market value of a holding of lands by an administrative body with special experience appears to me to be the kind of limited judicial power contemplated by Article 37."[7]

Finally, it should be noted that because of doubts which had been cast on the constitutionality of An Bord Uchtála, Article 37 was extended by constitutional amendment specifically in order to safeguard adoption orders against the possibility a challenge grounded on Article 34.1.[8]

Appointment and removal of members of tribunals

The type of institutional arrangements designed to create independent pedestals for judges[9] are largely absent in the case of tribunals. Thus, in the case of a typical tribunal, the chairman and other members will be selected by

[5] [1960] I.R. 263.
[6] High Court, May 22, 1980.
[7] *Ibid*. p. 9 of the judgment.
[8] Art. 37.2 was enacted by the Sixth Amendment of the Constitution Act 1979 to quieten doubts raised by the Supreme Court's decision in *M.* v. *An Bord Uchtála* [1977] I.R. 287.
[9] See Kelly, *op. cit.* pp. 354–358.

the Minister. The term of office is usually fixed at a maximum of three to five years. Members are generally eligible for reappointment.[10] However, in certain other cases, the appointment is intended as a full-time career post.[11]

Frequently no statutory qualifications are laid down for appointment but in some exceptional cases the chairman must be a lawyer. The two ordinary members of the Mining Board[12] must be property arbitrators, and it is assumed that some members of the Rent Tribunal[13] must have knowledge or experience of the valuation of property. There are also some examples of "balanced" or representative tribunals. This principle is adopted in the composition of the Labour Court[14] and the Employment Appeals Tribunal[15] where the employers and employees are represented equally. By convention one of the Appeals Commissioners is chosen from among the senior officials of the Revenue Commissioners while the other is a member of the Bar. The most sophisticated attempt in this direction involves An Bord Pleanála. Section 7 of the Local Government (Planning and Development) Act 1983 allows the Minister for the Environment to prescribe certain organisations[16] which are variously representative of particular interest groups. These groups are: professions or occupations relating to physical planning; organisations concerned with protection and preservation of the environment; business groups including those representing the construction industry; and community groups. The Minister is then required to choose one member of the Board from among the names nominated by each category of organisation. The fifth ordinary member is chosen from among the Minister for the Environment's own civil servants.[17]

Removal of members of tribunals is generally a matter for the responsible Minister. The power to remove members is generally confined to specific grounds, such as ill-health, stated misbehaviour or where the removal appears to the Minister to be necessary for the effective performance of the Board's functions.[18] In fact, dismissals are rare, and the most spectacular dismissals in recent times—that of the members of An Bord Pleanála in 1983—were brought about directly by an Act of the Oireachtas.[19]

---

[10] See, *e.g.* Minerals Development Act 1940, s.33; Adoption Act 1952, s.8 and First Sched. (Art. 2); Housing (Private Rented Dwellings) (Amendment) Act 1983, ss.2 and 3; Local Government (Planning and Development) Act 1983, ss.5 and 7; Pensions Act, First Sched.

[11] See, *e.g.* Controller of Patents, Designs and Trade Marks: see Patents Act 1964, s.78.

[12] Minerals Development Act 1979, s.41.

[13] Housing (Private Rented Dwellings) Regulations 1983 (S.I. 1983 No. 222), Art. 6(6).

[14] Industrial Relations Act 1969, s.2.

[15] Redundancy Payments Act 1967, s.39(4).

[16] The list of prescribed organisations is to be found in Local Government (Planning and Development) (An Bord Pleanála) Regulations 1983 (S.I. 1983 No. 285).

[17] s.7(2)(*e*) of the 1983 Act. Appointment of the Chairman of An Bord Pleanála is by way of similar, if not quite identical, process: see s.5 of the Act.

[18] See, *e.g.* Mineral Developments Act 1940, s.33(3) (Mining Board); Adoption Act 1952, s.3(1) (An Bord Uchtála); Local Government (Planning and Development) Act 1983, ss.4 and 7 (An Bord Pleanála); though see also, Pensions Act 1990, First Sched., para. 5.

[19] Local Government (Planning and Development) Act 1983, s.10. See further, p. 413.

4. The Social Welfare Appeals System[20]

A study of the detailed substantive operation of a tribunal would extend beyond the bounds of administrative law and into the particular substantive law field in which the tribunal was operating. However, in order to give some flavour of the operation of tribunals, we give, in this and the following Part, brief case-studies of two of the most important tribunals, focusing on structure rather than substance.

Each year over one million claims are made on the Minister for Social Welfare[21] in respect of such social welfare payments as: disability benefit; unemployment benefit and assistance; occupational injuries benefit and old-age pensions. The statutory basis for these vast administrative schemes is now consolidated in the Social Welfare Acts 1981–1990, under which entitlement to payment turns on the interpretation of such phrases as "not incapable of work and available for work" (unemployment benefit)[22]; "accident arising out of and in the course of employment" (occupational injury benefits)[23]; or whether a claimant has submitted to the necessary medical examinations (maternity allowance).[24]

For some purposes, there is or used to be a dichotomy between, on the one hand, social insurance schemes (where the benefits are in part financed out of contributions already made by the claimant) and, on the other hand, social assistance allowances (in respect of which no direct contributions have been paid). However, this dichotomy only has a slight impact on the system by which the schemes are administered: the administration of social insurance schemes and most social assistance schemes fall within the jurisdiction of the deciding officer, from which an appeal lies to the appeals officer.[25] Each

---

[20] The principal statutory provisions and regulations include the following: Social Welfare (Consolidation) Act 1981, Pt. VIII; Social Welfare (Amendment) Act 1990, ss.19–22; Social Welfare (Insurance Appeals) Regulations 1952 (S.I. 1952 No. 376); Social Welfare (Assistance Decisions and Appeals) Regulations (S.I. 1953 No. 9). These statutory instruments are continued in force by s.312 of the 1981 Act. See generally, Clark, "Social Welfare Insurance Appeals" (1978) 13 Ir. Jur.(N.S.) 265; Whyte and Cousins, "Reforming the Social Welfare Appeals System" (1989) 7 I.L.T.(N.S.) 198 and Ward, "Financial Consequences of Marital Breakdown" (Dublin, 1990), pp. 20–22.

[21] According to the Department of Social Welfare's Annual Report, *Statistical Information on Social Welfare Services 1988* (Pl. 6294), there were 1,327,260 beneficiaries (*i.e.* recipients and their dependants) in 1988.

[22] Social Welfare (Consolidation) Act 1981, s.29(4).

[23] 1981 Act, ss.42 and 43.

[24] *Ibid.* s.27.

[25] There are a number of other schemes which are administered by the Health Boards and which therefore fall outside these particular appeal procedures. These include: supplementary welfare allowances (Social Welfare (Consolidation) Act 1981, ss.119–222); infectious diseases maintenance allowance (Health Act 1947, s.41); domiciliary care allowances (Health Act 1970, s.61); and disabled person's maintenance allowance (Health Act 1970, s.69). For the summary appeal procedures operated by the Health Boards in the case of supplementary welfare allowances, see Ward, *op. cit.* 23. There does not appear to be any appeal mechanism available in the case of the other allowances operated by the Health Boards, although the more formal and expensive remedy of judicial review is always available in respect of decisions of Health Boards in relation to such allowances: see, *e.g. H.* v. *Eastern Health Board* [1988] I.R. 747. The payment of unemployment benefit or unemployment assistance to employees on strike is now a matter for the Social Welfare Tribunal: see Social Welfare (Consolidation) Act 1981, s.301B, as inserted by Social Welfare (No. 2) Act 1982, s.1 and Social Welfare (Social Welfare Tribunal) Regulations 1982

of these officers are designated officers, in the Department of Social Welfare.[26]

Deciding officer

In practice most applicants will, first, be advised by junior Department of Social Welfare officials as to their entitlement to the benefit which has been claimed. If the advice is in the negative, then the applicant can insist that a deciding officer adjudicate upon the claim. This officer may make various inquiries (*e.g.* to former employers of the applicant) but there is no oral hearing and, in general, no attempt is made to observe the rules of constitutional justice. It is clear, then, that the present practices are defective, at least where the effect of the decision of the deciding officer is to terminate payments to persons already in receipt of social welfare benefits or assistance. This emerges from the judgments of Barron J. in *The State (Hoolahan)* v. *Minister for Social Welfare*[27] and of O'Hanlon J. in *Thompson* v. *Minister for Social Welfare*.[28] In *Hoolahan*, the applicant was alleged to have fraudulently obtained social welfare benefits, but since the decision to disqualify her from benefit was based on facts which had not been brought to her attention, Barron J. held that the decision could not stand. He added that the claimant:

"Should know fully the extent of the case being made against her and that no decision should be made until she has been given proper opportunity to deal fully with a case."[29]

In *Thompson* v. *Minister for Social Welfare*, the deciding officer ruled that the applicant should be disqualified from receiving unemployment benefit for a six-week period because of the latter's refusal to participate in a career advice programme. O'Hanlon J. held that, in such circumstances, before a deciding officer terminates the payments of an applicant who has been in receipt of unemployment assistance for some time:

"He should inform the person concerned that the position is being reviewed by him; the grounds upon which he is considering disallowing further payment; and the person concerned should be given an opportunity to answer the case made against him."[30]

(S.I. 1982 No. 308). See generally, Kerr and Whyte, *Irish Trade Union Law* (Professional Books, 1985), pp. 371–376; Clark, "Towards the 'Just' Strike? Social Welfare Payments for Persons Affected by a Trade Dispute in the Republic of Ireland" (1985) 48 M.L.R. 569. The effect of the Social Welfare (No. 2) Act 1982, s.1 is to interpose a tribunal between the two existing appellate tiers, *viz.* the appeals officer and the High Court in respect of the question whether a person is disqualified from receiving unemployment benefit or assistance, by virtue of stoppage of work or a trade dispute.

[26] The deciding officer has a seldom-used power to refrain from deciding the case himself, but to seek the assistance of an appeals officer: Social Welfare (Consolidation) Act 1981; s.298(3).

[27] High Court, July 23, 1986.

[28] [1989] I.R. 618.

[29] *Ibid.* 621

[30] *Ibid.* However, the applicant subsequently sought and obtained an interview with the deciding officer. The officer explained why he proposed to review the applicant's entitlement and made inquiries of the applicant as to why he had refused to attend a training course. O'Hanlon J. held that, at this point, the deciding officer had sufficiently complied with fair procedures, so that a subsequent disqualification decision was not invalid.

Because of the failure of the deciding officer to satisfy these requirements, "however informally," his decision had to be set aside for non-compliance with constitutional justice. It is as yet too early to say whether this decision will presage a significant change in the procedures actually adopted by deciding officers.

Appeals officer

An appeal[31] against a refusal is supposed to be filed with the Chief Appeals Officer within 21 days, although, in practice, this time limit is not strictly adhered to as the Minister has a discretion to admit late claims. The appeal is initiated by a "notice of appeal" (which states the relevant facts and arguments on which the applicant proposes to rely) and accompanied by any docu-

[31] NUMBER OF APPEALS AGAINST DECISIONS OF DECIDING OFFICERS BY SCHEME 1988 (Pl. 6294 p.75)

Type of Appeal	Awaiting Decisions at beginning of January 1988	Received	Decided	Withdrawn	Sent on Enquiry during period	Awaiting Decision at end of December 1988
Insurability	35	161	96	5	51	44
Unemployment Benefit	316	2,196	2,298	31	—	183
Disability and Maternity Benefits, Invalidity Pension and Death Grants	333	3,228	2,639	4	548	370
Widow's and Orphan's Pensions (Contributory and Non-Contributory)	26	237	202	2	36	23
Old Age (Non-Contributory) and Blind Pension	105	1,527	1,142	4	395	91
Qualification Certificates (U.A. Acts)	432	8,413	6,901	23	1,495	426
Unemployment Assistance	304	2,338	2,444	31	—	167
Occupational Injuries Benefits	81	1,091	791	7	272	102
Deserted Wife's Allowance/Benefit	55	376	229	4	151	47
Unmarried Mother's Allowance	9	51	43	—	14	3
TOTALS	1,699	19,747	16,883	111	2,982	1,470
1984	1,094	19,349	15,747	91	2,508	2,097
1985	2,097	17,288	15,310	110	2,486	1,479
1986	1,479	18,095	15,075	77	2,657	1,765
1987	1,765	20,371	17,258	112	3,067	1,699

mentary evidence.[32] If a replying statement is filed, it will generally be confined to a summary of the original basis of the decision under appeal and the applicant will generally be permitted to have access to this document. The appeals officer hears the case *de novo*.[33]

The appeals officer is given a broad discretion to decide whether to grant an oral hearing save that the Minister has power to direct that a particular case shall be heard orally, where he considers that this is warranted in the circumstances.[34] In fact, oral hearings are held in over half of all appeals.[35] Each appeals officer decides an average of about 2,000 cases each year, and many oral hearings are disposed of in less than 15 minutes.

The decision as to whether to grant legal representation is at the discretion of the appeals officer.[36] In practice, legal representation is not very common[37] but, where it is permitted, solicitors and counsel are awarded costs in accordance with the scale rate. While constitutional justice does not require legal representation in all cases, the failure on the part of the appeals officer to permit representation in an appropriate case would probably amount to an unreasonable exercise of his discretion.[38]

The appeals officer has power to subpoena witnesses and to take evidence on oath.[39] Where a person required to attend or to produce documents fails to comply with such a request, the appeals officer may, on serving notice to such a person, apply to the District Court for an order requiring attendance or production of documents, as the case may be. Written evidence may also be admitted if the appeals officer thinks it "just and proper" to do so; however, this evidence ceases to have effect if "oral evidence of probative value is adduced which controverts the written statement so admitted."[40] However, one commentator has described the appeal proceedings as being more in the nature "of an interview of the claimant by the appeals officer, rather than the tribunal hearing which it should be."[41] The decision of the appeals officer is

---

[32] Social Welfare (Insurance Appeals) Regulations 1952 (S.I. 1952 No. 376), Arts. 6 and 7.

[33] 1981 Act, s.298 as substituted by Social Welfare Act 1990, s.19; Social Welfare (Assistance Decisions and Appeals) Regulations 1953 (S.I. 1953 No. 9, Art. 9(4).

[34] Formerly Social Welfare (Insurance Appeals) Regulations 1952 (S.I. 1952 No. 376) Art. 3; now: Social Welfare Act 1990, s.19(b). In *Kiely* v. *Minister for Social Welfare (No. 2)* [1977] I.R. 267, 278, Henchy J. stated that if there were "[U]nresolved conflicts in the documentary evidence, as to any matter essential to a ruling of the claim, the intention of these Regulations is that those conflicts shall be resolved by an oral hearing." But this approach tends to overlook the fact that in practice "[m]ost, if not all, of the documentary evidence will be adduced by the deciding officer who may fail to set out clearly the appellant's view of the appeal": Clark, "Social Welfare Insurance Appeals" (1978) 13 Ir. Jur.(N.S.) 265, 274.

[35] Clark, *loc. cit.* 273–277.

[36] Social Welfare (Insurance Appeals) Regulations 1952 (S.I. 1952 No. 376), Art. 11(1).

[37] According to Ward, *op. cit.* 58, only 12 per cent. of claimants in an admittedly small sample had legal representation before an appeals officer.

[38] *R.* v. *Home Secretary, ex p. Tarrant* [1985] Q.B. 251; *Flanagan* v. *University College, Dublin* [1988] I.R 724.

[39] Social Welfare (Consolidation) Act 1981, s.298(7)–(10).

[40] *Kiely* v. *Minister for Social Welfare* [1977] I.R. 267, 279. See Social Welfare (Insurance Appeals) Regulations 1952 (S.I. 1952 No. 376), Art. 11(5) which gives a discretion to the appeals officer to admit evidence in writing.

[41] Ward, *op. cit.* 21.

then sent to the Minister for Social Welfare. The applicant will then receive a memorandum of the Minister's decision. The memorandum is in standard form, and, in the case of unsuccessful appeals, sets forth a list of alternative reasons for the decision. The reasons which are inapplicable are deleted. The fact that appeals officers' decisions are not published means that there is no system of *stare decisis*, and this in turn leads to the operation of an appeals system "in which uniformity of decision-making is singularly absent."[42]

The Chief Appeals Officer is empowered to appoint an assessor to sit with an appeals officer in an appropriate case. For example, two assessors—one drawn from an employees' panel and the other from an employers' panel—sit on unemployment benefit appeals.[43] The role of the assessors is to assist the appeals officer with their knowledge of prevailing local employment conditions. This information is, of course, relevant in considering, for example, whether an applicant is making himself available for work. And where assessors have been appointed to deal with a particular case, section 298(12) provides that the appeal may not proceed in their absence unless all parties consent. This subsection is mandatory and failure to comply with this requirement will invalidate the decision.[44] The role of the medical assessors under the analogous Social Welfare (Occupational Injuries) Act 1966 was examined by the Supreme Court in *Kiely* v. *Minister for Social Welfare*.[45] In the view of Henchy J. (which appears to have adopted the procedure in a court of law, as a role model) the regulations envisaged that the medical assessors' role should be a strictly limited one. The assessors should not take any active part in the proceedings: their task was simply to give information on medical matters when requested to do so by the appeals officer.

Given the institutional bias of the appeals system, it may be questioned whether the procedures adopted are compatible with constitutional justice. If, as seems likely, the appeals officers are discharging judicial functions (of a limited nature under cover of Article 37), then a judicial standard of impartiality is required.[46] This high standard is scarcely met where the system is administered by civil servants working in the Department of Social Welfare whose independence is not guaranteed by law and who, perhaps, are unduly influenced by Departmental policy considerations.[47] It is true that some

---

[42] Clark, *loc. cit.* 382.
[43] Social Welfare (Consolidation) Act 1981, s.298(12) as amended by s.19(*e*) of the Social Welfare Act 1990; Social Welfare (Insurance Appeals) Regulations 1952 (S.I. 1952 No. 376), Art. 10(1).
[44] *Thompson* v. *Minister for Social Welfare* [1989] I.R. 618.
[45] [1977] I.R. 267. See Clark, *loc. cit.* 278–279.
[46] *O'Brien* v. *Bord na Móna* [1983] I.R. 265 and see pp. 453–454. Note, however, that in *The State (Calcul Ltd.)* v. *Appeal Commissioners*, High Court, December 1986, Barron J. ruled that the Appeal Commissioners for Income Tax were not discharging judicial functions.
[47] Clark, "Towards a 'Just' Strike? Social Welfare Payments for Persons Affected by a Trade Dispute in the Republic of Ireland" (1985) 48 M.L.R. 659 comments as follows (at 666): "Appeals officers provide an efficient method of internal administrative *review* but, given the status of the appeals officer—at the time of such appointment such a person is, and remains, employed within the Department of Social Welfare and holds office 'during the pleasure of the Minister'—it is unrealistic to regard this form of adjudication as an independent appeals mechanism." See further, pp. 235–236.

attempt was made by the Social Welfare Act 1990 to ameliorate this perceived lack of independence. Thus, the appeal now formally lies to the Chief Appeals Officer, instead of the Minister for Social Welfare. Moreover, it is the Chief Appeals Officer (instead of the Minister) who is entrusted with such diverse functions as assigning the appeals to other appeals officers; determining whether assessors should sit with an appeals officer in a particular case and referring questions of law to the High Court. A further innovation introduced by the 1990 Act is that the Chief Appeals Officer is obliged to produce an annual report on the working of the appeals officers, which report must be laid before both Houses of the Oireachtas. Again, section 19(b) of the 1990 Act empowers the Minister—who is also, be it noted, the respondent to the appeal—to overrule one of his appeals officers and direct that a particular appeal shall be determined by way of an oral hearing.

While these reforms go beyond the merely superficial, their significance may be overstated. The basic lack of even-handedness and impartiality, already identified, remain and it is only when the social welfare appeals system is remodelled along the lines of the An Bord Pleanála or the Valuation Tribunal that the independence of this system will be beyond question.

Review of appeals officers' decisions

First, section 300 of the Social Welfare (Consolidation) Act 1981 allows a deciding officer to review an earlier decision of a deciding officer if there is new evidence, or if the earlier decision was based on a mistake on a point of law or fact, or if there has been a change in circumstances. It is also open to an appeals officer to review the earlier decision of an appeals officer, though on slightly narrower grounds than in the case of a deciding officer. By virtue of these provisions, a deciding officer (or, where appropriate, an appeals officer) is entitled not only to increase but even to reduce or disallow payments, save that the latter order will not have retrospective effect, except in the case of fraud.

Secondly, section 299 of the Social Welfare (Consolidation) Act 1981 creates an appeal on a point of law[48] from a decision of an appeals officer to the High Court. However, read literally, the scope of this appeal would seem to be extraordinarily narrow in that every "question arising in relation to a claim for benefit" would be excluded, and the decision of the appeals officer rendered "final and conclusive."[49] As Lynch J. observed in *Kingham* v. *Minister for Social Welfare*,[50] such a literal interpretation would have the effect of excluding appeals in:

---

[48] The Chief Appeals Officer is entitled to refer "any question" arising from a decision of the appeals officer to the High Court (*i.e.* this reference is not confined to points of law): 1981 Act, s.299(*a*), as amended by s.20(*a*) of the Social Welfare Act 1990.

[49] Section 299 refers the reader on to s.298(6). S.111(*a*) is the principal provision to which s.298(6) applies, and s.111(*a*) refers to "every question arising in relation to a claim for benefit." The "final and conclusive" clause contained in s.298(6) could not, however, bar judicial review by the High Court: see pp. 374–378.

[50] High Court, November 25, 1985.

"the vast majority of questions that might arise under the provisions of t. 1981 Act, leaving only a minority of cases where persons claim not to be within the Act and therefore not liable to pay contributions under the Act nor entitled to benefits thereunder."

Indeed, section 298(6) of the 1981 Act goes even further and purports to exclude from judicial review (the formula "final and conclusive" is used) virtually all decisions of an appeals officer. It is significant that the scope of the decisions so excluded is defined to be coterminous with the extent of the decisions from which no appeal is allowed. In sum, apart from the negligible area identified in the passage quoted from *Kingham*, there would be neither appeal nor review. The demarcation line identified in *Kingham*, would appear to be based on the rather quaint view that there should be an appeal in all cases where the citizen was required to make payments to the State, but not where the appellant was a mere recipient of the State's largesse. In *Kingham's* case, Lynch J. reacted against such a construction of section 299, saying that the matter excluded should be construed narrowly so as not to oust the jurisdiction of the High Court "save where such ouster is clear." The apparent effect of *Kingham* is that an appeal now lies to the High Court by virtue of section 299 of the 1981 Act in respect of *all* decisions of an appeals officer, the provisions of section 298(6) notwithstanding.[51]

In *The State (Power)* v. *Moran*[52] Gannon J. ruled that an absence of probative evidence to support a decision of an appeals officer was not an error affecting jurisdiction, and the decision could not be impeached in certiorari proceedings. This restrictive interpretation of the scope of jurisdictional error is out of line with some of the modern authorities, and it is doubtful whether this decision represents good law.[53] However, in the subsequent decision of *Foley* v. *Moulton*[54] the same judge was at pains to stress that, in *Foley*, the appeals officer had based his decision on "evidence which was reasonably capable of supporting the determination he made,"[55] which, perhaps, may be said to raise the inference that Gannon J. would have quashed the decision had it not been so based. *Murphy* v. *Minister for Social Welfare*[56] provides some further evidence that the courts are now more willing to scrutinise decisions of deciding and appeals officers in judicial review application, for here Blayney J. had little hesitation in quashing a decision of an appeals officer who had answered "the wrong question" and, thereby erred in law. Similarly, as far as challenges to the validity of social welfare legislation on constitutional[57] and European Community law[58] grounds are concerned

---

[51] Note that in *Foley* v. *Moulton* [1989] I.L.R.M. 169 the respondents accepted that an appeal could lie to the High Court under ss.298–300 of the 1981 Act on all questions of law.
[52] [1976–1977] I.L.R.M. 20.
[53] See pp. 345–352.
[54] [1989] I.L.R.M. 169.
[55] *Ibid*. 176.
[56] [1987] I.R. 295.
[57] See, *e.g. H.* v. *Eastern Health Board* [1988] I.R. 624 and *Hyland* v. *Minister for Social Welfare* [1988] I.R. 624.
[58] See, *e.g. McDermott and Cotter* v. *Minister for Social Welfare* [1987] I.L.R.M. 324.

judicial caution has not been much in evidence. However, pulling in the other direction is the fact that the courts—admittedly mainly English courts[59]—have sometimes been unwilling to interfere with the decisions of specialists such as appeals officers,[60] especially if this means interfering with a long-standing interpretation of the relevant regulations.[61]

5. Independent Radio and Television Commission[62]

Introduction

The need for some form of regulation of broadcasting—which was early recognised as an even more potent form of mass communication than that provided by the printing press—led to the passing of the Wireless Telegraphy Act 1926. Employing the standard licensing technique (more fully explored in Part 7) sections 3 and 5 of the 1926 Act made the possession of "wireless telegraphy apparatus" (as now defined in section 2(1) of the Broadcasting and Wireless Telegraphy Act 1988) a criminal offence unless it was authorised by a licence granted by the then Minister for Posts and Telegraphs.

In fact, the first systematic Irish broadcasting service began, as "2RN" on New Year's Night, 1926. The unit providing this service was to remain a section within the Department of Posts and Telegraphs until 1960. Some gestures were made in the direction of its unusual nature and the need for some independence: the unit was placed under the control of a Director of Broadcasting and in 1953, he was fortified by the establishment of a non-statutory *Comhairle* of five persons, given temporary civil service appointments, who were to be responsible to the Minister for the general control and supervision of the service.[63]

The Broadcasting Authority Act 1960 at last established broadcasting on a footing independent of the Government[64] by constituting the Radio Éireann (from 1966, Radio Telefís Éireann) Authority as a state-sponsored body. Some modifications to RTE were effected by amending statutes, enacted in 1976 and 1990. Other aspects of RTE, including its relations with the Government

---

[59] But note the manner in which Gannon J. refused to disturb a finding by an appeals officer in *Foley* v. *Moulton* [1989] I.L.R.M. 169 to the effect that the claimant was co-habitating with a man and was thus disqualified from receiving a widow's pension by virtue of s.92(3) of the Social Welfare (Consolidation) Act 1981.
[60] "Where a real error of law is shown then this court will interfere, but it would in my opinion be wrong to set up this Court as in effect a court of appeal of fact from decisions of these specialised tribunals," *per* May J. in *R.* v. *National Insurance Commissioner, ex p. Michael* [1976] I.C.R. 90, 94 (D.C.), affirmed [1977] 1 W.L.R. 109 (C.A.). See also, *R.* v. *Industrial Injuries Commissioner, ex p. Amalgamated Engineering Union* [1966] 2 Q.B. 31; *R.* v. *Preston Supplementary Benefits Appeal Tribunal, ex p. Moore* [1975] 1 W.L.R. 624.
[61] *R.* v. *National Insurance Commissioner, ex p. Stratton* [1979] Q.B. 361, 369 (Lord Denning).
[62] See generally, Hall and McGovern, "Broadcasting and Wireless Telegraphy Act 1988 and Radio and Television Act 1988" (1988) *Irish Current Law Statutes Annotated* (Sweet and Maxwell); Hall and McGovern, "Regulation of the Media" (1986) 8 D.U.L.J. (N.S.) 1. This Part was written before the publication of any annual report by the Commission.
[63] L. O'Broin, *Just Like Yesterday* (Gill and MacMillan), pp.167–180.
[64] For the first decade or so, this independence was rather faltering: see J. M. Kelly "The Constitutional Position of RTE" (1967) 15 *Administration* 205; L. O'Broin, "The dismissal of the Irish Broadcasting Authority *E.B.U. Review*, March 1973, p. 24 and September, 1975, p. 39.

and the Order made under section 31 of the Broadcasting Authority Act 1960 (as amended) are covered elsewhere in this book.[65]

For present purposes, what is significant is that until the new settlement (in the late 1980s, described below) the licence to broadcast was granted only to the official services provided first by the Department and thereafter by RTE (notwithstanding unsuccessful applications by some pirate—pop stations). This *de facto* monopoly was threatened by the pirate broadcasters at first, in the 1960s, maritime, but by the 1980s, within the jurisdiction. Because of the popularity of the pirate stations with the electorate, especially its younger members, official action to repel boarders was sluggish and ineffectual. The policy followed by successive Ministers for Communication was to take legal action against unlicensed stations only if they were causing interference to authorised users of wireless telegraphy apparatus.[66] The suggestion was made[67] that the Minister's apparent policy of confining broadcasting to the official services amounted to an unjustified inhibition on other would-be broadcasters' freedom of expression (under Article 40.6.1) and also to a violation of their right to earn a livelihood (under Article 40.3.1). These points seem to have been raised but not settled in *Nova Media Ltd.* v. *Minister for Post and Telegraphs*.[68] Article 10.1 of the European Convention on Human Rights[69] might also be relevant, as would E.C. competition law. In addition, as explained, a failure properly to exercise a discretion—in this case, in regard to the grant of a licence—may be invalid.

Eventually, falteringly,[70] the legislature confronted the problem of providing a legal framework within which to exercise such control over private broadcasting as was considered necessary. The final settlement retained the requirement already mentioned of a licence to broadcast, under the 1926 Act (albeit that the Broadcasting and Wireless Telegraphy Act 1988 established enhanced penalties for unlicensed broadcasting: see below). The major innovation was the constitution of a *de luxe* tribunal, the Independent Radio and Television Commission, by the Radio and Television Act 1988. It is this Commission which bears the responsibility of allocating the franchises to private broadcasters and thereafter policing them. The Schedule to the Radio and Television Act 1988 provides that:

> "A person shall not be appointed to be a member of the Commission unless he has had experience of, or shown capacity in, media or commercial

[65] See pp.137–140 and 535–536.

[66] *Senate Debates*, Vol. 120, col. 787, June 21, 1988 (Mr. R. Burke, Minister for Communications).

[67] J. M. Kelly, "Are Our Broadcasting Structures Out of Date?" *Irish Broadcasting Review*, Summer 1978, p.5. *A contra*: L. McRedmond, "Irish Radio Controversy" *Irish Broadcasting Review*, Autumn 1978, p. 62. See also, *Cooke* v. *Minister for Communications, Irish Times Law Report*, Februar 20, 1989.

[68] [9184 I.L.R.M. 161, 167. See also, *Cooke* v. *Minister for Communications, Irish Times Law Report*, February 20, 1989.

[69] See, *e.g. Autronic AG* v. *Switzerland* (1990) 12 E.H.R.R. 485 (ban on reception of foreign satellite television by satellite dish "not necessary in a democratic society" and, hence, contrary to Art. 10(1)). But see *Groppera Radio AG* v. *Switzerland* (1990) 12 E.H.R.R. 321 (legislation banning foreign retransmissions justifiable where necessary to give effect to international broadcasting rules).

[70] There were a number of attempts to legislate before the 1988 Acts were passed. The history of these other measures is recorded in Hall and McGovern, Radio and Television Act 1988.

affairs, radio communications engineering, trade union affairs, administration or social, cultural, educational or community activities."

The franchises cover: one television programme service; a national radio service; and 20-odd regional radio services. The RTE services remain under the control of the RTE Authority, unaffected, so far as the law is concerned, by the new régime.

Licences and contracts

One particular point of interest in this regulatory system concerns the demarcation of control functions between the Commission and the Minister for Communications. Broadly speaking the Minister controls the technological matter of broadcasting frequency management, whilst the Commission is concerned with the broadcasters and the material broadcast. The reasons given by the Minister as to why the frequency management could not be transferred to the Commission so that both functions would be united in the same body were two-fold. In the first place, broadcasting frequencies are but one element of the radio frequency spectrum which also has to accommodate aeronautical, mobile or emergency communications and it is necessary for all elements on the spectrum to be vested in the same authority.[71] Secondly, the entire radio-communications area is governed by international treaties for which the Government is responsible.

It is the Commission which appears to have the determining voice. How the dual control is coordinated is as follows. First, as we shall see, the key organising concept is the "contract." The provisions in the Act regarding sound broadcasting contracts and the television programme service contract are similar save that the latter do not contemplate that the contractor itself will have to establish a transmitter. Accordingly in this account we shall concentrate on sound broadcasting. The provision in respect of sound contracts is as follows:

> "The Commission shall enter into contracts (in this Act referred to as 'sound broadcasting contracts') with persons (in this Act referred to as 'sound broadcasting contractors') under which the sound broadcasting contractors have, subject to the provisions of this Act, the right and duty to establish, maintain and operate sound broadcasting contract and to provide, as the sound broadcasting contract may specify, a sound broadcasting service."[72]

On the other hand, it is for the Minister to decide whether to issue a licence and to specify the transmitter and area of the country to which it relates and also the frequency on which it is to operate and "such [other] terms and con-

---

[71] *Senate Debates*, Vol. 120, col. 781. "In the vast majority of countries in the world this function is vested in central Government. The only practical alternative would be the American model of vesting responsibility for managing the whole of the spectrum in one body—the Federal Communications Commission in their case. To achieve that here one would effectively have to convert the Department of Communications into a semi-State body."
[72] Radio and Television Act 1988, ss.4(2)(a), 18(1).

ditions as [he] sees fit to attach to the licence."[73] The Minister may also vary any term or condition of a licence on any of a number of specified grounds, including the fact that "it appears to him to be necessary so to do in the interests of good radio frequency management."[74]

The yoke between the contract and the licence is constructed in this way: the Commission cannot authorise a broadcasting contractor to operate a transmitter and provide a broadcasting service pursuant to a sound broadcasting contract "unless and until the Minister has issued . . . to the Commission a licence in respect of the . . . transmitter to which the contract relates."[75] However when the licence has been issued by the Minister, provided its terms and conditions have been complied with, then the contract automatically conveys the benefits of the licence to the contractor.[76] (And, incidentally, any transmitter established under the licence shall also be deemed to be licensed for the purposes of the Wireless Telegraphy Act 1926.[77])

However, the licence is made to be valid for the same period as the contract: if the contract is terminated or suspended, then so too is the licence.[78] And, equally, any breach of a condition of the licence is to be treated as if it were a breach of a term of the contract.[79] In short, since the licence is, in the ways mentioned, tied to the contract, it is the Commission which, by its control over the contract, determines who has the contract-licence and for how long.

Allocating the contract

Section 17 of the Radio and Television Act lays it down that there may be only a single television programme service. However as far as sound broadcasting services are concerned, the first step is for the number and catchment area of such services to be determined. A fair degree of formality is required in regard to this process. According to section 5:

"(1) In order to secure the orderly development of sound broadcasting services and, having regard to the availability of radio frequencies for sound broadcasting, to allow for the establishment of a diversity of services in an area catering for a wide range of tastes including those of minority interests, the Commission shall as soon as may be after it has been established and may thereafter from time to time by notice published in at least one national newspaper, invite expressions of interest in the securing of contracts for sound broadcasting services under this Act. Such expressions of interest shall indicate in general terms the type of sevice that would be pro-

---

[73] *Ibid.* s.4(5).
[74] *Ibid.* s.7(2).
[75] *Ibid.* s.4(3).
[76] *Ibid.* s.4(5). Notice also that, by ss.4(6) and 14(5), every licence and contract is open to inspection by the public.
[77] *Ibid.* s.4(5).
[78] *Ibid.* s.4(4).
[79] *Ibid.* s.4(5).

vided and shall not be regarded as an application for a sound broadcasting contract.

(2) The Commission shall make a report of its findings under *subsection (1)* to the Minister who, having considered the report and after consultation with the Commission, shall specify the area (which area may consist of the whole or any part of the State) in relation to which applications for a sound broadcasting contract are to be invited and the Commission shall comply with such direction.

(3) The Minister, having regard to the report furnished by the Commission under *subsection (2)* and having regard to the availability of radio frequencies for sound broadcasting, may limit the number of areas which he may specify under that subsection."[80]

After this information-gathering exercise has been completed, the contracts must be allocated by the Commission. First of all, the Commission invites applications for a contract (whether television or sound) by advertisement published in at least one national newspaper and, where the catchment area of the contract is restricted to one part of the country, in one local newspaper circulating in that area.[81] The Commission specifies the procedure which is to be followed in its adjudication on the applications. At its initial award of contracts, in 1989 (in the case of sound broadcasting) and 1990 (in the case of television), it issued detailed specifications as to the types of information which each applicant should supply. These included: the applicant and his experience and management team; an advertising market analysis together with revenue targets; the types of programmes envisaged; production facilities; and the financial structure. Thereafter oral hearings were held at which the applicants could be cross examined on their submissions.

The criteria on which the Commission is to draw, in awarding contracts, are specified in section 6(2) of the Radio and Television Act, as follows:

"In the consideration of applications received by it and in determining the most suitable applicant to be awarded a sound broadcasting contract, the Commission shall have regard to:—

    (a) the character of the applicant or, if the applicant is a body corporate, the character of the body and its directors, manager, secretary or other similar officer and its members and the persons entitled to the beneficial ownership of its shares;

    (b) the adequacy of the expertise and experience and of the financial resources that will be available to each applicant and the extent to which the application accords with good economic principles;

    (c) the quality, range and type of the programmes proposed to be provided by each applicant or, if there is only one applicant, by that applicant;

. . . .

---

[80] There is an exemption from ss.5, 6 and 9(1)(c) in the case of temporary or institutional sound broadcasting: s.8(4).
[81] *Ibid.* s.5(5), (7).

    (h) the desirability of allowing any person, or group of persons, to have control of, or substantial interests in, an undue amount of the communications media in the area specified in the notice under *section 5(5)*;

    (i) the extent to which the service proposed—

        (i) serves recognisably local communities and is supported by the various interests in the Community,

        or

        (ii) serves communities of interest, and

    (j) any other matters which the Commission considers to be necessary to secure the orderly development of sound broadcasting services."

The Minister (or anyone else) has no authority to issue any directions. Thus it is for the Commission to decide on the successful applicant with the only assistance coming from the guidelines in the Act. Inevitably, this entails both policy decisions (for example whether to prefer drama to documentaries) and factual decisions (whether an applicant is likely to obtain the finance he anticipates). Since the Commission has such a wide policy discretion, it would be inappropriate for any appeal to exist[82] and none has been created. An application for judicial review of a decision to award to a particular applicant (probably brought by a disappointed applicant) remains a possibility. However save in an extreme case, success would seem unlikely: for each of the factors listed in the passage quoted involves what is very much a matter of opinion; again the trade off between them constitutes a further point of discretion; and the further discretion introduced by paragraph (j) counteracts the requirement, at the start of the provision quoted, that the Commission "shall have regard [sc. only] to the criteria specified in the list just quoted."

Contractor's duties

The sources of a contractor's duties are to be found in the Radio and Television Act, itself, and in the individual contracts. By the Act; all news and current affairs must be presented in an objective and impartial manner and without any expression of the broadcasters, own views[83] and nothing must be broadcast which offends against good taste or decency[84]—nor which violates the requirements already imposed on RTE, namely avoidance of material which might promote crime[85] and obedience to any direction made under section 31 of the Broadcasting Authority Act 1960 as amended.[86] The total times for advertising may not exceed 15 per cent. of the daily broadcasting time or

---

[82] See p. 8.
[83] *Ibid.* s.9(1)(a), (b). *Cf. Senate Debates*, Vol. 120, col. 790 ("There was some concern that such a provision could run counter to the 'freedom of expression' provisions of Article 40 of the Constitution but it is considered that the risk is small").
[84] *Ibid.* s.9(1)(d).
[85] *Ibid.*
[86] *Ibid.* s.12.

16 2/3 per cent. in any one hour.[87] The contractor must comply with a code governing standards and practices in advertising to be drawn up by the Commission.[88] A contractor must give "due and adequate consideration to any complaint made by a member of the public" and records of such complaints are to be kept and made available to the Commission, on request.[89] However, the Minister has not yet exercised his statutory power to make regulations giving jurisdiction to the Broadcasting Complaints Commission so that, in contrast to RTE, the contractor is left in the position (absent any intervention by the IRTC) of policing itself. A most significant provision—by virtue of its inherent importance and its cost to the contractor—is section 9(1)(c) which requires, in the case of sound broadcasting only, that a minimum of:

> "(i) not less than 20 per cent. of the broadcasting time,
>   and
> (ii) if the sound broadcasting service is provided for more than 12 hours in any one day, two hours of broadcasting time between 07.00 hours and 19.00 hours,

is devoted to the broadcasting of news and current affairs programmes; provided a derogation from this provision is not authorised by the Commission under *section 15*".[90]

Other significant matters are dealt with in the contract: section 14 provides as follows:

> "(1) Every sound broadcasting contract may contain such terms and conditions as the Commission thinks appropriate and specifies in the contract.
> (2) Without prejudice to the generality of subsection (1), the Commission may specify in a sound broadcasting contract all or any of the following terms or conditions:
>> (a) the period during which the contract shall continue in force;
>> (b) whether the contract may be renewed and, if so, the manner in which, the terms of which, and the period for which, the contract may be so renewed;
>> (c) a condition prohibiting the assignment of the contract or of any interest therein;
>> (d) if the sound broadcasting contractor be a company, a condition prohibiting any alteration in the Memorandum or Articles of Association of the company or in so much of that Memorandum or of those Articles as may be specified or prohibiting any material change in the ownership of the company;
>> (e) a condition requiring the sound broadcasting contractor to pro-

---

[87] *Ibid.* s.9(1)(c). This is deliberately fixed at a higher level than for RTE because private broadcasters enjoy no equivalent of the licence fee income: *Senate Debates*, Vol. 120, col. 791 (Mr. Burke).
[88] *Ibid.* s.10.
[89] *Ibid.* s.11.
[90] There is a statutory exemption from s.9(1)(c) in the case of temporary or institutional sound broadcasting: s.8(3).

vide the quality, range and type of programmes which he proposed to offer in his application for the award of the contract."

Revocations

A most significant question is: what happens if any of these conditions is broken. The central provision here is section 14(4)(a) of the Act which states:

"(4) Every broadcasting contract shall—
   (a) provide that the Commission may, at its discretion, suspend or terminate the contract—
     (i) if any false or misleading information was given to the Commission by or on behalf of the sound broadcasting contractor prior to the making of the contract,
     (ii) if the sound broadcasting contractor has, in the opinion of the Commission, committed serious or repeated breaches of his obligations under the . . . broadcasting contract or under this Act."

This provision has not yet been used (although concern has been expressed, informally, by the Commission, as to whether certain contractors are honouring the obligation that 20 per cent. of their programme content should be news). However, the following tentative comments may be offered. In the first place, in the precarious state of most stations at the moment, a suspension (unless it were for a negligible period) would have the same effect as a termination. In substance, then there is only a single sanction and that a very drastic one: the provision may be regarded as deficient in that it does not include a range of sanctions (*e.g.* fines, censure, etc.) to meet more or less serious infringements. Secondly, it is a little surprising that no procedural safeguards are articulated. However, since both the right to livelihood and the right to property are involved, there is no doubt that a court would expect a fairly stringent standard of constitutional justice to be observed by the Commission, before a contract could be "suspended" or terminated.

As noted already (1) a contract is made co-extensive with the accompanying licence; and (2) broadcasting without a licence is a criminal offence. It follows that if a contract is terminated, the licence falls with it and any further broadcasting would be a criminal offence just as must as if no licence had ever been granted.

As will be explained in Part 7 of this chapter, the courts have often been unwilling to impose meaningful sanctions on those convicted of regulatory offenses. Accordingly the draftsman of the Broadcasting and Wireless Telegraphy Act 1988 has displayed some ingenuity in devising strategies which will adequately discourage unlicensed broadcasting. In the first place, the maximum punishments for unlicensed broadcasting is increased from a maximum fine of £10[91] to a maximum of £800 and/or three months imprisonment, on summary conviction.[92] On conviction on indictment, the maximum punish-

---

[91] Wireless Telegraphy Act 1926, s.3(3).
[92] Broadcasting and Wireless Telegraphy Act 1988, s.12(1).

ments are £20,000 and/or two years imprisonment.[93] The same sanctions apply to a number of novel offences whose broad thrust is to discourage persons whose assistance is vital to a working broadcasting service. Thus it is now an offence for anyone to provide accommodation, equipment or programme material for unlicensed broadcasts, or to advertise by means of, or take part in, such broadcasts.[94] It is also an offence (though only punishable, on summary conviction, by a fine of up to £1,000) for anyone to allow their telephone service or electricity supply to be used to promote, further or facilitate a business engaged in making illegal broadcasts.[95]

The Act also enables the Minister to serve a *prohibition notice* on either Bord Telecom Éireann or the Electricity Supply Board requiring them not to provide telephone or electricity services, respectively, to premises in which illegal broadcasts are made.[96]

6. Statutory Inquiries

There are, generally speaking, two types of statutory inquiry. The first type of inquiry (and the one which is the more frequently availed of) is the "standard device for giving a fair hearing to objectors before the final decision is made on some question of government policy affecting citizens' rights or interests."[97]

The circumstances in which the first type of inquiry is a statutory requirement in regard to the taking of a decision include: the siting of a new burial ground[98] the removal or suspension of persons holding office under the Vocational Education Acts[99]; the removal of members of a local authority for failure to perform their duties[1] the making of a compulsory purchase order by a local authority[2] and the determination of certain planning appeals.[3]

The second type of inquiry is, in effect, a post mortem: the inquiry is given the task of investigating the causes of accidents, natural disasters or other matters of general public concern. The terms of reference of this type of inquiry—which usually involves fact-finding as to the causes of (say) a shipping collision and recommendations as to improvements for the future—will usually be "at large," simply because the conclusions of the inquiry cannot be anticipated in advance. The most dignified and high-powered example of this

[93] *Ibid.* s.18.
[94] *Ibid.* ss.3–6.
[95] *Ibid.* s.7.
[96] *Ibid.* s.6.
[97] Wade, *Administrative Law* (Oxford, 1988), p. 955.
[98] Public Health (Ireland) Act 1878, s.163.
[99] Vocational Education Act 1930, s.27(2).
[1] Local Government Act 1941, s.44. See also, Harbours Act 1946, s.164 (local inquiry into performance by harbour authority of their "powers, duties and functions" and other related matters).
[2] See, *e.g.* Housing Act 1966, s.76 and Third Sched. (Compulsory Purchase Order) Procedure.
[3] Local Government (Planning and Development) Act 1963, s.82 and Local Government (Planning and Development) Regulations 1977 (S.I. 1977 No. 65).

latter type of inquiry is one which is constituted under the Tribunals of Inquiry (Evidence) Acts 1921–1979.[4] However, there is also specialised legislation regulating accidents involving railways,[5] shipping[6] and aeroplanes.[7]

Both types of statutory inquiry may be regarded as having many of the characteristics of a tribunal for the procedures adopted before an inquiry and a tribunal are similar in that each of them approximates to that of a court. However, there are three differences between a tribunal and an inquiry. First, the latter's conclusions do not bind the Minister or other responsible decision-making authority,[8] though in practice it would be rare for the Minister to depart from the conclusions of at any rate, the first type of inquiry. Secondly, an inquiry is set up *ad hoc* for each episode examined; whereas a tribunal enjoys a continuous existence. Finally whilst a tribunal is a decision-making body, an inquiry may be regarded as an instrument of participation in government.

[4] Tribunals of Inquiry have been appointed to investigate such diverse matters as allegations against members of the Oireachtas (*Report of the Tribunal appointed by the Taoiseach on November 7, 1947* (P. No. 8576) (sale of Locke's distillery); *Report of the Tribunal appointed by the Taoiseach on 4 July 1975* (Prl. 4745) (allegations against Minister for Local Government)); Garda practices (*Coghlan shooting inquiry: Tribunal Report* (1928) J.34; *Death of Liam O'Mahony: Report of the Tribunal appointed by the Minister* (1967, Pr. 9790); *Report of the Tribunal of Inquiry: The "Kerry Babies" case* (1985, Pl. 3514); and natural disasters (*Report of the Tribunal of Inquiry: Disaster at Whiddy Island, Bantry, Co. Cork* (1980, Pl. 8911); *Report of the Tribunal of Inquiry: Fire at the Stardust, Artane, Dublin* (Pl. 853). The only other Tribunal of Inquiry appointed since 1922 concerned an investigation into the making of an RTE programme on moneylending: *Report of the Tribunal appointed by the Taoiseach on 22 December, 1969* (Prl. 1363). See generally, P. A. R. Hillyard, "The Use of Judges to Chair Social Inquiries" (1971) 6 Ir.Jur. 93.

[5] Regulation of Railways Act 1871, s.9. For a recent example of an inquiry held under the terms of this section, see *Report of the Investigation into the Accident on the CIE Railway at Buttevant, Co. Cork on 1 August, 1980* (Prl. 9698, 1981).

[6] Merchant Shipping Act 1894, s.465. This section was invoked by the Minister for the Marine to set up an inquiry chaired by a District Justice with nautical assessors charged with an investigation into the deaths of four lifeboat officers off Ballycotton, Co. Cork: see *The Irish Times*, September 24, 1990. For a case arising from this tragedy, see *Haussman* v. *Minister for the Marine*, High Court, January 25, 1991.

[7] Air Navigation and Transport Act 1936, s.60 and Air Navigation (Investigation of Accidents) Regulations 1957 (S.I. 1957 No. 19). For a recent example of an inquiry held pursuant to these provisions, see *Accident to Reims Cessna F.182 Q in the Blackstairs Mountains, Co. Wexford on 7 September, 1983* (Department of Communications, 1984).

[8] It is of interest to notice the reasons given by the Martin Report on Certain Aspects of Criminal Procedure (March, 1990) which recommended that persons who have been convicted of criminal offences and who have exhausted the normal appeals procedures should have their convictions re-examined not by a court but by a statutory inquiry. Those reasons were: (i) a departure from the rules of evidence might be necessary for a full investigation; but a departure from these rules by a court would be undesirable (p. 11); (ii) because of the wide-ranging nature of the inquiry, the inquisitorial mode of procedure is to be preferred to the accusatorial method, which is characteristic of a court (p. 12); (iii) before someone who had already unsuccessfully exercised his option of appealing to the Supreme Court could litigate any further within the court system a constitutional amendment would be necessary because the Supreme Court is the final court of appeal (Art. 34.4.1) (p. 11). Not mentioned as reasons but possibly relevant, all the same, are: (i) the court system's possible reluctance to confess that it had committed an injustice; (ii) the fact that court decisions are characteristically conclusive and not (as proposed in the Report) merely an expression of opinion as to whether doubt existed as to the propriety of the conviction, with the status of a recommendation as to whether Government should advise the President to grant a pardon. Of interest, in this last context, is the Committee's view that for an inquiry to go further than an expression of opinion would possibly amount to "a trespass into the judicial domain" (p. 16).

Procedure before an inquiry

As regards the procedure adopted at a statutory inquiry of either type, much will be left to the chairman of the tribunal, but he must act subject to the procedural requirements imposed by the particular statute and the·overriding requirements of constitutional justice. Normally, statutory inquiries take the form of public hearings where the witnesses give evidence under oath and are subject to cross-examination by the opposing parties.[9]

Accusatorial v. *Inquisitorial procedure*

Traditionally, it was thought that the principles of constitutional justice should not apply in the case of persons conducting preliminary statutory inquiries (*e.g.* such as where the report of an inspector requires confirmation by the decision-making authority). However, this argument has been rejected by the Irish courts. In *The State (Shannon Atlantic Fisheries Ltd.)* v. *McPolin*[10] an inspector had been appointed to investigate the causes of the wrecking of the applicant's fishing vessel. The inspector took depositions from members of the ship's crew, but he did not interview the owners of the vessel or give them an opportunity of refuting the allegations against them. The inspector's findings of fact impugned the good name and reputation of the shipowners and Finlay P. ruled that the inspector's report should be quashed for breach of the *audi alteram partem* rule. Finlay P. continued:

> "The fact that it is not the investigating officer but the Minister for Transport and Power who must decide, having regard to the content of the report, whether any further action should be taken by him in relation to prosecutions under the Act seems to me not to affect the true decision-making role of the person carrying out the preliminary inquiry."[11]

In the unusual case of *Re Haughey*[12] the Supreme Court had emphasised that the duty to observe fair procedures could arise despite the fact that the report of an inquiry did not of itself apportion liability or impose penalties. In *Haughey*, the plaintiff had sought leave to cross-examine witnesses appearing before the Dáil Committee of Public Accounts, and to have counsel appear on his behalf. Ó Dálaigh C.J. rejected the argument that Haughey was a mere witness before the Committee—he was in effect a party. His conduct and reputation were the very subject-matter of the investigation. In that situation he had the same rights as those guaranteed by Article 38.1 to accused persons facing trial, and basic fairness of procedures demanded that he be afforded the right to cross-examine (by counsel, if he wished), to call rebutting evidence and to make closing submissions. Without those rights, no person in the plaintiff's position could hope to defend his good name.

One might contrast this decision with that of the House of Lords in *Bushell*

---

[9] See, *e.g.* Local Government Act 1941, s.86.
[10] [1976] I.R. 93. The inquiry was held pursuant to s.465 of the Merchant Shipping Act 1894.
[11] [1976] I.R. 93, 98.
[12] [1971] I.R. 217. See also, *Mahon* v. *Air New Zealand Ltd.* [1984] A.C. 808.

v. *Environmental Secretary*.[13] *Bushell's* case concerned a statutory inquiry into whether a particular motorway should be constructed or not. The planning inspector who was chairman of the inquiry refused to allow the objectors to cross-examine witnesses as to the reliability of the Department of the Environment's predictions as to future traffic flow, or to query witnesses as to the need for such a motorway. The House of Lords ruled that the inspector had not acted contrary to natural justice as the objectors had been allowed to voice their opinions on these matters. Lord Diplock cautioned against the "over-judicialisation" of such inquiries, and he observed that it was fallacious to assume that cross-examination was the only procedure of ascertaining matters of fact and opinion. Perhaps these comments should be read in light of the fact that the proposed cross-examination concerned issues of policy. It may be surmised that Lord Diplock would have taken a different approach had the witnesses impugned the good name or reputation of the witnesses, or if there had been a conflict of evidence as to the essential facts at issue.

These cases recall the earlier discussion, in the context of tribunals, of the choice between the accusatorial and inquisitorial approaches.[14] It could be argued that in relation to inquiries, the inquisitorial approach with its higher regard for seeking the whole truth and its reduced emphasis on individual rights in regard to a narrow issue, is the more appropriate model.

The difficult question of whether the deciding authority is free to act on the basis of extrinsic evidence which was not before the parties at the inquiry is considered elsewhere.[15]

Attendance of witnesses, etc.

In the case of inquiries held at the instance of the Minister for the Environment (whether under the provisions of section 83 of the Local Government Act 1941 or any other Act), the inspector conducting the inquiry enjoys a statutory power to subpoena witnesses and to take evidence on oath.[16] Similar provisions exist in respect of other statutory inquiries.[17]

In the case of Tribunals of Inquiry, section 4 of the Tribunals of Inquiry (Evidence) (Amendment) Act 1979 provides that the Tribunal "may make such orders as it considers necessary for the purposes of its functions," and it is invested with all such "powers, rights and privileges of the High Court" in that regard.

Immunity from defamation proceedings

There is no general statutory provision which provides that statements made during the course of a statutory inquiry are privileged. Although the issue is not free from doubt, it would seem that the common law rule that statements during the course of judicial proceedings are absolutely privileged

---

[13] [1981] A.C. 75.
[14] See p. 235.
[15] See pp. 446–448.
[16] Local Government Act 1941, s.86.
[17] See, *e.g.* Regulation of Railways Act 1871, s.7(3); Air Navigation and Transport Act 1936, s.60.

extends to statutory inquiries which follow a quasi-judicial procedure.[18] Since a tribunal of inquiry is invested with the status of the High Court by virtue of section 4 of the Tribunals of Inquiry (Evidence) (Amendment) Act 1979, it would seem that statements made during the course of proceedings before the tribunal are absolutely privileged.[19]

Appointment of assessors

Statutory provision has been made for the appointment of assessors to assist in certain types of inquiries.[20] An assessor will generally be appointed to assist in the evaluation of complex scientific and technical evidence.[21]

Costs

Costs may be awarded against a local authority or other body in the case of inquiries held at the instance of the Minister for the Environment under the provisions of section 83 of the Local Government Act 1941 or any other Act.[22] The Minister may certify that the local authority or other body should make a contribution towards the costs and expenses reasonably incurred by any person (other than the local authority or other body) in relation to the inquiry. These provisions would certainly appear to be broad enough to cover most statutory inquiries.

In the case of Tribunals of Inquiry, the Tribunals of Inquiry (Evidence) (Amendment) Act 1979, section 6, enables the chairman of the tribunal to certify that the whole or part of the costs of any person appearing before the tribunal shall be borne by another party (generally the State).[23]

In some cases, however, there is no statutory authority to award costs to, or against, any person appearing before the inquiry. In *Condon* v. *C.I.E.*[24] Barrington J. ruled that a statutory inquiry constituted under the provisions of section 7 of the Railway Regulation Act 1871 did not have power to award costs. Section 7 provided that the persons conducting the formal investigation were to have all the powers of a court of summary jurisdiction as well as certain other additional powers. These additional powers did not include the power

---

[18] McMahon and Binchy, *The Irish Law of Torts* (Abingdon, 2nd ed.), p. 646. See also, *Trapp* v. *Mackie* [1979] 1 W.L.R. 377.

[19] By virtue of s.5 of the 1979 Act, statements made during the course of a hearing before a Tribunal of Inquiry are inadmissible in all subsequent criminal prosecutions (with the exception of perjury).

[20] Regulation of Railways Act 1871, s.7(i); Air Navigation (Investigation of Accidents) Regulations 1957 (S.I. No. 19 of 1957), Art. 7(2); Tribunal of Inquiry (Evidence) (Amendment) Act 1979, s.2.

[21] Assessors were appointed in the two recent Tribunals of Inquiry concerning natural disasters, *Whiddy Island* and *Stardust*. See p. 257, n. 4.

[22] Local Government Act 1941, s.83(2). A similar provision exists in relation to inquiries held pursuant to the Public Health (Ireland) Act 1878: see s.210 of the 1878 Act.

[23] The general tendency so far has been for the chairman to award costs in favour of the private parties (but not institutions such as local authorities or major companies) who were properly represented before the tribunal: see the comments of Costello J. at Chap. 24 of the Whiddy Island Report, and those of Lynch J. at Chap. 36 of the "Kerry Babies" Report.

[24] High Court, November 22, 1984. For the background to this case, see *Report of the Investigation into the Accident on the CIE Railway at Buttevant, Co. Cork on August 1, 1980* (1981, Pr. 9698).

to award costs, and, as Barrington J. noted, the power of courts of summary jurisdiction to award costs has always been strictly circumscribed.

In *Condon's* case itself, the plaintiff was an employee of CIE and he claimed that he had been "singled out" as the person principally responsible for a serious train crash at Buttevant Station, Co. Cork, in 1980. Since his good name and his livelihood were at stake, the plaintiff engaged solicitor and counsel to represent him at the inquiry. It was argued that if the inquiry had no jurisdiction to award him costs, a constitutional duty was imposed on the State by the terms of Article 40.3 to defray the cost of such representation. Barrington J. rejected this argument, saying that while the guarantee of fair procedures contained in Article 40.3 required that the plaintiff be allowed to defend himself, "it was quite another thing to say that the State must pay the costs of his defence."[25] However, as CIE had been negligent and responsible for the accident, Barrington J. found (1) that it was almost unthinkable that the Minister for Transport would not establish a statutory inquiry into the disaster and (2) that the plaintiff, as a person immediately involved in the events leading up to the disaster, would naturally seek to be legally represented before the inquiry. The judge concluded that, as the plaintiff "was placed in the position of needing such representation as a consequence of the negligence of CIE", this was a reasonably foreseeable consequence of such negligence. Under these circumstances he was entitled to recover the reasonable costs of being legally represented before the inquiry. Taken at its full width, *Condon* would lead to the rather extreme proposition that the person responsible for a particular accident will be liable to pay the legal costs of the other parties appearing before the inquiry, as this will generally be a reasonably foreseeable consequence of their negligence.

7. General Principles of Licensing

Introduction

Licensing[26] is one of the most common techniques by which the dirigiste State regulates activities which are potentially harmful to its citizens. Such

---

[25] Barrington J. followed the earlier decision of *K. Security Ltd.* v. *Ireland*, High Court, July 15, 1977 in this regard. In *K. Security*, Gannon J. held that the State was not under any constitutional duty to discharge the costs of the plaintiff company which had been legally represented at a tribunal of inquiry. (This was before the enactment of the Tribunal of Inquiry (Evidence) (Amendment) Act 1979, s.5 of which makes provision for the payment of the parties' costs by the State or other party appearing before the tribunal).

[26] The meaning explained in this paragraph describes the use of the term "licence" is used in public administration. As used in private law, the term also means permission but with the implication that the remedy for performing the action without permission is merely a civil wrong and not an offence.

Note that, in general, a licence involves permission to take some positive action or, more usually, series of actions (whether trading, practising a profession or possessing a potentially harmful object). By contrast, there may be a direction to *refrain* from doing some act or series of acts. Examples of this include: the making of a prohibition order under the Censorship of Publications Acts 1929–1967; and the making of an order by the Central Bank under section 21 of the Central Bank Act 1971 (as inserted by s.38 of the Central Bank Act 1989) directing that the holder of a banking licence shall

unlicensed activity is made a criminal offence (triable in the usual way) by specific legislation. However, the legislation also provides, implicity, that the activity in question is lawful so long as it is carried out within the terms of the licence issued by some official or quasi-official authority.

How does the Oireachtas decide which activities ought to be licensed? Broadly speaking (as will be seen from the examples given below), they involve acts which are not in themselves harmful in the same way as ordinary crimes (such as murder or larceny). Indeed, they are activities which, if carried out in the appropriate circumstances by a suitably qualified person, will usually be beneficial to the community. On the other hand, if performed by the wrong person or in the wrong circumstances (such as medical treatment carried out by an unqualified practitioner), they may be positively harmful.

A further contrast with traditional crimes is that licensing is preventative rather than curative. A licensing régime is not content to wait until a vendor of land has his money misappropriated by an auctioneer or estate agent. Rather, it seeks to strike at an earlier point in time by prosecuting unlicensed auctioneers and by seeking to ensure that only auctioneers of good character are granted a licence.[27]

We may commence by considering, first, the stage at which a licence is granted or withheld and, secondly, the enforcement stage.

Licensing stage

Consonant with the haphazard design of our system of government administration, the task of licensing may be vested in any one of at least five different types of agency. In the first place, this function may be vested in a court, generally the District Court, but occasionally the Circuit Court, and examples here include: selling intoxicating liquor[28]; running dance halls[29]; moneylending[30]; auctioneering[31] and pawnbroking.[32] Secondly, control over a number of activities is vested in the local authorities. These activities are generally in the environmental or public health field and include: land use[33]; discharge of

---

not carry on banking business. However, very little turns on this point of characterisation. For "the directing power" (to borrow U.S. parlance), see Stout, *Administrative Law in Ireland* (Dublin, 1985), pp. 373–419.

In some administrative regulatory systems, the onus is placed upon the private individual to "declare" or "certify" that what he is doing is not potentially injurious. For example, under ss.2, 3 and 12 of the Local Government (Multi-Storey Buildings) Act 1988, if a local authority serves notice on the owner of a building with five or more storeys, the owner must submit to the local authority a certificate signed by a "competent person" (a chartered engineer, etc.) certifying, *inter alia* that the building is constructed in accord with the appropriate codes of practice and standards. Failure to submit a certificate, or the submission of a false certificate, is an offence.

[27] See Auctioneering and Houseagents Acts 1947–1973.
[28] Licensing Acts 1933–1988. See further, Woods, *Guide to the Intoxicating Liquor Acts* (1974) and Supplement (1977); Woods, *District Court Guide* (1977), Vol. 1, Pt. XI.
[29] Public Dance-Halls Act 1935, s.2.
[30] Moneylenders Act 1933, s.6(2).
[31] Auctioneering and Houseagents Acts 1947–1973.
[32] Pawnbrokers Act 1964, s.10.
[33] Local Government (Planning and Development) Act 1963, s.26. See further, pp. 202–209.

effluent[34]; air pollution,[35] and running a caravan park[36] or abattoir.[37] Sometimes, however, local authorities are given licensing functions in matters of social concern to the community and the powers given to local authorities in respect of gaming halls under Part III of the Gaming and Lotteries Act 1956 provide the best example in this context. Thirdly, the licensing functions may be allocated to a Minister, as, for example, in the case of: road passenger licences[38]; livestock marts[39]; bull-breeding[40]; tour-operators[41]; the operation of licensed health insurance schemes[42] and insurance services.[43] Fourthly, in some cases, the allocation of licences has been considered sufficiently important to warrant the vesting of these functions in an autonomous agency. Thus, the Central Bank is the ultimate regulatory authority in respect of (commercial,[44] or trustee savings,[45]) banking licences and other financial services, including building societies.[46] Alternatively, an independent tribunal may be established solely for the purpose of licensing. Thus An Bord Pleanála deals with all planning appeals[47] and the Independent Radio and Television Commission distributes broadcasting franchises.[48] Fourthly, licences to practise professions (such as law,[49] medicine,[50] veterinary science,[51] nursing[52] or dentistry[53]) are issued by the respective professional body. Finally, licences which have a security or policing dimension (such as firearms,[54] bookmaking[55] and house-to-house and street collections[56]) are handled by the Gardaí. There are also licensing systems which fall outside any of these five categories, such as, for example, a licence to drive a taxi (which is dispensed by the Garda carriage office under the auspices of the Garda Commissioner)[57] or a supply certificate in respect of video recordings (which is granted by the Official Censor).[58]

---

[34] Local Government (Water Pollution) Act 1977, s.4(1)(*b*).
[35] Air Pollution Act 1987, Pt. III.
[36] Local Government (Sanitary Services) Act 1948, s.34(4).
[37] Abattoirs Act 1988, s.9.
[38] Road Transport Act 1932, ss.8–12.
[39] Livestock Marts Act 1967, s.3.
[40] Control of Bulls for Breeding Act 1985, s.3.
[41] Transport (Tour Operators and Travel Agents) Act 1982, s.6.
[42] Voluntary Health Insurance Act 1957, s.22.
[43] European Communities (Non-Life Insurance) Regulations 1976 (S.I. 1976 No. 115); European Communities (Life Assurance) Regulations 1984 (S.I. 1984 No. 57).
[44] Central Bank Acts 1971–1989.
[45] Trustee Savings Banks Act 1989, s.10.
[46] Building Societies Act 1989, ss.17 and 119 and Pt. IV.
[47] Local Government (Planning and Development) Act 1976, s.26. See pp. 206–208.
[48] Radio and Television Act 1988, ss.6 and 7. See Pt. 5.
[49] Solicitors Act 1954 (Incorporated Law Society of Ireland).
[50] Medical Practitioners Act 1978 (Medical Council).
[51] Veterinary Surgeons Act 1931 (Veterinary Council).
[52] Nurses Act 1985 (An Comhairle Altranais).
[53] Dentists Act 1985 (Dental Council).
[54] Firearms Acts 1925–1990.
[55] Betting Act 1931, s.6.
[56] Street and House to House Collections Act 1962, ss.5, 6, 9–11.
[57] Road Traffic (Public Service Vehicles) Regulations 1963 (S.I. 1963 No. 191), Art. 20.
[58] Video Recordings Act 1989, s.3(1).

Power to grant licences is always accompanied by powers to refuse the renewal of a licence or even to revoke it when prescribed violations of the terms of a licence are established. Revocation is regarded as an interference with the right to earn a livelihood.[59] Accordingly, powers to revoke, in the absolute discretion of the licensing authority, while once common,[60] are rarely, if ever, conferred today. Moreover, the governing legislation will invariably provide for some form of appeal against an adverse decision of the licensing authority. Sometimes the right of appeal will lie to another administrative agency,[61] but more often it will lie to the District Court[62] or even to the High Court.[63] In *Cashman* v. *Clifford*[64] Barron J. rejected the argument that, when hearing such appeals from licensing authorities, the courts were merely discharging administrative functions and were not thereby administering justice, under Article 34.1 of the Constitution. Here the applicant had challenged the validity of section 13 of the Betting Act 1931 which had established an appeal to the District Court against a decision of the Garda Superintendent refusing a licence, but had also provided by section 13(5) that only the Garda Síochána and the Revenue Commissioners and "no other person" were entitled to be heard on the appeal. Barron J. held that the exclusion of other potential objectors (such as the applicant, who was already a bookmaker in the area) represented an unconstitutional interference with the administration of justice. In the result, section 13(5) was found to be invalid.[65]

In any event, in addition to any form of (administrative or judicial) appeal, the revocation of a licence is subject to a fairly stringent application of the principles of judicial review of administrative action, including not only

[59] But as for whether a licence may be regarded as a form of property right enjoying constitutional protection, see pp. 274–276. For the statutory procedure to be followed in a revocation under the Livestock Marts Act 1967, see ss.3 and 6 of the Act.
[60] See, *e.g.* Road Transport Act 1932, s.17(3) ("The Minister may at any time on his own motion and at his absolute discretion revoke an occasional passenger licence"); Voluntary Health Insurance Act 1957, s.22(1) ("The Minister may, in his absolute discretion, revoke a health insurance licence.")
[61] See, *e.g.* Local Government (Planning and Development) Act 1976, s.14; Air Pollution Act 1987, s.34; Local Government (Water Pollution) Act 1977, s.20 (as inserted by s.15 of the Local Government (Water Pollution) (Amendment) Act 1990) (appeal lies in all cases to An Bord Pleanála); Video Recordings Act 1989, s.10 (appeal to Censorship of Films Appeals Board).
[62] See, *e.g.* Betting Act 1931, s.13; Street and House to House Collections Act 1962, s.13; Health (Nursing Homes) Act 1990, s.5.
[63] See, *e.g.* Central Bank Act 1971, s.21(3), as inserted by s.38 of the Central Bank Act 1989 (right of appeal to the High Court by holder of banking licence against order of Central Bank suspending carrying on of banking business); Transport (Tour Operators and Travel Agents) Act 1982, s.9(3) (appeal to the High Court against refusal or revocation of tour operator's licence by Minister).
[64] [1989] I.R. 122.
[65] Barron J. followed the earlier decision of the Supreme Court in *The State (McEldowney)* v. *Kelleher* [1983] I.R. 289, where that court had declared a section of the Street and House to House Collections Act 1962 (which had in effect purported to allow a Garda Superintendent to direct a District Justice to dismiss certain types of appeals against the Superintendent's refusal to grant a collecting licence) to be unconstitutional. However, in neither authority was the precise point mentioned in the text—whether Art. 34.1 of the Constitution applied where a court is exercising a regulatory function—really addressed.

substantive checks as to, for instance, reasonableness, but also the rules of constitutional justice. The same is true, although to a lesser extent, of the refusal of a renewal.

Because of the variety of different cases to which any licensing system will have to apply, the need for flexibility is particularly great. This need for flexibility is accommodated by empowering the licensing agency to grant a licence not only absolutely but also subject to specified conditions. In practice, licences are seldom, if ever, granted free of conditions.

Enforcement stage

In principle, there is less to say with regard to enforcement. As a general rule, the governing statute will provide for criminal offences triable summarily before the District Court or, on indictment, before the Circuit Court. In addition, the licensing agency will be given a special prosecuting role in summary prosecutions.[66] However, in practice, presumably because there is no readily identifiable victim, the punishments imposed tend to be small if not altogether derisory.[67] They rarely have a deterrent effect and may, indeed, be regarded as simply additional "overheads" of running the unlawful activity. Recent legislation tends to rely more heavily on civil remedies in aid of enforcement. Thus the licensing agency or some other person with *locus standi* is entitled to seek an injunction against the unlicensed operator. The best-known injunctions of this type are in the field of planning control, where such a remedy is specifically made available by section 27 of the Local Government (Planning and Development) Act 1976.[68]

However, it is also a cardinal legal principle that, in general, an injunction may be sought by or on behalf of the Attorney-General, to enforce a statutory obligation, even without explicit authorisation.[69] In this case, however, it is a vexed question as to whether a competitor has any remedy against an unlicensed rival in the absence of statutory provisions conferring such a right of objection. Certainly, a competitor has sufficient standing to seek judicial

---

[66] But not in prosecutions on indictment. In fact, the function of prosecuting on indictment in respect of all offences (apart from the few, responsibility for which remains with the Attorney General) is vested in the Director of Public Prosecutions: Prosecution of Offences Act 1974, s.3(1); Criminal Justice (Administration) Act 1924, s.9. This is not required by Art. 30, or any other Article, of the Constitution. However there appears to be a policy that the independent and specifically-established office of the D.P.P. should bear responsibility for all prosecutions on indictment.

[67] See, *e.g.* the comments of Costello J. in *Att.-Gen.* v *Paperlink Ltd.* [1984] I.L.R.M. 373, 392 and those of O'Hanlon J. in *Parsons* v. *Kavanagh* [1990] I.L.R.M. 560, 567 (where he referred to the unchanged monetary penalties provided by the Road Transport Acts 1932–1933 and with "the fall in the value of money in the meantime, they appear to me at the present time to be somewhat derisory as against possible breaches of the Acts.")

[68] See pp. 208–209. For a further example of a "statutory injunction," see Local Government Act 1977, s.11.

[69] "Whenever Parliament has enacted a law and given a particular remedy for breach of it, such remedy being in an inferior court, nevertheless, the High Court always has a reserve power to enforce the law so enacted by way of an injunction or other suitable remedy. The High Court has jurisdiction to ensure obedience to the law whenever it is just and convenient to do so," *per* Lord Denning in *Att.-Gen.* v. *Chaudry* [1971] 1 W.L.R. 1614, 1624. This statement was quoted with approval by Costello J. in *Att.-Gen.* v. *Paperlink Ltd.* [1984] I.L.R.M. 373 and see also, *Att.-Gen. (O'Duffy)* v. *Appleton* [1907] 1 I.R. 252.

R.T.C. LIBRARY LETTERKENNY

review of the decision actually to grant a licence to the rival where he alleges that the requisite statutory formalities have not been complied with.[70] It is also clear, as mentioned, that the Attorney-General may sue to restrain breaches of the law and this includes restraining the activities of an unlicensed operator. But what if the situation is the more common one in which there is no licence (or perhaps the licence has been struck down) and yet the business is trading: where the Attorney-General does not take action, can a private individual seek an injunction to restrain the activities of an unlicensed rival? Prior to the decision of O'Hanlon J. in *Parsons* v. *Kavanagh*,[71] it appeared— to judge from the traditional English authorities—that a licensed operator did not have standing to complain about the activities of an unlicensed rival. Thus, in *RCA Corporation* v. *Pollard*,[72] the English Court of Appeal held that as the Performers' Protection Acts 1958–1972 were not enacted for the benefit of the public at large, the plaintiff company could not seek an injunction against the defendants (who were allegedly trading in illegal copies of records in respect of which the plaintiff had exclusive rights) to restrain breaches of this legislation causing it financial loss. As Oliver L.J. stated:

"No case which has been cited to us has gone so far as to confer a cause of action where the damage complained of is merely economic damage as an incidental result of the breach of a prohibition in a statute not designed to protect the interests of a class to which the plaintiff belongs."[73]

However, in *Parsons* v. *Kavanagh*, O'Hanlon J. held that these common law principles must yield, in this jurisdiction, to the constitutional right to earn a livelihood. The plaintiff was a licensed operator of a passenger bus service and she sought an injunction to restrain the activities of an unlicensed competitor. While O'Hanlon J. held that the licensing régime of the Road Transport Act 1932 was enacted for the benefit of the public at large (so that a licensed operator could not sue at common law for breach of these provisions), this had to be considered in the light of the relevant constitutional guarantees:

"The constitutional right to earn one's livelihood by lawful means carries with it the entitlement to be protected against any unlawful activity on the part of another person which materially impairs or infringes that right."[74]

The judge went on to find that the defendants had engaged in unlawful activity which impaired "in a significant manner the plaintiff's exercise of her constitutional right to earn her livelihood by lawful means" and granted an injunction accordingly.

A further type of enforcement procedure may be provided by statute in the form of a "concretising" directive (often called a notice) by which the licensing authority must give the offender precise instructions as to how the law

[70] *Irish Permanent Building Society* v. *Caldwell (No. 2)* [1981] I.L.R.M. 242.
[71] [1990] I.L.R.M. 561.
[72] [1983] Ch. 135.
[73] *Ibid.* 153C. But see, *a contra*: *Re Island Records* [1978] 3 All E.R. 824 and *Rickless* v. *United Artists* [1987] 1 All E.R. 679.
[74] [1990] I.L.R.M. 561, 566.

(including any conditions attached to a licence) has been broken and what must be done to put matters right. Where such a notice is invoked, if and when its terms have been defied for a specified time period, then an offence is committed.[75]

Finally, the lack of a licence, where one is required, may have various consequences in private law. These consequences may amount to an indirect sanction against the failure to obtain a licence. A well-known example is the principle that a contract in respect of the unlicensed activity may not be enforceable.[76]

Having considered both the licensing and enforcement stages, we may now proceed to identify some more detailed characteristics of licensing legislation.

A licence is generally personal to the grantee and is not assignable

As a general rule, a licence is personal to the holder, since it was only granted on proof of the applicant's suitability of character, skill, qualifications, etc. Thus, for example, section 13(1) of the Abattoirs Act 1988 provides that:

"The holder of an abattoir licence shall not transfer the licence to any other person and any such purported transfer shall be void and of no effect."

Despite the fact that this principle of non-assignability is clear, there are occasional transgressions and thus, for example, it appears that taxi-plates are currently being freely traded as if they were commodities. There is, however, a second category of cases where the grant of the licence does not depend on the personal suitability or qualifications of the applicant but instead attaches to the land, business, etc., involved.[77] As we shall see, in this sort of case, the licence or permission may not be severed and sold independently. A grant of planning permission is an example in point, for section 29(5) of the Local Government (Planning and Development) Act 1963 provides that:

"Where permission to develop land or for the retention of a structure is granted . . . then, except as may otherwise be provided by the permission, the grant of permission shall enure for the benefit of the land or structure and of all persons for the time being interested therein, but without prejudice to the provisions of this Part of the Act with respect to the revocation and modification of permissions granted thereunder."

The planning permission attaches to the land (which will invariably make the land more valuable) and any subsequent purchaser will take the lands with

---

[75] Again an example is provided by the planning legislation: see enforcement notice and warning notices described at p. 208. For enforcement notices in the context of the Data Protection Act 1988, see p. 224, n. 32.

[76] See Cheshire and Fifoot, *Law of Contract* (11th ed.), pp. 334–341; *Re Moneylenders Act 1933 and Lynne, Applicants* v. *A.-G.* 74 I.L.T.R. 96.

[77] Such as registered bulls under s.3(1) of the Control of Bulls for Breeding Act 1985.

the benefit of that permission.[78] Indeed, such is the effect of section 29(5) that a planning permission has been judicially described as an "appendage to the title of the property."[79]

There is a third category of cases which combines elements of the first two by requiring both the existence of a licence attaching to the premises and the suitability of the applicant to hold the licence in question. This is the case with the Licensing Acts 1833–1988, which require attestation both as to the suitability of the licensed premises and the applicant before a licence is granted. Again, in the case of applicants seeking a special restaurant licence under Part II of the Intoxicating Liquor Act 1988 (which entitles restaurants to serve intoxicating liquor for consumption by patrons of the restaurant with their meals), even higher standards are required. The applicant must first establish the suitability of the restaurant to the satisfaction of Bord Fáilte: section 8(2) requires that the restaurant must, *inter alia*, be "well equipped, well furnished and provide comfortable seating in the dining area and waiting area" and must also provide "a high standard of catering" and "maintain a high standard of hygiene." Secondly, the applicant must also establish his own personal suitability, since by section 8(1), the Circuit Court may refuse to grant a licence on the grounds of "character, misconduct or unfitness of the applicant" or of the "unfitness or inconvenience of the premises."

As mentioned, where the licence attaches to the land, it cannot be sold independently from the land. This is illustrated by a series of decisions on the Licensing Acts 1833–1988, of which two recent cases may serve as examples. In *Re Sherry-Brennan*[80] a bankrupt publican was the owner of licensed premises in respect of which a judgment mortgage and other charges had been registered in the Land Registry. The premises were sold. However, the Official Assignee claimed to be entitled to retain the notional value of the licence (as reflected in the enhanced purchase price) for the benefit of the unsecured creditors, basing himself on the argument that the licence (as distinct from the premises itself) was not captured by the judgment mortgage and the other charges. Hamilton J. rejected this submission, stating that:

> "As a licence cannot be regarded as a property capable of separation from the licensed premises, I am satisfied that the licence is subject to the same charges and incumbrances as the property and hold that it is incapable of passing to the Official Assignee in priority to incumbrances registered against the property to which it is attached."[81]

---

[78] See, *e.g. Pine Valley Developments Ltd.* v. *Minister for the Environment* [1987] I.R. 23 where the plaintiffs purchased lands with the benefit of development permission for £550,000. The planning permission was ultimately found to be invalid and the plaintiffs sued the Minister for the Environment and Ireland for damages, since the true market value of the lands without the permission was far less. However, the action failed for other reasons: see pp. 647–648 and 652–653.

[79] *Readymix (Eire) Ltd.* v. *Dublin County Council*, Supreme Court, July 31, 1974, *per* Henchy J. at p. 4 of the judgment. The same judge made similar observations in *Pine Valley Developments Ltd.* v. *Minister for the Environment* [1987] I.R. 23, 42.

[80] [1979] I.L.R.M. 113.

[81] *Ibid.* 117. Hamilton J.'s reasoning was affirmed on appeal by the Supreme Court.

And in *Macklin* v. *Graecen & Co.*,[82] a specific performance action, the Supreme Court held that a purported sale of a seven-day publican's licence, in isolation from the premises, was void and inoperative. Griffin J. said:

> "For almost 100 years it has been accepted that a licence to sell intoxicating liquor is inalienable and must be attached to the premises. The law on the matter has been stated succinctly by O'Connor's, *Irish Justice of the Peace* as follows:— "The doctor cannot sell his degree, because it is attached to himself; on the other hand, the holder of a licence cannot sell the licence to any other person, unless such other person also buys the premises. The licence *per se* is inalienable. It must always, so long as it exists at all, remain attached to the premises.""[83]

This principle of non-assignability is reflected in the latest licensing system involving land, namely, milk reference quantities or quotas. As a general rule, it may be said that a milk quota is land-based[84] and that it attaches to the land. Article 7 of Council Regulation 857/84, as inserted by Article 4 of Council Regulation 590/85, provides that:

> "Where a [farm] holding is sold, leased or transferred by inheritance, all or part of the corresponding reference quantity shall be transferred to the purchaser, tenant or heir."

However, Article 7 simply states the general rule and there are some limited exceptions which permit the sale, or leasing, of milk quotas separately from the land itself.

A licence will generally only be granted for a limited duration

Since it is of the essence of licensing statutes that they are intended to provide and maintain essential standards regulating the conduct of trade, business or activity in the public interest, it follows that, in the absence of an express statutory provision to the contrary, a licence will generally be deemed

---

[82] [1983] I.R. 61.
[83] *Ibid.* 66. The quotation was from O'Connor's, *Irish Justice of the Peace* (1915), Vol. 2, p. 368. See also, *Brennan* v. *Dorney* (1887) 21 L.R.Ir. 353. In some cases, however, the legislation may permit the transfer of the licence to another authorised person (see, *e.g.* Pawnbrokers Act 1964, s.10 (providing for transfer of pawnbroking licence to another certified person with consent of Revenue Commissioners). However, where the licensing régime involves a trade or business, the governing statute will usually permit other persons (such as close relatives or personal representatives) to carry on the business of the licence-holder on a temporary basis in circumstances such as illness, incapacity, death, etc. So the Abattoirs Act 1988, s.13(2) provides that:

> "Where the holder of an abattoir licence dies, the licence shall continue in full force and effect for the benefit of the licence holder's personal representative, or, as the case may be, his spouse or any other member of his family, for the period of four months, or for the period then unexpired of the term of the licence, whichever is the longer, after the death of the licence holder and shall then expire."

[84] *Lawlor* v. *Minister for Agriculture* [1988] I.L.R.M. 400. See Geoghegan, "The Superlevy, Sales, Lease and Clawbacks" and Laffoy, "Milk Quotas as Security for Loans" in *Milk Quotas: Law and Practice* (Robinson ed.), (Irish Centre for European Law, 1989), pp. 21 and 27 respectively.

to have been granted for a limited duration. Moreover, simply because the licensing authority has seen fit to grant a licence in the past, it does not follow that the licensee will be taken to have a right to engage in the regulated activity in perpetuity.

Some statutes take care to state explicitly that the licence granted is not of indefinite duration. Thus section 3(5) of the Radio and Television Act 1988 provides that a sound broadcasting licence "shall be valid only for such period of time as a sound broadcasting contract between the [Independent Radio and Television] Commission is extant."

But what of the situation where the licensing provisions are not explicit on this? This was considered in *Dublin Corporation* v. *Judge O'Hanrahan*,[85] where a gaming licence had been granted by the respondent, in face of a statutory resolution passed by the applicants rescinding the licensing provisions of the Gaming and Lotteries Act 1956. The notice party sought to justify the decision on the basis that, once a gaming licence had been granted, it attached to the property in perpetuity and that the effect of the rescission resolution was simply to prevent the grant of new licences. Johnson J. agreed that there was nothing in the 1956 Act which expressly declared that the certificate in question was an annual certificate, but said that it was implicit in the statutory framework that a licence subsisted from year to year. Consequently the notice party's annual licence had lapsed and, because of the resolution, they were unable to apply for a new one. It would seem, therefore, that where the parent Act is not explicit on the question, the duration of the licence must be deduced from the surrounding statutory background.

Registration

It is noteworthy, that although the use of different nomenclature is not, of itself, decisive where the Oireachtas uses the word "registration" (as opposed to "licence"), it generally intends that the entry on the register[86] (subject always to a power of amendment or revocation or erasure) should be permanent or indefinite.

In this sense, registration is an act of recording which is required of persons carrying out certain types of activity, by some scheme of public administration, and which may be permitted as a matter of right, provided that certain (often formal) conditions are satisfied.[87]

The object of registration is often to facilitate monitoring and the legislation invariably provides that the register is open to the public for inspection

---

[85] [1988] I.R. 121. This view was confirmed by Griffin J. in *Re Camillo's Application* [1988] I.R. 104.

[86] The term, "registration" may also be used as a synonym for licensing (see s.10(3) and (4) of the Building Societies Act 1989; s.17(2) and (3) of the Data Protection Act 1988; and s.4 of the Health (Nursing Homes) Act 1990).

[87] See, *e.g.* Registration of Potato Growers and Potato Packers Act 1984; and Control of Bulls for Breeding Act 1985. In exceptional cases, the onus of compiling the register is put on the public authority rather than the person registered: see, for example, Local Government (Multi-Storey Buildings) Act 1988, s.2(1).

without a fee.[88] The expression, "registration", is usually employed by the legislation governing the professions and connotes an indefinite permission to practise the profession in question. One such example is provided by section 27(2) of the Medical Practitioners Act 1978 which provides that eligible persons:

> "shall . . . on making application in the form and manner determined by the [Medical] Council and on payment of the appropriate fee, be registered in the register."

This, of course, is without prejudice to a possible refusal to register the applicant on the grounds of unfitness to practise. Nevertheless, subject to these disciplinary provisions, an entry in the register is intended to be of indefinite duration and, indeed, provision is made: for the practitioner to apply to have his name removed from the register; and also for the Registrar to erase the name of a practitioner in the case of death. Similar provisions are contained in the Veterinary Surgeons Act 1931 and the 1978 Act, itself, has served as a model for other regulatory legislation, such as the Nurses Act 1985 and the Dentists Act 1978.

The scheme of the Solicitors Acts 1954–1960 is somewhat different in that each solicitor already on the rolls must apply annually for a practising certificate.[89] Although section 40 of the 1954 Act empowers the Incorporated Law Society to refuse to renew the practising certificate for what are essentially disciplinary reasons, nevertheless the entry on the register (again subject to the disciplinary provisions of the legislation of concerning refusals) lasts indefinitely and the necessity to obtain annually a practising certificate is little more than a revenue-raising mechanism for the Society.

Licensing legislation is principally regulatory, not anti-competitive

As a general rule, the object of regulatory legislation is to prescribe certain minimum standards in the public interest and not to protect the economic interests of existing licensees. Unless the legislation in question expressly allows the licensing authority to impose a restriction on the number of licences to be granted—as does section 6(1) of the Independent Radio and Television Act 1988[90]—then it is to be presumed that the licensing régime is to be based on *qualitative* and not *quantitative* criteria. This has been made clear by the Supreme Court in cases arising under the Livestock Marts Act 1967 and the Intoxicating Liquor Acts, and by the High Court in another case

---

[88] For some diverse examples, see *e.g.* Solicitors Act 1954, s.9(2) (roll of solicitors "available for public inspection during office hours without payment"); Local Government (Planning and Development) Act 1963, s.8 (register of planning permission); Local Government (Water Pollution) Act 1977, s.9 (register of licences granted) and Video Recordings Act 1989, s.14 (register of certificated video works). Occasionally, an inspection fee is prescribed, see, *e.g.* s.7(2) of the Insurance Act 1989 (which provides that the fee for inspection of the register under section 21 of the Insurance Act 1936 is not to exceed £10, unless the Minister for Industry & Commerce and the Minister for Finance otherwise direct).
[89] Solicitors Act 1954, s.48.
[90] At least as this provision was interpreted by Murphy J. in *Dublin and County Broadcasting Ltd.* v. *Independent Radio and Television Commission*, High Court, May 12, 1989. See, to similar effect, Intoxicating Liquor Act 1960, s.14 in *In the Matter of Thank God it's Friday Ltd.* [1990] I.L.R.M. 228.

271

involving the Intoxicating Liquor Acts. In the first of these, *East Donegal Co-operative Livestock Mart Ltd.* v. *Att.-Gen.*,[91] the plaintiffs attacked the licensing provisions of the Livestock Marts Act 1967 on the ground, *inter alia*, that they would enable the Minister to use his discretion to limit the number of marts in operation. This submission was rejected by Walsh J., who said that the object of the Act was directed to:

> "The proper conduct of the business concerned, the standard of hygiene and veterinary standards in relation to such places and to provision of adequate and suitable accommodation and facilities for such auctions. . . . Nowhere in the Act is there anything to indicate that one of the purposes of the Act is to limit or otherwise regulate the number of auction marts as distinct from regulating the way in which business is conducted in auction marts. In the absence of any such indication in the Act, the Minister is not authorised by the Act to limit the number of businesses. . . ."[92]

This approach was followed by the Supreme Court in *Re Application of Power Supermarkets Ltd.*,[93] where the court addressed the question of whether the Circuit Court could take the economic consequences to other publicans in the area into account in deciding whether or not to grant an off-licence to a major supermarket chain. Walsh J. said that this was an irrelevant factor in the exercise of the judge's discretion:

> "The object of the [Intoxicating Liquor Acts] was to safeguard the public interest by preventing a proliferation of licensed premises . . . and not to shelter existing publicans from competition . . . To decide that a licence ought not to be granted because the competition it would offer to existing licences would be economically disadvantageous to the holders of those licences is not a ground which is contemplated by the code and therefore is not one which can be said to be an exercise of judicial discretion."[94]

It is notable that while rejecting the argument founded on the economic consequences to other publicans, Walsh J. did accept (in the context of the Intoxicating Liquor Acts) the possibility of restriction of the number of licences provided that it was in "the public interest." The third case to be mentioned is *Re Connellan's Application*,[95] where an objection was raised to the grant of a declaration that the applicant's premises was fit to be licensed under section 15 of the Intoxicating Liquor Act 1960. The objectors intended to build a community centre immediately adjacent to the applicant's premises and the centre would only be economically viable if it had the sole right to sell intoxicating liquor in that area. However, Finlay J. said that this consideration was not one which could properly be taken into account by the Circuit Court:

> "No matter how much I might, as a matter of social policy, favour the pro-

---

[91] [1970] I.R. 317.
[92] *Ibid.* 342–343.
[93] [1988] I.R. 206.
[94] *Ibid.* 210–211.
[95] High Court, October 19, 1973.

vision of a community centre and favour a situation in which it could from a monopoly sale of intoxicating liquor in its own area fund itself in an economic and profitable way, I do not consider that the licensing code gives me a discretion to implement that view."[96]

The judge went on to observe that as the objects of the Licensing Acts were to restrict the proliferation of public houses and to increase standards generally, it was in these respects essentially "a negative or restrictive code" and could not properly be construed as "a positive weapon of social policy."

It might have been thought that, in certain circumstances, there could be a causative link between preventing excessive competition and maintaining adequate standards so that the use of licensing to prevent competition might be regarded as acceptable on the ground that it tended to maintain standards. However, the authorities just recounted suggest that such an argument has been—at least implicitly—rejected.

The refusal or revocation of a licence must be in the public interest and not a punishment

The refusal or revocation of a licence will generally only be justified where this is established as being itself directly in the public interest and not as a punitive measure. A good example of the application of this principle may be found in *Re Crowley*,[97] where the applicant solicitor had been refused a practising certificate by the Incorporated Law Society. It appeared that the applicant had engaged in "touting" for business on one occasion in the past and this was relied on by the Society as justification for the refusal of the certificate. Kingsmill Moore J. held that, save in cases where the solicitor is actually being charged with a disciplinary offence, the withdrawal of a certificate could only be justified where this was in the public interest. The judge went on to admit that there might be circumstances where the public interest required that a solicitor should be restrained from practising; but he added that:

"Such restraint is not a matter of discipline for past offences but of precaution lest future practice by the solicitor should prove dangerous to the public or profession in the future. The fact that a solicitor has misbehaved himself in the past may indeed be an element in arriving at a conclusion that he is likely to misbehave himself in the future and so . . . may form grounds for withholding a practising certificate, or issuing it subject to conditions; but, in such a case, the certificate is not to be withheld, or conditions imposed, as a discipline for past misdoing. Such action is only justified as a necessary precaution against the likelihood of future misdoing reasonably to be inferred from past conduct."[98]

This approach also finds support in the judgment of Walsh J. for the Supreme

---

[96] *Ibid.* p. 7 of the judgment.
[97] [1964] I.R. 106. See also, *Balkan Tours Ltd.* v. *Minister for Communications* [1988] I.L.R.M. 101.
[98] *Ibid.* 129.

Court, in a different context, in *Conroy* v. *Att.-Gen.*,[99] where it was held that the disqualification of a driver for drunk driving, coupled with the loss of a driving licence, was not, as such, a punishment. As Walsh J. explained:

> "One must not lose sight, however, of the real nature of the disqualification order which is that it is essentially a finding of unfitness of the person concerned to hold a driving licence."[1]

This implies that a licence can only be revoked on the basis of the present unfitness of the holder. And although such unfitness can be established by reference to past misconduct, the revocation is not intended to be a punishment, but simply a recognition that the public interest would not be served were the applicant to continue to hold the licence. Thus, in *Ingle* v. *O'Brien*[2] Pringle J. held that simply because the applicant taxi-driver was convicted in the District Court of carriage offences did not entitle the licensing authorities, *ipso facto*, to revoke the applicant's licence.

In other cases, the licensing legislation itself will stipulate the circumstances in which the licence will automatically lapse. Thus, section 28(1) of the Intoxicating Liquor Act 1927 provides that upon the recording of a third licensing conviction on a licence, the licence is thereby automatically forfeited.

Licences as property rights

In some contexts and by some judges, licences have been regarded as property rights or, at least, rights to earn a livelihood.[3] Consequently, licence protection has been provided from the arbitrary refusal or revocation of that right. Thus the applicant is entitled to a fair hearing before his application is refused or revoked,[4] he is entitled to reasons if the licence is refused[5] and, indeed, he may have acquired a legitimate expectation that the licence will be renewed.

On the other hand, a licence has often been regarded as, in the words of Carroll J. in *The State (Pheasantry Ltd.)* v. *Donnelly*,[6] merely "a privilege granted by statute and regulated for the public good."[7] The reason why this distinction matters is that the right of the Oireachtas to regulate in the area of privileges, in the public interest, is greater than in the case of property rights. In the *Pheasantry* case, the applicants challenged the constitutionality of section 28 of the Intoxicating Liquor Act 1927 whereby the licence attaching to licensed premises is forfeited when three convictions are duly recorded and indorsed on the licence. Carroll J. agreed that the property rights protected

---

[99] [1965] I.R. 411.
[1] *Ibid.* 441.
[2] (1975) 109 I.L.T.R. 7.
[3] See, *e.g. East Donegal Co-operatives Ltd.* v. *Att.-Gen.* [1970] I.R. 317 and *Moran* v. *Att.-Gen.* [1976] I.R. 400 and see p. 478.
[4] *International Fishing Vessel Ltd.* v. *Minister for Marine* [1989] I.R. 149.
[5] [1982] I.L.R.M. 512.
[6] *Ibid.* 516.
[7] *Ibid.*

by Article 40.3 included the licence in conjunction with the premises, but she could not agree that the forfeiture provisions were, thereby, unconstitutional:

> "The licence is a privilege granted by statute and regulated for the public good. It is, *ab initio*, subject to various conditions, one of which is the inherent possibility of automatic forfeiture under section 28. If the conditions necessary for statutory forfeiture are fulfilled, this is brought about through the licensee's own default. There is no constitutional right to a liquor licence or a renewal thereof. There are only such rights as are given by statute subject to limitations and conditions prescribed by statute."[8]

This reasoning finds support in the subsequent judgment of Barron J. in *Hand v. Dublin Corporation*,[9] where the plaintiffs challenged the constitutionality of section 6(4) of the Casual Trading Act 1980, which provided that the applicant for a casual trading licence must be refused a licence where he has been convicted of two or more street trading offences within the last five years. This provision was said to prescribe an unreasonable and disproportionate penalty, but Barron J. said:

> "Treating the grant of a licence under the Casual Trading Act 1980 as a certificate of fitness to trade under the provisions of that Act, it seems to me appropriate that the statute itself may set out the circumstances in which the privilege may be lost. Such circumstances must be reasonable . . .
> Undoubtedly, some of the offences which bring section 6(5) into effect may be relatively unimportant and its effect may have serious consequences in individual cases. However, the right to earn one's living by casual trading is given by the Act. It does not seem to me to be unreasonable for the Oireachtas, having granted the privilege, to deprive persons of it for conduct directly referable to the fitness of the person concerned to exercise the same privilege."[10]

The logical consequence of this reasoning is that the Oireachtas could constitutionally terminate a particular licensing system where this was established to be in the public interest and prohibit the previously licensed activity without payment of any compensation to the existing licence holders, even though such licensees might have invested heavily in that particular licensed business.

This latter point had, in fact, already been accepted by the courts in two earlier cases: *Private Motorists Protections Society Ltd. v. Att.-Gen.*[11] and *Cafolla v. Att.-Gen.*[12]

In the *Private Motorists* case, certain friendly societies had been permitted to continue to operate small-scale banking businesses by virtue of an exemption contained in the Central Bank Act 1971. However, by 1978 it appeared that many of these societies had begun to operate what were, in effect, unre-

---

[8] *Ibid.*
[9] [1989] I.R. 26. For further discussion of this case, see pp. 542–545.
[10] *Ibid.* 32. This judgment was approved by Griffin J. when the case went on appeal: Supreme Court, March 6, 1991.
[11] [1983] I.R. 339.
[12] [1985] I.R. 486.

gulated retail banking operations with doubtful liquidity ratios and lending bases. Section 5(2) of the Industrial and Provident Societies (Amendment) Act 1978 removed this exemption and gave the societies the option of either winding up their affairs within five years or else converting to limited companies and applying to the Central Bank for banking licences. Carroll J. accepted that the 1978 Act effected an interference with the plaintiff's property rights, but since such an interference was entirely justified in the public interest, it was not, in her view, thereby unconstitutional. She added that:

> "The fact the Society was given a privilege under the Central Bank Act 1971 exempting it at that time from the requirement of having to apply for a licence, if it continued to accept deposits, does not mean that this privilege can never be withdrawn or that its withdrawal should automatically give rise to compensation."[13]

In *Cafolla* v. *Att.-Gen.*, the plaintiff claimed that the failure of the Oireachtas to increase the stakes and prize money payable under the Gaming and Lotteries Act 1956 was an unconstitutional attack on his property right and right to earn a livelihood. This argument proved unacceptable to the Supreme Court. Finlay C.J. reasoned that if (as he held) the Oireachtas could validly terminate the licensing of gaming machines by local authorities without compensation, then the plaintiff could not complain if the Oireachtas tolerated the licensing of such machines subject to very rigid restrictions which substantially interfered with the profitability of the machines in question. However, it is significant that part of the reasoning in *Cafolla's* case turns on the fact that the plaintiff obtained a licence to do something that would have been unlawful at common law (*i.e.* before the licensing system was introduced). Nevertheless, different considerations must surely come into play where the Oireachtas decides to abandon an existing licensing system and prohibit entirely activities or occupations or professions which were perfectly lawful in their own right before such regulatory legislation was introduced. Would there not here be a more compelling constitutional for compensation in such circumstances?

It was probably a consequence of the reasoning in *PMPS* and *Cafolla* that when Dublin Corporation rescinded the operation of Part III of the Gaming and Lotteries Act 1956 in 1986 (thus effectively closing all existing gaming halls), the former licence holders refrained from making any claim for compensation.

The terms of the licence must be construed by reference to objective standards

Since a licence is a public document, the governing legislation often provides that the licence is open to public inspection or, even, that the terms of the licence must be publicly displayed.[14] A corollary of this is that the terms of the licence must be objectively construed and any private arrangements or

---

[13] [1983] I.R. 339, 354.
[14] See, *e.g.* Medical Practitioners Act 1978, s.26(4) ("Every person whose name is entered in the register shall . . . cause [his] certificate to be displayed at the place where he conducts the practice of medicine at all times during which his registration continues and at no other time.")

understandings as between the licensing authority and the licence holder are not admissible. This is illustrated by *Readymix (Éire) Ltd.* v. *Dublin County Council*,[15] where it was argued that the planning permission granted by the local authority should be construed as having merely the meaning or effect given to it by the planning officals and agreed to by the developer. The Supreme Court rejected that submission, with Henchy J. observing:

> "The Act does not in terms make the register the conclusive or exclusive evidence record of the nature and extent of a permission, but the scheme of the Act indicates that anybody who acts on the basis of the correctness of the particulars in the register is entitled to do so. Where the permission recorded in the register is self-contained, it will not be permissible to go outside it in construing it. But where the permission incorporates other documents, it is the combined effect of the permission and such documents which must be looked at in determining the proper scope of the per-mission. . . . Since the permission notified to an applicant and entered in the register is a public document, it must be construed objectively as such, and not in the light of subjective considerations special to the applicant or those responsible for the grant of permission."[16]

In sum, a licence is a self-contained public document and must be construed as such.

---

[15] Supreme Court, July 31, 1974.
[16] *Ibid.* p. 4 of the judgment. See also, *Jack Barrett Builders Ltd.* v. *Dublin County Council*, Supreme Court, July 28, 1983.

CHAPTER 7

THE OMBUDSMAN[1]

1. Introduction

The task of the Ombudsman is to secure redress when a person suffers harm or loss, through some act of governmental maladministration. The mistakes of large, hierarchical organisations are hard to correct, especially when they have been endorsed by senior management. It might be expected that the courts would undertake this task. In fact, as we shall see in Chapters 8–10, the structure of our law on the judicial review of administrative action is—perhaps inevitably—so designed as to exclude from its scope many cases of injustice arising from maladministration. Moreover, the High Court—and it usually is only the High Court which has jurisdiction—is an expensive and inaccessible place. The result is that relatively few instances of maladministration surface as court cases. Traditionally, public representatives have seen it as their principal duty to use their moral authority, behind the scenes, to remedy the grievances of individual constituents against governmental services, a fact reflected in the title of Basil Chubb's classic study of public representatives, "Going about persecuting civil servants . . . "[2] as well as in the very high number of representatives per head of population. There are,

---

[1] This chapter draws, to a limited degree, on Gwynn Morgan, "The Ombudsman Act" (1982) 17 Ir.Jur.(N.S.) 105. See also, J. F. Zimmerman, 'The Office of Ombudsman in Ireland" (1989) 27 *Administration* 258; F. C. White, *The Irish Ombudsman* (unpublished LL.M. thesis available for consultation in UCC Library). For the flavour and personality of the Ombudsman, see C. Clothier (former British Parliamentary Commissioner for Administration) [1986] *Public Law* 204.
[2] "Going about Persecuting Civil Servants: The Role of the Irish Parliamentary Representative" (1963) 11 *Political Studies* 272. *Cf.* the views of the Minister for Finance reported in *The Irish Times*, November 12, 1966 (and quoted by Kelly, "Administrative Discretion and the Courts" (1966) 1 Ir.Jur.(N.S.) 209, 211):

"There is hardly anyone without a direct personal link with someone, be he Minister, T.D., clergyman, county or borough councillor, who will interest himself in helping a citizen to have a grievance examined and, if possible, remedied. . . . My own experience is that members of the Dáil are extremely assiduous and persistent in taking up individual cases and raising them by way of that truly democratic device, the parliamentary question. . . . The basic reason therefore why we do not need an Ombudsman is that we already have so many unofficial but nevertheless effective ones."

Professor Kelly went on to comment on this passage as follows:

"In the large perspective of European social and legal history this utterance is a fascinating testimony to the survival in 20th century Ireland of the primitive system of clientship and patronage. This phenomenon was, in the distant past, a sure sign of a society where a weak man had no hope of justice without the aid of a strong one, and its general replacement in civilised countries by a regular, strong and impartial process of law is a major social milestone. It is disheart-

279

indeed, twice as many deputies per person in Ireland compared with any other EC State, apart from Greece. Yet this is not a desirable approach, either from the view-point of the effective and economic settlement of grievances or from the wider perspective of the health of the body politic. Finally, there are, it is true, tribunals to oversee government administration; but these only exist in a few areas.

The gaps and defects in these traditional institutions for remedying grievances suffered at the hands of officialdom mean that there remains a need for the sort of comprehensive, flexible, informal, free service which is offered by the Ombudsman. This need has been acknowledged outside Ireland too and there are now about 100 Ombudsmen in existence in States and provinces throughout the world.

The idea of an Irish Ombudsman was first suggested, authoritatively, as part of the package of reforms proposed by the Devlin Report.[3] Later, a debate was held in the Dáil,[4] which resulted in the constitution of an All-Party Informal Committee on Administrative Justice. This committee produced a report (the All-Party Report) in 1977, favouring the introduction of an Ombudsman.[5] Eventually, goaded by a Private Member's Bill put forward by the Opposition in 1979,[6] the Government published its own Bill, which was modelled fairly closely on the All-Party Report. This Bill became law, as the Ombudsman Act 1980, following an unusually constructive debate in the Oireachtas. However, the first incumbent of the office, who was appointed following consultation with the principal opposition party, did not take up office until January 3, 1984.[7]

ening to find this primitive doctrine being not alone practised, but also blandly preached from the topmost minaret of the Irish administrative structure.

All this would be unimportant if, in fact, the Minister's preferred system of controls were effective (as was claimed). But it is not, and in the nature of things cannot be. It is very probable that some ignorant poor old man, denied some modest grant or pension because of his own failure to make his position clear, will get redress without question if a deputy or parish priest writes a letter for him. But what machinery can these informal patrons invoke to extract from an unwilling Minister the real history behind a planning application?"
[3] Report of Public Services Organisation Review Group 1966–1969 (Prl. 792), App. I, pp. 447–458. The Devlin Committee's working paper on Administrative Law and Procedure proposed a "Commissioner for Administrative Justice," whose secondary role would be to act as an Ombudsman. His primary task would have been to watch over the extensive system of tribunals required by Devlin's chief proposal, which was to remove routine executive functions from control by Ministers and the Dáil, and vest them in executive units overseen by the tribunals.
[4] The motion was: "That Dail Éireann favours the appointment of an Ombudsman." See *Dáil Debates*, Vol. 280, cols. 1199–1206, 1257–1284, May 6 and 7, 1975.
[5] The Committee held 10 meetings in 1976 and 1977. It received three submissions including one (dated October 29, 1976) from a well-qualified group convened by the Institute of Public Administration and chaired by Mr. Justice Hamilton.
[6] Bill No. 20 of 1979.
[7] Following resolutions passed in the Dáil (October 25, 1983) and Senate (November 2, 1984). His warrant of appointment is dated November 8, 1983. The 1980 Act was brought into force as from July 7, 1983; Ombudsman Act 1980 (Commencement Day) Order 1983 (S.I. 1983 No. 424). See further, *Dáil Debates*, Vol. 345, col. 605 (October 25, 1983).

Constitutional setting

The Ombudsman must be, and be seen to be, independent of the Government or any other body or person. Thus he has been provided with a similar, though not identical, institutional pedestal to that occupied by the higher judiciary. The Act contains a declaration that: "[t]he Ombudsman shall be independent in the performance of his functions." He is to be appointed by the President, acting on a recommendation contained in a resolution passed by both Houses. No qualifications are laid down for the incumbent save that he must be no more than 61 years of age (at the time of *first* appointment), and must retire at the age of 67.[8] He cannot be a public representative, or a member of the Reserve Defence Force, or hold any other paid office or employment apart from that of Ombudsman. The Ombudsman may only be removed from office "for stated misbehaviour, incapacity or bankruptcy," and then only on resolutions passed by each House of the Oireachtas. The term of office is six years and a holder is eligible for a second or subsequent term. The Ombudsman is to be paid the same salary and expenses as a High Court judge.[9]

Finally, the Ombudsman derives some limited support for his independence from the fact that his civil servants are to be civil servants of the state,[10] and that he has his own separate vote in the Estimates.

It is eloquent of the significance of the new office that during the first six years of its existence, two episodes occurred which could plausibly be regarded as attempts to undermine its independence.

The first of these episodes concerned the need for adequate staffing. For one of the main factors governing the Ombudsman's efficacy and public image is the provision of sufficient staff to investigate complaints adequately and promptly and the size and grading of his staff is determined by the Minister for Finance.[10] Following the extension of his remit in 1985, the work of the Ombudsman's Office was divided into four units (dealing with complaints against, respectively: the civil service, local authorities, health boards, and Bord Telecom and An Post). Each unit consisted of one Senior Investigator (the equivalent of a Principal in the civil service) assisted by four Investigators (at Assistant Principal level). At the apex was the Director of the Office (at Assistant Secretary level).

In April 1987, the incoming Fianna Fáil Government's budget, reducing

---

[8] 1980 Act, s.2(3), (7). Yet the Government offered, as the reason for its hesitancy in appointing Mr. Mills for a second term (see further pp. 282–283) the fact that Mr. Mills would be 67 part way through his second term, although the statutory restriction is directed at the incumbent's age at the time of his appointment for his *first* term. This justification was coupled with the claim that s.2(3) and (7) was lacking in clarity: *Dáil Debates*, Vol. 394, cols. 1675 and 1816, December 14 and 15, 1989.

[9] *Ibids.* s.10(2), ss.2, 3. For the Ombudsman's Superannuation Scheme, made under s.3(2), see S.I. 1987 No. 70.

[10] *Ibid.* s.10(1)(*a*). The Minister for the Public Service is the "appropriate authority" for the purpose of the Civil Service Regulation Act 1956 but almost all his powers as such have been delegated to the Ombudsman: 1980 Act, s.10(4); Annual Report for 1985 (Pl. 3748) (hereafter "the 1985 Report"), Chap. 10.

the Ombudsman's vote by £100,000, or 13 per cent. of the previous year's figure, necessitated a reduction in staff of four investigators. In July, it was announced that the vote for 1988 would show a further reduction of £125,000. In the event, this meant that, in 1988, there had to be a total reduction of seven investigators whilst the Minister for Finance also refused to allow the replacement of the Director and one senior investigator, upon the resignation of the existing incumbents.

These reductions were explained by reference to the crisis in public expenditure and to cuts elsewhere in the public service. But it was noticeable that the cuts in other sections of the public service did not amputate nearly a half of the establishment. A fact which made the cuts appear particularly damaging was that (though, in the event, there was to be a reduction in complaints to the Ombudsman in 1988 and 1989) all that was known, at the time, was that the number of complaints for 1985–1987 had exceeded 5,000, each year, and that by the end of 1987, there was already a back-log of 2,000 or the equivalent of eight months' work for the (reduced) numbers of staff.

These reductions attracted a good deal of protest in the media and the Dáil and Senate.[11] The Ombudsman himself took to informing complainants that there was likely to be considerable delay in dealing with their complaints, and in November he made a special report on the matter—the only special report to issue so far—to the Houses of the Oireachtas. This report[12] commences: "It is necessary under the provisions of the Ombudsman Act to report that the Office of Ombudsman is unable, due to staff cutbacks, to fulfil the functions assigned to it by the Oireachtas."

In response, in mid-1988, the Department of Finance carried out a review of the Ombudsman's staffing needs. The recommendations of this review led to the Ombudsman being able to take on three investigators and to replace the senior investigator who had resigned. In addition, some staff were loaned to the office until the back-log of complaints—running at 2,000 cases at the end of 1988—had been reduced to manageable proportions.

The second occasion when political controversy surrounded the office was in late 1989, upon the making of an appointment of the office-holder for the second term.[13] Although the charter-Ombudsman, Mr. Michael Mills, had, in the privately-held and publicly-expressed views of politicians of all parties, done a good job, there were circumstances which led the opposition to claim, plausibly enough, that the Government intended to have someone else appointed. In fact, under opposition and public pressure and at the very last moment, the Government did propose a motion recommending that the President reappoint Mr. Mills. What is certain is that, in contrast to the appoint-

---

[11] See *The Irish Times*, January 4, 1988, February 11, 1988, June 4 and 7 1988, May 13, 1988; *Sunday Independent*, June 12, 1988, ("The Ombudsman and Hypocrisy"); *Cork Examiner*, November 6, 1988 ("Watchdog with no Teeth"); *Dáil Debates*, Vol. 380, col. 1423, May 12, 1988.

[12] Published as an Appendix to his 1987 Report (Pl. 5258). For special reports, see p. 303.

[13] See *Dáil Debates*, Vol. 394, cols. 1668–1676 and 1806–1820, December 14 and 15, 1989; *Sunday Tribune*, December 17, 1989. See also, n. 8.

ment for the first term of office, there was on this occasion no consultation with the opposition parties as to who should be proposed.

2. Jurisdiction

The restrictions upon the type of complaint which the Ombudsman is empowered[14] to scrutinise may be examined under five heads. First, the public bodies whose actions may be investigated must be one of those specified. Secondly, the action must have "adversely affected" some person. Thirdly, the complainant must have a sufficient interest in the matter. Fourthly, the action must have been taken in the performance of administrative functions. Finally, the action must bear one of the (seven) types of defect specified. These questions will now be examined *seriatim*.

Public bodies within field of investigation

The bodies against whom a complaint may be heard have always included all the Departments of State, but not the Government itself, or any of the public bodies listed in the Second Schedule.[15] Since April 1, 1985, the Ombudsman's bailiwick has been extended to include Bord Telecom Éireann, An Post, local authorities (excluding the "reserved functions" exercised by elected representatives) and health boards excluding:

> "[p]ersons when acting on behalf of health boards and (in the opinion of the Ombudsman) solely in the exercise of clinical judgment in connection with the diagnosis of illness or the care or treatment of a patient, whether formed by the person taking the action or by any other person."[16]

The Government may extend (or restrict) the Ombudsman's jurisdiction by making an order amending the First Schedule to the 1980 Act. Such an order is unusual in that it requires the approval of each House.[17]

It bears mentioning (in part because of the comparative references made throughout this chapter) that in the United Kingdom, the Ombudsman has proved to be a very fertile genus and the jurisdiction which, in Ireland, is vested in a single office is divided among a number of entities: the Parliamentary Commissioner for Administration; the English (and Welsh) Commissions for Local Administration; the Scottish Commissioner for Local Administration; (separate)

---

[14] Even where all five conditions are satisfied, the Ombudsman still has a discretion whether to exercise his jurisdiction: see 1980 Act, s.4(2) and (8) and Foulkes, "The Discretionary Provisions of the Parliamentary Commissioner Act 1967" (1971) 43 M.L.R. 377, 391–393.
[15] 1980 Act, s.4(2), (4) and First and Second Scheds. See also, Ombudsman Act 1980 (First Schedule) (Amendment) Order 1984 (S.I. 1984 No. 332); Ombudsman Act 1980 (First Schedule) (Amendment) Order 1985 (S.I. 1985 No. 66). For a complaint involving a Government decision, see 1988 Report (Pl. 5991), p. 71.
[16] Ombudsman Act 1980 (First Schedule) (Amendment) Order 1984 (S.I. 1984 No. 332); *Dáil Debates*, Vol. 356, cols. 852 *et seq.*, February 27, 1985. Before April 1985, Bord Telecom Éireann, the local authorities and health boards co-operated with the Ombudsman, though they were not formally within his jurisdiction.
[17] 1980 Act, s.4(10), as amended by Ombudsman (Amendment) Act 1984, s.1. See *Dáil Debates*, Vol. 356, cols. 1300 *et seq.*, November 7, 1984.

Health Commissioners for England, Wales and Scotland; the Northern Ireland Parliamentary Commissioner; and the Northern Ireland Commissioner for Complaints, the last two offices having been held, since 1973, by the same person. References to "the Ombudsman" in the British context should be understood as referring to the entire flock, save where the context directs otherwise.

"Adversely affected"

It must appear to the Ombudsman that the action has or may have "adversely affected" some person. This wide phrase is not defined and, as far as the Reports show, the concept has only been invoked once. This was in a case in which he came close to finding that a health board ought to have paid the costs of the complainant's treatment at the Mayo Clinic but then concluded:

> "[t]he financial costs had been met from a fund created by public subscription so no adverse financial effects were suffered by the complainant's family. In the circumstances, it was not open to me under the Ombudsman's Act to make a finding or recommendation on the question of finance."[18]

The same factor was the basis of the Ombudsman's defeat in *R. v. Local Commissioner, ex p. Eastleigh B.C.*,[19] a case which arose from the Ombudsman's finding that a local authority had failed properly to inspect a sewer. However, the Ombudsman had also observed that he could not affirm categorically that even a proper inspection would have revealed this particular defect. There was a division between the majority and the dissenting judge as to the interpretation of this observation. However, the Court of Appeal was unanimous that if (as the majority thought) the Ombudsman meant: "I cannot say whether the failure to inspect led to the expenditure, but as the council was at fault it would be fair that it should contribute to the cost of remedial measures," then the Ombudsman had exceeded his powers. The reason was that it could not be said that the complainant householder had been "adversely affected" as a result of the council's maladministration.

Complainant

If, as in almost all cases, the investigation is initiated by way of complaint (rather than by the Ombudsman of his own motion) the complainant must have, in the Ombudsman's opinion, "a . . . sufficient interest in the matter."[20]

The All-Party Committee realistically recommended that there should be

---

[18] 1987 Report, p. 54.
[19] [1988] Q.B. 855; M. Jones [1988] *Public Law* 608.
[20] 1980 Act, ss.4(2)(*a*), 4(3), 9.

no requirement that a complaint should be made by the victim himself.[21] It seems that the Ombudsman has taken the view that the provision enables him to take this position and to entertain complaints submitted by, for instance, social workers and professional advisers (only approximately 5 per cent. of complaints travel via public representatives). In addition, the person affected or the complainant must not be a Department or other body specified in the First or Second Schedule.[22] Indeed, the chief purposes of the Second Schedule which consists of a list of several public bodies, including state-sponsored bodies, is to extend the category of public authorities which may not make a complaint and, thus, to remove the possibility that the Ombudsman might be used as a forum for internecine warfare by public bodies (as has happened in Britain).

"Taken in the performance of administrative functions"

The requirement that the "action" be "taken in the performance of administrative functions"[23] is designed to exclude judicial or legislative decisions. Since, as already mentioned, the only bodies against whom the Ombudsman can hear complaints are Departments or other executive agencies, this requirement has been inserted largely *ex abundanti cautela*, but not entirely so. It does at least have the effect of excluding actions taken by the executive which are incidental to the judicial function, *e.g.* the involvement of the Department of Justice in extradition proceedings, or a Department deciding whether to prosecute for breach of some specialist legislation for which it is responsible. However, it is very clear that "quasi-judicial" decisions—broadly, those which have a high law content and which directly affect a single individual—are regarded as falling within the Ombudsman's jurisdiction, for instance, decisions in regard to housing grants or welfare benefits. As regards policy issues, notwithstanding the statutory restriction to "administrative functions," the Ombudsman has been prepared to appraise what might be called, at least, low-level policy questions.[24]

"The bad rule"

A more difficult question arises where the adverse consequences of an administrative action can be traced back, not to any error by the administrator, but to the content of a statute, statutory instrument or extra-legal rule (contained in, for example, a circular), which determined the way the administrative decision had to be taken. If it is the rule which is the source of, say, unfairness, has the Ombudsman jurisdiction? In the first place, where the maladministration is dictated by an Act of the Oireachtas or a common law

---

[21] Section VIII: " . . . since a significant proportion of those affected by administrative action may lack the skills or confidence to approach the Ombudsman themselves, they may feel more secure if the matters can be taken up on their behalf. . . . " See 1984 Report, p. 54 (where a social worker made a report on behalf of a deserted wife).

[22] 1980 Act, s.4(2)(*a*), 3(*a*), (9). See also, Ombudsman Act 1980 (Second Schedule) (Amendment) Order 1985 (S.I. 1985 No. 69) extending this Schedule.

[23] For definition of "action" (to include *inter alia* failure to act) and "function" see s.1.

[24] See further, pp. 288–290.

rule, the Ombudsman has no authority to deal with the case: all he can do is to state his opinion that the law is in need of reform and this will presumably be of some weight with a Government deciding whether to bring forward amending legislation. Indeed, large parts of the Ombudsman's Annual Reports are taken up with criticisms of various laws.[25]

The position is similar in regard to statutory instruments and administrative circulars since these are legislation or quasi-legislation,[26] rather than administration. However, as with other sources of law, while he cannot intervene in the instant case,[27] the Ombudsman feels free to comment on "the bad rule." Naturally, his pressure for change is more likely to bear fruit quickly than in cases where primary legislation would be required. One example of this arose from his criticisms of the procedure for the revision of rateable valuations by the Commissioners of Valuation.[28] One defect was that the date for the publication of revised rating valuation lists was December 1 so that, given the Christmas holiday period, the statutory period of 28 days within which an appeal to the Circuit Court had to be lodged was substantially reduced. The Minister for Finance acceded amicably—without challenge to the Ombudsman's authority, which was thus not tested—to the request to change the date for publication of lists from December 1 to November 1, although this change necessitated a statutory instrument.

The Ombudsman has also succeeded in getting Departments to issue or to amend circulars.[29] The second defect in the rateable valuations revision system, described in the last paragraph, concerned the function (which is vested in local authorities) of informing a person that the valuation of his premises has been increased so that he can decide whether he wishes to appeal. Certain local authorities did not inform the persons affected directly but simply placed a notice in a newspaper. The Ombudsman could not address himself directly to the local authorities concerned because this case occurred before local authorities were brought within his terms of reference. Instead, the Department of the Environment issued a circular suggesting to local authorities that they should notify ratepayers affected, personally by letter.

Types of defect

The British Parliamentary Commissioner Act 1967 relies heavily on a term which it does not define—"maladministration". In contrast, the Irish legislation does not use this term, yet provides what might be regarded as a definition of it: for section 4(2)(*b*) of the 1980 Act gives a list of defects which may attract the Ombudsman's attention.

---

[25] For examples, see p. 316.
[26] As to the classification of statutory instruments and circulars, see Chap. 2.
[27] See, *e.g.* 1988 Report, p. 27. For the British position on the doctrinal problem of the bad rule, see R. Gregory [1982] *Public Law* 49, 68–70.
[28] 1984 Report, pp. 41–42. See also, 1986 Report, p. 19; 1989 Report, p. 23.
[29] For examples, see 1984 Report, pp. 46–48; 1985 Report, pp. 27–28.

". . . the Ombudsman may investigate any action . . . where . . . it appears
to the Ombudsman

(*b*) that the action was or may have been:
   (i) taken without proper authority;
   (ii) taken on irrelevant grounds;
   (iii) the result of negligence or carelessness;
   (iv) based on erroneous or incomplete information;
   (v) improperly discriminatory;
   (vi) based on an undesirable administrative practice; or
   (vii) otherwise contrary to sound or fair administration."

In view of the vagueness of some of these categories; the discretion in their
application which is vested in the Ombudsman; and the informal attitude
adopted by the Ombudsman (whose Reports, it is worth noting, do not
usually identify individual statutory heads but refer, instead, to such notions
as "fairness"), there seems to be little point in a comprehensive scrutiny of
each type of defect. However, the following tentative observations may be
made. In the first place, as might be expected, there is a substantial overlap
between some of the items in the statutory catalogue and the grounds on
which a court would exercise its power of judicial review of an administrative
action.[30] Thus, head (v) "improperly discriminatory" is similar to Article
40.1[31] of the Constitution which would be available to a court reviewing an
administrative action. Again, heads (i) ("taken without proper authority")
and (ii) ("taken on irrelevant grounds") establish grounds which would also
be available in a court reviewing an administrative action. Take, for instance,
a complaint arising from the health boards' refusal to pay Disabled Persons'
Maintenance Allowance to persons attending secondary school because this
meant that they were not available for employment. The Ombudsman upheld
the complaint because the statute created an entitlement to payment provided
that three factors—which related to the applicant's age, means and level of
disability—were satisfied. In conventional legal parlance, the health boards
had taken irrelevant considerations into account.[32] However, the remaining
heads create wider powers than their judicial equivalents. Thus, in head (iii)
("the result of negligence or carelessness"), since negligence is mentioned,
"carelessness" must mean something in addition to negligence. It may be that
the "duty of care" or "remoteness of damage" elements do not have to be
established or, at least, not to the same standard as for negligence. In any
case, given the under-developed state of the law on public authority torts,[33] it
is useful to have a flexible alternative to negligence *stricto sensu*. And head

---

[30] The question of this overlap is discussed further, pp. 309–313.
[31] "All citizens shall, as human persons, be held equal before the law. This shall not be held to
mean that the State shall not in its enactment have due regard to differences of capacity, physical
and moral, and of social function."
[32] 1985 Report, p. 32. For taking into account irrelevant considerations see pp. and for a close
parallel to the facts in the text, in the context of judicial review, see *The State (Keller)* v. *Galway
Co. Co.* [1958] I.R. 142.
[33] See pp. 655–668.

(iv) ("based on erroneous or incomplete information") is clearly wider than the embryonic and limited "no-evidence" rule in the field of judicial review of administrative acts.[34] Likewise, as we shall see, head (vii) ("otherwise contrary to fair or sound administration") goes beyond constitutional justice.

The Ombudsman has been able to use this statutory catalogue to review complaints which a reasonable, informed person would regard as "maladministration", without legalism. The Annual Reports disclose that the Ombudsman has been prepared to intervene on such broad bases as consistency, equity and flexibility, as, for instance, in cases: where the Department of Agriculture refused to deal with an accountant as a professional representative of a farmer on the ground that it was departmental policy only to deal with solicitors[35]; where a local authority's method for valuing a house for a Housing Finance Agency loan was based only on site cost plus building cost per square metre, with the result that small houses in urban areas were undervalued[36]; where welfare payments had been made as from the date of certification of eligibility by the health board rather than the date of application[37]; where a widow's pension had been very substantially reduced in view of her "means" which were taken to include a judgment debt, which she had, in practice, very little hope of enforcing[38]; or where there was an absolute entitlement under the Urban Fuel Scheme which operates in 17 urban districts, whereas the National Fuel Scheme, which applied elsewhere, was discretionary.[39]

Fairness, merits and policy

It is also clear, from his annual reports, that the Ombudsman is more prepared than a court would be to review questions of merits or judgment.[40] Intertwined with this is the fact, noted in the preceding Part, that he is prepared to appraise questions which reach beyond administration to low-level policy.

These two matters are so closely related—and are not dissected in the Reports—so that it seems best to consider examples of them together. The first illustration arose from the fact that under the rubric of "fairness," the Ombudsman was prepared to intervene when a mother complained that the

[34] On which see de Smith, *op. cit.* pp. 126–141.
[35] 1985 Report, p. 65.
[36] *Ibid.* p. 53.
[37] *Ibid.* pp. 31, 52.
[38] 1989 Report, see pp. 73–74; see also, 1986 Report, p. 48.
[39] 1985 Report, p. 33.
[40] See p. 285. Notice that in England, it has been said that "maladministration . . . is concerned with the manner in which decisions . . . are reached . . . and implemented . . . and [has] nothing to do with the nature, quality or reasonableness of the decision itself" *R.* v. *Local Commissioner, ex p. Eastleigh B.C.* [1988] Q.B. 855, 863, *per* Lord Donaldson. See also *R.* v. *Local Commissioner, ex p. Bradford MCC* [1979] Q.B. 287, 311, 314, 318 and *R.* v. *Local Commissioner, ex p. Croydon LBC* [1989] 1 All E.R. 1033, 1043 j. It should be noted, though, that the British legislation bans the Ombudsman from investigating the "merits" of a decision taken without maladministration. Local Government Act 1974, s.34(3); Parliamentary Commissioner for Administration Act 1967, s.12(3). Also that the British Ombudsmen do not always adhere to this precept.

Department of Education bus route for taking children to school was so drawn that her five-year-old child had to walk one and a half miles to the bus, whilst certain older children were being picked up much closer to their homes. The Ombudsman put forward a proposal which, without extra overall cost, enabled the bus to collect the five-year-old closer to his home whilst requiring some older children to walk somewhat further. The Department of Social Welfare accepted his proposal.[41] The Ombudsman also condemned as a case of "Catch 22" a situation in which the Department of Social Welfare had refused to allow a complainant to register retrospectively as unemployed in respect of the five-week period during which the Department was hearing his appeal—which was ultimately rejected—against the termination of his disability benefit. The complainant was naturally unwilling to register prospectively as unemployed during this period for to do so would be to imply that he was capable of work and thus, possibly, to jeopardise his appeal on the disability benefit claim. The net result was that he had been unable to claim either benefit in respect of this period.[42]

Further examples include recommendations: that a health board allow the complainant access to the medical records of his infant son[43]; that a health board permit a relation of the mother (other than her husband) to be present at the birth of her child[44]; and that the Department of Foreign Affairs allow a joint passport to be issued for a one-year period only at a fee of £3 to an elderly couple (the one-year passport being a concession which had formerly been confined to individuals).[45] The final example to be mentioned concerns the situation of a local authority tenant who has purchased his house and then (possibly because his family has grown up) wishes to be rehoused again as a local authority tenant in a smaller house. In some cases, the complainant was required to surrender the original house, for which he has paid, to the local authority with no compensation. The Ombudsman recommended a re-examination "with a view to ensuring that the system operates on a basis that is consistent and fair to all concerned."[46]

A lot of policy differences, of course, come down in the end to money, especially so in this era of limited public resources. The Ombudsman has naturally been prepared to accept this as a factor justifying a public authority's action. For example, in one case concerning allegedly inadequate refuse collection arrangements, he found that "the Council's justification for those arrangements was reasonable in light of their financial constraints and I

---

[41] 1984 Report, p. 37.
[42] *Ibid.* p. 33.
[43] 1986 Report, p. 65.
[44] 1987 Report, p. 91.
[45] 1986 Report, p. 50. The Ombudsman's concern not to trench too far on policy matters is shown by his approach here: "I asked the Department if, at the time of initiating the concession it was *their clear intention* to exclude holders of a joint passport from availing of the concession. The Department considered the matter and decided that it would be the Minister's wish to interpret the rule in the most favourable way for those entitled to the concession." (Author's italics).
[46] 1987 Report, p. 30.

consider that it outweighed the inconvenience experienced by the complainant as a result of these arrangements."[47]

Other complaints have been found to fall on the other side of the line and, in appropriate cases, the Ombudsman has been prepared to recommend the payment of substantial sums of money, for example, in the case of orthodontic treatment[48]; and the education of a deaf child[49]; and under the Treatment Abroad Scheme.[50]

The Ombudsman has also accepted the need for a fairly administered queue in appropriate circumstances[51]:

> "I could not pursue other cases because the medical records available to me indicated that the health boards concerned were not unreasonable in putting the patients on a waiting list with other children requiring similar treatment, at a time when sufficient financial resources were not available to the boards to enable them to provide early treatment."

At any rate, as regards policy, the position would appear to be slightly different from that in the United Kingdom: take, for example, *R. v. Local Commissioner, ex p. Eastleigh B.C.*,[52] a case arising from a British Ombudsman's investigation of a local authority's inspection of the construction of a sewer. It was common cause among the judges of the Court of Appeal that the decision to inspect at only the four most important—and not at all—stages of the construction was a matter of policy and, so, outside the Ombudsman's jurisdiction, leaving him only to examine the execution of the inspections. One of the three judges, Taylor L.J., however, went further and held that even the question of whether an inspection required a "gradient test" to be made of every drain and sewer was also a matter of policy. It seems likely from his treatment of the complaints mentioned earlier that the Irish Ombudsman would, like his British cousin, have thought that he did have jurisdiction to appraise these "policy issues."

Even in cases where policy is not involved, it would seem implicit in both the nature of the Ombudsman's role and the list of deficiencies quoted earlier, that the Ombudsman only has authority to intervene where there is some specific defect in the process or reasoning leading up to the decision, rather than simply where he differs from the result. In short, he must not usurp the position of the body in which the decision in question has been vested. Thus,

---

[47] 1989 Report, p. 91, see also, 1987 Report, p. 32.
[48] 1989 Report, pp. 50–59. It is striking that this Report quotes from the board's response to the Ombudsman that:

> "[it] well be that the policy itself is open to criticism or even to legal challenge but that, of itself, it does not imply that it is necessarily a matter where change is incumbent on the Board as a result of the Ombudsman's observations."

The Ombudsman's Report, however, makes no comment on this contention.
[49] 1989 Report, p. 43.
[50] 1989 Report, p. 64; see also 1987 Report, p. 53.
[51] 1987 Report, p. 28; see also 1989 Report, p. 60.
[52] [1988] Q.B. 855. The division between the majority and the dissentient judge was not primarily about the demarcation line between policy and administration but rather about whether, as a matter of fact, the Ombudsman had crossed the line.

for instance, he rejected a complaint against the Revenue Commissioners. The facts were that the Commissioners had refused to grant a cartographer a tax exemption under the Finance Act 1969 for producing work which is "original and creative" and displays "cultural and artistic merit", had taken no account of evidence of his work's artistic merit. The Ombudsman's view was that:

> "Having studied and consulted on the case at length I came to the conclusion that no fault could be found with the efforts of the Revenue Commissioners to arrive at a decision in a fair and reasonable way. I might not agree with the decision but I have no authority to set up an alternative source of assessment to challenge the advice given to the Commissioners."[53]

In another case a dispute had arisen as to whether planning permission should be allowed for an access between two housing estates so as to shorten the children's journey to school, even though this access would disturb the privacy of the complainant who lived in one of the estates. The Ombudsman concluded that whatever decision was reached was bound to be unacceptable to one of the parties and that the local authority had "acted reasonably and with common sense." Accordingly, he did not recommend any change.[54]

At the same time, it has to be said that there have been a few cases in which the Ombudsman has upheld a complaint merely because he took a different view of the facts from the public body, for example as to whether the complainant was "available for work", in the context of a claim for unemployment benefit.[55] In such cases, the Ombudsman has come close to acting as an appeal court.

New facts

In a surprising number of cases, investigation—some of it very resourceful and imaginative—by a member of the Ombudsman's staff has led to the discovery of new facts or information, or cast a fresh light on the existing information, and this has led to a change of heart in the responsible authority. For example, the Department of Social Welfare had decided that the complainant was not available for employment except as an actor and that this constituted "unreasonable limitations on his availability for work" which was a statutory ground for terminating his unemployment benefit. The Ombudsman suggested various new factors to the appeals officer—including the fact that the complainant has previously worked as a car-park attendant and that this showed that he was willing to take any kind of work. Accordingly, the appeals officer reversed the original decision.[56] In another case, the Department of Health had refused to grant financial assistance in respect of medical treat-

---

[53] 1984 Report, p. 46. See also 1985 Report, p. 30.
[54] 1985 Report, p. 54.
[55] 1986 Report, p. 49; 1988 Report, p. 80 (whether complainant was sharing the house with another person, in the context of rent assessment for a local authority house).
[56] 1984 Report, pp. 49–50.

ment which he had received in London on the ground that the treatment had been available in Ireland free of charge. The Ombudsman was able to establish that at *the relevant time* the treatment had not been available. The Department reversed its decision and also reviewed its administrative arrangements for obtaining the relevant information (requirement of hospital consultant's certificate).[57] In one instructive case, the information given by an applicant for unemployment benefit, as a result of which his claim had been refused, was wrong—it had been supplied by the applicant only because he had misunderstood the form.[58] In yet another case, involving an application for a contributory widow's pension, it was discovered that the complainant had paid the appropriate number of social insurance contributions, but under her maiden name (something which the Department had not checked, although they had the complainant's maiden name). The complainant was awarded £13,000 back-payment plus £6,000 for loss of purchasing power.[59]

"Negligence or carelessness"

Another category of case (which could go under the head of "negligence or carelessness") included the "administrative bungling"[60] by which a wedding dress and two bridesmaid's dresses, which had been sent by registered post, were mislaid—though eventually recovered—a few days before the wedding. Following the intervention of the Ombudsman, An Post made an *ex gratia* payment of £80 to compensate for expenses (travelling and phone calls) incurred in searching for the dresses. In a more typical case, the Department of Social Welfare said that the complainant had a record of insufficient contributions for the payment of a contributory widow's pension. Following a request from the Ombudsman, the Department rechecked and discovered a second contribution record which brought her total of contributions up to the necessary level.[61]

A further set of cases involved the Land Registry's practice of returning original deeds in letters which have been registered at the lowest registered post fee so that the maximum compensation payable is £20, although the value of the loss would often be a great deal higher. In two complaints of this type,[62] the Ombudsman was informed that *"ex gratia* payments [are made] in appropriate circumstances after each case has been examined on its merits."

Procedure

As might be expected, a great number of complaints to the Ombudsman fall into a category which might broadly be called "procedure." Procedural

---

[57] 1985 Report, p. 47.
[58] 1988 Report, p. 55.
[59] *Ibid.* p. 63.
[60] 1984 Report, pp. 39–40. See further, p. 312.
[61] 1985 Report, pp. 56–57.
[62] 1987 Report, pp. 26–27.

defects include not only breach of the rules of constitutional justice[63] or the particular procedural regulations but also delay[64]; and bureaucratic bad manners shading into "the insolence of office." Speaking generally about the performance of the Revenue Commissioners, the Ombudsman made the following observation[65]:

> "Coping with the harsh economic realities of the eighties is a traumatic experience, particularly for widows and pensioners. Both are extremely vulnerable and dependent. When sharp cryptic demands for payments are issued from the computer system no account is taken of the age or circumstances of the recipient. The elderly are easily frightened and upset by authoritative demands for payment. It may be that such categories are difficult to identify but some thought should be given as to how the problem might be overcome in order to avoid unnecessary distress to the weak and elderly in our community."

A concrete case which is relevant in the present context involved an American citizen (there is, of course, no requirement that a complainant should be Irish) who arrived at Dublin Airport, on holiday with his golf clubs. Because he attempted to carry the clubs through the green channel, a customs officer decided that he was trying to smuggle them into the country and accordingly that they were liable to forfeiture. As a compromise, they were returned to the complainant on payment of £100 (import tax plus penalty). The Ombudsman recommended that, because there was a reasonable doubt about the complainant's intentions, the penalty should be refunded and that, if he subsequently removed the clubs from the country, the taxes should also be refunded. The Ombudsman also disapproved of two procedural features of the Customs authorities' treatment of the visitor: first, he had not been given a receipt for his golf clubs until he had asked for one; secondly, the customs officers had seized and opened a private letter of the visitor's, explaining this action on the ground that it might contain evidence. The Ombudsman's judgment was that there was insufficient justification for opening the letter and, further, that the (non-statutory) instructions governing the opening of such letters, issued by the Revenue Commissioners, had not been followed. The Ombudsman recommended that the instructions for opening personal letters be conveyed clearly to all customs staff.

Information about rights

Finally, in a number of complaints, the Ombudsman appears to have drawn upon a broad, though unspecified, principle that the State is under a positive

---

[63] e.g. "No attempt was made by the Department [of Education] at any time to give the parents an opportunity to present their case in direct consultation with officials of the Department: 1989 Report, p. 48.
[64] In 1984, 10 per cent. of all complaints to the Ombudsman involved delay. (See Chap. 7 of his Report). By s.1(1) of the 1980 Act, his jurisdiction includes "failure to act."
[65] 1984 Report, p. 18. See also, 1987 Report, p. 25.

duty to supply the citizen with relevant information about his rights, whether this involves legal advice or facts about his own personal situation.[66] There is of course only a fine line between this notion and the principle which has also been adopted by the Ombudsman[67] that a public authority must not mislead an individual. Thus the two principles may be discussed together. One finds in the Reports, as a general comment upon the performance of public bodies, strictures against: the use of "language which, although technically accurate is not capable of being understood by members of the public"[68]; Bord Telecom's predilection for "standard replies produced by word processor [which] do not respond to the specific point made by the complainant"[69]; and Disabled Persons Maintenance Allowance regulations which "are unsatisfactory in their lack of clarity."[70] At a specific level, there have been a number of cases in which welfare agencies have been censored for failing to mention to the complainant benefits or allowances which might have applied to him.[71] In such circumstances, the agency has granted the benefit or allowance with retrospective effect. In addition, as a result of the Ombudsman's prompting, the Department of Social Welfare now gives to farmers details of its assessment of their means where this assessment has led to a reduction in their social welfare payments.[72] Again, the Ombudsman has censured the Departments of State involved for their failure, over a period of five years, to reply to letters from a public servant, inquiring what her pension rights would be.[73] Another problem stemmed from section 37 of the Road Traffic Act 1961, under which a person can apply for the removal of a driving licence endorsement after he has had a clean licence for a *continuous* period of five years, *i.e.* if a new licence is necessary, there must be no gap between the two licences. The Department of the Environment agreed to the Ombudsman's suggestion that the explanatory leaflet provided by the Department should be amended to make it clear that, if a person in this situation has to obtain a new licence, he should ensure that the two licences are absolutely continuous.[74] In such cases as these, the Ombudsman shows no sympathy whatsoever with the well-established legal principle which was actually put to him unavailingly on one

---

[66] In Britain, during recent years advice cases have represented 20 per cent. of all the investigations published by the PCA in his selected case reports: Mowbray, "A Right to Official Advice." [1986] *Public Law* 68, 69.

[67] See further, pp. 312–313.

[68] 1986 Report, p. 15.

[69] *Ibid.* p. 23.

[70] 1988 Report, p. 25.

[71] 1985 Report, p. 23.

[72] 1987 Report, p. 68; 1988 Report, p. 65; 1989 Report, p. 73.

[73] 1985 Report, p. 63. *Cf.* Civil Service Executive Union Annual Report 1985–1986, App. 2, paras. 4.6 and 4.7. ("If an application [for a housing grant] is refused and the citizen disputes the refusal on certain grounds, the Department of the Environment will arrange for the matter to be investigated again by an officer of higher rank than the officer who carried out the first investigation. However, the citizen is not told that such a facility exists. Again, in instances such as this, the necessity for intervention by the Ombudsman's office would be reduced if the appeals system were formalised and the public made aware of their rights.")

[74] *Ibid.* p. 28.

occasion, by the Department of Social Welfare,[74a] that "ignorance of the law is no defence."

3. Exemptions from Jurisdiction

Even within the subject area thus staked out, six categories of case are exempted from the Ombudsman's jurisdiction.

(1) The Ombudsman is excluded where there is a right of appeal in respect of the decision of a court.[75] It is striking that, in contrast with the position in Britain, there is no provision preventing a potential complainant from going to the Ombudsman merely because he could have instituted legal proceedings (for example, judicial review of an administrative action) in a court in respect of the complaint.[76] However, the Ombudsman is, naturally, prevented from hearing a case where the person aggrieved has actually initiated "civil legal proceedings."[77] Even then, the Ombudsman will not be excluded if "the proceedings have . . . been dismissed for failure to disclose a cause of action or a complaint justiciable by that court."[78] This limitation upon the matters over which the Ombudsman has no jurisdiction evidently arises because (as noted *supra*), the grounds on which complaints may be made to the Ombudsman are wider than those which apply to a court, and it is thought to be harsh to prevent a case going to the Ombudsman on the basis that the case has been before a court, if the grounds of complaint anyway fall outside the court's jurisdiction. Pursuing a similar line of reasoning, it might be asked whether a complainant ought to lose his chance of going to the Ombudsman if his court case had failed because it was out of time, or because he had adopted the wrong procedure, or for any other reason unrelated to the merits. If the provision is read strictly, such a person would not be within the Ombudsman's jurisdiction. There is, however, an equitable proviso which permits the investigation of actions "if it appears to the Ombudsman that special circumstances make it proper to do so"[79] even though those actions would otherwise be excluded (under either this, or the next, exemption). This proviso would probably enable the Ombudsman to investigate in a case in which the court had turned the complainant away for some reason other than the merits of his claim.

(2) The Ombudsman has no jurisdiction over a decision from which an appeal lies to "a person other than a Department of State or other person specified in Part I of the First Schedule . . . ," irrespective of whether any appeal has actually been taken.[80] The effect of the phrase quoted is that, fol-

---

[74a] 1987 Report, p. 68.

[75] s.5(1)(*a*)(ii). But though a person is entitled to apply to the High Court for habeas corpus, he may still refer his grievance to the Ombudsman: see Gwynn Morgan, *loc. cit.* p. 110.

[76] See further, p. 310.

[77] s.5(1)(*a*)(ii). "Civil legal proceedings" is probably (if only from its context) intended to include both civil actions and applications for judicial review.

[78] *Ibid.*

[79] Proviso to s.5(1).

[80] s.5(1)(*a*)(ii), (iii).

lowing the recommendation of the All-Party Report,[81] the Ombudsman retains jurisdiction over decisions if the appeal lies to a Minister or civil servant[82] in a Department. Thus subject to the local remedies rule (see exemption 5 *infra*), the Ombudsman has jurisdiction over claims for social welfare benefit which are heard by deciding officers in the Department of Social Welfare or appeals from deciding officers which are heard by appeals officers, again within the Department.[83] By contrast, on the other side of the line, the exclusion of cases where there is an appeal to someone other than a Department means, for instance, that the Ombudsman is excluded from planning cases (either at the initial or appeal stage) because of the appeal to An Bord Pleanála. Similarly, he may not review decisions of the Revenue Commissioners where there is an appeal to the Appeals Commissioners. Nevertheless the Ombudsman has investigated a large number of complaints against the Revenue Commissioners in respect of other matters, for instance: delay in sending out tax rebates or statements of allowance; excessive zeal in investigating suspected evasion; or the Customs and Excise area, in respect of which there is no appeal.

(3) The Ombudsman does not have jurisdiction over actions relating to "national security or military activity or (in the opinion of the Ombudsman) arrangements regarding participation in organisations of states or governments"; "the administration of the law relating to aliens or naturalisation"; the exercise of the power of pardon and the administration of prisons or other similar institutions.[84] In addition, the Ombudsman is forbidden to investigate recruitment or appointment to any of the bodies listed in the First Schedule[85] or any matter relating to the terms or conditions upon which a person holds any office or employment in any of the bodies listed in the First or Second Schedule.[86] However, there is no ban on investigating the dismissal of a servant or officer nor (as there is in Britain) the making or terms of a commercial contract between a department and a private person.

(4) A Minister of the Government may prevent or restrain the Ombudsman from investigating any action of that Minister's Department (or of a person "whose business and functions are comprised" in that Department) simply by making a written request to that effect, setting out in full the reasons for the request.[87] The justification for this provision, offered by the Minister of State at the Department of the Public Service piloting the Bill through the Dáil, is the need to exclude from the Ombudsman's jurisdiction points of judgment

---

[81] All Party Report, s.VII, para. 12.

[82] See s.1(2).

[83] Notice that s.5(1)(*a*)(iii) is fortified by s.1(1) which defines "action" to include "decision" and section 1(2) which defines Department of State "to include not only a Minster but also his officers," *i.e.* civil servants. See also, s.5(2).

[84] s.5(1)(*b*), (*e*)(i), (ii) and (iii).

[85] s.5(1)(*c*).

[86] s.5(1)(*d*)(i). (In 1984 and 1985, 13 per cent. and 3 per cent., respectively, of all complaints made to the Ombudsman had to be excluded on the grounds that they involved the civil service personnel matters. Thereafter this figure diminished even further.

[87] s.5(3).

for which a Minister should be answerable only to the Dáil.[88] The safeguard, which is designed to prevent Ministers from drawing too freely on this blank cheque, is publicity: not only must the communication to the Ombudsman be in writing, but it must be passed on by the Ombudsman to the complainant and must also be recorded in the Reports which the Ombudsman has to lay before the Oireachtas.[89] This device has not yet been used.

(5) The Ombudsman has a jurisdiction not to hear a complaint if he considers that it is "trivial or vexatious"; that the complainant has not exhausted his local remedies; or that the subject-matter of the complaint has been, is being, or will be, sufficiently investigated in another investigation by the Ombudsman.[90]

(6) The complaint must be made within 12 months of the time of the action or—and this could be a significant extension—the time when the complainant became aware of the complaint, whichever is the later. However, an exception to this rule may be allowed where "it appears to the Ombudsman that special circumstances make it proper to do so."[91]

4. Procedure

An investigation (which must be "conducted otherwise than in public"[92]) may be initiated either by way of complaint or by the Ombudsman acting of his own motion if it appears to him that an investigation would be warranted.[93] No formality is necessary: even a simple phone call will suffice.[94]

Preliminary examination

First, the Ombudsman carries out a preliminary examination[95] at which a number of complaints are weeded out, for instance, because they involve social welfare claims by persons who clearly have not paid sufficient contributions; or because they seek to inveigle the Ombudsman to intervene in the merits of income tax disputes which are the preserve of the Appeals Com-

---

[88] *Dáil Debates*, Vol. 321, cols. 867–869 (May 28, 1980). See too All Party Report, ss.II, VII.
[89] ss.5(3), 6(7).
[90] s.4(5), (6).
[91] s.5(1), proviso. In addition the action must not have taken place before the commencement of the Act. s.5(1)(g). The Act was brought into force on July 7, 1983, by statutory order, made under s.12(2). S.5(2) provides that notwithstanding the time limits in the text, the Ombudsman may investigate insurability and entitlement to benefit under the Social Welfare Acts 1952–1979. Even apart from specific provision the Ombudsman observes a general "continuing effect" doctrine by which he is prepared to investigate circumstances or facts occurring before the time limit, if these are relevant to decisions taken after the time limits.
[92] s.8(1). This phrase may have been used in preference to "in private" so as to indicate that the Ombudsman retains a power to allow selected persons to attend.
[93] s.4(3)(b).
[94] In *R.* v. *Local Commissioner for Public Administration, ex p. Bradford MCC* [1979] Q.B. 287, 313 the argument that a complaint must specify the particular maladministration which led to the injustice to the complainant was rejected by a majority of the Court of Appeal.
[95] s.4(2). See also, s.4(5).

missioners.[96] Where the Ombudsman decides not to proceed with a complaint, then he must write to the complainant stating his reasons.[97]

The 1980 Act, section 8(3) provides that: "[s]ubject to the provisions of this Act, the procedure for conducting an investigation shall be such as the Ombudsman considers appropriate. . . . " And, indeed drawing on this freedom, more than 90 per cent. of the Ombudsman's cases are settled at the first and only stage, which the Act contemplates would be merely a preliminary examination. In the 1984 Report, this device was characterised as a "Review Procedure"[98] and explained as follows:

> "I have adopted a system of seeking to find a solution to many cases by way of a request to the Department involved for a review. Requests for a review are normally made in the context of our having conducted fairly detailed preliminary examination and having reached certain tentative conclusions as to the outcome. At the stage where I have established in my mind the nature of the likely recommendation, I sometimes ask the Department concerned if they would like to respond favourably along certain lines.
> The purpose of a review of this kind, which is widely used by Ombudsmen throughout the world, is to enable a Department to look again at a particular case in the light of new evidence or fresh argument. A review enables a Department to alter an earlier decision on its own initiative rather than to await a formal recommendation from the Ombudsman's Office when the opportunity will have been lost to act independently."

In later Reports, the Ombudsman has adverted to the two types of *modus operandi* (the preliminary examination, which may or may not be followed by a formal investigation), though without employing the useful term "Review Procedure," or, even, acknowledging that there has been some modification in the purpose of the preliminary examination from that contemplated by the 1980 Act. In his 1986 Report, the Ombudsman stated:[99]

> "At the preliminary examination stage relevant information and facts are obtained from the bodies concerned and, if necessary, additional information is sought from the complainant. The purpose of a preliminary examination is two-fold. First, it enables me to establish whether an investigation is warranted and second, it allows more straightforward complaints to be resolved without the need for a detailed formal investigation. The main advantage of this procedure is that I have an opportunity to consider if a complaint is well-founded before deciding whether or not to carry out a formal investigation.
> A formal investigation is undertaken only after detailed consideration of the issues involved in the case. The work involved in the investigation itself is painstaking and time-consuming. I could, for example, complete many

---

[96] *Cf.* Civil Service Executive Union Report for 1985–1986, App. 2, para. 3.3, complaining that provided a matter falls within his jurisdiction, "the Ombudsman's enquiries are becoming akin to representations by public representatives—*i.e.* almost all cases taken up without discrimination."
[97] s.6(1).
[98] Pl. 2909, pp. 9–10.
[99] 1986 Report, p. 13. See also, 1985 Report, p. 19.

preliminary examinations in the time it takes to carry out one formal investigation."

Related points of difference are that following an investigation (in contrast to a preliminary inquiry) the Ombudsman must notify, in writing, the head of the body concerned of its results and, also, may publish a report.[99a]

The Ombudsman has made formal agreements[1] as to procedure with the Departments of State, local authorities and health boards. These provide, in the first place, that a particular official—at the levels indicated—should act as a contact point with the Ombudsman: principal (Department of State); county secretary (local authority); programme manager (health board). On first receiving a complaint (assuming that it is not outside jurisdiction or manifestly unsustainable) the Ombudsman contacts, usually by letter but sometimes by phone, the appropriate official, who is supposed to ensure that a reply is furnished within one month. There may also be further exchanges. The matter may be concluded by the Ombudsman accepting that there has been no maladministration or that for some other reason there is no ground for the complaint. Alternatively, the public body complained against may accept from the Ombudsman what is, strictly speaking, at this stage merely a suggestion as to how the maladministration may be remedied. A further possible way in which a complaint may be resolved at this stage is through the Ombudsman writing to the head of the public body explaining that he is concluding the preliminary examination and suggesting that the public body review its performance along specified lines.

Formal investigation

Almost all complaints are concluded at the preliminary examination stage. However, a small number—of the order of a dozen each year—go on to what the 1980 Act calls simply an "investigation," though it is usually referred to, in the Ombudsman's annual reports, as a "formal investigation." Such investigations are expensive for the Ombudsman's office and, accordingly, he prefers to reserve them for complaints which are particularly serious, usually because there are a number of similar complaints.[1a] First of all, the Ombudsman directs, to the head of the organisation under scrutiny, a letter which must include an explanation of the complaint and a statement that the Ombudsman has completed a preliminary examination, has decided to proceed and is now commencing an investigation. The head of the organisation then replies giving his view of the matter. Next, the Ombudsman sends out two persons—usually an investigator and a senior investigator—to check documents, interview each person, etc. When an interview has been put in the form in which it is going to be used, it is checked with the interviewee, who may, at this point, for instance, suggest that something be omitted because it would cause him embarrassment, which suggestion would be taken seriously by the Ombudsman. When

---

[99a] 1980 Act, s.6(2), (7); 1989 Report, pp. 11–12.
[1] See also DPS Circular 30/83.
[1a] 1980 Act, s.6(2), (7). See also, 1988 Report, pp. 11–12.

the first draft of a report has been prepared, with no recommendations at this stage, it is sent to the head of the organisation for his comments. It is only after these have been considered that the Ombudsman completes his report and adds on a recommendation.[2]

As already mentioned, the statutory statement that the Ombudsman can choose his own procedure is qualified by the *caveat* "[s]ubject to the provisions of this Act." The principal provisions referred to consist of a formulation of the *audi alteram partem* rule: the public must have an opportunity to comment upon both the complaint and any adverse finding or criticism by the Ombudsman.[3] These statutory obligations are, we believe, satisfied, by the normal procedure which is described in the previous paragraph.

The Act gives the Ombudsman virtually full access to all relevant files for the purposes of a preliminary investigation or an examination. Considering the extent to which public authorities record information, it is one of the Ombudsman's most potent weapons that he may require any person who, in his opinion, possesses relevant information, or a relevant document or "thing," either to send the information, document or thing to the Ombudsman or, where appropriate, to attend before the Ombudsman to furnish the information, document or thing.[4]

There are only two curbs on the Ombudsman's access to information. The first is that the Ombudsman may not ask for information or a document which "relates to decisions and proceedings of the Government or of any of its committees."[5] And, for the purposes of determining whether information or a document does fall within this category, a certificate given by the Secretary to the Government is to be conclusive.[6] The second exception is only partial: it

---

[2] The Ombudsman's wide discretion in regard to procedure would allow him to hold oral hearings (s.8(3), (4)) but not a single hearing has yet (October 1985) been held. A former British Commissioner was reluctant to hold oral hearings: "because they are alien to the ombudsman tradition which seeks to solve disputes between citizens and state with the least degree of confrontation or formality. People in general do not want confrontation or to appear in anything resembling a court." C. Clothier (1984) L.S. Gaz. 3108, 3110.

[3] 1980 Act, ss.8(2), 6(6). This right probably extends to any public servant whose behaviour is criticised because he or she would probably be included in the word "person" in s.6(6). However, in practice, the Ombudsman avoids allocating responsibility to individual officials. See also, s.6(2), (4).

[4] s.7(1)(*a*). Failure to comply is not made an offence by the Act (whatever the common law position). It is assumed that public servants would not wish to jeopardise their careers by a refusal to comply. The basic principle that the Ombudsman may call for whatever evidence is relevant is buttressed by other rules: witnesses are entitled to the same privileges as High Court witnesses (s.7(1)) though in contrast to certain other Ombudsmen, he has no authority to administer an oath; a witness' evidence may not be used against him in criminal proceedings (s.7(6)); expenses of witnesses or complainant may be paid (s.7(5)); the Official Secrets Act 1963 is suspended in respect of examinations or investigations (s.7(4)); executive privilege is restricted to the rules stated in the next paragraph of the text (s.7(4)); the same protection created for a court by the contempt of court rules is extended to the Ombudsman, though no power is given to commit for contempt (s.7(3)); and information obtained by the Ombudsman can be disclosed only for the purpose of the Act or for proceedings under the Official Secrets Act and not for any other proceedings (s.9(1)).

[5] s.7(1)(*b*). This is the first statutory acknowledgment of the existence of Government committees.

[6] *Ibid.*

does not prevent information or a document from being given to the Ombudsman, but only from being disclosed by the Ombudsman to anyone else, even those involved in the complaint. It applies where any Minister of the Government has given notice, in writing, to the Ombudsman, that the disclosure of any document or information or class thereof would in his opinion and for the reasons stated in the notice, "be prejudicial to the public interest."[7]

Before the Ombudsman was established, there was a fear that these extensive powers of investigation would be used by a complainant whose real objective was to gather information to be used to fuel a court action. There seems in fact to be no evidence that the Office has been used for trials of this type. Indeed, the only matters which the Ombudsman is required to communicate to the complainant—and all he does transmit—are "the result of the investigation, the recommendation (if any) made by [the Ombudsman] . . . and the response (if any) made to it by the Department of State or other person to whom it was given."[8] If, as a result of the investigation, it does appear to the Ombudsman that the action had an adverse affect and that, otherwise too, it fell within his jurisdiction, then the Ombudsman may choose between three specified types of recommendation to the Department which took the decision, *viz.* that the action be reconsidered; that the reasons for it be given to the Ombudsman; or, finally, that measures or specified measures be taken to remedy, mitigate or alter the adverse effect of the action.[9] In some cases, there might have to be further sets of responses and recommendations in the dialogue.

Remedies

Apart from the three specified types of recommendation which have just been itemised, no further guidance is given, by the Act, as to the type of remedies to be granted. A very great deal is thus left to the discretion of the Ombudsman in consultation with the public body under investigation. Moreover, with one exception, described below, the Annual Reports do not yet show much in the way of clarification in this field. In at least one case, an apology was forthcoming (where the Motor Registration Office claimed that the complainant had been given too much change).[10] However, in the overwhelming majority of cases, the remedy is the payment of money and calculation of the amount is, in principle, straightforward: for example, it is the amount of the grant or benefit which the complainant was wrongfully denied or the amount by which his telephone bill was too high (though the precise assessment of this may require some give and take). The Ombudsman is not, of course, concerned with whether the public authority is legally obliged to pay the money. His objective is simply to achieve "a reasonable outcome,"[11] an inevitably inexact

---

[7] s.9(2)(*a*)(*c*). See also, s.9(2)(*b*).
[8] s.6(4).
[9] s.6(3).
[10] 1988 Report, pp. 78–79.
[11] 1989 Report, p. 13.

R.T.C. LIBRARY
LETTERKENNY

phrase which was used to explain the acceptance of a local authority's offer to pay a round figure of £1,000 to cover any possible defects in building work which a council engineer had certified as completed for the purpose of a grant. Potentially, the Ombudsman could be confronted with the entire gamut of problems regarding consequential loss, pecuniary loss, etc., which arise in the law of tort. What would happen, to take just one hypothetical example, in a situation in which a complainant had set up a business on the basis of (wrong) advice from a public servant that he was entitled to a grant. The grant is refused, and the business crashes. Is the complainant awarded: merely the value of the grant; the amount of his loss of capital money; and/or compensation for loss of profits?[12]

Interest

One particular situation which has frequently arisen is where the Ombudsman orders the payment of back money which should have been paid, say, several years before.[13] In these cases the Ombudsman may wish to include an amount to compensate for late payment. His ability to do this was at first opposed by the Department of Finance and the Government, their opposition being put on the basis of the principle that in making such a recommendation, the Ombudsman was trespassing in the field of policy; yet, surely, assuming that there has been an action involving maladministration, if payment in respect of it has been delayed, then the necessity for compensation for late payment flows fairly automatically from the Ombudsman's obligation to "remedy . . . the adverse affect [sic] of the action."[14] In any case, in 1986, following a threat by the Ombudsman to publish what would have been his first special report to the Oireachtas, a decision of the Government led to an agreement between the Ombudsman and the Department of Finance, providing for the payment of compensation in Social Welfare cases. (The Department of Finance also agreed that this precedent would be followed in cases in which payments by other Departments were excessively delayed.) By this agreement, the Department of Finance, whose sanction (either direct or delegated) is necessary for all departmental expenditure, delegated sanction to the Department of Social Welfare to pay compensation based on the movement of the Consumer Price Index, where a payment is made more than two years late.[15]

---

[12] In the U.K., the following comment has been offered on the Ombudsman's approach to one complaint: "the Commissioner is seeking to distinguish between financial losses directly attributable to the defective advice and those flowing from other sources. But this process of allocation is far from precise and the PCA has considerable leeway in making his calculations": Mowbray, "A Right of Official Advice" [1986] *Public Law* 68, 82.

[13] 1986 Report, pp. 16, 36 and 67. See also, 1984 Report, p. 42; 1985 Report, p. 8.

[14] s.6(3)(*b*).

[15] For this agreement, see 1986 Report, pp. 16, 36 "The Department of Finance have also supported my suggestion that there should be statutory provision for such payments as soon as practicable and they have asked the Department of Social Welfare to consider bringing forward statutory provisions to formalise the new arrangements."

Special Report

If the response to any recommendation is not "satisfactory" the Ombudsman's final sanction is to make a "special report" on the case to the Houses of the Oireachtas.[16]

This term is always used by the Ombudsman in the sense of a report which is separate from the annual report and which is laid before the Houses of the Oireachtas immediately after the public body's unsatisfactory response, thereby attracting greater publicity than a report which is merely included as part of the annual report. A special report has been threatened on a number of individual complaints but "in all [such] cases my recommendations were accepted and the need to make a special report to the Oireachtas did not arise."[17] The only one of these cases to be identified in the annual reports concerned the Department of Social Welfare's refusal to pay compensation for late payment described in the previous paragraph.

5. Legal Control of the Ombudsman

In view of the expansionist policy adopted by the present Ombudsman, it is worth stating that, like any other public authority, he is subject to the law. His jurisdiction and procedure are governed by public law. This means, as far as substantive law is concerned, that he is subject to the 1980 Act; the Constitution (including constitutional justice) and various general principles, such as the doctrine of reasonableness in the exercise of his various discretions.[18]

As regards the procedure by which these controls might be mobilised, it would be open to (say) a Department of State which wanted to stop the Ombudsman from investigating their activities, to move the High Court, by way of an application for judicial review seeking an order restraining such an investigation.[19] A second possibility is an action brought against the Ombudsman by a private individual whose complaint he had rejected. (In practice, this is unlikely, not least because if such a person were prepared for High Court litigation, then in almost all cases, it would be possible—and tactically better—to go directly against the erring public body.) In the early case of *Re Fletcher's Application*[20] the applicant sought leave to apply for an order of mandamus requiring the P.C.A. to investigate an allegation of neglect of duty against the Official Receiver acting as liquidator of a company. The appeal committee of the House of Lords refused leave to take the application to the House. The entire reason given was that "there was no jurisdiction to order the commission to investigate a complaint because [the British equivalent of section

---

[16] s.6(5), (7). The Ombudsman's functions under s.6(5), (7) (together with those in the personnel field) are the only ones which he is not empowered to delegate to his officers: s.10(3).

[17] 1986 Report, p. 5; 1989 Report, p. 11. As mentioned, at pp. 281–282, a special report was made on the cuts in the Ombudsman's staff: see 1987 Report, p. 119.

[18] For example, by s.4(2) of the 1980 Act, he has a discretion as to whether to investigage an action at all.

[19] For further information on the matters alluded to in this paragraph, see pp. 318–323 (Reach of Public Law); pp. 409–420 (Constitutional Justice); and pp. 565–591 (application for Judicial Review).

[20] [1970] 2 All E.R. 527.

303

4(2) of the Irish Ombudsman Act 1980] (which provides that the commissioner 'may' investigate certain matters) conferred on him a discretion whether to investigate or not."[21] This approach would be unlikely to be followed in contemporary Ireland because it runs contrary to the judicial zeitgeist that almost all discretions are open to review.[22] Nevertheless, for reasons to be explained below, it seems likely that it is only if the facts were extreme that a case against the Ombudsman would actually succeed.

Apart from *Fletcher*, British cases involving the Ombudsman have concerned the Commission for Local Administration. In one of these, *R. v. Local Commissioner for Administration, ex p. Eastleigh B.C.*,[23] the English High Court (Nolan J.) had grounded itself on the remarkable proposition that since Parliament had not thought it necessary to create a right of appeal against the Ombudsman's findings, then, in the absence of "impropriety," the courts ought not to provide the equivalent of such a right by means of judicial review. This view, which fundamentally misunderstands the nature of judicial review, was rejected by the Court of Appeal—unanimously, on this point. Lord Donaldson M.R. stated:

> "It is [the fact that there is no right of appeal], coupled with the public law character of the Ombudsman's office and powers, which is the foundation of the right to relief by way of judicial review."[24]

In the opposite direction, some body or person might refuse to co-operate with the Ombudsman. In that case, two remedies would be open to the Ombudsman: the first would be to invoke the sanctions of publicity, presumably through a special report. The alternative would be for the Ombudsman to have recourse to the courts, usually by way of an application for judicial review proceedings against the recalcitrant Minister or other public body.[25]

In any case, whether proceedings were taken against, or by, the Ombudsman, it is realistic to suppose that any private individual, or, *a fortiori*, any public body, which was opposing the Ombudsman would have an uphill battle. In the first place, the Ombudsman is popular with the public and the courts are not insensible to the feelings of the public. In addition, a court would be influenced by the reversal of its own normal role in a public law case. Ordinarily, its task is to consider whether to control a public body in the interest of an individual. In a case involving the Ombudsman, it would probably have to decide whether to restrain the Ombudsman from controlling a

---

[21] *Ibid.*

[22] See Chap. 10.5.

[23] [1988] Q.B. 855.

[24] *Ibid.* 866. This is not to say that the existence of an appeal always excludes review: see pp. 392–396 and pp. 605–609 (in Remedies—Discretion).

[25] It is suggested that the sanction envisaged by the Ombudsman in his Annual Report for 1989, p. 4 would be premature: "It might have been expected that . . . it would not be necessary . . . to draw [any public servants'] attention to the risk of contempt proceedings for their failure to respond adequately or in good time to this Office." But surely a coercive order, issued as a conclusion to judicial proceedings, would have had to be defied before contempt proceedings became a possibility.

public body in the interest of an individual. This would probably weight the scales in favour of the Ombudsman.[26]

Irrespective of whether court proceedings are on the cards, the Ombudsman is naturally bound to take a challenge to his jurisdiction seriously. Sometimes, legal advice has to be taken. There is no provision for a lawyer as a member of the Ombudsman's staff[27] and it would be inappropriate for him to go to the Attorney-General who would usually be advising the public body against whose action the Ombudsman wished to investigate. Accordingly, he takes legal advice from private practitioners.

In fact, so far, in all of the (few) complaints in which legal obstacles have been raised, the matter has been resolved—eventually—by agreement.[28] With one exception, this resolution has always been in favour of permitting the investigation to continue. Some of the challenges, most of which occurred in the first year of the Ombudsman's existence, arose from the novelty of the new office—an unwelcome novelty in some quarters—and plainly had little substance behind them. For instance, in spite of the fact that the 1980 Act is clearly to the contrary, an unsuccessful challenge was mounted by the Department of Social Welfare to the Ombudsman's authority to investigate the decisions of appeals officers.[28a] More substantial was the argument of the Department of Posts and Telegraphs when it claimed that the Ombudsman was not competent to investigate telephone accounts in respect of the period from July 1983, when the 1980 Act came into force, until December 1983, when the telephone service was transferred to Bord Telecom Éireann. Eventually the Bord permitted investigation, for this period, on an *ex gratia* basis.

However, the Ombudsman's progress was halted by a legal argument in one case.[29] The complaint related to a person who had been selected as a lecturer by a voluntary education committee, but whose appointment had not been sanctioned by the Department of Education because he did not have the normal qualifications, although he did have what might be regarded as equivalent, or even superior, qualifications. The first and unsuccessful legal ground of objection taken by the Department was that the action complained against had occurred before the Ombudsman Act commenced, thus contravening the requirement described in paragraph 6 of Part 3 above. However, as the Department eventually accepted, this argument failed on the facts, in that the complainant, upon learning of his rejection, had appealed and hence a final decision on his case was not reached until a date which was within the Ombudsman's jurisdiction.

---

[26] *Cf.* Lord Donaldson M.R. in *Eastleigh* stating: "judicial review of an Ombudsman's report . . . , bearing in mind the nature of his office and duties and the qualifications of those who hold that office, is inherently unlikely to succeed . . . " (at 867). And: "An ombudsman's report is neither a statute nor a judgment. It is a report to the council and to the ratepayers of the area. It has to be written in everyday language and convey a message. This report has been subjected to a microscopic and somewhat legalistic analysis which it was not intended to undergo." (at 866)

[27] Though for some years one of his investigators happened to be qualified as a solicitor.

[28] See 1984 Report, pp. 11–12; 1986 Report, p. 38.

[28a] s.5(1)(a)(iii) as read with ss.1(2) and 2. See further, p. 296.

[29] 1984 Report, pp. 11–12, 1985 Report, pp. 45–46.

The Department's second, and successful, objection concerned what appeared, at first, to the Ombudsman to be "a loophole in the general prohibition against examining complaints about recruitment or appointment."[29a] This most significant general prohibition is contained in section 5(1)(c) of the Act, which refers to "recruitment or appointment to any office or employment in a Department of State or by any other person specified in the *First Schedule* to this Act." Now Vocational Education Committees are neither Departments of State nor within the First Schedule so that, as far as this provision is concerned, the Ombudsman would have had jurisdiction. However, the Department of Education invoked two other subsections which persuaded the Ombudsman that he did not have jurisdiction. The first of these is section 4(4) by which "the Ombudsman shall not investigate an action taken by or on behalf of a person specified in the *Second Schedule* to this Act" which Schedule includes vocational educational committees. The other provision, section 1(3)(b), extends this provision. Its effect, in the present context, is that references to a vocational educational committee are taken to include the Department of Education as far as functions performed by the Department in relation to the VEC is concerned. In sum, the exclusion of the VEC also covers the Department acting in relation to the VEC.

6. Appraisal

It is worth emphasising some of the new institution's more novel features. The first of these is that while the Ombudsman's only formal sanction is a special report nevertheless he is not on a par with a deputy or local councillor making "representations."[30] At the same time, one should not fly to the

---

[29a] 1985 Report, p. 45.

[30] For the attitude of certain politicians and officials, see 1985 Report, p. 20; 1986 Report, pp. 3, 5 and 38; and 1989 Report, p. 4. On this subject, 1985 Report, p. 16 states: "[S]ome County Managers saw my role as making representations. Arising from this they considered that locally elected public representations might see my involvement as interfering with their traditional role and, indeed, some Managers felt that I was merely duplicating this role. My staff at all times stressed that this Office was not involved in making representations. The Ombudsman has been charged by the Oireachtas with the statutory function of investigating complaints . . . ."

Notice also the following statement by Lord Eastleigh in *Eastleigh* at 867, in which the Court of Appeal correctly rejected an extraordinary statement of the High Court (which appeared to suggest that the Ombudsman enjoyed only moral or political authority): "Next there is the suggestion [of the High Court] that the council should issue a statement disputing the right of the ombudsman to make his findings and that this would provide the council with an adequate remedy. Such an action would wholly undermine the system of Ombudsman's reports and would, in effect, provide for an appeal to the media against his findings. The parliamentary intention was that reports by ombudsmen would be loyally accepted by the local authorities concerned."

Finally, consider the attitude of the medical profession. Regarding medical records, a matter which arises in the context of investigations into health boards, 1985 Report, p. 15 states:

"The Director of my Office met with the Irish Medical Council and also with the Irish Medical Organisation to discuss this matter. Both bodies recognised my unconditional right to all records, medical and otherwise. Notwithstanding this, I was happy to assure them that I would request medical records only when I considered it absolutely necessary and that, in all such cases, I would satisfy myself that I had the permission of complainants before examining these records."

opposite extreme and deduce that there has been some fundamental shift on the legal plane, in the relationship between the individual public servant, the State and a member of the public affected by an official action. The 1980 Act contains no provision making the State or a public servant liable where there was no liability before 1980. The major conceptual innovation introduced by the Act is to provide a remedy against the public body in the case of maladministration, even if this falls short of a breach of law. The emphasis is on compensation and not punishment. It is true that the Act explicitly grants a right to constitutional justice to a "person" (which word, we consider, includes a public servant as well as a public body) against whom the Ombudsman is considering making an adverse "finding or criticism . . . in a statement, recommendation or report. . . . " Nevertheless, the legislation is not designed to pillory or even identify the "guilty" public servant, assuming (as will often not be the case) that there is a single culprit. And, in practice, the Ombudsman's attitude has manifestly been based upon the assumption that disciplining the responsible public servant is not his function and that any straying in such a direction would mean a risk of losing the co-operation of the public service upon which he depends.[31]

On the political, as opposed to the legal, plane, it is of course true that the entry of the Ombudsman upon the constitutional scene means a dilution of the pure milk of the individual ministerial responsibility doctrine, which holds that a Minister is responsible to the Dáil and only to the Dáil, for the performance of his Department. However this doctrine has always been a rather broken-backed one.[32]

There is no doubting the potency of the Ombudsman. To quote from the Annual Report for 1989[33]:

"Many of the complaints to the Office had previously been made through the normal channels by local representatives, Dáil Deputies and members of the Seanad. Despite the best efforts of politicians of all parties and strong representation to various sections of officialdom, the complaints remained unresolved—simply because the politicians did not have access to the relevant documentation.

With the passing of the Ombudsman Act 1980, politicians provided this authority to the Ombudsman and for the first time in the history of the State, the files of Government Departments and public bodies subject to remit were open to scrutiny by an independent office. The result was that many complaints which had gone unresolved for a long time were found to be justified and were settled in favour of the complainant."

---

[31] It follows that we respectfully disagree with the suggestion contained in the 1986 Report, pp. 3–4, that the establishment of the Ombudsman has altered the corporation sole system by which it is the Minister and not (save to a limited extent) the civil servant actually involved, who is legally responsible for what is done by the civil servant: see further, pp. 53–58.
[32] See pp. 54–57.
[33] Pl. 6877, p. 30.

Ombudsman v. the Courts

According to Professor Bradley writing about the British Ombudsman[34] "I am in no doubt that the Ombudsman's methods enable him to get closer to reconstructing the administrative history of a citizen's case than does High Court procedure. . . . " The reasons for this assessment apply in Ireland too. These reasons include the fact that the Ombudsman follows an inquisitorial, flexible and private process of inquiry with unrestricted access to departmental files; that this usually occurs in a non-confrontational milieu; and that the investigators are almost all themselves former public servants. Finally, the system for devising a remedy—the inter-play of recommendation from the Ombudsman and response from the public body—is more likely to yield a result satisfactory to all parties than would the polarised concepts administered in a court. Indeed, the Ombudsman has a very conciliatory manner. For example[35]:

> "I sought the views of the Department on the circumstances of this case. Initially, they were not well disposed toward the case but they agreed to consider it if the local authority processed the application in the normal way and submitted a full report on the matter to them.
> The local authority did this and I am glad to report that the Department paid the £5,000 grant to the complainants."

Only seldom has the goad of a special report had to be made explicit.

The Ombudsman himself has drawn no comparisons with the courts of law, but it seems probable that in many ways, besides the one just mentioned, he is superior to the courts. In the first place, his examination of a case involves no costs to the victim of maladministration, even where the complaint is unsuccessful. The complaint can be initiated informally, if the complainant is involved thereafter, this is usually done in the most unalarming way, often by an investigation interviewing the complainant at home.

The persona of the Ombudsman is very different from that of a court. He plainly sees himself as the tribune of the people—the Irish version of the Ombudsman is "Fear a 'Phobal" (literally, "the man of the People") although the translation used in the Act is simply "Ombudsman." Some 30 per cent. of all complaints to his office are from people who have encountered difficulty in obtaining benefits from the State's welfare systems.[36] Making no claim to icy impartiality, he leans towards whichever method of interpretation, whether literal or ultra-liberal, will be most favourable to the complainant (although, in this, he is not all that different from the situation existing in some courts). The office of Ombudsman has been deliberately designed and utilised to promote maximum usage. He projects a high public profile, with

---

[34] "Role of Ombudsman in Relation to Citizens' Rights" [1980] C.L.J. 304, 322.
[35] 1988 Report, p. 78. See also, for example, 1986 Report, p. 50.
[36] 1988 Report, p. 4.

substantial media publicity. A particular feature of his *modus operandi* is regional visits.[37]

He publishes attractively set out reports, with catchy headlines, within six months of the year to which they relate. It happens that in the great majority of cases which are described in the reports, some advantage is achieved for the complainant (although this is not true of overall complaints to the Ombudsman, as can be seen below). This no doubt helps to attract other complainants.[38]

Maladministration and the law

There is another ground on which the Ombudsman and the courts may be compared and that is in relation to their subject-matter. These, in fact, have a great deal in common. For, as will be demonstrated in succeeding paragraphs, to assert that the Ombudsman and the courts are involved in different types of regulation in that the Ombudsman is concerned with "maladministration" whereas the courts deal with judicial review or causes of action is merely playing with words.[39] Indeed so far from its being the Ombudsman's business "to operate beyond the frontier where the law stops"[40] (*e.g.* rudeness or delay), a substantial number of the complaints for which he has provided a remedy could have come before a court. In part, this is because during the past decade or so, the rising tide of public law has engulfed the island of "maladministration." This can be demonstrated by reference to: legitimate expectations[41]; the liability of public authorities[42]; the *audi alteram partem* rule[43]

[37] Such a visit consists of one or more investigators, heralded by a local advertising campaign, setting up a temporary office in either the Southern Capital or some provincial centre. Indeed during the period 1985–1986, a visit was made to each of the counties in the country. In addition to heightening the general public's awareness of the Ombudsman, this brought in a substantial number of complaints: about 1,000 (1985); 700 (1986), 500 (first half of 1987), 300 (1989). (Visits were suspended during the second half of 1987 and 1988 because of the staff cut-backs). The Ombudsman is of the opinion that few of these complaints would have reached him, were it not for the regional visits: " . . . there are many instances where the presentation of a complaint in writing or on the telephone is just not possible; in such instances the only option available to the individual is to call to my Office and have the matter discussed and examined by my staff. Individuals living outside the Dublin area are at a disadvantage. Regional visits represent an attempt to redress the balance." (1989 Report, p. 13); see also 1986 Report, p. 28; 1987 Report, p. 9, 1988 Report, p. 7.
[38] The 1989 Report, p. 71 states: "The cases chosen for this part of my report are mainly cases where I have been successful in having decisions of public servants reversed. I must emphasise that they are not meant to give an unbalanced view of the efficiency or effectiveness of any one organisation. They have been selected purely because they highlight interesting issues and they can be presented fairly and accurately in summary form."
[39] See further P. P. Craig, *Administrative Law* (2nd. ed.), pp. 111–113; Crawford [1985] *Public Law* 246, 262.
[40] A phrase used by Professor Wade in the 1967 and 1971 editions of *Administrative Law* but not in later editions.
[41] See 1985 Report, pp. 55; 1987 Report, p. 13, 17, 75, 80, 81, 88 and 96; 1988 Report, pp. 39, 70, 78; 1989 Report, pp. 82 and 86.
[42] See 1989 Report, p. 93—recipient of a grant complained that renovations which a council engineer certified, for the purposes of the grant, to have been completed, were unsatisfactory. ("Council decided, while not accepting any liability in the case, to pay £1,000 to cover any possible defects in the work"). See also, pp. 301–302.
[43] See 1989 Report, p. 41.

and the duty to give reasons for decisions[44]—each of which has been the subject of both Ombudsman and court decisions. In some cases, it is only in terminology that there is a difference from a court. Take, for instance, the following complaint involving what a court would call abuse of power. The complainant, who had purchased his house from the local authority, wished to alter the ownership of the house by adding his wife as joint owner. This transaction required the local authority's consent which was being withheld because the complainant had not paid his local service charges for a number of years. The complainant's solicitor referred the matter to the Ombudsman who found "that while the housing legislation gave local authorities power to refuse to grant a consent in certain specific circumstances, refusal to pay service charges was not an appropriate reason for such refusal."[45]

Again, the Reports disclose examples of such indisputably legal questions as: the interpretation of the Higher Education Grant Scheme (as to whether certain moneys should be treated as capital or income); or whether a step-parent's means were to be counted as the means of a "guardian"[46]; the use of a previous decision of the Supreme Court to characterise the complainant's treatment as a "hospital in-patient" service, as distinct from an "institutional service" and, therefore, available free of charge to a medical card holder[47]; and the conclusion "from my examination of the relevant legislation" that a Disabled Persons Maintenance Allowance is payable as from the date of application and not the date of award.[48] There have even been complaints on private law points such as: trespass to land (damage to a garden wall done by the Department of Posts)[49]; whether the complainant had been given too much change[50]; negligent conveyancing by a local authority[51]; and trespass to goods involving the unlawful seizure of a van by the Revenue Commissioners.[52]

In Britain, such an overlap has been regarded as undesirable in principle and section 5(2)(b) of the Parliamentary Commissioner Act 1967 provides that the Ombudsman shall not investigate administrative action "in respect of which the person aggrieved has or had a remedy by way of proceedings in any court of law." However, the Act goes on to permit an investigation where the Ombudsman is satisfied that it was not reasonable to expect the person aggrieved to go to court. In part because of the fluidity and uncertainty of this area of law, this discretion has been exercised generously. However, in recent years, the overlap has begun to attract attention. Mr. Yardley—a former Pro-

---

[44] See 1988 Report, p. 88 and 1985 Report, p. 23.
[45] 1989 Report, p. 89. See also 1988 Report, p. 25. Compare Chap. 11.4.
[46] 1987 Report, p. 71; 1989 Report, p. 85; 1985 Report, p. 28, respectively.
[47] 1988 Report, p. 84.
[48] 1985 Report, p. 31.
[49] 1987 Report, pp. 94–95, see also 1989 Report, p. 90.
[50] 1988 Report, p. 78.
[51] 1988 Report, p. 80.
[52] 1989 Report, pp. 34–38.

fessor of Public Law—who is now chairman of the English Commission for Local Administration has stated[53]:

> "We take the view, sir, that we are not dealing primarily with legality as opposed to illegality; we are dealing with, in a public sense in a public area, morality as opposed to immorality; reasonableness as opposed to unreasonableness."

Yet this rather begs the question which is under discussion here, namely, what is the Ombudsman to do if confronted with a complaint in respect of which some established law has settled the point. In a later English case, *R.* v. *Local Commissioner, ex p. Croydon L.B.C.*[54] which dealt to some extent with this point, Woolf L.J. stated[55]:

> "Issues whether an administrative tribunal has properly understood the relevant law and the legal obligations which it is under when conducting an inquiry are more appropriate for resolution by the High Court than by a commissioner, however eminent."

In Ireland, there is no equivalent to the English statutory provision excluding the Ombudsman in principle if the complainant would have had a court remedy. (This is, of course, characteristic of Irish impatience with constitutional dogma.) However, given the respective natures and responsibilities of the courts and the Ombudsman, the problem of overlap remains a topic worthy of discussion.

Does it matter if legal questions are decided by the Ombudsman? The answer is that in practice, it does not usually matter since most of this type of case will fall within one of the following three categories. The first and most significant of these categories is where (possibly after both the Ombudsman and the public body have taken legal advice) it is agreed that there is no dispute as to what the legal rule is so that the Ombudsman is simply following the law. Most of the complaints exemplified in the last two paragraphs do, in the end, fall within this class. Secondly, it is inevitable that there should be some overlap where the Ombudsman is dealing with one of the many complaints about which it is uncertain on which side of the line between breach of law and "maladministration" the complaint falls. A lot, indeed, is explained by the fact that public law is now so fluid and uncertain. Finally, it is acceptable that it should occur where little in the way of (say) money, or effect upon administrative organisation, is involved.

Nevertheless in the few legal cases falling outside these categories, there

---

[53] Select Committee on P.C.A.H.C. 448 (1985–86), Minutes of Evidence, p. 10, quoted by Crawford, *op. cit.*

[54] [1989] 1 All E.R. 1033.

[55] *Ibid.* 1045c. However, the judge went on actually to resolve the case on the following rather strange basis (at 1045f): "The problem in this case is that the commissioner apparently never appreciated that there was a conflict between his jurisdiction and that of the court. In my view he should have done so at least before he concluded his investigation and then he should have exercised his discretion whether to discontinue his investigation. However, as he indicates that if he had considered the question of discretion he would undoubtedly have decided to proceed, I would not be prepared to grant relief solely on this basis."

may be a difficulty of principle. For the conventional, court-centred view is that it is the courts which are the appropriate places to determine questions of law. And this conventional view is enshrined in the Constitution which states, in Article 34.1, that limited judicial powers apart, justice must be administered in a court of law. There is evidence in the Reports that the Ombudsman appreciates this limitation.[56]

The most acute form of this difficulty arises, of course, where the Ombudsman decides a legal issue differently from the courts. Take, as an example, those statutory immunities from tort action of which section 64(1) of the Postal and Telecommunications Act 1983 is an example. This provision gives An Post immunity from all liability in respect of any loss suffered in the use of a postal service. One complaint to the Ombudsman concerned a wedding dress which had been misplaced—though subsequently found—in the post.[57] The Ombudsman took the matter up as a case of "administrative bungling" and secured the payment of £80 to the bride to compensate her for expenses incurred in looking for the dress in Dublin, but no mention whatever was made of the following difficulty which inevitably arises where there are two jurisdictions which resolve a situation in different ways. The legislature has exercised its prerogative to determine (for policy reasons, be they good or bad, arising from the operation of the postal service) that a person who suffers loss through negligence in the postal service cannot recover against An Post. It would appear to be inconsistent to set up this statutory immunity against any person who sues for negligence before the courts but to allow it to be circumvented by another person who complains of "bungling" to the Ombudsman.

It may be objected that: the payment was made "strictly on an *ex gratia* basis"; the amount was trivial; in the practical world, there is less to this conceptual flaw than meets the eye; and, anyway, as Ralph Waldo Emerson said: "All mankind love a lover." Let us turn then to a second series of examples which is not open to any of these rebuttals. This is a series of a dozen or so cases[58] which can be put under the broad heading of legitimate expectations and misleading advice, shading off into a failure to supply relevant information. In many of these cases, the result would probably have been the same if an action had been brought before a court. One example[59] concerned the Department of Agriculture's refusal to pay the complainant-farmer, who had carried out certain farm development work, the full rate of a grant under the Farm Modernisation Scheme. The reason for this refusal was a change which had been made to the Scheme *after* the complainant's application had been approved. Following the Ombudsman's intervention, the Department agreed to pay the grant in full.

---

[56] 1988 Report, p. 26 ("I have refrained from making a recommendation in the case for the moment as there is a case before the Supreme Court involving similar circumstances and the same issues. In view of this I accept that the Health Boards should await the final judicial decision before deciding on the case I investigated . . . ").
[57] 1984 Report, p. 39; see also 1987 Report, p. 26.
[58] See pp. 293–295.
[59] 1987 Report, pp. 79–80.

However, in a minority of cases, the Ombudsman has probably gone further than would a court. One case concerned the loss of a letter carrying £100, which had been registered at the minimum fee of 95p for which the maximum compensation payable was £20. The critical point was that there was no notice on display to indicate the conditions regarding the sending of money by post. This omission meant, the Ombudsman found, that An Post should compensate the complainant for the entire amount lost.[60] Yet, in these circumstances, a court would have been most unlikely to have inferred a misrepresentation or estoppel from silence. In another case[61] incorrect information as to a housing grant scheme was given by a local authority employee in connection with the period for which the Housing Surrender Grant Scheme was to remain in operation. As a result, the complainant suffered the loss of a £5,000 grant. The Ombudsman recommended that the Department of the Environment pay this grant, although the complainant fell outside the terms of the scheme. Here the striking point is that, as the Ombudsman remarks in the Report[62]:

> "This case extended the principle outlined in my Annual Report of 1987. . . . In this case the incorrect information was given by one body relating to a scheme operated by another body and the second body was prepared to pay the grant although it was not directly involved in giving the incorrect information."

A court would not have given a remedy against the body which provided incorrect information. To take a further, and as yet hypothetical example, as we explain in Chapter 14, the law on legitimate expectations is a compromise between a number of conflicting policies, and among these is the principle that a public authority will not be permitted to fetter its discretionary power. Would the Ombudsman take this into account in an appropriate case? If he would not, is it fair that a plaintiff who takes his complaint to a court should be caught by this principle? As a general principle, it surely cannot be right to have two conflicting independent systems of jurisprudence.

Numbers of complaints[63]

In terms of sheer volume of complaints there is no doubt that the new office has been a success. The figures for complaints received are as follows: 2,267 (1984); 5,496 (1985); 5,691 (1986); 5,281 (1987); 3,164 (1988); and 2,948 (1989). The relatively low number in 1984 may be explained by the facts that it was the first year of the office and before the extension of its remit. In each year, the sum of complaints against Bord Telecom Éireann and the Department of State account for some 80 per cent. of the entire total, the remainder coming from the local authorities, closely followed by the health boards, with

---

[60] 1987 Report, p. 96.
[61] 1988 Report, pp. 77–78.
[62] *Ibid.*
[63] 1984 Report, Chaps. 5 and 12; 1985 Report, Chaps. 3 and 12; 1986 Report, Chaps. 2 and 10; 1987 Report, Chaps. 2 and 7; 1988 Report, Chaps. 2 and 6; 1989 Report, Chaps. 5 and 9.

An Post a long distance behind.[64] One unexpected feature of the figures is that for the years 1987–1989 the number of complaints against Telecom Éireann (almost all in respect of telephone bills)[65] slightly exceeded the total number of complaints against all the Departments of State. However, there was a fall from 1,270 in 1988 to 1,087 in 1989, partly due to the operation of itemised billing in the Limerick region (whence complaints fell dramatically) and it is likely that this trend will continue as itemised billing becomes more widely available. Out of the complaints against the Departments of State, about two-thirds are against the Department of Social Welfare and the next largest number is against the Revenue Commissioners.

The figures for 1985–1986 are exceptionally high by international standards.[66] The Ombudsman has suggested that the reduction in numbers of complaints for 1988–1989 to a figure of about 3,000, which is more in line with countries of similar size, may also be connected with the limited programme of regional visits and the recent long delays—each of which arose because of the staff reductions of 1987 and 1988. Complaints falling outside jurisdiction are also low by international standards. Apart from the first year when there were, *inter alia*, about 300 complaints from civil servants regarding personnel matters, complaints falling outside jurisdiction have been relatively few and were running at 6 per cent. in 1989.

[64]*COMPLAINTS RECEIVED WITHIN JURISDICTION*

	1984	1985	1986	1987	1988	1989
Civil Service	1,544	2,392	2,247	1,878	1,008	1,026
Telecom Éireann		1,377*	1,775	2,022	1,270	1,087
Local Authorities		521*	483	396	247	260
Health Boards		397*	422	311	196	237
An Post		59*	69	116	82	45
Total	1,544	4,746	4,996	4,723	2,803	2,655

(*Complaints as from April 1, 1985)

[65] A typical complaint out of a large group which presents few features of wider interest is the following: "A subscriber complained about the charges on an account in respect of a period in which he alleged the telephone had been locked away. He complained that the usage recorded could not be consistent with a private telephone. Telecom Éireann said that increased usage was first recorded on the line immediately following the conversion of the telephone from manual to automatic working. They also claimed that the telephone was used for business purposes. In the course of my examination of the case, I confirmed that the telephone was, in fact, used for business purposes. In the circumstances, I found no reason to make a recommendation in the complainant's favour." As can be seen from this example, until Bord Telecom Éireann introduces an itemised billing system, there is no unconrovertible method of establishing how many phone calls have been made. However, in 1985, the Board agreed on methods to streamline their investigation of complaints and, by 1991, an itemised billing had been introduced in several areas of the country.

Members of the Dáil Public Accounts Committee have suggested that any public body (and especially Bord Telecom Éireann since so many of the complaints were against it), against whom the Ombudsman makes an adverse finding, should pay a levy towards the cost of the Ombudsman's office: *The Irish Times*, July 8, 1988.

[66] The Irish complaints emanate from a population of 3·5 million. Compare this with recent figures for Denmark (1,650 complaints from a population of 5·1 millions); Sweden (3,374; 8·4 millions); New Zealand (1,906; 3·1 millions); and Finland (2,027; 4·9 millions): comparative figures from 1986 Report, p. 8.

The most important statistic, perhaps, is that of the cases determined in 1989, 20 per cent. were resolved in favour of the complainant. A further 27 per cent. were assisted in one way or another. The equivalent figures for the 1984–1988 period are 23 per cent. and 27 per cent. respectively. The category of "complainants assisted" covers cases in which, for instance, a complainant is told that he is not eligible for the benefit claimed but he may be eligible for another benefit—possibly a benefit administered by a health board, when a Social Welfare benefit was claimed. Another example: no maladministration is found so that the complainant is obliged to pay his telephone bill, nevertheless circumstances are such that payment by instalments are arranged. Often the assistance takes the form of "information provided" and such cases are almost as significant as those complaints resolved in the complainant's favour. They confirm one of the Ombudsman's major themes—the point, discussed earlier, that the public service should supply citizens with better quality information. As regards the majority of complainants, who are unsuccessful, these have at least the consolation of knowing that their grievance has received a thorough investigation by an independent agency—the poor man's equivalent of the Day in Court. In addition, such investigations enhance confidence in the public service by giving it an independent *imprimatur*.

Further testimony to the fact that the Ombudsman principle is an idea whose time has come is provided by the way in Ireland (as elsewhere) this constitutional species has multiplied and spread to fresh fields of activity.[67]

Uniformity

The Ombudsman is naturally alert to the need for him to observe consistency in his findings in similar situations. His decisions do demonstrate a fair measure of consistency, especially in regard to general principles such as delay or clear explanations. Occasionally, in his Reports, there are explicit references to previous decisions.[68] Reference back to previous decisions is also facilitated by the establishment in 1986 of a computerised system of digests of previous decisions.[69] A second aid to consistency is provided by communication with the Ombudsman offices of other states, mainly by way of the International Ombudsman Conference and the Interman Institute. Some members of the international community gave the

---

[67] s.94(1) of the Central Bank Act 1989 provides for the establishment of an Ombudsman for the major credit institutions. Goaded by this threat of a statutory Ombudsman, the banks and buildnational Ombudsing societies have announced the setting up of a voluntary complaints investigation scheme: *The Irish Times*, June 14, 1990. Notice also that: University College, Cork is the only university in Europe, apart from the University of Helsinki, to have a Student Ombudsman; in the case of the legal profession, s. 18.42 of the Fair Trade Commission Report, 1990 *Report of Study into Restrictive Practices in the Legal Profession* recommends the establishment of a Legal Ombudsman's Office. In 1989, the Progressive Democrats proposed a Private Member's Bill to establish a Health Ombudsman to investigate improper or wasteful decisions of public hospitals or health board administrators: see *Dáil Debates*: Vol. 390, col. 1901, May 23, 1989.
[68] 1988 Report, pp. 86 and 78. ("This case extended the principle I outlined in my Annual Report of 1987 relating to the giving of incorrect information by a public body.")
[69] 1986 Report, p. 29.

Ombudsman advice when the Irish Ombudsman was first established.[70] And there is the occasional reference in Reports to foreign approaches to such common problems as telephone bills[71] and compensation for the loss of purchasing power in the case of late payment.

Trouble-shooter

As well as his duty in respect of individual grievances, the Ombudsman has a second role, namely as a trouble-shooter over the entire range of Government administration. Obviously, there is a correlation between a vigorous discharge of this second function and a lack of too nice a concern for the policy-administration border which, if too punctiliously observed, would cramp an Ombudsman's style. The Irish Ombudsman (like his New Zealand colleague, but in contrast to the British P.C.A.[72]) has been alert to the potential of his office to act in the role of trouble-shooter. He has not been over-concerned with the policy-administration restriction and has been prepared—to quote a characterist phrase used by the present incumbent, in various public talks— "to push the boat out." His 1989 Report[73] summarises some 16 legislative or policy changes which have come about, partly or entirely, as a result of recommendations of the Ombudsman. For example: Social Welfare legislation has been amended to reduce discrimination against husbands and widowers; the Department of Social Welfare has agreed to change its practice to admit claims for unemployment from those on holiday outside the state[74]; the Finance Act 1986, included a provision by which it ceased to be a consequence of a deceased's having taken out comparatively small assurance policies on his children that his widow forfeited certain tax allowances; the Domicile and Recognition of Foreign Divorces Act 1986 uprooted the law of dependent domicile, ("the last barbarous relic of a woman's servitude"[75]) by which a woman whose "husband" had deserted her, gone abroad and obtained a divorce was deemed also to be domiciled abroad, with the consequence that the divorce was recognised and, thus, the wife might lose a welfare benefit. An Post agreed to reintroduce the facility of paying a television and radio licence by instalments; and Bord Telecom agreed to alter their billing system so that the issue of a first account to new subscribers should occur within six months in contrast to the long delay (up to 18 months in one case)

---

[70] 1984 Report, p. 27.

[71] 1986 Report, p. 24.

[72] See Harlow, "Ombudsman in Search of a Role" (1978) 41 M.L.R. 446.

[73] Pl. 6877, Chap. 2 and pp. 23 and 28.

[74] In at least one of the complaints of this type, the case was exacerbated by the fact that the holiday was in Northern Ireland. The Ombudsman commented, in his 1987 Report, p. 21: "It would seem reasonable in view of our often expressed attitude towards Northern Ireland that a person visiting Northern Ireland should not be regarded as 'absent from the State' for the purposes of social welfare payments."

[75] *Gray* v. *Formosa* [1963] P. 259, 267 (*per* Lord Denning); 1984 Report, p. 13; 1985 Report, p. 46. Note that this rule was held to be unconstitutional (quite independently of its legislative abrogation) by Barr J. in *C.M.* v. *T.M.* [1988] I.L.R.M. 456 on the ground that it infringed Art. 40.1 of the Constitution.

which had occurred in the past. In addition, the Ombudsman has encouraged public bodies to develop and publicise their own internal complaints procedure.[76] It will be noted that, as with the individual cases, many of these changes will be of most benefit to the poorer sections of the community. This is appropriate since other, better-off groups are often better equipped to make their own representations felt by the administrative machine, for example accountants' organisations lobbying the Revenue Commissioners for extra-statutory concessions or farmers' groups negotiating with the Department of Agriculture in regard to grants.

In this second role, the Ombudsman can counter a frequent failure of communication at the interface at which the citizen meets his Government. Thus the Ombudsman has described his duty as "giving the citizen a role in government administration."[77] It may be that the Ombudsman's most significant service will, in the long term, be to stimulate improvements which raise the level of public administration (quicker decisions; more flexibility; better explanations; good manners) and so reduce the amount of clientelism embedded in the Irish political system.

---

[76] 1985 Report, p. 30; 1987 Report, p. 34.
[77] See, *e.g. Senate Debates*, Vol. 94; col. 1593, July 2, 1980. For debates on 1984 Annual Report, see *Dáil Debates*, Vol. 364, cols. 483 *et seq.*, February 26, 1986; *Senate Debates*, Vol. 109, cols. 478 *et seq.* October 17 and November 7, 1985.

CHAPTER 8

FUNDAMENTAL PRINCIPLES OF JUDICIAL REVIEW

1. The Reach of Public Law: Public Bodies and Statutory Functions[1]

The expression public law is best defined simply by comparison with private law. Thus, whilst private law governs relations between private individuals (*e.g.* contract, tort, property law) by contrast, public law comprises rules which govern the relations between the Government and private individuals (though note that private law also applies in appropriate contexts to governments: a point which is developed below). Public law is more or less synonymous with administrative law but is used here in preference to administrative law because a wide, conceptual point is under consideration.

The question examined here—about the type of bodies and activities which fall within the reach of public law—could be asked in relation to all the different areas of law described elsewhere in this book. Thus one could, for instance, focus the query into the questions of which categories of public body: are within the Ombudsman's bailiwick[2]; are subject to the growing law on legitimate expectations[3]; or enjoy the privileges against disclosure, on public policy grounds, of confidential information in evidence before a court.[4] In fact, these comparatively specialised questions are examined within the context of each of the particular rules themselves. In this section, the examination is confined to what are far and away the most comprehensive segments of public law, namely: on the substantive side, the bloc of law known as judicial review of administrative action which is covered in Chapters 8–10 and, more briefly on the procedural side, the question of which bodies and what activities fall within the specialised régime known as an application for judicial review and prescribed by Order 84 of the Rules of the Superior Courts 1986.

Before the reformation in procedure, effected by this Order and described in Chapter 11, the general understanding was that in respect of certain types of entity on the fringe of the "public body" category (*e.g.* trade unions and universities) . . . there were two restrictions on the sweep of public law. In the first place, a litigant could proceed not by way of state-side order (the forerunner of the contemporary application for judicial review application) but only by the less convenient method of plenary proceedings for a declaration or injunction. Secondly, as regards the substantive law to which such border-

---

[1] The topical importance of public law in England has led to a lot of academic writing on the subject. See, *e.g.* Woolf, "Public Law—Private Law: Why the Divide?" [1986] *Public Law* 220; Oliver, "Is the *Ultra Vires* Rule the Basis of Judicial Review?" [1987] *Public Law* 543; Beatson, " 'Public' and 'Private' in English Administrative Law."
[2] See pp. 283–284.
[3] See Chap. 13.
[4] See pp. 729–735.

line candidates were subject, this law indisputably included constitutional jus-tice[5] as well as the body's own rules, charter, etc. In addition, it was com-monly believed that the Constitution with its requirements of non-discrimination, respect for the right to associate, work, etc., probably also applied.[6] If one stops at this point—as the traditional teaching would require[7]—then, so far as substantive law is concerned, trade unions would not be treated any differently from say private companies, which are also subject to constitutional justice, their own rules and the Constitution. In fact, it seems to be an open question whether the law goes further and holds that in the case of a trade union, a discretionary power granted by its own rules would be sub-ject to the principles concerning an abuse of a discretionary power (such as reasonableness, etc.), described in Chapter 10.

This substantive question has not been affected directly by the advent of the new application for judicial review and, as we shall see, later on in the present Part, still remains cloudy. The procedural issue might appear to have been changed, by the fact that a declaration or an injunction is now available by way of judicial review proceedings. Does it flow from this that bodies like trade unions which have always been subject to control by declaration, have thereby been drawn within the jurisdiction of the application for a judicial review? By way of rebuttal of this argument the obviously correct point may be urged that the applicability of a remedy ought not to be determined merely by its title. Yet if one adopts this view and thereby shifts the debate to the level of principle and practicability, then surely it makes sense that the jurisdiction of the judicial review application should be interpreted widely to embrace all bodies which affect the community and are subject to public law. This view would return us to the point which was left in doubt in the last paragraph, namely, whether bodies such as trade unions are subject to substantive public law in its entirety. If so, then the argument for subjecting them to the judicial review procedure is strengthened. But if not—if they are subjected to the restrictions, in the substantive law field, listed in the previous paragraph—then there is more to be said for their exclusion from the judicial review procedure.

The case law on the procedural-jurisdictional issue is more voluminous than that on the question of the demarcation in the substantive field; but still inconclusive. It is surveyed in Chapter 11, on Remedies.[8] We turn now to dis-cuss this demaracation in the substantive field.

There are a number of historical/political developments which have stretched public law from its pristine (and possibly unrealistic) simplicity to the uncertainties and anomalies of today. The first of these is that the scope of

---

[5] This was frequently based on the idea of an implied term that the union would observe a fair procedure being read into the contract between the members [or between the members and the union]? See, *e.g. Doyle* v. *Croke*, High Court, May 6, 1988, p. 17. On *Doyle*, see further, pp. 420–421.
[6] See further, Forde, *Constitutional Law of Ireland*, Chap. XXVI: "Non-Governmental Action."
[7] See Woolf, *op. cit.* 224–225.
[8] See pp. 573–578.

governmental power has increased so much that there are few islands of private right against which it does not, at least potentially, lap. For example private property may be compulsorily acquired and even if it is not, there are restrictions upon what may be done with it. Again, in the dirigiste State, governmental controls—through licensing, compulsory contractual terms, grants—can make such a big impact on activities within the private sector that it is difficult to know where one stops and the other begins.

Secondly, governmental power is articulated by a variety of forms. A utility, for instance, may be operated in the form of a Department of State; a state-sponsored body; or a private company in which the State may have a share-holding. Again, a private company with a monopoly or a trade union with a closed shop may dispose of a reservoir of power greater than many State organs.

It is a useful historical, base-line to note that because of the nature of judicial review most of the actions to which it was traditionally directed, were actions (purportedly) authorised by statute and discharged by bodies constituted by statute. Plainly there are two types of restriction here.[9] In the first place, as regards the body involved, the High Court could only exercise public law powers of control over a body which was grounded upon statute, statutory instrument or prerogative. Secondly, as to function being discharged control could only be exercised when the body was using statutory, as opposed to common law, powers. It remains to enlarge upon each of these two points, considering whether they are still correct.

(i) Which bodies are within the scope of public law: "public bodies"?

It used to be thought that such bodies had to be constituted by statute and have a "public" function. The classification of functions as "public" was, at base, ideological and, even more so, historical, rather than legal. Where the first condition—"constituted by statute"—was satisfied then it almost always happened that so, too, was the public function requirement. What was problematic was the question of non-statutory bodies whose functions were "public." The authority of such bodies might be based on "custom" or the agreement of the parties affected. As we shall see in a moment, less straightforward systems of legal support developed. Where such bodies had a significant effect upon the community, the realistic argument came to be made that public law should "move on from *ultra vires* rule to a concern for the protection of individuals, and for the control of power, rather than *powers*, or *vires*."[10] Two English cases in which this challenge to develop the law was accepted may be considered at this juncture. The first of these is *R. v. Criminal Injuries Compensation Board, ex p. Lain*,[11] where the applicant sought to

---

[9] There is a further point which might be thought to arise at this point, namely the type of legal instrument which is subject to public law discipline. However, this question, which mainly involves the issue of how circulars and kindred legal artefacts should be controlled, has already been considered in Chap. 2 on Sources.

[10] Oliver, *op. cit.* 543.

[11] [1967] 2 Q.B. 864.

quash a decision of the Board on the grounds of error on the face of the record. Although the Board was an extra-statutory tribunal, a Divisional Court of the English Queen's Bench held that it sufficed to bring it within the scope of judicial review that the Board was a body with a public character, set up by executive act to administer moneys voted by Parliament, according to an extra-statutory published scheme, while following a quasi-judicial procedure. It is symptomatic of the activist temper of Irish law and its lack of sympathy with technical doctrine that in the Irish equivalent of *Lain*, which is *The State (Hayes) v. Criminal Injuries Compensation Tribunal*,[12] it was actually conceded that the standard substantive and procedural rules of judicial review applied to the tribunal.

The other English case, *R. v. Panel on Take-overs and Mergers, ex p. Datafin plc*,[13] concerned a self-regulating unincorporated association which devised and operated the City Code on Take-overs, a non-statutory scheme. The Court of Appeal held that certiorari would issue to such a body (though, in the instant case, it exercised its discretion not to make an order). The kernel of the court's reasoning has been well summarised as follows[14]:

> "While the court excluded from judicial review and 'publicness' bodies whose *sole* source of power was a consensual submission, it pointed out that the power of self-regulatory bodies such as the Panel is not exclusively consensual. Rather it is a system whereby a group of people acting in concert use their collective power to force themselves *and others* to comply with a code of conduct of their own devising. But the existence of *de facto* power was insufficient in itself to make the Panel 'public' and amenable to judicial review. What was vital was that (a) the decision that there should be a central but non-statutory regulatory body for takeovers was a *government* decision and, (b) the non-statutory system was buttressed by a periphery of statutory powers and penalties which assume that the Panel is the centrepiece of the regulatory system. The test is thus whether *de facto* power is underpinned by either a government decision to have regulation by a non-statutory body or by statutory support or, as in the *Take-over Panel* case, by both."

Two points bear emphasis. In the first place, it will often happen that even where (as in the case of the Panel on Take-overs) there is an element, real or artificial, of consensus, nevertheless the body's activities will have an effect on those outside the consensus (*e.g.* shareholders, employees, customers). Secondly, it happened that in the two cases just mentioned there was an organisational link between the body and the Government. What is to happen if this link is absent even though the body is performing governmental-type functions (leaving aside the question of how this phrase is to be defined)? An example would be the regulation of a sport. Of bodies like An Bord Luthchleas na hÉireann (the Irish Athletics Board) it has been said, in England,

[12] [1982] I.L.R.M. 210, 211.
[13] [1987] Q.B. 815.
[14] Beatson, *op. cit.* 50–51.

that: "If they did not exist, the government might have to invent them."[15] Does it follow from this that they ought to be regarded as subject to public law?

Sources of power: statutory rather than common law

So far, we have talked about the formal origin of a body. The other question concerns the source of the power which it is exercising. For while public law deals only with public bodies, it is also true that public bodies are sometimes governed by private law, in such fields as property, contract and tort. As has been said: "Like public figures, at least in theory, public bodies are entitled to have a private life."[16] This is certainly a long-established doctrine. It links up with the Diceyan view that, save in exceptional cases when there is some specific reason to justify the contrary, public bodies should be subject to the same law as private individuals. When Dicey enunciated this influential principle, he did so over against his portrayal of the *droit administratif* which, supposedly, set a rather low standard by which to control the Executive. Now, paradoxically, what is happening, in some admittedly exceptional areas, is that the law has developed to such an extent that it now offers a more stringent control over public bodies than over private bodies. One area in which this has occurred is the area of legitimate expectations. Here, within a few years, principles have developed which, to a substantial degree, have superseded the normal rules on the formation of a contract, where it is a public authority which is the defendant.[17] However, outside this significant but limited area, it seems likely that there has been no shift in the traditional principle that, as a matter of strict law (whatever the position if political representations are involved) a public authority is subject to the same law as regards contract, property and (with some few exceptions) tort as any private individual.[18] This was illustrated in the recent case of *O'Neill* v. *Iarnród Éireann*[19] in which the Supreme Court showed a preference for refusing an application for

---

[15] Oliver, *op. cit.* 551. In view of *Law* v. *National Greyhound Racing Club* [1983] 1 W.L.R. 1302, it seems that in England, self-regulatory sports bodies are not subject to an application for judicial review. But it was assumed, without the point being raised, that the respondent was subject to a review application in *Quirke* v. *An Bord Luthchleas na hÉireann* [1988] I.R. 83.

[16] Woolf, *op. cit.* 223.

[17] See Chap. 13.

[18] At this point, we ought to consider a qualification: in Ireland (to a greater extent than in England) almost all public authorities—Ministers, National University of Ireland, etc., probably all local authorities (the doubt concerns non-county boroughs which predated and were only "recognised" by the Municipal Corporations Act 1854) are the creatures of statute rather than prerogative or custom. In some strict sense, therefore, their power, for example, to contract is statutory. For example, the Ministers and Secretaries Act 1924, s.2(1) states that: "Each of the Ministers . . . shall be a corporation sole . . . and may sue and . . . be sued . . . and may acquire, hold and dispose of land. . . . " However it seems unrealistic to argue that every time a civil servant, acting on behalf of a Minister, buys paper-clips, he is thereby exercising a discretionary statutory power and is engaging all the law as to reasonableness, etc. Such a contract would, however, be subject to the restriction of the *ultra vires* rule, in its narrower sense in that the paper-clips would have to be used to forward the Minister's statutory function see p. 59.

[19] [1991] I.L.R.M. 129. See also, *Murtagh* v. *Board of St. Emer's National School*, Supreme Court, March 7, 1991 (where Hederman J. held that most school disciplinary functions fall outside the scope of public law, and, hence the Ord. 84 remedies).

judicial review in respect of a contract of employment. Again in *Page Motors Ltd.* v. *Epsom & Ewell B.C.*,[20] it was held that the issue of whether the occupation of council land by gypsies constituted a nuisance by the Council did not raise questions of public law. The reason was that the duty of the Council arose in its capacity as an occupier of land and the nuisance had not arisen out of the exercise of a statutory power.

There is, of course, a case to be made for saying that, in exceptional circumstances, public authorities should be subject to an exceptionally strict régime such that they should be governed in their common law activities by special principles of public law as well as the ordinary private law. This argument focuses upon the fact that public authorities dispose of huge reservoirs of economic power by way, largely, of making contracts[21] and do so, moreover, in some sense, as a trustee for the community. They should not be free, therefore, to abuse the power which freedom of contract gives in order, for instance, either: to achieve policy objectives which would normally be effected by the exercise of the discretionary powers (a point to which we return below); or to alter the commercial or social ecology for others. An example of the second exception is most likely to arise in monopoly or near-monopoly conditions and the application of this principle in such conditions has been accepted, at any rate on the authority of a powerful *obiter dictum* in *McCord* v. *ESB*.[22] The subject of the *obiter dictum* (in these plenary proceedings seeking damages for breach of contract) was the ESB's standard form contract for the supply of electricity of which Henchy J. stated[23]:

> " . . . judicial self-control requires that I withhold adverse comments on certain terms of the contract, such as that which purports to give contractual force to the idea that notices of intended disconnection may be taken as having been delivered on the weekday following the day they were posted; or on even the final term of the contract by which 'the Board reserves to itself the right to add to, alter or amend any of the foregoing terms and conditions, *as it may think fit.*"

Commenting on this legal artefact, Henchy J. said[24]:

> "[The] contract . . . is what is nowadays called a contract of adhesion: it is a standardised mass contract which must be entered into, on a take it or leave it basis, by the occupier of every premises in which electricity is to be used. The would-be consumer has no standing to ask that a single iota of the draft contract presented to him be changed before he signs it. He must lump it or leave it. But, because for reasons that are too obvious to enumer-

---

[20] (1982) 80 L.G.R. 337; [1983] *Public law* 202.
[21] See pp. 113–116.
[22] [1980] I.L.R.M. 153.
[23] [1980] I.L.R.M. 161.
[24] [1980] I.L.R.M. 161–162.

ate, he cannot do without electricity, he is invariably forced by necessity into signing the contract, regardless of the fact that he may consider some of its terms arbitrary, or oppressive, or demonstrably unfair. He is compelled, from a position of weakness and necessity *vis-à-vis* a monopolist supplier of a vital commodity, to enter into what falls into the classification of a contract and which, as such, according to the theory of the common law which was evolved in the laissez-faire atmosphere of the nineteenth century, is to be treated by the courts as if it had emerged by choice from the forces of the market place, at the behest of parties who were at arm's length and had freedom of choice. The real facts show that such an approach is largely based on legal fictions. When a monopoly supplier of a vital public utility—which is what the Board is—forces on all its consumers a common form of contract, reserving to itself sweeping powers, including the power to vary the document unilaterally as it may think fit, such an instrument has less affinity with a freely negotiated interpersonal contract than with a set of by-laws or with any other form of autonomic legislation. As such, its terms may have to be construed not simply as contractual elements but as components of a piece of delegated legislation, the validity of which will depend on whether it has kept within the express or implied confines of the statutory delegation and, even if it has, whether the delegation granted or assumed is now consistent with the provisions of the Constitution of 1937. However, having regard to my conclusion that the contractual powers of the Board are in the nature of delegated legislation, and because a statute replacing the powers conferred on the Board by the 1927 Act may result from this case, it might not be out of place to refer to what was laid down by this Court in the following passage in its judgment in *Cityview Press Ltd.* v. *An Chomhairle Oiliúna.*"

The judge then went on to quote the well-known passage concerning the impact of Article 15.2.1 of the Constitution upon the type of delegated legislation which is permissible. In addition to this subsection of the Constitution, it seems reasonable to assume (from the tenor of the passage and the words " . . . keep[ing] within the express or implied confines of the statutory delegation") that the normal common law controls which apply to delegated legislation—reasonableness, etc.—would also operate in the present case. Indeed, O'Higgins C.J. stated in *McCord*[25]: " . . . these General Conditions emanating as they do exclusively from the appellant must be construed strictly and must be operated fairly and reasonably."

Let us turn now to the other exceptional area in which it is suggested that public law principles should apply to the making of contracts or the ownership of property, namely where these powers are used to implement some public policy, distinct from the usual commercial objectives which motivate any private person in entering a contract. One possible example which attracted a

---

[25] [1980] I.L.R.M. 155.

deal of political and academic[26] discussion, but, unfortunately, no case law, concerned the British Labour Government's incomes policy during the period 1975–1979. The programme implementing this policy was almost entirely without statutory means of support. It was, however, underpinned by a substantial sanction: for an undertaking to comply with the policy was a prerequisite for the award of almost all Government contracts.

Some indication of at least one Irish judge's attitude to this problem is shown by *Rice* v. *Dublin Corporation*.[27] The facts here were straightforward. A long lease, which included a covenant not to permit the premises on the land to be used for the sale of intoxicating liquor, had been granted by the defendant local authority to the plaintiff-lessees. The defendants' general policy was not to permit the sale of liquor in any premises, such as the present premises, on their new housing estates. Accordingly they had refused their consent to such sale and the plaintiff instituted proceedings for a declaration that the defendants had unreasonably withheld their consent. It is significant, both in the case and in the context of the present discussion, that it was held, by the Supreme Court, that the premises did not come within the public law statute, the Housing of the Working Classes Acts 1890–1921. Accordingly the question of the local authority's consent fell to be considered under section 57(2)(*a*) of the Landlord and Tenant Act 1931 which would apply equally to private or public landlords so that this might have been regarded as a private law case. This provision of the 1931 Act states that a landlord's consent is not to be "unreasonably withheld." The case was remitted to the High Court for the reasonableness of the defendants' consent to be assessed. The central passage, for present purposes, in Davitt J.'s judgment is as follows[28]:

> "The Corporation is responsible for the housing of a very large section of the population of Dublin and is likely to continue to be so responsible for many years to come . . . Very many people have no . . . real alternative to becoming tenants to the Corporation on one or other of its existing or contemplated housing estates. If the Corporation is successful in these appeals, and continues the policy of refusing to allow any licensed premises on its housing estates, it can effectively render large portions of the city "dry" areas. I am not here concerned with the question whether such a policy is or is not perfectly legitimate and commendable. I am concerned, I am afraid, with the question whether it is reasonable for the Corporation to carry out that policy in the way in which it is sought to be carried out in these cases. The Corporation has been placed in the position of being the owner of large estates, housing tens of thousands of people, through the expenditure of

---

[26] See Daintith, "Regulation by Contract: the New Prerogative" (1979) 32 C.L.P. 41; Ganz [1978] *Public Law* 333. For a case verging on this area, see *Wheeler* v. *Leicester City Council* [1985] 1 A.C. 1054 in which a local authority banned a rugby club from using local authority land as a pitch because members of the club were going to play rugby in South Africa. However, note that, in this case, the rugby pitch was held and administered under a statute (the Open Spaces' Act 1906) so that, as it happened, this did not involve the exercise of common law powers of land ownership.
[27] [1947] I.R. 425.
[28] [1947] I.R. 455–456.

large sums of money contributed by the public. Is it reasonable that they should use that position to deprive a large section of the city's population of the convenient exercise of legal right to purchase a certain commodity? If it is to be sought to make considerable areas of the city "dry" areas, compulsorily, and quite possibly against the wishes of many, if not the majority, of the inhabitants, should not this be done by means of appropriate legislation? If the liberties of citizens are to be interfered with, . . . is it not improper that this should be effected, . . . through the exercise by the Corporation of powers which, so far as such matters are concerned, it happens to possess quite fortuitously? It has been entrusted with such powers by the citizens for no such purpose. The policy which the Corporation is seeking to enforce may be a perfectly sound, proper, and reasonable one. It is a truism that a policy which is, in itself, sound may yet be enforced by improper means. In enforcing its policy in the way in which it seeks to enforce it in these particular instances the Corporation are in my opinion acting arbitrarily and unreasonably. I think the Corporation has unreasonably refused its consent in these cases."

Considering that this case was decided well before the Renaissance era of Irish public law, the issue presently under discussion emerges tolerably well from this passage. It seems plain that specially stringent standards, which would not be applied to a private landlord, are being invoked because the landowner is a public authority. This is justified on the basis that a public authority should not be allowed to use the power given by its ownership of the vast resources of public property, in monopoly conditions in regard to low-cost housing, to enforce a policy. The line of thought in *Rice*, indeed, goes beyond that which has been suggested in certain modern authorities in that it holds that the power of public authority leasing or contracting may not be used to pursue any policy whatsoever; and not merely that such powers should be subject to the same forms of control as are discretionary statutory powers. It is suggested that this difference may arise simply from the fact that *Rice* was decided in an era before the nature and control of even discretionary powers had been much considered by the courts. (This may be inferred from the fact that the contrast drawn in the latter part of the quotation is with legislation rather than discretionary powers). The essential point is that the court is applying a control which would not be enforced against a private landlord.

We have been pursuing the argument that the law has reached the stage of development in which there are, in certain specific situations, exceptions to the traditional general principle that a public authority is to be treated in the same way as a private body in the exercise of its common law powers. The remaining question, of course, is whether, exceptions apart, the general principle itself remains still standing. Recent Irish authority on this point is hard to find, possibly because it may be regarded as axiomatic. However, it is submitted here—briefly, since there appears to be no controversy about the matter—that, as a matter of policy, the principle ought to be retained. Consider the alternative. In the first place, it would introduce uncertainty into a fairly settled area if, as features of some new public law of contract (perhaps derived from the notion of mala fides) public authorities were made subject— to take a few hypothetical examples—to a particularly stringent doctrine of undue influence or remoteness of damage; or a duty of full disclosure (analagous to that which presently exists in regard to contracts *uberrimae fidei*). Secondly, such changes would be unfair to public authorities. For, while it is one thing to say, as Dicey did, that public authorities should not be above the law; it is another to state that public authorities should be at a disadvantage. For in a constitutional democracy, public authorities should be—and to a substantial degree, are—merely embodiments of community interests. To disadvantage public authorities is to give an advantage to those members of the community who do business with public authorities (or, in rare cases who compete with state-sponsored bodies) at the expense of other members of the community. There is no reason to suppose that this rather random change will be an improvement.

2. The Doctrine of Ultra Vires

Judicial review of administrative action is founded on the doctrine of *ultra vires*. Although the High Court possesses an inherent jurisdiction to supervise the activities of inferior courts,[29] tribunals and other public authorities, it is a cardinal principle (which is considered below) that this power of review may only be exercised in circumstances where the inferior body has exceeded its jurisdiction. The High Court, when exercising its powers of judicial review, is not concerned with the *merits*, but rather with the *legality* of the decision under review. In short, a finding of *ultra vires* is a prerequisite to judicial intervention by means of judicial review. To this there is one recognised exception: the court may quash a decision, otherwise within jurisdiction, which is flawed by the presence of an error "on the face of the record," *i.e.* where an error of law is patent.[30] The power to quash for error of law on the record is an historical anomaly which is now probably too well established to be disregarded. Where a decision exhibited a patent error of law, this irregularity is regarded "as an affront to the law which cannot be overlooked" and more "than judicial flesh and blood could resist."[31]

A decision which is vitiated by jurisdictional error is void, and will, save in exceptional cases, be declared to be void *ab initio* in the appropriate proceedings. Nevertheless such a decision—unless flagrantly illegal—remains valid

---

[29] The inferior courts are the District Court, the Circuit Court and the Special Criminal Court. The High Court, Court of Criminal Appeal and the Supreme Court are all superior courts of record and are not subject to judicial review: see *People (D.P.P.) v. Quilligan (No. 2)* [1989] I.R. 46, 57, *per* Henchy J.

[30] See pp. 354–358.

[31] Wade, *Administrative Law* (Oxford, 1988), pp. 303, 304. Professor Wade's account of the historical development of error on the face of the record (pp. 303–308) is excellent.

for all purposes unless and until it is set aside by the courts.[32] The public law remedies are discretionary in nature, and a quashing order will only be granted to a proper plaintiff with the requisite *locus standi* who can persuade the court to exercise its discretion in his favour.

No comprehensive account can be given of what errors will destroy the jurisdiction of a lower court or tribunal, thus rendering its decisions liable to be quashed. It is clear that an error committed in the course of an adjudication may go to jurisdiction,[33] but that said, the leading authorities do not disclose a governing principle which facilitates the classification of errors as "jurisdictional" as opposed to those which are merely errors committed within jurisdiction and which—unless they appear on the face of the record—stand immune from correction upon an application for judicial review. In truth, the common law doctrine of *ultra vires* is based on the artifice of statutory interpretation. The courts presume that Parliament did not intend that the donee of a statutory power should exercise that power in an unfair or arbitrary fashion. Thus the courts will intervene not only to restrain administrative action which contravenes some express statutory provision, but also where some implied condition of the Act—adherence to the rules of constitutional justice, or the doctrine of reasonableness—has been infringed. The common law principles of judicial review of administrative action are based upon this edifice of parliamentary intent and statutory interpretation.

In recent times, Irish courts have elevated these common law doctrines onto the constitutional plane. Legislation authorising administrative action which was arbitrary, unfair, or contrary to principles of fair procedures would plainly be unconstitutional.[34] The presumption of constitutionality requires that a constitutional interpretation be given to the impugned statutory provisions if this is at all possible. The presumption extends to proceedings, procedures, discretions and adjudications which are permitted, provided for or prescribed by an Act of the Oireachtas and, it means that, in these contexts, a statutory provision is entitled to the presumption:

> "That what is required, is allowed to be done, for the purpose of its implementation, will take place without breaching any of the requirements, express or implied of the Constitution. . . . If [the donee of the statutory power] exercised his discretion or his powers capriciously, partially or in a manifestly unfair manner it would be assumed that this could not have been contemplated or intended by the Oireachtas and his action would be restrained and corrected by the Courts."[35]

[32] *The State (Llewellyn)* v. *UaDonnachada* [1973] I.R. 151; *Campus Oil* v. *Minister for Industry and Energy* [1983] I.R. 88; *The State (Abenglen Properties Ltd.)* v. *Dublin Corporation* [1984] I.R. 381; *Hoffman-La Roche* v. *Trade Secretary* [1975] A.C. 295 and *C.W. Shipping Co. Ltd.* v. *Limerick Harbour Commrs.* [1989] I.L.R.M. 416. But *cf.* the comments of Lord Denning in *R.* v. *Paddington Valuation Officer, ex p. Peachy Properties Ltd.* [1966] 1 Q.B. 380, those of Lord Diplock in *Dunlop* v. *Woolahra M.C.* [1982] A.C. 158 and Walsh J. in *Mahon* v. *Shelley* [1990] 1 I.R. 36, 41. On this difficult subject, see pp. 378–388.
[33] *The State (Holland)* v. *Kennedy* [1977] I.R. 193.
[34] See, *e.g. Loftus* v. *Att.-Gen.* [1979] I.R. 221; *O'Brien* v. *Bord na Móna* [1983] I.R. 265.
[35] *Loftus* v. *Att.-Gen.* [1979] I.R. 221, 238, 241, *per* O'Higgins C.J.

The courts have used this principle to hold that the exercise of administrative discretion in an improper fashion,[36] or in a manner contrary to constitutional justice[37] is *ultra vires* the principal Act, while at the same time upholding the constitutionality of the parent legislation.

The modern tendency has been to increase the range of errors which affect the jurisdiction of administrative bodies and lower courts, almost to the point where all errors of law are assumed to destroy that jurisdiction. But this tendency—which is doubtless prompted by a judicial desire to protect the citizen against legally unjustifiable administrative actions—is often at odds with the legislative policy of allocating tasks to a specialised public body.[38] In view of this tension, and given the inherent difficulty in distinguishing satisfactorily between matters bearing on the merits and those relating to *vires* (or jurisdiction), the entire doctrine of jurisdictional review has become increasingly artificial and complex. It may be useful, therefore, to separate out by way of introduction the seven heads of judicial review. Four of these heads—(a), (d), (e) and (f)—will be examined in some detail later in this Part. The other three heads will only be mentioned in this Part since two of them—(b) and (c)—will be dealt with more extensively elsewhere in this book and the third—(e)—falls more properly into the field of constitutional law. (There is one other ground of judicial review—error on the face of the record—which is not dealt with here because it is not based on jurisdiction or *ultra vires*: see Part 4.)

(a) Correct authority. The power may only be exercised by the administrative authority in whom it was vested by the Oireachtas. One aspect of this is the *delegatus non potest delegare* principle: a power may only be delegated to a body or person other than that designated by the Oireachtas if this is authorised, expressly or by implication, by the legislation in question. Another aspect is that the authority must be properly appointed, properly constituted and, where relevant, properly qualified.[39] *Thompson* v. *Minister for Social Welfare*[40] provides a good recent example of this principle. Here O'Hanlon J. quashed a decision of a social welfare appeals officer, as that officer had not sat with the two assessors required by section 298(12) of the Social Welfare Act 1981 and the appellant had not consented to this course of action.

(b) Discretionary powers. The courts assume (unless the contrary is clearly established) that the Oireachtas did not intend to confer a discretionary power on public authorities which would enable them to act in an unreason-

---

[36] *Irish Family Planning Assoc. Ltd.* v. *Ryan* [1979] I.R. 295.
[37] *O'Brien* v. *Bord na Móna* [1983] I.R. 255.
[38] *R.* v. *Preston Supplementary Benefits Appeal Tribunal, ex p. Shine* [1975] 1 W.L.R. 624; *R.* v. *National Insurance Commissioner, ex p. Stratton* [1979] Q.B. 361. There are traces of this attitude in *Irish Permanent Building Society* v. *Caldwell* [1981] I.L.R.M. 242; *The State (Casey)* v. *Labour Court* (1984) 3 J.I.S.L.L. 135 and in the judgment of Henchy J. in *The State (Abenglen Properties Ltd.)* v. *Dublin Corporation* [1984] I.R. 381.
[39] *The State (Walshe)* v. *Murphy* [1981] I.R. 275; *Shelley* v. *Mahon* [1990] 1 I.R. 36 (convictions imposed by improperly qualified District Justices quashed). As far as the *delegatus* rule is concerned, see pp. 396–400.
[40] [1989] I.R. 618.

able or arbitrary fashion.[41] Consequently discretionary powers must be exercised reasonably and bona fide, relevant considerations taken into account and irrelevant considerations ignored. These matters are considered elsewhere.[42]

(c) Constitutional justice: see Chapter 9.

(d) Other formal and procedural requirements. Where an administrative authority violates the principles of natural justice or constitutional justice, its decisions will generally be quashed on an application of an aggrieved party. The position in the case of disregard of other procedural and formal requirements is not as clear-cut. In some cases procedural requirements have been found to be directory only, breach of which will not lead to the nullification of the administrative or judicial decision under challenge. These matters are considered elsewhere.[43]

(e) Unconstitutionality. Any administrative authority which acts in an unconstitutional fashion will thereby exceed jurisdiction.[44]

(f) Conditions precedent to jurisdiction. An administrative authority can only exercise its powers over subject-matter which falls within the description, as to facts and circumstances, specified in the authority's field of competence. In other words, some errors of fact made by an administrative authority can effect its jurisdiction, where that jurisdiction depends upon a condition whose existence must be established before the authority has power to act.

In *The State (Ferris)* v. *Employment Appeals Tribunal*[45] the respondent body declined to rule on the merits of an unfair dismissal case. The tribunal had erroneously concluded that wrongful dismissal proceedings arising out of the case were pending in the High Court, and that, as a result, it was precluded by section 15(3) of the Unfair Dismissals Act 1977 from ruling on the case. The tribunal's decision was quashed by the Supreme Court, for, as Henchy J. pointed out, the initiation of "a claim [for wrongful dismissal] as an objective fact must be proved before the Tribunal can exercise the jurisdiction given to it by section 15(3)." Since, in point of fact, no such common law claim for damages had been initiated, that order was invalid as being in excess of jurisdiction.

---

[41] *East Donegal Co-operatives Ltd.* v. *Att.-Gen.* [1970] I.R. 317; *Loftus* v. *Att.-Gen.* [1979] I.R. 221.
[42] See Chap. 10.
[43] See pp. 361–371.
[44] See the comments of Henchy J. in *The State (Holland)* v. *Kennedy* [1977] I.R. 193, 201 and *The State (Byrne)* v. *Frawley* [1978] I.R. 326, 345 and those of Walsh J. in *Shelley* v. *Mahon* [1990] 1 I.R. 36, 45. This appears to be such a self-evident proposition that there do not appear to be any cases where an argument to the contrary was even advanced, much less accepted.
[45] (1985) 4 J.I.S.S.L. 100. See also, *M.* v. *An Bord Uchtála* [1977] I.R. 287, where the existence of a valid consent to adoption by the natural mother was held by the Supreme Court to be a condition precedent to jurisdiction of the Board to make a valid adoption order.

Kennedy v. *Hearne*[46] is another recent example of a case in which certain facts were treated as jurisdictional. Here, through an administrative error, the Revenue Commissioners caused an enforcement notice in respect of unpaid income tax to be sent to the sheriff under section 485 of the Income Tax Act 1967. The Supreme Court held that such a notice was invalid, as the powers contained in that section could only be validly activated upon condition that there was an actual default in the payment of a levied tax. As Finlay C.J. explained:

> "The section must be construed as vesting in the Revenue Commissioners the power to issue a notice to the sheriff only in cases where an actual default of a levied tax has occurred. Where, as happened in this case, they issued such a notice where that default had not continued up to the time that the notice was issued, what they did was a nullity."[47]

It is easy to understand why the Supreme Court should hold that an actual default in the payment of tax was a condition precedent to the operation of a section with such potentially far-reaching consequences. In general, however, the difficulty is that there is no *a priori* method whereby the critical question of whether certain facts should be treated as jurisdictional may be determined. It is sometimes said that the facts necessary to give jurisdiction must be preliminary to, or collateral to, the merits of, the issue.[48] But even this formula gives rise to its own difficulties, as is well illustrated by a series of conflicting Irish decisions in licensing matters.[49]

In the first of these cases, *The State (Att.-Gen.)* v. *Durcan*,[50] the question arose as to whether a statutory provision stipulating that a licence for the sale of intoxicating liquors on premises could only be granted where these premises had been licensed for a five-year period. Davitt P. acknowledged the governing principle:

> "Where the legislature clearly provides that a Court is to have a limited jurisdiction dependent upon the existence of a certain state of affairs, the Court, before purporting to exercise its jurisdiction, will inquire and decide whether the requisite state of affairs does exist . . . If . . . the requisite state of affairs does not exist in fact, then what the Court does in purported exercise of its jurisdiction is done . . . in excess of jurisdiction."[51]

Nevertheless, Davitt P. concluded that the five-year licensing requirement was not a condition precedent to jurisdiction, since section 24 of the Courts

---

[46] [1988] I.R. 481.
[47] *Ibid.* 491.
[48] *R.* v. *Fulham Rent Tribunal, ex p. Zerek* [1951] 2 K.B. 1, 6, *per* Lord Goddard; *Re Doherty's Application* [1988] 1 N.I.J.B. 8, 29, *per* Kelly L.J.
[49] See also, the series of the "orchard" cases which plagued the Irish courts in the early part of this century culminating in *R. (Greenaway)* v. *Armagh JJ.* [1924] 2 I.R. 55.
[50] [1964] I.R. 279.
[51] *Ibid.* 289.

(Supplemental Provisions) Act 1961 conferred the Circuit Court with a full, unqualified jurisdiction in licensing matters and this must necessarily include:

> "Jurisdiction to determine all questions which have to be determined in deciding whether an application for a certificate leading to a new on-licence should or should not be granted. It seems to me that the prohibition contained in section 2(1) of the Licensing (Ireland) Act 1902 cannot deprive the Circuit Court of jurisdiction conclusively to determine . . . whether the premises in question were or were not licensed within the requisite five-year period."[52]

While Davitt P. held , correctly, it is suggested that the question was really one of statutory interpretation, combined with the essential legal policy of ensuring that inferior tribunals and courts do not usurp jurisdiction, yet it might be thought that the result arrived at was incorrect. Section 24 of the 1961 Act scarcely does more than declare the amplitude of the Circuit Court's jurisdiction and the Oireachtas cannot have intended that the Circuit Court would thereby be free to ignore the substantive constraints of the Licensing Acts. This reasoning was nonetheless followed by Finlay P. in *Re Riordan*[53] where he refused to quash a decision of the District Court granting a renewal of a publican's licence which had, unbeknown to the District Justice in question, actually been previously forfeited by operation of law. Finlay P. appears to have been influenced by the unfairness which an award of certiorari would have caused to the applicant in concluding that the existence of a subsisting publican's licence was not a condition precedent to the jurisdiction of the District Court to award a renewal of that licence.[54]

In contrast, the Northern Irish Court of Appeal took a different view in *Re Doherty's Application*.[55] In this case the relevant licensing legislation imposed a number of requirements where it was sought to obtain a renewal of a publican's licence. Chief among these was a requirement that licensed business be conducted on the premises in question and, secondly, that the premises be the same as those to which the original licence was granted. It was common case that, through inadvertence, these statutory requirements had not been complied with by the Resident Magistrate in granting the renewal of the licence. The issue was whether these errors affected his jurisdiction. Kelly L.J. answered this question in the affirmative, saying that compliance with these statutory requirements was a precondition to jurisdiction. The "main

---

[52] *Ibid.* 290.
[53] [1981] I.L.R.M. 2. See also, to the same effect *The State (Reddy)* v. *Johnston*, High Court, July 31, 1980.
[54] The error in question had occurred in 1973 and was not detected until some seven years later when the applicant (the wife of the original licence holder who had subsequently died) applied for a renewal of the licence. But the better way to deal with this problem would surely have been for the court to pronounce the error to have been *ultra vires*, but to refuse on discretionary grounds (delay, hardship, etc.) to quash the original District Court order granting a renewal of the licence.
[55] [1988] 1 N.I.J.B. 8.

question" which the magistrate was required to decide was whether the licence should be renewed, but the collateral questions were:

> "Whether the premises were the same as those originally licensed, [whether there] was a valid licence in existence and [whether] an on/off licensed business [had] been carried on during the previous twelve months. These collateral questions constitute the certain state of affairs which has to exist before a tribunal has jurisdiction."[56]

Kelly L.J.'s reasoning seems more persuasive than that of either Davitt P. or Finlay P. respectively, as otherwise the lower courts could, through legal error, grant licences in the face of the substantive restrictions on the exercise of that jurisdiction by the Licensing Acts. In view of the absence of any satisfactory method of determining what facts are collateral to jurisdiction, this divergence of judicial opinion indicates that this principle is a flexible doctrine which can be invoked to control, where necessary, an abuse or excess of power. However, the significance of this principle is declining in view of the modern tendency (described elsewhere[57]) to treat all major errors of law as destroying jurisdiction.

(g) Within the power conferred by statute. The administrative decision must fall within the substantive power conferred—whether expressly or by implication—by the statute.

There are numerous instances where an express statutory restriction has been violated by the administrative body in question and, save in cases where the requirement has been found to be merely directory,[58] the decision will invariably be set aside in such circumstances. Most of the cases in this area turn on questions of particular statutory interpretation. Nevertheless three modern examples may be cited for the purpose of illustration.

In *Meade* v. *Cork County Council*[59] the Minister for Local Government made an order pursuant to section 98(5) of the Housing Act 1966 approving the sale of the applicant's cottage subject to payment of an amount to the respondents in redemption of an annuity under the 1966 Act. In fact, this subsection did not authorise the repayment of an annuity and Griffin J. held that in purporting to make such a condition, the Minister had failed to comply with the express requirements of the 1966 Act. Another clear example is provided by *Reidy* v. *Minister for Agriculture and Food*[60] where, as a disciplinary measure, the applicant civil servant was not allowed to compete in competition for any civil service post for a two-year period. O'Hanlon J. set aside this decision, saying that there was no authority in either the Civil Service Regulation Acts 1956–1958, or the regulations made thereunder, for a disciplinary penalty of this kind. The final example is supplied by the judgment of

[56] *Ibid.* 29.
[57] See pp. 345–354.
[58] See pp. 361–371.
[59] Supreme Court, July 31, 1974.
[60] High Court, June 9, 1989.

Lardner J. in *Devitt* v. *Minister for Education*.[61] Section 23(2) of the Vocational Education Act 1930 requires the Minister to approve of any appointment submitted to her by a vocational education committee. Here a committee submitted the applicant's name for approval to a whole-time *permanent* post, but the Minister instead approved her appointment to a whole-time *temporary* post. Lardner J. quashed this decision, since the Act merely enabled the Minister to approve or disapprove of the appointment submitted to her: it did not enable her to approve the appointment of a candidate to a different type of post.

Incidental powers

However, in many of the reported cases, the real issue is whether the impugned administrative action is reasonably incidental to the express power and thus falls within the implied powers conferred by statute. The general rule remains that stated by Lord Selborne in *Att.-Gen.* v. *Great Eastern Ry. Co.*[62]:

"Whatever may fairly be regarded as incidental to or consequential upon, those things which the legislature has authorised, ought not (unless expressly prohibited) to be held by judicial construction, to be ultra vires."[63]

Thus, in *Dublin Corporation* v. *Raso*[64] it was held that the local authority were entitled to impose restrictions on the opening hours of a "fish and chips" shop under its powers under the Planning Acts because conditions restricting the amount of noise and preserving the residential character of the neighbourhood were reasonably incidental to the authority's powers to impose conditions for the "proper planning and development" of the area in question. Another example is provided by *Minister for Transport and Power* v. *Trans World Airlines Inc.*,[65] where the question arose as to whether the Minister was entitled to prescribe landing charges for Shannon Airport. In the High Court, O'Keefe P. found against the Minister on the ground that while the Air Navigation and Transport Act 1936 gave the Minister power to establish and operate an airport, it did not expressly authorise him to prescribe charges of this kind. The Supreme Court took a different view, with Walsh J. holding that the power to prescribe fees was impliedly authorised by the 1936 Act:

"I agree that the Minister is not essentially a trading corporation, but when a statutory provision expressly gives him a right to establish and maintain an airport . . . this power carries with it the inherent right to determine the

---

[61] [1989] I.L.R.M. 696.
[62] (1880) 5 App.Cas. 31, 473.
[63] *Ibid*. 478.
[64] [1976–1977] I.L.R.M. 139.
[65] Supreme Court, March 6, 1974.

conditions under which the aircraft will be permitted to use the airport and that would include the charges which may be made for the same."[66]

In other cases, the "reasonably incidental" principle is supplemented by the principle of effectiveness: *ut res magis valeat, quam pereat.* Thus, the courts will seek to avoid a construction of a statute which renders it ineffectual. This principle was applied in *McGlinchey* v. *Governor of Portlaoise Prison*[67] in order to uphold the validity of the Government order establishing the Special Criminal Court. Part V of the Offences against the State Act 1939 contains detailed requirements prescribing the composition, jurisdiction and procedure of the Special Criminal Court but it does not actually specify by whom the members of the court are to be appointed. While Lynch J. acknowledged that the relevant statutory provisions could have been more "felicitously drafted," he invoked the principle of effectiveness in order to uphold the validity of the order:

> "I have no doubt at all . . . but that a necessary inference arises that the Government is given power to establish the first Special Criminal Court following the making of the [Government's] proclamation, having regard to the mandatory terms of section 38(1) [of the 1939 Act] that such court should be established . . . ."[68]

It will be seen, therefore, that the *ultra vires* principle is not applied with unnecessary strictness and the courts will only intervene where the administrative action cannot fairly be said to be reasonably incidental to the statutory provisions.

However, pulling in the opposite direction to the "reasonably incidental" principle are certain specialised rules of statutory interpretation such as the presumption against unnecessary interference with common law or other vested rights; the strict construction of penal statutes and the need for express language in the case of taxing or revenue-raising statutes. These rules are in part but specialised examples of a more general principle of statutory interpretation: the presumption against unclear changes in the law. However, it will be convenient if the case law is considered under these separate headings.

Presumption against interference with common law or vested rights

The presumption that the Oireachtas does not intend to interfere with common law or other vested rights means that clear statutory language is called for where it is sought to interfere with such rights. This presumption is often

---

[66] *Ibid.* p. 11 of the judgment of Walsh J. But for cases on the other side of the line, see, *e.g. Waterford Corporation* v. *Murphy* [1920] 2 I.R. 165; *Irish Benefit Building Society* v. *Registrar of Friendly Societies* [1981] I.L.R.M. 73 (registrar given statutory power to ensure the "orderly and proper regulation of building society business"; held, this power relates only to matters of honesty, legality, administration and propriety and does not cover matters of business judgment such as the interest rate paid to shareholders); *McMeel* v. *Minister for Health* [1985] I.L.R.M. 616 (ministerial power to give directions concerning "arrangements for providing services" in hospitals contemplates positive action and not the discontinuance of hospital services).
[67] [1988] I.R. 671.
[68] *Ibid.* 681.

applicable in the case of regulatory or licensing statutes. Thus, in *Limerick Corporation* v. *Sheridan*[69] Davitt P. set aside an order of the local authority made under the Local Government (Sanitary Services) Act 1948 which had the effect of prohibiting the preserve of all temporary dwellings within their functional area. This order involved "such gratuitous interference with the common law rights of those affected" that it could not be justified by the mere general words of the 1948 Act and, in the absence of such clear statutory language, the order was condemned as *ultra vires*. Another example is provided by *C.W. Shipping Ltd.* v. *Limerick Harbour Commissioners*,[70] where the respondents sought to prevent the applicant tug owner from operating in the Shannon estuary without a licence. Section 53 of the Harbours Act 1946 gave the respondents licensing powers in respect of "lighters, ferry-boats or other small boats." O'Hanlon J. held tugs were not of the same genus as lighters or ferry-boats, so that the licensing requirements did not apply in the applicant's case. He further observed that the 1946 Act must be strictly construed bearing in mind the fact that the "ordinary common law rights to use the waters of the harbour as a highway . . . are being curtailed."[71]

Presumption against unnecessary interference with property rights

A particularly strong case of the presumption against interference with vested rights is the case of interference with property or other proprietary rights. This traditional common law presumption was placed in a constitutional perspective by Budd J. in *Dunraven Estates Ltd.* v. *Commissioners of Public Works*,[72] where speaking in the context of the validity of an arterial drainage scheme under the Arterial Drainage Act 1945 which the Commissioners proposed to carry out on the plaintiff's lands, he said:

"In the course of elucidating the interpretation of these sections, one has to bear in mind the constitutional position of the plaintiffs with regard to their lands, fisheries and other proprietary rights . . . There can be little doubt that an Act such as this, aimed at the improvement of large areas of land, is one for the benefit of the community, but the delimitation of property rights which is constitutionally permissible must be made with regard, as far as possible, to the property rights of citizens. The relevant articles of the Constitution do not, to take an extreme example, entitle the State to despoil a person of his property by taking a great deal more of it than is necessary for purposes connected with the common good . . . The Act of 1945 should be construed on the basis that it was not the intention of the legislature to deprive the plaintiffs of their property or interfere with it save and in so far as that was necessary for the common good and was in accordance with the Constitution."[73]

---

[69] (1956) 90 I.L.T.R. 59.
[70] [1989] I.L.R.M. 416.
[71] *Ibid.* 426.
[72] [1974] I.R. 113.
[73] *Ibid.* 132.

In the light of this rule of construction, Budd J. went to hold that section 6 of the Act (which required the Commissioners to provide the owner of the lands with full details of the proposed works so that he could make observations on these proposals) was mandatory and must be fully complied with as:

> "An owner must be in a position to know precisely what is proposed to be done to his property, be it land or fisheries or any other proprietary rights, and what precise interference is intended before he is in a position to make observations of any worth."[74]

Since the Commissioners had not provided sufficient details of their proposals, the impugned decision was held to be *ultra vires*.

This principle of strict construction was also applied by the Supreme Court in *Hussey* v. *Irish Land Commission*,[75] where the Commission was held to have acted *ultra vires* in acquiring land which was not required for immediate resale. The Land Acts authorised the Commission to acquire lands for the purposes of resale and it was argued that this empowered the Commission to create a stockpile of acquired lands, from which resales might take place from time to time. Henchy J. rejected this argument, saying that compulsory purchase legislation must be strictly construed. In the absence of express statutory language, the Commission's power of compulsory acquisition could not be construed as authorising them to build up a land bank.[76]

The context and background to the legislation is often relevant and these factors, together with the presumption, will often help to determine the exact scope of the regulatory legislation. An example of this is afforded by *U.S. Tobacco International Ltd.* v. *Minister for Health*,[77] where the Minister had declared certain forms of tobacco products to be restricted articles for the purposes of section 66 of the Health Act 1947. This section enabled the Minister to restrict the sale of "substances" involving the "risk of serious injury to health or body." This section might, at first sight, be thought to justify the restriction in question. However, Hamilton P. first drew attention to the fact that section 66 was contained in Part VI of the Act, which was stated to deal with "provisions in relation to medical and toilet preparations and certain other articles." Furthermore, section 66(3) allowed the Minister to grant a licence to a registered medical practitioner to deal in such restricted products. Hamilton P. considered that as the object of Part VI was to allow the Minister to restrict the sale and distribution of medicinal, toilet and other similar preparations which, if unrestricted and not under the control of a medical practitioner might cause injury to members of the public, the Minister could not

---

[74] *Ibid*. 134.
[75] Supreme Court, December 13, 1984.
[76] For a similar approach, see *Meaney* v. *Cashel U.D.C.* [1937] I.R. 56; *Hendron* v. *Dublin Corporation* [1943] I.R. 566.
[77] [1990] 1 I.R. 394.

rely on the section to restrict the sale of substances which were not of the same genus as medicinal and toilet preparations. The Minister could not rely on the general words of section 66 to restrict the sale of such tobacco products, as clear statutory authorisation for such a banning order would be required.

The need for express language in the case of taxing or revenue-raising statutes

One of the more entrenched presumptions of the common law is that taxes or charges may not be levied by the State or public authorities in the absence of express words, for as Atkin L.J. explained in *Att.-Gen.* v. *Wilts United Dairies Ltd.*[78]:

"The circumstances would be remarkable indeed which would induce the courts to believe that the Legislature had sacrificed all the well-known checks and precautions, and, not in express words, but merely by implication, has entrusted a Minister with undefined and limited powers of imposing charges upon the subject for purposes connected with his department."[79]

In this jurisdiction, this presumption is probably given express constitutional underpinning by the money Bill provisions of Articles 21 and 22, which ensure that general taxation or charges may not be levied save by means of an Act of the Oireachtas. The effect of this presumption is that even statutes authorising local taxation or charges must be couched in express language. A good example of the use of express language is section 26(2)(*h*) of the Local Government (Planning and Development) Act 1963 which provides expressly that planning authorities may impose the following conditions upon a grant of planning permission:

"Conditions for requiring contribution (either in one sum or by instalments) towards any expenditure (including expenditure on the acquisition of land) that is proposed to be incurred by any local authority in respect of works (including the provision of open spaces) facilitating the proposed developments [subject to stipulations providing for repayment in the event that the works in question are not completed within a specified period]."

The need for strict compliance with these statutory requirements is illustrated by *Bord na Móna* v. *An Bord Pleanála*,[80] where the plaintiffs had been granted planning permission for a factory subject to a condition that they should pay a contribution towards the cost of the reconstruction of certain roads. This contribution was to be paid immediately over a three-year period but there was no period specified in the condition within which the works

---

[78] (1922) 37 T.L.R. 884 (affirmed by the House of Lords (1922) 91 L.J.K.B. 897). But see now *R.* v. *Richmond upon Thames L.B.C.* ex p. *McCarthy and Stone* (Development) Ltd. [1990] 2 W.L.R. 1294.
[79] *Ibid.* See also, *Liverpool Corpn.* v. *Maiden (Arthur) Ltd.* [1938] 4 All E.R. 200.
[80] [1985] I.R. 205.

were to be carried out. Keane J. held these conditions to be *ultra vires* on two grounds. First, they frustrated the statutory right of the grantee of the permission, which was to wait for five years before implementing the permission. Secondly, the authority had not complied exactly with the terms of section 26(2)(*h*) of the 1963 Act, since they had not specified a time by which the works were to be completed. This was a significant omission, since:

> "It clearly would not be open to a planning authority to impose a condition requiring a contribution towards the cost of works which would facilitate a development, but expressly excluding any right on the part of the applicant to a refund of contributions in the event of the works not being done."[81]

But, in response to a third argument, Keane J. refused to condemn the condition on the ground that the proposed contribution would amount to the total cost of the relevant works, saying that this of itself was not objectionable. In view of the fact that a revenue-raising provision such as section 26 must be strictly construed, this conclusion seems questionable. The word "contribution" implies financial assistance towards the cost of local authority works, but would not seem to encompass payment of the full cost of these works.

The operation of this presumption can also be seen in the context of the cases arising under the Local Government (Financial Provisions) (No. 2) Act 1983, which authorises local authorities to charge for certain services provided by them. This legislation has been strictly construed by the courts and service charges have been held invalid where there is no clear statutory authorisation for the charge in question.[82] These cases are considered elsewhere.[83]

Strict construction of penal statutes

At common law there is a particularly strong presumption in favour of a statutory construction which protects individual liberty. This common law presumption must now, of course, be read in the light of constitutional provisions protecting such fundamental rights and which elevate the status of such rights to a somewhat higher legal plane. A modern restatement of this presumption (in which the notion of constitutionally-protected personal rights appears to be implicit) is to be found in the judgment of Henchy J. in *Director of Public Prosecutions* v. *Gaffney*[84] where, speaking in the context of a statutory power of arrest, he said:

> "The right to arrest without a warrant given by section 49(6) of the Road

---

[81] *Ibid.* 210. See Scannell, "Invalid Planning Conditions" (1986) 8 D.U.L.J.(N.S.) 96.
[82] See, *e.g. Louth County Council* v. *Mathews*, High Court, April 14, 1989; *Ballybay Meat Exports Ltd.* v. *Monaghan County Council* [1990] I.L.R.M. 864.
[83] At pp. 193–196.
[84] [1987] I.R. 177, 181.

Traffic Act 1961 [is a] substantial invasion of the personal rights enjoyed before the enactment of those provisions and there should not be attributed to Parliament an intention that such personal rights were to be curtailed further than the extent expressed in the statute."

3. Jurisdictional Review

Seven types of jurisdictional error have already been listed in Part 2. However, as mentioned, it is not every error of law committed by an administrative body or lower court which will affect the jurisdiction of that body so as to invalidate the resulting decision. The question of which errors are jurisdictional is an intractable one and is intrinsically linked to questions of statutory interpretation and judicial policy. While the various theories of jurisdictional error provide some guide to the extent of review, the matter is nonetheless not one of abstract logic, but, at root, judicial pragmatism, for it depends upon what degree of supervision the courts wish to exercise over decisions of administrative bodies and of lower courts. There have been several judicial suggestions that the courts will be reluctant to interfere with decisions of specialist tribunals, and, as far as the lower courts are concerned, there is some evidence that with the advent in 1924 of District and Circuit Courts staffed by professional judges, the High Court has been more reluctant to interfere with decisions of the lower courts. As Davitt P. said in *The State (Att.-Gen.) v. Durcan*[85]:

> "Since 1924 the superior courts in this country [have been] more reluctant to interfere on certiorari with the decisions of the District Court and the Circuit Court than was the King's Bench Division to correct the legal errors of the justices at Petty and Quarter Sessions. It is possible that that tribunal was on occasions inclined to act as if it were hearing appeals from the justices. It has, of course, to be remembered that generally speaking the justices possessed no legal qualifications or training; that, in licensing matters particularly, canvassing was a distinct possibility; and that in such matters there was no appeal from their decisions at Quarter Sessions."[86]

Nevertheless, this judicial policy must bear in mind that it is important that tribunals and lower courts do not wrongfully usurp jurisdiction and that errors of law must not go uncorrected. While not stating so openly, the courts have by and large sought to strike what they regard as the proper balance as between these competing considerations rather than seeking to decide the issues which arise by exclusive reference to any set formula or theory of jurisdictional review.

---

[85] [1964] I.R. 279.
[86] *Ibid.* 288–289. See also the comments of Gannon J. in *Clune* v. *Director of Public Prosecutions* [1981] I.L.R.M. 17, 20.

Something must be said at this stage about the evolution of various theories of jurisdiction.

The original jurisdiction doctrine

This theory held sway from the first half of the nineteenth century until very recently.[87] The crucial feature of this theory is that jurisdiction is determined at the "commencement, and not at the conclusion of, the inquiry."[88] If an administrative authority or lower court has "subject-matter" or "original" jurisdiction, it does not lose such jurisdiction even if there is no evidence to support its findings of fact.[89]

This was decided by a very strong Divisional Court in *R. (Martin)* v. *Mahoney*,[90] where it was held that a conviction under section 1 of the Betting House Act 1853 which was (admittedly) based on insufficient evidence could not be quashed on certiorari, since the absence of sufficient evidence did not affect the jurisdiction of the convicting magistrate; as Lord O'Brien L.C.J. remarked:

> "To grant certiorari merely on the ground of want of jurisdiction, because there was no evidence to warrant a conviction, confounds . . . want of jurisdiction with error in the exercise of it. The contention that mere want of evidence to authorize a conviction creates a cesser of jurisdiction, involves the unwarrantable proposition that a magistrate has . . . jurisdiction only to go right; and that, though he had jurisdiction to enter upon an inquiry, mere miscarriage in drawing an unwarrantable conclusion from the evidence, such as it was, makes the magistrate act without and in excess of jurisdiction."[91]

The wealth of erudition displayed in the judgments of Lord O'Brien, Palles C.B. and Gibson J., coupled with the reputation of these judges, seems to have almost hypnotised successive generations of judges, since the authority of the reasoning in this case remained unquestioned until very recently. Indeed, the emphasis on the original jurisdiction theory in *Mahoney's* case appears to have been so influential that even today many judges are reluctant to classify an error made in the course of exercising jurisdiction (such as misconstruing a statutory provision or admitting inadmissible evidence) as one which destroys that jurisdiction.

There are numerous Irish cases in which this doctrine has been followed and

---

[87] For an historical account of these developments, see Rubinstein, *Jurisdiction and Illegality* (Oxford, 1965), Chap. 4; Jaffe and Henderson, "Judicial Review and the Rule of Law: Historical Origins" (1956) 72 L.Q.R. 345 and Jaffe, "Constitutional and Jurisdictional Fact" (1957) 70 Harv.L.Rev. 953 and de Smith's *Judicial Review of Administrative Action* (4th ed.), pp. 108–119.
[88] *R.* v. *Bolton* (1841) 1 Q.B. 66, 74, *per* Lord Denman C.J.
[89] *R. (Martin)* v. *Mahoney* [1910] 2 I.R. 695. Such was the influence of the "original jurisdiction" theory that in *McDonald* v. *Bord na gCon (No. 3)*, High Court, January 13, 1966, Kenny J. held that the defendants had acted invalidly in breaching the *audi alteram partem* rule, but since they had original jurisdiction in the matter, they did not thereby exceed jurisdiction.
[90] [1910] 2 I.R. 695.
[91] *Ibid.* 707.

the following example from the mid-1950s illustrates how narrow the scope of review was to become as a result of it.

In *The State (Batchelor & Co.)* v. *O'Floinn*[92] the applicants sought to quash a search warrant issued under section 12 of the Merchandise Marks Act 1887. It was said that there was insufficient evidence before the respondent District Justice to justify the warrant. But O'Daly J. for the Supreme Court disposed of this argument by stating that it was well settled that providing the error did not appear on the face of the record, questions as to the sufficiency of evidence amounted to errors within jurisdiction. The District Justice clearly had jurisdiction to make an order under the Act, and he did not lose jurisdiction by making an error of this nature. In the view of O'Daly J., questions as to the sufficiency of evidence were the very matters committed to the jurisdiction of the District Justice. The result of this and other similar decisions was that the scope of review was rather narrow, and this could often lead to injustice, particularly in criminal cases.[93]

"Conditions precedent to jurisdiction"

One method of escaping the confines of this doctrine was to classify certain findings of fact as "collateral" or as "conditions precedent to jurisdiction."[94] Administrative authorities do not possess an inherent jurisdiction; their jurisdiction depends upon facts which must have an objective existence before the authority has power to act. Hence, any decision of the authority as to the boundaries of its jurisdiction could not be conclusive, as otherwise it would usurp power never conferred on it by the Oireachtas. If, for example, the Circuit Court has jurisdiction to hear ejectment cases where the rateable valuation of the premises does not exceed £60, that court cannot acquire jurisdiction by reason of an erroneous conclusion as to the rateable valuation of the premises.[95] In other words, an administrative authority cannot give itself a jurisdiction which it cannot have, and the High Court will enforce the *ultra vires* doctrine by insisting on the objective existence of certain facts upon which some jurisdiction depends.

The difficulty with this, of course, is that there does not appear to be any clear-cut method of determining which legal points or facts are "jurisdic-

---

[92] [1958] I.R. 155. See also, *R. (Limerick Corporation)* v. *Local Government Board* [1922] 2 I.R. 76; *R. (Dillon)* v. *Minister for Local Government* [1927] I.R. 474 and *McDonald* v. *Bord na gCon (No. 3)*, High Court, January 13, 1966.

[93] See, *e.g. The State (Lee-Kiddier)* v. *Dunleavy*, High Court, August 17, 1976 where McWilliam J. held that the question of whether there was sufficient evidence to support a conviction was not reviewable in certiorari proceedings, absent error on the face of the record. Contrast this with the observations of Kenny J. in *The State (Holland)* v. *Kennedy* [1977] I.R. 193 where he doubted whether the rule in *Mahoney* was compatible with Art. 38.1 of the Constitution which prescribes trial "in due course of law."

[94] Thus, in *The State (O'Neill)* v. *Shannon* [1931] I.R. 691 it was held that the principle of *Martin's* case only applied to decisions arrived at on the merits and was not relevant in the case of preliminary objections to jurisdiction.

[95] *The State (Att.-Gen.)* v. *Durcan* [1964] I.R. 279; *Harrington* v. *Judge Murphy* [1989] I.R. 207.

tional," and which are not.[96] In *The State (Davidson)* v. *Farrell*[97] Kingsmill Moore J. sought to answer this question by referring to the jurisdiction conferred—whether expressly or by necessary intendment—by statute on the authority concerned. In this case the applicant, a tenant in a controlled dwelling, sought to quash decisions of the District and Circuit Courts awarding her landlord certain sums as allowances in respect of the repair of the premises. She claimed that these decisions were flawed by jurisdictional error as a result of the misconstruction of the phrase "premises," as defined by the Rent Restrictions Act 1946. A majority of the Supreme Court concluded, following an examination of the 1946 Act, that the Oireachtas had intended to vest the District Court with jurisdiction to determine the basic rent and allowances. It was not a precondition to jurisdiction that the word "premises" be correctly construed, and as Kingsmill Moore J. explained:

> "The [District] Court may make an error in law in interpreting the word 'premises,' or an error in fact in determining that money has been expended when it has not, but these are errors within the jurisdiction conferred."[98]

Another example of this approach from this period is to be found in *The State (Att.-Gen.)* v. *McGivern*,[98a] where the Court refused to quash the granting of an exemption under section 5 of the Intoxicating Liquor Act 1927. The applicant had contended that dances at the local hotel could not constitute a "special occasion" within the meaning of the section. O'Daly J., having engaged in a rigorous examination of the statutory context, rejected the argument that this determination of what was a "special occasion" was a condition precedent to jurisdiction. The following passage contains one of the very few useful expositions of what constitutes a collateral fact or condition precedent to jurisdiction:

> "There is nothing in the structure of the sub-section to indicate that the Oireachtas is subtracting from the substantive jurisdiction of the [District] Justice the determination of what is a special occasion and placing it upon the pre-existing absolutes to jurisdiction. Moreover, the very nature of the subject matter is one of the strongest indications to the contrary. Matters collateral to jurisdiction are usually distinguished by their clear-cut and identifiable character, arising from the terms used or the appended definition. The words "special occasion" or "special event" have the very opposite character; they range over a wide variety of circumstances, their very imprecision is of itself a mark that their meaning is being committed to the Justice as part of his substantive jurisdiction."

[96] See, *e.g.* the division of judicial opinion in the "orchard" cases: *R. (De Vesci)* v. *Queen's Co. JJ.* [1908] 2 I.R. 365; *R. (D'Arcy)* v. *Carlow JJ.* [1916] 2 I.R. 313 and *R. (Greenaway)* v. *Armagh JJ.* [1924] 2 I.R. 55 and in the various licensing cases considered at pp. 332–334.
[97] [1960] I.R. 438. See also, *The State (Att.-Gen.)* v. *Durcan* [1964] I.R. 279 for a useful judicial discussion of this question.
[98] [1960] I.R. 438, 455.
[98a] Supreme Court, July 25, 1961.

But difficulties nevertheless remain. The concept of "collateral fact" is a malleable one—virtually any fact may be classified as "collateral" to jurisdiction. Moreover, this issue is not solely one of statutory interpretation. The essential legal policy behind the *ultra vires* doctrine is that it is vital that administrative authorities respect the principle of legality and have due regard to constitutional precepts of fairness. For these reasons the courts have recently tended to turn away from this theory of jurisdiction in order to increase the scope of review.

The modern doctrine of jurisdictional error

The modern trend is to treat all errors of law committed by lower courts or administrative tribunals as jurisdictional in character. There have also been suggestions that the courts may invervene to quash findings based on inadequate evidence.[99] But the law in this area is far from settled. Contradictory opinions have been expressed by eminent judges and the Supreme Court has yet to give an authoritative exposition on the subject of jurisdictional error. Earlier authorities such as *Farrell's* case have never been formally overruled, and are still on occasion relied on as good law.[1]

The leading Irish authority is *The State (Holland)* v. *Kennedy*.[2] The Children Act 1908 forbids the imposition of a prison sentence on a young person between the ages of 15 and 17 unless it is shown that he is of such an "unruly character" that he cannot be detained in an approved place of detention. The prosecutor had been convicted of a particularly serious assault. He was certified as of unruly character by the respondent District Justice, and she sentenced him to a period of imprisonment.

The Supreme Court held that the bare facts of this assault, unrelated to any previous evidence of a behavioural pattern, could not justify a conclusion that this young person would not be amenable to detention in a suitable institute. Turning to the question of whether an error of this nature was reviewable on certiorari, Henchy J. observed:

"Having considered the authorities, I am satisfied that this error was not within jurisdiction. [I]t does not necessarily follow that a court or tribunal . . . which commences a hearing within jurisdiction will be treated as

[99] *Kiely* v. *Minister for Social Welfare* [1971] I.R. 21; *The State (Holland)* v. *Kennedy* [1977] I.R. 193; *The State (Cork C.C.)* v. *Fawsitt (No. 2)*, Supreme Court, July 28, 1983; *The State (Casey)* v. *Labour Court* (1984) 3 J.I.S.S.L. 135; *M.* v. *M.* [1979] I.L.R.M. 160; *The State (Burke)* v. *Garvey*, [1979] I.L.R.M. 232; and *The State (McKeown)* v. *Scully* [1986] I.L.R.M. 133. The wrongful admission of evidence may also be a ground for intervention by way of judicial review: *The State (Keeney)* v. *O'Malley* [1986] I.L.R.M. 31. But there are also modern authorities which point in the opposite direction: *The State (Power)* v. *Moran* [1976–1977] I.L.R.M. 20 (decision based on evidence of little probative value not reviewable by certiorari); *The State (Shinkaruk)* v. *Carroll*, High Court, December 15, 1976 (wrongful exclusion of evidence not reviewable by certiorari); *Memorex World Trade Corporation* v. *Employment Appeals Tribunal*, High Court, November 25, 1988 (certiorari will not be granted on the basis "that there was want of evidence to support a finding").
[1] *The State (Lee-Kiddier)* v. *Dunleavy*, High Court, August 17, 1976; *The State (Cole)* v. *Labour Court* (1984) 3 J.I.S.S.L. 128.
[2] [1977] I.R. 193.

continuing to act within jurisdiction. For any number of reasons it may exceed jurisdiction and thereby make its decisions liable to be quashed on certiorari. For instance, it may fall into an unconstitutionality, or it may breach the requirements of natural justice, or it may fail to stay within the bounds of the jurisdiction conferred on it by statute. It is an error of the latter kind that prevents the impugned order in this case from being held to have been made within jurisdiction. It was necessarily the statutory intention that a legally supportable certificate to that effect is to be a condition precedent to the exercise of jurisdiction to impose a sentence of imprisonment. Otherwise the sentencing limitation could be nullified by disregarding what the law regards as essential for the making of the certificate. In the present case, the certificate, having been made without evidence, was as devoid of legal validity as if it had been made in disregard of uncontroverted evidence showing that the young person was not what he had been certified to be."[3]

An order of certiorari quashing the conviction and sentence was granted.

The precise significance of *Holland* is difficult to assess. The above passage contains some reasoning reminiscent of the collateral law or fact approach. But the judgment of Henchy J. suggests that errors of law committed by a lower court or tribunal in the course of a hearing will be deemed—almost as of course—to go to jurisdiction. Yet other passages in the judgments of Henchy and Kenny JJ. give the impression that the existence of a legally supportable certificate was a collateral fact—a condition precedent to jurisdiction which the District Justice had failed to satisfy. If the latter interpretation is correct, *Holland* represents no more than an application of principles approved in earlier decisions such as *The State (Davidson)* v. *Farrell*, and the case can hardly be said to have broken new ground.

The judgments in the two *Fawsitt* cases point towards wider scope for review. Both cases concerned an application by the local authority to enter upon certain lands in order to ascertain whether the lands were suitable for the setting up of a waste disposal site. The Circuit Court judge initially refused the application because he was not satisfied that the lands were not manifestly unsuitable. By contrast, the relevant statutory provision[4] only authorised the judge to refuse the request if he were satisfied that the lands were manifestly unsuitable. In *The State (Cork C.C.)* v. *Fawsitt*,[5] McMahon J. held that the Circuit Court judge had made an error of law in so holding, and that he had thereby stepped outside his jurisdiction. McMahon J. referred approvingly to the epoch-making decision of the House of Lords in *Anisminic Ltd.* v. *Foreign Compensation Commission*[6] ("an extreme example of an

---

[3] [1977] I.R. 193, 201.
[4] Public Health (Ireland) Act 1878, s.271.
[5] High Court, March 13, 1981. For another example of where "asking the wrong question" was held to be a jurisdictional defect, see *The State (McMahon)* v. *Minister for Education*, High Court, December 21, 1985.
[6] [1969] 2 A.C. 147.

error of law . . . being held to be jurisdictional")[7] and *The State (Holland)* v. *Kennedy* (which McMahon J. cited as an example of a case where an order of the District Court made without evidence was quashed). The tenor of McMahon J.'s judgment suggests that *every* error of law is to be deemed to affect jurisdiction.

The case was remitted to the Circuit Court judge following the quashing of the first order. On this occasion the Circuit Court found as a fact that the lands were "manifestly unsuitable" within the meaning of the statutory provisions, and the application to enter upon the lands was refused. Once again, the local authority sought to impeach this order in certiorari proceedings. On this occasion, the case reached the Supreme Court.[8]

The Supreme Court upheld the validity of the impugned order. Henchy J. noted that in the first case, the Circuit Court judge had stepped outside his jurisdiction because he had "answered the wrong question"—a question which the statutory provisions gave him no jurisdiction to answer. If he had decided that it was not necessary for the county council to enter upon the lands to carry out the preliminary tests

"[h]is orders would have been unassailable, because there was evidence to support such a finding so it could not be said that he acted without or in excess of jurisdiction."

In the present case, he had found as a fact that the lands were manifestly unsuitable for the purposes of a waste disposal site. The judge acted *intra vires*: he approached the evidence from a different standpoint, and he reached the same conclusion for a valid reason.

The first *Fawsitt* judgment (which now, of course, has the approval of the Supreme Court) is an example of an error of law which, up to relatively recently, would almost certainly have been treated as an error within jurisdiction.[9] Yet such errors are now condemned as *ultra vires*. In the light of the *Fawsitt* litigation, one may reasonably ask whether the time-honoured distinction between errors which go to jurisdiction and those which do not has been effectively abolished. Certainly, the Supreme Court has failed to establish criteria whereby the distinction (if any) between the two types of error may be established. With such judicial guidance absent, it is fair to assume that all major errors of law will be regarded as affecting jurisdiction. In addition, the *obiter* remarks of Henchy J. in *Fawsitt (No. 2)* imply that insufficiency of evidence to support a finding is itself an error of law going to jurisdiction, thus rendering the impugned order liable to be quashed.[10]

Yet the recent pronouncements by the Supreme Court on this question have not always been in favour of widening the scope of judicial review. The judgment of Henchy J. in *The State (Abenglen Properties Ltd.)* v. *Dublin Cor-*

---

[7] Wade, *Administrative Law* (Oxford, 1988), p. 299.
[8] *The State (Cork C.C.)* v. *Fawsitt (No. 2)*, July 28, 1983.
[9] See, *e.g. The State (Davidson)* v. *Farrell* [1960] I.R. 439.
[10] Contrast this with the observations of O'Daly J. in *The State (Batchelor & Co.)* v. *O'Floinn* [1958] I.R. 155 and those of Lord Sumner in *R.* v. *Nat Bell Liquors Ltd.* [1922] 2 A.C. 125, 151.

poration[11] demonstrates that the distinction between errors of law going to jurisdiction and those which do not retains a foothold in our law. In *Abenglen Properties*, the Supreme Court had been invited to quash an allegedly *ultra vires* planning permission. It was said that the respondents had acted *ultra vires* in attaching restrictive conditions to the grant of permission, and that the entire permission rested on an erroneous identification of the relevant development plan. To this submission Henchy J. replied by stating:

> "The alleged errors arose in the course of identifying and construing the Dublin City Development Plan. There is no doubt but that on a true reading of the relevant Acts and Regulations, the Corporation . . . had jurisdiction to identify and construe the relevant Dublin City Development Plan in its relation to Abenglen's application. If, therefore, they erred in either respect, they erred within jurisdiction, and any error they may have made does not appear on the face of the record."[12]

In these circumstances certiorari would only lie if the respondents had disregarded the principles of natural justice, and the alleged error of law was one within jurisdiction.

Henchy J.'s reasoning is similar to that employed by the former Supreme Court in *The State (Davidson)* v. *Farrell*: if a court or tribunal has "subject-matter" jurisdiction then it does not lose that jurisdiction by erring in the course of its adjudication, unless that error relates to a collateral fact, or where the rules of natural justice have been breached. It is difficult to reconcile this aspect of *Abenglen Properties* with other recent decisions such as *Holland, Fawsitt (No. 1)* and *Fawsitt (No. 2)*. It should, perhaps, be noted that Henchy J.'s was only one of three substantive judgments delivered by the Supreme Court and that the other judges reserved their position on this question. The reasoning of the court may also have been coloured by judicial perceptions as to the motives of the applicants in seeking this relief.

Barrington J. employed a more sophisticated and rather novel approach to this question in *Irish Permanent Building Society* v. *Caldwell*.[13] In this case the Registrar of Building Societies had misconstrued the relevant sections of the Building Societies Act 1976 when he came to register the Irish Life Building Society, and Barrington J. was satisfied that the Registrar had "asked himself the wrong question," and had erred in law in registering the Society's rules under the 1976 Act. But the judge did not think that the case turned on that point:

> "The real issue in the present case is whether, because of the Registrar's

---

[11] [1984] I.R. 381. Hederman J. joined in the judgment of Henchy J. The other three members of the court reserved their position on this question.

[12] [1984] I.R. 381, 399–400. This passage has served to resuscitate the distinction in this jurisdiction between errors of law affecting jurisdiction and those which do not. See, *e.g.* the judgment of Blayney J. in *The State (Keegan)* v. *Stardust Compensation Tribunal* [1986] I.R. 642, 650 where this passage was quoted with approval.

[13] [1981] I.L.R.M. 242. See also, the judgment of Finlay P. in *Re Riordan* [1981] I.L.R.M. 2 for a similar approach.

mistake of law, the incorporation of the building society is a nullity. It seems to me that the answer to this question is not to be found in abstract questions of law, but in ascertaining the intentions of the legislature in this particular statute."[14]

Barrington J. pointed out that the scheme of the Act was such that had the Registrar failed to reach a decision within the prescribed time, the Society would have been entitled to have been incorporated under the Acts, the defect in its rules notwithstanding. Furthermore, it was no longer required that the Registrar should be a person with legal qualification. He concluded that it would have been surprising:

"[I]f the incorporation of a society could be invalidated by an honest mistake such as was made by . . . the Registrar in the present case. If the law were otherwise people might in good faith deal with a society for many years only to find that because of some defect in the rules the society did not exist as a corporate body. . . . To hold that the society was not validly incorporated would clearly cause great damage to many innocent people, and I cannot accept that the Oireachtas intended that such a catastrophic result should ensue."[15]

It is instructive to compare *Caldwell* with *The State (Costello) v. Bofin*,[16] where a coroner's decision to adjourn an inquest *sine die* was quashed. The Supreme Court ruled that the Coroner's Act 1962 simply permitted the coroner to adjourn for a definite period of time, and that, as a result of this mere error of statutory construction, the coroner thereby exceeded his jurisdiction. The court appeared to assume that a mere error of construction automatically destroyed the coroner's jurisdiction. But was this not a case of an administrative authority making an "honest mistake," just as was the case with *Abenglen Properties* and *Caldwell*? All three cases involved errors of statutory construction, but why should such an error be deemed to be jurisdictional in one of these cases, but not in others?

Recent developments

The last few years have seen a continuation of this general judicial inconsistency and the lack of clear general principles governing the question of jurisdictional error. Indeed, this lack of consistency has been so prevalent that one suspects that the courts are prepared to characterise an error of law as being jurisdictional where this seems convenient often because it offers adventitious support for conclusions already reached. We may now consider some of the very recent cases.

Civil cases. In *The State (Keegan) v. Stardust Compensation Tribunal*,[17] the applicant sought to have a decision of the tribunal quashed on the ground that

---

[14] [1981] I.L.R.M. 248, 268.
[15] *Ibid.* 269–270.
[16] [1980] I.L.R.M. 223.
[17] [1986] I.R. 642.

insufficient regard had been paid to the medical reports concerning his case. Blayney J. referred with approval to passages from *R. (Martin)* v. *Mahoney*[18] (already discussed under the heading *The original jurisdiction doctrine*) and the judgment of Henchy J. in *Abenglen Properties* and said that the applicant complained of a "mere miscarriage in drawing an unwarrantable conclusion from the evidence" and that such an error of law did not affect jurisdiction:

> "The [applicant's] case is that the Tribunal ought to have decided on the basis of medical reports that [he] was entitled to an award. But even if the Tribunal was wrong, it did not mean that it exceeded its jurisdiction. What it did was to make an error within its jurisdiction."[19]

The Supreme Court did not deal with this issue on appeal, save to confirm (in contrast to Blayney J.) that had the tribunal acted unreasonably in law, it would have thereby affected its jurisdiction.

A similarly narrow view of the courts' powers of review emerges from the judgment of Carroll J. in *Memorex World Trade Corpn.* v. *Employment Appeals Tribunal.*[20] The applicant sought to quash a decision on the ground that there was insufficient evidence to support certain findings of the tribunal, but Carroll J. held such an error could not be reviewed by way of certiorari:

> "Lack of evidence does not create want of jurisdiction. This is long established law. Certiorari will not be granted on the basis that there was a lack of evidence to support a finding . . . If there was a want of evidence or it took into account extraneous matters, the [Tribunal] erred within jurisdiction."[21]

On the other hand, in *Att.-Gen.* v. *Sheedy*[22] the Supreme Court had little difficulty in characterising an error of statutory construction as one affecting jurisdiction. Here the Circuit Court judge had made an order forfeiting the gear and catch of the master of a fishing vessel convicted of offences under the Fisheries Act. This forfeiture order was now, for all practical purposes, unenforceable, because once surety had been provided as bail, the vessel departed from Irish waters. The Circuit Court judge, however, declined to make an order estreating the security in satisfaction of the forfeiture order. Murphy J. considered that any error on this point could not be corrected by way of certiorari, as the Circuit Court judge:

---

[18] [1910] 2 I.R. 695.

[19] [1986] I.R. 642, 648.

[20] High Court, November 25, 1988.

[21] *Ibid.* p. 2 of the judgment. Compare these observations with the earlier remarks of Carroll J. in *Dublin Corporation* v. *Murdon Ltd.* [1988] I.L.R.M. 86 where she held that the Circuit Court judge had erred in law in extending time for the purposes of an application for compensation under s.23 of the Malicious Injuries Act 1981. Carroll J. added (at 89) that this error went to jurisdiction:

> "The order of the Circuit Court cannot be classified as erring within jurisdiction. It does not involve the finding of facts. It concerns the exercise of a power not conferred on the Circuit Court by the statute. Therefore the order on the fact of it is made without jurisdiction."

[22] [1988] I.R. 226 (H.C.); [1990] 1 I.R. 70 (S.C.).

"Did have the requisite statutory power to deal with the proceedings before him and, in particular, to release the security provided. In those circumstances, it is difficult to see how the order could be reviewed by way of certiorari."[23]

The Supreme Court, however, took a different view as McCarthy J. said that by virtue of section 235 of the Fisheries (Amendment) Act 1983, the forfeiture order operated automatically on the surety and the Circuit Court's order was duly quashed. There is here nothing of the hesitancy about the court's power of review that is evident in the judgment of Blayney J. in *Keegan* and that of Carroll J. in *Memorex*. Yet an authoritative pronouncement on the scope of jurisdictional error in civil cases is still awaited.

Criminal cases. As we have seen, the courts are generally ready to expand the scope of review in criminal cases because they are reluctant to allow any significant legal errors to go uncorrected. But even in criminal cases, the scope of review has not been consistent.

In *Gill* v. *Connellan*[24] the applicant sought to quash a conviction in the District Court in circumstances where the respondent had wrongly prevented the applicant's solicitor from persisting with a certain line of cross-examination. Lynch J. considered that this error went to jurisdiction and duly quashed the conviction. By contrast, however, in *O'Broin* v. *Ruane*,[25] where cross-examination of a witness was incorrectly disallowed by a District Justice, Lynch J. refused to set aside the conviction, saying that the error was within jurisdiction:

"It is part of his function as the presiding justice to decide what evidence is admissible and to decide what sort of examination-in-chief and cross-examination may be pursued. Unless the error was so gross as to oust jurisdiction, which can be so in exceptional circumstances, the error would not justify the making of an order of certiorari."[26]

But the most restrictive approach to the scope of review by far is to be found in the judgment of O'Hanlon J. in *The State (Daly)* v. *Ruane*.[27] The applicant sought to quash a return for trial on the ground that the various essential proofs had not been established by the prosecution before the District Court, but O'Hanlon J. held that even if the District Justice had erred in the manner suggested, any such errors would be within jurisdiction. Having referred to several pre-*Anisminic* English authorities, he quoted the following passage from the judgment of Molony C.J. in *R.* v. *Murphy*[28] with approval:

"When the Court has jurisdiction to decide a matter, its jurisdiction is not ousted because it happens to give an erroneous decision and it certainly

[23] [1988] I.R. 226, 230–231.
[24] [1987] I.R. 541.
[25] [1989] I.R. 214.
[26] *Ibid.* 217.
[27] [1988] I.L.R.M. 117.
[28] [1921] 2 I.R. 190.

351

cannot be deemed to exceed or abuse its jurisdiction merely because it incidentally misconstrues a statute, or admits illegal evidence, or rejects legal evidence."[29]

This view of the courts' power of review is so narrow that it is difficult to see how it could possibly be accepted in the modern era. If one takes but one example: suppose a lower court wrongly convicts an accused on the basis of inadmissible evidence, can it seriously be contended that the High Court would have no power to quash that conviction on certiorari? In fact, as we have seen, the whole trend of the modern authorities is to treat such errors (such as a misconstruction of a statute or the wrongful admission or exclusion of evidence) as affecting jurisdiction. Finally, we may note that in *Russell* v. *Fanning*[30] Barr J. took a much broader view of the courts' power of review. The applicant sought to challenge an extradition warrant on the ground that there was no evidence to support certain findings made by the District Justice who made the order. Barr J. considered that even if the District Justice had so erred, such an error would be within jurisdiction for the purposes of certiorari proceedings and so not reviewable. However, Barr J. continued by saying that such an error would be reviewable in habeas corpus proceedings under Article 40 of the Constitution:

"Where it is appropriate to look again at the whole proceedings by way of judicial review and determine in the light of all the evidence now available whether it is proper that the extradition orders in question should have been made."[31]

While Barr J. is correct to advocate a wider power of review in criminal cases, the extent of the courts' powers should not turn on the remedy invoked and it seems more correct to say that the scope of review is just as broad in certiorari proceedings.

Recent English developments

The modern trend in English administrative law has been expressly to collapse the distinction between errors of law affecting jurisdiction and those which do not. This has been clear since the majority decision of the House of Lords in 1969 in *Anisminic Ltd.* v. *Foreign Compensation Commission*,[32] where it was held that the taking into account of an irrelevant consideration was sufficient to destroy jurisdiction. After some initial hesitancy, it was gradually recognised that the pre-1969 authorities on jurisdictional error had been superseded. This was made clear by Lord Diplock in two major cases, *Re Racal Communications Ltd.*[33] and *O'Reilly* v. *Mackman*.[34] In the former case, he explained that:

---

[29] *Ibid.* 226.
[30] [1988] I.R. 505.
[31] *Ibid.* 525.
[32] [1969] 1 A.C. 147.
[33] [1981] A.C. 374.
[34] [1983] 2 A.C. 237.

"The break-through made by *Anisminic* was that, as respects administrative tribunals and authorities, the old distinction between errors of law that went to jurisdiction and errors of law that did not, was for practical purposes abolished. Any error of law that could be shown to have been made by them in the course of reaching their decision on matters of fact or of administrative policy would result in their having asked themselves the wrong question with the result that the decision they reached would be a nullity."[35]

He went on to state that whereas there was a presumption that Parliament did not intend to confer administrative authorities with the power to determine their own jurisdiction, inferior courts might still have authority to make errors of law within jurisdiction.[36] In *O'Reilly* v. *Mackman*, however, Lord Diplock included lower courts along with administrative tribunals as bodies to which the old distinction would no longer apply.[37] It is now clear that, as a matter of English law at any rate, the distinction between errors of law affecting jurisdiction and those which do not has almost[38] been abolished.

Conclusions

No clear picture emerges from a consideration of the modern Irish cases, save that there is a trend towards treating all decisive errors of law as jurisdictional, especially in criminal cases. Part of the problem is that many of the Irish judges use the word "jurisdiction" in the narrow sense of "original jurisdiction" and are disinclined to accept the argument that this jurisdiction may be lost by reason of serious error of law. And while it has been long accepted by the Supreme Court that a tribunal may lose its jurisdiction by reason of legal error, since the decision in *The State (Holland)* v. *Kennedy*,[39] there has been no coherent judicial statement of principle on this difficult issue. Indeed, the other major judicial pronouncement, that of Henchy J. in *The State (Abenglen Properties Ltd.)* v. *Dublin Corporation*,[40] based as it was on incorrect analysis of the post-*Anisminic* English authorities, only served to revive the old distinction and gave inconsistent signals as to the scope of jurisdictional review. An authoritative review of these issues is clearly required.

Some indications of possible future developments in this area of the law are provided by *Tormey* v. *Attorney-General*.[41] In this case, speaking of a situation in which *exclusive* jurisdiction has been committed to a lower court or

---

[35] *Ibid.* 278.
[36] This presumption is a rebuttable one. Thus, in *R.* v. *Registrar of Companies, ex p. Central Bank of India* [1986] Q.B. 1114 it was held that an error of law made by the Registrar in registering certain securities for the purposes of the Companies Acts was not reviewable in certiorari proceedings. The need for certainty in commercial transactions meant Parliament must have intended that the Registrar could err in law and still remain within jurisdiction.
[37] See subsequent cases such as *R.* v. *Manchester Coroner, ex p. Tal* [1985] Q.B. 67 where the full significance of Lord Diplock's remarks is explained.
[38] Subject only to exceptional cases such as the *Central Bank of India*, n. 36 above.
[39] [1977] I.R. 193.
[40] [1984] I.R. 384.
[41] [1985] I.R. 289, 296–297.

administrative authority exercising judicial powers under cover of Article 37, Henchy J. observed that the High Court's full jurisdiction under Article 34.3.1 might be invoked so as to ensure that "the hearing and determination will be in accordance *with law*" (author's italics). The context of this observation was an explanation that even though the High Court did not have original jurisdiction, yet, nevertheless, it retained a complete supervisory control over lower courts and tribunals. Accordingly, this remark can be taken to mean that the High Court's power of review must be broad enough to allow it to quash at least for major errors of law committed by a lower court or administrative authority exercising exclusive jurisdiction. It may also be that the High Court may review decisions of lower courts or administrative authorities which have been based on insufficient evidence. Similar results might well be achieved through an extension of the constitutional principles of fair procedures and the right of access to the courts.[42] In any event, despite some recent inconsistent signals, our courts will probably find the trend towards increasing the scope of jurisdictional review to be well nigh irresistible.

4. Error on the Face of the Record

The jurisdiction to review for error on the face of the record is an anomalous one since the power to review is not based on jurisdiction or *ultra vires*.[43] Nevertheless, this power of review enables the High Court to quash a decision, otherwise within jurisdiction, if that decision contains an error of law,[44] provided that error appears on the face of the record.[45]

What is the record? Denning L.J. has provided us with a comprehensive answer:

> "[T]he record must contain at least the document which initiates the proceedings; the pleadings, if any; and the adjudication; but not the evidence, nor the reasons, unless the tribunal chooses to incorporate them. If the tribunal does state the reasons, and the reasons are wrong in law, certiorari lies to quash the decision.[46]

---

[42] For example, it could be argued that the constitutional guarantee of fair procedure requires that a decision be based on adequate, probative evidence, and Henchy J. has already argued along these lines in *M.* v. *M.* [1979] I.L.R.M. 160.

[43] This anomaly has sometimes led judges to hold that error on the face of the record must be a form of jurisdictional error: see the comments of Palles C.B. in *R. (Martin)* v. *Mahoney* [1910] 2 I.R. 695, 721. By the turn of the century the jurisdiction to quash for error of law on the face of the record had fallen into decline, and in England, the very existence of this jurisdiction was denied by the Court of Appeal in *Racecourse Betting Control Board* v. *Secretary of State for Air* [1944] Ch. 114. This jurisdiction was revived following the decision of the Court of Appeal in *R.* v. *Northumberland Compensation Appeal Tribunal, ex p. Shaw* [1952] 1 K.B. 338.

[44] But this jurisdiction does not extend to errors of fact: see *per* Carroll J. in *The State (C.I.E.)* v. *An Bord Pleanála*, High Court, February 12, 1984.

[45] Thus, in *R.* v. *Knightsbridge Crown Court, ex p. International Sporting Club Ltd.* [1982] Q.B. 304 a Divisional Court was evenly divided as to whether a particular error of law went to jurisdiction, but held that, as they were agreed the error of law appeared on the record, the decision could be quashed.

[46] *R.* v. *Northumberland Appeal Compensation Tribunal, ex p. Shaw* [1952] 1 K.B. 338, 352.

To this it may be objected that a court or tribunal could avoid review for error on the face of the record by the High Court by the simple expedient of refusing to make a judgment part of the final order or refusing to give any reason for a decision at all. But it is clear that English law, at any rate, has now progressed to the point whereby the reasons given orally for a decision are now regarded as forming part of the record, which is, when thus augmented, known as a "speaking order." Moreover, the English courts have strongly hinted that they have jurisdiction, at least in appropriate cases, to call for reasons to be given for the decision by the tribunal or lower court,[47] so that if these reasons exhibit an error of law, the resulting decision may be quashed as appearing on the "face" of the record, irrespective of whether that error would otherwise affect jurisdiction. This judicial expansion of what constitutes the record is probably due to two reasons. First, the supporting documentation (pleadings, transcripts, written reasons for decisions, etc.) is generally now more elaborate than was the case in the early part of this century when the jurisdiction to review for error on the record had fallen into decline. In addition, the facilities for recording spoken judgments is also nowadays far superior.[48] Secondly, the courts are nowadays loath to allow a decision containing an error of law to survive review and will tend to classify such error as either going to jurisdiction or appearing on the face of the record.

The scope of record is not uniform in all cases and the courts have expanded the concept of record if this is necessary to do justice. Thus, in *Re Stevenson's Application*[49] (where certiorari was sought to quash the grant of a bookmaker's licence), Carswell J. held that he could look at the affidavit filed by the notice party in order to supplement the record, saying that the notice party "must be taken" to have consented to the affidavit being used for this purpose.[50] Similar reasoning was applied by the Northern Irish Court of Appeal in *Re Weir and Higgins' Application*[51] where it was held that an affidavit by the respondent Taxing Master setting out the reasons for his decision formed part of the record. Lowry L.C.J. said that the court inclined to the view that:

> "When the lower deciding authority of its own motion files an affidavit setting out its reasons, it will be taken to have made it part of the record by incorporating therein the reasons for its decision. We would not be dissuaded from this opinion by the objection that the affidavit was not in being at the time when the order to be challenged was made, since this could frequently be said with regard to a speaking order."[52]

---

[47] "The Court has always had power to order an inferior tribunal to complete the record," *per* Denning L.J. in *R. v. Medical Appeal Tribunal, ex p. Gilmore* [1957] 1 Q.B. 574, 582–583. See also, *R. v. Knightsbridge Crown Court, ex p. International Sporting Club Ltd.* [1982] Q.B. 304.
[48] See the comments of Griffiths L.J. in *R. v. Knightsbridge Crown Court, ex p. International Sporting Club Ltd.* [1982] Q.B. 304.
[49] [1984] N.I. 373.
[50] *Ibid.* 386.
[51] [1988] 10 N.I.J.B.I.
[52] *Ibid.* 17.

However, where the respondents or notice party object, it appears that the court may not look at *the applicant's* affidavit in order to supplement the record, at least where the affidavit contains documentary material not otherwise before the court.[53]

In criminal cases, the record has been held to include the warrant, the formal records and the transcript of the trial.[54] In some cases, the scope of the record has been restricted by statute. The Summary Jurisdiction Act 1848 originally restricted the scope of the record for the purposes of summary convictions[55] and when the District Court was made a court of record by the Courts Act 1971, section 14 provided that the record, in cases of summary jurisdiction before that court, was confined to the formal court order signed by the District Justice. This means that external documentary material cannot be availed of in order to impeach an order of the District Court in such a case. Thus, in *Friel* v. *McMenamin*[56] the applicant sought to rely on the note of the respondent District Justice in order to challenge the conviction. Barron J. held that the respondent was under no obligation to supply the note, adding that section 14 of the 1971 Act would not allow "the note to be used to go behind the order."

In Ireland, there appears to be some confusion as to the scope of review for error of law on the face of the record, but it does not appear to be as broad as that suggested by the recent English and Northern Irish authorities. Yet again, however, the authorities are not easily reconcilable. In *Walsh* v. *Minister for Local Government*,[57] the former Supreme Court agreed that if the Minister had set out his reasons in arriving at a decision, these reasons would form part of the record, thus rendering the impugned decision liable to be quashed if the Minister had erred in law. In this case the applicant sought to quash a surcharge imposed by the local government auditor. The auditor's certificate was said to contain an error of law. The applicant exercised his statutory right of appeal to the respondent Minister, who issued a sealed order upholding the auditor's decision. The ministerial order mentioned—but it did not set out—the reasons give by the auditor. Murnaghan J. observed:

"We do not see how this [ministerial] order can in any sense be said to be a speaking order, stating the views of the Minister upon some point of law, so as to make an erroneous view of the law apparent on the record."[58]

[53] *R.* v. *Agricultural Lands Tribunal, ex p. Bracey* [1960] 2 All E.R. 518.
[54] *Re Tynan*, Supreme Court, December 21, 1963.
[55] This had the effect of limiting the opportunities of challenging summary convictions on the ground of error on the face of the record and, indeed, the 1848 Act was designed to counteract the then prevailing tendency to quash convictions exhibiting purely formal defects. As Lord Sumner explained in *R.* v. *Nat Bell Liquors Ltd.* [1922] 2 A.C. 128, 159:

> "The effect of [the 1848 Act] was not to make that which had been error, error no longer, but to remove all opportunity for detection. The face of the record 'spoke' no longer: it was the inscrutable face of the sphinx."

[56] [1990] I.L.R.M. 761.
[57] [1929] I.R. 377.
[58] *Ibid.* 404.

The court went on to hold that the Minister's order had not incorporated the reasons of the auditor so as to make these reasons the view of the law taken by the Minister.

In *The State (Attorney-General)* v. *Binchy*,[59] the former Supreme Court implied that the record in a criminal trial on indictment was confined to the formal record of the trial (*i.e.* only the official court documents, the verdict and record of conviction, if any). Yet, some three years later, the Supreme Court held in *Re Tynan*[60] that the record in such a case included the court orders and the transcript (thus rendering a conviction liable to be quashed if, for example, the judge erred in law in his summing-up). More recently, in *The State (Abenglen Properties Ltd.)* v. *Dublin Corporation*,[61] Henchy J. adopted a more restrictive attitude to this question. The judge implied that the record in planning cases is confined to the formal decision of the local authority or An Bord Pleanála, *i.e.* whether or not to grant planning permission.[62] An authoritative decision of our courts delineating the scope of review for error on the face of the record is clearly required.

It should be noted that traditionally certiorari was the only remedy which could correct an error of law on the face of the record.[63] The combined effect of Order 84, rules 18 and 19 of the Rules of the Superior Courts 1986 is to rob this procedural anomaly of any practical significance.[64] Order 84, rule 18 provides that all applications for certiorari, mandamus, prohibition or *quo warranto* shall be by way of an application for judicial review, and that this procedure may be invoked upon an application for a declaration or an injunction. Order 84, rule 19 states that on an application for judicial review any relief mentioned in rule 18 may be claimed "as an alternative or in addition to any other relief so mentioned" and, in any event, the court may grant any relief mentioned in rule 18 "which it considers appropriate notwithstanding that it has not been specifically claimed." In other words, the High Court would be empowered upon an application by way of judicial review for a declaration invalidating an administrative decision to grant an order of certiorari in lieu of such declaratory relief quashing that decision on the ground that it exhibited an error of law on the face of the record. But given the trend towards expansion in the scope of jurisdictional error, the entire issue may become rather academic, in that,

---

[59] [1964] I.R. 395.

[60] Supreme Court, December 20, 1963.

[61] [1984] I.R. 381.

[62] The judge appears to have overlooked the provisions of s.26(8) of the Local Government (Planning and Development) Act 1963 which provides that the conditions attached to the grant of a planning permission, together with the reasons given for the imposition of such conditions, form part of the record. See further, Hogan, "Remoulding Certiorari" (1982) 17 Ir.Jur.(N.S.) 32, 37–39.

[63] *Punton* v. *Ministry for Pensions (No. 2)* [1964] 1 W.L.R. 226. But *cf. King* v. *Att.-Gen.* [1981] I.R. 233, where a declaration was granted invalidating a conviction for error on the face of the record. The conviction had failed to show jurisdiction on its face, and this is a well-recognised ground for quashing for error of law on the face of the record: *The State (Carr)* v. *Youghal D.J.* [1945] I.R. 43; *The State (Leahy)* v. *Cork D.J.* [1945] I.R. 426 and *The State (Browne)* v. *Feran* [1967] I.R. 147.

[64] See further, p. 580.

henceforth, all errors may be treated as jurisdictional, whether or not they appear on the "record" of the impugned order.

5. Power or Duty?

The essence of a discretionary power is that it is enabling or permissive, whereas mandatory language (such as "shall" or "must") usually implies the existence of a statutory duty. By contrast the use of permissive language (such as "may" or "it shall be lawful") generally imports a discretionary power, as is illustrated by the leading authority in the common law world, *Julius* v. *Lord Bishop of Oxford*.[65] In this case, the relevant statutory provisions provided that "it shall be lawful" for a bishop to convene a commission of inquiry in case of alleged misconduct by a clergyman, either on the application of a complainant or of his own motion. The bishop refused to act on a complaint and the issue arose as to whether this refusal was lawful. The House of Lords concluded that this power was enabling only, since it was evident not only from the wording but also from the background and context of the statute that the bishop might use his own discretion and disallow complainants that were insubstantial or frivolous. Otherwise clergymen might be subjected to unjustified and vexatious complaints.

Similar reasoning has been employed in a variety of recent Irish cases. Thus, in *Duffy* v. *Dublin Corporation*[66] the question arose as to whether section 80 of the Dublin Improvement Act 1849 (which provided that "it shall be lawful" for the Corporation "to build and improve" a cattle market) was obligatory or simply created a power. Henchy J. referred with approval to *Julius* v. *Bishop of Oxford* and held that, when viewed in the context of the statute as a whole, these words were simply enabling. Express statutory language would have been required had it been intended to impose on the Corporation "a perpetual obligation to maintain and improve a market place, regardless of the costs to the ratepayers or the absence of public demand or its unsuitability."[67] In *Stafford* v. *Roadstone Ltd.*[68] Barrington J. rejected the argument that where an unauthorised use was made out the words "the High Court *may* . . . prohibit the continuance of the development or unauthorised use" (contained in section 27 of the Local Government (Planning and Development) Act 1963) obliged the court to grant an order. The Oireachtas presumably intended that this new jurisdiction would be exercised on principles similar to those governing injunctions and it could not have been intended that:

> "The High Court should have no discretion but to issue an injunction where the plaintiff has no interest in the lands in question and the breach of the planning law has been innocent or technical . . ."[69]

---

[65] (1880) L.R. 5 App.Cas. 214.
[66] [1974] I.R. 33.
[67] *Ibid.* 44.
[68] [1980] I.L.R.M. 1.
[69] *Ibid.* See also, *Bradley* v. *Meath County Council* [1991] I.L.R.M. 179 where Costello J. held that it was clear from the interchange of the words "may" and "shall" in s. 52 of the Public Health (Ireland) Act 1878 that a statutory duty to collect refuse only arose where the sanitary authority had been required to do so by ministerial order.

This question was also considered by the Supreme Court in *The State (Shee-han)* v. *Government of Ireland*,[70] where the construction of section 60(7) of the Civil Liability Act 1961 was at issue. Section 60(1) abolished the common law rule whereby a highway authority was not liable for acts of non-feasance, but section 60(7) was in the following terms:

"This section shall come into operation on such day, not earlier than the 1st day of April 1967 as may be fixed therefor by order made by the Government."

As no order had been made by 1986, the question arose as to whether the Government could be compelled by mandamus to make such an order. This in turn raised the issue of whether the words used were obligatory or permissive only. Henchy J. thought that the latter construction was the correct one:

"The uses of 'shall' and 'may,' both in the subsection and the section as a whole, point to the conclusion that the radical law-reform embodied in the section was intended not to come into effect before the 1st April 1967, and thereafter only on such day as *may* be fixed by an order made by the Government. Not, be it noted, on such day as *shall* be fixed by the Government. Limiting words such as 'as soon as may be' or 'as soon as convenient,' which are to be found in comparable statutory provisions, are markedly absent."[71]

Moreover, the passage quoted from *Sheehan* does not satisfactorily come to terms with the distinct, but related, issue, namely, that even permissive language conferring a discretion does not absolve the donee of that power from the obligation to exercise that discretion reasonably.

This reasoning may be contrasted with that of Griffin J. in *Bakht* v. *Medical Council*.[72] Section 27(2) of the Medical Practitioners Act 1978 provided for the registration of certain categories of doctors who had passed such examinations "as are specified . . . in rules made by the Council." Griffin J. rejected the submission that this subsection conferred a discretion and held that the section imposed a statutory duty on the Council to make such rules.

But while the use of permissive language will generally be held to mean that the statute merely confers an enabling power, there exists an important exception to this general rule in cases where a statutory body is given a discretionary power coupled with a duty to exercise this power in a particular way in prescribed circumstances. In other words, there are cases—exemplified by *Bakht*—in which, when applied to action of an administrative character, "may" means, in effect, "must." Thus, in *R. (Local Government Board)* v. *Guardians of the Letterkenny Union*,[73] it was held that the provisions of section 10 of the Vaccination (Amendment) Ireland Act 1879 were mandatory. This section pro-

---

[70] [1987] I.R. 550. See Hogan, "Judicial Review of an Executive Discretion" (1987) 9 D.U.L.J. (N.S.) 91.
[71] *Ibid.* 561.
[72] [1990] 1 I.R. 515. See also, *Philips* v. *Medical Council*, High Court, December 11, 1990.
[73] [1916] 2 I.R. 18.

vided that the guardians of any union "may direct proceedings" to be instituted for the "purpose of enforcing obedience" to the Vaccination Acts. The Letterkenny Union, apparently deferring to local opinion, had taken no action against some 290 defaulting parents, claiming that in doing so, they were exercising bona fide a discretion conferred by the Act. Cherry L.C.J. said:

> "It is settled law that provisions in a statute merely of a permissive character may impose a duty [and] it has been held that where a statute directs anything to be done which is for the public good, words of permission may be construed as mandatory in their operation."[74]

The background to the Act, coupled with the provision for the expense of the proceedings to be paid out of the rates, indicated that the legislature intended that a duty should be imposed "upon the guardians of enforcing the provisions of the Acts in all proper cases."

This principle has been applied by the Supreme Court in a series of cases. Thus, in *Dolan* v. *Neligan*,[75] Walsh J. held that the words "hereby authorised" in section 25 of the Customs Consolidation Act 1876 were mandatory. The Revenue Commissioners were empowered by this provision to repay overpaid customs duties and it had to be assumed:

> "That a statutory power authorising the repayment or the return of overpayments of customs duties authorises that repayment for the sake of justice or for the good of the person for whose benefit the provision exists. . . . Upon the [statutory] conditions [as to overpayment in error] being fulfilled, the person who has paid the duties is entitled to call for the repayment of the overpayments. In my view, the statute is not to be construed as merely conferring a discretion to return the overpayments when those other conditions have been satisfied."[76]

Likewise, in *Re Dunne's Application*,[77] Walsh J. held that the phrase in section 19(2) of the Intoxicating Liquor Act 1960 that the District Court "may order" the extinguishment of a seven-day publican's licence where certain statutory criteria were fulfilled was mandatory. The section was conferred for the benefit of persons holding hotel licences, who could, via the operation of the extinguishment procedure, have their existing licences converted to full licences. This fact, coupled with the absence of notice to potential objectors and the general informality of the procedure, led to the conclusion that, upon "the giving of the required proofs in the particular case," there was no discretion to refuse the order sought.

The converse principle may also be true, in that there are occasions in which the apparently mandatory language of the statute will nonetheless be held to connote a discretion, at least in cases touching on constitutional rights.

---

[74] *Ibid.* 24–25.
[75] [1967] I.R. 247.
[76] *Ibid.* 275, *per* Walsh J.
[77] [1968] I.R. 105.

An example here is *McMahon* v. *Leahy*[78] where the Supreme Court held that, despite the mandatory language of the Extradition Act 1965, the court retained a discretion to refuse extradition where this would infringe the accused's constitutional rights. Henchy J. said that a contrary construction would be tantamount to saying that the court's function was "mechanical, discretionless and without regard to the fact that its order would have an unconstitutional impact on the person sought to be extradited."[79]

6. Formal and Procedural Requirements

As we have seen, nearly every question pertaining to jurisdiction turns on a question of statutory interpretation. This is especially true in the case of the disregard of procedural and formal requirements laid down by statute. When the Oireachtas stipulates that certain formal and procedural requirements must be observed before an administrative decision is arrived at, it rarely states what consequences follow non-compliance with these statutory requirements. Of course, to this general rule there are exceptions: section 5 of the Adoption Act 1976, for example, states that an adoption order shall not be declared invalid solely on the ground that certain statutory prerequisites have not been complied with. Nevertheless, it is true to say that the courts are for the most part left to their own devices as far as the non-compliance with procedural requirements is concerned. Whether a statutory provision which on the face appears to be obligatory is to be regarded as truly mandatory or is merely to be regarded as directory in nature depends on the statutory intent and whether compliance with the provision can fairly be said to be essential to the general object intended to be secured by the Act.[80] The relevant test has been stated in the following terms:

> "If the requirement which has not been observed may fairly be said to be an integral and indispensable part of the statutory intendment, the courts will hold it to be truly mandatory, and will not excuse a departure from it. But if, on the other hand, what is apparently a requirement is in essence merely a direction which is not of the substance of the aim and scheme of the statute, non-compliance may be excused."[81]

But even in the case of directory provisions, the courts will not readily sanction a radical departure from what the legislature has ordained. Thus, even provisions which are directory as to *precise* compliance are generally manda-

---

[78] [1984] I.R. 525.
[79] *Ibid.* 541.
[80] *Monaghan U.D.C.* v. *Alf-A-Bet Promotions Ltd.* [1980] I.L.R.M. 64. See also, *The State (McCarthy)* v. *O'Donnell* [1945] I.R. 126.
[81] *The State (Elm Developments)* v. *An Bord Pleanála* [1981] I.L.R.M. 108, 110, *per* Henchy J. For a dubious application of similar principles see *Re Philip Clarke* [1950] I.R. 235. In *Connolly* v. *Sweeney* [1988] I.L.R.M. 483 McCarthy J. said (at 488) that he "would be slow to accept the underlying principle [in *Elm Developments*] in criminal cases."

tory as to *substantial* compliance.[82] On the other hand, courts are rarely impressed by defects of form, and will often excuse an irregularity where the "requirements of justice and the substance of the procedure have been observed."[83] Thus, in *Veterinary Council* v. *Corr*[84] the appellants had requested a case-stated from a decision of the Circuit Court. The relevant statutory provisions required that the case-stated be served on the respondents "at or before the time" that the case-stated was transmitted to the High Court. On the day that the case-stated was lodged in the High Court, a representative of the appellant's solicitors was delayed in court and found that the respondents' offices had closed. The case-stated was, however, delivered the following day. While the Supreme Court accepted that these statutory requirements were mandatory, Maguire C.J. held that, on these facts, there was sufficient compliance with the terms of the section.

In addition, in view of the fact that in nearly all cases the remedy sought will lie in the discretion of the court, there is increasing evidence that the crucial factor is probably whether the irregularity will cause real prejudice. If the party aggrieved cannot show that he has been "wrong-footed or damnified" or that the "spirit and purpose" of the statutory provisions have not been breached, then relief may be withheld on discretionary grounds.[85]

There are, however, no universal rules which can be used to determine whether a statutory provision is mandatory or directory—each will turn on the proper construction of the legislation in question, and the citation of authorities is not always especially helpful. Difficult issues of principle have been thrown up in recent Irish cases. *O'Mahony* v. *Arklow U.D.C.*[86] is one such case. The plaintiff, who was town clerk of Arklow, was suspended for certain irregularities in the performance of his duties. He was subsequently removed from office with the consent of the Minister for Local Government pursuant to section 26 of the Local Government Act 1941. That application provided that a written application to the Minister for his consent for such dismissal was necessary. No such letter was sent, though the Minister was generally kept informed of the situation and was aware of the dissatisfaction of the council with the plaintiff's performance as town clerk. Although the misconduct of the plaintiff was admitted to be such as would have justified dismissal, the validity of his dismissal was put at issue by the plaintiff.

The dismissal was upheld by a bare majority of the Supreme Court. Lavery J. was of the opinion that as the Minister was fully aware of the situation, and as the plaintiff was given every opportunity to explain his conduct, the irregu-

---

[82] *The State (Doyle)* v. *Carr* [1970] I.R. 87.

[83] *O'Mahony* v. *Arklow U.D.C.* [1965] I.R. 710, 735 (Lavery J.). See also, *The State (Toft)* v. *Galway Corporation* [1981] I.L.R.M. 439; *The State (Elm Developments Ltd.)* v. *An Bord Pleanála* [1981] I.L.R.M. 108; *The State (Coveney)* v. *Special Criminal Court* [1982] I.L.R.M. 284; *McGlinchey* v. *Governor of Portlaoise Prison* [1988] I.R. 671, 695 (Lynch J.); *Rhatigan* v. *Textiles Y Confecciones Europeas S.A.* [1990] 1 I.R. 126.

[84] [1953] I.R. 12.

[85] *The State (Elm Developments Ltd.)* v. *An Bord Pleanála* [1981] I.L.R.M. 108; *The State (Coveney)* v. *Special Criminal Court* [1982] I.L.R.M. 284.

[86] [1965] I.R. 710.

larities complained of were "defects of form and not of substance." He did
not think that the court should:

> "[P]arse and construe rules of procedure in a narrow and unreal way, look-
> ing for some flaw in procedure to invalidate a transaction where the
> requirements of justice and the substance of procedure have been
> observed."[87]

Kingsmill Moore J. in dissent considered that as the procedural requirements
of the Act had not been adhered to, this represented a fundamental procedural defect which invalidated the dismissal. This approach seems unduly narrow and rigid; the majority view that the dismissal should not be invalidated
as there was substantial compliance with the statutory requirements seems
preferable, given that the plaintiff was given every opportunity to prepare his
case—which was the very object of this procedural safeguard.

The conventional distinction between mandatory and directory provisions
has, perhaps, been somewhat blurred, however, by two Supreme Court
decisions even though the traditional language is employed in both cases. In
Monaghan U.D.C. v. *Alf-A-Bet Promotions Ltd.*[88] the respondent developer
sought planning permission which would enable him to convert a drapery
store into a betting office and an amusement arcade. The relevant regulations
required the developer to publish a notice in a newspaper stating the "nature
and extent of the development." The developer's notice referred only to
"alterations and improvements." The Supreme Court held that the notice did
not convey the nature and extent of the proposed development. Inclusion in
the notice of information as to the nature and extent of the proposed development was vital to the proper orientation of the statutory scheme for the grant
of planning permission. The misleading notice that was published was held to
be non-compliance with a mandatory provision, and such compliance was
held to be fatal to the developer's case. In view of the fact that planning permission could radically affect the rights and amenities of others, and substantially benefit or enrich the grantee of the permission, Henchy J. considered
that the courts should not countenance deviation from that which had been
deemed obligatory by the Oireachtas save on an application of the *de minimis*
rule:

> "What the legislature has prescribed in such circumstances as necessary
> should be treated as nothing short of necessary and deviations from the
> requirements must, before it can be overlooked, be shown, by the person
> seeking to have it excused, to be so trivial or so technical, or so peripheral,
> or otherwise so insubstantial that on the principle that it is the spirit rather

---

[87] *Ibid.* 735.
[88] [1980] I.L.R.M. 64. See Cooney (1982) 17 Ir.Jur.(N.S.) 346 and Scannell, "Planning Control:
Twenty Years On" (1982) 4 D.U.L.J.(N.S.) 41. See also, *Dunne Ltd.* v. *Dublin C.C.* [1974] I.R.
45; *McCabe* v. *Harding Investments Ltd.* [1984] I.L.R.M. 105 and *The State (Multi-Print Labels
Ltd.)* v. *Employment Appeals Tribunal* [1984] I.L.R.M. 545.

than the letter of the law that matters, the prescribed obligation has been substantially, and therefore adequately, complied with."[89]

This matter was further considered by the Supreme Court in *The State (Elm Developments Ltd.)* v. *An Bord Pleanála.*[90] A developer sought and obtained a grant of planning permission from a local authority. An appeal was lodged by local residents against the grant of such permission. The developer claimed that failure by the residents to state the grounds of appeal in writing at the actual time of filing a notice of appeal rendered such appeal a nullity in law. The court concluded that the requirement that the grounds of appeal be stated contemporaneously with the notice of appeal was directory rather than mandatory in nature. The purpose of the regulations was informative in nature: the Board was quite entitled to listen to points other than those mentioned in the grounds of appeal. Furthermore, in the instant case grounds of appeal had been furnished to the satisfaction of the Board within a few weeks of the appeal, and Henchy J. concluded that the developer could not say that he had been in any way "wrong-footed or damnified" or that the "spirit or purpose" of the Planning Acts and regulations had been breached. In addition, perhaps the fact that the courts are traditionally less zealous in classifying statutory provisions as mandatory where they have been ignored by a private individual rather than by a public body was also an (unarticulated) factor in this decision.

As stated, these cases tend to blur the conventional and traditional distinction between mandatory and directory provisions. The purpose of the conventional mandatory/directory distinction was to ensure that one party could not rely on a minor or technical breach of prescribed statutory requirements in order to invalidate an administrative decision. In practice, this convention distinction has proved difficult to draw and, increasingly, the courts seek to examine all the circumstances of the case in order to ascertain whether the disregard of procedural requirements in that particular context has caused real prejudice. If an applicant cannot show that he has been "wrong footed or damnified" by a breach of the prescribed procedure, then either the provisions in question will be classified as directory (so that, in fact, the decision-maker did not act *ultra vires*) or the courts will admit that there was an inadvertent excess of jurisdiction, but will refuse relief on discretionary grounds, since this breach did not prejudice the applicant. This trend is confirmed by an important decision of the Supreme Court, *Rhatigan* v. *Textiles Y Confecciones Europeas S.A.*[91] The plaintiff challenged the validity of an order made by the Master of the High Court providing for the enforcement of contested English judgments under the terms of the Jurisdiction of Courts and Enforcement of Judgments (European Communities) Act 1988 on the ground that the order did not state that the judgments in question were judgments of a Contracting State which is a party to the Convention. Griffin J. stated that in so far as there was any such

[89] [1980] I.L.R.M. 64, 69.
[90] [1981] I.L.R.M. 108.
[91] [1990] 1 I.R. 126.

requirement, it was governed by national—and not European Community—law. Accordingly, the "sanction for any failure to comply with such a [procedural] requirement" had to be determined by national law:

> "The Court must therefore ascertain where the balance of justice lies as between the parties—in other words, it must determine whether the interests of justice require that the plaintiff should be permitted to rely on the breach of the procedural requirements of the Master's order or whether Textiles should be permitted to enforce the order notwithstanding such breach."[92]

On this question, Griffin J. held that the "interests of justice overwhelmingly require that this conflict should be resolved in favour of Textiles." The plaintiff had contested these judgments in the English courts and he could not "have been under the slightest misapprehension" as to the origin of the foreign judgments which were the subject of the enforcement order.

Perhaps the best way of regarding these cases is to say that they demonstrate a change of emphasis. The courts will no longer pronounce a statutory provision to be either mandatory or directory in isolation from the facts of a particular case but will examine its effect on the parties to see if compliance has worked prejudice. Moreover, the courts seem more prepared to excuse non-compliance on the part of a private litigant than is the case with public bodies.

Having stated what appears to be the emerging general principles, it will be convenient if we now consider particular categories.

Legislation prescribing formal procedures

Where legislation requires that an administrative or judicial body must follow a set or prescribed procedure before arriving at its decision, non-compliance will often be fatal to the validity of an order, especially where the prescribed procedure is designed to ensure compliance with the requirements of a fair hearing. Thus, in *Ahern* v. *Kerry County Council*,[93] a councillor complained that the local authority had not complied with section 10(1) of the City and County Management (Amendment) Act 1955 in considering the estimates of expenditure for the following year. Section 10(1) requires the authority to consider all estimates of expenditure and Blayney J. held that it was not sufficient compliance for the councillors simply to consider some of the estimates. It followed that the resolution adopting the estimates was invalid, as Blayney J. said:

> "Once a statute prescribes what is to be done at a meeting, it seems to me that what is prescribed must be observed at the meeting by the local authority if the resolution that was passed at that meeting is to be valid."[94]

It will be noted that strict compliance with procedural requirements will be

---

[92] *Ibid.* 136.
[93] [1988] I.L.R.M. 382.
[94] *Ibid.* 396.

insisted on, even where those requirements go further than what is required by constitutional justice (as was the case here).[95]

This is further illustrated by *O'Flynn* v. *Mid-Western Health Board*,[96] where the applicant sought to quash a decision of the respondents to refer his case to the Minister for Health for the purpose of having a committee established under Article 8 of the Health Services Regulations 1971 to investigate certain complaints made against him. Barr J. noted that the regulations provided for a two-stage procedure to investigate such complaints. First, the chief executive of the health board was to consider the complaint against the doctor concerned and to invite him to respond. Secondly, it was only where the chief executive considered that a prima facie case had been made out that he could validly request the Minister to establish an investigating committee. Here Barr J. considered that as the applicants had not been supplied with sufficient details of the complaint to enable them to reply to these charges, the chief executive officer could not properly invoke the second stage of the procedure, since:

> "This is patently an important step which has potentially far-reaching consequences for the doctor in question. Article 24 clearly envisages that it ought not to be taken until the doctor has had an opportunity to consider the complaint and to respond to it. He cannot make a meaningful response if he is not fully informed as to the complaint alleged. Furthermore, the failure in the present case of the chief executive officer to inform the applicants fully of the details of the complaint made against them, resulted in the response which each made to him being necessarily incomplete. Thus, the chief executive officer could not reasonably arrive at a decision that it was proper to invite the Minister to appoint a committee of inquiry to investigate the alleged complaints."[97]

A similarly strict view will be taken where the formal procedures are designed to protect fundamental interests such as property rights. Thus, in *Dunraven Estates Ltd.* v. *Commissioners of Public Works*,[98] the Supreme Court held that the defendants were obliged to tender full particulars of their proposed arterial drainage works on the plaintiff's lands, as was required by sections 5 and 6 of the Arterial Drainage Act 1945. As Budd J. observed, the object of these sections was to enable an owner of land "to know precisely what is proposed to be done to his property." If he was not made aware of the

---

[95] Interestingly, the applicant had also complained that what transpired was also a breach of constitutional justice. But while Blayney J. accepted that the statutory formalities had not been complied with, he rejected the suggestion that there had also been a breach of constitutional justice, saying that as the applicant was actually present at the meeting, "it would be difficult to say" that the resolution was passed in breach of constitutional justice.

[96] [1989] I.R. 429.

[97] *Ibid.* 438–439. This decision was, however, reversed on appeal by the Supreme Court in its decision of February 26, 1991. Hedeman J. said that the chief executive officer did not have an "adjudicative role", but was rather intended to act as a filter, excluding groundless complaints. This characterisation of the officer's statutory role does not affect this aspect of Barr J.'s judgment.

[98] [1974] I.R. 113.

proposals, he would not be in a position to make "observations of any worth"[99] on these proposals and his statutory right to do so would be defeated. The Supreme Court accordingly concluded that these provisions were mandatory and must be strictly complied with.

The converse proposition is also true: if the formal requirements do not affect individual rights and are simply prescribed for the convenience of the authorities and for good administration generally, then they are likely to be classified as directory only. Thus, Finlay P. held in *Cahill* v. *Governor of Curragh Detention Barracks*[1] that prisoners cannot complain of breaches of the Prison Rules requiring the authorities to furnish Bibles in cells or have a serving medical officer appointed where these breaches do not in any way imperil his welfare or breach his constitutional rights. In a similar fashion, a Divisional High Court held in *McGlinchey* v. *Governor of Portlaoise Prison*[2] that the provisions of the Special Criminal Court Rules 1975 giving the court power to determine when and where to sit, etc., were administrative only and did not confer enforceable legal rights on persons coming before that court.

Legislation prescribing substantive requirements

Legislation prescribing substantive requirements is usually regarded as mandatory, unless it is clear from the statutory context that it was not so intended. Substantive requirements of this kind are designed to further a statutory purpose and if non-compliance with these requirements would frustrate those objectives, the provision will invariably be held to be mandatory. Again, some modern examples are illustrative.

In *M.* v. *An Bord Uchtála*[3] the Supreme Court held that as section 15(3) of the Adoption Act 1976 required a valid consent to be furnished by a natural mother prior to an adoption, non-compliance with this section was not a "mere procedural irregularity but must be regarded as being destructive of the power sought to be exercised." Again, in *The State (Elm Developments Ltd.)* v. *An Bord Pleanála*[4] Henchy J. held that statutory provisions requiring that an appeal to the Board be accompanied by a deposit and be in writing were mandatory:

> "The requirement that the appeal be in writing is so obviously basic to the institution of the appeal that it . . . must be considered to be mandatory. So also must the requirement that the written appeal state the subject-matter of the appeal, for the absence of such identification could lead to administrative confusion. The lodgment of a deposit with the appeal (perhaps not necessarily physically or contemporaneously with the appeal) would also seem to be an essential part of the statutory scheme, so as to discourage frivolous, delaying or otherwise worthless appeals."[5]

[99] *Ibid.* 134.
[1] [1980] I.L.R.M. 191.
[2] [1988] I.R. 671.
[3] [1977] I.R. 287.
[4] [1981] I.L.R.M. 108.
[5] *Ibid.*

Two other recent examples confirm this general trend. In *Thompson* v. *Minister for Social Welfare*[6] a social welfare appeals officer sat without the assessors required by section 298(12) of the Social Welfare (Consolidation) Act 1981. This failure to comply with an imperative statutory requirement was sufficient to warrant the quashing of the appeals officer's decision. Similarly, the requirements of section 23 of the Children Act 1908 (which obliges the District Court when making a fit person order to specify the religious persuasion of the child in the body of the order) were held to be mandatory in *The State (D.) v. G. (No. 2).*[7] Finlay C.J. said that this requirement was concerned "with the welfare of the child in a very fundamental matter and, as such, must be a mandatory provision."[8]

Time limits

A large proportion of the cases raising non-compliance with formal requirements occur in the context of time limits. No universal principles can be stated as to the consequences of non-compliance with such time limits, but four guiding principles in relation to time limits were stated as being relevant by Lord Lowry L.C.J. in *Dolan* v. *O'Hara.*[9] It will be convenient if we examine the case law in the light of these four principles.

"1. A time limit is likely to be imperative where no power to extend time is given and where no provision is made for what is to happen if the time limit is exceeded."

An example of this principle was given by Henchy J. in *The State (Elm Developments Ltd.)* v. *An Bord Pleanála*[10] where commenting on the 21-day appeal period for appeals prescribed by section 26(5) of the Local Government (Planning and Development) Act 1963, he said:

"The decision of a planning authority to grant a development permission . . . will become final if an appeal is not lodged within the time fixed by the Act. Since an extension of time is not provided for, the requirement as to time is mandatory, so that a departure from it cannot be excused."[11]

Of course, these are but working principles which, as might be expected, will not cater for every case. Thus, in *Irish Refining plc* v. *Commissioner of Valuation,*[12] the Supreme Court held that a six-month time limit prescribed by section 10 of the Annual Revision of Rateable Property (Ireland) (Amendment) Act 1860 was merely directory, despite the absence of any power to extend the time limit, since a contrary conclusion might produce an injustice.

[6] [1989] I.R. 618.
[7] [1990] I.L.R.M. 130.
[8] *Ibid.* 135.
[9] [1974] N.I. 125.
[10] [1981] I.L.R.M. 108.
[11] *Ibid.*
[12] [1990] 1 I.R. 568.

"2. Requirements in statutes which give jurisdiction are usually imperative."

This principle was illustrated in *Dolan* v. *O'Hara*[13] itself, where an obligation on the appellant to transmit a case-stated within a 14-day period was
held to be mandatory by the Northern Ireland Court of Appeal. Both Lord
Lowry L.C.J. and Jones L.J. observed that, as the section itself conferred jurisdiction and as there was no provision for an extension of time, only impossibility could excuse non-compliance with this mandatory provision. This
principle has also been applied to other statutory provisions, such as section
26(5) of the Local Government (Planning and Development) Act 1963[14] and
section 8 of the Unfair Dismissals Act 1977.[15]

"3. Where the act is to be done by a third party for the benefit of a person
who will be damnified by non-compliance, the requirement is more likely to
be directory."

This principle is well illustrated by several cases raising the issue of the six-
month limit for the signature of a case-stated by a District Justice prescribed
by rule 17 of the District Court Rules 1955. In *Prendergast* v. *Porter*,[16] the
District Justice had failed to sign the case-stated within this period and the
party opposing the case-stated claimed as a result that the appeal was not
maintainable. Davitt P. rejected this argument, saying that the time limit was
intended simply:

"to provide a period after which the Justice could clearly be said to have
neglected or refused to perform his duty . . . It never could have been the
intention to deprive a party of his right of appeal by way of case-stated."[17]

In *McMahon* v. *McClafferty*[18] Costello J. took a similar view, saying that Rule
55 was not mandatory and he held that a District Justice could sign the case-
stated after the six-month limit. Another example is afforded by the judgment
of the Supreme Court in *Irish Refining plc* v. *Commissioner of Valuation*,[19]
where the Circuit Court judge had not signed the case-stated within the 21-
day period prescribed by section 10 of the Annual Revision of Rateable Property (Ireland) (Amendment) Act 1860. Finlay C.J. held that the provision was
directory only, since any contrary interpretation would mean that the person
applying for the case-stated:

"Would be entirely at the mercy of the judge concerned and that, for practical purposes, it would be impossible for him, under a number of different
hypothetical circumstances, such as the absence from the country on vaca-
tion or illness of the judge, to prosecute his appeal by way of case-stated.

---

[13] [1974] N.I. 125.
[14] *The State (Elm Developments Ltd.)* v. *An Bord Pleanála* [1981] I.L.R.M. 108.
[15] *The State (I.B.M. Ltd.)* v. *Employment Appeals Tribunal* [1984] I.L.R.M. 31.
[16] [1961] I.R. 440.
[17] *Ibid.* 441–442.
[18] [1989] I.R. 68.
[19] [1990] 1 I.R. 568.

Such a manifestly unfair or unjust procedure should not, in my view, be assumed to have been the real intention of the legislature."[20]

"4. Impossibility may excuse non-compliance even where the requirement is imperative."

Clearly the courts will not readily countenance arguments such as impossibility or *force majeure* in the face of imperative statutory provisions, so it is hardly surprising that there are few authorities on this point. However, it does seem that this principle may apply where it has proved impossible to effect service on the other side within the requisite period or where every effort has been made to comply with the statutory provisions. In *Veterinary Council* v. *Corr,*[21] for example, the appellants attempted to serve a case-stated on the respondents on the last day permitted by the legislation, but found that the offices had closed. This was held by the Supreme Court to be a sufficient compliance with the (mandatory) statutory requirements.

Where non-compliance might affect third-party rights or the rights of the public

Where the non-compliance might affect third-party rights or the rights of the general public, then the provisions will generally be regarded as mandatory and the courts will be even more reluctant to excuse anything less than full and precise compliance with the statutory requirements. This is especially true of statutory requirements contained in planning, licensing and other regulatory legislation designed to protect the participation and other rights of third parties and the general public.

In *Monaghan U.D.C.* v. *Alf-A-Bet Promotions Ltd.*[22] the plaintiffs (who claimed to have secured planning permission by default under section 26(4) of the Local Government (Planning and Development) Act 1963) had failed— whether by inadvertence or otherwise—to state the true nature of the proposed development in their advertisement in the local newspapers, as required by Article 14 of the Local Government (Planning and Development) Regulations 1977. The Supreme Court held that the application was invalid, as the plaintiffs had not sufficiently complied with a mandatory provision. As Henchy J. observed:

"One of the primary purposes of the notification [in the newspaper] is defeated if the notice does not, at least in fair and general terms, state the nature and extent of the proposed development. Whether the unilluminating words used in this case ("alterations and reconstructions") were chosen deliberately for their vagueness or casually through inattention to the stated requirements of the regulations, they were so wanting in compliance with the spirit and purpose of the Act and the regulations, that the pub-

---

[20] *Ibid.* 577.
[21] [1953] I.R. 12. There is an interesting analysis of this decision in *Hughes* v. *Viner* [1985] 3 All E.R. 40.
[22] [1980] I.L.R.M. 64.

lished notice, and therefore the application, must be deemed to have been nullified . . . Such powers as have been given to planning authorities, tribunals or the courts to operate or review the operation of the planning laws should be exercised in such a way that the statutory intent in its essence will not be defeated, intentionally or unintentionally, by omissions, ambiguities, misstatements or other defaults in the purported compliance with the prescribed procedures."[23]

The courts' insistence on strict compliance with mandatory provisions where the interests of the public might be affected is also illustrated by *Dublin County Council* v. *Marren*.[24] The issue in this case was whether an applicant for planning permission had complied adequately with the relevant regulations which require the submission of such plans, drawings and other particulars as are necessary "to identify the land and to describe the work or structure to which the application relates." The applicant had previously applied unsuccessfully for planning permission in respect of certain premises. He made a fresh application some years later, but on this occasion he omitted to include details of plans and drawings. The reasons for this omission were, however, contained in the application itself, where he stated that the house plans were to be the same as in the previous application. While Barrington J. took the view that the planning officials were not in any way incommoded or prejudiced by this failure to comply precisely with the terms of the regulations, he observed that this was not simply a matter of *inter partes*. If it had been, he would have ruled that there had been substantial compliance and that any non-compliance was covered by the *de minimis* principle. But it was not simply an *inter partes* matter, as the relevant regulations contemplated that the application, together with the plans, drawings, etc., would be made available to the public. As it was possible that a member of the public might have been misled or incommoded by the failure to include the relevant drawings and plans, Barrington J. ruled that there had not been adequate compliance with the regulations.[25]

7. Waiver and Consent

The fundamental rule is that waiver and consent cannot confer jurisdiction. Closely related to this is the principle that public authorities cannot waive observance of the law by exercising a dispensing power. Accordingly, a plan-

---

[23] *Ibid.* 69.
[24] [1985] I.L.R.M. 593. See also, *R. (Byrne)* v. *Dublin JJ.* [1904] 2 I.R. 190 (21-day notice in Licensing Acts held to be mandatory, as otherwise "there might be frequent disputes as to whether the notice was given within a reasonable time or not," thus prejudicing the interests of the members of the public who might otherwise wish to lodge an objection in licensing matters).
[25] For an example of a purely *inter partes* matter in this context, see *The State (I.B.M. (Ireland) Ltd.)* v. *Employment Appeals Tribunal* [1984] I.L.R.M. 31.

ning authority is not at liberty to waive statutory requirements which are clearly imposed for the public benefit.[26] Nevertheless, the principle that waiver or consent cannot validate or modify *ultra vires* action must be treated with some reserve, for it is clear that waiver or consent may operate as a discretionary bar to relief.[27] The doctrines of waiver, acquiescence[28] and estoppel by conduct represent in varying degrees the idea that a plaintiff cannot approbate and reprobate. It has been stated that it would be inconsistent with the due administration of justice if a plaintiff "were allowed to reserve unto himself the right to argue later a point touching on the validity of a decision," should that decision prove adverse to his interests.[29]

The traditional rule has been put in the following terms by Lord Reid:

"[I]t is a fundamental principle that no consent can confer on a court or tribunal with limited statutory jurisdiction any power to act beyond that jurisdiction, or can estop the consenting party from subsequently maintaining that such court or tribunal lacks jurisdiction."[30]

Irish courts have been reluctant, however, to commit themselves unequivocally to such a position. In the leading case, *Corrigan* v. *Irish Land Commission*,[31] Henchy J. acknowledged that a totally new jurisdiction[32] could not be created by means of an estoppel. The crucial test was whether the court or tribunal had initiated jurisdiction to enter upon the inquiry. Once such jurisdiction was present, any errors committed in the course of the inquiry could be waived. In *Corrigan* itself it was clear that the Appeals Tribunal of the

---

[26] *Dublin Corporation* v. *McGrath* [1978] I.L.R.M. 208; *Morris* v. *Garvey* [1983] I.R. 319; *Western Fish Products Ltd.* v. *Perwith District Council* [1981] 2 All E.R. 204. But minor irregularities may, in some circumstances, be waived: *Wells* v. *Minister for Housing and Local Government* [1967] 1 W.L.R. 1000; *Lever Finance Ltd.* v. *Westminster Corporation* [1971] 1 Q.B. 222 and *Re Thompson's Application* [1985] N.I. 170.

[27] *The State (Byrne)* v. *Frawley* [1978] I.R. 326; *Corrigan* v. *Irish Land Commission* [1977] I.R. 317 and *The State (Cronin)* v. *Circuit Judge for the Western Court* [1937] I.R. 34.

[28] Acquiescence means "participation in proceedings without taking objection to the jurisdiction of the tribunal once the facts giving ground for raising the objection are fully known"; de Smith's *Judicial Review of Administrative Action* (London, 1980), p. 423.

[29] *Corrigan* v. *Irish Land Commission* [1977] I.R. 317, 325, *per* Henchy J. But see *The State (Gallagher, Shatter & Co.)* v. *de Valera* [1986] I.L.R.M. 3 where a solicitor's firm permitted a taxation of costs to proceed while maintaining an objection as to jurisdiction. The Supreme Court, *per* McCarthy J., held that there had been no waiver of jurisdictional objection: "[I]t does not appear to me that justice is served by determining a case of this kind aginst a solicitor because, whilst maintaining his objection, he thought it more practicable to allow the taxation to proceed, in the hope that the result would, in any event, be satisfactory. When, far from being short of satisfactory, it held him guilty of making a gross overcharge, in my view he is not to be defeated by a plea of waiver" ([1986] I.L.R.M. 9).

[30] *Essex Incorporated Church Union* v. *Essex C.C.* [1963] A.C. 808. See also, *The State (Byrne)* v. *Frawley* [1978] I.R. 326, 342, *per* O'Higgins C.J.

[31] [1977] I.R. 317. See also, *Re Creighton's Estate*, High Court, March 5, 1982; *The State (Grahame)* v. *Racing Board*, High Court, November 22, 1983.

[32] The word "jurisdiction" is used by Henchy J. in the restrictive sense of "jurisdiction to enter upon an inquiry." Contrast this with his judgment in *The State (Holland)* v. *Kennedy* [1977] I.R. 193 where the judge stated that for any number of reasons a tribunal which had jurisdiction at the start of an inquiry could lose that jurisdiction.

Land Commission plainly had jurisdiction to hear the plaintiff's appeal. The question was whether two particular lay commissioners were debarred from exercising that jurisdiction by reason of their prior dealing with the case. Henchy J. found that that point could be, and indeed had been, waived by the plaintiff when he accepted the tribunal as he found it composed on the day of the hearing.

In other cases, waiver and estoppel have been regarded as a bar to discretionary relief. In *R. (Kildare C.C.)* v. *Commissioner for Valuation*[33] the applicants sought to quash a revised valuation order made on appeal by a County Court. They allowed the appeal to proceed on the basis that there was jurisdiction in the County Court to revise the valuation: it was only when the decision of the Court did not prove as favourable to their interests as they had expected that they sought to question the jurisdiction of the tribunal. The former Irish Court of Appeal agreed that the adjudication of the County Court was *ultra vires*, but held nevertheless that the applicants were precluded by their conduct from obtaining the relief sought. A similar conclusion was reached in *The State (Byrne)* v. *Frawley*[34] where the Supreme Court held that the applicant by his conduct had approbated a jury selected in an unconstitutional fashion. He could not now be heard to say that the jury lacked competence to try him.

A litigant will generally be deemed to have waived objections based on the composition of a tribunal[35] or the procedure adopted if the jurisdictional question is not raised at the appropriate time in the proceedings. Persons who attend court hearings are deemed to have waived any possible irregularities which might exist.[36] In one case,[37] the applicant attended petty sessions and participated in the case to the extent of asking for an adjournment on a number of occasions. It was decided that he was deemed to have waived any possible irregularity, and that he had estopped himself by his conduct from obtaining certiorari. The Supreme Court ruled to like effect in *Re Tynan*[38] where the applicant had sought an order of prohibition restraining the District Court from dealing with an allegedly irregular summons. In the opinion of Walsh J. the conduct of the applicant in appearing at the District Court, his giving of evidence, and his failure to raise prompt objection were all consistent with the inference that he had waived the point.

---

[33] [1901] 2 I.R. 215. See also, *The State (McKay)* v. *Cork Circuit Judge* [1937] I.R. 650; *The State (Cronin)* v. *Circuit Judge for Western Circuit* [1937] I.R. 34; *R. (Dorris)* v. *Ministry of Health* [1954] N.I. 79.

[34] *The State (Byrne)* v. *Frawley* [1978] I.R. 326. See also, *Whelan* v. *R.* [1921] 1 I.R. 310. For cases where the plea of waiver was disallowed, see *The State (Redmond)* v. *Wexford Corporation* [1946] I.R. 409; *The State (Cole)* v. *Labour Court* (1984) 3 J.I.S.L.L. 128; *The State (Gallagher, Shatter & Co.)* v. *de Valera* [1986] I.L.R.M. 3 and *Browne* v. *An Bord Pleanála* [1989] I.L.R.M. 865.

[35] *Corrigan* v. *Irish Land Commission* [1977] I.R. 317.

[36] *Whelan* v. *R.* [1921] 1 I.R. 310; *The State (Grahame)* v. *Racing Board*, High Court, November 22, 1983.

[37] *R. (Sherlock)* v. *Cork JJ.* (1909) 42 I.L.T.R. 247.

[38] [1969] I.R. 1. See also, *Moore* v. *Gamgee* (1890) 25 Q.B.D. 244.

8. Statutory Restriction of Judicial Review

Full ouster clauses

The courts have never looked favourably on legislative attempts to curb the High Court's supervisory jurisdiction over decisions of lower courts and administrative bodies.[39] Even in the case of widely-drafted statutory[40] ouster clauses both the High Court[41] and the Supreme Court[42] have affirmed on many occasions that such clauses will not protect a decision which is *ultra vires*. However, it does seem that an ouster clause will have the limited effect of preventing the High Court from granting certiorari where the alleged defect is a non-jurisdictional error of law only.[43]

Furthermore, the constitutionality of legislative attempts to oust the High Court's power of review must be doubtful in light of the decision of the Supreme Court in *Tormey* v. *Attorney-General*.[44] In that case Henchy J. observed that Article 34.3.1,[45] when read in conjunction with Article 34.3.4 and Article 37, permitted the Oireachtas to vest lower courts or administrative tribunals with exclusive jurisdiction in respect of certain justiciable controversies, but where this had been done:

"[The] full jurisdiction [of the High Court] is there to be invoked—in proceedings such as habeas corpus, certiorari, prohibition, quo warranto, injunction or declaratory action—so as to ensure that the hearing and

---

[39] "[T]he courts should be reluctant to surrender their inherent right to enter on a question of what are prima facie justiciable matters," *per* Henchy J. in *The State (Pine Valley Developments Ltd.)* v. *Dublin C.C.* [1984] I.R. 417, 426. And see the strict manner in which the Supreme Court has construed such clauses in cases such as *Pine Valley* and *The State (Finglas Industrial Estates Ltd.)* v. *Dublin C.C.*, February 17, 1983.

[40] This reasoning applies *a fortiori* to non-statutory ouster clauses. In *Casey* v. *Minister for Agriculture*, High Court, February 6, 1987, McCarthy J. held that a provision of the (non-statutory) Bovine Brucellosis Eradication Scheme which had stipulated that the Minister's decision was "final" meant "final" only in the administrative sense: it could not exclude the supervisory jurisdiction of the High Court.

[41] *The State (O'Duffy)* v. *Bennett* [1935] I.R. 70; *The State (Hughes)* v. *Lennon* [1935] I.R. 128; *Murren* v. *Brennan* [1942] I.R. 466 and *The State (Horgan)* v. *Exported Livestock Board Ltd.* [1943] I.R. 581. See also, *R. (Conyngham)* v. *Pharmaceutical Society of Ireland* [1899] 2 I.R. 132; *Commissioners of Public Works* v. *Monaghan* [1909] 2 I.R. 718; *R. (Sinnott)* v. *Wexford Corporation* [1910] 2 I.R. 403 and *Waterford Corporation* v. *Murphy* [1920] 2 I.R. 165.

[42] *The State (McCarthy)* v. *O'Donnell* [1945] I.R. 126; *Brannigan* v. *Keady* [1959] I.R. 283 (*semble*). This was also the attitude of the House of Lords: see *Ansminic Ltd.* v. *Foreign Compensation Commission* [1969] 2 A.C. 147. But a different attitude prevails in the case of clauses imposing brief limitation periods: *R.* v. *Environment Secretary, ex p. Ostler* [1977] Q.B. 122; *Inver Resources Ltd.* v. *Limerick Corporation* [1988] I.L.R.M. 47.

[43] *R.* v. *Medical Appeal Tribunal, ex p. Gilmore* [1957] 1 Q.B. 574. But in *Gilmore* it was decided that the court may still intervene to quash for error of law on the face of the record even where the tribunal's decision is expressed to be "final."

[44] [1985] I.R. 289.

[45] Art. 34.3.1 vests the High Court with "full original jurisdiction" in respect of all matters and questions "whether of fact or law, civil or criminal." However, Art. 34.3.4 goes on to permit the Oireachtas to establish courts of "local and limited jurisdiction" and Art. 37 enables tribunals to exercise judicial functions of a limited nature in non-criminal matters.

determination will be in accordance with law. Save to the extent required by the terms of the Constitution itself, no justiciable matter may be excluded from the range of the original jurisdiction of the High Court."[46]

This is a clear indication that legislative ouster clauses are unconstitutional, at least where the lower court or tribunal has been vested with exclusive jurisdiction to determine particular justiciable controversies.[47]

Partial ouster clauses: brief limitation periods

Legislative provisions which, instead of attempting to effect a complete ouster of the High Court's supervisory jurisdiction, purport to impose brief limitation periods on the right to seek judicial review may stand on a different footing. While there is a definite trend away from complete ouster clauses on the part of the parliamentary draftsman, there are, however, some important partial ouster clauses which are regularly invoked. Partial ouster clauses (which generally take the form of very short limitation periods) may be defended—at least, in some cases—on the ground that, in the case of certain types of administrative decisions, there is an overwhelming need for a swift determination and finality.[48]

The most important clause of this kind is section 82(3A) of the Local Government (Planning and Development) Act 1963, which provides for a two-month time limit in any case where it is sought to challenge a decision of a planning authority or An Bord Pleanála. The unqualified nature of this two-month restriction is illustrated by *Inver Resources Ltd.* v. *Limerick Corporation*.[49] Here a planning permission had been granted to a non-existent company, but Barron J. held that this absence of jurisdiction could not now be questioned by reason of the fact that the application for judicial review was made outside the two-month period. While the applicant company was non-existent, the application for permission had been in reality on behalf of its principal shareholder and Barron J. was satisfied that the application "had substance or reality."

The question arises as to the constitutionality of this provision, especially where there is no judicial discretion to cater for "hard cases," such as where the applicants had no means of knowing of the facts giving rise to the application for judicial review until the time period had elapsed. In *Brady* v. *Donegal County Council*[50] Costello J. found this provision to be unconstitutional:

---

[46] [1985] I.R. 289, 296–297.
[47] See also, *Re Loftus Bryan's Estate* [1942] I.R. 185 and *O'Doherty* v. *Att.-Gen.* [1941] I.R. 569.
[48] "The public interest in (a) the establishment at an early date of certainty in the development decisions of planning authorities and (b) the avoidance of unnecessary costs and wasteful appeals is obviously a real one and could well justify the imposition of stringent time limits for the institution of court proceedings," *per* Costello J. in *Brady* v. *Donegal County Council* [1989] I.L.R.M. 282, 289.
[49] [1988] I.L.R.M. 47.
[50] [1989] I.L.R.M. 282.

while his decision was set aside by the Supreme Court on factual grounds[51] (and not on the merits), his reasoning casts considerable doubt on the validity of this subsection (and, indeed, by implication, other unqualified time bars of this kind). In this case, it appeared that the advertisement placed by the applicant for planning permission had not been published in a newspaper circulating in the area, as required by Article 14 of the 1977 Planning Regulations. Some neighbours sought to quash this permission, but found that they were a few days out of time to challenge its validity. On the basis of these assumed facts, Costello J. concluded that the subsection was unconstitutional. It is noteworthy that this conclusion was grounded not on Article 34.3.1 or Article 34.1 but rather on the notion that the sub-section amounted to an impermissible invasion of their property rights, contrary to Article 40.3.2:

> "If the plaintiff's ignorance of his own rights during the short limitation period is caused by the defendant's own wrong-doing and the law still imposes an absolute bar unaccompanied by any judicial discretion to raise it, there must be very compelling reasons indeed to justify such a rigorous limitation on the exercise of a constitutionally protected right. The public interest in the establishment at an early date of certainty in the development decisions of planning authorities . . . could well justify the imposition of stringent time limits for the institution of court proceedings. . . . Certainly the public interest would not be quite as well served by a law with the suggested saver as by the present law, but the loss of the public interest by the proposed modification would be slight while the gain in the protection of the plaintiff's constitutionally protected rights would be very considerable. I conclude, therefore, that the present serious restriction on the exercise of the plaintiff's constitutional rights imposed by the two-month limitation period cannot reasonably be justified."[52]

This reasoning would also seem to apply *a fortiori* to cases of permission obtained in bad faith or, even, perhaps, where the requirements of the 1977 Regulations were manifestly disregarded.

Conclusive evidence provisions[53]

These constitutional developments not only call into question the validity of "no certiorari" clauses, but also the many other statutory provisions which seek to exclude or restrict judicial review, indirectly, by providing that an

---

[51] Costello J. had not reached a final determination as to whether the planning notice itself was invalid. The Supreme Court pointed out, however, that if the facts were so that it were valid, then the applicants' challenge to the validity of the permission would fall *in limine* and there would be no need for the courts to pronounce on the constitutionality of s.82(3A) of the 1963 Act. The finding of unconstitutionality was therefore vacated and the matter remitted back to the High Court.
[52] [1989] I.L.R.M. 282, 288–289. Perhaps some of the force of this reasoning has been diluted by the subsequent decision of *Hegarty* v. *O'Loughran* [1990] I.L.R.M. 403 where the Supreme Court inclined to the view that a similarly unqualified three-year time limit prescribed by s.11(2)(b) of the Statute of Limitations 1957 was not unconstitutional.
[53] For an excellent analysis of this topic, see Pye, "The Section 104 Certificate of Registration— An Impenetrable Shield No More?" (1985) 3 I.L.T.(N.S.) 213. See also, Hogan, "Reflections on the Supreme Court's decision in *Tormey* v. *Attorney-General*" (1986) 8 D.U.L.J.(N.S.) 31.

administrative decision shall be "conclusive evidence" of the existence of certain facts or of the status of specified legal entities. Some important miscellaneous examples of this legislative device include section 2(1) of the Trade Union Act 1913[54] (which provides that the certificate of the Registrar of Friendly Societies is conclusive evidence of the status of a trade union); section 19(4) of the Offences Against the State Act 1939[55] (which provides that a Government suppression order under section 18 of that Act shall be conclusive evidence of the fact that the suppressed organisation is unlawful); section 104 of the Companies Act 1963[56] (which provides that the Registrar of Companies' certificate that a particular charge has complied with the registration requirements of Part IV of the 1963 Act shall be conclusive evidence of this fact) and, finally, section 31(1) of the Registration of Title Act 1964[57] (which states that the register shall be "conclusive evidence" of title, subject to the right of the Circuit or High Courts to order rectification of the register on the grounds of actual fraud or mistake).

It is true that in *Lombard & Ulster Banking Ltd.* v. *Amurec Ltd.*[58] a charge had been registered some 17 months after its actual creation. While the charge had been left undated at the date of its creation, a much later date was inserted shortly before it was submitted for registration to the Companies Office. Hamilton J. held that the validity of this charge could not now be challenged by a liquidator, as this was prohibited by the conclusive evidence provisions of section 104. The judge drew attention to the importance—from a commercial point of view—of the finality of the register, a factor which also weighed heavily with the English Court of Appeal in *R.* v. *Registrar of Companies, ex p. Central Bank of India*,[59] where the equivalent clause in the English Companies Act was held to preclude judicial review.

There would seem, however, to be a real risk that such "conclusive evidence" will be held either to be unconstitutional or otherwise ineffective, at least in certain types of cases. In *Maher* v. *Attorney-General*[60] the Supreme Court held that a "conclusive evidence" clause contained in the Road Traffic Act 1968 was unconstitutional, as it attempted to oust the jurisdiction of the courts to determine an essential ingredient (alcohol levels) of a criminal prosecution. Similar thinking prevailed with the European Court of Justice in *Johnston* v. *Chief Constable of the Royal Ulster Constabulary*,[61] where a "conclusive evidence" certificate issued by the Chief Constable pursuant to the provisions of Article 53(2) of the Sex Discrimination (Northern Ireland) Order 1976 purported to establish that the conditions for derogating from the equal treatment directive had been satisfied. The court held that such a clause

[54] See Kerr and Whyte, *Irish Trade Union Law* (Abingdon, 1985), pp. 42–48 where the constitutionality of this and other similar conclusive evidence clauses is discussed.
[55] See Hogan and Walker, *Political Violence and the Law in Ireland*, pp. 245–248.
[56] Ussher, *Company Law in Ireland* (London, 1986), pp. 467–471.
[57] Wylie, *Irish Land Law* (Abingdon, 1986), pp. 906–910.
[58] (1978) 112 I.L.T.R. 1.
[59] [1986] Q.B. 1114.
[60] [1973] I.R. 140.
[61] (Case 222/84) [1986] E.C.R. 1651.

was contrary to the "principle of effective judicial control," which itself "reflects a general principle of law which underlies the constitutional traditions common to the member states" and was therefore ineffective. All of this would seem to point to one of two conclusions. Either the "conclusive evidence" does not preclude judicial review, or, should it do so, it is unconstitutional as inconsistent with the High Court's full original jurisdiction under Article 34.3.1.

The only judgment directly on this issue, however, points in the other direction. In *Sloan* v. *Special Criminal Court*[62] the applicant challenged the validity of section 19(4) of the Offences against the State Act 1939, in so far as it provided that a suppression order made by the Government shall be "conclusive evidence" of the suppressed organisation's illegality. Costello J. could not accept this submission, saying that:

> "If an order is made under section 19(4), then the justiciable dispute is whether an accused is a member of an illegal organisation and not whether the organisation itself is illegal."[63]

It may be thought, however, that this analysis is incomplete and does not cater for the case where the accused admits membership of the suppressed organisation, but says that, by virtue of the changed circumstances of the organisation, it should no longer be regarded as illegal. The effect of the "conclusive evidence" provision of section 19(4) is that the accused is not permitted to raise this argument, yet the justiciable controversy would be (were it not for this purported statutory ouster) whether the organisation had, in fact, illegal objectives. Accordingly, it is difficult to see how this type of statutory provision (assuming it precludes judicial review) would survive constitutional challenge either on the ground that it infringes the High Court's full original jurisdiction as conferred by Article 34.3.1 (as this provision was interpreted in *Tormey* v. *Ireland*)[64] or that it constitutes an impermissible invasion of the judicial domain by the Oireachtas. Despite the remarks of Costello J. in *Sloan*, it remains to be seen, therefore, whether this form of "conclusive evidence" provision will survive future challenges.

9. Invalidity

General principles

As a general rule—which is subject to major exceptions—*ultra vires* decisions are null and void and have no legal consequences. The one important Irish case where there was an extended discussion of the nature of invalidity, *Murphy* v. *Att.-Gen.*,[65] arose in the special context of constitutional law, but a majority of the Supreme Court had little difficulty in holding that legislation

---

[62] High Court, July 14, 1989.
[63] *Ibid.* p. 6 of the judgment.
[64] [1985] I.R. 289.
[65] [1982] I.R. 241.

(and, by implication, *ultra vires* administrative acts) found to be unconstitutional must be deemed to be void *ab initio*. Henchy J. described this principle as one which was "inherent in the nature of such limited powers."[66] Another graphic example of the application of this principle is provided by *Shelley* v. *Mahon*,[67] where the Supreme Court held that a criminal conviction imposed by a person who was not a duly appointed District Justice was void and had been arrived at in breach of the applicant's constitutional rights. In this case, the irregularity had occurred because of an oversight as to the respondent's date of birth. The Courts Act (No. 2) 1988[68] had been passed with a view to curing this flaw retrospectively, although the Supreme Court found it was ineffective for this purpose. In the result, it was estimated that up to 100,000 judicial decisions[69] of convictions imposed by the respondent over a four-year period, before *Shelley* was decided, were liable to be set aside. Indeed, in a subsequent case, *Glavin* v. *Governor of the Training Unit, Mountjoy Prison*,[70] a conviction in the Circuit Court for robbery was quashed some four years later, since the return for trial to the Circuit Court had been made by Mr. Mahon at a time when he was not a qualified District Justice. The cases described so far have concerned laws which have been held to be unconstitutional. The conventional view is that a similar principle and exceptions apply to both this situation and the case of an administrative action (or, for that matter, delegated legislation) held to be *ultra vires* a statute. This assumption is borne out by the sequel to *Gilmer* v. *Incorporated Law Society of Ireland*,[71] when the Education Committee of the Incorporated Law Society was found to have unwittingly acted *ultra vires* in raising the competition standard for candidates attempting professional examinations. It was subsequently reported that the Society had reopened the cases of other similarly placed candidates and admitted them to its professional course.[72] This seems a reasonable assumption for the considerations behind both principle and exceptions are the same in each case. And, indeed, the language employed in Henchy J.'s judgment (*e.g.* the use of the word "invalidity") would seem apt to cover both types of case. Accordingly, it seems perfectly reasonable to treat the constitutional authorities as if they also applied, *mutatis mutandis*, to ordinary cases of *ultra vires*.

Exceptions and qualifications

However, cases such as *Shelley* and *Glavin* would appear to represent the high-water mark of the classic doctrine of invalidity, as the rule that *ultra vires* decisions are a nullity is itself subject to considerable qualification. As Costello J. explained in *O'Keefe* v. *An Bord Pleanála*.[73]

[66] *Ibid.*
[67] [1990] 1 I.R. 36.
[68] See Hogan (1988) I.C.L.S.A. 34/01.
[69] *The Irish Times*, March 9, 1990.
[70] High Court, May 12, 1990.
[71] [1989] I.L.R.M. 590.
[72] *The Irish Times*, May 14, 1988.
[73] High Court, July 31, 1990.

"It is usual to say that an *ultra vires* decision is void and a nullity. But it is clear that it is wrong to conclude that such decisions are completely devoid of legal consequences."[74]

This perceptive analysis is borne out by the fact that, with the possible exception of a flagrantly invalid decision, invalidity can only be established in legal proceedings.[75] If the court sets aside the impugned decision this will have retrospective effect, but until this is done it will enjoy a presumption of validity and the decision will be regarded as binding.[76] Moreover until this has occurred, it cannot be confidently anticipated that it will necessarily occur for even where invalidity has been established in the appropriate proceedings, the court may refuse to grant relief on public policy or discretionary grounds.[77] Again, there are sometimes statutory provisions which govern the consequences of invalidation,[78] or which prescribe a limitation period which serves to preclude judicial review once that time limit has expired,[79] or where the statutory context is such that, as Costello J. said in *O'Keefe*, the court must "give legal efficacy to an *ultra vires* decision . . . if the construction of the statute so requires." In short, invalidity is a relative concept and the courts have refrained from pushing that concept to extremes. Perhaps it is because the Irish courts have, in general, taken such a pragmatic approach that the void/voidable controversy which has plagued English administrative law has not given rise to the same difficulties in this jurisdiction.[80] *Irish Permanent Building Society* v. *Caldwell*[81] provides an interesting example of this pragmatic judicial attitude. Here Barrington J. refused to accept that the incorporation of a building society could be nullified by reason of an error on

---

[74] *Ibid.* p. 9 of the judgment.

[75] *Smith* v. *East Elloe R.D.C.* [1956] A.C. 736; *The State (Abenglen Properties Ltd.)* v. *Dublin Corporation* [1984] I.R. 381; *C.W. Shipping Ltd.* v. *Limerick Harbour Commissioners* [1989] I.L.R.M. 416. In the latter case, O'Hanlon J., speaking in the context of an allegedly invalid planning decision, said (at 426) that it was "unrealistic" to suggest that the developer should rely on legal advice as to its invalidity and proceed "to expend money in the belief that the courts will later uphold his view of the law, rather than that taken by the planning authority."

[76] *Hoffman-La Roche & Co.* v. *Secretary for Trade and Industry* [1975] A.C. 295; *Abenglen Properties, supra*; *Campus Oil* v. *Minister for Industry and Energy (No. 2)* [1983] I.R. 88, 107 (O'Higgins C.J.), and, in the special context of constitutional law, *The State (Llewellyn)* v. *UaDonnachada* [1973] I.R. 151; *Pesca Valentia Ltd.* v. *Minister for Fisheries* [1985] I.R. 193.

[77] See, *e.g. The State (Cussen)* v. *Brennan* [1981] I.R. 181; *Murphy* v. *Att.-Gen.* [1982] I.R. 341.

[78] See, *e.g.* Electoral Act 1923, s.9 (no election to be declared invalid where non-compliance with rules concerning secrecy and integrity of the ballot did not affect the result); Adoption Act 1976, s.6 (no child to be removed from custody of its adoptive parents solely on the grounds that adoption order was invalid).

[79] Housing Act 1966, s.78(2) (three-week time limit in respect of challenges to validity of a compulsory purchase order); Local Government (Planning and Development) Act 1963, s.42(3A) (two-month time limit in respect of challenges to the validity of a planning permission) and see *Inver Resources Ltd.* v. *Limerick Corporation* [1988] I.L.R.M. 47.

[80] See, *e.g. D.P.P.* v. *Head* [1959] A.C. 83; *R.* v. *Paddington Valuation Officer, ex p. Peachey Property Corporation Ltd.* [1966] 1 Q.B. 380; *Hoffman-La Roche & Co.* v. *Secretary of State for Trade and Industry* [1975] A.C. 295; *R.* v. *Environment Secretary, ex p. Ostler* [1977] Q.B. 122. But the English courts no longer view nullity as an absolute concept: *Calvin* v. *Carr* [1980] A.C. 574 and *London & Clydeside Estates Ltd.* v. *Aberdeen D.C.* [1980] 1 W.L.R. 182. See generally, Cane, "A Fresh Look at Punton's Case" (1980) 43 M.L.R. 264.

[81] [1981] I.L.R.M. 242. See also, *Re Riordan* [1981] I.L.R.M. 2 for a similar approach.

the part of the Registrar of Building Societies in construing the relevant legislation. Such a result would be "catastrophic," and the judge could not believe
that the Oireachtas intended that "an honest mistake" could have such drastic
consequences.

It remains to elaborate on these propositions. Take, first, the proposition
that, save in the case of a flagrantly invalid decision, an administrative act
enjoys a presumption of validity and will have legal consequences until it is set
aside. This fact has been recognised either expressly or by implication by
recent Irish decisions. For example, in *Re Comhaltas Ceolteoirí Éireann*,[82] the
applicants sought renewal of a certificate under the Registration of Clubs (Ireland) Act 1904. Local residents objected to the renewal before the District
Court, claiming, *inter alia*, that the club was being operated in breach of the
planning laws, since the planning permission granted by the local authority
was invalid. The District Justice stated a case as to whether he could hear evidence concerning the validity of this planning permission, but Finlay P. said
that, as a general rule, this could not be done:

> "A planning authority is a public authority with a decision-making capacity
> acting in accordance with statutory powers and duties. In my view, there is
> a rebuttable presumption that its acts are valid. A challenge to the validity
> of the acts of a planning authority can only be made by review on certiorari
> or by a substantive action seeking a declaration of invalidity [in the High
> Court]. To either form of proceeding, the planning authority . . . is an
> essential party . . . and it would be contrary to natural justice for a court to
> be called upon to adjudicate on the validity of the acts of the planning auth-
> ority in a case to which they were not a party. There is no method by which
> the planning authority can be made a party to this application for renewal."

To this general rule there was but one exception. Finlay P. suggested that if it
appeared to the District Justice that the document purporting to be a planning
permission did not emanate from the authority or which was not "executed or
signed by the planning authority," then he was bound to inquire further.
Comhaltas Ceolteoirí Éireann is a good example of how this general rule operates in practice and illustrates how decisions bearing "no brand of invalidity"
or flagrant illegality on their face must be regarded as valid until they are set
aside by either the High Court or Supreme Court.

The State (Abenglen Properties Ltd.) v. *Dublin Corporation*[83] provides
another example of this type of reasoning. Here Henchy J. said of an allegedly invalid planning permission which was good on its face that it remained a
"decision" for the purposes of the Planning Acts until it was set aside in the
appropriate proceedings. Similar thinking was employed by Costello J. in

---

[82] High Court, December 5, 1977. See also, the comments of O'Higgins C.J. in *Campus Oil Ltd.*
v. *Minister for Industry and Commerce* [1983] I.R. 88, 107: "The order which is challenged was
under the provisions of an Act of the Oireachtas. It is, therefore, valid and is to be regarded as a
part of the law of the land, unless and until its invalidity is established."
[83] [1984] I.R. 381.

O'Keefe v. *An Bord Pleanála*,[84] where he held that, at least in the context of the special statutory features of the Planning Acts, one could appeal an *ultra vires* decision of the planning authority to An Bord Pleanála. The judge drew attention to the special features of the Planning Acts, such as section 26 of the Local Government (Planning and Development) Act 1963, whereby An Bord Pleanála is required to determine the matter *de novo* and the Board's decision has the legal effect of annulling the decision of the planning authority and concluded that it followed that the statute should be construed as meaning that:

> "No defect in the proceedings before the planning authority should have any bearing, or impose legal constraints, on the proceedings before the Board. The Board had no jurisdiction to consider the validity from a legal point of view of the [planning authority's] decision and it seems to be contrary to the proper construction of the section now to hold that the Board lacked jurisdiction to entertain the appeal because the . . . decision was *ultra vires*. There is no logical inconsistency in this conclusion for it would mean that as a matter of law (a) the County Manager's order did not confer permission to develop, but (b) did enable the appeal machinery to be brought into operation—a result which seems to me to be a reasonable construction of the statute and to produce a sensible result."[85]

The very fact that the courts have found themselves obliged in appropriate cases to grant interlocutory relief to a person affected by the consequences of an administrative decision pending a challenge to its legality is itself indicative of the legal consequences in this interim period of a decision which may ultimately prove to be *ultra vires*. Thus, in *Pesca Valentia Ltd.* v. *Minister for Fisheries*,[86] Finlay C.J. said that the courts had power, in an appropriate case, to grant an interlocutory injunction restraining the implementation of administrative action which derived its authority from statutory provisions "which might eventually be held to be invalid having regard to the provisions of the Constitution." From this it may be inferred that the court recognised that administrative action which is not patently illegal will be presumed to be valid. As a result, it will have legal consequences during this interim period for the individual pending a decision as to its invalidity, unless interlocutory relief is granted.[87]

However, if an administrative act which is not flagrantly invalid enjoys a presumption of validity and has the force of law until quashed, how is it possible to assert, once that presumption has been displaced, and the decision

---

[84] High Court, July 31, 1990.
[85] *Ibid*. pp. 14–15 of the judgment.
[86] [1985] I.R. 193. See also, *Hoffmann-La Roche* v. *Department of Trade* [1975] A.C. 295 and, in the special context of European Community law, *R.* v. *Transport Secretary, ex p. Factortame Ltd.* [1990] 3 W.L.R. 818.
[87] In *O'Keefe* v. *An Bord Pleanála*, High Court, July 31, 1990, Costello J. appeared to hint that he agreed with this proposition but said that he could decide the issue which arose in that case by reference to a construction of the relevant provisions of the Planning Acts without having to deal with this larger issue.

quashed as *ultra vires*, that it was a legal nullity? Cane has provided a convincing answer to this apparent paradox by suggesting that *ultra vires* decisions, although void, are not nullities which never had any legal existence or force. In his view, when administrative decisions are invalidated by the courts, this invalidation has retrospective effect:

"[o]n this view acts done in pursuance of *ultra vires* decision would be treated as lawful until made unlawful by the quashing of the decision which supported them."[88]

Consequences of invalidity

R.T.C. LIBRARY
LETTERKENNY

One of the most difficult problems facing the courts is how to deal with the *de facto* consequences of *ultra vires* administrative action. The most obvious and, perhaps, most logical solution is to pronounce that all that was previously done under an unconstitutional statute or invalid decision to be simply *ultra vires* and to have had no legal effects. Yet the courts have understandably displayed a reluctance retroactively to interfere where this would cause manifest injustice, prejudice acquired rights or cause administrative chaos. The primary rule of redress was stated in the following terms by Henchy J. in *Murphy* v. *Att.-Gen.*[89]:

"Once it has been judicially established that a statutory provision [or administrative decision] is invalid, the condemned provision [or decision] will normally provide no legal justification for any acts done or left undone, or for transactions undertaken in pursuance of it; and the person damnified by the operation of the invalid provision will normally be accorded by the Courts all permitted and necessary redress."[90]

But this "primary rule" was subject to exceptions, especially where public policy factors or the need to avoid injustice to third parties justified the courts refusing to set aside the consequences of invalid administrative decisions. Thus, in *Murphy* itself, redress was limited to the small number of married couples who had instituted proceedings to challenge the operation of the Income Tax Act 1967. Even though these statutory provisions were held to have been unconstitutional *ab initio*, the vast majority of married couples were unable to recover moneys collected in this unconstitutional fashion. Henchy J. explained that the courts had only a limited power to undo what had been done:

"[T]he law has to recognise that there may be transcendent considerations which make such a course [of legal redress] undesirable, impractical or impossible. Over the centuries the law has come to recognise . . . that factors such as prescription . . . waiver, estoppel, laches, a statute of limitations, *res judicata*, or other matters (most of which may be grouped under the heading of public policy) may debar a person from obtaining redress in

[88] Cane, "A Fresh Look at Punton's Case" (1980) 43 M.L.R. 264, 272.
[89] [1982] I.R. 241.
[90] *Ibid.* 313.

the courts for injury . . . which would be justiciable and redressible if such considerations had not intervened."[91]

The sequel to *Murphy* was section 21 of the Finance Act 1980, which sought to impose the same burden of taxation on married couples for the tax years immediately prior to the date of the *Murphy* decision. The justification for this section was that persons who had been assessed for this unconstitutional tax but who, for some reason, had not paid it prior to the *Murphy* decision should now be treated in the same way as those who had already paid. This provision was, however, found to be unconstitutional in *Muckley* v. *Ireland*.[92] As Barrington J. observed, while Article 40 obliges the State to defend and vindicate the personal rights of the citizen as far as it was practicable to do so, in the *Murphy* case:

> "It was found to be impractical to vindicate the personal rights of the married couples who paid an invalid tax because directing the State to refund taxes unconstitutionally collected would have caused financial and administrative chaos."[93]

But the same public policy justifications stemming from the need to avoid administrative chaos were not present here, where the taxes were merely assessed, but never collected: "There is no impracticability in defending the citizen against exactions which the State has no authority to impose."[94] This reasoning was subsequently confirmed by the Supreme Court and *Muckley* would seem to exemplify Henchy J.'s "primary rule" of redress.

Yet, in the immediate aftermath of this decision, there were several judicial indications that it would require the most exceptional of circumstances before the courts would give retroactive effect to an earlier decision. In *Connors* v. *Delap*,[95] the applicant sought to quash a conviction imposed *in absentia* on the ground that the summons was defective in the light of the subsequently-announced decision of the Supreme Court in *The State (Clarke)* v. *Roche*.[96] Lynch J. admitted that, in view of the decision in *Clarke*, the summons was defective, but refused, on discretionary grounds, to quash the conviction and invoked the principles in *Murphy* as justification:

> "The Supreme Court made it clear that other citizens were not entitled in the light of [the] decision [in *Murphy*] to reopen past accounts. It seems to me that what the applicant seeks to do in this case is analogous to reopening past accounts. He seeks to rely on the subsequent . . . Supreme Court judgments in the case of *The State (Clarke)* v. *Roche* already referred to purely as a means of avoiding a liability which he [had already] chosen not to contest."[97]

[91] *Ibid.* 314.
[92] [1985] I.R. 472.
[93] *Ibid.* 482.
[94] *Ibid.*
[95] [1989] I.L.R.M. 93.
[96] [1986] I.R. 619.
[97] [1989] I.L.R.M. 93, 97–98.

Barr J. adopted this reasoning and, indeed, elaborated upon it, in *White* v. *Hussey*,[98] a case whose facts were on all fours with *Connors*. He refused to apply the *Clarke* decision retroactively, saying:

> "It seems to me that if the Supreme Court intended that its finding as to the invalidity of the erstwhile practice under which complaints were received and summonses issued by District Court clerks or Peace Commissioners was to be regarded as having retrospective effect then that conclusion would have been specifically stated in that judgment."[99]

This reasoning seems dubious. First, the fact that the Supreme Court in *Clarke* was silent as to the retrospective effect of its judgment would not seem to be a relevant factor, given that that Court had already stated in *Murphy* that the essential issue in such cases is whether discretionary relief should, in the light of the circumstances of the later case, now be granted. Secondly, all of the members of the Court in *Murphy* rejected the argument that the retro-spective consequences should depend on some arbitrary cut-off date decided by the courts, and Henchy J. spoke of the:

> "Arbitrariness and inequality, in breach of Article 40.1, that would result in a citizen's constitutional rights depending on the fortuity of when a court's decision would be pronounced."[1]

Finally, both Lynch J. and Barr J. appeared to regard certiorari as a purely discretionary remedy, whereas the true rule appears to be that certiorari lies *ex debito justitiae* in a criminal case such as this.[2]

A further instance of a judicial attempt to restrict the retroactive conse-quences of an earlier judgment comes—albeit in the very special context of European Community law—with the decision of Hamilton P. in *Cotter* v. *Minister for Social Welfare (No. 2)*.[3] Following the decision of the European Court of Justice in *McDermott and Cotter* v. *Minister for Social Welfare (No. 1)*[4] in 1987 which held that the EC Equality Directive had direct effect in Irish law since December 1984, the applicant sought declarations to the effect that she was entitled to be paid certain social welfare benefits between the months of December 1984 and March 1985. In other words, she sought to have the decision of the European Court applied retrospectively to the cir-cumstances of her case. Any such ruling would probably have had very large financial consequences, since thousands of other women were in a similar pos-ition, many with pending claims. In the light of these public policy consider-

---

[98] [1989] I.L.R.M. 109.
[99] *Ibid.* 112.
[1] [1982] I.R. 241, 311. Moreover, the Supreme Court has also accepted that its rulings *do* have retroactive effect, save that, due to acquiescence, effluxion of time and other factors it may not always be possible to grant relief: see *The State (Byrne)* v. *Frawley* [1978] I.R. 326. See also, *Finucane* v. *McMahon* [1990] 1 I.R. 165, 177, where Hamilton P. rejected an argument to the effect that judicial decisions should not apply retroactively.
[2] See pp. 609–610 and Collins, "*Ex Debito Justitiae?*" (1988) 10 D.U.L.J.(N.S.) 130.
[3] [1990] 2 C.M.L.R. 141. See generally, Whyte, *Sex Equality, Community Rights and Irish Social Welfare Law* (Dublin, 1988).
[4] (Case 265/85) [1987] I.L.R.M. 324.

ations, Hamilton P. refused to grant her such relief, and relying on the principles of *Murphy*, observed that the "equity of the case" was against her. This reasoning also seems dubious. First, the European Court[5] has now ruled that the issue of the retrospective effect of its own decisions is a matter for itself, and, that, in the absence of any express pronouncement to that effect contained in the original judgment, the judgment will have retrospective effect. Secondly, the reasoning in *Murphy* was premised, at least, in part, on the fact that the State had no advance knowledge of the unconstitutionality and altered its position accordingly. This factor was not present here, where the State had plenty of advance warning of the impact and legal consequences of the Equality Directive.

But the more recent cases have seen a swing away from this trend in favour, once again, of regarding nullification as the more general consequence of a finding of invalidity. This proposition has already been illustrated by the references, at the start of this Part,[6] to the facts in *Shelley* v. *Mahon*[7] and *Glavin* v. *Governor of the Training Unit, Mountjoy Prison*.[8]

Validating statutes

One of the ways in which the Oireachtas has sought to counteract the potential disruption to the legal system is by enacting validating statutes which seek to confer retrospective validity on invalid administrative decisions. Provided the Oireachtas did not enact retroactive penal sanctions, contrary to Article 15.5, it had been thought up to relatively recently that there were no constitutional restrictions on the power of the Oireachtas to enact such validating legislation. Indeed, the Military Service Pensions (Amendment) Act 1945 affords a good example of this *laissez-faire* attitude. In *The State (O'Shea)* v. *Minister for Defence*[9] the applicant obtained in the High Court an order of certiorari quashing a decision of the referee appointed under the Military Service Pensions Act 1934. It was accepted by Davitt J. that the referee had adopted an incorrect procedure in the light of a then recent Supreme Court decision in *The State (McCarthy)* v. *O'Donnell*.[10] The 1945

<hr>

[5] *Barra* v. *Belgium* (Case 309/85) [1988] 2 C.M.L.R. 409. Note that in *Carberry* v. *Minister for Social Welfare* [1990] 1 C.M.L.R. 29. Barron J. refused to follow the lead given by Hamilton P. in *Cotter* on the ground that it was clear from the subsequent decision in *Barra* that only the European Court itself had jurisdiction to pronounce on the retroactive effect of its rulings.
   The European Court itself has emphasised that it will require exceptional circumstances before the Court will countenance the non-retroactive application of a ruling: see *Defrenne* v. *SABENA (No. 2)* (Case 43/75) [1976] E.C.R. 455; *Blaizot* v. *University of Liege* (Case 42/86) [1989] 1 C.M.L.R. 57; *Barber* v. *Guardian Royal Exchange Assurance Group* (Case C 262/88) [1990] 2 C.M.L.R. 513. Generally the Court will only permit non-retroactivity where not to do so would be to interfere with third-party vested rights or where to undo past transactions would cause chaos. It was precisely for these reasons that the Court in *Defrenne* (equal pay); *Blaizot* (differential fees for university education) and *Barber* (discriminatory occupational pension schemes) refused to apply its ruling retroactively.
[6] See pp. 378–379.
[7] [1990] 1 I.R. 36.
[8] High Court, May 12, 1990. This approach was confirmed by the Supreme Court in judgments delivered on December 21, 1990.
[9] [1947] I.R. 49.
[10] [1945] I.R. 126.

Act, however, (which allowed the Minister to appeal to the Supreme Court against the High Court's order) and, furthermore, purported retrospectively to validate the procedure actually adopted by the referee in the applicant's case. When the case came before the Supreme Court, that court simply applied the new Act to the applicant's case and allowed the Minister's appeal. The reasoning of Maguire C.J. appears entirely oblivious to the separation of powers considerations that would almost certainly nowadays render legislation of this kind unconstitutional. Another example from this era is the Mental Treatment (Detention in Approved Institutions) Act 1961. This Act validated the detention of certain inmates in mental institutions where, by reason of a clerical oversight, the statutory procedures prescribed by the Mental Treatment Act 1945 had not been followed. Section 1(iii) of the Act provided, however, that:

> "No damages shall be recoverable by or on behalf of that person in respect merely of his detention during the same period ending on the passing of this Act."

A provision of this kind, which purported to deprive potential plaintiffs of their right to sue for false imprisonment, would clearly nowadays be regarded as highly suspect and open to constitutional attack on the ground that the State by its laws had failed to vindicate such a plaintiff's constitutional rights.

In the more recent legislation of this kind, a more sophisticated approach may be discerned on the part of the Oireachtas. Following a decision of the Supreme Court in *Garvey* v. *Ireland*[11] to the effect that the dismissal of a previous Garda Commissioner was invalid, the Oireachtas sought via section 1(1) of the Garda Síochána Act 1979 to validate the acts of his successor (who had been improperly appointed to replace Mr. Garvey following that latter's invalid dismissal). Section 1(2), however, contained a new form of saving clause of a kind that was later to become standard:

> "If, because of any validation expressed to be effected by subsection 1 . . . that subsection would, but for this subsection, conflict with a constitutional right of any person, the validation shall be subject to such limitation as is necessary to secure that it does not so conflict, but shall otherwise be of full force and effect."[12]

A similar clause was contained in section 6(2) of the Local Government (Planning and Development)(Amendment) Act 1982, where the Oireachtas sought to confirm the validity of certain planning permissions in the wake of the Supreme Court's decision in *The State (Pine Valley Developments Ltd.)* v.

---

[11] [1981] I.R. 75.
[12] Note that in *McHugh* v. *Garda Commissioner* [1986] I.R. 228 the Supreme Court accepted (although without any reference to the terms of the Garda Síochána Act 1979) that an order made by the then Commissioner of the Garda Síochána directing the holding of a sworn inquiry into the plaintiff's conduct as a member of the Gardaí was invalid, since the appointment of the then Commissioner to replace the former Commissioner, Mr. Garvey, was itself invalid.

Dublin County Council.[13] However, the saving clause contained in section 6(2) naturally[14] had the consequence that the applicants in the original proceedings, Pine Valley Developments Ltd., could not claim the benefit of this validating legislation, since this would clash with the constitutional rights of Dublin County Council, who had succeeded in establishing that such permission was invalid.

The interpretation of such clauses, in a much wider context than that presented by *Pine Valley*, was considered by the Supreme Court in *Shelley* v. *Mahon*,[15] where the applicant succeeded in having his conviction quashed on the ground that the respondent who purported to convict him was not a duly qualified judge at the time. Walsh J. (joined by Hederman J.) did not think that the saving clause contained in section 1(3) of the Courts (No. 2) Act 1988 had any relevance, since in his view the conviction was a nullity and an "unconstitutional procedure cannot subsequently be declared by the Oireachtas" to be valid. The other majority judges, Griffin and McCarthy JJ., took the view that the purported validation would have taken effect, save that any such validation would have conflicted with the constitutional right of the applicant to trial in due course of law, as guaranteed by Article 38.1. Accordingly, in their view, this validation became inoperative and the conviction was thus invalid. On the radical view adopted by Walsh and Hederman JJ., the effect of *Shelley* would appear that the power of the Oireachtas retrospectively to confer validity on what were originally invalid administrative or judicial decisions is very limited, since any such validation is likely to conflict with some other constitutional rights. On the other view taken by Griffin and McCarthy JJ. (and, it may be legitimate to add, by the dissenting judge, Costello J.), *Shelley* may come to be seen as a special case, turning on the applicant's right to trial in due course of law. On either view, it appears that the Oireachtas has a much freer hand where it seeks to validate an ordinary *ultra vires* act where that original invalidity does not stem from constitutional grounds.

10. Severance

General principles

In some cases, the condemned legislation or administrative decision may only be partially invalid. The question arises as to whether it is open to the court to excise offending sections of the Act, order or decision leaving the

---

[13] [1984] I.R. 407.

[14] The planning permission obtained by Pine Valley had been declared invalid in 1982: *The State (Pine Valley Developments Ltd.)* v. *Dublin County Council* [1984] I.R. 407. In the subsequent damages action (*Pine Valley Developments Ltd.* v. *Minister for Environment* [1987] I.R. 23) the Supreme Court pointed out that had the 1982 Act purported to reverse the effects of that decision as between the parties to the original action it would have been unconstitutional as an improper invasion of the judicial domain: see *Buckley* v. *Att.-Gen.* [1950] I.R. 67.

[15] [1990] 1 I.R. 36.

remainder valid. The classic statement of the courts' attitude to the question of severance is to be found in the judgment of Fitzgerald C.J. in *Maher* v. *Att.-Gen.*,[16] where speaking in the context of an unconstitutional statute, he said that, if, following the deletion of an unconstitutional portion of a statute:

> "The remainder may be held to stand independently and legally operable as representing the will of the legislature [then effect will be given to it]. But if what remains is so inextricably bound up with the part held invalid that the remainder cannot survive independently, or if the remainder would not represent the legislative intent, the remaining part will not be severed and given constitutional validity. . . . If, therefore, the Court were to sever part of a statutory provision as unconstitutional and seek to give validity to what is left so as to produce an effect at variance with legislative policy, the Court would be invading a domain exclusive to the legislature and thus exceeding the Court's competency."[17]

While these principles were enunciated in the context of an unconstitutional statute, it would seem that they are of general application.

Administrative decisions

Like principles have been applied in a series of administrative cases. In *The State (Sheehan)* v. *McMahon*,[18] a member of the Garda Síochána challenged the validity of certain disciplinary penalties imposed on him. The Supreme Court found that the Appeal Board acted *ultra vires* in declining to hear his appeal. But as the first tier of the procedure laid down by the regulations had been correctly observed, it did not follow that the error of the Appeal Board in thinking that they had no jurisdiction should be held to invalidate what had gone before. The court accordingly remitted the matter to the Appeal Board who could then hear the appeal. Similarly, in *The State (McKeown)* v. *Scully*[19] that part of the record which recorded a verdict of suicide was quashed as *ultra vires*, leaving untouched the other aspects of the verdict.

This question has also assumed relevance in planning cases where an invalid condition had been attached to the grant of a planning permission. In these cases, the court will quash the entire permission if what remains when shorn of the invalid condition is such that the planning authority would not have been willing to grant it in the first instance. As Keane J. observed in *Bord na Móna* v. *Bord Pleanála*:

> "[W]here the condition relates to planning considerations and is an essential feature of the permission granted, it would seem . . . wrong that the

---

[16] [1973] I.R. 140.
[17] *Ibid.* 147–148.
[18] [1976–1977] I.L.R.M. 305.
[19] [1986] I.L.R.M. 133. See also, *The State (Moloney)* v. *Minister for Industry and Commerce* [1954] I.R. 253 (severance of ministerial order). But severance is not possible in the case of a criminal conviction: *The State (Kiernan)* v. *deBúrca* [1963] I.R. 348.

permission should be treated as still effective, although shorn of an essential planning condition."[20]

In the *Bord na Móna* case, a condition requiring the contribution of a large sum of money towards the cost of restructuring a public road was held to be invalid. Keane J. was of the opinion that severance was not possible, and that the entire permission must fall. The offending condition could not be regarded as inessential or peripheral to the grant of the permission, and it would have been unjust to the defendants to enforce a permission stripped of such a vital condition. A similar attitude is to be found in the judgment of the Supreme Court in *The State (F.P.H. Properties S.A.)* v. *An Bord Pleanála*.[21] Here the applicants were granted planning permission to develop a house of significant historical and architectural interest, subject to conditions that the house be restored. McCarthy J. found that these conditions were invalid, but could the rest of the permission be upheld by means of severance? McCarthy J. did not think so, saying the permission could not stand "with the conditions severed from them," as to do otherwise "would be to rewrite the permission."

Delegated legislation and administrative circulars

Many of the cases on this topic have arisen in the special context of delegated legislation. In *Pigs and Bacon Commission* v. *McCarren & Co.*[22] where the plaintiffs were empowered by the Pigs and Bacon Acts 1935–1941 to fix the rate of an appropriate levy which pig producers were required to pay, save that the prior consent of the Minister for Agriculture was required for this purpose. Following reference by the High Court under Article 177 of the Treaty of Rome, the European Court of Justice held that inasmuch as the statutory scheme permitted the Commission to pay export bonuses and to engage in direct selling activities outside the State it was contrary to Community law. The Supreme Court rejected the argument that it was open to the Court to declare the rate of levy which would have been appropriate to finance those purposes and activities which would not offend against Community law. O'Higgins C.J. pointed out that the rate fixed:

"[Could] not be broken up, and the portion attributable to lawful purposes salvaged by severance. To do this would involve the Court, and not the plaintiff Commission in declaring a rate of levy. This, however, is not what the legislature authorises or permits, nor would a rate so declared [be compatible with the statutory scheme]."[23]

[20] [1985] I.R. 205, 211. See also, to like effect, *Killiney & Ballybrack Development Assoc.* v. *Minister for Local Government (No. 2)*, High Court, April 1, 1977 and, generally, *Potato Marketing Board* v. *Merricks* [1958] 2 Q.B. 316; *Kent C.C.* v. *Kingsway Investments (Kent) Ltd.* [1971] A.C. 72; *Dunkley* v. *Evans* [1981] 1 W.L.R. 1522; *Thames Water Authority* v. *Elmbridge B.C.* [1983] Q.B. 570; *R.* v. *Transport Secretary, ex p. G.L.C.* [1985] 3 All E.R. 300; *R.* v. *North Hertfordshire D.C., ex p. Cobbold* [1985] 3 All E.R. 486; *D.P.P.* v. *Hutchinson* [1990] 3 W.L.R. 196.
[21] [1987] I.R. 698.
[22] [1981] I.R. 451.
[23] [1981] I.R. 451, 469.

In that case it was impossible to effect a severance, with the result that the impugned orders were condemned as wholly *ultra vires*.

This issue was also considered by the Supreme Court in *The State (McLoughlin)* v. *Eastern Health Board*,[24] where regulations which sought to exclude certain persons who drew supplementary welfare benefits from obtaining fuel allowances were held to be *ultra vires*. Finlay C.J. relied on the principles enunciated in *Maher* to hold that severance was not possible, since this would be to expose the exchequer to substantial, unanticipated claims. In his concurring judgment, McCarthy J., however, appeared to attach significance to the provisions of Article 15.4.2 of the Constitution, which provides that:

"Every law enacted by the Oireachtas which is in any respect repugnant to this Constitution or to any provision thereof, shall, but to the extent only of such repugnancy, be invalid."

McCarthy J. observed that Article 15.4.2 did not apply to statutory instruments, at least where the defect was said to be merely *ultra vires*, as opposed to a defect arising from constitutional grounds. Where the statutory instrument was found to be *ultra vires* on non-constitutional grounds, there was "no constitutional provision to enable it to be restored [or] cleansed of the defect." He then continued:

"I greatly doubt if any statutory instrument can remain valid when any material portion of it has been condemned: I cannot identify any legal principle of construction to support judicial resuscitation of truncated subordinate legislation."[25]

In so far as McCarthy J. is suggesting that the courts cannot sever the good from the bad in the case of delegated legislation held to be *ultra vires*, at common law this would seem to be incorrect. As Finlay C.J. recognised for the majority in *McLoughlin*, the test enunciated in *Maher* is one of general application and can be applied to the severance of statutory instruments in cases of plain *ultra vires*. Moreover, the same technique is followed in British courts which are without the aid and comfort of any equivalent of Article 15.4.2. Nevertheless, there are some indications that McCarthy J.'s suggestions have taken root, for in *Howard* v. *Minister for Agriculture*,[26] Murphy J., following the *McLoughlin* principles, held that the entirety of the Tuberculosis (Attestation of the State and General Provisions) Order must fail, even though only a single (and rather inessential) feature of the order was actually found to be *ultra vires*.

The question of whether the severance principles can be applied to a par-

---

[24] [1986] I.R. 416.
[25] *Ibid.* 426.
[26] High Court, October 3, 1989.

tially invalid administrative circular was considered for the first time in *Greene* v. *Minister for Agriculture*.[27] In this case, the circular sought to implement an EC Directive providing for headage payments to farmers. However, the circular also imposed an off-farm income limit which was found by Murphy J. to be unconstitutional on the ground that this condition discriminated against married couples, contrary to Article 41 of the Constitution. Murphy J. considered that he could apply the standard severance principles to this case, even though, of course, the circular was not a "law" within the meaning of Article 15.4.2 and could not benefit from the restorative features of that provision. Nevertheless, the judge did not think that severance was possible since, just as in *McLoughlin*, the presence of the off-farm income limit served to restrict the numbers of farmers who could avail of the scheme:

> "The operation of the ministerial schemes without excluding therefrom the married couples who exceeded the income limit for the time being would be to operate a very different scheme from that which had been intended by the Minister."[28]

11. Appeals from Administrative Decisions

In some contexts the Oireachtas provides for a statutory right of appeal from a decision of an administrative body. The right of appeal is usually confined to an appeal on a point of law, although this need not necessarily be the case.[29] The appeal will generally lie to the High Court.[30] If, however, a right of appeal to the lower courts is granted by statute, the decision of the lower court on appeal may itself be quashed upon an application to the High Court for judicial review.[31]

The nature and scope of the court's jurisdiction on a statutory appeal is in all cases a matter of statutory construction. Nevertheless, it would be surprising if the Oireachtas, having created a statutory right of appeal, did not intend to vest the High Court with powers in addition to, and distinct from, the inherent powers of judicial review which it enjoys at common law. As Costello J. explained in *Dunne* v. *Minister for Fisheries*:

> "[It does not follow] that in every case the Court's jurisdiction on a statutory appeal is the same; in every case the statute itself must be construed. In construing a statute it does not seem to me helpful to apply by analogy

---

[27] [1990] I.L.R.M. 364.

[28] *Ibid.* 374.

[29] For example, some administrative bodies have power to state a case for the High Court: see Adoption Act 1952, s.20 (An Bord Uchtála); Local Government (Planning and Development) Act 1976, s.42 (An Bord Pleanála).

[30] But is not always the case: see, *e.g.* Income Tax Act 1967, s.429 (appeal on a point of law to the Circuit Court).

[31] See, *e.g.*, *The State (McEldowney)* v. *Kelleher* [1983] I.R. 289.

the rules of judicial review, since, by granting a statutory appeal, the legislature must have intended that the Court would have powers in addition to those already enjoyed at common law."[32]

From a conceptual point of view, this form of appeal must be contrasted with judicial review. This means that when the High Court exercises such an appellate jurisdiction it has, generally speaking, the power to alter or vary an administrative decision. In judicial review proceedings, the court is faced with the starker question: to quash (save where the order is severable) or not to quash. Moreover, even when an appeal is allowed, this will only have a prospective effect and will not call into question the legality of earlier administrative decisions. There is finally the distinction between "legality" which is all that can be examined on review and "merits" which are the proper province of an appeal. This has already been explained[33] and, with it, the fact that in practice there may not be a great deal of difference between the reach of the High Court's jurisdiction to hear appeals where these appeals are confined by statute to an appeal on a point of law and its supervisory jurisdiction over administrative bodies and the lower courts now that the reach of jurisdictional error has been so greatly expanded.[33a] In addition, one would be hard pressed to draw a satisfactory distinction between the scope of appellate review for errors of law and that of certiorari to quash for errors of law on the face of the record. But other important differences remain. In the first place, the remedies available on an application for judicial review are discretionary in nature.[34] Secondly, the High Court's power of judicial review is an inherent jurisdiction derived from Article 34.3.1, and it is doubtful whether this supervisory jurisdiction may be removed by statute.[35] In contrast, any appellate jurisdiction is entirely the creation of statute and there are no constitutional impediments to the abolition of such a jurisdiction. Thirdly, a finding of invalidity has effect *erga omnes*. In other words, there may be a large category of persons who, being similarly affected by the impugned legislation or administrative act, will be permitted to rely on this finding of invalidity.[36] In contrast, because of the nature of the circumstances in which an appeal has been created, a decision of the High Court on appeal is a ruling in an *inter partes* matter between the appellant and the administrative body concerned and such a decision will not necessarily have general significance. Finally, it would seem that in the case of a statutory appeal, the parties may be able to introduce even, which was not previously before the decision-maker, whereas in judicial review matters, such fresh evidence is inadmissible. This difference is explained by the fact that a statutory appeal is on the merits, whereas in

---

[32] [1984] I.R. 230, 237.
[33] See pp. 328–330.
[33a] See pp. 345–354.
[34] See pp. 595–611.
[35] *Tormey* v. *Att.-Gen.* [1985] I.R. 289 and see further, pp. 374–378.
[36] For a more extended discussion of the difference between appeal on the merits and judicial review, see Hogan, "Remoulding Certiorari" (1982) 17 Ir.Jur.(N.S.) 32, 48–54.

judicial review matters, the task of the High Court is to examine whether the lower court or tribunal erred in law based on the material then before it. As this form of review is not concerned with the merits, it may said that, as a matter of principle, it matters not that there is fresh evidence which has come to light showing that the impugned decision was wrong on the merits.

A good example of an appeal on a point of law is provided by section 428 of the Income Tax Act 1967 which allows such an appeal from the Appeal Commissioners to the High Court. The effect of this section was extensively discussed in *Mara* v. *Hummingbird Ltd.*[37] The Appeal Commissioners had found as a fact that Hummingbird's purchase and sale of development property was for investment purposes, and, accordingly, could not be regarded as a sale "in the course of trade."

In the Supreme Court, Kenny J. drew the distinction between findings of primary fact, and the inferences to be drawn from those facts. Findings of primary fact—in this case, for example, Hummingbird's intentions when purchasing the premises—should not be disturbed "unless there was no evidence whatever to support them." In the case of inferences of conclusions based on these primary facts, a different approach was called for. If these conclusions were based on the interpretation of documents, the court should reverse them, for it was in as good a position as the Appeal Commissioners to determine the meaning of these documents. The court should only reverse other conclusions based on primary facts if these conclusions are ones which could not reasonably have been drawn, or which are based on a mistaken view of the law. Kenny J. urged a cautious approach, noting that the Appeal Commissioners will often have evidence:

> "[S]ome of which supports the conclusion that the transaction under investigation was an adventure in the nature of trade and he will have some which points to the opposite conclusion. These are essentially matters of degree and his conclusions should not be disturbed (even if the court does not agree with them, for we are not retrying the case) unless they are such that a reasonable commissioner could not draw them, or they are based on a mistaken view of the law."[38]

The effect of this test is to allow effective control over unreasonable decisions, or decisions based on "no evidence" or a mistaken view of the law, while at the same time allowing the administrative authority a tolerable margin of error. While the extent of the court's appellate jurisdiction is always a

---

[37] [1982] I.L.R.M. 421. Kenny J., delivering the Supreme Court judgment, referred with approval to the speech of Lord Radcliffe in *Edwards* v. *Bairstow* [1956] A.C. 14. See also, *Rahill* v. *Brady* [1971] I.R. 69. The test enunciated in *Hummingbird* has been followed in a series of subsequent decisions. See, *e.g. Ó'hArgáin* v. *Beechpark Estates Ltd.* [1979] I.L.R.M. 57; *Re McElligott* [1985] I.L.R.M. 210; *MacCarthaigh* v. *D.* [1985] I.R. 73. For an application of these principles in the non-revenue context, see *Brewster* v. *Burke and the Minister for Labour* (1985) 4 J.I.S.L.L. 98.

[38] [1982] I.L.R.M. 421, 426.

matter of statutory construction, the principle enunciated in *Mara* can be readily adopted for other administrative appeals "on a point of law," *e.g.* under section 299(*b*) of the Social Welfare (Consolidation) Act 1981.

There are, however, statutory provisions which serve to confer even broader powers on the courts than simply an appeal on a "point of law." A typical example is section 11 of the Fisheries (Consolidation) Act 1959 which provides that, on appeal by a "person aggrieved," the High Court may "confirm or annul" a by-law made by the Minister for Fisheries. In *Dunne* v. *Minister for Fisheries*[39] Costello J. held that this section empowered the court to rule on the merits of the appeal and rejected the submission that the court could only interfere where it was established that the Minister had erred in law. The judge contrasted this section with other statutory appeal procedures, which restricted the appeal to an appeal on a point of law. When it transpired on the evidence given before him that the by-law made by the Minister revoking certain restrictions on drift-net fishing in the County Kerry ran counter to the "overwhelming scientific evidence," Costello J. concluded that the order should be annulled.

Another interesting example of the application of the court's appellate role is provided by *Balkan Tours Ltd.* v. *Minister for Communications.*[40] Section 3 of The Transport (Tour Operators and Travel Agents) Act 1982 gives the Minister power to revoke a tour agent's licence. This power had been exercised by the Minister in the present case, since there had been a history of a "careless, unbusinesslike approach" on the part of the applicants as far as the observance of their trading licences was concerned. One of the more serious breaches of these conditions lay in the fact that the applicants had apparently circulated their travel brochures to the public without ensuring that the correct tour operator's licence had been reproduced in the brochures. Since no satisfactory explanation had been forthcoming, Lynch J. concluded that the Minister had been correct "to revoke the licences at the time and in the circumstances when he did so." However, further evidence had come to light at the hearing before Lynch J. showing that this error had been principally the fault of the applicants' printers, who had "acted on their own initiative and without any instructions." This evidence had not been before the Minister and Lynch J. concluded that the effect of section 3 was that:

"The High Court is to ascertain all the relevant facts of the case, whether they were before the Minister or not and to give effect to them."[41]

The judge accordingly relied on this evidence to decide the appeal on the merits and he decided to allow the appeal on terms.

A slightly different form of appellate procedure is to be found in section 54(7) of the Fisheries Act 1980, which provides that "any person who is

[39] [1984] I.R. 230.
[40] [1988] I.L.R.M. 101.
[41] *Ibid.* 107.

aggrieved" by the making of a ministerial order designating an area as one in which it shall be lawful to engage in aquaculture, "may . . . appeal to the High Court against the order" within a 28-day period. This section was invoked in *Courtney* v. *Minister for the Marine*,[42] where local residents opposed on environmental grounds the making of such an order in respect of Smerwick Harbour, Co. Kerry. While O'Hanlon J. acknowledged that the court should be slow to interfere with a ministerial opinion, he took the view that the appeal envisaged by the section enabled the High Court to review the merits of the decision:

> "The court should be slow to interfere with a ministerial decision in a matter of this kind where a question of industrial development and a conflict with local interests is involved. However, the Act requires the High Court, once an appeal is taken, as permitted by the provisions of section 54, to assess again whether a designation should be made in regard to a particular locality or stretch of sea and to review the ministerial order which has already been made."[43]

O'Hanlon J. did proceed to set aside the order, but chiefly because he was not satisfied that the Minister had been fully informed on all the potential environmental aspects of the project at the time he made his decision.

12. Delegatus Non Potest Delegare

The general principle here is that a power must be exercised by the authority (*delegatus*) in which it has been vested by the legislature. It cannot be transferred (*delegare*) to any other person or body. A straightforward example is *O'Neill* v. *Beaumont Hospital Board*.[44] In this case, a certificate, stating that the plaintiff's services were unsatisfactory with the consequence that he could not be confirmed in his post as a hospital consultant, was declared by Murphy J. to be invalid. The reason for this decision was that the certificate had been issued by the chief executive officer of the hospital rather than by the (part-time) Board in which the statutory instrument constituting the hospital had vested this function.

In principle, the maxim may apply to all types of decision whether quasi-judicial, legislative, administrative or policy (discretionary) (which is why the subject is treated in this general chapter and not in the chapter on the control of discretionary powers). However the nature of the decision is undoubtedly one of the factors conditioning whether the rule applied in any particular situ-

---

[42] [1989] I.L.R.M. 605.
[43] *Ibid.* 611.
[44] [1990] I.L.R.M. 419. (This point was not taken in the Supreme Court). For unsuccessful *delegatus* arguments, see *Flynn* v. *An Post* [1987] I.R. 68, 75, 80–81; *Heneghan* v. *Western Regional Fisheries Board* [1986] I.L.R.M. 225, 228.

ation.[45] The principle is at its strictest in the case of court proceedings.[46] It is fairly stringently applied in the case of legislative, quasi-judicial or wide discretionary powers. However, the courts may allow some latitude in the case of routine administrative matters.[47] The essential point is that the maxim is merely a rule of statutory construction, rather than a rule of law and, in predicting its operation it has been said that[48]:

"Whether a person other than that named in the empowering statute is empowered to act will be dependent upon the entire statutory context, taking into account the nature of the subject matter, the degree of control retained by the person delegating and the types of person or body to whom the power is delegated."

But even with the tolerance which the attitudes, correctly summarised in this

---

[45] See de Smith, *Judicial Review of Administrative Action* (4th ed.), p. 298.

[46] In regard to courts, the decision of the Supreme Court in *The State (Clarke)* v. *Roche* [1986] I.R. 619 is relevant. This case is best known for a far-reaching *obiter dictum* (which is quoted below) in connection with Art. 34.1 and the administration of justice. However, the major point in the case was the *delegatus* principle. The case centred on the procedure for the issuing of a District Court summons. Under the relevant legislation (Petty Sessions (Ireland) Act 1851, ss.10, 11) a complaint could be made to, *inter alia*, a District Court clerk, who thereupon issued a summons. The point which was taken by counsel for the applicant was that there was no proof that the issue of a summons against the applicants had been made by the District Court clerk personally as opposed to some person under his general supervision and that, accordingly, the *delegatus* principle had been violated.

The success of this submission depended, in part, on a point which was accepted as beyond controversy by the court, namely, that in the case of a judicial, in contrast to an administrative, act, no delegation would be possible. It thus became relevant to ascertain whether "the activity of a District Court in deciding to issue a summons is not the carrying out of a judicial act but is rather the carrying out of an administrative or ministerial act" (at 640). Finlay C.J. concluded that the act was a judicial one for the purpose of non-delegation.

This would have been sufficient to determine the matter in the applicant's favour. However, having reached this finding, Finlay C.J. then went on to make what, it is submitted is a separate point, namely the speculation referred to earlier regarding Art. 34.1. Finlay C.J. stated (at 64):

"No argument in this case was submitted to the Court with regard to the consequences from the point of view of constitutional validity of a conclusion that the powers given to the Peace Commissioner and District Court clerk to receive a complaint and issue a summons constituted the carrying out of a judicial act in a criminal matter. I, therefore, express no view upon it, but would refer to the query raised by Walsh J. in his judgment in *The State (Lynch)* v. *Ballagh* [1986] I.R. 203 as to the constitutional validity of giving to a Peace Commissioner powers to grant bail."

It is suggested that this query, which was taken up and answered in the affirmative in subsequent High Court decisions (see pp. 384–385) was based on an identification of a "judicial act" for the purpose of the *delegatus* principle with an administration of justice in Art. 34.1. It is submitted that this identification is erroneous in view of the wide scope of the *delegatus* principle and the purpose of Art. 34.1. which is different from that of the *delegatus* principle. See also, *Rainey* v. *Delap* [1988] I.R. 470.

[47] *The State (Keller)* v. *Galway County Council* [1958] I.R. 142, 148 (chief medical officer can delegate physical examination of applicant for a grant, but not duty of forming the necessary opinion as to whether the applicant was substantially handicapped). See also, *Bridge* v. *R.* [1953] 1 D.L.R. 305; *Hookings* v. *Director of Civil Aviation* [1957] N.Z.L.R. 929. In the case of routine tasks performed by servants of a public authority, foreign courts have sometimes achieved this result by characterising the situation as involving the creation of an agency and so evading the *delegatus* principle: see de Smith, *op. cit.* pp. 301–303.

[48] Craig, *Administrative Law* (London, 1988), p. 306. See further, Willis, (1943) 21 Can.B.R. 257.

passage evince, the *delegatus* principle has immense and often unwelcome implications in an era of mass government which is executed in practice largely by anonymous public servants, rather than the chieftains in whom the function has been formally vested. The principle is, indeed, as might be guessed from its formulation, a survival from Roman law and fairly substantial exceptions to it have been developed in an attempt to reconcile it with modern conditions. The first of these applies only to the special, though common, case of the relationship between Ministers and civil servants: it is covered in Part 13 of this chapter. Secondly, a Government order may be made on the request of a Government Minister, delegating to his Minister of State all the Minister's powers and duties under a particular Act or, more narrowly, any particular statutory power.[49] Thirdly, at local government level, a county (or city) manager is empowered to delegate any of his functions to an assistant county (or city) manager, county secretary, town clerk, or officer approved by the Minister for the Environment, as an approved officer for the purposes of the delegation.[50]

Within the areas in which they operate, these exceptions are fairly far reaching (though the second and third categories are, of course, qualified by the terms of the order implementing them). The second and third exceptions are also, of course, examples of the *delegatus* principle being forced to bow before a statutory provision. There are numerous other statutory restrictions of the principle,[51] one of which is a formula which is often included in the constituent statutes of public bodies: "[the Agency] may perform any of its state functions through or by any of its officers and servants duly authorised by [the Agency] in that behalf."[52]

A further example concerns An Bord Pleanála which would be substantially affected by the *delegatus* principle since it exercises quasi-judicial functions over significant property rights, were it not for the following statutory dispensation:

"(a) Subject to *paragraphs (b)* and *(c)* of this subsection, the Board may perform or exercise any of its functions through or by any member of the Board or other person who, in either case, has been duly authorised by the Board in that behalf.

(b) *Paragraph (a)* of this subsection shall be construed as enabling a member of the Board finally to determine a particular case if, and only if,

---

[49] Ministers and Secretaries (Amendment) Act 1977, s.2. See, *e.g.* Public Service (Delegation of Ministerial Functions) Order (S.I. 1978 No. 117). See also, *Geraghty* v. *Minister for Local Government* [1976] I.R. 153, 154, 160.

[50] County Management Act 1940, s.13; City and County Management (Amendment) Act 1955, s.17; *Cassels* v. *Dublin Corporation* [1963] I.R. 193.

[51] See, e.g., Extradition (Amendment) Act 1987, s.5(1) (delegation of A.G.'s functions to D.P.P. in case of the former's "illness or absence").

[52] See, for example, *Ingle* v. *O'Brien* (1975) 109 I.L.T.R. 9 (power to revoke licence to drive taxis vested in Garda Commissioner but delegated, under authority contained in regulation, to Superintendent); *The State (Fagan)* v. *Governor of Mountjoy Prison*, High Court, March 6, 1978 (delegation by Prison Governor to Deputy Governor held to be authorised under Rules for the Government of Prisons 1947).

the case to which an authorisation under that paragraph relates has been considered at a meeting of the Board prior to the giving of the authorisation.

(c) *Paragraph (a)* of this subsection shall not be construed as enabling the Board to authorise a person who is not a member of the Board finally to determine any particular case with which the Board is concerned."[53]

However, such statutory dispensations are usually fairly specific and narrow so that, in certain areas of public administration, it may happen that there is a gap in the statutory patch-work, at which the *delegatus* principle will operate to strike down an administrative action for no better reason than legislative oversight.

Finally, three incidental points may be made, the first two of which involve merely the operation of the general principles of administrative law in association with an act of delegation.[54] In the first place, we ought to draw attention to the possibility of a waiver being deemed to authorise a delegation. For example, in *Flanagan* v. *University College, Dublin*[55] a University committee of discipline, in which the duty of disciplining students had been vested, took action solely on the recommendation of an independent expert from another institution from whom it had commissioned a report on an alleged case of plagiarism. This amounted, Barron J. held, to an improper delegation of its function by the committee of discipline. What is striking is that Barron J. appeared to suggest that if the student had given her "informed consent"[56] to the committee's total reliance on the opinion of the independent expert, then the delegation would have been proper. This appears to be the first suggestion that the *delegatus* principle may be waived. In its favour is the fact that, in an appropriate case, it appears to meet the justice of the situation. As against this, however, it may be argued that the *delegatus* principle is supposed to be a bulwark of good public administration having wider implications than its effects upon any particular individual.[57]

Secondly, where there is a statutory authority to delegate, then it will usually happen that this power will be discretionary. As such, like any substantive or any other procedural, discretionary power, it is subject to the general controls upon the exercise of discretionary powers, *e.g.* the requirement of reasonableness. An illustration of this occurred in the Northern Irish case of *Re Curran and McCann's Application*.[58] Here the Craigavon Borough Council had exercised its power, under section 18(*d*) of the Local Government Act (Northern Ireland) 1972, to appoint a committee consisting of all

---

[53] This particular example is the National College of Art and Design Act 1971, s.18 and its potency was accepted in *Gunn* v. *An Bord Cholaiste Náisiúnta*, Supreme Court, May 12, 1988. For a further example, see Electricity (Supply) Act 1927, s.9.

[54] For delegation coupled with the *audi alteram partem* rule, see pp. 452–454.

[55] [1988] I.R. 724, 727, 733.

[56] *Ibid*. 732.

[57] *Cf.* the brief discussion of waiver in the context of bias at pp. 372–373.

[58] [1985] N.I. 26. On reasonableness generally, see Chap. 11.

the Council members, apart from the two Sinn Féin councillors, and delegated almost all the functions of the Council to that committee. The object of this device was to exclude the Sinn Féin councillors from the work of the Council. However, Hutton J. held that the legislative intendment of the delegation provision was to promote the better management and regulation of the Council's business. Accordingly, in reliance on the general principle that a power given for one purpose cannot be exercised for another, Hutton J. struck down the resolution effecting the delegation since the purpose behind the resolution was not to further the better management of business.

The third point worth noting is that while the general question of the appropriate body to take an administrative action has usually arisen in the particular form of the correctness of a transfer of the power to take the action, it is perfectly possible that variations on these themes may occur. For example, in *McGabhann* v. *Incorporated Law Society of Ireland*[59] a query was raised by Blayney J. (though he did not determine the issue, since it had not been argued by the parties) as to the particular entity in which the power had been vested in the first place. It was clear from the relevant legislation that the Society's Educational Committee was to lay down the standard of proficiency to be achieved in the qualifying examination before a candidate could gain entry to the Society's training course; but unclear as to whether it was for the committee or the examiners to decide whether the student had actually passed. On the one hand, the regulations stated that: "the committee shall also consider and adjudicate upon the report of the examiners," but gave no authority to delegate.[60] On the other hand, according to Blayney J.:

> "the question might arise as to whether the committee, *having appointed examiners*, as it is given power to do under the regulations [just quoted], can reserve to itself what may necessarily be a function of the examiners, namely the decision as to whether a candidate has passed or not."[61]

13. Minister and Civil Servants

It would plainly be an impossible state of affairs if the law required a Minister, even with the assistance of his Minister for State, to keep in personal contact with each of the hundreds of decisions taken in his Department each day. In most cases, the *delegatus* doctrine can be side-stepped by regarding each civil servant as the *alter ego* of the Minister at the head of the Department. This is a principle which is known as the "*Carltona* doctrine." The principle that the powers vested in a Minister may be exercised, without any express act

---

[59] [1989] I.L.R.M. 854, 864–865.
[60] This is a significant point in view of the fact that after the *McGabhann* case the Committee actually purported to delegate to the examiners the power to determine whether a student had passed.
[61] [1989] I.L.R.M. 865.

of delegation, by responsible officials on his behalf is according to a recent English authority "a common law constitutional power, but one which is capable of being negatived or confined by express statutory provisions . . . or by clearly necessary implication." (The doctrine is buttressed, in form anyway, by the notion that the Minister bears political responsibility to the Dáil and legal responsibility, under the Ministers and Secretaries Act 1924, for all actions going on within his Department.)

The question of acceptance of the *Carltona*[62] doctrine has not been explicitly addressed in Ireland. However, in two judgments, Walsh J. has shown a tendency to reject it; whereas other judges have appeared to accept it. The first case was an interlocutory decision in *Murphy* v. *Dublin Corporation*.[63] It concerned an inspector's report to the Minister for Local Government upon an inquiry, chaired by the inspector as part of the compulsory order procedure under the Housing Act 1966. Through his visits to the site, observation of witnesses' demeanour, etc., an inspector, much more so than an ordinary departmental civil servant, has access to information and experience which could not be made available to his Minister. In spite of this, Walsh J. speaking *obiter*, for the Supreme Court, stated:

" . . . [T]he inspector's function is to convey to the Minister, if not a verbatim account of the entire of the proceedings before him, at least a fair and accurate account of what transpired. . . . The inspector has no advisory function nor has he any function to arrive at *a preliminary judgment which may or may not be confirmed or varied by the Minister. . . . If the Minister is influenced in his decision by the opinions of the inspector, . . . the Minister's decision will be open to review*" (author's italics).[64]

This passage was glossed by O'Keeffe P. in *Murphy* v. *Dublin Corporation (No. 2)* who said:

"I do not think for one moment that [Mr. Justice Walsh] intended to indi-

---

[62] *Carltona Ltd.* v. *Commissioners of Works* [1943] 2 All E.R. 560, 563; see also, *Point of Ayr Colleries Ltd.* v. *Lloyd-George* [1943] 2 All E.R. 546; *R.* v. *Skinner* [1968] 2 Q.B. 700; *Re Golden Chemical Products Ltd.* [1976] Ch. 300, 310; and *McKernan* v. *Governor of H.M. Prison* [1983] N.I. 83; *R.* v. *Secretary of State for the Home Department, ex p. Oladehinde* [1990] 2 All E.R. 367, 381h. In Britain, there is a narrow exception to the *Carltona* doctrine in that in cases involving personal liberty, the responsible Minister must truly bring his mind to bear on the issue: *Oladehinde*, at 381; Wade, *op. cit.* pp. 368; de Smith, *op. cit.* pp. 307–309. But *cf.* the comments of Hutton J. in *McKernan* v. *Governor of H.M. Prison* [1983] N.I. 83.
[63] [1972] I.R. 215. It is accepted that the inspector had the same relation to the Minister as he did, before the creation of Bord Pleanála, in a planning appeal: see *Geraghty* v. *Minister for Local Government* [1976] I.R. 168.
[64] [1971] I.R. 239. *Murphy* involved the Minister for Local Government's decision on whether to confirm a compulsory purchase order. However, it is accepted (see, *e.g. Geraghty* v. *Minister for Local Government* [1976] I.R. 168 (Walsh J.)) that the inspector had the same relation to the Minister in this situation as in a planning appeal. *Cf.* Local Government (Planning and Development) Act 1976, s.23 of which requires an inspector conducting an oral inquiry for the Minister (or Bord Pleanála) to include a recommendation which must be considered by the Minister (or Bord Pleanála).

cate that the Minister should not receive in the report of an inspector holding an inquiry of this kind views of the inspector derived from the consideration of the evidence—views which the Minister might or might not
accept."[65]

The second case is *Geraghty* v. *Minister for Local Government (No. 2)*[66]
which arose out of a planning appeal heard by the Minister (in the period
before the creation of An Bord Pleanála). An oral inquiry was held by an
inspector who was an official in the Department of Local Government. He
made a report on the hearing, recommending that the appeal be rejected for
reasons which he stated. This report was channelled through the routes normally followed by internal departmental documents and, as it went, gathered
accretions of suggestions, comments and additional information from various
civil servants. These included information which had been gained in another
appeal from the same locality and suggested alternative reasons which might
be given for rejecting the appeal. Eventually, the file reached the Parliamentary Secretary to whom the Minister's powers had been (properly) delegated
and he rejected the appeal. The Supreme Court was unanimous that the *audi
alteram partem* rule had been broken in that the plaintiff had no opportunity
to know about or comment upon the additional material added to the report
after the oral inquiry. The second issue—which is the relevant one here—
arose from the fact that the inspector and other civil servants had given their
views and that the Parliamentary Secretary appeared to have been influenced
by them. Did this violate the *delegatus non potest delegare* principle? Upon
this issue, differing views were expressed (although these differences were of
no significance to the actual decision). Walsh J. (with whom Budd J. concurred) said that a Minister could not regard himself as bound even by the
findings of fact made by an inspector holding an oral inquiry. Gannon J. (with
whom Griffin J. agreed) and Henchy J. each disagreed with this and stated
that the inspector could make (non-binding) recommendations as to the outcome which the Minister could take into account. In addition, they said that
the Minister, as a lay-person, could obtain expert advice on technical (*e.g.*
legal or planning) matters from his departmental civil servants or elsewhere.[67]

These differences are of considerable practical significance for upon their
resolution turns the question of how much scope is to be allowed to a civil servant and how much time and attention a Minister must actually give to a case
himself. The second practical question is what range of decisions would
attract the rule, followed by Walsh J., that it is the Minister himself who must
decide. It seems probable from the nature of the facts in *Murphy (No. 1) and*

---

[65] [1976] I.R. 144n. See the comments of O'Higgins J. on this point in *Geraghty* v. *Minister for
Local Government* [1976] I.R. 153, 162. See also, *per* Henchy J. in *Murphy* v. *Dublin Corporation* [1976] I.R. 143, 150: "[I]t was for the Minister to reach his own decision, unfettered by any
conclusion the inspector may have reached but on the basis of the same evidential material as was
before the inspector."
[66] [1976] I.R. 153.
[67] [1976] I.R. 171 (Walsh J.); 174–175 (Henchy J.); and 181–182 (Gannon J.).

Geraghty (No. 2) that the rule is confined to what are loosely called "quasi-judicial" decisions.[68]

Finally, with regard to the entire question of a Minister's dual personality, it is worth pointing out that the interlocutory decision in *Murphy* v. *Dublin Corporation (No. 1)* involved the issue of executive privilege against the disclosure of documents. It was against this background that Walsh J. made a distinction, which was critical to his reasoning, between a Minister exercising an executive power, and, on the other hand, a Minister, as "*persona designata*" undertaking a quasi-judicial function with a duty to observe constitutional justice and confined executive privilege narrowly to the former function. In the context of the *delegatus* principle, different considerations apply; yet in *Murphy (No. 2)* and *Geraghty, Murphy (No. 1)* appears to have been treated as an authority, without regard to this significant shift in context.

The policies underlying the two approaches are demonstrated in the following quotations. In *Murphy*, Walsh J. stated:

"[The Minister] is *persona designata* in that the holder of the office of the Minister for Local Government is the person designated for that function. If the Oireachtas had so enacted, the Act could just as easily have assigned the functions to the chairman of Coras Iompair Éireann or to the chairman of the Electricity Supply Board.[69]

By contrast, Lord Diplock said in *Bushell* v. *Secretary of State for the Environment*[70]:

"To treat the Minister in his decision-making capacity as someone separate and distinct from the department of government of which he is the political head and for whose actions he alone in constitutional theory is accountable to Parliament is to ignore not only practical realities but Parliament's inten-

---

[68] In addition to compulsory purchase order confirmation and residual planning matters, the following types of decision fall within the category of quasi-judicial decisions: decisions as to the superannuation rights of various categories of public servants: Minister for Finance. Superannuation and Pensions Act 1923, s.9: questions arising under any scheme of administering higher education grants: Minister for Education (Local Authorities (Higher Education Grants) Act 1968, s.7.); appeals against refusal by a health board of registration as food premises (Minister for Health) (Health Act 1970, s.6(2)); appeals against refusal by a local authority of registration as a person who may carry on dairying (Minister for Agriculture) (Milk and Dairies Act 1935, ss.21–23). As with some of the other decisions mentioned in this catalogue, the Minister's decision is said to be "final." But at least where the Minister is exercising judicial functions under cover of Art. 37 this cannot preclude judicial review of his decision: *Tormey* v. *Att.-Gen.* [1985] I.R. 289 and see pp. 374–375.

[69] [1972] I.R. 238. This passage was quoted with approval by O'Higgins J. in the High Court in *Geraghty*: see [1976] I.R. 160–161. See to similar effect, Walsh J. in *Geraghty (No. 2)* [1976] I.R. 189.

[70] [1981] A.C. 75, 95. See also, *McKernan* v. *Governor of H.M. Prison* [1983] N.I. 83, a case where an order authorising the solitary confinement of a prisoner was signed by a Minister of State. The relevant prison regulations required that the order be signed by either a member of the prison board of visitors, or the Secretary of State for Northern Ireland. Hutton J. (and affirmed by the Court of Appeal) rejected the argument that this was a matter which was peculiarly committed to the Secretary of State, saying that it was most unlikely that Parliament intended that a member of the board of visitors could sign an authority under the regulations, but that a Minister of State could not.

tion. Ministers come and go; departments, though their names may change from time to time, remain. Discretion in making administrative decisions is conferred on a Minister not as an individual but as the holder of an office in which he will have available to him in arriving at his decision the collective knowledge, experience and expertise of all those who serve the Crown in the department of which, for the time being, he is the political head. The collective knowledge, technical as well as factual, of the civil servants in the department and their collective expertise are to be treated as the Minister's own knowledge, his own expertise. It is they who in reality will have prepared the draft scheme for his approval; it is they who in the first instance will consider the objections to the scheme and the report of the inspector by whom any local inquiry has been held and it is they who will give to the Minister the benefits of their combined experience, technical knowledge and expert opinion on all matters raised in the objections and the report. This is an integral part of the decision-making process itself; it is not to be equiparated with the Minister receiving evidence himself, expert opinion or advice from sources outside the department after the local inquiry has been closed."

More recent Irish case law appears to have come down, albeit, *sub silento*, in favour of what is submitted is the commonsensical view expressed in this passage. In *Gallagher* v. *Corrigan*,[71] which concerned the disciplining of a prison officer, the facts were that the investigation of the applicant's transgression had all been done by a Higher Executive Officer in the Department of Justice; but no question whatsoever was taken as to whether the Minister could regard himself as bound by the official's views on the facts.

A similar point of omission could be made in regard to *Pok Sun Shun* v. *Ireland*[72] which, it may be noted, was a deportation case, *i.e.* it concerned a peculiarly significant and delicate area of personal rights in which the Minister's involvement has traditionally been required, even in the United Kingdom.[73] The relevant passage from the judgment of Costello J. is as follows:

"The procedures which are gone through as a matter of course, in this case, were described by Mr. O'Brien and Mr. Hanrahan, [civil servants in the aliens section of the Department of Justice] and it does appear that the reports were obtained from gardaí in relation to the activities of the plaintiff. The files, which eventually reached the Minister's department, had full information concerning the plaintiff's marital status and the number of children which he had, and the files contained reports of interviews which were held between Mr. O'Brien and Mr. Hanrahan and the plaintiff. The files went through what, I think, are normal channels. They contained obser-

---

[71] High Court, February 1, 1988. See pp. 441–442.
[72] [1986] I.L.R.M. 593.
[73] See *R.* v. *Secretary of State for the Home Department, ex p. Oladehinde* [1990] 2 All E.R. 367 a deportation case, in which the High Court held the deportation invalid for unauthorised delegation by the Secretary of State; but was reversed by the Court of Appeal.

vations on the plaintiff, and information from the respective officials and from the assistant secretary to the Minister."[74]

As can be seen from this passage, the facts in *Pok Sun Shun* were similar to those in *Geraghty (No. 2)*, yet nothing was said about the Minister's acceptance of his official's observations and findings. Broadly speaking then, it seems that the *Carltona* doctrine has been accepted—though only implicitly—by a majority of the judges.

14. Acting Under Dictation by Another Body

In the field next to the delegation of a decision by an authorised body to another body is a case in which the authorised body does take the decision in form, but in substance is merely rubber-stamping an instruction from another body.[75] A straightforward example of this occurred in *McLoughlin* v. *Minister for Social Welfare.*[76] Here the substantive point which has already been discussed was whether the appellant solicitor, employed in the Chief State Solicitor's Office, was to be classified as being in the employment of the State or of the civil service of the Government. The context in which this issue arose was that the appellant had claimed that he was not employed in the civil service of the State and accordingly was not an employed contributor for the purpose of making payments under the Social Welfare Act 1952. In deciding against the appellant, the appeal officer in the Department of Social Welfare said that he had received a minute from the Minister for Finance directing that the appellant was in the employment of the civil service of the Government and that he believed that he was bound to adhere to the Minister's direction.[77] That belief was characterised by O'Daly J. (as he then was) in the Supreme Court as:

" . . . [A]n abdication by him from his duty as an appeals officer. That duty is laid upon him by the Oireachtas and he is required to perform it as between the parties that appear before him fairly and freely as becomes anyone who is called upon to decide on matters of right and obligation."[78]

[74] [1986] I.L.R.M. 598.
[75] The two classes plainly overlap. For instance, *Geraghty* v. *Minister for Local Government* [1975] I.R. 300 could have been classified under the present heading, but, as against this, it is usual for the "dictation" to emanate from an internal source. As it happened, the "advice" in *Geraghty* was from civil servants to their Minister. In any event, nothing turns on the distinction.
[76] [1958] I.R. 1. Another aspect of the case is discussed at pp. 68–73. See also, *H. Lavender & Co. Ltd.* v. *Minister of Housing* [1975] 1 W.L.R. 1231.
[77] See also, *The State (Meade)* v. *Cork C.C.*, High Court, May 27, 1971 (local authority wrongly considering themselves bound by ministerial circular).
[78] [1958] I.R. 12. The phrase "natural justice" is also used by O'Daly J., but it is submitted that the more appropriate analysis is that adopted in the text. *The State (Kershaw)* v. *Eastern Health Board* [1985] I.L.R.M. 235 would also appear at first sight to engage the principle against acting under dictation. But Finlay P. made it plain that such was not the case: "The Minister has, of course, in addition a general administrative function with regard to the administration of the scheme for supplementary benefits which he himself has prescribed in the Regulations of 1977. In so far, therefore, as the circulars issued on his behalf on June 22, 1983, form advice and guidance to health boards carrying out the National Fuel Scheme it is clearly a proper and valid administrative act" ([1985] I.L.R.M. 239).

The principle thus robustly laid down in *McLoughlin* was followed in *The State (Rajan)* v. *Minister for Industry and Commerce*.[79] This case arose out of "directives" issued by the Controller of Patents, Designs and Trade Marks to members of his professional staff which were designed to reduce the arrears of applications in the Patent Office. These directives stated, *inter alia*, that if exactly the same patent application had already been accepted in another European Patent Office then that specification should be accepted in Ireland without any further checks as to matters such as "patentability" and "novelty", which the Act requires to be tested. The crucial point here is that this duty is vested not in the Controller but in members of his staff known as "examiners." For section 11(1) of the Patents Act 1964 states:

"When the complete specification has been filed in respect of an application for a patent, the application . . . shall be referred by the Controller to . . . an examiner . . . for examination."

In the light of this, Barron J. held that the Controller's instruction was invalid. First, he found that there is a statutory obligation to examine all applications for both patentability and novelty, irrespective of anything done abroad. Secondly, Barron J. states that it was "erroneous" for the Controller to believe:

" . . . that he has a general power of control over the Examiners even extending to telling them the extent of the investigation of applications which they are to perform. The examination is a statutory function and there is nothing in the relevant statutory powers giving him such a right either as *persona designata* or as head of the Patent Office."[80]

The point was strengthened by the fact that the 1964 Act in effect provides for an appeal from the examiner to the Controller, so making it even less appropriate for an examiner to be subject to instructions from the Controller.

One point of comparison may be made: *Rajan* was a more extreme case than *McLoughlin*. For in *Rajan* what was involved was interference with a statutory obligation imposed upon another person, as opposed to a discretion, as in *McLoughlin*. Thus, in *Rajan*, there was purported interference with a mandate from the legislature.

It will have been noted, that, in both *McLoughlin* and *Rajan*, there was little doubt that an instruction had been given; rather the live issue before the court was whether (as the applicant successfully submitted, in each case) the person receiving the instruction was independent, and not under the contol, of the person giving it. By contrast, in the third case, *The State (McCormack)* v. *Curran*,[81] what was mainly in contention was whether an instruction had been given. The facts of the case were rather unusual. The central provision in the case was Article 2 of the Third Schedule to the Northern Irish Criminal Law Jurisdiction Act 1975. This provides that where a person is accused before a Northern Irish

[79] [1988] I.L.R.M. 231.
[80] *Ibid.* 240.
[81] [1987] I.L.R.M. 225.

Court of an extra-territorial offence—that is, one committed in the Republic—then, provided that a warrant for his arrest for the same offence has been
issued in the Republic, the accused may not opt for trial in Northern Ireland.
In the present case, the applicant was awaiting trial before the Belfast Crown
Court but had intimated that he wished to be tried in the Republic. However,
in the Republic, no warrant had been sought in respect of the applicant.
Accordingly, in the instant proceedings, he sought an order against the
respondent that they seek a warrant for his arrest. The particular point of relevance, here, concerned the inter-action between the Chief Superintendent
and the D.P.P. The applicant alleged that the D.P.P. had issued a direction to
the Chief Superintendent not to apply for a warrant for the applicant's arrest.
The Supreme Court found that the applicant's case failed on the facts as there
was no evidence to show such an instruction. However, the analysis of the
relationship between the D.P.P. and the Garda Síochána is of interest. Walsh
J. stated, in the first place, that on the authority of the Supreme Court in *The
State (Collins)* v. *Ruane*[82]: "all members of the Garda Síochána in the exercise
of their duties are completely independent of the D.P.P. as he is completely
independent of them."[83] In consequence, if there had been any direction
from the D.P.P., it "would be devoid of legal effect."[84] The applicant's
second point was that there had been consultations at which the D.P.P. had
intimated to the Chief Superintendent that if he went ahead in procuring a
warrant, the D.P.P. would not put down an indictment. However, according
to Finlay C.J., such intimation would be "perfectly reasonable and proper,"[85]
since it is the D.P.P.'s function to decide whether to prosecute. In these circumstances, as Walsh J. stated, the Chief Superintendent "could not reasonably be expected to undertake proceedings which he might have had good
reason to believe would be abortive."[86]

[82] [1984] I.R. 39.
[83] [1987] I.L.R.M. 238.
[84] *Ibid.*
[85] [1987] I.L.R.M. 236.
[86] [1987] I.L.R.M. 239.

407

CHAPTER 9

CONSTITUTIONAL JUSTICE

Constitutional justice is an aspect of procedural law and procedural law looms especially large in the field of administrative law. The reason for this import- ance is that administrative law is directed to public authorities. One of the car- dinal features distinguishing public authorities from private persons—so the theory runs—is that public authorities are taken to be non-partisan and open to persuasion provided that all the relevant facts and arguments are placed before them. With a fair procedure, all the relevant matters are more likely to emerge and to be properly weighed by the decision-maker. Accordingly there is a causative link between proper procedure and the quality of the decision. In short, "[t]he whole theory of 'natural justice' is that ministers, though free to decide as they like, will in practice decide properly and responsibly once the facts have been fairly laid before them."[1] In addition, considering the minute rules which the judges apply to their own procedure in court, it is perhaps inevitable that they should regard fair procedure as a particularly important matter. To some extent, also, procedural rectitude has been regarded as com- pensation for the latitude which the courts have traditionally allowed to the merits of an administrative action. There are other reasons, too, for the importance of procedure and we shall return to this question in Part 6, below.

As a second preliminary, it should be emphasised that constitutional justice does not comprehend the whole of the procedural law in the field of public administration. For, in addition, each decision may have its own particular procedural rules.[2] Some examples of such rules have already been given in Chapter 8 (under the heading of "Formal and Procedural Provisions" for pro- cedural rules provide some graphic examples of this category). The special feature of constitutional justice is that it applies over such a wide field of pub- lic decision-making.

1. Constitutional Justice and Natural Justice

Natural justice

The best way of explaining constitutional justice is to begin with natural justice, which consists of two fundamental procedural rules, namely: that the

[1] Wade, "Quasi-Judicial and its Background" (1949) 10 Camb.L.J. 216, 217.
[2] See Lord Diplock's well-known restatement in *C.C.S.U.* v. *Minister for Civil Service* [1985] 1 A.C. 374, 411:

> "I have described the third head as 'procedural impropriety' rather than failure to observe basic rules of natural justice or failure to act with procedural fairness towards the person who will be affected by the decision. This is because susceptibility to judicial review under this head covers also failure by an administrative tribunal to observe procedural rules that are expressly laid down in the legislative instrument by which its jurisdiction is conferred, even where such failure does not involve any denial of natural justice."

decision-maker must not be biased; and, secondly, that anyone who may be adversely affected by a decision should not be condemned unheard; rather he should have the best possible chance to put his side of the case.

The title, in particular the epithet "natural," has attracted a certain amount of attention. According to Costello J. in *Nolan* v. *Irish Land Commission*:

" . . . [T]he adjective 'natural' before justice was not used to describe justice by reference to man in a state of nature or in primitive society. Rather it has been employed as part of a phrase which developed from a philosophical view of man's nature as that of a being endowed with reason and capable of ascertaining objective moral values. As pointed out by de Smith, *Judicial Review of Administrative Action* [now 4th Ed. at p. 157]: 'The term expresses the close relationship between the common law and moral principles and it has an impressive ancestry.' "[3]

This quotation draws attention to the universality of natural justice which can also be illustrated by the inclusion of the two principles of natural justice in the European Convention of Human Rights, which provides that: "In the determination of his civil rights and obligations or of any criminal charges against him, everyone is entitled to a fair and public *hearing* within a reasonable time by an *independent and impartial* tribunal established by law."[4] (Author's italics). In similar vein to the quotation from *Nolan*, O'Higgins C.J. has remarked:

"The application of [the principles of natural justice] to the different situations which competing interests in society create has never been capable of precise definition. For that reason they have been criticised and even rejected by those who believe precise definition to be the *sine qua non* of true law. They came to be recognised, however, at a time when society was emerging from the rule of might and force and when men looked for the protection of their rights in the oral sphere of justice and fairness. Natural justice, imprecise though the term may be, was something which came to be regarded as each man's protection against the arbitrary use of power."[5]

Constitutional Justice " . . . more than the two well-established principles . . . "

In 1965, natural justice in Ireland was reincarnated as constitutional justice. In what was obviously intended to be a seminal *obiter dictum*, Walsh J. stated:

"In the context of the Constitution, natural justice might be more appropriately termed constitutional justice and must be understood to import

[3] [1981] I.R. 23, 34. Costello J. was countering criticism of the term contained in *Green* v. *Blake* [1948] I.R. 242.
[4] Art. 6(1). See *Campbell* v. *United Kingdom* (1985) 7 E.H.H.R. 165 (guarantee of Art. 6(1) extends to adjudications of Prison Boards, at least in serious disciplinary cases).
[5] *Garvey* v. *Ireland* [1981] I.R. 75, 91.

more than the two well-established principles that no man shall be judge in his own cause, and *audi alteram partem*."[6]

There has been a striking lack of progress in divining what these additional factors comprise and the courts have sometimes appeared reluctant explicitly to recognise this reservoir of due process (possibly because of the width of natural justice *simpliciter*).

One candidate for inclusion under the umbrella of constitutional justice appeared in *M.* v. *M.*,[7] where Henchy J. stated that a trial judge was not entitled to disregard "the corroborated and unquestioned evidence of witnesses." To do so was not in accordance with the proper administration of justice. Other candidates for inclusion are a right to have an administrative decision based on probative evidence[8] and a requirement that the burden of proving facts, which, if established, would lead to a person being deprived of his livelihood, should be beyond reasonable doubt.[9] Other possibilities, the details of which are discussed below, are the right to a reasonably prompt decision and the right to reasons for a decision.[10]

At common law, a breach of natural justice was not in itself tortious.[11] However, it now seems probable that an infringement of the constitutional right to fair procedures may sound in damages.[12]

It is suggested that it is better to confine constitutional justice to procedural safeguards, and not, as is sometimes done, to apply the term so widely that it encompasses substantive rights, lest it become too imprecise a concept.[13]

---

[6] *Per* Walsh J. in *McDonald* v. *Bord na gCon* [1965] I.R. 217, 242. For a discussion of the significance of these remarks, see Casey, "Natural and Constitutional Justice—The Policeman's Lot Improved" (1979–1980) 2 D.U.L.J.(N.S.) 95 and Hogan, "Natural and Constitutional Justice: *Adieu* to *Laissez-Faire*" (1984) 19 Ir.Jur.(N.S.) 309.

[7] [1979] I.L.R.M. 160.

[8] *M.* v. *M.* [1979] I.L.R.M. 160; *R.* v. *Deputy Industrial Injuries Commissioner, ex p. Moore* [1965] 1 Q.B. 456; *Mahon* v. *Air New Zealand Ltd.* [1985] A.C. 808. But *cf. The State (Power)* v. *Moran*, [1976–1977] I.L.R.M. 20; *The State (Shinkaruk)* v. *Carroll*, High Court, December 15, 1976.

[9] *O'Donoghue* v. *Veterinary Council* [1975] I.R. 398, 404, *per* Kenny J. Note, however, that in *Banco Ambrosiano Spa.* v. *Ansbacher & Co. Ltd.* [1987] I.L.R.M. 669, Henchy J. rejected the notion that the criminal standard of proof was applicable in civil cases, even where serious allegations (such as fraud) were at issue.

[10] See pp. 465–470 and pp. 457–465 respectively.

[11] *Dunlop* v. *Woollahra M.C.* [1982] A.C. 158.

[12] While this issue has not yet been resolved, it would seem to follow from the breach of constitutional rights cases (such as *Glover* v. *B.L.N. Ltd.* [1973] I.R. 388 and *Kennedy* v. *Ireland* [1987] I.R. 587) that an infringement of the constitutional right to fair procedures should be actionable. Furthermore, the right to fair procedures may be classified as a "personal right" (and not a constitutional provision pertaining to (say) the structure of Government) and it thus passes the test prescribed by Murphy J. in *Greene* v. *Minister for Agriculture* [1989] 3 C.M.L.R. 830.

[13] In *The State (Gleeson)* v. *Minister for Defence* [1976] I.R. 280, 295 Henchy J. defined constitutional justice very widely to include a number of constitutional guarantees some of which are peculiar to criminal courts (*e.g.* the right to jury trial) and some of which are substantive (*e.g.* that unconstitutional laws should not be applied). He then commented: "Because of the wide scope of such constitutional guarantees . . . a plea of denial of constitutional justice lacks the correctness and particularity necessary to identify and bring into focus the precise constitutional issue which is being raised." However, this view of constitutional justice has largely fallen into disfavour: see Hogan, "Natural and Constitutional Justice: *Adieu* to *Laissez-Faire*" (1984) 19 Ir.Jur.(N.S.) 309.

Foundation in the Constitution

There is another point of contrast between constitutional and natural justice, namely that natural justice remains a mere common law (and therefore rebuttable) presumption to be applied, in appropriate contexts, in the interpretation of statutes. By contrast, constitutional justice is judicially regarded as implicit in Article 40.3 of the Constitution.[14] The reasoning seems to be that words like "respect" and "protect . . . from unjust attack" in Article 40.3 refer not only to substantive protection but also mean that even where substantive interference is permitted, it must be accompanied by a fair procedure. This difference in the sources of constitutional and natural justice is important. A British statute can if it uses clear enough words, exclude the rules of natural justice because of the absence of a written constitution.[15] By contrast, an Irish statute attempting to exclude the rules of constitutional justice in a situation where they would be appropriate would be unconstitutional.

A straightforward and (in that a nineteenth-century statute was involved) not untypical example of a statute being overridden by the principles of constitutional justice occurred in *Jaggers Restaurant Ltd.* v. *Ahearne*.[16] The case arose out of a Circuit Court order declaring that a liquor licence should be granted (under section 14 of the Intoxicating Liquor Act 1960) for a premises substituted for a demolished licensed premises. According to section 4 of the Licensing (Ireland) Act 1833 (which was the relevant provision regarding procedure) the only persons who could object to such a declaration were inhabitants of the civil parish in which the premises proposed to be licensed are situated. The Supreme Court unanimously refused to accept this restriction. Finlay C.J. stated[17]:

"Since in the instant case one of the matters which the applicant must prove is that the location of the premises in Fleet Street rather than on the site of the original premises in Sean McDermott Street is unlikely to have a materially adverse effect on the business carried on in any licensed premises in the neighbourhood, it must inevitably follow that the owner of any licensed premises carrying on business in the neighbourhood must have an immedi-

---

[14] *Re Haughey* [1971] I.R. 217; *Kiely* v. *Minister for Social Welfare (No. 2)* [1977] I.R. 267; *Garvey* v. *Ireland* [1981] I.R. 75; *Ryan* v. *V.I.P. Taxi Co-operative Ltd.* (High Court *ex tempore*) *Irish Times Law Report*, April 10, 1989; *Halal Meat Packers* v. *E.A.T.* [1990] I.L.R.M. 293, 307–309; *Glover* v. *B.L.N. Ltd.* [1973] I.R. 388.

[15] See, *e.g.* *O'Brien* v. *Bord na Móna* [1983] I.R. 255, 270–271 where Keane J. held that an enactment which created a situation where the decision-maker was a judge in his own cause would conflict with the constitutional guarantee of fair procedures, unless a different form of procedure was not practicable. By contrast in *Bushell* v. *Environment Secretary* [1981] A.C. 75 the fact that the Minister was the person to consider objections to a provisional motorway route he himself had prepared was beyond challenge because *it had been clearly established by statute*. Keane J. commenting on *Bushell's* case, said ([1983] I.R. 270) that it was "a reasonable inference" that the difference between the different approaches in the two jurisdictions was to be explained "by the absence in England of a written constitution containing express guarantees of fundamental rights and fair procedures in the protection of those rights." See also, *S.* v. *S.* [1983] I.R. 68.

[16] [1988] I.R. 308.

[17] *Ibid.* 315.

ate and obvious interest and right to oppose the licence in order to assert what by the sub-section is clearly intended to be a protection of his business interests.

It would be clearly contrary to any concept of fair procedure should such a person be prevented from being heard and represented on the hearing of the application for the licence. In so far as this interpretation of section 14 may appear to be inconsistent with any of the provisions of the Act of 1833 that Act must to this extent be deemed to have been amended."

This may also be illustrated by speculative reference to section 10 of the Local Government (Planning and Development) Act 1983. This Act abolished the original Bord Pleanála (replacing it with a differently constituted Bord) and also in effect, dismissed the members of the original Bord from office (section 10(1) states that they shall "cease to be . . . members"). These members then brought an action against Ireland which was settled out of court. Had the case proceeded to hearing, one of the plaintiff's strongest arguments would have been that their dismissal from office without being granted a hearing violated the *audi alteram partem* rule. If such a claim had arisen in Britain, the Crown could have pleaded that the dismissal was effected by Act of Parliament and there was no higher law to which the plaintiffs could appeal. In Ireland, no such defence was available.[18]

Moreover, even where no such clear-cut question has been involved, the Irish judges have given constitutional/natural justice a keener cutting edge than have their British counterparts. They have been prepared not only to strike down decisions for breach of constitutional justice but also, on the positive side, to suggest improvements in procedure which would meet the requirements of constitutional justice. For example, in *Nolan* v. *Irish Land Commission*,[19] the Supreme Court upholding the High Court, granted an injunction restraining the hearing of objections by the Land Commission to the compulsory acquisition of the plaintiff's land unless discovery and inspection of the Commission's documents were allowed. Costello J. in the High Court gave an explanation as to how the procedure should operate in this novel setting and this advice was approved in the Supreme Court. The same trend was manifest in the following extract, which has frequently been

---

[18] For another example, see *The State (Haverty)* v. *Bord Pleanála* [1987] I.R. 485 (where Murphy J. held that even on the assumption that the planning legislation did not require an objector to a planning application to be heard on an appeal by an unsuccessful applicant for permission, yet this was required by the constitutional requirement of fair procedures). An even more far-reaching use of constitutional justice might be adopted to repair what it is suggested is a major deficiency in our planning legislation, namely the inadequate provisions for notifying interested parties, such as neighbours, regarding a planning application (on which, see pp. 205–208). If a neighbour does not learn of an application in time to object, may he not argue that the rules of constitutional justice requires that he be genuinely (and not notionally) alerted to a decision which affects his own property rights. This is not exactly what was said, in the High Court, in *Brady* v. *Donegal C.C.* [1989] I.L.R.M. 282 examined at pp. 375–376 but this case would provide some support for such a submission.

[19] [1981] I.R. 23. For other examples, see *M.* v. *The Medical Council* [1984] I.R. 485; *O'Donoghue* v. *Veterinary Council* [1975] I.R. 398.

413

adopted in later cases, from Walsh J.'s judgment in *East Donegal Co-Operative Ltd*. v. *Attorney-General*[20]:

> "The presumption of constitutionality carries with it not only the presumption that the constitutional construction is the one intended by the Oireachtas but also that the Oireachtas intended that proceedings, procedures, discretions and adjudications which are permitted, provided for, or prescribed by an Act of the Oireachtas are to be conducted in accordance with the principles of constitutional justice."

Walsh J. went on to hold that constitutional justice would apply to an application to the Minister for Agriculture for a mart licence, under the Livestock Marts Act 1967, even though the wording of the Act would seem on the *expressio unius exclusio altero* principle of statutory interpretation, to militate against this result.

A number of cases involving court procedure further illustrate the potency of constitutional justice. The first is *S*. v. *S*.,[21] in which the High Court, in the name of "constitutional entitlement to fair procedures," uprooted the long-established common law rule in *Russell* v. *Russell*.[22] This rule, whose policy was to maintain the unity of the family, excluded any evidence from a wife which would tend to prove that a child born to her during wedlock was not the child of her husband. Again, in *O'Domhnaill* v. *Merrick*[23] the Supreme Court held, in effect, that notwithstanding the existence of the Statute of Limitations fixing precise time limits, the court retained, in addition, an inherent power to stay proceedings, where the passage of time could be taken to work an injustice. Finally, in *The State (McKeown)* v. *Scully*,[24] a case on the powers of a coroner, O'Hanlon J. said[25]:

> "If this construction of [the Coroners Act 1962, s.30] is incorrect and if it is permissible for a coroner's jury to bring in a verdict of suicide, then I would hold that there was a departure from the rules of natural and constitutional justice in the present case in failing to give the widow and deceased of the next of kin any opportunity to be heard before this very grave and damaging finding which was made against the deceased husband of the prosecutor. Had such opportunity been given they could reasonably have sought leave to be represented at the inquest, to have the witnesses cross-examined on their depositions, to address the jury; and to offer to make available to the coroner further evidence which might be of assistance at the inquest."

Constitutional justice has been grounded in Article 40.3 of the Constitution

[20] [1970] I.R. 317, 341. For a similar approach, see, *e.g. Hogan* v. *Minister for Justice* [1976–1977] I.L.R.M. 184; *Loftus* v. *Att.-Gen.* [1979] I.R. 221; *O'Brien* v. *Bord na Móna* [1983] I.R. 255 and *McCann* v. *Racing Board* [1983] I.L.R.M. 67.
[21] [1983] I.R. 68.
[22] [1924] A.C. 687.
[23] [1984] I.R. 151.
[24] [1986] I.L.R.M. 133.
[25] *Ibid*. 135.

which confers rights explicitly on "citizen[s]." Nevertheless it has been held by Barrington J. in *The State (McFadden)* v. *The Governor of Mountjoy Prison* [(*No. 1*,)][26] (a case arising out of extradition proceedings) that the duty to observe "basic fairness of procedures" applies even where aliens are involved. The reason according to Barrington J. is that[27]:

" . . . [W]hen the Constitution prescribes basic fairness of procedures in the administration of the law, it does so not only because citizens have rights, but also because the courts in the administration of justice are expected to observe certain forms of due process enshrined in the Constitution. Once the courts have seisin of a dispute, it is difficult to see how the standards they should apply in investigating it should, in fairness, be any different in the case of an alien than those to be applied in the case of a citizen."

Applies to all three arms of government

Whilst it is true that most constitutional justice cases emanate from the executive branch of government, it is an aspect of the rules' universality that they can apply, in appropriate circumstances, to each of the three arms of government: legislature; judicature; or executive.

The rules of constitutional justice regulate decisions affecting individuals directly and these are just the sort of decisions which are usually not taken by the Oireachtas. However, in appropriate circumstances constitutional justice has been extended even to the Oireachtas, as was demonstrated in the multi-faceted case of *Re Haughey*.[28] The aspect of the case which is relevant here is that it applied the *audi alteram partem* rule to an investigation by a committee of the legislature (specifically, the Dáil Public Accounts Committee).

At the opposite pole from the legislative function is the judicial function, which deals almost exclusively with individual decisions. But here procedure is regulated by a minute, specialised code of procedural and evidential law. For example, at the pre-trial stage in the Superior Courts, provision is made by the Rules of the Superior Courts, as to pleadings, interrogatories, discovery etc in order to ensure that litigants have an adequate opportunity to meet

---

[26] [1981] I.L.R.M. 113.

[27] *Ibid.* 122.

[28] [1971] I.R. 217, 263–264. Another episode involving a House of the Oreachtas occurred in 1991. The Senate Committee on Procedure and Privileges recommended to the House that Senator Norris be disciplined by being suspended from the service of the Senate for one week (T. 279 (Pl. 7181), March 14, 1990) and this recommendation was adopted (*Seanad Debates*, Vol. 124, cols. 772–804, March 15, 1990). The basis of Senator Norris' offence was an allegation he had made against the Cathaoirleach. Notwithstanding this, it was the Cathaoirleach who, in line with the usual practice, chaired both the Committee and the Senate, at the relevant times. In addition, Senator Norris, the Committee refused the Senator's request that he be allowed legal representation, to call witnesses, etc. Senator Norris was then granted leave by the High Court to apply for a judicial review of his disciplining by the Senate on the ground of violation of both the first and second rules of constitutional justice. As a result of the order made by the High Court, Senator Norris was reinstated and eventually his action was withdrawn before it had received a substantive hearing: see, especially, *Seanad Debates*, Vol. 124, cols. 1039–1145; Vol. 125, cols. 381–385, May 25, 1990.

their opponent's case.[29] Fair procedure in the courts is underpinned by such specialised constitutional provisions as Articles 38.1, 34.1, as well as 40.3.[30] This law is inspired by the same policy which underlies constitutional justice. However, it is not usual to classify procedural law or the law of evidence as part of constitutional justice. Nevertheless, constitutional or natural justice has, very occasionally been invoked *eo nomine*, to augment procedural law. One example which has been mentioned already is *McKeown*.[31] Another example is *N. v. K.*[32] in which Henchy J. suggested that constitutional justice may require separate representation for children in appropriate cases where their welfare is at stake. The same argument could be made in favour of representation rights for the prosecutrix in rape cases, in the not uncommon circumstances that the accused is claiming that she consented, thereby impugning her reputation. In addition, it is likely that in suitable cases, constitutional justice could be used as a device with which to extirpate some of the less justifiable results of the rule excluding hearsay evidence or to supply the omission of the Rules of Court which provide no system of discovery of documents before the District Court.[33] Such examples draw attention to the connection which exists between the principles of constitutional justice and the right of access to the courts, a continuum which was acknowledged in the following passage from *S. v. S.* (the facts of which are given above):

"The combined effect of Articles 34.1, 38.1 and 40.3 [of the Constitution] appears to me to guarantee (*inter alia*) something equivalent to the concept of 'due process' under the American Constitution in relation to causes and controversies litigated before the Court. . . . Just as the parties have a right of access to the courts when this is necessary to defend or vindicate life, person, good name or property rights, so they have *a constitutional right to fair procedures* when they get to court. . . . Because the rule in *Russell* v. *Russell* ran counter to [the] paramount public policy [of ascertaining truth and doing justice] and was calculated to defeat the due and

---

[29] Thus, in *Cooney* v. *Browne* [1984] I.R. 185, 191 Henchy J. said that the rules governing the delivery of particulars were essentially designed to ensure a fair hearing:

> " 'The object of particulars is to enable the party asking for them to know what case he has to meet, and so save unnecessary expense, and avoid allowing parties to be taken by surprise': *Spedding* v. *Fitzpatrick* (1888) 38 Ch.D. 410, 413. Thus, where the pleading is so general or so imprecise that the other side cannot know what case he will have to meet at the trial, he should be entitled to such particulars, as will inform him of the range of evidence . . . which he will have to deal with at the trial."

While Henchy J.'s comments were in the context of delivery of particulars, they could just as easily be applied, *mutatis mutandis*, to the whole panoply of High Court procedures, such as discovery, interrogatories, etc.

[30] Art. 38.1 provides that "No person shall be tried on any criminal charge save in due course of law." Art. 34.1 states that "Justice shall be administered in courts established by law. . . . "

[31] See p. 414. See also, *The State (Buchan)* v. *Coyne* [1936] I.R. 485; *The State (Killian)* v. *Minister for Justice* [1954] I.R. 207; *The State (Walshe)* v. *Murphy* [1981] I.R. 275 and *The State (O'Regan)* v. *Plunkett* [1984] I.L.R.M. 347.

[32] [1985] I.R. 733, 749.

[33] See *Nolan* v. *Irish Land Commission* [1981] I.R. 23 described at pp. 413–414.

proper administration of justice, I would hold that it ceased to have legal effect in the State after the enactment of the Constitution in 1937."[34]

The issue of the impact of constitutional justice upon court procedure also arose when, immediately following the enactment of the Companies (Amendment) Act 1990, the Goodman Group Plc applied *ex parte* to the High Court for the appointment of an examiner to the Group. The order was duly made by Hamilton P. [35] Because the order was made *ex parte* the creditors of Goodman Group were precluded from taking steps to realise their securities as against the Group, as, for example, seeking to have the company put into liquidation. The question of whether this *ex parte* procedure constituted a breach of the creditors' right to fair procedures was much discussed but never litigated. To this question, we shall return on the following page.

The general rule would appear to be that where a court makes a final order which affects the rights of interested parties, fair procedures means that both sides must be heard. Thus, to take but one example from many, in *The State (O' Sullivan)* v. *Buckley*,[36] the Supreme Court quashed an order of a District Justice where he had purported to grant, *ex parte*, an enlargement of time to allow an appeal to be taken to the Circuit Court. The Court added that, save for purely procedural orders (of which this was not one), persons discharging judicial functions must hear both sides before proceeding to make a final order.

These principles also apply to the High Court and the decision of the Supreme Court in *People* v. *Ellis*[37] is a good example. In this case O'Hanlon J. had discharged an earlier order of his and directed that a criminal lunatic be taken into custody. Although the defendant was legally represented at the hearing, his legal representatives were not given an opportunity to make submissions on legal issues. Finlay C.J. said that this omission "constituted a major breach of the constitutional guarantee of fair procedures to which the defendant was entitled."[38] Finlay C.J. also drew attention to the fact that O'Hanlon J. had purported to pronounce on constitutional issues, without having directed service of the proceedings on the Attorney General in the manner required by Order 60 of the Rules of the Superior Courts 1986. This omission alone raised "significant doubts and queries to the validity of the procedures leading to the making of this order."[39]

It is true that in *Butler* v. *Ruane*[40] the Supreme Court sanctioned the making of orders *ex parte*, such as giving the respondents additional time to file affidavits in judicial review matters, but the courts will (or, at least, should) never make *final* orders *ex parte*, in cases affecting legal rights or interests. So well established is this principle that it is not easy to find auth-

---

[34] [1983] I.R. 75, 80 (O'Hanlon J.).
[35] *The Irish Times*, August 30, 1990.
[36] (1967) 101 I.L.T.R. 152.
[37] [1990] 2 I.R. 291.
[38] *Ibid.* 303.
[39] *Ibid.*
[40] *Butler* v. *Ruane* [1989] I.L.R.M. 159.

orities for it. *The State (Rogers)* v. *Galvin*[41] does, however, afford such authority.

Here Hamilton J. had made an order *ex parte* releasing the applicant from custody. This Order was set aside by the Supreme Court. The provisions of Article 40.4.2 requiring the respondents to be given an opportunity to justify the detention in writing were, said Henchy J., mandatory because they were:

"A constitutional recognition of the rule of natural justice expressed in the maxim *audi alteram partem*. It guards against the risk that on an *ex parte* application . . . an unjustified release from custody may be made."[42]

The judge went on to doubt whether Order 84, rule 9 (which purported to allow the making of such orders) was actually *intra vires* the Superior Court Rules Committee inasmuch as it allowed the making of such orders *ex parte*. Because of these doubts, Order 84, rule 9 was deleted from the Rules of the Superior Courts when the new Rules were promulgated in 1986.

Returning to the facts of the Goodman episode, it seems clear that the *ex parte* order of Hamilton P. appointing the Examiner was not simply a procedural interlocutory order such as that in *Butler* v. *Ruane*. In *Butler*, the Supreme Court had held that the High Court was entitled to make an *ex parte* order allowing a respondent in judicial review proceedings further time to file affidavits and notice of opposition. An order appointing an examiner to a company is, in fact, a *final* order, albeit one of a definite duration. Moreover, there is no question but that the order trenches upon and affects many valuable rights of creditors since section 5(2) of the 1990 Act prevents a winding-up and execution against the company's property during the currency of the protection period. In these circumstances, constitutional justice would seem to require that the creditors be given a say as to whether an Examiner should be appointed.[43] If they are heard, they may be able to persuade the court to refuse the petition or to agree to some other course of action. But even irrespective of whether the result might have been otherwise, the failure to afford the creditors a hearing in the *Goodman* case would appear to have consti-

---

[41] [1983] I.R. 249. For another example, see *Re Zwann's Application* [1981] I.R. 395, 404.
[42] [1983] I.R. 249, 253.
[43] One possible way of refuting the breach of fair procedures argument might be to argue that the creditors would have the right to apply to the High Court to have the order of examinership vacated. This was suggested by Finlay C.J. in *Re R. Ltd.* [1989] I.R. 126, 133 where the appellants complained that the making *ex parte* of an order directing that oppression proceedings brought under s.205 of the Companies Act 1963 be heard *in camera* was a breach of fair procedures:

"Any conceivable disadvantage which could arise from the making of such an order *ex parte* is avoided by the procedure which was adopted in this case of giving an extremely early hearing to an application to set aside or remove the order. I would, therefore, reject the contention that the fact that the original order *in camera* was made *ex parte* vitiated the validity of the orders eventually made."

However, in the present context, it should be observed that (a) Finlay C.J.'s judgment was a dissenting one and that this point was not addressed by the majority; (b) an order directing a hearing *in camera* is in the nature of an interlocutory order rather than a final one; and (c) Finlay C.J. did not advert to the doctrine of *functus officio*, which, in the context of a *final* (as opposed to interlocutory) order, would seem to argue in favour of a direct appeal and would appear, as a general rule, to preclude the High Court from vacating such a final order.

tuted, no less than in *People* v. *Ellis*, a "major breach of the constitutional guarantee of fair procedures." While, of course, speed was of the essence in the *Goodman* case, this, of itself, cannot justify the making of a *final* order appointing an examiner *ex parte*, no more than urgency could justify the granting of a *final* (or even interlocutory) injunction on an *ex parte* basis. Fair procedures would seem to require, therefore, that the intitial appointment of an examiner is on an *interim* basis.[44] During this interim period, the interests of the company seeking protection would be adequately cared for, since by virtue of section 5(1) of the 1990 Act, court protection commences from the date of the presentation of the petition.

Nomenclature

At least two, and possibly three, different judicial attitudes to the relationship between constitutional and natural justice have emerged. The first takes the view that constitutional justice only applies where a possible breach of some constitutionally-protected interest, for example, a property right, is involved, whereas natural justice continues to exist to protect other rights or privileges created by statute, common law or contract.[45] A further refinement on this attitude has it that whilst constitutional and natural justice should be distinguished as just indicated, even natural justice should be read in the light of the Constitution, thereby giving rise to the dual concepts of constitutional justice and constitutionalised natural justice.[46] The other, simpler view is that constitutional justice has succeeded and subsumed natural justice. As McCarthy J. observed: "In my view the two principles of natural justice as they pre-existed the Constitution are now part of the human rights guaranteed by the Constitution."[47]

Both constitutional and natural justice are elastic and vague concepts and the differences between them contemplated in the seminal passage from *McDonald*, quoted *supra* have not developed significantly. Indeed in a number of cases, the phrase "constitutional and/or natural justice" has been used indiscriminately, not to say gaily.[48] Other judgments have betrayed impatience with the subtle difference between the two concepts.[49] Accordingly, we feel that a split-level procedural system only creates complication without adding anything to the stock of legal ideas or rules. Thus we shall nor-

[44] Such a procedure—which is akin to the appointment of a provisional liquidator under s.226 of the Companies Act 1963—was, in fact, adopted by Costello J. in a subsequent case arising under the 1990 Act: see *Re Heffernon Kearns Ltd.*, *The Irish Times*, October 13, 1990.
[45] *The State (Gleeson)* v. *Minister for Defence* [1976] I.R. 280; *Kiely* v. *Minister for Social Welfare* [1977] I.R. 287; *The State (Donnelly)* v. *Minister for Defence*, High Court, October 8, 1979; *Ní Bheoláin* v. *Dublin V.E.C.*, High Court, January 28, 1983.
[46] See *Gleeson, Kiely* and *Nolan* v. *Irish Land Commission* [1981] I.R. 23.
[47] *The State (Furey)* v. *Minister for Defence*, [1988] I.L.R.M. 89. This was the approach taken in *Garvey* v. *Ireland* [1981] I.R. 75 and *The State (Williams)* v. *Army Pensions Board* [1983] I.R. 308.
[48] *e.g. The State (Boyle)* v. *General Medical Services (Payment) Board* [1981] I.L.R.M. 14; *O'Brien* v. *Bord na Móna* [1983] I.R. 255.
[49] See, *e.g.* the comments of Costello J. in *Doupe* v. *Limerick Corporation* [1981] I.L.R.M. 456, 463 and *McHugh* v. *Garda Commissioner* [1985] I.L.R.M. 606.

mally speak only of constitutional justice. In addition, we shall take it that such variants as "basic fairness of procedures"[50] are synonymous with constitutional justice. Again, to the extent that ideas peculiar to court procedure, such as "due process" go beyond constitutional justice we shall not be concerned with them in a book whose primary focus is government administration, rather than court procedure.

2. Nemo Iudex in Causa Sua

Sources of bias

The principle that no person shall be a judge in his own cause is fundamental[51] and well established in both public and judicial administration. Possible sources of bias are infinitely varied and the following list is certainly not exhaustive. Moreover, the list is only intended for descriptive purpose since, with the possible exception of the first category, no legal consequences turn on the particular pigeon-hole to which a case is allocated:

(a) **Material interest.** The most obvious source of bias is financial (or material) interest of which *The People (Attorney-General) v. Singer*[52] is a straightforward example. In this case, the Court of Criminal Appeal ordered a re-trial on a fraud charge because the foreman of the jury had been an investor in the company which was the vehicle for the alleged fraud and was thus one of the victims. Interest was also found to have been present in *Connolly v. McConnell*,[53] a case arising out of the dismissal of a general secretary of a trade union on the authority of the executive Council of the union. This dismissal was found to be void, as some of the members of the union's executive council had financial or other interests in the outcome of the disciplinary hearing. For example, one of the charges involved the defendants disobedience to an order of the plaintiff trade union to pay a recoupment of expenses to a person who was actually a member of the executive council.

Again, in *Doyle v. Croke*[54] an employer, whose company was drifting towards liquidation paid £360,000 in settlement of an official strike. The strike

---

[50] This was the language used by the Supreme Court in *Re Haughey* [1971] I.R. 217. In *S. v. S.* [1983] I.R. 68, 80 O'Hanlon J. spoke of "a constitutional entitlement to fair procedures." See also, *Gunn* v. *National College of Art and Design* [1990] 2 I.R. 168, 179–181, *per* walsh J.; *O'Neill* v. *Beaumont Hospital*, [1990] I.L.R.M. 419, 437, *per* Finlay C.J.

[51] To impute bias against a judge may amount to a contempt of court: *Att.-Gen.* v. *Connolly* [1947] I.R. 213; *The State (D.P.P.)* v. *Walsh* [1981] I.R. 412; *R.* v. *Editor of New Statesman, ex p. D.P.P.* (1928) 44 T.L.R. 301. See Walker, "Scandalising in the Eighties" (1985) 101 L.Q.R. 359.

[52] [1975] I.R. 408n. (decided in 1963). In some cases, there is a statutory disqualification in cases of personal interest: see, *e.g.* s.155 of the Income Tax Act 1967 (special commissioner for income tax disqualified from adjudicating on his own personal tax liability).

[53] [1983] I.R. 172. Interest was found not to exist on the facts in *The State (Divito)* v. *Arklow U.D.C.* [1986] I.L.R.M. 123, where the respondent's refusal of a gaming licence to the applicant company was under challenge. Henchy J. found that there were no "financial or other connections" between the council and a rival company such as "would be likely to deflect the council from fairness or even-handedness in their dealings with the applicant—or such as would be likely to lead a reasonable person to think that the Council would thus act."

[54] High Court, May 6, 1988.

committee decided that this fund was to be divided equally among the former employees, who had adequately performed picket duty. As a result, the committee drew up a list of 150 persons (out of a work-force of about 270) who were to participate in the distribution of these monies. However, in a case brought by 83 of the disappointed employees, the procedure was held to be invalid because, *inter alia*, according to Costello J.:

"All the members of the strike committee were former employees of Irish Meat Producers Limited and as such had a financial interest in the settlement and, accordingly, a financial interest in the actual number of persons who would participate in it. It has not been suggested that they in fact allowed this interest to influence the decisions in which they were involved but the test to be applied is an objective one and a reasonable person could conclude that there was a risk that an even-handed decision might not be taken by a committee all of whose members had a financial interest in its outcome."[55]

An unsuccessful claim occurred in the case of *Dublin and County Broadcasting Ltd.* v. *Independent Radio and Television Commission*[56] which arose out of the allocation of contracts to provide sound broadcasting services, under the new broadcasting regime created by the Radio and Television Act 1988. To discharge the duty of selecting contractors, the Act constitutes the Radio and Television Commission, which is chaired by a former Supreme Court judge, Mr. Justice Henchy. In early 1989, the Commission awarded two contracts to broadcast in the Dublin City and County area. In the present action, which was brought by the only serious contender among the unsuccessful applicants, the plaintiff's major argument was that the Commission's decision in regard to the contract was void because Mr. O'Donovan, one of the ordinary members of the Commission, was biased, by virtue of both his pecuniary and his non-pecuniary interest in one of the successful companies, Radio 2000 Limited. The question of the non-pecuniary interest will be covered below. Before coming to the matter of Mr. O'Donovan's pecuniary interest, it is worth noting that, the High Court treated two general points as being beyond dispute. First, Murphy J. noted that, under the Act, the Commission must have seven to 10 members; yet he stated that if even one of the members were affected by bias, this would invalidate the Commission's decision.[57] Secondly, he accepted the conventional wisdom that pecuniary bias is a uniquely heinous departure from the rules of constitutional justice. It seems reasonable to infer from this that it is to be judged by a more austere standard.

Mr. O'Donovan's interest stemmed from the fact that he had been involved with E-Sat Television Ltd., which owned 70 per cent. of the shares in Radio 2000 Ltd. The pecuniary aspect of his involvement lay in the fact that he had owned some £30,000 worth of shares in E-Sat. However, about a year before

---

[55] *Ibid.* pp. 19–20.
[56] High Court, May 12, 1989.
[57] On this type of numbers point, see too *Connolly* v. *McConnell* [1983] I.R. 172.

the contract was awarded, he had sought to transfer these shares. In fact, as a matter of strict law concerning the assignment of shares, Murphy J. accepted that, unknown to Mr. O'Donovan, he had retained some residual legal (but not beneficial) rights in the shares. However, Murphy J.'s crucial finding on the facts was that:

"Mr. O'Donovan had sought to divest himself of his shares in E-Sat, and he bona fide believed he had successfully done so. I would also accept that the vast majority of people would believe that such was the case and he could not as a matter of law or honour resile from the action he had taken and he has shown no indication of any intention to do so. . . . [And although] as a matter of law, Mr. O'Donovan does have certain rights, . . . I could see a serious challenge being mounted if he were at this stage to seek to exercise those rights."[58]

Given these facts, the plaintiff's argument failed on the ground that "[the pecuniary loss or gain] must be a real possibility, and one which is known to the person exercising the judicial function, if it is to invalidate his decision."[59] Murphy J. was also probably influenced, in regard to both alleged sources of bias, by the fact that Mr. O'Donovan had made a frank and unforced admission of his interest.[60]

(b) Personal attitudes, relationships, beliefs. Bias may arise from the decision-maker's personal attitudes, relationships, or beliefs in the case. In a number of clear cases personal hostility has been found to be present. For example, in *R. (Donoghue)* v. *Cork County JJ.*[61] a conviction imposed by a magistrate who had remarked shortly after the case that he "would not leave any member of the [accused's] family in the district" was quashed on this

---

[58] *Ibid.* pp. 16–17. See too, *McDonough* v. *Minister for Defence* [1991] I.L.R.M. 115, 120, *per* Lavan J. "the Commanding Officer's decision to delegate Captain Holmes to conduct the interview [was unreasonable] having regard to the applicant's complaints against that Officer."]
[59] *Ibid.* pp. 15–16.
[60] For example, Mr. O'Donovan wrote two letters on the difficulty of his position to the chairman of the Commission, each of which is quoted in the judgment at pp. 6, 7. The letter of January 3, 1989, reads as follows:

"Dear Chairman,
  I have a problem and I need your wisdom. Having read the four applications for the National Radio franchise I formed the following conclusions. The application for Nova International could not be treated seriously. That left three applicants, two are of a very high standard and herein lies my problem. Century has Oliver Barry and James Stafford. Now Oliver Barry is an old friend of mine, an ex-RTE Authority member under my Chairmanship. Radio 2000's Chairman is Denis O'Brien and he is Chief Executive in E-Sat, and at one stage was engaged to my daugher. I am quite happy to give you an honest professional opinion on all the applications, but I do believe I am in a no-win situation provided either of these two win the franchise. How do you think I should approach this in the interest of the Commission, myself and the applicants."

At p. 8 Murphy J. states, in regard to these matters:

"The decision of the Chairman [Henchy J.] was that he took the view that Mr. O'Donovan's assistance should not be dispensed with and he wasn't disqualified and should not be debarred from the consideration of and implementation of the decisions." [*sic*]
[61] [1910] 2 I.R. 271.

ground. Similarly, in *R. (Kingston)* v. *Cork County JJ.*[62] an evicted farmer brought charges of assault against the purchaser of the farm. The charges arose out of a boycott which had been imposed on the purchaser by the United Irish League. The purchaser was convicted of assault by a magistrates' bench of four, including two members of the League, who had attended the meeting where the decision to impose the boycott had been taken. The High Court had little difficulty in quashing the conviction."

A case of what, the Supreme Court held, may have appeared to an "unprejudiced onlooker" as personal involvement occurred in *The State (Hegarty)* v. *Winters.*[63] Here an arbitrator appointed under the Acquisition of Land (Assessment of Compensation) Act 1919 was assessing the amount of compensation to be awarded to the applicant land owner for damage done to his land by a county council. The arbitrator went to inspect the land himself and was accompanied by the county council engineer with nobody to represent the applicant. The court quashed the arbitrator's award.

On the other side of the line from *Hegarty* was *Dublin and County Broadcasting Ltd.* Here it was claimed unsuccessfully that the Independent Radio and Television Commission's decision was vitiated, first by O's pecuniary interest (an argument examined above) and, secondly, by O's non-pecuniary interest. The High Court's treatment of this, second issue is of even wider significance than its claim under the first head of this case, in that it is so likely to recur. The reason is that the claim arose out of the inevitable difficulty in discovering, in a relatively small state like Ireland, a respected figure within a particular specialised field who yet has no links with any of the parties to the issue which he is obliged to decide. In the case of the Commission, section 1(5) of the Schedule to its constituent statute, the Radio and Television Act 1988 provides that no one may be appointed as a member "unless he has experience of or has shown a capacity in media or commission affairs, radio communications, engineering, trade union affairs, administration or social, cultural, educational or communications activities."

In view of this statutory requirement, it is not so surprising that one of the members should have had a connection with one of the applicants. Indeed, in O's case, he himself said in evidence, that, out of 13 applications to the Commission, he knew the promoters of 12 of them. However, the ground on which the plaintiff's case rested was O's former involvement with E-Stat, which owned 70 per cent. of the shares in one of the successful applicants for a radio service contract. O had been promoter of E-Stat and until about six months before the Commission had awarded the contract to the company, he had been its chairman and a director. He resigned at that time because of a serious disagreement with his promoter and effective partner, who was also the chief executive of Radio 2000 Ltd. and at one time engaged to his

---

[62] [1910] 2 I.R. 658. See also, *R. (Harrington)* v. *Clare J.J.* [1918] 2 I.R. 116. For cases on the other side of the line, see *R. (Findlater)* v. *Dublin JJ.* [1904] 2 I.R. 75 and *R. (Tavener)* v. *Tyrone JJ.* [1909] 2 I.R. 763.

[63] [1956] I.R. 320. For a more extreme example than *Hegarty*, see *The State (Horgan)* v. *Exported Livestock Insurance Board* [1943] I.R. 600.

daughter. Nevertheless, the judge decisively rejected the plaintiff's case on the following brief ground:

"It seems to me that in the nature of the functions he was discharging that there was no real likelihood of bias and that no right-minded man would have thought so. . . . Mr. O'Donovan was in a position to bring an independent mind to bear on the problems which the Commission was called on to address."[64]

In assessing this decision, two points bear emphasis. First, as already mentioned, in the context of pecuniary interest, the judge was impressed by O's frank and spontaneous disclosure of his interest. Secondly, and more generally, the background to the Commission—namely the likelihood of some form of connection with the broadcasting world leads presumably to some relaxation of standard, in contrast with that which would be appropriate for (say) a court. A similar point, will be noted below in the section on "Prior involvement and pre-judgment."[65]

An instance of personal reputation or professional pride, as a source of bias, could just possibly arise out of the arrangements for compensation payable in the case of an error in the Land Registry. It is the Registrar himself who must adjudicate upon a claim for compensation arising out of loss to a land-owner caused by error, misstatement, misdescription, etc., of officials of the Registry or even the Registrar himself. Although it is the Minister for Finance who actually pays the compensation, it has been judicially remarked " . . . it seems very desirable that the adjudicator should be chosen from outside the Land Registry."[66]

McMahon J. gave an instance of bias arising from the decision-maker's personal observation in *The State (Fagan)* v. *Governor of Mountjoy Prison*.[67] Here the validity of certain disciplinary punishments imposed by a deputy prison governor were under challenge:

"If . . . the Deputy Governor had witnessed some of the events to which the charges related I could understand an objection to his sitting in judgment since it would be difficult for the prisoner to deal with and to be heard in relation to the impression of the facts which may have been formed by the Deputy Governor as distinct from the evidence given by prison officers at the inquiry."

However, McMahon J. ruled that this claim failed on its facts.

Another obvious category of bias would be party political advantage in the context of a Minister (usually the Minister for Environment) taking decisions in regard to elections. The point was raised obliquely in *Dillon* v. *Minister for*

[64] High Court, May 12, 1988 at p. 18.
[65] See pp. 428–429.
[66] *Application of Sean Leonard*, High Court (D'Arcy, J.) June 30, 1981; Supreme Court, December 15, 1982 (adverse comment on this arrangement); McAllister, *Registration of Title* (Incorporated Council of Law Reporting for Ireland, Dublin, 1973), p. 302. See also, B. Fitzgerald, *Land Registry Practice* (Round Hall Press, Dublin, 1989), p. 248.
[67] High Court, March 6, 1978.

Posts and Telegraphs[68] in which the plaintiff was a Dáil candidate yet the Minister would not allow him to circulate his election brochure free of charge to the voters on the ground that some of the material which it contained did not relate to the election. Henchy J. alluded to the possibility of a conflict of interest in the following brief passage:

" . . . [T]he expression 'matter relating to the election only' should be liberally construed. This is particularly so when, as in this case, the person seeking to block the free postal circulation of the plaintiff's election brochure is a member of the Dáil and whose party leader is seeking re-election to the Dáil in the same constituency as the plaintiff has chosen to contest."

It is necessary, at this point, briefly to recall the category of material interest in order to examine a situation which straddles two categories. There is one type of material interest which will usually be regarded as too remote to be significant. It is most likely to be suggested in the area of domestic tribunals in which the decision-maker and the person affected by the decision are each members of the same profession, trade or industry and, consequently, the alleged wrong doing of the person affected may have some effect on the financial interest or possibly reputation of the decision-maker. Take, for example, the following passage from the judgment of Kingsmill Moore J. in *In re Solicitors Act, 1954*:

"It is true that in a hearing before the Committee a solicitor will not have the protections he would receive in a Court of justice. Complainant, tribunal and the person who conducts the complaint are inextricably interconnected. Moreover the circumstances are such as to make it difficult for the tribunal to be impartial. In many cases the person against whom a complaint is made will be a solicitor with whom members of the tribunal have had professional dealings which may have predisposed them in his favour or against him. All of the members are liable to contribute yearly to a compensation fund established under the Act to relieve or mitigate losses sustained in consequence of dishonesty of solicitors and the amount of contribution may be increased if found necessary (ss. 69, 70) so that there might be a tendency to bear hardly on a solicitor charged with dishonesty. Although the character and standing of the members is such that they can be expected to resist and rise superior to any influences which might affect their impartiality, and it is not suggested that they do not so do, the tribunal is not constituted in a manner best calculated to provide the security against bias and partiality which a Court of justice affords. In the opinion of the Court these considerations, though advanced by the appellants, are not in point. If the Committee are not administering justice, the Constitution imposes no restrictions on the composition of the body."[69]

---

[68] Supreme Court, June 3, 1981. The type of point discussed in the text does not appear to have been canvassed in *The State (Lynch)* v. *Cooney* [1982] I.R. 337.
[69] [1960] I.R. 239, 272. See also, *McCann* v. *The Racing Board* [1983] I.L.R.M. 67, 75 and *Dublin and County Broadcasting Ltd.* at 14–15.

What is odd is that in none of the admittedly few cases in this area was the point raised that the powerful pull of professional brotherhood may make the domestic government unduly favourable to the member of the fraternity who is said to have fallen by the way side. "Dog doesn't eat dog!" The reasonable outsider might well regard this as a far more powerful influence than the possibilities canvassed in the passage just quoted. In addition, the passage refers to the compensation fund but does not consider the argument that a finding of unprofessional conduct would facilitate a claim against the fund and, so, might be thought to bias members of the Disciplinary Committee against such a funding. Two further points may be made here. First, there is certainly no authority to suggest that the law on bias is sufficiently accommodating to balance two sources of bias against each other, and so discount, interests pulling in opposite directions for instance, in the present area, professional brotherhood versus increased contributions to the compensation fund. Such a random approach would fly in the face of the principle in this area. The other and more important point is the doctrine of necessity, described below, which is a major qualifying factor: for the Solicitors Act, 1954 requires the Disciplinary Committee to be composed exclusively of practising solicitors. Accordingly the doctrine would be an answer to any claim of bias. At the same time, the possible source of bias under discussion might indicate that no solicitor from the same part of the country or (if relevant) the same speciality as the accused should be included on the Committee.

There is a presumption that judges and administrators will discharge their function fairly and impartially. Thus, it has been held that a member of a society for the prevention of cruelty to animals may hear a prosecution brought by a member of the society.[70] Persons or bodies not exercising judicial powers are entitled to reach a provisional or tentative conclusion in respect of a dispute, and it will generally suffice if such a tribunal approaches its task with an open mind, and a "will to reach an honest conclusion after hearing what was urged on either side." This statement was made in *McGrath and O'Ruairc* v. *Trustees of Maynooth College*,[71] a case which, it may be thought, goes to the very limits of tolerance for a tribunal's procedure. The facts were that two university lecturers had been removed from office by the trustees of the seminary at which they taught. The plaintiffs had questioned certain aspects of Church teaching. Thus the trustees were bound to have "firm views" on this question, and might very well "have had strong views." Nevertheless, it seems to have been held that even if there were a marked disagreement as to belief between the trustees and the plaintiffs, coupled with an element of pre-judgment, this would not have precluded the trustees from giving a fair hearing. Moreover, as the plaintiffs had elected not to attend the hearing, rather oddly, the Supreme Court refused to listen to any complaints

---

[70] *R.* v. *Deal JJ.* (1881) 45 L.T. 439. See also, *Allison* v. *General Medical Council* [1894] 1 Q.B. 750 and *R.* v. *Muluihilj* [1990] 1 W.L.R. 438.
[71] [1979] I.L.R.M. 166. All the quotations in the text are drawn from Griffin J.'s judgment. See also, *R. (Campbell College)* v. *Department of Education* [1982] N.I.125; *Re Wislang* [1984] N.I. 69; *Murtagh* v. *St Emer's National School* High Court, November 27, 1989, p. 6.

concerning the impartiality of the trustees. The outcome was different in *The State (McGeough)* v. *Louth C.C.*[72] where the applicant complained of a county manager's refusal to give his consent to the sale of a labourer's cottage. This consent was required by the Labourer's Act 1936. It was clear that the county manager disapproved of the sale of such cottages; indeed the refusal of the present application was the twelfth consecutive refusal. The manager's refusal was struck down on the grounds, of *inter alia*, bias. It may be possible to reconcile *McGeough* with *McGrath and O'Ruairc* on the grounds that first, the county manager had gone beyond the stage of holding "firm views" to the point of no longer having an "open mind." Secondly, the plaintiffs in *McGrath and O'Ruairc* had submitted to this contractual jurisdiction, whereas in *McGeough* the county manager had been invested with statutory powers which he was bound to exercise fairly.

(c) Loyalty to the institution. It might be anticipated that the servants of an institution might be so committed to the objectives of that institution, that they might be incapable of holding the balance fairly between these objectives and other interests. This argument which anyway makes the assumption that the objectives of what is after all, a public body are rather one-sided has been rejected:

> "It would be manifestly impossible for [public bodies] to discharge their particular responsibilities in an efficient and sensible manner if every such decision could be successfully challenged by a litigant on the ground that the official who made it was actuated by a conscientious desire to advance the authority's interests rather than a spirit of judicial detachment. . . . [A] decision is not vitiated simply because the official who made it can be said to have a natural bias in favour of advancing the interest of the authority whose interest he is there to serve; but if, in addition, he exercises an administrative discretion 'capriciously, partially or in a manifestly unfair manner' his action would be restrained and corrected by the Courts."[73]

Another unsuccessful submission of this type occurred in *Flynn* v. *Director of Public Prosecutions.*[74] Here the plaintiff-postman had been suspended by An Post for various offences committed at work. He first brought successful proceedings against An Post seeking, *inter alia*, a declaration that his suspension

---

[72] (1973) 107 I.L.T.R. 13. On the question of a closed mind, see *Franklin* v. *Minister for Town and Country Planning* [1948] A.C. 87.
[73] *O'Brien* v. *Bord na Móna* [1983] I.R. 255, 269, quoting O'Higgins C.J. in *Loftus* v. *Att.-Gen.* [1979] I.R. 229. See also, *Collins* v. *County Cork V.E.C.*, High Court, May 26, 1982.
[74] [1986] I.L.R.M. 290. See also, *The State (McEldowney)* v. *Kelleher* [1983]; I.R. 289 *cf.* the comments of Keane J. in *The State (Comer)* v. *Minister of Justice*, High Court, December 19, 1980 where he said that the principle of *nemo iudex* "could not be literally applied" to an adjudication by the prison authorities as to whether a prison officer was guilty of neglect of his duties. Keane J. is probably suggesting here that some allowances must be made for a degree of institutional bias which may tend to creep into this assessment by the authorities. See Hogan, "Judicial Independence and Mandatory Orders" (1983) 5 D.U.L.J.(N.S.) 114. Costello J. was reversed by the Supreme Court, but nothing was said on this point.

was *ultra vires*.[75] Next, he was prosecuted on indictment in respect of the offences. The plaintiff's case, in respect of this prosecution, was grounded on the fact that the D.P.P. had appointed An Post's solicitor, S., to act in the prosecution of the plaintiff. This, the plaintiff argued, violated his right to a fair trial (the argument, in this case, being put on the basis of Article 38.1) in view of S's commitment to his employer and the action which the plaintiff was bringing against it. The Supreme Court rejected this argument on the ground that: "[t]here are no conceivable grounds for supposing that Mr. S, a responsible solicitor against whom no allegation of mala fides is made, would act in some improper manner so as unjustly to prosecute the plaintiff."[76]

(d) Prior involvement and pre-judgment of the issues. This source will often be interwoven with (c) institutional bias, since prior involvement will often arise because some institution is so structured that the same person is concerned at two stages of the decision-making process. It may also overlap with (b) personal attitudes, relationships, beliefs.[77]

As a matter of principle it seems objectionable that a decision-maker exercising quasi-judicial functions should sit with an appellate body to hear an appeal against his own decision. Statutory recognition of this is to be found in section 24 of the Courts of Justice Act 1924 which prohibits the judge who heard a case from sitting as a member of the court of appeal when the case at which he presided is being considered. Contrast this with section 14 of the Charities Act 1961 which provides that any judicial members of the charity Commissioners are not to be disqualified, on that account from hearing charity cases.

Statute aside, there have been a number of cases within this category of the *Nemo iudex* principle. Usually, the involvement arises from the fact that some institution is so structured that the same person is involved at two stages of the same serpentine bureaucratic process. An example is *Heneghan* v. *Western Regional Fisheries Board*[78] in which the dismissal of a fisheries inspector was set aside because the prime mover in the dismissal process had acted as "witness, prosecutor, judge, jury and appeal court."[79] A slightly less extreme

---

[75] On which, see pp. 466–467.
[76] [1986] I.L.R.M. 295. Yet, in later proceedings, arising out of the same episode, *Flynn* v. *An Post* [1987] I.R. 68, McCarthy J., who had sat on the Court in the instant case, remarked: "In my view, [the present] case shows that [the D.P.P.'s retention of An Post's solicitor] though legally proper, may, in practice, be unwise." (p. 84). One of the specific factors inspiring this remark is probably identified in the passage quoted in the text above n. 30, pp. 466–467, *infra*.
[77] An example of this way be the hypothetical case mentioned by McMahon J. in *The State (Fagan)* v. *Governor of Mountjoy Prison*, High Court, March 6, 1978: see p. 424.
[78] [1986] I.L.R.M. 225. Upheld in the Supreme Court: see *O'Neill and Bova Genetics Ltd.* v. *Irish Hereford Breed Society Ltd.*, High Court, October 2, 1990, p. 25 of the judgment.
[79] *Ibid.* 224.

case is *Flanagan* v. *University College, Dublin*,[80] a University disciplinary case. Before the three-member committee of discipline, the Registrar of the University acted as prosecutor and expressed the opinion that the case was a clear one. The accused student and her two representatives were then asked to retire. The committee, the Registrar and his principal assistant remained. When the student and her representatives returned, they were informed that the alleged plagiarism would be sent to an independent expert to assess, a course to which she agreed. The choice of an independent assessor was left to the Registrar as was both the consultation with the relevant Professors who assisted in this choice and the correspondence with the assessor. The applicant was not involved in the selection process. All this was stigmatised as bias by Barron J. in the High Court. Again in *R. (Snaith)* v. *Ulster Polytechnic*,[81] the applicant's dismissal was quashed as the members of the committee who had taken the initial decision to dismiss sat with the Governors of the College when the appeal was heard.

Another example occurred in *Turner* v. *Pilotage Committee of Dublin Pilotage Authority*.[82] Here following a collision, the responsible pilotage committee had set up an inquiry tribunal to establish the facts which led up to the accident. The inquiry tribunal, which consisted of four members of the pilotage committee plus two non-members, reached certain significant findings which were against the applicant. At this tribunal, in the view of Barron J. in the High Court, the rules of constitutional justice were not observed: "the five persons [including the applicant] were interviewed individually. None was made aware of the evidence which the others had given nor obviously was there any opportunity for cross-examination."[83] The tribunal reported to the full pilotage committee and after the committee had met, its secretary wrote to the applicant requesting him to appear before a meeting of the committee, explicity, in order to consider the taking of disciplinary action against him, including the revocation or suspension, of his pilotage licence. Barron J. granted the applicant's request for an order to restrain the resumed hearing. The strongest ground for this request was that, by this stage, the committee would have prejudged the issue. Finding for the applicant Barron J. stated:

"The proposed tribunal could not be independent. Four members have already decided the facts; another four members have already considered evidence which has neither been available to the Applicant nor the subject of cross-examination on his behalf. Having regard to all these factors, I am satisfied that the pilotage committee is not at present entitled to entertain the proceedings."[84]

---

[80] [1988] I.R. 724. On *Flanagan*, see also, pp. 450–451.
[81] [1981] N.I. 28. See also, *Cooper* v. *Wilson* [1937] 2 K.B. 309; *R.* v. *Kent Police Authority, ex p. Godden* [1971] 2 Q.B. 662; *R.* v. *Barnsley M.B.C., ex p. Hook* [1976] 1 W.L.R. 1052.
[82] High Court, June 14, 1988. for further examples of pre-judgment amounting to bias, see *O'Neill* v. *Beaumount* 1990 I.L.R.M. 419; *O'Neill* v. *Irish Hereford*, High Court, October 2, 1990, pp. 22–27.
[83] High Court, June 14, 1988, p. 2 of the judgment.
[84] *Ibid.* p. 10 of the judgment.

Standards of bias

An extremely, and it is suggested unreasonably, stringent standard was set by Kenny J. in *O'Donoghue* v. *Veterinary Council*,[85] which took the form of an appeal by a veterinary surgeon to the High Court from a finding by the Veterinary Council that he had been guilty of unprofessional conduct. The first stage in the procedure for the investigation of alleged misconduct was an assessment by the Standing and Penal Cases Committee of the Council. Next, the council convened a special committee of inquiry to investigate the allegations and it reached the unanimous opinion that the appellant was guilty. Finally, the Council considered the transcript of the evidence before the special committee and decided that the facts proved by the special committee had been proved to their satisfaction. The alleged misconduct consisted of duplicating blood tests for brucellosis and the real victim was the person paying for the tests, namely the Minister for Agriculture. However, the Attorney-General had advised the Minister not to act as complainant himself because some members of the Council were veterinarians employed in his Department. In these circumstances N, a member of the council agreed to allow his name to be used as complainant. He took no part in the case against the petitioner: the solicitors who nominally acted for N were in fact instructed by the registrar of the Council and he had not been a member of the special committee which had investigated the allegation. However, N was one of the 13 members of the Council present when the Council met and confirmed the special committee's decision and fixed the petitioner's punishment. In these circumstances, although the judge characterised N as a "nominal complainant" (the real complainant being the Minister) he held that the *nemo iudex* rule was violated and the Council's decision must be cancelled.

The outcome in *O'Donoghue* could be explained on the basis that the Veterinary Council was trying the appellant for a disciplinary offence and was, thus, following the authority of *Re Solicitors Act* 1954[86] administering justice, or, at least, discharging a quasi-judicial function. Such an analysis would bring *O'Donoghue* within the judicial/administrative functions dichotomy adopted in the *O'Brien-Collins* line of authority, outlined in the following paragraphs, and thus reconcile *O'Donoghue* with the view adopted by the majority of judges. However, considering the tenor of the judgment in *O'Donoghue*—the emphasis laid on the need for justice to be seen to be done—coupled with Kenny J.'s dissent in *Corrigan* (below), it is more realistic to regard *O'Donoghue* as representing a minority view, namely that a very rigorous standard of *nemo iudex* should be adopted.

[85] [1975] I.R. 398. The obvious question which this decision suggests is how a claim of bias against the Veterinary Council can be avoided when a complaint to the Council emanates from the Minster for Agriculture. The answer given by Kenny J, at the end of his judgment (at p. 407) is that:

> . . . those who are in the full-time employment of the State and are working in the Department of Agriculture and Fisheries should not go forward for election to the Council. Similarly, the person nominated by the Minister to the Council should not be an official of his but should be a veterinary surgeon in private practice.

[86] [1960] I.R. 239.

The majority of the judges have taken a view which entails distinguishing between judicial or quasi-judicial and, on the other hand, administrative functions and applying a less strict form of the rule against bias in the case of administrative functions. This point is illustrated by the leading case of *O'Brien* v. *Bord na Móna*.[87] The plaintiff challenged the compulsory acquisition of a large portion of his farm. In the system of compulsory acquisition created by the Turf Development Act 1946, both the drawing up of a provisional list of land to be acquired and the hearing of objections to the inclusion of land on that list is vested in the defendant. It was argued that the fact that the Board had drawn up the provisional list meant that it might be thought of as prejudiced at the second stage of the hearing, in that it would be predisposed to uphold its own earlier decision. Following a review of the provisions of the Act, the Supreme Court concluded that the Board's functions were administrative in nature as they entailed the "balancing of the desirability of the production of turf on the one hand, and the interest of an individual owner of land on the other. . . . " Accordingly, whilst the Board could not act from "an indirect or improper motive or without due fairness of procedure," yet a less stringent standard was required than in the case of persons or bodies exercising judicial functions.

A similar distinction has been drawn by Murphy J. in *Collins* v. *County Cork Vocational Education Committee*.[88] The central point of the case was the plaintiff's claim that the resolution of the defendant body suspending him from his duties as headmaster of a vocational school was void. It was said that the Committee was biased because of the prior involvement by some members of the Committee in the case, and the existence of a conflict of interest. Murphy J. found it necessary to distinguish between: "[t]he application of the rules of natural justice where it is sought to set up an independent tribunal and other cases in which a particular function is by the terms of a statute, order or agreement conferred on *a designated body*." The judge observed that were the position otherwise, then "the supervision and administration of any organisation involving a number of office holders would be quite impossible." While Murphy J. accepted that there was a likelihood of bias in the case of one member of the committee, who had previously made representations about the plaintiff's conduct, and that the other members had been exposed to a relatively one-sided account of events, yet he concluded that:

> "[S]ome real or apparent conflict of interest may arise and must be accepted as inherent in the discharge of the duties of the statutory body. . . . Certainly there would be no justification or authority for transferring that function to another body even if it should have the merit of total independence and a demonstrable freedom from any form of bias."

[87] [1983] I.R. 255. See Coffey, "Procedural Curbs on powers of Compulsory Acquisition" (1984) 6 D.U.L.J.(N.S.) 152.
[88] High Court, May 26, 1982. This decision was affirmed by the Supreme Court on March 18, 1983, but this point was not dealt with. For another authority along the same lines, see *McCann* v. *Racing Board* [1983] I.L.R.M. 67; *O'Neill* v. *Beaumont Hospital* [1990] I.L.R.M. 419, 437.

A point which is explicit in the quotations from *Collins*, and which clearly must also have been a factor in *O'Brien*, is that, given the respective statutory structure of the VEC and Bord na Móna some appearance of possible bias was inevitable. It is reasonable to assume that underlying these two decisions was the doctrine of necessity[89] which states that, in general, the no bias rule will not be permitted to destroy the only tribunal with authority to decide an issue. It is possible to distinguish this line of authority from *Re Grogan's Application*.[90] Here the applicant was a prisoner and his main submission was that disciplinary proceedings against him violated the first rule of natural justice in that the Governor had retired with the Board of Visitors when it considered its decision. Carswell J. found, as a fact, that the Governor did not take any part in the decision-making process and only remained with the Board for a few seconds in order to answer one question put to him by the Board. Nevertheless, Carswell J. quashed the adjudication of the Board:

" . . . a person in the Governor's position should not act in such a way that a reasonable outsider might think that the fairness of the proceedings had been prejudiced. Although the applicant did not raise the matter at the time, it obviously made an impression upon his mind, and in my opinion not unreasonably so."[91]

The outcome in *Grogan* can be distinguished from *Collins* and *O'Brien* on the ground that *Grogan* involved what Murphy J. in the passage quoted from *Collins*, called "an independent tribunal [as contrasted with] *a designated body*." Or, as the same point was put in *Grogan*: "the courts have insisted on a high standard of purity on the issue of possible bias of tribunals hearing such matters as charges of disciplinary offences."[92]

It is less easy to justify a series of cases involving the Land Commission. The procedure before the Commission is in two stages and in each of these cases, Commissioners who initially certified that the lands were suitable for acquisition had sat as a member of the tribunal which, at the later stage, decided whether to confirm the initial decision. (There are four Commissioners, two only of whom are involved at each stage so that, in most circumstances, it is unnecessary for the same Commissioner to be involved at both stages). In the first of these cases, *Corrigan v. Irish Land Commission*[93] a majority of the Supreme Court, with Kenny J. dissenting, ruled that an appellant, who with full knowledge of the facts had made no objection to the membership of an Appeal Tribunal composed of the two lay Commissioners, who had certified that his land was required for the relief of congestion, was estopped by his conduct from raising the issue of bias.

Similar facts arose in *The State (Curran) v. Irish Land Commission*[94] where

---

[89] On this point, see further, pp. 435–437.
[90] [1988] 8 N.I.J.B. 88.
[91] *Ibid*. 92.
[92] *Ibid*. 90.
[93] [1977] I.R. 317.
[94] High Court, June 12, 1978.

a provisional list for the acquisition of lands for resale was signed by two lay Commissioners. The appeal was heard by the two other lay commissioners who had no prior involvement in the case. These two commissioners could not agree on this matter, and they felt obliged to reconstitute the appeal with three Commissioners, one of whom would have to be one of the Commissioners who originally issued the certificate. At this point, the appellant sought an order of prohibition restraining the reconstituted panel from hearing the appeal. Doyle J. adverted to the dissent of Kenny J. in *Corrigan*, and noted that the majority of the Supreme Court in that case did not rule the question of bias. Nevertheless, he felt obliged to defer to earlier rulings—which are not extant in written form—of previous Judicial Commissioners upholding this practice. Similarly, in *Re Creighton's Estate*[95] where the same point was at issue D'Arcy J. ruled that the matter was not *res integra* and reluctantly followed these earlier rulings.

Corrigan may be justified on the narrow ground of waiver (examined below) and, on its particular circumstances, *Curran* may be supported by invoking the doctrine of necessity. However it seems, from the tenor of the judgment in these cases and from the decisions in *Re Creighton's Estate* and the other (unnamed) cases, that they were intended to lay down a broader rule, namely, that the no bias principle is not broken when a Land Commissioner is involved at the two stages, even though there are no extenuating circumstances. This line of case is surprising and is certainly out of step with other authority which has been exemplified.

Formulations of the test for bias

It should be noted that bias does not necessarily mean "a corrupt state of mind,"[96] and this is one of the features which distinguishes bias from mala fides, though admittedly there is a great deal of overlap between the two concepts. Bias may be conscious or unconscious.

Two formulations of the test vie with each other in the common law world. The principal test is whether there is a "real likelihood" of bias. The alternative test is whether there is a reasonable suspicion of bias, and this stricter test is prompted by a desire on the part of its judicial adherents to maintain public confidence in the administration of justice (a consideration usually expressed as: 'justice must not only be done; it must be seen to be done').[97]

From a logical perspective, it is difficult to see the difference between the two tests since the reasonable person would only suspect bias where there was a real likelihood of such occurring. In fact, both tests really involve questions of degree, and the difference between them is slight. The reasonable suspicion test is largely concerned with outward appearances whereas the alternative test focuses on the court's own view of the realities of the situation. In

---

[95] High Court, March 5, 1982.
[96] *R. (de Vesci)* v. *Queen's Co. JJ.* [1908] 2 I.R. 285. For mala fides, see pp. 511–512.
[97] See *R.* v. *Sussex JJ., ex p. McCarthy* [1924] 1 K.B. 256.

most cases, however, it is probably correct to say that the courts have employed the reasonable suspicion test where they wanted to set a higher standard of impartiality. One such case may have been *The State (Hegarty)* v. *Winters*[98]—the facts of which have already been recounted. In the High Court, Davitt P. upheld the arbitrator's award, saying that mere suspicion of bias was not enough. However, the award was quashed by the Supreme Court because the actions of the arbitrator in the words of Maguire C.J. might have given rise to *the suspicion* that justice was not being done. Another example is provided by Kenny J.'s judgment in *O'Donoghue*[99] and (dissenting) in *Corrigan* v. *Irish Land Commission*[1] where he employed the test of reasonable suspicion, but, in contrast, one of the majority judges, Griffin J., spoke of the need to establish a real likelihood of bias. It is likely that the outcome of a case would depend less on which formula is used and more on such factors as the type of tribunal or administrative agency involved; the nature of the decision and the source of bias. Indeed, many of the most recent Irish cases have been decided without reference to either test.[2] However, in *Dublin & County Broadcasting Ltd.*, the two tests were effectively conflated. Murphy J. stated:

> "Certainly it does seem to me the question of bias must be determined on the basis of what a right-minded person would think of the likelihood, of the real likelihood of prejudice, and not on the basis of a suspicion which might dwell in the mind of a person who is ill-informed and did not seek to direct his mind properly to the facts. . . . I entirely accept it would be irrelevant and immaterial if in a case such as the present it was established as a matter of fact that bias was non-operative, or that the particular person accused of the bias was out-voted or whatever. If it is shown that there are on the facts circumstances which would lead a right-minded person to conclude that there was a real likelihood of bias, that this would be sufficient to invalidate the proceedings of the Tribunal."[3]

---

[98] [1956] I.R. 320. For the facts of this case, see p. 423. See also, *Killiney & Ballybrack Residents Assoc.* v. *Minister for Local Government (No. 1)* (1978) 112 I.L.T.R. 9 and *The State (Cole)* v. *Labour Court* (1984) 2 J.I.S.L.L. 128.

[99] [1975] I.R. 405–407, though there is some reference to the other test at 405. For other examples of the reasonable man test leading to a finding of bias, see *Doyle* v. *Croke* and *O'Neill* v. *Beaumont Hospital* [1990] I.L.R.M. 419, 438.

[1] [1977] I.R. 317.

[2] See, *e.g. The State (Curran)* v. *Irish Land Commission*, High Court, June 12, 1978; *Collins* v. *County Cork V.E.C.*, High Court, May 26, 1982; *O'Brien* v. *Bord na Móna* [1983] I.R. 255 (S.C.). In *The State (Divito)* v. *Arklow U.D.C.* [1986] I.L.R.M. 123, Henchy J. cited both tests without differentiating between them. The pre-independence cases had all plumped solidly for the "real likelihood" test: *R. (Ellis)* v. *Dublin JJ.* [1894] 2 I.R. 527; *R. (Findlater)* v. *Tyrone JJ.* [1909] 2 I.R. 763; *R. (Kingston)* v. *Cork JJ.* [1910] 2 I.R. 658; *R. (de Vesci)* v. *Queen's Co. JJ.* [1908] 2 I.R. 285; *R. (Donoghue)* v. *Cork JJ.* [1910] 2 I.R. 272. There is some support for the suspicion test in *R. (Giant's Causeway Tram Co.)* v. *Antrim JJ.* [1895] 2 I.R. 603. See Sweeney, "Lord O'Brien's Doctrine of Bias" (1972) 7 Ir.Jur.(N.S.) 17.

[3] High Court, May 12, 1989 at p. 13 of the judgment. Compare Murphy J.'s judgment in *O'Neill* v. *Irish Hereford*, High Court, October 2, 1990, pp. 19–22.

One of the difficulties raised by this passage is the question of how well-informed the "reasonable man" must be taken to be. On the one hand, according to the passage, he must not be "ill informed." But, on the other hand, it seems that there are certain "matters of fact (such as that the bias was non-operative) which he must be taken not to know." Where is the line to be drawn? In England, there is authority for the rather odd proposition that the reasonable man should be taken to know all the matters which, whether known to the public generally or not, were in evidence on the hearing of the application for review,[4] but this important practical issue does not appear to have been addressed in this jurisdiction. What is striking, however, is that on the facts, in *Dublin & County Broadcasting Ltd.*, Murphy J. was influenced by the circumstance that the person allegedly affected by bias had sought to transfer his shares, several months before the relevant time. This private transaction was accepted as crucial, with no attempt to consider whether the "reasonable man" would have known of it.

It may be said, by way of summary, that in the area of bias, most Irish judges have proved uncharacteristically charitable towards the difficulties of public authorities.

Rule of necessity

Throughout the common law world, the no bias rule gives way to necessity in that the disqualification of the adjudicator will not be permitted to destroy the only tribunal with power to decide. Consider, for example, *O'Byrne* v. *Minister for Finance*[5] in which the High Court and Supreme Court were obliged to pass judgment on the constitutionality of legislation rendering them (and their judicial brethren) liable to income tax on their salaries. In the High Court, Dixon J. had proceeded with the case explicity because there was no other tribunal to which, under the law, recourse could be had on a matter of this kind. Another example occurred in *Attorney-General (Humphreys)* v.

---

[4] *R.* v. *West Yorkshire Coroner ex p. Smith, The Times*, November 6, 1982; *R.* v. *Liverpool City Justices ex p. Topping* [1983] All E.R. 490, 491. See Craig *Administrative Law* (2nd ed.), pp. 236–237.
[5] [1959] I.R. 1 where the doctrine was "applied if not expressly invoked" (*O'Neill* v. *Irish Hereford*, High Court, October 2, 1990). In *Collins* v. *County Cork V.E.C.*, High Court, May 26, 1982. Murphy J. said that it was the "clear constitutional duty" of the Supreme Court to decide the *O'-Byrne* case, "notwithstanding the interest which the members of the Court had in the outcome." See also, Kelly, *The Irish Constitution*, (Dublin, 1984), p. 226 for an explanation of the composition of the Supreme Court in *The State (Killian)* v. *Minister for Justice* [1954] I.R. 207. *O'Byrne* was followed in *Irish Hereford* (at p. 26) and, in less acute circumstances, in *Flynn* v. *Allen* High Court, May 2, 1988. Noting that the defendants in the action were Benchers of Kings Inn, Lynch J. stated (at p. 3):
"I am, of course, as is every other High Court Judge and Judge of the Supreme Court, a Bencher of the King's Inns and I am conscious of the fact that in one sense I myself could be said to be a defendant in these matters.
Be that as it may, the matter has to come to be decided by some Judge of the High Court and it has come before me and I must not shirk my duty of dealing with it.
I have been referred to the decisions of the High Court and the Supreme Court in the case of *O'Byrne* v. *Minister for Finance and the Attorney General*, [1959] I.R. 1 [and of course the difficulty that arises here arose there. The necessity for proceeding notwithstanding that unfortunate difficulty was emphasised and I accept that that is so and that I should and must deal with the matter."

Governors of Erasmus Smith's Schools,[6] a relator action involving a charitable trust administered by the defendants. Cherry L.J. commenced his judgment in the Irish Court of Appeal with the following apologia:

"I am in a rather difficult position in adjudicating upon this case, in as much as I was Attorney-General when the writ was fiated. I would have preferred not to have been a member of the Court which had to decide this appeal, but as all the Judges of the Court except Lord Justice Holmes and myself are Governors of the Schools, a Court could not otherwise have been formed."[7]

Clearly the necessity exemption will be strictly applied. For instance in *The State (Curran) v. Irish Land Commission*[7a] (already described) in which the two lay Commissioners disagreed as to whether the provisional list should be confirmed so that it was necessary to re-list the case before a tribunal of three Commissioners. Given that there were only four Commissioners, this would have necessitated enlisting the services of one of the Commissioners who had signed the original acquisition certificate. The resulting decision was held valid. However Doyle J. opined, *obiter*, that the argument of necessity could not have excused the respondents in other circumstances since the Land Act 1950 allowed for the appointment of a temporary replacement where a lay commissioner is temporarily disabled from fulfilling his function on account of illness, absence "or other sufficient reason." Similarly, in *R. (Snaith) v. Ulster Polytechnic*[8] the dismissal procedure laid down in the University statutes required, first, that the initial decision should be taken by a sub-committee of 11 Governors and secondly, that on appeal, this decision must be upheld by a two-thirds majority of the Governors of whom there were 42 in all. This arrangement plainly breached the "no bias" rule. Given the numbers of Governors involved at each level, it would have been very difficult if not impossible to work this system without some overlap of personnel. However, Hutton J. ruled that the necessity doctrine did not apply because the difficulty arose "from the scheme for termination of appointments which the Governors themselves had provided [in the statutes]" rather than from some externally-imposed instrument. Yet a further example is afforded by *O'Neill v. Beaumont Hospital*.[9] In this case, as a result of a finding of bias, the Supreme Court granted an injunction restraining the Chairman and two other members of the Hospital Board from taking part in any meeting which would consider whether to retain the plaintiff as a consultant.[9a] The Court declined, however, to grant an injunction in the terms sought by the plaintiff, which would have restrained any meeting of the Board. The first reason for this was that the

---

[6] [1910] 1 I.R. 325. See also, *Dimes v. Grand Junction Canal Co.* (1852) 3 H.L.C. 759; *Tolputt (N.) & Co. Ltd. v. Mole* [1911] 1 K.B. 836.
[7] [1910] I.R. 325, 332.
[7a] High Court, June 12, 1978. See also, pp. 432–433.
[8] [1981] N.I. 28.
[9] [1990] I.L.R.M. 419.
[9a] Followed on this point in *O'Neill v. Irish Hereford*, High Court, October 2, 1990, pp. 28–30.

other members of the Board had not committed themselves to a fixed position in advance of the meeting in the same way as had the Chairman and the two members who were enjoined. The other reason was the doctrine of necessity, whose application in the instant case was explained by Finlay C.J. as follows:

"It is not a dominant doctrine, it could never defeat a real fear and a real reasonable fear [sic] of bias or injustice but it is a consideration in relation to the question of the entire Board being prohibited, for if that were to be done there can be no other machinery by which something which is of great importance both to the Board of the Hospital and to the plaintiff and I might add, to the public who will attend the Hospital, namely the continuance or noncontinuance of the plaintiff's services in the hospital, can be determined in accordance with the terms of the probationary agreement."[10]

The rule of necessity is probably compatible with constitutional justice. For, as has been seen, constitutional justice is grounded in Article 40.3 the rights contained in which are not absolute but qualified by such phrases as "far as practicable" and "as best it may." And, as Murphy J. observed in *Collins* v. *County Cork Vocational Education Committee*, the courts cannot conjure up a new tribunal to take the place of a tribunal which has been held unconstitutional. Thus in some cases chaos would result if the *nemo iudex* rule were applied at its full width. On the other hand even, in England, the rule of necessity may not operate to enable an adjudicator to sit where actual bias can be shown and this qualification presumably applies in Ireland.[11]

Waiver

The right to object to a breach of the *nemo iudex* principle may be waived by a party with full knowledge of the facts which entitle him to raise a complaint.[12] The rule has been stated to be as follows:

"[W]here a decision is challenged on the grounds of bias in the tribunal which gave it, [the] Court will not interfere where it appears that the fact or suspicion of bias was present to the mind of the challenging party at the hearing before the tribunal, and the point as to bias or suspected bias was not made by or on his behalf at the hearing by the tribunal."[13]

Exceptions to the rule exist where the complainant is so taken by surprise that he forgets to make an objection or where the court deems it proper to interfere because of the scandalous state of affairs involved.[14]

Bias is a particularly heinous defect (more so than failure to give a hearing) which may lead to a general erosion of confidence in public or judicial admin-

[10] *Ibid.* 440.
[11] See *de Smith, op. cit.* p. 276.
[12] *Corrigan* v. *Irish Land Commission* [1977] I.R. 317 distinguished in *O'Neill* v. *Irish Hereford*, at pp. 31–32 on the ground that the plaintiff did not have knowledge of all the relevant circumstances; *The State (Cole)* v. *Labour Court* (1984) 3 J.I.S.L.L. 128. See also, pp. 470–471.
[13] *Per* Sir James Campbell C.J. in *R. (Harrington)* v. *Clare JJ.* [1918] 2 I.R. 116. See also, *Corrigan's* case, *supra*, and *The State (Grahame)* v. *Racing Board*, High Court, November 22, 1983.
[14] *R. (Giants Causeway Tram Co.)* v. *Antrim JJ.* [1895] 2 I.R. 603; *R. (Poe)* v. *Close JJ.* (1906) 40 I.L.T.R. 121; *R. (Harrington)* v. *Clare JJ.* [1918] 2 I.R. 116.

istration. In addition, bias or the possibility of bias, is a matter peculiarly within the knowledge of the deciding authority, giving rise in other contexts, to a duty to declare an interest.[15] Moreover, it is a particularly embarrassing matter to have to raise in front of the person whom it is alleged is partial. Such factors underlay the dissenting judgment of Kenny J. in *Corrigan* v. *Irish Land Commission*. In his view, the no bias rule is founded on public policy—the desire to maintain respect for the administration of justice—and thus it is not competent for the parties to waive this rule. Nevertheless the prevailing consensus seems to be in favour, for practical reasons, of a wide concept of waiver in the context of bias. As Henchy J. remarked in *Corrigan* v. *Irish Land Commission*:

> "It would obviously be inconsistent with the due administration of justice if a litigant were to be allowed to conceal a complaint of that nature in the hope that the tribunal will decide in his favour, while reserving to himself the right, if the tribunal gives an adverse decision, to raise the complaint of disqualification."[16]

In the case law considered so far, waiver occurs because of some action (or inaction) of the plaintiff *at the time* of the dispute. A distinct category of waiver exists where in the case of, for example, a trade union or other so-called voluntary association, the plaintiff is regarded as having consented to the defect of which he wishes to complain, simply by virtue of having joined the union or association, in the first place. This may be a rather far-reaching and unrealistic notion, but it was nevertheless adopted by Lardner J. in *I.D.A.T.U.* v. *Carroll*[17] (the facts of which are described below) in the situation, it is true, not of a trade union and a member, but in the different situation of the I.C.T.U. and a member union. In *Carroll*, Lardner J. stated in an *ex tempore* judgment[18]:

> "In the present case, the court is concerned with Congress, an association of trade unions and its members who are trade unions who have negotiated and freely accepted its rules. There is nothing in the evidence before me to suggest that there was any inequality between the plaintiff union and Congress at the time this constitution was adopted. Having regard to the fact that the clause complained of is part of the Constitution of Congress, which was freely accepted by the plaintiff, I am not satisfied by [plaintiff's] counsel's submission that this clause is contrary to natural justice."

Withdrawal of suspect members

One obvious way of avoiding trouble, which may be available where the decision has yet to be taken and where the deciding body has a number of members, is suggested by *I.D.A.T.U.* v. *Carroll*. Here the General Secretary

---

[15] *R. (Malone)* v. *Tyrone JJ.* 3 N.I.J.R. 77; *The State (Cole)* v. *Labour Court* (1984) 3 J.I.S.L.L. 128 (*semble*).
[16] [1977] I.R. p. 326.
[17] [1988] I.L.R.M. 713.
[18] *Ibid.* 719.

of the plaintiff union had made a number of derogatory references to trade unions. Accordingly the plaintiff had been informed that unless it disassociated itself from its General Secretary's remarks it would be required to show cause before the executive council of the Irish Congress of Trade Unions as to why it should not be suspended from Congress. The plaintiff's response was to seek an injunction to restrain the defendant from passing or considering any sanction upon the plaintiff. One of the plaintiff's submissions was grounded on bias in that, in Lardner J.'s summary of the argument:

"The Irish Transport and General Workers Union and the Federated Workers Union of Ireland who were each members of I.C.T.U. cater to some extent for the same category of workers as are catered for by the plaintiff union. A conflict of interests was suggested here. It was suggested that these unions might secure an advantage in this situation and if any of their representatives sat on the executive council, that would be in breach of the rules of natural justice."[19]

One of the reasons why Lardner J. rejected this argument was that:

"I note that the executive council consists of a president, a vice-president, a treasurer and 24 members elected by the annual delegate conference. Seven is a quorum. When this matter was raised, counsel on behalf of the defendants undertook that no member of the executive council who had any direct interest in the matter of the kind mentioned by Mr. Donnelly, the plaintiff's president, would sit or take part in the deliberations of the executive council dealing with this matter."[20]

Again in *O'Neill* mentioned earlier (at pp. 435–437), the outcome was the grant of an injunction but one which prevented only the chairman and two other members of the Board from taking part in a meeting to consider the plaintiff's fate.

3. Audi Alteram Partem

Introduction

It is trite law that tribunals and administrative agencies are not required to follow the same strict rules of evidence and procedure as a court of law.[21] Thus, for instance, Henchy J. observed in *Kiely* v. *Minister for Social Welfare (No. 2)*:

"Tribunals exercising quasi-judicial functions are frequently allowed to act informally to receive unsworn evidence, to act on hearsay, to depart from the rules of evidence, to ignore court room procedures, and the like."[22]

[19] *Ibid*. 718.
[20] *Ibid*. 718–719.
[21] *McElroy* v. *Mortished*, High Court, June 17, 1949; *Fitzpatrick* v. *Wymes* [1976] I.R. 301; *The State (Boyle)* v. *General Medical Services (Payment) Board* [1981] I.L.R.M. 14; *Re McNally's Application* [1985] N.I. 17.
[22] [1977] I.R. 276, 281.

439

As might be expected from the inexact, pragmatic nature of constitutional justice, the same standard does not apply in all areas for "domestic and administrative tribunals take many forms and determine many different kinds of issues and no hard and fast rules can be laid down. . . . ."[23] At one end of the scale, Costello J. stated:

> "The courts must not interfere officiously in the affairs of private associations such as trade unions and must only do so in clear cases to prevent or remedy some manifest injustice. And when considering what procedures can properly be regarded as fair it must consider procedures which would be appropriate to the type of organisation or association which is to adopt them and the nature and scope of the decision to which they relate."[24]

And, at the other end of the scale, in *Flanagan* v. *University College, Dublin*[25] in which a disciplinary committee was punishing a student for plagiarism, the High Court set a particularly stringent standard:

> "The present case is one in which the effect of an adverse decision would have far-reaching consequences for the applicant. Clearly, the charge of plagiarism is a charge of cheating and as such the most serious academic breach of discipline possible. It is also criminal in its nature. In my view, the procedures must approach those of a court hearing. . . . "[26]

The *audi alteram partem* rule embraces two types of obligation (although as there is a substantial overlap and as nothing turns on the distinction, it is not observed rigorously in the following account). First, the person to be affected by the decision must be alerted to it and given details of it. Secondly, he must be allowed appropriate facilities to make the best possible case in reply.

Let us take some examples of what may broadly be thought of as the first type of obligation. The first example, *Ryan* v. *V.I.P. Co-operative Society Ltd.*,[27] arose out of the suspension of a taxi-driver by his Co-operative for allegedly abusing some passengers. These passengers had not been present at the hearing. In holding the suspension to be invalid, Lardner J. first made a general remark and then went on to identify certain procedural deficiencies. He had:

> "full sympathy with the objectives of the society which were to maintain a high standard of quality of service to their customers. But despite the fact that they were a small co-operative, they had to observe certain minimal

---

[23] *Russell* v. *Duke of Norfolk* [1949] 1 All E.R. 109, 118, quoted with approval by Henchy J. in *Kiely* v. *Minister for Social Welfare* [1977] I.R. 267.
[24] *Doyle* v. *Croke*, High Court, May 6, 1988. See, to like effect: *The State (Keegan)* v. *The Stardust Victims Compensation Tribunal* [1986] I.R. 642; *McGowan* v. *Wren* [1988] I.L.R.M. 744; *Ryan* v. *VIP Taxi Co-operatives* High Court, January 20, 1989, reported *Irish Times*, Law Report, April 10, 1989.
[25] [1988] I.R. 724. See, to like effect, *McDonough* v. *Minister for Defence* [1991] I.L.R.M. 115.
[26] [1988] I.R. 731.
[27] See n. 24, *supra*.

obligations in relation to the conduct of disciplinary hearings . . . the applicant was entitled to be furnished with the names and addresses of the complainants. He was entitled to specific details of the complaints. The society should have sent someone to interview the complainants and to have secured a detailed testimony of the allegations made against the applicant. The applicant was also entitled to be told all relevant matters which might have assisted him properly to prepare his defence. Finally, the applicant was entitled to be given details of any other reasons which may have been taken into account by the committee in reaching their decision."

Again, in *The State (Gleeson)* v. *Minister for Defence*[28] it was held that the summary dismissal of a member of the defence forces was invalid. Henchy J. said that:

"The requirements of natural justice imposed an inescapable duty on the army authorities, before discharging the prosecutor from the army for the misconduct relied on, to give him due notice of the intention to discharge him of the statutory reason for the proposed discharge, and of the essential facts and findings alleged to constitute that reason; and to give him a reasonable opportunity of presenting his response to that notice. All that was dispensed with in this case."[29]

Certain cases have set a rather high standard of explicitness and formality in regard to the warning which the public authority must give to the person affected. An example is *Gallagher* v. *Corrigan*[30] which arose out of the purported disciplining of four prison officers—the applicants in the case—following on the escape of a prisoner from St. Patrick's Institution. Blayney J. posed the following question:

"Was [the *audi alteram partem* rule] complied with? In my opinion it was not. None of the applicants was aware until informed by the Deputy Governor on the 19th November 1986 that he had been found to have been negligent, that a charge of negligence was being brought against him. It was submitted by Mr. McGuinness that the reports of Chief Officer O'Sullivan, dated the 1st November 1986, which were furnished to the applicants, endorsed by the Deputy Governor 'for explanation please' constituted charges of negligence. In my opinion they did not. They were not addressed to the applicants. They were addressed to the Deputy Governor. The only part that was addressed to the applicants was the endorsement of the Deputy Governor 'for explanation please.' The purpose was clearly to

---

[28] [1976] I.R. 281. *Gleeson* was followed by Hamilton J. in *Hogan* v. *Minister for Justice*, [1976–1977] I.L.R.M. 184 and *The State (Furey)* v. *Minister for Defence* [1988] I.L.R.M. 89. *Gleeson*, was however, distinguished in *The State (Duffy)* v. *Minister for Defence* [1979] I.L.R.M. 65 and *The State (Donnelly)* v. *Minister for Defence*, High Court, October 8, 1979.

[29] *Ibid.* 296. This passage was quoted with approval by Hamilton J. in *Hogan* v. *Minister for Justice.* [1976–1977] I.L.R.M. 184.

[30] High Court, February 1, 1988.

obtain from each of the applicants, and from the other six officers who were also asked for an explanation, information which when pieced together would enable the Deputy Governor to come to a conclusion as to how the escape occurred. It was part of the investigation he was carrying out and which was still going on as was indicated by his report of the 3rd November 1986 to the Department of Justice, in which he said he would forward a further report when his investigations were complete. The applicants may have had reason to believe that if they did not give a satisfactory explanation of how they had performed their duties on the day of the escape, they might be charged with negligence, but *they had no reason to believe that such a charge had been preferred against them.*"[31] (Author's italics).

The last sentence takes on added point when one bears in mind the content of the reports which each applicant had received. One of these reports (that of the first applicant) may be quoted to illustrate their suggestively damning character:

"1. Anthony Gallagher
I am to report that on Friday the 31st October 1986 officer A. Gallagher was on duty in the visiting box. At approx. 4.15 p.m. on the termination of inmate Kenneth Noonan's visit this inmate was allowed to leave the visiting box and escape via the main gate."[32]

In face of this, it might be assumed, by a lay-person of average intelligence who had some explanation of his conduct to offer that it would be prudent to offer it. However, Blayney J. rejected such a common sensical approach and required something more akin to a formal charge.

The paragraph of the judgment dealing with the need for a charge is succeeded by the following:

"Even if they had reason to construe the reports in this way, the Deputy Governor was still at fault in failing at any time to inform them of the nature of the evidence against them, and in failing to give them an opportunity to speak and adduce evidence on their behalf. All that happened after they had supplied the explanations sought in the reports was that they received some further queries. At no time were they informed of the nature of the evidence against them or given an opportunity of making their defence."[33]

This passage illustrates the fact that the person affected must be positively offered an opportunity to make his defence: he is not expected to take the initiative by seeking out the decision-maker and proffering his side of the story.

---

[31] *Ibid.* pp. 13–14 of the judgment.
[32] *Ibid.* pp. 2–3 of the judgment.
[33] *Ibid.* p. 14 of the judgment.

At the same time, it must be commented there is only a very fine line between this line of law and the doctrine of waiver.[34]

The person affected must also be told (or, perhaps, be aware *aliunde*) of the significance of the decision for him. No difficulty should usually arise here (unless an unreasonably high standard of precise knowledge is required). However this was the point on which the applicant-athlete succeeded in *Quirke* v. *Bord Luthchleas na hÉireann*.[35] After his event, in spite of being asked to do so by an athletics official, the applicant had failed to return to the drug testing room to give the required sample, but instead had left the sports ground. A few days later he was asked to give a written explanation for this failure and offered an explantion which, according to Barr J., was "patently untenable and . . . unacceptable."[36] However, there were two crucial points in the applicant's favour. The first was that he should have been made aware when being asked to undergo the drug test that he would be liable to suspension if he failed to take the test. The other alternative was that, at the later stage, the applicant did not know that a formal complaint was being made against him to the national committee of the respondent athletics board and that it was to this that he was being required to furnish an explanation: Barr J. stated:

"[The respondent Bord's officials] request to the applicant to furnish a written explanation of his failure to submit a urine sample of dope-testing does not discharge the onus on B.L.E. [the respondent's] in that regard. If Mr. Quirke had been told that a formal complaint was being made to the national committee of B.L.E. and that he was required to furnish an explanation in writing by way of defence to the charge, he might also have referred to the fact that the [International Amateur Athletics Federation] notice had not been given to him as required by the regulations nor had he been informed *aliunde* that the dope-testing was being carried out under the I.A.A.F. rules and that he was liable to suspension if he failed to submit to the test."[37]

It is perhaps, unfortunate that nothing further was said about the possibility that the applicant might have "been informed *aliunde* . . . ." The significance of this alternative is that there must have been at least a possibility that the applicant was aware of certain facts which may have been common knowledge within the top-class athletic fraternity, namely the content of the I.A.A.F. notice and the fact that the applicant would be liable to suspension if he failed to submit to the test. It is uncertain from the passage whether it was necessary for the applicant to have been informed by the respondent or whether it sufficed if he knew from any source. If the second alternative be correct, then it is unfortunate that the factual question of the applicant's state of knowledge was not explored at the trial, if necessary, by oral evidence.

---

[34] On waiver, see pp. 470–471.
[35] [1988] I.R. 83.
[36] *Ibid.* 87.
[37] *Ibid.* 88.

R.T.C. LIBRARY, LETTERKENNY

However, another line of authorities has taken a less formal and, it is suggested, more realistic approach. One example is *Doupe* v. *Limerick Corporation*[38] in which the plaintiff had been refused a licence to operate an abbatoir by the defendant local authority. Rejecting one of the plaintiff's arguments, Costello J. stated:

"But there is no doubt that he was told the substance of the case against his application and it seems to me that he had ample opportunity before any final decision was reached to approach the council with an expert view, if one could be obtained, which challenged the conclusion that in the interests of public health weekly killings should be limited as the Chief Medical Officer required. But he did not avail of this opportunity, and he maintained his refusal to accept the recommended limitation. There was, of course, no formal 'hearing' of his application—but none was needed. He was, albeit informally, given notice of the advice the council had obtained and he was afforded an adequate opportunity to answer the objection raised."[39]

Again, in *Ní Bheoláin* v. *City of Dublin V.E.C.*[40] Carroll J. stated:

"If it can fairly be said that the person suspended knew or ought to have known that the act or conduct which led to the suspension could, in all the circumstances, have that result (either because of prior warnings or because the act per se was blatantly provocative) then in my opinion there is no breach of constitutional guarantees, as, for example, in the *Collins case* where the plaintiff blatantly refused to carry out his duty.

In my opinion the plaintiff was being ingenuous when she said in her letter of the December 17, 1976, (say) to discipline that she failed to see what was required of her. It must have been or should have been obvious to her that her conduct in refusing to communicate verbally with [her Head of Department] and her general attitude to him was at the root of the problem."[41]

Logically enough, too, the Supreme Court (*per* McCarthy J.) has stated that:

"[i]f . . . there are valid reasons for [the Minister's] decision based upon matters of which he has notified the applicants and given them ample opportunity to make representations, the fact that there are other reasons

---

[38] [1981] I.L.R.M. 456. See also, *The State (Curtin)* v. *Minister for Health* [1953] I.R. 93, 99; *The State (Murphy)* v. *Kielt* [1984] I.R. 458 and *Gallagher* v. *The Revenue Commissioners* High Court, January 11, 1991 where Blayney J. said at p. 8

"I am satisfied that when the plaintiff was suspended he must have known that it was because of the matters in respect of which he had been interviewed. He could not have come to any other conclusion. In the circumstances, I consider that the fundamentals of justice did not require that the defendants should inform him expressly of their reasons for suspending him, and accordingly in my opionion his suspension initially was valid."

[39] *Ibid.* 464.
[40] High Court, January 28, 1983.
[41] *Ibid.* pp. 36–37 of the judgment.

of which he has not given them notice, does not, in my view, invalidate his decision."[42]

A public authority's duty to give notice is not confined to details of the case against him. In *Flanagan* v. *University College, Dublin*, for example, Barron J. having made the point that the applicant was entitled to legal representation, continued: " . . . she should have been informed, in sufficient time to enable her to prepare her defence, of such right and of any other rights given to her by the rules governing the procedure of the disciplinary tribunal."[43] Although this was only a brief unconsidered part of *Flanagan*, it could, if developed, become a significant part of the law.

The public authority's duty to give notice to the person who may be affected by its decisions extends to all relevant information. This was once more, illustrated in *The State (Williams)* v. *Army Pensions Board*,[44] which arose out of a claim by the applicant, who was an army widow, for a pension. The substantive issue for decision by the Board was whether her husband's death had been caused by service with a United Nations force. His medical records, which were the most important evidence in the case were in the custody of the Army medical authorities. They were made available to, and considered by, the Board, but the applicant was not allowed to see and comment upon them. The Supreme Court held that the Board's procedure was defective in that the applicant was not allowed access to her husband's medical records. Henchy J. said:

> "Mrs. Williams was unfairly and unjustifiably prevented from rebutting, if that was possible, the conclusion reached by the Board. There may be cases where, for reasons such as state security or other considerations of public policy, the Board may be privileged from disclosing . . . the evidence before them. But this is not one of them. Counsel for the Board and the Minister has frankly and fairly conceded that the only reason for non-disclosure is the claim of the Board to be entitled to adhere to their settled practice."[45]

Two incidental comments may be made on this passage. First, the two rules of constitutional justice often march together since the failure to allow one side to put its case properly looks like bias.[46] This presumably is the reason for the reference to "one-sidedness" in the opening sentence of the passage. Secondly, the last sentence in the passage quoted illustrates once more that the staff of certain tribunals and administrative agencies have not taken on board recent developments in the field of judicial review of administrative

---

[42] *International Fishing Vessels Ltd.* v. *Minister for Marine (No. 2)* Supreme Court, February 22, 1991 p. 9.

[43] [1988] I.R. 724, 731. See also, *Cooney* v. *An Post*, High Court, April 6, 1990, p. 28.

[44] [1983] I.R. 308. See also, *Maunsell* v. *Minister for Education* [1940] I.R. 213; *The State (Hussey)* v. *Irish Land Commission* [1983] I.L.R.M. 407; *The State (Boyd)* v. *An Bord Pleanála*, High Court, February 21, 1983; *Nolan* v. *Irish Land Commission* [1981] I.R. 23.

[45] [1983] I.R. 313.

[46] See *per* O'Higgins C.J. in *Nolan* v. *Irish Land Commission* [1981] I.R. 23, 36: "If one party comes to the hearing with the scales of justice tilted against them because of a procedural defect then the requirements of justice are not satisfied."

actions.[47] Between them and the courts, there is almost what might be called a culture clash.[48] The individual affected is entitled to be given information not only as to facts, but also as to any policy or principles in the light of which his case is to be decided so as to have "the opportunity of conforming with or contesting such a principle or policy."[49]

We turn now to deal with more specific problems in the operation of the *audi alteram partem* rule, most of which relate to the second category identified above, namely that the person should have the necessary facilities to make the best possible case on his behalf.

Information obtained outside the hearing

One form of denial of *audi alteram partem* occurs when although some type of hearing (whether oral or written) has been allowed, the decision-maker relies upon information or argument, which has been obtained outside that hearing and not disclosed to the party adversely affected by it. Four illustrations of this fairly common situation will be given before the merits are briefly examined. The first illustration occurred in *Killiney and Ballybrack* v. *Minister for Local Government (No. 1)*[50] which arose from a planning appeal in which one of the factual issues was whether the sewerage disposal facilities in the area of the proposed development were already overloaded. There was a direct conflict of evidence at the oral inquiry as to whether raw sewerage was to be found on the foreshore near the development. After the inquiry had been concluded, the inspector examined the foreshore on his own and included a record of his findings in his report to the Minister who was, at the time of the case, responsible for deciding planning appeals. In the High Court, Finlay P. invalidated the Minister's decision because it was based on evidence which had not been disclosed to the party concerned, who thus had no opportunity to reply to it.

The second case is *The State (Polymark Ltd.)* v. *I.T.G.W.U.*[51] in which the facts relevant to the present point were that an employer had made a submission before the Labour Court that, in the circumstances of the particular case, the Court had no jurisdiction to entertain an appeal from the Equality Officer. In response to this submission, the Labour Court adjourned the case in order to seek legal advice from the registrar and, having received it, con-

---

[47] *Cf. Flanagan* v. *University College Dublin* [1988] I.R. 724, 732, *per* Barron J.
"The failure to apply proper procedures arises, as the Registrar accepted, because this committee has always sat in his experience to deal with cases where guilt, if not admitted, cannot reasonably be denied. This is aggravated by the absence of any published college regulations under which the committee purported to act."

[48] An attempt to mitigate this clash, in the British context, has been made by the publication of a pamphlet, designed for the lay-civil servant and entitled "The Judge Over your Shoulder. Judicial Review of Administrative Decisions": see [1987] *Public Law* 485.

[49] *The State (McGeough)* v. *Louth C.C.* (1973) 107 I.L.T.R. 13, 28, *per* O'Daly J. See also, *Mahon* v. *Air New Zealand* [1984] A.C. 808.

[50] (1978) 112 I.L.T.R. 9. The facts in *The State (Hegarty)* v. *Winters* [1956] I.R. 320 were similar to those of the *Killiney* case, save that in *Hegarty* the successful party had accompanied the decision-maker to the inspection, and, accordingly, The Supreme Court treated the case as an instance of the no-bias rule. On *Hegarty*, see p. 423.

[51] [1987] I.L.R.M. 357.

tinued with the case. In the High Court, the applicant employer complained of the fact that his counsel before the Labour Court had not been made aware of the advice given or afforded an opportunity of commenting upon it. Blayney J. decided the case on the basis that even if this were correct he would, since no useful purpose would be served,[52] exercise his discretion against granting a remedy. However for the future, it is significant that it appears from the following passage, that the applicant's contention was correct in principle. Blayney J. stated:

> "It might be of assistance for the future, however, if I were to indicate what procedure the Labour Court could safely adopt if similar circumstances arise again. They should first inform the parties of their intention to ask the registrar for legal advice; then, having obtained the advice, they should, at a resumed hearing, inform the parties of the nature of the advice they had obtained and give the parties an opportunity of making submissions in regard to it, and finally, having heard the submissions, the members of the court should, on their own, without further reference to the registrar, arrive at their own conclusion on the issue."[53]

Another authority on the same issue is *Kiely* v. *Minister for Social Welfare (No. 2)*[54] which arose after the appellant's husband had suffered an accident at work which caused severe burns and led eventually to depression. A few months later he died and the appellant, K, claimed a death benefit under the Social Welfare (Occupational Injuries) Act 1966. Her claim was heard by the deciding officer and, on appeal, the appeals officer, in the Department of Social Welfare. Before the appeals officers, the principal issue—on which the medical expert giving evidence for K disagreed with the Minister for Social Welfare's medical adviser—was whether it was possible for a heart attack to have been caused by depression and, thus, to be connected with her husband's employment. This question was settled against K by the appeals officer. Her arguments, on appeal to the High and Supreme Courts, all related to the procedure which he had followed. The first of the three grounds on which K succeeded before the Supreme Court involved a defect of the type under discussion here. During the interval between the hearing of the appeal and the notification of the decision nearly two months later, the medical assessor wrote a letter to the appeals officer giving new evidence as to why depression could not cause a heart attack. This evidence included the bulletin of an international medical symposium and the practice of actuaries in assessing "life mortality in relation to anxiety states." In explaining why this evidence had been obtained in breach of the rules of constitutional justice, Henchy J. stated briefly that the assessor's function is "to act as a medical dictionary and not as a medical report."

A fourth example of the same broad situation occurred in the case of

---

[52] See pp. 603–605.
[53] *Ibid*. 363.
[54] [1977] I.R. 287. *Cf. Horan* v. *An Post*, High Court, January 18, 1991, pp. 9–11.

Geraghty v. *Minister for Local Government (No. 2)*[55] details of which have already been given in a different context. The relevant point here is that some of the information on which the decision regarding the plaintiff's planning appeal had been taken was material (reports on other appeals from the same area) which the plaintiff had not seen and had not had the opportunity to comment upon. This was one of the grounds on which the plaintiff succeeded in having the decision quashed.

These cases illustrate a difficulty which is likely to loom large in the future. It arises from a contrast of cultures: first, a large part of the *raison d'être* of specialised tribunals is that the tribunal, unlike a court, has the ability and opportunity to accumulate a wealth of specialised knowledge, information and expertise. This indeed is said to be one of its advantages over a court. To some extent, therefore a tribunal's decision is the result not only of the evidence adduced by the parties at a particular hearing: it is also the product of the tribunal's own expertise, which has been brought to bear upon the evidence. However, this attitude collides with a rule which is central to all judicial or quasi-judicial adjudication, namely that a decision must be made in accordance only with evidence introduced at the hearing, tested by the opposing sides and forming part of the record. And thus, the categories of material of which judicial or official notice may be taken is severely limited. Outside Ireland, various tests have been proposed for resolving these two conflicting tensions.[56] First, a distinction has been made according to whether a tribunal is using its expertise as a substitute for evidence or only for the purpose of evaluating the evidence that has already been presented. This test, which of course involves a difficult question of degree, would seem to accord with the distinction drawn, in *Kiely (No. 2)* between a medical dictionary and a medical report. However, it might be argued that the court misapplied its own test in *Kiely* in that a medical report is personal to a specific patient, whereas the issue in that case (whether depression is capable of causing a heart attack) was a general question which could have been appropriately dealt with in a medical dictionary. Another test, in use elsewhere, distinguishes between the general accumulated experience of the decision-maker, which need not be shown to an applicant, and material obtained from an identifiable source. Comparing the Irish cases with this test, it seems clear that *Killiney and Ballybrack (No. 1)* and *Polymark* are in line with them, but it may be argued that the material relied on by the Minister and his department in *Geraghty (No. 2)* or by the appeals officer in *Kiely (No. 2)* might have been classified as "accumulated experience." In short, here, as elsewhere, the Irish law enforces a particularly, and possibly unnecessarily, stringent standard. Here, too, it may be that the courts are sub-consciously imposing upon the procedures of a tribunal the same mores which a court must observe in its own procedure.

---

[55] [1976] I.R. 153. See p. 402.
[56] See de Smith's, *Judicial Review of Administrative Action* (London, 1980), pp. 203–207; Flick, *Natural Justice* (Melbourne, 1979), Chap. 4.

Right to an oral hearing, right to summon witness and right to cross-examine

Plainly whilst these issues may need to be considered independently, there is often a substantial connection between them. In any case, with each of them, as with other aspects of the *audi alteram partem* rule it may be misleading to speak of a"right" since in such an amorphous area, entitlement to the advantage sought will depend on all the circumstances of the case.[57] On the question of when they apply, de Smith states:

"In the absence of clear statutory guidance on the matter, one who is entitled to the protection of the *audi alteram partem* rule is now prima facie entitled to put his case orally; but in a number of contexts the courts have held natural justice to have been satisfied by an opportunity to make written representations to the deciding body, and there are still many situations where a person will be able to present his case adequately in this way."[58]

The case of *Re Haughey*,[59] which arose out of the Dáil Committee of Public Accounts investigation into the expenditure of the grant in aid for Northern Ireland relief, is instructive in the context of a right to call witnesses or to cross-examine opposing witnesses. During the course of the Committee's investigations, a senior Garda Officer made a number of serious allegations against Mr. Haughey. These accusations lay at the heart of the Committee's investigation, so much so, the Court considered, that he might be regarded as being in an analogous position to a party in a court case, at any rate, so far as his good name was concerned. Emphasising this factor, Ó'Dálaigh C.J., writing for the Supreme Court majority, held that the Committee ought to have granted Mr. Haughey the following procedural safeguards:

"(a) that he should be furnished with a copy of the evidence which reflected on his good name; (b) that he should be allowed to cross-examine, by counsel his accuser or accusers; (c) that he should be allowed to give rebutting evidence; and (d) that he should be permitted to address, again by counsel, the Committee in his own defence."[59a]

[57] See, *e.g.* the comments of Keane J. in *Williams* v. *Army Pensions Board* [1981] I.L.R.M. 379, 382: "Whether [there must be an oral hearing] in any particular case must depend on the circumstances of that case. . . . The application in the present case was capable of being dealt with fairly . . . in the manner actually adopted by [the Board]." Webster J. made similar comments in relation to prisoner's right to call witness and cross-examine, etc., before a board of prison visitors in *R.* v. *Home Secretary, ex p. Tarrant* [1985] Q.B. 251.

[58] de Smith, *op. cit.* p. 201. As far as appeals to An Bord Pleanála are concerned, it is clear that the Board has a discretion as to whether to allow an oral hearing save in the case of appeals specified by regulation: Local Government (Planning and Development) Act 1983, s.15. No such regulations have yet been made. See also, *Kiely* v. *Minister for Social Welfare (No. 2)* [1977] I.R. 267, 278.

[59] [1971] I.R. 217. Failure to permit cross-examination was held to be a breach of *audi alteram partem* in *Kiely* v. *Minister for Social Welfare* [1977] I.R. 287 where this right was granted to the other side. As Keane J. observed in *The State (Boyle)* v. *General Medical Services (Payment) Board* [1981] I.L.R.M. 14, *Kiely* turns on the lack of even-handedness displayed by the appeals officer, and it would be wrong to deduce any comprehensive right to cross-examine from the facts of this case.

[59a] *Ibid.* 263. See also, *Turner* v. *Pilotage Committee of Dublin Pilotage Authority*, High Court, June 14, 1988, pp. 2 and 5.

A case on the other side of what it is suggested is the same line from that drawn in *Haughey* was *The State (Boyle)* v. *General Medical Services (Payment) Board*[60] which stemmed from an investigation which had established that the applicant doctor's claims for remuneration, under the "choice of doctor" scheme were excessive. Under the agreement on which the scheme was based, the applicant could, as he did, complain to an appeal committee. His appeal was rejected following an oral hearing. The committee based its decision on, *inter alia*, statistical data concerning the average number of home visits in the area in which the applicant practiced. The applicant requested that the expert who had compiled the data should be made available for cross-examination before the committee. This request was refused. Keane J. held that this refusal did not constitute a violation of constitutional justice because when the applicant had received a copy of the data he had not raised any specific issue as to its reliability, which required oral evidence in order to be resolved.

Flanagan v. *University College, Dublin*[61] is notable in a number of respects, among them, Barron J's assumption that the applicant was entitled to the rights under discussion here. The applicant in *Flanagan* was a student who had studied for a Diploma in Applied Social Science. She took honours in her written papers but the lecturer supervising her work suspected that she had copied parts of the essay, which was the other requirement of the Diploma. The matter was referred to the Registrar, as a breach of discipline. The Registrar wrote to the applicant asking her to appear before a committee of discipline but giving her no indication of the nature of the breach. The applicant made several attempts to find out from the Registrar what was alleged against her. Eventually some three weeks after the responsible lecturer had read her essay, she was told, over the telephone, about the allegation. The committee of discipline met six days later. Of the procedure which the committe should have followed, Barron J. stated[62]:

> "In my view, the procedures must approach those of a court hearing. The applicant should have received in writing details of offence. . . . At the hearing itself, she should have been able to hear the evidence against her, to challenge that evidence on cross-examination, and to present her own evidence.
>
> Unfortunately, there was a total failure on the part of the college to allow the applicant these rights. There was no attempt to make the applicant aware of the exact nature of the charge against her. It was not until her second telephone call to Miss Donnelly that she was made aware that it related to her choice of case history in her examination essay. Nor was she given an adequate opportunity to prepare her case or to present it. The refusal to permit her representation of her own choosing was a virtual

[60] [1981] I.L.R.M. 14. But *cf. R.* v. *Hull Prison Visitors, ex p. St. Germain (No. 2)* [1979] 1 W.L.R. 1401.
[61] [1988] I.R. 724.
[62] *Ibid.* 731.

denial of the former and the absence of anyone to give evidence against her at the hearing before the committee was a denial of one aspect of the latter. It gave her no opportunity either to discover how the case against her was being put or to test its strength by cross-examination."

As a result of this hearing, the committee decided to refer the matter of the applicant's guilt to an independent expert. This was held to be improper for a number of reasons. In the first place, whilst the committee secured the applicant's consent to this course of action, they did so on the basis that the independent assessor would be a university lecturer in human behaviour. However, before the High Court, the applicant claimed—and Barron J. appears to have accepted the claim—that the assessor did not fall within this category. Secondly, when the Registrar's officer purported to send on a copy of the assessor's report, a significant paragraph was omitted from it. Thirdly, the applicant's request for a postponement of the reconvened meeting of the disciplinary committee was refused.

Representation

Where there is an oral hearing, its practical value may depend on whether the individual is represented by an experienced, though not necessarily legally qualified, advocate. As against this, it will often happen that the advocate is a lawyer and it is often said that the involvement of lawyers has, in the long run, the effect of protracting and complicating the proceedings, to no advantage.[63] However, in other jurisdictions the tide appears to be running in favour of a right to be represented.[64] In Ireland, the position is still in doubt. In *McGrath and O'Ruairc* v. *Trustees of Maynooth College*,[65] which involved the dismissal of two University lecturers, the Supreme Court said that there was a right to be represented by a lawyer though not as the plaintiffs preferred, by their trade union representatives. But on the other hand, in two recent disciplinary cases,[66] a claim for representation was refused. This claim, did however, succeed in *Flanagan* v. *University College, Dublin* where, under the relevant procedural regulations, a student could only be represented by the Dean of Women's Studies and/or the President of the Student's Union, neither of whom the applicant knew. In *Flanagan*, with its grave consequences for the applicant and its rather nuanced evidence, the High Court regarded the offer of representation by these personages as inadequate. Barron J. rejected as "obviously fallacious"[67] the argument that since the applicant, who was a social worker, was educated, articulate and experienced in writing case

---

[63] *Report of the Committee on Civil Legal Aid and Advice* (1978, Prl. 2574), p. 50.
[64] *R.* v. *Home Secretary, ex p. Tarrant* [1985] Q.B. 251, and see de Smith, *op. cit.* p. 213 and Jackson, *Natural Justice* (London, 1979), pp. 73–79.
[65] [1979] I.L.R.M. 166
[66] *The State (Gallagher)* v. *Governor of Portlaoise Prison*, High Court, May 18, 1977 (prison discipline); *The State (Smullen)* v. *Duffy* [1980] I.L.R.M. 46 (school expulsion).
[67] [1988] I.R. 732. *Flanagan* was followed in *Gallagher* v. *The Revenue Commissioners* High Court, January 11, 1991 in which it was held by Blayney J. that the disciplinary charges against the applicant were so serious as to warrant an entitlement to legal representation (at pp. 13–14)

reports and putting forward their contents to case conferences, she would be well equipped to make her own case. Barron J. also rejected the idea that plagiarism is essentially a simple matter: the three experts who had examined Miss Flanagan's thesis had each made different judgments on it. Of the two recent disciplinary cases alluded to, earlier in this paragraph, Barron J. distinguished the first, *Smullen*—and it is suggested he could equally well have distinguished *Gallagher*—on the ground that: "the procedures adopted were fair and that what the school did was reasonable having regard to its magisterial responsibility and its obligation to enforce and maintain discipline. No element of such responsibility or duty exists in the present case."[68] On the subject of representation, it may be best to say only that the deciding authority should always genuinely consider whether the circumstances are such that it is necessary in the interests of justice.[69]

For in Ireland, there has been no equivalent of the test enunciated in Britain (in *R.* v. *Secretary of State for the Home Department, ex p. Tarrant*[70]) as to the factors to be taken into account when a board of prison visitors is exercising its discretion to permit legal representation to a prisoner charged before it with offences against prison discipline. In *Tarrant*, this list, which might, subject to appropriate modifications, be applied in other contexts, included the following items:

"1. The seriousness of the charge and of the potential penalty . . . 2. Whether any points of law are likely to arise . . . 3. The capacity of a particular prisoner to present his own case . . . 4. Procedural difficulties . . . 5. The need for reasonable speed in making their adjudication . . . 6. The need for fairness as between prisoners and as between prisoners and prison officers."[71]

Deciding without hearing

It frequently happens that the decision-making and information-gathering functions are divorced from each other, as for instance where the body in which a decision has been vested, either instructs its officials, or constitutes a sub-committee, to conduct interviews, examine records, etc. The question arises as to how far this process can go before it is held that the individuals affected have not been allowed a fair hearing because the decision maker has not itself heard the case. In England, it has been said that " . . . the general principle is that the greater the judicial element involved the more likely it is that the decision-maker must also hear."[72] One context in which this situation has arisen, in Ireland, is the decision as to a planning appeal or the confirmation of a compulsory purchase order, which is vested in Bord Pleanála or the Minister for the Environment, respectively. The decision often requires a

---

[68] *Ibid.*
[69] See *Tarrant* and *Enderby Town F.C.* v. *Football Association* [1971] Ch. 598.
[70] [1985] Q.B. 25 approved by the House of Lords in *Hone* v. *Maze Prison Board of Visitors* [1988] A.C. 379
[71] [1985] Q.B. 285.
[72] P. P. Craig, *Administrative Law.* (2nd ed.), p. 223

hearing at the site, which is chaired by an inspector and is not attended by the Board or Minister. Nevertheless, it has been agreed, in the *Murphy/Geraghty* line of cases,[73] that this procedure is valid, provided that the inspector gives the Minister "if not a verbatim account . . . at least a fair and accurate account of what transpired and one which gives accurately to the Minister the evidence and the submissions of each party . . ."[74]

In *Hession* v. *Irish Land Commission*,[75] the respondent landowner's objection to the inclusion of his farmland on the ILC's provisional list was heard before two lay Commissioners. However, the case was adjourned for two years. At the adjourned hearing, where one of the Commissioners had been replaced by another Commissioner, the respondent's objection was rejected. The Supreme Court held that this result must have been based at least in part upon evidence given at the initial hearing, and accordingly the decision was void. The case is unsatisfactory in that the court did not find whether there was any record (or if so, what quality of record) of the initial hearing before the reconstituted lay Commissioners or whether there was any other factor to distinguish the case from the *Murphy/Geraghty* line of authority, which was not even mentioned.

However, *Hession* is in line with the principle stated by Gibson L.J. in *Re McNally's Application*:

"[W]here all or part of the evidence has been given, the participation thereafter in the adjudication or determination by a person, who, though otherwise qualified to sit, did not hear that evidence, will invalidate the decision."[76]

In *McNally*, a Prison Board had sat on an earlier occasion to determine whether a prisoner who faced serious disciplinary charges should be entitled to legal aid, though in order to decide that point it was found necessary to hear evidence from certain prison officers as to the extent of their injuries. At a later stage a differently composed panel heard the substantive case, and the applicant was adjudged guilty of these offences. However, on the facts, Gibson L.J. found that these procedures did not amount to a breach of natural justice. The reason was that the later proceedings were not simply a continuance of the earlier partly heard case, but were rather "a complete hearing of every aspect of the substantive issue."

The final case bearing on this area is *O'Brien* v. *Bord na Móna*[77] which involved the compulsory acquisition of the plaintiff farmer's bogland. The

---

[73] *Murphy* v. *Dublin Corporation* [1972] I.R. 215. See, to like effect, *Murphy* v. *Dublin Corporation (No. 2)* [1976] I.R. 143; *Geraghty* v. *Minister for Local Government* [1976] I.R. 153. There were some differences between the judges, but this was on another point, namely, the operation of the *delegatus* principle. These cases are discussed at pp. 401–404.

[74] *Murphy* v. *Dublin Corporation* [1972] I.R. 239.

[75] [1978] I.R. 322.

[76] [1985] N.I. 17, 22. See also, *R. (Dobbyn)* v. *Belfast JJ.* [1917] 2 I.R. 297; *R. (Department of Agriculture)* v. *Londonderry JJ.* [1917] 2 I.R. 283.

[77] [1983] I.R. 255.

plaintiff had submitted to one of the Board's officials that the Board need only take a leasehold interest, with the land reverting to him after all the turf had been removed. Because of the Board's long-established policy of acquiring the fee simple interest, the official did not even bother to transmit this information to the Board. In the situation under discussion, there is often a close interaction between the *audi alteram partem* rule and the *delegatus non potest delegare* principle.[78] Thus in *O'Brien*, the Supreme Court dealt first with the argument that there had been no breach of the *audi alteram* rule because the decision had been delegated to the official who had received the plaintiff's submission. It held that even had there been a delegation (though there was, on the facts, no sign of one) the decision would still have been invalid because determinations regarding compulsory acquisition are not capable of being delegated to officials. The court then turned to the alternative issue and held that the *audi alteram* rule had been broken by the official's failure to relay the plaintiff's submission to the board of Bord na Móna (in which the decision was vested).[79]

O'Brien was distinguished by Carroll J. in the High Court in *ESB* v. *Gormley*[80] which involved the placing of an electric line upon the defendant's land. The defendant relied, *inter alia*, upon the fact that her objections had not been relayed to the ESB Board. Carroll J. rejected this argument and distinguished *O'Brien* primarily because the line had already been finally decided by the Board before the defendant acquired the land; and it was permissible for the Board to delegate to its officials negotiations with landowners and decisions regarding the relatively minor issue of the position of intermediate pylons.

Confirmation of a decision

It is a significant principle that an absence of constitutional justice at the intial decision-making stage is not cured by the provision of an appellate stage at which the rules are observed. This principle is discussed in Part 5 below. Here it is proposed to discuss a significant restriction on this principle. For it has recently come to be accepted, that where a "provisional" decision is taken without observing the *audi alteram* rule, this defect can be remedied if the person affected has the chance to put his side of the case before the decision is made permanent. In short, the process can sometimes be characterised as a single decision, (as opposed to a discrete decision, followed by an appeal) for the purposes of the constitutional justice principles. The effect of this characterisation would be avoid the principle explained at the start of the paragraph.

---

[78] On which, see pp. 396–400.
[79] The court rejected the argument that since the plaintiff's argument would have been so unlikely to sway the Board, this breach did not matter (see further pp. 499–500). The court's decision, at this stage, could also have been put on the ground that the Board's decision [against the plaintiff] would have been founded on an inflexible rule of policy: see pp. 545–548.
[80] [1985] I.R. 129. Carroll J. was reversed, on other grounds, by the Supreme Court: see [1985] I.R. 144.

The first case to be examined is *The State (Duffy)* v. *Minister for Defence*[81] which arose out of the discharge of a petty officer from the Navy. The appellant, who was one of the few people in the history of the Navy to fail to get his engine-room artificer certificate, had been warned by his commanding officer that he was going to be discharged, to which he replied that he was "going to do something about this."[82] His commanding officer told him that he was free to do so and ensured that the decision was not implemented for seven days so that the applicant could make whatever representations he wished. In fact, none were made. Reversing D'Arcy J. in the High Court, Henchy J. for the Supreme Court drew a distinction between "the decision to proceed to discharge" and "the actual discharge" seven days later and held that the fact that the applicant could have made representations during this period of delay, constituted adequate compliance with the *audi alteram partem* rule. Henchy J. thus implicitly rejected the possibility that the commanding officer might, at the final stage, be biased by loyalty to his own previous decision.[83]

Gammell v. *Dublin County Council*[84] involved an order prohibiting the erection of temporary dwellings which had been made under the Local Government (Sanitary Services) Act 1948, in respect of the plaintiff's caravan site, by the defendant council. The plaintiff was not aware of the inspection of her site by the local authority and health board experts on whose certificate the local authority relied in making the order. Following the procedure under the 1948 Act, a notice that the order had been made and that any person aggrieved had 14 days in which to apply to the Minister for the Environment, asking for the order to be annulled, was published in a newspaper circulating locally. On such an application the order could then be annulled or confirmed by the Minister. Carroll J. held that this opportunity to make representations to the Minister sufficed for compliance with the *audi alteram partem* rule (notwithstanding that the plaintiff had not seen the newspaper notice, a point to which we return in the next section).

Although Carroll J. did adopt a lengthy passage from the judgment in *Duffy* as part of her reasoning, there was an important point at which *Gammell*

---

[81] [1979] I.L.R.M. 65. (distinguished in *The State (Murphy)* v. *Kielt* [1984] I.R. 465, 478; *The State (Murphy)* v. *Governor of St. Patrick's Institution* [1985] I.R. 141,147). For a similar case to *Duffy* see *The State (Donnelly)* v. *Minister for Defence*, High Court, October 8, 1979. In *The State (McCann)* v. *The Racing Board* [1983] I.L.R.M. 67 which involved the revocation of a course betting permit by the Board, Barron J. distinguished between the Board's "decid[ing] whether matters alleged justified . . . revocation" and "the ultimate decision of the Board . . . before the . . . revocation takes effect." The words quoted confirm the distinction drawn in *Duffy* and in the later case of *Gammell* v. *Dublin County Council* [1983] I.L.R.M. 413 discussed *infra*. Other cases in which the situation under discussion might appear to arise, but was not mentioned by the court, are *The State (Boyle)* v. *General Medical Services (Payment) Board* [1981] I.L.R.M. 14 and *The State (Williams)* v. *Army Pensions Board* [1983] I.R. 308.

[82] *Cf.* "I will do such things, What they are yet I know not, but they shall be the terrors of the earth"—*King Lear*, Act II.

[83] It is submitted in regard to both *Duffy* and *Donnelly* that it may be unrealistic to assume that, in a strict military hierarchy, a superior officer who has taken up the definite position that a subordinate ought to be dismissed will resile from that position because of arguments advanced by the subordinate.

[84] [1983] I.L.R.M. 413.

differed from *Duffy*, namely, that in *Gammell* the confirmation was to be given by a body other than the body which had taken the initial decision. This made the confirmation look more like an appeal and required the High Court to confront a question not mentioned in *Duffy*, *viz.* how to distinguish the structure of the administrative process in *Gammell* from the *Ingle/Moran*[85] line of authority. Both *Ingle* and *Moran* had held that a failure to allow a person affected by a decision the right to make his case at the time of the initial decision would not be cured by the provision of an appellate stage at which this right was allowed. Carroll J. drew an important distinction in the following passage:

> "However, in this case we are not dealing with an order effective when made and an appeal therefrom to an appellate body. Under section 31 of the [1948] Act the order has no effect until the person aggrieved has been given an opportunity of stating reasons why it should not come into effect. There is no "appeal" to the Minister from an operative order. There is machinery set up under the section whereby an aggrieved party can make representations why the order should not come into operation. If successful, the order is annulled by the Minister and it never becomes operative. This is very different to the *Ingle* case and the *Moran* case where the revocation of the licence became operative immediately and of necessity there had to be a time lag between the revocation and the determination of an appeal in the District Court. Is there any real distinction between machinery which provides for an order to be made with delayed effect giving an opportunity to interested parties to make representations for annulment which, if successful, will result in the order never becoming operative and machinery which gives an opportunity to interested parties to make representations why an order should not be made, which, if successful, will result in the order never being made. . . .
> The fact that the representations are to be made to the Minister and are so the body making the order does not seem to me to be invidious in any respect. In fact, even though the County Council would not appear to be inhibited from acting, it seems preferable that representation should be made to the Minister who can avoid the criticism which might be levelled at the County Council that they are judges in their own cause."[86]

It is submitted that this is a practicable and useful distinction,[87] which can also

---

[85] *Ingle* v. *O'Brien* (1975) 109 I.L.T.R. 4; *Moran* v. *Att.-Gen.* [1976] I.R. 400. On which, see pp 500–501.
[86] [1983] I.L.R.M. 413, 417–418.
[87] For which some support may be found in *O'Brien* v. *Bord na Móna* [1983] I.R. 268 (See pp. 430–431) in which the plaintiff's case was that the body which had taken a provisional decision as regards a compulsory order would be biased, by the provisional decision, when it came to the stage of confirmation, and, consequently, that there should be an "appeal against the making of a compulsory acquisition order, or . . . confirmation by an external authority . . . ." ([1983] I.R. 281). It seems to have been assumed in both the High Court (which upheld the plaintiff's claims) and the Supreme Court (which, admittedly, rejected the plaintiff's case) that either confirmation or an appeal to an external authority would cure the defect arising from any bias in the original

be applied in other areas. Take, for instance, applications for planning per-mission[88]: considered in isolation, the procedure before a local planning auth-ority might appear to violate the *audi alteram partem* rule in that (confining the discussion to the applicant for planning permission and not examining the position of objectors)[89] the applicant is not told of the authority's provisional thinking on his application, much less allowed any opportunity to make rep-resentations in regard to it. On the other hand, there is ample constitutional justice at the rehearing on appeal to An Bord Pleanála. The crucial question thus is whether the initial application stage is to be examined in isolation or whether it is to be considered together with the proceedings before An Bord Pleanála. In other words, is the structure of the decision-making system anal-ogous to that involved in *Gammell* or does the provision of an appeal fail to cure the initial defect? It is submitted that the two systems are similar and thus that the planning application system does not violate the *audi alteram partem* rule. The key factor is that (as with the prohibition order) a local plan-ning authority decision granting permission does not come into effect until the appeal has been heard or, if no appeal is taken, until the period for appealing has elapsed.[90] Thus to adapt the test laid down in the passage from *Gammell* already quoted: " . . . [the planning authority's decision to grant planning permission] has no effect until the person aggrieved has been given an oppor-tunity of stating reasons why it should not come into effect. There is no appeal to the [Bord] from an *operative* order. . . . "

Duty to give reasons

It used to be the law that in the absence of a statutory requirement, consti-tutional justice does not require that an administrative body should give reasons for its final[91] decision.[92] And that seems to remain the position in England[93] though it must be said that in England the common law may not be so important because there the Tribunals and Inquiries Act 1971, section 12(1) (*cf.* United States (Federal Administrative Procedure Act, section 8(b))

decision. There is some support here for the idea that an appeal may be treated as being equivalent to a confirmation for the purposes of constitutional justice. The same distinction was also drawn, in the context of Art. 34.1, in *Re Solicitors Act 1954 and D. a solicitor* (1961) 95 I.L.T.R. 60.

[88] However the specific planning situation should be considered in the light of the *Frenchchurch Properties* case: see p 484, n. 9.

[89] On which see *The State (Stanford)* v. *Dun Laoghaire Corporation*, Supreme Court, February 20, 1981. However it might be made a point of distinction that in the planning situation, it is the private individual rather that the public body (as in *Gammell*) which is denied permission to do something.

[90] Local Government (Planning and Development) Act 1963, s.26(9), as amended by s.20 of the Local Government (Planning and Development) Act 1983.

[91] As contrasted with the duty to give reasons for a provisional decision which may arise as part of the narrow *audi alteram partem* rule: see pp. 439–445.

[92] *Kiely* v. *Minister for Social Welfare (No. 2)* [1977] I.R. 267, 274; *The State (Cole)* v. *Labour Court* (1984) 3 *J.S.L.L.* 128 (though here there appears to be some qualification: a party could "request the Court to give its decision in such a way that an appeal on a point of law could be taken.")

[93] See, for example, Wade, *op. cit.* 547. For monographs on the law of England and other com-mon law jurisdictions, see G. A. Flick, "Administraive Adjudications and the duty to give reasons" [1978] *Public Law* 16; M. Akehurst, "Statement of Reasons for Judicial and Adminis-trative Reasons" (1970) 33 M.L.R. 154; Woolf, *Protection of the Public—A New Challenge* (The Hamlyn Lectures for 1989), pp. 92–97.

imposes a duty to give reasons upon a large number of tribunals. In Ireland, as often, change has been left to the judges.[94] The fact that the following recent authorities[95] are not only unanimous but that they come from widely differing and representative sections of the administrative scene (public service employment; the Criminal Injuries Compensation Tribunal; trade licensing; trade mark appeals; and a planning application determined by local authority councillors) makes their authority that much more impressive. Equally, it is noteworthy that they are agreed upon a significant limitation upon the right to reasons, namely that there must first be a challenge to the decision-maker as to his reasons.

The first case in this line of authority is *The State (Daly)* v. *Minister for Agriculture*[96] which dealt with the dismissal of a probationer civil servant under section 7 of the Civil Service Regulation Act 1956, as amended by section 3 of the Civil Service Regulation (Amendment) Act 1958. This provision states that where a civil servant is serving a probationary period, if the "appropriate authority is satisfied that he has failed to fulfil the conditions of probation. . . . " the authority shall terminate the service of such civil servant. Here the applicant had been dismissed with no indication of the ground for his dismissal; nor had any been given during the hearing before the High Court. The State's strongest authority was *Broomfield* v. *Minister for Justice*[97] which concerned the dismissal of a civil servant, under the same statutory authority. In *Broomfield*, Costello J. had stated that in contrast with an office-holder, a probationer's service may be ended:

"for the very obvious reason that his employing authority may consider the probationer unsuited for permanent employment and without any specific charge of any acts of misconduct the employing authority keeps to himself the right not to appoint the probationer on a full-time basis."[98]

However, in *Daly*, Barron J. held that *Broomfield* had been implicitly overruled by Henchy J.'s observation in *State (Lynch)* v. *Cooney*[99] that:

" . . . [any] opinion formed by the Minister [under the statutory authority] must be one which is bona fide held and factually sustainable and not unreasonable. The court must ensure that the material upon which the Minister acted is capable of supporting his decision. Since the Minister has failed to disclose the material upon which he acted or the reasons for his action there is no matter from which the court can determine whether or not such material was capable of supporting his decision. Since the Minister

---

[94] Though see (Devlin) *Report on Public Services Organisation Review*, Pub. 792, App. 1, p. 456 ("Each notice of decision . . . should give the reason or reasons for the decision.")
[95] See also, *Garda Representative Association* v. *Ireland* [1989] I.R. 193; *Pok Sun Shun* v. *Ireland* [1986] I.L.R.M. 593, 599 (confining itself to cases where rights of appeal exist under statute); *Breen* v. *Minister for Defence* Supreme Court, July 20, 1990, p. 10 of the judgment.
[96] [1987] I.R. 165.
[97] High Court, April 10, 1981.
[98] *Ibid.* p. 5 of the judgment.
[99] [1982] I.R. 337, 361.

continues to refuse to supply this material, it must be presumed that there was no such material.

In the result therefore the Minister was entitled to dispense with the services of the prosecutor without warning him that he proposed to act in that manner. However, once his decision was challenged, he was obliged to disclose to the prosecutor the material upon which he had acted and to give his reasons for so doing."

In *Daly*, Barron J. found for the applicant on the basis that since the Minister continued to withhold the material, it must be presumed that there was no material.

The second case, *The State (Creedon)* v. *The Criminal Injuries Compensation Tribunal*[1] is in a sense a narrower authority than *Daly* in that, first, the Supreme Court placed some reliance on the fact that the Tribunal's functions are "quasi-judicial" (so far as such categories are useful[2]) and, secondly, the reasons point may be regarded as an auxiliary to the main issue.[3]

However, Finlay C.J.'s statement was quite trenchant. He considered that:

"for a tribunal of this nature, even though it is not of statutory origin and is set up as an administrative decision by the Government, to reach a conclusion rejecting in full the claim of an applicant before it and not give any reason for that rejection, is not an acceptable and proper form of procedure. Merely, as was done in this case, to reject the application and when that rejection was challenged subsequently to maintain a silence as to the reason for it, does not appear to me to be consistent with the proper administration of functions which are of a quasi-judicial nature."[4]

In *International Fishing Ltd.* v. *Minister for the Marine*[5] what was at stake was the Minister's refusal, following oral and written communication between the Minister and the applicant, to renew the applicant's sea-fishing boat licence. The applicant had breached a condition which had been attached to its previous licence and which provided that at least 75 per cent. of its crew should be either Irish citizens or nationals of an EC state. In response to a solicitor's letter asking for more detailed reasons, the Minister had refused "as a matter of policy" to give any reasons.

Counsel for the Minister argued that while the Minister was obliged to act fairly, this did not include a duty to give reasons: however, Blayney J. followed *Creedon* (although characterising the Minister's function as "not quasi-judicial") and *Daly* and held that the Minister was under a duty to give reasons.

---

[1] [1989] I.R. 51. *Creedon* was cited with approval in *O'Keeffe* v. *An Bord Pleanála* High Court, July 31, 1990, Supreme Court, February 15, 1991. However, the Supreme Court held, reversing the High Court, that adequate reasons had in fact been given.

[2] For the meaning of quasi-judicial, see pp. 485–486.

[3] For this, see pp. 505–506.

[4] [1989] I.R. 51, 54–55.

[5] [1989] I.R. 149. For the sequel to this case, see *International Fishing Vessels Ltd.* v. *Minister for the Marine* (*No. 2*), Supreme Court, February 22, 1991.

The next case, *Anheuser Busch Inc.* v. *Controller of Patents Design and Trade Marks*[6] depends rather heavily on the statutory context in which it was set. The applicant wished to appeal to the High Court from a decision of the respondent not to remove a mark from the Register of Trade Marks. The main basis of the decision was a statutory provision which made it clear that once an appeal has been brought then the Controller can be directed, by the court, to state the reasons for his decision. According to Barron J.: "It seems to me to follow [from this provision] that in judicial review proceedings such a direction should be made, where appropriate, before the appeal has been commenced."[7] For present purposes what is significant is that this deduction followed more easily, by virtue of the court's view (stated more fully in a passage quoted *infra*) that fair procedure includes a duty to give reasons.

A striking feature of these authorities is that in each case, the right to reasons was grounded in the fact that the decision for which reasons were sought was reviewable (not least because of the Constitution, Article 34.3.1°) and that, in order to make this right efficacious, reasons must be provided. In *Daly*, Barron J. stated:

" . . . the Minister was entitled to dispense with the services of the applicant without warning him that he proposed to act in that manner. However, once his decision was challenged, he was obliged to disclose to the applicant the material and to give his reasons for so doing."[8]

And, in *Creedon*, Finlay C.J. stated:

"No [adequate] reason was afforded by the Tribunal to the applicant for the failure of her claim, although the Tribunal was made aware, shortly after its determination of the matter, that its decision was being challenged in the High Court.
The Law
 . . . Once the Courts have a jurisdiction, and if that jurisdiction is invoked, an obligation to enquire into and, if necessary, correct the decisions and activities of a tribunal of this description, it would appear necessary for the proper carrying out of that jurisdiction that the courts should be able to ascertain the reasons by which the tribunal came to its determination.

Apart from that, I am satisfied that the requirement which applies to this Tribunal, as it would to a court, that justice should appear to be done, necessitates that the unsuccessful applicant before it, should be made aware in general and broad terms of the grounds on which he or she has failed."[9]

In *International Fishing*, Blayney J. stated:

"It is common case that the Minister's decision is reviewable by the court. Accordingly, the applicant has the right to have it reviewed. But in refusing

[6] [1987] I.R. 329.
[7] *Ibid.* 332.
[8] [1987] I.R. 165, 172.
[9] [1988] I.R. 51, 54–55.

to give his reasons for his decision the Minister places a serious obstacle in the way of the exercise of that right. He deprives the applicant of the material it needs in order to be able to form a view to whether grounds exist on which the Minister's decision might be quashed. As a result, the applicant is at a great disadvantage, firstly, in reaching a decision as to whether to challenge the Minister's decision or not, and secondly, if he does decide to challenge it, in actually doing so, since the absence of reasons would make it very much more difficult to succeed. A procedure which places an applicant at such a disadvantage could not in my opinion be termed a fair procedure, particularly where the decision which the applicant wishes to challenge is of such crucial importance to the applicant in its business."[10]

Finally, account may be taken of a passage from the judgment of Finlay C.J. in *P. and F. Sharpe* v. *Dublin City and County Manager*.[11] The passage is as follows:

"The necessity for the elected members in the case of any direction under section 4 [of the City and County Management (Amendment) Act 1955] concerning the granting or refusing of a planning permission to act in a judicial manner would inter alia involve an obligation to ensure that an adequate note was taken, not necessarily verbatim but of sufficient detail to permit a court upon review to be able to ascertain the material on which the decision had been reached."[12]

There is a significant divergence between *Creedon* and the other three decisions. For the passages from *Daly* state explicitly, and the passages from *International Fishing Vessels Ltd.* and *P. and F. Sharpe* indicate implicitly, that the duty to disclose reasons only arises if and when the person affected by a decision indicates a serious intention to challenge it by judicial review or, where possible, appeal. To elaborate: the facts of these cases and the wording of the judgments seem to suggest that the duty arises only as and when the person affected has asked the deciding authority for reasons and has indicated that he is at least seriously considering the possibility of review or an appeal. It is, of course, reasonable to suppose that if an aggrieved party intended to invoke a forum other than a court (*e.g.* the Ombudsman; *quaere*: the political process?) that the duty would be extended by analogy to cover these possibilities too. The striking point is that it is only in *Creedon* (in the final paragraph of the message quoted above) that the view was expressed that the duty to give reasons applies independently of any likelihood of challenge. And, even in *Creedon*, care was taken to confine this *obiter dictum* to tribunals, as opposed to, say, a Minister: (" . . . the requirement which applies to this Tri-

---

[10] [1989] I.R. 149, 155. For a very similar passage in *Anheuser Busch Inc.*, see [1987] I.R. 331.
[11] [1989] I.L.R.M. 565. See also, *McLoughlin* v. *Minister for Social Welfare* [1958] I.R. 1; *Kiely* v. *Minister for Social Welfare (No. 1)* [1971] I.R. 21; *Kiely* v. *Minister for Social Welfare (No. 2)* [1977] I.R. 297; *McKinley* v. *Minister for Defence* [1977] I.R. 139, 142; *Thompson* v. *Minister for Social Welfare* [1989] I.R. 618.
[12] *Ibid.* 579.

bunal, as it would to a court . . . "). As an aside, it should be noted that here is a recent statement of what has never been doubted, namely that courts bear a duty to give reasoned decisions.

It is appropriate here to mention the main channel of the *audi alteram partem* principle. For this precept, of course, requires that, as part of the obligation to facilitate the person likely to be affected by a decision in making his case, certain types of information should be given to him.[13] Among this information will often be what might amount to the provisional reasons why it is anticipated that the issue may go against him. Where this is the case, it will frequently be clear that the reasons which finally motivated the deciding authority were the same as those mentioned or implied at the earlier stage of the decision-making process. Oddly enough, the link between the duty to give a person affected notice of the case against him and the duty to give reasons for the final decision has seldom been scrutinised in this jurisdiction or, so far as we know, elsewhere. The question, is whether an adequate performance of the duty to give notice of the case against a person will, on the assumption that the reasons are the same at each stage, also satisfy the duty to give reasons at the final stage.[14] The tentative and conditional answer proposed here is that the test should be: whether the person affected is in a position to know (albeit indirectly) with reasonable certainty the reasons so as to enable him to decide whether to initiate an application for judicial review and, if necessary, to assist the High Court in determining such an application. Obviously, it will depend on the circumstances whether this requires extra information as to the deciding authority's findings as to: law, discretion, policy; basic facts; or "ultimate" facts (*i.e.* facts expressed in the language of the statute).[15]

To assess the possibility raised in *Creedon* that reasons for a decision must be given for some purpose other than review proceedings, we ought briefly to examine the advantages and disadvantages of a duty to give reasons. Apart from the fact that the giving of reasons would facilitate any review or appeal, the advantages appear to be twofold. In the first place: "a decision is apt to be better if the reasons for it have to be set out in writing because the reasons are then more likely to have been properly thought out."[16]

Secondly, reasons would give, to the person immediately affected and the public generally, confidence that the decision had been properly taken. The

---

[13] See pp. 439–445.
[14] One rare and slightly tantalising example of this line of thought being placed before a court appears to occur in the summary of counsel for the state's submission given in *International Fishing Vessels Ltd.* v. *Minister for Marine* ([1989] I.R. 154). "The Minister had made clear what material was before him. What the applicant was seeking was a formal statement by the Minister of his position." However, Blayney J.'s response to this argument (quoted in the text *infra*, pp. 461–462) is too general to advance the argument on this point.
[15] It has been held in the context of reasons required by statute [Local Government (Planning and Development) Act 1976, s.39(9)] for planning decisions, that the reasons given in support of conditions attached to the grant of planning permission must be logically capable of justifying the imposition of that condition: *Killiney and Ballybrack Residents Assoc. Ltd.* v. *Minister for Local Government (No. 2)* [1978] I.L.R.M. 78.
[16] *The Franks Report*, 1957 (Cmnd. 218), para. 98.

important point is the limitation which presently appears (in Irish law, though not in respect of the category of cases in which the duty applies, at all, in English law) to limit the duty to give reasons to situations in which there is an imminent appeal or review. As a result of this limitation, the present Irish law might seem not to bear these two advantages. As against this, however, as will be explained in Part 5 of this chapter, the decision-maker's obligation, under the rubric of the general *audi alteram partem* rule, to indicate tentatively the reasons why he is thinking of finding against the person affected will, in many situations, compensate for the lack of reasons at the final stage.

As regards the disadvantages of a duty to give reasons, an Australian authority has written:

"At least two arguments have been advanced against the giving of reasons. First, the giving of reasons would impose additional administrative burdens and might well be an undue drain on the resources of an agency. Such burdens may even result in the giving of canned reasons. Secondly, reasons may hinder the manner in which a discretion is exercised and it may be thought that some discretions should be uncontrollable. But considerations of administrative expediency should not mitigate principles of fairness and few, if any, discretions should be uncontrollable."[17]

To judge by their pro-individual stance in other contexts, Irish judges are likely to sympathise with the comment contained in the final sentence of this extract and not to be much impressed by the first of the two arguments advanced in the passage. On the other hand, (as mentioned earlier), in many situations the actual gains conferred by the imposition of a duty to give reasons at the final stage will not be significant. In view of these indefinite considerations, it is difficult to predict whether, over the next few years, the duty to give reasons will remain confined to situations in which an appeal or review is imminent or whether this limitation will be dropped or as seems more likely qualified. What can be said is that an extensive duty to give reasons would have significant consequential effects in such neighbouring fields as: estoppel, *res judicata*, the control of discretionary powers and the following of precedent in regard to administrative actions.

Closely related to the duty to give reasons would be a requirement that a decision-making authority should, in order to facilitate judicial review of its decision, indicate to the person affected, the materials which were before it when the decision was taken. Such a duty has not yet been fully established. It was first raised (on what might seem a rather unconclusive fashion) in *Sharpe*.[18] However, in *O'Keeffe* v. *An Bord Pleanála*,[19] the High Court drew

---

[17] Flick, *op. cit.* p. 19.
[18] [1989] I.L.R.M. 579. Though note that in the later case of *O'Keeffe* v. *An Bord Pleanála* (on which see n. 19 below), the *Sharpe* passage was treated as authoritative, in both the High Court and the Supreme Court.
[19] High Court, July 31, 1990; Supreme Court, February 15, 1991.

upon *Sharpe* as part of the basis for its finding that the Board's decision was procedurally void because *inter alia* of the Board's failure to keep minutes or to list the material before it. Although on the facts of the case, the Supreme Court (speaking per Finlay C.J.) reversed the High Court; in doing so, it made a number of points, which may be significant for the development of the law. The most important of these is that it implied that there could in principle be an obligation on a public body to indicate the materials which were before it, so as to facilitate judicial review. However this was qualified in two respects. In the first place, the question of whether the mode by which this duty was discharged could only be the provision of the minutes of a meeting would very much depend upon the circumstances[20]:

> "The requirement that a decision-making authority should keep minutes sufficient to allow proof of the material before it in the event of judical review, which is contained in the decision of this Court in *Sharpe* v. *The Dublin City Manager*, must, I am satisfied, be read in its precise terms in the light of the body and the decision which was concened in that case. In that case, what was at issue was the decision of the elected members meeting as the Dublin County Council. Such a meeting would of necessity involve the making of presentations, speeches, possibly the reading of documents by various members of the County Council. All that was avaialbe to the Court in that case was certain reports which were submitted and apparently read into the proceedings of the County Council at the particular meeting with which the Court was concerned, which came from the technical officers of the County Council. In order to obtain satisfactory proof of the material before the members when they resolved, as they did, to direct the granting of planning permission, it would have been necessary to establish what other material was before them and open for their consideration, and the only practical manner in which that could predictably be done would be by minutes of the meeting.
>
> That decision should not be taken, in my view, to mean that minutes contemporaneously made of the meeting of members of a board or of a tribunal are a necessary or the only method of establishing the material that was before them.
>
> In this case it would have been sufficient for this purpose if it were possible to establish the documents which in addition to the inspector's report and that of Mr. Enders were considered by the Board in the form of a list of the documents and the avaiablity of copies of them to the Applicant in a judicial review."

The Chief Justice then went on to mention a second restriction. This stems from the fact that, earlier in his judgment, he had held that the onus is upon the applicant of establishing the nature of the material which was before the

---

[20] Supreme Court, February 15, 1991, pp. 32–34.

decision-maker, a matter which will be explored in the following chapter.[21] It follows from this that before an applicant could complain of a want of material, he must have formally called upon the public body to supply the necessary information. This precondition was not satisified in the instant case because[22]:

" . . . no request was made by letter, by any form of motion or by seeking any form of interlocutory order of any description by the plaintiff to the defendants to establish by affidavit or by other means the material which was before the Board before it reached its decision on the planning appeal."

No general doctrine of delay

Two leading British authorities agree in admitting delay by the public authority[23] to the charmed circle of general factors which will vitiate a decision, although only on rather guarded terms. According to de Smith: "[the idea of substantive fairness] . . . includes a duty . . . not . . . to delay the making of a decision to the prejudice of fundamental rights."[24] Sir William Wade states: "Delay in performing a legal duty may also amount to an abuse which the law will remedy."[25]

It seems likely—though the case law does not permit one to be dogmatic about the point—that in Ireland, too, delay, of itself, is not a ground of invalidity[26] although it is probably so, if a plaintiff can point to some prejudice which flows from it. This was the approach adopted in the *ex tempore* judgment of Gannon J. in *McGowan* v. *Wren*.[27] The facts were that in September 1985 a sworn inquiry, under the Garda disciplinary regulations, was held to examine allegations that the plaintiffs-Gardaí had committed a breach of discipline (the date of which is not given in the report). Owing to certain irregularities in the documents before it, the inquiry was discontinued. Another fresh inquiry to examine the same allegation was fixed for September 1987. The plaintiffs then applied unsuccessfully to the High Court to quash the Garda Commissioner's decision to appoint the second Board of Inquiry. On the delay point, Gannon J. said:

---

[21] See pp. 507–508.

[22] Supreme Court, February 15, 1991 at p. 34 of the judgment of Finlay C.J.

[23] For a court's discretion to refuse a remedy where the litigant delays, see pp. 597–603.

[24] de Smith, *op. cit.* p. 346.

[25] *Administrative Law* (Oxford, 1988), p. 439. All but one of Wade's authorities are from the 1980s. These two English authorities also agree in categorising it, or at any rate squeezing it in, under the rubric of abuse of discretionary power. It is respectfully suggested that it is inappropriate to confine this vitiating factor to the exercise of a discretion, excluding (say) payment of a welfare benefit, hearing a planning appeal; or court proceedings. It is suggested too that delay is a matter of procedure or at least process, as opposed to substance. Possibly the more appropriate rubric for it, in the Irish framework, is the additional territory annexed by constitutional justice beyond the bounds of natural justice. This matter of classification is not perhaps of first importance and has received no attention in the few Irish cases on delay.

[26] Though a number of the Ombudsman's cases have involved delay: see p. 293.

[27] [1988] I.L.R.M. 744. See, to like effect, *Gallagher* v. *The Revenue Commissioners*, High Court, January 11, 1991, p. 10 of the judgment of Blayney J.

"[At the first inquiry board] no one had considered the applicants' side of the case but they [had] heard the case to be made against [them]. They are not suggesting that they are failing in recollection since the alleged events occurred. If there is any disadvantage in the delay, it must lie in the presentation of the investigation and not a disadvantage to the applicants. I do not think that there are any grounds in delay upon which the applicants may rely for the relief sought."[28]

Another point taken by the plaintiffs will often be found in association with delay. It was that there had already been one set of abortive proceedings brought against the plaintiffs. Again, Gannon J. took a pragmatic, non-dogmatic line, refusing an order, on the ground that the plaintiffs had suffered no disadvantage by reason of the previous proceedings.

Another claim based on delay was made in the rather extreme circumstances of *Flynn* v. *An Post*.[29] The plaintiff had been suspended from duty without pay in May 1984 because he was suspected of stealing letters and parcels. He had remained suspended for nearly three years until the Supreme Court decision in the instant case, in 1987. He lived on social welfare benefits and a distress fund organised by his union. In July 1984 the Director of Public Prosecutions decided to prosecute the plaintiff on indictment. The solicitor for An Post, who was also acting for the D.P.P., then wrote to the plaintiff to say that An Post would not bring the disciplinary action against the plaintiff until the criminal trial was over. The critical fact in the case was that, at this and at all other stages, the plaintiff wished to press ahead with the disciplinary investigation. However, according to McCarthy J., with whose judgment three of the other judges concurred:

"In the High Court [in the instant case] it was held that the plaintiff's right to silence might be lost or he might be otherwise prejudiced in the criminal trial if the investigation had proceeded. Without expressing any view as to the nature of an alleged right to silence, in my judgment, if an accused in a criminal proceeding wishes to embark upon a course which may damage him in the manner suggested, it is no function of his employer, who is not the prosecutor (although the confusion of the two is understandable because of the D.P.P.'s choice of solicitor) to protect him from the consequences of such a course. There may be circumstances in which it would be proper to postpone an investigation pending a criminal trial; I am unable to prescribe them in a case where an employee is suspended without pay and wants the investigation to proceed; in so far as the observations of Woolf J. in *Reg.* v. *British Broadcasting Corporation ex parte Lavelle* [1983] 1 W.L.R. 23 at p. 36 suggests that it is a matter of ordinary discretion, weigh-

[28] *Ibid.* 745–746.
[29] [1987] I.R. 68. See also, *Cosgrove* v. *The Legal Aid Board* High Court, October 17, 1990, pp. 2, 24 and 25 where Gannon J. granted a declaration that the Board was obliged to consider the applicant's claim for civil legal aid within a reasonable tune.

ing in the balance of several relevant factors, I would not accept it as a correct statement of the law applicable in this country."[30]

The plaintiff's criminal trial, which resulted in his acquittal on all charges, was held in November 1985. The provision under which he was suspended, section 13 of the Civil Service Regulation Act 1956, simply states that: "A suspending authority may suspend a civil servant. . . . " In the circumstances, McCarthy J. held that:

"To construe section 13 of the Act of 1956 as authorising a suspending authority to suspend without pay an employee of the company for a period of eighteen months does not appear to me to be a reasonable construction of the section nor one permissible within the constitutional framework."[31]

McCarthy J. went on to hold that the suspension ceased to be valid in August 1984, which was the date when An Post should have been ready to proceed with the formal investigation if they had not postponed the proceedings until the criminal trial was concluded. Accordingly he made a declaration to that effect and a consequential order for the payment of the plaintiff's salary from August 1984 to date.

Flynn could be read as supporting the proposition that any unjustifiable delay renders a decision or procedure invalid.[32] Alternatively, it could be taken as confirming the narrower view hazarded at the start of this section, namely that delay only renders a decision invalid where the delay has caused prejudice to the applicant. On this latter analysis, the way in which the applicant in *Flynn* had been prejudiced is that his suspension had forced him to live

---

[30] *Ibid.* 82. On the delay point, the dissenting judge, Henchy J. was broadly in agreement with the other judges. However, he did comtemplate (at 76–77) that there might be circumstances in which although an employee waives his rights as defendant-to-be he could not necessarily plead delay (*e.g.* if a strike were likely if dismissal occurred before the trial).

For the purposes of the future development of the law, the delay-point is the more important part of *Flynn*. However, the point on which majority members of the court and Henchy J divided is also of some practical interest. This point arose out of the fact that, in July 1984, the plaintiff had initiated the present plenary proceedings, claiming, *inter alia,* a declaration that his suspension was *ultra vires*. This fact was the ground of Henchy J.'s dissent in *Flynn*, where he stated that it was "reasonable and proper for An Post to postpone the inquiry, for it might have proved to be unnecessary, futile and in conflict with the jurisdiction of the High Court." [at 77–78] Rejecting this argument, McCarthy J., effectively writing for the majority, stated: "that the matters about which the enquiry would be concerned were wholly removed from the matters under consideration in the action itself." [at 84]. This surely underestimates the respect that all other institutions are required to pay to courts and also the surprising turn which court cases often take.

[31] *Ibid.* 83.

[32] There may also be some support for this proposition in *O'Flynn* v. *The Mid Western Health Board* [1989] I.R. 429, 439. The case involved complaints against medical practitioners participating in the general medical services scheme (see p. 366). Whilst not making any finding regarding delay in the instant case, Barr J. stated:

" . . . injustice might well result if there is unreasonable delay on the part of a health board in notifying a general medical practitioner of complaints made against him. He should be given an opportunity to investigate and answer such charges as soon as practicable after they have been made to the health board."

(*Cf.* same judge in *Cannon* v. *Minister for the Marine* [1991] I.L.R.M. 261, 265–267, Counsel conceded delay of six months unreasonable. Barr J. raised possibility of damages but provided that delay had caused loss).

without wages for a long period. *Flynn* was interpreted by Costello J. in this second sense and then distinguished, on the facts, in *Myers* v. *Commissioner of the Garda Siochana.*[33] The factual background to *Myers* was similar to that in *Flynn*. In *Myers*, the applicant's superiors had become concerned at the number of executed warrants (to the aggregate value of £2,664) which had been issued in respect of District Court fines and held by the applicant for collection. As a result, in early 1984, summonses were issued against the applicant involving charges of embezzlement, false pretences and forgery. The applicant was not tried until November 1986 when, in respect of all counts, either he was acquitted or charges were withdrawn by the Director of Public Prosecutions. After the summonses had been issued and thereafter up to the date of the present proceedings, the applicant had been suspended, under the Garda Síochána (Discipline) Regulations 1971, for repeated periods of three months. Soon after the applicant's acquittal, the procedure for an investigation into the alleged breaches of discipline, arising out of the matters on which he had been acquitted, was initiated. In September 1987 the applicant launched the instant proceedings.

His first claim was that, following *Flynn*, his continued suspension for over two years pending the outcome of the criminal prosecution was unconstitutionally unfair. This submission was rejected—and *Flynn* distinguished—on two grounds. In the first place, it had been a cardinal point, in *Flynn*, that the suspended employee had demanded that an internal inquiry be held, notwithstanding the pending criminal prosecution. By contrast, in *Myers*, Costello J. held:

"In the absence of a request that an immediate disciplinary inquiry be held the Garda authorities acted in my judgment fairly in postponing the inquiry and suspending him on a suspension allowance, as to hold an inquiry (which would certainly have required him to give evidence so as to avoid dismissal) before the criminal charges were heard might well have been prejudicial to the applicant."[34]

The other point of distinction was that in *Myers* the applicant has been receiving suspension pay of two-thirds of his basic salary; whereas the applicant in *Flynn* had received nothing from his employers.

The applicant's second claim (of which there was no equivalent in *Flynn*) related not to the suspension itself, but to the disciplinary proceedings which had been initiated after the termination of the criminal prosecution. The applicant sought an order to prohibit these proceedings. The first basis for this claim was delay and it is noteworthy that in rejecting it, Costello J. said:

"Whilst the Supreme Court in *Flynn* was not required to decide that the proposed internal inquiry should be prohibited on the ground of delay it is to be noted that notwithstanding the considerable time that had elapsed between the first suspension and the date on which the inquiry could have been held the Court contemplated that such an inquiry could with propriety take place. No arguments have been advanced to show that the delay in this

[33] High Court, January 22, 1988.
[34] *Ibid.* p. 6 of the judgment.

case has caused such prejudice that a disciplinary inquiry now would be unfair or to establish that to hold an inquiry after a three year delay would in itself amount to a breach of the applicant's constitutional right to fair procedures."[35]

The other ground on which the applicant claimed that the disciplinary proceedings should be discontinued also failed. Costello J. stated:

"Nor have any submissions been advanced to support the claim . . . that the proposed inquiry is invalid because it would amount 'to double jeopardy'—for good reason, because the *Flynn case* clearly shows that the dismissal of criminal charges against an employee is not in itself a bar to subsequent disciplinary proceedings arising out of the same set of facts, and no special circumstances creating such a bar have been shown to exist in this case."[36]

Speaking very broadly, the fate of this latter argument is in line with the finding in *McGowan* (the facts of which were mentioned above) that the fact that one set of abortive disciplinary proceedings had already been initiated was no necessary reason for holding that a second set was invalid.

There is one other case in which a plea of delay succeeded, although it probably involved too specialised an area for any worthwhile general principle to emerge. This is the case of *Van Nierop* v. *Commissioners for Public Works*[37] which involved a notice of compulsory acquisition and the ensuing notice to treat, under the Fishery Harbour Centres Act 1968. There had been about 15 years' delay between the first notice and the present action and it was conceded, even by the Commissioners, that this could mean that the notices ceased to be valid (even though no time limit was fixed by the Act). This appears to have been grounded on the basis of equity and/or the intention of the legislature.

Court cases

It would, thus, be premature to enunciate any general doctrine of undue delay in regard to administrative decisions. However, in what is conventionally regarded as the more important area of court cases, pleas of delay have been more successful. In the civil field, take for instance, *O'Keefe* v. *Commissioners of Public Works*.[38] In this case, the plaintiff sought to bring an action for damages in respect of an industrial accident which had occurred some 24 years earlier. Although a plenary summons had been issued within the three-year limitation period, the plaintiff took no steps to proceed with the action until some 17 years later. During that period he had accepted lump sum compensation from the defendants in discharge of all liability under the

---

[35] *Ibid.* pp. 6–7 of the judgment.
[36] *Ibid.* p. 7 of the judgment.
[37] [1990] 2 I.R. 189. See, to similar effect, *Grace Grice* v. *Dudley Corporation* [1958] Ch. 329, 339. *A contra*: *P.J. Smyth* v. *Dublin Corporation* 89 I.L.T.R. 1.
[38] Supreme Court, March 24, 1980. See, to similar effect, *O'Domhnaill* v. *Merrick* [1984] I.R. 151, 157–158 and *Toal* v. *Duignan (No. 2)* [1991] I.L.R.M. 140, 142–143.

Workmen's Compensation Acts. Henchy J. took the view that the plaintiff should be estopped from proceeding with his claim, as a hearing in these circumstances would be contrary to natural justice:

> "Natural justice requires that both parties to an action be heard before the decision can be said to have legal validity. Where one party, by his words or conduct . . . has put it beyond the capacity of that other party to be effectively heard, in the sense of presenting the potentially successful case which his opponent's conduct has put beyond his reach, the court will hold the party thus in default to be estopped from bringing the matter to a hearing. The reason is that a hearing in those circumstances would lack the mutuality and fairness which are necessary for the due administration of justice."

In the criminal field, the right to trial in due course of law (established by Article 38.1) has been held by the Supreme Court, in *The State (O'Connell)* v. *Fawsitt* to include the right to an expeditious trial.[39] This case entailed an assault charge which was to have been heard by the Circuit Court some four years after the incident from which it allegedly arose. On the facts, this delay had led to a concrete prejudice in the form of the non-availability of a defence witness. However it is significant that the Supreme Court made it clear that, even without this factor, it would have granted the order restraining the prosecution from continuing. The court also indicated, *obiter*, that it would apply the general principle quoted at the start of this paragraph, whether the trial was (as in the instant case) a trial on indictment or summary proceedings.

Waiver

The question of waiver, by the individual affected, is an important issue which has received even less attention in the context of the *audi alteram partem* rule than in other contexts.[40] For example, in *Gammell* v. *Dublin County Council*[41] Carroll J. held that if the statutory machinery permits an aggrieved party to make representations to the Minister before the order prohibiting the erection of any temporary dwelling came into effect, then the procedure conforms to the *audi alteram partem* rule. The only notice of the order before the period for the making of representations expired was a notice in *The Irish Press*, which the plaintiff said (and the defendant accepted) she had never seen. No point was taken in this case as to whether the plaintiff ought to have been individually served with notice and it seems plain from the result that the court must have assumed without discussion that the plaintiff had waived her right to make

[39] [1986] I.R. 362, 379. See, to similar effect, *D.P.P.* v. *Gill* [1980] I.R. 263; *The State (D.P.P.)* v. *Esmonde*, High Court July 30, 1984. *A contra*: *Maher* v. *Carroll*, High Court, August 8, 1986, in which a delay argument failed in regard to summary proceedings on the ground that the legislature had considered the matter and had prescribed, in s.10(4) of the Petty Sessions (Ireland) Act 1851, a relatively short period for making the complaint such provision being taken to mean, *inter alia*, "that the trial will be heard with reasonable expedition. . . . "
[40] On the issue of waiver and *nemo iudex*, see pp. 437–438.
[41] [1983] I.L.R.M. 413. For facts in *Gammell*, see pp. 455–457.

representations. By contrast, in *O'Brien* v. *Bord na Móna*,[42] the High and Supreme Court explicitly left open the possibility that waiver would only be deemed to have occurred on actual notice or following the sending of an individual, specific notification. (On the facts of *O'Brien*, this question did not arise since it was admitted that the plaintiff had received actual notice by way of the newspaper advertisement.) Again, in *Glover* v. *B.L.N. Ltd.*[43] a case involving the removal of an office-holder whose office was founded on contract, Walsh J. explicitly left open the question, which did not arise on the facts of the case, of the extent to which the rules of natural justice could have been excluded by express provision in the contract. (It should be noted that in this situation the renunciation of rights would have occurred at an earlier stage than in *Gammell*). Thus it must be admitted that the standard of informed consent necessary for a waiver has not yet been authoritatively determined. In *Flanagan*, it was stated that the plaintiff's "informed consent"[44] would have been required to validate the selection of an independent moderator to determine whether her thesis included plagiarism.

4. Types of Decisions which Attract the Rules of Constitutional Justice

It is generally assumed that the rules of natural justice are co-extensive in their application.[45] This assumption is questionable, given the differing nature and function of the rules. Bias is a particularly heinous defect likely to lead to a general erosion of confidence in the administrative system, whereas the failure to grant a hearing does not appear to be such a fundamental flaw. Reflecting this broader reach, the no-bias limb of constitutional justice shades off into the rule against exercise of discretionary power in bad faith,[46] with the result that the rule against bias applies in some form to almost all decisions by public authorities. In contrast, the *audi alteram partem* rule of its nature applies to a more limited range of decisions—essentially decisions raising issues of fact or law rather than matters of policy. Again, it has been stated that the rules of natural justice do not apply where this would defeat the object of the administrative power.[47] Of its nature, this restriction is more likely to apply to *audi alteram partem* than to the no-bias rule. However,

---

[42] [1983] I.R. 255, 276 (Keane J.) and 287 (Finlay P.). See also *Re Mountcharles's Estate* [1935] I.R. 163, where the only notice of Land Commission decisions determining ownership of mining rights was that published in *Iris Oifigiúil*. Finding that these procedures were in breach of *audi alteram partem*, Kennedy C.J. commented ironically ([1935] I.R. 166): "[T]he Land Commission purported to give themselves power to determine questions submitted by the Minister behind the backs of interested parties . . . while the very fact of such "determination" is not brought to their notice unless they happen to be members of that comparatively small and very select class of persons, the regular readers of *Iris Oifigiúil*."

[43] [1973] I.R. 388, 425. See further, pp. 474–476. *Cf. The State (Boyle)* v. *General Medical Services (Payments) Board* [1981] I.L.R.M. 14, 15.

[44] [1989] I.L.R.M. 469, 476.

[45] Clarke, "Natural Justice: Substance or Shadow?" [1975] *Public Law* 27.

[46] See pp. 511–512. For a good example of where the wrongful exercise of discretionary power was regarded as tantamount to bias: see *The State (McGeough)* v. *Louth C.C.* (1973) 107 I.L.T.R. 13.

[47] *O'Callaghan* v. *Commissioners of Public Works* [1985] I.L.R.M. 364.

these *caveats* notwithstanding, both rules will generally apply to the situations described in this Part.

The following classification of the relevant cases, by reference to the type of administrative decision involved, inevitably entails some degree of overlap.

Public and private employment

Historically, there were two distinctions of crucial importance for employment law. Office-holders (or officers) were distinguished from employees (servants), and, secondly, the category of office-holders was divided into two classes according to whether the holder was dismissible at pleasure or whether he could only be removed for cause. It was only the office-holder removable for cause who enjoyed the protection of the natural justice principles.

It seems likely that the second distinction, at least, is no longer part of the law. In *Garvey* v. *Ireland*[48] the Commissioner of the Garda Síochána argued successfully that his summary dismissal from office by the Government was contrary to natural justice. Of the four judges who comprised the majority, O'Higgins C.J. (with whom Parke J. agreed) decided that the office was not held merely at pleasure, but also concluded that this distinction was no longer significant. Henchy and Griffin JJ. classified the office as one held at pleasure, yet found that the rules of natural justice applied to any decision to dismiss.

It is, however, less certain whether the distinction between an office-holder and an employee has ceased to be significant in the present context.[49] The office is the legal form for a "superior" post (which was, in past centuries, even regarded as a property-right of the holder). An office is a position to which certain important duties are attached, usually of a more or less public character, with its holder likely to be better qualified and freer from day-to-day control than a servant. It thus plays a pivotal part in the administration of government, whether at central or local level, or sometimes in the administration of a company or other corporation. In addition:

"[An office] is created by Act of the National Parliament, charter, statutory regulation, articles of association of a company or of a body corporate formed under the authority of a statute, deed of trust, grant or by prescription."[50]

By contrast, the master-servant relationship is usually founded exclusively upon a contract. It should be stressed, though, that even an office-holder may—and usually does—have a contract, which fixes a great part of his conditions. Finally, a servant may occupy a temporary, personal post whilst an office:

"[M]ust have a sufficient degree of continuance to admit of its being held by

---

[48] [1981] I.R. 75.
[49] There are of course many other contexts in which the distinction is significant. The distinction still appears to have relevance as far as the court's power to order reinstatement in cases of wrongful dismissal is concerned (but *cf. Glover* v. *B.L.N. Ltd.* [1973] I.R. 388, 427) and also for tax purposes: *Edwards* v. *Clinch* [1982] A.C. 845.
[50] *Per* Kenny J. in *Glover* v. *B.L.N. Ltd.* [1973] I.R 388, 414.

472

successful incumbents . . . it cannot be limited to the tenure of one man, for if it were so, it would lack that independent existence which to my mind the word 'office' imports."[51]

The continuing validity of the distinction between an officer and an employee in the context of the *audi alteram* rule was questioned by the Supreme Court in *Glover* v. *B.L.N. Ltd.*,[52] which arose from the dismissal of a company director for alleged misconduct. The dismissal was invalidated as the plaintiff had not been given a fair hearing by the board of the company. In the High Court, Kenny J. adopted the traditional British view that the rules of natural justice apply to the removal of an office-holder but not a servant, and held that the rules applied in the instant case because the plaintiff was characterised as being an office-holder. However, Walsh J., writing on behalf of the Supreme Court majority, stated:

"[O]nce the matter is governed by the terms of a contract between the parties, it is immaterial whether the employee concerned is deemed to be a servant or an officer . . . [because] public policy and the dictates of constitutional justice require that statutes, regulations or agreements setting up machinery for taking decisions which may affect right or impose liabilities should be construed as providing for fair procedures."[53]

However, *Glover* leaves a number of loose ends. In the first place, the contract of service in the case included a clause which expressly stated that a hearing would take place prior to any dismissal for misconduct, thus making it possible for the court to impute a term to the effect that any such hearing or inquiry should be fairly conducted. Consequently the *excursus* into the broader reaches of constitutional justice was *obiter*. Secondly, Walsh J. explicitly left open the questions of the situation where the relationship between the parties was not grounded in either contract or statute and the extent to which the rules could be excluded by express agreement. Finally, and most significantly, the passage quoted depends upon the impregnation of contract law by constitutional principles. However, several recent decisions[54] show that there was some judicial reluctance—at High Court level at any rate—to follow this innovatory approach.

In *Lupton* v. *Allied Irish Banks Ltd.*[55] it was contended that *Glover* was an authority for the proposition that constitutional justice applies to *all* employees. While Murphy J. was not obliged to decide this point, he doubted whether Walsh J. had equated the position of an employee with that of an officer. He then proceeded to confine the authority of *Glover* to its own facts,

---

[51] *Per* Lord Wilberforce in *Edwards* v. *Clinch* [1982] A.C. 845, 860.

[52] [1973] I.R. 388. See O'Reilly, "The Constitution and the Law of Contract" (1973) 8 Ir.-Jur.(N.S.) 197.

[53] [1973] I.R. 425, 427. See, to like effect, the comments of McWilliam J. in *Garvey* v. *Ireland* [1981] I.R. 75, 82.

[54] In addition to those to be mentioned in the text, these include: *Heneghan* v. *The Western Regional Fisheries Board* [1986] I.L.R.M. 225, 228; *Connolly* v. *McConnell* [1983] I.R. 172, 178.

[55] (1983) 2 J.I.S.S.L. 107. For other cases invoking the officer/employee dichotomy, see *N.E.E.T.U.* v. *McConnell* (1983) 2 J.I.S.S.L. 97 and *Connolly* v. *McConnell* [1983] I.R. 172.

i.e. a case where the contract of service already envisaged that the office-holder would get natural justice. Murphy J. took the same approach in *Farrell* v. *Minister for Defence*[56] where the summary dismissal of a civilian maintenance man in the employment of the defendant was upheld. Unlike *Glover*, the contract of employment contained no express or implied term compelling the employer to conduct an investigation prior to dismissal. Counsel for the plaintiff was then forced to contend that in virtue of the constitutional guarantee of fair procedures the rules of natural justice should apply. Pending "an authoritative review of the law" Murphy J. was content to apply settled principles: the plaintiff was an employee, not an office-holder, and he was not entitled to natural justice. If, however, the dismissal was in breach of some term in his contract then the employee was entitled to recover damages. The same reasoning commended itself to Costello J. in *Gunn* v. *National College of Art and Design*,[57] a case arising out of the dismissal of a member of the full-time teaching staff for alleged financial irregularities in relation to a builder who had done work for the College. The judge concluded that the teacher-employer relationship was one governed by contract, and not by "the principles of administrative law developed to deal with office-holders in the public service." Thus the defendants were not bound to apply the rules of natural justice (although they had in fact done so, having written several admirable letters inquiring whether there were any representations which the plaintiff wished to make on the allegations against him).

To summarise, then, the state which the law had reached following this recent line of High Court decisions: first, there was the centuries-long period during which the classic distinction between the office-holder and an ordinary employee had held sway; next, the entire policy underlying this distinction was questioned, specifically, by the Supreme Court judgments in *Glover* and, to a lesser extent, in *Garvey*; and, more generally, by the entire *Zeitgeist* of contemporary Irish law, against ancient dogmas and in favour of individual rights; thirdly, the four High Court judgments, each, apart from *Gunn* and *Heneghan*, decided by Murphy J., re-established the old distinction. The judges in these cases were naturally pressed, by counsel for the plaintiff, with the authority of *Glover*. This case was distinguished by confining it to its own facts, namely where there was a term in the contract under which the officer/employee was entitled to the benefit of constitutional justice. Murphy J. stated in *Farrell*, that "in the absence of any authoritative review of the law" he was content to apply the settled law represented by the dictum of Lord Reid in *Ridge* v. *Baldwin* which had been approved by Kenny J. in *Glover*.

The gauntlet, thus thrown down, was picked up by the Supreme Court in *Gunn*,[58] which appears to have finally extirpated the distinction between an employee and an office-holder. At the same time, it must be said that there were two features of the case which slightly undermine its authority as a pre-

---

[56] (1985) 4 J.I.S.S.L. 105.
[57] High Court, October 29, 1985.
[58] [1990] 2 I.R. 168. Followed, though without being cited, in *Hickey* v. *The Eastern Health Board*, Supreme Court, July 20, 1990 at p. 8 of the judgment of O'Flaherty J.

cedent. First, Walsh J. made it clear that on the facts in *Gunn* a disciplinary scheme *had* been incorporated in the relationship between the National College and its staff. Secondly, Walsh J. held that the plaintiff was, in any case, an office-holder by virtue of section 1(3). (This provision states that : "an officer of An Bord includes . . . a member of the academic staff of the College.") McCarthy J., the only other judge to give a written judgment, also reasoned that as the plaintiff was a member of the academic staff, consequently he must be an officer. Strictly speaking these factors may render what the Supreme Court had to say on the question of the officer-employee distinction, *obiter*. On the other hand, the Court's statements on this matter were well-considered and intended to be followed. Walsh J. stated:

> "There is one other matter I wish to refer to in order to clear up what appears to be misapprehension concerning the application of the rules of natural justice or of constitutional justice. The application of these rules does not depend upon whether the person concerned is an office-holder as distinct from being an employee of some other kind. I mention this because it is a subject which is referred to in the course of the judgment of [Costello J.] in his reference to *Glover* v. *B.L.N. Ltd.* The quality of justice does not depend on such distinctions. It appears to me that the misunderstanding has arisen by reason of the great reliance which Mr. Justice Kenny in the High Court appeared to have placed upon the speech of Lord Reid in the English House of Lords decision of *Ridge* v. *Baldwin* [1964] A.C. 40. In that case the person who had been dismissed was a Chief Constable and was the holder of a statutory office. He could only have been dismissed from it in accordance with particular statutory provisions. The persons who had the power to dismiss him were not his employers in the strict sense. Because of that fact and that he was by statutory instrument designated as an 'officer' as distinct from another type of employee, it was held that the particular statutory provisions referable to the dismissal of an officer had not been complied with. As was pointed out in the majority judgment of this Court in *Glover* v. *B.L.N. Ltd.* the question of whether the plaintiff in that case was an officer or a servant was irrelevant, as the case fell to be decided not upon that distinction but upon the actual terms of the contract between Mr. Glover and his employers. In the present case, the agreed procedures are those set out in the Agreement with the Federated Workers Union of Ireland, and they did not in any way depend upon whether the employee in question was an officer or not. In any case where there is no particular procedure prescribed either by agreement between the parties or by statute and where the case falls to be determined by the application of the principles of natural justice, they are applicable without regard to the status of the person entitled to benefit from them."[59]

McCarthy J. agreed, offering the observation that "[t]hese principles [of

---

[59] *Ibid.* 181.

constitutional justice] are not the monopoly of any particular class."[60] In face of these statements, it is suggested that only a court heedless of the fundamental precepts of precedent and the hierarchy of the court system would seek to resurrect this stubborn distinction. Moreover, in *O'Neill* v. *Beaumont Hospital*[61] it was assumed by Finlay C.J. that the rules of constitutional justice applied to the dismissal of a consultant who was employed under "Common Consultant's Contract" which was characterised "as far as legal status of it is [concerned as] an individual contractual document reached as an agreement between the consultant, Mr. O'Neill and the Board of this Hospital."[62]

So much for authority. As regards principle, it is submitted that the *Glover-Gunn* line is the more desirable. On policy grounds, the modern view is that all means of livelihood are so important to the person to whom they belong (and often more important, in these times, to the "servant") that dismissal should require a fair procedure.[63] On the technical plane, the distinction between an office-holder and a servant is "abstruse and verging on the asinine or bizarre."[64] Indeed in *Gunn*, the Supreme Court reversed the High Court on the question of whether the plaintiff was an officer, without either court offering a very rigorous analysis of the problem. Moreover, it is usually the case that even with an office-holder, the bulk of the terms of employment are fixed by contract, rather than statute, deed of trust, etc., a factor which erodes the basis of the distinction.

Unfair Dismissals Act 1977

In any case, these doubts and difficulties will often be of only academic interest because of the 1977 Act which brings in the right to sue for unfair dismissal: for it is now accepted that a fair dismissal requires the observance of the rules of natural justice.[65] There are, however, two restrictions on the impact of the 1977 Act. First, the natural justice rules, derived as a gloss on the statute, may have a different content from that of common law/constitutional natural justice, in that for instance, under the Act, it is necessary to balance up procedural and substantive justice. Secondly, the Act's protection extends among public sector employees, to all employees of semi-state bodies (apart from AnCo trainees and apprentices) and to the servants of local authorities, vocational education committees and health boards. However, about one-fifth of the working population, most of whom are in public employment,

---

[60] *Ibid.* 183.
[61] [1990] I.L.R.M. 419. *Gunn* was also followed in *Cooney* v. *An Post*, High Court, April 6, 1990, p. 27.
[62] *Ibid.* 435.
[63] Thus, the justifications given in *Garvey* for the application of the rules of natural justice (*e.g.* avoiding any injustice caused through acting on an *ex parte* view of the facts) are equally applicable in the case of employees/office-holders working in the private sector.
[64] de Smith, *op. cit.* p. 228. The distinction appears to have a rather fitful existence in England: see de Smith, *op. cit.* pp. 227–233; Wade, *op. cit.* pp. 566–568.
[65] See, *e.g. Warner-Lambert* v. *Tormey* UD 255/1978; *Hynes* v. *Frederick Inns* UD 172/1978 and the cases cited at p. 245 and in Redmond, *Dismissal Law in the Republic of Ireland* (Dublin, 1982), pp. 160–169 and Modden and Kerr, *Unfair Dismissal Cases and Commentary* (Dublin, 1990), Chap. 6.

are expressly excluded from the Act's field of operation.[66] Most, but not all, of those excluded have some other form of procedural protection against dismissal. Thus, for instance of those excluded: officers of local authorities have a special statutory fair dismissal system under the Local Government Act 1941[67]; members of the Defence Forces and of the Garda Síochána are officeholders, hence, certainly, may only be removed in accordance with the principles of constitutional justice[68] and relevant disciplinary regulations; and it seems likely that civil servants are in the same position.[69]

Membership of trade unions, professional bodies or clubs

As the relationship between the member and the institution concerned is often grounded ultimately in contract, one is again faced with the question of how the rules of constitutional justice may be interpolated. A conceptually satisfactory answer to this difficult question has yet to be given, but for the moment the courts are content to construe the contract of membership as containing an implied term that fair procedures will be observed.[70] Different considerations, of course, arise in the case of professional bodies exercising *statutory powers*, and there can be no question but that the rules of constitutional justice are applicable to the exercise of such powers.

As illustrated in the two preceding Parts of this chapter, the content and stringency of the rules of constitutional justice vary enormously depending on 'the circumstances'. Thus, for example, it is likely that the classification into quasi-judicial and administrative functions,[71] in the context of the *nemo iudex* rule, would operate so that a less rigorous rule would apply, at least in regard to trade unions and clubs. It is clear, however, that disciplinary action by a trade union,[72] professional body[73] or club[74] cannot be conducted on a summary, *ex parte* basis and the courts have set aside disciplinary actions which did not observe the rules of natural justice or where the requirements of the association's own constitution or rules relating to notice had not been complied with.[75] This has been extended even to suspension from a sporting

---

[66] s.2(1). s.2(1)(*h*) actually excludes "a person employed by or under the State other than persons designated for the time being under s.17 of the Industrial Relations Act 1969." The qualification "other than" catches some 8,000 people, mostly industrial civil servants.

[67] ss.24 and 25. See *Dáil Debates*, Vol. 294, col. 480 (November 23, 1976). For an example of the 1941 Act in operation, see *O'Mahony* v. *Arklow U.D.C.* [1965] I.R. 710.

[68] *The State (Gleeson)* v. *Minister for Defence* [1976] I.R. 280, 294.

[69] The position of civil servants has already been dealt with at pp. 80–85.

[70] *Fisher* v. *Keane* (1878) 11 Ch.D. 353; *Dawkins* v. *Antrobus* (1881) 17 Ch.D. 615; *Flynn* v. *Grt. N. Ry. Co.* (1955) 89 I.L.T.R. 46; *Doyle* v. *Croke*, High Court, May 6, 1988. See pp. 420–421.

[71] See pp. 485–486.

[72] *Kilkenny* v. *Irish Engineering and Foundry Worker's Union* (1939) Ir.Jur.Rep. 52; *N.E.E.T.U.* v. *McConnell* (1983) 2 J.I.S.L.L. 97; *Connolly* v. *McConnell* [1983] I.R. 172. See also, Kerr and Whyte, *Irish Trade Union Law* (Abingdon, 1985), pp. 113–121.

[73] *Manning* v. *Incorporated Law Society for Ireland*, High Court, March 8, 1980; *Re M., a doctor* [1984] I.R. 479; *The State (Boyle)* v. *General Medical Services (Payment) Board* [1981] I.L.R.M. 14; *O'Donoghue* v. *Veterinary Council* [1975] I.R. 398; *Kerrigan* v. *An Bord Altranais*, Supreme Court, March 20, 1990.

[74] *Forde* v. *Fottrell* (1930) 64 I.L.T.R. 89; *Goggins* v *Feeney* (1949) 83 I.L.T.R. 181; *Ahern* v. *Molyneux* [1965] Ir.Jur.Rep. 59; *Cotter* v. *Sullivan*, High Court, April 23, 1980.

[75] *Doyle* v. *Griffin* [1937] I.R. 93.

organisation provided that it "involv[ed] the imposition of a substantial sanc-tion."[76] which was, in the case from which this quotation was taken, the dis-qualification of an international shot-putter from all competition, including the Olympic Games, for 18 months. Clauses in such constitutions or rules which provide for automatic forfeiture of membership are probably void as contrary to public policy.[77] This has been the conclusion of the English courts, and given that the Constitution may inform notions of public policy, such reasoning would also seem to apply *a fortiori* in this jurisdiction.

A general exception (which is elaborated *infra*) but which is of particular relevance here is that the rules of constitutional justice do not usually apply to suspensions from membership for a temporary period.[78]

Licensing and commercial regulation

The application of the rules of natural justice in this area stems from the desire to protect an individual's livelihood and business interests.This may be illustrated by the fairly typical case of *Doupe* v. *Limerick Corporation*.[79] The plaintiff had been refused permission to operate an abattoir by the defendant body. The gist of their objections was that the scale of the proposed operation posed environmental and health risks. Costello J. observed that the *audi alteram partem* principle did not require that every administrative order which may adversely affect rights "must be preceded by a judicial type hearing involving the examination and cross-examination of witnesses." The plaintiff had been informally told of the nature of the council's objections and Costello J. concluded that he had "ample opportunity" to seek expert advice (if such could be obtained) challenging the council's view that the scale of the pro-posal posed serious health risks. In the circumstances, the rules of consti-tutional justice had been observed. But one could imagine other cases (such as where the revocation of an existing licence would be tantamount to the deprivation of a means of livelihood) where a more exacting procedural stan-dard would be required.[80] The rules of constitutional justice have also been applied: to the revocation or suspension of a taxi driver's licence[81] or a betting permit for a bookmaker[82]; the licensing of agricultural marts[83]; the censorship of publications[84]; and the granting of a liquor licence in substitution for demo-lished licensed premises.[85]

---

[76] *Quirke* v. *Bord Luthchleas na hÉireann* [1988] I.R. 83, 88.
[77] *Edwards* v. *S.O.G.A.T.* [1971] Ch. 354. But *cf. Moran* v. *Workers Union of Ireland* [1943] I.R. 485.
[78] See pp. 492–493.
[79] [1981] I.L.R.M. 456.
[80] See, *e.g. Ingle* v. *O'Brien* (1975) 109 I.L.T.R. 9; *Moran* v. *Att.-Gen.* [1976] I.R. 400; *The State (Grahame)* v. *Racing Board*, High Court, November 22, 1983.
[81] *Ingle* v. *O'Brien* (1975) 109 I.L.T.R. 7; *Moran* v. *Att.-Gen.* [1976] I.R. 400.
[82] *McDonald* v. *Bord na gCon* [1965] I.R. 217; *The State (Grahame)* v. *Racing Board*, High Court, November 22, 1983.
[83] *East Donegal Co-Operative Ltd.* v. *Attorney-General* [1970] I.R. 317. See also, *Gammell* v. *Dublin C.C.* [1983] I.L.R.M. 413 (licensing of temporary dwellings.)
[84] *Irish Family Planning Assoc.* v. *Ryan* [1979] I.R. 295.
[85] *Jaggers Restaurant Ltd.* v. *Ahearne* [1988] I.R. 308.

Discipline

Two of the leading cases in this area have already been surveyed. In the first, *The State (Gleeson)* v. *Minister for Defence*,[86] the applicant had been summarily dismissed from the Defence Forces following an incident involving a group of soldiers of which he was one. This discharge was quashed by the Supreme Court, as the applicant had not been given an opportunity to meet the case against him or of dealing with the reason for his discharge. By contrast, in *The State (Duffy)* v. *Minister for Defence*,[87] the applicant had been dismissed from the Navy on the ground of inefficiency. The applicant's argument founded on breach of constitutional justice was rejected and *Gleeson* distinguished because the applicant had been warned as to why his position was in danger and allowed an opportunity to reply. A further point of distinction which is of particular relevance in discipline cases is that the procedural standards which must be met in cases involving alleged misconduct are higher than in the case of discharges on the grounds of inefficiency.[88]

The particular feature of interest in this area involves doubt over the extent to which one former principle retains vitality, namely the notion that in a disciplined organisation the need for unquestioning obedience to the commands of a superior was regarded as outweighing the advantages of constitutional justice.[89] Even the question of what is a "disciplined organisation" for this purpose is not clear-cut; but it may reasonably be regarded as constituting a spectrum running from (at the top) the prisons and the Defence Forces taking in, next, the Gardai, the fire services and the schools and then tailing off at the universities. However, over-precision in this area would be very unrealistic. The most that can be said is that, while there is no longer anything like a firm rule, this notion still retains some vitality; it is a factor which, in certain circumstances, will influence certain judges.

There is, for instance, High Court authority accepting the argument that

---

[86] [1976] I.R. 286. See p. 441. This decision has been applied in *Hogan* v. *Minister for Justice* [1976–1977] I.L.R.M. 184. and *The State (Furey)* v. *Minister for Defence* [1988] I.L.R.M. 89.

[87] [1979] I.L.R.M. 165 on which, see p. 455. See also, *The State (McGarrity)* v. *Deputy Garda Commissioner* (1978) 112 I.L.T.R. 25 (no obligation to give hearing to recruit Garda who was discharged at the end of his probationary period); *Delaney* v. *Garvey*, High Court, March 14, 1978. *Sed quaere* whether *McGarrity* is applicable in the case of a recruit discharged at the end of probationary period on the grounds of misconduct, *Chief Constable of N. Wales Police* v. *Evans* [1982] 1 W.L.R. 1155; *O'Rourke* v. *Miller* (1985) 58 A.L.R. 269.

[88] This point was not mentioned in *Duffy*. In both *Gleeson* and *Collins* v. *County Cork V.E.C.*, High Court, May 26, 1982 it was said that higher procedural standards were required where some specific act of misconduct or negligence is involved. See also *McDonough* v. *Minister for Defence* [1991] I.L.R.M. 115. In *Hickey* v. *The Eastern Health Board* Supreme Court, July 20, 1990, it appears to have been held that the rules of constitutional justice did not apply in a case where the applicant had been selected as the person to be made redundant, by the non-renewal of a temporary, part-time contract, in circumstances where there were other staff-members who had entered employment after her; yet who were not selected for redundancy. It was a supporting point in *Hickey* (at p. 9) that the applicant had not been removed for misconduct.

[89] *R.* v. *Army Council, ex p. Ravenscroft* [1917] 2 K.B. 504; *Ex p. Fry* [1954] 1 W.L.R. 730. *Cf.* "Their's not to make reply, Their's not to reason why, Their's but to do and die." (Tennyson, *The Charge of the Light Brigade*.)

special considerations apply in relation to the power of the state to dispense with the services of members of the Defence Forces, of the Garda Síochána and of the prison service "because it is of vital concern to the community as a whole that the members of these services should be completely trustworthy."[90] This factor played a part in *The State (Donnelly) v. Minister for Defence*[91] and in *The State (Jordan) v. Garda Commissioner.*[92] In *Donnelly* the applicant had been discharged from the Defence Forces as he was considered to have been a security risk. Some of the incidents in which the applicant was allegedly involved—such as the theft of a machine gun—were so serious that his commanding officer considered that they would warrant a discharge if no satisfactory explanation was forthcoming. Finlay P. agreed that the fact that the officer had drafted an application for Donnelly's discharge was "suspicious," but he was satisfied that this was simply a recommendation and that the matter would not have been carried any further if the applicant had given a satisfactory explanation of the incidents in question. Accordingly, Finlay P. ruled that there was a no bias or prejudgment of the issue on the part of the commanding officer. The judge also took the view that in the subsequent interviews the applicant had been given an adequate opportunity to make his own case. Nor was Finlay P. impressed by the argument that the applicant had never been convicted of any offences, whether under military law or the ordinary criminal law, since there was a "clear public necessity" that the military authorities should have the discretion to remove persons considered to be a security risk. Similar reasoning prevailed in *Jordan*, where a summary dismissal of a detective Garda was upheld. The applicant had been charged with the assault of a suspect (who was later to die while in police custody), but was acquitted following a trial in the Circuit Criminal Court. O'Hanlon J. considered that his defence in the criminal proceedings was such as to be tantamount to an admission that he had deceived the members of the Gardai who were investigating this incident by suppressing and concealing vital information. In these circumstances, and in view of the need to maintain public confidence in the members of the Force, it was held that the Garda Commissioner was entitled to dispense with the applicant's services without the need for a formal inquiry.

As against this, in *Garvey v. Ireland*, the Supreme Court majority firmly rejected the argument:

" . . . [T]hat the confidential and sensitive relationship that must necessarily exist between the Government of the day and the head of the national police force requires that the statutory right to remove a Commissioner from office at any time should not be interpreted as being shackled by an obligation to give a reason for its exercise. . . ."[93]

---

[90] *The State (Jordan) v. Garda Commissioner* [1987] I.L.R.M. 107, *per* O'Hanlon J.
[91] High Court, October 9, 1979.
[92] [1987] I.L.R.M. 107.
[93] [1981] I.R. 75, 102, *per* Henchy J.

Likewise, in *Gallagher* v. *Corrigan*,[94] which involved the disciplining of prison officers by the Deputy Governor, Blayney J. stated:

"I consider that the Deputy Governor, acting on behalf of the Governor, was discharging a quasi-judicial function. He had to weigh up evidence and come to a decision, and the sanction he imposed, reprimand with entry, was one which was intended to remain permanently on the Applicants' record and could obviously prejudice them in their careers. In addition, his decision included a recommendation that the Applicants should forfeit two increments, a recommendation which would obviously carry great weight with the Minister, and even though not an actual sanction in itself, was very close to being such. In view of this I consider that the Deputy Governor was not exercising powers which were merely magisterial."[95]

A compromise on the application of constitutional justice in the field of discipline is to say that, at any rate where fundamental interests are not at stake, the standard of constitutional justice may be relaxed in the case of a disciplinary body. For example, in *The State (Gallagher)* v. *Governor of Portlaoise Prison*[96] the applicant's privileges (such as associations with other prisoners and the receipt of letters) had been suspended following a hearing before the Governor when he had been found guilty of relatively minor disciplinary offences. Finlay P. rejected the argument that legal representation was required in this situation: Gallagher had been afforded an opportunity to speak on his own behalf and that sufficed. The judge also referred to the "partly magisterial" nature of the prison governor's functions and seemed to imply that it would be wrong for the courts to impose anything but the most rudimentary procedural standards in the context of prison discipline. This reluctance to exercise a supervisory jurisdiction over disciplinary awards is also to be found in *The State (Smullen)* v. *Duffy*.[97] This case arose following the effective expulsion of the participants in a gang fight at a community school. Although one of the boys involved had not been interviewed prior to his expulsion as he was in hospital, Finlay P. refused to find that this amounted to a breach of constitutional justice. He said that it was essential, in order to maintain peace and discipline within the school that the headmaster should be free to take immediate action. (It may also have been relevant that,

---

[94] High Court, February 1, 1988.
[95] *Ibid.* p. 11 of the judgment.
[96] High Court, May 18, 1977. See also, *The State (Gallagher)* v. *Governor of Portlaoise Prison*, High Court, April 25, 1983 in which, in regard to the withholding, by the Governor, of letters to bank managers, Mr. Tony Gregory T.D., and the Registrars of the High Court and the Supreme Court, McMahon J. said at p. 3 of the transcript: "I am satisfied that in dealing with the prisoner's letters, the Governor was not acting judicially and had no obligation to afford the prisoner a hearing. The Governor's decisions did not involve any disputed questions of fact and were based on his own views as to the requirements of security of the prison." Though note that in *Murtagh* v. *St. Emer's National School*, High Court, November 27, 1989 in spite of the extreme facts, Barron J. appeared to accept that the rules applied to a three days' suspension (though it indicated that the court might exercise its discretion to refuse relief on the ground of the trivial nature of the complaint). However, see now p. 493, n. 42.
[97] [1980] I.L.R.M. 82.

on the merits, the applicant appeared to have had no case.) All in all, it seems that it is only where there had been a substantial breach of natural justice in such cases that the courts will intervene.

The cases examined so far could, many of them, have been classified under an earlier heading since the sanction was dismissal. It is questionable whether the rules of natural justice apply at all where the punishment involved is the involuntary transfer of personnel. Such transfers are regarded as administrative decisions, and this fact when coupled with the public interest in maintaining the efficiency of the security forces, means that it would probably require something akin to mala fides before such an administrative decision could be successfully challenged.[98] Similarly, natural justice does not require a hearing prior to the suspension of a member of the Garda Síochána in the interests of good administration pending a fuller disciplinary hearing, even though financial loss may be caused as a result.[99]

Temporary release and parole

Two cases concerned the parole/release of prisoners, under the Prisoners (Temporary Release) Rules 1960.[1] In neither case was anything said about the notion, just examined, that constitutional justice should be applied in a less stringent form in certain types of disciplinary case. Possibly, the reason for this was that the fundamental right of liberty was involved. In the first of these cases, *The State (Murphy)* v. *Kielt*,[2] after serving four months, the prosecutor had been released for the remainder of his sentence. The release was subject to certain conditions including keeping the peace and being of good behaviour during the period of his release. However, whilst on release, the prosecutor was arrested and charged with attempted murder. The Governor "probably acting in a commonsense manner,"[3] treated the arrest on this serious charge as automatically terminating the temporary release. The High Court and, on appeal, the Supreme Court held that this termination was invalid for failure to observe the *audi alteram partem* rule, especially bearing in mind that charges are frequently dropped or not proceeded with. McCarthy J. remarked that while the suspicion regarding the person arrested must be assumed to be based on reasonable grounds, nevertheless the prisoner must be allowed the opportunity of contesting those grounds. Griffin J. added that: "[the grant and termination of a temporary release] are clearly acts which are administrative in nature. An informal procedure is all that is required provided that such procedure is conducted fairly."[4]

---

[98] *The State (Boyle)* v. *Governor of the Military Detention Barracks* [1980] I.L.R.M. 242; *The State (Smith & Fox)* v. *Governor of Military Detention Barracks* [1980] I.L.R.M. 208 (prison transfer cases); *Corliss* v. *Ireland*, High Court, July 23, 1984 (transfer of Gardaí). For *Reidy* v. *Minister for Agriculture*, High Court, June 1989, see p. 85.
[99] *McHugh* v. *Garda Commissioner* [1985] I.L.R.M. 606, 609–610. But *cf. Ní Bheoláin* v. *Dublin V.E.C.*, High Court, January 28, 1983 (natural justice applies to suspension without pay), and *Flynn* v. *An Post* [1987] I.R. 68. This topic is examined in more detail at pp. 466–467.
[1] S.I. 1960 No. 167.
[2] [1984] I.R. 458.
[3] *Ibid*. 462.
[4] *Ibid*. 472.

By contrast what had happened in *Ryan* v. *Governor of Limerick Prison*[5] was not that a release was terminated; but that no release was granted. In September 1988 the applicant had been granted a series of brief temporary releases, culminating in one from September 30 to October 7, accompanied by indications that his release might be definite, such as information from a welfare officer that he would be making monthly reports on the applicant to the Department of Justice and that the applicant's wife should return her prisoner's allowance book since he had been released from prison. However the applicant's release was not renewed after October 7 (because, so he was informed by the Governor, there had been a rise in the crime rate in Limerick). In one of the very few cases in which it has ever been held that the rules of constitutional justice did not apply, Murphy J. distinguished sharply between the termination of a release and the refusal of a release (as on the facts here). In the later case, no right to constitutional justice arose because "[t]he temporary release is a privilege or concession to which a person in custody has no right and indeed it has never been argued . . . that he should be heard in relation to any consideration given to the exercise of such a concession in his favour."[6] It is just possible, in the future, that, if the legitimate expectation doctrine[7] continues its present onward and unrestricted march, this passage may need to be reconsidered.

Property and planning

Even at times and in jurisdictions where the bounds of natural justice have been narrowly set, there has never been any doubt that the rules of natural justice apply to state interference with property rights.[8] Thus, the rules have been applied to compulsory purchase orders, and land acquisition pro-

---

[5] [1988] I.R. 198.
[6] *Ibid.* 199. Murphy J. then went on to make a related point (at 198–199):
" . . . a practice appears to have evolved of prison governors . . . granting temporary release for short periods. I think it reasonable to assume that this practice has been adopted by prison governors . . . to overcome or circumvent the problems identified in [*Murphy*]. By abbreviating the duration of temporary releases the prison governor sets himself the task of determining whether or not a fresh release should be granted rather than having to decide whether an existing one should be terminated. Obviously this procedure has the attraction that the former course does not involve any hearing or enquiry . . . whereas the latter does , . . Because this procedural change has such a dramatic effect I felt it appropriate to consider whether it constituted such a device as amounted to an abuse of the applicant's constitutional rights in the present case. In my view the answer must be in the negative. The temporary release is a privilege or concession to which a person in custody has no right. The fact that the release may be renewed on a number of occasions and not renewed subsequently does not confer any additional or new right on the prisoner."
[7] See Chap. 13.
[8] *Re Mountcharles' Estate* [1934] I.R. 754; *Foley* v. *Irish Land Commission* [1952] I.R. 118; *Re Roscrea Meat Products Estate* [1958] I.R. 47; *The State (Costello)* v. *Irish Land Commission* [1959] I.R. 353; *Clarke* v. *Irish Land Commission* [1976] I.R. 375; *Nolan* v. *Irish Land Commission* [1981] I.R. 23; *The State (Hussey)* v. *Irish Land Commission* [1983] I.L.R.M. 407; *O'-Brien* v. *Bord na Móna* [1983] I.R. 255. See also, *Irish Land Commission* v. *Hession* [1978] I.R. 322 (decision of Land Commission set aside where Commissioners acted on the basis of evidence not properly before them).

cedures; decisions of planning authorities and An Bord Pleanála[9] and the making of a preservation order by the Commissioners of Public Works.[10]

An interesting and novel application of the principles of natural justice is to be found in *The State (Philpott)* v. *Registrar of Titles*.[11] The applicant, who was the registered owner of certain freehold property, was informed that the respondent had entered an inhibition on the folio, which prevented all dealings with the land save with the consent of the respondent.[12] The applicant was engaged in the process of selling the lands in question when this inhibition had been entered without prior warning or notice. The Registrar had acted following correspondence with certain third parties in which the third parties claimed certain rights over the lands. Gannon J. ruled that because of the grave nature of the interference in the land, natural justice required that persons affected by the entry of an inhibition should be given prior notice and an opportunity to show cause why it should not be entered. The judge accepted that in order to protect the common fund, it would be "imprudent or impractical" to give the owner prior notice and a hearing in urgent cases. He held, however, that the instant case did not fall within this category and, accordingly, quashed the Registrar's decision. It is self-evident that this decision will be of great significance, not only to the Land Registry, but also for other systems of registration.[13]

Payments of grants, benefits and pensions

Irish courts have largely abandoned the formerly-held notion that the rules of constitutional justice did not apply to discretionary payments, such as grants, benefits or pensions, if the applicant had no statutory entitlement to them. A good example of the modern attitude is to be found in *The State (McConnell)* v. *Eastern Health Board*.[14] In this case an applicant who was entitled to a disability allowance had married, and his spouse was also in

[9] *Killiney and Ballybrack Residents Assoc.* v. *Minister for Local Government* (1978) 112 I.L.T.R. 69. *Geraghty* v. *Minister for Local Government* [1976] I.R. 153; *The State (Genport Ltd.)* v. *An Bord Pleanála* [1983] I.L.R.M. 12; *The State (Boyd)* v. *An Bord Pleanála*, High Court, February 18, 1983; *The State (C.I.E.)* v. *An Bord Pleanála*, Supreme Court, December 12, 1984; *The State (Hussey & Kenny)* v. *An Bord Pleanála*, Supreme Court, December 20, 1984 and *Frenchchurch Properties Ltd.* v. *Wexford C.C.*, High Court, April 12, 1991 (where Lynch J. said (at pp. 22–23) that generally a planning authority "is not obliged to enter into a dialogue . . . or to indicate in advance to an applicant the authority's thinking or views before deciding on the application"). However, the judgment goes on to qualify this remark.
[10] *O'Callaghan* v. *Commissioners of Public Works* [1985] I.L.R.M. 364.
[11] [1986] I.L.R.M. 499. For another case on property rights, see *Clancy* v. *Ireland* [1988] I.R. 326 described at p. 493.
[12] s.120 of the Registration of Title Act 1964 provides that the state will pay compensation to persons who suffer loss by reason of official errors in registration or entries obtained by fraud or forgery. S.121 of the Act enables the Registrar to take action by means of the entry of a caution to protect the state from possible claims.
[13] *e.g.* the registration of company charges under p. IV of the Companies Act 1963. See *R.* v. *Registrar of Companies, ex p. Easal Commodities Ltd.* [1986] Q.B. 1114 and Pye, "Certificate of Registration—An Impenetrable Shield No More?" (1985) 3 I.L.T.(N.S.) 213.
[14] High Court, June 1, 1983. See also, *McLoughlin* v. *Minister for Social Welfare* [1958] I.R. 1; *Kiely* v. *Minister for Social Welfare* [1971] I.R. 21; *Kiely* v. *Minister for Social Welfare (No. 2)* [1977] I.R. 297; *McKinley* v. *Minister for Defence* [1988] I.R. 139, 142.

receipt of unemployment benefit. Under the relevant regulations, a person in receipt of a disability allowance was obliged to inform the Health Board of any material change in their circumstances. The applicant was unaware of this obligation, and the fact of his marriage only came to the attention of the Health Board some 18 months later, resulting in a substantial overpayment of the disability allowance to the applicant. Hamilton J. quashed the respondent's decision to recoup the overpayment by means of weekly deductions from the applicant's allowance on the ground that no adequate opportunity had been given to the applicant to make representations prior to this decision; nor had he been afforded the opportunity to consider a report from the Department of Social Welfare concerning the case.

Legitimate expectations

This is a recently developed ground on which to apply the rules. It will be later described in Chapter 13.

General principle

Thus far, an attempt has been made to pigeon-hole most of the cases in which the constitutional justice principles have been said to apply. The next question is whether there is any general principle which would indicate the common ground shared by these cases and so assist a lawyer advising a client to predict whether the principles apply to new areas. The short answer is that the Irish courts have spent little time in looking for a guiding principle and, in any case, such a search would be inherently unlikely to be successful. Traditionally, the English courts invoked the quasi-judicial/administrative distinction to solve this problem. At the root of this classification lay the feeling that it was only decisions which were analogous to those taken by judges in courts which attracted the rules of natural justice. The reason was that these rules are, in essence, similar to the rules of procedure and evidence applied in a court. Thus, the rules of natural justice applied to quasi-judicial, but not administrative, decisions. Straightaway, this raises the difficulty of deciding precisely which decisions of government administration are to be regarded as analogous to decisions by courts, *i.e.* quasi-judicial. In England, various tests have been used (sometimes separately, sometimes in combination). First, does the test to be applied by the deciding body to require the determination of contested facts and/or the application of some fairly precise standard, as opposed to the exercise of a discretion. Secondly, reliance has been placed on the "trappings of the court" test: for instance, has the body taking the decision the power to summon witnesses and administer oaths? Does it usually sit in public?[15]

The administrative/quasi-judicial function classification has been used in the Irish case law, principally in regard to the first rule of constitutional justice but also, occasionally, in regard to the second rule as, for example, in *The*

---

[15] See pp. 233–234.

State (Williams) v. *Army Pensions Board.*[16] Here the Supreme Court classified the Board's decision as quasi-judicial because it was not exercising a discretion to award a widow's benefit, but was applying a fairly well-defined
statutory test, namely, whether a person's death was due to disease arising
during service with the United Nations. However, it is significant that, in *Williams*, Keane J. in the High Court differed from the Supreme Court in that he
classified the relevant function as "administrative" but then went on to say:

" . . . [I]t is clear from an abundance of recent authority, that even purely
administrative acts of persons such as [the Army Pensions Board and the
Minister for Defence] may be affected by the requirements of natural and
constitutional justice."[17]

A simpler test as to whether the rules apply is whether any serious individual interest is directly affected by a government action. The noticeable point
which emerges from the case law is that the rules have almost always been
held to apply (although, it may be, with a lower standard) even in a case like
East Donegal Co-Operatives Ltd. v. *Attorney-General*[18] which involved a discretionary decision. Indeed, it is remarkable how seldom the respondent has
even bothered to argue that the rules do not apply, confining himself instead
to arguments about the content of constitutional justice. For example, the
argument that a discretionary social welfare benefit is only a privilege is not
even mentioned in the judgments in the *Kiely* cases.[19]

However, apart from certain decisions of the D.P.P. and cases of waiver
which have been dealt with elsewhere, there are at least seven areas which
may be exempt from the rules. They are as follows:

(i) Legislation

It has just been stated the rules apply where any individual interest is
directly affected. However, as was demonstrated in the leading case of *Listowel U.D.C.* v. *McDonagh*,[20] the no-bias rule applies to delegated legislation, albeit in the attenuated form of the rule against mala fides. Thus, as
the New Zealand courts have made clear, it is sufficient that the donees of the
power to make delegated legislation approach the matter with an open mind
and genuinely satisfy themselves that the statutory criteria have been complied with.[21] They are not precluded from having a prior opinion. The pos-

---

[16] [1983] I.R. 308. For other examples, see *Re Roscrea Meat Products Estate* [1958] I.R. 47; *The State (Shannon Atlantic Fisheries Ltd.)* v. *McPolin* [1976] I.R. 93, 98; *Geraghty* v. *Minister for Local Government* [1976] I.R. 153; *Connolly* v. *McConnell* [1983] I.R. 172; *The State (Genport Ltd.)* v. *An Bord Pleanála* [1983] I.L.R.M. 12; *The State (Gallagher)* v. *Governor of Portlaoise Prison*, High Court, April 25, 1983. In some cases the courts have not used the term quasi-judicial, but have spoken instead of "a duty to act judicially": *McDonald* v. *Bord na gCon* [1965] I.R. 217; *O'Brien* v. *Bord na Móna* [1983] I.R. 255. This is only a terminological difference.
[17] [1981] I.L.R.M. at 382. See, to similar effect, *Flanagan* v. *U.C.D.* [1988] I.R. 724, 730 (University disciplinary committee "not a judicial body [but] under a duty to act judicially.")
[18] [1970] I.R. 317.
[19] On which, see p. 447
[20] [1968] I.R. 312.
[21] *Creednz Inc.* v. *Governor-General* [1981] 1 N.Z.L.R. 172.

ition is less definite in regard to the *audi alteram partem* rule. The rationale usually given for excluding legislative decisions from the scope of the rules is that the *audi alteram partem* rule, at any rate, is more appropriate where a compact range of facts is in issue—for example, in a dismissal case, whether an employee was dishonest—and less appropriate when a broader range of acts and considerations, for example, the economy or some other national interest, is concerned. In addition, of course, the fact that the principal type of legislation is an Act of Parliament, where all interests are supposedly represented and which is traditionally not subject to control by the courts during the process of legislation, has traditionally encouraged courts to avoid this area. (However, as a matter of practice rather than law, departments of state customarily consult interest groups about the content of draft bills). Traditionally, legislative decisions were taken as being beyond the reach of the rule.[22] This orthodoxy was confirmed by McMahon J. in the High Court in *Cassidy* v. *Minister for Industry and Commerce*[23] where he held, without discussion, that the rule did not apply to require consultation with a vintners' association before the making of a statutory instrument fixing maximum prices for the sale of intoxicating liquor in the Dundalk area.

On the other hand, in some cases involving delegated legislation, it has been decided or assumed (although again without any discussion of the difficulties) that the maker was under a duty to consult interested parties. For example, in *Burke* v. *Minister for Labour*[24] a Joint Labour Committee had fixed minimum wages for persons working in the hotel industry by means of an order made under the Industrial Relations Act 1946. Employers were obliged under pain of criminal sanction to respect this order and to comply with its terms. The employers' representatives wished to adduce evidence as to the real cost to the employers of the board and lodging provided for their employees, but the Committee went ahead and fixed minimum wages without regard to this evidence. The Supreme Court was of opinion that the Committee's refusal to admit such evidence rendered the order invalid. In the view of Henchy J.:

"Where Parliament has delegated functions of this nature, it is to be necessarily inferred as part of the legislative intention that the body which makes the orders will exercise its functions, not only with constitutional propriety and due regard to natural justice, but also within the framework of the

---

[22] *Bates* v. *Lord Hailsham* [1972] 1 W.L.R. 1373; *Essex C.C.* v. *Minister for Housing* (1967) 66 L.G.R. 23.
[23] [1978] I.R. 297. This point was not dealt with by the Supreme Court who found for the plaintiff on another ground: see pp. 522–523.
[24] [1979] I.R. 354. In *The State (Lynch)* v. *Cooney* [1982] I.R. 337 the Supreme Court appears to have accepted that the Minister could have been under a duty to consult with interested parties prior to the making of a banning order by way of statutory instrument under s.31 of the Broadcasting Authority Act 1960. However, the Minister's failure to do this was excused by the Supreme Court in view of the fact that given the circumstances of the case there was no time to hear the other side. In *U.S. International Tobacco Co. Ltd.* v. *Att.-Gen.* [1990] 1 I.R. 394. Hamilton P. reserved the question of whether the plaintiff company (whose products were the subject of an *ultra vires* banning order under the Health Act 1947) were entitled to be heard in advance of the making of such a statutory instrument.

terms and objects of the relevant Act and with basic fairness, reasonableness and good faith. The absoluteness of the delegation is susceptible of unjust and tyrannous abuse unless its operation is thus confined; so it is entirely proper to ascribe to the Oireachtas (being the Parliament of a State which is constitutionally bound to protect, by its laws, its citizens from unjust attack) an intention that the delegated functions must be exercised within those limitations."[25]

It may be that *Burke* has not laid down any general principle: the order which was invalidated in that case and the other cases cited on the previous page only applied to a small narrowly-defined category of situations and may be regarded as involving an administrative decision passed under the guise of delegated legislation. It is, perhaps, only in such unusual cases that the makers of delegated legislation are under a duty to observe the *audi alteram partem* rule.

(ii) Policy

In regard to the question of whether the *audi alteram partem* rule does or should apply, much the same issues are raised if the decision being taken involves policy rather than legislation (as might be expected since legislation is of course a special category of policy). Some of the underlying issues, which have been little discussed here, are teased out in the following passage by a British writer, Peter Cane, who begins by summarising the work of Lon Fuller who had advanced the view that natural justice was not suitable for dealing with what Professor Fuller called:

" . . . 'polycentric' disputes, that is disputes requiring account to be taken of a large number of interlocking and interacting interests and considerations. Fuller gave several examples of polycentric problems: how to divide between two art galleries 'in equal shares' a collection of paintings left by will; the task of establishing levels of wages and prices in a centrally controlled economy; . . .

The essential feature of the judicial process which makes it unsuitable to deal with polycentric problems is its bipolar and adversary nature. It is designed for one party to put forward a proposition which the other party denies or opposes. For example, the plaintiff asserts that he owns Blackacre and the defendant denies it; or the plaintiff asserts that he is entitled to compensation from the defendant and the latter denies it. None of Fuller's examples lends itself to being dealt with in this all-or-nothing way. For example one of the galleries might want the Picasso if it also gets the Cezanne but not the Turner; but it would not insist on the Picasso if it got the Turner; but would want both if it did not get the Cezanne. The other gallery might have an equally complex set of preferences, and the greater the number of works involved, the more complex the preference sets might become. Again, the workers in an industry might claim a wage increase of £X, and their employers might resist it and offer £Y; but the interests of

[25] [1979] I.R. 354, 361–362.

another part of the economy might be affected in such a way by either proposal that neither is acceptable.

. . . A good example in the administrative law context of a polycentric
problem is provided by a motorway inquiry. The ramifications of the
decision whether to build a motorway or not are enormous. At stake are
not only the interests of potential motorway users and of persons whose
land might be compulsorily acquired to provide a path for the motorway;
also involved are the inhabitants of villages and towns which will be
relieved of through-traffic by the motorway; British Rail may have an interest in inhibiting the development of alternative means for the transport of
goods; improved transport and communications facilities provided by the
motorway may benefit some businesses at the expense of others; and
motorways have, of course, serious environmental effects which lovers of
the countryside and people who live near the proposed route will be
anxious to avoid. Not only would accommodation and compromise
between these various interests be desirable, but also it may be that the best
solution would be some alternative to a motorway, or some alternative
route not already considered. The complexity of the issues involved makes
the model of bipolar adversary presentation of fixed positions by parties in
conflict seem inappropriate to the sound resolution of the issues involved.
And since the adversary model of dispute settlement is inappropriate, so
too is a standard of the validity of particular decisions on such issues which
rests on the rules of natural justice."[26]

A policy question may arise either in regard to a specific single case (as, for
instance, in the example discussed in the passage of the paintings) or in regard
to a potentially unlimited category of persons or situations which happen to
come within the boundaries of the decision (as, for instance, the wages
example). Nothing very much turns upon this distinction. (Indeed it is hard to
decide within which category the motorway example falls.) However, what
can perhaps be said is that cases within the second category look, and are,
rather closer to legislation than individual decisions and thus, as a general
principle, should be less likely to attract the rules of constitutional justice.

Unfortunately what little Irish case law there is in this areas focuses on only
a narrow and particular corner of it, namely policy-making by way of resolution of members or representatives.

The first case is *Ahern* v. *Kerry C.C.*[27] The issue here concerned the internal
proceedings of a local authority, albeit proceedings which were required by
statute (section 10 of the City and County Management (Amendment) Act
1955). The proceedings involved a motion that the estimates and ates proposed by the county manager should be adopted forthwith, although only a
single group of the estimates had been discussed. However the plaintiff-
councillor's argument on this point failed on the ground that the councillor

---

[26] *An Introduction to Administrative Law* (Clarendon Law Series, 1985), pp. 100–101. Professor
Fuller's article will be found at (1978) 92 Harv.L.Rev. 252.
[27] [1988] I.L.R.M. 392, 398.

had been present at the meeting and had an opportunity to speak and vote on the motion. What is of interest here is that it was assumed that constitutional justice did apply to the decision to adopt the estimates.

However, as this point was assumed without discussion, the other two cases in this area—both trade union cases—may be regarded as more authoritative. The first of these is *Rodgers* v. *I.T.G.W.U.*[28]; which arose out of an agreement reached between the Cork dockers and their employers, and related to the provision of pension rights coupled with a universal compulsory retiring age. This led to the passage, at a meeting of the Dockers Section, No. 9 Branch, Cork, of the Defendant Union of a motion which resolved that members of the Section must retire upon reaching the age of 65. The plaintiff, who was an over-age docker, based his argument on the ground that he had not been given notice that the subject of compulsory retirement would be discussed. The significant point is that Finlay P. held that the plaintiff had a right to know that compulsory retirement was to be discussed. The President grounded this right upon the following reasoning:

> "The constitutional right to the formation of trade unions [under Art. 40.6. iii] involves, of necessity, the right to join or not to join existing trade unions. See the *Educational Company of Ireland Ltd.* v. *Fitzpatrick*. It is, in my view, a necessary corollary of the right to join and become a member of a trade union that the right must extend to taking part in the democratic process provided by it and in particular to taking part in the decision making processes within the rules of the trade union."[29]

In the second case, *Doyle* v. *Croke*[30] the plaintiffs were members of the I.T.G.W.U. and former employees of a company which had gone into liquidation. A strike committee had been set up mainly to negotiate redundancy payments greater than the statutory minimum on behalf of the employees all of whom were members of the defendant-union. The strike committee organised a picket against the employer's premises.

Two resolutions were passed at meetings of union members. The first, in June, laid it down that workers who thenceforth did not perform satisfactory picket duty would not be represented by the strike committee in pursuance of redundancy payments or permitted to participate in any lump sum which might be obtained from the employer. However, Costello J. found that, for whatever practical reason of difficulty in keeping count of who in fact had completed the requisite six-hour picket shift, compliance with the resolution's terms was not required when it came to compiling the list of those entitled to share in the settlement of the union's claim. The second meeting was held in November. Prior to the meeting, the strike committee had drawn up the list

[28] [1978] I.L.R.M. 51.

[29] *Ibid.* Immediately after this passage, Finlay P. went on to suggest (although the point did not arise on the facts of the instant case) that the plaintiff's right to participate in the decision-making processes of the union could be restricted by the terms of the union rule book. This has been criticised on the ground that waiver of constitutional rights requires free and informed consent: Kerr and Whyte, *Irish Trade Union* (Professional Books Ltd., 1985), p. 26.

[30] High Court, May 6, 1988.

already mentioned of 150 employees (out of a total of 270 involved) among whom it was proposed to divide the settlement of £380,000. And it was submitted by the defendants that the resolution passed at the November meeting could be relied upon both as impliedly validating the June resolution (the defects of which are examined in the next paragraph) and also as approving the list, notwithstanding the fact that it was not compiled in accord with the June resolution. The 83 plaintiffs in the case were among the employees who were not to share in the settlement moneys. In the first place, Costello J. found that the plaintiffs had not been given adequate notice in respect of either resolution. Notice of the June meeting had been posted in the hut erected for members on picket duty but there was no reference to the business to be transacted and, in particular, there was no reference that a resolution would be discussed affecting members' rights. Again, some of the members did not do picket duty and, whilst a large number of these members saw either the notice or learnt of the June meeting by word of mouth, a significant number did not know that it was to be held. As regards the November meeting, only those 150 members of the union who were on the list were notified that the meeting was to be held. Other members learnt of the meeting and attended but were informed that they would not be permitted to vote at it.

Thus, in *Doyle*, as in *Rodgers*, the central question was whether "the right to fair procedures" (the phrase, constitutional justice not being used in either case though it seems that no significance was attached to this) extended to resolutions passed at trade union meetings. Costello J. grounded his decision that it did so apply upon three bases. The first was Article 40.6.1. iii (the constitutional rights of association) as interpreted in *Rodgers*, a case which was quoted with approval. The second was Lord Denning M.R.'s well-known observation in *Breen* v. *A.E.U.*[31] that (as it was summarised in *Doyle*): "even though the rules of a union might provide committees with wide discretionary powers . . . the contract between the members would be construed as containing an implied term that the discretion would be exercised fairly."[32] Thirdly, Costello J. invoked the generalised guarantee to the citizen of basic fairness of procedures established in *Re Haughey*.[33]

By way of summing up, one should ask what light these two trade union cases shed upon the question of whether constitutional justice applied to policy-resolutions? What, to give an example, if the decision under review was concerned with a trade union resolution authorising a strike in which the complainant was not himself involved? The full-blooded application of the *Rodgers ratio*—which was based on the idea of democratic processes in a trade union—might well lead to the idea that *audi alteram partem* should apply. As against this, on the facts of both *Rodgers* and *Doyle*, the plaintiff's own significant material interests were peculiarly engaged in the resolution. Indeed in *Doyle*, the resolution might be regarded as constituting, with its application, a single transaction which substantially disadvantaged the plain-

[31] [1971] 2 Q.B. 175, 190.
[32] At 17.
[33] [1971] I.R. 217, 264. See p. 415.

tiffs. It is very significant that in the more convincing of the judgments—that in *Doyle*—Costello J. was careful to restrict the scope of his *ratio* to what was necessary to "protect individual members against procedures which might be unfair to them" or to "decision[s] materially affecting the members' rights."[34] It appears then, from both these careful formulae and the peculiar facts of the cases, that there are restrictions upon the resolutions to which the rules apply.

Thus in regard to policy decisions which affect only individuals (as distinct from quasi-legislative actions) it seems that it is now too late in the day to argue that such decisions do not attract the rules. Even in regard to the deportation of a (non-EEC) alien, it seems that the *audi alteram partem* rule probably has to be followed.[35]

(iii) Suspension

Generally speaking, the rules of constitutional justice do not apply to suspensions. For instance, in *Rochford* v. *Storey*,[36] the plaintiffs had been suspended from membership of a trade union sporting club following a dispute over the plaintiff's eligibility for membership. The suspensions had been imposed when the plaintiffs had failed to attend a meeting at which they had been requested to produce evidence of their entitlement to become full members of the club. Even though O'Hanlon J. concluded that natural justice was complied with when the plaintiffs had been put on notice by letter that the validity of their membership was in dispute, he was also of opinion that the decision to suspend did not attract the rules. The reason was that this was not a suspension inflicted by way of punishment; but rather a suspension made as a holding operation pending enquiries. The same distinction was adopted by Barr J. in *Quirke* v. *Bord Luthchleas na hEireann*[37]:

" . . . the suspension of a member by a body such as B.L.E. or a trade union or professional association may take two different forms. On the one hand, it may be imposed as a holding operation pending the investigation of a complaint. Such a suspension does not imply that there has been a finding of any misbehaviour or breach of rules by the suspended person, but merely that an allegation of some such impropriety or misconduct has been made against the member in question. On the other hand, a suspension may be imposed not as a holding operation pending the outcome of an inquiry, but as a penalty by way of punishment of a member who has been

[34] At pp. 13, 16.

[35] *Abdelkefi* v. *Minister for Justice* [1984] I.L.R.M. 138; *Ghneim* v. *Minister for Justice, Irish Times*, September 2, 1989 (although here there was also a large element of legitimate expectation). *A contra*: *Pok Sun Shun* v. *Ireland* [1986] I.L.R.M. 593, 599 where Costello J. held that because of "the special control of aliens which every State must exercise" natural justice did not require the Minister for Justice to inform an applicant of the information on the files and give him an opportunity to comment before refusing a certificate of naturalisation under the provisions of the Irish Citizenship and Nationality Act 1956. The tenor of *Fajujonu* v. *Minister for Justice* [1990] I.L.R.M. 234 (see pp. 537–538) is all in favour of there being such a right although, on the facts of the case, the question did not arise.

[36] High Court, November 4, 1982. See also, *McHugh* v. *Garda Commissioner* [1985] I.L.R.M. 606.

[37] [1988] I.R. 83, 87.

found guilty of misconduct or breach of rules. The importance of the distinction is that where a suspension is imposed by way of punishment, it follows that the body in question has found its member guilty of significant misconduct or breach of rules."

However, in line with this passage, it has also been held in Ireland that the rules would apply where the suspension would have the effect of interfering with the affected individual's livelihood, as where he is suspended without pay or where the suspension imputes grave misconduct.[38] In addition, as explained already,[39] there is an argument that fair procedure may also require that the final, substantive decision should be taken with as little delay as possible so that the person affected is not kept in suspense longer than is necessary.

Clancy v. *Ireland*[40] involved a situation which was analogous to temporary suspension. The case concerned the constitutionality of the Offences against the State (Amendment) Act 1985. The 1985 Act provides a scheme for dealing with property which, but for the Offences Against the State Act 1939 (which has the automatic effect of vesting such property in the Minister for Justice) would be the property of an "unlawful organisation" under the 1939 Act. Under the 1985 Act, if the Minister for Justice is of opinion that certain moneys held by a bank is property of this kind, then he is given certain draconian powers: he is empowered to freeze those moneys and cause the bank to pay them into the High Court. The significant point is that the statute permits this to be done— and it had been done in the present case—entirely without notice to the account holder. However, it was open to anyone to reclaim the funds on the basis that the moneys belong to them and not to an illegal organisation. What saved the Act from unconstitutionality was that this claim was to be brought in the High Court, where the claimant is, of course, entitled to a fair hearing. The result in *Clancy* is in line with the law on temporary suspension in that here too what was involved was a provisional interference—in this case with property rights—but before it could be made permanent, the owner was allowed a hearing.

(iv) Trivial cases

One of the most fundamental ideas in the law is that the courts, especially the High Court will not interfere where the individual interest affected by a decision is too trivial to warrant such attention (a notion expressed in the maxim, *de minimis non curat lex*). This principle would have an obvious application in an attempt to invoke constitutional justice to control the operation of (say) a sports or social club. It has, however, not been much considered in Irish law[41] and was not, for example, discussed in *Rochford* v.

---

[38] *Flynn* v. *An Post* [1987] I.R. 68; *Ní Bheoláin* v. *Dublin V.E.C.*, High Court, January 28, 1983; *Collins* v. *Cork V.E.C.*, Supreme Court, March 18, 1983; *The State (Donegal V.E.C.) v. Minister for Education* [1985] I.R. 56.
[39] See pp. 465–469.
[40] [1988] I.R. 326.
[41] But see the comments of Hederman J. in *Murtagh* v. *Board of St. Emer's National School*, Supreme Court, March 7, 1991: "A three day suspension for an admitted breach of discipline would be no more reviewable by the High Court than, for example, the ordering of a pupil . . . to write out lines. . . ."

Storey—it would not, of course, have been relevant in *Quirke* v. *Bord Luthchleas na hÉireann* for the reason that what was involved in that case was the disqualification of an international athlete.

(v) Margin of appreciation

As is demonstrated at several points in this chapter, the constitutional justice rules allow a considerable margin of appreciation and the courts have held that within these broad limits (and subject, of course, to any particular procedural regulations) it is for the deciding agency itself to exercise "a certain discretion as to the manner in which it conducts the proceedings."[42] However, following the general principles which govern the exercise of any discretion, substantive or procedural, such a discretion must be genuinely exercised and it must be exercised fairly and reasonably.[43] Another type of exemption which exists in England—but which is probably not part of Irish law—stems from the idea that where a tribunal or other public authority has formulated a comprehensive, detailed code of procedure, the onus on a person who seeks to establish that this code is inconsistent with natural justice is very heavy.[44] By contrast, in Ireland, constitutional justice is not just a general norm of statutory interpretation; it also, as has been seen, enjoys the support of Article 40.3 of the Constitution, and thus the courts will readily inject the rules of constitutional justice into even a comprehensive procedural code.[45]

(vi) Countervailing factors

In a number of cases, some of which have already been described, countervailing factors have been said to justify a failure to observe the rules of constitutional justice (or, more correctly, just the *audi alteram partem* limb).[46] Examples of such countervailing policies include the fact that the rule would cause a delay or otherwise defeat the object of the public authority's action[47] or that it was impossible for the public authority to contact the person affected to elicit his representations.[48] A graphic illustration occurred in *O'Callaghan* v. *Commissioners of Public Works*.[49] The plaintiff was a farmer who

---

[42] *The State (Boyle)* v. *General Medical Services (Payments) Board* [1981] I.L.R.M. 14, 16, *per* Keane J. See also *The State (Genport Ltd.)* [1983] I.L.R.M. 12, 16.
[43] *Irish Family Planning Assoc.* v. *Ryan* [1979] I.R. 295. Note the significant differences in tone between O'Higgins C.J. (S.C.) and that of Hamilton J. (H.C.).
[44] Evans, "Some Limits to the Scope of Natural Justice" (1973) 36 M.L.R. 439. There is some Irish support for this point of view (see, *e.g. The State (Fagan)* v. *Governor of Mountjoy Prison*, High Court, March 6, 1978) but generally the courts will, if necessary, superimpose constitutional standards on the terms of a statute: see, *e.g. O'Domhnaill* v. *Merrick* [1984] I.R. 151 and *Toai* v. *Duignan* [1991] I.L.R.M. 140.
[45] See, *e.g. East Donegal Co-Operatives Ltd.* v. *Att.-Gen.* [1970] I.R. 317; *Kiely* v. *Minister for Social Welfare (No. 2)* [1977] I.R. 267.
[46] *e.g. The State (Donnelly)* v. *Minister for Defence*, High Court, October 9, 1979; *The State (Jordan)* v. *Garda Commissioner* [1987] I.L.R.M. (need to maintain public confidence in integrity of members of Defence Forces and Gardai).
[47] *The State (Lynch)* v. *Cooney* [1982] I.R. 337. *The State (Philpott)* v. *Registrar of Titles* [1986] I.L.R.M. 499.
[48] *Irish Family Planning Assoc. Ltd.* v. *Ryan* [1979] I.R. 295, 313–314, *per* O'Higgins C.J.
[49] [1985] I.L.R.M. 364.

owned a 2,000-year-old promontory fort which had been listed as a "national monument" under the National Monuments Acts 1930–1954. Ignoring the order, he instructed an agricultural contractor to plough up the land near the fort. Soon the ploughing had to be temporarily abandoned. The reason for this was damage to the plough. However, the imminent resumption of the work led the Commissioners to Public Works to make a preservation order which extended the Commissioners' powers to protect the fort. The Supreme Court rejected the argument that the Commissioners ought to have allowed the plaintiff farmer an opportunity to put forward any objection he might have had to the making of the preservation order. O'Higgins C.J. said:

> "Here an emergency had been created by the plaintiff's own action in defiance of his legal obligations. If the Commissioners had hesitated in acting as they did, the monument which it was their duty to preserve would have been seriously damaged or destroyed. Further, it was not possible to contact the plaintiff, because his address was not then known and did not become known to the Commissioners until sometime later."[50]

Again, in *The State (Lynch)* v. *Cooney* O'Higgins C.J. justified the Minister for Post and Telegraph's refusal to apply the *audi alteram partem* rule before making a regulation which, *inter alia*, banned the applicant from making a party political broadcast on the ground that "the time was short and a decision was urgent. There was no opportunity for debate or parley and, indeed, to permit or seek such might, in the circumstances, have defeated the very object and purpose of the section."[51] This suggests that there is a reservoir of discretionary power to which the principles of constitutional justice do not apply, which is wider than the specific examples mentioned in the previous paragraph. If this reading is correct, it is obviously pregnant with considerable possibilities for the future. It is also noteworthy that the courts have chosen to create a distinct category of exemption rather than simply to exercise their long-established discretion to refuse to grant relief.[52]

(vii) Private transactions and arrangements

As illustrated earlier,[53] there is no doubt that the constitutional justice precepts apply to cases of deprivation of livelihood, even in the private law field. This fact suggests the question of whether constitutional justice applies generally to private law transactions and arrangements. A mechanism for its importation is readily available in the form of the well-established notion that constitutional justice can be regarded, in appropriate circumstances, as an implicit term in a contract and this could presumably, with equal logic, be extended to other purely private law transactions such as an instrument constituting a settlement. However, whilst this area is almost bereft of helpful

---

[50] [1985] I.L.R.M. 373–374.
[51] [1982] I.R. 337, 365. See also his comments in *Irish Family Planning Assoc.* v. *Ryan* [1979] I.R. 295, 313. See too, *The State (Smullen)* v. *Duffy* [1980] I.L.R.M. 46.
[52] On which see Chap. 11.5.
[53] See pp. 472–477.

(Irish or English) authority, judicial or academic, it is suggested that, absent exceptional areas such as the livelihood cases, constitutional justice does not apply in the private law arena. It was stated, emphatically, in a Northern Irish case that[54]:

> "As a matter of company law, the rules of natural justice have no application to the decision of the members in general meeting. Such members are free to vote as their own individual interests and inclinations may require."

Again, in *Hounslow L.B.C.* v. *Twickenham Garden Developments Ltd.*,[55] a case in which an architect had given notice, under the normal term in a building contract, that the contractor had failed to proceed with the work regularly and diligently, the English High Court found that the principles of natural justice did not apply to an architect's notice. Megarry J. stated: "The principles of natural justice are of wide application and great importance but they must be confined within proper limits and not allowed to run wild."[56] This last quotation suggests that in England short shrift would be given to suggestions that, for instance: objects of a power of appointment must be heard before the donee of the power chooses among them; that a testator should solicit representations from a fond relative whom he intends to 'leave out' of the will; or that a tenant must be heard before a landlord issues a notice to quit. It would seem that this would also be true of this jurisdiction: the imposition of a formalised fair procedure is more appropriate when one is dealing with a powerful public or quasi-public body than with a private company or individual. There is a further point supporting this observation: as mentioned at the very start of this chapter, there is an intimate connection between natural or constitutional justice and, on the other hand, substantive controls imposed upon a decision-maker, as regards for example, "reasonableness" (covered in the next chapter). If, as is the case, persons governed exclusively by private law are not subject to these substantive controls—may indeed be as whimsical or capricious as they wish—then it would be anomalous if they were to be subjected to constitutional justice. The very fact that one is unable to find authorities in which the point has even been argued, much less accepted by the courts, is indicative of the fact that the rules of constitutional justice do not apply generally in the private law field.

5. Concluding Comment

It is useful to illustrate the difficulties inherent in constitutional justice by way of the *Kiely* saga. Mrs. Kiely's claim for a widow's benefit was rejected by a deciding officer and, on appeal, by the appeals officer in the Department of

---

[54] *Hawthorn* v. *Ulster Flying Club Ltd.* [1986] N.I.J.B. 56, 94. However, on the facts of the case, Murray J. held that the rules applied to a decision to expel a member; *a contra: Gaiman* v. *National Association for Mental Health* [1970] 2 All E.R. 362.
[55] [1970] 3 All E.R. 326.
[56] *Ibid.* 347.

Social Welfare; the appeals officer's decision was struck down on review by the High Court[57]; the case was reheard by a second appeals officer who decided against the claimant; this decision was struck down in the Supreme Court[58]; the question was then decided by a third appeals officer, who reached the same decision as his two colleagues, and this time there was no review so that the decision was effective. It might well be asked rhetorically: who benefited from this substantial expenditure of legal costs and court time? Nor is the *Kiely* saga unique. The law reports are replete with judicial statements, offered, as consolation prizes, in cases in which some administrative action has been condemned for violation of constitutional justice, to the effect that the public authority may repeat the process, even reaching the same conclusion, provided only that the proper procedure is followed on the subsequent occasion.[59]

Neither the advantages nor the disadvantages of constitutional justice have yet been researched empirically. However, it seems reasonable to make the following assumptions: first, that greater procedural complexity increases delay and expense[60]; secondly, that the rules promote excessive caution among public servants, particularly at the lower levels where the officials cannot reasonably be expected to be familiar with the novel, and sometimes rather artificial, requirements of constitutional justice. To take the example of an official charged with the duty of awarding a licence: he will know that it is more likely that the refusal of a licence will be challenged by a disappointed applicant than that an erroneous award of a licence will be challenged by a competitor or other member of the public. In view of this, there is a pressure, which is contrary to the public interest, upon the administrator to grant the licence. One of the consequences of the constitutional justice rules is to increase this pressure by imposing something analogous to the procedures of a law court in the very different circumstances of a tribunal or public authority. A British Government Lawyer has remarked that:

> "while presently public administration is honest there is a risk that, as a result of judicial review, people will go through a charade: applicants to put themselves in the best possible position and the authority to defend themselves."[61]

As against this, constitutional justice is taken to carry four advantages. In the first place, an impartial decision-maker and an opportunity for the person affected to put forward his comments both help to promote an "appropriate" result. (The decision may be too subjective to speak of the *correct result*). As Megarry J. remarked in a notable passage:

[57] *Keily* v. *Minister for Social Welfare* [1971] I.R. 21.
[58] *Kiely* v. *Minister for Social Welfare (No. 2)* [1977] I.R. 267.
[59] See, *e.g. Quirke* v. *Burd Luthchleas na hEireann* [1988] I.R. 83, 88, *per* Barr J.
[60] For a rare judicial acknowledgment of these difficulties, see the comments of Megarry J. in *McInnes* v. *Onslow-Fane* [1978] 1 W.L.R. 1520.
[61] Referred to in Woolf, *Protection of the Public—A New Challenge*, p. 18. In Cork, junior staff in the Department of Social Welfare are warned that they are "walking through a legal minefield."

"As everyone who has anything to do with the law well knows, the path of the law is strewn with examples of open and shut cases which, somehow, were not; of unanswerable charges which, in the event, were completely answered; of inexplicable conduct which was fully explained; of fixed and unalterable determinations that, by discussion, suffered a change."[62]

A hearing means that the risk of injustice caused by acting on an *ex parte* view of the situation will have been obviated. Even if the facts or arguments adduced by the person affected do not cause the decision to be reversed, they may lead to its being varied and thus, for instance, it has been held, in cases involving disciplinary punishments, that there is a right to be heard in mitigation.[63] It has been said that " . . . the holder's office being such a crucial part of his life, basic fairness requires that he should not be sundered from it without first being given a meaningful opportunity of being heard, if only *ad misericordiam*."[64]

Secondly, the duty to give reasons for a public authority's proposed decision (which is included in the *audi alteram partem* rule) might disclose to the person affected that the decision was being taken on grounds, or in circumstances, which rendered it substantially invalid. In such a case, the rule would assist the person affected by giving him information which would enable him to launch an action for judicial review on substantive grounds or, perhaps, to refer the matter to the Ombudsman or a T.D. or to seek some other sanction. The point was put eloquently in the following passage from Henchy J.'s judgment in *Garvey* v. *Ireland*:

"If, by maintaining an obscuring silence, a Government could render their act of dismissal impenetrable as to its reasons and unreviewable as to its method, an office-holder such as the plaintiff could have his livelihood snatched from him, his chosen career snuffed out, his pension prospects dashed and his reputation irretrievably tarnished, without any hope of redress, no matter how unjustified or unfair his dismissal might be. I doubt if it would be even contended that the statutory power of removal from office could validly be used to dismiss a person for an unconstitutional reason (for example, because of his race, creed or colour); yet if such were to happen, and suddenness and silence were to be allowed to curtain off the dismissal from judicial scrutiny, the dismissed person, far from getting the constitutionally guaranteed protection from unjust attack, would be aban-

---

[62] *John* v. *Rees* [1970] Ch. 345, 402.

[63] *R. (Hennessy)* v. *Department of Education* [1980] N.I. 109; *The State (Grahame)* v. *Racing Board*, High Court, November 22, 1983.

[64] *Garvey* v. *Ireland* [1981] I.R. 75, 102. Henchy J. pointed out that, in the context of a removal from office, another benefit of the *audi alteram partem* rule is that it requires the ground on which the office-holder was removed to be authoritatively stated, and that this may be less discreditable than the grounds which might otherwise be suspected. For an earlier Supreme Court decision denying that natural justice extends to *ad misericordiam* pleas, see *The State (Costello)* v. *Irish Land Commission* [1959] I.R. 353.

doned to the consequence of an unjust, unconstitutional and ruinous decision."[65]

Thirdly, it is a matter of satisfaction and dignity to the individual that he should have his say before a decision is taken against him by a governmental agency. (This is the equivalent, in the administrative sphere, of "the day in court"). In *R. (Smyth)* v. *C. Antrim Coroner*[66] it was sought to quash the verdict returned by a coroner's jury on the grounds that, in breach of the relevant regulations, the coroner had failed to sum up the evidence to the jury. Quashing the verdict, Kelly J. conceded that another jury, hearing the same evidence and assisted by a proper and adequate summing up of it by the coroner, might come to exactly the same verdict; but held that the next-of-kin were entitled "to have their unhappiness tempered by the knowledge that such a verdict was reached by a considered and regular inquiry."

Finally, an open consistent procedure in which the state agency taking the decision is seen to be impartial is necessary to maintain the confidence of the general public in the institutions of government. For example, in a case where the failure of a Joint Labour Committee to hear certain relevant evidence was found to be contrary to the principle of *audi alteram partem*, Henchy J. adverted to the dangers of the "no merits" argument:

"Even if such evidence would have made no difference, the Committee by rejecting it unheard and unconsidered, left themselves open to the imputation of bias, unfairness and prejudice."[67]

The relative importance which is to be assigned to the disadvantages and to each of the distinct advantages is relevant in considering two policy questions. The first issue, which has divided the judiciary in a number of jurisdictions, and which has arisen mainly in the context of the *audi alteram partem* limb of constitutional justice, is whether a failure to follow the rules is fatal where it is clear that the case was correctly decided, albeit by way of a wrongful procedure.

In Ireland, too, diametrically opposing views have been given to this conundrum, though usually without much in the way of discussion or consideration of precedent. In *Glover* v. *B.L.N. Ltd.*,[68] the majority brushed aside the submission that, if a hearing had been held, there was nothing the plaintiff could have said anyway, with Walsh J. remarking:

"This proposition only has to be stated to be rejected. The obligation to give a fair hearing to the guilty is just as great as the obligation to give a fair hearing to the innocent."[69]

The dissenting judge in *Glover*, Fitzgerald J., was equally strong and terse in

[65] [1981] I.R. 75, 101.
[66] [1980] N.I. 123.
[67] *Burke* v. *Minister for Labour* [1979] I.R. 354, 362. See also the comments of O'Donnell L.J. in *R. (Hennessy)* v. *Department of the Environment* [1980] N.I. 109.
[69] [1973] I.R. 388.
[69] *Ibid.* 429.

the opposite sense. Again, in *O'Brien* v. *Bord na Moná*,[70] Finlay P. stated on behalf of the Supreme Court that:

"A necessity for the observance of natural justice in the process of compulsory acquisition of property is too fundamental and important to be supplied by proof that objections would have been rejected if they had been entertained."[71]

By contrast, in *Corrigan* v. *Irish Land Commission*,[72] another case on compulsory acquisition of land, Henchy J. considered that there was an "overriding reason" why in the circumstances of this case the doctrine of estoppel by conduct should apply: this was that it was inconceivable on the facts "that a fresh hearing could have any result other than a finding adverse to the appellant."

Even overlooking the preliminary difficulty of a court being sure that the applicant had an impossible case, this is a difficult question. The most that can be said is that a judge will be more likely to strike down the decision impugned if he assigns importance to the advantages of "the day in court" and confidence in public administration and less likely to do so if he regards these advantages as trivial and outweighed by the disadvantages which were mentioned at the start of this Part. In addition, the more serious the consequences for the aggrieved party, the less likely the courts are to refuse relief.[73]

It is, of course, always possible for the court to avoid laying down any general principle and, instead, to determine the outcome of the case by refusing relief on discretionary grounds and this approach has often been adopted.[74]

The second policy question arising in this area concerns the effect of an appeal: where a decision is taken in breach of the rules of constitutional justice, is this defect cured where a right of appeal is exercised to a court (or other body) in which the rules are observed. It has been decided that an

[70] [1983] I.R. 266. See Coffey, "Procedural Curbs on Powers of Compulsory Acquisition" (1984) 6 D.U.L.J.(N.S.) 152. For other authorities along the same lines, see *Maunsell* v. *Minister for Education* [1940] I.R. 213; *General Medical Council* v. *Spackman* [1943] A.C. 627; *Ridge* v. *Baldwin* [1964] A.C. 40; *The State (Crothers)* v. *Kelly* [1978] I.L.R.M. 167 and see generally Clark, "Natural Justice: Substance or Shadow?" [1975] *Public Law* 27.
[71] [1983] I.R. 287.
[72] [1977] I.R. 317, 327. See also, to like effect: *Ward* v. *Bradford Corporation* (1970) 70 L.G.R. 27; *Glynn* v. *Keele University* [1971] 1 W.L.R. 487; *Irish Family Planning Assoc.* v. *Ryan* [1979] I.R. 295, 319; *R. (McPherson)* v. *Ministry of Education* [1980] N.I. 115n; *Cheall* v. *A.P.E.X.* [1983] 2 A.C. 109; and *Green* v. *South Eastern Health Board*, High Court (Barron J.) December 11, 1987. Note also the comments of Lord Denning in *R.* v. *Home Secretary, ex p. Mughal* [1974] Q.B. 313, 325. "Only too often the people who have done wrong seek to invoke the rules of natural justice in order to avoid the consequences."
[73] See, *e.g. R. (Hennessy)* v. *Department of the Environment* [1980] N.I. 109; *O'Brien* v. *Bord na Mona* [1983] I.R. 255.
[74] *Fulbrook* v. *Berkshire Magistrates' Courts* (1970) 69 L.G.R. 75; *Ward* v. *Bradford Corporation* (1971) 70 L.G.R. 27; *Glynn* v. *Keele University* [1971] 1 W.L.R. 487; *R. (McPherson)* v. *Department of Education* [1980] N.I. 115n. On the question of the discretionary character of the remedies, see further, Chap. 11.5.

appeal does not cure the flaw in the original decision.[75] However, the significance of this ruling has been reduced by the gloss introduced, in *Gammell* v. *Dublin C.C.*,[76] namely that certain categories of "appeal" can be treated as part of the initial decision.

---

[76] *Leary* v. *National Union of Vehicle Builders* [1971] Ch. 34; *Ingle* v. *O'Brien* (1975) 109 I.L.T.R. 9; *Moran* v. *Att.-Gen.* [1976] I.R. 400; *Irish Family Planning Assoc.* v. *Ryan* [1979] I.R. 295. *A contra, The State (Stanbridge)* v. *Mahon* [1979] I.R. 217; *Calvin* v. *Carr* [1980] A.C. 574 and *The State (Collins)* v. *Ruane* [1984] I.R. 105, 124, *per* Henchy J. and *Halal Meat Packers Ltd.* v. *E.A.T.* [1990] I.L.R.M. 293, 309.

[77] [1983] I.L.R.M. 413. See further, pp. 454–457.

R.T.C. LIBRARY
LETTERKENNY

CHAPTER 10

CONTROL OF DISCRETIONARY POWERS

1. Discretionary Power

There is a distinction between decisions involving the resolution of disputed questions of fact coupled with the application of pre-existing law (or, at least, a guideline) and, on the other hand, those involving the exercise of discretionary power. The first type of decision is quintessentially the domain of a court or tribunal, though, often and on a quite random basis, it may be vested in a Minister or local authority.[1] The second type of decision—that is where a discretionary or policy function is being exercised—may be illustrated by the following examples:

"On the application of . . . a person who proposes to carry on the business of a livestock mart . . . in such form . . . as the Minister [for Agriculture] may direct, the Minister may, at his discretion, grant or refuse to grant a licence authorising the carrying on of the business of a livestock mart . . ."[2]

"A sanitary authority may by order prohibit the erection . . . of temporary dwellings on any land or water in their sanitary district if they are of opinion that such erection . . . would be prejudicial to public health. . . ."[3]

In spite of the apparent *carte blanche* which expressions like " . . . may, at his discretion . . . 'or' . . . if they are of opinion . . . " appear to bestow, discretionary powers are subject to the general requirements requiring the decision-maker to observe both the *vires* of the parent statute (explained in Chapter 8) and certain additional controls which form the subject-matter of this chapter. These controls are grouped under the headings of: abuse (or excess) of discretionary powers, covered in Part 2; and failure to exercise a discretion described in Part 4. In addition, certain glosses deriving in part from the Constitution, which have made an appearance in the past few years are described in Part 3, under the title Modern Extensions. By way of conclusion to this chapter, Part 5 offers some comments on the broad question of whether any discretionary powers are unreviewable.

There is a distinction, in principle, between the exercise of a discretionary power and a statutory duty[4] imposed on a public authority (breach of which sounds in damages) in that the latter attracts strict liability whereas the former

---

[1] See pp. 224–231.
[2] Livestock Marts Act 1967, s. 3(1) examined in *East Donegal Co-Operatives Ltd.* v. *Att.-Gen.* [1970] I.R. 317 described at pp. 539–541.
[3] Local Government (Sanitary Services) Act 1948, s.31(1) involved in *Listowel U.D.C.* v. *McDonagh* [1968] I.R. 312 (see pp. 514–515) and *Corporation of Limerick* v. *Sheridan* (1956) 90 I.L.T.R. 59 (see p. 548).
[4] For breach of statutory duty, see pp. 647–649.

is discretionary. In practice, there are types of statutory duty[5] which are so broad and vague that the judicial task of determining their extent, in order to decide whether there has been a breach, comes close to the exercise of determining the considerations which are relevant to the exercise of a discretionary power so as to decide whether there has been an abuse of power.

The difficulty of delineating the law in this area is increased by the fact that:

"The scope of review may be conditioned by a variety of factors: the wording of the discretionary power, the subject-matter to which it is related, the character of the authority to which it is entrusted, the purpose for which it is conferred, the particular circumstances in which it has in fact been exercised, the materials available to the court, and in the last analysis whether a court is of the opinion that judicial intervention would be in the public interest. . . . Broadly speaking, however, one can say that the courts will show special restraint in applying tests of legality where (i) a power is exercisable in 'emergency' conditions . . . ; or (iii) the 'policy content of the power is large and its exercise affects large numbers of people. Their reluctance to intervene is likely to diminish the more closely the wording and content of the power approximate to those of a discretion typically exercised by a tribunal.' "[6]

These daunting observations show how wary the reader should be of generalisations in this field.

2. Abuse of Discretionary Power

The classic exposition of the principles traditionally restraining abuse of power by public authorities (these principles are cast in the mould of specialised rules of statutory interpretation) was given by Lord Greene in *Associated Provincial Picture Houses Ltd.* v. *Wednesbury Corporation*[7]:

"When an executive discretion is entrusted by Parliament to a body such as the local authority in this case, what appears to be an exercise of that discretion can only be challenged in the courts in a strictly limited class of case. As I have said, it must always be remembered that the court is not a court of appeal. When discretion of this kind is granted the law recognises certain principles upon which that discretion must be exercised, but within the four corners of those principles the discretion, in my opinion, is an absolute one and cannot be questioned in any court of law. . . . I am not sure myself whether the permissible grounds of attack cannot be defined under a single head. It has been perhaps a little bit confusing to find a series of grounds set out. Bad faith, dishonesty—those, of course, stand by themselves—un-

---

[5] *e.g.* see *O'Reilly* v. *Limerick Corporation* [1989] I.L.R.M. 181, 189–191.
[6] de Smith, *op. cit.* pp. 281, 297. Item (ii) in Professor de Smith's catalogue refers to immigration, expulsion and deportation cases; it is omitted because seemingly it does not apply here; see *The State (Kugan)* v. *Station Sergeant, Fitzgibbon St.* [1986] I.L.R.M. 95 (pp. 517–518 and 536–538).
[7] [1948] 1 K.B. 223, 230.

reasonableness, attention given to extraneous circumstances, disregard of public policy and things like that have all been referred to, according to the facts of individual cases, as being matters which are relevant to the question. If they cannot all be confined under one head, they at any rate, I think, overlap to a very great extent. For instance, we have heard in this case a great deal about the meaning of the word 'unreasonable.' . . . It has frequently been used and is frequently used as a general description of the things that must not be done. For instance, a person entrusted with a discretion must, so to speak, direct himself properly in law. He must call his own attention to the matters which he is bound to consider. He must exclude from his consideration matters which are irrelevant to what he has to consider. If he does not obey those rules, he may truly be said, and often is said, to be acting 'unreasonably.' Similarly, there may be something so absurd that no sensible person could ever dream that it lay within the powers of the authority. Warrington L.J. in *Short* v. *Poole Corporation*[8] gave the example of the red-haired teacher, dismissed because she had red hair. That is unreasonable in one sense. In another sense it is taking into consideration extraneous matters. It is so unreasonable that it might almost be described as being done in bad faith; and, in fact, all these things run into one another."

One crucial precept which emerges from this passage is that a court reviewing a discretionary action is not to substitute its own view of the merits for that of the public body in which the legislature has vested the decision. As has been said[9]:

Judicial review is concerned, not with the decision, but with the decision-making process. Unless that restriction on the power of the court is observed, the court will in my view, under the guise of preventing the abuse of power, be itself guilty of usurping power."

An analogy can usefully be drawn between the reviewing court's position and that of an appeal court which is asked to upset a jury verdict: the question is not what the court itself would have done had it been taking the initial decision, but rather whether no reasonable public body could have reached such a decision. Especially is this true where the applicant's contribution would require the reviewing court to investigate disputed facts. An illustration of this—though the point was not made explicitly in the judgments—is provided by *The State (Keegan)* v. *The Stardust Victims Compensation Tribunal*.[10] Here the facts were that whilst the applicant's wife had been awarded compensation for nervous shock caused by the death of their two daughters in the Stardust tragedy, his own claim for compensation for nervous shock had been rejected by the Tribunal. The applicant's application for review was rejected, by the

---

[8] [1926] Ch. 66, 90–91.
[9] *Chief Constable of the North Wales Police* v. *Evans* [1982] 1 W.L.R. 1155, 1173–74, quoted with approval in *The State (Keegan)* v. *The Stardust Victims Compensation Tribunal* [1986] I.R. 642, 661.
[10] [1987] I.L.R.M. 202.

Supreme Court, on the ground that since the Tribunal had before it oral evidence, which was not available to the Court, it would be impossible for the Court to say that the Tribunal was wrong in reaching the conclusion that there were essential differences between the applicant's case and that of his wife.

Secondly, abuse of power can be subdivided into different aspects which yet overlap to a considerable degree. It is to an examination, seriatim, of these three aspects—bad faith, taking into account irrelevant considerations or pursuing an improper purpose, unreasonableness—that we shall return after certain general matters have been examined. This examination will show that while the principles in the passage quoted from *Wednesbury* are well established, they have to be so generally stated that their application in concrete situations often gives rise to controversy.

Whilst Lord Greene's judgment in *Wednesbury* has been quoted extensively both because of its exemplary clarity and because of its influence for at least four decades in most parts of the common law world, it must be emphasised that the law has not stood still. In the first place, the formulae set out in the judgment ("unreasonableness," "public policy," etc.) have proved sufficiently elastic to accommodate far-reaching changes in judicial outlook. Take, for example, the outcome of *Wednesbury* itself. The defendant was a local authority which was empowered to grant licences for Sunday entertainment at the cinema subject to such conditions as it thought fit. The plaintiff picture-house owner was granted a licence but subject to the condition that no children under 15 be admitted to a Sunday performance with or without an adult. This condition was challenged. The challenge failed and the Court of Appeal evidently regarded it as a very feeble case. Yet, even apart from the wide social and religious difference between Britain in the 1940s (with its Lord's Day observance tendency) and Ireland in the 1990s (with its televisions and videos), it seems quite likely that the plaintiff would have succeeded had he come before a court with the same facts, at the present day, *a fortiori* if it were an Irish court. The reason for this surmise is that given the existence of Sunday opening at all, it appears by today's standard of "reasonablesness", an unreasonable exercise of discretion to do as the defendant had done, namely to prevent any person below the age of 15, even if accompanied by an adult, from watching any film, however innocuous. Judicial recognition of the change in standards is provided by the following extract from O'Hanlon J.'s judgment in the High Court in *P. & F. Sharpe Ltd.* v. *Dublin City and County Manager*[11]:

"In *Wednesbury* . . . Lord Greene M.R. said:

'It is true to say that if a decision on a competent matter is so unreasonable that no reasonable authority could ever have come to it, then the courts can interfere . . . but to prove a case of that kind would require something overwhelming.'

[11] [1989] I.L.R.M. 565, 571. Notice, though, that in the area of subordinate legislation the rather extreme standard ("manifest arbitrariness, injustice or partiality") laid down in *Mixnam's Properties* v. *Chertsey U.D.C.* [1964] 1 Q.B. 214, 237–238 has been cited recently with approval in *Cassidy* v. *Minister for Industry and Commerce* [1978] I.R. 297, 311 and *McGabhann* v. *Incorporated Law Society of Ireland* [1989] I.L.R.M. 854, 862. See pp. 522–524.

The requirement of 'overwhelming' proof of unreasonablenes has not, however, been demanded in a series of later cases referred to in de Smith's *Judicial Review of Administrative Action*, 4th ed., at p. 354, and it appears to me to be open to the courts to regard as invalid a decision made in exercise of a statutory discretion, if they conclude that no reasonable authority could have come to it."

However, notwithstanding the incremental change permitted by the *Wednesbury* formula which has just been described, by the mid-Eighties it was thought by many lawyers that a more radical and explicit modification was required. In response, a second source of change has begun to emerge. It is this subject which we shall consider in the next Part of this chapter, under the heading "Modern Extensions." However, it should be emphasised that these changes will not affect the outcome in most cases and that, side by side with these as yet embryonic developments, *Wednesbury* remains of substantial contemporary importance, as witness the number of modern cases which have found a niche within this, rather than the next Part.

A substantial practical problem often arises in cases in this area, namely the difficulty of establishing such essential facts as bad faith or, where these have not been divulged, the reasons on which a decision is based. The obvious sources of information include: the minutes of a decision-making meeting; affidavits of participants at such a meeting; or public statements made by the responsible authority. Again, in a characteristic passage in *East Donegal Co-Operatives Ltd.* v. *Attorney-General*, Walsh J. noted the existence of such devices as discovery and interrogatories and then issued the following warning: " . . . the resources of the Courts . . . are not so limited that they could facilitate . . . the concealment of an infringement of constitutional rights or the masking of injustice."[12] Another recourse for an appellant, frustrated by an absence of hard information, is that if there is an absence of explanation or elucidation, a court is entitled to infer the worst from a discrepancy between the decision taken and the decision which could have been expected if the proper guidelines had been observed.[13] There is, thus, an obvious relation-

---

[12] [1970] I.R. 317, 349.

[13] *The State (McGough)* v. *Louth County Council* (1973) 107 I.L.T.R. 13, 25; *Padfield* v. *Minister for Agriculture* [1968] A.C. 1032, 1061. Note that the proposition stated in the text is probably not supported by *P. & F. Sharpe Ltd.* v. *Dublin County Council* [1989] I.L.R.M. 565 (the facts of which are given at pp. 172–174 and 461). Here, rejecting, on behalf of the Supreme Court, the argument that the Council's decision was unreasonable Finlay C.J. stated: (at 579).

"It appears to me that both in the High Court and in this Court there is a very great difficulty in reaching a conclusion as to what the material was which was before the elected members at the time of their two discussions concerning this resolution and was considered by them prior to deciding to pass the resolution . . .

It seems likely that for this issue to have been satisfactorily determined in the High Court the procedure adopted in this particular application for judicial review of proceeding on affidavits only was incorrect and insufficient and that what would have been required was an oral hearing preceded by simple pleadings. If I were satisfied that it had been established that the only matters which were before the elected members when they passed this resolution were the reports of the county manager and his engineering staff, I would incline to the view that the resolution would be so unreasonable as to fall within the category dealt with in *State (Keegan)*

507

ship between a court making such an inference and the duty to give reasons.[14] This arises from the fact that, in appropriate circumstances, a decision may be either struck down for failure to give reasons or, alternatively, if no reasons are given, a court may be prepared to assume the worst as regards the public authority's motivation and, so, to strike down for abuse of a discretionary power.

The absence of reasons was at least a strong supporting factor in the case of *Breen* v. *Minister for Defence*.[15] Here the facts were that the respondent Minister had exercised his statutory discretion to reduce the applicant's army pension because of the fact that the applicant had obtained civil damages for the injury which had led the pension being awarded. The Minister's decision was based on the fact that the damages award was for £60,000. This failed to take into account such factors as: the applicant's legal costs; delay in receiving the award; expenditure by the applicant in reliance on receiving the entire award and a pension. As a result of these deductions the applicant had only ever been in possession of roughly half the award. Representations based on these points were put to the Minister, without effecting any change. The Supreme Court speaking, *per* O'Flaherty J, stated[16]:

"The Minister having carefully, as he said, considered the representations, nonetheless, has not stated how he reacted to the information that he received about the dire straits in which this unfortunate man found himself.

I am far from saying that every administrative decision must be accompanied by elaborate reasons such as would be appropriate to a judgment but the citizen's sense of resentment and frustration can be readily understood in circumstances where he has presented what he thinks is a viable case and has been met simply be a blanket refusal to change by the administrative decision-maker. Unfortunately, the decision arrived at appears to fly in the face of what the justice of the case required.

I would hold that the Minister's decision was unreasonable because the stark fact is that the appellant never received the sum of £60,000."

The question of motive is, of course, a peculiarly difficult issue of fact. It is nowhere more difficult than where the administrative authority's motives are

---

v. *Stardust Compensation Tribunal* [1986] I.R. 642. I am not satisfied on the facts as found in this case that that was the only information before the elected members. I would, therefore, uphold the conclusion reached by the learned trial judge in the High Court that he was unable to decide on the information before him, and in this context the onus would appear to be on the Appellants, that the decision was unreasonable."

In the last sentence, the Chief Justice implicitly rejects the notion that the decision should be regarded as invalid (or at least that there is a presumption that it is unreasonable) if given without reasons. Yet later on (at 581), Finlay C.J. states that the local authority is under a duty to state reasons.

[14] For the duty to state reasons, see pp. 457–463.

[15] Supreme Court, July 20, 1990. For another example; see *R* v. *Civil Service Appeals Board, ex p. Cunningham, The Guardian*, March 13, 1991.

[16] *Breen* v. *Minister for Defence* pp. 10–12 of the judgment.

mixed (a situation which is considered here because it could arise in regard to more than one of the sub-heads of abuse). Since in real life this is not a rare occurrence, it is surprising that there is such a dearth of Irish case law on the subject. Where an authority has sought to achieve unauthorised as well as authorised purposes, the question of what test should be used to determine the validity of its act has been characterised as "a legal porcupine which bristles with difficulties as soon as it is touched."[17] A straightforward example occurred in *Cassidy* v. *Minister for Industry and Commerce*[18] in which the plaintiff's case, on the present point, failed because, as Henchy J. stated:

> "The evidence forces me to the conclusion that the primary and dominant purpose of the Minister in making these orders was to eliminate unwarranted price increases (a proper purpose) and that, while he also had as his aim the return of the publicans to the voluntary practice of not making price increases without giving him prior notice (an improper purpose) that aim was merely subsidiary and consequential to the dominant and permitted purpose."[19]

The facts were on the other side of the same line in the Northern Irish case of *Re Murray's Application*.[20] This case involved a chief constable's power to transfer police officers and to change their duties. The proper purpose of this power, it was accepted, was to promote the efficiency of the police force. In the instant case, this was not the chief constable's only purpose and it was established that he was also pursuing an unauthorised purpose, namely that of disciplining the officers who were transferred and whose duties had been changed. Carswell J. held that the transfer order was invalid and adopted—admittedly in a case involving rather suspicious facts—the most stringent of the tests which have been employed elsewhere in the common law world. Whilst refusing to find that punishment was the predominant motive for the transfer, he held that it sufficed, if the applicant could establish that this was one of the chief constable's purposes.

The question of plurality of purposes has also arisen in the rather particular circumstances of criminal procedure. In *People (Director of Public Prosecutions)* v. *Howley*[21] the accused had been arrested under section 30 of the Offences against the State Act 1939 in respect of the offence of cattle maiming. This offence under the Malicious Damage Act 1861 is a scheduled offence under the 1939 Act and, hence, a suspect may be detained for a period of up to 48 hours if arrested under section 30.[22] However, the cattle-maiming incident had occurred over a year prior to the accused's arrest and

---

[17] de Smith, *op. cit.* p. 329.
[18] [1978] I.R. 297. See also, *Murphy* v. *Dublin Corporation* [1976] I.R. 143; *Hussey* v. *Irish Land Commission*, Supreme Court, December 13, 1984; *The State (Bouzagou)* v. *The Station Sergeant, Fitzgibbon St. Garda Station* [1986] I.L.R.M. 95.
[19] *Ibid.* 308–309.
[20] [1987] 12 N.I.J.B. 2.
[21] [1989] I.L.R.M. 624.
[22] For a fuller treatment of the arrest and scheduling powers under this section, see Hogan and Walker, *Political Violence and the Law in Ireland* (Manchester, 1989), pp. 192–200.

he submitted—with good reason, it might be thought—that this was merely a colourable device to permit his detention in respect of the (non-scheduled) offence of murder. The accused was suspected of the murder of a young woman (which had taken place over a year before the cattle-maiming incident) and it was argued that in reality it was the murder which was uppermost in the mind of the Gardái when they arrested him. In the Central Criminal Court, Barron J. ruled that the arrest was valid, saying that he had come to the conclusion that: "The Garda Síochána, while they were also investigating to a greater or lesser extent the murder suspect, were also seeking to detect the culprit in the cattle-maiming offence."[23] Barron J. accepted that it sufficed if the desire to investigate the cattle maiming was "genuine"; it did not also have to be the dominant motive.

Howley might, incidentally, have been of interest in an entirely different and more general context, namely, whether criminal procedure is broadly subject to the same substantive principles of judicial review as are other administrative actions of organs of the state. One British commentator has said that "where a constable has exercised a statutory discretion, his action is now in principle subject to challenge under public law"[24] and the correctness of this view in this jurisdiction (at least in relation to the discretionary powers of arrest conferred by section 30 of the 1939 Act) would appear to have been borne out by a series of judicial decisions.[25] As Walsh J. explained in *People (Director of Public Prosecutions)* v. *Quilligan*:

> "Whether or not the Garda has the required suspicion is itself a question of fact, because if he has not, then the action taken by virtue of section 30 and purported pursuant to section 30 would be illegal. Furthermore, the suspicion must be *bona fide* held and not unreasonable—see the views of this Court in *The State (Lynch)* v. *Cooney* when dealing with the "opinion" formed by the Minister in question. The "suspicion" of a member of the Garda in relation to section 30 is not beyond judicial review as is clearly established by the decision of this Court in *The State (Trimbole)* v. *Governor of Mountjoy Prison* [1985] I.R. 550."[26]

In *Howley*, however, the Supreme Court seemed suspicious of this line of argument. Walsh J. referred "to the English administrative law decisions [on plurality of purposes] cited to the court" but thought them of little assistance:

> "While in similar circumstances a court here might well arrive at the same conclusion in such an instance the subject matter of those decisions is so totally different from the point before this Court that, in my view, they are of no assistance in this case. What is before this Court is a much more fundamental point, namely whether somebody has been deprived of his liberty in accordance with law or has been deprived of his liberty in circumstances

---

[23] Quoted by Walsh J. (at 633).
[24] Lustgarten, *The Governance of the Police* (London, 1986), p. 68.
[25] See, *e.g. The State (Bowes)* v. *Fitzpatrick* [1978] I.L.R.M. 195; *D.P.P.* v. *Gilmore* [1981] I.L.R.M. 102, 105 and *The State (Trimbole)* v. *Governor of Mountjoy Prison* [1985] I.R. 550.
[26] [1986] I.R. 495, 507.

which render unlawful the deprivation of liberty and that therefore he has been the victim of violation of his constitutional right to liberty. Either his detention is lawful or it is not. There is no intermediate position. There can be no question of competing or predominant issues which can determine that question."[27]

This appears to suggest that criminal procedure is to be treated as a thing apart from all other administrative actions on the basis that the most important constitutional right of all—liberty—is involved. This, of course, is a major conceptual question on which Walsh J.'s remarks represent the first, rather than the last, word. However, it may be observed that it is not uncommon for fundamental rights—such as liberty—to be affected by administrative action and that judicial review offers a flexible instrument for reconciling individual rights of varying importance with the community interest, within a wide range of statutory régimes. It would seem undesirable to shun this relatively well-developed system of law and to seek to build an alternative specialised edifice for criminal procedure.

The passage from *Howley* also appears to suggest that the validity of an arrest must be capable of being objectively ascertained without any reference to the motives of the policemen concerned. But this can scarcely be correct, since it is trite law that any discretionary power (whether it be conferred by statute or the common law) can only be exercised for the purpose for which it is conferred and that an improper motive can invalidate what would otherwise be a valid exercise of that power. Indeed, a splendid example of this principle also in the context of an arrest under section 30 of the 1939 Act is provided by the earlier decision on *The State (Bowes)* v. *Fitzpatrick*.[28] Here the applicant had been arrested under section 30, ostensibly in respect of the scheduled offence of malicious damage to a weapon. But this damage to the weapon had occurred in the course of a murder and Finlay P. had little difficulty in concluding that, by reason of the predominant motive of the Gardái involved, the arrest of the applicant was not bona fide:

> "I am satisfied . . . that the arrest of the accused under section 30 of the [1939 Act], which on the candid evidence of Detective Sergeant Maguire was ultimately or in reality for the purpose of enabling him to be interrogated in respect of the alleged murder, was only made on suspicion of the commission of the offence of malicious damage as a colourable device to bring what is in reality and plain truth a murder investigation within the ambit of section 30 of the Offences against the State Act 1939."[29]

Bad faith (mala fides)

Bad faith (frequently known as mala fides or fraud) exists where a public body "intends to achieve an object other than that for which he believes the

---

[27] [1989] I.L.R.M. 624, 635.
[28] [1978] I.L.R.M. 195.
[29] *Ibid.* 196.

power to have been conferred."[30] Thus bad faith includes, but is wider than, the concept of "malice" which should be used only where the repository of the discretionary power is motivated by personal animosity against a person or persons affected by it. In the other direction, bad faith may be distinguished from bias (covered in Chapter 9.2) in that bias may have an objective existence, without any element of consciousness similar to the *criminal* law concept of *mens rea*; whereas the essence of bad faith is dishonesty.[31]

Straightaway, two features emerge: first, cases in which bad faith is established are inevitably rare. Courts naturally shrink from labelling elected representatives and/or public officials as dishonest.[32] Moreover, public bodies are often made up of groups of people with differing levels of information about the subject-matter and with varying outlooks, motivations and political allegiances. Against this background, it will often be difficult to bring home a charge of bad faith because of the need to prove something akin to the criminal law concept of *mens rea*. Secondly, if a court concludes that a discretionary decision is the product of the consideration of irrelevant factors or is unreasonable, then it will be held invalid, even if there is no element of bad faith. Thus it will usually be otiose to try to establish bad faith. One exception to this observation would occur in an action where a plaintiff is suing for the as yet undeveloped tort of misfeasance of public office as bad faith is a necessary element of this tort.[33] Again, bad faith is regarded as particularly heinous so that the consequences of such a finding are more far-reaching than with other defects and this has an effect, for example, on the exercise of a court's discretion to send a remedy or the interpretation of a statutory clause purporting to exclude judicial review.[34] Another exception involves cases where the subject-matter of the power and other circumstances are such that exercise of the power is beyond the reach of judicial review, for "honest abuse of power," yet the courts would be prepared to intervene, it seems reasonable to suppose, if bad faith could be established.

Irish case law tends to bear out these general propositions. It is seldom that bad faith has been alleged before a court, never mind established. Take, for example, *The State (O'Mahony)* v. *South Cork Board of Public Health*[35] where

---

[30] de Smith, *op. cit.* p. 335.
[31] Thus because of the finding of "pique" in *O'Mahony*, the case is put (at p. 513) under the heading of bad faith; whereas there is no reason to regard the similar case of *McGeough* as involving dishonesty and it is accordingly classified as a case of bias (see p. 427). Little usually turns on this point of characterisation. For bias, see p. 433.
[32] See *Smith* v. *East Elloe U.D.C.* [1956] A.C. 736, 767 quoted with approval in *Listowel U.D.C.* v. *McDonagh* [1968] I.R. 312, 317 and *P. & F. Sharpe* at 570.
[33] See pp. 643–647. See also, *Roncarelli* v. *Dupleiss* (1959) 16 D.L.R. (2d) 689, 705; *Dunlop* v. *Woollahra M.C.* [1982] A.C. 158; *Bourgoin S.A.* v. *Ministry of Agriculture* [1986] Q.B. 716; *Pine Valley Developments Ltd.* v. *Minister for Environment* [1987] I.R. 23.
[34] For the court's discretion and exclusion clauses, see further pp. 595–611 and pp. 374–378.
[35] For bad faith in extradition law, see, *e.g. The State (Hully)* v. *Hynes* (1966) 100 I.L.T.R. 145 (real purpose of effort to secure prosecutor was to charge him with revenue offences); *Ellis* v. *O'Dea* [1990] I.L.R.M. 87, 93 (real purpose to make applicant available for interrogation: hypothetical remark).

the applicant was a tenant of the Board whose application to purchase the cottage in which she was living (as she was entitled to do under a statutory scheme) had been rejected by the respondent.[36] There had been bad blood between the parties for some time. According to Maguire P.:

> "The obligation to repair rested on the landlords. The applicant was active in carrying out repairs to the cottage and had sought to make the respondents responsible for the expense of repairs which she claimed to have done by reason of the default of the respondents. In this she was partially successful. Reading between the lines of the affidavits, it would appear that the Board was annoyed because she had taken on herself to do repairs to her cottage and more annoyed still because she had obtained a decree against them for £18 in respect of these repairs. . . . Mere pique at an unfavourable judgment in the High Court seems to me to be no justification for attempting to deprive the applicant of her legal rights."[37]

What is notable is that, although opining that the authority's decision had been taken through "mere pique," the High Court formally classified the case as one of taking extraneous considerations into account and "failure to consider the tenant's application."

The State (Cogley) v. *Dublin Corporation*,[38] is an even more striking case. The facts were these: the prosecutor's application for planning permission having been refused by the Corporation, he appealed successfully to the Minister for Local Government. The remaining stage of the planning procedure was to seek the planning authority's approval and this was granted by the assistant city manager. However, subsequently, the elected members of the Corporation, using their power under section 30 of the Local Government (Planning and Development) Act 1963,[39] passed a resolution revoking the permission which had been granted by the Minister. The possibility of bad faith was raised, but rejected, with some distaste, by Teevan J., in the following remarkable passage[40]:

> "If it could be shown that the resolution was not a bona fide exercise by the Corporation of their authority, and was no more than a colourable device to nullify the Minister's order, then perhaps relief should be granted to the prosecutor. There are some circumstances which excite suspicion of mala

---

[36] [1941] Ir.Jur.Rep. 79. For another case in which what looked like at least a prima facie case of bad faith received short shrift, see *The State (Divito)* v. *Arklow U.D.C.* [1986] I.L.R.M. 123. (Respondent local authority passed a resolution under the Gaming and Lotteries Act 1956, the result of which was that anyone with premises in the relevant area was entitled to apply to the District Court for a gaming licence. The applicant applied unsuccessfully for a licence, his application being opposed by the local authority. Before he could reapply, the local authority revoked its resolution under the 1956 Act.)
[37] [1941] Ir.Jur.Rep. 81–83.
[38] [1970] I.R. 244.
[39] Amended by the Local Government (Planning and Development) Act 1976, s.39(i) which *inter alia* reversed the effect of *Cogley*.
[40] [1970] I.R. 249–250.

fides. The meeting was convened at about the time when grant of approval should have issued, that is to say, as soon as might be after the expiration of one month from notification of the decision to grant approval or from August 18, 1968; it was carried by the smallest possible majority by means of the casting vote of the Lord Mayor . . . ; and it would seem that the reasons for the revocation quoted in, and grounding, the resolution were such as must have been in mind when the application for outline permission was first made and declined by the Corporation, and on the hearing of the appeal to the Minister. However, these features are no more than suspicions or, I should say, possible suspicions; and it would be very unjust to base any conclusion on them impugning the honour of the members of the Corporation in their approach to the very complex and anxious problems of town planning. . . .

Perhaps I have dwelt too much on this aspect of the case for, while the submission was put forward by the prosecutor's counsel, it was not developed to any appreciable extent—doubtless because he would have felt it unfair to do so in the absence of precise probative facts."

It is also notable that in what seemed a strong case, the High Court should have taken the unusual course of refusing to grant the applicant even a conditional order and, so, obliging him to appeal to the Supreme Court before the substantive stage of the case could be heard.

However, about a year before *Cogley* was decided, the Supreme Court had made it clear in *Listowel U.D.C.* v. *McDonagh*[41] that mala fides is "a well recognised ground of challenge." By the Local Government (Sanitary Services) Act 1948 a sanitary authority is empowered: '[to] prohibit the erection . . . of temporary dwellings . . . if they are of opinion that such erection . . . would be prejudicial to public health . . . " Purporting to act under this power, Listowel U.D.C. made an order banning the construction of temporary dwellings on a number of named streets. The defendant was convicted and fined 10 shillings for contravening this order. His principal line of defence was to argue that the order had not been made bona fide in that the sanitary authority did not genuinely hold the necessary opinion. The prosecution submitted that such an argument could only be heard in judicial view proceedings; they could not be in collateral proceedings,[42] such as, in the instant

[41] [1968] I.R. 312, 318.
[42] On which see p. 328. The following planning cases involve sufficiently broad considerations to be mentioned here. In *The State (Fitzgerald)* v. *An Bord Pleanála* [1985] I.L.R.M. 117, the Supreme Court struck down the respondent's grant of planning permission to retain a building erected without permission. The reason given, by the board for its decision was its opinion that the degree of injury and departure from the original structure for which an earlier permission had been given was not such as to warrant the removal of the structure. The Supreme Court took the view that these were irrelevant factors. *Quaere* whether the Court's decision would have been different had the Court considered the argument that for Bord Pleanála not to grant permission would have violated the doctrine of proportionality (on which, see pp. 541–544. Again, in *Flanagan* v. *Galway County Council* [1990] 2 I.R. 66 Blayney J. quashed a grant of planning permission which had been awarded because the councillors were swayed by the applicant's personal circumstances. *Flanagan* was followed in similar circumstances, by Blayney J., in *Griffin* v. *Galway County Council*, High Court, Otober 25, 1990.

case, a criminal prosecution. The Supreme Court rejected this argument, holding that the defendant was free to adduce evidence before the Circuit Court (to which the case had gone on appeal) as to what transpired at the council meeting which considered the passing of the by-law; what views were expressed by members and officials of the Council; and the veracity of the opinion they expressed. In the result, the Circuit Court found as a matter of fact, that the order had been made bona fide.[43]

Improper purposes and irrelevant considerations

"Improper purpose" in this context refers to the fact that, in enacting a statute, the legislature is assumed to have had a definable purpose(s) or object(s).[44] True to the idea that they are implementing the mandate of the legislature, the courts seek to ensure that the power contained in the measure is used only for the "proper purpose."

A simple example was given in *Cassidy* v. *Minister for Industry and Commerce*.[45] Henchy J. stated that the purpose of price control orders made under the Prices Act 1958–1972 is "to maintain stability of prices generally."[46] The judge hypothesised an order which, by setting the same maximum prices in lounge bars as in public bars, made it uneconomic to run lounge bars and, thus, by design, drove them out of business. He considered that such an order would be invalid because the power conferred by the statute would have been used for a purpose for which it was not intended by the legislature.

With knowledge of the proper purpose (a difficulty to which we return *infra*) and making certain assumptions,[47] the court then deduces the consider-

---

[43] The applicants put in evidence a council memorandum entitled "The itinerant problem." However, nine councillors swore that they were concerned only with health matters and their evidence was accepted.

[44] Naturally the decision-maker must take care, where more than one range of purposes may seem apt, to select the correct range. This observation is prompted by *McDonough* v. *Minister for Defence* [1991] I.L.R.M. 115, which concerned the discipling of a naval driver by being "grounded", *i.e.* being barred from driving any vehicle other than the tractor—with a resultant loss of pay. One of Lavan J.'s findings drew on a rarified notion which is slouching towards the Four Courts to be born and which had already been adopted in *The People (D.P.P.)* v. *McCaughey*, Supreme Court, November 20, 1989, in the context of a punishment fixed by a court, for an offence of dangerous driving. In *McDonough*, it seems to have been held that the applicant's disqualification should have been considered not from the perspective of punishing the applicant but from the distinct perspective of what risks would be involved for the public in permitting the applicant to go on driving.

[45] [1978] I.R. 297, 310. See also, *Minister for Industry and Commerce* v. *White*, High Court, February 16, 1981. For other examples see *Corporation of Limerick* v. *Sheridan* (1956) 90 I.L.T.R. 59, 63–64. (Local Government (Sanitary Services) Act 1948, s.31 was being used, in effect, to constitute the Corporation as a licensing authority, although there were other sections in the 1948 Act which were specifically designed to do that.); *Latchford* v. *Minister for Industry and Commerce* [1950] I.R. 33 (disqualification from baking subsidy on ground of criminal conviction, which was held to be an irrelevant factor): see p. 688); *The State (Keller)* v. *Galway Co.Co.* [1958] I.R. 142 (disabled person's allowance refused on ground that applicant capable of doing any job when test was whether he could do job of same kind for which he would be suited, if he were not handicapped; *The State (Melbarien Enterprises Ltd.)* v. *Revenue Commissioners* [1986] I.L.R.M. 476, 482 (tax clearance certificate refused because a company with connections with the applicant company owed arrears of tax): see p. 47.

[46] Prices Act 1958, s.22A inserted by Prices (Amendment) Act 1965, s.1(1).

[47] See p. 519–521.

ations which the public authority should have in mind when it is exercising a discretionary power created by the measure. It follows, therefore, that there is an intimate relationship between the rules that relevant considerations must be taken into account and irrelevant considerations excluded and, on the other hand, the rule that the proper purpose must be observed when a discretionary power is being exercised. Accordingly, there seems to be little point in discussing the cases in separate compartments ('Pursuing an improper purpose' distinguished from 'taking into account an irrlevant consideration') depending upon which label has been used. Instead, our selection of specimen cases is arranged according to the criterion of whether or not the statute creating the discretionary power explicitly states its purpose or explicitly identifies the considerations which must be taken into account in exercising the discretion.[48] It must be admitted, however, that even where such guidelines exist, they may be insufficiently precise to settle specific cases beyond a doubt.

An example of a statutory power, the relevant factors in relation to which were fairly plainly indicated, was considered in *The State (Cussen)* v. *Brennan.*[49] This case arose out of the selection, by the Local Appointment Commissioners (of whom Mr. Brennan was one) of a consultant paediatrician. It was established that, as far as paediatrics was concerned, the L.A.C. had judged the applicant to be slightly ahead of his nearest rival but that the rival candidate's knowledge of the Irish language had tipped the balance in his favour. According to the relevant statutory provision (Health Act 1970, section 18), it was for the Minister for Health to lay down the qualifications for the job. The Minister had duly done this and a knowledge of Irish was not among the qualifications which he had specified. Consequently the L.A.C. had taken irrelevant considerations into account.[50]

The most sophisticated formulation of factors which are to guide the exercise of a discretionary (it may be better to style it "a semi-discretionary")[51] power is to be found in the Planning Code. According to the Local Govern-

---

[48] This ground of distinction is explored in Taylor, "Judicial Review of Improper Purposes and Irrelevant Consideration" (1976) Camb.L.J. 272, 277 who argues that "Where the reasons [for action envisaged by the legislature] are enumerated in the empowering provision the technique used in most reported cases under the rubric 'irrelevant factors' is appropriate. Where there is a discretion as to reasons, the 'improper purpose' is the one to be used." *A contra*: Hanks v. *Minister of Housing and Local Government* [1963] 1 Q.B. 999, 1020.

[49] [1981] I.R. 181.

[50] However the court exercised its discretion not to send an order because of undue delay on the part of the applicant (see pp. 598–599). The Local Authority (Officers and Employees) Act 1983, s.2 effectively reversed the legal rule established in *Cussen* by providing that the LAC may take into account a knowledge of the Irish language.

[51] On the spectrum running from an apparently unlimited discretion to, at the other end, a decision determined by precise rules, there is an infinite variety of gradations. In particular, there is no sharp distinction between a public authority exercising a discretion in respect of which he must be guided by specified factors, as in *Cussen* and, on the other hand, a tribunal applying a standard involving a question of appreciation (see, *e.g. Irish Benefit Building Society* v. *Registrar of Building Societies* [1981] I.L.R.M. 73, 75) or even a court exercising certain functions, *e.g.* granting a liquor licence (*Re Licensing Acts and Centennial Properties*, High Court, December 20, 1980).

ment (Planning and Development) Act 1963, section 26(1), in dealing with a planning application, a local planning authority is:

" . . . [R]estricted to considering the proper planning and development of the area of the authority (including the preservation and improvement of the amenities thereof), regard being had to the provisions of the development plan, the provisions of any special amenity area relating to the said area and the matters referred to in subsection (2) of this section."

Subsection (2) then goes on to empower the planning authority "without prejudice to the generality" of subsection (1) to impose a number of specified conditions among them. The use made in practice of this significant statutory power has already been described.[52]

Thus far cases have been examined in which the relevant statute provided an explicit statement of the factors which the public authority must take into account. Let us consider the situation arising when even this limited assistance is not available. Take first, two deportation cases, with contrasting results but each involving the statutory power to refuse an immigrant leave to land. In the first case, *The State (Kugan)* v. *Station Sergeant, Fitzgibbon St. Garda Station,*[53] deportation arose from refusal of entry based on the applicant's inadequate knowledge of English. This, Egan J. held in effect, was an

---

[52] At pp. 205–206. What is very curious, in the present context, is the line of three cases, which have appeared to subject development by a local authority to something like the standard statutory controls over development, notwithstanding s. 4(1) of the Local Government (Planning and Development) Act 1963 which plainly states that development by a local authority within its own territorial area is exempted development. The cases referred to have usually arisen from protests by neighbours against attempts by local authorities to construct halting sites for travelling people. In the first of these cases, *O'Leary* v. *Dublin County Council* [1988] I.R. 150, O'Hanlon J. held that such a "development" contravened the development plan (thereby violating s. 39(1) of the 1963 Act, which provides that a local planning authority may not contravene the development plan). Next, in *Wilkinson* v. *Dublin County Council* High Court, September 7, 1990 at p. 9, Costello J. held that a site would not be developed as a halting site on the ground that, even on the assumption that it did not violate the development plan, it should still be prevented because it was not consistent with "the proper planning and development of the area". Thirdly, in *Ferris* v. *Dublin County Council* Supreme Court, November 7, 1990 (as in *Wilkinson*) the Court rejected the possibility that the proposed halting site violated the development plan; yet went on to examine the possibility that it would constitute "a bad planning decision" and eventually concluded that, while the temporary provision which was proposed would not be "unreasonable . . . as a matter of proper planning and development" (at p. 11), this would probably not be true of a permanent site.

There would seem to be no warrant for a court to fly in the face of an explicit statutory provision (as did the second and third of the cases, just summarised) and it is remarkable that there was little or no discussion on this point. A local authority's decision to establish a halting site on its own land involves the exercise of discretion in regard to its own common law property rights. Now it is certainly arguable that a court may exercise control over a local authority's discretion in regard to its common law (as contradistinguished from statutory) rights: see pp. 323–328. However, there is no reason why such control should mimic the planning law from whose scope the local authority had been excluded. Moreover such controls should be based on a wider range of factors than are to be found in the planning-environment field and should include matters like the local authority's obligations to help all elements of the community; need to keep the roads free of insanitary, unofficial camp sites and other non-planning factors.

The line of cases under discussion above are discussed from the narrow, planning perspective at pp. 203–206.

[53] [1986] I.L.R.M. 95.

irrelevant factor. In the contrasting case, *The State (Bouzagou)* v. *Station Sergeant, Fitzgibbon St. Garda Station*,[54] a decision to refuse entry on the ground that the immigration officer believed that the applicant would be unable to support himself was upheld.

In these cases (not untypically) little explanation was given of the process of teasing 'the relevant considerations' out of the general tenor of the statute creating the discretionary power. Something of the difficulties entailed in this process emerges from the *locus classicus*, *East Donegal Co-Operatives Ltd.* v. *Attorney-General*[55] in which the Supreme Court scrutinised the Livestock Marts Act 1967, in order to decide a claim by a group of agricultural mart owners that the Act was unconstitutional. The Act bestows considerable discretionary power on the Minister for Agriculture enabling him to control marts, through the grant (whether absolutely or subject to conditions) or the revocation, of licences. In spite of the wide discretionary language in which these powers are couched, Walsh J. stated that:

"The words of the Act, and in particularly the general words, cannot be read in isolation and their content is to be derived from their context. Therefore words or phrases which at first sight might appear to be wide and general may be cut down in their construction when examined against the objects of the Act which are to be derived from a study of the Act as a whole including the long title."

Specifically:

"The provisions of section 6 [of the 1967 Act] throw considerable light upon the purposes, objects and scope of the Act because they refer specifically to the power of the Minister for Agriculture and Fisheries being directed towards the proper conduct of the businesses concerned, the standards in relation to such places and to the provision of adequate and suitable accomodation and facilities for such auctions. Section 6 also provides for the making of regulations dealing with what might be referred to as the mechanics of sale such as book-keeping, accommodation, hygiene, etc. . . . The type of conditions which the Minister may impose [on the grant of a mart licence] would include the site of the mart so as to ensure that, for example, it was not too near a place of worship or a particular road traffic hazard, or conditions aimed at the restriction of the carrying on of business at certain hours or on certain days so as to prevent interference with the activities of persons not connected with the mart, or conditions which indeed might be designed to facilitate the carrying on of business at the particular mart by preventing it being carried on at times which, by reason of particular local conditions or activities, would be detrimental to

---

[54] [1985] I.R. 426. The applicant also failed in *Gilmore* v. *Mitchell*, High Court, April 18, 1988 (Court agreed that the locality in which a Garda is stationed may be a relevant matter in determining a charge of conduct likely to bring discredit on the force.)
[55] [1970] I.R. 317. See also, *Doupe* v. *Limerick Corporation* [1981] I.L.R.M. 456, 461.

the business itself and to the persons having stock for sale at the mart or to persons resorting there for the purpose of purchasing livestock."[56]

Walsh J. added:

"Nowhere in the Act is there anything to indicate that one of the purposes of the Act is to limit or otherwise regulate the number of auction marts as distinct from regulating the way in which business is conducted in auction marts. In the absence of any such indication in the Act, the Minister is not authorised by the Act to limit the number of businesses of the type defined in section 1."[57]

The first sentence in this passage—dealing with control of numbers of marts—may be questioned. Assume that it could be shown that, in a particular area, there was a causal connection between the number of marts and their profitabiity and, on the other hand, a matter such as hygiene which is admittedly within the Act. On that assumption, could it not be argued that the Minister was empowered to refuse an application for a mart in order to maintain existing marts in profit and hence to enable them to maintain the necessary level of hygiene rather than to permit cut-throat competition in which standards of hygiene might fall?

General policy assumptions

So far we have examined cases in which the "relevant considerations" or "proper purposes/objectives" have been deduced by the courts from a study of the particular statute. In addition, there are certain general policy assumptions which the courts bring to their task and which have become well-established in the case law.

First, it is said that: "Parliament does not intend to deprive the subject of his common law rights except by express words or necessary implication."[58] Thus, for example, there are rebuttable presumptions that a statute does not authorise either any interference with general property rights[59] or the imposition of any money charge.[60] However these are matters which need not be considered since they have already been explored.[61]

Secondly, local authorities were originally regarded as being somewhat in the position of "trustees" in relation to their ratepayers and, hence, as owing them a "fiduciary" duty to observe business-like principles in regard to the expenditure of money. This principle severely restricts the powers of local authorities in relation to discretionary acts of expenditure. It has been relied upon, for example, in cases establishing that, in deciding to which contractor

---

[56] [1970] I.R. 317, 341–343.
[57] *Ibid.* 342. See further, pp. 271–273.
[58] de Smith, *op. cit.* p. 99.
[59] See, *e.g. Limerick Corporation* v. *Sheridan* (1956) 90 I.L.T.R. 59, 64.
[60] *City Brick and Terra Cotta Co. Ltd.* v. *Belfast Corporation* [1958] N.I. 44, 70. For the high constitutional principle that taxation may only be levied with the consent of the Dáil: see Gwynn Morgan, *op. cit.* p. 117.
[61] See pp. 335–340.

to award a public works contract, a local authority is obliged to take at least some account of the prices of the various tenders submitted to it.[62]

The doubt about the present status of this concept arises from the fact that the number of ratepayers and the significance of rates, as part of the income of local authorities, have both been substantially reduced by the elimination of domestic and agricultural rates, so that we are left only with business rate-payers.[63] Even apart from this recent change, the principle is open to criticism on the ground that it raises, but does not help in answering, the question of the balance to be drawn between the interests of ratepayers and of non-ratepayers. Moreover "value for money" would seem to be so obvious a factor as not to require supporting on any antecedent notion of "trusteeship".

Thirdly, again in the field of local government, there is also a rule that powers may only be exercised by a local authority for the good of its own territorial area. A straightforward example of this principle in action occurred in *Murphy* v. *Dublin Corporation (No. 2)*[64] which involved a compulsory purchase order made by the defendants. The Supreme Court struck down the order because it found that the Corporation had made it, in part at least,[65] in order to meet the needs of another housing authority, namely Dublin County Council. A further instance of what may be regarded as a judicial assumption about the general policy underlying certain types of discretionary powers occurred in *In re an Application by Cook.*[66] This was a Northern Ireland Court of Appeal case brought by some Alliance Party councillors on Belfast City councillors in response to certain actions taken by the Unionist majority on the Council in opposition to the Anglo-Irish Agreement of 1985. The applicants' first line of argument was to claim that opposition to the Agreement was not a matter of local government and as such was *ultra vires* in the narrow sense (or "illegal" in the *GCHQ* parlance which is explained below.)[67] This argument was rejected on the ground that the actions were *intra vires* the Council in that the working of the Agreement could affect functions, for example, transport, parks and recreation, which are either functions, or incidental to the functions, of the Council. The second set of arguments concerned *ultra vires*, in the wider sense with which we are concerned in this chapter, in that one of the actions taken by the Council was to pass a resolution to refrain from almost all Council and Committee meetings and, instead, to delegate the Council's to the Town Clerk. Accepting the applicants' argument on this point, Lord Lowry C.J. stated[68]:

"The Council's decision was from the local government standpoint and

---

[62] See generally, *The State (Raftis)* v. *Leonard* [1960] I.R. 381; *Bromley L.B.C.* v. *G.L.C.* [1983] 1 A.C. 768; H. A. Street, *Law Relating to Local Government* (Dublin, 1954), pp. 1263–1264 and cases cited therein; Kelly, "Local Authority Contracts, Tenders and Mandamus" (1967) 2 Ir. Jur.(N.S.) 7.
[63] See pp. 181–183.
[64] [1976] I.R. 143.
[65] On plurality of purposes see also pp. 508–511.
[66] [1986] N.I. J.B. 43.
[67] See pp. 334–335 and 529–530.
[68] [1986] 1 N.I. J.B. 93.

we emphasise those words, (*the local government standpoint*) the negation of all the principles according to which local government is carried on through discussion and debate among elected representatives, culminating in decisions on a wide variety of important matters. To say this is not to call in question the ability of the Town Clerk; but to leave all these matters to a paid official, no matter how competent, is simply not the way to carry on local government. It is in fact completely unreasonable in the *Wednesbury* sense . . . It is the activity of the elected representatives which is the essence of local government, as distinct from giving the whole matter into the hands of the Town Clerk to make all the decisions and transact all the business of which he is legally capable.''

Finally, it has been stated (as a make-weight, rather than a *ratio decidendi*) that it is permissible for a public authority to be influenced by "the declared wishes of responsible members of the community."[69]

Reasonableness

As Lord Greene pointed out in the extract from his judgment in *Wednesbury Corporation*—quoted *supra*—reasonableness can be used, widely, to cover almost all forms of abuse of power. Used more narrowly and, therefore, more usefully, it refers to a decision which departs so radically from the normal standards of cost, convenience, morality, respect for individual rights, etc. that no reasonable public authority could have come to it. In this sense, reasonableness was traditionally seldom used by the courts because it entails deciding questions of judgment in highly political areas, where courts prefer not to tread. An unreasonable decision is usually reached because the responsible public authority took into account irrelevant considerations, failed to take into account relevant considerations; or pursued an improper purpose.[70] Accordingly, it can usually be struck down on one of these grounds, thereby enabling a court to avoid the public controversy which may be stirred up if a court labels the decision of a public and, it may be an elected, body as unreasonable. However, these risks notwithstanding,[71] in recent years Irish courts have been less shy of this head.

---

[69] *The State (Divito)* v. *Arklow U.D.C.* [1986] I.L.R.M. 123; *a contra: The State (McGeough)* v. *Louth C.C.* (1973) 107 I.L.T.R. 13, 17, 18, 26. The cases may be reconcilable on the basis that the council resolution in *McGeough* flew in the face of the statute's policy: see 427. For the contradictory relationship between this factor and the rule against fettering a discretion, see *Bromley* v. *G.L.C.* [1983] 1 A.C. 768.

[70] Notice, for example, the following extract from *O'Keeffe* v. *An Bord Pleanála*, High Court, July 31, 1990, where Costello J. said (at p. 24):

"It seems to me that I am driven to the conclusion that the Board acted ultra vires because either (a) it took matters into consideration which, although, perhaps furnishing a rational explanation for its decision were not connected with considerations relating to the proper planning and development of the area, or alternatively, (b), it reached a conclusion which no reasonable planning authority applying the standards of reason and commonsense as laid down by the Supreme Court could have reached, namely that the proposed development was consistent with the proper planning and development of the area. It follows that its decision must be quashed."

[71] See McAuslan, "Administrative Law, Collective Consumption and Judicial Policy" (1983) 45 M.L.R. 1.

Consider first *Cassidy* v. *Minister for Industry and Commerce*,[72] which arose out of the creation of a maximum prices order in respect of bars in Dundalk, by which the same maxima were fixed for drinks sold in both public and lounge bars. The chief reason given by the Supreme Court for striking down the order was unreasonableness. Giving the principal judgment, Henchy J. first adopted the test for unreasonableness enunciated by Diplock L.J. in *Mixnam's Properties* v. *Chertsey U.D.C.*,[73] namely that there must be " . . . such manifest arbitrariness, injustice or partiality that a court would say: 'Parliament never intended to give authority to make such rules.' " It bears noting that although the *Mixnam's* test (laid down in a delegated legislation case) is couched in rather extreme language, notwithstanding this, plenty of applicants have succeeded in cases in which it has been invoked. Probably, one should pay more attention to the facts and result in each case rather than the language of the test. In any event, in *Cassidy*, having quoted *Mixnam's* case with approval, Henchy J. went on to state:

> "Applied here [this test] produces the conclusion that Parliament could not have intended that licences of lounge bars would be treated so oppressively and unfairly by maximum-price orders. If the Minister had made a maximum-price order which forbade hotel owners to sell drink in their hotels at prices higher than those fixed for public bars, it would be generally accepted that such an order would be oppressive and unfair. The capital outlay and overhead expenses necessarily involved in the residential and other features of hotels are such that to force their drink prices down to those chargeable in a public bar would in many cases be ruinously unfair . . . if the orders are construed as not distinguishing lounge bars in any way, and as forcing their prices down to those of public bars, they fail unreasonably to have regard to the fact that owners of lounge bars, like hoteliers, are entitled because of capital outlay and overhead expenses, to separate treatment in the matter of drink prices . . .."[74]

Henchy J.'s judgment in *Cassidy* was invoked in *The State (Kenny)* v. *Minister for Social Welfare*,[75] a case which, like *Cassidy*, could be regarded as

---

[72] [1978] I.R. 297. For other cases on unreasonableness see *Limerick Corporation* v. *Sheridan* (1956) 90 I.L.I.R. 59, 64; *Greaney* v. *Scully* [1981] I.L.R.M. 340; *Lawlor* v. *Minister for Agriculture* [1988] I.L.R.M. 400, 418; *Stroker* v. *Doherty* [1989] I.R. 440, 444–445; *Harvey* v. *Minister for Social Welfare* [1990] I.L.R.M. 185; *Belfast Corporation* v. *Daly* [1963] N.I. 78 and *Philips* v. *The Medical Council*, High Court, December 11, 1990 (requirement that seven years practice as a doctor must be consecutive to entitle applicant to full registration under the Medical practitioners Act 1978 held to involve "manifest injustice" (at p. 45)).
[73] [1964] 1 Q.B. 214, 237.
[74] [1978] I.R. 311.
[75] [1986] I.R. 693. Previous to this decision the Ombudsman had received complaints from a number of divorced women who had been refused a Deserted Wife's Allowance. In the then existing state of the law, he had been unable to make a finding of maladministration. However, as a result of *Kenny*, in cases where the divorce was recognised in Ireland, some of these women were able to claim Unmarried Mother's Allowance: see *Annual Report of the Ombudsman for 1987* (P1.5258), p. 20.

involving discrimination. The Social Welfare (Consolidation) Act 1981 provides that a welfare payment should be made to an "unmarried mother." The
central point in the case was that this expression was defined, by the relevant
regulations, to cover a woman "if, not being or *having been* a married
woman, she is the mother of a child . . . " (Authors italics). The consequence
of this was that whilst the effect of all parts of the legislation, taken as a
whole, was that while mothers, who were deserted wives, prisoner's wives, or
unmarried, were entitled to these payments, by contrast, mothers who had
been married but whose marriage had been dissolved, even by a court of competent jurisdiction, were excluded from this bounty. The applicant was a
member of this category. Finding in her favour, Egan J. stated:

> "Could Parliament have intended that one single class of mother should be
> excluded from the same benefits as those to which other classes of mother
> would be entitled? Was it intended that such a mother should be punished
> together with her child or children because her marriage had been dis-
> solved? I think not. To repeat the words of Henchy J. it would be "oppress-
> ive" and "unfair."[76]

Another example is provided by the decision of the Supreme Court in
Doyle v. *An Taoiseach*[77] in which the plaintiffs successfully challenged the
validity of a 2 per cent. levy on the price of live cattle established by a statutory instrument made under the Finance Act 1966. While the levy was
intended to bring farmers into the tax net, it was the proprietors of slaughter-
houses or, in the case of exported animals, exporters, who were made primarily liable for the levy. This anomaly had the result that the farmer escaped
liability for the operation of the levy. Had the levy been payable at the time
when an animal was sold for slaughter or for export, this unfairness could
have been avoided. As Henchy J. put it:

> "But in the case of exporters, the sale price was not the value of the levy; it
> was the value of the animal at the pier-head. This value might be, and fre-
> quently was, higher than the sale price. The exporter, therefore, became
> directly liable for a levy of an amount which he could not recover in full
> from the farmer, because he could not identify the seller of the animal; or,
> even when he could, because it would not be practicable to seek to recover
> the full amount of the levy; or because it was not possible for the exporter
> to assess at the time of purchase what the amount of the levy would be
> when the animal would arrive at the pier-head."[78]

These anomalies led the Supreme Court to conclude that the relevant statutory instruments were void for unreasonableness. The results produced by
these orders were so "untargeted, indiscriminate and unfair" and so removed
from their primary policy which, as was admitted by the defendants, was to

---

[76] *Ibid.* 696.
[77] [1986] I.L.R.M. 693.
[78] *Ibid.* 714–715.

tax farmers that the delegated legislation must be deemed to have been made in excess "of the impliedly intended scope of the delegation."[78a]

Plainly on the other side of the line was *McGabhann* v. *Incorporated Law Society of Ireland*[79] in which one of the issues was whether the respondents could impose, as a standard to be attained in an examination a pass mark of either 50 per cent. in each of five subjects or, in the case of a candidate who failed to achieve that standard in no more than two subjects, an aggregate pass mark of 250 marks in all five subjects. Rejecting an attack on the rules setting this standard, Blayney J. said:

> "Could it be said that the committee, in laying down this standard, was guilty of *manifest arbitrariness, injustice or partiality?* In my opinion it could not. There was no arbitrariness or partiality about it because it was a fixed standard which applied equally to all the candidates taking the examination. Nor could it be said to be unjust. An absolute standard of 50 per cent. in each subject would have been very rigid. To permit a candidate to pass who had fallen below 50 per cent. in no more than two subjects was a reasonable modification to introduce and in order to ensure a certain overall standard there had to be some minimum aggregate specified. And for this aggregate to be unjust, it seems to me it would have to be shown that it was fixed excessively high. But such is not the case. The figure of 250 simply requires an average equal to the pass mark. I am satisfied therefore that the standard was not unreasonable and so was lawful."[80]

In *Warnock* v. *The Revenue Commissioners*[81] the plaintiff-accountants claimed that a notice issued by the Revenue Commissioners (under section 59 of the Finance Act 1974) to provide certain information regarding the accountants' clients' affairs was unduly "burdensome and oppressive" in that compliance would involve an excessive amount of the accountants' staff time. The claim failed on the facts, although Costello J. appears to have accepted that, in extreme enough circumstances, the claim would have succeeded.

"Fundamentally at variance with reason and common sense . . ."

Recently, there has been some judicial discussion of the definition of 'reasonableness,' without, it is suggested, making any major change of substance in this segment of the law. The discussion was triggered by Lord Diplock's judgment in *Council of Civil Service Unions* v. *Minister for the Civil Service*[82] ("the *GCHQ* case") in which he proposed to rechristen reasonableness as "irrationality" and offered a redefinition. It is not clear whether (as appears from reading the judgment) Lord Diplock intended to impose a narrower definition than had prevailed hitherto. This point will be explored

---

[78a] *Ibid.*
[79] [1989] I.L.R.M. 854.
[80] *Ibid.* 862–863. (Authors' italics.)
[81] [1986] I.L.R.M. 37.
[82] [1985] A.C. 374, 410. For further discussion of this judgment, see pp. 529–533.

further in the following Part of this chapter. In any case, any such narrowing, like the wording of the redefinition, has been implicitly rejected by Henchy J. in *The State (Keegan)* v. *The Stardust Victims Compensation Tribunal* (the facts of which have already been given and are not, in any case, relevant in appreciating the law in the case).[83] Henchy J. (with whom the other members of the court agreed on this point) offered his own reformulation of *Wednesbury* reasonableness:

"The *Wednesbury* test of unreasonableness or irrationality has been considered in a number of subsequent cases and has been qualified to some extent. For example, in *Council of Civil Service Unions* v. *Minister for the Civil Service*, Lord Diplock said of the *Wednesbury* test:

'It applies to a decision which is so outrageous in its defiance of logic or of accepted moral standards that no sensible person who had applied his mind to the question to be decided could have arrived at it.'

For my part, I would be slow to test unreasonableness by seeing if the decision accords with logic. Many examples could be given of reputable decisions and of substantive laws which reject logic in favour of other considerations. I think in any event that it is only a particular aspect of logic that could be applicable in testing the validity of a decision when it is subjected to judicial review on the ground of unreasonableness, namely, whether the conclusion reached in the decision can be said to flow from the premises. If it plainly does not, it stands to be condemned on the less technical and more understandable test of whether it is fundamentally at variance with reason and common sense.

As to the suggestion that the unreasonableness of a decision should be decided by the extent to which it fails to accord with *accepted moral* standards, I would be equally slow to accept that criterion. The concept of accepted moral standards represents a vague, elusive and changing body of standards which in a pluralist society is sometimes difficult to ascertain and is sometimes inappropriate or irrelevant to the decision in question (as it is to the decision in question in this case). The ethical or moral postulates of our Constitution will, of course, make certain decisions invalid for being repugnant to the Constitution, but in most cases a decision falls to be quashed for unreasonableness, not because of the extent to which it has departed from accepted moral standards (or positive morality), but because it is indefensible for being in the teeth of plain reason and common sense. I would myself consider that the test of unreasonableness or irrationality in judicial renview lies in considering whether the impugned decision plainly and unambiguously flies in the face of fundamental reason and common sense. If it does, then the decision-maker should be held to have acted *ultra vires*, for the necessarily implied constitutional limitation of jurisdiction in all decision-making which affects rights or duties requires, *inter alia*, that

83 [1986] I.R. 642.

525

the decision-maker must not flagrantly reject or disregard fundamental reason or common sense in reaching his decision."[84]

However it should be emphasised that reasonableness will not always be a matter merely of sensible reasoning; not infrequently there will have to be a component based on morals or values. Such a component can, as Henchy J. stated, be drawn from the Constitution, augmented by what he called "common sense,"[85] which can be taken to include community values. Henchy J.'s reformulation appears to offer a sensible and balanced approach and, not surprisingly, the *Keegan* formula has been quoted with approval, in a number of recent Irish cases.[86] However it has to be emphasised again that whatever form of words is used, the fundamental problem remains namely to set a reasonable balance between permitting some latitude to a public body invested with a discretionary power and, on the other hand, preventing really abnormal exercises of discretion; and also to try to ensure that this balance does not vary too much from judge to judge. Take for example, *Stroker* v *Doherty*,[87] which involved an unsuccessful attempt to overturn a decision of the Gardaí disciplinary Appeal Board. The Board had affirmed a decision that the applicant had been guilty of a breach of discipline of bringing the Gardaí into disrepute in that when off duty in a public house, he had made lewd statements about his wife to an acquaintance. The Supreme Court reversed the High Court. McCarthy J. quoted the *Keegan* formula and then stated[87a]:

"Applying that test to the circumstances of this case, I am not prepared to hold that the conclusion of the Appeal Board involved a rejection or disregard of fundamental reason or common sense. There are, no doubt, many who would consider the incident in question as tasteless and offensive but irrelevant to An Garda Siochana as such, whatever about its relevance

[84] *Ibid.* 658. Finally C.J. commented on this passage in *O'Keeffe* v. *An Bord Pleanála*, Supreme Court, February 15, 1991, p. 15:

"I am satisfied that these three different methods of expressing the circumstances under which a court can intervene are not in any way inconsistent one with the other, but rather complement each other and constitute not only a correct but a comprehensive description of the circumstances under which a court may, according to our law, intervene in such a decision on the basis of unreasonableness or irrationality."

[85] *Cf.* Oscar Wilde, "that uncommon thing called commonsense."
[86] *E.g. Breen* v. *Minister for Defence* Supreme Court, July 20, 1990, p. 11; *O'Keeffe* v. *Bord Pleanála*, High Court, July 31, 1990, pp. 22–23 and Supreme Court, February 15, 1991, pp. 14–15; *Ferris* v. *Dublin County Council*, Supreme Court, November 7, 1990, at pp. 9–10. (In *Ferris*, Finlay C.J. also rejected the submission that a higher standard of reasonableness should be set for a public body where no appeal is provided). Two other cases (*The State (Creedon)* v. *Criminal Injuries Compensation Tribunal* [1989] I.L.R.M. 104 and *Hill* v. *Criminal Injuries Compensation Tribunal* [1990] I.L.R.M. 36) in which this test featured were not classic examples of "unreasonableness" in that both, a tribunal administering a (non-statutory) scheme was involved and it appeared as if an error as to facts and calculations, rather than exercise of discretion, had been made. However, the concept of "irrationality" (which may apply to a broader range of decisions than "unreasonableness" might seem to be especially apt in regard to these cases.
[87] Supreme Court, July 26, 1990.
[87a] *Ibid.* pp. 7–8. See, to similar effect, Griffin J. at p. 6.

to the individual Garda; there are some who would consider that what a Garda says off duty and in plain clothes is strictly his own business; there are others who would consider that, in a small country community, members of the Gardái should be setting an example of decent conduct. Quot homines tot sententiae.

It follows that the appeal in respect of this breach should be allowed."

The result was that the public authority's decision was not struck down, illustrating the unexceptionable point that the reformulated test, just like the *Wednesbury* principle, permits a margin of appreciation to the public authority.

A Change of Course

However what is more striking is that in two recent cases, the Supreme Court, speaking per Finlay C.J. in each case, appears to have gone further and, it would seem, for reasons of policy rather than anything to do with the *Keegan* reformulation, to have narrowed the grounds on which the exercise of discretionary power will be struck down. The facts of the first of these to be mentioned, *P. & F. Sharpe* v. *Dublin City and County Manager*[88] have already been given. All that need be mentioned here is that one of the points at issue was the validity of a grant of planning permission by the elected councillors of a local authority. This had been made in the face of opposition from the local authority staff based on the ground that the development would be a danger to traffic. Rejecting the submission that the grant of planning permission was invalid, Finlay C.J. stated:

"If I were satisfied that it had been established that the only matters which were before the elected members when they passed this resolution were the reports of the county manager and his engineering staff, I would incline to the view that the resolution would be so unreasonable as to fall within the category dealt with in *State (Keegan)* v. *Stardust Compensation Tribunal . . .* I am not satisfied on the facts as found in this case that that was the only information before the elected members. I would, therefore, uphold the conclusion reached by the learned trial judge in the High Court that he was unable to decide on the information before him, and in this context the onus would appear to be on the appellants, that the decision was unreasonable."[89]

The other case in this line of authority is *O'Keeffe* v *An Bord Pleanála*.[90] Here the respondent had granted planning permission for the erection of a long wave radio transmitting station, including a 300 metre high mast. This permission had been given in the face of recommendations against the grant of permission, contained in reports drawn up by the Board's inspector and a technical inspector, respectively. The reports emphasised the effects of elec-

---

[88] [1989] I.L.R.M. 565. See further at pp. 172–174.
[89] *Ibid*. 579.
[90] Supreme Court, February, 1991 reversing High Court, July 31, 1990.

tro-magnetic interference on an area of radius 7 kilometre around the development, in which 5,000 people lived. The outcome of the case is not especially significant since on the view of the facts, adopted by the Supreme Court[91], there was ample evidence in the reports which justified the Board in rejecting the inspector's recommendations. Much more striking is the tone of the following passage: from Finlay C.J.'s judgment[92]:

" . . . the circumstances under which the Court can intervene on the basis of irrationality with the decision-maker [sic] involved in an administrative function are limited and rare. It is of importance and, I would think, of assistance to consider not only as was done by Henchy J. in the *Stardust* case the circumstances under which the Court can and should intervene, but also in brief terms and not necessarily comprehensively, to consider the circumstances under which the Court cannot intervene.

The Court cannot interfere with the decision of an administrative decision-making authority merely on the grounds that:

(a) it is satisfied that on the facts as found it would have raised different inferences and conclusions, or

(b) it is satisfied that the case against the decision made by the authority was much stronger than the case for it.

These considerations described by counsel on behalf of the appellants as the height of the fence against judicial intervention by way of review on the grounds of irrationality of decision are of particular importance in relation to questions of the decisions of planning authorities.

Under the provisions of the Planning Acts the Legislature has unequivocally and firmly placed questions of planning, questions of the balance between development and the environment and the proper convenience and amenities of an area within the jurisdiction of the planning authorities and the Board which are expected to have special skill, comptence and experience in planning questions. The Court is not vested with that jurisdiction, nor is it expected to, nor can it, exercise discretion with regard to planning matters.

I am satisfied that in order for an appellant for judicial review to satisfy a court that the decision-making authority has acted irrationally in the sense which I have outlined above so that the court can intervene and quash its decision, it is necessary that the applicant should establish to the satisfaction of the court that the decision-making authority had before it no relevant material which would support its decision.

As was indicated by this Court in the case of *Sharpe* v. *The Dublin City Manager*, the onus of establishing all that material is on the applicant for

---

[91] It appears probable that *O'Keeffe* should be classified as a case in which the applicant's claim was, in substance, that there was no evidence by which to sustain essential facts rather than one in which the final decision was irrational. However the differences are rather nuancé and the Court certainly discussed it as if it were in the second category and, accordingly, it is classified as being in this category in the text.

[92] Supreme Court, February 15, 1991, pp. 17–19.

judicial review, and if he fails in that onus he must fail in his claim for review."

The consistency between *O'Keeffe* and *Sharpe* is noteworthy for whilst the passage from *O'Keeffe*, just quoted, depended in part upon the fact that the case concerned, to quote again, bodies "which are expected to have special skill, competence and experience in planning questions", *Sharpe* could not have been a more different case in that it involved a section 4 resolution by which some councillors had effectively overturned the decision reached by the professional experts of the local authority. Yet in each case, the fundamental ruling was that, however odd an administrative decision, it is the person wishing to upset the decision who bears the onus of adducing evidence regarding the material on which the body has grounded its decision. It also bears emphasis that, at a general policy level, there is a divergence between this ruling and the view, noted earlier that it is the public body which bears the onus of giving reasons to justify an apparently irrational decision.

Tending in the same direction as the point emphasised in the previous paragraph is the observation made towards the start of the passage quoted, that "the circumstances under which the court can intervene on the basis of irrationality . . . are limited and rare."[93]

It is too early to say definitely whether the *Sharpe–O'Keeffe* line of authority marks a turning of the tide, which at least since the *East Donegal Co-operatives Ltd*, has been so strongly in favour of the individual aggrieved by the exercise of a discretionary power. However, these cases do seem to indicate at least a change of emphasis.

3. The Future: An Excursus

New departure in Britain

Wednesbury was reported in 1948 and, in its pragmatism, diffidence and vagueness, it is very much a product of its time, which may be regarded as the pre-Renaissance era in judicial review of administrative action. It was to be expected then that the energetic judicial statesmen of the present generation of English judges would attempt at least a restatement of the *Wednesbury* principles and this duly came (along with much else) in the *GCHQ* case. Lord Diplock stated:

"Judicial review has I think developed to a stage today when without reiterating any analysis of the steps by which the development has come about, one can conveniently classify under three heads the grounds upon which administrative action is subject to control by judicial review. The first

---

[93] Contrast with this observation the passage from the High Court judgment *P & F Sharpe Ltd.* [1989] I.L.R.M. 570 which is quoted at pp. 506–507.

ground I would call 'illegality,' the second 'irrationality' and the third 'procedural impropriety.' "[94]

It is the second head—irrationality—which has captured the lion's share of the attention. Lord Diplock went on to say of it:

"By 'irrationality' I mean what can by now be succinctly referred to as '*Wednesbury* unreasonableness' (*Associated Provincial Picture Houses Ltd.* v. *Wednesbury Corporation* [1948] 1 K.B. 223). It applies to a decision which is so outrageous in its defiance of logic or of accepted moral standards that no sensible person who had applied his mind to the question to be decided could have arrived at it. Whether a decision falls within this category is a question that judges by their training and experience should be well equipped to answer, or else there would be something badly wrong with our judicial system. . . . "

There were two sets of responses to this reorganisation of judicial review along functional lines. The first, the Irish judicial reaction, has already been examined, in the previous Part: to summarise it, in *Keegan*, Henchy J. appears to have regarded *GCHQ* as requiring a more extreme level of unreasonableness—irrationality than did the older *Wednesbury* test. However, the British academic fall-out from *GCHQ* was less literal and more wide-ranging.[95] This second response is worthy of examination here because, notwithstanding *Keegan*, as we shall see below, post-*GHCQ* developments may be of influence in the future tenor of Irish law. To appreciate the significance of *GCHQ* in Britain, one must recall that in Britain, the major constitutional foundation is the "sovereignty of Parliament" doctrine. It is this dogma which has inspired the conceptual strait-jacket of the *ultra vires* doctrine within which, until *GCHQ*, all restrictions on administrative actions (save for error of law on the face of the record) had had to be accommodated. Thus all such restrictions had to be justified by reference to an imputed legislative intent.

Against this background, it was more awkward for a court to invoke, as a controlling factor upon an administrative action, any factor which could not, however artificially, be justified by reference to the particular legislation involved. It is true that there were some exceptions, examples of which were considered earlier under the head of "General Policy Assumptions." But the fact remains that the *ultra vires* doctrine meant that a court felt less free to take into account considerations and values which, although they were objectively significant, could not in some way be linked to the legislation.

Whatever its precise meaning, Lord Diplock's restatement in the *GCHQ* case has certainly acted as a catalyst. In view of the feature of British law noted in the preceding paragraph, it is not surprising that some British com-

[94] [1985] A.C. 410.
[95] Jowell and Lester, "Beyond *Wednesbury*: Substantive Principles of Administrative Law" [1987] *Public Law* 368. See also, "Proportionality: Neither Novel Nor Dangerous" in Jowell and Oliver (eds.) *New Directions in Judicial Review* (Stevens, 1988); Gearty, "Administrative Law in the 1980s (1987) 9 D.U.L.J.(N.S.) 91; Allan, "Pragmatism and Theory in Public Law" (1988) 104 L.Q.R. 422; P. P. Craig, *Administrative Law* (2nd ed., 1989), pp. 296–304.

mentators should emphasise the reclassification of the relevant law into "illegality" and "irrationality." They implicitly reject the narrow bounds which had been attributed to the category of "irrationality" by Henchy J. in *Keegan*. They argue that, whilst "illegality" is concerned with the infidelity of an official action to a statutory purpose and, thus, is tied to the intention of the legislature, by contrast, "irrationality," now fortified by classification as an independent and distinct category, provides a device which emancipates a reviewing court to give greater weight to objectively significant considerations. Among these considerations are: bad administrative practice, such as unfairness or unjustifiable inconsistency; vagueness or lack of certainty in the effect of a decision or standard and unjustifiable violation of fundamental rights. Among the sources of such fundamental rights are the European Convention on Human Rights.[96]

In *GCHQ*, some support was given to those who saw Lord Diplock's statement as more than a mere restatement, by the following tantalising remark, which Lord Diplock made in the course of the seminal passage from his judgment:

"That is not to say that further development on a case by case basis may not in course of time add further grounds. I have in mind particularly the possible adoption in the future of the principle of 'proportionality' which is

---

[96] The European Convention was invoked in the Northern Irish case of *Re Curran and McCann's Application* [1985] N.I. 261. In this part of the case (for the other parts, see pp. 200–201 and pp. 399–400) the question was whether it would be lawful for Craigavon Borough Council to exclude Sinn Féin councillors from council meetings on the ground that members of a party which, as a matter of policy, supports terrorism, should not be permitted to sit in the Council. This question was considered, in the first place, on the assumption that the protective and self-defensive powers of a council did include the power to exclude members of a party which, outside the council chamber, proclaims a policy of violence. The applicants argument was that—to use the language of *GCHQ* (though in fact, the court used the language of *Wednesbury*-reasonableness)—the Council's action was "irrational". In response, Hutton J. quoted from Lord Denning's judgment in *R.* v. *Chief Immigration Officer* [1976] 3 All E.R. 843, 847e.

"The position, as I understand it, is that if there is any ambiguity in our statutes or uncertainty in our law, then these courts can look to the Convention as an aid to clear up the ambiguity and uncertainty, seeking always to bring them into harmony with it."

Hutton J. went on to quote Article 17 of the Convention which states:

"Nothing in this Convention may be interpreted as implying for any State, group or person any right to engage in any activity or perform any act aimed at the destruction of any of the rights and freedoms set forth herein . . . "

Possibly because he did not apply the Convention directly, Hutton J. did not take the point that Article 17 was negative in effect. Rather, he adopted Article 17 as the main source of support for his finding that the Council would not be unreasonable in excluding Sinn Féin councillors if it had the power to do so.

A further aspect of this point was the applicant's contention that the exclusion was unreasonable because the Sinn Féin councillor's purpose in the Council Chamber was not to advocate violence but to discuss matters such as roads, houses, etc. This point was rejected on the ground that whatever their content, Council Chamber speeches would be intended to gather support for Sinn Féin. This was the same argument which was used by the Supreme Court in *The State (Lynch)* v. *Cooney* [1982] I.R. 337, 336 and extracts were quoted, with approval, from O'Higgins C.J.'s judgment in that case.

recognised in the administrative law of several of our fellow members of the European Economic Community."[97]

In short, there must be some sort of balance between the injury to an individual's interest caused by an administrative measure and the consequential gain to the polity. Now, hitherto, *proportionalité* had not existed as an explicit category in Anglo-Irish law although it did exist in Continental law.[98] In Germany, for example, the principle has been applied in cases involving the expulsion of foreigners who have been convicted of an offence. The expulsion of a person who had committed a violent crime was upheld[99]; but the expulsion of someone who had committed a traffic offence was quashed.[1] Again, in France, the *proportionalité* doctrine has given birth (in the planning and compulsory acquisition field) to *le bilan cout avantages* (a balance of costs and benefits). This stemmed from a compulsory acquisition case in which the Conseil d'Etat had stated that a Minister could not declare an acquisition to be in the public interest unless "the interference with private property, the financial cost, and where they arose, the attendant social inconveniences are not excessive having regard to the needs of the operation."[2] The doctrine plays a central part in the jurisprudence of both the European Court of Justice and the European Court of Human Rights. In a case before the former, an attack on a Council Regulation which made skimmed milk powder compulsory for the feeding of livestock (in order to reduce surpluses of the powder) succeeded because the powder cost users three times the price of vegetable feeding stuffs.[3]

Yet, as can be seen from these unsurprising examples, proportionality is a significant concept in any kind of just reasoning and, also to make a point to which we must return, an essential component of "reasonableness." Accordingly, whilst it is only just coming to be accepted as a discrete category in English law, yet it has always played a significant if unacknowledged part. A well-known example, drawn from the pre-*GCHQ* era, is *R.* v. *Barnsley M.B.C., ex p. Hook*,[4] in which the local authority suspended a stallholder's licence because he had been guilty of misconduct in that he had urinated in the street and sworn at an official who remonstrated with him. The Court of Appeal

---

[97] [1985] A.C. 410. However, the doctrine suffered a blow in *R.* v. *Home Secretary ex p. Brind* [1990] 1 All E.R. 469; [1991] 1 All E.R. 720.
[98] See Jowell and Lester, "Proportionality: Neither Novel Nor Dangerous" in Jowell and Oliver (eds.) *New Directions in Judicial Review*, (Stevens and Sons, London 1988) from which the examples given in this paragraph of the text are drawn.
[99] 59 B. VerwGE 105 and 112.
[1] 60 B VerwGE 75.
[2] *Ville Novvelle Est* C. E. Mai 28, 1971. Rec. 410, Concl. Braibant.
[3] *Bela-Muhle Josef Bergmann* v. *Grows-Farm* (Case 114/76) [1977] E.C.R. 1211. See also, *Fromonçais S.A.* v. *FORMA* (Case 66/82) [1983] E.C.R. 395 where the Court of Justice stated:

> "In order to establish whether a provision of Community law is consonant with the principle of proportionality it is necessary to establish, in the first place, whether the means it employs to achieve its aim correspond to the importance of the aim and in the second place whether they are necessary for its achievement."

For a recent discussion of the proportionality doctrine in a Community Law context, see *O'Brien* v. *Ireland* [1990] I.L.R.M. 466.
[4] [1976] 1 W.L.R. 1052.

struck down the suspension because of breach of the *audi alteram partem* rule. However, two of the three judges offered it as an alternative ground that in the words of Lord Denning "the punishment is altogether excessive and out of proportion to the occasion."[4a]

One can perhaps conclude this discussion of contemporary developments, some of them with a whiff of *leges ferenda*, in Britain by rehearsing the advantages and drawbacks which have been ascribed to it. The advantages, it is claimed, are twofold. In the first place, it renders the judiciary less restricted in developing a range of more appropriate, comprehensive and precise principles by which to police the exercise of administrative powers. Secondly and this is a related point—the existence of such principles would enable a court to give a better reasoned explanation as to why a decision was struck down or upheld. There would be less suspicion of judicial subjectivity within the *Wednesbury* cocoon: a court would be better able than if it were wielding the blunt instrument of *Wednesbury*-reasonableness to articulate reasons which would repulse the accusation of simply following (consciously or unconsciously) its own beliefs. It seems that Irish courts, anyway, have seldom been concerned with the long-term dangers of such accusations; but they may nevertheless, be a danger.

It would be hard to quarrel with such admirable objectives. However, one should not overestimate the extent of the change, even in a jurisdiction in which it had been universally accepted by the judiciary.[5]

For the *Wednesbury* catalogue, boldly used, would catch most of the deficiences which come within the proposed new law. Reasonableness, for instance, would encompass unfairness, violation of fundamental rights, or lack of proportionality. The proposed head of unjustifiable discrimination could probably have been accommodated within "taking into account an irrelevant factor," or bad faith. Nevertheless the changes do advance beyond a change of labels in that they free the judges from the restrictive associations of the *ultra vires* rule. They make explicit what was unstated before and so give greater self-confidence to judges.

As a practical matter, especially in a jurisdiction such as England, where the judges lack what one Irish judge speaking extra-judicially called "the secure foot-hold" of a written constitution, this development can in a sense be used as a substitute for a written constitution. However, the hard questions about the proper balance between freedom and control in the context of the courts' supervision of administrative actions—questions of values or appreciation rather than techique—remain. One distinguished and even-handed British commentator has remarked[6]:

[4a] *Ibid.* 1057–1058. See also Sir John Pennycuick at 1063.

[5] And one should note parenthetically that in England, to date, most of the enthusiasm for these new developments has come from academic commentators, who have analysed judgments in the light of the new learning, rather than from actual use of the new concepts by the judges; see the two articles by Professor Jowell and Mr. Lester cited at p. 530, n. 95.

[6] P. P. Craig, *Administrative Law* (1989), pp. 299–300. The "*Bromley* decision" refers to *Bromley L.B.C.* v. *G.L.C.* [1983] A.C. 768 and the arguments which Mr. Craig is appraising are to be found in Jowell and Lester, "Proportionality: Neither Novel nor Dangerous." (See n. 98).

"The argument has been made that proportionality underlies decisions as diverse as those relating to the legitimacy of planning conditions or local transport policy, disciplinary actions or sex discrimination. The effect of such an argument is however to view proportionality as a more general concept of fairness. If the concept is viewed in this broad way, then its application to any of the diverse areas mentioned above is scarcely more self-executing or clearcut than usage of terms, such as reasonableness, which it seeks to replace. For example to categorise the *Bromley* decision as one which has a 'hidden notion of proportionality,' requiring a balance between the benefits to transport users against the burdens to ratepayers, does not resolve any of the crucially difficult issues in the case. Any answer requires evaluation of the purpose of the legislation; a normative judgment on the strength of property interests and user interests; and some criterion as to what balance between them 'means.' The term proportionality does moreover *not* resolve in and of itself the actual standard of review. When the above questions concerning the *Bromley* case have been answered there is still the further crucial question as to how far the authority can deviate from what the *court* believes to be the correct proportionate balance between the respective interests . . .

[T]he application of substantive principles will require the proper articulation of a background political theory which will serve to explain why a particular principle is said to produce or demand a particular result in a given case. This point requires brief exposition. Intellectual honesty may well require a better explanation as to why an act is unreasonable than that which has been provided by the courts using traditional techniques of review. Concepts such as proportionality or legal certainty may be able to provide a more finely tuned approach. These concepts are not however self-executing, that much is readily apparent from the previous analysis. If the call for the development of substantive principles is to be pursued, then the scale of the undertaking must be fully appreciated. It requires, in all but the most self-evident cases, the recognition that the content which is given to concepts such as proportionality will be dependent upon the identification of the particular political theory which is said to warrant the conclusion which is being drawn."

Impact of the Constitution

For present purposes, of course, the major question raised by the preceding excursus is what relevance it has for Ireland. The answer, it is tentatively suggested, is that it is of substantial indirect relevance. It is not directly relevant because of the major distinction between the British and Irish Constitutions, namely that in Britain, Parliament is sovereign (the central significance of which, in the present area of law, was explained above); whereas, in Ireland, the basic rule is that the Constitution prevails over all other sources of law. The Constitution provides a reservoir of desiderata which the courts should take into account in addition to the parent legislation and, in some cases, even as overriding the parent legislation. Accordingly, it is suggested that for the

Irish courts to take on board the new English law, in an undigested form, would be to obfuscate the law by adding a fifth wheel to the chariot and creating (when coupled with the traditional common law and the Constitution) a very weighty superstructure of concepts for the amount of case law which these concepts are designed to organise. However, on the other hand as we shall see, the Constitution, like every such instrument, is suggestive, rather than fully articulate and so leaves a great deal to judicial interpretation. Thus in reaching their interpretation, Irish judges may, in ploughing what is sometimes virgin territory, derive valuable assistance from English thinking (judicial or academic) given that the two polities have such basic similarities, both in their societies and their governmental machines.[7]

Let us turn now to see what use has actually been made of the Constitution in the context of judicial review of administration or delegated legislation. Before enumerating the three ways in which the Constitution has been used, it ought to be noted that it is now accepted that constitutional provisions apply not only to "laws" (*i.e.* Acts of the Oireachtas) but also to administrative actions and statutory instruments.[8] In some cases, this is done directly. In other cases, it is done by way of the device known as "the presumption of constitutionality." This means that legislation tends to be given a narrow interpretation in order to save the constitutionality of the Act. This has two results: first, the Act is upheld; but secondly, in view of the narrower interpretation given to the Act, some administrative action performed under it is more likely to be struck down as *ultra vires*.[9]

The first, most straightforward, and probably most useful way in which the Constitution can be used, is as a reservoir of specific values and desiderata; (as it happens one of the ways in which the *GCHQ* diaspora is supposed to have enriched English Law). A capital example of this is *The State (Lynch)* v. *Cooney*.[10] The concrete question in this case was the validity of an order, made by the Minister for Posts and Telegraphs, at the time of the February 1982 General Election, directing RTE not to broadcast any programme, including a party political broadcast, inviting support for Provisional Sinn Féin. This order purported to be made under the Broadcasting Authority Act 1960, section 31, inserted by the Broadcasting Authority (Amendment) Act 1976. Under this section:

---

[7] No doubt, the English courts could learn from considering Irish authorities in regard to a number of areas covered in this book, but in fact such authorities have seldom been cited in English courts.

[8] See, *e.g. The State (Quinn)* v. *Ryan* [1965] I.R. 70, 130; *Dillane* v. *Ireland* [1980] I.L.R.M. 167.

[9] For further explanation, see Casey, *Constitutional Law of Ireland*, pp. 285–288.

[10] [1982] I.R. 337. See Gearty (1982) 4 D.U.L.J.(N.S.) 95. In the High Court O'Hanlon J. had ruled that the section was unconstitutional as in his opinion it purported to confer an unreviewable discretionary power on the Minister which might be used to override the rights to free speech protected by Art. 40.6.1. This reasoning is similar to that employed by Kenny J. in *Macauley* v. *Minister for Posts and Telegraphs* [1966] I.R. 345. S.2(1) of the Ministers and Secretaries Act 1924 required that the Attorney-General grant his *fiat* before an action could be commenced against a Minister of State. Kenny J. ruled that the power conferred by s.2(1) was not reviewable by the courts, and, on that basis, he proceeded to invalidate the subsection as it impeded the citizen's right of access to the courts protected by Art. 40.3.

"Where the Minister is of the opinion that the broadcasting of . . . any matter of a particular class would be likely to promote or incite to crime or would tend to undermine the authority of the State, he may by order direct the authority to refrain from broadcasting . . . any matter of the particular class, and the authority shall comply with the order."

The principal question was whether this section was unconstitutional for contravention of Article 40.6.1 which protects the right to free expression which is subject to the exception that the State must "endeavour to ensure that organs of public opinion . . . shall not be used to undermine public order or morality. . . ."

On a literal reading, section 31 is extremely wide: absent bad faith, it would indeed give the Minister the power to determine his own *vires*. Following this interpretation, which had been applied in earlier Supreme Court authorities, the High Court held that it was unconstitutional because, in contrast with the exemption to Article 40.6.1 just quoted, the test for the existence of the power created by the section was subjective and, hence, virtually unreviewable. It is striking that the Supreme Court not only reversed the High Court but also disavowed two of its own previous decisions.[11] O'Higgins C.J.'s judgment was based on a particularly strong application of the presumption of constitutionality. Adopting this approach, the judge was able to read the wording of section 31 in an objective sense so bringing it into line with Article 40.6.1 and upholding the section's constitutionality.

The second and final stage in the Supreme Court's reasoning was to examine whether the order, made by the Minister, banning Sinn Féin from the air-waves was *intra vires* the reduced power created by the court's reading of section 31. Having examined evidence of the organisation's policy—"to disestablish both States, North and South"—the Court held that the Minister was fully justified—indeed, Henchy J. stated that it would have been "perverse" not to hold the opinion prescribed by section 31. Accordingly the order was held to be *intra vires*.

In addition, there have been a number of immigration/deportation cases in which Articles 41 and 42 of the Constitution (The Family and Education) were invoked. In three cases which came before the High Court—*The State (Bouzagou) v. Fitzgibbon St. Garda Station*[12]; *Pok Sun Shum v. Ireland*[13]; and *Osheku v. Ireland*[14] the applicants/plaintiffs sought unsuccessfully to rely on Articles 41 and 42 as grounds for restraining the Minister for Justice from exercising his discretion to deport (*Pok Sun Shun* and *Osheku*) or to refuse entry to (*Bouzagou*) an alien. In the case of deportation, the Minister's discretion is ample, being conditioned upon whether "he deems it to be condu-

---

[11] O'Higgins C.J. said ([1982] I.R. 360): "While the opinion of the former Supreme Court expressed in 1940 (*Re Article 26 and the Offences against the State (Amendment) Bill 1940* [1940] I.R. 470) and 1957 (*Re O'Laighleis* [1960] I.R. 93) reflected what was then current judicial orthodoxy, judicial thinking has since undergone a change."
[12] [1986] I.L.R.M. 98.
[13] [1986] I.L.R.M. 593.
[14] [1987] I.L.R.M. 330.

cive to the public good [to deport]."[15] (The relevant wording was fairly similar in *Bouzagou*). In each case, the alien was married to an Irish citizen (though in *Bouzagou* at least, this point was not critical since it was said that the rights recognised by Articles 41 and 42 are not confined to citizens). In each case, a number of related claims drawn from the Constitution were made. The most representative of these was the submission that, as a result of the Constitution, the Irish citizen was entitled to the society of her spouse or parent within the State and that this constitutional right effectively restricted the Minister's discretion. For present purposes, it is significant that, in each case, the High Court appears to have accepted that, if the rights bestowed by Articles 41 and 42 were absolute, the submission would have succeeded on the ground that the Minister's order was unconstitutional. These submissions failed as a matter of constitutional law (something which is, only of incidental interest here). The decision in each case was based on the notion that there is an exception to the rights of the family under Article 41, for as Gannon J. said in *Osheku*:

"That it is in the interest of the common good of a State that it should have control of the entry of aliens, their departure, and their activities and duration of stay within the State is and has been recognised universally and from earliest times. There are fundamental rights of the State itself as well as fundamental rights of the individual citizens, and the protection of the former may involve restrictions in circumstances of necessity on the latter. The integrity of the State constituted as it is of the collective body of its citizens within the national territory must be defended and vindicated by the organs of the State and by the citizens so that there may be true social order within the territory and concord maintained with other nations in accordance with the objectives in the preamble to the Constitution."[16]

In parenthesis, one should note that notion of the "fundamental rights of the state" is one that may be significant in the future development of administrative law, since the central focus of the subject is the boundary between state and individual rights.

However, in a fourth case, *Fajujonu* v. *Minister for Justice*,[17] admittedly, in somewhat different factual circumstances—the Supreme Court sounded a different emphasis from that of the High Court. The facts of *Fajujonu* were that the first two applicants were aliens, a husband and wife, who had some years previously come to reside in Ireland. The third applicant was their daughter who had been born in Ireland and was, therefore, an Irish citizen. The family had lived illegally within the State and, in these proceedings, they sought an order that the first applicant—the father—should not be deported. Deportation would have meant that the daughter would be faced with the dilemma of either being compulsorily separated from her parents, in breach of her con-

---

[15] Aliens Order 1946, S.R. and O. 1946 No. 395 as amended by the Aliens (Amendment) Order, S.I. 1975 No. 128.
[16] [1987] I.L.R.M. 342.
[17] [1990] I.L.R.M. 234.

stitutional family rights, or, alternatively, being forced to leave the State of which she was a citizen. It was significant—and a point of contrast with the High Court cases—that although the parents were illegal immigrants, they had otherwise done nothing wrong. The resolution of the matter reached by the Supreme Court (which could well be regarded as a warning shot across the Minister for Justice's bows) was that the Minister should only deport the first applicant if he were "satisfied that for good and sufficient reason the 'common good' required it."[18]

A further example is that there must be no religious discrimination[19] and, in particular, that the State, in providing aid for schools, must not "discriminate" between schools.

Nor is this just a matter of fundamental rights *per se*: other constitutional provisions may also be relevant. A straightforward example is Article 15.2.1 (the Oreachtas has "the sole and exclusive power of making laws. . . . ") As explained in more detail above, this was used in *Cooke* v. *Walsh*[20] to strike down regulations made by the Minister of Health, which purported to exclude persons, otherwise entitled under the Health Act 1970 to free medical services, from such entitlement where their injuries were sustained as a result of a road accident and where they were entitled to compensation for their injuries.

The other two ways in which the Constitution may be used are less specific. The second way consists simply of refounding upon the Constitution the traditional common law power to review for: reasonableness, taking irrelevant considerations into account, etc., and, so, giving them a higher status. The instances in which the legislature will actually try to uproot the courts' power of judicial review—and hence in which the statute is held unconstitutional— are few. Accordingly the major practical value of this development is that it encourages the judges to be somewhat bolder in reviewing administrative actions than if they were dependent upon the presumed intention of the legislature[21] The major statement[22] of this source of judicial review is to be found in Henchy J.'s separate, assenting judgment in *The State (Lynch)* v. *Cooney*. We have already mentioned *Lynch* in the context of the other judges' *ratio*, which was grounded on the specific constitutional provision establishing free speech, which was under attack in that case. Henchy J.'s judgment took a wider view based on personal rights (from the expansiveness of the thinking, it is possible that it is not confined to personal rights which are protected by the Constitution). The seminal passage is as follows:

"I conceive the present state of evolution of administrative law in the courts on this topic to be that when a statute confers a decision-making power

---

[18] *Ibid.* 239. The entire quotation is in the text at p. 542, infra.
[19] See, *e.g. Quinn's Supermarket* v. *Att.-Gen.* [1972] I.R. 1; *Mulloy* v. *Minister for Education* [1975] I.R. 88; *M.* v. *An Bord Uchtala* [1975] I.R. 81.
[20] [1984] I.L.R.M. 208. See further, pp. 13–16.
[21] See p. 530.
[22] See also, *Garvey* v. *Ireland* [1981] I.R. 75, 97; *The State (Daly)* v. *Minister for Agriculture* [1987] I.R. 165, 172 (Barron J.)

affecting personal rights on a non-judicial person or body, conditional on that person or body reaching a prescribed opinion or conclusion based on a subjective assessment, a person who shows that a personal right of his has been breached or is liable to be breached by a decision purporting to be made in exercise of that power has standing to seek, and the High Court jurisdiction to give, a ruling as to whether the precondition for the valid exercise of the power has been complied with in a way that brings the decision within the express or necessarily implied range of the power conferred by the statute. It is to be presumed that when Parliament conferred the power it intended it to be exercised only in a manner that would be in conformity with the Constitution and within the limitations of the power as it is to be gathered from the statutory scheme or design. This means, amongst other things, not only that the power must be exercised in good faith, but that the opinion or other subjective conclusion set as a precondition for the valid exercise of the power must be reached by a route that does not make the exercise unlawful—such as by misinterpreting the law, or by misapplying it through taking into consideration irrelevant matters of fact, or through ignoring relevant matters. Otherwise, the exercise of the power will be held to be invalid for being *ultra vires*."[23]

The passage gives a constitutional foundation to the restatement of the general common law which is contained in the final two sentences. The decision in the case may be taken as involving a rejection of the plain words of a statute and, in this, it is certainly in line with recent developments, even in Britain, where the judges do not have the aid and comfort of a written constitution.[24]

The third aspect of the Constitution which needs to be examined is Article 40.1 by which: "All citizens shall, as human persons, be held equal before the law [subject to certain specified exceptions]. . . . "[25] Various passages from *East Donegal* dealing with what may be called "common law abuse of power" have already been quoted. It is notable that, in *East Donegal*, the Supreme Court (Walsh J.) also deduced similar law from Article 40.1.[26] The frequent references to the judgment of the President of the High Court, in the following extract from Walsh J.'s judgment, arise from the fact that Walsh J. was addressing himself to arguments which had found favour in the High Court:

---

[23] [1982] I.R. 330, See also, *D.P.P.* v. *Gilmore* [1981] I.L.R.M. 102, 105 (Henchy J.).

[24] Henchy J. quoted de Smith's *Judicial Review of Administrative Action* (4th ed., 1980), p. 326 with approval: "[T]he courts will not readily be deterred by subjectively worded statutory formulae from determining whether acts done avowedly in pursuance of statutory powers bear an adequate relationship to the purposes prescribed by the statute" ([1982] I.R. 380). The law has come a long way since decisions such as *Liversidge* v. *Anderson* [1942] A.C. 206 where an objectively worded statutory provision was read in a subjective fashion by the majority. For in *Lynch*, a subjectively-worded statutory provision was read in an objective sense.

[25] On which, see Forde, "Equality and the Constitution" (1982) 18 Ir.Jur.(N.S.) 295; Kelly, *op. cit.* pp. 446–466.

[26] Notice also that, in *East Donegal*, the Minister's power to exclude any particular business from the scope of the licensing system was held unconstitutional. In an inadequately explained passage at pp. 349–351, it is unclear whether this result is founded on Art. 40.1 or Art. 15.2.1.

"The learned President of the High Court in his judgment considered that the plaintiffs' claim that the power of the Minister to attach conditions to licences and to amend or to revoke such conditions gave the Minister an uncontrolled discretion which, in the words of the President, 'could be so exercised within the limits of the legislation as to amount to a breach of the guarantee contained in Article 40, s.1, of the Constitution.' The President continued as follows: 'It becomes obvious at once that the attachment of conditions to licences is subject to no such safe-guards as are provided in the case of the refusal or revocation of a licence.' The President went on to say later in that portion of his judgment that 'The contrast with the provisions of section 3(6), and the following subsections is so marked that one is compelled to accept the contention of the plaintiffs that it was intended that the conditions might be arbitrarily imposed, and that such arbitrary imposition of conditions was carefully left free from review. In this respect I have concluded that the legislation *can* be operated within its lawful limits so as to differentiate between citizens in a manner which does not reflect differences of capacity, physical or moral or of social function and accordingly this provision of the legislation, in my view, does offend against the provisions of the Constitution.' . . . It is quite true that conditions need not be uniform for all licences for the reasons already given in this judgment, and that in many cases, they are by their nature necessarily peculiar to an individual applicant. However, it is not valid to infer that the legislation, because it made provision for such a scheme of administration or imposition of conditions, authorised the exercise of that function in a manner amounting to a breach of a right guaranteed by the Constitution. The conditions must be of the character already indicated in this judgment and they must be related to the objects of the Act in the way already indicated."[27]

The question which arises now is this: given the existence of the well-developed common law rules, how does Article 40.1 strengthen the law in this area? To follow this issue, it must be appreciated that equality cannot exist in the abstract. There must be some yardstick by which to classify individuals, situations, etc., as equal or unequal. There are two ways of approaching this problem.

(1) "Equality" means equal treatment, taking as the standard for what constitutes equal cases, the objects of the statute (*supra*). *East Donegal* itself was an example of this type.[28] As is stated in the passage quoted, the conditions imposed could differ from licence-holder A to licence-holder B, provided that they were justifiable by reference to the object of the Act. Whilst this involves no radical advance on the common law, it does help to give a sharper focus to discrimination as a head of review and thus, for example, to smooth the pas-

---

[27] [1970] I.R. 347–348.
[28] See also, *Cassidy* v. *Minister for Industry and Commerce* [1978] I.R. 297, where although Art. 40.1 is not mentioned explicitly, Henchy J. refers to "unfair, unequal and arbitrary treatment" and "discrimination", *The State (Keegan)* v. *Stardust Compensation Tribunal* [1986] I.R. 642, 658.

sage of the doctrine of *proportionalité* (which is considered below) into Irish law.[29]

(2) There must be no arbitrary or unjustifiable discrimination even if this is explicitly authorised by the statute.

The difference between categories (1) and (2) is that in (1) the standard the court is applying is deduced from the statute; whereas in (2), the standard is based on what the court itself, independently of the statute, regards as arbitrary. The difficulty in (2) is thus to decide what constitutes arbitrary discrimination. This is really a question for constitutional, rather than administrative, law. All that can be said here is that it would certainly include discrimination on the grounds of political allegiance, race, sex, illegitimacy, or of being an itinerant and that we know, from the wording of Article 40.1 itself that the concept excludes, "enactments [which] have due regard to differences of capacity, physical and moral, and of social function."

So far as Article 40.1 represents an advance on the common law, it derives from head (2), specifically from the fact that the provision bans arbitrary administrative actions even where these are authorised by the parent statute. Attention should be drawn, however, to the restrictive interpretation given to "as human beings" which has restricted the scope of application of Article 40.1.[30]

However, in assessing Article 40.1, it has to be said that in the present context, as also in the context of invalidating laws,[31] little use (explicit or, as far as can be seen, implicit) has so far been made of it,[32] apart from its invocation in *East Donegal*, a case which could anyway have been decided on common law principles. Even in *Cassidy* v. *Minister for Industry and Commerce* and the cases which followed it, in invoking "unfair, unequal and arbitrary treatment" and (implicitly) discrimination, no reference was made to Article 40.1.

Proportionality

Perhaps the most likely concrete use to which Article 40.1 might be put is as a vehicle for the introduction of the principle of proportionality into Irish law (though as indicated at pages 531–533 it appears to have entered English law without any such aid). The reason for making this connection is that the idea of equal treatment before the law draws with it the idea that, if there are any differences in treatment, that these are only justifiable if they bear some sensible proportion to differences in circumstances. And this is, in a nutshell, the principle of proportionality. In addition we ought to note that, irrespective of Article 40.1, where substantive rights given by the Constitution (and given the existence of the ubiquitous "personal rights" in Article 40.3.1, this is a wide category) are concerned, some notion of proportionality is always involved. This arises

---

[29] *Cf. C.C.S.U.* v. *Minister for Civil Service* [1985] A.C. 374, 410 (Lord Diplock).
[30] The case law is in Kelly, *loc. cit.*
[31] Casey, *op. cit.* p. 347.
[32] Though it is just arguable that Barron J. had Art. 40.1 in mind in *Purcell* v. *Attorney-General*, High Court, November 14, 1989, a case in which it was held to be invalid to enforce a taxing statute (Farm Tax Act 1985) against some only of the persons within its scope.

from the fact that some constitutionally-authorised exemption from the right will also be involved. In reconciling the two, it is always assumed that, in the circumstances of the particular case, there must be a balance between the significance of the purpose served by the law or administrative action and, on the other hand, the damage to the constitutional right which is caused. A recent, explicit statement of this is to be found in *Fajujonu* v. *Minister for Justice*, the facts of which have already been given, in which Walsh J. stated[33]:

> "In my view, he [the Minister for Justice] would have to be satisfied, for stated reasons, that the interests of the common good of the people of Ireland and of the protection of the State and its society are so predominant and so overwhelming in the circumstances of the case that an action which can have the effect of breaking up this family [*sc.* deportation] is not so disproportionate to the aim sought to be achieved as to be unsustainable."

There was, however, no reference to proportionality *per se* in *Fajujonu* and, what is more important, the scope of the case may be regarded as restricted in that it dealt with rights protected by the Constitution.

Also of significance here—although it involved an appeal rather than a review—is the case of *Balkan Tours* v *Minister for Communications*[34]. This case was an appeal to the High Court from the Minister's revocation of a tour operator's licence. The rather brief basis of Lynch J.'s decision was that "the revocation of the licences would cause damage to the plaintiffs which would be disproportionate to their default . . . "[35]

Hand v *Dublin Corporation*,[36] although a somewhat confused case, does involve some discussion of the doctrine of proportionality in the context of judicial review. *Hand*, the facts of which are given below, involved the refusal of a licence under the Casual Trading Act 1980. Here Barron J. recounted the law enunciated in the *Hook* case[37] and then went on to state non-commitally:

> "The principle of proportionality exists in the administrative law of other member states of the European Community. Lord Diplock in *Council of Civil Service Unions* v. *Minister for Civil Service* [1985] A.C. 374, 410 refers to the possible adoption in the future into English law of this principle. The principle itself, that there should be an obligation on an administrative authority when exercising a discretionary power to maintain a proper balance between any adverse effects which its decision might have on the rights, liberties or interests of persons and the purpose pursued by that authority, is one annexed to Recommendation No. R (80) 2 adopted by the Committee of Ministers of the Council of Europe on the 11th March, 1980. Nevertheless, this principle, even if adopted in this jurisdiction, applies only in the exercise of administrative powers. As such it could be applied to the exercise of the Minister's discretion under the Act. Different consider-

---

[33] [1990] I.L.R.M. 242. For the facts, see pp. 537–538.
[34] [1988] I.L.R.M. 101.
[35] *Ibid.* 108.
[36] [1989] I.R. 26.
[37] [1976] 1 W.L.R. 1052, 1057, 1063. See p. 543.

ations apply in relation to section 4(6) since it is the Oireachtas which has imposed the sanction."[38]

Since the defendant local authority was not relying on an exercise of the Minister's discretion, there was no need for Barron J. to take this point further and he did not do so.

To appreciate the other aspect of *Hand*, one needs to know that the case centred on section 4(5) of the Casual Trading Act 1980. The Act makes casual trading an offence unless it is authorised by a licence which is issued by a local authority. Unfortunately the provision at the centre of the case had been drafted badly. The first submission of the plaintiff, who had been refused a licence by Dublin Corporation, was that the provision was "so uncertain as to its meaning that it must be disregarded."[39] It appears from the fact that Barron J. did not condemn this proposition that he accepted it, as a matter of law. In any event, he went on to find that, on the facts, it did not apply because he was able to interpret the provision. The judge held that the provision meant that if an applicant for a licence had at least two convictions under the Act and, secondly, if a period of at least five years had not elapsed since the most recent of his convictions, then the authority was precluded from granting a licence. Both conditions applied to the plaintiff and, accordingly, she had not been granted a licence.

The plaintiff's main contention was, however, that the provisions in question were unconstitutional in that the penalty imposed—which in effect deprives them of earning their living—was a punishment out of proportion to the nature of the offence. In the passage quoted earlier, Barron J. had held that, even assuming that the principle of proportionality, as such, existed in Irish law, it could only apply to an administrative action and not where, as in the instant case, the outcome about which complaint was made resulted from the mandatory application of a statutory provision. However, the judge, went on to consider, in the following passage, whether in an appropriate case, he would have been prepared to hold the section unconstitutional[40]:

> "Treating the grant of a licence under the Casual Trading Act, 1980, as a certificate of fitness to trade under the provisions of that Act, it seems to me that it is appropriate that the statute itself may set out the circumstances in which the privilege may be lost. *Such circumstances must however be reasonable.* Can it be said to be unreasonable on the part of the Oireachtas to provide that a casual trading licence shall not be given to a person who has already at the date of application two convictions for offences under the Act?
>
> *It is said to be unreasonable because the penalty is out of proportion to the offence.* The offence is the commission of two offences, which may be trivial in their nature, whereas the penalty is the right to earn one's living. Undoubtedly some of the offences which may bring s.5, subs. 6 into effect

---

[38] [1989] I.R. 29. The Supreme Court judgment (of March 7, 1991) appears to agree very briefly (at p. 19) with the view that the doctrine of proportionality could not have been relevant on the facts of *Hand*.
[39] *Ibid.*
[40] *Ibid.* 130.

may be relatively unimportant and its effect may have serious consequences in individual cases. However, the right to earn one's living by casual trading is given by the Act. It does not seem to be unreasonable for the Oireachtas, having granted that privilege, to deprive persons of it for conduct directly referable to the fitness of the person concerned to exercise that same privilege. That, in my view, is the position here." (Authors' italics)

In assessing the significance of this passage, various comments may be made. First, since either striking down legislation, (or possibly reading down legislation by the presumption of constitutionality), was involved here, the source of this "reasonableness" or proportionality must be the Constitution. (The Constitution was mentioned in the submission of counsel for the applicant.) While the exact Constitutional provision was not identified, the most appropriate provision would appear to be Article 40.1. As has been already explained, Barron J. had earlier said in his judgment in *Hand* that the principle of proportionality, if it existed at all in Irish law (which was left as an open point) could only apply to administrative actions and not to legislation. This distinction depends, it is suggested, upon a fairly unimportant point of semantics. For, if there is in Irish law some principle which is in substance similar to that of proportionality and which is derived from the Constitution then the terminology is unimportant. And if it is derived from the Constitution it would (whatever its title) presumably apply to administrative actions (or delegated legislation) as well as to Acts of the Oireachtas.

The substantive question remains, namely whether *Hand* acknowledges the existence of some notion akin to proportionality, in Irish law. The most that can be said is that this seems to be accepted, at least for the sake of argument, in particular in the opening sentence of the second paragraph of the passage quoted. The remainder of this paragraph then goes on to reject the relevance of any such principle on the facts of the case on a ground which is not of general interest, namely that casual trading is a "privilege" granted by act of the Oireachtas.[41]

Thus the principle of proportionality appears to have won a foothold in Irish law by way of *Cassidy, Fajujonu, Balkan Tours* and *Hand*. A great deal remains to be ironed out in future cases.

---

[41] On the facts in *Hand*, the judge did not strike down the provision requiring the refusal of a licence. However, the reasoning in the quotation seems to depend critically on Barron J.'s premise, *viz.* that "the right to earn one's living by casual trading is given by the Act." The correctness of this may be open to doubt: as Professor Kelly has written: "The truth, historically, in this State or in any other must be that once upon a time everyone was free to sell drink, lay bets or travel in a vehicle . . . ." See Kelly, *The Irish Constitution* (Dublin 1984), p. 401. Moreover the passage quoted was preceded by a discussion of *Conroy* v. *Attorney-General* [1965] I.R. 411. In this well-known case, a rather different issue was involved. This was the question of whether disqualification from driving a motor vehicle was to be counted in assessing the severity of an offence for the purpose of determining whether the offence was a "minor offence" (Article 38.5) so that there was no right to be tried by jury. Against this background, it was remarked by Kenny J. in *Conroy* that if the disqualification were "unreasonable" then this would mean that it should be regarded as penal, and hence could be counted for the purpose of Article 38.5. But all this is a long way from the context in which unreasonableness was significant in *Hand* (where no jury was involved). The view that this argument was relevant in *Hand* was accepted at p. 16 of the Supreme Court judgment.

4. Failure to Exercise a Discretion

Whereas "abuse of discretion" refers to a wrongly-exercised discretion, failure to exercise a discretion means that a public body vested with a discretionary power has incapacitated itself from being able to exercise its discretion at all. More specifically, there are at least six ways in which this undesirable result may be brought about, *viz.*: by delegating the decision to another body; by acting on the dictation of another body; by some previous agreement, representation, etc.; by a general blanket policy in the area; by taking the decision over such a broad area that all elements of it cannot have been adequately scrutinised; or by "rubber-stamping" a decision. The first two heads have already been discussed in Chapter 8.12 and 14, since they apply generally to all types of decision and are not peculiar to discretionary powers. The third head is examined in Chapter 13.2. Accordingly here we shall deal only with the remaining four ways in which a body may disable itself from exercising its discretion freely and fully.

Adhering to an inflexible policy rule[42]

Various dangers attend on a discretionary power, for instance, the danger of being, or seeming, arbitrary, partial, inconsistent or unpredictable. One way of avoiding these dangers is to proclaim and follow some precise and rational policy-rule in the exercise of the discretion. Such a solution carries its own difficulty, namely that, to the extent that the rule is rigidly followed, it emphasises a single policy and shuts out consideration of all others and thus neutralises the discretion which it was the intention of the legislature to create. Thus, on some pure plane, one would expect that where a discretionary decision is taken in accordance with a rule, it would therefore be invalid. On the other hand, common sense suggests that, in view of the desirability of avoiding arbitrariness and the other defects mentioned, the law should lean far over to accommodate such rules of practice. The result of these conflicting tensions is that there is a principle banning policy rules, but it is subject to a fairly wide exception.

Straightforward illustrations of the principle occurred in recent cases decided by Finlay P. In *Re N, a solicitor*,[43] the applicant had fallen into some difficulties in running his practice, and he subsequently failed to apply for a practising certificate. The Incorporated Law Society had a rule of practice that, in such circumstances, an applicant is bound to spend a year as an assistant solicitor in a solicitor's office before being considered for a full practising certificate and thus when N did apply for a certificate, he was refused a full certificate. Finlay P. held that the rule unduly fettered the discretion of the Society, and prevented full consideration of the merits of the applicant's case. While the Society was entitled to have a policy, it could not be applied to all cases in an inflexible manner. Finlay P. accordingly reversed the order made

---

[42] See [1976] *Public Law* 332 (D. J. Galligan).
[43] High Court, June 30, 1980. See also, *Rice* v. *Dublin Corporation* [1947] I.R. 425, 455–456; *East Donegal* v. *Att.-Gen.* [1970] I.R. 317, 344; *Norris* v. *Att.-Gen.* [1984] I.R. 36, 81 (McCarthy J.), *Cosgrove* v. *The Legal Aid Board* High Court, October 17, 1990, pp. 2 and 25; *Frenchchurch Properties Ltd.* v. *Wexford County Council*, High Court, April 12, 1991, pp. 19–20.

by the Society, saying that the Society may have paid insufficient regard "to the likely effect on a prospective employer of an applicant of the age of this applicant seeking employment and not carrying a full unqualified certificate."

In the second case, *The State (Kershaw)* v. *Eastern Health Board*,[44] the applicant was in receipt of unemployment benefit, but was still experiencing financial difficulties, *inter alia*, because her husband had deserted her. She applied for a supplementary welfare allowance in respect of fuel which was operated by the respondents under the terms of the Social Welfare (Consolidation) Act 1981. If the applicant could establish that her means were insufficient to meet her needs and those of her dependent children, then she enjoyed a right under the 1981 Act to a supplementary welfare allowance. However, her application was refused because under the terms of a ministerial circular she was ineligible for consideration since she was already in receipt of unemployment benefit. Finlay P. declared the circular invalid and quashed the decision based on it because the circular "purport[ed] to exclude absolutely" the health board's discretion to consider whether the applicant's means were sufficient for her needs.

On the other side of the line was *British Oxygen* v. *Board of Trade*.[45] The Board had a statutory discretion to make industrial capital grants: it had adopted a blanket policy of not giving grants towards expenditure of less than £25 per individual unit. British Oxygen had invested over £4 million, but the individual unit cost was only £20. The House of Lords held that particularly where a large number of similar decisions is involved, an administrative authority is entitled to evolve a precise policy. The only *caveat* is that the deciding agency must not totally ignore an argument that although a particular case fell outside the policy rule, yet it might be treated as an exception and the discretion exercised in its favour. On the facts, the House of Lords held rather surprisingly, that this requirement had been observed. The same idea has been expressed in the following classic passage from *R.* v. *Port of London, ex p. Kynoch*[46]:

> "There are on the one hand cases where a tribunal in the honest exercise of its discretion has adopted a policy, and without refusing to hear an applicant intimates to him what its policy is, and that after hearing him it will in accordance with its policy decide against him, *unless there is something exceptional in his case.* . . . On the other hand there are cases where the tribunal has passed a rule or come to a determination not to hear any application of a particular character by whomsoever made. There is a wide distinction to be drawn between the two classes."

It can thus be seen that, in England, at least, the exception has substantially diluted the principle banning "a policy-rule."

A similar exception probably exists in Ireland. For example, where limited

---

[44] [1985] I.L.R.M. 235. (For the question of why the case did not engage the principle against "acting under dictation . . . " see p. 405, n. 780). See also, *Att.-Gen. (ex rel. Tilley)* v. *Wandsworth L.B.C.* [1981] 1 W.L.R. 854.
[45] [1971] A.C. 610.
[46] [1919] 1 K.B. 176, 184. See also, *Re Findlay* [1985] A.C. 318.

resources, like corporation houses, are being distributed, the system often adopted is to give credit to those whose name has been longest on the waiting list. The question arises whether such a waiting list is valid, a question which was relevant, though it was not directly addressed, in *McDonald* v. *Dublin Corporation*[47] and *McNamee* v. *Buncrana U.D.C.*[48]

In *McDonald*, the Supreme Court, *per* O'Higgins C.J. had held that where a person is in need of housing, there is a duty on the relevant housing authority at least to consider whether their needs outweigh those of other applicants even if the other applicants have been waiting longer. However, especially when *McDonald* is read in the light of O'Higgins C.J.'s later comment in *McNamee* on his judgment in *McDonald*, it seems that the idea of the waiting list is not entirely condemned. O'Higgins C.J. said in *McNamee*:

> "It was not intended to suggest [in *McDonald*] that a housing authority need not have regard as a matter of priority to those in its functional area who have been resident or domiciled there for a particular period of time."[49]

On this interpretation, what was being said in *McDonald* (which involved rather an extreme case) was only that in a strong enough case—that is, strong in the context of the purposes of the Housing Act 1966—the housing authority must be prepared to override the dictates of the waiting list; and not that the waiting list may always, or even usually, be ignored. In short, a policy rule was permitted. On this analysis, there is a good deal in common between *McDonald-McNamee* and the passage quoted *infra* from *Kynoch*.

One can reconcile *N* and *Kershaw* with this line of authority on the basis that these two cases involved situations which were so exceptional that the Incorporated Law Society and the Eastern Health Board, respectively, should have been prepared at least to consider a departure from their usual rule of practice. That said, there is bound to be a margin of appreciation in the word "exceptional" and it seems likely that the House of Lords in *British Oxygen* required a higher standard of "exceptional circumstances" before they would intervene than did the High Court in *N* and *Kershaw*.

There remains a further related point: in spite of the substantial relaxation of the principle banning policy rules, it must surely follow from the law explained in Part 2 of this chapter, that for a policy rule to be permissible, its content must not fly in the face of the policies envisaged by the relevant statute. An example is afforded by the multi-faceted case of *The State (McGeough)* v. *Lough County Council*[50] in which the applicant complained successfully of a county manager's refusal to give his consent, required under the Labourers Act 1936, to the sale of the applicant's labourer's cottage. This refusal was motivated, in part, by a general resolution passed by the Council expressing disfavour of any such sale. Leaving aside the fact that the decision

---

[47] Supreme Court, July 23, 1980. For other issues in *McDonald* and *McNamee*, see pp. 210–211.
[48] [1983] I.R. 213.
[49] *Ibid.* 220.
[50] (1973) 107 I.L.T.R. 13, 19.

was vested not in the Council, but in the county manager,[51] one of the grounds on which the applicant succeeded was that the purpose of the 1936 Act was taken to be that the owner of a cottage should be allowed to sell it save in the exceptional cases in which the manager's consent was withheld, whereas the council resolution purported to ban sales in any circumstances whatsoever. The resolution was thus "wholly improper as an attempt on [the Council's] part to amend the statutory conditions on which purchasers hold their cottages."[52]

Failing to address the specific issue[53]

Consider a discretionary power taking the following form: "If it appears to the Minister that [a particular state of affairs is so] then the Minister may exercise [such a power in connection with that state of affairs]." What the rule presently under discussion means is that the Minister will only be regarded as having properly exercised his discretion if he has genuinely considered whether the requisite state of affairs exists in relation to all the areas which are affected by his exercise of the power. Thus, if the power is exercised over a very broad area, a court is liable to say that the Minister cannot be sure that the requisite state of affairs genuinely exists in relation to the entire area caught by the Minister's decision. Two examples[54] of this rule in operation in modern Irish law may be cited of which the first is *Limerick Corporation* v. *Sheridan*,[55] the facts of which have already been given. To recapitulate, the relevant statutory provision allowed the Corporation to prohibit temporary dwellings on any land where their "erection would be prejudicial to public health." The Corporation made an order affecting almost the entire area of the county borough. One of the grounds on which the order was struck down was that the area covered was so large that the court thought it unlikely that the Corporation could have formed the requisite opinion with respect to *all* parts of the land caught by the order.

The second example is the case of *Roche* v. *Minister for Industry and Commerce*[56] which concerned a mineral acquisition order made by the Minister in respect of "all minerals . . . under the land described in the Schedule to this Order . . . " The order was made under the Minerals Development Act 1940, section 14(1) by which:

"Whenever it appears to the Minister that there are minerals on or under any land and that such minerals are not being worked . . . and the Minister is of opinion that it is desirable in the public interest, with a view to the exploitation of such minerals, that the working of such minerals should be

---

[51] For "acting under the dictation of another body," see *McGeough* (1973) 107 I.L.T.R. 13, 19 and see generally pp. 405–407.
[52] (1973) 107 I.L.T.R. 18, 20, 24–26, 28.
[53] This rubric seems not to be used in the British textbooks.
[54] For another example, see *The State (Minister for Local Government)* v. *Ennis U.D.C.* [1939] I.R. 258, 260.
[55] (1956) 90 I.L.T.R. 59.
[56] [1978] I.R. 149.

controlled by the State, the Minister . . . may by order . . . compulsorily acquire such minerals."

Dealing with the rule we are illustrating, Henchy J. said, in *Roche*:

" . . . [T]he Minister must make an appraisal of the situation in the light of the particular mineral substances which he invoked . . . and must consider whether it is desirable in the public interest, with a view to their exploitation, that the working of them should be controlled by the State . . . the acquisition orders in question here [are] bad for they are blanket orders to cover "all minerals" under the land . . . and thereby show a want of the discrimination and appraisal necessary on the part of the Minster to comply with the . . . prerequisites set out in the subsection."[57]

Rubber-stamping

Finally, we should describe a rule which involves a fairly similar situation. This rubric covers the straightforward notion that a discretionary power must be exercised in substance and not merely in form. One illustration is provided by a case which has already been mentioned in Chapter 3, namely *Inspector of Taxes' Association* v. *Minister for the Public Service*.[58] Up to 1960 a staff association known as the Association of Inspectors of Taxes represented Inspectors of Taxes (Technical). In 1960 the expansion of the PAYE scheme to cover all employees necessitated the appointment of extra staff to the Revenue Commissioners. A number of additional Inspectors of Taxes were appointed, who; possessed no technical qualifications; were not granted a commission by the Minister and were designated "Inspectors of Taxes (Clerical)." However, the Minister refused to create a separate grade for these new Inspectors. The plaintiff association was formed in 1980 to represent the interests of Inspectors of Taxes (Technical) only and not the Inspector of Taxes (Clerical). The association sought recognition from the Minister for the Public Service in order to be allowed to participate in the public service Conciliation and Arbitration Scheme. This claim depended upon the argument that there should be separate gradings for Technical and Clerical Inspectors. When this argument was rejected, the association challenged the decision on the ground that the Minister had not really examined the possibility of regrading, but instead had merely looked back to the refusal by the Minister for Finance (the predecessor of the Minister for the Public Service) in 1960, of an earlier request that a distinct grade for Clerical Inspectors be established. Rejecting this argument, Finlay C.J. held that before taking the 1980 decision:

"[The Minister had gone] in detail into the existing situation in 1980 of the various categories of Inspectors of Taxes; the work that they carried out; and the material factors which might be appropriate if a re-grading of them had been contemplated."

---

[57] *Ibid.* 156.
[58] [1986] I.L.R.M. 296. See also, pp. 94–95.

Finlay C.J. concluded that the Minister had come to a considered decision on the application to regrade, and that decision could not be attacked as unreasonable.

Further examples are afforded by *The State (Thornhill)* v. *Minister for Defence*[59] and *Rederij Kennemerland N.V.* v. *Att.-Gen.*[60] The former case concerned a wound pension which is payable as a result of a disablement due to a wound attributable to army service. Under section 13 of the Army Pensions Act 1923, if (as had occurred in the instant case) any claimant for a pension has been able to recover civil damages from any person in respect of the wound, then the Minister may "having regard to the amount of that compensation, either terminate the pension or allowance or reduce the amount thereof." In the Supreme Court, Finlay C.J. dealt with the correct approach to be adopted by the Minister towards the exercise of his discretion as follows:

> "[The statute] does not mean that the Army Pensions Board assesses the pension in accordance with the appropriate schedules and that, it having done so and the Minister having approved of that assessment, there should be an automatic subsuming of the pension into what is calculated to be the annuity purchasable by the lump sum of compensation. The Minister's function is to take the compensation into consideration; he may consider it inappropriate to abate the mathematical calculation of the pension at all; he may only consider it appropriate to abate it by reference to the loss of earnings content or some other specific element of the compensation received, or he may consider it appropriate to abate it by a relatively small amount only. The statutory function of the Minister is to make a *bona fide* individual decision in each such case."[61]

In *Rederij Kennemerland*, a Peace Commissioner made out a detention order under the Fisheries (Consolidation) Act 1959. The Commissioner apparently acquiesced in the form of order prepared by the Attorney-General's office and he did not exercise any independent judicial judgment in the matter. While this case more properly falls to be considered under the rubric of "Acting under Dictation,"[62] it is notable that in quashing the order, Gannon J. said of the Peace Commissioner that he did no more than "provide by his presence and signature the formal appearances of compliances with the statutory requirements."[63]

What is probably a further illustration of this notion can be drawn from *Fajujonu* v. *Minister for Justice*,[64] the facts of which have already been given. Here the appeal was formally dismissed, but, at the same time, the Supreme Court enunciated some definitive views as to how they expected the Minister to treat the Fajujonu family in the future. Finlay C.J. stated:

---

[59] [1986] I.R. 1 followed in *McKinley* v. *The Minister for Defence* [1988] I.R. 139 and also in *Breen* v. *Minister for Defence* Supreme Court, July 20, 1990.
[60] [1989] I.L.R.M. 821.
[61] [1986] I.R. 12.
[62] See pp. 405–407.
[63] [1989] I.L.R.M. 821, 839.
[64] [1990] I.L.R.M. 234.

"[T]here is not any finding [of fact] that the existence of important family rights in the children of this marriage have been ignored. . . . Neither, however, is there a finding nor any evidence, it would appear to me, to support a finding of a careful consideration of those rights and a particular importance attached to them by reason of their constitutional origin. In any event the position of the family itself, the exercise by it of its rights to remain as a family unit and the exigencies of the common good which may be affected by the continued residence in the State of the first and second-named plaintiffs, are all matters which must of necessity, have been subject to at least the possibility, of very substantial change since this matter was investigated in 1984.

In these circumstances, I am satisfied that the protection of the constitutional rights which arise in this case require a fresh consideration now by the Minister for Justice, having due regard to the important constitutional rights which are involved . . . I am, however, satisfied also that if, having had due regard to those considerations and having conducted such inquiry as may be appropriate as to the facts and factors now affecting the whole situation in a fair and proper manner, the Minister is satisfied that for good and sufficient reason the common good requires that the residence of these parents within the State should be terminated, even though that has the necessary consequence that in order to remain as a family unit the three children must also leave the State, that this is an order he is entitled to make pursuant to the Act of 1935."[65]

This passage can be taken as an example of the idea under discussion, namely that a discretionary power must be scrupulously exercised, especially where constitutional rights are involved.

5. Are There Unreviewable Discretionary Powers?

Writing in 1966, Professor Kelly stated that:

" . . . provided an authority entrusted with administrative discretion keeps inside its *vires* and (where appropriate) commits no open breach of natural justice it may act as foolishly, unreasonably or even unfairly as it likes and the Courts cannot (or at any rate will not) interfere."[66]

Commenting on this statement only five years later, the same writer made *amende honorable*:

"In the light of four subsequent Irish decisions, it is clear that this point of view, whatever justification it may have had in 1966, does not now correctly state Irish law on the matter; . . . the Courts have, within the last three

---

[65] *Ibid.* 238–239.
[66] Kelly, "Administrative Discretion and the Courts" (1966) 1 Ir.Jur.(N.S.), 209, 210. Note, however, such cases as *The State (McGeough)* v. *Louth C.C.* (1973) 107 I.L.T.R. 13 which was decided in 1956 but not reported until 1973, and *The State (O'Mahoney)* v. *South Cork Board of Public Health* [1941] Ir.Jur.Rep. 79.

years, explicitly marked out bridgeheads from which the exercise of statutory discretion can be controlled on more penetrating criteria than mere *vires* (as traditionally understood) or natural justice."[67]

The preceding parts of this chapter consist largely of an account of the break-out from these bridgeheads.

The islands of immunity from judicial review which continue to remain above the waterline are few and each of them has to be justified by cogent reasons. Before going on to examine these exceptional areas, it is appropriate to describe some illustrations of the general proposition, namely that the tide of judicial review has been steadily rising.

To begin then, a number of instances of judicial intervention in situations which might previously have been thought to present non-justiciable issues may be given. In *Re Haughey*[68] it is striking that the Supreme Court was prepared to consider whether the Dáil Public Accounts Committee had transgressed the boundaries fixed for it by the Dáil Standing Orders (though without explicitly considering the question of whether the court was empowered to intervene in the internal proceedings of the Oireachtas).[69] In *Re Article 26 and the Emergency Powers Bill 1976*,[70] the Supreme Court expressly reserved for consideration the question of whether it had jurisdiction to review a declaration of emergency passed by both Houses of the Oireachtas, despite the fact that, to judge by the clear words and purpose of Article 28.3.3, it was intended that the Oireachtas should have the final say on this question. Again, in *Inspector of Taxes* v. *Minister for the Public Service*[71] the Supreme Court stated that a decision of the Minister in regard to grading, which affects the salary and career prospects of certain civil servants, is, like any other administrative action, open to review. Other decisions indicate that the exercise of certain prosecutorial discretions may be subject to review. In *The State (O'Callaghan)* v. *O'hUadaigh*[72] Finlay P. accepted that the power of the Director of Public Prosecutions to enter a *nolle prosequi* was reviewable and in *Norris* v. *Attorney-General*[73] McCarthy J. suggested that a positive

---

[67] Kelly, "Judicial Review of Administrative Action: New Irish Trends" (1971) 6 Ir.Jur.(N.S.) 40. The four subsequent Irish decisions referred to were: *Listowel U.D.C.* v. *McDonagh* [1968] I.R. 312; *Central Dublin Development Assoc.* v. *Att.-Gen.* (1975) 109 I.L.T.R. 69; *Kiely* v. *Minister for Social Welfare* [1971] I.R. 21 and *East Donegal Co-Operatives Ltd.* v. *Att.-Gen.* [1970] I.R. 317.
[68] [1971] I.R. 217. See also the abortive *Norris* proceedings described at p. 415, n. 28.
[69] See *O'Crowley* v. *Minister for Finance* [1935] I.R. 536 for an affirmation of the traditional rule that the courts will not scrutinise the internal workings of Parliament.
[70] [1977] I.R. 159. See Gwynn Morgan, "The Emergency Powers Bill Reference—II" (1979)14 Ir.Jur.(N.S.) 252, 256–262.
[71] [1986] I.L.R.M. 296 *contra*, High Court, March 24, 1983, p. 31. See pp. 549–550.
[72] [1977] I.R. 42. In *Raymond* v. *Att.-Gen.* [1982] Q.B. 839, 847 Shaw L.J. observed that "Unless [the D.P.P.'s decision] is manifestly such that it could not be honestly and reasonably arrived at, it cannot . . . be impugned." *Cf.* also *Flynn* v. *D.P.P.* [1986] I.L.R.M. 290. Note that in *The State (Killian)* v. *Att.-Gen.* (1958) 92 I.L.T.R. 182 the former Supreme Court ruled that the entry of a *nolle prosequi* by the Attorney-General could not be subject to judicial review. The exact precedential status of this decision in the light of *O'Callaghan* and *Flynn* is unclear. For cases on the D.P.P.'s authority to order a transfer to the Special Criminal Court, see pp. 558–561.
[73] [1984] I.R. 36, 81.

decision not to prosecute in respect of all crimes of a particular nature would be unlawful, and, by implication, subject to review. In *The State (McCormack)* v. *Curran*[74] Walsh J. stated that it was: "The common law duty of a policeman to bring criminals to justice and a refusal by a policeman on notice not to pursue a criminal [would be] a common law misdemeanour." It is by now well established that it is open to a judge to overrule governmental claims to the non-disclosure of evidence before a court.[75]

A Northern Irish example of this judicial trend is provided by *R.* v. *Governor of Maze Prison, ex p. McKiernan.*[76] In a similar case, *R.* v. *Deputy Governor of Camphill Prison, ex p. King,*[77] the English Court of Appeal had ruled that considerations of public policy and administrative convenience dictated that decisions of prison governors in regard to discipline should be immune from judicial review. The Northern Ireland Court of Appeal declined to follow this decision in *McKiernan's* case. Both Lowry L.C.J. and O'Donnell L.J. were unimpressed by arguments that the availability of judicial review in these circumstances would undermine prison discipline and would be contrary to the public interest. As Lowry L.C.J. eloquently put it:

"[It would be] quite unreasonable and contrary to the public interest in a civilised State that a [prison governor] should, in his judicial capacity, exercise an autocratic power and enjoy a freedom from High Court supervision which are denied both to the Board of Visitors and to all inferior courts."[78]

A little later this conflict between the Northern Ireland and English Courts of Appeal was resolved, by the House of Lords, in *Leech* v. *Deputy Governor of Parkhurst Prison,*[79] in favour of the view taken in Belfast. The significant part of the case was an examination of three possible exceptions to the general principle that judicial review applies to every exercise of a power conferred by statute which affects the rights of legitimate expectation of a citizen. First, Lord Bridge dismissed the "thin end of the wedge" argument that jurisdiction should be declined because of the danger that judicial review would be spread to every other area of prison administration. Such a trend, he said, could be controlled by an exercise of the court's discretion to refuse a remedy for claims within jurisdiction but without substance. Secondly, Lord Bridge dismissed the suggestion that a prisoner has an adequate alternative remedy to judicial review, in the form of the right to petition the Home Secretary. The third counter argument to be addressed was grounded on the claim that judicial review might lead to an undermining of the Governor's authority.

---

[74] [1987] I.L.R.M. 225, 239. See Finlay C.J.'s variation at 236.
[75] See Chap. 14.6 or 7. It bears noting that while this result was grounded on Art. 34.1 of the Constitution by the Supreme Court, in *Murphy* v. *Dublin Corporation* [1972] I.R. 215, the High Court in the same case had laid down the same principle (at 227) using the standard common law rules for the control of a discretionary power.
[76] [1986] N.I. 385.
[77] [1985] Q.B. 735.
[78] [1985] N.I. 385, 388.
[79] [1988] A.C. 533.

This argument was rejected as being a matter for the legislature, and as contradicting another important public policy, namely that in favour of the citizen's right of access to the courts.

In this jurisdiction the power of the courts to review disciplinary decisions of this kind appears to be taken as almost axiomatic. Thus, in *Gallagher* v. *Corrigan*[80] Blayney J. readily accepted, *obiter*, that judicial review would lie to control disciplinary decisions taken by prison authorities, whether it be in respect of prisoners or prison officers:

> "There is obviously a considerable difference between the Governor's exercising discipline over prisoners and his exercising discipline over his officers, but it seems to me that it would be anomalous . . . that prisoners should be entitled to the protection of the rules of natural and constitutional justice, but that prison officers should not . . . The Governor in exercising his powers of discipline over prison officers is also discharging a function which is partly magisterial and partly of a judicial or decision-making character, with the consequence that he must comply with the rules of natural and constitutional justice."[81]

Indeed, apart from the cases involving the exercise of a prosecutorial discretion, which are considered, *infra*, the only case in which the power of review has been seriously doubted or undermined is *The State (Sheehan)* v. *Government of Ireland*,[82] where the applicant sought judicial review of the Government's failure to bring into force section 60(1) of the Civil Liability Act 1961, which abolishes the common law rule that a highway authority cannot be held liable for non-feasance or non-repair of the public highway. Section 60(7) provided that no commencement order could be made for a date prior to April 1, 1967, and in the High Court Costello J. thought that the subsection vested the Government with a discretion as to when it was to be brought into force. This discretion was, however, one which was not "open-ended," but rather subject to review:

> "Whilst no time limit is imposed, and to that extent some discretion in the exercise of the power is given to the Government, it seems to me that if Parliament intended (as I think it clearly did) that the law should be reformed, it did not intend to confer a discretion which would permit that intention to be frustrated. This means that the discretion given by s.60(7) is a limited one, and that it should be construed as requiring the Government to make an order within a reasonable time after the 1st April 1967. Obviously a reasonable time has long since passed and, in my opinion, the Government is shown to have failed to carry out its statutory duty."[83]

The Supreme Court, however, took a different view of this matter. Henchy

---

[80] High Court, February 1, 1988.
[81] *Ibid*. pp. 12–13 of the judgment.
[82] [1987] I.R. 550. See Hogan, "Judicial Review of an Executive Discretion" (1987) 9 D.U.L.J. (N.S.) 91.
[83] *Ibid*. 556.

J. held that the subsection conferred on the Government what, in effect, is an unreviewable discretionary power:

> "The use of 'shall' and 'may,' both in the subsection and in the section as a whole, point to the conclusion that the radical law-reform embodied in the section was not intended to come into effect before the 1st April 1967 and thereafter only on such day as *may* be fixed by the Government. Not, be it noted, on such date as *shall* be fixed by the Government. Limiting words such as 'as soon as may be' or 'as soon as convenient,' which are to be found in comparable statutory provisions, are markedly absent."[84]

The judge concluded that all of this pointed to a parliamentary recognition of that fact that:

> "[The] important law reform to be effected by the section was not to take effect unless and until the Government became satisfied that, in the light of factors such as the necessary deployment of financial and other resources, the postulated reform would come into effect. The discretion vested in the Government to bring the section into operation on a date after 1st April 1967 *was not limited in any way as to time or otherwise.*"[85]

These passages would seem to suggest that the Oireachtas may, if it sees fit to do so, invest the Government (or a Minister or an administrative agency) with an unreviewable discretionary power, provided that the statutory language is sufficiently clear. Yet this would seem to fly in the face of the fundamental tenor of our modern administrative law. Thus, for example, O'Higgins C.J. observed in *Garvey* v. *Ireland*[86] that administrative powers could not be exercised "unjustly or unfairly" and added that this applied to "the Government as to any other authority within the State to which is given the power to take action which may infringe on the rights of others."[87] Walsh J. had expressed similar views some nine years earlier in *East Donegal Co-Operative Livestock Marts Ltd.* v. *Attorney-General*[88]:

> "All the powers granted to the Minister by s.3 [of the Livestock Marts Act 1967] which are preceded or followed by the words 'at his discretion' or 'as he shall see fit' are powers which may be exercised only within the boundaries of the stated objects of the Act; they are powers which cast upon the Minister the duty of acting fairly and judicially in accordance with the principles of natural justice, and they do not give him an absolute or an unqualified or an arbitrary power to grant or refuse at his will."

It is true that the Supreme Court was concerned in these cases with the exercise of a discretionary power which affected a personal right or interest, but there is nothing to suggest that this principle is not applicable to the exer-

---

[84] *Ibid.* 561.
[85] *Ibid.*
[86] [1981] I.R. 75.
[87] *Ibid.* 97.
[88] [1970] I.R. 317. See, to similar effect, Henchy J., himself, in *The State (Lynch)* v. *Cooney* [1982] I.R. 337, 380 quoted at pp. 538–539.

cise of an executive discretion in a case such as the present one. As Costello J. noted, the legislative intention that the law should be reformed was clear. Such executive inertia over such a long period would seem plainly at variance with this intention.

Henchy J.'s observations in relation to the language of section 60 are also difficult to accept. He concluded that there was no duty to bring the sub-section into effect because section 60 referred to such commencement day "as *may* be fixed by the Government." In his view, the absence of words which would tend to limit the ambit of the Government's discretion such as "shall"; "as soon as may be" or "as soon as convenient"—was decisive. The invocation of what amounts to the *expressio unius* principle seems misplaced in this statutory context. It was clearly intended that the Government should be given a discretion in the matter, but the use of the word "may" for this purpose probably results from the use of a convenient statutory formula to which no special significance should be attached.[89] As McCarthy J. pointed out in a persuasive dissenting judgment:

> "If the formula, of itself, gives a discretion to the appropriate authority to postpone indefinitely the bringing into force of the statute . . . then it would follow that much of the legislation of 1961, for instance, might never have been brought into force."[90]

The approach of the majority seems unduly cautious and unadventurous, especially when contrasted not only with the judgment of McCarthy J., but also with the judgment of Hodgson J. in *R. v. Secretary of State for the Environment, ex p. Greater London Council.*[91] Here the Secretary of State had refused to exercise his power to make regulations under the Act, as the British Government of the day had by then decided that the Greater London Council should be abolished. Despite the permissive language of section 18 ("may make regulations . . . "), Hodgson J. held that the Secretary of State

---

[89] One commentator distinguishes between various statutory commencement formulae, including those that are mandatory ("shall") and those which are permissive ("may"): see Bennion, *Statutory Interpretation* (London, 1984). But he concludes (at p. 416) that even in the case of permissive formulae:

> "[W]henever Parliament passes an Act it intends, unless the contrary intention appears, that all its provisions shall be brought into force within a reasonable time. There is no reason in principle why this matter of public law should be treated as withheld from the supervisory jurisdiction of the High Court."

[90] [1987] I.R. 550, 563. The same (or similar) formulae are still in use today. For example: s.2 of the Air Pollution Act 1987; s.2 of the Labour Services Act 1987; s.27(4) of the National Monuments (Amendment) Act 1987 and s.1(2) of the Safety, Health and Welfare (Off-Shore Installations) Act 1987 all provide that the relevant Minister "may" make an order bringing the Act into force. It is true that Henchy J. agreed (at 561) that if, on a "true reading of s. 60(7)," the Government were bound to bring the section into force, it would, of course, "be unconstitutional for the Government to achieve by their prolonged inactivity the virtual repeal of the section." However, to judge by the standards of *Sheehan*, it would seem that there are few cases involving an executive discretion to which this statement would be applicable, as in such instances the Government or the appropriate Minister would not be bound, apparently, to bring the Act into operation.

[91] *The Times*, December 2, 1983.

had abused his discretionary powers to make regulations "considered by Parliament to be necessary" for the proper functioning of sections 8 and 9. He continued:

> "Parliament is supreme, and the Act is an Act of Parliament. Until Parliament amends or repeals it, it remains the will of Parliament. The fact that the executive of the day do not want to do something which it is required by an Act of Parliament to do is nothing to the question: and if that executive because of no other reason than its own political posture exercises its discretion in a way contrary to the intention of Parliament as expressed in the legislation then the courts can and will intervene."

These principles would seem to be appropriate to the present case, where successive Governments have, in effect, flouted the will of the Oireachtas. Indeed, the only inference which can be drawn is that successive Governments did not want to do something which they were required by an Act of Parliament to do. But, as Hodgson J. remarked in the *Greater London Council* case, that "is nothing to the question." The approach of the majority in *Sheehan* in effect allows the Government to violate the principles of the separation of powers in that it has secured through its inaction the effective repeal of an important piece of law reform.

Quite apart from exceptional cases such as *Sheehan*, attempts have been made—though, it must be said, only rarely and then not in recent statutes—to put certain powers or decisions beyond the courts' power of review by the use of appropriately-worded statutory formulae. One example is section 22 of the Voluntary Health Insurance Act 1957 by which the Minister for Health "may, *in his absolute discretion* grant or refuse to grant to any person a . . . health insurance licence." Another example is afforded by section 34 of the Offences Against the State Act 1939 by which, save in capital cases, the Government "may, *at their absolute discretion*, at any time remit in whole or in part or modify (by way of mitigation only) or defer any punishment imposed by a Special Criminal Court." (Authors' italics) It is suggested that, especially since, as explained above, judicial review has now been given a constitutional pedestal, its removal could not be effected by any statutory formulae.[92]

The question of whether a court would regard the statutory language as precluding judicial review would depend more on the nature of the subject-matter and other circumstances than the wording of the provision. Thus, to take the health insurance licence example just quoted, there seems scant chance that a court would treat itself as debarred from the area of insurance licensing. The same might not be true of the remission of punishment example in view of its historical links with the prerogative and the fact that its entire purpose is to empower the executive to alter what has already been done by the court system.

As explained already, the dominant judicial view would appear to be that

---

[92] In a sense, the "absolute discretion" is an indirect attempt to create an ouster clause. For ouster clauses, see pp. 374–378.

all discretionary powers are reviewable unless the Constitution itself grants an exemption. One clear constitutional exemption is expressly provided for by Article 13.8.1 which states that the President shall not be answerable to "any court for the exercise and performance of the powers and functions of his office." In *Draper* v. *Ireland*,[93] the Supreme Court struck out the President from proceedings in which it was sought to prevent him from dissolving the Dáil on the advice of the Taoiseach. O'Higgins C.J. described the attempt to join the President as defendant as being in "open defiance" of Article 13.8.1. However, a different view was taken in *The State (Walshe)* v. *Murphy*[94] where an order of certiorari was granted on the grounds that the District Justice who convicted the applicant had been invalidly appointed. It had been argued that, as the President had appointed the District Justice, to review the validity of the appointment was tantamount to impugning an official act of the President. This potentially far-reaching argument was rejected by a Divisional High Court. Finlay P. suggested that the constitutional immunity does not exist in the case of judicial examination of a function which requires the President's intervention for its effectiveness in law, but which in fact is "the decision and act of the Executive." The need to choose between *Draper* and *Walshe* would arise, for instance, if some person sought to challenge, on the ground that it involves the application of an inflexible policy rule the exercise by the President (on the advice of the Government) of his "prerogative of mercy" so as to commute capital punishment to 40 years' imprisonment in all cases of capital murder from 1954 until capital punishment was removed by the Criminal Justice Act, 1990.

In some cases an immunity from judicial review may be regarded as having been implicitly conferred by the Constitution. This argument, to which we return below, seems to be the only satisfactory explanation of the line of cases which formerly held that the power of the Director of Public Prosecutions to order the transfer of trials to the Special Criminal Court is unreviewable. Article 38.3.1 expressly permits the creation of such courts, and vests the Oireachtas with a plenary legislative power to regulate their "constitution, powers, jurisdiction and procedure." The Offences against the State Act 1939 now vests the Director of Public Prosecutions with power to order the trial of accused persons before the Special Criminal Court once he is satisfied that in his opinion the ordinary courts are inadequate "to secure the effective administration of justice and the preservation of public peace and order in relation to the trial of such person on such a charge."[95] The High Court ruled in

---

[93] *The Irish Times*, May 14, 1981. In *O'Malley* v. *An Taoiseach* [1990] I.L.R.M. 461 an attempt to enjoin the Taoiseach not to advise the President to dissolve the Dáil was struck out, in effect, as an attempt to interfere indirectly with the President: As Hamilton P. said (at 465);

"the Courts have no jurisdiction to place any impediment between the President and his constitutional advisor in this important matter, which is solely the prerogative of the President."

[94] [1981] I.R. 275.
[95] For an account of the relevant provisions, see Casey, *The Office of the Attorney-General in Ireland* (Dublin, 1980), pp. 128–133.

Savage v. *D.P.P.*[96] (Finlay P.) and *Judge* v. *D.P.P.* (Carroll J.)[97] that once the D.P.P. bona fide holds that opinion, then the matter is not subject to any further review.

Both cases stress the security difficulties which made it impractical for the Director of Public Prosecutions to disclose the reasons for his decision.[98] In *Judge* Carroll J. was unimpressed by the argument that such an investigation might be held *in camera*, presumably because she considered that even an *in camera* investigation would involve the danger of a "leak" of highly sensitive information. In *The State (Lynch)* v. *Cooney*[99]—another "security" case—the Supreme Court was willing to review a banning order issued by the Minister for Posts and Telegraphs under the Broadcasting Authority Acts. This discrepancy between *Judge* and *Lynch* is probably explicable by reference to the differing nature of the decision under review and of the range of information on which it would probably turn. In regard to the prosecution of terrorist offenders, much of this information is likely to be confidential, whereas the decision in *Lynch*, involving the public impact of Sinn Féin policies upon the Irish television audience, would be less likely to involve such sensitive material. But in any event, the utilitarian basis of *Savage* and *Judge*, coupled with a desire not to discommode the prosecuting authorities in such a sensitive matter, is out of line with the general judicial trend in favour of review.[1]

However some slight change may have come as a result of *The State (McCormack)* v. *Curran*.[2] The facts in *McCormack* have already been given.[3] Here it is relevant only to say that the case arose out of the applicant's attempt to oblige the Director of Public Prosecutions to prosecute him in Ireland in order to frustrate a criminal prosecution which was pending against him in Belfast Crown Court. The question was whether the discretion to prosecute of the Director of Public Prosecutions was open to review. Barr J.

---

[96] [1982] I.L.R.M. 385, 389. See also, *Re McCurtain* [1941] I.R. 83.
[97] [1984] I.L.R.M. 224. The Supreme Court had earlier reserved this question: see *Re Article 26 and the Criminal Law (Jurisdiction) Bill 1975* [1977] I.R. 129; *The State (Littlejohn)* v. *Governor of Mountjoy Prison*, Supreme Court, March 18, 1976.
[98] See, *e.g. Savage* at 389:

> "If the contention made [by] the plaintiffs was correct . . . it would be necessary for the Director in order to uphold the certificate he issued and for the Special Criminal Court to have jurisdiction over the case which on his certificate has been sent forward for trial by it to reveal in open court in litigation at the instance of the accused person himself all the information, knowledge and facts upon which he formed his opinion. This would obviously, as a practical matter, entirely make impossible the operation of Part V of the Act of 1939 for the trial of any non-scheduled offence by the Special Criminal Court whilst it is established and in existence. The revealing of such information in open court under conditions under which persons are seeking to overthrow the established organs of the State would be a security impossibility and to interpret section 46(2) of the Act of 1939 so as to make that necessary would be to vitiate the entire purpose of that subsection."

[99] [1982] I.R. 337.
[1] The decisions in *Savage* and *Judge* have both come in for considerable criticism: see Byrne (1981) 16 Ir.Jur.(N.S.) 86; (1984) 6 D.U.L.J.(N.S.) 177 and Pye (1985) 3 I.L.T.(N.S.) 65.
[2] [1987] I.L.R.M.225.
[3] See pp. 406–407.

rejected this submission, and, following *Savage*, held that the exercise of discretion was unreviewable. However, in the Supreme Court, (not uncharacteristically) no reference was made to any authorities and, instead, Finlay C.J. stated, with no preliminary discussion:

> "In regard to the DPP I reject also the submission that he has only got a discretion as to whether to prosecute or not to prosecute in any particular case related exclusively to the probative value of the evidence laid before him. Again, I am satisfied that there are many other factors which may be appropriate and proper for him to take into consideration. I do not consider that it would be wise or helpful to seek to list them in any exclusive way. If, of course, it can be demonstrated that he reaches a decision *mala fide* or influenced by an improper motive or improper policy then his decision would be reviewable by a court. To that extent I reject the contention again made on behalf of this respondent that his decisions were not as a matter of public policy ever reviewable by a court."[4]

Walsh J. also appeared to acknowledge that there could be review if the Director's "opinion was either perverse or inspired by improper motives."[5]

Two comments may be made in regard to *McCormack*. First, contrasting the situation in *McCormack* with that in *Savage* and *Judge*, it may be observed that *McCormack* was a more likely candidate for a policy holding that there should be a bar on judicial review, because, in addition to the security element (which was common to all three cases) there was an international dimension which included a comparison of the possibilities of prosecuting cases in Belfast as against Dublin. If in an area such as this, the ban against judicial review could be lifted, in however restricted a way, there can be few other areas in which it can, consistently, be retained.

However, secondly and more importantly, it seems likely from the guarded language of the Supreme Court's formulations in *McCormack* that what was contemplated was not the full sweep of judicial review which applies generally to discretionary powers, but rather a power of review which was restricted to something akin to mala fides. That this may be so appears from the Chief Justice's reference to "a decision mala fides or . . . improper motive or improper policy" and Walsh J.'s use of the rather extreme term "perverse." This, certainly, was the view taken by Lynch J. in the most recent authority in this area: *Foley v. Director of Public Prosecutions*,[6] yet another case on the Director of Public Prosecution's power to order the transfer of trials to the Special Criminal Court. Here Lynch J. was reported as stating:

> " . . . while there might seem to be a slight conflict between the judgment of Mr. Justice Finlay, as President of the High Court, in *Savage's* case and

[4] [1987] I.L.R.M. 237.
[5] *Ibid.* 239.
[6] *Irish Times Law Reports*, September 25, 1989.

his judgment as Chief Justice in *McCormack's* case it seems that in reality the latter was a development of the former and an expansion of it.

> . . . the net result of the judgments in these cases was that the decision of the Director of Public Prosecutions in issuing certificates under the Offences Against the State Act 1939 was not reviewable, unless the applicant had established a prima facie case of some irregularity of a serious nature such as to amount to some impropriety of some sort or other. The onus of establishing such an irregularity must rest on the applicant."

Lynch J. went on to state that he was:

> " . . . satisfied that no prima facie case of mala fides had been made out against the respondent with regard to this matter. He said that he was satisfied that the facts appearing from the affidavit and documents did not exclude the reasonable possibility of a proper and valid decision by the respondent not to prosecute the applicant in the ordinary Courts but to transfer his trial instead to the Special Criminal Court. That being so, the respondent could not be called upon to explain his decision or to give the reasons for it, nor the source of the information from which it was based."

It may be tentatively suggested, then, that this debate may be of more importance on the conceptual than the practical plane. For it seems likely that even were the courts to assume a power of review in cases involving fundamental state interests (*e.g.* review of a declaration of emergency under Article 28.3.3), the courts would only intervene in the most extreme cases.[7]

Another area which, unusually, does involve something of the same unusually wide and difficult range of policy factors as *McCormack* is created by section 2 of the Extradition (Amendment) Act 1987 (which established a new section 44B of the Extradition Act 1965). This provision now requires the Attorney-General to direct that a particular warrant shall not be indorsed unless:

> " . . . the Attorney General, having considered such information as he deems appropriate, is of opinion that:
> (a) there is a clear intention to prosecute . . . the person named or described in the warrant concerned for the offence specified therein . . . and
> (b) such intention is founded on the existence of sufficient evidence."

The obvious question which arises from this provision is whether the Attorney-General's decision is subject to review. The effect of the gloss on *McCormack* introduced in *Foley* may be that the Attorney-General would be obliged to disclose, in open court, the material on which he had reached his decision (subject to any claim for executive privilege) if, but only if, the appli-

---

[7] See the graduated scale of review applied in the prison transfer cases: *The State (Smith and Fox)* v. *Governor of the Curragh Military Barracks* [1980] I.L.R.M. 208; *The State (Boyle)* v. *Governor of the Curragh Military Barracks* [1980] I.L.R.M. 242.

cant had succeeded in establishing a prima facie case as to mala fides or improper motive.[8]

On this interpretation, there is some consistency between these areas of the law and the related field of the Director of Public Prosecution's power to issue a *nolle prosequi.*

Carroll J. also advanced a second, constitutional argument to bolster her conclusion in *Judge* (described at page 559). She felt that "no analogy could be drawn" between the opinion of the Director of Public Prosecutions under legislation authorised under Article 38.3, and the exercise of a power by a Minister under an ordinary Act of the Oireachtas. The inference, perhaps, to be drawn here is that Carroll J. felt that this matter had been entirely committed to the Oireachtas by Article 38.3.1, and that judicial scrutiny of the exercise of the Director of Public Prosecution's powers would be a breach of the separation of powers. In this instance, the conclusion hardly follows from the stated premise, for if Article 38.3.1 is one of the permitted exceptions to jury trial guaranteed in Article 38.5, must there not be "some protections implicit in the Constitution itself which requires that it cannot be avoided by the exercise of an unreviewable power?"[9]

However, Carroll J.'s second argument in *Judge* does at least serve to raise the issue of whether the "political question" (as it is known in the United States), exists in Ireland. This is a residual category of issues—some, but not all, having a strongly political flavour—which the courts have decided, for various historical or policy reasons, to treat as non-justiciable.[10] Obviously one of the policies underlying the political question is an aspect of the separation of powers, which has not received much attention here, namely that the courts should confine themselves to the judicial function and not interfere in the functions of other organs of government.[11] The contrasting principle,

---

[8] One detailed point which should be noted is that this material would presumably anyway have to be disclosed at the trial in the U.K. of the person to be sent back. This is a distinguishing point from *Savage, Judge* and *Foley* (although not *McCormack*) where the question to be determined by the Director of Public Prosecutions was rather different from that which would emerge in open court at the applicant's trial. This might be a point of distinction from these authorities.

[9] Byrne (1984) 6 D.U.L.J.(N.S.) 177, 183.

[10] According to the U.S. *locus classicus* on the subject, *Baker* v. *Carr* (1962) 369 U.S. 186, 217, a political question arises where one or more of the following situations exist:

"a textually demonstrable constitutional commitment of the issue to a coordinate political department; or a lack of judicially discoverable and manageable standards for resolving it; or the impossibility of deciding without an initial policy determination of a kind clearly for non-judicial discretion; the impossibility of a court's undertaking independent resolution without expressing lack of the respect due coordinate branches of government; . . . the potentiality of embarrassment from multifarious pronouncements by various departments on one question.

[11] On broad Separation of Powers principles the courts will refrain from interfering with the process of legislation: *O'Crowley* v. *Minister for Finance* [1935] I.R. 536; *Halpin* v. *Att.-Gen.* [1936] I.R. 226; *Wireless Dealers Assoc.* v. *Fair Trade Commission*, Supreme Court, March 7, 1956; *Roche* v. *Ireland*, High Court, June 16, 1983 and *Finn* v. *Att.-Gen.* [1983] I.R. 154. Yet judicial intervention will be forthcoming if the constitutionally required stages of law-making have not been carried out: *R. (O'Brien)* v. *Governor of the North Dublin Military Barracks* [1924] 1 I.R. 32; *Victoria* v. *Commonwealth* (1975) 7 A.L.R. 1; *Western Australia* v. *Commonwealth* (1975) 7 A.L.R. 159.

which has taken precedence, is rather the notion that, as Walsh J. stated in *Crotty* v. *An Taoiseach*[12] "to the judicial organ of government alone is given the power to decide if there has been a breach of constitutional restraints." The strength of this principle—and also, the lack of judicial interest in any political question doctrine—was demonstrated recently in *Crotty* itself. The plaintiff had sought a declaration and injunction restraining the Government from ratifying the Single European Act (SEA) which was a treaty, signed by members of the European Community (EC), the criticial parts of which provided for improved co-operation in the sphere of foreign policy. The plaintiff's argument was that since Article 29.4 vests the Government with the power to conduct foreign affairs, it is not open to the State to fetter the Government's authority by a treaty which would oblige it to make foreign policy with a greater measure of co-operation with other Member States of the EC. The aspect of this multi-faceted case, which is relevant here, is that neither the majority nor the dissenting judges so much as adverted to the "political question" doctrine. It might have been thought that such an argument would have been apt; not only were foreign affairs involved, but the basis of *Crotty* was the hobgoblin of sovereignty and its alleged erosion. In a world of highly qualified sovereigns, this is an issue *par excellence* of political judgment.[13]

Plainly the issue of the constitutionality of a major act of foreign policy is at a considerable remove from the normal province of administrative law. However, it seems fair to extrapolate from the fact that there is no place for the political question, even in what might be thought to be such a natural situation as that disclosed in *Crotty*, to the proposition that it is unlikely to find a welcome in any of the more usual actions controlled by administrative law.

---

[12] [1987] I.R. 713. See also (on the constitutional aspect of the case) Hogan, "The Supreme Court and the Single European Act" (1987) 22 Ir.Jur. 55.
[13] The same point could be illustrated by the absence of any reference to the "political question" doctrine in *McGimpsey* v. *Ireland* [1988] I.R. 567 (H.C.); [1990] 1 I.R. 110 (S.C.).

CHAPTER 11

REMEDIES

1. Introduction

Prior to October 1986 a person aggrieved by a decision of an administrative body or lower court had a wide variety of remedies open to him. In addition to the principal State side orders of certiorari, prohibition and mandamus,[1] the private law remedies of the declaration and injunction could also have been invoked. These two sets of remedies differed in the scope of their application, depending on the nature of the decision, defect or public body involved. Writing in 1966, Griffith and Street commented as follows:

"The remedies, for no practical reason are plural; some of them cannot be used if another remedy is available; the lines between them are imprecise and shifting [and] the judges employ vague concepts (which they do not define) in marking the boundaries of each remedy."[2]

Prior to the coming into force of the new Rules of the Superior Courts in October 1986[3] if an applicant sought the wrong remedy, no relief could be granted to him because he had asked for the improper order.[4] Under the ancien régime, the former State side orders could be awarded in lieu of each other, but were not interchangeable remedies with the private law remedies. What this meant, in practice, was that if, say, an applicant had sought certiorari, but the court was of the view that mandamus was more appropriate, then the latter remedy could be awarded. However, if on an application for certiorari it transpired that the applicant had a good case on the merits, yet the restrictions on the scope of certiorari were such that it was not available, then no remedy could be awarded. In such a situation the litigant would be required to brace himself for a fresh set of plenary proceedings, where the wider rem-

---

[1] The other State side orders are habeas corpus (or an application for an inquiry under Art. 40.4.2, as it is more properly described) and quo warranto. The remedy of habeas corpus falls outside the scope of this book, but see Kelly, *The Irish Constitution* (Dublin, 1984). Quo warranto proceedings are now virtually obsolete, and there has been only one reported case involving quo warranto since 1922: *The State (Lycester)* v. *Hegarty* (1941) 75 I.L.T.R. 121, where the powers of the Master of the High Court in such proceedings are discussed. The modern practice is to seek a declaration that an office-holder has been invalidly appointed rather than to proceed by way of quo warranto: see *Glynn* v. *Roscomon C.C.* (1959) 93 I.L.T.R. 149. Proceedings by way of quo warranto must now be brought as an application for judicial review: see Ord. 84, r. 18(1) of the new Rules of the Superior Courts.

[2] Griffith and Street, *Principles of Administrative Law* (London, 1966), p. 236.

[3] S.I. 1986 No. 15. These Rules come into force on October 1, 1986. For an account of the previous State side practice, see Law Reform Commission Working Paper No. 8, *Judicial Review of Administrative Action: The Problem of Remedies* (1979) and Graham, "Judicial Review: Where to Reform" (1984) 6 D.U.L.J. (N.S.) 25. The new Rules very largely follow the scheme of reform as proposed by the Law Reform Commission in their working paper.

[4] As, for example, happened in cases such as *The State (Colquhoun)* v. *D'Arcy* [1936] I.R. 641 and *O'Doherty* v. *Att.-Gen.* [1941] I.R. 569.

565

edy of the declaration might be available. To take the converse example, the circumstances could be such that a litigant might initiate proceedings by way of plenary summons for a declaration, only to be turned away with the bitter-sweet news that although he had a good case on the merits, yet since one of the State side orders would have been available, he should have sought that order: the rationale for such a decision was that since the State side orders were the specialised form of proceedings for a public law matter, the normally private law remedies of a declaration or injunction should only have been sought if no State side order was apt for the case. Such blots on the legal system occurred but rarely. However, the very possibility of a catastrophe of this type, especially when coupled with the vagaries of the field of operation of the former State side orders, which might appeal more to one judge rather than another, increased even further the usual hazards of litigation.

The principal innovatory feature of the new judicial review procedure is the creation of a new comprehensive procedure (known as an "application for judicial review") which enables an aggrieved party to test the legality of administrative action in the High Court. The major objective behind the creation of this new procedure is to obviate the possibility that a good case on the merits will be lost because of the wrong choice of remedy, since all the individual remedies available on an application for judicial review are now interchangeable.[5]

There seems to be very little to choose—in terms of practical consequences—between one remedy and another. Accordingly, while such a course would have been beyond the competence of the Superior Courts Rules Committee, it may be asked: would anything have been lost if the six traditional remedies had been replaced by a single comprehensive remedy (which might have been called, like the principal remedy for judicial review in the United States Federal Courts, the "petition for review")? The answer would seem to be in the negative, although some may have feared that if the traditional orders were amputated, some violence might have been done to the substantive law of judicial review[6] (which originally developed in the interstices of the prerogative writs) and possibly also to the law on standing and discretion.

The new Rules also make provision for such matters as time limits[7]; *locus standi*[8]; discovery and interrogatories[9] and interim relief.[10]

Given the far-reaching dimensions of the changes brought about by Order 84, it remains to be seen whether these changes can truly be said to be *intra vires* the Superior Court Rules Committee. The Committee is confined to

---

[5] Because the effect of Ord. 84, r. 19 is that the various remedies are now interchangeable.

[6] See pp. 597–603.

[7] Ord. 84, r. 21(1) imposes a general time limit of three months (six months where the relief claimed is certiorari) from the date "when grounds for the application first arose." The court has a discretion to extend these time limits. See pp. 597–598.

[8] Ord. 84, r. 20(4) provides that the High Court shall not grant leave unless it considers that the applicant has a "sufficient interest" in the matter to which the application relates. See pp. 611–626.

[9] Ord. 84, r. 25. See p. 570.

[10] Ord. 84, r. 20(7). See pp. 591–592.

making rules dealing with "pleading and practice and procedure generally"[11] and the precaution has been taken in other jurisdictions to put precisely the sort of change effected by Order 84 on a statutory footing.[12] Two commentators have marshalled powerful arguments in support of their view that the changes effected by Order 84 are, in fact, *intra vires*:

> "Taking care not to abolish *quo warranto*, Ord. 84 does not seem to have made any substantive change in the definition, content, or application of the remedies available on an application for judicial review."[13]

Yet the correctness of this view may turn on the manner in which Order 84 is interpreted in practice.[14] Or, to put it another way, the fact that the Order 84 changes lack a statutory backing may induce the courts to take a narrower view of the changes thereby effected than might otherwise be the case. Three examples may be given.

First, it would not seem to be open to the Committee to prescribe via the new Order 84 (whether expressly or by implication) an *exclusive* procedure as far as applications for judicial review are concerned. The right to challenge an administrative decision in the High Court by means of plenary summons is a substantive right which may not be taken away save by clear statutory language.[15]

Secondly, the time limits imposed by Order 84, rule 21 are quite strict, although the High Court has power to extend these time limits where there is "good reason" to do so. But the ordinary time limit for declaratory actions prescribed by the Statute of Limitations 1957 is six years and it must be doubtful—especially given the restriction imposed by Article 15.2.1 of the Constitution—whether it is open to the Committee to prescribe what in effect is a radically different limitation period, by Rules of Court.[16]

---

[11] s. 36 of the Courts of Justice Act 1924 (as applied by ss. 14 and 48 of the Courts (Supplemental Provisions) Act 1961).

[12] See, *e.g.* Judicature (Northern Ireland) Act 1978, ss. 18-21 and Supreme Court Act 1981, s.31 (England and Wales). The Law Reform Commission in their Working Paper No. 8 (1979) *Judicial Review of Administrative Action: The Problem of Remedies* also recommended (at p. 79) that these changes be made by means of legislation.

[13] Collins & O'Reilly, *op.cit.* p. 76. But *cf.* the comments of Lord Denning in *O'Reilly* v. *Mackman* [1983] A.C. 237, 256:

> "When the Rules Committee made R.S.C., Ord. 53 some of us on the Committee had doubts about whether some of it was not *ultra vires*, but we took the risk because it was so desirable."

[14] Of course, it is not as yet completely clear as to whether Ord. 84 has, in fact, prescribed such an exclusive procedure, although the judgment of Costello J. in *O'Donnell* v. *Dún Laoghaire Corporation (No.2)* [1991] I.L.R.M. 301, suggests strongly that it does not. However, it may be surmised that the absence of legislation will make the Irish courts much more reluctant to adopt the *O'Reilly* v. *Mackman* approach (see pp. 586–590). As to whether Ord. 84, r.20(7)(a) has altered substantive law (and is thus *ultra vires*) as far the granting of substantive relief is concerned, see p. 592.

[15] See *Pyx Granite Ltd.* v. *Ministry of Housing* [1960] A.C. 260, 286, *per* Lord Simonds.

[16] Collins & O'Reilly, *op.cit.* correctly observe (at 70) that "time limits have always been a feature of remedies by way of judicial review." But this of itself cannot be conclusive in considering whether the very existence of such time-limits is *intra vires* the Superior Court Rule Committee.

Finally, the power contained in Order 84, rule 26(5) to remit the matter to the original court, tribunal or authority in the wake of an order of certiorari also seems questionable. It is true that in many cases, the effect of an order will be to quash the decision and, in those circumstances, there is no objection in law to the recommencement of proceedings before that body.[17] However, in many cases, Order 84, rule 26(5) will operate in the same manner as an order for retrial. Yet, the power to order a retrial is generally held to be a matter of substantive law and this would seem to cast doubts on the *vires* of this particular change.[18]

2. Certiorari, Prohibition and Mandamus

Certiorari lies to quash a decision of a public body which has been arrived at in excess of jurisdiction, whereas prohibition is sought to refrain that body from doing something which would be in excess of its jurisdiction. There is no real difference in principle between the two remedies, save that prohibition may be invoked at an earlier stage. The difference is thus almost exclusively one of tense. By contrast, the principal function of mandamus arises where a public body has failed to take action. Its purpose is to secure the performance of a duty imposed on a public body either by statute or by common law. We must now consider (i) the procedure for an application for judicial review introduced by the new Rules of the Superior Courts and (ii) the scope of these remedies.

(i) *Applications for judicial review: practice and procedure*

The procedure in relation to applications for certiorari, prohibition and mandamus is governed by Order 84, rule 18(1) which provides that:

"An application for an order of certiorari, mandamus, prohibition or *quo warranto* shall be made by way of application for judicial review in accordance with the provisions of this Order."

Order 84, rule 20(1) requires that no application for judicial review shall be

---

[17] See *Bord na Moná* v. *An Bord Pleánala* [1985] I.R. 260 where Keane J. found certain conditions attached to a planning permission by a local authority and confirmed by An Bord Pleánala to be invalid with the result that the permission fell in its entirety. The possibility of a remittal back to An Bord Pleánala to allow them to make a fresh order on the appeal was canvassed during the course of the hearing, but Keane J. said that (at 211) "it was accepted that there was no *statutory basis for such a course*" (emphasis supplied).

[18] See *People (Director of Public Prosecutions) Qulligan (No. 2)* [1989] I.R. 46, 53–54, where Henchy J. held that Ord. 87, r.2 of the Rules of the Superior Court 1986 could not have vested the Supreme Court with a jurisdiction to order retrial following a successful appeal by the prosecution against an acquittal by direction in the High Court:

"If that construction of the Rules were the correct one, it would, in my opinion, have to be declared *ultra vires* for the vesting in the Supreme Court of such a jurisdiction . . . would go far beyond 'pleading, practice and procedure generally' and would amount to a radical change in the substantive law."

made unless the prior leave of the court has been obtained.[19] An application for leave must be made by motion *ex parte* by a notice containing, *inter alia*, details of the relief sought and the grounds on which it is sought, and an affidavit verifying the facts relied on.[20] The court may permit an application for leave to be amended on such terms (if any) as it thinks fit.[21] Leave will not be granted unless the applicant has a "sufficient interest in the matter" to which the application relates.[22] If the court grants leave, it may impose such terms as to costs as it thinks fit, and may require an undertaking as to damages.[23]

The requirement as to leave is a most important feature. It serves as a "filtering device" and guards against unmeritorious claims that a particular decision is invalid.[24] This two-stage procedure also means that the High Court no longer has power to grant an absolute order of certiorari, prohibition or mandamus following an *ex parte* application.[25]

It has been said of certiorari, prohibition and mandamus that they afford a:

"[S]peedy and effective remedy to a person aggrieved by a clear excess of jurisdiction by an inferior tribunal. But they are not designed to raise issues of fact for the High Court to determine *de novo* . . . ."[26]

Thus, where a case turned on disputed facts, this used to pose difficulties for an applicant for State side relief. One way around these difficulties was to

---

[19] Ord. 84, r. 20(1). For an excellent account of practice and procedure in this area see Collins & O'Reilly, *op. cit.* pp. 82–93. The requirement for leave corresponds to the former practice on the State side whereby the applicant was required to seek a conditional order. If a conditional order was granted, an application was brought by motion to make the order absolute and the respondent was required to show cause why it should not be: see Ord. 84, rr. 9, 25 and 37 of the R.S.C. 1962. Under this procedure, the applicant, if refused a conditional order, had the right to go around all the High Court judges in pursuit of his remedy: *The State (Richardson)* v. *Governor of Mountjoy Prison* [1980] I.L.R.M. 82. Very significantly, it would seem that an applicant may still move from judge to judge if he is refused leave to apply for judicial review. An appeal against the *refusal* of leave to apply will lie to the Supreme Court by virtue of the general provisions of Art. 34.4.3. It is more doubtful as to whether the *respondents* could appeal a decision *to grant leave to the applicant: cf.* the comments of McCarthy J. in *The State (Hughes)* v. *O'Hanrahan* [1986] I.L.R.M. 218, 221 doubting whether anyone (other than the applicants) can appeal against an order *ex parte*.
[20] Ord. 84, r. 20(2). The court is entitled to refuse relief on discretionary grounds if material facts are suppressed in the affidavit: *R. (Bryson)* v. *Lisnaskea Guardians* [1918] 2 I.R. 258; *The State (Nicolaou)* v. *An Bord Uchtála* [1966] I.R. 567 and *Cork Corporation* v. *O'Connell* [1982] I.L.R.M. 505.
[21] Ord. 84, r. 23(2). But the grant of leave to amend can only be done at "the hearing of the motion or summons" and not earlier: *Ahern* v. *Minister for Industry and Commerce (No.2)* [1990] 1 I.R. 55.
[22] Ord. 84, r. 20(4). This matter is considered further at pp. 612–614.
[23] Ord. 84, r. 20(6).
[24] This was one of the principal reasons given by the House of Lords in *O'Reilly* v. *Mackman* [1983] 2 A.C. 237 as to why challenges to administrative action brought by plenary summons (as in the case of a declaration or injunction), and which thus circumvented the requirement for leave, should be struck out as an abuse of process.
[25] See Ord. 84, rr. 9, 28 and 38 of the R.S.C. 1962. This power was exercised in unusual cases where no proper defence to the granting of an absolute order *ex parte* could be made out: see *The State (Att.-Gen.)* v. *Coghlan*, High Court, May 10, 1974 and *Re Zwann's Application* [1981] I.R. 395.
[26] *R.* v. *Fulham Rent Tribunal, ex p. Zerek* [1951] 2 K.B. 1, 11, *per* Devlin J.

apply to cross-examine deponents on their affidavits, and this practice received the approval of the Supreme Court.[27] In addition, while discovery was available,[28] however, there was no procedure for serving interrogatories, or for obtaining interlocutory relief pending the determination of the application. It was for these reasons that where issues of fact were raised in a challenge to the validity of administrative action litigants tended to proceed by way of plenary hearings and seek an injunction or a declaration.[29] These procedural restrictions have now been removed. One may now apply for discovery or interrogatories,[30] and granting of leave to apply for judicial review will generally[31] operate as a stay of the proceedings to which the application relates. The court may also direct that the application for judicial review shall be made by plenary summons, instead of by originating notice of motion.[32] Any such notice of motion must be served on all persons directly affected within 14 days after the grant of leave, or within "such other period as the court may direct."[33] In default of service, the stay of proceedings shall lapse.[34]

The effect of a similar provision contained in the former Rules of Court was considered by Finlay P. in *The State (Fitzsimons)* v. *Kearney*.[35] In this case a conditional order of certiorari had not been served within the prescribed time limit owing to an oversight. The applicant then sought, pursuant to Order 108, rule 7[36] an extension of time for service of the conditional order. Finlay

---

[27] *The State (Furey)* v. *Minister for Defence* [1989] I.L.R.M. 89.

[28] Ord. 31 of the R.S.C. 1962 gave the court power to order discovery "in any cause or matter," and there was no objection to the use of this power in State side applications: *The State (McGarrity)* v. *Deputy Garda Commissioner* (1978) 112 I.L.T.R. 25.

[29] See the comments of Henchy J. in *M.* v. *An Bord Uchtála* [1977] I.R. 287, 297. The use of the plenary procedure in the wake of the new Rules does not *per se* amount to an abuse of process: but the principles pertaining to delay, etc., as far as judicial review proceedings will apply, *mutatis mutandis*, to plenary actions: see *O'Donnell* v. *Dún Laoghaire Corporation* [1991] I.L.R.M. 301.

[30] Ord. 84, r. 25.

[31] Ord. 84, r. 20(7)(*a*) provides that upon an application for judicial review by way of certiorari or prohibition, the grant of leave will, if the court so directs, operate as a stay of the proceedings until the determination of the application or until further order. If other relief is sought, Ord. 84, r. 20(7)(*b*) empowers the court to grant such interim relief "as could be granted in an action begun by plenary summons." See pp. 591–592.

[32] Ord. 84, r. 22(1). The court also has a power, upon an application for prohibition or quo warranto, to direct a plenary hearing with directions as to pleadings, discovery, etc.: see Ord. 84, r. 26(7) Where liberty is granted to proceed by way of plenary summons, then "the action should be presented by the plaintiff on oral evidence unless the court directs by order a hearing on affidavit or accepts from the parties an expressly agreed statement of the facts": *per* Finlay C.J. in *O'Keeffe* v *An Bord Pleanála*, Supreme Court, February 15, 1991, p. 38.

[33] Ord. 84, r. 22(3). In the case of a motion on notice, it shall be returnable for the first available motion day after the expiry of 10 days from the date of service, unless the court otherwise directs. An affidavit of service must be filed prior to the hearing of the motion or summons: see Ord. 84, r. 22(5).

[34] Ord. 84, r. 22(3).

[35] [1981] I.R. 406. See also, *The State (Flynn & O'Flaherty Ltd.)* v. *Dublin Corporation* [1983] I.L.R.M. 125.

[36] Ord. 108, r. 7 of the 1962 Rules gave the court a special power to enlarge or abridge time. A similar power is contained in Ord. 122, r. 7 of the 1986 Rules.

P. concluded that he had no jurisdiction to grant the extension of time sought. The purpose of the Order 84 procedure was to ensure a rapid determination of the validity of the impugned order, and, accordingly, it was an exception to the general provision contained in Order 108, rule 7. In short, the High Court had no jurisdiction to extend the period of time for service once the time had elapsed. The period for service could be extended by the court when making the conditional order, or *before* the expiry of the prescribed period. If, however, the conditional order (or, under the new Rules, a grant of leave) is not served within the prescribed period, or such period as fixed by the court, then the order stands discharged, and there can be no extension.

Any respondent who intends to oppose the application for judicial review by way of notice of opposition[37] must file in the Central Office a statement setting out concisely the grounds for such opposition and, if any facts are relied on, an affidavit verifying such facts.[38] A copy of such statement or affidavit must be served on all parties within seven days from the date of service of the notice of motion, or such other period as the court may direct.[39] In practice, this seven-day period has proved to be unrealistic and applications to extend time for the filing of a notice of opposition are very common. In *Butler* v. *Ruane*[40] McCarthy J. held that such an order could be made *ex parte*, although he thought that in some cases, the judge hearing the application for an extension:

"[W]ould, if the circumstances so require, refuse to grant the order sought *ex parte* and direct that the motion be brought on notice."[41]

(ii) *Scope of the remedies*

Recent litigation has shown that certiorari, prohibition and mandamus are remedies of great scope and flexibility. Nevertheless, these remedies are not universal in their scope, as the following discussion will show. Notwithstanding the changes effected by Order 84, we follow tradition and begin our discussion with the oft-quoted dictum of Atkin L.J. in *R.* v. *Electricity Commissioners, ex p. London Electricity Joint Committee Co. (1920) Ltd.*:

"Whenever any body of persons having legal authority to determine questions affecting the rights of subjects, and having the duty to act judicially, act in excess of legal authority, they are subject to the controlling jurisdiction [of the High Court]."[42]

---

[37] If the court has directed that the application for judicial review be made by way of plenary summons under Ord. 84, r. 22(1), the respondent will presumably conduct his defence as if in a plenary action. There is, however, no specific provision for this in the Rules (save in the case of applications for prohibition or quo warranto, for which see Ord. 84, r. 26(7)).
[38] Ord. 84, r. 22(4).
[39] *Ibid.*
[40] [1989] I.L.R.M. 159.
[41] *Ibid.* 161.
[42] [1924] 1 K.B. 171, 205.

However, as we shall see, the law has not stood still since 1924 when these words were first uttered, and further discussion will show that each of these restrictions has been either removed or rendered less inflexible.

"Any body of persons having legal authority." These public law remedies will issue in respect of any individual or body of persons exercising statutory authority, restrictions which have already been discussed in a more general context in Chapter 8.1 under the heading. "The Reach of Public Law."[43] This means that persons or bodies drawing their authority from contract or from the consent of their members fall outside the scope of these remedies, and the declaration and injunction are the most suitable remedies in such a situation.[44] For example, in *The State (Colquhoun)* v. *D'Arcy*[45] it was held that the General Synod of the Church of Ireland could not be restrained by prohibition as the Synod derived its authority, not from the common law or statute, but from contract and the consent of its members. The second aspect is that public law remedies may not be used to challenge decisions even of public bodies where these do not relate to the exercise of public law functions. In other words, the public law remedies will not lie where the circumstances of the case are governed by private law. Thus, in *R. (Butler)* v. *Navan U.D.C.*[46] the Supreme Court refused to grant mandamus to compel the respondents to carry out their statutory duty to repair a graveyard wall. Fitzgibbon J. observed that the application was misconceived because it was an attempt to secure the "performance of an alleged private right" and not the performance of any public duty.

However, as we shall see in the following account of the case law, the courts have often not kept these two aspects separate and have conflated them by speaking generally (for example) of "the correct interpretation of Order 84, does it apply to public law only or is it applicable also in private law?"[47]

Unfortunately, recent case law on the reach of Order 84 shows two divergent lines of authority. In the first place, there have been several recent cases where a more relaxed attitude to this critical jurisdictional issue was taken

---

[43] Thus, prohibition will not lie to a tribunal usurping legal authority (*R. (Kelly)* v. *Maguire and Sheil* [1923] 2 I.R. 58) or whose authority is derived from contract or consent (*The State (Colquhoun)* v. *D'Arcy* [1936] I.R. 641). As for whether judicial review will lie to extra statutory tribunals, see pp. 222 and 575.

[44] It would also appear that probably, in such a situation, the application for a declaration and injunction must be commenced by way of plenary summons (and not by way of an application for judicial review under Ord. 84, r. 18(2)) in this situation: see *Murphy* v. *Turf Club* [1989] I.R. 172; *R.* v. *B.B.C., ex p. Lavelle* [1983] 1 W.L.R. 23; *Law* v. *National Greyhound Racing Club Ltd.* [1983] 1 W.L.R. 1302. Both *Lavelle* and *Law* deal with s.31(2) of the English Supreme Court Act 1981, and the language of our Ord. 84, r. 18(2) corresponds almost exactly with that of s.31(2) of the English Act.

[45] [1936] I.R. 641.

[46] [1926] I.R. 466. See also, *R. (Lynham)* v. *Cork C.C.* (1901) 35 I.L.T.R. 167.

[47] *O'Neill* v *Iarnród Éireann* [1991] I.L.R.M. 129, 133, *per* Hedeman J.

where public employees (such as Gardaí) or Members of the Defence Forces have been permitted to use public law remedies as a means of challenging their dismissal. Yet it is at least arguable that the dismissal of public employees is governed by ordinary contract and that an application for certiorari or similar relief in such cases is misconceived.[48]

In England, there has been a definite tendency to extend the scope of judicial review in recent years. In *R. v. Panel of Take-overs and Mergers, ex p. Datafin plc*[49]; for instance, the English Court of Appeal held that judicial review lies to review decisions of the Panel of Take-overs and Mergers. The Panel is, of course, self-regulating, but it was put in place as an alternative to a statutory tribunal and its very existence enjoys official approval and support. This was enough for the Court of Appeal to hold that judicial review did lie, since Sir John Donaldson M.R. said that the court would have to bear in mind the "immense power *de facto*" wielded by the Panel and thus "recognise the realities of executive power . . . in defence of the citizenry."[50] A similar attitude was taken in *R. v. General Council of the Bar, ex p. Percival*[51] where the applicant (a distinguished Queen's Counsel in active practice) sought judicial review of the Professional Conduct Committee's (a sub-committee of the General Council) decision to proceed with the charge of a breach of proper professional conduct against a former colleague. The applicant maintained that his former colleague should have been charged with the more serious charge of professional misconduct. While the General Council was not established on a statutory footing, and despite the fact that an appeal lay to the Visitors of the Inns of Court (who were normally three High Court judges), Watkins L.J. held that judicial review would lie:

"The General Council . . . was fulfilling the role of prosecutor exercising discretion in the sifting and assessment of complaints and empowered by its own rules, when certain conditions were fulfilled, to prosecute that complaint before the disciplinary tribunal as an adjudicating body exercising powers delegated by the judges. The Professional Practices Committee, to whom those functions were delegated, had to carry them out in accordance with their own rules. Consequently its acts and omissions could be challenged by way of judicial review."[52]

One of the recent Irish cases in which the matter was discussed is *Murtagh*

---

[48] But, as against that, the decision to dismiss in the Garda and Defence Force cases (*e.g. The State (Gleeson) v. Minister for Defence* [1976] I.R. 280) has been taken pursuant to a statutory power, and this gives the cases a sufficient public dimension to bring them within the reach of certiorari: see Hogan, "Public Law Remedies and Judicial Review in the Context of Employment Law" (1985) 4 J.I.S.L.L. 9 and *R. v. East Berkshire Health Authority, ex p. Walsh* [1985] Q.B. 152 and *R. v. Home Secretary, ex p. Benwell* [1985] Q.B. 554. See pp. 90, n. 55 and 321–323.
[49] [1987] 1 Q.B. 815.
[50] *Ibid.* 838–839.
[51] [1990] 3 W.L.R. 323.
[52] *Ibid*, 335.

v. *Board of Governors of St. Emer's School*,[53] where Barron J. said that Order 84 was "intended to avoid submissions that the moving party had adopted the wrong procedure."[54] In *Murtagh* certiorari was sought to quash a minor disciplinary punishment imposed on a schoolboy attending national school. The respondents raised the issue as to whether certiorari would lie, but Barron J. found for the applicant on this point. Stressing that the body whose decision it is sought to quash "must be discharging a function of a public nature affecting private rights" and must also be under a duty "to act fairly in arriving at the decision," Barron J. said that the questions of discipline in national schools were not in the private domain:

"The school is a national school under the Department of Education. Rules formulated by the Department with the concurrence of the Minister for Finance govern every aspect of its existence. This includes school discipline. . . . The provisions for discipline [in the respondents' school] are no different in character from any other of the Rules governing these schools. They are not consensual in nature. Nor do they become so because, where different schools may have adopted different codes of discipline, one school rather than another is chosen. In each case, the parameters of the code are governed by the Rules."[55]

Barron J.'s analysis of the public law element of the Rules for the National Schools is undoubtedly correct and can be reconciled with *O'hUallacháin*, considered in the following paragraph, on the ground that the deed of trust involved in that case is a private law instrument with a well-established private law régime for its enforcement. And yet this demarcation can give rise to serious anomalies. For example, does it follow from this demarcation that a declaratory action by way of plenary summons is probably the only remedy available to a student expelled from university for serious misconduct, since this disciplinary jurisdiction is consensual and probably does not have its origins in public law? The gravity of this punishment of expulsion from university vastly exceeds that imposed in *Murtagh*, so it would be strange if the expeditious and cheaper remedy of judicial review were available in the latter case only.

On the other hand, there are three modern cases which squarely address this issue and which uphold the traditional limitations upon the scope of certiorari: *Ó hUallacháin* v. *Burke*,[56] *Murphy* v. *The Turf Club*[57] and *O'Neill* v.

---

[53] High Court, November 27, 1989. See also, *The State (Smullen)* v. *Duffy* [1980] I.L.R.M. 46 where a similar point does not appear to have been argued. Note, however, that decisions of the Educational Committee of the Incorporated Law Society have been held to be amenable to judicial review, since such decisions were taken pursuant to the Solicitors Act 1954 and the statutory instruments made thereunder: see *Gilmer* v. *Incorporated Law Society of Ireland* [1989] I.L.R.M. 590 and *MacGabhann* v. *Incorporated Law Society of Ireland* [1989] I.L.R.M. 854.

[54] At p. 5. He thought that Ord. 84, r. 22(1) and Ord. 84, r. 26(5) in particular were "designed to this end." Doubts were, however, expressed on this point by the Supreme Court on appeal: March 7, 1991.

[55] At p. 4. The Rules for the National Schools do not, of course, have any legal status as such and must be regarded as a form of elaborate administrative circular: see pp. 39–45.

[56] [1988] I.L.R.M. 693.

[57] [1989] I.R. 172.

Iarnród Éireann.[58] There have also been judicial dicta from the Supreme Court which point in this general direction. *ÓhUallacháin* concerned the administration of a secondary school governed by a deed of trust. Did certiorari lie to quash a decision of the school management to limit the intake of pupils on the ground that the imposition of such a quota was unreasonable in law? Murphy J. not only held that the quota was not unreasonable in the circumstances of the case, but expressed considerable doubts as to whether judicial review would lie. While he refrained from expressing a final view of the "serious questions" as to jurisdiction which arose, he distinguished *The State (Hayes)* v. *Criminal Injuries Compensation Board*[59] (in which it had been conceded by the State that the High Court had jurisdiction to review the operation of an extra-statutory tribunal) on the ground that:

> "I doubt whether one can validly equate the deed of trust in the present case with the publication of a ministerial scheme . . . The deed of trust is a binding legal instrument which can be invoked and enforced at the behest of the parties thereto . . . The relationship . . . between the students and the board of management are . . . matters to be determined in accordance with private law.[60]

In *Murphy* v. *The Turf Club*[61] proceedings had been commenced by way of judicial review to challenge the revocation of a racehorse trainer's licence. While the Turf Club enjoys certain statutory functions,[62] those functions were held to be immaterial, as on the instant occasion, the Turf Club was exercising supervisory powers derived from contract Barr J. said:

> "[The Turf Club] in purporting to revoke the applicant's training licence . . . was not exercising a public law function. On the contrary, its

---

[58] [1991] I.L.R.M. 129.

[59] [1982] I.L.R.M. 210. In *Bowes* v. *Motor Insurers' Bureau of Ireland* [1989] I.R. 225, 228 Finlay C.J. said that decisions of the Board (which is an extra-statutory body charged with administering the agreement made between the insurance companies and the Minister for the Environment) "could only be reviewed by the courts . . . in accordance with the principles of judicial review." This short passage would seem to suggest that decisions of the Board under this agreement are governed by principles of public law and that, accordingly, such decisions of the Board can be challenged by way of judicial review.

[60] [1989] I.L.R.M. 702. But *cf.* the views expressed by Barron J. in *Murtagh* v. *Board of Management of St. Emer's National School*, High Court, November 27, 1989, holding that a disciplinary punishment imposed on a primary school student was amenable to judicial review.

[61] [1989] I.R. 175. See also, *Law* v. *National Greyhound Racing Club Ltd.* [1983] 1 W.L.R. 1302 and *R.* v. *Disciplinary Committee of the Turf Club, ex p. Massingberd-Mundy, The Times*, January 3, 1990. Likewise, despite the fact that political parties are intimately involved in the electoral process and that the legal regulation of elections has a "public law" element, the disaffiliation of a candidate by a political party has been held not to be amenable to judicial review, since the relationship between the candidate and the party is a matter of private agreement: *Re Lyle's Application* [1987] 7 N.I.J.B. 24.

[62] Although Barr J. did not refer to these statutory provisions by name, they include such statutory powers as the power to exclude persons from race meetings: Racing and Racecourses Act 1945, s.39. It would seem therefore that a body such as the Turf Club finds itself in the anomalous position whereby it can be amenable to judicial review for one purpose (such as the exercise of statutory powers to exclude persons from a race meeting) and not for others (such as the suspension of a jockey).

decision was that of a domestic tribunal exercising a regulatory function over the applicant, being an interested party who had voluntarily submitted to its jurisdiction."[63]

The applicant was therefore left to pursue his remedies for breach of contract against the Turf Club. While Barr J.'s judgment may be regarded as restating the orthodox view, is it not somewhat unrealistic to regard Turf Club's jurisdiction as "voluntary," given that it enjoys a monopoly in respect of the granting of a horse-trainer's licence?

These troublesome matters were considered by the Supreme Court in a number of recent cases. Although none of these cases constitutes a perfect authority, their consistency is significant. The strongest authority is *O'Neill* v. *Iarnród Éireann*.[64] The facts were that the respondent-employer had dismissed the applicant-employee in circumstances which amounted, so Barr J. found in the High Court, to a breach of constitutional justice and the duty to observe fair procedures. However, Barr J. held that the applicant was not entitled to apply for judicial review. The reason was that the relationship between the applicant and the respondent was founded in a contractual relationship of master and servant.

In the Supreme Court in *O'Neill*, counsel for the applicant relied on cases such as: *Murtagh*; *Ryan* v. *VIP Taxi Co-operative Society Ltd.*[65]; *Flanagan* v. *University College, Dublin*[66]; *MacGabhann* v. *Incorporated Law Society of Ireland*,[67] but the Court nevertheless upheld the approach of the High Court. Hederman J. stated: "I am satisfied that relief sought under Order 84 lies only against public authorities in respect of the duties conferred upon them by law [*sc.* statute]."[68] And, addressing the argument that the judicial review procedure applied in the instant case just because constitutional justice was involved, Hederman J. added:

"I am . . . satisfied that a constitutional issue of justice and fairness which may arise between private parties can only be determined by ordinary Court procedure. See, for example, *Glover* v. *B.L.N. Ltd.*".[69] Finlay C.J. took the same approach and quoted from his judgment in *O'Neill* v. *Beaumont Hospital Board*[70] where he had said:

"The basis of an application for judicial review concerning the decision by an employer provided for specifically in a contract of employment with a

---

[63] [1989] I.R. 172, 174–175.
[64] [1991] I.L.R.M. 129. See also, *Shalvey* v. *Bord Telecom Eireann*, High Court, July 8, 1989, where Lardner J. held judicial review would not lie in respect of an internal disciplinary decision taken by the respondents, since this matter was not regulated by the Postal and Telecommunications Services Act 1983.
[65] *The Irish Times*, April 10, 1989.
[66] [1988] I.R. 724.
[67] [1989] I.L.R.M. 854.
[68] [1991] I.L.R.M. 129, 133.
[69] *Ibid.*
[70] [1990] I.L.R.M. 419.

person who is employed by that employer must be doubtful, but the respondents . . . have conceded that it is appropriate."[71]

The third member of the court in *O'Neill* v. *Iarnród Éireann* was McCarthy J., who stated: "I am far from satisfied that procedure by way of judicial review is applicable in the circumstances of this case or that it should be granted where alternative remedies are available".[72] He also referred to an earlier *ex parte* appeal: *Gupta* v. *Trinity College, Dublin*[72a] where he had previously expressed reservations about the application of judicial review to the decision of the relevant body of Trinity College in that case. Here, be it noted, is an example of a practice adverted to earlier, namely the conflation of a case on the nature of the body under review with a case on the source of the power, under review.

The authority of *O'Neill* v. *Iarnród Éireann* is weakened by the fact that the judgments were delivered in the context of an *ex parte* appeal and that, as a result of this, a majority of the Court considered that it would be incorrect to cut out the applicant at this preliminary stage from his opportunity of relief by way of judicial review. Nevertheless, there is no doubting the strength or unanimity of the views expressed. While these authorities undoubtedly represent the current law, the following two comments may be made on this vexed area of the area which has already been discussed at a more conceptual level in Chapter 8, under the heading "The Reach of Public Law."

First, as a matter of certainty and practicability in the law's operation, it is a matter for regret that this form of public law/private law characterisation should still be a feature of judicial review applications. As Carswell J. succintly put it in a Northern Irish context:

> "It does not seem to me consistent with the development of the law since the fusion of law and equity that the claimant's choice of remedy should be made to possess such a degree of importance; and it seems to me quite undesirable that litigants should be subjected unnecessarily to the hazards of having to make a correct guess in which court to pursue their claims."[73]

Secondly, from the point of principle, does it make any sense to distinguish, for example, between the decisions of, say, different educational institutions on the basis of their legal origin? The essential point is that in each case they wield a substantial degree of educational power over the individual and often do so, on what is, in practice, close to a monopoly basis. On this view, it seems preferable, first, that they should all be subject to the same form of supervision by the courts, and, secondly, that that form should be an application for judicial review.[74]

---

[71] *Ibid*, 437.
[72] [1991] I.L.R.M. 129, 135.
[72a] Supreme Court, April 14, 1990.
[73] *Re Western Health and Social Services Board's Application* [1988] 4 N.I.J.B. 36, 54.
[74] This is a vexed question. In *Flanagan* v. *University College, Dublin* [1988] I.R. 724 certiorari was granted to quash such a disciplinary punishment and the procedural issue of whether judicial review would lie was not raised. The issue might also have been addressed in *Kenny* v.

However, when one turns from the question of what is a public body to the issue of whether a particular power is to be classified as "public" and hence, subject to judicial review, there may be a genuine basis for a more discriminating attitude. Such an attitude would, as was done in *O'Neill* v. *Iarnród Éireann* regard statutory powers as exceptional, far-reaching and, therefore, "public" and, so, to be treated differently from a contract of employment (or any other commercial contract) on the basis that a contract of employment with a public body does not warrant different treatment from a contract with a private employer.

Judicial review does not apply to the Superior Courts.

One other important limitation to the scope of judicial review is that it is not available to review a decision of a Superior Court of record.[75] Thus, decisions of the High Court, Court of Criminal Appeal and the Supreme Court cannot be reviewed in this way. The High Court's power of judicial review is an inherent one which is designed to ensure that inferior courts,[76] tribunals[77] and other bodies exercising public functions do not exceed their jurisdiction. However, judicial review will lie to quash decisions of officers such as the Master of the High Court[78] or a Taxing Master,[79] as it has been

Kelly [1988] I.R. 457 (a judicial review case involving U.C.D. admissions policy), but this procedural objection was only raised at the hearing and Barron J. said that, at this stage, it was too late to raise this point.
There have been some English cases where certiorari was said to lie to quash a punishment of this kind (*e.g. R.* v. *Aston University Senate, ex p. Roffey* [1969] 2 Q.B. 538), but this was doubted by Russell L.J. in *Herring* v. *Templeman* [1973] 3 All E.R. 569, 585. There was a suggestion in *R.* v. *Disciplinary Committee of the Jockey Club, ex p. Massingberd-Mundy, The Times*, January 3, 1990, that the fact that the Jockey Club was established by Royal Charter might be enough to make it amenable to judicial review. Perhaps the fact that both the University of Dublin and the constituent colleges of the National University of Ireland were established by Royal Charter (in the latter case by charter under the Irish Universities Act 1908) might be sufficient for this purpose. However, in *Malone* v. *Queen's University, Belfast* [1988] 3 N.I.J.B. 9, 29 these facts were said by Kelly L.J. to be "so remote and indirect that it can not realistically be said to bring in any significant element of public law." In any event, it is undesirable that the availability of judicial review should turn on such fine points.
[75] "The High Court, whether sitting as the Central Criminal Court or otherwise, is not an inferior court subject to coercive orders such as mandamus," *per* Henchy J. in *People (D.P.P.)* v. *Quilligan (No. 2)* [1989] I.R. 46, 57. See also, *Re A Company* [1981] A.C. 374.
[76] The Special Criminal Court ranks as an inferior court for this purpose, despite that fact that in recent years it has been the practice for a High Court judge to preside over that Court. There have been numerous examples of applications for judicial review of decisions of the Special Criminal Court, but in no case has it been argued that judicial review will not lie to quash its decisions. For an example of where a decision of the Special Criminal Court was quashed by certiorari, see *The State (D.P.P.)* v. *Special Criminal Court*, High Court, May 18, 1983.
[77] Judicial review will, of course, also lie where a High Court judge is presiding over a tribunal, where he is not sitting as a High Court judge as such: *Baldwin & Francis Ltd.* v. *Patents Appeal Tribunal* [1959] A.C. 663. Thus, for example, there was no suggestion in *The State (Keegan)* v. *Stardust Compensation Tribunal* [1986] I.R. 642 that a decision of that tribunal (of which Barrington J. was the chairman) could not be quashed by certiorari.
[78] *Elwyn (Cottons) Ltd.* v. *Master of the High Court* [1989] I.R. 14 (mandamus lies to compel the Master of the High Court to grant protective measures under the Jurisdiction of Courts and Enforcement of Judgments (European Communities) Act 1988).
[79] *The State (Gallagher, Shatter & Co.)* v. *de Valera*, High Court, December 9, 1983 (certiorari lies to quash decision of the Taxing Master as to costs). While this decision was reversed on its

held that the High Court is not thereby making an order against itself or any other "Superior Court," but rather against an officer "attached" to the High Court.

"Determining questions affecting the rights of subjects . . . " It was traditionally understood that the public law remedies would only lie to review something in the nature of a determination or decision. The determination does not have to be absolutely final, but there are cases which hold that a requirement that the decision be approved by another person or body prevents the orders from issuing.[80] Allied to this is the notion that the public law remedies will not lie to a body whose sole function is to make a recommendation, and that the impugned determination must affect rights or impose liabilities.[81] The modern tendency, however, is to eschew a rigid classification of whether a determination is "binding," "conclusive" or whether the "legal rights" of the citizen have been affected. The courts are apt to examine whether the applicant has suffered a real or possible prejudice and to see whether he has a sufficient interest in the matter.

In *The State (Shannon Atlantic Fisheries Ltd.)* v. *McPolin*[82] Finlay P. quashed a report which followed a statutory inquiry. The report was sent to the Minister for Transport and Power, who was obliged to decide whether a prosecution was called for. The investigating officer had not observed the precepts of natural justice when compiling his report concerning the wrecking of the prosecutor's fishing vessel, and Finlay P. held that the applicants were entitled to have the report quashed on this account. It was irrelevant that the applicants could no longer be charged with offences arising out of this incident,[83] they were rightly concerned with the findings of fact made in the report which affected their reputation as ship owners. Cases such as *McPolin* show that the concept of the "determination of rights" is loosely construed. It cannot be said that a preliminary report in and of itself affects legal rights or imposes liabilities. But the critical factor is often whether the applicants were prejudiced in the contested determination, and whether they would obtain a real benefit were the determination to be quashed.[84]

---

facts by the Supreme Court ([1987] I.L.R.M. 3), there was no suggestion that judicial review would not lie to quash his decision. Certiorari was also granted in *The State (Gallagher, Shatter & Co.)* v. *de Valera (No. 2)*, Supreme Court, February 14, 1990. But *cf. Re Weir and Higgins' Application* (1988) 10 N.I.J.B. 4.
[80] *Re Local Government Board, ex p. Kingstown Commissioners* (1886) 18 L.R.Ir. 509; *R. v. St. Lawrence's Hospital, ex p. Pritchard* [1953] 1 W.L.R. 1158.
[81] *The State (St. Stephen's Green Club)* v. *Labour Court* [1961] I.R. 85; and the comments of Murnaghan J. in *The State (Pharmaceutical Society)* v. *Fair Trade Commission* (1965) 99 I.L.T.R. 24, 31–32 (no prohibition to respondent body as it could not affect individual rights or liabilities).
[82] [1976] I.R. 93.
[83] The six-month time limit for summary prosecutions imposed by s.10(4) of the Petty Sessions (Ireland) Act 1851 had expired.
[84] This has been the attitude taken in cases such as *The State (Hayes)* v. *Criminal Injuries Compensation Board* [1982] I.L.R.M. 210 (certiorari lies to review decisions of extra-statutory body) and *The State (Melbarien Enterprises Ltd.)* v. *Revenue Commissioners* [1985] I.R. 706 (certiorari lies to review refusal to grant tax clearance certificate, *i.e.* a purely administrative decision not taken pursuant to statutory power).

"Having the duty to act judicially." In *The State (Crowley)* v. *Irish Land Commission*[85] the Supreme Court accepted that not all administrative decisions were subject to review by way of prohibition or certiorari. The administrative body concerned had to be under a duty to act judicially[86] before such remedies could issue. Maguire C.J. said that an administrative body acted judicially when it was required to consider the facts and circumstances of the case before it could reach a decision imposing liability or affecting the rights of others.

But this requirement does not in practice greatly restrict the scope of certiorari or prohibition. First, the duty to act judicially is implied where there is a power to affect rights or impose liabilities.[87] Secondly, mandamus will issue in cases even where there is no duty to act judicially, and this reflects the fact that until nearly the end of the nineteenth century, mandamus was used to enforce administrative and ministerial duties of every description.[88] Certiorari, prohibition and mandamus are interchangeable remedies for all practical purposes. There is nothing to prevent a court granting an order of certiorari *in lieu* of mandamus in a case where the decision-maker was under no duty to act judicially even where this relief was not actually sought.[89]

"Act in excess of legal authority." Notwithstanding this qualification, traditionally, certiorari enjoyed one distinct procedural advantage over and above the other remedies. It would lie to review not only *ultra vires* decisions, but it would also quash for error on the face of the record.[90] The effect of the new Order 84, rule 19 is to empower the court to quash for error on the face of the record in all applications for judicial review.

Special features of mandamus

Mandamus is, technically, a recognised statutory remedy in that section 28(8) of the Supreme Court of Judicature (Ireland) Act 1877 permits an interlocutory order of mandamus to be granted in all cases "where it is just and convenient to do so." Thus, unlike certiorari and prohibition, it was theoreti-

---

[85] [1951] I.R. 250.

[86] O'Higgins C.J. appeared to insist upon this requirement in *The State (Abenglen Properties Ltd.)* v. *Dublin Corporation* [1984] I.R. 381, 392, as did Hamilton P. in *Byrne* v. *Grey* [1988] I.R. 31, 40, and Barr J. in *Egan* v. *Minister for Defence*, High Court, November 24, 1988.

[87] *Ridge* v. *Baldwin* [1964] A.C. 40; *R.* v. *Hillingdon B.C., ex p. Royco Homes Ltd.* [1974] Q.B. 720. *The State (Conlan)* v. *Military Service Pensions Referee* [1947] I.R. 264 (certiorari does not lie to review ministerial decision to request respondent referee to review the grant of a military service pension, as Minister under no duty to act judicially) is one of the very few cases in which the applicant has failed to satisfy this requirement. It also appears that certiorari cannot be used to mount a direct challenge to the validity of a statute or delegated legislation, as no duty to act judicially arises in the case of the exercise of a legislative function: *Re Local Government Board, ex p. Kingstown Commissioners* (1886) 18 L.R.Ir. 509. Of course, certiorari can be used to mount an indirect collateral challenge to the validity of such legislation: see Hogan, "Challenging the Validity of an Act of the Oireachtas by way of Certiorari" (1982) 4 D.U.L.J.(N.S.) 130.

[88] Wade, *Administrative Law* (Oxford, 1988), pp. 649–653.

[89] Note that in *O'Reilly* v. *Mackman* [1983] 2 A.C. 237, the House of Lords ruled that the duty to act judicially was no longer to be required in the case of applications for certiorari or prohibition.

[90] Thus, a declaration could not be awarded to quash for error on the face of the record: *Punton* v. *Ministry for Pensions (No. 2)* [1964] 1 W.L.R. 226.

cally possible to obtain interim relief in mandamus cases even prior to the 1986 Rules of Court, although the facility does not seem to have been ever availed of in practice. Curiously enough, the Rules of Court have always assimilated the practice and procedure of mandamus applications to that of interpleader actions, and this feature of mandamus is retained in the new Order 84, rule 25(2). Consequently, discovery and interrogatories have always been available in applications for mandamus, and, in a suitable case, the applicant is entitled to a jury trial.[91] Any applicant for mandamus must first call on the administrative body concerned to do its duty, and this must have been refused.[92] The requirement that there be "a demand and refusal" has much to commend it: it makes sense that the administrative body concerned is given the chance to mend its hand before the aggrieved citizen resorts to litigation. But the courts do not insist upon this requirement where it is unsuitable.[93]

In addition to its usual remit to enforce a duty which had not been discharged, mandamus has another less obvious function: in cases where the impugned order was classified as being administrative (as opposed to judicial)[94] in character, certiorari was not available and mandamus was granted in its place. The rationale was that in such cases no valid decision was deemed to exist, so that mandamus could lie to command the decision-maker to arrive at a decision. This practice was known as "certiorarified mandamus," and it was developed at a time when it was thought that certiorari would not lie in respect of purely administrative decisions. It was necessarily implicit in the grant of mandamus—that is, an order to the deciding official to determine the matter according to law—that the impugned decision was a nullity. In *The State (Keller)* v. *Galway C.C.*,[95] for example, Davitt P. held that mandamus should issue to a medical officer who had taken irrelevant considerations into account when rejecting an application for a disability allowance, saying that:

> "[W]here an inferior tribunal whose duty it is to hear and determine certain questions according to law takes into consideration, and allows its determination to be affected by, matters which it has no right to take into account, it can be held to have declined jurisdiction; and may be required on mandamus to hear and determine the issue properly according to law."[96]

---

[91] Ord. 36, r. 7 (which applies to interpleader and, consequently, to mandamus proceedings) allows the court to order a jury trial where there is a contested issue of fact. A jury trial on an issue of fact was ordered in *The State (Modern Homes (Ire.) Ltd.* v. *Dublin Corporation* [1953] I.R. 202.

[92] "It is an established rule that the prosecutor must make a specific demand for the performance of the public duty in question, and it must be shown that this demand has been refused, or has been followed by conduct which the Court considers as tantamount to a refusal," *per* Fitzgibbon J. in *R. (Butler)* v. *Navan U.D.C.* [1926] I.R. 466, 470–471. See also, *The State (Modern Homes (Ire.) Ltd.*v. *Dublin Corporation* [1953] I.R. 202 (refusal of applicant's demand inferred where respondents "made positive decisions to continue with existing law").

[93] *R.* v. *Hanley Revising Barrister* [1912] 3 K.B. 518.

[94] This form of mandamus will not lie where the decision-making authority is exercising judicial (or quasi-judicial) functions: see *R. (Spain)* v. *Income Tax Commissioners* [1934] I.R. 27.

[95] [1958] I.R. 142. See also, *R. (Clonmel Lunatic Asylum)* v. *Considine* [1917] 2 I.R. 1.

[96] [1958] I.R. 142, 150.

Despite the procedural improvements effected by the new Rules, this form of certiorarified mandamus may still be used as a means of review in the rare cases where certiorari would not appear to be available (*e.g.* administrative decisions where there is no duty to act judicially).

Mandamus is, of course, the most appropriate remedy where the enforcement of a statutory duty is sought. The statutory duty in question must, however, be "clearly and unambiguously expressed in the statute,"[97] before mandamus will issue. *Anheuser Busch Inc.* v. *Controller of Patents, Design and Trade Marks*[98] and *Elwyn (Cottons) Ltd.* v. *Master of the High Court*[99] are two recent examples of cases where such an unambiguous statutory duty was found to exist. In the former case, Barron J. granted an order of mandamus compelling the Controller to state his reasons for his failure to remove a particular trade mark on the grounds of non-use. Barron J. considered that section 56 of the Trade Marks Act 1963 enabled the High Court to direct the Controller to furnish such reasons so as to enable the applicants to appeal against his decision and granted an order of mandamus accordingly. And in *Elwyn Cottons*, O'Hanlon J. held that section 11(3) of the Jurisdiction of Courts and Enforcement of Judgments (European Communities) Act 1988 did oblige the respondent Master to grant protective measures in favour of the applicant for an enforcement order of a foreign judgment once such an enforcement order had been made. Accordingly, O'Hanlon J. granted an order of mandamus direct to the respondent to grant such protective measures. By contrast, in *The State (Finglas Industrial Estates Ltd.)* v. *Dublin C.C.*,[1] the Supreme Court held that mandamus would not lie to compel the respondents to accept a contrbution towards the construction of sewerage facilities in the absence of such a statutory duty. Similarly, in *The State (Sheehan)* v. *Government of Ireland*,[2] a majority of the Supreme Court held that the language of section 60(7) of the Civil Liability Act 1961 did not, on its true construction, impose an obligation on the Government to bring that section into force with the result that mandamus would not lie to compel this to be done.

3. Declaration and Injunction

Although it is not a purely public law remedy, the declaratory action has come to occupy a special place in our public law, chiefly because of the restrictions which hitherto restricted the scope of certiorari. A declaratory judgment declares the rights or the legal position of the parties to an action. Such a judgment is not of itself coercive, although the litigant may safely assume that public bodies will respect and obey such judgments. The declaratory action is of comparatively modern vintage, for the common law viewed non-coercive remedies with disfavour. As far as Ireland is concerned, the declaratory

---

[97] *The State (Sheehan)* v. *Government of Ireland* [1987] I.R. 550, 562, *per* Henchy J.
[98] [1987] I.R. 329.
[99] [1989] I.R. 14.
[1] Supreme Court, February 17, 1983.
[2] [1987] I.R. 550. See further, pp. 554–557.

action has its origins in the Chancery (Ireland) Act 1867, section 155 of which stated that no action should be open to the objection that a merely declaratory decree or order was sought thereby, and that it should be possible for the court to make binding declarations of right whether any consequential relief is or could be claimed, or not.[3] The wording of section 155 is substantially reproduced in Order 19, rule 29 of the Rules of the Superior Court.

The power of the High Court to grant an injunction derives from section 28(8) of the Supreme Court of Judicature (Ireland) Act 1877,[4] which enabled the court to grant this remedy in all cases where it appeared just and convenient to do so. Despite the generality of the language used, this subsection did not extend the reach of the injunction to claims for which no remedy had previously existed either at law or in equity, nor were the principles governing the grant of an injunction substantially altered.

Apart from the fact that the declaration is a non-coercive remedy (whereas, as we have seen, the effect of certiorari is positively to quash the impugned decision or order), there are but few factors which influence the litigant's choice as between these two remedies and the distinctions between them are comparatively minor. For example, as a matter of practice, due to the wording to Order 84, rule 20(7)(a) of the Rules of the Superior Courts 1986, it seems possible for an applicant to obtain interlocutory relief on an *ex parte* basis in the case of certiorari, whereas this is not true where declaration or an injunction is sought. Secondly, the language of Order 84, rule 18(2) appear to imply that the declaration and injunction are only secondary remedies compared to certiorari and prohibition and there is here a suggestion that the courts should only grant such relief if the granting of certiorari or prohibition would be for some reason inappropriate. As against this, certiorari will only lie to quash a decision or order. Accordingly, where a litigant wishes to challenge the decision taken pursuant to either primary or delegated legislation and he claims such legislation is invalid, he cannot use certiorari to mount a *direct* challenge to the validity of the legislation. If certiorari is employed, the litigant must either directly challenge the decision itself, reserving unto himself the right to argue that the legislation is invalid during the course of the hearing or (and which is now much more common in practice) seek a declaration (perhaps in tandem with certiorari) that the legislation itself is invalid, as the declaratory remedy is uniquely suited to a direct challenge to the validity of such legislation. However, given the court's power to substitute remedies, this may be academic.

---

[3] But note that in *Guaranty Trust Co. of N.Y.* v. *Hannay & Co.* [1915] 2 K.B. 536, 568, Bankes L.J. asserted that the courts had always possessed a residual jurisdiction to grant declaratory judgments. This statement was made, however, in the context of an action to have Rules of Court permitting the granting of declarations declared *ultra vires*. Naturally the Rules would have been *ultra vires* if they did not amount to procedural improvements of a jurisdiction which already existed.

[4] As applied to the present High Court by s.8(2) of the Courts (Supplemental Provisions) Act 1961. S.28(8) of the 1877 Act only refers in terms to the granting of an interlocutory order, but this subsection encompasses the grant of a final order: *Beddow* v. *Beddow* (1878) 9 Ch.D. 89, 93, *per* Jessel M.R.

We must now consider (i) the new judicial review procedure in so far as it relates to the declaration and injunction and (ii) the scope of these remedies.

(i) *The judicial review procedure*[5]

A litigant seeking declaratory or injunctive relief may commence his action by plenary summons in the ordinary fashion. But if the respondent is a public body, a declaration or an injunction may now be sought through an application for judicial review. Order 84, rule 18(2) of the new Rules of the Superior Court provides:

> "An application for a declaration or an injunction may be made by way of an application for judicial review, and on such an application the Court may grant the declaration or application claimed if it considers that, having regard to—
> (*a*) the nature of the matters in respect of which relief may be granted by way of an order of mandamus, prohibition, certiorari or quo warranto
> (*b*) the nature of the persons and bodies against whom relief may be granted by way of such order, and
> (*c*) all the circumstances of the case,
> it would be just and convenient for the declaration or injunction to be granted on an application for judicial review."

Pandion Haliaetus Ltd. v. *Revenue Commissioners*[6] provides a good example of the operation of Order 84, rule 18(2) in practice. Here the applicant company sought repayment of a substantial sum which had been withheld by the Revenue Commissioners on the ground that the company was involved in a "sham" tax avoidance scheme. Blayney J. rejected that contention and held that the company was entitled to a repayment of this sum. The Revenue Commissioners had taken the position that even if this were so, Pandion should appeal the Inspector of Taxes' determination. Pandion, in response, had contended on the basis of an earlier determination by an Inspector of Taxes that it was entitled to a repayment and that an appeal would, accordingly, be pointless. Blayney J. accepted this latter submission and observed that Pandion had "no method of enforcing repayment apart from claiming the declaration sought." Accordingly, Blayney J. held that it was "just and convenient" within the meaning of Order 84, rule 18(2) that a declaration in respect of the payments due should be granted by him to resolve the deadlock:

> "The determination in the present case is clearly being sought in a context of judicial review which is one of the matters to which I should have regard under clauses (a) and (b) [of r. 18(2)]. As to the circumstances of the case to which I should also have regard . . . I am satisfied that Pandion is entitled to a repayment. But if no declaration were made, there would be a

---

[5] See Collins & O'Reilly, *op. cit.* pp. 72–75.
[6] [1987] I.R. 309.

stalemate . . . In these circumstances, it seems to me to be eminently just and reasonable that the declaration should be made."[7]

It is to be noted that unlike Order 84, rule 18(1) (which, of course, relates to the purely public law remedies of certiorari, prohibition and mandamus), Order 84, rule 18(2) is discretionary in nature. ("An application for a declaration . . . may be made by way of an application for judicial review . . ..") The litigant is *apparently* given a choice: he may apply for a declaration or an injunction by way of an application for judicial review or he may, as in the pre-1986 era, commence the proceedings by way of plenary summons. But the litigant's choice is not an unrestricted one; in the first place, it would seem likely that the application for judicial review is only available where the proceedings relate to the exercise of public law powers by a public body, *i.e.* the matter must be one coming within the traditional scope of the purely public law remedies of certiorari, prohibition and mandamus.[8] An example should illustrate this point:

A local authority fails to honour its contractual obligation to purchase certain products from X Company Ltd. X Company Ltd. seeks a declaration that the local authority are in breach of contract. X Company Ltd. *cannot* proceed by way of an application for judicial review, for although the respondent is a public body, the matter does not relate to the exercise of the authority's public law functions, but is governed by ordinary principles of contract. X Company Ltd. must commence declaratory proceedings by way of plenary summons. If the company proceeds by way of an application for judicial review, the court may, instead of refusing the application, order the proceedings to continue as if they had been begun by plenary summons.[9]

Secondly, consider the converse case, *i.e.* where public functions are involved:

A local authority refuses to grant Y a licence under the Casual Trading Act 1980. Y seeks a declaration that this refusal is invalid. Since Y's claim relates to the exercise of public law powers by a public body, then of course, the declaratory action *may* proceed by way of an application for judicial review. It appears that in this jurisdiction, Y may, alternatively, commence the proceedings by way of plenary summons, save that questions of an abuse of process may arise where the litigant's motivation is to circumvent the stricter time limits and other safeguards provided for in Order 84 by proceedings by way of plenary summons.

It should be noted that there is no converse power to that contained in Order

[7] *Ibid.* 321.
[8] It is true that this restriction appears to be crumbling in regard to certiorari: see pp. 572–579. And if it ceases in regard to certiorari, what justification has it in regard to declaration, given that declaration and certiorari are now virtually identical, on judicial review?
[9] Ord. 84, r. 26(5). There is, however, no converse power allowing proceedings begun by plenary summons to proceed as if on an application for judicial review.

84, rule 26(5) whereby proceedings, commenced by way of judicial review, may be ordered to continue as if they had begun by way of plenary summons.[10] It is not immediately obvious why the courts should not have the power to "convert" an action commenced by way of plenary summons into an application for judicial review. It may be that, were such a power to exist, it would facilitate litigants who wished to circumvent the inherent restrictions in the Order 84 procedure (the need for leave, strict time limits, etc.) by commencing their action by way of plenary summons and for these reasons, the Superior Court Rules Committee deliberately elected to allow conversion in one direction only. But if this is so, that would be another powerful argument in favour of the approach favoured by the English courts, namely that Order 84 creates a special self-contained procedure for challenging administrative decisions and that, as a general rule, any challenges to such a decision must be brought in this fashion. It is to this important issue that we now turn.

The English law on this point was established by *O'Reilly* v. *Mackman*[11] in which certain prisoners commenced declaratory proceedings by plenary summons against a prison board of visitors. They sought declarations to the effect that the board of visitors had acted contrary to natural justice and that disciplinary punishments imposed by them were invalid. As this complaint was likely to raise many disputed issues of fact, it was decided to proceed by way of plenary action rather than by way of an application for judicial review. The House of Lords held that the actions should be struck out as an abuse of process.

In *O'Reilly*, Lord Diplock pointed out that whereas formerly the courts had, by concession, encouraged the use of the declaration and injunction in public law cases in order to permit litigants to avoid the procedural defects which then attached to the purely public law remedies of certiorari, prohibition and mandamus, this concession should now be withdrawn in view of the removal of those procedural defects by the new Rules of Court. More importantly, the new judicial review procedures contained certain safeguards designed to protect public bodies from vexatious and unmeritorious claims. An applicant for judicial review must obtain leave from the High Court, and conditions may be attached to the grant of leave. The applicant must, from

---

[10] In *R.* v. *East Berkshire Health Authority, ex p. Walsh* [1985] Q.B. 152, 166 Sir John Donaldson M.R. described the equivalent English rule in the following terms:

> "This is an anti-technicality rule. It is designed to preserve the position of an applicant for relief who finds that the basis of that relief is private law rather than public law. It is not designed to allow him to amend and to claim different relief."

This passage is probably too restrictive as far as practice in this jurisdiction is concerned. Ord. 84, r. 26(5) is often invoked in practice to enable judicial review cases presenting complex legal and factual issues to proceed by way of plenary summons.

[11] [1983] 2 A.C. 237. For largely critical comment see Wade, "Procedure and Prerogative in Public Law" (1985) 101 L.Q.R. 180. Lord Diplock's judgment in *O'Reilly* is described by Sir William Wade (at 86) as an opinion of "notable range and synthesising power." While one cannot but concur, many will nevertheless agree with Professor Jolowicz's observation that *O'Reilly* v. *Mackman* represented a "singularly unfortunate step back to the technicalities of a by-gone age": see "The Forms of Action Disinterred" (1983) C.L.J. 15, 18.

the outset, put his case on affidavit, and cannot rely on merely unsworn allegations in the pleadings. What is of special importance is that there is such a
short time-limit. This means that the judicial review procedure provides for a
speedy and expeditious determination of the validity of administrative action,
in contrast to the delays that may be caused in the case of an action commenced by plenary summons. Such delays would be particularly unwelcome
in such diverse areas as extradition, planning and adoption. As Lord Diplock
explained:

> "So to delay the judge's decision [as to whether to grant leave] would
> defeat the public policy that underlies the grant of those protections: *viz.*
> the need, in the interest of good administration and of third parties who
> may be indirectly affected by the decision, for speedy certainty as to
> whether it has the effect of a decision which is valid in public law. An action
> for a declaration and an injunction need not be commenced until the very
> end of the limitation period . . . and the plaintiffs are not required to sup-
> port their allegations by evidence on oath until the actual trial. The period
> of uncertainty as to the validity of a decision that has been challenged or
> allegations that may eventually turn out to be baseless or unsupported by
> evidence on oath, may thus be strung out for a very lengthy period . . .
> Unless such an act can be struck out summarily at the outset as an abuse of
> the process of the court, the whole purpose of the public policy to which the
> change [in the Rules] was directed would be defeated."[12]

Given the similarities between the two systems of judicial review in both Ireland and England, there is much to be said in favour of the reasoning in
O'Reilly applying in Ireland, especially in view of the fact that any other result
would mean that the safeguards now contained in Order 84 which are
designed to protect public authorities could be circumvented by the use of an
alternative procedure.

But while it is impossible to take issue with the principle underlying Lord
Diplock's reasoning, its practical operation has wreaked havoc ever since. A
whole new process of characterisation of claims has become necessary and the
decision in *O'Reilly* has been made subject to numerous exceptions.[13] It may
even be said that the whole object of the reforms has been defeated by the
decision. The new rules were designed to ease the path of public law litigants
and to ensure that a meritorious application was not lost by reason of the
wrong choice of remedy. In Britain, however, many litigants have found in

---

[12] [1983] 2 A.C. 237, 284.
[13] The judicially-created exceptions include the following:

- where there is no objection: *Gillick* v. *West Norfolk Area Health Authority* [1986] A.C.
  112.
- where the invalidity arises by way of defence: *Davy* v. *Spelthorne B.C.* [1984] A.C. 264.
- where the issues arise collaterally in a claim for the infringement of a right of the plaintiff
  arising under private law: *Wandsworth L.B.C.* v. *Winder* [1985] A.C. 461.

the wake of *O'Reilly* v. *Mackman* that their applications for judicial review have been struck out by reason of the wrong choice of proceedings.[14] In fact, this result is actually now more frequent than ever was the case prior to the introduction of the new Rules in England in 1977, when the procedural reforms, designed to avoid precisely this result, came into force. In sum, perhaps, operating the *O'Reilly* gloss on the new system would entail drawing a demarcation line between public and private law and thus admitting by the back door the curse of characterisation which had just been ceremoniously expelled at the front door. Moreover, it does not appear that, under the pre-1986 Rules, public authorities were, in fact, unduly troubled by the prospect of having to defend actions for declarations or injunctions commenced by plenary summons.[15]

The courts in this jurisdiction have shown no enthusiasm for *O'Reilly* v. *Mackman* and there have been several important actions where the applicant commenced his action by way of plenary summons, yet this fact went unremarked.[16] Barron J. has commented (albeit in the context of whether certiorari would lie in a matter allegedly private in nature) that the object of Order 84 was "intended to avoid submissions that the moving party had adopted the wrong procedure",[17] a view which argues stongly against the adoption of *O'Reilly* v. *Mackman*. However, it was not until the judgment of Costello J. in *O'Donnell* v. *Dún Laoghaire Corporation (No. 2)*[18] that the matter received full consideration by an Irish court. Here the plaintiffs successfully established that certain water charges imposed by the defendants some years previously were invalid. It was argued that it was an abuse of process for the plaintiffs to proceed by way of plenary action, especially since the action had been commenced outside the three months time-limit prescribed by order 84, rule 21(1).

Costello J. rejected this submission and was unwilling to following the reasoning in *O'Reilly* v. *Mackman*. First, he held that Order 84 did not prescribe an exclusive procedure and nor did he consider that the public interest required that Order 84 should be construed in this restrictive manner. However, he then went to hold that the safeguards contained in Order 84 should be

---

[14] See, *e.g.* cases such as *R.* v. *Home Secretary, ex p. Dew* [1987] 1 W.L.R. 881 for a striking example of current English practice.

[15] In *M.* v. *An Bord Uchtála* [1977] I.R. 287 proceedings challenging the validity of an adoption order were begun by plenary summons some four years after the making of the order. There was no suggestion by the Supreme Court that this procedure was inappropriate. Henchy J. stated (at 297) that:

> "They might have sought [to apply] to have the adoption order quashed on certiorari. Instead, they chose to apply for a declaratory order, doubtless because they wished to have the case fully presented on a plenary hearing."

[16] These cases are too numerous to mention, but notable examples include *Crotty* v. *An Taoiseach* [1987] I.R. 713 (challenge to the validity of ratification of the Single European Act) and *McGimpsey* v. *Ireland* [1988] I.R. 567 (challenge to the Anglo-Irish Agreement).

[17] *Murtagh* v. *Board of Governors of St. Emer's School*, High Court, November 27, 1989, p. 4.

[18] [1991] I.L.R.M. 301.

applied, *mutatis mutandis*, to actions against public authorities commenced by plenary summons:

> "In considering the effects of delay in a plenary action there are now persuasive reasons for adopting the principles enshrined in Ord. 84, r. 21 relating to delay in applications for judicial review, so that if the plenary action is not brought within the three months from the date of which the cause of action arose, the court would normally refuse relief unless it is satisfied that had the claim been brought under Ord. 84, time would have been extended. The Superior Court Rules Committee considered that there were good reasons why public authorities should be protected in the manner afforded by Ord. 84, r. 21 when claims for declaratory relief were made in applications for judicial review and I think exactly the same considerations apply when the same form of relief is sought in a plenary action. Furthermore, it is not desireable that the form of action should determine the relief to be granted and this might well be the result in a significant number of cases if one set of principles on the question of delay was applied in applications for judicial review and another in plenary actions claiming the same remedy."[19]

Because he felt that the Order 84 safeguards could be applied to plenary actions against public authorities, Costello J. concluded that:

> "The apprehended use of plenary actions as a device to defeat the protections given by Ord. 84 is not a real danger and does not justify the court in concluding that proceedings by plenary action for declaratory relief must be an abuse of process."[20]

The approach of Costello J. seems the most sensible one to date and is certainly preferable to the inherent difficulties posed by *O'Reilly* v. *Mackman*. Yet even this does not meet all of Lord Diplock's objections: what, for example, of the plaintiff who side-steps the requirement to obtain leave to apply for judicial review and simply commences a plenary action, as, in certain circumstances, this might amount to an abuse of process? This dichotomy will remain for so long as the Rules of the Superior Courts contain in-built special safeguards for public authorities, since for so long as these safeguards remain, litigants will seek to circumvent them by resorting to plenary actions.

One way to avoid this dilemma would have been to establish a single comprehensive form of action in all cases, irrespective of whether they involve public or private law. The speed and other advantages attaching to the present system of judicial review could have been preserved if the Rules of Court had provided for a special summary procedure (perhaps along the lines of the present special summons procedure with affidavit evidence and expedited hearings) in cases involving public authorities, with power to transfer the case to plenary hearing where this was warranted by the complexity of the facts or

[19] *Ibid.* 314–315.
[20] *Ibid.* 315.

legal issues at stake. Another, ad hoc way of avoiding the dilemma would be for a court to invoke its inherent jurisdiction to refuse to hear a case. Thus, a court before which plenary proceedings had been initiated might refuse to hear the proceedings if they were an abuse of process in that they were an attempt to avoid (say) the stringent time-limits laid down for the judicial review procedure.[21]

Side by side with this, the Irish courts increasingly encourage litigants in public law cases to proceed by way of plenary summons rather than by way of judicial review. There is certainly something to be said for this approach in cases raising complex issues of fact. (However, even this attitude brings its own attendant problems in those cases where there is only a net issue of law for it may deprive the applicant of a speedy and cheap resolution of the issues.)

(iii) *The scope of declaration and injunction*

While the power of the courts to grant declaratory relief has been stated "to be almost unlimited," it has always been understood to be confined to the context of defining the "rights of the two parties" to the action.[22] Thus, the court will not make declarations in respect of non-justiciable matters or in respect of matters of "morality and the like which fall short of being rights in law."[23] It is well settled that the court may refuse relief not only on grounds such as delay, acquiescence and the like,[24] but also on the grounds that the action is not yet ripe for determination, *i.e.* that it is speculative, premature[25] and raises hypothetical questions.[26]

However, two possible technical restrictions on the scope of the declaration have been removed by the new Rules of Court. Given that a declaration is, technically speaking, a final order, the courts were not prepared to make an interlocutory declaration.[27] Order 84, rule 25(1) now empowers the court to grant interlocutory relief on an application for judicial review. It was also formerly the case that the courts would not grant a declaration to quash for error of

---

[21] In this context, notice the reasoning of Costello J. in *Cavern Systems Ltd.* v. *Clontarf Residents' Association* [1984] I.L.R.M. 24, itself a case with unusual facts. S.82(3A) of the Local Government (Planning and Development) Act 1963 provides for a two-month limitation period in the case of challenges to the validity of a planning decision. Here the plaintiffs had commenced declaratory proceedings *within* the required two-month period, but these proceedings had not been served on the defendants. Costello J. held (at 29) that in view of the fact that s.82(3A) was designed to ensure that proceedings should be promptly initiated so that "uncertainty about future development be dispelled at the earliest possible date," it was an abuse of process to institute (but not serve) such proceedings in the absence of reasonable explanation for this course of action.

[22] *Hanson* v. *Radcliffe U.D.C.* [1922] 2 Ch. 490, 507, *per* Lord Sterndale M.R.

[23] *Malone* v. *Commissioner of Police (No. 2)* [1979] Ch. 344, 352, *per* Megarry V.-C.

[24] *Ibid.* 349–351.

[25] *Blythe* v. *Att.-Gen. (No. 2)* [1936] I.R. 549 and *Dyson* v. *Att.-Gen* [1911] 1 K.B. 410. The issue of ripeness is considered at pp. 624–626.

[26] *Halligan* v. *Davis* [1930] I.R. 237; *Re Bernato* [1949] Ch. 258.

[27] *Hill* v. *C.A. Parsons Ltd.* [1972] Ch. 305, 324, *per* Stamp L.J. and n. 36, *infra.*

law on the face of the record.[28] This restriction on the scope of the declaration is no longer of any practical significance, for Order 84, rule 19 enables the High Court upon an application for judicial review to grant an order of certiorari for this purpose *in lieu* of a declaration, notwithstanding that such relief has not been specifically claimed.

While the injunction is a remedy of wide scope, it will only be granted as an auxiliary remedy where the plaintiff already has an independent cause of action cognisable at law or equity.[29]

An injunction may be prohibitory[30] (*i.e.* restraining the commission of a wrongful act) or mandatory[31] (*i.e.* commanding the performance of a legal duty) in nature. The use of the injunction as a public law remedy has been somewhat curtailed by the alternative remedies of prohibition and mandamus. Such procedural advantages as the injunction enjoyed over the purely public law remedies have now been removed by the new Rules of Court.[32]

4. Ancillary Orders

The power to stay

Order 84, rule 20(7) provides that:

"Where leave to apply for judicial review is granted then—
(a) if the relief sought is an order of prohibition or certiorari and the Court so directs, the grant shall operate as a stay of the proceedings to which the application relates until the determination of the application or until the Court otherwise orders;
(b) if any other relief is sought, the Court may at any time grant in the proceedings such interim relief as could be granted in an action begun by plenary summons."

The effect of Order 84, rule 20(7)(a) would seem to be that the High Court is empowered to grant the equivalent of an interlocutory injunction after a purely *ex parte* hearing. This would appear to be the natural construction of

---

[28] *Punton* v. *Ministry of Pensions (No. 2)* [1964] 1 W.L.R. 226. But the Supreme Court has already granted one such declaration: see *King* v. *Att.-Gen.* [1981] I.R. 233.
[29] *The Siskina* [1979] A.C. 210; *Caudron* v. *Air Zaire* [1985] I.R. 716. An injunction cannot be granted where the case does not raise justiciable issues: see, *e.g. Finn* v. *Att.-Gen.* [1983] I.R. 154.
[30] A special form of prohibitory injunction, known as a *quia timet* injunction, may also be granted in unusual cases to restrain anticipated future wrongful acts: see *Att.-Gen. (Boswell)* v. *Rathmines and Pembroke Joint Hospital Board* [1904] 1 I.R. 161; *McGrane* v. *Louth C.C.*, High Court, December 9, 1983.
[31] For a recent example, see *Campus Oil Ltd.* v. *Minister for Industry and Commerce (No. 2)* [1983] I.R. 88.
[32] These procedural advantages included: the availability of interim relief, discovery and interrogatories (not all of which were available upon an application for certiorari, prohibition or mandamus); and the fact that an application for declaratory and injunctive relief, together with a claim for damages, could be combined in the one set of proceedings.

the sub-rule and it has been so interpreted in practice.[33] But if this construction is correct, then doubts must arise as to whether this sub-rule is *ultra vires* inasmuch as it changes the substantive law pertaining to interlocutory relief. The normal practice is, of course, that interim relief (which generally lasts for a matter of days at most) may be granted on an *ex parte* basis, but thereafter the plaintiff must apply on notice for an interlocutory injunction[34] and, indeed, this practice is expressly preserved as far as relief under Order 84, rule 20(7)(b) is concerned.[35] However, under Order 84, rule 20(7)(a), the applicant who seeks certiorari or prohibition is entitled to a stay (where the High Court so directs) until the hearing of the application or until the court otherwise orders. As already noted, such a stay is in practice equivalent to an interlocutory injunction and it would thus be on the respondents to bring a motion to have such an order discharged. This, of course, reverses the burden of proof by placing the onus on the respondents. It also means that applicants seeking certiorari or prohibition have a distinct procedural advantage in contrast to cases where only an injunction is sought. This again is an undesirable departure, inasmuch as one of the intentions behind the Order 84 procedure was to equalise the status of each individual remedy.

Remittal

One innovatory feature of the 1986 Rules is Order 84, rule 26(4) which provides:

"Where the relief sought is an order of certiorari and the Court is satisfied

---

[33] As pointed out by Collins & O'Reilly, *op. cit.* p. 92, practice varies in this regard, but the granting of a stay under r. 20(7)(a) at leave stage pending the hearing of the application is quite common. In *Murphy* v. *Turf Club* [1989] I.R. 171, 173 Barr J. refers to the fact that he stayed the suspension of the applicant's training licence for a nine-day period following the granting of leave to apply for certiorari. This would seem to suggest an attempt to assimilate the practice regarding the granting of stays to that of the normal practice with injunctions. Note also that in *Garda Representative Body* v. *Ireland*, Supreme Court, December 18, 1987, Finlay C.J. said in an *ex tempore* judgment that the ordinary principles governing interlocutory injunction applied to the granting of interlocutory relief under Ord. 84, r. 20(7)(b). However, it may be that these words apply only to r. 20(7)(b) and that the different wording of r. 20(7)(a) will compel the courts to arrive at a different result.

[34] See Keane, *Equity and the Law of Trusts and the Republic of Ireland* (Dublin, 1988), para. 15.27.

[35] It is not, of course, possible to obtain an interlocutory order of mandamus or a declaration, but the court has power to grant interim relief by way of injunction where mandamus or a declaration is the substantive relief sought. For a case (with unusual facts) where an interim *Mareva* injunction was granted on an application for mandamus, see *Elwyn (Cottons) Ltd.* v. *Pearle Designs Ltd.* [1989] I.R. 9, 13, *per* Carroll J. and *Elwyn (Cottons) Ltd.* v. *Master of the High Court* [1989] I.R. 14, 15. In certain very unusual cases a declaration may be granted in interlocutory proceedings: *International General Electric Co. of New York Ltd.* v. *Commissioners of Customs and Excise* [1962] Ch. 784; *Clarke* v. *Chadburn* [1985] 1 All E.R. 211. But, as Upjohn L.J. observed (at 789) in the *General Electric* case, this jurisdiction is to be "sparingly exercised" and, moreover, if such relief is granted in interlocutory proceedings "it finally determines and declares the rights of the parties and it is not open to further review save on appeal." Upjohn L.J. added (at 790) that he could not see "how there could be such an animal . . . as an interim declaratory order which does not finally determine the rights of the parties."

that there are grounds for quashing the decision to which the application relates, the Court may, in addition to quashing it, remit the matter to the Court, tribunal or authority concerned with a direction to reconsider it and reach a decision in accordance with the findings of the Court.''

This is clearly a provision of utility which can obviate the need for an order of mandamus or, indeed, spare the parties the cost of instituting fresh proceedings. An example of this last category may be drawn from the facts of the 1984 case of *Bord na Móna* v. *Bord Pleanála*.[36] Keane J. quashed a planning permission granted by An Bord Pleánala on appeal because of the existence of an invalid condition. Keane J. held that he had no jurisdiction to remit the matter to An Bord Pleánala and so the applicant for planning permission (who, after all, had won the action) was obliged to apply afresh to the local planning authority. Under the 1986 Rules, the matter could now simply be remitted to An Bord Pleánala without further ado. However, there is no statutory grounding for this power and, again it may be questioned as to whether this new rule is *intra vires* the powers of the Superior Court Rules Committee.[37]

The first reported case in which this power appears to have been exercised is *Comerford* v. *O'Malley*.[38] Under the Casual Trading Act 1980 an appeal may be taken to the Circuit Court against the making of by-laws by a local authority under that Act. The respondent Circuit judge did approve the order and by-laws in question, but Egan J. found that some of the by-laws were *ultra vires* the Act. Egan J. found that he had no power to vary the Circuit judge's decision by excluding the *ultra vires* by-laws because to do so would be to assume functions reserved to the Circuit Court. However, apparently acting under Order 84, rule 26(4), he felt able to remit the matter directly to the Circuit Court instead of leaving it to be commenced again at the local authority level. Blayney J. adopted a similar approach in *Ahern* v. *Kerry County Council*,[39] where having quashed a resolution to adopt certain expenditure on the ground that the estimates were not properly considered by the local authority in accordance with section 10 of the City and County Management (Amendment) Act 1955, he remitted the matter to the County Council in accordance with Order 84, rule 26(4). Yet another example is provided by *Singh* v. *Ruane*[40] where Barron J. set aside the applicant's conviction on the ground that he had been wrongly prevented from adducing certain evidence. The judge concluded that the matter should be remitted to the District Court, since this was not a case where the prosecution could obtain an unfair advantage by reason of rehearing:

"If there has been no valid adjudication, then there can be no objection to

---

[36] [1985] I.R. 205.
[37] See pp. 566–568.
[38] [1987] I.L.R.M. 595.
[39] [1988] I.L.R.M. 392.
[40] [1990] I.L.R.M. 62.

the matter being remitted for determination. There may be cases such as *The State (Keeney)* v. *O'Malley*[41] in which the order of certiorari would dispose of the matter finally . . . The effect of [that] decision was that on the admissible evidence the applicant was entitled to be acquitted. If, in those circumstances, the retrial had been permitted, the applicant would have been faced with different evidence which might have justified a conviction. The prosecution could have obtained a valid conviction on the first occasion if it had proved its case [and] ordering a retrial would have given it a second opportunity to do so."[42]

Since there was no "cat and mouse" element in the present case, Barron J. accordingly remitted the case for reconsideration to the District Court.

Costs

While the costs of proceedings lie in the discretion of the court, these will usually follow the event.[43] This is not always the case, for in some cases raising general points of importance, the courts have been prepared to award costs to the losing applicant.[44] There is also a general judicial reluctance to award costs against an impecunious applicant in judicial review proceedings, even where no important point of principle is at issue.

The applicant will also generally be entitled to the costs of the initial *ex parte* application for judicial review, even where the respondent does not contest the actual making of the order. This emerges from *Ó Murchú* v. *Cláraitheoir na gCuideachtaí*,[45] where the applicant had obtained leave to apply for an order of mandamus against the Registrar of Companies and the Minister for Industry and Commerce. The Minister had promulgated a statutory instrument under the Companies Acts 1963–1983, but, at the date of the application, an Irish language copy was not available, despite her request for such a copy. However, a copy did become available shortly after the order granting leave had been made and the question then arose as to whether the applicant was entitled to the initial costs of her application. O'Hanlon J. held that as she had a constitutional right to conduct her affairs in Irish if she wished, it was "reasonable for her to commence these proceedings in order to obtain the

---

[41] [1986] I.L.R.M. 31.

[42] [1990] I.L.R.M. 62, 63–64. See also, *Director of Public Prosecutions* v. *Johnson* [1988] I.L.R.M. 747 and *Dawson* v. *Hamill* [1989] I.R. 275.

[43] Ord. 99, r. 1(1). No court fees are payable in judicial review proceedings involving certiorari and mandamus: see Supreme Court and High Court (Fees) Order 1982 (S.I. No. 43 of 1982), para. 8. The provisions of the Attorney-General's scheme involving legal aid, in certain types of judicial review proceedings, may also apply: see Collins & O'Reilly, *op. cit.* p. 53.

[44] While this practice is quite common in constitutional actions (see, *e.g.*, *Norris* v. *Att.-Gen.* [1984] I.R. 36), there is quite a number of examples in "ordinary" judicial review proceedings, see, *e.g. Butler* v. *Ruane* [1989] I.L.R.M. 159; *Director of Public Prosecutions* v. *Nolan* [1989] I.L.R.M. 39 and *MacGabhann* v. *Incorporated Law Society of Ireland* [1989] I.L.R.M. 854 (part costs only).

[45] High Court, June 20, 1988.

relief she sought from the High Court"[46] and, accordingly, he granted her the costs of the original *ex parte* application.

To this rule, however, there is a most important exception. No order for costs may be made against a respondent who is a member of the judiciary in judicial review proceedings where the error was made bona fide and the application was unopposed. This long-standing rule was reaffirmed by the Supreme Court in *McIwraith* v. *Fawsitt*.[47] The respondent Circuit Court judge had extended time for the hearing of an appeal by the applicant's employers from the Employment Appeals Tribunal and in doing so, he exceeded his jurisdiction. The applicant obtained leave to seek certiorari to quash the order. However, matters did not proceed any further since the main dispute, as between the applicant and his employers, was settled before the judicial review proceedings came on. The Supreme Court held that the applicant was not entitled to the costs of the initial *ex parte* application, with Finlay C.J. saying that:

> "[U]nder no circumstances should the High Court upon application to it for judicial review with regard to either a decision of a District Justice or of a Circuit Court judge award costs to a successful applicant in a case where there is no question of impropriety or *mala fide* on the part of the judge concerned and where he has not sought to defend an order which apparently is invalid. For that reason, I am satisfied that the practice which I understood to have been usual in the High Court of adding as a further respondent in judicial review proceedings the other contesting party so as to create a *legitimus contradictor* for any issue that may arise in the event that the Circuit Court judge or District Justice does not seek to defend the order should be universally followed."[48]

It is hard to see why members of the judiciary should stand in this privileged position as regards costs. Nevertheless, it should be possible for an applicant to circumvent the restrictive nature of this rule by adding a further respondent, such as (where appropriate) Ireland, the Attorney-General or the Director of Public Prosecutions, as was suggested by Finlay C.J.

5. The Discretionary Nature of the Remedies

The public law remedies, together with the declaration and injunction are discretionary remedies. It is clear that this discretion is to be exercised on

---

[46] This part of the judgment reads in the original (at 4):

"agus go rabh sé reasúnta na himeachta seo do chur ar bun d'fhonn faoiseamh do lorg ón Ard-Chúirt."

[47] [1990] I.L.R.M. 1. Finlay C.J. expressly followed the decision of the former Supreme Court in *The State (Prendergast)* v. *Rochford*, July 1, 1952. In that case, Maguire C.J. in turn had followed the decision of Palles C.B. in *R. (King)* v. *Londonderry JJ.* (1912) 46 I.L.T.R. 105. For other pre-1922 examples of this practice, see *Hynes* v. *Clare JJ.* (1911) 45 I.L.T.R. 76 (costs awarded where contumacy on part of justices) and *R. (Roche)* v. *Clare JJ.* (1912) 46 I.L.T.R. 80.
[48] [1990] I.L.R.M. 4.

settled principles, regardless of the form of proceedings.[49] Although the grounds on which relief may be denied are not closed,[50] we must now consider the discretionary bars[51] to relief which are most frequently encountered.

(i) *Lack of good faith and general conduct of the applicant*

All applications for judicial review require the utmost good faith and full disclosure of all material facts on the part of the applicant.[52] This is because the initial application is *ex parte*, there is usually no oral evidence and because of the generally weighty issues raised by the application. Accordingly, relief may be withheld where the applicant has been guilty of gross exaggeration in his affidavits or where relevant evidence has been suppressed.[53] For example, in *The State (Vozza)* v. *Ó'Floinn*,[54] the applicant (who was of Italian origin) sought to quash his conviction for larceny on the grounds that he had not been informed of his right to jury trial and, secondly, that he did not understand the court procedure. A Divisional High Court refused to quash the conviction, on the grounds that the applicant had disentitled himself to relief by reason of his "grossly exaggerated and unrealistic" affidavits. In the Supreme Court, Kingsmill Moore J. agreed that Vozza had probably "exaggerated his capacity not to understand English," but doubted whether he was able fully to understand court procedure. Moreover, Vozza had not suppressed facts in respect of not being informed about his right to jury trial and so there were no grounds for refusing him relief on this basis. A similar argument was rejected by the Supreme Court in *The State (Furey)* v. *Minister for Defence*.[55] Here the applicant had failed to reveal certain minor disciplinary offences when seeking to quash his dismissal from the Defence Forces, but McCarthy J. was prepared to ignore this lack of candour in the circumstances, especially as the Defence Forces themselves had wrongly classified his record as "unsatisfactory" instead of "fair."

---

[49] See the comments of Henchy J. in *The State (Nicoloau)* v. *An Bord Uchtála* [1966] I.R. 567, 618 and in *M.* v. *An Bord Uchtála* [1977] I.R. 287, 297.
[50] See the comments of Byrne & Binchy, *Annual Review of Irish Law 1988* (Dublin, 1989), pp. 32–33 that "in recent years discretionary grounds for refusing relief have become more widespread in Irish law. . . . "
[51] At common law it was clear that the Attorney-General could not be refused relief on discretionary grounds (such as delay): see, *e.g. Re an Application for Certiorari* [1965] N.I. 67. Murnaghan J. made a similar observation in *The State (Kerry C.C.)* v. *Minister for Local Government* [1933] I.R. 517, 546. But, as Lord McDermott L.C.J. explained (at 70–71) in *Re an Application for Certiorari*, this rule was derived from the fact that the Attorney-General had a privileged position as representing the Crown. In view of this rationale and the general reasoning in *Byrne* v. *Ireland* [1972] I.R. 241, it must be doubtful whether such a rule has survived the enactment of the Constitution: see p. 724. Note that in *Director of Public Prosecutions* v. *Macklin* [1989] I.L.R.M. 113 the Director of Public Prosecutions was denied certiorari on discretionary grounds, but the point was not canvassed before Lardner J.
[52] *Cork Corporation* v. *O'Connell* [1982] I.L.R.M. 505.
[53] *R.* v. *Kensington I.T.C.* [1917] 1 K.B. 486; *R. (Bryson)* v. *Lisnaskea Guardians* [1918] 2 I.R. 258; *The State (Vozza)* v. *O'Floinn* [1957] I.R. 227; *The State (Nicolaou)* v. *An Bord Uchtála* [1966] I.R. 567, 610 (Henchy J.) and *Cork Corporation* v. *O'Connell* [1982] I.L.R.M. 505, 508, *per* Griffin J.
[54] [1957] I.R. 227.
[55] [1988] I.L.R.M. 89.

The court will also have regard to the general conduct of the applicant[56] and the reasons for the application.[57] Thus, in *Ahern* v. *Minister for Industry & Commerce (No. 2)*[58] the applicant was placed on compulsory sick leave following his "unreasonable refusal to see a psychiatrist." Blayney J. held that this decision was invalid, but refused to quash the decision because of the applicant's unreasonable behaviour, which was compounded by his persistent allegations (which Blayney J. found to be wholly unfounded) that his superiors were not acting bona fide. Nevertheless, the discretion to refuse relief on this ground where a proper case has been made out is but sparingly exercised. *Re Hogan's Application*[59] is a good example of this judicial attitude. Here Carswell J. found that the applicant (who was a Sinn Féin councillor) had been invalidly excluded from her council seat and that a council resolution to that effect was *ultra vires*. Carswell J. was invited to refuse to grant relief on the ground that:

> "[I]t ill behoves an active Sinn Féin supporter to come to court and ask it to order a council to resume meeting and proceed with ordinary democratic processes [and that the applicant] was seeking relief of a political nature on behalf of one faction seeking to take political advantage over another."[60]

The judge, however, declined to refuse relief on this ground:

> "[The applicant] and her party may well desire to see their political opponents discomfited, but this is not the only case where this may follow as the result of a legitimate application for judicial review . . . Notwithstanding the known aims and policies of Sinn Féin, its members are not debarred by law from standing for election and taking their seats as district councillors. It would in consequence be wrong in my judgment to bar the applicant, because she is a member of Sinn Féin, from seeking redress against a council which is in breach of statutory duty when she has made out a proper case to be granted it."[61]

(ii) *Delay*

Order 84, rule 21(1) provides that all applications for judicial review "shall be made promptly" and in any event within three months from the date when the grounds for the application first arose, or six months when the relief sought is certiorari. The court has a discretion to extend these time limits

---

[56] *Ex p. Fry* [1954] 1 W.L.R. 730; *Fulbrook* v. *Berkshire Magistrates' Court* (1970) 69 L.G.R. 75; *Murtagh* v. *Board of Governors of St. Emer's National School*, High Court, November 27, 1989; *Condon* v. *Minister for Agriculture*, High Court, October 12, 1990.
[57] *The State (Abenglen Properties Ltd.)* v. *Dublin Corporation* [1984] I.R. 384 (attempt to obtain benefit "not contemplated" by the planning code); *The State (Conlon Construction Co. Ltd.)* v. *Cork C.C.*, High Court, July 31, 1975; *R. (Burns)* v. *Tyrone JJ.* [1961] N.I. 167; *R.* v. *Monopolies Commission, ex p. Argyll plc* [1986] 1 W.L.R. 763 (rival company attempting to obtain advantage from procedural defect in Commission's ruling).
[58] High Court, July 29, 1990. See pp. 83–85.
[59] [1986] 5 N.I.J.B. 81.
[60] *Ibid.* 101.
[61] *Ibid.* 102.

where "there is a good reason"[61a] for doing so. The decision of the Superior Court Rules Committee to impose such relatively short time limits was somewhat surprising given that the Law Reform Commission had recommended that the issue of delay should be left entirely to the discretion of the court. Nevertheless, the discretion as to whether to extend time is a flexible one. As Costello J. explained in *O'Donnell* v. *Laoghaire Corporation (No. 2)*,[62] the phrase "good reasons" is one:

"Of wide import which it would be futile to attempt to define precisely. However, in considering whether or not there are good reasons for extending the time, I think it is clear that the test must be an objective one and the court should not extend the time merely because an aggrieved plaintiff believed that he or she was justified in delaying the institution of proceedings. What the plaintiff has to show (and I think the onus under Ord. 84, r. 21 is on the plaintiff) is that there are reasons which both explain the delay and afford a justifiable excuse for the delay."[63]

Prior to the adoption of the new Rules, the general attitude of the courts had been to ask whether the delay had been such as to affect prejudicially the rights of third parties. In cases where there was prejudice, periods of as short as four months had been held to disentitle the applicant to relief "to which he was otherwise entitled *ex debito justitiae.*"[64] (However in the surprising decision of *M.* v. *An Bord Uchtála*[65] the Supreme Court declared an adoption order to be invalid for want of jurisdiction, despite a delay of over three years and despite the fact that the child had spent all of its sentient life with its parents). On the other side of the line, delay of itself is not a ground for refusing relief, where the applicant has suffered a "public wrong" at the hands of the State or its agents. This emerged from the Supreme Court's decision in 1984 in *The State (Furey)* v. *Minister for Defence.*[66] Although these certiorari proceedings were not commenced until more than four years from the date of the applicant's dismissal from the Defence Forces,[67] the Court granted the

---

[61a] However, where the appropriate time-limit prescribed by Ord. 84, r. 21(1) has expired, then, *per* Hederman J. in *O'Flynn* v. *Mid-Western Health Board*, Supreme Court, February 26, 1991, pp. 28–29:

"the judge should be furnished with the reasons for the delay in the grounding affidavit and he should decide whether there are grounds for excusing the delay. Even if leave is granted at the *ex parte* stage, nonetheless, when the trial judge comes to hear the matter he must adjudicate upon whether the delay was reasonable and such as may be excused or not."

[62] [1991] I.L.R.M. 301.
[63] *Ibid.* 315.
[64] *The State (Cussen)* v. *Brennan* [1981] I.R. 181; *R. (Rainey)* v. *Belfast Recorder* (1937) 71 I.L.T.R. 272. See Hogan, "Discretion and Judicial Review of Administrative Action" (1980) 15 Ir.Jur.(N.S.) 118.
[65] [1977] I.R. 287. See also, *The State (D.P.P.)* v. *ÓhUuadaigh*, High Court, January 30, 1984; *The State (Murphy)* v. *Kielt* [1984] I.R. 458 (delay on the part of applicant for certiorari not such as to prejudice respondent or other third party); *The State (Gleeson)* v. *Martin* [1985] I.L.R.M. 578.
[66] [1988] I.L.R.M. 89. See Hogan, "Natural and Constitutional Justice: Adieu to Laissez-Faire" (1984) 19 Ir.Jur.(N.S.) 309.
[67] See n. 59, *supra.*

order sought, as the applicant had been unaware of his right to challenge the validity of the dismissal as being contrary to the rules of natural justice. McCarthy J. said that he could see no reason:

> "[W]hy delay, however long, should, of itself, disentitle to certiorari any applicant for that remedy who can demonstrate that a public wrong has been done to him—that, for instance, a conviction has been obtained without jurisdiction, or that otherwise the State has wronged him and that wrong continues to mark or mar his life."[68]

As far as criminal cases are concerned, the general principle appears to be that the applicant cannot be precluded by his delay from challenging a conviction made in excess of jurisdiction or which is bad on its face[69] but this principle applies to convictions only and not to orders of return for trial.[70] It has also been doubted whether even gross laches would prevent an order of prohibition from issuing to restrain an inferior court from proceeding with a criminal trial where it had no jurisdiction.[71] Thus, presumably the fact that the applicant had suffered a "public wrong"—*e.g.* invalid dismissal from State employment, or conviction imposed without jurisdiction—would of itself be a "good reason" for the High Court to extend the time limits contained in Order 84, rule 21(1).

There is some evidence that the new Rules have brought about a stricter judicial attitude to the issue of delay on the part of some members of the High Court, even in cases where the validity of a conviction is under challenge.[72] In the first place, there is authority for the view that an applicant who has not moved "promptly" for judicial review may find that he is out of time, *even* where the application has been brought within the six months' time limit. In *Director of Public Prosecutions* v. *Macklin*[73] the applicant sought to have certain orders of a District Justice quashed. Lardner J. accepted that the respondent had acted *ultra vires*, but pointed to the fact that the Director had not

---

[68] [1988] I.L.R.M. 100. McCarthy J. distinguished *The State (Cussen)* v. *Brennan* [1981] I.R. 181 on the basis that in *Furey* (unlike *Cussen*) the granting of certiorari would not prejudice third party rights. Note also the comments of McCarthy J. in *O'Flynn* v. *Mid-Western Health Board*, Supreme Court, February 26, 1991, p. 6:

> "There is ample ground for saying that both in principle and in precedent, an application for judicial review should not fail merely because it is out of time . . . In principle, it is right to relieve against delay in challenging an administrative decision where the delay has not prejudiced third parties."

Here the applicant had waited some eight months before applying for judicial review and McCarthy J. found that they had deliberately temporised before applying to the High Court. In the circumstances, he concluded that they had been guilty of undue delay.

[69] *The State (Kelly)* v. *District Justice for Bandon* [1947] I.R. 258; *The State (Furey)* v. *Minister for Defence* [1988] I.L.R.M. 88. But *cf.* the comments of Henchy J. to the contrary in *The State (Abenglen Properties Ltd.* v. *Dublin Corporation* [1984] I.R. 384, 403.

[70] *The State (Walsh)* v. *Maguire* [1979] I.R. 372; *The State (Coveney)* v. *Special Criminal Court* [1982] I.L.R.M. 284.

[71] *The State (Coveney)* v. *Special Criminal Court* [1982] I.L.R.M. 284, 289, *per* Finlay P.

[72] See Hogan, "Time Limits and Judicial Review Applications" (1988) 82 Gaz. of I.L.S.I. 237 and Collins & O'Reilly, *op. cit.* pp. 93–96.

[73] [1989] I.L.R.M. 113.

acted "promptly" within the meaning of Order 84, rule 21(1) inasmuch as he had delayed almost six months in making the application. As there was no explanation for this delay, Lardner J. refused to grant the orders of certiorari sought. And if an explanation is required of an applicant who, although within time, has not been prompt in seeking judicial review, this appears to apply, *a fortiori*, to cases where the delay is greater than six months. This was the view of both the English Court of Appeal and House of Lords in *R. v. Dairy Quota Tribunal, ex p. Caswell.*[74] The applicants were farmers who were required to pay super-levy charges following a misconstruction of the relevant regulations in their case by the Dairy Quota Tribunal. However, they had delayed by up to two years in applying for judicial review. Thus, despite the applicant's success on the merits of the case, the Court of Appeal refused to quash the Tribunal's decision because of the undue delay. Lloyd L.J. said that it was not open to an applicant who was outside the three-month limit to argue that there was no undue delay. The Court could, of course, grant the applicant an extension if there was "good reason" to do so, such as where he had a good case on the merits. But even then, the Court is obliged to consider whether the granting of relief would substantially prejudice the rights of third parties or "would be detrimental to good administration." Lloyd L.J. held that the delay would be prejudicial to good administration, since a substantial number of applicants during a five-year period might thereby be entitled to reapply for an additional quota if the Caswells were to succeed in obtaining relief. Although these views were endorsed by Lord Goff in the House of Lords, this seems an unduly harsh attitude to take and quite unnecessarily overprotective of public authorities.

In this jurisdiction, unexplained delay beyond the six months' period is likely to be fatal for the applicant's chances of success. In *Connors v. Delap,*[75] Lynch J. considered that he should exercise his discretion against an applicant who was relying on a technical point and who had waited some 18 months before challenging his District Court conviction. This approach was followed by Barr J. in refusing relief in *White v. Hussey,*[76] where again the defect in the conviction was of a technical character and the delay approached 14 months. The question of undue delay was again considered by Barr J. in *Solan v. Director of Public Prosecutions.*[77] Here the applicant sought to challenge District Court convictions imposed some 18 months previously. Barr J. could not accept that, in view of the decision in *Furey*, certiorari should issue *ex debito*

---

[74] [1989] 1 W.L.R. 1089 (C.A.); [1990] 2 W.L.R. 1320 (H.L.). A similar view had been taken in *R. v. Stratford-on-Avon D.C., ex p. Jackson* [1985] 1 W.L.R. 1319. It is important to bear in mind that these time limits are prescribed by s.31(6) of the (English) Supreme Court Act 1981 and that the wording of this subsection is very different from that contained in Ord. 84, r. 21(1). Accordingly, as Costello J. remarked in *O'Donnell v. Dún Laoghaire Corporation* [1991] I.L.R.M. 301, the English authorities on delay should be viewed with some caution.
[75] [1989] I.L.R.M. 93.
[76] [1989] I.L.R.M. 109.
[77] [1989] I.L.R.M. 491. See Collins, "*Ex Debito Justitiae?*" (1988) 10 D.U.L.J.(N.S.) 130 for a critique of these decisions.

justitiae. There were, he thought, three reasons why this case fell outside the ambit of McCarthy J.'s reasoning:

"First, in *Furey's* case the applicant put before the court in evidence a detailed explanation for his delay in seeking relief by way of judicial review, whereas no evidence whatever has been given by or on behalf of Mr. Solan to justify his delay in that regard. In the absence of evidence explaining delay, there is no basis on which the court can exercise its discretion to grant an extension of time for making the applications. Secondly, Mr. Furey's application was regarded as having substantial merit *per se*, whereas there is no evidence to suggest that Mr. Solan may not have been properly convicted on the merits . . . Thirdly, Mr. Furey's only remedy was by way of judicial review [whereas Mr. Solan may appeal to the Circuit Court]."[78]

Despite these differences the fact remains that the applicant's conviction was invalid; yet mere lapse of time was enough to shut his application for certiorari. Decisions such as *Connors* and *Solan* show a move away from the long-standing principle that a person aggrieved by an *ultra vires* decision is entitled to a quashing order *ex debito justitiae.* Indeed, part of the problem stems from the fact that the Superior Court Rules Committee elected to follow the more restrictive approach as to delay adopted in England.[79] It would have been preferable instead to follow the recommendations of the Law Reform Commission who thought there should be no fixed time limits and that the question of delay should be a matter for the discretion of the court, subject always to the doctrine of laches.[80]

However, where excusing circumstances have been found, periods of delay beyond the six months have generally been overlooked in the absence of prejudice to the respondents. In *Murphy* v. *Minister for Social Welfare*,[81] Blayney J. was prepared to extend time in circumstances where an appeals officer had erred in law in determining that the applicant was not in insurable employment, despite the fact that there had been a delay of up to 15 months in seeking relief. There was no evidence that the respondent was prejudiced by the delay and, rather like the facts of *Furey*, the applicant had entered into correspondence with the respondents with a view to making alternative arrangements with respect to his pension contributions. The same judge took a similar view in *Corrigan* v. *Gallagher*.[82] Here the increments of several prison officers had been forfeited following related decisions of the prison authorities and the Minister for Justice that the officers had been negligent in the performance of their duties. While the challenge to the Minister's decision had been brought within the six months' period, the applicants were out of

---

[78] [1989] I.L.R.M. 491, 493–494.
[79] But, of course, as has already been emphasised elsewhere (at pp. 597–599), Ord. 53, r. 4 of the English Rules (which deals with delay) follows s.31(6) of the Supreme Court Act 1981. In contrast, there is no statutory parallel to s.31(6) in this jurisdiction.
[80] At p. 81 of the Report.
[81] [1987] I.R. 295.
[82] High Court, February 2, 1988.

time by some two weeks in respect of the decision of the prison authorities. Blayney J. considered that the decisions in question had been arrived at in breach of the *audi alteram partem* rule and granted the orders of certiorari sought. He thought that there was "good reason" within the meaning of Order 84, rule 21(1) to extend the time. Both decisions were interlinked and it:

> "would not seem reasonable, given that the decisions implementing the recommendations of the sanctions could be attacked, to refuse to allow to be attacked also the decision [of the prison authorities] recommending the sanction, particularly as the applications in regard to those decisions were only two weeks outside the six-month period."[83]

Blayney J. also drew attention to the fact that the applicants may have been misled in certain respects by the respondents, a factor contributing further to the delay. This trend was powerfully reinforced by the judgment of Costello J. in *O'Donnell* v *Dún Laoghaire Corporation (No.2)*.[84] In 1989 the plaintiff commenced a plenary action whereby he sought to challenge water charges imposed by the Corporation between 1983 and 1985 and it was argued that relief should be denied on discretionary grounds because of this delay. Costello J. firstly held that there were "good reasons" within the meaning of Order 84. rule 21 for the plaintiff delaying until June 1988, since prior to that date, the plaintiff:

> "Did not undertake the burden of instituting proceedings because he believed that the legality issue could be adjudicated upon in proceedings instituted by the Corporation either against him or other householders who, he was aware, had raised the validity of the orders in other proceedings."[85]

After June 1988, the defendants began to turn off the water supply of the houses of persons (including the plaintiff) who had failed to pay the disputed water charges. However, during the 1988-1989 period, the plaintiff enlisted the support of no less than three public representatives in an effort to settle this dispute. Costello J., applying the principles of *Furey*, said that this constituted a "reasonable explanation" for this further delay, adding that:

> "No third parties have acquired rights which it would be unjust to injure by making the declaratory order the plaintiff seeks. Whilst it is true that the declaratory order may cause the defendants' administrative and, perhaps, financial problems, I do not think that they are such as to justify the court refusing the plaintiff relief to which otherwise he would be entitled."[86]

This judgment, together with those of Blayney J. in *Murphy* and *Corrigan*, are more in harmony with the principles laid down in *Furey* than are the views

---

[83] At pp. 21–22 of his judgment. See also, *Byrne* v. *Grey* [1988] I.R. 31 and *Berkley* v. *Edwards* [1988] I.R. 217.
[84] [1991] I.L.R.M. 301.
[85] *Ibid.* 316.
[86] *Ibid.* 318.

of Lynch J. and Barr J. in cases such as *Connors, White* and *Solan*. It may be that while the new Order 84, rule 21 originally led some members of the High Court to believe that a stricter approach to delay was now called for, the subsequent cases appear to suggest a return to the *Furey* principles.

(iii) *Acquiescence and waiver*

The courts will not allow the creation of a wholly new jurisdiction through acquiesence or waiver.[87] Nevertheless, acquiescence and waiver may disentitle the applicant to relief. In *R. (Kildare C.C.)* v. *Commissioner of Valuation*[88] the applicant appealed to the County Court against a valuation revision. It was only when the decision of the County Court proved not to be as favourable as expected that the applicant claimed that the County Court had no jurisdiction in the matter. The Court of Appeal ruled that, even assuming that the County Court had acted without jurisdiction, relief should be refused on discretionary grounds. Holmes L.J. said that he found it difficult to conceive of a "stronger case of estoppel by conduct."[89] Similarly in *The State (Byrne)* v. *Frawley*[90] the applicant's failure to raise certain alleged irregularities in his trial when appealing to the Court of Criminal Appeal was found to be prima facie evidence of acquiescence. Participation (or continued participation) in proceedings may constitute acquiescence where the party seeking to challenge the decision was aware of the full facts and failed to take objection to the composition or procedure of the tribunal.[91] The right to object to an irregularity of procedure or breach of natural justice may also be lost by waiver.[92]

(iv) *Where no useful and legitimate purpose would be served*

The court will not make an order which cannot now be implemented or which would be illegal.[93] Nor will relief be granted where this would simply cause further delay[94] or would confer no practical benefit on the applicant or where no legitimate purpose would be served. There have been several recent

---

[87] *Corrigan* v. *Irish Land Commission* [1977] I.R. 317, 325, *per* Henchy J.; *The State (Byrne)* v. *Frawley* [1978] I.R. 326, 342, *per* O'Higgins C.J. See pp. 371–373 and 672–677.

[88] [1901] 2 I.R. 215. See also, *R. (Mathews)* v. *Petticrew* (1886) 18 L.R.Ir. 342; *The State (McKay)* v. *Cork Circuit Judge* [1937] I.R. 650 and *R. (Doris)* v. *Ministry for Health* [1954] N.I. 79.

[89] The *Kildare* case was distinguished by Barron J. in *Browne* v. *An Bord Pleanála* [1989] I.L.R.M. 865.

[90] [1978] I.R. 326.

[91] *The State (Cronin)* v. *Circuit Judge for Western Circuit* [1937] I.R. 34; *The State (Redmond)* v. *Wexford Corporation* [1946] I.R. 409. But the principle does not apply where the applicant is unaware of the full facts, or has been taken by surprise: *R. (Harrington)* v. *Clare JJ.* (1918) 2 I.R. 116; *The State (McDonagh)* v. *Sheerin* [1981] I.L.R.M. 149; *The State (Cole)* v. *Labour Court* (1984) 3 J.I.S.L.L. 128.

[92] *Corrigan* v. *Irish Land Commission* [1977] I.R. 317.

[93] *The State (Modern Homes (Ire.) Ltd.)* v. *Dublin Corporation* [1953] I.R. 202; *The State (Foxrock Development Co. Ltd.)* v. *Dublin C.C.*, High Court, February 5, 1980; *The State (Pine Valley Developments Ltd.)* v. *Dublin County Council* [1984] I.L.R. 407.

[94] *Fulbrook* v. *Berkshire Magistrates' Court* (1970) 69 L.G.R. 85; *The State (Walsh)* v. *Maguire* [1979] I.R. 372; *R.* v. *Monopolies Commission, ex p. Argyll plc.* [1986] 1 W.L.R. 763, where Sir John Donaldson M.R. emphasised (at 774) the need for "speed of decision, particularly in the financial field."

examples of the refusal of relief on this ground. For example, in *The State (Abenglen Properties Ltd.)* v. *Dublin Corporation*[95] the Supreme Court refused to quash the granting of a planning permission when it became clear that the applicants could not obtain the default planning permission which they had sought. In *Farrell* v. *Farelly*,[96] O'Hanlon J. held that even if the search warrants, issued by a Peace Commissioner under section 42 of the Larceny Act 1916 and used to search the applicant's house, were invalid, he would refuse certiorari. The reason was that both the applicants had subsequently been convicted and the quashing of the warrants would serve no useful purpose, as this would not have affected the admissibility of the evidence. And in another search warrant case, *Byrne* v. *Grey*,[97] Hamilton P. refused to grant relief where the sole object of the quashing order was to secure the exclusion of evidence obtained on foot of that search. Such exclusion was for the court of trial and the court should not grant relief by way of judicial review where this would be to anticipate the rulings of the trial court.

The courts have sometimes recognised the clearing of an applicant's name as a useful purpose. Thus, in *The State (Furey)* v. *Minister for Defence*[98] certiorari was granted to quash an ignominious dismissal from the Defence Forces. Even though the applicant's probationary period had long since expired, McCarthy J. rejected the argument that a quashing order would serve no useful purpose on the grounds that an order would allow him to vindicate his reputation.

Relief will not be granted if the remedy would not serve any legitimate purpose. This ground of refusal is more difficult to identify, but there have been cases where the courts have held that they will not facilitate a litigant who seeks relief for an unmeritorious or ulterior purpose. There are elements of such thinking in *Abenglen Properties* and also in the judgment of Henchy J. in *The State (Doyle)* v. *Carr*[99] Here the applicant established that the District Court order providing for a transfer of a publican's licence on an interim basis was invalid. However, the publican had long since acquired a perfectly valid full licence and this of itself was a ground for refusing to quash an order which was now spent. However, reading between the lines of the judgment of Henchy J., it may be that relief was also refused because it appeared that the application was simply a strategem designed and sought to discomfit a business rival.

---

[95] [1984] I.R. 384. See also, *The State (Doyle)* v. *Carr* [1970] I.R. 87 and *R. (Campbell College)* v. *Department of Education.*[1982] N.I. 123.
[96] [1988] I.R. 201.
[97] [1988] I.R. 31.
[98] [1988] I.L.R.M. 89. See also, *The State (Shannon Atlantic Fisheries Ltd.)* v. *McPolin* [1976] I.R. 93 (where Finlay P. quashed an inspector's report which contained findings critical of the applicants, even though the time limit for the prosecution of any offences on foot of the report had expired) and *Mulhall* v. *O'Donnell* [1989] I.L.R.M. 367. In the latter case, Murphy J. quashed an order made by a District Justice under the Probation of Offenders Act 1907. Such an order "was a very serious reflection on the character of a defendant" and it was understandable "that if such an order is wrongly made, a defendant would seek to have it set aside."
[99] [1970] I.R. 69.

Another example is, perhaps, provided by *Re McGlinchey's Application*[1] where Lowry L.C.J. refused to quash an extradition order which was long since spent. It was plain that the quashing of the order at this remove would not provide the applicant with any legal advantage for the purpose of proceedings in Northern Ireland, but the applicant argued that this might assist him in pending criminal proceedings in the Republic. Lord Lowry, however, thought that it would be improper to grant relief as this might be thought "to interfere with proceedings in another jurisdiction."

In some cases the court will withhold relief in discretion in order to allow the administrative body concerned time to comply with its judgment. In *The State (Richardson)* v. *Governor of Mountjoy Prison*[2] Barrington J. concluded that the hygiene facilities provided in the womens' section of Mountjoy Prison were so inadequate that the State had failed in its constitutional duty to vindicate the applicant prisoner's right to bodily integrity. Nevertheless, the judge granted a short adjournment to allow the recommendations for the improvement of facilities to be implemented.[3]

(v) *Availability of alternate remedies*

The existence of an alternative remedy does not of itself debar an application for judicial review. The question is essentially one for the discretion of the court and regard will be had to the adequacy of the alternate remedy[4] and to all the circumstances of the case.[5] In *The State (Abenglen Properties Ltd)* v. *Dublin Corporation*[6] the Supreme Court had appeared to lean in favour of the "exhaustion of remedies" requirement. The applicant company had sought certiorari to quash certain conditions attached by the respondent to the grant of planning permission, thus by-passing the possible appeal to An Bord Pleanála which the relevant legislation made available for them. It was said that the applicants were entitled to a ruling by the High Court as to the *vires* of these conditions and that the legality of the conditions was not within the capacity of An Bord Pleanála. While it appears that the applicant's evident desire to obtain a benefit "not contemplated by the planning code" may have coloured the court's attitude, Henchy J. said that where the Oireachtas had provided

---

[1] [1987] 3 N.I.J.B. 1.
[2] [1980] I.L.R.M. 82. See also, *R.* v. *Greater London Council, ex p. Blackburn* [1976] 1 W.L.R. 550.
[3] Another interesting example is furnished by the decision of Costello J. in *The State (Sheehan)* v. *Government of Ireland* [1987] I.R. 550, where he gave the Government five months to make an order bringing into force s.60(1) of the Civil Liability Act 1961. His decision was, however, reversed by the Supreme Court.
[4] *The State (Stanbridge)* v. *Mahon* [1979] I.R. 214; *The State (Glover)* v. *McCarthy* [1981] I.L.R.M. 47; *The State (Pheasantry Ltd.)* v. *Donnelly* [1982] I.L.R.M. 512; *Aprile* v. *Naas U.D.C.*, High Court, November 22, 1983; *The State (Redmond)* v. *Delap*, High Court, July 31, 1984; *The State (Abenglen Properties Ltd.)* v. *Dublin Corporation* [1984] I.R. 384; *The State (McInerney Properties Ltd.)* v. *Dublin C.C.* [1985] I.L.R.M. 513; *Creedon* v. *Dublin Corporation* [1984] I.R. 427 and *The State (Wilson)* v. *Neilan* [1985] I.R. 89.
[5] *The State (Litzouw)* v. *Johnson* [1981] I.L.R.M. 273.
[6] [1984] I.R. 384.

"a self-contained administrative scheme,"[7] the courts should not intervene by way of judicial review where—as in the instant case—the statutory appellate procedure was adequate to meet the complaint on which the application was grounded.

This approach has been followed in a series of cases. Thus, in *Nova Colour Graphic Supplies Ltd.* v. *Employment Appeals Tribunal*[8] Barron J. held that as the issues arising out of an unfair dismissal case would be reheard *de novo* by the Circuit Court (where the applicant's appeal was pending), this procedure was more appropriate than an application for judicial review. A similar view was taken by Costello J. in *O'Connor* v. *Kerry County Council*,[9] where the applicant had challenged the validity of an enforcement notice served under the Local Government (Planning and Development) Act 1963. Costello J. refused the relief sought, saying that an appeal to An Bord Pleanála was a more appropriate remedy than judicial review. Essentially, the same policy was applied in a different situation in *Byrne* v. *Grey*[10] in which Hamilton P. refused to grant certiorari to quash an invalid search warrant on the grounds that the real object of the application was to seek to exclude certain evidence and the ruling on admissibility was best left to the court of trial. Accordingly, relief was refused on discretionary grounds. The approach adopted in *Abenglen* is also the view taken—both traditionally and in trenchantly worded recent cases—in England.[11]

The approach taken in *Abenglen* and subsequent cases has now been put in doubt as a result of the Supreme Court's decision in *P. & F. Sharpe Ltd.* v. *Dublin City and County Manager*.[12] The applicant sought permission to build an access road on to a new dual carriageway, but the respondent indicated that, for reasons of traffic safety, he was unwilling to accede to this request. He further declined to comply with a resolution passed under section 4 of the City and County Management (Amendment) Act 1955 on the grounds that it was unlawful. The applicants sought an order of mandamus compelling the respondents to comply with the resolution. The Supreme Court refused to

---

[7] [1984] I.R. 405. The applicants had sought to have the planning permission with its oppressive conditions quashed. Once that order was secured, they then proposed to argue that the planning authority had made "no decision" within the time limits envisaged by the Local Government (Planning and Development) Act 1963 and then claim entitlement to a default planning permission under s.26(4)(a)(iii) so that they would obtain the permission they had originally sought, shorn of any conditions. Henchy J. described this process of reasoning as "totally unacceptable": [1984] I.R. 400. See the same judge's views in *The State (Collins)* v. *Ruane* [1984] I.R. 105, where he indicated that a person convicted in the District Court should normally appeal to the Circuit Court before applying for judicial review, even where the complaint was that natural justice had been breached at first instance.
[8] [1987] I.R. 426. A similar view was taken by Carroll J. in *Memorex World Trade Corpn.* v. *Employment Appeals Tribunal* [1990] 2 I.R. 184 but *cf. Mythen* v. *Employment Appeals Tribunal* [1989] I.L.R.M. 884, *infra*.
[9] [1989] I.L.R.M. 660.
[10] [1988] I.R. 31.
[11] "Judicial review will not be granted" said May L.J. "save in the most exceptional circumstances": *R.* v. *Chief Constable of Merseyside Police, ex p. Calveley* [1986] Q.B. 424, 435. And in *R.* v. *Inland Revenue Commissioners, ex p. Preston* [1985] A.C. 835, 862 Lord Templeman stated bluntly that "judicial review should not be granted where an alternative remedy is available."
[12] [1989] I.L.R.M. 565.

grant an order of mandamus on the grounds that the resolution in question was a nullity, but did grant certiorari to quash the respondent's refusal to grant permission for the access road. The respondents had argued that as the applicants had appealed to An Bord Pleanála against the decision to refuse permission, they should be confined to that remedy and certiorari should be refused on discretionary grounds. Finlay C.J. did not accept this contention:

> "The powers of An Bord Pleanála on the making of an appeal to it would be entirely confined to the consideration of the matters before it on the basis of proper planning and development of the area and it would have no jurisdiction to consider the question of the validity, from a legal point of view, of the purported decision by the county manager. It would not, therefore, be just for the [applicants] to be deprived of their right to have that decision quashed for want of validity."[13]

This, however, is precisely the argument which had been advanced by the applicants in *Abenglen* who had sought an authoritative ruling from the High Court as to the validity (as opposed to the *merits*) of the conditions attached by the planning authority. One difficulty arising from *P. & F. Sharpe* is that the law as to appellate remedies is still left uncertain inasmuch as Finlay C.J. purported to distinguish (as opposed to overrule) this aspect of *Abenglen*. If anything, the argument against granting relief in *P. & F. Sharpe* was even stronger than in *Abenglen*, inasmuch as the applicants had also concurrently sought to appeal to An Bord Pleanála in addition to commencing judicial review proceedings; whereas in *Abenglen* an appeal was available, but not actually exercised. It used to be trite law that a relief would not be granted where an alternative remedy has been invoked and is pending[14] or where an applicant has deliberately pursued an alternate remedy in the belief that this course of action was in his best interests.[15] The advantages, in terms of consistency and orderly decision-making among state organs are obvious and it is suggested that this facet, at least, of the rather unconsidered finding in *Sharpe* will not be followed.

This *Sharpe* approach was apparently followed in *Mythen* v. *Employment Appeals Tribunal*[16] where Barrington J. quashed a decision of the respondents on the ground that it had misapplied the Transfer of Undertakings Directive. Barrington J. did not think that certiorari could be refused on the ground that the applicant should have applied to the Circuit Court:

---

[13] *Ibid.* 581.
[14] *The State (Roche)* v. *Delap* [1980] I.R. 170; *The State (Wilson)* v. *Neilan* [1985] I.R. 89. But *cf. The State (Cunningham)* v. *O'Floinn* [1960] I.R. 198. Note that Ord. 84, r. 20(5) provides that where certiorari is sought to quash an order which may be the subject of an appeal, the court may adjourn the application for leave until the "appeal is determined or the time for appealing has expired."
[15] *The State (Conlon Construction Co. Ltd.)* v. *Cork C.C.*, High Court, July 31, 1975. But the mere fact that alternative remedies have been invoked does not of itself preclude an application for judicial review when the pursuit of these alternative remedies proves to be unsuccessful: *The State (Ryan)* v. *Revenue Commissioners* [1934] I.R. 1; *The State (Vozza)* v. *O'Floinn* [1957] I.R. 227; *The State (N.C.E. Ltd.)* v. *Dublin C.C.* [1979] I.L.R.M. 249.
[16] [1989] I.L.R.M. 844.

"[T]he Tribunal erred as to its jurisdiction in refusing to entertain the applicant's claim. The applicant is entitled to have the matter investigated by a judge of first instance [and this] is particularly true in a case such as the present where there is an allegation of victimisation and where the date of the agreement to sell the business, the date of the expiration of the applicant's employment and the date and circumstances of the selection of workers to be made redundant may all be interrelated and of vital importance."[17]

It is interesting to note that Barrington J. described the substantive issue raised by the applicant as "a very important and difficult point."

A distinct point is that, there is a strong, though not unanimous, line of authority that the exhaustion requirement will not now be insisted upon where the complaint relates to a breach of constitutional justice.[18] This is perhaps partly because of the particularly grievous nature of the error.

Upon these divergent authorities, two comments may be offered. In the first place, the two lines of authority are presumably grounded on different policy views in that the *Abenglen* line takes the view that if the applicant has a fair, full trial on the merits available to him, on appeal, then he has little to complain about. The alternative, *Sharpe* view is that the applicant is entitled to a proper decision at the initial stage without being put to the trauma, delay and expense of an appeal. The second comment is to suggest that a partial reconciliation may be made between the two views by focusing on the basic assumption of whether the appeal does indeed put the applicant in as good a position as he would have been in, had the initial decision been *intra vires* and valid. The adequacy of the alternative remedy is a matter mentioned in the introductory remarks to this Part and its significance is attested in many authorities. Something of this approach is adopted in the passage from *Mythen* just quoted. It is stated even more explicitly in *Gill* v. *Connellan*,[19] a case where the applicant was convicted in the District Court in circumstances where the solicitor was not afforded an adequate opportunity to make legal submissions. While Lynch J. accepted that, as a general rule, the proper course was to exhaust appellate remedies, the present case was different[19a]:

"Neither the facts nor the law have been adequately heard in the District Court. On appeal to the Circuit Court, therefore, the appeal could hardly be said to be by way of rehearing—the case would more truly be heard for the first time. The applicant and his solicitor would be deprived of the poss-

---

[17] *Ibid.* 853. This view can scarcely be reconciled with the approach of Barron J. in *Nova Colour Graphic Supplies* nor that of Carroll J. in *Memorex.* However Lynch J. adopted similar views in *Gill* v. *Connellan* [1987] I.R. 541.
[18] A view adopted in the following authorities: *Leary* v. *National Union of Vehicle Builders* [1971] Ch. 34; *Ingle* v. *O'Brien* (1975) 109 I.L.T.R. 6; *Moran* v. *Att.-Gen.* [1976] I.R. 400; *Irish Family Planning Assoc. Ltd.* v. *Ryan* [1979] I.R. 295; *The State (Grahame)* v. *Racing Board*, High Court, November 22, 1983. *A contra Memorex*; *Ruane*.
[19] [1987] I.R. 541.
[19a] *Ibid.* 548.

ible advantages of having gone over the whole facts and law and of having heard the submissions and cross-examination by the prosecuting Superintendent in the District Court."

Since the appellate body involved in both *Abenglen* and *Sharpe* was the same (An Bord Pleanála), these two cases seem hardly capable of being reconciled. However it may be that some consistency can be built upon a reasonable principle by considering, in any concrete case, exactly how comprehensive and appropriate an appeal is provided.

General attitudes to the exercise of discretion

Up to quite recently it was considered to be settled law that a person aggrieved by *ultra vires* administrative action had a prima facie entitlement to relief.[20] It was true that the applicant's right to relief might be lost on account of his delay, bad conduct, etc., but, generally speaking, this would only happen where to grant relief would prejudice the rights or interests of the administrative body concerned or third parties, *i.e.* relief would issue *ex debito justitiae*.[21]

A slightly different test appears to have been formulated by a majority of the Supreme Court in *The State (Abenglen Properties Ltd.)* v. *Dublin Corporation*.[22] This case presented a challenge to the validity of certain conditions attached to the grant of planning permission. Relief was refused on the grounds that the applicants had failed to exhaust alternative remedies and that an order of certiorari would serve no useful purpose in the circumstances of the case. But Henchy J. for the majority appeared to go further when he stated that the grant of certiorari in civil cases was purely discretionary. However, in *The State (Furey)* v. *Minister for Defence*,[23] a majority of the Supreme Court reverted to the more orthodox position by stating that a person aggrieved by *ultra vires* administrative action was entitled to relief *ex debito justitiae*. It was not enough to show, for example, that there had been undue delay on the part of the applicant. McCarthy J.'s judgment implies that the respondents would have to establish that it would now be unfair to them or

[20] *R. (Bridgeman)* v. *Drury* [1894] 2 I.R. 489; *R. (Kildare C.C.)* v. *Commissioner for Valuation* [1901] 2 I.R. 215; *The State (Kerry C.C.)* v. *Minister for Local Government* [1933] I.R. 517; *The State (Doyle)* v. *Carr* [1970] I.R. 87 and *M.* v. *An Bord Uchtála* [1977] I.R. 287 (judgment of Henchy J.) A "person aggrieved" (on which see Part 6) was defined as someone whose legal rights or interests were affected by the impugned order: *R.* v. *Thames Magistrates' Court, ex p. Greenbaum* (1957) 55 L.G.R. 129; *The State (Toft)* v. *Galway Corporation* [1981] I.L.R.M. 439.
[21] As happened in cases such as *The State (Cussen)* v. *Brennan* [1981] I.R. 181 (applicant's delay caused third parties to change position in the belief that he would not challenge *ultra vires* appointment; held, it would now be unfair to third parties to grant applicant the relief sought) and *R.* v. *Monopolies Commission, ex p. Argyll plc* [1986] 1 W.L.R. 793.
[22] [1984] I.R. 384. See Hogan, "Remoulding Certiorari: A Critique of *The State (Abenglen Properties Ltd.)* v. *Dublin Corporation* (1982) 17 Ir.Jur.(N.S.) 32 and Jackson, "Certiorari, Alternative Remedies and Judicial Discretion" (1983) 5 D.U.L.J.(N.S.) 100.
[23] [1988] I.L.R.M. 87. Note that in *The State (R. F. Gallagher, Shatter & Co.)* v. *de Valera*, High Court, December 9, 1983, Costello J. stated that the test laid down by Henchy J. in *Abenglen Properties* was that while "aggrieved persons are entitled to certiorari only on a discretionary basis . . . if the requirements of justice and fairness justified the making of the order then it should be made."

third parties or that there were other exceptional circumstances present in the case before the court would be justified in refusing relief. Although the difference between *Abenglen* and *Furey* is largely one of emphasis, the *Furey* decision did appear to indicate a return to traditional principles on the part of the Supreme Court.

Subsequently, however, there have been a number of High Court decisions which appear to be incompatible with *Furey* although it may be significant that in each of these cases the applicant sought to raise technical points all arising out of the Supreme Court's decision in *The State (Clarke)* v. *Roche*.[24] In *Connors* v. *Delap*[25] the applicant sought to challenge a conviction for driving a motor vehicle without insurance on the ground that the summons issued by the District Court clerk was defective. Lynch J. pointed out that the reason why the applicant had failed to answer the summons and appear before the District Court was because "he did not wish to face up to charges to which he knew he had no defence." Accordingly, he did not think that certiorari should issue to quash a conviction based on a technically defective summons:

"If I were to make an order of certiorari in favour of the applicant based on the technical points on which he relies, it would clearly deprive the people of Ireland of the just retribution to which they are entitled in respect of the crime committed by the applicant . . . Certiorari is a discretionary remedy. In the present case the applicant has no merits on the substance of the case and is also late in bringing his application. . . ."[26]

White v. *Hussey*[27] was a decision arising out of a similar set of facts and Barr J. clearly endorsed the approach which Lynch J. had taken in *Connors*:

"The relief which the applicant seeks is a discretionary remedy. It seems to me that in deciding whether or not discretion should be exercised in his favour, it is proper I should take all of the relevant circumstances into account and then decide whether justice requires that the convictions complained of should be set aside."[28]

Barr J. thought that in determining this issue:

"[R]egard must be had to the interests of the people of Ireland who are entitled to redress where the facts establish, or clearly imply, that the applicant was in fact guilty of the offences the subject-matter of the conviction

---

[24] [1986] I.R. 619. In this case the Supreme Court held, *inter alia*, that s.10 of the Petty Sessions (Ireland) Act 1851 required that a District Court clerk or Peace Commissioner should personally consider and adjudicate upon an application for a summons under that Act. This in practice meant that all computer summonses were invalid, since there had not been an individual adjudication prior to the issue of the summonses. This decision gave rise to a veritable flood of applications for judicial review and necessitated the immediate passage of the Courts (No. 3) Act 1986 (for commentary, see Hogan (1986) I.C.L.S.A. 33/01 – 33/09).

[25] [1989] I.L.R.M. 93.

[26] *Ibid*. 97–98.

[27] [1989] I.L.R.M. 109.

[28] *Ibid*. 111.

which he challenges on a technical ground that has no relevance to the merits of the case."[29]

These views would appear clearly to be incompatible with *Vozza* and *Furey*. It would seem that yet another pronouncement by the Supreme Court on this question will be necessary before the matter can be regarded as having been authoritatively decided one way or the other.

6. Locus Standi

The current law on *locus standi* is currently in a state of flux. The modern tendency of the Irish courts is to move away from a technical approach to *locus standi* towards a rationalisation of standing requirements based on considerations relating to the general administration of justice, and the separation of powers.[30] Further proof that the current trend is away from the technical approach to standing is supplied by recent dicta to the effect that the standing rules are merely rules of practice (which may be relaxed if there are "weighty countervailing considerations" justifying a departure from the ordinary rules), and that these requirements are the same regardless of the form of the proceedings.[31] The new Order 84, rule 20(4) states that leave to apply for judicial review shall not be granted unless the applicant "has a sufficient interest in the matter to which the application relates." As noted *infra* the effect of a similar change in the English Rules of Court has been stated to permit an *actio popularis* (or "citizen's action") in suitable cases.[32] It seems probable (from the judicial silence on the point) that the change in the Irish rules has not had a similar, or indeed any, effect.

The traditional standing rules

At common law, the standing rules varied depending on the character of the remedies. The public law remedies of certiorari and prohibition always contained an element of the *actio popularis*, as the purpose of these remedies was not merely to avoid injustice *inter partes*, but also to maintain order in the legal system.[33] It was thus open to anyone—even a stranger to the proceed-

---

[29] *Ibid.* 113.
[30] See the judgment of Henchy J. in *Cahill* v. *Sutton* [1980] I.R. 269.
[31] *Cahill* v. *Sutton* [1980] I.R. 269, 285, *per* Henchy J.; *The State (Lynch)* v. *Cooney* [1982] I.R. 337, 369, *per* Walsh J.
[32] Wade, *Administrative Law* (Oxford, 1988), p. 704.
[33] Yardley, "Certiorari and the Problem of *Locus Standi*" (1955) 71 L.Q.R. 388; "Prohibition and Mandamus and the Problem of *Locus Standi*" (1957) 73 L.Q.R. 534. The *locus standi* requirements for mandamus have always been somewhat stricter than in the case of the other public law remedies: *R.* v. *Lewisham Union* [1897] 1 Q.B. 498 (existence of specific legal right); *R. (I.U.D.W.C.)* v. *Rathmines U.D.C.* [1928] I.R. 260 ("legal right" (Hanna J.), "specific interest in performance of duty" (O'Byrne J.)). But for a less restrictive approach, see *The State (Modern Homes (Ire.) Ltd.)* v. *Dublin Corporation* [1953] I.R. 202; *The State (A.C.C. Ltd.)* v. *Navan U.D.C.*, High Court, February 22, 1980.

ings—to apply for certiorari or prohibition. In practice, however, relief was hardly even given to anyone other than a "person aggrieved."[34]

A stricter approach was taken in the case of the declaration and the injunction, and here standing rules reflected the fact that these remedies were derived from private law. An applicant was required to show the existence of a legal right or other cognisable interest which was affected or threatened.[35] A recent example of this restrictive approach is provided by *Irish Permanent Building Society Ltd.* v. *Caldwell (No. 1)*,[36] where the plaintiffs had challenged the decision of the Registrar of Building Societies to register a new building society. The defendants brought a motion seeking to have the plaintiffs' claim struck out on the grounds that they had not alleged that they suffered or would suffer peculiar injury as a result of this allegedly invalid decision. Although Keane J. refused to strike out the claim on the grounds that the matter deserved "full and unhurried consideration," he did hint strongly that the infringement, or threatened infringement, of some legal right or interest was a prerequisite in declaratory proceedings of this nature.[37]

However the law, in respect of both sets of remedies, has long moved away from the stricter, technical requirement of a legal right to the notion that the applicant should have suffered some prejudice going beyond that felt by most other members of the community. That this is so was stated in the major Supreme Court case of *Cahill* v. *Sutton*,[38] which confirmed and articulated an existing trend, rather than marking a new departure.

Preliminary points

However, before returning to explore this central issue further, we should attempt to clear away three preliminary points. In the first place, whatever about the historical position set out in the previous paragraph, the standing requirements are the same whether the court is dealing with the three remedies which originated on State side or the two which originated in the Courts of Equity. That this is so had been accepted even before the new system was introduced.[39] It has surely been put beyond any doubt by the advent of the new regime. The policy of the new Rules is to achieve uniformity between the remedies. This is confirmed by the wording of Order 84, rule 20(4): "The Court shall not grant leave unless it considers that the applicant has a sufficient

---

[34] In cases such as *The State (Kerry C.C.)* v. *Minister for Local Government* [1933] I.R. 517; *The State (Doyle)* v. *Carr* [1970] I.R. 87 and *The State (Toft)* v. *Galway Corporation* [1981] I.L.R.M. 439, certiorari was refused to applicants who were not "persons aggrieved."

[35] *Weir* v. *Fermanagh C.C.* [1913] 1 I.R. 193; *Gregory* v. *Camden L.B.C.* [1966] 1 W.L.R. 899; *Gouriet* v. *U.P.O.W.* [1978] A.C. 435.

[36] [1979] I.L.R.M. 273. But *cf. Martin* v. *Dublin Corporation*, High Court, November 14, 1977.

[37] The plaintiffs subsequently amended their pleadings to include a claim that they had suffered loss and damage: see *Irish Permanent Building Society* v. *Caldwell (No. 2)* [1981] I.L.R.M. 242. This view must now be taken to have been superseded by the judgment of the Supreme Court in *Society for the Protection of Unborn Children (Ire.) Ltd.* v. *Coogan* [1990] I.L.R.M. 70.

[38] [1980] I.R. 269. For a perceptive analysis of this case and subsequent developments, see Sherlock, "Understanding Standing: *Locus Standi* in Irish Constitutional Law" (1987) *Public Law* 345.

[39] See, *e.g. The State (Lynch)* v. *Cooney* [1982] I.R. 337, 369, *per* Walsh J. See also, *Irish Permanent Building Society* v. *Caldwell (No. 2)* [1981] I.L.R.M. 242.

interest in the matter. . . . " This provision applies to all applications for judicial review (including cases presenting constitutional challenges) irrespective of the form of the proceedings. This must mean that the *locus standi* requirements do not vary from remedy to remedy. Secondly, it has now been stated judicially on several occasions, that the standing requirements are the same, even though the application for judicial review involves the constitutionality of a law or an executive or administrative action, rather than merely the *vires* of an administrative action with no such constitutional issues.[40] It is significant that whereas *Cahill* v. *Sutton* was a case involving the constitutionality of a law, yet the principle it laid down has been widely followed in cases falling within either of the other two categories.

The third and final preliminary point is the fact that the issue of standing is distinct from that of the merits or strength of an applicant's case. This orthodoxy would hardly be worth stating were it not for the fact that in Britain the House of Lords has seized upon the analogous changes to Order 84 as a ground for rejecting the traditional view: *Inland Revenue Commissioners* v. *National Federation of Self-Employed and Small Businesses Ltd.*[41] This case concerned an application for judicial review of the respondent's decision to grant an amnesty to a group of printing workers who for many years had defrauded the Inland Revenue and evaded tax. The House of Lords ruled that it could not be shown that the Revenue had acted *ultra vires* in granting such an amnesty, and, accordingly, it could not be said that the Federation had a "sufficient interest" in the application. If, however, there were grounds for thinking that the Revenue had acted improperly, then the Federation would have had standing to complain. The approach taken in this case, or, at any rate in the more radical judgments of Lords Diplock and Scarman, appears to merge the hitherto distinct concepts of standing and merits by creating a two-stage process. At the leave stage, it is only the hopeless or meddlesome applicants who may be rejected on this ground. At the substantive hearing, the issue of standing has to be considered in the light of the nature of the powers and duties of the public authority and the character of the alleged illegality. The corollary of the decision is that if an applicant can show that an administrative body is acting improperly, then he will be deemed to have "sufficient interest" to maintain the application, however remote his personal interest. This is, in effect, to permit an *actio popularis* in a suitable case.

There is no reason to expect the Irish courts to draw upon Order 84, (which

---

[40] *The State (Sheehan)* v. *Government of Ireland* [1987] I.R. 550, 557, *per* Costello J. (who thought that it was "to be expected" that the test in each case "should be formulated somewhat differently"); *Duggan* v. *An Taoiseach* [1989] I.L.R.M. 710, 725, *per* Hamilton P. (quoted at p. 618). However, *Society for the Protection of Unborn Children (Ireland) Ltd.* v. *Coogan* [1990] I.L.R.M. 70, 73 (Finlay C.J.), 77 (Walsh J.) gives some cause to suggest that the standing requirements may be stricter where it is a law, rather than an administrative or executive action, whose constitutionality is at stake. Humphreys and O'Dowd, "*Locus Standi* to Enforce the Constitution" (1990) 3 I.L.T.(N.S.) 14, 15 suggest that the fact that the courts cannot fill the statutory vacuum created by the invalidation of legislation argues in favour of stricter standing rules in cases challenging the constitutionality of legislation.

[41] [1982] A.C. 617. *A contra*: *R* v. *Secretary of State for the Environment ex p. Rose* [1990] 2 W.L.R. 186.

does expressly require "a sufficient interest,") in order to follow this English authority and effectively abolish the standing rule. Every case has treated the issue of standing independently from the merits[42] and the reasoning for this was based firmly in *Cahill* on the need to safeguard the proper administration of justice (against the officious man of straw); to prevent the abuse of the power of judicial review; and to uphold the principle of the separation of powers. In addition, it was said in *Cahill* that a case brought by a litigant with no direct interest would tend to lack in Henchy J.'s words "the force and urgency of reality."[43] In response to these arguments, it has been said that a standing rule is "constitutionally inspired but not constitutionally compelled."[44] It is among a package of devices which enable a judge to refuse to address the merits of a constitutional claim. At base then, the content of a standing rule depends upon a judge's view of the proper place of judicial review in a constitutional polity.

Cahill v. *Sutton*

Cahill was the first modern Irish case thoroughly to address the issue of *locus standi*. It involved a medical negligence claim in which the plaintiff was time barred under the Statute of Limitations 1957, section 11(2)(b). Before the Supreme Court, the plaintiff challenged the Statute on the ground that it contained no exception to protect the right to litigate of an injured person who had only become aware of the facts on which his claim was based after the period of limitation had expired. The essential point for present purposes was that the plaintiff was not herself such a person since at all material times she was aware of all the facts necessary to ground her claim. In sum, said Henchy J.:

" . . . the plaintiff is seeking to be allowed to conjure up, invoke and champion the putative constitutional rights of a hypothetical third party, so that the provisions of s.11, subs. 2(b), may be declared unconstitutional on the basis of that constitutional *jus tertii*—thus allowing the plaintiff to march through the resulting gap in the statute."[45]

Only two of the five unanimous judges who heard *Cahill* gave substantive

---

[42] *Cahill* v. *Sutton* [1980] I.R. 269; *The State (Lynch)* v. *Cooney* [1982] I.R. 337 and *Norris* v. *Att.-Gen.* [1984] I.R. 36. But note that in *Lynch* Walsh J. said ([1982] I.R. 369):

"[Rules of standing) must be flexible so as to be individually applicable to the particular facts of any given case. Such a question cannot be regarded as a preliminary point unless there is an admission of all the facts necessary to decide the issue. In the absence of any admission in any case where the point is raised, it is necessary for the court to enter into a sufficient examination of the facts and, having heard them, to decide whether or not a sufficient interest has been established."

[43] [1980] I.R. 269, 282–283. Though note that in *Norris* v. *Att.-Gen.* [1984] I.R. 36, 91 McCarthy J. remarked apropos of what might be termed the "busybody" basis of *Cahill* "from 1937–1980, I doubt if the court records reveal many, or even any, instances of such officious interference."
[44] Sherlock, *loc. cit.* 266–269, where these ideas are developed.
[45] [1980] I.R. 280.

Locus Standi

judgments. The tenor of O'Higgins C.J.'s fairly brief judgment and Henchy J.'s judgment are in accord. However, as Henchy J. gave the more elaborate consideration to the standing topic, which was the main point, it is his treatment which is generally regarded as the more authoritative. In holding that Ms. Cahill had no standing to make the only argument which could assist her, Henchy J. stated:

> "[An applicant] must show that the impact of the impugned law on his personal situation discloses an injury or prejudice which he has either suffered or is in imminent danger of suffering.
>
> This rule, however, being but a rule of practice must, like all such rules, be subject to expansion, exception or qualification when the justice of the case so requires. Since the paramount consideration in the exercise of the jurisdiction of the Courts to review legislation in the light of the Constitution is to ensure that persons entitled to the benefit of a constitutional right will not be prejudiced through being wrongfully deprived of it, there will be cases where the want of the normal *locus standi* on the part of the person questioning the constitutionality of the statute may be overlooked if, in the circumstances of the case, there is a transcendent need to assert against the statute the constitutional provision that has been invoked. For example, while the challenger may lack the personal standing normally required, those prejudicially affected by the impugned statute may not be in a position to assert adequately, or in time, their constitutional rights. In such a case the court might decide to ignore the want of normal personal standing on the part of the litigant before it. Likewise, the absence of a prejudice or injury peculiar to the challenger might be overlooked, in the discretion of the court, if the impugned provision is directed at or operable against a grouping which includes the challenger, or with whom the challenger may be said to have a common interest—particularly in cases where, because of the nature of the subject-matter, it is difficult to segregate those affected from those not affected by the challenged provision."[46]

Two comments may be made on this passage. First, what may be taken as the general rule, which is contained in the first paragraph, describes the plaintiff's title to sue as "injury or prejudice." Later in the judgment, it was said that he must "stand in real or imminent danger of being adversely affected."[47] These formulations are, of course, much broader than the traditional standard (at any rate for the remedies of declaration or injunction). Secondly, Henchy J. acknowledged that the rule was flexible and embraced a number of exceptions "when the justice of the case so requires." Given the entire range of public cases which the standing rule must accommodate, it is inevitable that the rule should be broad and flexible.[48]

R.T.C. LIBRARY LETTERKENNY

[46] *Ibid.* 284–285.
[47] *Ibid.* 286.
[48] *The State (Lynch)* v. *Cooney* [1982] I.R. 337, 369, *per* Walsh J.

615

Post-Cahill cases

The question is: how has *Cahill* fared in subsequent cases? It is certainly true that it has been quoted with approval in almost every case on standing.[49] This formal obeisance, of course, does not necessarily mean that it has been influential upon later judgments. In the post-*Cahill* era, the few cases in which the rules of standing have prevented an issue from being examined on the merits are cases in which the claim may be regarded as opportunist and unmeritorious.[50] Of course, this is no bad thing. But it does make it difficult to assess the impact of *Cahill*. It is suggested, nevertheless, that the following review of recent case law in this area demonstrates that (with the possible exception of *ESB* v. *Gormley*[51]) the cases accord reasonably well with the flexible *Cahill* principles.

The first significant decision after *Cahill* was *The State (Lynch)* v. *Cooney* in which the question of *locus standi* arose in the context of a ministerial ban made under the provisions of section 31 of the Broadcasting (Authority) Act 1960. The ministerial order purported to prevent Radio Telefis Éireann from broadcasting a party political broadcast on behalf of Sinn Féin which, under RTE's guidelines, agreed with all the major parties, for the allocation of party political broadcasts, was entitled to one such broadcast. The Supreme Court was unanimously of the view that the organisation's representatives had sufficient interest to challenge the validity of the ban in certiorari proceedings. As Walsh J. put it, irrespective of whether the applicants had a "right" or a mere "privilege," they had suffered a loss and had been affected in a material way. According to O'Higgins C.J.[52]:

> "In such circumstances the respondent and his party were deprived of a benefit lawfully accorded to them in the first instance and, in my view, were entitled to complain if the deprivation were unlawful."[53]

The more difficult question, of course, would have been if the applicant had not been a member of the political party affected but a mere member of the electorate, arguing that he had been unlawfully denied his opportunity to hear all points of view in the forthcoming election. Case law reviewed later[54] suggested that such a claim would not have been turned away simply on the ground that the applicant was no worse off than the other two million or so electors, provided the application was bona fide and there was no other more obvious plaintiff. However as against this, the point may be made that there would have been more obvious plaintiffs in the person of party officials or members.

---

[49] A notable exception being *Norris* v. *Att.-Gen.* [1984] I.R. 36, 91 where McCarthy J. described *Cahill* as a case "he was bound reluctantly to follow."

[50] See Sherlock, *loc. cit.* 264.

[51] [1985] I.R. 129.

[52] [1982] I.R. 337.

[53] *Ibid.* 362–363.

[54] As suggested by the judgments in cases such as *Crotty* v. *An Taoiseach* [1987] I.R. 713; *Society for the Protection of Unborn Children (Ireland) Ltd.* v. *Coogan* [1990] I.L.R.M. 70 and *McGimpsey* v. *Ireland* [1990] 1 I.R. 110.

There have been at least three other straightforward applications of the *Cahill* principle. In *The State (King)* v. *Minister for Justice*[55] (which actually pre-dates *Cahill*) the applicants obtained an order of mandamus commanding the Minister to exercise his statutory powers, under the Court Houses (Provision and Maintenance) Act 1935 to renew and repair Waterford Courthouse. Rather surprisingly, Doyle J. rejected the argument that the applicants (one of whom was President of the Waterford Law Society) had standing as representatives of the Society which Doyle J. noted was "an unincorporated body whose membership includes most, if not all, of the solicitors practising in the city and county of Waterford."

However, Doyle J. went on to hold that the applicants had standing in their own right:

> "Both gentlemen carry on an extensive practice in the Waterford court and may, therefore, be regarded as having a particular personal interest in the provision of proper court accommodation to enable them to earn their livelihood."[56]

In *Ahern* v. *Kerry County Concil*[57] Blayney J. held that the applicant had standing in his capacity as a member of the Council to challenge the validity of a resolution to adopt estimates. Here, perhaps, it was assumed that, absent some special qualfication—such as membership of the Council or being a ratepayer[58]—an ordinary private individual would lack the necessary *locus standi* to challenge the validity of estimates adopted by the County Council. Another example of this approach is afforded by the decision of Hamilton P. in *Duggan* v. *An Taoiseach*.[59] The applicants had been appointed to the office of the Farm Tax Commissioner under the Farm Tax Act 1985. While these appointments were not permanent, it was understood that they would last for at least five years. Following a change of Government, the new Minister for Finance announced that this tax was no longer to be collected, although no repealing legislation was ever introduced. When the applicants were informed that their appointments had been terminated, they sought orders declaring

---

[55] [1984] I.R. 169.
[56] *Ibid.* 175.
[57] [1988] I.L.R.M. 392. Blayney J. followed the decision of the Northern Ireland Court of Appeal in *Re Cooke's Application* (1986) 1 N.I.J.B. 43.
[58] Some difficulty in connection with the category of ratepayer standing arises from the fact that it is now only business rates which are actually levied: see pp. 181–182. However, the technique by which domestic rates were abolished is that the rating authority "shall make an allowance to the peron so rated by them . . . and such allowance shall equal in amount the rate in the pound . . . and accordingly the rate so made shall be abated . . . ": Local Government (Financial Provisions) Act 1978, s.3(1). This oblique technique which creates non-rate paying rate payers has been necessary to retain rateable valuations for such secondary purposes as determining Circuit Court jurisdiction and rate-payer standing. Perhaps the better solution would be to allow any local residents standing in an action against his or her local authority. *Cf.* the words of Lord Denning in *R.* v. *Greater London Council, ex p. Blackburn* [1976] 1 W.L.R. 550. If this solution is not adopted, the law would be distinguishing between non-rate paying rate payers and other persons which would probably violate Art. 40.1.
[59] [1989] I.L.R.M. 710.

unlawful: (i) the Government's decision to suspend the operation of the Act; and (ii) the termination of their appointments to the Farm Tax Office.

Hamilton P. first referred to *Cahill* v. *Sutton* and said that the observations of Henchy J. applied to the present case:

> "These observations . . . relate to the *locus standi* of a person seeking to challenge an enactment of the Oireachtas as being repugnant to the Constitution but apply, in my opinion, with equal validity to the status of a person or persons challenging an act of the executive. A person or persons challenging an act of the executive must show that his or their interests have been adversely affected or stand in real or imminent danger of being adversely affected by the action of the executive."[60]

The applicants' case was that they had a legitimate expectation to continue their work in the Farm Tax Office until that work had been completed or until the work of the Farm Tax Office upon which they were engaged was terminated in accordance with law. Accordingly, Hamilton P. held that the applicants had *locus standi* to challenge this decision. However, the judge continued by ruling that the applicants had no standing to seek the wider declarations sought, such as that the Government's decision to direct suspension of collection of the tax was also unlawful.

Duggan was a case where the applicants lacked standing only in respect of the wider declarations as to the unlawfulness of the Government's actions and these were anyway unnecessary in their case. But it would be surprising if a high-minded litigant with the general public interest in mind—such as the plaintiff in *Crotty* v. *An Taoiseach*[61]—were to be denied standing in a case such as this. If every citizen has "an interest in ensuring that the fundamental law of the State is observed,"[62] does this not extend to cases where the Government has attempted to suspend the operation of a law in an unconstitutional manner?

The State (Sheehan) v. *Government of Ireland*[63] was another case in which the standing issue was discussed. Here the applicant sought an order compelling the Government to bring into force section 60(1) of the Civil Liability Act 1961 which abolishes the non-feasance rule with prospective effect. Mr. Sheehan had been injured by tripping on a pavement and, anticipating that his claim might be defeated by the non-feasance rule, commenced mandamus proceedings. His standing to do so was strenuously contested by the respondents, on the basis that as the section only has prospective force, it could avail the applicant nothing even if it were brought into effect.

In the High Court, Costello J. applied the standard test in mandamus proceedings: has it been established the applicant suffered prejudice to an extent greater than the members of the public? (The judge considered that while

---

[60] *Ibid.* 724–725.
[61] [1987] I.R. 713.
[62] *Society for the Protection of Unborn Children (Ireland) Ltd.* v. *Coogan* [1990] I.L.R.M. 70, 75, *per* Walsh J.
[63] [1987] I.R. 550.

this test was "formulated somewhat differently" than the *Cahill* v. *Sutton* principles, it was "not very different.")[64] Costello J. went on to hold that the applicant had satisfied this test, despite the fact that the making of the order would not relieve the prejudice in his own case:

"He has an interest in the operation of the Act which is not just that which all citizens have in the enforcement of the law. He is an aggrieved citizen who may have suffered the loss of a substantial amount of money due to the Government's failure to carry out its duties. It seems to me that this gives him a special interest in the matter, and that the court's rules of standing should not shut out a complainant with such an interest from asking that the court's supervisory functions be exercised. Secondly, it was pointed out that should Mr. Sheehan be able to establish that the Corporation has been guilty of non-feasance but not of misfeasance with the result that his claim against the Corporation fails, then an action for damages would lie against the Government for its failure to carry out its statutory function. Whilst expressing no concluded view on the force of this contention, it is obviously not a frivolous or insubstantial one. It is clear therefore that Mr. Sheehan has an interest (which other members of the public do not share) in establishing the Government's dereliction of duty. This can be done in these proceedings and so, in my view, he is thus afforded an interest which is sufficient to justify him bringing them."[65]

One may characterise these two points by saying, of the first, that it amounts to extending the law somewhat by recognising that the applicant had a "special interest," albeit not in the conventional material sense, but because he had a legitimate reason for being aggrieved, namely, the fact that he could not be compensated for his injuries. The second reason, although for some reason offered more tentatively by Costello J., is well in line with the present law. It amounts to saying that the applicant has an interest, namely that success might facilitate him in bringing an action for breach of statutory duty.

On appeal, a majority of the Supreme Court rejected the applicant's case on other grounds. However, McCarthy J. in his dissent agreed with Costello J.'s conclusion on *locus standi*, as otherwise no private individual would have

---

[64] *Ibid.* 557. Costello J. added that:

"[T]he test in *Cahill* v. *Sutton* (where prejudice to the personal situation of the plaintiff would be sufficient) is not very different to that in *The State (Modern Homes (Ire.) Ltd.* v. *Dublin Corporation* (in which prejudice to an extent greater to the members of the public was required) and I think that I am entitled to follow the earlier judgment and consider whether the [applicant] herein has a 'sufficient interest' in the performance by the Government of its duty under the Act of 1961 to justify his claim in these proceedings."

[65] *Ibid.* 558. Costello J. also cautioned that:

". . . our courts should now look with considerable caution on earlier authorities which have now been discarded by the House of Lords and which may have formed the basis of earlier decisions in this country."

619

had standing to maintain the proceedings.[66] This may be regarded as a reason either for according standing to the applicant on more or less the same basis as the exceptional constitutional cases referred to later, or more logically, for modifying the strict common law rules as to the need for relator proceedings, as has now occurred in *Society for the Protection of Unborn Children (Ireland) Ltd.* v. *Coogan*.[67]

A more problematic case was *E.S.B.* v. *Gormley*[68] in which the defendant was allowed to challenge the validity of a planning permission on the grounds that the advertisement indicating an intention to apply for permission (which is required by section 26(1) of the Local Government (Planning and Development) Act 1963), was defective. It had been argued that as the defendant had acquired the lands *after* the planning permission was granted, she was not prejudiced or affected by this irregularity.

This argument was accepted by Carroll J. in the High Court but rejected in the Supreme Court, where Finlay C.J. stated:

"[locus standi] does not depend upon the person making such challenge being able to demonstrate that the non-compliance directly affected him or her. Such a challenge can properly be made *by any person who is affected by the permission granted* and if made, and if non-compliance is established, then the permission is invalid not by reason of prejudice or disadvantage to the person challenging it but by reason of a want of power and jurisdiction in the planning authority to exercise their right of granting or refusing permission . . . ."[69]

Admittedly there are parts of this passage (notably the first sentence and the second part of the second sentence) which appear to contradict *Cahill* and to jutify the summary in the head note in the Irish Reports: " . . . as a member of the public who was affected by the planning permission granted, the defendant was entitled to challenge the validity of that permission . . .." Perhaps it is more correct to read this passage in the light of the facts of the case, namely that Mrs. Gormley was peculiarly affected by the fact that she had previously bought the land from P., the land-owner at the time the advertisement appeared. Plainly, on the narrowest view, P. would have had standing as the land-owner. Had the application for planning permission been properly advertised, P. might have objected and permission not been granted. This would have been very much in the defendant's interest and, accordingly, Mrs. Gormley as his successor in title was entitled to complain that the application had not been properly advertised. Even in private law, there are many situations in which a land-owner is affected by burdens or benefits, which were

---

[66] Henchy J. did observe (at 560), however, that the applicant was "lacking in that special interest in the outcome of the mandamus proceedings." This comment might be thought to imply that Costello J. was wrong to hold that the applicant had the necessary standing to maintain the proceedings.

[67] [1990] I.L.R.M. 70. For an interesting account of this case, see Humphreys and O'Dowd, "Locus Standi to Enforce the Constitution" (1990) 8 I.L.T.(N.S.) 14.

[68] [1985] I.R. 129.

[69] *Ibid.* 157.

annexed to the land during the time of his predecessor in title, and it does not seem an unreasonable extension of *Cahill* to adopt a similar view in public law.

Exceptional constitutional cases

We must now turn to three major constitutional cases which might be regarded as constituting special cases justifying an exception to the *Cahill* principles. In *Crotty* v. *An Taoiseach*,[70] where the plaintiff had challenged the validity of the ratification of the Single European Act, the Supreme Court found for him on the standing issue. If the Single European Act were to be ratified, it would affect every citizen and, accordingly, the plaintiff had *locus standi* "to challenge the Act notwithstanding his failure to prove the threat of any special injury or prejudice to him, as distinct from any other citizen, arising from the Act."[71] This approach was followed by Barrington J. in the High Court in *McGimpsey* v. *Ireland*,[72] where the constitutionality of the Anglo-Irish Agreement was at issue. He found that the plaintiffs had standing to challenge the Agreement as they "were patently sincere and serious people who have raised an important constitutional issue which affects them and thousands of others on both sides of the border"[73] a view subsequently accepted (although with some reservations) by the Supreme Court on appeal. This attitude was confirmed by the Supreme Court in *Society for the Protection of Unborn Children (Ireland) Ltd.* v. *Coogan*.[74] Here the plaintiff Society sought an injunction restraining the dissemination of a student handbook containing information on abortion services, claiming that this booklet infringed Article 40.3.3. Finlay C.J. first observed that the plaintiffs merely sought to restrain what it claimed was a threatened breach of the Constitution by the defendants, so that there was no question of a challenge to the validity of any statutory provision. The test in such a case was:

> "[T]hat of a *bona fide* concern and interest, interest being used in the sense of proximity or an objective interest. To ascertain whether such *bona fide* concern and interest exist in a particular case it is of special importance to consider the nature of the constitutional right sought to be protected. In this case, the right is the right to life of an unborn child in its mother's womb. The threat to that constitutional right which it is sought to avoid is the death of the child. In respect of such a threat, there can never be a victim or potential victim who can sue."[75]

In comparing these recent decisions on standing with the *Cahill* v. *Sutton* principles, the most obvious point relates to the *Coogan* case. In *Cahill*, Henchy J. stated that, by way of exception to the general rule, a litigant could

---

[70] [1987] I.R. 713.
[71] *Ibid.* 766.
[72] [1988] I.R. 567 (H.C.); [1990] 1 I.R. 110 (S.C.).
[73] *Ibid.* 580.
[74] [1990] I.L.R.M. 70.
[75] *Ibid.* 73.

have standing even though "he lack[ed] the personal standing normally required if those prejudicially affected by the impugned statute [are] not in a position to assert adequately . . . their constitutional rights."[76] As observed by the Supreme Court in *Coogan*; what clearer case could be found of a "being" not capable of asserting its constitutional right than that of a foetus whose mother was contemplating an abortion? As Walsh J. said:

> "When the unborn life is threatened by the parent or parents with the encouragement or assistance of other persons, there is an obvious need for somebody to assert the interest of the unborn. In the present case the plaintiffs have . . . shown a genuine interest in the protection of unborn life and it was reasonable on their part to raise the issue as representing the interest of unborn lives."[77]

Alternatively, one may group *Coogan* with *Crotty* and *McGimpsey* as involving examples of what Henchy J. in *Cahill* called a "transcendent need to assert against the statute the constitutional provisions . . ."[78] This is clearly a very broad exemption, since it cannot be every constitutional point which warrants a suspension of the normal standing rules. The great question which will now be briefly examined, is what common threads may be discerned running through the three cases under review. It may be suggested that the following requirements are necessary to bring a case within this exception to the usual *Cahill* principles.

First, it must be reasonable to assume that there is no one who has standing in the classic sense of being directly and materially affected by the allegedly unconstitutional law or the administrative action which is said to be invalid. As Walsh J. remarked in *Coogan*:

> "[E]ven in cases where it is sought to invalidate a legislative provision the Court will, where the circumstances warrant it, permit a person whose personal interest is not directly or indirectly, presently, or in the future, threatened, to maintain proceedings if the circumstances are such that the public interest warrants it. In this context, the public interest must be taken in the widest sense."[79]

This exceptional head of standing is more likely to arise in cases such as where it said that there has been a breach of constitutional provisions setting out the powers and functions of the State, rather than raising individual constitutional rights. *Crotty* and *McGimpsey* clearly fall into this category. Another example is provided by cases such as *O'Donovan* v. *Attorney-*

---

[76] [1980] I.R. 269. These cases should be regarded as examples of exceptions to the primary *Cahill* v. *Sutton* rules, rather than as qualifying or retreating from, these principles. As Walsh J. remarked in *Coogan* ([1990] I.L.R.M. 78) the decision in *Cahill* "is not of such sweeping application as is sometimes thought."
[77] [1990] I.L.R.M. 79.
[78] [1980] I.R. 269, 285.
[79] [1990] I.L.R.M. 70, 78.

General[80] and *O'Malley* v. *An Taoiseach*[81] which raised the issue of whether there had ben a fair distribution of Dáil seats.

The other requirement is that the litigants should have serious interest in the matter, the formula used in *McGimpsey* "being patently sincere and serious" and in *Coogan* "bona fide concern and interest." The assumption here is that if that dreaded figure, the meddlesome and crank litigant, is not to be excluded by the test of material interest, then he must be excluded in some other way. One way in which the seriousness of the litigant might be shown would be if the litigant were, or were a member of, a representative association, as in the *Coogan* case. Another possibility is that, as mentioned in *McGimpsey*, there should be a large number of persons affected by the action or law, of which complaint was made. It remains to be seen whether it is essential that a large section of the population must be affected or whether, as seems more probable, this is merely one type of evidence of the seriousness of the litigant's case.

One further difficulty which was raised by the Supreme Court in *McGimpsey* pertains to the motivation of the plaintiffs. Plainly, as distinguished members of the Official Unionist party of Northern Ireland, the plaintiffs had standing in the narrow sense to be explained in the next section as they were concerned about the signing of the Anglo-Irish Agreement. The difficulty lies in the particular constitutional argument on which they principally relied, *viz.*, the jurisdictional claim in respect of Northern Ireland contained in Articles 2 and 3 of the Constitution which, as Unionists, they naturally found offensive. Although the Supreme Court decided that their case should be heard on the merits, Finlay C.J. had considerable reservations as to whether a claim of this kind could be entertained:

> "As a general proposition, it would appear to me that one would have to entertain considerable doubt as to whether any citizen would have the *locus standi* to challenge the constitutional validity of an act of the executive or of a statute of the Oireachtas for the specific and sole purpose of achieving an objective directly contrary to the purpose of the constitutional provisions invoked."[82]

Indeed, one might observe that the McGimpseys' relation to Articles 2 and 3 was roughly analogous to that between Mrs. Cahill and the defect which she wished to rely upon in the Statute of Limitations. This in turn raises the question of the distinction between *locus standi* and *jus tertii*.

---

[80] [1961] I.R. 114.
[81] [1990] I.L.R.M. 460.
[82] [1990] 1 I.R. 110. McCarthy J., however, thought (at 123) that "one does not determine *locus standi* by motive, but rather by objective assessment of rights and the means of protecting them." He was, however, minded to deny the plaintiffs standing on the ground that only citizens could challenge an Agreement of this kind. Similar sentiments are to be found in the judgment of Gannon J. in *Rederei Kennermerland N.V.* v. *Att.-Gen.* [1989] I.L.R.M. 821.

Jus tertii

The concept of *jus tertii* has not yet been treated judicially as a separate category. The distinction between the two concepts is that *locus standi* involves the litigant's status in relation to the administrative action (or law) and its consequences, whilst *jus tertii* refers to his position *vis-à-vis* the particular defect of which complaint is made. Strictly speaking, as is acknowledged in Henchy J.'s judgment (quoted at page 614), *Cahill* was a *jus tertii* case in that the plaintiff was certainly affected by the law; but not by the constitutional infirmity of which she complained. Another example is the plaintiff's argument in *Norris* v. *Attorney-General*,[83] that since the sections of the Offences Against the Person Act 1861 applied, *inter alia*, to married persons, they constituted a violation of marital privacy. The High Court and Supreme Court agreed that the plaintiff had general standing to attack the constitutionality of the impugned provisions. However, since his evidence showed that he would never marry, the courts declined to permit him to rely on arguments based on marital privacy. The exception was the dissenting judge, McCarthy J., who defined *locus standi* narrowly as "the status . . . to maintain the action and not the right to advance arguments of a particular kind, unrelated to the facts of the case. . . ."[84] He held that once standing (in the narrow sense in which he defined it) had been established, there was no restriction on the type of arguments which could be adduced to support a litigant's case. However, this is an exceptional view. In other cases, no distinction has been drawn between situations which, strictly speaking, involve a *jus tertii* and those which involve *locus standi* in the narrow sense, both categories being lumped together under the broad head of *locus standi*. Moreover, the important point is that a similar test has been applied, (save in *McGimpsey*) whichever category was involved: the litigant is required to have an "interest" in both the administrative action (and its consequences) and in the particular defect of which he complains.

Ripeness

There is another theoretical distinction which need only be examined briefly since its existence, independent of standing, has scarcely been examined by the courts. This is the requirement of ripeness, by which a litigant whose interest is likely to be affected by an administrative action or law may not initiate proceedings until the threat has actually materialised or, at any rate, the public body in question has taken concrete steps. He may not, in short, take action in respect of an abstraction or a hypothesis.

This issue (which necessarily is usually associated with the declaratory remedy) arose in *Blythe* v. *Attorney-General (No. 2)*.[85] Here the plaintiffs had formed an organisation known as "The League of Youth" but, anticipating an executive ban, sought a declaration to the effect that the organisation was a

---

[83] [1984] I.R. 36. For further examples, see *L'Henryenat* v. *Ireland* [1983] I.R. 193 and *Madigan* v. *Att.-Gen.* [1986] I.L.R.M. 136.
[84] [1984] I.R. 36, 90.
[85] [1936] I.R. 549.

lawful one. Johnston J. held that the making of a declaratory order lay in the discretion of the court and that jurisdiction must be exercised "judicially" and "cautiously". He added that:

> "It is only *binding* declarations that can be made. That must mean a declaration that is *binding* upon some one else who can, and who, in the opinion of the Court, ought to be bound."[86]

The present case was premature and Johnston J. considered that the case was not a proper one for the exercise of his discretion. In view of the fact that the plaintiffs appeared to have a genuine apprehension that such a ban might be imposed, this seems an unduly narrow approach to take. The issue of ripeness also arose in *East Donegal Co-operative Ltd.* v. *Att.-Gen.*[87] where it was, in fact, discussed under the heading of *locus standi*. The plaintiffs were mart-owners who sought a declaration that the Livestock Marts Act 1967 which had established a licensing system for marts was unconstitutional. They clearly had the necessary *locus standi* in the strict sense of the term to challenge this régime, but the key issue was whether they had taken the action prematurely. Their licences had not been revoked, nor the conduct of their business otherwise interfered with. The Supreme Court, however, concluded that the plaintiffs did have a genuine apprehension that their business activities might be interfered with and that, accordingly, the action was not premature. The rationale for this decision was later expressed by Walsh J. in the following terms:

> "This Court . . . in *East Donegal* expressly rejected the contention that it was necessary for a plaintiff to show that the provisions of the legislation impugned applied not only to the activities in which he was currently engaged but that their application has 'affected his interests adversely.' This decides that a person does not to have to wait to be injured. Once again, the question of sufficiency of interest will depend upon the circumstances of the case and upon what appears to be the extent or nature of the impact of the impugned law on the [applicant's] position."[88]

Similarly, Henchy J. in *Cahill* referred to "an injury or prejudice which he has either suffered or is in imminent danger of suffering."[89] As with *jus tertii* and *locus standi*, the courts have adopted the sensible view with regard to ripeness

---

[86] *Ibid.* 554.
[87] [1970] I.R. 317.
[88] In *The State (Lynch)* v. *Cooney* [1982] I.R. 337, 371. See also, *Curtis* v. *Att.-Gen.* [1985] I.R. 458, 462 where Carroll J. said that:

> "It is not necessary that a determination adversely affecting rights must first be made before a constitutional challenge cn be started. It is sufficient if there is a reasonable apprehension of such determination."

[89] [1980] I.R. 269, 286.

that sufficiency of interest is such a loose, expansive category that there is no value in attempting to draw demarcation lines within it.

7. Relator Actions

The Attorney-General may sue *ex officio* to enforce the law, and no special injury need be shown in such proceedings.[90] The Attorney-General may also sue at the relation (*i.e.* at the instance) of some members of the public in order to stop a breach of the law. The use of the relator action enables a private individual to sue where he might otherwise not have the necessary *locus standi*. In effect, the relator action is a form of *actio popularis*, which is subject to the control of the Attorney-General. However, the Attorney-General is at all times the plaintiff in a relator action:

"It has been settled beyond the possibility of question that the Attorney-General alone is plaintiff. It is true that he generally permits the relator to select a solicitor to conduct the case; but such person is not the solicitor of the relator, but of the Attorney-General, who remains *dominus litis* throughout the proceedings."[91]

Nevertheless, where an undertaking as to damages has been given by the relator, the relator alone will be liable on foot of that undertaking.[92] The grant of the Attorney-General's consent (or "*fiat*") to the relator action simply means that the relator has been conferred with the necessary standing in order to permit him to litigate an arguable case, and does not necessarily imply approval of the proceedings.

Traditionally, by virtue of his role as *parens patriae*, the Attorney-General was regarded as enjoying an *exclusive* role in the enforcement of public rights.[93]

As an example of this, take the facts of *Irish Permanent Building Society Ltd.* v. *Caldwell (No. 1)*[94] which have been mentioned, *supra*.[95] In this case, Keane J. hinted very strongly that the plaintiff would have to be able to show that the decision infringed some *private* right which it enjoyed[96] as the protection of *public* rights was the exclusive preserve of the Attorney-General, or a plaintiff suing at his relation:

---

[90] *Att.-Gen. (O'Duffy)* v. *Appleton* [1907] 1 I.R. 252; *Att.-Gen.* v. *Paperlink Ltd.* [1984] I.L.R.M. 373.

[91] *Att.-Gen. (Humphreys)* v. *Governors of Erasmus Smith's Schools* [1910] 1 I.R. 325, 331, *per* Cherry L.J. (as Attorney-General alone is plaintiff, relator (who was not a barrister) not entitled to appear personally to argue case).

[92] *Att.-Gen. (Martin)* v. *Dublin Corporation* [1983] I.L.R.M. 254.

[93] *Moore* v. *Att.-Gen. for Irish Free State* [1930] I.R. 471; *Gouriet* v. *Union of Post Office Workers* [1978] A.C. 435; *Irish Permanent Building Society Ltd.* v. *Caldwell (No. 1)* [1979] I.L.R.M. 273 and see Casey, *The Office of the Attorney General in Ireland* (Dublin, 1980), pp. 145–157.

[94] [1979] I.L.R.M. 273.

[95] See p. 612.

[96] The plaintiffs subsequently amended their pleadings and averred that the registration of the rival building society had caused them loss and damage: *Irish Permanent Building Society Ltd.* v. *Caldwell (No. 2)* [1981] I.L.R.M. 242.

"I cannot detect any fundamental difference between the law in this country and [the law as stated in England in *Gouriet*] . . . It is at least argu-able that the limitations recognised by the common law on the right of a pri-vate citizen to assert a right public in its nature, without the intervention of the Attorney-General, were not . . . in any way affected by the enactment of the present Constitution."[97]

However the obverse of the widening of standing rules in the context of high constitutional matters established by cases such as *Crotty, McGimpsey* and *Coogan* is the termination of the Attorney's traditional monopoly to enforce public rights. If the standing rules are widened, there is less need to call upon the Attorney-General. It is clear from recent cases that the tra-ditional views expressed in *Caldwell* no longer hold sway at least where funda-mental constitutional rights are concerned. The first of the modern cases to be considered is *Att.-Gen. (Society for the Protection of Unborn Children (Ire-land) Ltd.) v. Open-Door Counselling Ltd.*[98] Here the plaintiff who had orig-inally commenced proceedings without the intervention of the Attorney-General sought to restrain the defendants' counselling activities which, it was claimed, provided active assistance for women seeking to avail of abortion facilities in Great Britain, contrary to Article 40.3.3 of the Constitution. The Attorney-General was subsequently joined at the close of pleadings. It was clear that the plaintiff had *locus standi ex relatione* the Attorney-General, but, in a subsequent judgment, Hamilton P. was required to decide the issue of the costs incurred *prior* to the joining of the Attorney-General. This in turn raised the question of whether the Society would independently have had standing without the benefit of the Attorney-General's intervention. Hamil-ton P. ruled that it was not necessary for the Society to have obtained the *fiat*:

"[H]aving regard to the obvious fact that the unborn themselves cannot seek the protection of the court, the obligation which rests on all organs of government to support the right to life of the unborn must and should be extended to all persons, artificial and real. In bringing these proceedings, the Society was fulfilling this obligation and I have no doubt but that they had *locus standi* to maintain these proceedings."[99]

This question was even more directly at issue in a subsequent case involving the Society: *Society for the Protection of Unborn Children (Ireland) Ltd. v.*

---

[97] [1979] I.L.R.M. 275–276. This view must now be regarded as having been superseded by the judgment of the Supreme Court in *Society for the Protection of Unborn Children (Ireland) Ltd. v. Coogan* [1990] I.L.R.M. 70.
[98] [1988] I.R. 593.
[99] Hamilton P. said in the High Court ([1988] I.R. 604):

"The public interests are committed to the care of the Attorney-General. He is entitled to sue to restrain the commission of an unlawful act, to protect and vindicate a right acknowledged by the Constitution and to prevent the corruption of public morals. I am satisfied that the Attorney-General has the *locus standi* to maintain these proceedings and that when the Attorney-General sues with a relator, the relator need have no personal interest in the subject except his interest as a member of the public: see *Att.-Gen. v. Logan* [1891] 2 Q.B. 100."

Coogan.[1] Here the Society sought to restrain the dissemination of a student publication containing information on abortion services which again was said to infringe Article 40.3.3. On this occasion the Society had not invoked the Attorney-General's protection, but Carroll J. ruled in a very short, *ex tempore* judgment that, without his *fiat*, the Society had no *locus standi* to maintain the proceedings.[2]

The Supreme Court, however, took a different view. Finlay C.J. said that the contention that only the Attorney-General could sue to protect a constitutional right of this nature would represent "a major curtailment of the duty and power of the courts to defend and uphold the Constitution."[3] The Society had the requisite standing, as it had a bona fide and legitimate interest in the outcome of the proceedings.

In a powerful concurring judgment, Walsh J. first observed that:

"The question at issue in the present case is not one of a public right in the classical sense (and I do not subscribe to the view that only the Attorney-General can sue in respect of such public rights) but it is a very unique private right . . . which there is a public interest in preserving . . . It is a right guaranteed by public law, as it is part of the fundamental law of the State by reason of being incorporated into the Constitution. In my view, every member of the public has an interest in seeing that the fundamental law of the State is not defeated."[4]

It was equally clear that the Attorney-General enjoyed no exclusive right to vindicate these constitutional rights:

"[T]he Attorney-General by virtue of his constitutional office also has cast upon him in the appropriate case the duty of defending the Constitution and vindicating the rights conferred or guaranteed by it. He has therefore a sufficient interest at all times to represent the public interest in the protection of the right in question, but not the exclusive right to move in the matter."[5]

Walsh J. also drew attention to the fact that the Attorney-General might be required to defend the actions of either the executive or the Oireachtas:

"If some Department of State or some public health authority with the

---

[1] [1989] I.L.R.M. 526 (H.C.); [1990] I.L.R.M. 70 (S.C.).
[2] She said that ([1989] I.L.R.M. 527):

"The plaintiff has assumed the self appointed role of policing the Supreme Court judgment. In my opinion, it has no right to seek undertakings from citizens and it is the Attorney-General who is the proper party to move in such a case".

[3] [1990] I.L.R.M. 73.
[4] *Ibid.* 75. Griffin J. reserved the question of the role of the Attorney-General and "on the extent or limits" of *Cahill* v. *Sutton* [1980] I.R. 269, but agreed that the Society had standing, as they had a *"bona fide* interest and concern for the unborn."
[5] *Ibid.* 77.

approval, if not the encouragement, of the executive power, were to engage in activities which this Court in the *Open Door Counselling* case restrained as being a violation of the Constitution, it would be an intolerable situation if the defence or vindication of constitutional rights was to be confined to the very officer of State who had been entrusted with the task of defending such impugned activities."[6]

It is clear from the judgment of Walsh J. that these observations are of general application and the decision in *Coogan* does not turn on the constitutional nature of the rights protected by Article 40.3.3. Indeed, O'Hanlon J. appeared to arrive at a similar conclusion in *Parsons* v. *Kavanagh*,[7] where the plaintiff had sought an injunction to restrain the actions of the defendants who were apparently engaged in operating a bus service in competition with her, without having obtained the necessary licence under the Road Transport Act 1932. Although the 1932 Act was passed for the benefit of the public rather than individual licence holders, the plaintiff was entitled to an injunction restraining "unlawful activity which impaired in a significant manner the exercise of her constitutional right to her living by lawful means."[8] Here again we see that the Attorney-General is not accorded any exclusive right to assert the public interest, provided that the private plaintiff can point to an actual or threatened infringement of a constitutional right. It is on the basis of this proviso that this case may be reconciled with the *Cahill* principles examined in the last Part. Moreover, there are recent explicit judicial statements to suggest the Attorney-General does not enjoy an exclusive function to enforce the law, even where constitutional rights are not at stake. In *Coogan*, Walsh J. said that he did not "subscribe to the view" that the Attorney-General enjoyed an exclusive right to enforce public rights.[9] A similar view was hinted at by McCarthy J. in *Att.-Gen. (McGarry)* v. *Sligo County Council*,[10] where the plaintiffs had obtained the *fiat* of the Attorney-General in proceedings whereby they sought to restrain the defendant from constructing a refuse

---

[6] *Ibid.* 75. Barrington J. had also drawn attention to this possible anomaly in *Irish Permanent Building Society* v. *Caldwell (No. 2)* [1981] I.L.R.M. 242. The Attorney-General had refused his *fiat* to the plaintiffs, yet, following discovery of documents, they learned that the Attorney-General had actually advised the defendants as to the conduct of the litigation. McCarthy J. also adverted to this in *The State (Sheehan)* v. *Government of Ireland* [1987] I.R. 550, where the applicant had sought mandamus to compel the Government to bring into force s.60(1) of the Civil Liability Act 1961. Dealing with the argument that the applicant had no standing and that only the Attorney-General could assert such a right, McCarthy J. said ([1987] I.R. 562–563):

"If the prosecutor, or another in like position, does not have *locus standi*, then who has? In theory, the Attorney-General could assert the public right and seek the relief claimed; in practice, this has no reality. The Attorney-General is legal adviser to the Government and presumably, has advised the Government that it is not under the legal obligation for which the prosecutor contends."

[7] [1990] I.L.R.M. 560.
[8] *Ibid.* 567.
[9] [1990] I.L.R.M. 75.
[10] [1989] I.L.R.M. 768.

dump in the vicinity of a national monument. While the issue did not arise for consideration, McCarthy J. said that he must not be taken as "supporting or otherwise" the view of McWilliam J. in the High Court "that it was necessary to bring these proceedings as a relator action."[11]

However, it is worth noting a minority view in *Coogan*, as both Carroll J. in the High Court and McCarthy J. in the Supreme Court expressed concern at the prospect of private individuals or pressure groups being equipped to police the activities of other private persons by commencing litigation which is founded on some political, ideological or religious motivation, rather than some personal grievance which is justiciable at law. Accordingly, McCarthy J. in his dissenting judgment sought to restate the traditional rule that ordinarily it is the Attorney-General, as the defender of public rights, who can enforce public rights. However, he addressed the concerns voiced by the majority judges by proposing two exceptions to the general rule:

"If the Government, through the legislature or otherwise, were to act so as to breach [Art. 40.3.3], it must *a priori* be open to any citizen to call the judicial organ of government in aid. If the feared breach is through the act of some other person or body, immediacy may require personal initiation of the suit. The only requirement in either case would be a *bona fide* intent . . ."[12]

McCarthy J. added that he differed only from the majority in what "may properly be permitted" thereafter:

"In my view, it is the Attorney-General, and he alone, who can in such a case validly pursue that claim to protect the right of the unborn to judgment."[13]

Finally, two queries may be raised with regard to the Attorney's decision to grant or not grant his consent to a relator action. However, this may be done very briefly. For, if, as has just been argued, the standing rules in regard to constitutional and public matters have been substantially relaxed, then the Attorney's decision in this field is of less significance than formerly. The first is whether, as is the case in England, the Attorney's decision to grant his consent is immune from judicial review. Professor Casey has argued that it is open to the Irish courts to hold that the Attorney-General's consent is no more unfettered than that of a Minister, and that if the Attorney-General's

---

[11] *Ibid.* 773. See also, *Martin* v. *Dublin Corporation*, High Court, November 14, 1977, where Costello J. granted an interlocutory injunction to restrain building operations on a site which the plaintiff, a distinguished Professor of Medieval History, claimed was a national monument. The Corporation had argued that the plaintiff lacked *locus standi*, but Costello J. disagreed, saying that he thought that, at the trial of the action, the plaintiff would be able to establish that the general approach of the courts in constitutional cases should be followed in cases where a citizen claimed that a public body was not carrying out the law.
[12] [1990] I.L.R.M. 70, 83.
[13] *Ibid.*

consent is unreviewable, this will be "a situation unique in Irish law."[14] As things stand, it is not possible to predict with confidence what attitude Irish courts will take to the question of the reviewability (or otherwise) of the Attorney-General's decision: this is a matter which must await judicial resolution.

Secondly, despite our relatively relaxed standing rules, there is still a rule regarding standing and, accordingly, cases may occur from time to time which do not come within existing *Cahill* v. *Sutton* exceptions and where the intervention of the Attorney-General may still be required. Could Mrs. Cahill, for example, have either sought or compelled the Attorney-General to intervene on her behalf to argue the constitutionality of section 11(2)(b) of the Statute of Limitations 1957? One may expect that, in practice, the majority of such cases which fall outside the exceptions will not involve fundamental constitutional issues and are unlikely to be situations in which the Attorney-General will feel impelled to intervene.

Thirdly, the discussion so far has concerned the Attorney-General's *exclusive* right to intervene. As already suggested, this has been shrunk by the expansion of the private citizen's right to take action. However, this does not affect the fact that the Attorney-General retains a right to intervene in a wide area touching on public rights, albeit this is no longer exclusive to him. In practice, this means that even where a private citizen has standing, but elects not to do so, the Attorney may intervene.

Finally, we may ask whether relator proceedings have survived the enactment of the Constitution. As we have seen, the issue of standing is primarily a question for the courts and the standing requirements have been formulated with the interests of proper administration of justice in mind. Thus, on the one hand, the courts will not allow unrestricted standing (as this might lead to a possible abuse of the judicial power). Accordingly, a procedure whereby a non-judicial personage such as the Attorney-General could effectively confer standing on a plaintiff might appear to be an unconstitutional interference with the administration of justice. Moreover, the very fact that the Attorney-General is supposed to act judicially and weigh up evidence before deciding to grant his fiat might lead one to suppose that he was exercising judicial powers which are not of a limited nature, contrary to Article 34.1, although it may be noted that analogous arguments have been rejected by the courts in the context of the Attorney's functions under the Extradition (Amendment) Act 1987.[15] The equivalent argument may not necessarily work in reverse. In the days of a strict standing rule, it was the judges themselves who imposed such limitation. Accordingly, an Attorney-General who refused to assist a litigant,

---

[14] *The Office of the Attorney General in Ireland* (Dublin, 1980) at p. 156. Professor Casey rests his argument on cases such as *East Donegal Co-operatives Ltd.* v. *Att.-Gen.* [1970] I.R. 317 which stress that all exercises of administrative discretion should, in principle, be open to review. Contrast *Macauley* v. *Minister for Posts and Telegraphs* [1966] I.R. 345, 346 ("[T]he Attorney-General is free to grant or withhold his *fiat* . . . for any reason and if he decides to withhold it, no proceedings to review his decision can successfully be brought in the courts.")

[15] *Wheeler* v. *Culligan* [1989] I.R. 344.

with no individual interest, to circumvent a strict standing rule, could hardly be said to be interfering with the administration of justice by the courts. Finally, one ought to note a judicial observation which provides some sustenance for the present line of thought. In *Coogan*, Walsh J. remarked:

> "[T]here must be some doubt on the question of whether any statute could validly seek to exclude members of the public from calling in aid the judicial power in defence of the public interest in the vindication of constitutional rights."[16]

---

[16] [1990] I.L.R.M. 77.

CHAPTER 12

DAMAGES

1. Damages and Judicial Review

Prior to the introduction of the new Rules of Court in 1986 it was not possible to combine a claim for damages with an application for a State side order, although such a claim could be combined with an application for a declaration or injunction. If damages were sought, it was necessary to commence separate proceedings.[1] It may be surmised that prior to the procedural changes effected by the new Rules in 1986 many litigants were content to secure the invalidation of the impugned administrative act, and were not prepared to commence separate proceedings in order to press their claim for damages. The new Rules of Court seek to rectify this procedural anomaly by providing for a new unified judicial review procedure. The new Order 84, rule 24 empowers the court to grant damages in addition to, or in lieu of, a State side order, or a declaration or an injunction. Order 84, rule 24 provides as follows:

"(1) On an application for judicial review the Court may, subject to paragraph (2), award damages to an applicant if

    (a) he has included in the statement in support of his application for leave under [Ord. 84, r. 20(3)] a claim for damages arising for any matter to which the application relates, and

    (b) the Court is satisfied that, if the claim had been made in a civil action against any respondent or respondents begun by the applicant at the time of making this application, he would have been awarded damages.

  (2) Order 19, rules 5 and 7[2] shall apply to a statement relating to a claim for damages as it applies to a pleading."

The effect of these changes has been to make it easier for applicants to

---

[1] Law Reform Commission, *Judicial Review of Administrative Action*, Working Paper No. 8, 1979, pp. 4–5.

[2] Ord. 19, r. 5 provides in relevant part that:

> "In all cases alleging a wrong within the meaning of the Civil Liability Acts 1961–1964, particulars of such wrong, any personal injuries suffered and any items of special damage shall be set out in the statement of claim or counterclaim and particulars of any contributory negligence shall be set out in the defence."

Ord. 19, r. 7 deals with particulars. In effect, this means that all claims for damages in an application for judicial review must be fully pleaded in a manner analogous to that required in a plenary hearing. In *Duggan* v. *An Taoiseach* [1989] I.L.R.M. 710, 731 Hamilton P. required that the plaintiffs "submit a statement of claim setting forth the loss which they alleged they have and are likely to suffer" before a judge of the High Court could assess the damages to which they were entitled by reason of a breach of their legitimate expectations.

633

recover damages in respect of wrongful administrative action and such claims are now made with increasing frequency.

One practical problem which is likely to arise is whether it is possible to proceed via the Order 84 procedure where the applicant's claim is *solely* for damages. The strict language of Order 84, rule 24(1)(a) would seem to suggest a negative answer to this query, as the wording of this rule appears to imply that the court's jurisdiction to award damages presupposes the independent existence of an application for judicial review. In other words the remedy of damages is only *ancillary* to the principal remedies of certiorari, prohibition, declaration, etc. and this would seem to imply that the judicial review procedure should not be availed of where damages are the principal remedy sought by the applicant. Yet this construction of Order 84, rule 24(1)(a) would seem to give rise to its own difficulties.

Assume that an applicant wishes to claim damages by way of an application for judicial review for false imprisonment and breach of constitutional rights following an unlawful arrest under section 30 of the Offences against the State Act 1939 on the ground that the extension order authorising a further 24 hours detention was unlawful.[3] It is, of course, open to him to proceed by way of plenary summons, but for reasons of speed and convenience he elects to seek damages by way of judicial review. The applicant will certainly encounter procedural difficulties if he merely seeks damages, but with a view to circumventing these problems, he may be advised to apply for an order of certiorari quashing the extension order. Such an application for certiorari is not vexatious or spurious if the applicant genuinely wishes to demonstrate the invalidity of this extension order. But what if the application for certiorari is included simply to circumvent possible procedural difficulties? In such a case are the courts to bar the applicant's path and direct that he proceed by way of plenary summons rather than on an application for judicial review? A further difficulty is illustrated by the English case of *R.* v *Home Secretary ex p. Dew.*[4] Here a prisoner sought mandamus to compel the prison authorities to provide him with adequate medical treatment and damages for negligence. After the initial *ex parte* application had been made, the prison authorities undertook to provide the required medical treatment so that the applicant was left with his claim for damages. In those circumstances, Neill J. ruled that the claim for damages could not proceed and struck out the judicial review proceedings. It would be undesirable if the equivalent rule in this jurisdiction were to be interpreted so narrowly, but given its wording, such a conclusion would seem almost inevitable.

2. Common Law Defences to Actions in Tort

As a general proposition, it is true to say that neither the State nor any other public authority enjoys any special position in the law of torts. The general

---

[3] See *People* v. *Byrne* [1987] I.R. 363.
[4] [1987] 1 W.L.R. 881.

law—trespass, negligence, nuisance, breach of statutory duty, etc.,—applies in substantially the same way as to a private person. This is an important aspect of the rule of law and damages actions are an effective means of securing judicial protection against unlawful administrative action.

Most of the special immunities and exemptions for public bodies, which are considered presently, are statutory in origin. However, one common law exception is the immunity enjoyed by local authorities in respect of damage caused by non-repair of the highway. The principle that a local authority is not liable for an injury to a user of the highway caused by a hole in the road resulting from failure to repair can be traced back to *Russell* v. *The Men Dwelling in the County of Devon.*[5] The basis of this immunity is that at common law the duty of repairing highways fell on the community, (though by virtue of a statute of 1612,[6] this duty was imposed on the parish). Because the inhabitants were not a corporation they could not be sued collectively and therefore no action lay against them in respect of their failure to carry out their duty. Despite the changes wrought by the Local Government (Ireland) Act 1898—most notably the imposition, by section 82, on every county and district council of the duty of keeping the road in good condition and repair—the position remained the same.[7] The distinction between non-feasance and misfeasance has been judicially described as both "unsatisfactory"[8] and "anomalous,"[9] but was regarded as sufficiently well-established to warrant its abrogation by statute. Section 60 of the Civil Liability Act 1961 provides in sub-section (1) that:

> "A local authority shall be liable for damages caused as a result of their failure to maintain adequately a public road."

Subsection (7), however, provides that the section is to come into operation on such day, not earlier than April 1, 1967, as might be fixed by order of the Government, and no such order has yet been made. In *The State (Sheehan)* v. *Government of Ireland*[10] Costello J. held that the Government had failed in its statutory duty and made an order of mandamus directed against the Government compelling them to bring section 60 into effect.[11] A majority of

---

[5] (1788) 2 T.R. 667.
[6] 11, 12 & 13 Jac. 1, c. 7 (Ir.), following the lines of the 1555 English statute (2 & 3 Ph. & M., c. 8).
[7] *Harbinson* v. *Armagh C.C.* [1902] 2 I.R. 538. The reasons for this restrictive approach were explained by Johnson J. (at 560–561):

> "To create such a liability a legislative enactment in express and affirmative terms is necessary, which should show that the Legislature in transferring the duty to this corporate body intended to change the nature and extent of their liability. . . . I do not find anything in these enactments . . . which shows . . . any intention of the Legislature to impose on the corporate county council or on the ratepayers whom they represent a new liability which did not previously exist at common law or by statute, for non-feasance. . . . "

[8] *Kelly* v. *Mayo C.C.* [1964] I.R. 315, 324, *per* Kingsmill Moore J.
[9] *O'Brien* v. *Waterford C.C.* [1926] I.R. 1, 8, per Murnaghan J.
[10] [1987] I.R. 550. This case is further discussed at pp. 554–557.
[11] This order was stayed for a six-month period to allow an appeal to be taken to the Supreme Court.

the Supreme Court, however, took a different view, with Henchy J. holding in effect that the discretion vested in the Government was unreviewable.[12]

It is nonetheless possible, despite the result in *Sheehan*, that, given recent developments in the general law of civil liability,[13] the Supreme Court would react favourably to arguments that road authorities are not immune from liability in respect of negligent non-feasance. Since *Purtill* v. *Athlone U.D.C.*,[14] the Irish courts have steadily recognised the existence of a duty of care in situations where formerly it had been held that the defendant was exempt from responsibility (*e.g.* liability of occupier to trespasser,[15] liability of builder to second purchaser,[16] liability of animal owners[17]) and the rule would seem to be at variance with the march of the modern law of negligence. Moreover, the immunity would also appear to be constitutionally suspect. Might not a plaintiff injured in an accident due to a hole in the road and unable to recover compensation because of the non-feasance principle, claim that the State has failed to vindicate fully, as required by Article 40.3 of the Constitution of Ireland, his right to bodily integrity and the right to litigate a jusiciable controversy? Such a claim would be merely the invocation, in the context of a local authority, of the principles established in *Byrne* v. *Ireland*.[18]

A wider principle is the rule that at common law, where a statute authorises the doing of a particular act, then no action will lie at the suit of any person if the inevitable consequence of the act is to cause damage, provided, of course, that it is done without negligence.[19] In *Kelly* v. *Dublin C.C.*[20] the defendant local authority had made use of a vacant site beside the plaintiff's cottage for the purpose of storing vehicles and materials used in an extensive road construction project. The plaintiffs claimed that these activities amounted to an actionable nuisance, but the defendants argued that they enjoyed statutory

---

[12] *Ibid.* 561. Note that in Northern Ireland the law was changed by the Roads (Liability of Road Authorities for Neglect) Act (Northern Ireland) 1966. Section 1(1) of this Act abrogated any rule of law which operated to exempt road authorities from liability for non-repair of roads. The law was further amended by the Roads (Northern Ireland) Order 1980, Art. 8(1), which imposes an express duty on the Department of Environment to maintain all roads and to provide such maintenance compounds as it think fit. In *McKernan* v. *McGeown and Department of the Environment* [1983] N.I. 167, Gibson L.J. said, however, that there was no difference between the nature and extent of liability under the 1966 Act and the 1980 Order. As to liability under the 1966 Act, see *Lagan* v. *Department of the Environment* [1978] N.I. 120.
[13] In *Forsyth* v. *Evans* [1980] N.I. 230 Kelly J. said that he was attracted "to the view that the neighbour principle of *Donoghue* v. *Stevenson* [1932] A.C. 562 might be applied having regard to modern day conditions and their extensive user." He was satisfied that there was "a sufficient relationship of proximity or neighbourhood" between a highway authority and the drivers and passengers of motor vehicles on highways. He considered, however, that there were sufficient considerations of public policy which justified the non-extension of the neighbour principle in this situation. (The case concerned the Department of the Environment's failure to minimise the hazards of weather on road surfaces).
[14] [1968] I.R. 205.
[15] *McNamara* v. *E.S.B.* [1975] I.R. 1.
[16] *Ward* v. *McMaster* [1985] I.R. 29. See Kerr (1985) 7 D.U.L.J. (N.S.) 109.
[17] *Gillick* v. *O'Reilly* [1984] I.L.R.M. 402.
[18] [1972] I.R. 241.
[19] *Geddis* v. *Proprietors of the Bann Reservoir* (1873) 3 App.Cas. 430; *Allen* v. *Gulf Oil Refining Ltd.* [1981] A.C. 1001.
[20] High Court, February 21, 1986.

protection under the Local Government Act 1925. O'Hanlon J. found that the activities in question amounted to a nuisance which was not authorised by the 1925 Act. While the 1925 Act afforded protection to the defendant's road construction work, it did not extend to the provision and use of a depot for vehicles and materials. In any event, O'Hanlon J. held that the defendants had not shown that the nuisance was an inevitable result of the exercise of the statutory powers. There was no evidence to show that the Council had no reasonable alternative but to use this particular site for these purposes.

Where the damage is caused not by acting in pursuance of statutory functions, but by going beyond them, then the remedy and the calculation of damages has to be dealt with by the general law. So, for example, in *Red Cow Service Station Ltd.* v. *Murphy International Ltd. and Bord Gáis Éireann*[21] it was held that, while under section 27(1)(*d*) of the Gas Act 1976 Bord Gáis Éireann has the power to dig or break or interfere with any road, if they acted negligently, *e.g.* broke a telephone cable and caused damage to the plaintiff beyond what was essential and necessary, they could not claim the protection of the Act. The 1976 Act provides a particular remedy and method of computation for any loss caused by the operation of the Act.

The principle that *intra vires* administrative decisions are not actionable has its most important application in cases where public bodies are authorised to commit what might otherwise be a nuisance. In *Allen* v. *Gulf Oil Refining Ltd.*[22] a private Act of Parliament had authorised the defendant to construct a refinery but it did not specifically authorise the operation of the refinery, and some neighbours who complained of excessive smell, vibration and noise sued in nuisance. The House of Lords ruled that the operation of the refinery was authorised at least by necessary implication—and as a result the plaintiffs had no remedy in so far as the nuisance complained of was the inevitable result of the authorised operation.

It is difficult to believe that an Irish court would reach the same conclusion were it faced with a case on similar facts. If the Act had plainly extinguished the landowner's right to sue in respect of such a nuisance, an Irish court would probably rule that such provisions amounted to an unconstitutional attack on his right to sue in court or to recover compensation in respect of this state interference with their property rights.[23] If the statute were silent in the matter, the court would probably apply the presumption of constitutionality in order to rule that there was no overt legislative intention to act in an uncon-

---

[21] (1985) 3 I.L.T. (N.S.) 15. In *Collins* v. *Gypsum Industries Ltd.* [1975] I.R. 321, the plaintiffs had claimed damages for personal injuries under the Mineral Development Act 1940. The Supreme Court held, however, that the 1940 Act provided for a scheme of compensation in respect of damage to land caused by mining operations and it did not extend to personal injuries. The proper forum for pursuing such a claim for personal injuries was that provided by the ordinary courts. See also, *Tate & Lyle Food Distribution Co. Ltd.* v. *Greater London Council* [1983] 2 A.C. 509.

[22] [1981] A.C. 1001.

[23] Unless, of course, this was a case where the requirements of social justice and the exigencies of the common good did not require the payment of compensation: see *O'Callaghan* v. *Commissioners of Public Works* [1985] I.L.R.M. 364.

stitutional fashion, and that the Oireachtas did not intend to deprive the plaintiff of his right to sue in nuisance.

3. Statutory Rules of Immunity for Particular Sectors

There are, however, special rules creating immunity for particular areas of governmental action. As these exceptions are heterogenuous, they may be considered separately.

(i) *Treatment of the mentally ill*

Leave of the High Court is required where it is sought to institute civil proceedings against a health board in respect of acts purporting to have been done in pursuance of the Mental Treatment Act 1945 (which is a comprehensive statute providing for the treatment of mental disturbance and the care of persons suffering therefrom: see *In Re Phillip Clarke*).[24] The 1945 Act, section 260(1), which provides for the requirement of leave, goes on to state that such leave shall only be granted where the High Court is satisfied that there are substantial grounds for contending that the person against whom the proceedings are to be brought acted in bad faith or without reasonable care. The meaning of "substantial grounds" was considered by the Supreme Court in *O'Dowd* v. *North Western Health Board*,[25] where O'Higgins C.J. said that the section did no more than require the applicant:

> "To discharge the same onus of proof as he would be required to discharge in pursuing a claim for damages for a tort outside the Act, but to discharge it at an earlier point in time."[26]

In this case, a majority of the Supreme Court held that a mental patient who had been discharged after only six days of custody had not established "substantial grounds" within the meaning of section 260. It was true that the initial medical diagnosis was that the plaintiff was unlikely to recover within six months, but both O'Higgins C.J. and Griffin J. considered that on the facts, there was nothing to suggest that this diagnosis had been incorrect or had been arrived at in a negligent fashion.

(ii) *Postal and telecommunications services*

Special provision is also made by section 64 of the Postal and Telecommunications Services Act 1983 which provides that *An Post* shall be immune from all liability in respect of any loss or damage suffered by a person in the use of a postal service by reason of (i) failure or delay in providing, operating or maintaining a postal service, or, (ii) failure, interruption, suspension or restriction of a postal service. Similarly, members of staff are immune from civil liability except at the suit of An Post itself in respect of any such loss or damage. Section 88 of the 1983 Act provides a similar immunity to Bord Tele-

---

[24] [1950] I.R. 235.
[25] [1983] I.L.R.M. 186.
[26] *Ibid*. 190. See also, *Murphy* v. *Greene*, Supreme Court, December 18, 1990.

com Éireann in respect of loss or damage suffered by reason of failure, etc., of a telecommunications service or any error or omission in a directory published by Bord Telecom itself or any telegrams or telex messages transmitted by the company.[27]

(iii) *Special Criminal Court*

Article 38.3 of the Constitution allows for the establishment of special courts where the ordinary courts "are inadequate to secure the effective administration of justice and the preservation of public peace and order." Part V of the Offences against the State Act 1939 regulates, *inter alia*, the composition, practice and procedure of the Special Criminal Court. Since the ordinary constitutional guarantees do not apply to this Court and in view of its extraordinary nature, it is, perhaps, not surprising that section 53(1) of the 1939 Act should provide *ex abundante cautela*[28] that:

> "No action, prosecution, or other proceeding, civil or criminal, shall lie against any member of a Special Criminal Court in respect of any order made, conviction or sentence pronounced, or other thing done by that Court or in respect of anything done by such member in the course of the performance of his duties or the exercise of his powers as a member of that Court, whether such thing was or was not necessary to the performance of such duties or the exercise of such powers."

Section 53(2) confers an immunity from defamation in respect of anything "written or said by [a witness] in giving evidence before a Special Criminal Court" and section 53(3) provides for a complete immunity in respect of anything done by a registrar, clerk or servant of the court in the performance of their duties, irrespective of "whether such thing was or was not necessary to the performance of such duties."

(iv) *Defence Forces*

Section 111 of the Defence Act 1954 provides that, where any action is commenced against any person for any act done in pursuance, execution or intended execution of the Act or in respect of any alleged neglect or default in the execution of the Act, the action must be brought in the High Court and

---

[27] The British Post Office enjoys a similar immunity which is of long standing and now contained in the British Telecommunications Act 1981, s.29. For cases where the Post Office has been permitted to avail of these generous statutory immunities, see *Triefus & Co. Ltd.* v. *Post Office* [1957] Q.B. 353; *Stephen Harold & Co. Ltd.* v. *Post Office* [1977] 1 W.L.R. 1171 and *American Express Co.* v. *British Airports Board* [1983] 1 W.L.R. 701. A similar immunity which was enjoyed by British Telecom was repealed by the Telecommunications Act 1984. Wade, *Administrative Law* (6th ed.), pp. 106, 107 sees "no good reason" for such immunities and thinks it surprising that they "are still tolerated."

[28] The Special Criminal Court would in any case presumably benefit from the common law immunity attaching to judicial acts, in so far as that immunity has survived the enactment of the Constitution: see pp. 716–717. For a full discussion of the jurisdiction and work of the Special Criminal Court, see Hogan and Walker, *Political Violence and the Law in Ireland* (Manchester, 1989), pp. 227–244.

must be instituted within six months of the act, neglect or default complained of. This provision is modelled on the Public Authorities (Protection) Act 1893 which provided that any action, prosecution or proceeding against any person for any act done in pursuance, execution or intended execution of any, *inter alia*, public duty or authority should not lie or be instituted unless it was commenced within six months after the act, neglect or default complained of. The 1893 Act, however, was repealed by the Public Authorities (Judicial Proceedings) Act 1954 and actions against public authorities, other than the Defence Forces, are now subject to the general provisions of the Statute of Limitations 1957. In *Ryan* v. *Ireland*[29] the Supreme Court held that section 111 had no relevance to a case where it was alleged that officers of the Defence Forces had been guilty of *common law* negligence in the performance of their duties.

(v) *Fire services*

A complete immunity is given by section 36 of the Fire Services Act 1981[30] to fire and sanitary authorities who are discharging their fire safety, fire fighting and fire protection functions under this Act. This section provides:

"No action or other proceeding shall lie or be maintainable against the Minister, or against a fire authority or a sanitary authority or any officer or servant of, or person engaged by, any such authority for recovery of damages in respect of injury to persons or property alleged to have been caused or contributed to by the failure to comply with any functions conferred by this Act."

(vi) *Miscellaneous*

An interesting example of an immunity for certain foreign customs officials is provided by section 6 of the Air Navigation and Transport (Pre-Inspection) Act 1986 (A statutory formulation of state immunity). This legislation allows the United States Immigration and Naturalization Service to carry out in Ireland the inspection required, under United States law, relating to immigration and public health of all persons travelling thereto by air. Section 6(1) now provides that:

"A citizen of the United States, who is a permanent employee of the government of the United States and is assigned to carry out duties at a pre-inspection facility, shall not be amenable to the jurisdiction of the judicial

---

[29] [1989] I.R. 177.

[30] This immunity was originally contained in s.5(2) of the Fire Brigade Act 1940 (which was repealed and replaced by the Fire Services Act 1981) and the reasons for the immunity were given as follows by the Parliamentary Secretary for Local Government at the Committee Stage of the Bill: *Dáil Debates*, Vol. 78, col. 7145 (February 21, 1940).

"If damage caused by the outbreak of a particular fire could be made the basis of a claim against the local authority, it is considered that public funds might be liable to be applied towards compensation which can at present be obtained only on the basis of a contractual arrangement between a private person and an insurance company."

or administrative authorities of the State in respect of acts performed by him in the exercise of his duties . . . ."

Another recent example is provided by section 61 of the Safety, Health and Welfare at Work Act 1989 which confers a complete immunity on the National Authority for Occupational Safety and Health.

4. Constitutionality of Statutory Rules of Immunity

The issue of whether it is competent for the Oireachtas to establish special rules of immunity or even to confer complete immunity from suit is something which has never been directly judicially considered. The Supreme Court's decision in *Byrne* v. *Ireland*[31] would seem to suggest that such immunities are constitutionally vulnerable, as being inconsistent with the State's obligation under Article 40.3 to defend and vindicate individual personal rights. This is reinforced by *Ryan* v. *Ireland*,[32] where the Supreme Court held that common law immunities relieving the Defence Forces from liability in respect of injuries to soldiers engaged on active service were unconstitutional. If such is the case, then surely a shadow must hang over the validity of section 36 of the Fire Services Act 1981, at least in so far as it precludes a fireman from suing a fire authority in respect of the negligent discharge of their statutory duties under the 1981 Act. It is difficult to see how such an immunity could survive if an analogous common law immunity enjoyed by the Defence Forces has been condemned as unconstitutional. And while it is easy to understand the legislative intention to favour the rescue services and to ensure that they will not be hampered by the threat of legal action, the absolute nature of this immunity seems hard to justify. Again, what of the fire authority which through some gross act of negligence on its part, failed to answer a distress call? Certainly major constitutional issues would be raised should the authority seek to fall back in such circumstances on the provisions of section 36 of the 1981 Act in order to defend itself against an action for negligence.

One way of justifying such immunities might be to adopt the reasoning in *Pine Valley* and say that, the personal rights guarantees contained in Article 40.3 are not absolute and that the Oireachtas has to balance the common good against them and that in some instances no action will lie for negligence or breach of duty. Such an immunity might, therefore, be justified on the basis of public policy grounds either in order to protect persons performing an essential social service (such as firemen) or some implied constitutional value (such as the independence of persons performing judicial or quasi-judicial functions). However, arguments along these lines were emphatically rejected in *Ryan* (even if the reasoning in this case appears to be out of line with *Pine Valley* a decision which was not even mentioned in the judgment of Finlay C.J.) and this must cast some doubt over the validity of many of the statutory

---

[31] [1972] I.R. 241.
[32] [1989] I.R. 177.

immunities already referred to. One possible compromise would be that not all special rules of immunity or quasi-immunity are *per se* unconstitutional, but a complete and absolute immunity (such as that contained in sections 64 and 88 of the Postal and Telecommunications Services Act 1983) seem susceptible to a successful constitutional challenge.

5. Governmental Liability and Judicial Control of Administrative Action

It is a cardinal principle that there is no *direct* relationship between the power of the court to annul an administrative act and liability to pay damages or monetary compensation. When a court annuls an administrative act on procedural grounds, that decision is deemed to be *ultra vires* and void *ab initio*. However, it does not follow that a declaration of invalidity of an administrative decision in and of itself gives rise to a cause of action in damages. It seems that an invalid administrative act will sound in damages only if:

(i) it involves the commission of a recognised tort, such as false imprisonment, trespass or negligence;

(ii) where the invalid act was motivated by malice or the authority knew that it did not have the power which it purports to exercise, *i.e.* the tort of misfeasance of public office;

(iii) there is a breach of statutory duty; or

(iv) the invalid act amounts to an infringement of a personal constitutional right or a breach of the plaintiff's legitimate expectations.

It remains to consider each of these categories.

(i) *The commission of a recognised tort*

There are many heterogeneous examples of cases where either the State or public officials have been found liable for recognised torts such as false imprisonment, trespass or negligence, following a finding that the relevant decisions in question have been found to be *ultra vires*. In *Gildea* v. *Hipwell*,[33] for example, the Governor of Sligo Prison was held liable in damages for false imprisonment for wrongfully detaining the plaintiff pursuant to an invalid arrest warrant. Likewise in *McGowan* v. *Farrell*[34] the State was held vicariously liable for false imprisonment, following the wrongful arrest of the plaintiff by a Garda who did not realise that an outstanding fine had, in fact, been paid. There are also numerous examples where either individual Garda

[33] [1942] I.R. 489. The question arises as to whether the prison governor could now rely on the *Pine Valley* defence, *viz.* that he was discharging a public duty in good faith without notice of the invalidity.

[34] *The Irish Times*, February 15, 1975. See also, *McIntyre* v. *Lewis*, Supreme Court, December 18, 1990.

or the State itself have been liable for wrongful arrest.[35] Strangely enough, there do not appear to be any reported cases of either the State or public officials being found liable in trespass, but presumably such officials would be liable in trespass where they searched a dwelling on foot of an invalid search warrant.

Liability in negligence is dealt with elsewhere.[36]

(ii) *Misfeasance of public office*

Quite independently of any developments on the constitutional front, Irish law recognises the tort of "misfeasance in public office," although there are but few authorities directly in point. The tort of misfeasance in public office is committed where an act is performed by a public official, either maliciously, or with actual knowledge that it is committed without jurisdiction, and is so done with the known consequence that it would injure the plaintiff.[37] Two cases which deal with related questions are *Johnston* v. *Meldon*[38] and *Ó Conghaile* v. *Wallace*.[39]

In *Johnston* the plaintiff, who had been convicted by magistrates of a statutory offence of unlawful fishing, was fined and imprisoned, in default of payment of the fine. The plaintiff had set up a defence of a bona fide claim to fish where he did, and had raised an issue as to the ownership of the fisheries where the acts complained of had taken place. The conviction was accordingly quashed on the grounds that the plaintiff had raised a question of title which the magistrates had no jurisdiction to decide. However, the Court of Exchequer held that, *absent* malice, the plaintiff's claim for false imprisonment must fail even though the conviction had been quashed. The magistrates had fallen into legal error in the course of an adjudication in respect of a matter which they had authority to decide, but this of itself was not actionable. But the Court implied that the result might have been different if the magistrates had actual knowledge of the irregularity. This principle was confirmed by the Supreme Court in *Ó Conghaile* v. *Wallace*, where Fitzgibbon J. stated that where a public official acts in good faith on foot of an order of a court or tribunal of competent jurisdiction, he is protected against an action for damages in respect of anything done by him before that order is quashed for procedural impropriety. Again, the Court intimated that different considerations would arise if the official had actual knowledge of the irregularity,

---

[35] See, *e.g. Lynch* v. *Fitzgerald* [1938] I.R. 382 where a detective was held personally liable in an action under the Fatal Accident Act 1846.

[36] At pp. 655–668.

[37] It is difficult to improve on the following definition of the tort given by Smith J. in *Farrington* v. *Thomson* (1959) V.R. 286, 293:

"[I]f a public official does an act which, to his knowledge, amounts to an abuse of his office, and he thereby causes damage to another person, then an action in tort for misfeasance of public office will lie at the suit of that other person."

See also, *Roncarelli* v. *Duplessis* (1959) 16 D.L.R. (2d) 689 and *David* v. *Abdul Cader* [1963] 1 W.L.R. 834.

[38] (1891) 30 L.R.Ir. 13.

[39] [1938] I.R. 526.

or where the court or tribunal which made the order was not one of competent jurisdiction.[40]

This entire question appears to have been considered in any detail in only four Irish cases. In *McDonald* v. *Bord na gCon (No. 3)*,[41] disciplinary action was taken against a greyhound owner by the members of the Control Committee of the Dogs Board. The Control Committee was established by a statutory instrument made under the Greyhound Industry Act 1958. Kenny J. found that this establishment order was actually invalid and it followed that the exclusion order which they purported to make was also *ultra vires*. But did this finding of invalidity of itself entitle the plaintiff to succeed in his claim for damages? Kenny J. answered this question in the negative, saying first that he accepted the proposition that:

"[A] member of a corporate body or of an unincorporated association who is expelled from it is entitled to recover damages if his expulsion is not in accordance with the rules of the body of which he is a member because his expulsion amounts to a breach of contract. I also accept the proposition that a violation of a legal right committed knowingly is a legal wrong for which damages may be awarded if there is no sufficient justification for it. But . . . this does not assist the plaintiff because there was never a contract between the plaintiff and the Board and because the members of the Board acted honestly and without malice."[42]

In addition, the judge continued:

"I think that the law . . . is that anyone who has been damaged by such a tribunal acting in a matter in which it had no jurisdiction is entitled to damages for usurpation of jurisdiction. . . . I emphasis that [this only] relates to the position where they had no jurisdiction to make the award or punishment which they did."[43]

But, somewhat surprisingly, Kenny J. held that even on this basis, the plaintiff's claim in the instant case failed because the Board had acted within the jurisdiction as far as the issue of damages was concerned:

"The order is invalid, not because the Board had not jurisdiction to make it, but because the procedure which they adopted was incorrect. I think that it is incorrect to speak of what they did as *ultra vires*. If the members of the Board had carried out the investigation into the alterations in the identity card and if they had heard the plaintiff, the Board would not have exceeded

[40] *Ibid.* 555. Fitzgibbon J. observed that:

"There is, however, authority for the proposition that officers are supposed, or presumed, to know the general jurisdiction of the tribunals whose orders they are bound to prepare or execute, and that they may be liable in trespass if they prepare or execute an order which shows upon its face that it is outside the general jurisdiction of the tribunal which professed to make it."

[41] High Court, January 13, 1966.
[42] *Ibid.* pp. 39–40 of the judgment.
[43] *Ibid.* p. 4.

its jurisdiction in making the order. It follows, in my opinion, that the plaintiff is not entitled to damages against the Board. Moreover, I do not think that the members of the Control Committee knew or had any means of knowing that they had no jurisdiction to deal with the matter. The regulations have all the sign of having been prepared by someone with legal qualifications and the members of the committee acted reasonably in assuming that the regulations were valid."[44]

Taken together, these two passages seem to suggest that, first, an order made by a tribunal who had no jurisdiction whatever to deal with the matter (in the sense of having no "original" jurisdiction) can give rise to liability in damages irrespective (it seems) of the knowledge of the members of the tribunal and, secondly, that in all other cases, something akin to malice must be proved in order to establish liability for the tort of misfeasance of public office.

A similar view appears to have been taken in the more recent cases. In the first of these, *Corliss* v. *Ireland*,[45] the plaintiffs, who were detective police officers, sued for defamation and the question arose as to whether the pleadings disclosed a reasonable cause of action. The defamation was said to have arisen by reason of the fact that the plaintiffs had been transferred by the Garda Commissioner under section 8(1) of the Police Forces Amalgamation Act 1923 from the Crimes Section of the Technical Bureau of the Garda Síochána to alternative duties, thereby giving rise to the implication that they were not fit for their original duties. Hamilton J. held that the pleadings did disclose a cause of action, as they raised the question of whether the Commissioner had acted bona fide and he agreed that if it could be established that the transfer order was malicious—as opposed merely to establishing that it was invalid—then liability in damages could arise. The onus of proof was on the plaintiffs, but he added that:

"Want of probable cause and malice are not necessarily unrelated and independent. The absence of just cause may go to prove malice, and similarly, the presence of oblique or dishonest motives may go to show the absence of probable cause. Malice may be inferred from recklessness and circumstances from which it may be inferred need not be extrinsic to the circumstances in which the act is done or to the manner of doing it."[46]

---

[44] *Ibid.* Kenny J.'s view that an incorrect procedure does not result in an *ultra vires* action would, however, certainly not now be accepted as good law (see, *e.g. The State (Holland)* v. *Kennedy* [1977] I.R. 193, 201, *per* Henchy J.). However, he is correct in attempting to draw a distinction (as far as the issue of damages is concerned) between lack of *original* jurisdiction (where the entire procedure is *coram non judice* and a nullity) and an error (such as denial of natural justice or the misconstruction of a statutory provision) made in the course of the hearing by a tribunal or court with original jurisdiction in the matter. This distinction was also elaborated upon at some length by Fitzgibbon J. in his somewhat obscure judgment in *O'Conghaile* v. *Wallace* [1938] I.R. 565. As a matter of general principle, misfeasance of public office would seem to be easier to establish where the proceedings were entirely *coram non judice* as this, perhaps, may give rise to the inference that the persons purporting to exercise jurisdiction knew, or ought to have known, of the lack of jurisdiction.

[45] High Court, July 23, 1984.

[46] *Ibid.* pp. 16–17 of the judgment, quoting from the Lord-Justice Clerk in *Robertson* v. *Keith* 1936 S.C. 36, 37.

More recently, the Supreme Court suggested in *Pine Valley Developments Ltd.* v. *Minister for the Environment*[47] that liability could arise where the decision was coupled with malice. In this case, the Minister for the Environment had granted on appeal a planning permission which the Supreme Court held to be *ultra vires*.[48] This resulted in an estimated loss of some IR£1.5 million to the plaintiffs, who then commenced proceedings claiming damages as against the Minister. While the *ultra vires* act of itself did not give rise to liability, Finlay C.J. agreed that the presence of malice or knowledge of the lack of *vires* would give rise to liability in damages. The question of misfeasance, however, did not arise on the facts, for the evidence showed that the Minister had acted on the basis of legal advice prior to granting the planning permission. Accordingly, his actions could not possibly:

> "constitute such a gross abuse of power or wholly unreasonable exercise of power as to lead to an inference that he was aware that he was exercising a power which he did not possess. The only evidence led in this case quite clearly indicates to the contrary and that the Minister was of the belief that he was exercising a power which he possessed."[49]

This matter was also explored by O'Hanlon J. in *C.W. Shipping Co.* v. *Limerick Harbour Commissioners*.[50] Here the applicants had sought to provide towage services for the Limerick estuary, but the respondents had refused to grant them a licence for this purpose under the provisions of the Harbours Act 1946. O'Hanlon J. held that the respondents had erred in law in that he found that the 1946 Act did not apply to tugs, and, hence, that the applicants were not required to apply for a licence. O'Hanlon J. was happy to apply the principles contained in Lord Diplock's judgment in *Dunlop* v. *Woollahra Municipal Council*,[51] save that he did not concur with Lord Diplock's "unrealistic" view that the person whose interests are affected by the impugned order "can afford to ignore it and proceed as though it had never been passed." In the present case, for example, local shipping agents were reluctant to engage the services of tugs once it became known that the respondents contended that a

---

[47] [1987] I.R. 23. In his judgment, Henchy J. expressly approved of the reasoning in two leading recent authorities: *Dunlop* v. *Woollahra Municipal Council* [1982] A.C. 158 and *Burgoin S.A.* v. *Ministry of Agriculture* [1986] Q.B. 716.

[48] *The State (Pine Valley Developments Ltd.)* v. *Dublin C.C.* [1984] I.R. 407. The Supreme Court held that the Minister had no power to contravene the planning authority's development plan when exercising his statutory powers of appeal in planning cases.

[49] [1987] I.R. 36. The Court of Justice of the European Communities takes a similar view in cases arising under Art. 215 of the Treaty of Rome. Mere illegality causing loss is not, of itself, enough, as liability will only arise "exceptionally" in cases "in which the institution concerned has manifestly and gravely disregarded the limits on the exercise of its powers": *G.R. Amylum N.V. & Tunnel Refineries Ltd.* v. *Council & Commission* (Cases 116 & 124/77) [1979] E.C.R. 3497. Analagous principles have been established by the U.S. Supreme Court:

> "Government officials performing discretionary functions generally are shielded from liability for civil damages in so far as their conduct does not violate clearly established statutory or constitutional rights of which a reasonable person would have known."

Harlow v. *Fitzgerald*, 457 U.S. 800, 814–815, *per* Powell J.

[50] [1989] I.L.R.M. 416. See also, *Micosta S.A.* v. *Shetlands Islands Council* 1986 S.L.T. 193.

[51] [1982] A.C. 158.

licence was necessary for towage services. Nevertheless, the claim for damages failed, as O'Hanlon J. held that there should be no liability in damages merely because they had misconstrued the relevant statutory provisions:

> "I do not find any evidence suggesting that they acted maliciously, or in pursuance of a conspiracy to inflict damage on the applicant, or that there was any abuse of public office on their part."[52]

Although the applicants do not appear to have claimed damages for breach of constitutional rights, it is unlikely that the result would have been otherwise if this had been done.[53] The infliction of pecuniary loss as a result of an *ultra vires* act does not entitle the plaintiff *per se* to damages for breach of constitutional rights.

Though each of these cases tend in the same direction, it is worth noting that in none of them were the motives necessary to establish an action for misfeasance of public office found to exist. As a practical matter it is manifest that this would be a most difficult case to establish. Indeed, there is no reported post-1922 case in which this particular tort has been made out.

(iii) *Breach of statutory duty*

A plaintiff may also seek damages in respect of breach of statutory duty. Given that a showing of negligence has no bearing on the question of whether a plaintiff is entitled to succeed, the imposition of liability for breach of statutory duty is really another form of strict liability. The major problem in this area is whether breach of the statute gives rise to a private right of action. Very occasionally the statute will state explicitly that breach of the statute does[54] or does not[55] do so. Generally, however, the statute will be silent on the matter, and the courts will engage in the fictitious exercise of imputing legislative intent in order to determine breach of the statute will give rise to a civil action.[56]

If the duty is owed to the public at large, then no action for breach of that duty will lie. Thus, in *Pine Valley Developments Ltd.* v. *Minister for the*

---

[52] [1989] I.L.R.M. 426. See also, *O'Donnell* v. *Dún Laoghaire Corporation* [1991] I.L.R.M. 301 (wrongful suspension of water supply to plaintiff's home, but no liability as no recognised tort thereby committed and actions not motivated by malice).

[53] As mere unlawful administrative action causing pecuniary loss does not of itself appear to constitute a breach of the plaintiff's property rights or his right to earn a livelihood: see *per* Costello J. in *Moyne* v. *Londonderry Port and Harbour Commissioners* [1986] I.R. 299, 317. But *cf. Parsons* v. *Kavanagh* [1990] I.L.R.M. 560 where O'Hanlon J. granted an injunction restraining the defendant from operating unlicensed bus services. The plaintiff was the holder of a licence under the Road Transport Act 1932 and O'Hanlon J. said that she was entitled to an injunction against "unlawful activity which impaired in a significant manner the plaintiff's exercise of her constitutional right to earn her living by lawful means."

[54] See, *e.g.* Air Navigation and Transport Act 1936, s.21 (right of action for damage caused by aircraft to persons or property).

[55] See, *e.g.* Transport Act 1958, s.7(3) (No action will lie for failure by C.I.E. to comply with its own statutory duty to provide a "reasonable, efficient and economical transport service").

[56] See generally, McMahon & Binchy, *The Irish Law of Torts* (Dublin, 1990), pp. 373–388 and Salmond & Heuston, *Law of Torts* (London, 1987), pp. 273–289.

Environment[57] the Supreme Court held no action for breach of statutory duty would lie against the defendant Minister who had granted a planning permission (which was subsequently found to be invalid) to the plaintiffs. Finlay C.J. said:

"The Minister in making his purported decision to grant outline planning permission was exercising a decision-making function vested in him for the discharge of a public purpose or duty. The statutory duty thus arising must, however, in law, be clearly distinguished from duties imposed by statute on persons or bodies for the specific protection of the rights of individuals which are deemed to be absolute and breach of which may lead to an action for damages."[58]

On the other side of the line was *Moyne* v. *Londonderry Port and Harbour Commissioners*[59] where Costello J. found that the breach of the statutory duties imposed on the defendants by the provisions of the Londonderry Port and Harbour Act 1854 to keep certain harbours open gave rise to an action for damages at the suit of members of the public living in the locality:

"[It] is clear that the statute with which this case is concerned is strikingly different from that class of statutes which the courts held concerned a duty to the public only. Here it cannot reasonably be argued that the duty to maintain the pier was imposed for the benefit of the Irish public generally. The benefit which was being afforded by the pier was being conferred primarily on a definable class of persons, namely those living in the clearly defined geographical area of the Inishowen peninsula, and particularly those living and working on its eastern seaboard."[60]

Again, one must question whether these settled techniques of statutory interpretation have survived the enactment of the Constitution of Ireland in the case of statutes enacted after the coming into force of the Constitution. Barrington J. has pointed out that this method of statutory interpretation owes its origins to the fact that:

---

[57] [1987] I.R. 23.
[58] *Ibid.* 36. See also, *Walsh* v. *Kilkenny C.C.* [1978] I.L.R.M. 1 and *Siney* v. *Dublin Corporation* [1980] I.R. 400 for a similar approach. But *cf. O'Neill* v. *Clare C.C.* [1983] I.L.R.M. 141 (planning authority liable in damages in respect of wilful refusal to grant planning permission in circumstances where they were statutorily obliged to do so and *Bakht* v. *Medical Council* [1990] 1 I.R. 515 (where the plaintiff was awarded £12,500 damages in respect of his loss of earnings for one year during which period he could not practise medicine by reason of the wrongful failure of the Medical Council to adopt the necessary registration rules under the Medical Practitioners Act 1978.)
[59] [1986] I.R. 299.
[60] *Ibid.* 314. See also, *Waterford Harbour Commissioners* v. *British Railway Board* [1979] I.L.R.M. 296 where the Supreme Court held that the provisions of s.70 of the Fishguard and Rosslare Railways and Harbours Act 1898 (which imposed an obligation on the defendants to maintain a shipping service from Waterford to Fishguard in Wales) enabled the plaintiff harbour authority to maintain an action for breach of statutory duty when this service was terminated. As O'Higgins C.J. observed (at 341), the statutory provision in question was intended to benefit not only the general public but had also been enacted for the protection and benefit of the harbour authority.

"The British Parliament is a sovereign legislature and the right of the individual plaintiffs are to be ascertained by finding out what was the intention of Parliament in the particular case. If the Parliament intended to provide a remedy for the individual plaintiff in the courts, then he has a remedy. If it did not intend to provide a remedy, then he has not. But in our jurisdiction the citizen would appear to have a remedy, by virtue of the provisions of Article 40.3, if he has or may suffer damage as a result of a breach of the law in circumstances which amount to an injustice."[61]

In future, therefore, the answer to the question of whether breach of statutory duty gives rise to an action in damages may depend not on the presumed legislative intent as ascertained by a construction of the relevant statutory provisions, but rather by reference to whether the absence of such a remedy would infringe the constitutional rights of the plaintiff. Admittedly, the question of what precisely are the constitutional rights will depend on the statutory context. Nevertheless, this approach appears to have won favour with O'Hanlon J. in *Parsons* v. *Kavanagh*.[62] Here, the plaintiff was the holder of a licence under the Road Transport Act 1932 and she sought an injunction to restrain the defendant from operating an unlicensed bus service. While O'Hanlon J. concluded that the licensing régime established by the 1932 Act was for the benefit of the public at large, so that the plaintiff accordingly could not sue in her own right for breach of statutory duty, she was nevertheless entitled to an injunction. O'Hanlon J. concluded that she had a constitutional right to earn her livelihood by lawful means and that this right was infringed by the defendant's conduct.

(iv) *Breach of constitutional rights*

Article 40.3.1. provides that the State "guarantees in its laws to respect, and, as far as practicable, by its laws to defend and vindicate the personal rights of the citizen."

It has been suggested that Article 40.3 may have transformed the law of torts by supplanting the recognized torts such as assault, battery, libel and false imprisonment, and replacing them "by an innominate claim for infringement of constitutional rights."[63] A slightly less radical view is to say that the State could be said to have adequately defended and vindicated the citizen's personal rights:

"by providing the law of tort as the forum for the vindication of interests by means of damage actions, and that it is only where the common law remedies are inadequate or non-existent that an action based on the Constitution would lie."[64]

---

[61] *Irish Permanent Building Society* v. *Caldwell (No. 2)* [1981] I.L.R.M. 242, 254.
[62] [1990] I.L.R.M. 560.
[63] Heuston, "Personal Rights under the Irish Constitution" (1976) 11 Ir.Jur. (N.S.) 205.
[64] Cooney & Kerr, "Constitutional Aspects of Irish Tort Law" (1981) 3 D.U.L.J. (N.S.) 1, 2.

There would seem to be judicial support for both points of view,[65] but the latter would now appear to prevail. In practice, this means that the Constitution may be invoked only where the ordinary law of torts has been shown to be inadequate or ineffective to protect constitutional rights. As Henchy J. recently observed:

"The implementation of those constitutional rights is primarily a matter for the State and the courts are entitled to intervene only when there has been a failure to implement or, where the implementation relied on is plainly inadequate, to effectuate the constitutional guarantee in question. . . . A person may, of course, in the absence of a common law or statutory cause of action, sue directly for a breach of a constitutional right (see *Meskell* v. *C.I.E.*); but when he founds his action on an existing tort, he is normally confined to the limitations of the tort. It might be different if it could be shown that the tort in question is basically ineffective to protect his constitutional rights."[66]

Nevertheless, there are several recent cases where the plaintiffs recovered damages from the State[67] for breach of constitutional rights. In *Kearney* v. *Ireland*[68] a prisoner was awarded damages for breach of his constitutional right to communicate when his incoming mail was wrongly stopped by prison officials taking unofficial industrial action. Similarly, in *Kennedy* v. *Ireland*[69] the phones of the plaintiffs were illegally intercepted by agents of the Minister for Justice. Hamilton P. awarded each plaintiff substantial damages for breach of their constitutional right to privacy. Finally, in *McHugh* v. *Commissioner of the Garda Síochána*,[70] the Supreme Court held that the protection afforded to the plaintiff's property rights by Article 40.3.2. required that the State compensate him in respect of the legal costs which he incurred as a result of a statutory disciplinary inquiry which, it subsequently transpired, was invalid.

But if these cases suggested that the consequences of *ultra vires* administrative action might be transformed by the development of the doctrine of

---

[65] For the former view, see Walsh J. in *Meskell* v. *Coras Iompair Eireann* [1973] I.R. 121, 133 where he said that an action for breach of constitutional rights could be brought even though such action might not "fit into any of the ordinary forms of action in either common law or equity." The latter view is best expressed by Henchy J. in *Hanrahan* v. *Merck, Sharp & Dohme Ltd.* [1988] I.L.R.M. 629, 636.
[66] *Hanrahan* [1988] I.L.R.M. 629, 636.
[67] A plaintiff may, of course, also recover damages in an appropriate case against a *private* defendant, for "uniquely, the Irish Constitution confers a right of action for breach of constitutionally protected rights against persons other than the State and its officials" (*P.H.* v. *John Murphy & Sons Ltd.* [1987] I.R. 621, 626, *per* Costello J.). Thus, there have been a number of cases where infant plaintiffs have recovered damages against a trade union whose members engaged in industrial action, thus depriving the children of their constitutional right to free primary education under Art. 42 of the Constitution: see *Hayes* v. *Ireland* [1987] I.L.R.M. 651 and *Conway* v. *Ireland* Supreme Court, February 13, 1991.
[68] [1986] I.R. 116.
[69] [1987] I.R. 587. For a fuller account of this case, together with a discussion of the damages issue, see Hogan, "Free speech, privacy and the press in Ireland" [1987] *Public Law* 509.
[70] [1986] I.R. 228.

constitutional wrongs, a more cautious attitude seems presently to prevail. In *Moyne* v. *Londonderry Port and Harbour Commissioners*,[71] Costello J. held (without elaborating) that a breach of a statutory duty causing a loss of business profit was not of itself an actionable breach of a constitutional right:

> "The infliction of a pecuniary loss does not in itself establish that an infringement of the constitutionally protected right to earn a livelihood has taken place."[72]

In *Greene* v. *Minister for Agriculture*[73] Murphy J. held that damages could only be obtained in respect of a breach of a *personal* constitutional right. Here, the Minister had infringed Article 41.3.1. (which provides that the State "pledges to protect the institution of marriage, on which the family is founded and to protect it against attack") by implementing the provisions of a European Community directive dealing with headage payment grants in a manner which discriminated against married couples. Murphy J. said that as the breach was that of a general pledge contained in the Constitution and did not relate to a personal constitutional right (such as, for example the right to liberty), the plaintiffs could not recover.[74] While the desire to draw the line at some point is, perhaps, understandable, it introduces a new element of characterisation into this question of recovery for breach of constitutional rights. Take, as an example of this difficulty, Article 44.2.3:

> "The State shall not impose any disabilities or make any discrimination on the ground of religious profession, belief or status."

This is clearly a general pledge, but it would also appear to confer a per-

---

[71] [1986] I.R. 299.
[72] *Ibid.* 317.
[73] [1989] 3 C.M.L.R. 830. The case concerned the manner in which the Minister had implemented Directive 75/286/EEC. The Minister had provided that farmers and their spouses whose off-farm income exceeded a certain maximum were precluded from obtaining certain headage payment grants. Murphy J. held that by including the off-farm income of spouses (but not, *e.g.* the off-farm income earned by the common-law wife of the applicant farmer) the Minister had violated the constitutional guarantee to protect the family as contained in Art. 41.3.1.
[74] Thus, Murphy J. could say (at 841):

> "The plaintiffs in the present case . . . cannot establish the infringement of a personal constitutional right. The only right which they can assert successfully is the general right of the citizens to the performance by the State of its obligation 'to guard with special care the institution of marriage." Whilst I accept that citizens are entitled to ensure that that duty is honoured, the duty cast on the State does create a corresponding right in the individual citizen so that a breach of the duty would necessarily constitute an infringement of any right of his."

See also, *Nolan* v. *Minister for the Environment* [1989] I.R. 357 where the Minister had given consent to an unlawful planning development. Costello J. held (at 364) that the plaintiffs were not entitled to damages for breach of constitutional rights:

> "[N]o such constitutional requirement can exist because what was involved in this case was the consent to the commission of an illegal act, and the Constitution would not impose a duty to give notice of a proposal to allow an illegal act to be committed. As no constitutional duty to adopt fair procedures existed in the particular circumstances of this case of relevance to the plaintiffs there was no correlative constitutional right vested in them to receive notice and be given an opportunity to make representations."

sonal right so as to entitle a person aggrieved by a breach thereof to damages in respect of that breach.

A further significant restriction on this scope of liability is that a plea of breach of constitutional rights cannot apparently be used to circumvent the inherent limitations of the tort of misfeasance of public office or the quasi-immunities enjoyed by persons discharging public office. This emerges from the Supreme Court decision in *Pine Valley Developments Ltd.* v. *Minister for the Environment*,[75] where the plaintiffs sued for damages in respect of a breach of their property rights following a ruling by the Supreme Court that a planning permission granted to them by the defendant Minister was invalid. However, Finlay C.J. observed that:

"[T]he State may have to balance its protection of the right as against other obligations arising from regard for the common good."[76]

The Chief Justice continued:

"I am satisfied that it would be reasonable to regard as a requirement of the common good an immunity for persons in whom are vested statutory powers of decision from claims for compensation where they act bona fide and without negligence. Such an immunity would contribute to the efficient exercise of such statutory powers and would, it seems to me, tend to avoid indecisiveness and delay, which might otherwise be involved."[77]

And while the reasoning of Henchy J. in his concurring judgment contained a slightly different emphasis, he added that:

"[T]he exemption of the State from liability is not alone not an unconstitutionality, but is in harmony with the due operation of the organs of government established under the Constitution."[78]

In effect, the Court appears to have created a quasi-immunity in favour of persons discharging public duties affecting the rights or liberties of others, thus effectively emasculating the potential scope of liability for breach of constitutional rights in this area. But why should this be so? Finlay C.J. said that, were it otherwise, this would lead to "an inevitable paralysis of the capacity for decisive action in the administration of public office."[79] But this reasoning

---

[75] [1987] I.R. 23.
[76] *Ibid.* 38, quoting from the judgment of O'Higgins C.J. in *Moynihan* v. *Greensmyth* [1977] I.R. 56, 71.
[77] *Ibid.*
[78] *Ibid.* 43.
[79] *Ibid.* 38. It is interesting to note that Lord Keith also expressed similar sentiments in *Rowling* v. *Takaro Properties Ltd.* [1988] A.C. 473 where he said (at 502) that:

"It is to be hoped that, as a general rule, imposition of liability in negligence will lead to a higher standard of care in the performance of the relevant type of act; but sometimes not only may this not be so, but the imposition of liability may lead to harmful consequences. . . . [A] danger may exist in cases such as the present, because, once it became known that liability in negligence may be imposed on the ground that a minister has misconstrued a statute and so acted *ultra vires*, the cautious civil servant may go to extreme lengths in ensuring that legal advice or even the opinion of the court, is obtained before decisions are taken, thereby leading to unnecessary delay in a considerable number of cases."

seems old-fashioned and contrary to modern principles of liability. In every other area of tort law, the imposition of higher standards is viewed as salutary and practically every immunity from liability has disappeared.[80] Moreover, it seems curious that whereas in *Byrne* v. *Ireland*[81] the State's immunity from suit was found to be unconstitutional, the result of *Pine Valley* appears to be the creation of a new constitutional quasi-immunity. A further complication is provided by the later decision of the Supreme Court in *Ryan* v. *Ireland*, where Finlay C.J. said that any immunity enjoyed by the State at common law in respect of negligent acts committed by military personnel during the course of armed hostilities or armed conflict would be unconstitutional as inconsistent with the personal rights of the injured soldier. A fresh reappraisal of the relationship between the Constitution and the law of torts and the extent to which the Oireachtas can create new immunities or quasi-immunities would seem to be called for.

6. Statutory Right to Compensation

We have seen that there is no general right to obtain compensation or damages in respect of administrative decisions which have been properly taken within jurisdiction. However, a *statutory* right to compensation exists in respect of certain administrative decisions. Such a statutory right arises, for example, where land has been acquired by an administrative body or where the value of land has been reduced by certain types of planning decisions. The right to compensation only extends to damage authorised by legislation. Unauthorised damage may give rise to an action for damages in tort, but it will not give rise to a claim under the relevant statutory provisions.[82] There are many administrative decisions which affect legal rights or interests in respect of which no statutory right to compensation exists: for example, the power of a local authority to require measures to be taken to prevent water pollution[83] or to order the demolition of a dangerous house[84] fall into this category. It would be out of place to provide a full list of administrative

---

[80] This is in contrast with the prevailing judicial attitude to the question of professional negligence. In *Roche* v. *Pielow* [1985] I.R. 232 the Supreme Court held that a solicitor was guilty of professional negligence, even though he had not departed from what was then accepted conveyancing practice, as it ought to have realised (*per* Henchy J. at 254) "that the practice in question was fraught with danger for his client and was readily avoidable or remediable." The thinking here is that the imposition of such liability will have a salutary effect on professional standards and will ensure that solicitors (and other professionals) are sufficiently careful in the discharge of their duties. Yet cases such as *Pine Valley* and *Takaro Properties* show no willingness to accept that the potential imposition of such liability for negligent administrative errors might have a similar effect on administrators and others discharging public functions or quasi-judicial duties.
[81] [1972] I.R. 241.
[82] *Red Cow Service Station Ltd.* v. *Bord Gáis Éireann* (1985) 3 I.L.T.(N.S.) 15.
[83] Local Government (Water Pollution) Act 1977.
[84] Local Government (Sanitary Services) Act 1964.

decisions in respect of which no compensation is payable[85] but the general principle is that no provision for compensation is made in respect of administrative decisions which can be objectively shown to be in the public interest unless this would impose an undue burden on the individual citizen.

These principles may have to be re-examined in the light of the provisions of Article 40.3 and Article 43 of the Constitution. Article 40.3 requires the State by its laws to protect "as best it may from unjust attack" and in the case "of injustice done" to vindicate the property rights of every citizen. Article 43, while protecting the institution of private property rights permits the delimitation of such rights "with a view to reconciling their exercise with the exigencies of the common good."[86] The interpretation of these separate provisions is fraught with uncertainty, but the following propositions can be put forward with some confidence:

(i) Article 40.3 protects individual rights over particular items of real and personal property, while Article 43 deals with the institution of private property.[87]

(ii) If the action of the State authorities can be justified by reference to Article 43, then such action cannot by definition be regarded as an "unjust attack" on the individual's property rights as protected by Article 40.3;[88] and

(iii) It is for the courts to say whether the delimitation of property rights is actually required by social justice and the exigencies of the common good, *i.e.* whether this general regulation of particular property rights can be justified under Article 43.[89]

While the case law is in the course of development, it will be seen that the relevant legislation dealing with the right to compensation may have to be reassessed in the light of cases such as *Electricity Supply Board* v. *Gormley,*[90] where the Supreme Court held that, where a statutory scheme of compensation was established to compensate landowners for an interference with their land, the property rights guarantees contained in Articles 40.3 and 43 of the Constitution required that such legislation provide for assessment of compensation by an independent arbitrator.

In particular, it must be doubted whether general techniques of statutory interpretation are applicable in the light of such constitutional provisions. The general principle established by the English courts is that no action will lie in

---

[85] Examples include Local Government (Planning and Development) Act 1963 (no compensation payable for certain types of planning refusals); National Monuments Acts 1930–1964 (no compensation for reduction in land values caused by imposition of preservation order on national monuments).

[86] For a general account of these provisions, see Kelly, *op cit.* pp. 644–661 and Casey, *op cit.* pp. 523–545.

[87] *Blake* v. *Attorney General* [1982] I.R. 117.

[88] *Dreher* v. *Irish Land Commission* [1984] I.L.R.M. 94; *O'Callaghan* v. *Commissioners for Public Works* [1985] I.L.R.M. 364.

[89] *Buckley* v. *Attorney General* [1950] I.R. 67; *Electricity Supply Board* v. *Gormley* [1985] I.R. 129.

[90] [1985] I.R. 129.

respect of acts done under lawful authority; nor will a public authority be liable in tort where the injury complained of is the inevitable consequence of that which has been legislatively ordained. In *Allen* v. *Gulf Oil Refining Ltd*,[91] the House of Lords applied these principles to hold that as the construction of a particular oil refinery was authorised by legislation, that Act had—at least by necessary implication—authorised the operation of the refinery—and that neighbours who complained of the smell, noise and vibration had no cause of action in so far as the nuisance complained of was the inevitable consequence of the operation of the refinery. It is difficult to believe that an Irish court would reach the same conclusion were it faced with a case with similar facts. If the statute plainly extinguished neighbouring landowners' rights to sue in respect of such nuisance, an Irish court would probably rule that such provisions amounted to an unconstitutional attack[92] on the plaintiff's rights to sue in tort,[93] (which itself is a species of the property right protected by Article 40.3) or to recover compensation in respect of this State interference with their property rights. If the statute was silent on the matter, an Irish court, applying the presumption of constitutionality, would probably rule that as there was no overt legislative intention to act in an unconstitutional fashion, it must be presumed that the legislature did not intend to deprive the plaintiffs refinery. In short, cases such as *Gormley* show that there may have to be a complete reappraisal of the general principles of law governing the citizen's right to recover damages or compensation in respect of administrative decisions which injuriously affect his property rights. It is true that a great many statutes already confer a right to compensation, but even where no such express right has been granted the effect of Articles 40.3 and 43 of the Constitution is probably such as to oblige the courts to imply such a right, or, at the very least, judicially create the right to sue the administrative body concerned in tort.

7. Liability for the Negligent Exercise of Discretionary Public Powers

As mentioned already, public authorities are subject to broadly the same common law of tortious liability as private individuals or companies. They (or their servants or agents) must: drive carefully; observe the appropriate duties of an employer or occupier; and if they dig a trench, ensure that it is guarded so that no one will fall into it. The only public law issue which arises in relation to such issues is whether, as a result of some special rule, a defence is available to a public authority which would not be available to a private individual. The issue

---

[91] [1981] A.C. 1001. See also, *Kelly* v. *Dublin C.C.*, High Court, February 21, 1986 (Council liable for damages caused by storing of vehicles in neighbouring depot, as nuisance not shown to have been "inevitable result of the exercise of statutory powers").

[92] Unless, of course, it could be said that such interference was justified by considerations pertaining to the common good, such as to result in no violation of their constitutional rights.

[93] On the ground that otherwise existing tort law would be "plainly inadequate" (to use the language of Henchy J. in *Hanrahan* v. *Merck, Sharp and Dohme Ltd.* [1988] I.L.R.M. 629, 636) to vindicate the landowner's constitutional rights.

to be discussed next, namely, liability for the negligent exercise of a discretionary power, is not such a defence. Rather it concerns a function peculiar to public authorities, negligence in regard to which calls for special discussion.

The issue as to what extent public bodies may be liable for the negligent exercise of their discretionary powers, as contrasted with a mere operational decision or action, is one which has beset the courts of the common law world for the last 15 years or so, but especially since the decision of the House of Lords in *Anns* v. *Merton L.B.C.*[94] In this case, a block of flats developed cracks because, apparently, it had been built on inadequate foundations. The question of whether the local authority could be liable in negligence for its failure to exercise their discretionary statutory power to inspect the foundations was among the preliminary issues raised. Lord Wilberforce set out what has come to be known as the "two-tier test."[95] The first requirement was that there could not be liability for the negligent exercise of a discretionary power "unless the act complained of lies outside the ambit of the power," *i.e.* a showing of *ultra vires* was a prerequisite to liability for the negligent exercise (or non-exercise) of a discretionary public power.[96] This requirement was included in order to accommodate the fact that as the legislature saw fit to invest the public body with a discretionary power, it presumably intended to allow it some margin of appreciation. Once *ultra vires* was established, then, in principle, a plaintiff could sue, provided he could satisfy the normal requirements of the tort of negligence. At this point the second stage of Lord Wilberforce's test came into play and the fact that the subject-matter of the case involved a discretionary power rather than an operational matter was again significant. For the more operational the power may be, the easier it is to superimpose a common law duty of care, since liability is determined in accordance with the ordinary law of negligence.[97] By contrast, in the case of a discretionary power, the

---

[94] [1978] A.C. 728. *Anns* represented the culmination of judicial thinking contained in cases such as *Dorset Yacht Co.* v. *Home Office* [1970] A.C. 1004 and *Dutton* v. *Bognor Regis U.D.C.* [1972] 1 Q.B. 373.

[95] *Ibid.* 753–758. Somewhat confusingly, Lord Wilberforce also enunciated a separate "two-tier" test based on proximity and public policy considerations in relation to liability in negligence generally. This test is distinct from the special two-tier test of liability which he sought to apply in the area of negligent exercise of discretionary powers.

[96] The Council inspector had apparently acted *ultra vires* the discretion vested in him by not ensuring that the plans and foundations were in accordance with the building by-laws. The assumed facts (*Anns* was tried on a preliminary point of law) were consistent with his having been negligent either in not inspecting the foundations, or in the manner in which the inspection was actually carried out.

[97] Lord Wilberforce referred to *Indian Towing Co.* v. *U.S.* 350 U.S. 61 (1955), where a decision to *build* a lighthouse was classified as a "policy" decision, but the failure to keep the lighthouse in working order was described as "operational negligence." And while Blayney J. did not employ this terminology in *Burke* v. *Dublin Corporation* [1990] 1 I.R. 18, he did appear to differentiate as far as liability was concerned between the Corporation's decision to purchase a new and cheaper form of heating system for certain tenants (a form of policy decision) and the actual maintenance of the system in good working order (an operational matter). But *cf.* the comments of Costello J. in *Ward* v. *McMaster* [1985] I.R. 29, 47 where he described the policy/operational distinction as one of "degree" and "certainly one which may be difficult to make with precision in many cases."

question of the persons to whom a duty of care is owed is much more open-ended and it is more difficult to establish in the case of any particular plaintiff.

Considerable doubts have been expressed in several important English and Privy Council[98] decisions about Lord Wilberforce's formula especially in regard to the issue of whether a duty of care is owed. These doubts appear to cast a cloud over the entirety of the reasoning in *Anns*, including those aspects of Lord Wilberforce's judgment which deal exclusively with liability arising from the negligent exercise of discretionary power. In certain types of context, courts have been reluctant to hold that public authorities owe the general public a duty of care[99] and, even in the case of *ultra vires* acts, the courts are unwilling to impose liability where these public functions have been discharged in good faith.[1] Secondly, it is now evident that the question of whether a duty of care is to be imposed on the public body for the negligent exercise of a discretionary power depends, at least in part, upon the relevant statutory context.[2] This, in turn, has tended to assimilate the test for negligence to that of liability for breach of statutory duty, namely, was the plaintiff a member of the class of persons which the statute was designed to protect? Finally, it must be borne in mind in any analysis of the case-law that the different approaches to this problem and the judicial pronouncements thereon cannot always be reconciled.[3] In this respect, there is a similarity between this area and contemporary developments in the general law of negligence[4], where, for instance, the recent economic loss cases have reduced the law in this area to an uncertain state (not uncommon at a time of flux) and, in turn, have tended to cast doubt on Lord Wilberforce's expansive judgment in *Anns*.

It bears remarking, however, that though nearly all the cases presently to be considered may certainly be classified under the rubric of negligent exercise of discretionary power, yet they almost all fall within a rather small sub-field of this area, namely the regulation of private, commercial activity such as building and planning matters. This means that apart from exceptional cases such as *McMahon* v. *Ireland*,[5] the wider aspects of a potentially vast field remain uncharted by judicial decision or even, to a large extent, academic comment. We have not yet gone much beyond the range of policy decisions similar to those which may arise in the private law field, where, for instance: a hospital's policy is not to adopt a particular surgical technique; or a stock-broker's

---

[98] Thus, in *Yuen Kun Yeu* v. *Att.-Gen. of Hong Kong* [1988] A.C. 175 Lord Keith could say (at 191) that the two-tier test had been "elevated to a degree of importance greater than it merits, and greater perhaps than its author intended." The same judge made similar remarks in *Rowling* v. *Takaro Properties Ltd.* [1988] A.C. 473.

[99] See, *e.g. Pine Valley Developments Ltd.* v. *Minister for Environment* [1987] I.R. 23; *Yuen Kun Yeu* v. *Att.-Gen. for Hong Kong* [1988] A.C. 175; and *McMahon* v. *Ireland* [1988] I.L.R.M. 610.

[1] See, *e.g.* the decisions in *Pine Valley*; *McMahon*; *Rowling* v. *Takaro Properties Ltd.* [1988] A.C. 473; and *Jones* v. *Department of Employment* [1989] Q.B. 1.

[2] This was the approach adopted by the House of Lords in *Governors of Peabody Donation Fund* v. *Sir Lindsay Parkinson & Co. Ltd.* [1985] A.C. 210 and by McCarthy J. in *Sunderland* v. *McGreavey* [1990] I.L.R.M. 658.

[3] A fact readily acknowledged by Henchy J. in *Ward* v. *McMaster* [1988] I.R. 337, 341.

[4] See, *e.g.* D. & F. *Estates Ltd.* v. *Church Commissioners* [1989] A.C. 177.

[5] [1989] I.L.R.M. 610.

policy is not to buy a share in a particular type of undertaking. Thus, we have not yet encountered cases raising broader issues, such as: where a victim of a motor-accident claims that this accident was caused by the highway authority's failure to construct a by-pass; or where a trader argues that the decision to turn the road on which his shop is located into a one-way street was negligent, thereby causing him financial loss; or, yet again, where an exporter claims that the government's decision to withdraw export credit insurance for a particular project because of the uncertain political and financial climate in the foreign country for which the goods were destined was negligently arrived at. Clearly, the plaintiff in each such example would face an up-hill task to establish liability. Not only would the courts be reluctant to impose a duty of care on the public authority in question, but they might elect to reject such claims by a heavy emphasis on the *ultra vires* test, or some other modern re-formulation of the *Anns* conditions. Nevertheless, it seems likely that claims of this kind will, at least, be presented with increasing frequency over the next decade.

Since an understanding of the developments in other common law jurisdictions following the decision in *Anns* is essential in any consideration of this issue, it will be convenient if we first assess the response in those jurisdictions to *Anns* before analysing the more recent Irish decisions.

The retreat from Anns

While, in the immediate aftermath of *Anns*, Lord Wilberforce's judgment was acclaimed as a masterly analysis of liability in negligence in general and that of public authorities in particular, it was quickly felt that *Anns* had unduly widened the scope of public authority liability. This consequences of this expansionism were quickly seen in one of the first major post-*Anns* decisions, *Acrecrest Ltd.* v. *W.S. Hattrell & Partners*.[6] Here the English Court of Appeal held that a local authority owed a duty of care in the exercise of its statutory supervision functions to a building developer. Accordingly, it held the authority liable for financial loss where an inspector had failed to insist on sufficiently deep foundations, even though there was no question of any apprehended injury to the health or safety of the developer.

However, in *Peabody Donation Fund* v. *Sir Lindsay Parkinson & Co.*,[7] the House of Lords held that *Acrecrest* was wrongly decided and that the Court of Appeal had misapplied *Anns*. The facts of *Peabody* were very similar to those of *Acrecrest*. The plaintiffs had engaged in a large-scale building project and they were obliged by statute to deposit drainage plans with the defendant local authority. The local authority approved plans which had been drawn up by the plaintiff's architects. Later it transpired that the plans were defective, and the plaintiffs incurred substantial losses as a result. It was claimed that the local authority should have activated their statutory enforcement powers and

6 [1983] Q.B. 260. *Cf. Weir* v. *Dún Laoghaire Corporation* [1983] I.R. 242 at p. 661.
7 [1985] A.C. 210.

that they were accordingly negligent in failing to ensure that the plaintiffs adhered to their original plans.

The House of Lords rejected the claim. Lord Keith accepted that the plaintiffs' loss was a reasonably foreseeable consequence of the local authority's inaction. Nevertheless, he held that in the light of the purpose of the statutory powers, no duty of care was owed to the plaintiffs by the local authority. The purpose of the enforcement powers was to safeguard the occupiers of houses within the authority's functional area and to protect the public interest: they were not designed to protect developers such as the plaintiff from the economic loss which they might suffer as a result of their own failure to comply with the relevant building regulations. Lord Keith added that there had been "a tendency in some recent cases" to treat passages from Lord Wilberforce's judgment in *Anns* "as being themselves of a definitive character," but he observed that this was "a temptation which should be resisted." A duty of care should only be imposed where "it was just and reasonable to do so"[8] and a mere relationship of proximity between the parties did not of itself suffice. Further evidence of judicial discomfort with *Anns* is evidenced by the fact that Lord Keith made no mention of the *ultra vires* test as a prerequisite to liability.

This trend was continued by cases such as *Investors in Industry Commercial Properties Ltd.* v. *South Bedfordshire D.C.*[9] and *Curran* v. *Northern Ireland Co-Ownership Housing Association Ltd.*[10] In the former case, the English Court of Appeal held that the original owner was normally owed no duty of care by the local authority, since he himself was under a duty to comply with the building laws. In any case, even if the owner was not personally negligent, it would be neither "just nor reasonable" to impose liability on a local authority. In *Curran*, the plaintiffs had purchased their house with the assistance of a mortgage from the Northern Ireland Housing Executive, a statutory authority responsible for the provision of housing accommodation and the general improvement of the housing stock. An extension to the house had been constructed, also with the benefit of a grant from the Housing Executive. The House of Lords decided that the Executive did not owe the plaintiffs a duty of care, saying that a contrary conclusion would be "bizarre." As Lord Bridge explained, in so far as there was any statutory duty on the Executive: " . . . the purpose of imposing any such duty is for the protection of the public revenue, not of the recipients of the grant. . . . "[11]

Finally, in *Yuen Kun Yeu* v. *Att.-Gen. for Hong Kong*[12] the Privy Council emphasised that the *Anns* test of itself was no longer a safe guide on the question of the very existence of a duty of care. Here the plaintiffs had lost substantial sums of money following the collapse of a deposit-taking company. It was said that the authorities had been negligent in failing to exercise their

---

[8] *Ibid.* 241.
[9] [1986] Q.B. 1034.
[10] [1987] A.C. 718.
[11] *Ibid.* 728. Compare this decision with *Ward* v. *McMaster* [1988] I.R. 337.
[12] [1988] A.C. 175.

statutory powers in order to safeguard the interests of the depositors with the company. Lord Keith said first that the *Anns* test had been "elevated to a degree of importance greater than it merits and greater perhaps than its author intended."[13] He proceeded by emphasising that foreseeability of harm did not of itself have the effect of bringing into being "a relationship apt to give rise to a duty of care." Here the Commissioner of deposit-taking companies had no day-to-day control over the management of any company and it might be:

> "[a] very delicate choice whether the best course was to deregister a company forthwith or to allow it to continue in business with some hope that, after appropriate measures by the management, its financial position would improve."[14]

Lord Fraser concluded that, in the circumstances, there was no "special relationship" between the Commissioner and those "unascertained members of the public who might in future become exposed to the risk of financial loss through depositing money with the company" as to give rise to a duty of care.

It is clear, therefore, that the reasoning in *Anns* has been to an extent, at least, disowned. The English courts have been reluctant to impose liability in the case of "discretionary" (as opposed to "operational") decisions and, in any event, liability will only be imposed where this is "just and reasonable." As we shall see, the Irish courts have arrived at a rather different result.

The Approach of the Irish Courts

A wide variety of approaches have been taken by the Irish courts to this question over the last decade and so it is difficult to ascertain any fixed pattern as far as judicial reasoning is concerned.

In the first major case of its kind, *Siney* v. *Dublin Corporation*,[15] the plaintiff had been allocated a flat by the defendant. It transpired that it was unfit for human habitation. However, it is not clear whether the inspection was taken pursuant to the authority's statutory powers or its statutory duties. If, as seems likely, the inspection was taken pursuant to a statutory power, then according to the *Anns* test, it would have been necessary to show that the authority's inspectors acted "outside any delegated discretion either as to the making of an inspection or as to the manner in which the inspection was made."[16] But although *Anns* was referred to with approval, no mention was made of the *ultra vires* requirement. And so, in finding that the local authority

---

[13] *Ibid.* 191. Indeed, the wider "two-tier" test for liability in negligence generally enunciated by Lord Wilberforce in *Anns* has now been overruled by the House of Lords: *Murphy* v. *Brentwood D.C.* [1990] 3 W.L.R. 414. But McCarthy J. has said *Cuard* v. *McMaster* [1988] I.R. 337, 347) that he would not seek to dilute the words of Lord Wilberforce.

[14] *Ibid.* 195.

[15] [1980] I.R. 400. See also, *Coleman* v. *Dundalk U.D.C.*, Supreme Court, July 17, 1987; and *Burke* v. *Dublin Corporation* [1990] 1 I.R. 18. For an account of *Siney*, see Clark & Kerr, "Council Housing, Implied Terms and Negligence—A Critique of *Siney* v. *Dublin Corporation*" (1980) 15 Ir. Jur. (N.S.) 32.

[16] Kerr & Clarke, *loc. cit.* p. 51.

was negligent, the Supreme Court appears to have applied the standard common law principles of liability—the neighbourhood principle enunciated in *Donoghue* v. *Stevenson*.[17]

The reasoning of the Supreme Court majority in *Weir* v. *Dún Laoghaire Corporation*[18] is even more curious. Here the plaintiff had tripped and fallen on a public road as a result of a difference in road levels caused by the construction of a bus lay-by. No warning of this difference in level had been given, although the entire tarmacadam roadway had appeared level. There was thus clear evidence of negligence on the part of those engaged in constructing the lay-by. The local authority had granted planning permission to a development company to build a shopping centre nearby and it had been a condition of this permission that the bus lay-by be built. The lay-by was constructed with the "knowledge and approval" of the defendant local authority.

A majority of the Supreme Court ruled that the local authority was liable in negligence. O'Higgins C.J. appeared to emphasise the fact that the local authority had insisted on the construction of the lay-by, and that the work was carried on with the knowledge and approval of the local authority in their capacity both as planning authority and highway authority. The tenor of this remarkable judgment suggests that because the local authority insisted on the condition, it must have in a sense "authorised" the work with the result that the construction company came to be regarded as the local authority's servants or agents. Griffin J. delivered a trenchant dissent:

> "[S]o to extend the liability of a highway authority for the acts of a contractor engaged by a developer in doing work for which the latter had obtained planning permission, and equating this liability with that of the authority for acts of a contractor engaged by them, is warranted neither by principle nor authority."[19]

Weir is not an entirely satisfactory decision because it ignores, *inter alia*, the public law nature of a local authority's powers and functions. Just as in *Siney*, no mention was made of the *ultra vires* requirement, and no authorities were referred to in the judgments of the Supreme Court. It is also interesting to note that the result in *Weir* is the exact opposite to that arrived at by the House of Lords in *Peabody*. In both cases building developers sought to escape the consequences of their own negligence (or that of their agents) by claiming that a local authority was negligent in not activating its statutory powers. In direct contrast to the result in *Peabody*, the Supreme Court in *Weir* appears to have held that a local authority owes a duty of care in the discharge of its statutory functions to the grantee of a planning permission to protect him from the consequences of his own negligence. This is a remark-

---

[17] [1932] A.C. 652. According to Lord Wilberforce in *Anns*, if liability for the negligent exercise of a discretionary power is based solely on the neighbour principle this is to neglect an essential factor: "[T]hat the local authority is a public body discharging duties under statute; its powers and duties are definable in terms of public not private law" ([1978] A.C. 754).
[18] [1983] I.R. 242.
[19] [1983] I.R. 248.

able proposition and one which—the decision in *Weir* notwithstanding—a future Supreme Court is unlikely to endorse, as is evident from the judgment of McCarthy J. in *Sunderland* v. *McGreavey*[19a].

The judgment of Costello J. in *Ward* v. *McMaster*[20] represents a more considered approach to this problem. In this case the plaintiff had purchased a new house which turned out to be grossly sub-standard structurally and a health risk. Proceedings were then instituted against the builder and the local authority. There were two aspects of the claim against the local authority. The plaintiff had applied to the council for a loan of £12,000 under the provisions of the Housing Act 1966 to enable him to purchase the house.[21] The council sent a valuer who reported that it was in good repair and that its market value was £25,000. The plaintiff alleged that this valuation was negligently carried out and that the council was vicariously liable.

Costello J. found that the valuer had no professional qualification relating to building construction and was employed simply to place a market value on the property. The standard of care required of him was merely that of an ordinary skilled auctioneer, and he had not been negligent. The plaintiff successfully alleged, however, that the Council was directly liable in that it had broken the common law duty of care owed to him in carrying out its statutory functions. The council had a statutory power under the 1966 Act to grant a loan to the plaintiff and a statutory duty by virtue of the relevant regulations[22] to inspect the property before granting a loan. In carrying out the inspection a duty to act with care arose, a duty which was broken by authorising an inspection by someone who lacked the necessary qualification to ascertain reasonably discoverable defects. Costello J. had no doubt, on the authority of cases such as *Anns* and *Siney* that a common law duty of care based on the principle established in *Donoghue* v. *Stevenson* might exist when statutory functions were being performed. Following a review of the relevant authorities, including *Peabody*, Costello J. concluded that the relevant principles in cases of this kind were as follows:

"(a) When deciding whether a local authority exercising statutory functions is under a common law duty of care the court must firstly ascertain whether a relationship of proximity existed between the parties such that in the reasonable contemplation of the authority carelessness on their part might cause loss. But all the circumstances of the case must in addition be considered, including the statutory provisions under which the authority is acting. Of particular significance in this connection is the purpose for which the statutory powers were conferred and whether or not the plaintiff is in the class of persons which the statute was designed to assist.

(b) It is material in all cases for the court in reaching its decision on the

---

[19a] [1990] I.L.R.M. 658.
[20] [1985] I.R. 29 (H.C.).
[21] s.39 of the Housing Act 1966 provides that a local authority may lend money to a person for the purpose of acquiring or constructing a house.
[22] Housing Authorities (Loans for Acquisition or Construction of Houses) Regulations 1972 (S.I. 1972 No. 29).

existence and scope of the alleged duty to consider whether it is just and reasonable that a common law duty of care as alleged should in all the circumstances exist."[23]

Applying these principles to the facts as found, Costello J. concluded that, although the plaintiff did not expressly inform any member of the Council's staff that he was relying on their valuation and although the Council carried it out for its own purposes and to comply with its statutory obligations, the council ought to have been aware that it was probable that the plaintiff, a person of limited means, would not have gone to the expense of having the house examined by a professionally qualified person and would have relied on the inspection which he knew would be carried out for the purpose of the loan application. There was therefore a sufficient relationship of proximity and there was nothing in the dealings between the parties which restricted or limited the duties in any way. In particular, no warning against relying on the proposed valuation was given.[24] As to the scope of the duty, Costello J. concluded that the Council should have ensured that the person carrying out the valuation would be competent to discover reasonably ascertainable defects which would materially affect its market value.

The judge did not attempt to draw any sharp distinction between "powers" and "duties" for the purposes of liability. He also declined to pay too much regard to the distinction drawn by Lord Wilberforce in *Anns* between "discretionary" and "operational" decisions, concluding that the matter was essentially a question of whether it was "just and reasonable" in the circumstances that a common law duty of care as alleged should exist.[25] The Council appealed to the Supreme Court against the finding of liability, but prior to the hearing of that appeal, there were two other important decisions of the High Court which merit consideration.

In *Sunderland* v. *McGreavey*,[26] the plaintiffs had purchased a house from a builder and owner of the site. When the house proved to be hopelessly defective and unfit for human habitation due to flooding and a defective drainage system, the plaintiffs sued the local authority on the ground that it was the authority which had granted both planning and retention permission for the house, and, as such they owed him a duty of care. Lardner J. followed the reasoning of Costello J. in *Ward* v. *McMaster*, first examining the statutory background to the exercise of the authority's statutory functions:

---

[23] [1985] I.R. 29, 49–50.
[24] But note that in *Harris* v. *Wyre Forest D.C.*, a companion case to *Smith* v. *Bush* [1989] 3 W.L.R. 790, the House of Lords held that an attempted disclaimer of liability in respect of a valuation supplied by the local authority was ineffective for this purpose. A duty of care was owed by the valuer and the local authority to the prospective mortgagee and, therefore, any attempted repudiation of liability was found to be an "unfair contract term" within the meaning of the Unfair Contract Terms Act 1977. Lord Templeman thought it neither fair nor reasonable "for building societies and valuers to agree together to impose on purchasers the risk of loss arising as a result of incompetence or carelessness on the part of valuers." It may be, therefore, that any attempt by a local authority to exclude liability in respect of the provision of such a service would be void under s.40 of the Sale of Goods and Supply of Services Act 1980.
[25] For McCarthy J.'s view of this, on the appeal, see p. 665.
[26] [1987] I.R. 372.

R.T.C. LIBRARY
LETTERKENNY

"[The relevant provisions of the Planning Acts] are intended to assist in the implementation of the proper development of the planning authority's area in accordance with the development plan. . . . They do not seem to be concerned with such matters as the specification or design of particular septic tanks or soak-away areas which might appropriately be the subject of local authority building regulations, nor I think are they concerned with the protection of individual houses against flooding due a locally high-water table."[27]

Having regard to this, in addition to factors such as that the local authority had not adopted building regulations and the way in which the plaintiff's claim against the local authority was framed by reference:

"[C]hiefly to the erection of a dwellinghouse in an area allegedly liable to flooding and with a drainage system which was incapable of function, I have come to the conclusion that, in regard to the matters complained of by the plaintiffs, a relationship of proximity did not exist between Louth County Council and the plaintiffs; that the purposes for which these powers are conferred are quite different and distinct from and did not comprehend the subject-matter of the plaintiffs' complaints which more properly fall within the appropriate area of building regulations. In all the circumstances, I conclude that in considering whether to grant the original planning permission and the ultimate permission for the retention of the dwelling house Louth County Council did not owe the plaintiffs a common law duty of care in regard to the matters complained of and that to hold otherwise would not be just or reasonable in the circumstances."[28]

Quite irrespective of the test one might care to apply to the facts of such a case (be it the *Anns* formulation or the "just and reasonable" test), Lardner J.'s decision would seem to be correct. Clearly any decision bearing on the question of planning permission is largely a question of planning policy and a decision to grant planning permission cannot in any sense be taken as warranting the soundness of any subsequent construction on the site.

The judgment of Blayney J. in *McMahon* v. *Ireland*[29] is along similar lines. The facts were similar to those of *Yuen Kun Yeu*: the plaintiff had lost money following the collapse of a deposit-taking institution which, taking advantage of an exemption in the Central Bank Act 1971 which it then enjoyed, had carried on a form of banking business. It was claimed that both the Ministers for Finance and Industry and Commerce, on the one hand, and the Registrar of

---

[27] *Ibid*. 389.
[28] *Ibid*. 390.
[29] [1988] I.L.R.M. 610. See McGrath (1987) 9 D.U.L.J. (N.S.) 163. But the Oireachtas is clearly taking no chances, for s.17(9) of the Building Societies Act 1989 now provides as follows:

"The grant of an authorisation to a society by or under this section shall not constitute a warranty as to the solvency of the society to which it is granted and the State or the Central Bank . . . shall not be liable in respect of any losses incurred through the insolvency of a society to which an authorisation is deemed granted under this section or granted by the Bank."

Friendly Societies, on the other, were negligent in failing to ensure that the legislation was amended so as to end this particular exemption. Blayney J. found that neither Minister was responsible for the initial exemption; nor did they owe the plaintiff a duty of care to bring a Bill before the Oireachtas to seek to have the 1971 Act amended. Blayney J. considered that the position of the Registrar of Friendly Societies was analogous, in principle, and in several points of detail, to that of the Commissioner of deposit-taking companies in *Yuen Kun Yeu* and he followed the reasoning of the Privy Council to hold that the Registrar owed the plaintiffs no duty of care. And while Blayney J. did not expressly say so, *McMahon* stands out from the other negligence cases which have arisen (mostly in the planning or bulding field) in that it involved a public authority decision which was plainly at the discretionary end of the spectrum. It is in regard to this type of policy decision that liability in negligence is most difficult to establish.

In 1988 the entire question was exhaustively examined by the Supreme Court when delivering judgment on the appeal from Costello J. in *Ward* v. *McMaster*[30] Henchy J. (with whom Finlay C.J. and Griffin J. concurred) considered that while the Council were plainly in breach of their public duty, it was for the plaintiffs to show that there was sufficient proximity between the parties to give rise to a duty of care. This they had done:

> "The consequences to the plaintiff of a failure on their part to value the house properly should have been anticipated by the council in view of factors such as, that in order to qualify for the loan, the plaintiff had to show that he was unable to obtain the loan from a commercial agency . . . and that his circumstances were such that he would otherwise need to be re-housed by the council. A borrower of that degree of indigence could not have been reasonably expected to incur the further expense of getting a structural survey of the house done."[31]

McCarthy J. (with whom Finlay C.J. (again) and Walsh J. concurred) spoke in similar language, but stressed that he would not "seek to dilute the words of Lord Wilberforce" in *Anns*. McCarthy J. said that whilst Costello J. had rested his conclusion on the "fair and reasonable test," he preferred to express the duty as arising from the "proximity of the parties, the foreseeability of the damage and the absence of any compelling exemption based on public policy."[32] While McCarthy J. did not rule out the public policy issues, he considered that "such a consideration must be a very powerful one" if it is to be used to deny "an injured party his right to redress at the expense of the person or body that injured him."[33] On the critical issue of whether there was sufficient proximity between the parties, McCarthy J. said:

> "This proximity had its origin in the Housing Act 1966 and the consequent

[30] [1988] I.R. 337. See Kerr (1988) 10 D.U.L.J. (N.S.) 182.
[31] *Ibid*. 342.
[32] *Ibid*. 349.
[33] *Ibid*. 347.

loan scheme. This Act imposed a statutory duty upon the County Council and it was in the carrying out of that statutory duty that the alleged negligence took place. It is a simple application of the principle of *Donoghue* v. *Stevenson*, confirmed in *Anns* and implicit in *Siney*, that the relationship between the party and the plaintiff and the County Council created a duty to take reasonable care arising from the public duty of the County Council under the statute. The statute did not create a private duty, but such arose from the relationship between the parties."[34]

Moreover, the loss was reasonably foreseeable, as it did not require "much imagination" on the part of the officers of the Council to contemplate that a purchaser under the scheme would both lack the personal means of having an expert examination and "might well think" that the very circumstances of the Council investing its money in the house was "a badge of quality."[35]

What is striking about the decision in *Ward* is that there was scant mention of a consideration regarded as central by the House of Lords in *Curran* v. *Northern Ireland Housing Executive*,[36] a case with similar facts. Addressing the contention that the Housing Executive owed the plaintiff borrower a duty of care, Lord Bridge remarked that any duty imposed on the Executive was:

"[T]o satisfy themselves that the grant-aided works have been properly executed, it seems to me clear that the purpose of imposing any such duty is for the protection of the public revenue, not the recipients of the grant or their successors in title."[37]

Finally, in 1990, the Supreme Court agreed with Lardner J.'s analysis in *Sunderland* v. *McGreavey*[38] and dismissed the plaintiff's appeal. In holding that planning authorities did not owe purchasers or occupiers a duty of care to ensure that a particular dwelling was structurally sound and suitable for human habitation, McCarthy J. distinguished between cases such as *Siney* and *Ward* on the one hand and the present case on the other:

"The fundamental difference between what may be called planning . . . and housing legislation is that the first is regulatory or licensing according to the requirements of the proper planning and development, but the second is a provision in a social context for those who are unable to provide for themselves. If they are unable to provide for themselves, then the duty on the provider reaches the role that would be taken by professional advisers

[34] *Ibid*. 351.
[35] *Ibid. Cf.* the comments of Lord Griffiths in *Smith* v. *Bush* [1989] 2 W.L.R. 790, 811:

"[T]his is a decision in respect of a dwelling house of modest value in which it is widely recognised by surveyors that purchasers are in fact relying on their skill and care."

Lord Griffiths expressly reserved his position in respect of valuations of "quite different types of property for mortgage purposes, such as industrial property, large blocks of flats or very expensive houses." However, it is clear from *Ward* v. *McMaster* that the decision in that case turned in part on the fact that the plaintiffs were of modest means.
[36] [1987] A.C. 718.
[37] *Ibid*. 728.
[38] [1990] I.L.R.M. 658.

engaged on behalf of the beneficiary. This is in marked contrast to the watchdog role that is created under the Planning Act, a watchdog role that is for the benefit of the public at large."[39]

If the plaintiff's argument were correct, it would mean that planning authorities and An Bord Pleanála would be under a duty of care to inspect dwelling houses before deciding to grant permission. McCarthy J. mentioned these potential consequences not "in terrorem," but rather to seek to identify "on a reasonable approach the intention of the legislature in enacting the relevant parts of the 1963 Act." The judge concluded that:

> "The Act in conferring statutory powers on planning authorities imposed on them a duty towards the public at large. In my view, in conferring these powers, the Oireachtas did not include a purpose of protecting persons who occupy buildings erected in the functional area of planning authorities from the sort of damage which the plaintiffs suffered, That being so, the Council, in the exercise of those powers, owed no duty of care at common law to the plaintiffs."[40]

It may be remarked in passing that McCarthy J. appears to have employed the "ascertain the intention of the legislature" test in determining the liability of the planning authority. This approach is very similar to that employed by Lord Fraser in *Peabody Donation Fund* v. *Sir Lindsay Parkinson & Co.*[41] and is marked contrast to the "two-tier" test which was accepted in McCarthy J.'s judgment in *Ward* v. *McMaster*.

So far as the results in the five recent cases[42] are concerned, the following summary may be offered. One case (*McMahon*) was untypical in that the decision at issue was so close to the discretionary end of the spectrum. There have been few cases in this area in any jurisdiction and very few have been successful. A second case (*Sunderland*) was manifestly a rather forlorn attempt on the part of the plaintiff to ascribe liability to the local authority. In the remaining three cases (*Siney*, *Weir* and *Ward*) the plaintiff won and it is significant that the last two of these involved similar situations to those resolved by the House of Lords (in *Peabody* and *Curran*, respectively) in favour of the local authority. These results—in which the tenor of the Irish decisions is in contrast not only with British but with other foreign decisions—display the Irish courts' marked preference for the individual plaintiff. In any area where any test is bound to include a large margin of judicial appreciation, previous results may be a better guide to future decisions than any stated formula.

---

[39] *Ibid.* 658.
[40] *Ibid.*
[41] [1985] A.C. 210.
[42] See also, *Ryan* v. *Ireland (No. 2)*, High Court, October 19, 1989 (the sequel to *Ryan* v. *Ireland* [1989] I.R. 177) where Barr J. found that officers of the Defence Forces had been negligent at an "operational level" in not taking adequate steps to protect Irish troops serving with the UN forces in the Lebanon from the possibility of attack by militia groups. The plaintiff was awarded £198,354 in damages.

However, in as much as formulae do afford a predictable guide, it is worthy of note that the only attempts at such a formulation occurred in *Ward* v. *McMaster*. In the High Court, Costello J. declined to pay too much regard to the distinction between "discretionary" and "operational" decisions. In the Supreme Court, while not seeking to dilute the *Anns* formula, McCarthy J. was plainly more concerned with that facet of the *Anns* test which emphasises the potential duty of care to the individual. McCarthy J. did also, however, examine the other limb of the *Anns* test, namely, the *ultra vires* requirement which does provide some protection for the public authority. Counsel for the Council had put his argument grounded on this limb thus:

"The omission held to be culpable arose from a decision of policy or discretion which was not open to question by the courts in an action such as this. It was, it is said, a policy decision within the discretion of the County Council not to have any inspection other than that which produced a valuer's certificate: to carry out inspections in every instance through an engineer or like qualified person would greatly reduce the amount of money available in loans with consequent damage to the true purpose . . . of the Housing Act."[43]

McCarthy J., however, could not accept this submission:

"The monetary argument does not bear critical examination. The County Council would not be required to have an engineering inspection in any case in which the relevant house is newly built since procedures for grants involve inspections at the material times with regard to such things as foundations etc., whilst the house is being built. Likewise, houses of significant age would not require inspections to deal with defects arising from subsidence; visual inspection by a relatively unqualified person would be quite adequate to disclose such defects. In any event, I see no bar to the County Council expressly excluding any representations to be inferred from the fact that it sanctions a particular loan. Having regard to this conclusion, it is not necessary for me to express an opinion as to whether or not so-called policy considerations are, in that context, free from review in the Courts in an action of this kind."[44]

This passage shows the Supreme Court as just leaving open the possibility that, in an appropriate case, it might be proper to take into account the discretion accorded by the Oireachtas to the public authority. This view might possibly be recognised either by making policy considerations effectively—to borrow McCarthy J.'s phrase—"free from review"; or through the use of some other device, such as the *ultra vires* requirement employed by Lord Wilberforce in *Anns*.

---

[43] [1988] I.R. 337, 346.
[44] *Ibid.*

8. Liability in Contract

Neither the State nor public authorities enjoy any immunity in respect of the ordinary law of contract. While it is true that certain principles of administrative law operate to restrict the power of public bodies to enter into legally binding contracts—thus, public bodies may not contract so as to fetter their discretionary powers,[45] or, in some cases, so as to create an estoppel[46]. However, there are no special rules applicable to contracts entered into by public bodies. These matters are considered, as indicated, in other chapters of the book.

9. Liability in Quasi-contract[47]

The general rule here is that money paid voluntarily under a mistake of law—as opposed to mistake of fact—is not recoverable. The rigour of this rule is tempered by the fact that a mistake of law has sometimes been characterised as a mistake of fact. Furthermore, the courts will often hold that the payment is not a voluntary one, and is thus recoverable, if the parties were not on equal terms, and the defendants were responsible for the mistake. It is this latter principle which enables the courts to hold public bodies liable to make restitution where the money has been had and received by such a body *colore officii*.[48]

Thus in *Rogers* v. *Louth C.C.*[49] the Supreme Court held that the plaintiff was entitled to recover an excessive sum demanded *colore officii* by the defendants as the price of the redemption of an annuity due to them under the provisions of the Housing Act 1966.[50] The Court held that the payment was not a "voluntary" one, for as Griffin J. explained:

> "The parties were not on equal terms. The defendants had the power, if they thought fit, to withhold payment for the redemption of the annuity; they were prepared to allow the plaintiff to redeem it but only on the conditions imposed by them, which included exacting a payment in excess of that permitted by statute. The plaintiff [had no] reason to think that she was not liable to pay the sum demanded by the defendants for the redemption of the annuity. In my view, the defendants were primarily responsible for the mistake. . . ."[51]

The same principle holds true in the case of payments unlawfully demanded, *colore officii*, by a public body. Payments of this nature, such as taxes[52] or

---

[45] See Chap. 10.
[46] See p. 674
[47] See further, Goff and Jones, *The Law of Restitution* (1986), Chaps. 3 and 9.
[48] *I.e.* where a public official demands payment of moneys by virtue of his office for a charge which the law enables him to demand and enforce.
[49] [1981] I.R. 265.
[50] The plaintiff was the personal representative of the deceased. A cottage had previously been vested in the deceased in fee simple free incumbrances, but subject to an annual annuity due to the defendants.
[51] [1981] I.R. 271. See also, *Dolan* v. *Neligan* [1967] I.R. 247.
[52] *Murphy* v. *Att.-Gen.* [1982] I.R. 241, 317, *per* Henchy J.

licence fees[53] are regarded as having been demanded under duress, so that whether the action is framed at common law or in equity, such payments are recoverable *in the absence of countervailing circumstances.* In *Murphy* v. *Attorney-General*[54] the Supreme Court permitted only limited recoupment of tax collected under a statute that had subsequently been declared to be unconstitutional on the grounds that it would now be inequitable to compel the State to make restitution. The State had been led to believe, by the protracted absence of a claim to the contrary, that it was legally and constitutionally entitled to spend the taxes thus collected. In the view of Henchy J.:

> "[T]he position had become so altered, the logistics of reparation so weighted and distorted by factors such as inflation and interest, the prima facie right of the taxpayers to be recouped so devalued by the fact that, as members of the community . . . they had benefited from the taxes thus collected, that it would be inequitable, unjust and unreal to expect the State to make full restitution."[55]

Thus, the Court held that laches on the part of the general body of taxpayers, and altered circumstances, made it inequitable to compel restitution save to those taxpayers who had instituted proceedings challenging the constitutionality of the collection system. The Court held that the right to recover taxes which were illegally collected could be quickly extinguished by laches. *Murphy* shows that, generally speaking, only limited recoupment of the monies collected will be possible where taxes or levies have been illegally exacted.

---

[53] *Mason* v. *New South Wales* (1959) 102 C.L.R. 108; *Bell Bros. Property Ltd.* v. *Shire of Serpentine Jarrahdale* (1969) 121 C.L.R. 137. But *cf. William Whitley Ltd.* v. *The King* (1909) 101 L.T. 741 where this proposition was doubted. However, in *Woolwich Equitable Building Society* v. *I.R.C.*, *The Times*, May 26, 1991, Glidewell L.J. said that there was a prima facie right to recover sums so unlawfully demanded and that *William Whitley* was probably wrongly decided.
[54] [1982] I.R. 241. See also, pp. 383–386.
[55] [1982] I.R. 320.

CHAPTER 13

LEGITIMATE EXPECTATIONS AND ESTOPPEL

1. Introduction

When the first edition of this book was written in 1986, the principle of legitimate expectations scarcely received a mention. Yet this principle, which was to receive the *imprimatur* of the Supreme Court in its decision in *Webb* v. *Ireland*[1] in December 1987, has launched a host of subsequent cases. There is, perhaps, no other principle which has so rapidly given rise to so much litigation or which has so quickly become embedded in the fabric of the legal system. The principle is one which originally developed in German administrative law (*"Vertrauensschutz"*)[2] and was later recognised as a general principle of law by the European Court of Justice.[3] The principle of legitimate expectations was subsequently transplanted into our legal system via judgments of the Court of Justice and the House of Lords.[4] It is clear, therefore, that developments in the United Kingdom and in the European Communities generally will have a considerable influence on the future progress of this principle in this jurisdiction.

It will be readily appreciated that the doctrine of legitimate expectations has very close affinities with that of promissory estoppel and, indeed, there are judicial dicta to the effect that these doctrines are more or less interchangeable.[5] While these dicta probably go too far and do not recognise

[1] [1988] I.R. 353. There has been a considerable amount of academic writing on this topic, see, *e.g.* Baldwin and Horne, "Expectations in a Joyless Landscape" (1986) 49 M.L.R. 685 and Forsyth, "The Provenance and Protection of Legitimate Expectations" (1988) Camb.L.J. 238.
[2] Literally, "protection of confidence." But this literal translation is apt to be misleading, since it might appear to correspond with the equitable doctrine of breach of confidence and the words "legitimate expectations" are used instead. The use of the noun *Vertrauen* in this context implies that a trust or confidence will be honoured or protected (as in *"ein Vertrauen wird verschutzt"*) by a public body, thus conveying the idea that principles of good administration require that a public body should honour its promises and undertakings. See generally, Usher, "The Influence of National Concepts on Decisions of the European Court" (1976) 1 E.L.Rev. 359; Forsyth, *loc. cit.* and Delany, "The Doctrine of Legitimate Expectation in Irish Law" (1990) 12 D.U.L.J. (N.S.).
[3] See, *e.g. EVGF* v. *Mackprang* (Case 2/75) [1975] E.C.R. 607 and Hartley, *The Foundations of European Community Law* (Oxford, 1988), pp. 142–143. The classic case is now, of course, *Mulder* v. *Minister van Landbouwen en Visserij* (Case 120/86) [1989] 2 C.M.L.R. 1 where the Court of Justice held that a milk producer who had been encouraged by provisions of a Community Regulation to suspend the marketing of milk for a limited period could not, following the expiry of that period, be subjected to new restrictions which specifically prejudiced him as far as future milk production was concerned. See generally on this issue, Sharpston, "Legitimate Expectations and Economic Reality" (1990) 15 E.L.Rev. 103.
[4] *Council of Civil Service Unions* v. *Minister for the Civil Service* (the GCHQ case) [1985] A.C. 319.
[5] See, *e.g.* the comments of Finlay C.J. in *Webb* v. *Ireland* [1988] I.R. 353, 384 and those of Murphy J. in *Garda Representative Association* v. *Ireland* [1989] I.R. 193. In November 1986 (*i.e.* over a year prior to the Supreme Court's decision in *Webb*) Murphy J. refused to accept that the doctrine of legitimate expectations formed part of our law: see *Goldrick* v. *Dublin Corporation* (1987) 6 J.I.S.L.L. 156.

important differences between the two principles, nevertheless they do show the close relationship between them. In any event, the courts have shown an increasing willingness to hold a public authority to an earlier promise, representation or practice, irrespective of which of the doctrines the decision is grounded upon. We shall postpone our comparison of the two doctrines until Part 6, by which stage the case law in this field will have been surveyed.

2. Legitimate Expectations, Estoppel and the Ultra Vires Principle

One significant feature which the two doctrines share is that they are each potentially in conflict with the major principle of public law, namely the *ultra vires* rule: a public authority cannot give itself a jurisdiction it does not possess. It cannot do this by a mistaken conclusion as to the extent of its own powers and neither can it do so by creating an estoppel or a legitimate expectation.

The leading Irish authority in which the *ultra vires* prevailed over an argument founded upon estoppel is *Re Green Dale Building Co.*[6] The significant point here is that under the Housing Act 1966, a notice to treat in relation to land purchases may only be served after the compulsory purchase order has become operative and a c.p.o. does not take effect pending the determination of proceedings which challenge its validity.[7] In this case, a notice to treat was served by a local authority in 1972 but this notice was invalid as proceedings had been commenced by a third party challenging the validity of the compulsory purchase order. That order did, however, take effect in 1975 after the third-party proceedings had been dismissed. The housing authority immediately served a second notice to treat. The value of Green Dale's land was less in 1975 than it had been in 1972. Accordingly, the company wished to rely on the first notice to treat. Thus, they contended that, the non-compliance with the requirements of the Housing Act notwithstanding, the authority should be estopped from relying on the invalidity of the first notice because:

(i) the authority had represented that the first notice had been validly served; and

(ii) the company had, relying on the validity of that representation, acted to their detriment by treating the lands as sterile from 1972, and by submitting to an abortive arbitration to assess the compensation payable.

The Supreme Court rejected the submission that the doctrine of promissory estoppel could have any application in cases of this nature. Henchy J. reasoned that it would entirely destroy the doctrine of *ultra vires* if the donee of a statutory power could extend his power by creating an estoppel. The judge noted that the company was seeking to estop the local authority from asserting that it had acted in breach of an express or implied prohibition or restriction of function in a statute. To permit an estoppel in these circum-

---

[6] [1977] I.R. 256.
[7] Housing Act 1966, s.79(1).

stances would require the court acting to defy the will of the Oireachtas as set out in the statute.[8]

This point had earlier been made by Kenny J. in *Re Parke Davis & Co.'s T.M. Application*.[9] Here the Controller of Trade Marks had refused to register the mark in respect of particular pharmaceutical products in Part A of the Register on the grounds of lack of distinctiveness. It was contended that because the Controller had previously registered a particular mark (belonging to an entirely different company) of this nature in Part A, he was estopped from raising the distinctiveness argument. This was firmly rejected by Kenny J.:

> "The Controller is a public official on whom many duties are imposed by the Trade Marks Act 1963: one of those is to ensure that all marks which are put on the register gets this privilege by complying with the law. He also has a discretion to refuse to accept a mark if he thinks it undesirable that it should be on the register. He cannot be estopped by anything which his predecessors or he might have done from exercising his judgment on each application."[10]

Thus, it is clear that previous decisions of the Controller cannot create an estoppel and it would seem that similar arguments would nowadays be deployed to defeat a claim based on legitimate expectations.

More often what is involved is an express agreement or representation on which the plaintiff seeks to ground a claim to an estoppel or a legitimate expectation whilst the defendant public authority replies by arguing that it would be *ultra vires* to fetter its discretionary power by an agreement of any kind. In some cases, the reverse happens: the agreement is honoured and it is some third party who seeks judicial review of the action honouring the agreement by claiming that it is *ultra vires* because it is not a free exercise of a discretionary power.

For a classic example of a case in which the Crown (in effect, the State) was allowed to break an explicit agreement, deliberately made, consider *Reder-*

---

[8] *Green Dale* was followed in *Dublin Corporation* v. *McGrath* [1978] I.L.R.M. 208. In *Morris* v. *Garvey* [1983] I.R. 319 the Supreme Court ordered the demolition of an unauthorised development in proceedings taken pursuant to s.27 of the Local Government (Planning and Development) Act 1976, despite the fact that the respondent had been assured by a planning official that the planning permission was not necessary in respect of the development. Henchy J. commented thus: "If he wishes to retain the unpermitted walls, the respondent should have applied for a fresh development permission—thus enabling the applicant, or any member of the public to raise such objection as might be thought warranted. In such circumstances the opinion of a planning official—no matter how genuinely given—cannot be allowed to defeat the rights of the public . . . " ([1983] I.R. 324–325). The reasoning in *Green Dale* was also followed by Lardner J. in *Devitt* v. *Minister for Education* [1989] I.L.R.M. 639 in holding that a representation made in an administrative circular could not estop the respondent Minister in the performance of her statutory functions and similar views were expressed by Blayney J. in *Power* v. *Minister for Social Welfare* [1987] I.R. 307 and by Costello J. in *Nolan* v. *Minister for Environment* [1989] I.R. 357.
[9] [1976] F.S.R. 195.
[10] *Ibid*. 197.

eiaktiebolaget Amphitrite v. *The King.*[11] Here, certain neutral shipowners sued on foot of an undertaking given by the British Government that if a particular ship was sent to the United Kingdom laden with a particular cargo, she would not be detained under the blockade regulations then in force. Rowlatt J. dismissed their petition of right, describing the arrangements as one whereby:

> "[T]he Government purported to give an assurance as to what its executive action would be in the future in relation to a particular ship in the event of her coming to this country with a particular kind of cargo. And that is . . . not a contract for the breach of which damages can be sued for in a court of law. It was merely an expression of intention to act in a particular way in a certain event . . . [I]t is not competent for the Government to fetter its future executive action which must necessarily be determined by the needs of the community when the question arises. It cannot by contract hamper its freedom of action in matters which concern the welfare of the State."[12]

This reasoning was followed by Fitzgibbon J. in *Kenny* v. *Cosgrave*,[13] where the plaintiff sought to rely on a promise made to him by W. T. Cosgrave, then President of the Executive Council. Mr. Cosgrave apparently represented to him that if the plaintiff (who was a builder) refused to compromise with his striking employees, then the Executive Council would reimburse him for any losses thereby incurred by him. The plaintiff acted on this assurance to his detriment, and duly sued Mr. Cosgrave, personally. Because he chose to sue Mr. Cosgrave,[14] his action was struck out, as disclosing no reasonable cause of action. However, the relevant point here is that even if the action had been brought against the Executive Council, it would have been bound to fail on the ground that the Government cannot fetter its future executive action.[15]

In more recent times, other attempts have been made to ground actions upon assurances given by public officials. A good illustration of this is provided by *Nova Media Services Ltd.* v. *Minister for Posts and Telegraphs.*[16] Here the plaintiffs operated an illegal radio station without a licence. When their equipment was seized by officials from the Department, the plaintiffs sought an interlocutory injunction restraining the defendant from interfering with their broadcasting activities pending the outcome of a challenge to the constitutional validity of the broadcasting legislation. The plaintiff argued that the official inaction and tacit co-operation from the Minister, public representatives and State agencies had encouraged them "to enter into and to expand the particular business in which they are now engaged." Murphy J. expressed sympathy with their dilemma, but said that:

[11] [1921] 3 K.B. 300. *Red. Amphitrite* has been referred to as their lordship's contribution to the war effort.
[12] *Ibid.*
[13] [1926] I.R. 517.
[14] On this point, see p. 714.
[15] *Ibid.* 527.
[16] [1984] I.L.R.M. 161.

"If the position is that persons in authority are prepared to make use of and co-operate with illegal radio broadcasts, it is not surprising that the owners of those stations should assume that they have an immunity from the law or that, at the very least, the law would not be enforced against them. However, the effect of a statute is clear. It does not wither away from lack of use and it cannot be repealed, waived or abandoned, even by the express decision or agreement of the Executive or any administrator and still less by an explicit representation by public representatives or State agencies."[17]

It should be emphasised that what was involved here was not, as in *Red. Amphitrite*, a commitment to exercise a discretionary power in a particular way but rather a promise to ignore a statute, moreover a statute creating a criminal offence. Seen in this light, the outcome was altogether unsurprising.

There is no doubt but that if the *ultra vires* principle is strictly applied, it is capable of causing considerable injustice and, incidentally, largely stifling the legitimate expectation—estoppel doctrine at birth in the public law field. As will be demonstrated by the survey of the case law in Part 3, the law in this area remains immature and in particular no satisfactory accommodation has been found between the conflicting tensions of the *ultra vires* principle and the legitimate expectation—estoppel doctrine. Indeed, the determination which tension is to prevail varies from judge to judge. In the past, one compromise which was suggested was to confine the legitimate expectation—estoppel doctrine to procedural rights.[18] But as we shall see, this limitation, if it ever existed, has long gone. Another stopping point, which was accepted *obiter* by Henchy J. in *Green Dale Building Co.*, would be an exception which debarred a public authority from relying on a mere irregularity which it ought in fairness to have overlooked, but any such exceptions have been confined to technicalities.[19]

Henchy J. did not explain why technicalities represented an exception to the rule. It might be an example of the application of the *de minimis* principle. But perhaps the exception represents a wider principle which would allow an estoppel in respect of *ultra vires* action where the injustice to the plaintiff was not outweighed by any tangible public benefit.[20] Indeed, the very fact that a public body sees fit to resile from an earlier promise might itself amount to an abuse of discretionary powers and, hence, itself amount to an *ultra vires* act. Such a balancing of interests would surely be acceptable given that the object of the *ultra vires* rule is to protect the public inter-

---

[17] *Ibid.* 169.
[18] *R.* v. *Liverpool Corporation, ex p. Liverpool Taxi Fleet Operators Assoc.* [1972] 2 Q.B. 299; *GCHQ* case, and *Att.-Gen. of Hong Kong* v. *Ng Yuen Shiu* [1983] 2 A.C. 629. On the later case see pp. 683–684.
[19] *e.g. Wells* v. *Minister for Housing and Local Government* [1967] 1 W.L.R. 1000; *Lever Finance Ltd.* v. *Westminster L.B.C.* [1971] 1 Q.B. 222. But even these authorities are considered doubtful in light of more recent developments, see *Western Fish Products Ltd.* v. *Penwith District Council* [1981] 2 All E.R. 204 and *Rootkin* v. *Kent County Council* [1981] 1 W.L.R. 1186.
[20] Craig, *Administrative Law* (London, 1989), pp. 470–483.

est.[21] It could also be said that the mere fact that the public authority has acted *ultra vires* should not of itself be decisive, and that regard must be had to other considerations.[22]

Against this, it has been suggested that a public body should be bound by *ultra vires* representations by its authorised agents when that body is acting in a proprietary rather than in a governmental or administrative capacity.[23] This proposition has a certain superficial attractiveness, but its application involves the difficulty of characterisation, namely, the distinction between what is a governmental and what is a proprietary function which is not easy to draw.

At another level, the doctrine of estoppel might be allowed to apply to representations which were beyond the powers of the official who gave the assurance but which were not actually *ultra vires* the public body itself. Such an approach has obvious affinities with the "internal management rule" in company law[24] and appears to have been adopted—albeit without elaborate discussion—by Barron J. in *Kenny* v. *Kelly*.[25] Here the applicant had sought a deferral of a place offered to her by University College, Dublin. An administrative official informed the applicant's father that her request for a deferral for one year had been granted. As it happened, the official who had communicated that information had misconstrued her instructions, but, of course, the granting of such a deferral was not *ultra vires* the respondents. Barron J. held that this representation was binding, since if the official had misrepresented her instructions, this "does not entitle the respondent to deny her apparent authority to bind the respondent."[26]

Nevertheless, this approach would be of assistance only in a limited class of cases. In *Dublin Corporation* v. *McGrath*,[27] for example, the defendant submitted that the planning authority was estopped from denying the existence of planning permission in respect of an unauthorised structure. It appeared that an agent of the authority had given verbal permission for the construction of a garage which was subsequently erected by the defendant. The plea of estoppel failed, for, as McMahon J. observed, not only did the agent not have power to make such a representation, but such a representation was also *ultra vires* the planning authority itself.

If the courts propose to adhere rigidly to this "jurisdictional principle," then there is much to be said for compensating individuals who have relied to

---

[21] The courts regularly engage in such reasoning when exercising their discretion whether to invalidate administrative decisions: see, *e.g. The State (Cussen)* v. *Brennan* [1981] I.R. 181.
[22] Craig, *Administrative Law* (London, 1989), pp. 476–478.
[23] Craig, *op. cit.* p. 479.
[24] See Ussher, *Irish Company Law* (London, 1986), pp. 152–153.
[25] [1988] I.R. 457.
[26] *Ibid.* 462. *Cf.* the views of Costello J. in *Nolan* v. *Minister for Environment* [1989] I.R. 357 who did not think that the Minister could be bound by the views expressed by a local authority engineer in the course of a planning inquiry. A further point in *Kelly* was whether a university is a "public body" for this purpose (see further pp. 577–578). Barron J. held that the respondents had not disputed the applicant's entitlement to proceed by way of judicial review in sufficient time and went on to treat University College, Dublin as a "public body" for the purposes of this case.
[27] [1978] I.L.R.M. 208.

their detriment on an *ultra vires* representation.[28] It may be that the eventual solution which the courts will adopt is to find the public authority liable under the principle of *Hedley Byrne & Co. Ltd.* v. *Heller & Partners Ltd.*,[29] *i.e.* liability in negligence for careless misrepresentations resulting in pure financial loss to the misrepresentee, even though no contractual or recognised fiduciary relationship between the parties exists. In addition, such cases would seem to come within the ambit of the Ombudsman's power.[30]

3. Legitimate Expectations and Estoppel: Current Developments

The impetus for the present developments in the law has largely come from the decision of the House of Lords in *Council of Civil Service Unions* v. *Minister for the Public Service* ("the *GCHQ* case")[31] and that of the Supreme Court in *Webb* v. *Ireland.*

In the former case, the majority of employees working at Government Communications Headquarters, a highly sensitive defence establishment, belonged to a trade union. There was a long-standing practice whereby all matters pertaining to the terms and conditions of employment were the subject of prior consultation between the management and the unions. The British Government, fearing that industrial action at GCHQ was impairing defence readiness, unilaterally revised the conditions of employment for GCHQ employees by providing that they would no longer be eligible to join any trade union other than a departmental staff association recognised by the director of GCHQ

The House of Lords ruled, in the first place, that the exercise of prerogative powers was amenable to judicial review. The speeches of Lords Fraser and Diplock were notable, secondly, for the fact that they were willing to classify the practice of the consultation as a legitimate expectation enjoyed by the GCHQ employees and to hold that, in principle, the rules of natural justice had to be complied with when such an expectation was not going to be honoured. Lord Fraser said:

---

[28] Gould, (1971) 85 L.Q.R. 15, 18.

[29] [1964] A.C. 465.

[30] The Ombudsman Act 1980, s.4(2) provides, *inter alia*, that the Ombudsman may investigate any action where it appears to him that the action was, or may have been, taken "without proper authority" or as "the result of negligence or carelessness": see p. 287 and pp. 293–295.

[31] [1985] A.C. 374. This is not the first time that the phrase "legitimate expectations" has been used by the English courts, but *GCHQ* is regarded as the first major case in which the concept received the seal of approval of the House of Lords. Lord Denning had used this phrase in contrasting a legitimate expectation with a "mere privilege" in *Schmidt* v. *Home Secretary* [1969] 2 Ch. 149 (an aliens' expulsion case). Forsyth, *loc. cit.* comments that Lord Denning informed him in a private letter that he felt sure that the concept of legitimate expectations "came out of my own head and not from any continental or other source." The phrase was also used in a number of prison cases where prisoners sought to challenge loss of remission (*R.* v. *Hull Prison Board, ex p. St. Germain (No. 2)* [1979] 1 W.L.R. 1041 and *O'Reilly* v. *Mackman* [1983] 2 A.C. 237) and in cases where it was said that a public body should adhere to a settled procedure (*R.* v. *Liverpool Corporation*; *Att.-Gen. of Hong Kong* v. *Ng Yuen Shiu*: fuller references are given at pp. 675 and 682–683.

"Legitimate, or reasonable, expectation may arise either from an express promise given on behalf of a public authority or from the existence of a regular practice which the claimant can reasonably expect to continue."[32]

Lord Diplock added:

"[The] civil servants employed at GCHQ who were members of national trade unions had, at best, . . . a legitimate expectation that they would continue to enjoy the benefits of such membership and of representation by those trade unions in any consultations and negotiations with representatives of the management of that government department as to changes in any term of their employment. So, but again *prima facie* only, they were entitled, as a matter of public policy under the head of 'procedural impropriety,' before administrative action was taken on a decision to withdraw that benefit, to have communicated to the national trade unions by which they had theretofore been represented the reason for such withdrawal, and for such unions to be given an opportunity to comment on it."[33]

Lord Diplock went on to hold that, on the facts of the instant case, this prima facie right to consultation had to yield to the interests of national security. For the Government had decided to take action unilaterally, just because advance notice to the unions might very well lead to the kind of industrial action which the decision barring trade union membership to GCHQ employees was designed to prevent.

A further impetus was provided by the decision of the Supreme Court in *Webb* v. *Ireland*.[34] The plaintiffs were the finders of a hoard of treasure containing exceptionally valuable specimens of early Christian art. These articles were handed over for safe-keeping to the Director of the National Museum who assured the plaintiffs that they would be honourably treated. The plaintiffs' claim for recovery of the treasure failed, but they succeeded in their claim that they had a legitimate expectation that they would be honourably treated and that the State had failed to honour that assurance. Finlay C.J. put the matter thus:

"It would appear that the doctrine of 'legitimate expectations,' sometimes described as 'reasonable expectations' has not in those terms been the subject of any decisions of our courts. However, the doctrine connoted by such expressions is but an aspect of the well-recognised concept of promissory estoppel . . . whereby a promise or representation as to intention may in certain circumstances be held binding on the representor or promisor. The nature and extent of that doctrine in circumstances such as those of this case has been expressed as follows by Lord Denning M.R. in *Amalgamated Property Co.* v. *Texas Bank*:

---

[32] [1985] A.C. 401.
[33] *Ibid.* 412.
[34] [1988] I.R. 353. For an interesting account of some of the issues which arose in this multi-facetted case, see Kelly, "Hidden Treasure and the Constitution" (1988) 10 D.U.L.J. (N.S.) 5.

'When the parties to a transaction proceed on the basis of an underlying assumption—either of law or of fact—whether due to misrepresentation or mistake makes no difference—on which they have conducted the dealings between them—neither of them will be allowed to go back on that assumption when it would be unfair or unjust to allow him to do so. If one of them does seek to go back on it, the courts will give the other such remedy as the equity of the case demands.' "[35]

The plaintiffs had argued that the long-standing practice of the National Museum of paying rewards to finders of such treasure was enough to create a legitimate expectation to fair compensation in their favour, but Finlay C.J. did not find it necessary to rule on this point. In his view:

"[T]he plaintiff's claim for compensation rests solidly on the fact that the assurance given to Mr. Webb that he would be honourably treated (which should be held to mean that he would be reasonably rewarded) was an integral part of the transaction whereby he deposited the hoard in the National Museum. It would be inequitable and unjust if the State were to be allowed to repudiate that assurance and give only a meagre and disproportionate award."[36]

Thus analysed, the *Webb* decision would seem to have been an instance of a generous application of the doctrine of promissory estoppel, rather than presaging a radical new development in the law. Moreover, this judgment was given in the context of a case in which no statutory powers of the State were involved and, accordingly, where there was no potential conflict between the plaintiff's legitimate expectations and the doctrine that the exercise of statutory powers may not be fettered by estoppel. But it is also worth noting that the rights at issue in *Webb* were substantive rights, whereas the legitimate expectation recognised in *GCHQ* was procedural only—the right to advance consultation. In any event, the decision in *Webb* has given rise to a host of new cases and, as might be expected from an area of law in the early stages of its development, many doctrinal questions have yet to be adequately resolved. We turn now to analyse three of these points.

What conduct or practice gives rise to an expectation or estoppel?

It is self-evident that an expectation or an estoppel may be grounded upon an explicit statement of the person who is seeking to rely upon it. However, the facts seldom present themselves in such a convenient form. More commonly, the question which is posed is whether some conduct or settled practice will suffice.

It may be noted that in *Webb*, Finlay C.J. did not find it necessary to decide whether the long-standing practice adopted by the National Museum of pay-

[35] *Ibid.* 384. The quotation from Lord Denning is at [1982] Q.B. 84, 122.
[36] *Ibid.* 385.

ing *ex gratia* sums to the finders of treasure trove could *of itself* give rise to a legitimate expectation which would be enforceable against the State. The question has subsequently arisen as to whether a regular practice, of itself, can give rise to a legitimate expectation, as suggested by Lord Fraser in the *GCHQ* case.

This very question was considered by Blayney J. in *Wiley* v. *Revenue Commissioners.*[37] The respondents operated a scheme whereby disabled drivers could obtain a refund of excise duty and value added tax levied on motor vehicles where it was established that the owner was disabled and that the vehicle was otherwise exempt for road tax under section 43(1) of the Finance Act 1968. This statutory exemption was granted where the driver could show that he was disabled to the extent that he was "wholly, or almost wholly, without the use of each of his legs." The applicant had certain physical disabilities which prevented him driving an ordinary motor car, but it was conceded his disability did not correspond to the criteria which would entitle him to a refund or exemption. Nevertheless, on two occasions the applicant applied for, and was granted, a refund of excise duty and VAT. By the time of the applicant's third application for a refund, the respondents had altered their practice in that they required not only a certificate of exemption from road tax, but also a copy of the medical certificate on which the road tax exemption was granted. As the medical certificate disclosed that the applicant did not satisfy the exemption criteria, his application was refused.

As we shall see, the present question was not the major issue at stake in *Wiley*. However, it is worth noting that Blayney J. stated that: "the doing of something on two occasions only could not constitute a practice" and then went on to observe that:

> "[T]he granting of a refund of the excise duty to eligible persons under the scheme could be held to constitute a regular practice which such persons could reasonably expect would continue. Accordingly if, without notice, the Revenue Commissioners were to cease operating the scheme, or were to change it so that persons formerly eligible lost their eligibility, I consider that in that case, the principle of legitimate expectations would apply so as to give such persons a remedy by way of judicial review if they had suffered loss by reason of the cessation or alteration of the scheme without their being given notice. But such is not the situation in the present case."[38]

A slightly different point arose in *Egan* v. *Minister for Defence.*[39] The applicant was an aircraft pilot with the Air Corps, but because of the large number of such pilots who were leaving the Defence Forces in order to fly with commercial airlines, the Minister refused him permission to retire prematurely. It was claimed that the applicant had a legitimate expec-

---

[37] [1989] I.R. 350.
[38] *Ibid.* 356.
[39] High Court, November 24, 1988.

tation that such permission would be granted, but Barr J. could not accept this:

> "Even if I were to proceed from the premise . . . that in 1966 when the applicant joined the army, there was a long-established and universally recognised practice that officers of five years' standing and upwards who apply to the Minister for permission to retire early were duly given leave to do so and that that practice continued until mid-1988, it would not derogate from the Minister's statutory right to refuse permission on reasonable grounds in any particular case. Such a practice, however firmly entrenched it may have been in the life of the permanent Defence Forces, did not amount to an implied promise or representation (as envisaged by Finlay C.J. in *Webb* v. *Ireland*) made by the Minister to the officer corps that permission to retire would be granted in each and every case."[40]

In contrast, however, a claim of this kind did succeed in *Duggan* v. *An Taoiseach*[41] where the applicant civil servants challenged a decision of the Government to transfer them from the Farm Tax Office to another department following the purported suspension of the operation of the Farm Tax Act 1985. It was held, in the first place, that because of the unusual nature of the applicants' transfer to the Farm Tax Office, and because the Office was established for a specific purpose and for a limited period, they could not have had any expectation that they would be allowed to remain in those posts on a permanent basis. Secondly, however, the applicants did have a legitimate expectation that they would continue in the post to which they had been appointed in an acting capacity until the work of the Office was either completed or terminated in accordance with law. Hamilton P., thus, held that the (unlawful) decision of the Government to suspend the operation of the Farm Tax Office constituted an infringement of the applicant's legitimate expectations. A further example of conduct giving rise to a legitimate expectation is supplied by *Ghneim* v. *Minister for Justice*,[42] a case decided by the same judge. Here the applicant was a Libyan national who had illegally remained in Ireland beyond the time period stipulated by his entry visa. He had, however, applied in March 1988 for permission to stay to complete his studies in Ireland and, at the date of the hearing in September 1989, this request was still under consideration. Hamilton P. went so far as to hold that this delay in informing the applicant of a decision in his case was such that he had developed a reasonable expectation that his request that he be permitted to complete his studies would be granted. Hamilton P. accordingly granted an injunction restraining the Minister from taking steps to force the applicant to leave the jurisdiction until the latter had a reasonable time to complete his studies.[43]

---

[40] *Ibid.* pp. 15–16 of the judgment. A similar claim was made in *The State (Rajan)* v. *Minister for Industry & Commerce* [1988] I.L.R.M. 231, 242 to the effect that established disciplinary practices were not followed in the applicant's case and that his legitimate expectations were accordingly violated, This claim was found by Barron J. not to arise on the facts of the case.
[41] [1989] I.L.R.M. 710.
[42] *The Irish Times*, September 2, 1989.
[43] Which Hamilton P. considered as being 12 months from the date of the hearing.

Is an assurance or representation of itself enough to give rise to a legitimate expectation?

There have been three decisions of the High Court which hold that a mere representation *of itself* will not give rise to a legitimate expectation, as there must be something approaching reliance or change of circumstances so as to make it unfair or inequitable for the representor to renege on an assurance.[44]

In the first of these cases, *Garda Representative Association* v. *Ireland*[45] the plaintiffs sought to rely on an assurance given by the Minister for Justice in the Dáil that certain overtime payments would not be abolished without consultation with the representative associations. Murphy J. held that this could not form the basis of a legitimate expectation, "as there [was] no evidence that the plaintiffs relied upon the Minister's statement."[46] In addition, any such representation must be unqualified and unambiguous. This point was made by Lardner J. in *Devitt* v. *Minister for Education*[47] where the plaintiff had submitted that since the Minister had allowed the applicant to apply for a permanent teaching post, she could not turn around and appoint the applicant to a mere temporary post. In the absence of an "unqualified assurance" (such as had been given in *Webb*), Lardner J. did not think that the applicant had acquired a legitimate expectation that she would be appointed to a permanent position:

> "There are really only two matters alleged as involving the Minister . . . [First] the fact that an inspector of the Department of Education sat on the board which interviewed the applicant and [secondly] the letter from the Department in reply to the applicant's inquiry as to the point of the salary scale at which the applicant had left her previous teaching appointment and would re-enter it if appointed. None of these matters appear to involve any assurance by the Minister of the kind contended for by the applicant."[48]

And in *Cosgrove* v. *Legal Aid Board*,[49] the applicant argued that she had acquired a legitimate expectation by reason of the general representations made concerning the legal aid scheme that the Board would deal promptly with her application for assistance. While Gannon J. acknowledged that while the "existence of the scheme and the nature of its purpose and its availability" may have given rise to expectations, she had not acquired a legitimate expec-

---

[44] There is also a separate line of authority to the effect that the claim for breach of legitimate expectation will not arise where the promise made by the representor was never communicated to the applicant. Thus, in *Nolan* v. *Minister for Environment* [1989] I.R. 357 Costello J. held that the applicant could not rely on an alleged representation in a letter sent to her local residents' association in the absence of evidence that this representation was communicated to her at the relevant time. Likewise in *Devitt* v. *Minister for Education* [1989] I.L.R.M. 639 Lardner J. held that the applicant could not rely on the terms of a memorandum issued by the Minister to local authorities, since it had never been intended to communicate this information to the public at large.
[45] [1989] I.R. 193.
[46] *Ibid.* 205.
[47] [1989] I.L.R.M. 639. See p. 689.
[48] *Ibid.* 650–651.
[49] High Court, October 14, 1990.

tation in this regard since there was no evidence that she had acted to her detriment.

This approach seems somewhat unadventurous, representing an unwillingness on the part of at least some High Court judges to recognise the principle of legitimate expectations as being anything more than a species of the doctrine of promissory estoppel. The differences between these two principles are examined at Part 6 below. There are at least some cases where a mere representation from a public official should be enough to create a legitimate expectation, even where there is no element of reliance. This is well illustrated by a decision of the Privy Council in *Att.-Gen. of Hong Kong* v. *Ng Yeun Shiu*.[50] In this case the Government of Hong Kong had announced that certain illegal immigrants who were otherwise liable to deportation without a hearing would be interviewed individually and that each case would be treated on its merits. A removal order was subsequently made against Mr. Ng before he had been given an opportunity of putting forward all the circumstances of his case. Lord Fraser held that the Government had failed to honour the promise which it had made to the illegal immigrants, including Mr. Ng. The deportation order was quashed and Lord Fraser explained that:

> "The justification for the doctrine of [legitimate expectations] is primarily that, when a public authority has promised to follow a certain procedure, it is in the interests of good administration that it should act fairly and should implement its promise, so long as implementation does not interfere with its statutory duty."[51]

The commitment in *Ng Yeun Shiu* was in regard to procedure. However, this was not true of *R.* v. *Home Secretary, ex p. Ruddock*,[52] where the applicant sought to quash a decision of the British Home Secretary. Successive Home Secretaries had made public criteria and guidelines indicating the manner in which they proposed to exercise their discretion (as to phone-tapping). Taylor J. said that "it would be hard to imagine a stronger case of expectation" which arose from both an express promise on behalf of a public authority and the "existence of a regular practice which the claimant can reasonably expect to continue."[53]

In both *Ng* and *Ruddock* there was no sense in which the applicants had relied to their detriment or changed their position on the strength of the official representations in question. Rather, the explanation for the existence of the legitimate expectation lay in the fact that, as Lord Fraser explained in *Ng*, it was in the "interests of good administration that it should act fairly and

---

[50] [1983] 2 A.C. 629.
[51] *Ibid.* 638. Thus, in *Gaw* v. *Commissioner of Corrections* (1986) Can.Admin.L.R. 137, one Canadian judge (Dube J.) has used language which finds a ready response in the present Irish political and sporting climate:

> "One does not change the rules in the middle of the game, especially where the rights of persons are at play."

[52] [1987] 2 All E.R. 518.
[53] *Ibid.*

should implement its promise." As much could have been said in the *Garda Representative Association* case and *Devitt*.

When is an expectation "legitimate"?

The major reason why the plaintiff failed in *Wiley* was Blayney J.'s finding that it was necessary for the applicant to show not only that he had an expectation that he would receive the refund; but also that such an expectation was a legitimate one:

> "I am prepared to accept that [the applicant] had an expectation that he would get a refund. This arose from the fact that he had got such a refund on two previous occasions. But I am unable to accept that his expectation could be said to be a legitimate expectation. It did not derive from his having been eligible under the scheme to get the refund since it is now conceded that he was not. . . . [I]t is only [where the applicant] considered that he was entitled to the refund that he could have a legitimate expectation of getting it again. Otherwise, at best, all he could have believed was that he had a good chance of getting it because he had got it twice before. And no doubt that would have been a reasonable belief. But it fell far short of being a legitimate expectation. . . . Such expectation as he had could only have been the result of a failure to appreciate what any reasonable person ought to have known [about the relevant criteria] and for that reason could not in my opinion constitute a legitimate expectation. And, of course, if he did in fact know what it seems to me he ought to have known, there could be no question of his having any real expectation, let alone a legitimate one."[54]

A slightly different point is exemplified by *Cannon* v. *Minister for Marine*.[55] Here the applicant had applied in 1986 for a licence for a particular boat which he hoped to purchase and the licence was duly granted. It then transpired that he could not afford that particular boat. The Minister then allowed the applicant, on a concessionary basis, an opportunity to purchase another vessel of similar size and indicated that he would also grant a licence in respect of such a vessel. The applicant delayed for a two year period before he contemplated purchasing such a vessel, but was then refused a licence. Barr J. acknowledged that the applicant had acquired an expectation that the licence would be granted, but this could not be regarded as a legitimate one:

> "I am satisfied that neither party ever envisaged that the Minister's concession was intended to be open-ended. I apprehend that when it was made both parties assumed that it was to apply for a reasonable period to enable the applicant to find a suitable alternative vessel. There is no evidence to suggest that either party contemplated that it might take upwards of two years to do so."[56]

[54] [1989] I.R. 350, 355.
[55] [1991] I.L.R.M. 261.
[56] *Ibid*. 267.

Reasons justifying a change of position

Even where the citizen has acquired a legitimate expectation, the public body is probably entitled to resile from its previous practice or representation where there are objective reasons which justify this change of position. If this is correct, the effect of the doctrine of legitimate expectations is only to protect the citizen against an arbitrary change of position by a public authority.

This very point had been made in the *GCHQ* case itself, where objective considerations of national security were found to justify a departure from previous practice. Similarly, the judgment of Barr J. in *Egan v. Minister for Defence*[57] provides a good illustration of these principles. Here the plaintiff was an officer in the Air Corps who sought the Minister's permission (as is required by the Defence Act 1954) for early retirement (in order to take up a position with a private airline). Barr J. found that there was, in fact, no settled practice giving rise to a legitimate expectation on the part of the plaintiff. Significantly, however, Barr J. added that even if the Minister had departed from previous practice, this would not have been either unfair or unjust in the circumstances:

"The criterion is whether the Minister's decision is reasonable having regard to the circumstances of the particular case. He is entitled . . . to take account of special circumstances such as those which occurred in 1988 when, within a short period of time, he was faced with numerous applications for early retirement from the Air Corps. . . . This created a new situation, and, in the interest of maintaining a viable Air Corps, he was entitled to deal with the matter as he did."[58]

Accordingly, a public body is entitled to change its position where new factors or objective alterations in circumstances will justify it in so doing and this remains true even though the private citizen had a legitimate expectation that the public body would adhere to the previous practice.

Limitation upon a statutory power

There are other limits to the scope of legitimate expectations. Principles discussed in Part II would seem to require that the doctrine could not be invoked to limit the scope of a statutory power or, indeed, to prevent the enactment or enforcement of legislation. Quite apart from cases such as *Nova Media Services Ltd. v. Minister for Posts and Telegraphs*,[59] or *Nolan v. Minister for the Environment*,[60] both *Devitt v. Minister for Education*[61] and *Pesca Valentia Ltd. v. Minister for Fisheries*[62] provide post-*Webb* examples of this limitation. In *Pesca Valentia* it was argued that the conduct of certain semi-state agencies such as the Industrial Development Authority gave rise to a legitimate expec-

[57] High Court, November 24, 1988.
[58] *Ibid.* pp. 15–16 of the judgment.
[59] [1984] I.L.R.M. 161. See pp. 674–675.
[60] [1989] I.R. 357.
[61] [1989] I.L.R.M. 639.
[62] High Court, June 6, 1989.

tation on the part of the plaintiffs that no fundamental legislative changes would be made affecting their right to fish.[63] Keane J. rejected this contention:

> "[W]hile the plaintiffs were undoubtedly encouraged in their project by semi-state bodies, they were not given any assurance that the law regulating fishing would never be altered so as adversely to affect them nor, if such an assurance had been given, could any legal rights have grown from it. No such 'estoppel' could conceivably operate so as to prevent the Oireachtas from legislating or the executive from implementing the legislation when enacted."[64]

A similar conclusion was reached by Lardner J. in *Devitt*, where he said that no legitimate expectation could restrict a Minister from exercising the full scope of her statutory powers under the Vocational Education Act 1930.

However, it is surprising that there have been at least two cases in which the courts have been prepared to allow a legitimate expectation to prevail against a statute. The first of these is *Waterford Harbour Commissioners* v. *British Railway Board*[65] where the Supreme Court effectively held that a statutory provision had been allowed to fall into disuse. The facts were that the defendants were under a statutory duty imposed by section 70 of the Fishguard and Rosslare Railways and Harbours Act 1898 to provide a daily steamer service between Waterford and the Welsh coast. Political considerations, changed commercial trends and the advent of war all combined to undermine the viability of the provision of a daily service. The parties reached an agreement in 1939 (which was extended and renegotiated on several occasions) and, as a result, the defendants agreed to provide a thrice-weekly service while the plaintiffs undertook not to sue for damages for breach of statutory duty. When the defendants gave notice of intention to discontinue the service in 1977, the plaintiffs sued for damages for breach of statutory duty and for breach of contract. A majority of the Supreme Court held that while the plaintiffs could sue for breach of contract, they were now estopped from pursuing the claim for breach of statutory duty, since by their conduct they had led the defendants to believe that their statutory obligations were "moribund or dead." Henchy J. added:

> "Thus, so far as the plaintiffs were concerned, from 1939 to 1977, section 70 had been allowed to become a dead letter. In the circumstances, the plaintiffs are estopped from reverting to the position they were in when they could justifiably have said that section 70 should be complied with."[66]

One special feature of this case is that this rare pre-*Webb* example of a successful plea of legitimate expectation was founded not upon practice but,

---

[63] For facts, see pp. 722–723.
[64] At p. 10 of the judgment. It remains an open question whether state-sponsored bodies attract the legitimate expectations doctrine: see pp. 320–321.
[65] [1979] I.L.R.M. 296.
[66] *Ibid.* 353.

initially, upon a formal agreement not to sue for damages, which had been renewed on several occasions over a 40-year period.

The second case is *Conroy* v. *Garda Commissioner*.[67] The facts were that the plaintiff had been injured in the course of his duties as a member of the Garda Síochána. He duly commenced proceedings under the Garda Síochána (Compensation) Acts. It was agreed between the parties that the case for compensation would be heard on the basis that the plaintiff would retire from the Gardái on a 100 per cent. disability pension and Finlay P. made his award to the plaintiff on that basis. It was subsequently determined that the plaintiff was entitled only to a 66 per cent. pension and fresh proceedings were then commenced claiming that he had now a legitimate expectation that he would receive a 100 per cent. disability pension.

Hamilton P. first dealt with the estoppel argument and rejected the contention that the plaintiff could be awarded a full disability pension by agreement:

"[T]he payment of a special pension is governed by the statutes, statutory orders and regulations relating to the pensions of members of An Garda Síochána and the procedures therein set forth must be followed. Consequently, I am satisfied that it was not open to the respondent in the Garda Síochána (Compensation) Act proceedings, or any person acting on his behalf to enter into an enforceable agreement with the applicant to grant him a special pension on the basis of 100 per cent. disability and that no enforceable agreement with regard thereto was entered into."[68]

Despite the failure of the estoppel argument, the plaintiff had nonetheless acquired a legitimate expectation that he would receive a full pension. The reason was that the sum awarded by Finlay P. in the earlier compensation proceedings would almost certainly have been greater had he but known that the plaintiff would only have received a 66 per cent. pension. According to Hamilton P.:

"The matter was dealt with by [Finlay P.] on the basis that the plaintiff would be entitled to and would be awarded a special pension based on 100 per cent. disability. The actuarial evidence before him was based on this assumption and counsel appearing on behalf of the Minister for the Public Service did not object to this or in any way suggest that the plaintiff would not be awarded a special pension based on 100 per cent. disability. In the events which have happened the plaintiff in those proceeding had, in my opinion, a legitimate expectation or reasonable expectation that he would have been awarded a 100 per cent. disability pension."[69]

Thus, on one view, an estoppel was allowed to prevail against the terms of a statutory provision. This flies in the face of the well-established orthodoxy, restated for example in *Nova Media Services*, that a statutory provision cannot be allowed to be "repealed, waived or abandoned" by decision or agreement.

---

[67] [1989] I.R. 140.
[68] *Ibid*. 144.
[69] *Ibid*. 147.

As against this, *Conroy* can be classified as a case where the plaintiff was compensated—via the legitimate expectations doctrine—for the earlier mistake.

4. Administrative Circulars and Legitimate Expectations[70]

The cases disclose that one of the most common ways in which legitimate expectations have been created is by way of an administrative circular. An early example of this is provided by *Latchford* v. *Minister for Industry and Commerce*,[71] which concerned a ministerial scheme providing for the payment of subsidies to bakers. This published scheme contained certain conditions, with all of which the plaintiffs had complied. The Minister refused to sanction the payment of the subsidy on the ground that the plaintiffs had been convicted of an offence relating to the sale of bread. The published conditions, however, did not disqualify a claimant on this ground. The Supreme Court accordingly made a declaration that the Minister was not entitled to withhold payment of the subsidy, with Murnaghan J. commenting:

> "After having made and published the conditions on which the payment of subsidy would be made, the Minister can alter these conditions from time to time; but until altered or withdrawn, the conditions apply, and persons who have complied with the conditions are entitled to claim that they have qualified for payment of the subsidy."[72]

This is a classic example of where an administrative circular may be said to have created legitimate expectations, although, of course, the Supreme Court did not use this language as such.

Another instance is provided by *Staunton* v. *St. Lawrence's Hospital*,[73] where the defendants had acted on foot of a Departmental circular issued by the Department of Health and arranged for the payment of special salary increases to certain consultants. The Department subsequently sought to issue a new circular revoking these special increases, but by this stage the hospital had entered into a new contract with the plaintiff which provided for these special payments. The hospital then claimed the cost of these additional payments from the State. It was common case that there was no statutory obligation imposed on the Minister for Health to make the reimbursements claimed by the hospital. Nevertheless, Lardner J. concluded that the State was bound by the terms of the original circular:

> "When the hospital acted in accordance with, and in reliance upon its terms, clause 12 [of the circular] gave rise to a contractual obligation which bound the Minister to adjust . . . the hospital's financial allocation to the extent that was necessary to cover the additional cost incurred by the hospital in respect of the common contract made with the plaintiff."[74]

---

[70] On administrative circulars, see further, pp. 39–50.
[71] [1950] I.R. 33.
[72] *Ibid*. 40–41.
[73] High Court, February 21, 1986.
[74] *Ibid*. pp. 9–10 of the judgment.

While this case may also be readily classified as one of legitimate expectations arising from reliance upon the terms of an administrative circular, it is really a case of promissory estoppel. The hospital had acted, to its detriment, upon a representation made by the Department and was allowed to use the estoppel not merely as a "shield," but also as a cause of action in itself to recover the moneys in question from the State.

But suppose that in *Latchford* the scheme had been superimposed on a statutory provision which had provided that the Minister may pay the subsidy in such circumstances "as he deems fit and proper." It is at this point that the doctrine of legitimate expectations runs up against the principle (discussed in Part II) that there can be no estoppel in respect of the exercise of statutory powers.

Such a situation is illustrated by the facts of *Devitt* v. *Minister for Education*.[75] In this case, one of the arguments in which was explained in the previous Part, the applicant had been appointed to a permanent teaching post by the County Dublin Vocational Education Committee. Under section 23 of the Vocational Education Act 1930, an application for a full-time position was to be made in the first instance to the appropriate Vocational Education Committee. The Committee's appointment was, in turn, subject to the Minister's approval. A ministerial circular entitled Memorandum V7 issued in 1967 appeared to indicate that the Minister would abide by the Committee's decision, provided the person in question was duly qualified and there was satisfactory evidence of age, health and character. In this case, the Minister— in an apparent effort to reduce the number of teaching posts created by Vocational Education Committees—invoked her powers under section 23(2) of the 1930 Act and refused to give her consent to the appointment. It was argued that the Minister was confined to the matters referred to in the circular and could not invoke other matters in seeking to exercise his discretion. Lardner J. could not accept this submission:

"No doubt in relation to the exercise of this statutory discretion the Minister may adopt general rules or procedures to guide himself [*sic*] or to notify other concerned parties as to the manner in which he will exercise his discretion provided that they are relevant to the exercise of his powers and are reasonable. But he is not in my view entitled by such rules or procedures to limit the scope of the discretion entrusted to him or disable himself from the full exercise of it. Nor in my judgment may such a practice be relied upon by the applicant as estopping a Minister from the full exercise of the discretion vested in her by the Act."[76]

---

[75] [1989] I.L.R.M. 639. Contrast this reasoning with that of the English Court of Appeal in *R.* v. *Home Secretary, ex p. Khan* [1985] 1 All E.R. 40 where it was held that the Home Secretary was bound to follow the procedures set out in a circular issued by him concerning the entry of children into the United Kingdom for adoption purposes. He was not entitled to depart from those procedures without affording those affected an opportunity to be heard. Lardner J. considered that *Khan* was distinguishable on the grounds (i) that the circular had not been issued to the general public; and (ii) the legitimate expectation contended for would be incompatible with the Minister's statutory duty.

[76] *Ibid.* 649.

5. Advance Rulings, etc., from the Revenue Commissioners and Legitimate Expectations

The administration of our tax laws would also seem likely to prove a fertile source of legitimate expectation claims. For it has long been a significant feature of tax practice in this jurisdiction that the Revenue Commissioners will give what have come to be known as "advance rulings"[77] on tax planning schemes, *i.e.* indicate their position in advance on whether a particular scheme will avoid a tax liability.[78] A second practice exists whereby the Revenue Commissioners will grant extra-statutory concessions to mitigate the rigour of the revenue code, although (in contrast to the practice prevailing in the United Kingdom) such concessions are not published. The reason for this refusal to publish is that the Revenue Commissioners assert that extra-statutory concessions exist on an individual basis and that general concessions are not allowed and, therefore, do not exist. The Commission on Taxation in its *Fifth Report* expressed dissatisfaction with this attitude, saying that if the interpretation of a particular piece of legislation amounts to the granting of an extra-statutory concession, then the same interpretation should apply in all similar situations.[79] Finally, there are occasional statements of practice by the Revenue Commissioners indicating generally what attitude they will take in regard to the interpretation and application of certain legislation. The Commission on Taxation concluded that the Revenue Commissioners were reticent to acknowledge the existence of these practices. Hard information on Revenue practice was difficult to come by and, in addition, the decentralisation of the Office of the Revenue Commissioners meant that there were inconsistencies in the operation of such practices.[80]

[77] The term "advance ruling" was defined by the Commission on Taxation in their *Fifth Report* (p. 47) as "a statement by the Revenue Commissioners on how they will interpret legislative provisions in a given situation." In contrast, in *Pandion Haliaetus Ltd.* v. *Revenue Commissioners* [1987] I.R. 309, Blayney J. appeared to be less enamoured of the term, saying ([1989] I.R. at 317) that there was no justification for attributing "the connotation of a final irreversible decision," as this term "advance ruling" was "not a term of art."

[78] Reardon, "The Operation of the Revenue Commissioners in Relation to Inland Revenue Matters" (Unpublished LL.M. thesis, University College, Cork, 1989) comments as follows (pp. 123–124):
"There is no general clearance or rulings procedure for transactions. The only exceptions are cases in which incentive reliefs for projects with which the Industrial Development Authority or another State agency is associated: see the White Paper, "Industrial Policy" (July, 1984), para. 8.5. The policy behind this exception is to attract foreign industry and investment to Ireland. So the general rule is that the Revenue Commissioners do not give advance rulings which are binding on Inspectors of Taxes when the latter come to compute tax liability, grant exemptions, reliefs or allowances or issue notices of assessment in individual cases. The reasons for this were outlined by the Revenue Commissioners to the Commission on Taxation (see *Fifth Report*, at para. 3.9) as follows:
(i) the volume of work to which this would give rise would be enormous;
(ii) the facts put before the Revenue Commissioners are often inconsistent with the final position;
(iii) the Revenue Commissioners could be liable for damages if the courts overturned their opinion; and
(iv) they do not wish to facilitate tax avoidance."

[79] *Ibid.* para. 3.18.

[80] *Ibid.* paras. 3.6 and 3.7.

There would seem to be room for the operation of the doctrine of legitimate expectations in any of these three areas so as to prevent the Revenue officials from reneging on prior representations or from unilaterally altering settled practices or from treating similarly situated taxpayers in an inconsistent fashion. However, as in other areas, this doctrine must be reconciled with the conflicting principle that the Revenue Commissioners, like other public officials, cannot be estopped in the exercise of their statutory powers.

This entire matter was considered by the House of Lords in *R. v. Inland Revenue Commissioners, ex p. Preston*.[81] The applicant had engaged in a series of sophisticated tax avoidance manoeuvres which had attracted the attention of the respondents. In 1978, the applicant arranged a settlement of his tax affairs, but as part of this arrangement, he was required to provide full information concerning certain share dealings. It subsequently transpired that the information supplied was, in Lord Templeman's words, "woefully inadequate" and in 1982, the respondents decided to reopen the earlier settlement. Was this a breach of the applicant's legitimate expectations or otherwise an abuse of power?

Lord Templeman agreed that, in principle, judicial review would lie in a case of this sort where the Commissioners had sought unilaterally to renege on an earlier representation:

"In principle, I see no reason why the appellant should not be entitled to judicial review of a decision taken by the commissioners if that decision is unfair to the appellant because the conduct of the commissioners is equivalent to a breach of contract or breach of representation. Such a decision falls within the ambit of an abuse of power for which in the present case judicial review is the sole remedy and an appropriate remedy."[82]

However, on the facts of the particular case, the claim failed because the applicant had not kept his side of the bargain: he had not disclosed relevant information in the manner requested by the respondents, so that it was not now unfair for the respondents to reopen earlier transactions.

A similar conclusion was arrived at by Blayney J. in *Pandion Haliaetus Ltd. v. Revenue Commissioners*.[83] Here the Revenue Commissioners were asked for, and gave, their views on the tax implications of certain patent licensing transactions. However, as had happened in *Preston*, the judge was satisfied that the respondents had not been given full details of the schemes as actually adopted by the applicant companies, so that the applicants could not rely on official correspondence "as being binding rulings or expressions of opinion in relation to the tax implications of the scheme."[84] However, what is more significant is that the judge went on to doubt whether such "advance rulings" could be binding:

"[The applicant's case] assumes that when the Revenue Commissioners

[81] [1985] A.C. 835.
[82] *Ibid.* 864–865.
[83] [1987] I.R. 307.
[84] *Ibid.* 318.

give a taxpayer an opinion on some query submitted to them, the tax-payer's Inspector is bound by that opinion and must act in accordance with it. I cannot see any legal basis for this. The Revenue Commissioners are not the agents of the Inspector of Taxes. And they would have to be his agents, acting with his authority, if their opinion was to bind him. . . . [N]either can be identified with the other. Accordingly, an Inspector is not bound by a prior opinion expressed to the taxpayer by the Revenue Commissioners. So, in the present case, even if the Revenue Commissioners had expressed opinions beforehand on the actual transaction which took place, it does not follow that the Inspector would have been bound by that opinion."[85]

Even making allowance for the fact that *Pandion Haliaetus* was decided a few months before *Webb*, this approach seems nonetheless unduly narrow and formalistic. Even if there is no formal relationship of agency between the Commissioners and an individual Inspector, this fact would not appear to be crucial. There was, after all, no formal relationship of agency between the Director of the National Museum and the State in *Webb*, yet the former's "unqualified assurance" was sufficient to bind the latter. It would seem quite wrong and unfair if a similar assurance given by the Commissioners could, without further justification, be unilaterally reneged upon by an individual Inspector and, in this respect, the wider view adopted by Lord Templeman in *Preston* is to be preferred.[85a]

6. The Distinction between Legitimate Expectations and Promissory Estoppel

In practice, these two principles may be regarded as convergent. So, for example, in *Kenny* v. *Kelly*[86] the applicant had been given an assurance that she could defer taking up a place at the Arts Faculty in University College, Dublin until the following academic year. Barron J. held that "whichever legal approach is adopted," the respondents were precluded by both the doctrine of legitimate expectations and that of promissory estoppel from reneging on that assurance. Barron J. added that:

"The principle of promissory estoppel upon which [*Webb*] was based applies equally in the present case. . . . The promise of a deferral was in effect a promise not to require the applicant to register and pay the balance of her fees in 1986, but a promise to permit her to do so instead in 1987. Such a promise to delay the enforcement of legal rights is of the essence of the doctrine of promissory estoppel as it has developed."[87]

There have been other judicial assertions which have gone so far as to state that the doctrine of legitimate expectations does not really represent an

[85] *Ibid.* 319. On this question of formal independence, see p. 406.
[85a] A better example of the situation under discussion might be the view that the D.P.P. could not be estopped from prosecuting because of an immunity purportedly granted by the Government.
[86] [1988] I.R. 457.
[87] *Ibid.* 463.

advance on the principle of promissory estoppel. In *Webb* v. *Ireland*, Finlay C.J. said that:

"It would appear that the doctrine of 'legitimate expectation' . . . has not in those terms been the subject of any decision of our courts. However, the doctrine connoted by such expressions is but an aspect of the well recognised equitable concept of promissory estoppel . . . whereby a promise or representation as to intention may in certain circumstances be held to be binding on the representor or promisor."[88]

Barr J. referred to this passage in *Cannon* v. *Minister for the Marine*[89] and added:

"An analysis of the foregoing statement of the law establishes that the concept of legitimate expectation being derived from an equitable doctrine, must be reviewed in the light of equitable principles. The test is whether in all the circumstances it would be unfair or unjust to allow a party to resile from a position created or adopted by him which at the time gave rise to a legitimate expectation in the mind of another that that situation would continue and might be acted upon by him to his advantage."[90]

This more conservative view was echoed by Murphy J. in his judgment in *Garda Representative Association* v. *Ireland*,[91] where he said that the Supreme Court in *Webb* had been "reluctant to recognise this doctrine [of promissory estoppel] as a new and separate doctrine within our legal system."[92]

However, despite the fact that both principles have appeared to work in parallel in cases such as *Webb*, *Garda Representative Association* and *Kenny*, there would appear to be some important doctrinal differences which have yet to be discussed, much less fully explored by the courts. The following analysis of these doctrinal differences between the principles of promissory estoppel and legitimate expectations is, accordingly, tentatively advanced.

(1) Strictly speaking, the principle of promissory estoppel can only apply to suspend or vary the legal rights already existing between the parties by virtue of a contractual or other similar relationship. This contractual element was clearly present in cases such as *Kenny* v. *Kelly*. Even in cases such as *Webb* (where there was, admittedly, no such contractual relationship) the relationship of bailor/bailee between the parties was sufficient to allow—on even the most orthodox view of the law—for the application of the promissory estoppel doctrine. Such a relationship is not, however, essential in the case of legitimate expectations as evidenced by cases where the plaintiff has sought to rely on

---

[88] [1988] I.R. 353, 384.
[89] [1991] I.L.R.M. 261.
[90] *Ibid.* 266.
[91] [1989] I.R. 193.
[92] *Ibid.* at 203.

the settled practices of a public body or representations made by it to the public in general and not necessarily to particular individuals.

(2) There must be an element of reliance or acting to one's detriment in order to give rise to a promissory estoppel. This would not seem to be essential in the case of legitimate expectations, which, focussing upon the behaviour of the decision-maker holds that the interests of consistency, good administration and equal treatment (it may be that Article 40.1 of the Constitution will some day be invoked here) may, in an appropriate case, of themselves require—without any element of reliance—that the decision-maker abide by its previous practice or representation. This point was made by the Privy Council in *Ng*, where the representation made to the illegal immigrants was held to be enforceable for this reason, even though all the elements required to found a promissory estoppel might not have been present in such a case. To take another example: suppose the Government were formally to undertake to release certain prisoners if they, in turn, undertook to renounce violence? In this example, there is no contractual or analogous relationship between the parties and it would be difficult to say that the prisoners acted to their detriment (in the sense that "detriment" is traditionally understood by the law of contract) so as to give rise to a promissory estoppel. However, in an appropriate case,[93] the courts could well hold such a promise to be legally binding by virtue of the doctrine of legitimate expectations?[94] The Irish courts have yet, however, to address this important issue.

(3) There is another reason why a claim of legitimate expectation applies to a wider category of cases than does a plea of estoppel. It arises from the fact that, of its nature, estoppel operates only if the author of the misrepresentation is himself involved in the case usually, it happens, as the defendant. By contrast, with a legitimate expectation, the author of the misrepresentation, who created the expectation, may be a third party to the case. In most of the decided cases, this factor made no difference since it happened that the author of the misrepresentation was a party to the case. However, there is a decision in which it might have been of significance. This is the *Pandion Haliaetus* case, the facts of

---

[93] Of course, one excludes from consideration, on public policy grounds, cases where the Government acted under duress or threats, such as where a promise to release a prisoner was made following a hostage-taking incident or kidnapping. One also excludes any argument founded on the possible notion that the power of pardon is not subject to judicial review on which see Chap. 10.5.
[94] In 1957 the Government made such a promise to internees who were interned under the Offences against the State (Amendment) Act 1940 in return for an undertaking not to engage in violent or unconstitutional activity. Interestingly enough, in *Lawless* v. *Ireland (No. 3)* [1978] 1 E.H.R.R. 15, 34 (decided in 1961) the European Court of Human Rights made the following observations:

"In a democratic country such as Ireland, the existence of this guarantee of release given publicly by the Government constituted a legal obligation on the Government to release all persons who have the undertaking."

See *O'Reilly* v. *Mackman* [1983] 2 A.C. 217, 275 (quoted at p. 696).

which have just been described. Here, it appears from the language of the passage quoted that Blayney J. analysed the situation as involving a plea of estoppel with legitimate expectation not being considered. On this analysis, he went on to reject the plaintiff's argument on the basis that the representation was given by the Revenue Commissioners, a separate entity from the Inspector of Taxes, who was the defendant in the case.

(4) By contrast, the next point of difference would seem to make it easier to establish a plea of estoppel. For if a public body makes an unambiguous representation to a private individual who then alters his position such as to give rise to a promissory estoppel, then it would seem to be irrelevant that, subsequently, new factors have come to light since then which would, objectively speaking, justify the body in question in changing its position or resiling from its representation.[95] The same would not, however, seem to be true of legitimate expectations. For example, had the defendants in *Egan* v. *Minister for Defence*[96] made a representation to the plaintiff giving rise to a promissory estoppel, then it would have been no answer for the Minister to say that new factors had subsequently emerged which justified him in resiling from that promise. However, as we have seen, Barr J. was of the view that, even if there was a practice giving rise to a legitimate expectation, new factors (such as the increasing depletion of Air Corps personnel) would have justified the Minister in departing from that practice. Similar thinking is to be found in the speeches of the House of Lords in *GCHQ*, where new supervening national security considerations were found to justify a departure from the previous practice giving rise to a legitimate expectation.

(5) It would seem that the doctrine of legitimate expectations is a principle whose operation is confined to the public law sphere and that it cannot be invoked in a *purely private law dispute*,[97] even if the defendant were a public authority. This point does not appear to have received judicial consideration in this jurisdiction, but it seems to follow from the first principles summarised in the preceding paragraphs, particularly from the principle, examined in paragraph 2, *viz.* that the principle of legitimate expectations contains an additional element over and above that of promissory estoppel, namely, that it is in the interests of fairness and good administration that a public body should not lightly or arbi-

---

[95] As opposed to circumstances which were known to at least one of the parties at the date of the transaction which is said to give rise to the promissory estoppel: see, *e.g. D. & C. Builders Ltd.* v. *Rees* [1966] 2 Q.B. 617. Here the defendants (who were fully aware of the plaintiffs' precarious financial position) had unfairly extracted a promise from them to accept a smaller sum in respect of certain debts. The English Court of Appeal found that, in the circumstances, it would not be inequitable for the plaintiffs to go back on their promise and they could sue for the balance of the debts. The decision would almost certainly have gone the other way if the defendants could have shown (i) that their precarious financial situation had arisen *after* the original promise had been made and (ii) they had altered their circumstances in reliance on that promise.
[96] High Court, November 24, 1988.
[97] See further, pp. 683–684.

trarily resile from a previous representation. By contrast, and subject only to the doctrine of promissory estoppel, a private citizen or undertaking is, in general, free to be as arbitrary as he pleases in his dealings. He is, for instance free (apart from the possibility of a constitutional action) to vary his prices from one customer to another. Lord Diplock was very much alive to this private law/public law dichotomy in *O'Reilly* v. *Mackman*,[98] where the plaintiff prisoners challenged a disciplinary decision forfeiting remission of sentence:

"So far as private law is concerned, all that each appellant had was a legitimate expectation, based upon his knowledge of what is the general practice, that he would be granted the maximum remission. . . . In public law, as distinguished from private law, however, such legitimate expectation gave to each appellant a sufficient interest to challenge the legality of the adverse disciplinary award made against him by the board. . . . "[99]

7. Res Judicata and Functus Officio

One particular specialised species of estoppel is *res judicata*. The doctrine of *res judicata*, in relation to the judgment of a court, has been defined in the following manner by Holmes L.J.:

"A judgment not appealed from binds the parties and privies for all time by what appears on its face; and if it can be shown that, in the course of the action that resulted in the judgment, a certain definite material issue not set forth in the judgment itself was raised by the parties and determined judicially or by consent, it would be contrary to public policy to allow the same parties to re-agitate the same matter in subsequent legal proceedings."[1]

The two aspects of *res judicata* are contained in this passage. First, a "cause of action" estoppel precludes the same parties from relitigating an action which has been finally determined by a court of competent jurisdiction—this is *res judicata* "in its most essential form."[2] Secondly, an "issue estoppel" (or "constructive *res judicata*") prevents the parties to the earlier proceedings litigating an essential feature—"a certain definite material issue"—of the earlier decision.[3]

The doctrine of *res judicata* has hitherto had a limited application in regard to administrative decisions.[4] Such decisions rarely fulfil the required *probanda* for *res judicata*: they do not deal with matters of status[5] and generally

[98] [1983] 2 A.C. 237.
[99] *Ibid.* 275.
[1] *Irish Land Commission* v. *Ryan* [1900] 2 I.R. 565, 584. For a general discussion of this topic see Spencer Bower, Turner, *Res Judicata* (London, 1969).
[2] Spencer Bower, Turner, *op. cit.* p. 149.
[3] *D.* v. *C.* [1984] I.L.R.M. 173; *Hoystead* v. *Federal Taxation Commissioner* [1926] A.C. 155.
[4] Ganz, "Estoppel and Res Judicata in Administrative Law" [1965] *Public Law* 237.
[5] *McMahon* v. *Leahy* [1984] I.R. 525 (prior extradition order).

do not involve a *lis* between private individuals.[6] More fundamentally, a rigid application of the doctrine might conflict with two essential principles of administrative law: that jurisdiction cannot be created by estoppel, and that statutory powers and duties may not be fettered.[7] Subject to all these qualifications, the doctrine of *res judicata* is not confined to courts of law but may also apply to tribunals and administrative authorities with powers to make binding determinations.[8]

That *res judicata* can only have a limited application in administrative law is well illustrated by a series of important decisions concerning rating and taxation. In *Society of Medical Officers of Health* v. *Hope*[9] a medical society successfully claimed before a Lands Tribunal that it was entitled to an exemption from rates. Some years later, a fresh valuation list was drawn up. Upon a further attempt being made to assess the society, *res judicata* was pleaded before the Lands Tribunal. Although it was conceded that there had been no material change of circumstances, the House of Lords ruled that no such estoppel arose. Emphasis was placed on the limited nature of the tribunal's jurisdiction, and Lord Radcliffe observed that the tribunal's jurisdiction was to decide the liability of a person "for a defined and terminable period." Put another way, the tribunal had a public duty to make a correct assessment on the ratepayer on each occasion, and no estoppel could be raised to prevent the tribunal from carrying out its duties under the statute. A similar conclusion was reached by a majority of the Supreme Court in *Kildare C.C.* v. *Keogh*.[10] Walsh J. pointed out that the doctrine of *res judicata* was inapplicable to rating cases, as the question of liability for rates for one year was always to be treated as inherently a different question to that of liability for another year, even though "there might be an identity on the question of law involved."

It is sometimes sought to explain away the above decisions by saying that "administrative" as opposed to "judicial" decisions were involved.[11] But such

---

[6] *R.* v. *Fulham Rent Tribunal, ex p. Zerek* [1951] 2 K.B. 1, 11, *per* Devlin J.

[7] *Bradshaw* v. *M'Mullan* [1920] 2 I.R. 412 (prior court settlement contrary to Local Government (Ireland) Act 1898; plea of *res judicata* failed as one cannot give "judicial effect to a transaction which the statute expressly forbids" (Lord Shaw)), and see also the comments of Walsh J. in *Kildare C.C.* v. *Keogh* [1971] I.R. 330, 343; "It would be contrary to public policy that an erroneous construction of a statute should be perpetuated so as to decide successive claims between the same parties." However, this rationale has been rejected by Lord Bridge in *Thrasyvoulou* v. *Secretary of State for Environment* [1990] 2 W.L.R. 1, 8.

[8] *Athlone Woollen Mills Ltd.* v. *Athlone U.D.C.* [1950] I.R. 1; *Thrasyvoulou* v. *Secretary of State for Environment* [1990] 2 W.L.R. 1 and *Crown Estate Commrs.* v. *Dorset County Council* [1990] 2 W.L.R. 89.

[9] [1960] A.C. 551.

[10] [1971] I.R. 330, following the Privy Council decision in *Caffoor* v. *Colombo Income Tax Commissioner* [1961] A.C. 584 where it was held that a tribunal's determination that a certain trust was charitable was conclusive only for the relevant *year of assessment*. The doctrine of *res judicata* did not prevent the tribunal from reopening this question in any subsequent years. But in England, Millett J. has said that these tax and rating cases should be regarded as *sui generis* and anomalous and should not be regarded as detracting from the possible application of *res judicata* to administrative law in an appropriate case: *Crown Estate Commissioners* v. *Dorset County Council* [1990] 2 W.L.R. 89, 99.

[11] Ganz, *loc. cit.* deals with these arguments, and rebuts them in a convincing fashion.

technical arguments are unconvincing, for *res judicata* may operate once a tribunal has power to determine an issue. The true principle is, as Lord Keith pointed out in *Hope's* case, that no estoppel can prevent a public body from carrying out its public duty. This principle was recognised by O'Hanlon J. in *Aprile* v. *Naas U.D.C.*[12] where he declined to apply the doctrine of *res judicata* to a decision of a planning authority. The applicant applied for retention permission in respect of an amusement centre. This application was refused by the respondent planning authority on the grounds that the proposed amusement centre would constitute a traffic hazard, and as such would be contrary to the proper planning and development of the area. The applicant took steps to deal with these objections, and he made a further application for permission. Once again, the application was refused, but on this occasion the planning authority gave new grounds for the refusal.

O'Hanlon J. held that the doctrine of *res judicata* was inapplicable in the circumstances of the case. In his view, no estoppel could operate to prevent the authority from carrying out its statutory duty:

"If a fresh application is later made in relation to the development of the same lands, there is an obligation on the planning authority, whenever it is called upon to deal with the application, to consider it *de novo* and to have regard to all aspects of the proper planning and development of the area as of that time, in granting or refusing the application."

However, in a major decision, *Thrasyvoulou* v. *Secretary of State for the Environment*,[13] the House of Lords has confirmed that while the principle of *res judicata* does not apply to the *refusal* of planning permission—since such a refusal does not serve to create a legal right to such permission in favour of the applicant—the converse is *not* true.[14] In other words, adjudicative decisions which have been resolved in favour of the private citizen can, in principle, attract the doctrine of *res judicata*. As Lord Bridge explained, the public policy behind *res judicata* was of such fundamental importance that its application could not be confined to private law litigation:

"In principle, [*res judicata*] must apply equally to adjudications in the field of public law. In relation to adjudications subject to a comprehensive self-contained statutory code, the presumption, in my opinion, must be that where the statute has created a specific jurisdiction for the determination of any issue which establishes the existence of a legal right, the principle of *res*

---

[12] High Court, November 22, 1983. But *cf. Dublin C.C.* v. *Tallaght Blocks Co. Ltd.*, Supreme Court, May 17, 1983 where Hederman J. stated that where a developer applied for planning permission in respect of an unauthorised structure and was refused, he could not later be heard to argue that permission for the development was not required.

[13] [1990] 2 W.L.R. 1.

[14] Lord Bridge rationalised this apparent dichotomy in the following terms:

"A decision to grant planning permission creates, of course, rights which such a grant confers. But a decision to withhold planning permission resolves no issue of legal right whatever. It is no more than a decision that in existing circumstances and in light of existing planning policies the development in question is not one which it would be appropriate to permit. Consequently, in my view, such a decision cannot give rise to an estoppel *per rem judicatam.*"

judicata applies to give finality to that determination unless an intention to exclude that principle can properly be inferred as a matter of construction of the relevant statutory provisions."[15]

Lord Bridge acknowledged that a statutory body could not, by estoppel, fetter the exercise of its statutory powers, but said that the principles underlying *res judicata* were so different from that which underlies estoppel by representation that the authorities on estoppel in public law had "no relevance" for this purpose.

If Lord Bridge's analysis is followed in this jurisdiction, this would seem to leave room for a much greater application of the doctrine of *res judicata* in administrative cases than had hitherto been thought possible.[16] The potential application of this principle to decisions of administrative bodies exercising limited judicial powers under cover of Article 37 is obvious, provided, of course, that such decisions create legal rights in favour of the applicant (such as by granting a licence or permission) and this principle may be applied more widely to all administrative adjudications involving a decision in the nature of a *lis*. This, perhaps, would only as it should be, since it would be most unfair that administrative bodies should be allowed to resile from the implications of a previous adjudication in favour of an individual citizen.

The *res judicata* doctrine must not be confused with the situation where the decision-taker has become *functus officio*. If a public authority has statutory power to determine some question its decision will generally be final and irrevocable. This is not because of the operation of *res judicata*, but rather because the authority lacks jurisdiction to alter its original decision and has become *functus officio*.[17] The *functus officio* doctrine is likely to become more significant in the future.

8. Judicial Review and Res Judicata

We turn now to a different focus of attention: we are concerned not with the original decision taken by a public authority, but with the situation in which such a decision has been subject to judicial review. The question is whether the High (or Supreme) Court decision in the judicial review proceedings attracts the *res judicata* doctrine. It would seem that, up to recently at any rate, *res judicata* was inapplicable in cases where the public law remedies of certiorari, prohibition and mandamus had been refused (as opposed to being granted). These remedies were primarily regarded as being concerned with

---

[15] *Ibid.* 8. See also, to the like effect, *Crown Estate Commissioners* v. *Dorset County Council* [1990] 2 W.L.R. 89.

[16] It is only in very exceptional circumstances (such as that disclosed in the *Athlone Woollen Mills* case) that the doctrine of *res judicata* has been applied to decisions of planning authorities in this jurisdiction. However, in *The State (Kenny and Hussey)* v. *An Bord Pleanála*, Supreme Court, December 20, 1984, McCarthy J. observed that while he did not have to determine whether *res judicata* applied to planning decisions, he found it difficult to see how a planning authority could be permitted "to come to a different view when circumstances do not change." For a similar approach, see *O'Dea* v. *Minister for Local Government* (1957) 91 I.L.T.R. 169.

[17] *Re 56 Denton Road* [1952] 2 All E.R. 799. See also, *Re Lynham's Estate* [1928] I.R. 127.

the maintenance of order in the legal system. It was argued that they did not purport finally to determine the *private* rights of the parties *inter se*, and it was said that the court was merely required to decide "whether there had been a plain excess of jurisdiction or not."[18] Therefore, where the High Court or Supreme Court had, for example, refused to quash a decision of the Rent Tribunal in *certiorari* proceedings, it would still have been open to the landlord to argue in subsequent civil proceedings that in fact no tenancy had existed and that the Rent Tribunal acted *ultra vires* in assuming jurisdiction. The fact that neither the High Court nor Supreme Court was prepared to quash this order could not be conclusive of the jurisdictional issue, which could then be tried *de novo* on oral evidence before the court which was seised of the landlord's application for (say) possession.

The basis for this principle was that the High Court could not readily assess the conflicting evidence simply on the basis of the affidavits tendered in the old form of State side proceedings. (It is just for this reason that *res judicata* does apply where relief was refused following a plenary hearing in the case of an application for a declaration, injunction or damages). But it may be that this rationale had been undermined by the new Order 84, rule 25(1), which allows the court to conduct an oral hearing (including cross-examination of deponents on their affidavits) in an application for judicial review. If the court can thus inquire and determine *de novo* on oral evidence whether the facts giving rise to the tribunal's jurisdiction exist, can there be any sound reason why the refusal of certiorari, prohibition or mandamus should not attract the rule of *res judicata*?

---

[18] *R.* v. *Fulham Rent Tribunal, ex p. Zerek* [1952] 2 K.B. 11, 13, *per* Devlin J.

CHAPTER 14

THE STATE IN LITIGATION

1. Patrimony of the Prerogative

In the United Kingdom, the prerogative has been said to embrace "those rights and capacities which the King alone enjoys in contradistinction to others."[1] In the United Kingdom many of the former prerogative rights have been uprooted, qualified or superseded by statute, or shrivelled by desuetude. Nevertheless, the prerogative still covers a diverse bundle of rights, powers, privileges etc., most of which are exercised by the Crown on the advice of the responsible ministers.[2] In Ireland, by contrast, the prerogative has been largely superseded in that much of the ground which the prerogative covers in the United Kingdom is regulated by the Constitution or to a lesser extent, by statute. Thus, for instance, when the President appoints or removes Ministers or dissolves the Dáil, he does so on the authority of Articles 13.1 and 13.2 and 28.9.4, respectively. Again, the prerogative of mercy has been overtaken by the right of pardon and remission of punishment vested in the President by Article 13.6; whilst the prerogative to declare war is now grounded in Article 28.3.1 (which reserves this right to the Dáil). In the case of certain of the other prerogatives, their content is such as actually to conflict with the Constitution. Take, for example, the leading case of *Byrne* v. *Ireland*[3] which arose because the plaintiff had been injured when she fell into a trench dug by or, more probably, on the authority of, the Minister for Posts and Telegraphs. The State sought to defend itself by calling in aid the supposed prerogative of immunity from tort action. However, the Supreme Court held this prerogative to be unconstitutional. According to the narrower alternative ratio (the other ratio is covered below[4] in the following paragraphs) the reason for this was that this immunity interfered unjustifiably with the right to litigate a justiciable controversy (under Article 40.3.1). Another example is provided by a series of cases which held that, since the Central Fund of the Irish Exchequer does not have the character of a royal fund, it cannot attract the prerogative of priority of debts due to the State in case of an insolvency.[5] Again the prerogative of the Crown to enforce payment of a

---

[1] Blackstone, *Commentaries*, Vol.1, p. 239. See also, Wade, "Procedure and Prerogative in Public Law" (1985) 101 L.Q.R. 180.
[2] On the prerogative generally, see de Smith, *Constitutional and Administrative Law* (Penguin Books, 3rd. ed.), Chap. 4 and Wade, *Administrative Law* (Oxford, 1988), pp. 240–245.
[3] [1972] I.R. 241.
[4] See pp. 702–703, and 711–712.
[5] *Re P.C., an Arranging Debtor* [1939] I.R. 306; *Re Irish Mutual Employers Association Ltd.* [1955] I.R. 176.

judgment debtor by securing the arrest and imprisonment of the debtor is scarcely compatible with Article 40.4.1[6]

Pre-*Byrne*, it had, however been accepted[7]—although without much discussion—that, save for cases, where it had been superseded by, or was in conflict with, the Constitution or a statute, the prerogative had managed to navigate the rapids of 1922 and 1937. In short, it had been assumed that there was nothing in the nature or source of the prerogative to prevent its continued existence, as it continues to exist for instance in such former-colony Republics as Zambia. However, *Byrne*, now confirmed by the Supreme Court, in *Webb* v. *Ireland*,[8] gave the quietus to that notion. Nevertheless a brief summary of the present status of the prerogative, which represents such an important stage in the evolution of the law covered in the remainder of this chapter, remains relevant.

The view that the prerogative had survived the enactment of the Constitution of the Irish Free State in 1922 was based, in the first instance, upon Article 49.1 of the Constitution which provides that:

"All powers, functions, rights and prerogatives whatsoever exercisable in or in respect of Saorstát Éireann immediately before the 11th day of December, 1936, whether in virtue of the Constitution then in force or otherwise, by the authority in which the executive power of Saorstát Éireann was then vested are hereby declared to belong to the people."

This provision makes the inquiry turn on the antecedent question of whether the prerogative existed in Saorstát Éireann before December 11, 1936. The significance of this date lies in the fact that it was the day when the Irish Free State Constitution was amended to extirpate the King (formerly the head of state in whom all executive authority was vested under Articles 41, 51, 55, 60 and 68 of the Irish Free State Constitution). Prior to *Byrne*, it had been assumed that the presence of the King drew with it the prerogative. This argument was rejected by the majority in *Byrne* on two grounds. First, it was said that the King's powers could be confined to those actually specified in the 1922 Constitution: there was no necessary reason why they had to be identical with those which the Crown enjoyed in the United Kingdom or in pre-Independence Ireland. There is, however a different argument for saying that the prerogative came over into independent Ireland. It is that "[The prerogative]

---

[6] In *The State (Coombes)* v. *Furlong*, High Court, February 1, 1963, Davitt P. appeared to doubt whether this particular prerogative had survived "the constitutional changes of 1922 and 1937."
[7] In *Cooper* v. *Att.-Gen.* [1935] I.R. 425, 440 Johnson J. had said that "the prerogative rights of the Crown were carried over as part of the law of the Irish Free State by Article 73 of the [1922] Constitution." See also, *Re Mahony, a Bankrupt* [1926] I.R. 202; *Galway County Council* v. *Minister for Finance* [1931] I.R. 215; and *Re Irish Mutual Employers Association Ltd.* [1955] I.R. 176 for similar expressions of judicial opinion.
[8] [1988] I.R. 353. For criticism of this decision, see Kelly, "Hidden Treasure and the Constitution" (1988) 10 D.U.L.J. (N.S.) 5 and Gwynn Morgan, "Constitutional Interpretation" (1988) 10 D.U.L.J. (N.S.) 24.

was part of the common law which was applied to the Irish Free State by Article 73".[9] In regard to this argument, the kernel of the Court's argument is contained in the following extract from Walsh J's judgment[10]:

" . . . the basis of the Crown prerogative(s) in English law was that the King was the personification of the State. Article 2 of the Constitution of the Irish Free State declared that all the powers of government and all authority, legislative, executive and judicial, in Ireland were derived from the people of Ireland and that the same should be exercised in the Irish Free State through the organisations established by or under and in accord with that Constitution. The basis of the prerogative of the English Crown was quite inconsistent with the declaration contained in that Article. The King enjoyed a personal pre-eminence; perfection was ascribed to him."

(Article 2 is not reproduced separately here since it is quoted practically *verbatim* by Walsh J.)

This passage merits two observations. First, it might have seemed more realisitic to regard Article 2 as a statement of political principle, as a generalised warning to Irish Governments that they held their power "on trust" for the People along the lines of the generally accepted Lockeian, "Social Contract" theory of limited government; and also as a warning to the British Crown that as governmental authority came ultimately from the People, it was not for the British to start trying to take power away from the Irish Free State or to interfere with it in any way.

Secondly, leaving aside this criticism, the effect of Article 2 is to stipulate (i) that all powers of government flow in some sense from the People and, (ii) that these powers may only be exercised by the independent Irish organs of government. As to the content of the powers of government, little is said. In view of this, Article 2 could have been interpreted as not affecting the content of these powers but rather as relocating the basis of State authority from the King to the people and as shifting the mode of its exercise from the King to the organs established by the Irish Constitution.

At a broader level, Professor Kelly has criticised not so much the reasoning, as the conclusion, in *Byrne*. He summarises his views, characteristically cogently, in the following passage:

" . . . the statutory usage of the Irish Free State, positive and negative, together with the opinions of judges who played a part in drafting its Constitution, together with the record of what actually was done in those years in such matters as pardons, passports, and precedence of counsel, suggest that the Crown and its prerogative were understood to have survived into the newly independent Irish State, as part of the common law, under Article 73, so far as such survival was not, in letter or in spirit, inconsistent

---

[9] *Cork County Council* v. *Commissioners of Public Works* [1945] I.R. 561, 578, *per* O'Byrne J.
[10] [1972] I.R. 241, 272.

with some specific dimension of the new Constitution. I think that for us today, 50 or 60 years later, to take the line that our fathers and grandfathers in legal and official life quite misunderstood the nature of the machine they were not only operating but had also in fact constructed is to adopt an unreal and intellectually unamiable position."[11]

Irrespective of such criticisms, however, it is clear, now that the prerogative is not part of the Irish constitutional legal scene. This means that the State is without certain pockets of legitimate authority the need for which is likely to arise unexpectedly or in an emergency, when there might be no time for the passage of legislation. Examples (drawn from English Law) include the rules: permitting the seizure or destruction of private property, in time of war or imminent danger (albeit on payment of compensation); affording a significant component in martial law; and enabling the State to create corporations, without statutory authority.[12]

The question of the continued existence of the prerogative of treasure trove came up for consideration by the Supreme Court in *Webb* v. *Ireland*. The plaintiffs in this case were the finders of an exceptionally valuable hoard of early Christian objects who had handed over the artefacts to the National Museum for safe-keeping.[13] They were dissatisfied with the £10,000 compensation offered to them by the State and commenced proceedings seeking the delivery up by the State of these objects. The State pleaded that it was not a mere bailee, but that by reason of the prerogative of treasure trove, it had acquired a superior title to that of the plaintiffs.

The Supreme Court, affirming the reasoning of Walsh J. in *Byrne*, held that none of the royal prerogatives had survived the enactment of the Constitution. Nor was it possible, said Finlay C.J., to distinguish between the prerogative of sovereign immunity "which could be traced to the royal dignity of the King" and a prerogative of treasure trove which it was stated:

"[C]ould be traced or related not to the dignity of his person, but his position as sovereign or ruler. Such a distinction does not alter the view that I have expressed with regard to the effect of the Constitution of 1922, and appears to me to ignore the essential point which is that by virtue of the provisions of the Constitution of 1922 what was being created was a brand new sovereign State and that the function, power or position of the King in that sovereign State was such only as was vested in him by that Constitution and by the State created by it."[14]

While this meant that no part of the prerogative had survived, Finlay C.J. nevertheless went on to hold that the State did enjoy a right to a modern form

---

[11] Kelly, *loc. cit.* 14–15.
[12] Wade, *op. cit.* 240–245. .
[13] The find was described by Blayney J. as "one of the most significant discoveries of early Christian art ever made." The hoard was valued by him in a separate judgment at £5,536,000.
[14] [1988] I.R. 382.

of the treasure trove prerogative by virtue of Article 5, which proclaims that: "Ireland is a sovereign, democratic State."[15] Finlay C.J. stated:

> "[O]ne of the most important national assets belonging to the people is their heritage and knowledge of its true origins and the buildings and objects which constitute keys to their ancient history . . . [A] necessary ingredient of sovereignty in a modern state and certainly in this State, having regard to the terms of the Constitution, with an emphasis on its historical origins and a constant concern for the common good is and should be an ownership by the State of objects which constitute antiquities of importance and which have no known owner."[16]

The net effect of *Byrne-Webb*, therefore, while confirming that none of the prerogative rights have survived at common law, is to allow the State to assert the equivalent of such prerogative rights, *provided* that such rights can be shown to derive expressly or impliedly from the Constitution or which can be given a republican pedigree. Examples of the latter type of prerogative include the State's exemption from statute, since this rule was rationalised in *Byrne* v. *Ireland* as a rule which although:

> "[S]ometimes called a prerogative right . . . is, in fact, nothing more than a reservation, or exception, introduced for the public benefit, and equally applicable to all governments."[17]

These remarks were anticipated in the case of public interest immunity (or "executive privilege") from disclosure of documents as early as 1925 by Meredith J. in *Leen* v. *President of the Executive Council*.[18] Dealing with the suggestion that only the Crown could claim executive privilege, Meredith J. remarked:

> "[This privilege] appears to me to be broad based upon the public interest. . . . This privilege has roots in the general conception of State interests and the functions of Courts of Justice, which make it independent of the particular type of constitution under the body of law which recognises that principle is administered."[19]

A narrower and more convincing example of the same phenomenon—the

---

[15] Morgan, *loc. cit.* predicts that the "broadness and vagueness of the concept of sovereignty [contained in Art. 5] make it likely to be used as an aid when the post-1922 existence of the former prerogatives come before the Courts."

[16] [1988] I.R. 383. But it is not easy to see why State's ownership of such artefacts should be deemed to be an *inherent* feature of the State's sovereignty. A majority of the Court (Finlay C.J., Henchy and Griffin JJ.) also held the phrase "all royalties" contained in Art. 10.3 was broad enough to include artefacts, such as the Derrynaflan chalice. Walsh and McCarthy JJ. dissented strongly from this latter conclusion, with the former saying (at 393) that the word "royalties" was to be construed as referring to "the sums paid or payable for the use or exploration of the natural resources."

[17] [1972] I.R. 241, 287, *per* Walsh J., quoting from the judgment of Story J. in *United States* v. *Hoar* (1821) 6 Mason 311.

[18] [1926] I.R. 456.

[19] *Ibid.* 463.

re-location of a former prerogative on a more acceptable basis—concerns the right to a passport. Whilst this has as its origin in the prerogative[20] it seems likely that the present administrative arrangements would be upheld as a means of giving effect to the citizen's constitutional right to travel abroad.[21]

In any event, the general effect of *Byrne-Webb* is that whilst the prerogative has been formally expelled, certain former prerogatives may yet be admitted to the post-1922 polity. For this to occur, such prerogatives must comply with two conditions. The first of these, has always existed. It is a rational and relatively predictable condition, namely that the prerogative should not conflict with the Constitution. The effect of *Byrne-Webb* is to add a second—and, it is suggested—a vague and unnecessary condition. This has been articulated by reference to such subjective factors as the public interest (*Leen*); legislative intention (*Byrne*) (see page 726); and sovereignty (*Webb*).

2. The State as Juristic Person

In holding in *Bryne* v. *Ireland* that the State could be sued in tort, the Supreme Court necessarily confirmed that the State had legal personality. It is true that the significance of this is reduced to some extent by the fact that most central government functions are vested in Ministers who have been designated as corporations sole by the Ministers and Secretaries Act 1924. In addition, Article 28.2 makes a grant of the executive power of the State to the Government. however, this constitutional provision is carefully made "subject to the provisions of this Constitution" which suggests that the State retains in itself executive power for some purposes and this alone would be a ground on which to suggest that the State has some legal personality. It is also significant that it is the State and not the responsible Minister who is vicariously responsible for a tort committed by a civil servant, although the position in contract is less clear. The significance of this is that this common law responsibility is among the reasons why the State's legal personality is an important matter.

However, one further preliminary point which is of importance arises from the fact that in Britain there are two ways of defining the prerogative. The first is to restrict the prerogative to those powers which are unique to the Crown. The alternative and wider approach (and which is more common in practice) is to treat the prerogative as embracing "every power of the Crown

[20] This is certainly the position in England: "[T]here is no doubt that passports are issued under the royal prerogative in the discretion of the Secretary of State," *per* O'Connor L.J. in *R.* v. *Foreign Secretary, ex p. Everett* [1989] Q.B. 811, 817. Finlay P. took a similar view in *The State (M.)* v. *Minister for Foreign Affairs* [1979] I.R. 73, 76 where he said that the "granting or withholding of a passport does not appear to have been of statutory origin but would appear to have derived originally from the Crown prerogative."
[21] As recognised in *The State (M.)* v. *Minister for Foreign Affairs* [1979] I.R. 73 and *P.I.* v. *Ireland* [1989] I.L.R.M. 810.

which is non-statutory."[22] If the latter approach is adopted,[23] certain difficulties are presented by reason of the Supreme Court's decision in *Byrne* and *Webb* to the effect that the prerogative did not survive the constitutional changes after 1922, namely, that the State would be lacking in even the legal personality and attributes which are possessed by the ordinary artificial legal person, since this very personality is taken at common law to derive from the prerogative.[24] Such a suggestion, however, would serve only to confuse the character of the Irish State with that of the United Kingdom. In the United Kingdom it is the Crown, a corporation sole, whose character and capacities were initially determined by the prerogative, which acts as the State. In Ireland, the State is the creation of the people and designed according to the (admittedly rather vague) specifications of the Constitution.[25] The most that could ever have been claimed for the prerogative in Ireland is that, entering the polity via the bridges of Article 73 of the 1922 Constitution and Article 49.1 of the present Constitution, it might have contributed certain auxiliary rights and privileges to the capabilities of the State, rather than actually establishing it and shaping it. However, as we have seen as a result of *Byrne* and *Webb*, it has now been determined that the prerogative did not survive beyond 1922.

It seems clear, therefore, that the State's legal personality is independent of the prerogative and not in any sense contigent on its survival. The question then is whether the State has all the usual powers of a legal person to: sue and be sued; establish companies; expend money and generally bear similar legal rights and duties to those of an ordinary artificial person. These are now matters to be determined by the Constitution, as interpreted by case law. However, it is true that:

> "[T]he Constitution gives no express answer [to the question of the State's legal personality], nor to questions about the State's legal capacities or privileges. These answers must be elaborated from the narrow base of Article 5, with the help of some other indications."[26]

Nor does statute offer any real assistance, for the only statutory provisions even to allude to this matter are sections 10 and 11 of the State Property Act 1954, which confer extensive powers on the Minister for Finance in relation to the sale, exchange, transfer and leasing of State lands. And insofar as the

---

[22] Dicey, *Law of the Constitution* (10th ed.), p. 425, quoted by Wade, "Procedure and Prerogative in Public Law" (1985) 101 L.Q.R. 180, 191. See also, Wade, *op. cit.* 241–242. To Sir William Wade belongs the credit for pointing out the difficulties with the second approach.

[23] The prerogative was defined by Kennedy C.J. in *In Re K., an arranging debtor* [1927] I.R. 260, 270 as "the residue of discretionary or arbitrary power which at any given time is legally left in the hands of the Crown." Similar views are to be found in *R. v. Criminal Injuries Compensation Tribunal ex p. Lain* [1967] 2 Q.B. 864, 881, *per* Diplock L.J. and *Council of Civil Service Unions* v. *Minister for the Public Service* [1985] A.C. 374. Note, however, that in *R. v. Panel on Take-Overs ex p. Datafin Plc* [1987] Q.B. 815, 848 Lloyd L.J. accepted the narrower definition of the prerogative urged by Sir William Wade.

[24] Halsbury, *Laws of England* (4th ed.), para. 931.

[25] *Byrne* v. *Ireland* [1972] I.R. 241.

[26] Kelly, *The Irish Constitution* (Dublin, 1984), p. 21.

1954 Act says anything about the present issue, it implies a lack of confidence about the State's capacity to hold, lease and convey real property. However, the 1954 Act was passed in an era long before *Byrne* v. *Ireland* and the rapid modern development of constitutional thought.

The stronger line of argument, which has found favour in the few cases on this topic, is founded on the rights and duties on the high constitutional plane with which the Constitution endows the State. These include the capacity to own natural resources, lands, minerals and waters (Article 10); the power to commit itself to international agreements and international organisations (Article 29.4 and 5); the duty to provide for free primary education (Article 42.4) as well, of course, as the State's liability in tort, which was stated in *Byrne* to be founded on Article 40.3. Surely it would be strange, indeed, if the State were not also endowed with an adequate legal personality on the mundane level of making grants, entering contracts etc., to equip it to implement these rights and bear these duties?[27] This line of thought finds expression in the following example of judicial statesmanship taken from the judgment of Kingsmill Moore J. in *Comyn* v. *Attorney General*[28]:

> "There is at least one point on which general agreement may be found, namely, the practical necessity of endowing the State with some form of legal personality . . . Ultimately, the nature and attributes of the State must be found in the wording of the Constitution. It is, however, not unreasonable to assume that those who framed, and those who debated, the Constitution were familiar with current opinions as to the nature of the State . . . The Constitution has told us a great deal about the State, its organisation, its rights, its obligations and its attributes; but still it has not attempted to define its juristic nature. Is it a corporation? Is it, as has been suggested, an unincorporated association? Is it neither of these, but a legal *persona* of a new type and *sui generis*? These questions may provide much food for discussion in future cases. It is not necessary, and it would be dangerous, to attempt a full or final answer. For the purposes of this case, all that is necessary is to find that the State is conceived of as a juristic person or entity having as one of its many attributes the capacity to hold property. It may; or may not, be a corporation. It may be a conception entirely new to English and Irish law; but I hold that it is a juristic person and can hold property."[29]

Thus, if—as has been judicially confirmed—the State is a juristic person (whether in virtue of Article 5 or otherwise), then it would seem to follow that the State must thereby enjoy the ordinary legal capacity of an artificial person. Accordingly, the State's right to make contracts, establish companies, etc., would seem to be derived from this juristic status and the non-survival of the prerogative has no bearing on this issue.

[27] See Casey, *Constitutional Law in Ireland* (London, 1987), pp. 197–199.
[28] [1950] I.R. 142.
[29] *Ibid*. 160–161.

3. Liability of the State and Ministers

The purpose of this part to outline the relationship between the State, ministers and the civil service as these have been created (the word is used advisedly as some artificiality is involved here) by the courts in the context of tort and contract litigation.

There are two bases to the central executive organ's capacity to sue and to be sued, and the relationship between these two bases has not yet been clarified. The first basis is the Ministers and Secretaries Act 1924, section 2(1) of which provides:

"Each of the Ministers, heads of the respective departments of State . . . shall be a corporation sole under his style or name aforesaid . . . and shall have perpetual succession and an official seal . . . and may sue . . . and be sued."

The purposes of making each of the Ministers a corporation sole have been explained as follows by Sullivan P. in *Carolan* v. *Minister for Defence*[30] (a case in which the plaintiff claimed damages for personal injuries sustained through the alleged negligence of a soldier driving an Army lorry):

"1. to secure continuity of title and obviate the need for the transfer of State property, rights and obligations from a Minister to his successor; 2. to secure that persons contracting with the Government through any of its Departments should have the ordinary remedy of action available in case of breach of contract; 3. to enable a Minister to be sued in his corporate capacity for a wrongful act done by him as such Minister or by his orders and directions. I cannot think that the legislature intended to go further and create by this section a liability in each Minister for all the wrongful acts or defaults of all the persons employed in his Department. . . ."[31]

Comment is unnecessary on the first of these functions; the third is considered below and the second will be examined immediately.

Contract

The second function mentioned in the quotation enables the Minister to be sued in contract in the ordinary way, rather than, as formerly, having to proceed by way of the Petition of Right (Ireland) Act 1873. At common law, the existence of the prerogative ensured that neither the Crown nor its servants could be sued upon a contract. As Phillimore J. said in *Graham* v. *Public Works Commissioners*:

"The Crown cannot be sued; and that being so, neither can the subject take action indirectly against the Crown by suing a servant of the Crown upon a contract made by the servant as agent of the Crown."[32]

---

[30] [1927] I.R. 62.
[31] *Ibid* 69.
[32] [1901] 2 K.B. 781, 789–90.

But even at common law it was clear that certain public officials could, in Phillimore J.'s words, be designated "as agents of the Crown but with a power of contracting as principals" (*i.e.* not merely as agents) and the same principles govern modern public contracts in this jurisdiction, with the exception, of course, that the prerogative immunity is no longer applicable.

It is, of course, as in private law, a precondition of liability that the contract was made by a person (usually a civil servant) who can be regarded as the agent of the Minister. The question of agency featured in *Grenham* v. *Minister for Defence*[33] in which Hanna J. held that army officers, who had commandeered motor vehicles for military purposes during the Civil War, were not agents of the Minister so as to make him liable on the contract. However, because of the unusual facts of the case and the brevity of the judgment, *Grenham* cannot be regarded as having significant precedential value. This case does raise the more general question of whether an action arising out of a contract made by a civil servant should be brought against the State or against the Minister for the Department in which the civil servant worked. It would seem that the contract should be brought against the Minister and this is buttressed by the fact that Government contracts are always made in the name of the appropriate Minister. In effect, the Minister is—to adapt Phillimore J.'s formulation—an agent of the State but with the power of contracting as principal. Moreover, the fact that a civil servant, is, in law, a servant of the State, rather than the Minister does not prevent him from also being the agent of his Minister (whose *alter ego* he is always said to be in the conventional, slightly imprecise usage). While the question is not of great significance, so long as it remains unresolved, the prudent plaintiff will join both the State and the relevant Minister as defendants.

Tort

Byrne v. *Ireland* is the basis of liability in tort. Until *Byrne* v. *Ireland*, the general rule was that neither the State nor any of its organs could be liable for an action in tort. Historically, the British Crown was immune from actions in tort (whether directly or vicariously, through the behaviour of Crown servants),[34] both because of the principle that the King could do no wrong and because of the King's disability to command himself to appear before his own courts. In tort, in contrast to contract, this relic persisted into the twentieth century. In *Carolan* v. *Minister for Defence*,[35] Sullivan P. held that section 2 of the Minister and Secretaries Act 1924 was intended not to alter the position because its objective was only to allow:

"a Minister to be sued in his corporate capacity for a wrongful act done by him as such Minister, or by his orders or directions, I cannot think that the Legislature intended to go further, and create by this section a liability in

[33] [1926] I.R. 54.
[34] See, *e.g. Murphy* v. *Soady* [1903] 2 I.R. 213, where the Commissioners of Public Works were allowed to invoke Crown immunity in action for negligence.
[35] [1927] I.R. 62.

each Minister for all wrongful acts or defaults of all the persons employed in his Department."[36]

The evident injustice of this situation was ameliorated in particular areas by statute. For instance, section 59 of the Civil Liability Act 1961 provides that where a wrong is committed through the use of a motor vehicle belonging to the State, and driven by a person acting in the course of his employment, then the Minister for Finance is liable. There were other legislative interventions[37] and further legislative reform to abolish the general principle of state immunity[38] (as had happened elsewhere) was promised. In addition, there was a scheme of *ex gratia* payments[39] but this could not be regarded as a satisfactory substitute for all action against the State.

However, the most far-reaching developments were to come via the judiciary. In 1962 the High Court refused to stay an action claiming damages for negligence brought by a State employee against the Attorney General representing the "People of Ireland."[40] In 1965, in *Macauley* v. *Minister for Posts and Telegraphs*,[41] Kenny J. said that in his view the State could be sued "whenever this is necessary to vindicate or assert the rights of a citizen." Accordingly, the requirement in section 2(1) of the Ministers and Secretaries Act 1924 (which required the *fiat* of the Attorney General before proceedings could be instituted against the Minister) was held to be unconstitutional. Finally, in *Byrne* v. *Ireland*, as already mentioned, the Supreme Court ruled that the doctrine of sovereign or state immunity had not survived the enactment of the Constitution of Ireland. Both Walsh and Budd JJ. (who delivered the majority judgments) held first that the prerogative, of which state immunity was a part, had not survived the enactment of the Constitution. Secondly, in respect of state immunity itself, it was held that, even if the State was internally sovereign, this did not necessarily mean that it was immune from actions before its own courts and, indeed, such result was expressly excluded by certain provisions of the Constitution. For instance, Article 42.4 declares that the State is to provide for free primary education. This sub-article carried the necessary implication that if the State failed in this obligation, it could be sued in respect of such continued default. Similarly, Article 40.3 guarantees, the citizen right of access to the courts and the right to sue in respect of a justiciable controversy. Moreover, it was emphasised that there was a critical difference between the State in Ireland and the Crown in the United Kingdom which

---

[36] *Ibid.* 69. In fact, the *Dáil Debates* reveals that the intention was to abolish the State's immunity. See the comments of the Attorney-General (Hugh Kennedy, subsequently Chief Justice) at *Dáil Debates* Vol. 5, col. 1498 (December 16, 1923) cited in Kelly, *The Irish Constitution* (Dublin, 1984), p. 699.
[37] See Osborough, "The Demise of the State's Immunity in Tort" (1973) 8 Ir.Jur. (N.S.) 274, 278–279.
[38] See Osborough, *loc. cit.* 281–282 referring to s.64 of the Workman's Compensation Act 1934; the Garda Síochána Acts 1941–1945, and ss.3, 100 and 118 of the Factories Act 1955.
[39] *Programme of Law Reform* (January 1962), p. 7. See also, *Dáil Debates*, Vol. 215, col. 1858 (May 20, 1965).
[40] Kelly, *op. cit.* p. 703–704.
[41] [1966] I.R. 345.

sufficed to explain why the former was liable in tort while at common law, the Crown was above the law. The difference is that whereas in the United Kingdom the Crown personifies the State and is the sovereign authority, in Ireland it is the people, and not the State, who are sovereign.

In *Byrne*, it had not been open to the plaintiff to sue the Minister, since *Carolan* v. *Minister for Defence* had decided that both the Minister and civil servants were fellow employees of the State. The judgments in *Byrne* confirmed this rule and, consequently, a Minister cannot be made vicariously liable for the tortious acts of civil servants in his Department. As Walsh J. explained:

> "All . . . persons employed in the various Departments of the Government and the other Departments of State, whether they be in the civil service or not, are in the service of the State . . . and the State is liable for damages done by such person in carrying out the affairs of the State so long as that person is acting within the terms of his employment."[42]

Unfortunately, *Byrne*, like many another epoch-making authority, leaves many questions unanswered. First of all, if would seem that this decision has not effected an implied repeal of the earlier statutory provisions which granted limited statutory rights to sue specified Ministers. For example, in the case of a person injured by the negligent use of a vehicle used in the service of the State, the aggrieved party may still either sue the Minister for Finance by virtue of the Civil Liability Act 1961,[43] or the State itself under the principle enunciated in *Byrne*. Secondly, is it possible to enact legislation which would modify the effects of the *Byrne* decision? Such legislation might provide, for example, that injured parties could only sue the Minister for Finance, and not the State, or that a special limitation period would apply to actions against the State. Such alternative arrangements would not unfairly impinge on a person's right to litigate a justiciable controversey. But it is doubtful whether legislation which sought to tamper with the principle enunciated with *Byrne*— such as legislation placing an upper limit on the quantum of damages recoverable in actions against the State or which precluded recovery in respect of certain types of economic loss—would survive constitutional challenge.

Another query raised by *Byrne* is the relationship between the new liability which the case created and the existing basis for suing the central state authority (*i.e.* the right to sue Ministers of State created by section 2 of the 1924 Act). Reference has already been made to one question raised by *Byrne*, namely, whether breach of contract actions should be brought against the State or the responsible Minister. A similar question arises in relation to tort actions. In the first place; as stated already, it is quite clear that where the tort was actually committed by a civil servant, the Minister cannot usually be held to be responsible.

However, Sullivan P. in *Carolan* v. *Minister for Defence* acknowledged that

---

[42] [1972] I.R. 241.
[43] Originally Road Traffic Act 1933, s.116. The Minister for Finance is not, however, liable where the State employee is not acting within the course of his employment: *Murray* v. *Minister for Finance*, Supreme Court, April 22, 1982 (off-duty policeman).

one of the functions of section 2 was to enable the Minister to be sued "in his corporate capacity for a wrongful act done by him as Minister, or by his orders or directions."[44] What this probably means is that the Minister cannot be held *vicariously* liable for the torts of his civil servants, but this does not affect his *direct* liability in tort. There is an important distinction between the direct liability of a Minister for the acts of his civil servants and vicarious liability for the torts committed by them. If a plaintiff contends that the Minister *ordered or authorised* the civil servant to commit the action complained of, or that the Minister was careless in selecting or supervising the employee, then this is an allegation of direct or personal liability on the part of the Minister and the action can proceed under section 2(1) of the 1924 Act.[45] On the other hand, vicarious liability arises when the law attaches liability to the employer for the employee's torts even where the employer is not personally at fault. For this category of liability, as already mentioned, the appropriate defendant is the State.

Personal responsibility of Minister or public servant

However, the cardinal and historical principle that, if the plaintiff prefers, the responsible public servant or ministerial incumbent may be sued personally, in place of the State or the Minister as corporation sole, remains correct. Thus, in *Lynch* v. *Fitzgerald*[46] the detectives who had unlawfully killed the son of the plaintiff during the course of suppressing a riot were found to be personally liable in an action under the Fatal Accidents Act 1846.

It is also worth emphasising that the Minister, *qua* corporation sole is a separate legal entity from the incumbent at any particular time. *Sheil* v. *Attorney-General*[47] is a good illustration of this principle. The plaintiff had been a train-bearer to the former Master of the Rolls, and upon the abolition of that judicial office in 1924, he was granted a declaration against the Attorney-General to the effect that he was entitled to compensation under Article 10 of the Anglo-Irish Treaty 1921, to be paid out of monies voted by the Oireachtas. Costs of the action were awarded against the Attorney-General. However, it was against Mr. John Costello personally, the then holder of the office, that the plaintiff sought to enforce this part of the judgment. The original judgment was then rectified to make it clear that the costs, as well as the compensation, were also entitled to come from funds appropriated by the Oireachtas.

---

[44] [1927] I.R. 68–69.
[45] In cases of direct liability, it is the Minister's negligence which is the basis of the action and it is not crucial that the employee in question was negligent. On this general question, see McMahon & Binchy, *Irish Law of Torts* (Dublin, 1990), pp. 748–61.
[46] [1938] I.R. 382. This case was, of course, decided in the pre-*Byrne* era and so the State was immune. And, for the reasons set out in *Carolan's* case, the plaintiff could not sue the Minister for Justice, as the Minister and the detectives were both fellow servants of the State and thus the doctrine of *respondeat superior* could not apply. See also, *Gildea* v. *Hipwell* [1942] I.R. 489 (prison governor personally liable for false imprisonment) and *Liversidge* v. *Anderson* [1942] A.C. 206, 210–211 (action for false imprisonment against British Home Secretary).
[47] (1928) 62 I.L.T.S.J. 199 (referred to in Casey, *The Office of the Attorney-General in Ireland* (Dublin, 1980), pp. 161–162.

The distinction between the office and the office-holder is also significant in contract actions. In *Kenny* v. *Cosgrave*[48] the President of the Executive Council had told an employer whose workers were on strike that it was essential that the strikers' demands be resisted. The President promised that the Executive Council would also indemnify him against any financial loss which resulted from this resistance. The action failed before the Supreme Court on a number of grounds, which included the fact that Mr. Cosgrave had been sued personally and neither a Minister nor a civil servant can be held *personally* liable on a State contract.

Vicarious liability of the State

Irrespective of the possibly academic point that public servants may be sued personally, their liability is of obvious importance since (just as with any other employer) the State's liability is usually vicarious and is thus contingent upon proof of the employee's individual negligence. Public officials, while not as such carrying on a business or profession, necessarily hold themselves out as having special knowledge and authority in their field of activity. If they make a decision or give specific advice regarding the application of departmental (and, in the case of a Minister, of Governmental) policy, in circumstances where they should know that their advice will be relied on, it would be consistent with general principles of negligence for the Irish courts to hold that they are under a duty to be reasonably careful. Nevertheless, assuming that such a duty of care does exist, it would seem that liability under this heading will be difficult to establish not least because of the various special defences which Ministers and other public officials have sometimes been held to enjoy. In *Pine Valley Developments Ltd.* v. *Minister for the Environment*[49] the Supreme Court held that the defendant Minister must be acquitted of negligence where he had acted on the basis of legal advice. The plaintiffs had suffered considerable financial loss as a result of the invalidation of a planning permission which had been granted to them by the defendant. The evidence showed, however, that the Minister's legal advisers believed that he had power to grant such permission and the Court held that, in such circumstances, no liability could attach. As Finlay C.J. said:

> "If a Minister of State, granted as a *persona designata* a specific duty and function to make his decisions under a statutory code . . . exercises his decision *bona fide*, having obtained and followed the legal advice of the permanent legal advisers attached to his Department, I cannot see how he could be said to have been negligent if the law eventually proves to be otherwise than they have advised him and if by reason of that he makes an order which is invalid or *ultra vires*."[50]

The Supreme Court was, however, less than clear as to the precise extent of a Minister's duty in general. Henchy J. (with whom Griffin and Lardner JJ.

---

[48] [1926] I.R. 517.
[49] [1987] I.R. 23.
[50] *Ibid.* 35.

agreed) expressly stated that the Minister's duty was to give "his decision with the care and circumspection to be expected from a reasonably careful Minister." But Finlay C.J. (Hederman J. concurring), with whom Griffin and Lardner JJ. also agreed, appeared to enumerate a different test, referring with approval to a dictum of Lord Moulton in *Everett* v. *Griffiths*[51] to the effect that the Minister's duty was merely to make a decision honestly and in good faith.[52]

A further query which this case leaves unanswered, of course, is what is the position if the legal advice tendered to the Minister had been negligent? This, of course, was not the case in *Pine Valley*, because the advice then given to the Minister represented the common understanding of the legal profession at the time when it was given. However, had these facts been otherwise and assuming that the negligent advice had been given by a civil servant (as opposed to a private practitioner) there would appear in principle to be no reason why the State should not have been made vicariously liable for the negligent advice.

This matter was also considered by Blayney J. in *McMahon* v. *Ireland*.[53] Here the suggestion was that the Minister for Finance and the Minister for Industry and Commerce were negligent in allowing an under-capitalised friendly society (which ultimately became insolvent, leaving unsecured and unpaid creditors) to continue in operation what in effect was a banking business outside the control of the Central Bank.[54] Blayney J. found that there was no cause of action *vis-à-vis* the Ministers:

"Neither [Minister] was responsible for the initial exemption [from the scope of the Central Bank Acts] of which the plaintiff complains. It was contained in a statute enacted by the Oireachtas. And it could not be contended that either Minister owed the plaintiff a duty of care to have the Central Bank Act amended so as to prevent industrial provident societies from taking deposits."[55]

But while Blayney J. appears to have demonstrated a willingness to test the ministerial activity by reference to standard principles of negligence, he concluded his judgment by saying that the principles of quasi-immunity enjoyed by persons discharging quasi-judicial functions which were recognised by *Pine*

[51] [1921] 1 A.C. 631, 695.
[52] [1987] I.R. 23, 38. *Cf. Jones* v. *Department of Environment* [1989] Q.B. 1 where the English Court of Appeal held that a social security officer did not owe a claimant a common law duty of care in calculating social security entitlements. Glidewell L.J. said (at 22) that, as a matter of general principle:

"[I]f a government department or officer, charged with the making of decisions whether certain payments should be made, is subject to a statutory right of appeals against his decisions, he owes no duty of care in private law. Misfeasance apart, he is only susceptible in public law to judicial review or to the right of appeal provided by the statute under which he makes his decision."

[53] [1988] I.L.R.M. 610. See MacGrath (1987) 9 D.U.L.J. (N.S.) 163.
[54] Friendly societies had been exempted from the requirement to hold banking licences under the Central Bank Act 1971.
[55] [1988] I.L.R.M. 612.

Valley would have been applicable to the present case and would, in any event, have been enough to defeat the plaintiff's claim.[56]

4. Vicarious Liability of the State for Actions of Judges, Gardaí, Prison Officers and Members of the Defence Forces

The question of just who is a servant of the State for the purposes of the decision in *Byrne* remains to be considered. This, in some ways, is linked into the question of special defences, for in some cases, the servants will enjoy an immunity or quasi-immunity (usually statutory in origin) in their own right. Save in the case of judges, whose immunity if it exists derives from the Constitution, the topic of statutory defences will be left to be covered in Chapter 12.2.

(i) *Judges*

Clearly the judiciary are not civil servants nor employees of the Government, but there is no reason why they should not be regarded as servants of the State for the purposes of vicarious liability, since the courts are organs of the State.

At common law, judges enjoyed immunity from suit in respect in judicial acts.[57] It may be asked whether this common law immunity is compatible with constitutional principles and has survived the decision in *Byrne*. The immunity is founded on public policy. As Lord Salmon explained in *Sutcliffe* v. *Thackrah*[58]:

"It is well settled that judges, barristers, solicitors, jurors and witnesses enjoy an absolute immunity in respect of any civil action being brought against them in respect of anything they say or do in court during the course of the trial. . . . The law recognises that, on balance of convenience, public policy demands that they shall have such an immunity. It is of great public importance that they shall all perform their functions free from fear that disgruntled and possibly impecunious persons who have lost their cause or been convicted may subsequently harass them with litigation."[59]

Indeed, as Murnaghan J. observed in the High Court in *Byrne* v. *Ireland*, any other conclusion might lead to obvious difficulties:

"It would be very invidious if the High Court had to entertain an action against the State based on an allegation against the Supreme Court."[60]

At common law, judges, acting in their judicial capacity, are not liable in

---

[56] While Blayney J. only applied the *Pine Valley* principles in the case of the claim against the Registrar of Friendly Societies (who, it is said, had been negligent in failing to take action under s.16 of the Industrial and Friendly Societies (Amendment) Act 1978 to direct the company to cease accepting deposits), it is implicit in his judgment that he would have been prepared to apply these principles to the case of the two Ministers had this been required.
[57] *Tughan* v. *Craig* [1918] 1 I.R. 245; *Macauley* v. *Wyse-Power* (1943) 77 I.L.T.R. 61.
[58] [1974] A.C. 727.
[59] *Ibid.* 757.
[60] [1972] I.R. 241, 253.

tort. Moreover, the defence of absolute privilege attaches to all statements made by judges during judicial proceedings.[61] As against this, the State is required by Article 40.3 of the Constitution, by its laws, to defend and vindicate the personal rights of the citizen, which include the right to litigate a justiciable controversy.[62]

On the other hand, it is well settled that the most fundamental rule of constitutional interpretation is that the Constitution must be read as a whole and that its several provisions "must not be looked at in isolation, but be treated as interlocking parts of the general constitutional scheme."[63] And immunity from suit in respect of judicial acts would appear to be latent in Articles 34 and 35, which guarantee the administration of justice by judges and judicial independence. Given that the courts lean against an interpretation which perverts "any of the fundamental purposes of the Constituton," it is probable that the constitutional right to litigate a justiciable controversy will have to give way to this judicial immunity from suit and such a possibility is accommodated in Article 40.3.1 by the words "so far as it is practicable . . . ." This is strongly suggested by the reasoning of the Supreme Court in *Pine Valley Developments Ltd.* v. *Minister for the Environment.*[64] If persons discharging a quasi-judicial function enjoy an immunity from suit provided that they act "negligently and bona fide,"[65] then it would not be difficult for the courts to hold that persons discharging judicial functions enjoy a complete immunity from suit in respect of acts done in the course of their judicial duties, as their judicial independence would otherwise be compromised. However, the requirements of judicial independence may be solved by the executive indemnifying individual members of the judiciary as has been suggested in the different context of an order for costs;[66] this suggestion might be extended to ensure that the judiciary would be indemnified against an order for damages. This would tend to preserve the independence of the judiciary, while ensuring that the personal rights of the individual to litigate a justiciable controversy were adequately respected. On the other hand, considerations pertaining to public confidence, judicial esteem and the very propriety of stigmatizing another judicial decision as negligent may make it unlikely that this suggestion will ever be taken up.

(ii) *The police and prison officers*

It is now clear that both the Gardaí and prison officers are servants of the State. This would appear to follow from the fact that the State has been held responsible under the doctrine of *respondeat superior* for the wrongful acts of Gardaí and prison officers acting within the scope of their employment in accordance with the principles enunciated in *Byrne*. This emerges from a

[61] *Macauley* v. *Wyse-Power* (1943) 77 I.L.T.R. 61.
[62] *O'Brien* v. *Keogh* [1972] I.R. 144. See also, Kelly, *1987 Supplement to the Irish Constitution.*
[63] *Tormey* v. *Ireland* [1985] I.R. 289, 296, *per* Henchy J.
[64] [1987] I.R. 23.
[65] *Ibid.* 38, *per* Finlay C.J.
[66] A suggestion made by Finlay C.J. in *MacIlwraith* v. *Fawsitt* [1990] I.L.R.M. 1. See p. 595.

number of recent cases. For example, in *Dowman* v. *Ireland*[67] the State was held to be vicariously liable for the tort of false imprisonment following an unlawful arrest effected by members of the Gardaí. In *McKevitt* v. *Ireland*[68] the plaintiff, who had been arrested while drunk and incapable, subsequently set fire to his cell. The plaintiff alleged negligence against the members of the Garda Síochána and, vicariously, as against the State. While the Supreme Court directed a new trial on all issues, there was no suggestion that the State would not be vicariously liable for the torts of members of the Gardaí.

This matter was also considered by Costello J. in *Kearney* v. *Minister for Justice*,[69] which concerned the liability of the State for constitutional wrongs committed by prison officers. In this case, the plaintiff's mail was stopped by reason of unofficial action taken by prison officials. Costello J. held that although these actions did not amount to a tort at common law, they did constitute a breach of the plaintiff's constitutional right to communicate. On the question of the State's vicarious liability, the judge had this to say:

"The wrong that was committed in this case was an unjustified infringement of a constitutional right, not a tort; and it was committed by a servant of the State and, accordingly, Ireland can be sued in respect of it: see *Byrne* v. *Ireland. . . .* [T]he State is clearly liable for such a wrong when it can be shown that had the wrong been a tort, vicarious liability would attach to the State. The wrongful act in this case was obviously connected with the functions for which the prison officers or officers who committed it were employed, and even though the act was not authorised I cannot hold that it was performed outside the scope of his or their employment. The plaintiff is therefore entitled to be awarded damages against the State."[70]

This reasoning would appear to apply, *mutatis mutandis*, to the Gardaí and ensure that the State is vicariously liable for torts or constitutional wrongs committed by members of the force within the scope of their employment.

(iii) *Members of the Defence Forces*

Members of the Defence Forces are regarded as servants of the State for the purposes of the *Byrne* decision, and in the series of cases which followed this decision, the State did not attempt to dispute this point. However, in *Ryan* v. *Ireland*,[71] the Supreme Court was given the opportunity of considering the liability of the State in respect of tortious acts committed by officers

[67] [1986] I.L.R.M. 111. See also, *McIntyre* v. *Lewis*, Supreme Court, December 17, 1990 (State vicariously liable on the facts for assaults, false imprisonment and malicious prosecution committed by Gardaí in course of employment.)
[68] [1987] I.L.R.M. 541.
[69] [1986] I.R. 116.
[70] *Ibid.* 122. *Cf. McHugh* v. *Garda Commissioner* [1986] I.R. 228 where Finlay C.J. accepted (at 233) that Ireland was vicariously liable for a breach of constitutional rights committed by the Garda Commissioner.
[71] [1989] I.R. 177. See also, *Groves* v. *Commonwealth of Australia* (1981) 150 C.L.R. 113, where the High Court of Australia held that the Commonwealth could be vicariously liable for damages for personal injury suffered by a serving member of the armed forces and caused by the negligence of a fellow member of the armed forces while on duty in peace time.

while engaged in active service. The plaintiff was a member of the Irish contingent which formed part of the United Nations International Force serving in the Lebanon. In April 1979 a member of Christian Militia had been shot dead outside an Irish Army post and it appears that the militia were determined to seek revenge on the members of the Irish contingent. Although there were clear signals that such an attack was being planned, the plaintiff was ordered to take a rest in a portacabin shelter which had not been sandbagged. His position was attacked after he had gone to sleep and he was seriously injured by a mortar which struck his portacabin. There was evidence of negligent preparations to meet the attack and the Supreme Court was asked to consider:

(i) whether at common law the State enjoyed an immunity from suit in respect of negligent acts committed by serving officers on active service; and

(ii) if the answer to this was in the affirmative, whether such an immunity was consistent with the provisions of the Constitution.

Dealing with the first question, Finlay C.J. observed that Article 28.3 of the Constitution gives the Oireachtas extensive powers to deal with war and the preservation of the State in time of war and that the Constitution may not be invoked to invalidate "legislation expressed to be for such purpose." He concluded that these provisions made it impossible to accept:

" . . . the application of a common law doctrine arising from necessity to ensure the safety of the State during a period of war or armed rebellion which has the effect of abrogating constitutional rights. In so far, therefore, as the principle apparently supporting some of the decisions to which we have been referred is the question of the dominant priority in regard to the defence of the State, such decisions would not appear to be applicable and cannot be applied to the question of service with the United Nations force . . . I, therefore, conclude that an immunity from suit, or the negation of any duty of care to, a serving soldier in respect of operations consisting of armed conflict or hostilities has not been established as part of our common law."[72]

And, as to the second question, even if such an immunity had existed at common law, it would not have survived the enactment of the Constitution:

"I conclude that in the blanket form which has been contended for [such an immunity] would be inconsistent with the guarantees by the State to respect, defend and vindicate the rights of the citizens contained in Article 40.3.1 and Article 40.3.2 of the Constitution."[73]

---

[72] [1989] I.R. 182.
[73] *Ibid.* 182–183.

5. Procedural Aspects of Litigation Involving the State

(i) *Litigation involving the State and Government*

The procedural aspects of suing the State were considered by the Supreme Court in *Byrne* v. *Ireland*.[74] The State's power or right to defend itself is one which can be exercised only by or on the authority of Government (by virtue of the provisions of Article 49.2 of the Constitution). Walsh J. said that, if it was the Attorney-General's opinion that the Government should authorise the defence by the State of the claim brought against it, the defence was a matter of public interest and was properly financed out of public monies. If the Government did not wish to authorise the defence then the Attorney-General would not defend the case and in that case the correct procedure would be to sue the State and to join the Attorney-General in order to effect service upon the Attorney-General for both parties. (It is not quite clear why it is necessary to *join* the Attoney-General). If the claim should succeed, judgment would be against the State and not against the Attorney-General because the Attorney-General had only been joined in a representative capacity as the law officer of State designated by the Constitution.[75] As a result, Ireland must be joined as a defendant in any proceedings where there is a claim for either a liquidated or unliquidated sum and it does not for this purpose suffice merely to nominate the Attorney-General as the defendant.[76]

So far we have spoken of the State as defendant, but there is no reason why the State may not sue as plaintiff in its own right. One such case is *Ireland* v. *Mulvey*,[77] where the State commenced proceedings against the defendants claiming that it had title by virtue of Article 5 of the Constitution in respect of an eight-century cross. Hamilton P. granted Ireland an interlocutory injunction restraining the defendants from removing the cross out of the jurisdiction.

A related question which sometimes arises is whether the Government can, as such, sue and be sued in its own right and whether it has legal personality for this purpose. A practice has emerged whereby all the individual members of the Government have been sued in cases involving the actions of the Government: see, *e.g. Crotty* v. *An Taoiseach*.[78] However, the Government was sued as such in *The State (Sheehan)* v. *Government of Ireland*[79] and no objection was taken to that course of action. Of course, in *Sheehan*, the applicant's complaint related to the failure to bring section 60(1) of the Civil Liability Act 1961 into force and that duty was imposed on the *Government* by statute. Different considerations may arise as to the propriety of suing the Government, in cases where no such statutory (or, indeed, constitutional) obligation has been imposed. Accordingly, this procedural point may still cause difficulties for a plaintiff wishing to sue the Government for breach of

[74] [1972] I.R. 241.
[75] *Ibid.* 289. See also, *Sheil* v. *Attorney General* (1928) 62 I.L.T.S.J. 199.
[76] *Murphy* v. *Attorney General* [1982] I.R. 241, 315–316, *per* Henchy J.
[77] *The Irish Times*, November 11, 1989.
[78] [1987] I.R. 713.
[79] [1987] I.R. 550.

contract, to take but one example. Nevertheless, in view of the fact that the Government has been vested with specific constitutional and statutory functions, perhaps the better view is that it is a legal person, at any event, for some purposes.

(ii) *Enforcement of judgments*

The Supreme Court in *Byrne* v. *Ireland* did not consider how a decree for the plaintiff would be executed or enforced. Walsh J. however, did comment that "an order for mandamus to compel compliance with the judgment would be an appropriate step and not without precedent."[80] Budd J. said that he took it for granted that the necessary monies to meet the decree would be provided. "That would only be what would be normally expected in a State governed according to the rule of law and there would seem to be no reason to believe that the State would not honour its legal obligations."[81] If it had been necessary to come to a final decision on this point, he thought that "the ordinary procedure of execution by way of levy or enforcement by mandamus would both seem to be appropriate."[82] While enforcement may be straightforward in the case of a successful plaintiff who is an Irish citizen, it has been suggested that it may be less so in a case where the plaintiff is a citizen or legal person of a foreign jurisdiction.[83]

(iii) *Mandamus*

At common law the writ of mandamus did not lie against a Minister of the Crown and in Northern Ireland it has been held that an application for mandamus against the Minister for Home Affairs was unsustainable.[84] In the Republic, however, this immunity has not survived and in *The State (King)* v. *Minister for Justice*[85] Doyle J. granted an order of mandamus commanding the Minister to exercise the statutory duties imposed on him by section 6(1) of the Courthouses (Provisions and Maintenance) Act 1935, namely, to direct the Commissioners of Public Works in Ireland to execute such repairs and to do such other work as may be necessary or proper to put the court accommodation at Waterford into proper repair and condition. Doyle J. relied on the majority decision of the Supreme Court in *Byrne* v. *Ireland* in holding that the survival of such an immunity would be inconsistent with the general tenor of the Constitution in that there "is no power, institution, or person in the land free of the law save where such immunity is expressed, or provided for, in the Constitution itself."[86] This view was also accepted as correct by Costello J. in *The State (Sheehan)* v. *Government of Ireland*,[87] where counsel for the Government had submitted that mandamus would not lie against the Govern-

---

[80] [1972] I.R. 241, 289.
[81] *Ibid.* 307.
[82] *Ibid.* On monetary awards, see further, Part 7 of this chapter.
[83] Kelly, *op. cit.* p. 707.
[84] *R. (Diamond and Fleming)* v. *Warnock* [1946] N.I. 171.
[85] [1984] I.R. 169.
[86] *Ibid.* 176, quoting from the judgment of Walsh J. in *Byrne* v. *Ireland* [1972] I.R. 241, 281.
[87] [1987] I.R. 550.

ment. Costello J. thought that this submission was based on the proposition that:

"In English law since a prerogative order emanates from the Crown it cannot lie against the Crown. But there is no analogy between the law of Ireland and England on this topic. An order of mandamus made now by an Irish court is not a prerogative writ of mandamus which, before the establishment of the State, was the means by which the courts enforced observance of statutory duties . . . and under the Constitution the Government which it establishes is not the successor to the Crown. There is no constitutional reason, therefore, which would prohibit the making of an order of mandamus against the Government."[88]

Accordingly, therefore, any vestigial immunity which might hitherto have attached in respect of mandamus to Ministers, the Government or even, it would seem, Ireland itself, has now been judicially removed. As against this, however, there remains the awkward fact (see below) that the Supreme Court has refused to grant an injunction against the State. There is very little policy justification for distinguishing between a mandamus and an injunction in this context and, accordingly, the matter cannot be regarded as absolutely beyond doubt.

(iv) *Injunctions*

As for injunctions, the Supreme Court has ruled, in *Pesca Valentia Ltd.* v. *Minister for Fisheries*[89] that it is not appropriate that any injunction should ever be given against *Ireland*. Instead, the practice is to grant injunctions against the relevant Minister. No reasons were given for this conclusion by Finlay C.J. in his judgment in *Pesca Valentia*[90] and this immunity would seem

---

[88] *Ibid.* 555.

[89] [1985] I.R. 193. *Cf. R.* v. *Transport Secretary, ex p. Factortame Ltd.* [1989] 2 W.L.R. 997, 1021 where Lord Bridge, speaking for a unanimous House of Lords, said that, apart from any possible exceptions under European Community law: "[A]s a matter of English law, [there is no] jurisdiction to grant interim injunctions against the Crown."

[90] In this case, the plaintiffs had commenced proceedings challenging the constitutionality of the Fisheries (Amendment) Act 1983, which imposed nationality quotas as a condition of a fishing licence. This was said to infringe the plaintiff company's constitutional rights to property and to earn a livelihood and was also said to be contrary to European Community law. In the event, however, the plaintiff's challenge was unsuccessful before the Court of Justice of the European Communities: [1988] 1 C.M.L.R. 188.

There was an interesting sequel to this case in that the State attempted to recover damages on foot of the undertaking given by the plaintiff company at the time that they were awarded an injunction. In *Pesca Valentia Ltd.* v. *Minister for Fisheries (No. 2)*, High Court, June 6, 1989, Keane J. held that the State could not recover damages on foot of this undertaking. It was contended that the fish caught by the plaintiffs were in some sense the "property of Ireland and that Ireland was entitled to be compensated for their loss." Quite apart from the fact that Ireland was not bound by the terms of the injunction (and, thus, Keane J. thought, should not properly be entitled to recover on foot of an undertaking), the fish caught, were prior to their catch, animals *ferae naturae* "which did not belong to any one" and hence the State had not established any loss on this account. Keane J. identified the real loss as the defendant's inability "to police the fishing regime lawfully established by the Oireachtas during the period in question." If damages were to be awarded on this basis, it would be in effect to impose a penalty on the plaintiff rather than compensate the defendants. Keane J. thought that as the defendants had never been tried by

difficult to justify. If Ireland can be liable for damages, why should it enjoy an immunity for another form of remedy, such as an injunction? This is especially so, given that it now seems that mandamus (a very similar form of remedy to an injunction) will lie against Ireland.

An injunction may be granted (against a party other than *Ireland*) in certain circumstances to restrain the operation of an Act of the Oireachtas or to restrain the ratification of a Treaty, although it is now clear that such relief will not be readily given. In *Pesca Valentia*, the Supreme Court held that the duty of the courts to protect persons against the invasion of their constitutional rights or against unconstitutional action meant that there must exist a jurisdiction to restrain, in an appropriate case, the operation of a statutory provision pending a challenge to its validity. As Finlay C.J. observed:

"It would seem wholly inconsistent with that duty if the Court were to be without power in an appropriate case to restrain by injunction an action against a person which found its authority in a statutory provision which might eventually be held to be invalid having regard the Constitution."[91]

The Chief Justice continued by hinting that this power would be more readily exercised where a penal statute was under challenge. Accordingly, the Supreme Court granted an injunction restraining the prosecution of the plaintiff company under the Fisheries (Amendment) Act 1983 pending the outcome of a constitutional challenge. A spectacular example of the exercise of this power may be found in *Crotty* v. *An Taoiseach*[92] where Barrington J. and, subsequently, the Supreme Court, granted an injunction restraining the Government from ratifying the Single European Act pending the outcome of the plaintiff's constitutional challenge to the validity of such a ratification.

More recently, however, the courts have signalled an unwillingness to grant such interlocutory relief and an apparent retreat from the principles enshrined in *Pesca Valentia*. In *Cooke* v. *Minister for Communications*,[93] with no apparent consideration of *Pesca Valentia*, the Supreme Court refused to grant an injunction to the proprietor of an unlicensed radio station restraining the Minister from invoking his statutory powers to direct the termination of elec-

judge and jury on these charges, "such a procedure would seem to be constitutionally suspect in the highest degree."
[91] [1985] I.R. 201. See also, *Dublin District Milk Board* v. *Golden Vale Co-operative Creameries Ltd*. High Court, April 3, 1987 where Costello J. refused to grant an injunction restraining the operation of the Milk (Regulation of Supply and Price) Act 1936 pending a challenge to its validity on EC law grounds.
[92] [1987] I.R. 713.
[93] *Irish Times Law Report*, February 20, 1989. See also, the comments of Murphy J. in *Nova Media Services Ltd.* v. *Minister for Posts and Telegraphs* [1984] I.L.R.M. 161, 169 (a case with facts similar to those in *Cooke*):

"In principle . . . it may be that in certain circumstances the courts might in the proper exercise of their discretion refuse to grant an injunction . . . to secure compliance with a statutory provision by members of the public pending a decision by the courts as to the constitutionality of the particular statute, but . . . it would only be in the most extraordinary circumstances that the courts would intervene to prevent the Minister or the Government agencies from exercising a function conferred upon him or them by the express terms of a statute made for the control of a public resource and for the benefit of the public good."

tricity and telecommunications supplies, pending a challenge as to the constitutional propriety of the Independent Radio and Television Act 1988, which established such a licensing régime. Walsh J. said that:

> "Where an existing statute rendered an activity illegal, the court would not by injunction restrain the imposition of preventive measures authorised by the statute, even where a challenge to the constitutional validity of the said statute was pending."

And in *Grange Developments Ltd. v. Dublin County Council (No. 4)*[94] Murphy J. refused to grant an injunction staying the enforcement of an arbitrator's award of compensation in favour of the plaintiffs under the Local Government (Planning and Development) Act 1963 pending a challenge to the validity of the compensation provisions of that Act. Murphy J. agreed that an injunction to restrain the operation of contested statutory provisions could be granted in an appropriate case, but he thought that such relief should only be granted in exceptional cases. The present case did not fit into that category, as the County Council could not show that they would suffer irreparable loss. The sum of money paid by way of compensation was readily ascertainable and was repayable in the event of the impugned provisions being declared unconstitutional.

(v) *Miscellaneous*

At common law the Crown enjoyed a variety of procedural privileges derived from the prerogative.[95] Thus, neither laches nor delay could be imputed to the Crown[96] and the courts would not deny relief on discretionary grounds to the Attorney-General.[97] Moreover, the courts did not require the Attorney-General to tender an undertaking as to damages where he sought an injunction.[98] The absence of recent case-law on these issues makes it difficult to offer any firm views, but, in principle, it would seem that these rules, derived as they are from the prerogative, are unlikely to have survived for the benefit of the State. This is especially so, given that the entire tenor of *Byrne v. Ireland* is such as to suggest that the State should stand on an equal footing with all other litigants and should not enjoy procedural privileges not available to the private litigant.

---

[94] [1989] I.R. 337. This decision was confirmed by the Supreme Court in a brief *ex tempore* judgment delivered on March 20, 1989. See also, *Staunton v. Voluntary Health Insurance Board*, High Court, February 23, 1989.
[95] Halsbury, *Laws of England* (4th ed.), para. 931.
[96] *Re an Application for Certiorari* [1965] N.I. 67.
[97] *The State (Kerry County Council) v. Minister for Local Government* [1933] I.R. 517, 546, *per* Murnaghan J.
[98] *Hoffman-La Roche & Co. A.G. v. Trade Secretary* [1975] A.C. 295. The House of Lords held that the rule that an injunction could not be required of the Crown where it was sued in a proprietary capacity had been abolished by the Crown Proceedings Act 1947, but the privileged position of the Crown in cases where it was seeking an injunction to enforce the law remained unaffected by this legislative change. It is likely that a similar distinction would be adopted by the Irish courts, even in the absence of any equivalent legislation.

6. State Exemption from Statute

As usually stated, this exemption means that the State is not "bound" (*i.e.* affected to its disadvantage) by a statute unless it is referred to either expressly or by necessary implication. An early example is provided by *Galway County Council* v. *Minister for Finance*[99] where one of the issues was whether the defendant Minister was free to set off as against the plaintiff's claim, an overpayment which he had made to them eight years earlier. The County Council submitted in reply that the Minister's claim was not statute-barred. Johnson J. was unimpressed by this argument:

> "[T]he Minister relies on preprogative rights and contends that the sub-section has no applicability to a claim such as the present, there being no indication in the subsection that it was the intention of the Legislature to bind the Crown or the State. There has been no doubt and it has not been argued in the present case to the contrary, that the prerogative and pre-rogative right can be relied upon by the Irish Free State, and is part of the law of the land, . . . I can see nothing in [the subsection] that suggests that it was intended to have any applicability to the Crown or the State and, I think, therefore, that the defendant is entitled to rely on this set-off. . . ."[1]

In *Irish Land Commission* v. *Ruane*[2] the High Court applied the rule that the exemption may be excluded by necessary implication. The statutory provision in question in that case, the Increase of Rent and Mortgage Interest (Restriction) Act 1923, restricted the right of the landlord to recover possession unless "the dwelling house is reasonably required for the purpose of the execution of the duties . . . of any Government Department or . . . any local authority or statutory undertaking." Both Johnston and Gavan Duffy JJ. appear to have assumed[3] that this provision only applied where the Department, local authority or statutory undertaking was the landlord, and, accordingly, that the provision would be redundant if it were excluded in the case of State property. However, in *Fitzsimons* v. *Menkin*,[4] a majority of the Supreme Court ruled that the provision was of general application, and would apply even in the case of a private landlord. Although such a situation would seem likely to be rare, the Supreme Court held in the later case of *Cork County Council* v. *Commissioners of Public Works*[5] that this change of interpretation destroyed the premise on which the judgment in *Ruane* was founded, and meant that, in the usual way, the State was exempt from the

---

[99] [1931] I.R. 215.

[1] *Ibid.* 232. See now s.3(1) of the Statute of Limitations 1957, which provides that the Statute shall apply to "proceedings by or against a State authority in the same manner as if that State authority were a private individual." See also, *Dáil Debates*, Vol. 318, cols. 240–247 (February 20, 1980) (restriction on application to State of Landlord and Tenant (Amendment) Act 1980 though see also Landlord and Tenant (Amendment) Act 1984, s.14).

[2] [1938] I.R. 148.

[3] Certainly this was the view taken of their judgments by the Supreme Court in *Cork County Council* v. *Commissioners of Public Works* [1945] I.R. 561.

[4] [1938] I.R. 805.

[5] [1945] I.R. 561.

application of the 1923 Act. The question of whether the State was bound by the Local Government (Rates on Small Dwellings) Act 1928 which made provision for the rating of the owners of dwellings below a specified rateable value, in lieu of the occupiers, also arose in the *Cork County Council* case. A majority of the Supreme Court rejected the argument that it was a necessary implication in the construction of the Act that it should be held to bind the State merely because, in the words of O'Byrne J., "the opposite construction would have the effect of leaving certain houses free from liability."[6] The Court accordingly held the houses owned by the defendant Commissioners were exempt from rates.

All three members of the Supreme Court accepted that the exemption of the State from the application of statutes had survived the enactment of the Constitution. However, there are clear hints in the judgments of O'Byrne and Black JJ. that this exemption could be rationalised in terms of a principle of statutory construction rather than a privilege derived from concepts of a regal personality.[7] Walsh J. was to fasten on to this approach in *Byrne* v. *Ireland*,[8] and he quoted with approval from the judgment of Story J. in *United States* v. *Hoar*:

> "*But independently of any doctrine founded on the notion of prerogative, the same construction of statutes of this sort ought to prevail, founded upon the legislative intention.* Where the government is not expressly or by necessary implication included, it ought to be clear from the nature of the mischiefs to be redressed, or the language used, that the government itself was in contemplation of the legislature, before a court of law would be authorised to put such an interpretation before any statute. In general, acts of the legislature are meant to regulate and direct the acts and rights of citizens; and in most cases the reasoning applicable to them applies with very different, and often contrary force to the government itself. It appears to me, therefore, to be a safe rule founded in the principles of the common law, that the general words of statute ought not to include the government, or affect its rights, unless that construction be clear and undisputable upon the text of the Act."[9]

Leaving aside the question of the relationship between this principle and the prerogative, this passage also throws light on an important issue of substance. In the first place, *United States* v. *Hoar* was decided in 1821, at the time when statute law was rarer than today and when governmental actions were excep-

---

[6] *Ibid.* 581.
[7] Thus, Black J. observed: "Much time was devoted to discussing the true nature of this right and to combating the supposition that so far as it still exists, it is inseparable from the institution of kingship. If that were so, one would not expect to find such a right recognised for over a century by the Courts of the United States of America where the institution of kingship has no existence . . . ." ([1945] I.R. 587).
[8] [1972] I.R. 241.
[9] (1822) 6 Fed.Cas. 329 quoted in *Byrne* (at 278). The sentence in italics had been omitted by O'Byrne J. when he was quoting from the judgment of Story J. in *Hoar*. Walsh J. described this sentence as "vital," because it rationalised the principle expressed by Story J.

tional and in an entirely different category from those of individuals. This latter point is reflected in Story J.'s remark that "the reasoning applicable to the acts and rights of citizens applies with very different and often contrary force to the government itself." Should it not follow that, in modern times when governmental actions are commonplace, that the State exemption should only apply if the statutory provision is appropriate to attract it?[10] This argument draws some support from the earlier part of the quoted passage where Story J. said that the State should be bound, not only where it is expressly or implicitly included, but also if it is clear, from the purposes of the Act or its language, that the Legislature intended the State to be included. In other words, the question of the applicability of statutes to the State should be determined *solely* by reference to standard principles of statutory construction. This is a slightly different test from the contemporary "necessary implication" standard, because the latter is rooted in a common law presumption *against* the application of statutes to the State.[11] Were this presumption to be dispensed with, the State's exemption from the application of statutes would be thereby narrowed. Such a consequence would be more consistent with the rule of law, and the courts' general approach to constitutional issues with their emphasis on individual rights and justice.[12] Decisions such as *Ruane* and the *Cork County Council* case have tended to adopt the wider view of the State's exemption from the application of statutes, usually[13] without considering the narrower approach advocated here. To adopt the narrower approach would involve a departure, although one which finds support in the judgment of Story J. in *United States* v. *Hoar* as approved by Walsh J. in *Byrne*.

It has also found more recent support in other foreign jurisdictions. Take, for instance, *Lord Advocate* v. *Strathclyde Regional Council*[14] which concerned the question of whether an obstruction on the public road was free of control by the planning legislation by virtue of the fact that it had been created by the Ministry of Defence. The Inner House of the Scottish Court of Session held that in Scots (and, at any rate, modern English) law, the rule only applied to statutory provisions which if they caught the Crown, would prejudicially affect the Crown by divesting it of some of its existing rights, interests or privileges; whereas, on the facts of the case, the Crown had no right to occupy the public road. The kernel of Lord Emslie's judgment is as follows[15]:

---

[10] Professor Street has demonstrated that in the 16th century, where the statute touched upon the rights of subjects generally, then the Crown would normally be bound unless it affected the prerogative rights of the King. See H. A. Street, *Government Liability; a Comparative Study* (Cambridge, 1953), Chap. vi; P. W. Hogg, *Liability of the Crown in Australia, New Zealand and the United Kingdom* (Melbourne, 1971).

[11] See, *e.g. per* Jessel M.R. in *Postmaster General* v. *Bonham* (1878) 10 Ch.D. 595, 601 where he said that one must find "clear and strong words" to alter the prerogative exemption.

[12] Keane J. has suggested extra-judicially that this exemption may violate the constitutional guarantee of equality contained in Art. 40.1. See Keane, "The 1963 Planning Act—Twenty Years On" (1983) 5 D.U.L.J. (N.S.) 92.

[13] [1989] 3 W.L.R. 346.

[14] 1988 S.L.T. 546.

[15] *Ibid.* 552–553.

" . . . the rule of construction of universal application emerged in an age when the Crown was virtually unfettered in the exercise of arbitrary power and when anything enacted in a statute would be likely to constitute a derogation of its position. . . . The special rule of construction of universal application was, it appears to me, designed to protect the Crown against divestiture of any of its rights, privileges or interests. In the centuries since that rule was formulated however, enormous changes have taken place in the position of the Crown which today personifies the executive government of the country in all its activities and no longer exercises arbitrary power in all things. That being so, I can see no justification in principle for the universal application of the special rule, designed for the protection of the Crown in 17th century circumstances, in the quite different circumstances of the 20th century. There is no longer an 'antecedent improbability' that the Crown would agree to be bound by any statutory provisions. Such an 'antecedent improbability' can only be identified where particular statutory provisions would bind the Crown to its prejudice. In modern times, in my opinion, the application of the special rule is only required for the protection of the Crown where it is necessary to construe statutory provisions which would be likely, if applied to the Crown, to encroach upon its rights, interests and privileges."

However, notwithstanding this, on appeal, the House of Lords founding largely on English authority and on the notion that the same legislative should be subject to the same rule of construction, irrespective of the jurisdiction involved, reaffirmed,[16] the wider rule, namely that the Crown is not bound unless identified, expressly or by necessary implication.

The rule has been expelled, with bell, book and candle from India, in *State of West Bengal* v. *Corporation of Calcutta*[17] a case heard by a full bench of nine judges in order to reconsider the correctness of an earlier precedent. The case involved the conviction of the State of West Bengal for the offence of carrying on a daily market without a licence. The State had defended itself, before the High Court, on the ground that the legislation requiring the licence—the Calcutta Municipal Act 1951—must be presumed not to apply to a State. The High Court, however, held that the State was bound by the 1951 Act because it had been acting in a commercial, as opposed to a sovereign, role. This judgment was upheld, by an 8–1 majority, in the Supreme Court, on three alternative grounds. In the first place, the Court scrutinised the critical expression "law in force" in Article 372 of the Indian Constitution (exactly the same phrase as is used in Article 50.1 of the Irish Constitution) by which the pre-Independence law was imported into the post-Independence polity. It held (in contrast to the decision in *United States* v. *Hoar*, the relevant passage from which was quoted above) that this language was not apt to embrace a principle of statutory construction because there is an essential difference

[16] [1989] 3 W.L.R. 1346.
[17] [1967] A.I.R. 997.

728

between a law and a canon of construction. Accordingly, this principle could not have become part of Indian law. Secondly, Subba Rao C.J. stated:

> "There are many reasons why the said rule of construction is inconsistent with and incongruous in the present set-up. We have no Crown: the archaic rule based on the perogative and perfection of the Crown has no relevance to a democratic republic: it is inconsistent with the rule of law based on the doctrine of equality. It introduces conflicts and discrimination. . . . The normal construction, namely, that the general Act applies to citizens as well as to States unless it expressly or by necessary implication exempts the State from its operation, steers clear of all the said anomalies. It prima facie applies to all States and subjects alike, a construction consistent with the philosophy of equality enshrined in our Constitution. This natural approach avoids the archaic rule and moves with the modern trends. This will not cause hardship to the State. The State can make an Act, if it chooses, providing for its exemption from its operation."[18]

Finally, simply, but unanswerably, Bachawat, J. stated

> "In interpreting a statute, it is the duty of the Court to give effect to the expressed intentions of the legislature. There is no compelling reason why the Courts in India should not give full effect to the general words of a statute on the basis of some artificial rule of construction prevailing in England."[19]

The final question relates to what is meant by "the State" in the present context. In view of its origin in the prerogative, it presumably includes the State and Ministers, but excludes local authorities[20] and formally independent bodies such as state sponsored bodies. However, administrative bodies such as the Commissioners of Public Works have been permitted to rely on the exemption where such bodies are dealing with State property.[21]

7. Privilege Against the Disclosure of Official Documents

Traditionally it was the law that Ministers could not be compelled by court order to produce documents for inspection or even to disclose the existence of a document. This applied in all litigation, irrespective of whether the Minister or the State was a party to it. All that was necessary for the exercise of this privilege was an affadavit claiming it, signed by the responsible Minister or one of his senior civil servants. Plainly there were two elements to this privilege:

(i) There was a public interest in maintaining the confidentiality of certain official documents; and

---

[18] *Ibid.* 1007–1008.
[19] *Ibid.* 1019.
[20] But *cf.* Johnston J. in *Galway County Council* v. *Minister for Finance* [1931] I.R. 215.
[21] *Irish Land Commission* v. *Ruane* [1938] I.R. 148; *Cork County Council* v. *Commissioners of Public Works* [1945] I.R. 561.

(ii) It was for the responsible Minister, and not the court, to decide whether this interest outweighed the public interest in the fair administration of justice.

As has been remarked, " . . . the newly independent State, having shaken off the yolk of the Crown, embraced with enthusiasm many of its privileges."[22] The privilege was invoked to protect: communications between the Executive Council and the Shaw Commission which investigated the destruction of Ballyheigue Castle[23]; advices and minutes given to the Minister for Local Government in regard to the Electoral (Amendment) Act 1959[24] and, in a prosecution for "showing for gain an indecent and profane performance" the instructions, given by their superiors, to the detectives who watched the play.[25]

The law was authoritatively changed in *Murphy* v. *Dublin Corporation*,[26] a case which arose in the wake of objections raised by the plaintiff to a proposed compulsory purchase order in respect of his lands. A public inquiry was held in accordance with the usual procedure, and the planning inspector sent a report of the proceedings to the Minister. In dealing with the Minister's claim for privilege in respect of the report, Walsh J. stated:

"Under the Constitution the administration of justice is committed solely to the judiciary in the exercise of their powers. . . . Power to compel the attendance of witnesses and the production of evidence is an inherent part of the judicial power of government of the State and is the ultimate safeguard of justice in the State. If . . . conflict arises during the exercise of judicial power then, in my view, it is the judicial power which will decide which public interest shall prevail. This does not mean that the court will always decide that the interest of the litigant shall prevail. It is for the court to decide which is the superior interest in the circumstances of the particular case and to determine the matter accordingly."[27]

Thus the courts still retain a discretion to preserve the confidential nature of official documents in the public interest, but this matter may not be constitutionally remitted to a non-judicial personage.[28] That, of course, is not to say

---

[22] Russell, "A Privilege of the State" (1967) 2 Ir.Jur. (N.S.) 88. This prescient article reviewed the former law and predicted its demise.

[23] *Leen* v. *President of the Executive Council* [1926] I.R. 456.

[24] *O'Donovan* v. *Minister for Local Government* [1961] I.R. 114.

[25] *Att.-Gen.* v. *Simpson* [1959] I.R. 335. In *Kenny* v. *Minister for Defence* (1942) Ir.Jur.Rep. 81 (an action in contract concerning the construction of army huts), Maguire P. observed that the Minister was entitled to claim privilege in respect of "documents of a confidential nature." In more recent times a prison governor was allowed to claim privilege in respect of confidential information concerning a planned prison escape: see *The State (Comerford)* v. *Governor of Mountjoy Prison* [1981] I.L.R.M. 86.

[26] [1972] I.R. 215. See also, *O'Leary* v. *Minister for Industry and Commerce* [1966] I.R. 676 and *Dolan* v. *Neligan* [1967] I.R. 247.

[27] [1972] I.R. 225, 233–234. It is noteworthy that the High Court (Kenny J. at 227) would also have created judicial control over the Minister's discretion.

[28] In contrast, note the late S. A. de Smith's view that judges are poorly equipped to hold the balance between these two aspects of the public interest; de Smith, *op. cit.* p. 40, n. 57.

that the courts will not be reluctant to overrule official claims for privilege, especially in sensitive areas concerning the security or safety of the State.[29] But as Walsh J. remarked:

"It may well be that it would be rare or infrequent for a court after its own examination, to arrive at a different conclusion from that expressed by the Minister, but that is a far remove from accepting without question the judgment of the Minister."[30]

McWilliam J. made a similar point in *Hunt* v. *Roscommon Vocational Education Committee*,[31] where the substantive action involved a claim for wrongful dismissal by a former headmaster of a vocational school. The Minister for Education claimed privilege in respect of documents containing the opinions expressed by individual civil servants on the case. The judge observed that the claim for privilege depended on whether there was "a likelihood of injury to the State or the public service by the production of the documents." This interest had to be balanced against that of the fair administration of justice, and the task of the court was to decide as between the merits of these competing interests. As far as the instant case was concerned, the claim of privilege failed, as it had not even been alleged that disclosure of the documents would be detrimental to the public interest. Nor was it any answer to say that the civil service administration might be adversely affected if there was an appreciation by officers of the Department that their memoranda might subsequently be read out in court.

There have been several recent examples of cases where public interest immunity was claimed. In *Silver Hill Duckling Co. Ltd.* v. *Minister for Agriculture*,[32] the plaintiffs had commenced proceedings seeking compensation in respect of an outbreak of avian influenza in their flock of ducks. They claimed that the Minister had been negligent in the exercise of their statutory powers in ordering the destruction of a large quantity of their ducks. Privilege was claimed in respect of, *inter alia*, minutes of meetings of the Standing Veterinary Committee of the European Community in Brussels where the outbreaks of avian influenza were discussed. O'Hanlon J. held that, in the circumstances, no question of public interest privilege could possibly arise. A similar view was taken by Costello J. in *Fitzpatrick* v. *Independent Newspapers plc*,[33] where he held that documents pertaining to a statutory inquiry carried out by Bord na gCon were not privileged, as he could not see "how the production of these particular documents would be adverse to the public interest" or how "their production would injure the proper functioning of the service which

---

[29] See, *e.g. Comerford's* case, n. 47, *supra* and *People* v. *Ferguson*, Court of Criminal Appeal, October 27, 1975.
[30] [1972] I.R. 236. See also, *Geraghty* v. *Minister for Local Government* [1975] I.R. 300; *Folens and Co.* v. *Minister for Education* [1981] I.L.R.M. 21; and *Incorporated Law Society of Ireland* v. *Minister for Justice* [1987] I.L.R.M. 42.
[31] High Court, May 1, 1981.
[32] [1987] I.R. 289. See also *Dublin Meatpackers Ltd.* v. *Ireland, The Irish Times*, April 13, 1989 (no privilege for diplomatic exchanges with U.K. officials concerning operation of beef slaughtering scheme).
[33] [1988] I.R. 132.

the Board is required by statute to provide." This trend was continued by both Lardner J. in *Ahern* v. *Minister for Industry & Commerce*[34] and Blayney J. in *P.M.P.S. Ltd.* v. *P.M.P.A. Ltd.*[35]

The applicant in *Ahern* was an established officer in the Patent Office who sought judicial review to challenge certain disciplinary action taken by the Minister. The respondent objected to the production of confidential reports prepared by the applicant's immediate superiors on the grounds that:

> "[D]isclosure of them would considerably interfere with the day-to-day running of a Civil Service Department and would breach fundamental concepts of confidentiality which pertain to the ability of officers to report on the conduct of officers they supervise."[36]

Lardner J. could not accept these submissions, as the reports in question were prepared simply with the particular applicant in mind. As the reports were highly relevant to the applicant's case and as Lardner J. was not satisfied that production of the reports would have the consequences feared by the respondent, he accordingly disallowed the claim of privilege. In *P.M.P.S. Ltd.* v. *P.M.P.A. Ltd.*, the liquidator of a friendly society sought discovery of documents pertaining to an investigation carried out on behalf of the Registrar prior to the collapse of the society in question. Blayney J. rejected the argument that the inspector's functions and civil service morale would be undermined if privilege could not be claimed:

> "Nobody interrogated by the inspector could be under any illusion that information obtained by him would be confidential. . . . Nor can I accept either that responsible civil servants would be any less likely to speak with the Registrar if the memorandum was disclosed to the liquidator."[37]

O'Mahony v. *Ireland*[38] is, however, one case which falls on the other side of the line. Here the plaintiff, who was a soldier with the Irish UN contingent in the Lebanon, claimed damages for negligence against the State. It was said that Irish army officers had permitted him and his two colleagues to be placed under the control of an officer who was not a member of the UN interim force, thereby causing him to fall into the hands of the irregular Christian Militia. His colleagues were killed and he was seriously injured as a result. A separate court of inquiry was conducted by the Irish Defence Forces and by the UN force itself. Barrington J. upheld the claim of public interest privilege. It was not unreasonable for the Minister for Defence to provide that the court of inquiry organised by the Defence Forces should be confidential:

> "having regard to the nature of the work which a court of inquiry could do and the possible security implications. . . . The privilege, therefore, was properly claimed."

[34] High Court, March 4, 1988.
[35] [1990] 1 I.R. 284.
[36] High Court, March 4, 1988, p. 3, of the judgment.
[37] [1990] 1 I.R. 287.
[38] *The Irish Times*, June 28, 1989.

With regard to the UN inquiry, Barrington J. said that the report had been passed on to the Irish Government in circumstances of confidentiality:

> "The Government had taken the view that it was under a duty to preserve the confidence. This was a reasonable attitude and the privilege was properly claimed."

The procedure to be followed in adjudicating upon a claim for privilege is a most important matter. In the first place, where a document is relevant, the burden of proving that it is privileged rests on the State. It may be possible for the court to decide the claim without an inspection.[39] However, before any inspection is ordered, the affidavit must be clear and must sustain at least a prima facie case that the documents are privileged. In one case McWilliam J. complained that to ask the court "to examine all these documents under the circumstances of the present case seems to me to be getting very close to asking the Court to prepare . . . the affadavit of discovery."[40] In some cases it will be necessary for the court to inspect the documents, possibly *in camera*, in order to decide whether to order discovery.

There are four points which require further elaboration.

(a) No "class" grounds. There is one significant point on which modern Irish law differs from that prevailing in Britain. In Britain, the courts are still prepared, in certain circumstances, to allow privilege in respect of a document not only on the grounds of its own particular content, but also on the grounds that it belongs to a class of documents, some or most of whose members will have a confidential content. The thinking underlying "class privilege" is that official documents of certain categories are so sensitive that they would not be fearlessly and candidly written if there were any possibility that they might be made public.[41] However, the concept of privilege on class grounds was rejected by the Supreme Court in *Murphy* as inconsistent with the principle of judicial independence enshrined in Article 34.1.

(b) Criminal proceedings. In *Murphy*, Walsh J. had been careful to refrain from expressing any opinion as to the scope of executive privilege in criminal proceedings. But it was this very point which was at issue in *D.P.P. (Hanley)* v. *Holly*.[42] At a hearing in the District Court of a charge of unlawful assault, the defence called upon the investigating Garda to produce his report of the incident. Privilege was claimed by the State, and this claim was upheld by the District Justice.

Keane J. held that this conclusion was incorrect. In the light of the prin-

---

[39] See generally, *Murphy* v. *Dublin Corporation* [1972] I.R. 234–235. It has been said that any interested person and not just the State may assert a claim for immunity; the point could even be taken by a court of its own motion. See *Rodgers* v. *Secretary of State for Home Department* [1973] A.C. 388, 400, 406, 408, 412.

[40] *Hunt* v. *Roscommon V.E.C.*, High Court, May 1, 1981. See also, *Murphy* v. *Dublin Corporation* [1972] I.R. 237.

[41] *e.g. Burmah Oil* v. *Bank of England* [1980] A.C. 1090.

[42] [1984] I.L.R.M. 149. The result had been anticipated by an academic commentator: O'Connor, "The Privilege of Non-Disclosure and Informers" (1980) 15 Ir.Jur. (N.S.) 111.

The State in Litigation

ciples enunciated by Walsh J. in *Murphy*, he was satisfied that a general claim of privilege in the case of police communications failed "because as a class their admission would be against the public interest is no longer sustainable."[43] To succeed it would have been necessary for the Garda authorities to advance a specific ground of possible damage to the public interest which might result from the disclosure of such documents, although Keane J. remarked that in the circumstances of the case it seemed "highly unlikely that any such ground exists."[44]

In *People* v. *Eccles*[45] the Court of Criminal Appeal held that the privilege claim was on the other side of the line from *Holly*. The Court ruled that, in the exceptional circumstances of the case, the disclosure of confidential Garda information would have been contrary to the public interest. The defendants were charged with capital murder (and other serious offences). They had been arrested under section 30 of the Offences against the State Act 1939, and an extension order had been served on them permitting their detention for up to 48 hours. The Chief Superintendent who had caused the extension order to be served on the defendants claimed that he had received information which suggested that one of the defendants should be detained for a further 24 hour period. The Chief Superintendent claimed privilege when asked to reveal the source of this information. Hederman J. ruled that the Special Criminal Court was correct to uphold the claim of privilege:

> "The Chief Superintendent was entitled to claim privilege in respect of both the source, and the nature of the source, of the sensitive, confidential information he received in respect of the applicant. Normally a member of the Garda Síochána cannot claim privilege in respect of information received from a fellow member of the force simply by virtue of its being such a communication. The circumstances in this case, however, were exceptional. [Privilege was claimed] on the ground that . . . 'it would be dangerous to identify whether the source was civilian or police.' This he was clearly entitled to do."[46]

(c) Extension of privilege to all public interest cases. In *Murphy's* case, Walsh J. emphasised the point that "executive privilege only applied to a Minister who was exercising "the executive powers of government of the State." If this observation is taken at its face value, it would appear to restrict the immunity to Ministers exercising their executive function.[47] But if the immunity has now (in fact, since *Leen's* case in 1926; see page 705) been

[43] See also, *People* v. *Ferguson*, Court of Criminal Appeal, October 27, 1975.
[44] Keane J. regarded *Att.-Gen.* v. *Simpson* [1959] I.R. 105 as having been impliedly overruled by *Murphy* v. *Dublin Corporation*.
[45] Court of Criminal Appeal, February 10, 1986.
[46] *Ibid.* pp. 34–35 of the judgment. See also, *Gormley* v. *Ireland*, High Court, March 7, 1991 (general disclosure of documentation concerning plaintiff's internment, save for "highly confidential" Garda Correspondence) and *Director of Fair Trade* v. *Sugar Distributors Ltd.*, High Court, November 26, 1990.
[47] As opposed to when the Minister has merely acted as a *persona designata*, as in *Murphy* v. *Dublin Corporation*.

severed from the prerogative, and put on the basis of public interest, it seems arbitrary and unnecessary to confine the immunity in this narrow fashion. And there is evidence that the immunity is not so confined. For example, in *The State (Williams)* v. *Army Pensions Board*,[48] Henchy J. assumed that privilege could be claimed, in a suitable case, in respect of the Board's documents. Again, in *Geraghty* v. *Dublin Corporation*,[49] the immunity was allowed to protect some of the documents for which it was claimed, although that case involved a Minister hearing a planning appeal, and thus taking a quasi-judicial—as opposed to executive—function. Most recently in *O'Mahony* v. *Ireland* a report of a UN inquiry benefitted from the privilege. There is also a line of British authority to like effect. In *D.* v. *National Society for the Prevention of Cruelty to Children*,[50] the House of Lords held that the defendant body (a private, charitable body which did, however, enjoy official status to the extent of being an "authorised person" for the purpose of bringing child care proceedings under the relevant English legislation) was entitled to claim immunity on the grounds of public interest in respect of members of the public who had given information to them concerning child abuse.

(d) Does the right to a fair hearing require the disclosure of documents? The dictates of constitutional justice will often require the disclosure of relevant evidence, and this is especially so where the decision-maker is exercising quasi-judicial functions. In *O'Leary* v. *Minister for Industry and Commerce*[51] a bridge in the neighbourhood of the plaintiff's farm had been submerged by the Electricity Supply Board in the course of the construction of a hydro-electric scheme. The Board was required by the relevant legislation to build a new bridge unless the defendant Minister determined that in the circumstances this was not necessary. Privilege was claimed in respect of memoranda and other communications exchanged between the Board and the Minister. ÓDálaigh C.J. observed that the minister had been cast in a quasi-judicial role and that he was required to make "an objective finding in effect as between the parties." The communications of the Board to the Minister were not those of an adviser in relation to the discharge of a statutory duty, but were rather "the representations of a party with an interest." The *audi alteram partem* principle therefore required that such circumstances be disclosed.[52] However, the rule will not always require that such disclosure of relevant documents be made: there will be situations where the constitutional

---

[48] [1983] I.R. 308.
[49] [1975] I.R. 300.
[50] [1978] A.C. 171. See also, *Director of Fair Trading* v. *Sugar Distributors Ltd.*, High Court, November 26, 1990 (Director entitled to treat complaint that Restrictive Practices Orders violated as confidential and public interest required non-disclosure).
[51] [1966] I.R. 676.
[52] Non-disclosure of documents was also found to breach the *audi alteram partem* rule in *Geraghty* v. *Minister for Local Government* [1975] I.R. 300 and *The State (Williams)* v. *Army Pensions Board* [1983] I.R. 308.

guarantee of fair procedures, which, of course, is not absolute, may have to yield to the need to preserve confidential information.[53]

8. Obligations Conditional on the Dáil's Approval

It used to be thought that the voting of funds by Parliament was a condition precedent to the validity of contracts to which the State is a party. This view, which is founded on the high constitutional principle that the consent of Parliament is necessary for the expenditure of public monies, derives principally from the old case of *Churchward* v. *R.* and, in particular from an unnecessarily wide statement in that case from Shea J.[54] The wide propositions suggested in *Churchward's* case was rejected in *New South Wales* v. *Bardolph*.[55] It has now been accepted that the result in *Churchward* depended on the peculiar fact of the case, namely that the contract in the case expressly provided that payment, for the carriage of mails between Dover and the Continent were to be made out of monies voted by Paliament and no such monies were voted. Thus, in foreign jurisdictions, *Churchward* is now regarded as an authority only for the unexceptionable proposition that a contract[56] may be expressly made subject to parliamentary appropriation, whether by statute, constitutional provision or, as in *Churchward*, by express words.[57]

In Ireland, the *Churchward* doctrine was explicitly relied upon just after independence in the case of *Kenny* v. *Cosgrave*.[58] Here the President of the Executive Council had told an employer whose workers were on strike that it was essential that the employer resist the demands and had promised that the Executive Council would indemnify him against any financial loss which ensued from this resistance. The promise was not honoured and the plaintiff sued for damages. Even on the assumption that there was a contract between the plaintiff and the Executive Council, his claim was rejected on the grounds that the Executive Council could not "make a binding contract to pay public money without the authority of the Oireachtas [*sc.* given in advance]."

The authority of the decision is, however, weakened by the fact that Fitzgibbon J. speaking for the Supreme Court, also rested his decision on the doctrine that the Executive may not make a contract which fetters its discretionary power[59] and apparently failed to perceive that he was dealing

---

[53] Thus, in *The State (Williams)* v. *Army Pensions Board* [1983] I.R. 308 the respondent Board's failure to disclose certain medical evidence in their possession was found to be a breach of constitutional justice. Henchy J. observed that there might well be other cases where for reasons such as "State security or other considerations of public policy," the Board might be privileged from disclosing, or making full disclosure of, the evidence before them.

[54] (1865) L.R. 1 Q.B. 173.

[55] (1934) 52 C.L.R. 455.

[56] And not just, of course, contracts. See, for example, in *Conroy* v. *Minister for Defence* [1934] I.R. 679 (Supreme Court granted a declaration that the Minister was bound to take steps for the payment of a pension to the plaintiff).

[57] See generally, Hogg, *Liability of the Crown in Australia, New Zealand and the United Kingdom* (Melbourne, 1971), Chap. 5; Turpin, *Government Contracts* (London, 1972), Chap. 1 and Street, *Governmental Liability* (Cambridge, 1953), Chap. 3.

[58] [1926] I.R. 517.

[59] See further, p. 674.

with separate rules.[60] It is submitted, however, that the principal reason why *Kenny* does not represent present-day law is the wealth of authority against it. *Bardolph's* case has already been briefly noted. The Irish authorities commence with *Leyden* v. *Attorney-General*[61] which was decided just before *Kenny*. The plaintiff, in *Leyden*, sought certain declarations in respect of his salary under a contract employing him as a teacher. His claim was resisted by the defendants on the grounds that a contract with a government department was involved, for the payment of which no grant had been made by the Oireachtas. Here the Supreme Court distinguished *Churchward* on the ground that the remedy sought was only a declaration of the plaintiff's rights. However, Murnaghan J. also observed that: "[*Churchward's*] doctrine will require a careful scrutiny before it is given such a wide application as was here contended for."[62] *Maunsell* v. *Minister for Education*[63] was a similar case to *Leyden* (save that no contract was involved) in that a teacher was suing for a declaration of his right to salary based on the Rules and Regulations of the Commissioners of National Education in Ireland. In *Maunsell* Gavin Duffy J. rejected an argument based on the *Churchward* doctrine with some *hauteur* founding himself, in part, on Article 34.3.1, which gives the High Court full original jurisdiction:

> "Finally, I am solemnly assured that I can give no relief to the plaintiff . . . because the Executive cannot bind itself in law by a promise to pay . . . I cannot entertain any suggestion that a public servant, the conditions of whose remuneration are in dispute is precluded from invoking the jurisdiction of the High Court to declare his rights until an Appropriation Act has been enacted providing his Department with money to pay him, however necessary it may be to prove that such an Act has been passed before an order for payment is made."[64]

The final qualifying clause in this passage[65] recalls the doctrine which is now generally accepted in Britain and elsewhere in the Commonwealth: namely, that whilst parliamentary appropriation is not necessary to the validity of a contract, before the monies can actually be paid, there must be properly authorised funds available. This point is not peculiar to contract, for there are many cases (such as actions in tort) where the problem of enforcing an action against the State could also theoretically arise. The question is, of course,

---

[60] [1926] I.R. 528, where Fitzgibbon J. cited *Rederiaktiebolaget Amphitritie* v. *The King* [1921] 3 K.B. 500 in support of the proposition that the Government could not by contract fetter its discretion to act in the public interest as it saw fit.
[61] [1926] I.R. 334.
[62] *Ibid.* 367. See also, *Att.-Gen.* v. *Great Southern Ry. Co.* [1925] A.C. 754, a case with an Irish connection, discussed by Street, *op. cit.* pp. 88–89.
[63] [1940] I.R. 213. Certain other cases such as *Kildare County Council* v. *Minister for Finance* [1931] I.R. 215 and *Latchford* v. *Minister for Industry and Commerce* [1950] I.R. 33, involved (it was claimed) a statutory debt in respect of which funds had already been approved by the Oireachtas (by an Appropriation Act or in some other way) and thus did not raise the problem examined in the text.
[64] [1940] I.R. 236–237.
[65] See also, to like effect, *Leyden* v. *Att.-Gen.* [1926] I.R. 334.

most unlikely ever to arise in practice since it may be assumed that the State will fulfil its legal obligations. Where a monetary judgment against the State is concerned, a specific parliamentary vote will not usually be necessary to meet the judgment, as there will usually be an appropriate existing vote from which the money can be taken (provided, of course, that the Dáil has not expressly forbidden this). And even if there is no such vote, it may be assumed that the Government would bring the necessary supplementary estimate before the Dáil, and that the Dáil would pass it.

However, in view of the question's inherent constitutional interest, we may briefly examine what would happen if the Dáil failed to vote the necessary funds to meet the State's obligations. In Britain, the common law rule that no form of execution was available against the Crown was an aspect of the prerogative, and founded on the fiction that the King could do not wrong.[66] It is plain from *Byrne* that this doctrine did not survive in Ireland. However, there is another fundamental constitutional principle which may be a barrier in the case of damages: Articles 11 and 21 make it clear that all State expenditure must be authorised by the Dáil.[67] There is, accordingly, some authority for the proposition that any form of enforcement which required a monetary payment would constitute an interference with this principle.[68] Take, for example, *Conroy* v. *Minister for Defence*,[69] in which the Supreme Court granted a declaration that the Minister was bound to take steps for the payment of a pension to the plaintiff, and that under the terms of the Military Service (Pensions) Act 1924, he had no authority to question the plaintiff's entitlement. The Act had stipulated that no person could receive a military service pension unless money for this purpose had been voted by the Oireachtas. This meant, according to Kennedy C.J., that it was the duty of the Minister for Defence to submit the particulars of the pensions granted by him to the Oireachtas "so that the moneys [could] be voted accordingly *if the Oireachtas so please[d]*" (authors' italics). It should be noted that even in this traditional authority the Minister was put under an obligation to execute his part of the parliamentary process.

---

[66] See Wade, *op. cit.* p. 809. In *Crowley* v. *Ireland* [1980] I.R. 102, Kenny J. (at 129) expressly refrained from giving an opinion on "the difficult question as to whether damages may be awarded against a Minister of State or against Ireland for failure to perform a duty imposed by the Constitution." But see now, *Kearney* v. *Ireland* [1986] I.R. 116 (State vicariously liable for damages arising from employees' wrongful breach of prisoner's constitutional rights).

[67] See also, the comments of Gannon J. in *K. Security Ltd.* v. *Ireland*, High Court, July 15, 1977.

[68] It is also just possible that any enforcement involving monetary payment would be held to constitute an interference with the business of the Oireachtas, and would run up against Art. 15 (parliamentary privilege). However as parliamentary privilege is so much less extensive in Ireland than in Britain, this seems unlikely.

[69] [1934] I.R. 679.

LOCAL GOVERNMENT ACT 1991

As was stated at page 165 of the text, the 1990 local government elections were postponed pending a review of the local government system by a committee of experts under the chairmanship of Dr. Tom Barrington. This committee duly reported in March 1991: see *Local Government Reorganisation and Reform* (P1. 7918). While there was little time for legislative action between the date of publication of the report and June 1991, the rescheduled date for the local elections, the Oireachtas nonetheless passed the Local Government Act 1991. While the Act is only the first of four promised Local Government Bills, the 1991 Act may nevertheless be fairly regarded as one of the most far-reaching pieces of local government reform since 1922. It does not, however, tackle the more vexed question of local authority financing. Unfortunately, only the main features of the Act may be highlighted in this context.

Relaxation of the ultra vires rule

Section 6 effects a major relaxation of the *ultra vires* rule (treated at pages 175–178 of the text) insofar as it affects local authorities. Section 6(1) provides that:

"(a) A local authority may, subject to the provisions of this section, engage in such activities or do such things in accordance with law (including the incurring of expenditure) as it considers necessary or desirable to promote the interests of the local community.

(b) For the purposes of this section a measure, activity or thing shall be deemed to promote the interests of the local community if it promotes, directly or indirectly, the social, economic, environmental, recreational, cultural, community or general development of the area (or any part thereof) of the local authority concerned or of the local community (or any group consisting of members thereof)."

Section 6(4) provides that the exercise of powers under this section shall be a reserved function, while section 6(6) precludes the authority from exercising its powers under this section to perform tasks that "would prejudice or duplicate activity arising from performance of a statutory function by any person in the functional area of the authority" or which would involve "wasteful or unnecessary expenditure by the local authority."

Local Authorities to have regard to certain matters in performance of their functions

Section 7(1) is an entirely novel section which requires local authorities when performing their statutory functions to have regard to certain matters such as: the availability and effective use of resources, maintenance of essential services, achievement of reasonable balance between functional programmes, Governmental or Ministerial policy and the need for co-ordination, co-operation and consultation between public bodies. Section 7(2) provides, however, that "a local authority shall perform those functions which it is by law required to provide and this section shall not be regarded as affecting any such requirement." This section might yet have considerable relevance in those cases (described at pages 655–668 of the text) where the authority is sued for the alleged negligent exercise of its statutory functions. Where the authority elects (assuming, of course, that it has a discretion in the matter) for policy reasons, for example, not to inspect the foundations of houses, it may possibly be more readily able to justify its stance on the ground that it needs to conserve its resources in order that it may provide other, more essential, services which it has decided to provide.

Transfer of functions

Section 9(1)(a) allows the Government to make an order transferring the functions of a Minister or the Government (other than a function which is required by the Constitution to be performed by a Minister of the Government) where, the function:

> ". . . could be performed effectively by local authorities of a specified class or classes and is a function relating to the provision of a public service in the functional area of local authorities of that class or those classes to local authorities of that class or those classes."

This section may, however, give rise to problems of characterisation, including, for example, the question of what are the executive powers of the Government within the meaning of Article 28 of the Constitution.

Reserved functions

Section 44(1) provides that it shall be the general function of the members of the local authority to determine by resolution the policy of the local authority "in accordance with and subject to the provisions of the enactments relating to that authority." Section 44(2) allows the Minister for the Environment to declare by order that certain specified functions shall be reserved functions for the purposes of the City and County Management Acts 1940–1955: see pages 166–171 of the text.

Section 4 in the planning context

The Barrington Committee recommended (at page 48 of the Report) that the section 4 procedure (section 4, City and County Management (Amendment) Act 1955, described at pages 171–175 of the text) should not apply to planning decisions, because:

(1) of the existence of an independent appeals tribunal; and
(2) in accordance with the "general reserved/executive framework, decisions on individual cases should rest with the executive."

The Government could not see fit to accept this recommendation in its entirety, but sections 44 and 45 of the 1991 Act substantially restrict the operation of section 4 in the planning context.

Section 44 amends section 4 of the 1955 Act so as to require that, in the case of a resolution under section 4 in planning matters, the required notice in relation to the resolution must be signed by not less than three-quarters of the total number of the members elected for the electoral area or areas concerned and that it shall be necessary for the passing of such a resolution, that not less than three-quarters of the total number of members of the local authority vote in favour.

Section 45 is a consequential section which amends section 26 of the Local Government (Planning and Development) Act 1963 to provide that it will be necessary for the passing of a resolution under section 26(3), in relation to a resolution that would materially contravene the development plan, that not less than three-quarters of the total number of the members of the planning authority vote in favour. These two amendments in requiring three-quarters majority vote of the total members (together with, in the case of section 44 three-quarters support of the total members in whose area the land is situate) radically change section 4 of the 1955 Act which, of course, merely requires a simple majority of the members attending the meeting, providing that figure is greater than one-third of the total number of members of the authority.

SUBJECT INDEX

743

Bord Telecom Éireann—*cont.*
  statutory rules of immunity, 638–639, 642
  supply to illegal radio stations, 256
Bord Uchtála, An, (Adoption Board), 105,
    229
  adoption orders, 231, 239
  constitutionality, 239
  judicial functions, 229
Borough corporations, 161–162 175
Breach of constitutional rights,
  See under Constitutional rights.
Breach of statutory duty, 635, 642, 647–649
Bristow J., 118
Britain. *See under* United Kingdom.
British and Irish Steam Packet Company, 119,
    134
British Council on Tribunals, 234
Broadcasting, 119–120, 248–250. *See also*
    RTE.
  Broadcasting Complaints Commission, 139,
    149*n*, 254
  frequency management, 250
  private broadcasting contracts, 249–256. *See
    also* Independent Radio and Television
    Commission.
  RTE monopoly, 249
  unlicensed broadcasting, 249
  penalties for, 255–256
Broadcasting Complaints Commission, 139,
    149*n*, 254
Broadcasting franchises and licences. *See
    under* Independent Radio and Television
    Commission.
Bus Átha Cliath, 146
Bus Éireann, 146
By-laws, 33–34. *See also* Delegated
    legislation.
  definition, 33, 167*n*
  evidence of, 33
  judicial control of, 34
  local authorities' powers, 33
  making of, a reserved function, 167
  Minister's powers in relation to, 216
  regulations, distinguished from, 33

CIE (Córas Iompair Éireann), 118, 119, 122,
    134
  Ministerial intervention in disputes, 131–132
  reorganisation, 146
Cabinet. *See under* Government.
Cahill v. *Sutton*
  locus standi test, 612, 614–615, 616, 619*n*,
    620, 621
Carltona doctrine, 88, 400–405
  individual ministerial responsibility and,
    56–57
Case stated,
  challenge to delegated legislation, 30
Casual trading licences, 275, 543
Ceimici Teoranta, 119
  auditors, 142

Censorship of Films Board, 221
Censorship of Publications Board, 221,
    232–233
Censorship of Publications Appeals Board,
    233
Central Bank, 127*n*, 128, 143
  licensing functions, 263, 276
Central Statistics Office, 65
Certiorari, 342, 350, 565, 568. *See also* Judicial
    review; Judicial review procedure;
    Remedies.
  application procedure, 568–571
  declaration, and, 583
  locus standi, 611–612. *See also* Locus standi.
  orders *ex debito justitiae*, 385, 601
  remittal, power of, 568, 592–593
  scope of, 571, 572–573, 574–575
    See also Remedies.
  stay of proceedings 591–592
Charitable purposes,
  rates exemption, 189–192
Chief Appeals Officer, 245, 246
Chief executives,
  executive offices, of, 65
  state-sponsored bodies, of, 143–144
    Consultative Group, 150
    salaries, restrictions on, 117
Chubb, Basil, 279
Circulars. *See under* Administrative rules and
    circulars.
Citizens' rights,
  right to information on, 293–295
City County Manager. *See under* Management
    system.
Civil Liability,
  non-feasance, 635–636
Civil proceedings,
  jurisdictional review, scope of, 349–351
Civil servants. *See also* Civil Service.
  appearance on radio or television, 102
  appointment and selection, 75–80
    basic recruitment posts, 77–80
    Civil Service Commissioners, 77–79
    competitions for posts, 76, 76*n*, 78–79
    excluded positions, 79–80
    higher posts, 76
    married women, reappointment of, 79–80
    personal political advisers, 79
    promotional posts, 75–76
    public interest exemption, 79
    recertification, 76
    selection process, 77–79
    senior appointments, 76
    Top Level Appointments Committee,
      63–64, 76–77
  communication of official information, 102
    confidentiality, duty of, 102
    Official Secrets Act, 102
  conciliation and arbitration scheme
    See under Civil service.
  conflict of interest, 99*n*

Education service, 105. *See also* Schools;
    Universities.
Efficiency Audit Group, 66, 67
Elections,
    Constitutional right to stand for, 99–100
    local. *See under* Local elections.
Electricity Supply Board. *See under* ESB.
Employment,
    civil servants. *See under* Civil servants.
    discipline
        constitutional justice and, 479–480, 482
    dismissals. *See under* Dismissals.
    judicial review, application of, 576–577
    office-holders and employees, distinction
        between, 472–476
Employment Appeals Tribunal, 221, 222,
    221*n*, 228, 232
    composition of, 240
Enforcement,
    licensing legislation, 265–267
    planning control, 208–209
Environment, Department of the, 146*n*
    circulars 40, 45*n*
Environmental Impact Assessment Directive,
    18, 44–45
Equality,
    discretionary powers, exercise of, 539–541
    proportionality, principle of, 541
Errors of fact, 331–332, 354*n*
Errors of law, 21, 345–349, 349–352. *See also*
    Errors on the face of the Record;
    Jurisdictional errors; Jurisdictional
    Review.
    appeals on point of law, 392–395
Errors on the face of the record, 328,
    329, 393
    criminal cases, 356, 357
    judicial review, 354–358
    record, scope of, 354–357
    remedies 357, 590–591
    speaking order, 355, 356
Estimates, 140
Estoppel, 671–700. *See also* Legitimate
    expectations; Promissory estoppel; *Res
    judicata*.
    cause of action estoppel, 696
    conduct, by, 372, 373, 603
    discretionary bar to relief, as, 372, 373
    issue estoppel, 696
European Communities,
    directives. *See under* European Community
        directives.
    free movement of workers/goods
        public service exemption, 109–110
    proportionality, doctrine of, 532*n*
    regulations, 17*n*
    state monopolies, 155–157
    state-sponsored bodies, 109–113
European Community Directives,
    binding nature of, 17
    duty of State to implement, 17, 18

European Community Directives—*cont.*
    Environmental Impact Assessment, 18,
        44–45
    implementation measures, 16–19, 39–40
        Act of Oireachtas, by, 18
        circular, by, 44–45
        Ministerial regulations, 17–19, 37
    non-implementation or inaccurate
        translation
        whether operational against state bodies,
            110–113
    parliamentary scrutiny, 34
        Joint Committee on Secondary
            Legislation of the European
            Communities, 37–39
    public works contracts, 115
    retrospectivity, 38–39
    state-sponsored bodies, binding on, 110–113
European Convention on Human Rights, 531
    natural justice, 410
European court of Justice,
    legitimate expectations doctrine, 671
    proportionality doctrine, 532
    retrospectivity of decisions, 386
Evidence. *See also* Discovery; Interrogatories
    by-laws, of, 33
    delegated legislation, of, 23*n*, 24
Ex debito justitiae orders, 385, 601, 609
Ex parte applications,
    final orders, 417–419
Excess of jurisdiction, 568, 700. *See also*
    Certiorari; Prohibition.
Executive. *See under* Government.
Executive functions (local government), 8,
    165, 166–171. *See also* Management
    system.
Executive offices,
    proposals for, 64–65
Executive privilege, 12, 21, 403, 705, 729–735
    audi alteram partem and, 735
    class grounds, 733
    criminal proceedings, 733–734
    government ministers, 729–735
    public interest immunity, 729–730, 731,
        734–735
Expectation. *See under* Legitimate
    expectations.
Extra-statutory tribunals, 321–323, 573, 575

FÁS (Foras Áiseanna Sathaoir), 145–146
Fair procedures. *See also* Constitutional
    justice.
    due process, 411, 415, 416, 420
    remedy for breach of, 411
    right to, 25, 45, 411*n*, 412–415
        aliens, 415
    statutory inquiries, 258–259, 261
False imprisonment, 387, 634, 642, 643
Farm Tax Office, 617–618, 681
Farm Tax Tribunal, 221*n*
Fianna Fáil Government (1987–9), 145

Subject Index

Grants, payment of,
decisions bound by constitutional justice,
484–485

Habeas corpus, 565n
Halting sites. *See under* Travelling
community.
Harbour boards, 105
Haughey, Charles (Taoiseach), 62, 67
Health boards, 105, 163, 164. *See also*
Minister for Health.
judicial review of decisions, 241n
Ombudsman's jurisdiction in relation to,
283
medical card schemes, 20
social welfare schemes, 241n
Health service,
ombudsman proposal, 315n
Hearing, 410
failure to grant, 471
natural justice, rules of. *See under Audi
alteram partem.*
Bias
Henry VIII clauses, 19–20, 60n
High Court jurisdiction,
full original jurisdiction, 374–375
powers of review, 328, 354, 392, 393
restrictions on. *See under* Ouster clauses.
social welfare appeals, 246–247
statutory appeals, in, 392–396
Highway authority,
non-repair, liability for, 635, 636
Hospitals,
rating exemption for, 192
Housing, 209–214, 547. *See also* Housing
Authority, Rent Tribunal.
building programme, 211
closing order, 213–214
demolition of habitable house, 214
demolition order, 213–214
fitness for human habitation, implied
warranty as to, 211–213
overcrowding, 210n, 213
powers and duties of housing authority,
209–213
travelling community, sites for, 166n, 204,
210–211
unfit houses, 211–213
Housing authority,
duty of care, 662–663, 665–666
negligent exercise of statutory functions,
660–661
policy decisions, 668
powers and duties, 209–213
Housing Finance Agency Ltd., 141

IDA (Industrial Development authority), 114,
122n, 146n
Iarnród Éireann (Irish Rail), 146
Illegality, 530, 531
Immigration. *See under* Aliens, control of.

Immunities,
common law
non-feasance, 635–636
statutory authorisation, 636–638
statutory rules of immunity, 635, 638–641
constitutional quasi-immunities,
652–653
constitutionality of, 641–642, 652–653
defence forces, 639–640, 641
fire services, 640, 641
mental treatment, 638
miscellaneous, 640–641
postal and telecommunication services,
638–639, 642
Special Criminal Court, 639
Improper purposes, 506, 515–519
Incidental powers, 335–336
Incorporated Law Society, 3, 114, 545–546
disciplinary functions, 237, 273, 425, 426
practising certificates, 271, 273
Independent Radio and Television
Commission, 137, 138, 221, 249–256, 263,
421, 423
allocation of contracts, 251–253
complaints, 254
duration of licences, 270
duties of contractor, 253–255
franchises, 249, 250
membership of, 249–250
Minister's functions and, 250–251
procedure, 251–253
revocation of contracts, 255–256
terms of contracts, 254–255
Individual decisions, 7–8, 9
Individual Ministerial responsibility, 54–57,
64, 67, 307
Carltona doctrine, 56–57
consequences, 55–57
duty to answer Dáil questions, 56–57
judicial review, and, 56
Ombudsman and, 307
White Paper proposals (1985), 64–65
Industrial civil servants, 68n
Industrial Credit Corporation, 119, 126n, 130,
145
Industrial Development Association. *See
under* IDA.
Inferior courts, 328n, 578n
High Court's powers of review, 328, 578
Inflexible policy rules, 229
adherence to, in exercise of discretion,
545–548
Injunction, 565, 566, 583
discretionary nature of, 595
licensing, enforcing, 265
locus standi, 612
mandatory, 591
new judicial review procedure, 320, 584–590
O'Reilly v. *Mackman*, 586–589
plenary summons, actions begun by, 584,
585, 586–590

755

Subject Index

Subject Index

Licensing—*cont.*
broadcasting licences, 250–256
constitutional justice, bound by, 478
constitutional rights and, 264,
266, 274–276
court, by, 262
directing power, 261*n*
enforcement, 265–267
injunctions, 265–266
locus standi, 265–266
notices, 266–267
Garda Síochána, by, 263
general principles, 261–262
intoxicating liquor licences, 268–269,
272–273, 332–334, 344
judicial review of decisions, 264–265
licences,
attached to land or business, 267–269
construction of terms of, 276–277
duration of, 269–270
non–assignability of, 267–269
personal to grantee, 267
property rights, as, 264*n*, 274–276
public documents, as, 276–277
refusal or revocation of, 264–265,
273–276
transfer of, 267, 269
licensing stage, 262–265
local authorities, by, 262–263
Minister, by, 263
objects of legislation, 271–273
professions, by, 263, 271
registration and, 270–271
regulatory nature of legislation, 271–273
Licensing Acts 1833–1988, 268
Licensing authorities, 262–263
Limitation periods. *See under* Time limits.
Limited judicial functions,
Tribunals, 236–239
Local Appointments Commission, 78, 105,
164
appointment of County/City Manager, 165
staff of, 72
Local authorities, 3, 5. *See also* Local finance;
Local government.
borrowing powers, 215–216
by-laws. *See under* By-laws.
central government controls, 215–218
decisions
appeals to Minister from, 216
development by, 517*n*
discretionary powers, exercise of, 519–520,
660–667. *See also* Discretionary
powers.
dismissals, 477
duty of care 661, 662–664, 665–667
estimates, challenge of,
locus standi, 617
estimates meetings, 197–199
exercise of discretionary powers, 178
finance. *See under* Local finance.

Local authorities—*cont.*
functions and powers, 201–202
delegation of, 167–168, 200–201
gaming licences, 214–215, 263
housing. *See under* Housing.
licensing, 262–263
planning. *See under* Planning control.
specimen functions, 201–202
general competence, 176*n*
meetings, 196–199
conduct of, 196–197
estimates meetings, 197–199
exclusion/suspension of councillors,
199–200
standing orders, 197
misfeasance, 635
negligent exercise of discretionary powers,
660–667
non-feasance, liability for, 635, 636
removal of elected members, 217
reserved functions
by-laws, making of, 167
delegation of, 167–168
executive functions and, 166-170
exercise of, 168
Local elections,
franchise, extension of, 162–163, 163*n*
postponement powers of Minister,
217–218
Local finance. *See also* Local authorities;
Local government.
audit system, 178–181
borrowing, 215–216
estimates
challenge to, 365, 617
meetings, 197–199
preparation of, 165
grand jury cess, 161
illegal payments 179, 180
local taxation, 194
power to levy, 168
poor law rates, 162
rate support grants, 215
rates. *See under* Rating system.
service charges. *See under* Service charges.
surcharge, 179, 180–181
travelling community
provision of sites for, 166*n*, 204, 210–211
ultra vires payments, 180–181
unnecessary or extravagant payments, 181
White Paper, 1972, 183*n*
Local Finance and Taxation (White Paper
1972), 183*n*
Local government. *See also* Local authorities;
Local finance.
borough corporations, 161–162
central government controls, 215–218
centralisation, 164
compulsory acquisition, 175, 176
county council system, 162, 163
elections. *See under* Local elections.

759

Subject Index

Local government—*cont.*
  finance. *See under* Local finance; Rating
    system; Service charges.
  franchise, extension of, 162–163
  grand jury system, 161, 162
  health functions, removal of, 163, 164
  historical development, 161–165
    1898 Act, 162–163
    post–1922 developments, 163–165
  housing function. *See under* Housing.
  management system. *See under*
    Management system.
  Minister for the Environment, powers of,
    215–218
  officers and employees
    appointment of, 163–164
  planning functions. *See under* Planning.
  poor law system, 161, 162, 163
  rates. *See under* Rating system.
  reorganisation and reforms, 162–165, 739
    Health Act 1970, 164
    White Paper, 1971, 164
  reserved/executive functions, 8, 165,
    166–171
  rural district councils, 162, 163
  ultra vires rule. *See under* Local authorities.
Local Government Act 1990, under, 739
  power of Minister to add to, 166
  reserved/executive functions, 165, 166–170
  section 4 resolutions, 171–175
    illegal payments, 179
    planning matters, 173–175, 740–741
  surcharge 178, 180–181
  ultra vires, doctrine of, 164, 175–178
    consequences of acts, 176
    council resolutions, 177
    expenditure, 180–181
    incidental powers, 176–178
    modification of rule, 176, 739
    service charges, 178, 195–196
  voting procedures, 197
Local government auditor, 179–180
  appeals against decisions, 179
  exercise of functions, 179–180
  power to surcharge, 180–181
Local Government Board, 162
Local Government Reorganisation (White
  Paper 1971), 164*n*
Local Loan Fund, 216
Local taxation, 194. *See also* Local finance;
  Rating system.
Locus standi, 329, 566, 611–626
  actio popularis, 611, 613
  aggrieved citizen, 619, 621
  Cahill v. *Sutton* test, 612, 614–615, 616,
    619*n*, 620, 621–622
    post-*Cahill* cases, 616–621
  constitutional challenges, 613, 615, 618,
    621–623
    exceptional cases, 621–623
    motive, 623

Locus standi—*cont.*
  constitutional challenges—*cont.*
    public interest, 622
    serious interest, 623
  constitutional rights, enforcement of,
    627–629, 632
  current trends, 611
  historical position, 611–612
  injury or prejudice, 615, 618–619, 620
  jus tertii and, distinction between, 623, 624
  legal right, 612
  legitimate expectation, 618
  merits of case, distinct from, 613
  new judicial review procedure, 612–614
  planning cases, 620
  planning injunctions, in, 209
  public interest, 632
  public rights, enforcement of, 626–630
  relator actions and, 626–632
  ripeness, 624–626
  special interest, 619, 620*n*
  standing requirements, 612–613
  sufficient interest, 612–614, 625
Lynch, Jack (Taoiseach), 132

McSharry, Ray (Minister for Finance), 136
Mala fides. See under Bad faith.
Maladministration,
  defects within Ombudsman's jurisdiction,
    286–288
  individual ministerial responsibility and,
    54–57
  redress for, 279–280
    Ombudsman v. the Courts, 309–313
    and *see under* Ombudsman
  types of, 286–288
Malice,
  misfeasance of public office, 645–647
Management system (local government), 164,
  165–175
  appointment and removal of Manager, 165
  assistant managers, 165*n*, 166
  executive functions, 8, 165, 166–171
    delegation of, 165*n*, 166
    information to councillors, 170–171
    performance of, 166, 169–170
    planning permission, 203
    reserved functions and, 166–170
    section four resolutions, 171–175,
      740–741
  local policy, contribution to, 170
  managerial order, 170
  suspension of Manager, 165
Mandamus, 565, 568. *See also* Judicial review.
  application procedure, 568–571
  certiorarified mandamus, 581–582
  demand and refusal, requirement of, 581
  discovery, 581
  enforcement of statutory duty, for, 582
  Government and Ministers, availability
    against, 721–722

760

Prerogative, 109
  Byrne-Webb decisions, 701–706, 707
  Constitution and, 701–706, 707
  non-survival of, 704, 705, 707
  procedural privileges, 724
  sovereign immunity, 704, 711
  State exemption from statute, 705, 725–729
  treasure trove, of, 704–705
  United Kingdom, in, 701, 706–707
President of Ireland, 53, 558
  staff of, as Civil servants of the State, 73
Presumptions of statutory construction
  See under Statutory interpretation
Price controls, 114
Primary legislation. *See also* Legislation.
  source of administrative law, as, 20, 21
Prior involvement,
  source of bias, as, 428–429, 431
Prison service,
  discipline, 229–230, 428, 480, 481, 553–554
  temporary release and parole, 482–483
  tortious actions of officers
    vicarious liability of State for, 717–718
Private bodies,
  discharging public functions, 3
Private broadcasting. *See under* Independent
  Radio and Television Commission.
Private law, 3, 4. *See also* Declaration;
  Injunction.
  legitimate expectation doctrine inapplicable
    to, 695–696
  public bodies, application to, 323–324,
    327–328
  public law, applicability of, 572
  public law contrasted with, 319
  remedies, 565, 566
  transactions and arrangements
    constitutional justice and, 495–496
Private persons,
  public rights, locus standi to enforce,
    626–630
Private sector,
  worker participation, 136
Privatisation, 151–154
  Golden Share schemes, 153–154
Privilege. *See also* Executive privilege.
  inquiries, statements made during, 259–260
  Tribunal proceedings, 234
Privy Council, 4, 5
Procedural codes, 409
  constitutional justice, application of, 494
Procedural defects,
  Ombudsman's jurisdiction, within, 292–293
Procedural impropriety, 409n, 530, 643
Procedural law, 42–45, 409. *See also*
  Constitutional justice.
Procedural privileges, 724
Procedural requirements,
  mandatory/directory provisions, 361–371
  non-compliance with, 361–371
    formal procedures, 365–367

Procedural requirements—*cont.*
  non-compliance with—*cont.*
    substantive requirements, 367–368
    third-party rights, 370–371
    time limits, 368–370
  ultra vires doctrine, 331
Professional bodies, 3. *See also* Domestic
  tribunals; Incorporated Law Society;
  Medical Council; Veterinary Council.
  disciplinary tribunals, 222–223, 237–238,
    425–426
  constitutional justice, bound by, 3, 477–478
  licensing 263, 273
  non-commercial state bodies, as, 122–123
  registration, 270–271
Professionalism.
  public service, in, 4
Programme for Economic and Social Progress
  (1990), 145n
Programme for National Recovery, 145,
  146–147, 148
Progressive Democrats, 145
Prohibition, 565, 568. *See also* Judicial review.
  application procedure, 568–571
  locus standi, 611–612. *See also* Locus standi.
  scope of remedy. *See under* Remedies.
  stay of proceedings 591–592
Promissory estoppel,
  administrative circular, arising from, 689
  conduct giving rise to, 679–684
  legitimate expectations and, 671–672, 678,
    683
    distinction between, 692–696
  statutory powers, and, 685, 689
  ultra vires principle, and, 672–677
  Webb v. *Ireland*, 678–679
Property rights,
  compensation for interference with,
    654–655
  licences as, 264n, 274–276
  presumption against unnecessary
    interference with, 337–339
  state interference with,
    constitutional justice and, 483–484, 493
Property valuation. *See under* Rating system.
Proportionality, doctrine of, 531–534, 541–544
Provisional decisions, 454–457
Public Accounts Committee, 415, 552
  *Special Report on the Future Role of the
    Comptroller and Auditor General and
    the Committee of Public Accounts*,
    141–142, 158–160
Public bodies, 107, 108. *See also* Departments
  of State; Government; Local authorities;
  Ministers; State-sponsored bodies.
  breach of statutory duty, 635, 637
  common law powers
    applicability of public law to, 32–328, 572
    policies, implementing, 325–7
    private law, governed by, 323–324,
      327–328

State servants, 69, 70. *See also* Civil servants.
  civil servants of the Government or of the
    State, 70, 72, 73–75
  non-civil servant State servants, 72–73
  vicarious liability of State for, 73
State side orders, 319, 565, 566. *See also*
    Certiorari; Mandamus; Prohibition.
  conditional orders, 569*n*, 570–571
State-sponsored bodies, 3, 5, 23, 103–157. *See
    also* Public bodies.
  accountability, 131, 141–142, 158–160
  annual report and accounts, 131
  audit of accounts, 141–142
    audit reports, 160
    Public Accounts Committee Special
      Report, 142, 158–160
  board
    chairman, 143
    Chief Executive and, 143–144
    duties of, 142
    membership, 143
    members/directors, appointment,
      127–128
    members/directors, dismissal, 128–129
  central control over wages, 116
  Chief Executives, 143–144
    salaries, Government involvement in, 117
  contracts, law applicable to, 324–325. *See
    also* Contracts.
  co-ordination between, 150–51
  commercial bodies, 118–122. *See also*
    Commercial state-sponsored bodies.
  commissions, compared with, 105–106
  consumer protection, 149
  control by Minister, 127–140, 148–149
    balance of authority, 131–133
    conflict of interests, 137–138
    practical examples of relationship,
      133–138
    social policy, 134
    special controls on RTE, 138–140
  control by Oireachtas, 140–142
    Joint Oireachtas Committees, 122*n*,
      140–141, 149*n*
  cross–subsidisation, 121–122
  definition, 103*n*, 104–105
  dissolution, 129
  diversification, 147
  EC law and, 109
    free movement of goods/workers,
      109–110
    non-implemented directives, 110–113
  economic performance in 1980's, 144
  executive salaries, Govt. restrictions, 117
  finance, 129–131
    borrowing limits, 149–150
    breaking even, 130–131
    guarantees for loans, 130
    investment criteria, 150
    performance, 145
    pricing policy, 150

State-sponsored bodies—*cont.*
  functional classification, 116–124
  government contracts procedures, 114–116
  government control, 133–134, 137–138
    intervention, 136–137
    policy directions, 132–133, 133–134
  government policy towards, 144–157
    greater discrimination, 146
    increased flexibility, 146–147
  information to be given to Minister, 131
  joint ventures, 146, 147, 148
  legal form, 124–127
    enabling statute, 124–125
    statutory company, 124–125, 126, 128,
      131
    statutory corporation, 124, 126–127, 128
    ultra vires doctrine, 125, 127
  legal status, 107–113
  Ministerial intervention in disputes, 131–132
  monopolies, 120–121, 137–138, 154–157
    EC competition rules, 155–157
  new state bodies, 146
  non-commercial, 116–117, 122–124. *See also*
    Non-commercial state bodies.
  numbers employed, 103, 134
  political interference, 136
  prerogative rights and, 109
  Prevention of Corruption Act, 108
  privatisation, 151–154
    golden share scheme, 153–154
  Programme for National Recovery, 145,
    146–147, 148
  public authorities, whether, 107–109
  rationalisation, 145–146
  senior officials, 143
  shareholding, 131
  social obligations, 122
  staff of, 105
  State, whether part of, 109, 110–112
  wage controls, 116
  worker participation, 134–136
Stationery Office, 114
  publication of statutory instruments, 23
Statute,
  exemption of State from, 725–729
Statute law. *See under* Legislation.
Statutory appeals, 392–396
  point of law, on, 392–395
Statutory companies, 124–125, 126, 128, 131
Statutory corporations, 124, 126–127, 127,
    128, 175
Statutory duty,
  breach of, 635, 642, 647–649
  discretionary powers and, 358–361, 503–504
  enforcement by mandamus, 582
  negligent exercise of, 637
Statutory inquiries. *See under* Inquiries.
Statutory instruments. *See under* Delegated
    legislation.
Statutory Instruments Act 1947, 22–25, 32, 49,
    88